City Crime Rankings

Crime in Metropolitan America

14th Edition

Kathleen O'Leary Morgan and Scott Morgan, Editors

A Division of Congressional Quarterly Inc.
Washington, D.C.

CQ Press
2300 N Street, NW, Suite 800
Washington, DC 20037

Phone: 202-729-1900; toll-free, 1-866-4CQ-PRESS (1-866-427-7737)

Web: www.cqpress.com

Cover photo: Photos.com

∞ The paper used in this publication exceeds the requirements of the American National Standard for Information Sciences--Permanence of Paper for Printed Library Materials, ANSI Z39.48-1992.

Printed and bound in the United States of America

11 10 09 08 07 1 2 3 4 5

ISBN 978-0-87289-820-2

PREFACE

Final data for 2006 from the Federal Bureau of Investigation (FBI) provide a mixed report of crime in the United States. For the fourth consecutive year, property crimes decreased in both numbers and rates. Numbers and rates of violent crimes, however, increased for the second year in a row.

The data released by the FBI on September 24, 2007, show that the nation's property crime rate dropped 2.8 percent while its violent crime rate rose 1 percent from 2005 to 2006. Specific rates for murder, robbery, and burglary increased, but rates for rape, aggravated assault, larceny-theft, and motor vehicle theft have decreased since 2005.

The 14th edition of *City Crime Rankings* analyzes these latest FBI crime statistics and ranks U.S. cities with populations of 75,000 or more and metropolitan areas by type of crime and measures of overall safety. This book features a thorough collection of data presented in 90 tables that allow for easy comparisons of crime numbers, rates, and trends throughout the country.

Important Notes about *City Crime Rankings*

City Crime Rankings, 14th edition, is organized into five sections. The first section announces the winners of the Safest City and Metro Area Awards, our annual survey that assesses the 2006 FBI crime data and ranks cities and metro areas by overall safety. This year's competition compares the incidence of crime in 378 cities throughout the United States. Complete results and an explanation of survey methodology can be found on pages 1 to 16.

Also included in this new edition is a revised overview of 2006 crime in the United States. This second section presents definitions, facts, and caveats that provide important background information about the numbers presented in *City Crime Rankings,* 14th edition.

The third section reports statistics for metropolitan areas. Forty tables, presented in both alphabetical and rank order, compare 350 U.S. metropolitan areas in numbers of crimes, crime rates, and crime trends over periods of one year and five years. The metropolitan areas must meet two criteria for inclusion: first, their central city or cities must have submitted 12 months of data in 2006; second, at least 75 percent of all law enforcement agencies located in the metro area must have reported crime statistics for 2006. The metro areas not meeting these requirements and therefore excluded from this edition of *City Crime Rankings* are listed on page 16.

The fourth section features city crime ranking tables. It covers cities with populations of 75,000 or more that reported crime data to the FBI for 2006. In all, this 14th edition provides data and rankings for 390 cities. Researchers will find crime numbers, rates, and percent changes in crime rates over one year and five years for each city. In addition, we report the numbers and rates of police officers patrolling the streets of these cities.

The sections covering the city and metropolitan area statistics feature the same layout. Each table spans four pages. The first two pages of each table display the cities and metro areas in alphabetical order; the third and fourth pages display them in rank order.

The fifth and final section of *City Crime Rankings* offers appendixes consisting of population tables for cities and metro areas as well as cross-reference tools describing which cities and counties make up specific metro areas. It also includes a table that summarizes rates for each crime category for the past 20 years. This examination of national trends provides yet another perspective of crime in the 50 United States.

All statistics in this edition are derived from *Crime in the United States 2006,* an annual publication from the FBI. These statistics are collected under the Uniform Crime Reporting (UCR) Program, a nationwide effort under which 17,500 city, county, and state law enforcement agencies report data on crimes committed in their jurisdictions. In 2006, approximately 94 percent of Americans lived in areas participating in the UCR program. For more information, log on to www.fbi.gov/ucr/cius2006/index.html.

The 2006 statistics presented in *City Crime Rankings* are the most recent non-preliminary, full-year numbers available from the FBI. All rankings appearing in this book are reported in order from highest to lowest. In case of a tie, the rankings are listed alphabetically. Parentheses indicate negative numbers and rates. Data reported as "NA" are not available or could not be calculated. The national totals and rates appearing at the top of each table are for the entire United States, including both metropolitan and nonmetropolitan areas. Specific totals for metropolitan areas and larger cities are provided in the Appendix.

A Cautionary Note about Rankings

We recognize that some members of the criminal justice community view our crime rankings as controversial. The FBI and many criminologists caution against crime rankings of any type. They correctly point out that crime levels are affected by many factors, such as population density, population composition (particularly the concentration of youth), climate, economic conditions, cultural factors, family cohesiveness, education levels, strength of local law enforcement agencies, citizens' attitudes toward crime, and citizens' crime reporting practices. As a result, crime rankings are often deemed "simplistic" or "incomplete."

However, the criticism is largely based on the fact that there are reasons for the differences in crime rates, not that the rates are incompatible. This would be somewhat akin to deciding not to compare athletes on their speed in the 40-yard dash because of physical or training differences. Such differences help explain the different speeds but do not invalidate the comparisons.

We agree that it is important to exercise caution with crime rankings and certainly do not wish to be irresponsible in our presentation of these data. However, we also believe that our rankings tell an interesting and very important story regarding the incidence of crime in this country. Annual rankings not only allow for comparisons among different cities and metro areas; they enable local leaders and concerned citizens to track their community's progress in addressing crime problems from one year to the next.

We ask our readers to use and learn from these crime rankings while understanding that city size is just one of many factors used in assessing crime in the United States.

Exciting Changes for Morgan Quitno Press

This 14th edition of *City Crime Rankings* ushers in a new and exciting era for our company and our readers. Effective May 2007, Morgan Quitno's reference books are now published by CQ Press of Washington, D.C. A division of Congressional Quarterly Inc., CQ Press is the premier publisher of books, directories, periodicals, and electronic products on American government and politics.

While our publishing structure has changed, our commitment to bringing the highest quality publications to our customers has not. We look forward to providing researchers with top notch reference titles for many years to come.

- THE EDITORS

TABLE OF CONTENTS

TABLE OF CONTENTS (continued)

TABLE OF CONTENTS (continued)

SAFEST CITY and SAFEST METROPOLITAN AREA

The citizens and leaders of Mission Viejo, CA, are very patient. After a ten-year wait, this southern California city at last has achieved the honor of America's Safest City.

Mission Viejo has ranked as one of the top ten safest cities in all the years it has participated in our survey. Certainly it has earned its Safest City stripes: it reports no murders for 2006, boasts the nation's lowest rape rate, and has the third-lowest aggravated assault, violent crime, and property crime rates among cities with populations of 75,000 or more. Joining Mission Viejo at the top of the Safest City rankings are Clarkstown, NY; Brick, NJ; Amherst, NY; and Sugar Land, TX.

At the opposite end of the crime scale, Detroit returns as the nation's most dangerous city. The Motor City last held this title in 2003 and has hovered in the number-two spot every year since then. Detroit has the second-highest murder, aggravated assault, and motor vehicle theft rates among cities of 75,000 people or more. Its violent crime rate is also the third-highest in the nation. However, Detroit has made some progress: the city's rape rate has dropped 9 percent since 2002 and its aggravated assault rate has decreased in the past year. Rounding out the list of the nation's top five most dangerous cities are St. Louis, MO; Flint, MI; Oakland, CA; and Camden, NJ.

Our Safest Metropolitan Area competition includes both Metropolitan Statistical Areas (MSAs) and Metropolitan Divisions (MDs), which are subdivisions of MSAs. This year, America's Safest Metropolitan Area is the Logan region of Utah and Idaho. The other metro areas atop the list are Eau Claire, WI; State College, PA; Bangor, ME; and Appleton, WI.

For the fourth consecutive year, the Detroit-Livonia-Dearborn, MI, metropolitan division appears at the bottom of the Safest Metropolitan Area rankings. Right behind the Detroit region are Memphis, TN-MS-AR; Las Vegas-Paradise, NV; Flint, MI; and Pine Bluff, AR.

Methodology

The methodology used to determine the Safest City and Safest Metro Area awards has been used in *City Crime Rankings* since 1999. First, crime rates for six basic crime categories—murder, rape, robbery, aggravated assault, burglary, and motor vehicle theft—were plugged into a formula that measures how a particular city or metro area compares to the national average for a given crime category. The results for each of the six crimes were added together to yield a final score for each city and metro area. These scores were then ranked from lowest to highest to establish which cities and metropolitan areas were safest and most dangerous.

All crimes are weighted equally under our current methodology. A number of years ago, we weighted each of the six crimes based on the results of a telephone survey that determined which crimes were of greatest concern to Americans. The polls seemed to indicate that most Americans believe crimes such as burglary are more likely to happen in their lives than more heinous crimes such as murder. Thus, burglary received the highest weight and murder the lowest weight in the formula.

Our current methodology seeks to strike a balance between the crimes most people would consider worst and those crimes that affect the most people. We now measure a city or metro area's crime record against the national average. The farther below the national average a city or metro area falls, the higher (and better) it will rank in the final Safest Cities and Metropolitan Areas list; the farther above the national average it falls, the lower (and worse) a city or metro will rank.

Our survey includes all cities with a population of 75,000 or more that reported data to the FBI for the six categories of crime. Any city or metro area missing data was disqualified from the competition. Chicago, Minneapolis, and other cities in Illinois and Minnesota are among the major cities not included this year due to data collection discrepancies (see Missing Cities and Metro Areas on page 16). There was no population minimum required for metropolitan areas.

The tables that follow display final scores and complete rankings for 378 cities and 333 metro areas. Results are presented in both alphabetical and rank order.

Community safety is a top concern for most Americans, and our Safest City and Metro Area crime rankings generate more controversy than any of our other surveys. Our hope is that these rankings bring about a meaningful debate among citizens, community leaders, and police regarding crime in the United States.

Congratulations to the citizens of Mission Viejo and the Logan metro area!

- THE EDITORS

AMERICA'S SAFEST CITY

14th ANNUAL

SAFEST CITY

Overall Top 25 and Bottom 25
(out of 378 cities)

SAFEST 25:		MOST DANGEROUS 25:	
1	Mission Viejo, CA	1	Detroit, MI
2	Clarkstown, NY	2	St. Louis, MO
3	Brick Twnshp, NJ	3	Flint, MI
4	Amherst, NY	4	Oakland, CA
5	Sugar Land, TX	5	Camden, NJ
6	Colonie, NY	6	Birmingham, AL
7	Thousand Oaks, CA	7	North Charleston, SC
8	Newton, MA	8	Memphis, TN
9	Toms River Twnshp, NJ	9	Richmond, CA
10	Lake Forest, CA	10	Cleveland, OH
11	Irvine, CA	11	Orlando, FL
12	Orem, UT	12	Baltimore, MD
13	Round Rock, TX	13	Little Rock, AR
14	Cary, NC	14	Compton, CA
15	Greece, NY	15	Youngstown, OH
16	Chino Hills, CA	16	Cincinnati, OH
17	Coral Springs, FL	17	Gary, IN
18	Troy, MI	18	Kansas City, MO
19	Farmington Hills, MI	19	Dayton, OH
20	Centennial, CO	20	Newark, NJ
21	Glendale, CA	21	Philadelphia, PA
22	Broken Arrow, OK	22	Atlanta, GA
23	Parma, OH	23	Jackson, MS
24	Sterling Heights, MI	24	Buffalo, NY
25	Simi Valley, CA	25	Kansas City, KS

SAFEST CITY

Rankings by Population Categories

CITIES OF 500,000 OR MORE POPULATION: (33 cities)

Safest 10:		Most Dangerous 10:	
1	Honolulu, HI	1	Detroit, MI
2	El Paso, TX	2	Memphis, TN
3	San Jose, CA	3	Baltimore, MD
4	New York, NY	4	Philadelphia, PA
5	Austin, TX	5	Washington, DC
6	San Diego, CA	6	Dallas, TX
7	San Antonio, TX	7	Milwaukee, WI
8	Louisville, KY	8	Houston, TX
9	Fort Worth, TX	9	Indianapolis, IN
10	Portland, OR	10	Columbus, OH

CITIES OF 100,000 TO 499,999 POPULATION: (216 cities)

Safest 10:		Most Dangerous 10:	
1	Amherst, NY	1	St. Louis, MO
2	Thousand Oaks, CA	2	Flint, MI
3	Irvine, CA	3	Oakland, CA
4	Cary, NC	4	Birmingham, AL
5	Coral Springs, FL	5	Richmond, CA
6	Centennial, CO	6	Cleveland, OH
7	Glendale, CA	7	Orlando, FL
8	Sterling Heights, MI	8	Little Rock, AR
9	Simi Valley, CA	9	Cincinnati, OH
10	Sunnyvale, CA	10	Kansas City, MO

CITIES OF 75,000 TO 99,999 POPULATION: (129 cities)

Safest 10:		Most Dangerous 10:	
1	Mission Viejo, CA	1	Camden, NJ
2	Clarkstown, NY	2	North Charleston, SC
3	Brick Twnshp, NJ	3	Compton, CA
4	Sugar Land, TX	4	Youngstown, OH
5	Colonie, NY	5	Gary, IN
6	Newton, MA	6	Reading, PA
7	Toms River Twnshp, NJ	7	Trenton, NJ
8	Lake Forest, CA	8	West Palm Beach, FL
9	Orem, UT	9	Canton, OH
10	Round Rock, TX	10	Macon, GA

14th Annual

America's Safest City Award*

RANK	CITY	SCORE
169	Abilene, TX	7.03
275	Albany, GA	76.37
273	Albany, NY	74.78
295	Albuquerque, NM	87.20
87	Alexandria, VA	(30.93)
99	Alhambra, CA	(24.24)
311	Allentown, PA	104.24
229	Amarillo, TX	46.88
4	Amherst, NY	(75.44)
141	Anaheim, CA	(6.73)
254	Anchorage, AK	59.58
57	Ann Arbor, MI	(45.54)
241	Antioch, CA	52.42
208	Arlington, TX	34.89
54	Arvada, CO	(47.37)
155	Athens-Clarke, GA	2.12
357	Atlanta, GA	189.86
225	Aurora, CO	43.60
NA	Aurora, IL**	NA
173	Austin, TX	8.79
207	Bakersfield, CA	34.88
179	Baldwin Park, CA	12.49
367	Baltimore, MD	236.73
351	Baton Rouge, LA	179.55
296	Beaumont, TX	88.11
47	Beaverton, OR	(50.64)
76	Bellevue, WA	(35.70)
209	Bellflower, CA	34.93
109	Bellingham, WA	(19.65)
236	Berkeley, CA	50.37
64	Billings, MT	(42.08)
373	Birmingham, AL	268.82
NA	Bloomington, MN**	NA
67	Boca Raton, FL	(40.81)
127	Boise, ID	(13.57)
316	Boston, MA	112.08
61	Boulder, CO	(43.98)
3	Brick Twnshp, NJ	(78.66)
324	Bridgeport, CT	129.64
NA	Brockton, MA**	NA
22	Broken Arrow, OK	(58.87)
128	Brownsville, TX	(13.43)
104	Buena Park, CA	(21.53)
355	Buffalo, NY	187.84
62	Burbank, CA	(43.73)
97	Cambridge, MA	(26.82)
374	Camden, NJ	323.81
50	Canton Twnshp, MI	(49.08)
336	Canton, OH	143.42
116	Cape Coral, FL	(17.55)
65	Carlsbad, CA	(41.04)
70	Carrollton, TX	(39.61)
255	Carson, CA	59.59
14	Cary, NC	(68.64)
122	Cedar Rapids, IA	(15.78)
20	Centennial, CO	(61.32)
117	Chandler, AZ	(17.13)
282	Charleston, SC	80.08
329	Charlotte, NC	132.08
318	Chattanooga, TN	120.15
58	Cheektowaga, NY	(44.95)
101	Chesapeake, VA	(23.18)
NA	Chicago, IL**	NA
16	Chino Hills, CA	(63.23)

RANK	CITY	SCORE
84	Chino, CA	(32.15)
180	Chula Vista, CA	12.83
363	Cincinnati, OH	218.29
2	Clarkstown, NY	(80.96)
206	Clarksville, TN	34.26
190	Clearwater, FL	18.84
369	Cleveland, OH	244.41
45	Clifton, NJ	(51.35)
73	Clinton Twnshp, MI	(36.70)
63	Clovis, CA	(42.40)
6	Colonie, NY	(74.55)
199	Colorado Springs, CO	25.39
102	Columbia, MO	(22.65)
263	Columbia, SC	66.48
248	Columbus, GA	56.19
331	Columbus, OH	135.97
365	Compton, CA	223.58
160	Concord, CA	4.48
17	Coral Springs, FL	(61.96)
75	Corona, CA	(36.24)
205	Corpus Christi, TX	34.07
100	Costa Mesa, CA	(23.35)
37	Cranston, RI	(52.60)
345	Dallas, TX	154.58
81	Daly City, CA	(32.46)
51	Danbury, CT	(49.07)
88	Davie, FL	(29.87)
360	Dayton, OH	201.49
186	Dearborn, MI	16.78
194	Deerfield Beach, FL	20.70
89	Denton, TX	(29.65)
292	Denver, CO	83.96
191	Des Moines, IA	19.99
378	Detroit, MI	407.15
175	Downey, CA	10.22
NA	Duluth, MN**	NA
276	Durham, NC	76.63
52	Edison Twnshp, NJ	(48.87)
35	Edmond, OK	(52.90)
200	El Cajon, CA	26.34
165	El Monte, CA	5.68
130	El Paso, TX	(11.97)
265	Elizabeth, NJ	69.36
163	Erie, PA	5.63
153	Escondido, CA	0.46
147	Eugene, OR	(2.08)
167	Evansville, IN	5.98
313	Everett, WA	105.51
198	Fairfield, CA	25.18
115	Fargo, ND	(17.71)
19	Farmington Hills, MI	(61.67)
320	Fayetteville, NC	124.93
239	Federal Way, WA	51.54
376	Flint, MI	380.98
149	Fontana, CA	(1.26)
95	Fort Collins, CO	(27.16)
306	Fort Lauderdale, FL	97.38
310	Fort Smith, AR	103.05
156	Fort Wayne, IN	2.70
227	Fort Worth, TX	44.03
92	Fremont, CA	(28.66)
269	Fresno, CA	70.44
111	Fullerton, CA	(19.52)
278	Gainesville, FL	77.21

RANK	CITY	SCORE
124	Garden Grove, CA	(14.91)
83	Garland, TX	(32.18)
362	Gary, IN	214.03
36	Gilbert, AZ	(52.65)
261	Glendale, AZ	64.73
21	Glendale, CA	(59.23)
168	Grand Prairie, TX	6.81
268	Grand Rapids, MI	70.38
15	Greece, NY	(68.48)
161	Greeley, CO	4.76
134	Green Bay, WI	(9.41)
287	Greensboro, NC	82.29
230	Gresham, OR	47.44
41	Hamilton Twnshp, NJ	(52.40)
259	Hammond, IN	62.37
145	Hampton, VA	(2.71)
348	Hartford, CT	159.30
233	Hawthorne, CA	48.50
238	Hayward, CA	51.26
106	Henderson, NV	(21.12)
157	Hesperia, CA	2.93
152	Hialeah, FL	0.11
257	High Point, NC	62.33
74	Hillsboro, OR	(36.51)
193	Hollywood, FL	20.47
118	Honolulu, HI	(16.87)
335	Houston, TX	141.34
38	Huntington Beach, CA	(52.57)
303	Huntsville, AL	93.15
215	Independence, MO	37.56
334	Indianapolis, IN	140.65
328	Inglewood, CA	131.39
11	Irvine, CA	(71.05)
140	Irving, TX	(6.94)
264	Jacksonville, FL	67.11
356	Jackson, MS	188.81
293	Jersey City, NJ	84.98
NA	Joliet, IL**	NA
354	Kansas City, KS	187.55
361	Kansas City, MO	203.43
136	Kenosha, WI	(8.54)
319	Kent, WA	120.74
272	Killeen, TX	74.09
285	Knoxville, TN	81.60
289	Lafayette, LA	82.81
10	Lake Forest, CA	(71.66)
211	Lakeland, FL	35.18
146	Lakewood, CA	(2.44)
201	Lakewood, CO	26.96
299	Lancaster, CA	90.19
270	Lansing, MI	72.11
202	Laredo, TX	30.76
148	Largo, FL	(2.03)
221	Las Cruces, NM	40.97
321	Las Vegas, NV	126.89
166	Lawrence, KS	5.83
298	Lawton, OK	89.99
27	Lee's Summit, MO	(57.10)
94	Lewisville, TX	(27.23)
171	Lexington, KY	8.38
126	Lincoln, NE	(14.32)
366	Little Rock, AR	233.84
53	Livermore, CA	(48.62)
31	Livonia, MI	(55.24)

RANK	CITY	SCORE
217	Long Beach, CA	38.28
300	Longview, TX	91.60
244	Los Angeles, CA	53.49
218	Louisville, KY	39.20
246	Lowell, MA	54.62
243	Lubbock, TX	52.43
247	Lynn, MA	54.96
333	Macon, GA	140.51
110	Madison, WI	(19.57)
108	Manchester, NH	(20.60)
86	McAllen, TX	(30.99)
66	McKinney, TX	(41.02)
228	Melbourne, FL	46.44
371	Memphis, TN	245.56
189	Mesa, AZ	18.37
112	Mesquite, TX	(19.49)
326	Miami Beach, FL	129.68
353	Miami Gardens, FL	181.41
344	Miami, FL	151.97
143	Midland, TX	(4.64)
343	Milwaukee, WI	151.65
NA	Minneapolis, MN**	NA
162	Miramar, FL	5.18
1	Mission Viejo, CA	(82.11)
240	Mobile, AL	52.37
223	Modesto, CA	43.02
267	Montgomery, AL	69.80
231	Moreno Valley, CA	47.97
210	Murfreesboro, TN	35.17
44	Murrieta, CA	(51.47)
91	Napa, CA	(28.87)
NA	Naperville, IL**	NA
28	Nashua, NH	(56.08)
323	Nashville, TN	128.68
279	New Bedford, MA	78.08
314	New Orleans, LA	106.70
142	New York, NY	(6.00)
359	Newark, NJ	197.32
26	Newport Beach, CA	(57.33)
251	Newport News, VA	56.62
8	Newton, MA	(73.54)
249	Norfolk, VA	56.53
103	Norman, OK	(22.34)
372	North Charleston, SC	254.25
317	North Las Vegas, NV	112.71
183	Norwalk, CA	13.23
375	Oakland, CA	338.87
144	Oceanside, CA	(3.12)
120	Odessa, TX	(16.53)
181	Ogden, UT	12.85
304	Oklahoma City, OK	94.48
82	Olathe, KS	(32.34)
222	Omaha, NE	41.95
226	Ontario, CA	43.82
40	Orange, CA	(52.42)
12	Orem, UT	(70.63)
368	Orlando, FL	237.38
32	Overland Park, KS	(54.69)
139	Oxnard, CA	(7.14)
188	Palm Bay, FL	17.13
234	Palmdale, CA	48.68
23	Parma, OH	(58.81)
133	Pasadena, CA	(9.65)
129	Pasadena, TX	(12.06)
290	Paterson, NJ	82.83
48	Pembroke Pines, FL	(49.43)
107	Peoria, AZ	(21.08)
NA	Peoria, IL**	NA
358	Philadelphia, PA	192.94
315	Phoenix, AZ	110.45
312	Pittsburgh, PA	105.33
55	Plano, TX	(45.75)
90	Plantation, FL	(29.36)
250	Pomona, CA	56.56
302	Pompano Beach, FL	92.47
80	Port St. Lucie, FL	(33.42)
232	Portland, OR	48.48
274	Portsmouth, VA	75.76
220	Providence, RI	40.05
39	Provo, UT	(52.48)
203	Pueblo, CO	31.42
78	Quincy, MA	(34.51)
212	Racine, WI	37.01
174	Raleigh, NC	9.80
60	Rancho Cucamon., CA	(44.29)
347	Reading, PA	159.19
184	Redding, CA	14.53
260	Reno, NV	63.45
253	Rialto, CA	59.44
69	Richardson, TX	(39.90)
370	Richmond, CA	245.07
350	Richmond, VA	175.16
204	Riverside, CA	32.52
288	Roanoke, VA	82.31
NA	Rochester, MN**	NA
349	Rochester, NY	170.74
327	Rockford, IL	131.22
114	Roseville, CA	(18.89)
30	Roswell, GA	(55.96)
13	Round Rock, TX	(69.44)
338	Sacramento, CA	147.25
176	Salem, OR	11.02
219	Salinas, CA	39.52
271	Salt Lake City, UT	73.66
154	San Angelo, TX	1.65
216	San Antonio, TX	38.22
337	San Bernardino, CA	145.75
197	San Diego, CA	25.13
280	San Francisco, CA	78.35
138	San Jose, CA	(7.62)
297	San Leandro, CA	88.98
71	San Mateo, CA	(38.71)
34	Sandy, UT	(53.43)
187	Santa Ana, CA	16.87
113	Santa Barbara, CA	(19.25)
68	Santa Clara, CA	(40.47)
49	Santa Clarita, CA	(49.20)
195	Santa Maria, CA	22.82
177	Santa Monica, CA	12.31
151	Santa Rosa, CA	(0.36)
235	Savannah, GA	48.82
93	Scottsdale, AZ	(27.99)
266	Seattle, WA	69.55
322	Shreveport, LA	127.75
25	Simi Valley, CA	(58.50)
132	Sioux City, IA	(11.02)
135	Sioux Falls, SD	(8.65)
123	Somerville, MA	(15.52)
308	South Bend, IN	98.79
252	South Gate, CA	58.30
286	Southfield, MI	81.82
182	Sparks, NV	13.08
131	Spokane Valley, WA	(11.45)
245	Spokane, WA	54.14
NA	Springfield, IL**	NA
341	Springfield, MA	150.73
214	Springfield, MO	37.54
24	Sterling Heights, MI	(58.53)
342	Stockton, CA	151.08
377	St. Louis, MO	406.15
NA	St. Paul, MN**	NA
325	St. Petersburg, FL	129.67
150	Suffolk, VA	(0.62)
5	Sugar Land, TX	(75.43)
29	Sunnyvale, CA	(56.06)
119	Sunrise, FL	(16.87)
33	Surprise, AZ	(54.03)
283	Syracuse, NY	80.72
346	Tacoma, WA	156.29
291	Tallahassee, FL	83.65
305	Tampa, FL	97.14
77	Temecula, CA	(35.68)
262	Tempe, AZ	65.59
170	Thornton, CO	7.17
7	Thousand Oaks, CA	(73.78)
332	Toledo, OH	136.72
9	Toms River Twnshp, NJ	(72.70)
213	Topeka, KS	37.15
59	Torrance, CA	(44.75)
46	Tracy, CA	(50.97)
340	Trenton, NJ	150.30
18	Troy, MI	(61.84)
309	Tucson, AZ	99.53
330	Tulsa, OK	133.33
294	Tuscaloosa, AL	85.77
164	Tyler, TX	5.64
96	Upper Darby Twnshp, PA	(26.87)
72	Vacaville, CA	(37.79)
284	Vallejo, CA	81.41
158	Vancouver, WA	3.29
85	Ventura, CA	(31.02)
237	Victorville, CA	50.40
79	Virginia Beach, VA	(34.31)
277	Visalia, CA	76.73
159	Vista, CA	3.55
256	Waco, TX	60.28
242	Warren, MI	52.43
42	Warwick, RI	(52.21)
352	Washington, DC	181.30
185	Waterbury, CT	15.00
137	West Covina, CA	(7.87)
56	West Jordan, UT	(45.72)
339	West Palm Beach, FL	148.45
178	West Valley, UT	12.33
172	Westland, MI	8.71
98	Westminster, CA	(26.75)
125	Westminster, CO	(14.71)
121	Whittier, CA	(16.48)
192	Wichita Falls, TX	20.27
257	Wichita, KS	62.33
301	Wilmington, NC	92.42
307	Winston-Salem, NC	97.81
43	Woodbridge Twnshp, NJ	(51.75)
224	Worcester, MA	43.50
281	Yakima, WA	79.66
105	Yonkers, NY	(21.22)
364	Youngstown, OH	221.96
196	Yuma, AZ	25.12

Source: CQ Press using data from F.B.I. "Crime in the United States 2006"

**Includes murder, rape, robbery, aggravated assault, burglary, and motor vehicle theft. A negative score (in parentheses) indicates a composite crime number below the national rate, a positive number is above the national rate. **Not available.*

14th Annual

America's Safest City Award (continued)*

RANK	CITY	SCORE
1	Mission Viejo, CA	(82.11)
2	Clarkstown, NY	(80.96)
3	Brick Twnshp, NJ	(78.66)
4	Amherst, NY	(75.44)
5	Sugar Land, TX	(75.43)
6	Colonie, NY	(74.55)
7	Thousand Oaks, CA	(73.78)
8	Newton, MA	(73.54)
9	Toms River Twnshp, NJ	(72.70)
10	Lake Forest, CA	(71.66)
11	Irvine, CA	(71.05)
12	Orem, UT	(70.63)
13	Round Rock, TX	(69.44)
14	Cary, NC	(68.64)
15	Greece, NY	(68.48)
16	Chino Hills, CA	(63.23)
17	Coral Springs, FL	(61.96)
18	Troy, MI	(61.84)
19	Farmington Hills, MI	(61.67)
20	Centennial, CO	(61.32)
21	Glendale, CA	(59.23)
22	Broken Arrow, OK	(58.87)
23	Parma, OH	(58.81)
24	Sterling Heights, MI	(58.53)
25	Simi Valley, CA	(58.50)
26	Newport Beach, CA	(57.33)
27	Lee's Summit, MO	(57.10)
28	Nashua, NH	(56.08)
29	Sunnyvale, CA	(56.06)
30	Roswell, GA	(55.96)
31	Livonia, MI	(55.24)
32	Overland Park, KS	(54.69)
33	Surprise, AZ	(54.03)
34	Sandy, UT	(53.43)
35	Edmond, OK	(52.90)
36	Gilbert, AZ	(52.65)
37	Cranston, RI	(52.60)
38	Huntington Beach, CA	(52.57)
39	Provo, UT	(52.48)
40	Orange, CA	(52.42)
41	Hamilton Twnshp, NJ	(52.40)
42	Warwick, RI	(52.21)
43	Woodbridge Twnshp, NJ	(51.75)
44	Murrieta, CA	(51.47)
45	Clifton, NJ	(51.35)
46	Tracy, CA	(50.97)
47	Beaverton, OR	(50.64)
48	Pembroke Pines, FL	(49.43)
49	Santa Clarita, CA	(49.20)
50	Canton Twnshp, MI	(49.08)
51	Danbury, CT	(49.07)
52	Edison Twnshp, NJ	(48.87)
53	Livermore, CA	(48.62)
54	Arvada, CO	(47.37)
55	Plano, TX	(45.75)
56	West Jordan, UT	(45.72)
57	Ann Arbor, MI	(45.54)
58	Cheektowaga, NY	(44.95)
59	Torrance, CA	(44.75)
60	Rancho Cucamon., CA	(44.29)
61	Boulder, CO	(43.98)
62	Burbank, CA	(43.73)
63	Clovis, CA	(42.40)
64	Billings, MT	(42.08)
65	Carlsbad, CA	(41.04)
66	McKinney, TX	(41.02)
67	Boca Raton, FL	(40.81)
68	Santa Clara, CA	(40.47)
69	Richardson, TX	(39.90)
70	Carrollton, TX	(39.61)
71	San Mateo, CA	(38.71)
72	Vacaville, CA	(37.79)
73	Clinton Twnshp, MI	(36.70)
74	Hillsboro, OR	(36.51)
75	Corona, CA	(36.24)
76	Bellevue, WA	(35.70)
77	Temecula, CA	(35.68)
78	Quincy, MA	(34.51)
79	Virginia Beach, VA	(34.31)
80	Port St. Lucie, FL	(33.42)
81	Daly City, CA	(32.46)
82	Olathe, KS	(32.34)
83	Garland, TX	(32.18)
84	Chino, CA	(32.15)
85	Ventura, CA	(31.02)
86	McAllen, TX	(30.99)
87	Alexandria, VA	(30.93)
88	Davie, FL	(29.87)
89	Denton, TX	(29.65)
90	Plantation, FL	(29.36)
91	Napa, CA	(28.87)
92	Fremont, CA	(28.66)
93	Scottsdale, AZ	(27.99)
94	Lewisville, TX	(27.23)
95	Fort Collins, CO	(27.16)
96	Upper Darby Twnshp, PA	(26.87)
97	Cambridge, MA	(26.82)
98	Westminster, CA	(26.75)
99	Alhambra, CA	(24.24)
100	Costa Mesa, CA	(23.35)
101	Chesapeake, VA	(23.18)
102	Columbia, MO	(22.65)
103	Norman, OK	(22.34)
104	Buena Park, CA	(21.53)
105	Yonkers, NY	(21.22)
106	Henderson, NV	(21.12)
107	Peoria, AZ	(21.08)
108	Manchester, NH	(20.60)
109	Bellingham, WA	(19.65)
110	Madison, WI	(19.57)
111	Fullerton, CA	(19.52)
112	Mesquite, TX	(19.49)
113	Santa Barbara, CA	(19.25)
114	Roseville, CA	(18.89)
115	Fargo, ND	(17.71)
116	Cape Coral, FL	(17.55)
117	Chandler, AZ	(17.13)
118	Honolulu, HI	(16.87)
119	Sunrise, FL	(16.87)
120	Odessa, TX	(16.53)
121	Whittier, CA	(16.48)
122	Cedar Rapids, IA	(15.78)
123	Somerville, MA	(15.52)
124	Garden Grove, CA	(14.91)
125	Westminster, CO	(14.71)
126	Lincoln, NE	(14.32)
127	Boise, ID	(13.57)
128	Brownsville, TX	(13.43)
129	Pasadena, TX	(12.06)
130	El Paso, TX	(11.97)
131	Spokane Valley, WA	(11.45)
132	Sioux City, IA	(11.02)
133	Pasadena, CA	(9.65)
134	Green Bay, WI	(9.41)
135	Sioux Falls, SD	(8.65)
136	Kenosha, WI	(8.54)
137	West Covina, CA	(7.87)
138	San Jose, CA	(7.62)
139	Oxnard, CA	(7.14)
140	Irving, TX	(6.94)
141	Anaheim, CA	(6.73)
142	New York, NY	(6.00)
143	Midland, TX	(4.64)
144	Oceanside, CA	(3.12)
145	Hampton, VA	(2.71)
146	Lakewood, CA	(2.44)
147	Eugene, OR	(2.08)
148	Largo, FL	(2.03)
149	Fontana, CA	(1.26)
150	Suffolk, VA	(0.62)
151	Santa Rosa, CA	(0.36)
152	Hialeah, FL	0.11
153	Escondido, CA	0.46
154	San Angelo, TX	1.65
155	Athens-Clarke, GA	2.12
156	Fort Wayne, IN	2.70
157	Hesperia, CA	2.93
158	Vancouver, WA	3.29
159	Vista, CA	3.55
160	Concord, CA	4.48
161	Greeley, CO	4.76
162	Miramar, FL	5.18
163	Erie, PA	5.63
164	Tyler, TX	5.64
165	El Monte, CA	5.68
166	Lawrence, KS	5.83
167	Evansville, IN	5.98
168	Grand Prairie, TX	6.81
169	Abilene, TX	7.03
170	Thornton, CO	7.17
171	Lexington, KY	8.38
172	Westland, MI	8.71
173	Austin, TX	8.79
174	Raleigh, NC	9.80
175	Downey, CA	10.22
176	Salem, OR	11.02
177	Santa Monica, CA	12.31
178	West Valley, UT	12.33
179	Baldwin Park, CA	12.49
180	Chula Vista, CA	12.83
181	Ogden, UT	12.85
182	Sparks, NV	13.08
183	Norwalk, CA	13.23
184	Redding, CA	14.53
185	Waterbury, CT	15.00
186	Dearborn, MI	16.78
187	Santa Ana, CA	16.87
188	Palm Bay, FL	17.13
189	Mesa, AZ	18.37
190	Clearwater, FL	18.84
191	Des Moines, IA	19.99
192	Wichita Falls, TX	20.27

RANK	CITY	SCORE
193	Hollywood, FL	20.47
194	Deerfield Beach, FL	20.70
195	Santa Maria, CA	22.82
196	Yuma, AZ	25.12
197	San Diego, CA	25.13
198	Fairfield, CA	25.18
199	Colorado Springs, CO	25.39
200	El Cajon, CA	26.34
201	Lakewood, CO	26.96
202	Laredo, TX	30.76
203	Pueblo, CO	31.42
204	Riverside, CA	32.52
205	Corpus Christi, TX	34.07
206	Clarksville, TN	34.26
207	Bakersfield, CA	34.88
208	Arlington, TX	34.89
209	Bellflower, CA	34.93
210	Murfreesboro, TN	35.17
211	Lakeland, FL	35.18
212	Racine, WI	37.01
213	Topeka, KS	37.15
214	Springfield, MO	37.54
215	Independence, MO	37.56
216	San Antonio, TX	38.22
217	Long Beach, CA	38.28
218	Louisville, KY	39.20
219	Salinas, CA	39.52
220	Providence, RI	40.05
221	Las Cruces, NM	40.97
222	Omaha, NE	41.95
223	Modesto, CA	43.02
224	Worcester, MA	43.50
225	Aurora, CO	43.60
226	Ontario, CA	43.82
227	Fort Worth, TX	44.03
228	Melbourne, FL	46.44
229	Amarillo, TX	46.88
230	Gresham, OR	47.44
231	Moreno Valley, CA	47.97
232	Portland, OR	48.48
233	Hawthorne, CA	48.50
234	Palmdale, CA	48.68
235	Savannah, GA	48.82
236	Berkeley, CA	50.37
237	Victorville, CA	50.40
238	Hayward, CA	51.26
239	Federal Way, WA	51.54
240	Mobile, AL	52.37
241	Antioch, CA	52.42
242	Warren, MI	52.43
243	Lubbock, TX	52.43
244	Los Angeles, CA	53.49
245	Spokane, WA	54.14
246	Lowell, MA	54.62
247	Lynn, MA	54.96
248	Columbus, GA	56.19
249	Norfolk, VA	56.53
250	Pomona, CA	56.56
251	Newport News, VA	56.62
252	South Gate, CA	58.30
253	Rialto, CA	59.44
254	Anchorage, AK	59.58
255	Carson, CA	59.59
256	Waco, TX	60.28
257	High Point, NC	62.33
257	Wichita, KS	62.33

RANK	CITY	SCORE
259	Hammond, IN	62.37
260	Reno, NV	63.45
261	Glendale, AZ	64.73
262	Tempe, AZ	65.59
263	Columbia, SC	66.48
264	Jacksonville, FL	67.11
265	Elizabeth, NJ	69.36
266	Seattle, WA	69.55
267	Montgomery, AL	69.80
268	Grand Rapids, MI	70.38
269	Fresno, CA	70.44
270	Lansing, MI	72.11
271	Salt Lake City, UT	73.66
272	Killeen, TX	74.09
273	Albany, NY	74.78
274	Portsmouth, VA	75.76
275	Albany, GA	76.37
276	Durham, NC	76.63
277	Visalia, CA	76.73
278	Gainesville, FL	77.21
279	New Bedford, MA	78.08
280	San Francisco, CA	78.35
281	Yakima, WA	79.66
282	Charleston, SC	80.08
283	Syracuse, NY	80.72
284	Vallejo, CA	81.41
285	Knoxville, TN	81.60
286	Southfield, MI	81.82
287	Greensboro, NC	82.29
288	Roanoke, VA	82.31
289	Lafayette, LA	82.81
290	Paterson, NJ	82.83
291	Tallahassee, FL	83.65
292	Denver, CO	83.96
293	Jersey City, NJ	84.98
294	Tuscaloosa, AL	85.77
295	Albuquerque, NM	87.20
296	Beaumont, TX	88.11
297	San Leandro, CA	88.98
298	Lawton, OK	89.99
299	Lancaster, CA	90.19
300	Longview, TX	91.60
301	Wilmington, NC	92.42
302	Pompano Beach, FL	92.47
303	Huntsville, AL	93.15
304	Oklahoma City, OK	94.48
305	Tampa, FL	97.14
306	Fort Lauderdale, FL	97.38
307	Winston-Salem, NC	97.81
308	South Bend, IN	98.79
309	Tucson, AZ	99.53
310	Fort Smith, AR	103.05
311	Allentown, PA	104.24
312	Pittsburgh, PA	105.33
313	Everett, WA	105.51
314	New Orleans, LA	106.70
315	Phoenix, AZ	110.45
316	Boston, MA	112.08
317	North Las Vegas, NV	112.71
318	Chattanooga, TN	120.15
319	Kent, WA	120.74
320	Fayetteville, NC	124.93
321	Las Vegas, NV	126.89
322	Shreveport, LA	127.75
323	Nashville, TN	128.68
324	Bridgeport, CT	129.64

RANK	CITY	SCORE
325	St. Petersburg, FL	129.67
326	Miami Beach, FL	129.68
327	Rockford, IL	131.22
328	Inglewood, CA	131.39
329	Charlotte, NC	132.08
330	Tulsa, OK	133.33
331	Columbus, OH	135.97
332	Toledo, OH	136.72
333	Macon, GA	140.51
334	Indianapolis, IN	140.65
335	Houston, TX	141.34
336	Canton, OH	143.42
337	San Bernardino, CA	145.75
338	Sacramento, CA	147.25
339	West Palm Beach, FL	148.45
340	Trenton, NJ	150.30
341	Springfield, MA	150.73
342	Stockton, CA	151.08
343	Milwaukee, WI	151.65
344	Miami, FL	151.97
345	Dallas, TX	154.58
346	Tacoma, WA	156.29
347	Reading, PA	159.19
348	Hartford, CT	159.30
349	Rochester, NY	170.74
350	Richmond, VA	175.16
351	Baton Rouge, LA	179.55
352	Washington, DC	181.30
353	Miami Gardens, FL	181.41
354	Kansas City, KS	187.55
355	Buffalo, NY	187.84
356	Jackson, MS	188.81
357	Atlanta, GA	189.86
358	Philadelphia, PA	192.94
359	Newark, NJ	197.32
360	Dayton, OH	201.49
361	Kansas City, MO	203.43
362	Gary, IN	214.03
363	Cincinnati, OH	218.29
364	Youngstown, OH	221.96
365	Compton, CA	223.58
366	Little Rock, AR	233.84
367	Baltimore, MD	236.73
368	Orlando, FL	237.38
369	Cleveland, OH	244.41
370	Richmond, CA	245.07
371	Memphis, TN	245.56
372	North Charleston, SC	254.25
373	Birmingham, AL	268.82
374	Camden, NJ	323.81
375	Oakland, CA	338.87
376	Flint, MI	380.98
377	St. Louis, MO	406.15
378	Detroit, MI	407.15
NA	Aurora, IL**	NA
NA	Bloomington, MN**	NA
NA	Brockton, MA**	NA
NA	Chicago, IL**	NA
NA	Duluth, MN**	NA
NA	Joliet, IL**	NA
NA	Minneapolis, MN**	NA
NA	Naperville, IL**	NA
NA	Peoria, IL**	NA
NA	Rochester, MN**	NA
NA	Springfield, IL**	NA
NA	St. Paul, MN**	NA

Source: CQ Press using data from F.B.I. "Crime in the United States 2006"

**Includes murder, rape, robbery, aggravated assault, burglary, and motor vehicle theft. A negative score (in parentheses) indicates a composite crime number below the national rate, a positive number is above the national rate. **Not available.*

AMERICA'S SAFEST METROPOLITAN AREA

14th ANNUAL

14th Annual

Safest Metropolitan Area Award*

RANK	METROPOLITAN AREA	SCORE
158	Abilene, TX	(10.19)
76	Albany-Schenectady-Troy, NY	(35.82)
201	Albany, GA	3.21
318	Albuquerque, NM	65.01
321	Alexandria, LA	66.59
71	Altoona, PA	(37.00)
248	Amarillo, TX	21.04
40	Ames, IA	(44.86)
311	Anchorage, AK	57.08
289	Anderson, SC	39.08
98	Ann Arbor, MI	(30.73)
5	Appleton, WI	(66.53)
111	Asheville, NC	(26.54)
157	Athens-Clarke County, GA	(10.30)
NA	Atlanta, GA**	NA
227	Atlantic City, NJ	14.22
222	Augusta, GA-SC	11.90
119	Austin-Round Rock, TX	(25.15)
279	Bakersfield, CA	33.88
303	Baltimore-Towson, MD	47.00
4	Bangor, ME	(67.88)
NA	Barnstable Town, MA**	NA
315	Baton Rouge, LA	62.51
295	Battle Creek, MI	42.78
110	Bay City, MI	(26.89)
229	Beaumont-Port Arthur, TX	15.17
102	Bellingham, WA	(28.86)
54	Bend, OR	(40.90)
48	Bethesda-Frederick, MD M.D.	(43.87)
31	Billings, MT	(48.96)
25	Binghamton, NY	(53.64)
297	Birmingham-Hoover, AL	43.23
27	Bismarck, ND	(53.32)
84	Blacksburg, VA	(33.64)
52	Bloomington, IN	(41.42)
101	Boise City-Nampa, ID	(28.89)
150	Bowling Green, KY	(12.54)
196	Bremerton-Silverdale, WA	2.16
151	Brownsville-Harlingen, TX	(12.26)
249	Brunswick, GA	21.06
200	Buffalo-Niagara Falls, NY	2.76
161	Burlington, NC	(7.57)
121	Camden, NJ M.D.	(24.96)
256	Cape Coral-Fort Myers, FL	24.48
39	Carson City, NV	(45.36)
81	Casper, WY	(34.88)
41	Cedar Rapids, IA	(44.84)
314	Charleston-North Charleston, SC	60.60
170	Charleston, WV	(4.81)
NA	Charlotte-Gastonia, NC-SC**	NA
64	Charlottesville, VA	(38.69)
220	Chattanooga, TN-GA	9.57
55	Cheyenne, WY	(40.80)
NA	Chicago, IL**	NA
209	Chico, CA	6.07
178	Cincinnati-Middletown, OH-KY-IN	(2.35)
195	Clarksville, TN-KY	1.27
217	Cleveland-Elyria-Mentor, OH	8.89
146	Cleveland, TN	(13.77)
120	Coeur d'Alene, ID	(24.99)
176	College Station-Bryan, TX	(2.55)
207	Colorado Springs, CO	5.50
90	Columbia, MO	(32.40)
253	Columbia, SC	22.67
247	Columbus, GA-AL	20.97
38	Columbus, IN	(45.58)
268	Columbus, OH	29.18
239	Corpus Christi, TX	18.60
82	Cumberland, MD-WV	(34.49)
238	Dallas (greater), TX	17.86
257	Dallas-Plano-Irving, TX M.D.	25.20
77	Dalton, GA	(35.57)
63	Danville, VA	(38.75)
210	Daytona Beach, FL	6.48
189	Dayton, OH	(0.43)
131	Decatur, AL	(20.39)
218	Denver-Aurora, CO	9.07
86	Des Moines-West Des Moines, IA	(33.55)
316	Detroit (greater), MI	62.68
333	Detroit-Livonia-Dearborn, MI M.D.	176.50
192	Dothan, AL	0.28
221	Dover, DE	10.10
49	Dubuque, IA	(43.60)
NA	Duluth, MN-WI**	NA
243	Durham, NC	20.38
2	Eau Claire, WI	(71.06)
10	Edison, NJ M.D.	(61.36)
197	El Centro, CA	2.36
141	El Paso, TX	(14.77)
7	Elizabethtown, KY	(64.06)
139	Elkhart-Goshen, IN	(16.12)
26	Elmira, NY	(53.47)
68	Erie, PA	(37.65)
145	Eugene-Springfield, OR	(13.81)
56	Evansville, IN-KY	(40.24)
NA	Fairbanks, AK**	NA
NA	Fargo, ND-MN**	NA
203	Farmington, NM	3.48
132	Fayetteville, AR-MO	(19.89)
299	Fayetteville, NC	44.19
154	Flagstaff, AZ	(11.32)
330	Flint, MI	95.34
313	Florence, SC	59.69
20	Fond du Lac, WI	(55.67)
58	Fort Collins-Loveland, CO	(39.79)
205	Fort Lauderdale, FL M.D.	5.03
206	Fort Smith, AR-OK	5.33
99	Fort Walton Beach, FL	(29.39)
94	Fort Wayne, IN	(31.26)
202	Fort Worth-Arlington, TX M.D.	3.41
282	Fresno, CA	35.16
263	Gadsden, AL	26.69
310	Gainesville, FL	55.58
65	Gainesville, GA	(38.16)
15	Glens Falls, NY	(58.87)
185	Goldsboro, NC	(1.53)
NA	Grand Forks, ND-MN**	NA
117	Grand Junction, CO	(25.30)
160	Grand Rapids-Wyoming, MI	(9.02)
21	Great Falls, MT	(54.39)
126	Greeley, CO	(22.24)
23	Green Bay, WI	(54.09)
233	Greensboro-High Point, NC	16.15
274	Greenville, NC	33.10
246	Greenville, SC	20.75
61	Hagerstown-Martinsburg, MD-WV	(38.96)
112	Hanford-Corcoran, CA	(26.50)
70	Harrisburg-Carlisle, PA	(37.01)
28	Harrisonburg, VA	(51.48)
109	Hartford, CT	(27.05)
204	Hattiesburg, MS	4.25
46	Holland-Grand Haven, MI	(44.01)
138	Honolulu, HI	(16.87)
306	Hot Springs, AR	51.70
183	Houma, LA	(1.68)
301	Houston, TX	46.75
78	Huntington-Ashland, WV-KY-OH	(35.25)
250	Huntsville, AL	21.14
103	Idaho Falls, ID	(28.80)
286	Indianapolis, IN	37.57
42	Iowa City, IA	(44.78)
11	Ithaca, NY	(61.32)
NA	Jacksonville, FL**	NA
155	Jacksonville, NC	(11.27)
156	Jackson, MI	(11.09)
294	Jackson, MS	42.74
319	Jackson, TN	65.23
96	Janesville, WI	(30.81)
66	Jefferson City, MO	(38.08)
123	Johnson City, TN	(23.26)
32	Johnstown, PA	(48.56)
266	Jonesboro, AR	28.35
170	Joplin, MO	(4.81)
188	Kalamazoo-Portage, MI	(0.61)
276	Kansas City, MO-KS	33.49
88	Kennewick-Richland-Pasco, WA	(33.14)
NA	Killeen-Temple-Fort Hood, TX**	NA
140	Kingsport, TN-VA	(15.35)
33	Kingston, NY	(48.41)
177	Knoxville, TN	(2.40)
127	Kokomo, IN	(21.96)
NA	La Crosse, WI-MN**	NA
67	Lafayette, IN	(37.97)
317	Lake Charles, LA	63.75
194	Lake Havasu City-Kingman, AZ	1.24
216	Lakeland, FL	8.37
44	Lancaster, PA	(44.29)
152	Lansing-East Lansing, MI	(11.48)
265	Laredo, TX	27.85
180	Las Cruces, NM	(2.07)
331	Las Vegas-Paradise, NV	104.04

Note: All listings are for Metropolitan Statistical Areas (M.S.A.s) except for those ending with "M.D." Listings with "M.D." are Metropolitan Divisions which are smaller parts of ten large M.S.A.s. See explanatory note at beginning of metropolitan area section on page 23.

Alpha Order - Metro Area (continued)

RANK	METROPOLITAN AREA	SCORE
199	Lawrence, KS	2.56
312	Lawton, OK	59.12
74	Lebanon, PA	(36.04)
22	Lewiston-Auburn, ME	(54.30)
13	Lewiston, ID-WA	(59.95)
142	Lexington-Fayette, KY	(14.40)
264	Lima, OH	26.89
124	Lincoln, NE	(23.20)
325	Little Rock, AR	84.54
1	Logan, UT-ID	(72.45)
262	Longview, TX	26.65
270	Longview, WA	29.95
273	Los Angeles County, CA M.D.	32.29
231	Los Angeles (greater), CA	15.85
168	Louisville, KY-IN	(5.26)
284	Lubbock, TX	36.52
34	Lynchburg, VA	(48.18)
300	Macon, GA	45.56
164	Madera, CA	(6.70)
36	Madison, WI	(47.02)
14	Manchester-Nashua, NH	(59.11)
143	Mansfield, OH	(14.39)
147	McAllen-Edinburg-Mission, TX	(13.23)
35	Medford, OR	(48.06)
332	Memphis, TN-MS-AR	126.00
271	Merced, CA	31.05
292	Miami (greater), FL	40.53
324	Miami-Dade County, FL M.D.	70.55
106	Michigan City-La Porte, IN	(28.04)
153	Midland, TX	(11.33)
230	Milwaukee, WI	15.18
NA	Minneapolis-St. Paul, MN-WI**	NA
57	Missoula, MT	(40.23)
267	Mobile, AL	28.61
278	Modesto, CA	33.86
245	Monroe, LA	20.60
43	Monroe, MI	(44.74)
252	Montgomery, AL	22.20
80	Morgantown, WV	(34.92)
97	Morristown, TN	(30.79)
162	Mount Vernon-Anacortes, WA	(7.54)
148	Muncie, IN	(13.19)
225	Muskegon-Norton Shores, MI	13.43
327	Myrtle Beach, SC	85.29
72	Napa, CA	(36.16)
79	Naples-Marco Island, FL	(35.03)
275	Nashville-Davidson, TN	33.19
8	Nassau-Suffolk, NY M.D.	(62.57)
308	New Orleans, LA	54.64
107	New York (greater), NY-NJ-PA	(27.45)
137	New York-W. Plains NY-NJ M.D.	(16.95)
181	Newark-Union, NJ-PA M.D.	(1.96)
187	Niles-Benton Harbor, MI	(0.69)
323	Oakland-Fremont, CA M.D.	68.09
226	Ocala, FL	13.60
89	Ocean City, NJ	(33.07)
115	Odessa, TX	(25.98)
29	Ogden-Clearfield, UT	(50.16)
269	Oklahoma City, OK	29.54
87	Olympia, WA	(33.38)
191	Omaha-Council Bluffs, NE-IA	0.26
309	Orlando, FL	54.93
12	Oshkosh-Neenah, WI	(60.47)
51	Oxnard-Thousand Oaks, CA	(41.47)
211	Palm Bay-Melbourne, FL	6.71
50	Palm Coast, FL	(42.36)
237	Panama City-Lynn Haven, FL	17.80
219	Pascagoula, MS	9.40
208	Pensacola, FL	5.59
255	Philadelphia (greater) PA-NJ-DE	23.05
291	Philadelphia, PA M.D.	40.05
298	Phoenix-Mesa-Scottsdale, AZ	43.89
329	Pine Bluff, AR	87.51
95	Pittsburgh, PA	(31.17)
128	Pittsfield, MA	(21.72)
53	Pocatello, ID	(41.00)
166	Port St. Lucie, FL	(6.04)
136	Portland-Vancouver, OR-WA	(17.24)
19	Portland, ME	(56.32)
24	Poughkeepsie, NY	(54.06)
105	Prescott, AZ	(28.15)
6	Provo-Orem, UT	(64.59)
186	Pueblo, CO	(1.12)
84	Punta Gorda, FL	(33.64)
83	Racine, WI	(33.96)
116	Raleigh-Cary, NC	(25.58)
108	Rapid City, SD	(27.39)
130	Reading, PA	(21.37)
169	Redding, CA	(5.23)
244	Reno-Sparks, NV	20.42
167	Richmond, VA	(5.28)
241	Riverside-San Bernardino, CA	19.47
129	Roanoke, VA	(21.41)
NA	Rochester, MN**	NA
134	Rochester, NY	(18.85)
296	Rocky Mount, NC	43.10
175	Rome, GA	(3.12)
287	Sacramento, CA	37.87
328	Saginaw, MI	85.98
122	Salem, OR	(24.61)
174	Salinas, CA	(3.39)
304	Salisbury, MD	48.57
163	Salt Lake City, UT	(6.73)
159	San Angelo, TX	(9.62)
223	San Antonio, TX	12.90
212	San Diego, CA	7.17
302	San Francisco (greater), CA	46.85
232	San Francisco-S. Mateo, CA M.D.	15.94
118	San Jose, CA	(25.22)
60	San Luis Obispo, CA	(39.05)
45	Sandusky, OH	(44.15)
62	Santa Ana-Anaheim, CA M.D.	(38.83)
114	Santa Barbara-Santa Maria, CA	(25.99)
184	Santa Cruz-Watsonville, CA	(1.55)
259	Santa Fe, NM	25.41
113	Santa Rosa-Petaluma, CA	(26.29)
214	Sarasota-Bradenton-Venice, FL	7.90
NA	Savannah, GA**	NA
59	Scranton--Wilkes-Barre, PA	(39.74)
260	Seattle (greater), WA	25.56
251	Seattle-Bellevue, WA M.D.	21.39
125	Sebastian-Vero Beach, FL	(22.31)
18	Sheboygan, WI	(57.98)
47	Sherman-Denison, TX	(44.01)
326	Shreveport-Bossier City, LA	85.17
73	Sioux City, IA-NE-SD	(36.14)
92	Sioux Falls, SD	(31.81)
182	South Bend-Mishawaka, IN-MI	(1.86)
254	Spartanburg, SC	23.01
198	Spokane, WA	2.40
NA	Springfield, MA**	NA
133	Springfield, MO	(19.65)
280	Springfield, OH	34.46
3	State College, PA	(68.57)
322	Stockton, CA	67.88
NA	St. Cloud, MN**	NA
75	St. Joseph, MO-KS	(36.01)
213	St. Louis, MO-IL	7.56
320	Sumter, SC	66.39
69	Syracuse, NY	(37.26)
290	Tacoma, WA M.D.	39.25
285	Tallahassee, FL	37.34
258	Tampa-St Petersburg, FL	25.27
293	Texarkana, TX-Texarkana, AR	40.63
261	Toledo, OH	26.33
190	Topeka, KS	0.19
149	Trenton-Ewing, NJ	(13.17)
305	Tucson, AZ	48.60
272	Tulsa, OK	32.10
283	Tuscaloosa, AL	36.11
144	Tyler, TX	(13.91)
30	Utica-Rome, NY	(49.10)
135	Valdosta, GA	(18.82)
234	Vallejo-Fairfield, CA	16.24
172	Victoria, TX	(4.27)
288	Vineland, NJ	37.93
178	Virginia Beach-Norfolk, VA-NC	(2.35)
307	Visalia-Porterville, CA	53.45
235	Waco, TX	17.52
100	Warner Robins, GA	(29.22)
104	Warren-Farmington Hills, MI M.D.	(28.69)
193	Washington (greater) DC-VA-MD	0.74
224	Washington, DC-VA-MD-WV M.D.	13.15
91	Waterloo-Cedar Falls, IA	(32.13)
9	Wausau, WI	(62.36)
37	Wenatchee, WA	(46.49)
277	West Palm Beach, FL M.D.	33.67
16	Wheeling, WV-OH	(58.79)
165	Wichita Falls, TX	(6.08)
242	Wichita, KS	19.75
17	Williamsport, PA	(58.77)
228	Wilmington, DE-MD-NJ M.D.	14.58
236	Wilmington, NC	17.72
93	Winchester, VA-WV	(31.53)
240	Winston-Salem, NC	18.66
NA	Worcester, MA**	NA
281	Yakima, WA	34.47
215	Yuba City, CA	8.05
173	Yuma, AZ	(3.94)

Source: CQ Press using data from Federal Bureau of Investigation "Crime in the United States 2006" (Uniform Crime Reports, September 24, 2007)

**Includes murder, rape, robbery, aggravated assault, burglary, and motor vehicle theft. A negative score (in parentheses) indicates a composite crime number below the national rate, a positive number is above the national rate. **Not available.*

14th Annual

Safest Metropolitan Area Award (continued)*

RANK	METROPOLITAN AREA	SCORE
1	Logan, UT-ID	(72.45)
2	Eau Claire, WI	(71.06)
3	State College, PA	(68.57)
4	Bangor, ME	(67.88)
5	Appleton, WI	(66.53)
6	Provo-Orem, UT	(64.59)
7	Elizabethtown, KY	(64.06)
8	Nassau-Suffolk, NY M.D.	(62.57)
9	Wausau, WI	(62.36)
10	Edison, NJ M.D.	(61.36)
11	Ithaca, NY	(61.32)
12	Oshkosh-Neenah, WI	(60.47)
13	Lewiston, ID-WA	(59.95)
14	Manchester-Nashua, NH	(59.11)
15	Glens Falls, NY	(58.87)
16	Wheeling, WV-OH	(58.79)
17	Williamsport, PA	(58.77)
18	Sheboygan, WI	(57.98)
19	Portland, ME	(56.32)
20	Fond du Lac, WI	(55.67)
21	Great Falls, MT	(54.39)
22	Lewiston-Auburn, ME	(54.30)
23	Green Bay, WI	(54.09)
24	Poughkeepsie, NY	(54.06)
25	Binghamton, NY	(53.64)
26	Elmira, NY	(53.47)
27	Bismarck, ND	(53.32)
28	Harrisonburg, VA	(51.48)
29	Ogden-Clearfield, UT	(50.16)
30	Utica-Rome, NY	(49.10)
31	Billings, MT	(48.96)
32	Johnstown, PA	(48.56)
33	Kingston, NY	(48.41)
34	Lynchburg, VA	(48.18)
35	Medford, OR	(48.06)
36	Madison, WI	(47.02)
37	Wenatchee, WA	(46.49)
38	Columbus, IN	(45.58)
39	Carson City, NV	(45.36)
40	Ames, IA	(44.86)
41	Cedar Rapids, IA	(44.84)
42	Iowa City, IA	(44.78)
43	Monroe, MI	(44.74)
44	Lancaster, PA	(44.29)
45	Sandusky, OH	(44.15)
46	Holland-Grand Haven, MI	(44.01)
47	Sherman-Denison, TX	(44.01)
48	Bethesda-Frederick, MD M.D.	(43.87)
49	Dubuque, IA	(43.60)
50	Palm Coast, FL	(42.36)
51	Oxnard-Thousand Oaks, CA	(41.47)
52	Bloomington, IN	(41.42)
53	Pocatello, ID	(41.00)
54	Bend, OR	(40.90)
55	Cheyenne, WY	(40.80)
56	Evansville, IN-KY	(40.24)
57	Missoula, MT	(40.23)
58	Fort Collins-Loveland, CO	(39.79)
59	Scranton--Wilkes-Barre, PA	(39.74)
60	San Luis Obispo, CA	(39.05)
61	Hagerstown-Martinsburg, MD-WV	(38.96)
62	Santa Ana-Anaheim, CA M.D.	(38.83)
63	Danville, VA	(38.75)
64	Charlottesville, VA	(38.69)
65	Gainesville, GA	(38.16)
66	Jefferson City, MO	(38.08)
67	Lafayette, IN	(37.97)
68	Erie, PA	(37.65)
69	Syracuse, NY	(37.26)
70	Harrisburg-Carlisle, PA	(37.01)
71	Altoona, PA	(37.00)
72	Napa, CA	(36.16)
73	Sioux City, IA-NE-SD	(36.14)
74	Lebanon, PA	(36.04)
75	St. Joseph, MO-KS	(36.01)
76	Albany-Schenectady-Troy, NY	(35.82)
77	Dalton, GA	(35.57)
78	Huntington-Ashland, WV-KY-OH	(35.25)
79	Naples-Marco Island, FL	(35.03)
80	Morgantown, WV	(34.92)
81	Casper, WY	(34.88)
82	Cumberland, MD-WV	(34.49)
83	Racine, WI	(33.96)
84	Blacksburg, VA	(33.64)
84	Punta Gorda, FL	(33.64)
86	Des Moines-West Des Moines, IA	(33.55)
87	Olympia, WA	(33.38)
88	Kennewick-Richland-Pasco, WA	(33.14)
89	Ocean City, NJ	(33.07)
90	Columbia, MO	(32.40)
91	Waterloo-Cedar Falls, IA	(32.13)
92	Sioux Falls, SD	(31.81)
93	Winchester, VA-WV	(31.53)
94	Fort Wayne, IN	(31.26)
95	Pittsburgh, PA	(31.17)
96	Janesville, WI	(30.81)
97	Morristown, TN	(30.79)
98	Ann Arbor, MI	(30.73)
99	Fort Walton Beach, FL	(29.39)
100	Warner Robins, GA	(29.22)
101	Boise City-Nampa, ID	(28.89)
102	Bellingham, WA	(28.86)
103	Idaho Falls, ID	(28.80)
104	Warren-Farmington Hills, MI M.D.	(28.69)
105	Prescott, AZ	(28.15)
106	Michigan City-La Porte, IN	(28.04)
107	New York (greater), NY-NJ-PA	(27.45)
108	Rapid City, SD	(27.39)
109	Hartford, CT	(27.05)
110	Bay City, MI	(26.89)
111	Asheville, NC	(26.54)
112	Hanford-Corcoran, CA	(26.50)
113	Santa Rosa-Petaluma, CA	(26.29)
114	Santa Barbara-Santa Maria, CA	(25.99)
115	Odessa, TX	(25.98)
116	Raleigh-Cary, NC	(25.58)
117	Grand Junction, CO	(25.30)
118	San Jose, CA	(25.22)
119	Austin-Round Rock, TX	(25.15)
120	Coeur d'Alene, ID	(24.99)
121	Camden, NJ M.D.	(24.96)
122	Salem, OR	(24.61)
123	Johnson City, TN	(23.26)
124	Lincoln, NE	(23.20)
125	Sebastian-Vero Beach, FL	(22.31)
126	Greeley, CO	(22.24)
127	Kokomo, IN	(21.96)
128	Pittsfield, MA	(21.72)
129	Roanoke, VA	(21.41)
130	Reading, PA	(21.37)
131	Decatur, AL	(20.39)
132	Fayetteville, AR-MO	(19.89)
133	Springfield, MO	(19.65)
134	Rochester, NY	(18.85)
135	Valdosta, GA	(18.82)
136	Portland-Vancouver, OR-WA	(17.24)
137	New York-W. Plains NY-NJ M.D.	(16.95)
138	Honolulu, HI	(16.87)
139	Elkhart-Goshen, IN	(16.12)
140	Kingsport, TN-VA	(15.35)
141	El Paso, TX	(14.77)
142	Lexington-Fayette, KY	(14.40)
143	Mansfield, OH	(14.39)
144	Tyler, TX	(13.91)
145	Eugene-Springfield, OR	(13.81)
146	Cleveland, TN	(13.77)
147	McAllen-Edinburg-Mission, TX	(13.23)
148	Muncie, IN	(13.19)
149	Trenton-Ewing, NJ	(13.17)
150	Bowling Green, KY	(12.54)
151	Brownsville-Harlingen, TX	(12.26)
152	Lansing-East Lansing, MI	(11.48)
153	Midland, TX	(11.33)
154	Flagstaff, AZ	(11.32)
155	Jacksonville, NC	(11.27)
156	Jackson, MI	(11.09)
157	Athens-Clarke County, GA	(10.30)
158	Abilene, TX	(10.19)
159	San Angelo, TX	(9.62)
160	Grand Rapids-Wyoming, MI	(9.02)
161	Burlington, NC	(7.57)
162	Mount Vernon-Anacortes, WA	(7.54)
163	Salt Lake City, UT	(6.73)
164	Madera, CA	(6.70)
165	Wichita Falls, TX	(6.08)
166	Port St. Lucie, FL	(6.04)
167	Richmond, VA	(5.28)
168	Louisville, KY-IN	(5.26)
169	Redding, CA	(5.23)
170	Charleston, WV	(4.81)
170	Joplin, MO	(4.81)

Note: All listings are for Metropolitan Statistical Areas (M.S.A.s) except for those ending with "M.D." Listings with "M.D." are Metropolitan Divisions which are smaller parts of ten large M.S.A.s. See explanatory note at beginning of metropolitan area section on page 23.

RANK	METROPOLITAN AREA	SCORE
172	Victoria, TX	(4.27)
173	Yuma, AZ	(3.94)
174	Salinas, CA	(3.39)
175	Rome, GA	(3.12)
176	College Station-Bryan, TX	(2.55)
177	Knoxville, TN	(2.40)
178	Cincinnati-Middletown, OH-KY-IN	(2.35)
178	Virginia Beach-Norfolk, VA-NC	(2.35)
180	Las Cruces, NM	(2.07)
181	Newark-Union, NJ-PA M.D.	(1.96)
182	South Bend-Mishawaka, IN-MI	(1.86)
183	Houma, LA	(1.68)
184	Santa Cruz-Watsonville, CA	(1.55)
185	Goldsboro, NC	(1.53)
186	Pueblo, CO	(1.12)
187	Niles-Benton Harbor, MI	(0.69)
188	Kalamazoo-Portage, MI	(0.61)
189	Dayton, OH	(0.43)
190	Topeka, KS	0.19
191	Omaha-Council Bluffs, NE-IA	0.26
192	Dothan, AL	0.28
193	Washington (greater) DC-VA-MD	0.74
194	Lake Havasu City-Kingman, AZ	1.24
195	Clarksville, TN-KY	1.27
196	Bremerton-Silverdale, WA	2.16
197	El Centro, CA	2.36
198	Spokane, WA	2.40
199	Lawrence, KS	2.56
200	Buffalo-Niagara Falls, NY	2.76
201	Albany, GA	3.21
202	Fort Worth-Arlington, TX M.D.	3.41
203	Farmington, NM	3.48
204	Hattiesburg, MS	4.25
205	Fort Lauderdale, FL M.D.	5.03
206	Fort Smith, AR-OK	5.33
207	Colorado Springs, CO	5.50
208	Pensacola, FL	5.59
209	Chico, CA	6.07
210	Daytona Beach, FL	6.48
211	Palm Bay-Melbourne, FL	6.71
212	San Diego, CA	7.17
213	St. Louis, MO-IL	7.56
214	Sarasota-Bradenton-Venice, FL	7.90
215	Yuba City, CA	8.05
216	Lakeland, FL	8.37
217	Cleveland-Elyria-Mentor, OH	8.89
218	Denver-Aurora, CO	9.07
219	Pascagoula, MS	9.40
220	Chattanooga, TN-GA	9.57
221	Dover, DE	10.10
222	Augusta, GA-SC	11.90
223	San Antonio, TX	12.90
224	Washington, DC-VA-MD-WV M.D.	13.15
225	Muskegon-Norton Shores, MI	13.43
226	Ocala, FL	13.60
227	Atlantic City, NJ	14.22
228	Wilmington, DE-MD-NJ M.D.	14.58
229	Beaumont-Port Arthur, TX	15.17
230	Milwaukee, WI	15.18
231	Los Angeles (greater), CA	15.85

RANK	METROPOLITAN AREA	SCORE
232	San Francisco-S. Mateo, CA M.D.	15.94
233	Greensboro-High Point, NC	16.15
234	Vallejo-Fairfield, CA	16.24
235	Waco, TX	17.52
236	Wilmington, NC	17.72
237	Panama City-Lynn Haven, FL	17.80
238	Dallas (greater), TX	17.86
239	Corpus Christi, TX	18.60
240	Winston-Salem, NC	18.66
241	Riverside-San Bernardino, CA	19.47
242	Wichita, KS	19.75
243	Durham, NC	20.38
244	Reno-Sparks, NV	20.42
245	Monroe, LA	20.60
246	Greenville, SC	20.75
247	Columbus, GA-AL	20.97
248	Amarillo, TX	21.04
249	Brunswick, GA	21.06
250	Huntsville, AL	21.14
251	Seattle-Bellevue, WA M.D.	21.39
252	Montgomery, AL	22.20
253	Columbia, SC	22.67
254	Spartanburg, SC	23.01
255	Philadelphia (greater) PA-NJ-DE	23.05
256	Cape Coral-Fort Myers, FL	24.48
257	Dallas-Plano-Irving, TX M.D.	25.20
258	Tampa-St Petersburg, FL	25.27
259	Santa Fe, NM	25.41
260	Seattle (greater), WA	25.56
261	Toledo, OH	26.33
262	Longview, TX	26.65
263	Gadsden, AL	26.69
264	Lima, OH	26.89
265	Laredo, TX	27.85
266	Jonesboro, AR	28.35
267	Mobile, AL	28.61
268	Columbus, OH	29.18
269	Oklahoma City, OK	29.54
270	Longview, WA	29.95
271	Merced, CA	31.05
272	Tulsa, OK	32.10
273	Los Angeles County, CA M.D.	32.29
274	Greenville, NC	33.10
275	Nashville-Davidson, TN	33.19
276	Kansas City, MO-KS	33.49
277	West Palm Beach, FL M.D.	33.67
278	Modesto, CA	33.86
279	Bakersfield, CA	33.88
280	Springfield, OH	34.46
281	Yakima, WA	34.47
282	Fresno, CA	35.16
283	Tuscaloosa, AL	36.11
284	Lubbock, TX	36.52
285	Tallahassee, FL	37.34
286	Indianapolis, IN	37.57
287	Sacramento, CA	37.87
288	Vineland, NJ	37.93
289	Anderson, SC	39.08
290	Tacoma, WA M.D.	39.25
291	Philadelphia, PA M.D.	40.05

RANK	METROPOLITAN AREA	SCORE
292	Miami (greater), FL	40.53
293	Texarkana, TX-Texarkana, AR	40.63
294	Jackson, MS	42.74
295	Battle Creek, MI	42.78
296	Rocky Mount, NC	43.10
297	Birmingham-Hoover, AL	43.23
298	Phoenix-Mesa-Scottsdale, AZ	43.89
299	Fayetteville, NC	44.19
300	Macon, GA	45.56
301	Houston, TX	46.75
302	San Francisco (greater), CA	46.85
303	Baltimore-Towson, MD	47.00
304	Salisbury, MD	48.57
305	Tucson, AZ	48.60
306	Hot Springs, AR	51.70
307	Visalia-Porterville, CA	53.45
308	New Orleans, LA	54.64
309	Orlando, FL	54.93
310	Gainesville, FL	55.58
311	Anchorage, AK	57.08
312	Lawton, OK	59.12
313	Florence, SC	59.69
314	Charleston-North Charleston, SC	60.60
315	Baton Rouge, LA	62.51
316	Detroit (greater), MI	62.68
317	Lake Charles, LA	63.75
318	Albuquerque, NM	65.01
319	Jackson, TN	65.23
320	Sumter, SC	66.39
321	Alexandria, LA	66.59
322	Stockton, CA	67.88
323	Oakland-Fremont, CA M.D.	68.09
324	Miami-Dade County, FL M.D.	70.55
325	Little Rock, AR	84.54
326	Shreveport-Bossier City, LA	85.17
327	Myrtle Beach, SC	85.29
328	Saginaw, MI	85.98
329	Pine Bluff, AR	87.51
330	Flint, MI	95.34
331	Las Vegas-Paradise, NV	104.04
332	Memphis, TN-MS-AR	126.00
333	Detroit-Livonia-Dearborn, MI M.D.	176.50
NA	Atlanta, GA**	NA
NA	Barnstable Town, MA**	NA
NA	Charlotte-Gastonia, NC-SC**	NA
NA	Chicago, IL**	NA
NA	Duluth, MN-WI**	NA
NA	Fairbanks, AK**	NA
NA	Fargo, ND-MN**	NA
NA	Grand Forks, ND-MN**	NA
NA	Jacksonville, FL**	NA
NA	Killeen-Temple-Fort Hood, TX**	NA
NA	La Crosse, WI-MN**	NA
NA	Minneapolis-St. Paul, MN-WI**	NA
NA	Rochester, MN**	NA
NA	Savannah, GA**	NA
NA	Springfield, MA**	NA
NA	St. Cloud, MN**	NA
NA	Worcester, MA**	NA

Source: CQ Press using data from Federal Bureau of Investigation "Crime in the United States 2006" (Uniform Crime Reports, September 24, 2007)

**Includes murder, rape, robbery, aggravated assault, burglary, and motor vehicle theft. A negative score (in parentheses) indicates a composite crime number below the national rate, a positive number is above the national rate. **Not available.*

Missing Cities and Metro Areas

In order to be included in the 14th Annual Safest City and Safest Metropolitan Area Award rankings, cities and metro areas must report data for six crime categories: murder, rape, robbery, aggravated assault, burglary, and motor vehicle theft. Complete crime information for 2006 was not available for a number of cities and metropolitan areas. These details are outlined below.

Cities. The data collection method used by the states of Illinois and Minnesota for the offense of forcible rape did not meet the Federal Bureau of Investigation's Uniform Crime Reporting (UCR) guidelines in 2006 (Rockford, IL, is an exception). As those rape numbers are not available, the following cities are not included in our Safest City rankings: Aurora, IL; Chicago, IL; Joliet, IL; Naperville, IL; Peoria, IL; Springfield, IL; Bloomington, MN; Duluth, MN; Minneapolis, MN; Rochester, MN; and St Paul, MN.

In addition, aggravated assault data were not available for Brockton, MA, making this city ineligible for the Safest City Award rankings.

The FBI did not report crime data for 16 other cities with populations larger than 75,000. Crime statistics for these cities were unavailable for a number of reasons, ranging from general reporting difficulties and computer issues to changes in reporting systems. Below is a list of cities with populations greater than 75,000 (according to the U.S. Census Bureau) but for which no information was available in the FBI's 2006 Uniform Crime Report.

Akron, OH	Citrus Heights, IL	Elgin, IL	Longmont, CO
Augusta, GA	Davenport, IA	Elk Grove, CA	New Haven, CT
Avondale, AZ	Decatur, IL	Evanston, IL	Norwalk, CT
Cicero, IL	Deltona, FL	Fall River, MA	Stamford, CT

Metropolitan areas. As explained above, forcible rape data were not available for metropolitan areas in Minnesota and Illinois. Rape statistics for Killeen-Temple-Fort Hood, TX, also did not meet UCR guidelines and therefore were not reported. Burglary data were not available for the Atlanta-Sandy Springs-Marietta, GA, metro area. Aggravated assault statistics were not reported for Barnstable Town, MA; Springfield, MA; Worcester, MA; Charlotte-Gastonia-Concord, NC-SC; Jacksonville, FL; and Savannah, GA.

The FBI did not report 2006 crime data for these metropolitan areas: Akron, OH; Allentown-Bethlehem-Easton, PA-NJ; Anderson, IN; Anniston-Oxford, AL; Auburn-Opelika, AL; Bloomington-Normal, IL; Boston-Cambridge-Quincy, MA; Boulder, CO: Bridgeport-Stamford-Norwalk, CT; Burlington-South Burlington, VT; Canton-Massillon, OH; Champaign-Urbana, IL; Chicago-Naperville-Joliet, IL-IN-WI; Corvallis, OR; Danville, IL; Davenport-Moline-Rock Island, IA-IL; Decatur, IL; Florence-Muscle Shoals, AL; Gulfport-Biloxi, MS; Hickory-Lenoir-Morganton, NC; Hinesville-Fort Stewart, GA; Kankakee-Bradley, IL; Lafayette, LA; New Haven-Milford, CT; Norwich-New London, CT; Owensboro, KY; Parkersburg-Marietta-Vienna, WV-OH; Peoria, IL; Providence-New Bedford-Fall River, RI-MA; Rockford, IL; St. George, UT; Springfield, IL; Terre Haute, IN; Weirton-Steubenville, WV-OH; York-Hanover, PA; and Youngstown-Warren-Boardman, OH-PA.

An Overview of 2006 Crime

Final data from the Federal Bureau of Investigation (FBI) indicate that violent crime increased in 2006, while property crime fell. Incidents of violent crime rose 1.9 percent from 2005 to 2006, and the nation's violent crime rate rose 1 percent. Conversely, property crime numbers declined 1.9 percent in that same one-year period, and the property crime rate dropped 2.8 percent. This overview provides definitions, basic facts, and brief summaries about violent crime and property crime, as well as their subcategories, as they occurred in 2006. Also included here is a statistical overview of the police officers serving the nation's cities.

Total Crime and Changes in the UCR Program

Crimes are reported by police agencies to the FBI as part of the Uniform Crime Reporting (UCR) Program. Approximately 17,500 city, county, and state law enforcement agencies participate in the program. Law enforcement agencies active in the program represented 94 percent of the total U.S. population in 2006.

The crimes tracked by the UCR program include violent crimes of murder, rape, robbery, and aggravated assault, and property crimes of burglary, larceny and theft, and motor vehicle theft. These numbers are also called "Crime Index" offenses; the Crime Index is simply the total of the seven main offense categories. The FBI discontinued use of this measure in 2004, its officials and advisory board of criminologists having concluded that the index was no longer a true indicator of crime. They contend that the Crime Index was inflated by a high number of larceny-thefts, which account for nearly 60 percent of reported crime, therefore diminishing the focus on more serious but less frequently committed offenses, such as murder and rape. The consensus of the FBI and its advisory groups was that the Crime Index no longer served its purpose and that a more meaningful index should be developed, which it has not yet done.

While the FBI considers whether it will replace the Crime Index, *City Crime Rankings* continues to provide crime numbers, rates, and trends for U.S. cities and metropolitan areas as a service to readers. However, with these data we offer a cautionary note that 88 percent of reported crimes are larceny-thefts and other property crimes, while the remaining 12 percent consist of violent crimes of murder, rape, robbery, and aggravated assault.

A crime occurred in the United States every 2.8 seconds in 2006, for a total of 11,401,313 offenses. Larcenies and thefts accounted for 57.9 percent of these offenses, burglaries accounted for 19.1 percent, motor vehicle thefts for 10.5 percent, aggravated assaults for 7.6 percent, robberies for 3.9 percent, forcible rapes for 0.8 percent, and murders for 0.1 percent. The 2006 total crime rate of 3808 crimes per 100,000 people is 2.3 percent lower than in 2005.

Violent Crime

Violent crimes include offenses of murder, forcible rape, robbery, and aggravated assault. A total of 1,417,745 such crimes were committed in 2006. Of these, 60.7 percent were aggravated assaults, 31.6 percent were robberies, 6.5 percent were forcible rapes, and 1.2 percent were murders. The 2006 national violent crime rate was 473.5 violent crimes per 100,000 population, a 1 percent increase from 2005.

Five- and ten-year trends show the 2006 violent crime rate was 4.2 percent lower than it was in 2002 and 22.5 percent lower than in 1997. Actual numbers of violent crimes were lower as well, down 0.4 percent from 2002 and 13.3 percent from 1997.

Among those violent crimes for which weapons information was available, firearms were involved in 67.9 percent of murders, 42.2 percent of robberies, and 21.9 percent of aggravated assaults.

Murder

Murder and nonnegligent manslaughter, as defined by the FBI, involve the willful (nonnegligent) killing of one human being by another. Up 0.8 percent from 2005, the national murder rate in 2006 was 5.7 murders per 100,000 population, or 17,034 murders total. Five-year trends show the 2006 murder rate was 1 percent higher than in 2002. A ten-year comparison shows a drop of 16.3 percent from levels recorded in 1997.

Of those murders for which complete weapons data were available, 67.9 percent involved firearms. FBI data showed that 16.3 percent of murders were committed in conjunction with felonious activities such as robberies, drug deals, and rapes. Strangers committed slightly more than 23 percent of murders in 2006. Nearly 79 percent of murder victims were male, 47.1 percent were white, and 50.2 percent were black.

Gary, Indiana had the highest murder rate in 2006. Gary's murder rate of 48.3 murders per 100,000 population was well above the national rate of 5.7 murders per 100,000 population.

Forcible Rape

Forcible rape, as defined by the FBI, is the carnal knowledge of a female forcibly and against her will. While the definition includes assaults or attempts to commit rape by force or threat of force, it does not include statutory rape (without force) or other sex offenses.

An estimated 60.9 of every 100,000 females in the United States were reported rape victims in 2006. Although the FBI's definition of rape is limited to female victims, the 2006 national rape rate of 30.9 per 100,000 applies to the entire U.S. population, both males and females. This national rape rate was 3 percent lower than in 2005 and 6.6 percent lower than in 2002. A rape occurred every 5.7 minutes in 2006.

A total of 92,455 rapes were reported to the FBI by law enforcement agencies in 2006. Of that total, 91.9 percent constituted rapes by force. The remainder included attempts or assaults to commit forcible rape.

Robbery

Robbery is the taking or attempt to take anything by force or threat of force. The 447,403 robberies that occurred in 2006 represented an increase of 7.2 percent from levels recorded in 2005. The national rate of 149.4 robberies per 100,000 people is higher as well, having increased 6.1 percent from 2005.

The average dollar loss per robbery was $1,268. Banks lost an average of $4,330 per robbery. Forty-five percent of robberies occurred on streets or highways, 21.9 percent took place in commercial establishments, 14.3 percent were at residences, and 2.1 percent were at banks. The remaining robbery locations were termed "miscellaneous."

Firearms of various types were used in 42.2 percent of robberies in 2006. Strong-arm tactics were used in 39.9 percent of robberies, knives or cutting instruments were used in 8.6 percent, and other dangerous weapons were involved in the remaining 9.2 percent.

Aggravated Assault

Aggravated assault is the unlawful attack by one person upon another for the purpose of inflicting severe bodily injury. This type of assault usually involves the use of a dangerous weapon. The FBI aggravated assault data includes attempts.

The 860,853 aggravated assaults that occurred in 2006 represent a 0.2 percent decrease from 2005 levels. The nation's 2006 rate of 287.5 aggravated assaults per 100,000 population is a 1.1 percent decrease from 2005. Aggravated assault rates fell 7.1 percent from 2002 levels and 24.8 percent from 1997 levels.

Assailants chose a variety of weapons with which to carry out their attacks in 2006. Slightly more than 34.5 percent of assaults were committed with blunt objects (e.g., clubs), 24.8 percent with "personal weapons" (e.g., hands or feet), 21.9 percent with firearms, and 18.7 percent with knives. An assault occurred every 36.6 seconds in 2006.

Property Crime

Property crime includes the crimes of burglary, larceny-theft, motor vehicle theft, and arson. These offenses involve the taking of money or property, but there is no force or threat of force against the victims. While arson is considered a property crime, data for arson offenses are not included in this book. The vast majority of crimes committed in the United States are property crimes; in 2006 they accounted for approximately 88 percent of all crimes reported.

A property crime occurred every 3.2 seconds in the United States in 2006, for a total of 9,983,568 offenses. The national property crime rate measured 3,334.5 property crimes per 100,000 population. Property crime decreased from 2005 to 2006 in both number and rate: the number of property crimes fell 1.9 percent from 2005, while the rate decreased 2.8 percent. Five-year trends show that property crime rates decreased 8.2 percent from 2002. A ten-year comparison shows a decline of 22.7 percent from 1997.

Property crimes accounted for an estimated $17.6 billion in losses in 2006. Larceny-thefts accounted for 66.2 percent of all property crimes, burglaries for 21.9 percent, and motor vehicle thefts for 11.9 percent.

Burglary

Burglary is defined as the unlawful entry of a structure to commit a felony or theft. The use of force to gain entry is not required for an offense to be classified as burglary. The FBI tracks data for three types of burglaries: forcible entry, unlawful entry where no force is used, and attempted forcible entry. Burglary accounted for 21.9 percent of the estimated number of property crimes committed in 2006.

A total of 2,183,746 burglaries were reported in 2006. The year's burglary rate of 729.4 burglaries per 100,000 population is 0.3 percent higher than in 2005. Five- and ten-year trends show that burglary rates have decreased 2.4 percent since 2002 and decreased 20.6 percent since 1997.

The majority of burglaries in 2006 were residential and the majority of those--63.1 percent--occurred during the daytime. By comparison, 56.7 percent of nonresidential burglaries occurred at night. A burglary occurred every 14.4 seconds in 2006, with an average dollar loss of $1,834 per incident.

Larceny and Theft

Larceny and theft is the unlawful taking of property from another person. It includes crimes such as shoplifting, pick-pocketing, purse-snatching, thefts from motor vehicles, thefts of motor vehicle parts and accessories, and bicycle thefts. No use of force, violence, or fraud is involved in these offenses. This category does not include embezzlement, "con" games, forgery, or worthless check writing.

A total of 6,607,013 thefts occurred in 2006, down 2.6 percent from 2005. This number represents 57.9 percent of the total number of crimes reported for the year. The national rate of 2,206.8 larcenies and thefts per 100,000 population represents a 3.5 percent decrease from 2005 levels. Five- and ten-year trends show that larceny-theft rates have decreased 10 percent since 2002 and are down 23.7 percent from 1997.

The average value of property stolen in 2006 was $855, an 11.9 percent increase from the 2005 value of $764.

Motor Vehicle Theft

The motor vehicle theft category includes the stealing of automobiles, trucks, buses, motorcycles, motor scooters, snowmobiles, etc. The definition does not include the taking of a motor vehicle for temporary use by those persons having lawful access to the vehicle.

A total of 1,192,809 motor vehicle thefts were committed in 2006. This represents a 3.5 percent decrease from 2005. The national rate of 398.4 vehicles stolen per 100,000 population represents a decrease of 4.4 percent from the prior year.

A motor vehicle theft occurred every 26.4 seconds in 2006. The total estimated value of these thefts was $7.9 billion, or an average of $6,649 per stolen vehicle. Automobiles were the most frequently stolen vehicle type, accounting for 73.5 percent of all those stolen.

Police Officers

Nationwide, a total of 683,396 sworn police officers were on the job in 2006, with an additional 303,729 civilian employees assisting. This equates to 2.4 full-time officers per 1,000 population.

Only police officers on each city's primary police force are reported in this volume. Many cities have a number of overlapping law enforcement agencies. For example, New York City has its Transit Police, Port Authority Police, and officials in other special law enforcement agencies. Those officers are not covered in *City Crime Rankings*.

Miscellaneous Notes Regarding City and Metro Crime Data

- 2006 crime statistics are not comparable to previous years' data for these cities with populations greater than 75,000: Rockford, IL; Fort Wayne, IN; Des Moines, IA; El Paso, TX; St. Joseph, MO; and Kansas City, MO. Accordingly, one- and five-year crime rate trends are not available for these cities.

- 2006 crime statistics are not comparable to previous years' data for these metro areas: Abilene, TX; Des Moines-West Des Moines, IA; Durham, NC; Fort Wayne, IN; Hattiesburg, MS; Jacksonville, NC; Kansas City, MO-KS; Lexington-Fayette, KY; and Washington-Arlington-Alexandria, DC-VA-MD-WV. As a result, one- and five-year trends are not available for these metro areas.

- The population estimates reported in *City Crime Rankings,* 14th Edition, are provided by the FBI. These estimates sometimes differ from those reported by the U.S. Census Bureau.

- Forcible rape data reported to the Uniform Crime Reporting (UCR) Program by the states of Illinois (with the exception of Rockford) and Minnesota were not in accordance with national UCR guidelines. Therefore, these numbers are not available for cities and metro areas in these two states.

- Larceny-theft data are not reported for Tucson, AZ, because they did not meet UCR guidelines. Thus this information, as well as property crime statistics, is not available for this city.

- The Hamilton Township, NJ, data are for Mercer County.

- Honolulu, HI, has a combined city-county government. Therefore, the population and crime data provided in this book include areas outside the principal city of Honolulu.

- Indianapolis, IN, crime and population data include Marion County.

- Charlotte, NC, crime and population data include Mecklenburg County.

- Louisville, KY, data include offenses reported by the Louisville and Jefferson County Police Departments.

- Las Vegas, NV, has a metropolitan police department and its crime and population numbers include areas outside of the principal city of Las Vegas.

- Savannah, GA, crime and population data include Chatham County.

- Toms River Township, NJ was formerly known as Dover Township.

- The population shown for the city of Mobile, AL, includes 56,876 inhabitants from the jurisdiction of the Mobile County Sheriff's Department.

- A number of Metropolitan Statistical Areas (MSAs) were altered as a result of the 2000 census. Consequently, five-year crime rate comparisons can not be calculated for these metro areas. We have made every effort to check comparability, but readers are advised to use caution when interpreting tables showing percent changes in crime rates for metro areas from 2002 to 2006.

- *City Crime Rankings,* 14th Edition, also provides rankings for Metropolitan Divisions (MDs). These are subdivisions of eleven large Metropolitan Statistical Areas.

METROPOLITAN AREA CRIME STATISTICS

Please note the following for tables 1 through 40 and 85 through 87:

- All listings are for Metropolitan Statistical Areas (M.S.A.s) except for those ending with "M.D."
- Listings with "M.D." are Metropolitan Divisions which are smaller parts of eleven large M.S.A.s. These eleven M.S.A.s, further divided into M.D.s, are indicated by the word "(greater)" following the name.
- An example is Dallas (greater) which includes the two M.D.s of Dallas-Plano and Fort Worth-Arlington. The data for the M.D.s are included in the data of the overall M.S.A.
- Statistics for principal cities alone begin on page 185.

1. Crimes in 2006

National Total = 11,401,313 Crimes*

RANK	METROPOLITAN AREA	CRIMES
223	Abilene, TX	6,379
89	Albany-Schenectady-Troy, NY	26,514
196	Albany, GA	7,847
58	Albuquerque, NM	45,314
185	Alexandria, LA	8,855
297	Altoona, PA	3,578
147	Amarillo, TX	13,601
325	Ames, IA	2,345
129	Anchorage, AK	15,624
175	Anderson, SC	9,376
165	Ann Arbor, MI	10,602
260	Appleton, WI	5,201
149	Asheville, NC	13,108
188	Athens-Clarke County, GA	8,452
NA	Atlanta, GA**	NA
157	Atlantic City, NJ	12,053
91	Augusta, GA-SC	26,315
47	Austin-Round Rock, TX	64,049
68	Bakersfield, CA	37,653
24	Baltimore-Towson, MD	114,685
271	Bangor, ME	4,737
NA	Barnstable Town, MA**	NA
65	Baton Rouge, LA	40,312
216	Battle Creek, MI	6,811
309	Bay City, MI	3,099
116	Beaumont-Port Arthur, TX	17,906
178	Bellingham, WA	9,272
252	Bend, OR	5,424
81	Bethesda-Frederick, MD M.D.	31,071
246	Billings, MT	5,599
213	Binghamton, NY	6,967
54	Birmingham-Hoover, AL	53,662
323	Bismarck, ND	2,415
280	Blacksburg, VA	4,321
243	Bloomington, IN	5,718
121	Boise City-Nampa, ID	16,803
291	Bowling Green, KY	4,048
204	Bremerton-Silverdale, WA	7,535
109	Brownsville-Harlingen, TX	19,970
259	Brunswick, GA	5,238
67	Buffalo-Niagara Falls, NY	39,608
221	Burlington, NC	6,537
69	Camden, NJ M.D.	37,513
99	Cape Coral-Fort Myers, FL	23,200
333	Carson City, NV	1,442
302	Casper, WY	3,355
191	Cedar Rapids, IA	7,972
80	Charleston-North Charleston, SC	31,280
151	Charleston, WV	12,556
NA	Charlotte-Gastonia, NC-SC**	NA
234	Charlottesville, VA	6,056
93	Chattanooga, TN-GA	24,291
310	Cheyenne, WY	3,082
NA	Chicago, IL**	NA
194	Chico, CA	7,894
36	Cincinnati-Middletown, OH-KY-IN	84,191
182	Clarksville, TN-KY	9,045
38	Cleveland-Elyria-Mentor, OH	76,437
286	Cleveland, TN	4,150
283	Coeur d'Alene, ID	4,252
179	College Station-Bryan, TX	9,234
92	Colorado Springs, CO	25,657
257	Columbia, MO	5,311
78	Columbia, SC	32,085
118	Columbus, GA-AL	17,621
305	Columbus, IN	3,220
34	Columbus, OH	87,687
87	Corpus Christi, TX	27,381
308	Cumberland, MD-WV	3,100
4	Dallas (greater), TX	296,427
10	Dallas-Plano-Irving, TX M.D.	199,082
267	Dalton, GA	4,880
313	Danville, VA	3,042
105	Daytona Beach, FL	21,855
75	Dayton, OH	34,372
232	Decatur, AL	6,074
28	Denver-Aurora, CO	98,860
100	Des Moines-West Des Moines, IA	22,998
11	Detroit (greater), MI	194,786
21	Detroit-Livonia-Dearborn, MI M.D.	123,833
253	Dothan, AL	5,406
254	Dover, DE	5,404
324	Dubuque, IA	2,348
NA	Duluth, MN-WI**	NA
95	Durham, NC	23,865
289	Eau Claire, WI	4,055
57	Edison, NJ M.D.	48,082
211	El Centro, CA	7,051
90	El Paso, TX	26,460
328	Elizabethtown, KY	2,088
203	Elkhart-Goshen, IN	7,564
322	Elmira, NY	2,580
218	Erie, PA	6,619
125	Eugene-Springfield, OR	16,197
161	Evansville, IN-KY	10,955
326	Fairbanks, AK	2,203
NA	Fargo, ND-MN**	NA
294	Farmington, NM	3,711
142	Fayetteville, AR-MO	14,226
98	Fayetteville, NC	23,337
225	Flagstaff, AZ	6,350
102	Flint, MI	22,483
145	Florence, SC	13,857
331	Fond du Lac, WI	2,041
180	Fort Collins-Loveland, CO	9,151
40	Fort Lauderdale, FL M.D.	75,314
159	Fort Smith, AR-OK	11,267
232	Fort Walton Beach, FL	6,074
143	Fort Wayne, IN	14,214
29	Fort Worth-Arlington, TX M.D.	97,345
59	Fresno, CA	44,332
247	Gadsden, AL	5,595
146	Gainesville, FL	13,641
250	Gainesville, GA	5,521
317	Glens Falls, NY	2,871
249	Goldsboro, NC	5,548
NA	Grand Forks, ND-MN**	NA
265	Grand Junction, CO	5,022
84	Grand Rapids-Wyoming, MI	28,306
306	Great Falls, MT	3,189
181	Greeley, CO	9,070
205	Green Bay, WI	7,534
72	Greensboro-High Point, NC	35,104
183	Greenville, NC	8,911
88	Greenville, SC	27,328
209	Hagerstown-Martinsburg, MD-WV	7,300
285	Hanford-Corcoran, CA	4,158
148	Harrisburg-Carlisle, PA	13,391
329	Harrisonburg, VA	2,050
74	Hartford, CT	34,711
269	Hattiesburg, MS	4,784
245	Holland-Grand Haven, MI	5,601
63	Honolulu, HI	41,055
199	Hot Springs, AR	7,661
190	Houma, LA	8,237
7	Houston, TX	262,244
169	Huntington-Ashland, WV-KY-OH	9,989
110	Huntsville, AL	19,106
298	Idaho Falls, ID	3,553
37	Indianapolis, IN	77,995
303	Iowa City, IA	3,327
319	Ithaca, NY	2,724
NA	Jacksonville, FL**	NA
251	Jacksonville, NC	5,489
242	Jackson, MI	5,743
96	Jackson, MS	23,574
217	Jackson, TN	6,783
227	Janesville, WI	6,263
290	Jefferson City, MO	4,052
210	Johnson City, TN	7,067
296	Johnstown, PA	3,619
231	Jonesboro, AR	6,083
193	Joplin, MO	7,896
139	Kalamazoo-Portage, MI	14,426
32	Kansas City, MO-KS	93,612
192	Kennewick-Richland-Pasco, WA	7,904
NA	Killeen-Temple-Fort Hood, TX**	NA
156	Kingsport, TN-VA	12,088
293	Kingston, NY	3,918
86	Knoxville, TN	27,436
279	Kokomo, IN	4,350
NA	La Crosse, WI-MN**	NA
229	Lafayette, IN	6,229
166	Lake Charles, LA	10,543
172	Lake Havasu City-Kingman, AZ	9,634
94	Lakeland, FL	24,031
152	Lancaster, PA	12,502
135	Lansing-East Lansing, MI	14,778
141	Laredo, TX	14,242
215	Las Cruces, NM	6,901
30	Las Vegas-Paradise, NV	94,783

Note: All listings are for Metropolitan Statistical Areas (M.S.A.s) except for those ending with "M.D." Listings with "M.D." are Metropolitan Divisions which are smaller parts of eleven large M.S.A.s. See explanatory note at beginning of metropolitan area section on page 23.

RANK	METROPOLITAN AREA	CRIMES
226	Lawrence, KS	6,307
240	Lawton, OK	5,954
315	Lebanon, PA	2,967
316	Lewiston-Auburn, ME	2,938
330	Lewiston, ID-WA	2,049
119	Lexington-Fayette, KY	17,597
270	Lima, OH	4,744
138	Lincoln, NE	14,609
61	Little Rock, AR	42,596
332	Logan, UT-ID	1,965
163	Longview, TX	10,781
248	Longview, WA	5,559
3	Los Angeles County, CA M.D.	334,378
2	Los Angeles (greater), CA	410,347
55	Louisville, KY-IN	49,507
126	Lubbock, TX	16,095
258	Lynchburg, VA	5,294
130	Macon, GA	15,607
281	Madera, CA	4,255
122	Madison, WI	16,694
184	Manchester-Nashua, NH	8,910
220	Mansfield, OH	6,563
76	McAllen-Edinburg-Mission, TX	34,117
219	Medford, OR	6,600
33	Memphis, TN-MS-AR	92,650
164	Merced, CA	10,611
5	Miami (greater), FL	284,395
17	Miami-Dade County, FL M.D.	145,346
266	Michigan City-La Porte, IN	4,978
272	Midland, TX	4,699
43	Milwaukee, WI	68,420
NA	Minneapolis-St. Paul, MN-WI**	NA
288	Missoula, MT	4,061
103	Mobile, AL	22,185
85	Modesto, CA	28,286
173	Monroe, LA	9,542
287	Monroe, MI	4,091
112	Montgomery, AL	18,539
312	Morgantown, WV	3,058
264	Morristown, TN	5,032
214	Mount Vernon-Anacortes, WA	6,948
276	Muncie, IN	4,511
174	Muskegon-Norton Shores, MI	9,481
120	Myrtle Beach, SC	17,256
295	Napa, CA	3,696
201	Naples-Marco Island, FL	7,576
44	Nashville-Davidson, TN	67,707
52	Nassau-Suffolk, NY M.D.	53,844
56	New Orleans, LA	48,632
1	New York (greater), NY-NJ-PA	440,209
6	New York-W. Plains NY-NJ M.D.	278,828
50	Newark-Union, NJ-PA M.D.	59,455
235	Niles-Benton Harbor, MI	6,047
23	Oakland-Fremont, CA M.D.	120,051
168	Ocala, FL	10,390
263	Ocean City, NJ	5,053
255	Odessa, TX	5,394
128	Ogden-Clearfield, UT	15,712
49	Oklahoma City, OK	59,853
189	Olympia, WA	8,392
70	Omaha-Council Bluffs, NE-IA	36,754
27	Orlando, FL	102,229
292	Oshkosh-Neenah, WI	4,027
111	Oxnard-Thousand Oaks, CA	18,813
104	Palm Bay-Melbourne, FL	21,904
327	Palm Coast, FL	2,137
197	Panama City-Lynn Haven, FL	7,785
212	Pascagoula, MS	6,999
114	Pensacola, FL	18,255
9	Philadelphia (greater) PA-NJ-DE	207,849
18	Philadelphia, PA M.D.	142,026
8	Phoenix-Mesa-Scottsdale, AZ	216,212
236	Pine Bluff, AR	6,041
45	Pittsburgh, PA	64,348
299	Pittsfield, MA	3,534
319	Pocatello, ID	2,724
140	Port St. Lucie, FL	14,409
35	Portland-Vancouver, OR-WA	84,548
144	Portland, ME	14,209
137	Poughkeepsie, NY	14,638
228	Prescott, AZ	6,234
154	Provo-Orem, UT	12,117
187	Pueblo, CO	8,562
230	Punta Gorda, FL	6,193
208	Racine, WI	7,342
79	Raleigh-Cary, NC	31,919
304	Rapid City, SD	3,226
158	Reading, PA	11,845
244	Redding, CA	5,634
113	Reno-Sparks, NV	18,412
66	Richmond, VA	39,753
15	Riverside-San Bernardino, CA	154,679
171	Roanoke, VA	9,693
NA	Rochester, MN**	NA
73	Rochester, NY	34,858
186	Rocky Mount, NC	8,729
274	Rome, GA	4,545
31	Sacramento, CA	94,093
176	Saginaw, MI	9,340
124	Salem, OR	16,284
133	Salinas, CA	15,132
224	Salisbury, MD	6,356
51	Salt Lake City, UT	55,496
256	San Angelo, TX	5,351
25	San Antonio, TX	108,832
26	San Diego, CA	106,932
12	San Francisco (greater), CA	191,314
41	San Francisco-S. Mateo, CA M.D.	71,263
53	San Jose, CA	53,724
206	San Luis Obispo, CA	7,447
307	Sandusky, OH	3,147
39	Santa Ana-Anaheim, CA M.D.	75,969
162	Santa Barbara-Santa Maria, CA	10,844
160	Santa Cruz-Watsonville, CA	11,019
239	Santa Fe, NM	5,971
153	Santa Rosa-Petaluma, CA	12,246
77	Sarasota-Bradenton-Venice, FL	32,821
NA	Savannah, GA**	NA
134	Scranton--Wilkes-Barre, PA	14,917
14	Seattle (greater), WA	176,751
19	Seattle-Bellevue, WA M.D.	133,682
278	Sebastian-Vero Beach, FL	4,422
300	Sheboygan, WI	3,468
282	Sherman-Denison, TX	4,254
101	Shreveport-Bossier City, LA	22,747
275	Sioux City, IA-NE-SD	4,519
273	Sioux Falls, SD	4,681
132	South Bend-Mishawaka, IN-MI	15,460
136	Spartanburg, SC	14,659
107	Spokane, WA	20,226
NA	Springfield, MA**	NA
108	Springfield, MO	19,974
177	Springfield, OH	9,278
314	State College, PA	2,996
62	Stockton, CA	42,281
NA	St. Cloud, MN**	NA
262	St. Joseph, MO-KS	5,160
22	St. Louis, MO-IL	120,281
238	Sumter, SC	5,974
115	Syracuse, NY	18,158
60	Tacoma, WA M.D.	43,069
131	Tallahassee, FL	15,538
20	Tampa-St Petersburg, FL	132,847
222	Texarkana, TX-Texarkana, AR	6,409
71	Toledo, OH	36,345
150	Topeka, KS	12,726
170	Trenton-Ewing, NJ	9,867
NA	Tucson, AZ**	NA
64	Tulsa, OK	40,354
167	Tuscaloosa, AL	10,395
195	Tyler, TX	7,869
202	Utica-Rome, NY	7,575
241	Valdosta, GA	5,929
117	Vallejo-Fairfield, CA	17,660
277	Victoria, TX	4,459
207	Vineland, NJ	7,440
46	Virginia Beach-Norfolk, VA-NC	64,309
106	Visalia-Porterville, CA	21,768
155	Waco, TX	12,102
268	Warner Robins, GA	4,821
42	Warren-Farmington Hills, MI M.D.	70,953
13	Washington (greater) DC-VA-MD	177,617
16	Washington, DC-VA-MD-WV M.D.	146,546
261	Waterloo-Cedar Falls, IA	5,191
321	Wausau, WI	2,687
284	Wenatchee, WA	4,160
48	West Palm Beach, FL M.D.	63,735
318	Wheeling, WV-OH	2,830
200	Wichita Falls, TX	7,653
82	Wichita, KS	30,252
311	Williamsport, PA	3,074
83	Wilmington, DE-MD-NJ M.D.	28,310
123	Wilmington, NC	16,558
301	Winchester, VA-WV	3,431
97	Winston-Salem, NC	23,432
NA	Worcester, MA**	NA
127	Yakima, WA	15,730
237	Yuba City, CA	6,001
198	Yuma, AZ	7,762

Source: CQ Press using data from Federal Bureau of Investigation
"Crime in the United States 2006" (Uniform Crime Reports, September 24, 2007)
**Includes murder, rape, robbery, aggravated assault, burglary, larceny-theft, and motor vehicle theft.*
***Not available.*

1. Crimes in 2006 (continued)

National Total = 11,401,313 Crimes*

RANK	METROPOLITAN AREA	CRIMES
1	New York (greater), NY-NJ-PA	440,209
2	Los Angeles (greater), CA	410,347
3	Los Angeles County, CA M.D.	334,378
4	Dallas (greater), TX	296,427
5	Miami (greater), FL	284,395
6	New York-W. Plains NY-NJ M.D.	278,828
7	Houston, TX	262,244
8	Phoenix-Mesa-Scottsdale, AZ	216,212
9	Philadelphia (greater) PA-NJ-DE	207,849
10	Dallas-Plano-Irving, TX M.D.	199,082
11	Detroit (greater), MI	194,786
12	San Francisco (greater), CA	191,314
13	Washington (greater) DC-VA-MD	177,617
14	Seattle (greater), WA	176,751
15	Riverside-San Bernardino, CA	154,679
16	Washington, DC-VA-MD-WV M.D.	146,546
17	Miami-Dade County, FL M.D.	145,346
18	Philadelphia, PA M.D.	142,026
19	Seattle-Bellevue, WA M.D.	133,682
20	Tampa-St Petersburg, FL	132,847
21	Detroit-Livonia-Dearborn, MI M.D.	123,833
22	St. Louis, MO-IL	120,281
23	Oakland-Fremont, CA M.D.	120,051
24	Baltimore-Towson, MD	114,685
25	San Antonio, TX	108,832
26	San Diego, CA	106,932
27	Orlando, FL	102,229
28	Denver-Aurora, CO	98,860
29	Fort Worth-Arlington, TX M.D.	97,345
30	Las Vegas-Paradise, NV	94,783
31	Sacramento, CA	94,093
32	Kansas City, MO-KS	93,612
33	Memphis, TN-MS-AR	92,650
34	Columbus, OH	87,687
35	Portland-Vancouver, OR-WA	84,548
36	Cincinnati-Middletown, OH-KY-IN	84,191
37	Indianapolis, IN	77,995
38	Cleveland-Elyria-Mentor, OH	76,437
39	Santa Ana-Anaheim, CA M.D.	75,969
40	Fort Lauderdale, FL M.D.	75,314
41	San Francisco-S. Mateo, CA M.D.	71,263
42	Warren-Farmington Hills, MI M.D.	70,953
43	Milwaukee, WI	68,420
44	Nashville-Davidson, TN	67,707
45	Pittsburgh, PA	64,348
46	Virginia Beach-Norfolk, VA-NC	64,309
47	Austin-Round Rock, TX	64,049
48	West Palm Beach, FL M.D.	63,735
49	Oklahoma City, OK	59,853
50	Newark-Union, NJ-PA M.D.	59,455
51	Salt Lake City, UT	55,496
52	Nassau-Suffolk, NY M.D.	53,844
53	San Jose, CA	53,724
54	Birmingham-Hoover, AL	53,662
55	Louisville, KY-IN	49,507
56	New Orleans, LA	48,632
57	Edison, NJ M.D.	48,082
58	Albuquerque, NM	45,314
59	Fresno, CA	44,332
60	Tacoma, WA M.D.	43,069
61	Little Rock, AR	42,596
62	Stockton, CA	42,281
63	Honolulu, HI	41,055
64	Tulsa, OK	40,354
65	Baton Rouge, LA	40,312
66	Richmond, VA	39,753
67	Buffalo-Niagara Falls, NY	39,608
68	Bakersfield, CA	37,653
69	Camden, NJ M.D.	37,513
70	Omaha-Council Bluffs, NE-IA	36,754
71	Toledo, OH	36,345
72	Greensboro-High Point, NC	35,104
73	Rochester, NY	34,858
74	Hartford, CT	34,711
75	Dayton, OH	34,372
76	McAllen-Edinburg-Mission, TX	34,117
77	Sarasota-Bradenton-Venice, FL	32,821
78	Columbia, SC	32,085
79	Raleigh-Cary, NC	31,919
80	Charleston-North Charleston, SC	31,280
81	Bethesda-Frederick, MD M.D.	31,071
82	Wichita, KS	30,252
83	Wilmington, DE-MD-NJ M.D.	28,310
84	Grand Rapids-Wyoming, MI	28,306
85	Modesto, CA	28,286
86	Knoxville, TN	27,436
87	Corpus Christi, TX	27,381
88	Greenville, SC	27,328
89	Albany-Schenectady-Troy, NY	26,514
90	El Paso, TX	26,460
91	Augusta, GA-SC	26,315
92	Colorado Springs, CO	25,657
93	Chattanooga, TN-GA	24,291
94	Lakeland, FL	24,031
95	Durham, NC	23,865
96	Jackson, MS	23,574
97	Winston-Salem, NC	23,432
98	Fayetteville, NC	23,337
99	Cape Coral-Fort Myers, FL	23,200
100	Des Moines-West Des Moines, IA	22,998
101	Shreveport-Bossier City, LA	22,747
102	Flint, MI	22,483
103	Mobile, AL	22,185
104	Palm Bay-Melbourne, FL	21,904
105	Daytona Beach, FL	21,855
106	Visalia-Porterville, CA	21,768
107	Spokane, WA	20,226
108	Springfield, MO	19,974
109	Brownsville-Harlingen, TX	19,970
110	Huntsville, AL	19,106
111	Oxnard-Thousand Oaks, CA	18,813
112	Montgomery, AL	18,539
113	Reno-Sparks, NV	18,412
114	Pensacola, FL	18,255
115	Syracuse, NY	18,158
116	Beaumont-Port Arthur, TX	17,906
117	Vallejo-Fairfield, CA	17,660
118	Columbus, GA-AL	17,621
119	Lexington-Fayette, KY	17,597
120	Myrtle Beach, SC	17,256
121	Boise City-Nampa, ID	16,803
122	Madison, WI	16,694
123	Wilmington, NC	16,558
124	Salem, OR	16,284
125	Eugene-Springfield, OR	16,197
126	Lubbock, TX	16,095
127	Yakima, WA	15,730
128	Ogden-Clearfield, UT	15,712
129	Anchorage, AK	15,624
130	Macon, GA	15,607
131	Tallahassee, FL	15,538
132	South Bend-Mishawaka, IN-MI	15,460
133	Salinas, CA	15,132
134	Scranton--Wilkes-Barre, PA	14,917
135	Lansing-East Lansing, MI	14,778
136	Spartanburg, SC	14,659
137	Poughkeepsie, NY	14,638
138	Lincoln, NE	14,609
139	Kalamazoo-Portage, MI	14,426
140	Port St. Lucie, FL	14,409
141	Laredo, TX	14,242
142	Fayetteville, AR-MO	14,226
143	Fort Wayne, IN	14,214
144	Portland, ME	14,209
145	Florence, SC	13,857
146	Gainesville, FL	13,641
147	Amarillo, TX	13,601
148	Harrisburg-Carlisle, PA	13,391
149	Asheville, NC	13,108
150	Topeka, KS	12,726
151	Charleston, WV	12,556
152	Lancaster, PA	12,502
153	Santa Rosa-Petaluma, CA	12,246
154	Provo-Orem, UT	12,117
155	Waco, TX	12,102
156	Kingsport, TN-VA	12,088
157	Atlantic City, NJ	12,053
158	Reading, PA	11,845
159	Fort Smith, AR-OK	11,267
160	Santa Cruz-Watsonville, CA	11,019
161	Evansville, IN-KY	10,955
162	Santa Barbara-Santa Maria, CA	10,844
163	Longview, TX	10,781
164	Merced, CA	10,611
165	Ann Arbor, MI	10,602
166	Lake Charles, LA	10,543
167	Tuscaloosa, AL	10,395
168	Ocala, FL	10,390
169	Huntington-Ashland, WV-KY-OH	9,989
170	Trenton-Ewing, NJ	9,867
171	Roanoke, VA	9,693

Note: All listings are for Metropolitan Statistical Areas (M.S.A.s) except for those ending with "M.D." Listings with "M.D." are Metropolitan Divisions which are smaller parts of eleven large M.S.A.s. See explanatory note at beginning of metropolitan area section on page 23.

RANK	METROPOLITAN AREA	CRIMES
172	Lake Havasu City-Kingman, AZ	9,634
173	Monroe, LA	9,542
174	Muskegon-Norton Shores, MI	9,481
175	Anderson, SC	9,376
176	Saginaw, MI	9,340
177	Springfield, OH	9,278
178	Bellingham, WA	9,272
179	College Station-Bryan, TX	9,234
180	Fort Collins-Loveland, CO	9,151
181	Greeley, CO	9,070
182	Clarksville, TN-KY	9,045
183	Greenville, NC	8,911
184	Manchester-Nashua, NH	8,910
185	Alexandria, LA	8,855
186	Rocky Mount, NC	8,729
187	Pueblo, CO	8,562
188	Athens-Clarke County, GA	8,452
189	Olympia, WA	8,392
190	Houma, LA	8,237
191	Cedar Rapids, IA	7,972
192	Kennewick-Richland-Pasco, WA	7,904
193	Joplin, MO	7,896
194	Chico, CA	7,894
195	Tyler, TX	7,869
196	Albany, GA	7,847
197	Panama City-Lynn Haven, FL	7,785
198	Yuma, AZ	7,762
199	Hot Springs, AR	7,661
200	Wichita Falls, TX	7,653
201	Naples-Marco Island, FL	7,576
202	Utica-Rome, NY	7,575
203	Elkhart-Goshen, IN	7,564
204	Bremerton-Silverdale, WA	7,535
205	Green Bay, WI	7,534
206	San Luis Obispo, CA	7,447
207	Vineland, NJ	7,440
208	Racine, WI	7,342
209	Hagerstown-Martinsburg, MD-WV	7,300
210	Johnson City, TN	7,067
211	El Centro, CA	7,051
212	Pascagoula, MS	6,999
213	Binghamton, NY	6,967
214	Mount Vernon-Anacortes, WA	6,948
215	Las Cruces, NM	6,901
216	Battle Creek, MI	6,811
217	Jackson, TN	6,783
218	Erie, PA	6,619
219	Medford, OR	6,600
220	Mansfield, OH	6,563
221	Burlington, NC	6,537
222	Texarkana, TX-Texarkana, AR	6,409
223	Abilene, TX	6,379
224	Salisbury, MD	6,356
225	Flagstaff, AZ	6,350
226	Lawrence, KS	6,307
227	Janesville, WI	6,263
228	Prescott, AZ	6,234
229	Lafayette, IN	6,229
230	Punta Gorda, FL	6,193
231	Jonesboro, AR	6,083
232	Decatur, AL	6,074
232	Fort Walton Beach, FL	6,074
234	Charlottesville, VA	6,056
235	Niles-Benton Harbor, MI	6,047
236	Pine Bluff, AR	6,041
237	Yuba City, CA	6,001
238	Sumter, SC	5,974
239	Santa Fe, NM	5,971
240	Lawton, OK	5,954
241	Valdosta, GA	5,929
242	Jackson, MI	5,743
243	Bloomington, IN	5,718
244	Redding, CA	5,634
245	Holland-Grand Haven, MI	5,601
246	Billings, MT	5,599
247	Gadsden, AL	5,595
248	Longview, WA	5,559
249	Goldsboro, NC	5,548
250	Gainesville, GA	5,521
251	Jacksonville, NC	5,489
252	Bend, OR	5,424
253	Dothan, AL	5,406
254	Dover, DE	5,404
255	Odessa, TX	5,394
256	San Angelo, TX	5,351
257	Columbia, MO	5,311
258	Lynchburg, VA	5,294
259	Brunswick, GA	5,238
260	Appleton, WI	5,201
261	Waterloo-Cedar Falls, IA	5,191
262	St. Joseph, MO-KS	5,160
263	Ocean City, NJ	5,053
264	Morristown, TN	5,032
265	Grand Junction, CO	5,022
266	Michigan City-La Porte, IN	4,978
267	Dalton, GA	4,880
268	Warner Robins, GA	4,821
269	Hattiesburg, MS	4,784
270	Lima, OH	4,744
271	Bangor, ME	4,737
272	Midland, TX	4,699
273	Sioux Falls, SD	4,681
274	Rome, GA	4,545
275	Sioux City, IA-NE-SD	4,519
276	Muncie, IN	4,511
277	Victoria, TX	4,459
278	Sebastian-Vero Beach, FL	4,422
279	Kokomo, IN	4,350
280	Blacksburg, VA	4,321
281	Madera, CA	4,255
282	Sherman-Denison, TX	4,254
283	Coeur d'Alene, ID	4,252
284	Wenatchee, WA	4,160
285	Hanford-Corcoran, CA	4,158
286	Cleveland, TN	4,150
287	Monroe, MI	4,091
288	Missoula, MT	4,061
289	Eau Claire, WI	4,055
290	Jefferson City, MO	4,052
291	Bowling Green, KY	4,048
292	Oshkosh-Neenah, WI	4,027
293	Kingston, NY	3,918
294	Farmington, NM	3,711
295	Napa, CA	3,696
296	Johnstown, PA	3,619
297	Altoona, PA	3,578
298	Idaho Falls, ID	3,553
299	Pittsfield, MA	3,534
300	Sheboygan, WI	3,468
301	Winchester, VA-WV	3,431
302	Casper, WY	3,355
303	Iowa City, IA	3,327
304	Rapid City, SD	3,226
305	Columbus, IN	3,220
306	Great Falls, MT	3,189
307	Sandusky, OH	3,147
308	Cumberland, MD-WV	3,100
309	Bay City, MI	3,099
310	Cheyenne, WY	3,082
311	Williamsport, PA	3,074
312	Morgantown, WV	3,058
313	Danville, VA	3,042
314	State College, PA	2,996
315	Lebanon, PA	2,967
316	Lewiston-Auburn, ME	2,938
317	Glens Falls, NY	2,871
318	Wheeling, WV-OH	2,830
319	Ithaca, NY	2,724
319	Pocatello, ID	2,724
321	Wausau, WI	2,687
322	Elmira, NY	2,580
323	Bismarck, ND	2,415
324	Dubuque, IA	2,348
325	Ames, IA	2,345
326	Fairbanks, AK	2,203
327	Palm Coast, FL	2,137
328	Elizabethtown, KY	2,088
329	Harrisonburg, VA	2,050
330	Lewiston, ID-WA	2,049
331	Fond du Lac, WI	2,041
332	Logan, UT-ID	1,965
333	Carson City, NV	1,442
NA	Atlanta, GA**	NA
NA	Barnstable Town, MA**	NA
NA	Charlotte-Gastonia, NC-SC**	NA
NA	Chicago, IL**	NA
NA	Duluth, MN-WI**	NA
NA	Fargo, ND-MN**	NA
NA	Grand Forks, ND-MN**	NA
NA	Jacksonville, FL**	NA
NA	Killeen-Temple-Fort Hood, TX**	NA
NA	La Crosse, WI-MN**	NA
NA	Minneapolis-St. Paul, MN-WI**	NA
NA	Rochester, MN**	NA
NA	Savannah, GA**	NA
NA	Springfield, MA**	NA
NA	St. Cloud, MN**	NA
NA	Tucson, AZ**	NA
NA	Worcester, MA**	NA

Source: CQ Press using data from Federal Bureau of Investigation "Crime in the United States 2006" (Uniform Crime Reports, September 24, 2007)

**Includes murder, rape, robbery, aggravated assault, burglary, larceny-theft, and motor vehicle theft.*

***Not available.*

2. Crime Rate in 2006

National Rate = 3,808.0 Crimes per 100,000 Population*

RANK	METROPOLITAN AREA	RATE	RANK	METROPOLITAN AREA	RATE	RANK	METROPOLITAN AREA	RATE
174	Abilene, TX	3,918.8	207	Cleveland-Elyria-Mentor, OH	3,590.5	317	Glens Falls, NY	2,227.0
248	Albany-Schenectady-Troy, NY	3,115.0	187	Cleveland, TN	3,793.1	100	Goldsboro, NC	4,752.8
109	Albany, GA	4,668.8	238	Coeur d'Alene, ID	3,245.7	NA	Grand Forks, ND-MN**	NA
29	Albuquerque, NM	5,602.7	102	College Station-Bryan, TX	4,732.7	186	Grand Junction, CO	3,795.1
11	Alexandria, LA	6,313.7	143	Colorado Springs, CO	4,286.1	197	Grand Rapids-Wyoming, MI	3,679.7
274	Altoona, PA	2,819.4	222	Columbia, MO	3,439.7	168	Great Falls, MT	3,969.8
35	Amarillo, TX	5,541.7	111	Columbia, SC	4,579.6	178	Greeley, CO	3,888.2
265	Ames, IA	2,917.5	20	Columbus, GA-AL	6,028.5	302	Green Bay, WI	2,523.3
49	Anchorage, AK	5,298.7	139	Columbus, IN	4,349.7	72	Greensboro-High Point, NC	5,102.6
50	Anderson, SC	5,260.3	68	Columbus, OH	5,125.8	45	Greenville, NC	5,373.2
250	Ann Arbor, MI	3,109.2	10	Corpus Christi, TX	6,438.5	116	Greenville, SC	4,551.3
310	Appleton, WI	2,408.6	255	Cumberland, MD-WV	3,072.6	267	Hagerstown-Martinsburg, MD-WV	2,899.2
236	Asheville, NC	3,271.5	81	Dallas (greater), TX	4,953.3	270	Hanford-Corcoran, CA	2,873.3
107	Athens-Clarke County, GA	4,677.2	78	Dallas-Plano-Irving, TX M.D.	4,972.7	298	Harrisburg-Carlisle, PA	2,564.0
NA	Atlanta, GA**	NA	208	Dalton, GA	3,590.1	330	Harrisonburg, VA	1,817.4
131	Atlantic City, NJ	4,444.0	277	Danville, VA	2,788.9	220	Hartford, CT	3,464.5
86	Augusta, GA-SC	4,926.7	132	Daytona Beach, FL	4,385.7	201	Hattiesburg, MS	3,640.9
142	Austin-Round Rock, TX	4,288.0	159	Dayton, OH	4,069.6	320	Holland-Grand Haven, MI	2,198.5
85	Bakersfield, CA	4,930.8	162	Decatur, AL	4,057.8	124	Honolulu, HI	4,498.3
140	Baltimore-Towson, MD	4,306.7	155	Denver-Aurora, CO	4,111.2	1	Hot Springs, AR	8,096.7
240	Bangor, ME	3,220.8	133	Des Moines-West Des Moines, IA	4,378.7	136	Houma, LA	4,352.3
NA	Barnstable Town, MA**	NA	138	Detroit (greater), MI	4,350.6	94	Houston, TX	4,829.8
24	Baton Rouge, LA	5,795.8	14	Detroit-Livonia-Dearborn, MI M.D.	6,212.7	218	Huntington-Ashland, WV-KY-OH	3,481.8
88	Battle Creek, MI	4,905.5	172	Dothan, AL	3,922.3	64	Huntsville, AL	5,136.1
272	Bay City, MI	2,849.5	194	Dover, DE	3,709.8	256	Idaho Falls, ID	3,052.3
117	Beaumont-Port Arthur, TX	4,540.1	299	Dubuque, IA	2,548.9	103	Indianapolis, IN	4,722.8
79	Bellingham, WA	4,968.3	NA	Duluth, MN-WI**	NA	311	Iowa City, IA	2,389.0
189	Bend, OR	3,774.5	66	Durham, NC	5,129.0	284	Ithaca, NY	2,716.3
287	Bethesda-Frederick, MD M.D.	2,698.5	294	Eau Claire, WI	2,622.8	NA	Jacksonville, FL**	NA
188	Billings, MT	3,783.2	324	Edison, NJ M.D.	2,085.5	214	Jacksonville, NC	3,530.3
275	Binghamton, NY	2,797.0	127	El Centro, CA	4,484.6	215	Jackson, MI	3,518.6
90	Birmingham-Hoover, AL	4,878.5	210	El Paso, TX	3,565.8	119	Jackson, MS	4,527.4
307	Bismarck, ND	2,434.0	329	Elizabethtown, KY	1,872.4	18	Jackson, TN	6,041.9
273	Blacksburg, VA	2,832.3	182	Elkhart-Goshen, IN	3,846.3	171	Janesville, WI	3,961.0
242	Bloomington, IN	3,196.5	269	Elmira, NY	2,874.6	276	Jefferson City, MO	2,796.1
260	Boise City-Nampa, ID	3,009.0	313	Erie, PA	2,358.1	196	Johnson City, TN	3,693.2
203	Bowling Green, KY	3,618.8	98	Eugene-Springfield, OR	4,754.4	306	Johnstown, PA	2,441.9
254	Bremerton-Silverdale, WA	3,078.1	249	Evansville, IN-KY	3,112.8	46	Jonesboro, AR	5,365.9
65	Brownsville-Harlingen, TX	5,133.2	NA	Fairbanks, AK**	NA	104	Joplin, MO	4,717.1
61	Brunswick, GA	5,155.9	NA	Fargo, ND-MN**	NA	118	Kalamazoo-Portage, MI	4,528.6
221	Buffalo-Niagara Falls, NY	3,441.8	266	Farmington, NM	2,900.9	97	Kansas City, MO-KS	4,771.9
115	Burlington, NC	4,560.6	219	Fayetteville, AR-MO	3,472.9	216	Kennewick-Richland-Pasco, WA	3,516.6
261	Camden, NJ M.D.	3,008.6	6	Fayetteville, NC	6,621.7	NA	Killeen-Temple-Fort Hood, TX**	NA
149	Cape Coral-Fort Myers, FL	4,188.1	NA	Flagstaff, AZ**	NA	170	Kingsport, TN-VA	3,964.9
305	Carson City, NV	2,489.0	75	Flint, MI	5,077.7	322	Kingston, NY	2,138.8
99	Casper, WY	4,753.3	4	Florence, SC	6,875.9	153	Knoxville, TN	4,133.6
241	Cedar Rapids, IA	3,218.2	326	Fond du Lac, WI	2,047.2	145	Kokomo, IN	4,263.2
58	Charleston-North Charleston, SC	5,177.5	232	Fort Collins-Loveland, CO	3,302.8	NA	La Crosse, WI-MN**	NA
156	Charleston, WV	4,093.8	152	Fort Lauderdale, FL M.D.	4,166.5	225	Lafayette, IN	3,375.2
NA	Charlotte-Gastonia, NC-SC**	NA	175	Fort Smith, AR-OK	3,911.9	25	Lake Charles, LA	5,704.7
244	Charlottesville, VA	3,182.3	234	Fort Walton Beach, FL	3,278.9	80	Lake Havasu City-Kingman, AZ	4,956.9
92	Chattanooga, TN-GA	4,847.4	217	Fort Wayne, IN	3,491.6	135	Lakeland, FL	4,352.9
209	Cheyenne, WY	3,578.9	87	Fort Worth-Arlington, TX M.D.	4,914.1	300	Lancaster, PA	2,546.3
NA	Chicago, IL**	NA	76	Fresno, CA	5,006.5	237	Lansing-East Lansing, MI	3,253.8
199	Chico, CA	3,652.7	44	Gadsden, AL	5,373.5	15	Laredo, TX	6,163.7
163	Cincinnati-Middletown, OH-KY-IN	4,055.3	31	Gainesville, FL	5,583.6	206	Las Cruces, NM	3,594.0
198	Clarksville, TN-KY	3,671.5	239	Gainesville, GA	3,226.9	48	Las Vegas-Paradise, NV	5,361.9

Note: All listings are for Metropolitan Statistical Areas (M.S.A.s) except for those ending with "M.D." Listings with "M.D." are Metropolitan Divisions which are smaller parts of eleven large M.S.A.s. See explanatory note at beginning of metropolitan area section on page 23.

Alpha Order - Metro Area (continued)

RANK	METROPOLITAN AREA	RATE
16	Lawrence, KS	6,085.5
52	Lawton, OK	5,249.4
312	Lebanon, PA	2,360.6
283	Lewiston-Auburn, ME	2,719.2
223	Lewiston, ID-WA	3,388.8
161	Lexington-Fayette, KY	4,061.6
130	Lima, OH	4,460.2
59	Lincoln, NE	5,160.7
8	Little Rock, AR	6,547.1
331	Logan, UT-ID	1,724.6
55	Longview, TX	5,202.9
28	Longview, WA	5,615.3
230	Los Angeles County, CA M.D.	3,335.4
246	Los Angeles (greater), CA	3,146.8
160	Louisville, KY-IN	4,065.8
17	Lubbock, TX	6,043.8
318	Lynchburg, VA	2,212.6
7	Macon, GA	6,611.6
263	Madera, CA	2,953.3
252	Madison, WI	3,097.2
319	Manchester-Nashua, NH	2,212.0
69	Mansfield, OH	5,123.1
89	McAllen-Edinburg-Mission, TX	4,891.4
231	Medford, OR	3,324.5
3	Memphis, TN-MS-AR	7,275.5
137	Merced, CA	4,350.8
60	Miami (greater), FL	5,158.1
21	Miami-Dade County, FL M.D.	6,015.8
128	Michigan City-La Porte, IN	4,474.8
190	Midland, TX	3,764.9
122	Milwaukee, WI	4,506.1
NA	Minneapolis-St. Paul, MN-WI**	NA
165	Missoula, MT	4,019.0
38	Mobile, AL	5,477.0
34	Modesto, CA	5,545.6
22	Monroe, LA	5,882.3
292	Monroe, MI	2,664.3
63	Montgomery, AL	5,142.9
291	Morgantown, WV	2,668.4
185	Morristown, TN	3,805.3
19	Mount Vernon-Anacortes, WA	6,035.7
181	Muncie, IN	3,851.2
41	Muskegon-Norton Shores, MI	5,414.1
2	Myrtle Beach, SC	7,485.6
281	Napa, CA	2,759.0
308	Naples-Marco Island, FL	2,424.9
105	Nashville-Davidson, TN	4,699.7
327	Nassau-Suffolk, NY M.D.	1,912.4
177	New Orleans, LA	3,888.8
314	New York (greater), NY-NJ-PA	2,343.4
309	New York-W. Plains NY-NJ M.D.	2,422.6
280	Newark-Union, NJ-PA M.D.	2,759.4
192	Niles-Benton Harbor, MI	3,728.0
95	Oakland-Fremont, CA M.D.	4,823.5
226	Ocala, FL	3,367.2
74	Ocean City, NJ	5,085.4
150	Odessa, TX	4,184.9
247	Ogden-Clearfield, UT	3,125.5
67	Oklahoma City, OK	5,128.7
205	Olympia, WA	3,604.8
125	Omaha-Council Bluffs, NE-IA	4,495.5
56	Orlando, FL	5,200.2
304	Oshkosh-Neenah, WI	2,515.8
315	Oxnard-Thousand Oaks, CA	2,342.0
164	Palm Bay-Melbourne, FL	4,054.7
282	Palm Coast, FL	2,750.3
101	Panama City-Lynn Haven, FL	4,738.8
129	Pascagoula, MS	4,468.4
158	Pensacola, FL	4,081.2
211	Philadelphia (greater) PA-NJ-DE	3,562.6
200	Philadelphia, PA M.D.	3,647.6
43	Phoenix-Mesa-Scottsdale, AZ	5,388.0
26	Pine Bluff, AR	5,695.8
288	Pittsburgh, PA	2,694.5
293	Pittsfield, MA	2,663.9
253	Pocatello, ID	3,090.0
193	Port St. Lucie, FL	3,718.9
169	Portland-Vancouver, OR-WA	3,968.4
279	Portland, ME	2,763.0
321	Poughkeepsie, NY	2,186.3
258	Prescott, AZ	3,021.8
297	Provo-Orem, UT	2,591.3
33	Pueblo, CO	5,553.1
179	Punta Gorda, FL	3,865.9
191	Racine, WI	3,737.7
233	Raleigh-Cary, NC	3,295.3
285	Rapid City, SD	2,708.3
262	Reading, PA	2,986.2
251	Redding, CA	3,103.7
120	Reno-Sparks, NV	4,522.6
228	Richmond, VA	3,348.0
173	Riverside-San Bernardino, CA	3,920.7
235	Roanoke, VA	3,275.8
NA	Rochester, MN**	NA
229	Rochester, NY	3,345.9
23	Rocky Mount, NC	5,881.7
108	Rome, GA	4,674.9
112	Sacramento, CA	4,566.1
126	Saginaw, MI	4,493.9
144	Salem, OR	4,266.0
202	Salinas, CA	3,639.2
39	Salisbury, MD	5,452.7
57	Salt Lake City, UT	5,195.3
83	San Angelo, TX	4,938.5
30	San Antonio, TX	5,600.2
204	San Diego, CA	3,612.7
113	San Francisco (greater), CA	4,565.8
148	San Francisco-S. Mateo, CA M.D.	4,189.0
257	San Jose, CA	3,033.9
268	San Luis Obispo, CA	2,888.9
167	Sandusky, OH	3,995.6
303	Santa Ana-Anaheim, CA M.D.	2,519.7
290	Santa Barbara-Santa Maria, CA	2,681.7
134	Santa Cruz-Watsonville, CA	4,374.1
151	Santa Fe, NM	4,182.3
295	Santa Rosa-Petaluma, CA	2,601.7
96	Sarasota-Bradenton-Venice, FL	4,795.6
NA	Savannah, GA**	NA
286	Scranton--Wilkes-Barre, PA	2,707.1
40	Seattle (greater), WA	5,424.5
47	Seattle-Bellevue, WA M.D.	5,365.3
224	Sebastian-Vero Beach, FL	3,381.7
259	Sheboygan, WI	3,014.9
213	Sherman-Denison, TX	3,540.7
13	Shreveport-Bossier City, LA	6,262.1
245	Sioux City, IA-NE-SD	3,152.1
316	Sioux Falls, SD	2,234.2
93	South Bend-Mishawaka, IN-MI	4,834.5
42	Spartanburg, SC	5,410.1
121	Spokane, WA	4,511.9
NA	Springfield, MA**	NA
77	Springfield, MO	4,980.6
9	Springfield, OH	6,508.6
323	State College, PA	2,129.6
12	Stockton, CA	6,309.7
NA	St. Cloud, MN**	NA
147	St. Joseph, MO-KS	4,200.2
141	St. Louis, MO-IL	4,297.3
32	Sumter, SC	5,575.0
278	Syracuse, NY	2,778.6
27	Tacoma, WA M.D.	5,617.1
114	Tallahassee, FL	4,562.8
84	Tampa-St Petersburg, FL	4,934.3
106	Texarkana, TX-Texarkana, AR	4,682.6
36	Toledo, OH	5,527.8
37	Topeka, KS	5,516.4
289	Trenton-Ewing, NJ	2,692.0
NA	Tucson, AZ**	NA
123	Tulsa, OK	4,506.0
54	Tuscaloosa, AL	5,232.4
166	Tyler, TX	4,014.9
301	Utica-Rome, NY	2,536.2
110	Valdosta, GA	4,639.7
146	Vallejo-Fairfield, CA	4,252.3
183	Victoria, TX	3,825.3
91	Vineland, NJ	4,851.1
180	Virginia Beach-Norfolk, VA-NC	3,864.7
51	Visalia-Porterville, CA	5,250.7
53	Waco, TX	5,238.1
195	Warner Robins, GA	3,702.3
271	Warren-Farmington Hills, MI M.D.	2,856.5
227	Washington (greater) DC-VA-MD	3,366.7
212	Washington, DC-VA-MD-WV M.D.	3,553.3
243	Waterloo-Cedar Falls, IA	3,189.5
325	Wausau, WI	2,076.3
176	Wenatchee, WA	3,903.6
82	West Palm Beach, FL M.D.	4,940.9
328	Wheeling, WV-OH	1,901.4
73	Wichita Falls, TX	5,087.7
71	Wichita, KS	5,117.0
296	Williamsport, PA	2,594.1
157	Wilmington, DE-MD-NJ M.D.	4,081.4
62	Wilmington, NC	5,151.3
264	Winchester, VA-WV	2,926.9
70	Winston-Salem, NC	5,120.8
NA	Worcester, MA**	NA
5	Yakima, WA	6,677.5
184	Yuba City, CA	3,811.7
154	Yuma, AZ	4,124.3

Source: CQ Press using data from Federal Bureau of Investigation "Crime in the United States 2006" (Uniform Crime Reports, September 24, 2007)

**Includes murder, rape, robbery, aggravated assault, burglary, larceny-theft, and motor vehicle theft.*

***Not available.*

2. Crime Rate in 2006 (continued)

National Rate = 3,808.0 Crimes per 100,000 Population*

RANK	METROPOLITAN AREA	RATE
1	Hot Springs, AR	8,096.7
2	Myrtle Beach, SC	7,485.6
3	Memphis, TN-MS-AR	7,275.5
4	Florence, SC	6,875.9
5	Yakima, WA	6,677.5
6	Fayetteville, NC	6,621.7
7	Macon, GA	6,611.6
8	Little Rock, AR	6,547.1
9	Springfield, OH	6,508.6
10	Corpus Christi, TX	6,438.5
11	Alexandria, LA	6,313.7
12	Stockton, CA	6,309.7
13	Shreveport-Bossier City, LA	6,262.1
14	Detroit-Livonia-Dearborn, MI M.D.	6,212.7
15	Laredo, TX	6,163.7
16	Lawrence, KS	6,085.5
17	Lubbock, TX	6,043.8
18	Jackson, TN	6,041.9
19	Mount Vernon-Anacortes, WA	6,035.7
20	Columbus, GA-AL	6,028.5
21	Miami-Dade County, FL M.D.	6,015.8
22	Monroe, LA	5,882.3
23	Rocky Mount, NC	5,881.7
24	Baton Rouge, LA	5,795.8
25	Lake Charles, LA	5,704.7
26	Pine Bluff, AR	5,695.8
27	Tacoma, WA M.D.	5,617.1
28	Longview, WA	5,615.3
29	Albuquerque, NM	5,602.7
30	San Antonio, TX	5,600.2
31	Gainesville, FL	5,583.6
32	Sumter, SC	5,575.0
33	Pueblo, CO	5,553.1
34	Modesto, CA	5,545.6
35	Amarillo, TX	5,541.7
36	Toledo, OH	5,527.8
37	Topeka, KS	5,516.4
38	Mobile, AL	5,477.0
39	Salisbury, MD	5,452.7
40	Seattle (greater), WA	5,424.5
41	Muskegon-Norton Shores, MI	5,414.1
42	Spartanburg, SC	5,410.1
43	Phoenix-Mesa-Scottsdale, AZ	5,388.0
44	Gadsden, AL	5,373.5
45	Greenville, NC	5,373.2
46	Jonesboro, AR	5,365.9
47	Seattle-Bellevue, WA M.D.	5,365.3
48	Las Vegas-Paradise, NV	5,361.9
49	Anchorage, AK	5,298.7
50	Anderson, SC	5,260.3
51	Visalia-Porterville, CA	5,250.7
52	Lawton, OK	5,249.4
53	Waco, TX	5,238.1
54	Tuscaloosa, AL	5,232.4
55	Longview, TX	5,202.9
56	Orlando, FL	5,200.2
57	Salt Lake City, UT	5,195.3
58	Charleston-North Charleston, SC	5,177.5
59	Lincoln, NE	5,160.7
60	Miami (greater), FL	5,158.1
61	Brunswick, GA	5,155.9
62	Wilmington, NC	5,151.3
63	Montgomery, AL	5,142.9
64	Huntsville, AL	5,136.1
65	Brownsville-Harlingen, TX	5,133.2
66	Durham, NC	5,129.0
67	Oklahoma City, OK	5,128.7
68	Columbus, OH	5,125.8
69	Mansfield, OH	5,123.1
70	Winston-Salem, NC	5,120.8
71	Wichita, KS	5,117.0
72	Greensboro-High Point, NC	5,102.6
73	Wichita Falls, TX	5,087.7
74	Ocean City, NJ	5,085.4
75	Flint, MI	5,077.7
76	Fresno, CA	5,006.5
77	Springfield, MO	4,980.6
78	Dallas-Plano-Irving, TX M.D.	4,972.7
79	Bellingham, WA	4,968.3
80	Lake Havasu City-Kingman, AZ	4,956.9
81	Dallas (greater), TX	4,953.3
82	West Palm Beach, FL M.D.	4,940.9
83	San Angelo, TX	4,938.5
84	Tampa-St Petersburg, FL	4,934.3
85	Bakersfield, CA	4,930.8
86	Augusta, GA-SC	4,926.7
87	Fort Worth-Arlington, TX M.D.	4,914.1
88	Battle Creek, MI	4,905.5
89	McAllen-Edinburg-Mission, TX	4,891.4
90	Birmingham-Hoover, AL	4,878.5
91	Vineland, NJ	4,851.1
92	Chattanooga, TN-GA	4,847.4
93	South Bend-Mishawaka, IN-MI	4,834.5
94	Houston, TX	4,829.8
95	Oakland-Fremont, CA M.D.	4,823.5
96	Sarasota-Bradenton-Venice, FL	4,795.6
97	Kansas City, MO-KS	4,771.9
98	Eugene-Springfield, OR	4,754.4
99	Casper, WY	4,753.3
100	Goldsboro, NC	4,752.8
101	Panama City-Lynn Haven, FL	4,738.8
102	College Station-Bryan, TX	4,732.7
103	Indianapolis, IN	4,722.8
104	Joplin, MO	4,717.1
105	Nashville-Davidson, TN	4,699.7
106	Texarkana, TX-Texarkana, AR	4,682.6
107	Athens-Clarke County, GA	4,677.2
108	Rome, GA	4,674.9
109	Albany, GA	4,668.8
110	Valdosta, GA	4,639.7
111	Columbia, SC	4,579.6
112	Sacramento, CA	4,566.1
113	San Francisco (greater), CA	4,565.8
114	Tallahassee, FL	4,562.8
115	Burlington, NC	4,560.6
116	Greenville, SC	4,551.3
117	Beaumont-Port Arthur, TX	4,540.1
118	Kalamazoo-Portage, MI	4,528.6
119	Jackson, MS	4,527.4
120	Reno-Sparks, NV	4,522.6
121	Spokane, WA	4,511.9
122	Milwaukee, WI	4,506.1
123	Tulsa, OK	4,506.0
124	Honolulu, HI	4,498.3
125	Omaha-Council Bluffs, NE-IA	4,495.5
126	Saginaw, MI	4,493.9
127	El Centro, CA	4,484.6
128	Michigan City-La Porte, IN	4,474.8
129	Pascagoula, MS	4,468.4
130	Lima, OH	4,460.2
131	Atlantic City, NJ	4,444.0
132	Daytona Beach, FL	4,385.7
133	Des Moines-West Des Moines, IA	4,378.7
134	Santa Cruz-Watsonville, CA	4,374.1
135	Lakeland, FL	4,352.9
136	Houma, LA	4,352.3
137	Merced, CA	4,350.8
138	Detroit (greater), MI	4,350.6
139	Columbus, IN	4,349.7
140	Baltimore-Towson, MD	4,306.7
141	St. Louis, MO-IL	4,297.3
142	Austin-Round Rock, TX	4,288.0
143	Colorado Springs, CO	4,286.1
144	Salem, OR	4,266.0
145	Kokomo, IN	4,263.2
146	Vallejo-Fairfield, CA	4,252.3
147	St. Joseph, MO-KS	4,200.2
148	San Francisco-S. Mateo, CA M.D.	4,189.0
149	Cape Coral-Fort Myers, FL	4,188.1
150	Odessa, TX	4,184.9
151	Santa Fe, NM	4,182.3
152	Fort Lauderdale, FL M.D.	4,166.5
153	Knoxville, TN	4,133.6
154	Yuma, AZ	4,124.3
155	Denver-Aurora, CO	4,111.2
156	Charleston, WV	4,093.8
157	Wilmington, DE-MD-NJ M.D.	4,081.4
158	Pensacola, FL	4,081.2
159	Dayton, OH	4,069.6
160	Louisville, KY-IN	4,065.8
161	Lexington-Fayette, KY	4,061.6
162	Decatur, AL	4,057.8
163	Cincinnati-Middletown, OH-KY-IN	4,055.3
164	Palm Bay-Melbourne, FL	4,054.7
165	Missoula, MT	4,019.0
166	Tyler, TX	4,014.9
167	Sandusky, OH	3,995.6
168	Great Falls, MT	3,969.8
169	Portland-Vancouver, OR-WA	3,968.4
170	Kingsport, TN-VA	3,964.9
171	Janesville, WI	3,961.0

Note: All listings are for Metropolitan Statistical Areas (M.S.A.s) except for those ending with "M.D." Listings with "M.D." are Metropolitan Divisions which are smaller parts of eleven large M.S.A.s. See explanatory note at beginning of metropolitan area section on page 23.

Rank Order - Metro Area (continued)

RANK	METROPOLITAN AREA	RATE
172	Dothan, AL	3,922.3
173	Riverside-San Bernardino, CA	3,920.7
174	Abilene, TX	3,918.8
175	Fort Smith, AR-OK	3,911.9
176	Wenatchee, WA	3,903.6
177	New Orleans, LA	3,888.8
178	Greeley, CO	3,888.2
179	Punta Gorda, FL	3,865.9
180	Virginia Beach-Norfolk, VA-NC	3,864.7
181	Muncie, IN	3,851.2
182	Elkhart-Goshen, IN	3,846.3
183	Victoria, TX	3,825.3
184	Yuba City, CA	3,811.7
185	Morristown, TN	3,805.3
186	Grand Junction, CO	3,795.1
187	Cleveland, TN	3,793.1
188	Billings, MT	3,783.2
189	Bend, OR	3,774.5
190	Midland, TX	3,764.9
191	Racine, WI	3,737.7
192	Niles-Benton Harbor, MI	3,728.0
193	Port St. Lucie, FL	3,718.9
194	Dover, DE	3,709.8
195	Warner Robins, GA	3,702.3
196	Johnson City, TN	3,693.2
197	Grand Rapids-Wyoming, MI	3,679.7
198	Clarksville, TN-KY	3,671.5
199	Chico, CA	3,652.7
200	Philadelphia, PA M.D.	3,647.6
201	Hattiesburg, MS	3,640.9
202	Salinas, CA	3,639.2
203	Bowling Green, KY	3,618.8
204	San Diego, CA	3,612.7
205	Olympia, WA	3,604.8
206	Las Cruces, NM	3,594.0
207	Cleveland-Elyria-Mentor, OH	3,590.5
208	Dalton, GA	3,590.1
209	Cheyenne, WY	3,578.9
210	El Paso, TX	3,565.8
211	Philadelphia (greater) PA-NJ-DE	3,562.6
212	Washington, DC-VA-MD-WV M.D.	3,553.3
213	Sherman-Denison, TX	3,540.7
214	Jacksonville, NC	3,530.3
215	Jackson, MI	3,518.6
216	Kennewick-Richland-Pasco, WA	3,516.6
217	Fort Wayne, IN	3,491.6
218	Huntington-Ashland, WV-KY-OH	3,481.8
219	Fayetteville, AR-MO	3,472.9
220	Hartford, CT	3,464.5
221	Buffalo-Niagara Falls, NY	3,441.8
222	Columbia, MO	3,439.7
223	Lewiston, ID-WA	3,388.8
224	Sebastian-Vero Beach, FL	3,381.7
225	Lafayette, IN	3,375.2
226	Ocala, FL	3,367.2
227	Washington (greater) DC-VA-MD	3,366.7
228	Richmond, VA	3,348.0
229	Rochester, NY	3,345.9
230	Los Angeles County, CA M.D.	3,335.4
231	Medford, OR	3,324.5
232	Fort Collins-Loveland, CO	3,302.8
233	Raleigh-Cary, NC	3,295.3
234	Fort Walton Beach, FL	3,278.9
235	Roanoke, VA	3,275.8
236	Asheville, NC	3,271.5
237	Lansing-East Lansing, MI	3,253.8
238	Coeur d'Alene, ID	3,245.7
239	Gainesville, GA	3,226.9
240	Bangor, ME	3,220.8
241	Cedar Rapids, IA	3,218.2
242	Bloomington, IN	3,196.5
243	Waterloo-Cedar Falls, IA	3,189.5
244	Charlottesville, VA	3,182.3
245	Sioux City, IA-NE-SD	3,152.1
246	Los Angeles (greater), CA	3,146.8
247	Ogden-Clearfield, UT	3,125.5
248	Albany-Schenectady-Troy, NY	3,115.0
249	Evansville, IN-KY	3,112.8
250	Ann Arbor, MI	3,109.2
251	Redding, CA	3,103.7
252	Madison, WI	3,097.2
253	Pocatello, ID	3,090.0
254	Bremerton-Silverdale, WA	3,078.1
255	Cumberland, MD-WV	3,072.6
256	Idaho Falls, ID	3,052.3
257	San Jose, CA	3,033.9
258	Prescott, AZ	3,021.8
259	Sheboygan, WI	3,014.9
260	Boise City-Nampa, ID	3,009.0
261	Camden, NJ M.D.	3,008.6
262	Reading, PA	2,986.2
263	Madera, CA	2,953.3
264	Winchester, VA-WV	2,926.9
265	Ames, IA	2,917.5
266	Farmington, NM	2,900.9
267	Hagerstown-Martinsburg, MD-WV	2,899.2
268	San Luis Obispo, CA	2,888.9
269	Elmira, NY	2,874.6
270	Hanford-Corcoran, CA	2,873.3
271	Warren-Farmington Hills, MI M.D.	2,856.5
272	Bay City, MI	2,849.5
273	Blacksburg, VA	2,832.3
274	Altoona, PA	2,819.4
275	Binghamton, NY	2,797.0
276	Jefferson City, MO	2,796.1
277	Danville, VA	2,788.9
278	Syracuse, NY	2,778.6
279	Portland, ME	2,763.0
280	Newark-Union, NJ-PA M.D.	2,759.4
281	Napa, CA	2,759.0
282	Palm Coast, FL	2,750.3
283	Lewiston-Auburn, ME	2,719.2
284	Ithaca, NY	2,716.3
285	Rapid City, SD	2,708.3
286	Scranton--Wilkes-Barre, PA	2,707.1
287	Bethesda-Frederick, MD M.D.	2,698.5
288	Pittsburgh, PA	2,694.5
289	Trenton-Ewing, NJ	2,692.0
290	Santa Barbara-Santa Maria, CA	2,681.7
291	Morgantown, WV	2,668.4
292	Monroe, MI	2,664.3
293	Pittsfield, MA	2,663.9
294	Eau Claire, WI	2,622.8
295	Santa Rosa-Petaluma, CA	2,601.7
296	Williamsport, PA	2,594.1
297	Provo-Orem, UT	2,591.3
298	Harrisburg-Carlisle, PA	2,564.0
299	Dubuque, IA	2,548.9
300	Lancaster, PA	2,546.3
301	Utica-Rome, NY	2,536.2
302	Green Bay, WI	2,523.3
303	Santa Ana-Anaheim, CA M.D.	2,519.7
304	Oshkosh-Neenah, WI	2,515.8
305	Carson City, NV	2,489.0
306	Johnstown, PA	2,441.9
307	Bismarck, ND	2,434.0
308	Naples-Marco Island, FL	2,424.9
309	New York-W. Plains NY-NJ M.D.	2,422.6
310	Appleton, WI	2,408.6
311	Iowa City, IA	2,389.0
312	Lebanon, PA	2,360.6
313	Erie, PA	2,358.1
314	New York (greater), NY-NJ-PA	2,343.4
315	Oxnard-Thousand Oaks, CA	2,342.0
316	Sioux Falls, SD	2,234.2
317	Glens Falls, NY	2,227.0
318	Lynchburg, VA	2,212.6
319	Manchester-Nashua, NH	2,212.0
320	Holland-Grand Haven, MI	2,198.5
321	Poughkeepsie, NY	2,186.3
322	Kingston, NY	2,138.8
323	State College, PA	2,129.6
324	Edison, NJ M.D.	2,085.5
325	Wausau, WI	2,076.3
326	Fond du Lac, WI	2,047.2
327	Nassau-Suffolk, NY M.D.	1,912.4
328	Wheeling, WV-OH	1,901.4
329	Elizabethtown, KY	1,872.4
330	Harrisonburg, VA	1,817.4
331	Logan, UT-ID	1,724.6
NA	Atlanta, GA**	NA
NA	Barnstable Town, MA**	NA
NA	Charlotte-Gastonia, NC-SC**	NA
NA	Chicago, IL**	NA
NA	Duluth, MN-WI**	NA
NA	Fairbanks, AK**	NA
NA	Fargo, ND-MN**	NA
NA	Flagstaff, AZ**	NA
NA	Grand Forks, ND-MN**	NA
NA	Jacksonville, FL**	NA
NA	Killeen-Temple-Fort Hood, TX**	NA
NA	La Crosse, WI-MN**	NA
NA	Minneapolis-St. Paul, MN-WI**	NA
NA	Rochester, MN**	NA
NA	Savannah, GA**	NA
NA	Springfield, MA**	NA
NA	St. Cloud, MN**	NA
NA	Tucson, AZ**	NA
NA	Worcester, MA**	NA

Source: CQ Press using data from Federal Bureau of Investigation "Crime in the United States 2006" (Uniform Crime Reports, September 24, 2007)

**Includes murder, rape, robbery, aggravated assault, burglary, larceny-theft, and motor vehicle theft.*

***Not available.*

3. Percent Change in Crime Rate: 2005 to 2006

National Percent Change = 2.4% Decrease*

RANK	METROPOLITAN AREA	% CHANGE
NA	Abilene, TX**	NA
75	Albany-Schenectady-Troy, NY	2.9
52	Albany, GA	5.3
164	Albuquerque, NM	(2.6)
16	Alexandria, LA	9.4
63	Altoona, PA	4.4
244	Amarillo, TX	(8.0)
134	Ames, IA	(0.7)
52	Anchorage, AK	5.3
219	Anderson, SC	(6.3)
230	Ann Arbor, MI	(6.8)
38	Appleton, WI	6.9
234	Asheville, NC	(7.2)
56	Athens-Clarke County, GA	5.1
NA	Atlanta, GA**	NA
145	Atlantic City, NJ	(1.5)
118	Augusta, GA-SC	0.3
186	Austin-Round Rock, TX	(4.3)
178	Bakersfield, CA	(3.7)
123	Baltimore-Towson, MD	0.0
15	Bangor, ME	9.7
NA	Barnstable Town, MA**	NA
41	Baton Rouge, LA	6.5
109	Battle Creek, MI	0.8
181	Bay City, MI	(3.9)
263	Beaumont-Port Arthur, TX	(10.0)
250	Bellingham, WA	(8.8)
293	Bend, OR	(17.9)
49	Bethesda-Frederick, MD M.D.	5.5
302	Billings, MT	(21.5)
61	Binghamton, NY	4.6
NA	Birmingham-Hoover, AL**	NA
55	Bismarck, ND	5.2
143	Blacksburg, VA	(1.4)
10	Bloomington, IN	11.0
NA	Boise City-Nampa, ID**	NA
173	Bowling Green, KY	(3.5)
227	Bremerton-Silverdale, WA	(6.7)
230	Brownsville-Harlingen, TX	(6.8)
139	Brunswick, GA	(1.2)
161	Buffalo-Niagara Falls, NY	(2.5)
94	Burlington, NC	1.4
59	Camden, NJ M.D.	4.8
85	Cape Coral-Fort Myers, FL	2.1
290	Carson City, NV	(17.3)
196	Casper, WY	(5.2)
201	Cedar Rapids, IA	(5.4)
139	Charleston-North Charleston, SC	(1.2)
253	Charleston, WV	(9.0)
NA	Charlotte-Gastonia, NC-SC**	NA
32	Charlottesville, VA	7.7
233	Chattanooga, TN-GA	(7.0)
225	Cheyenne, WY	(6.6)
NA	Chicago, IL**	NA
170	Chico, CA	(3.2)
118	Cincinnati-Middletown, OH-KY-IN	0.3
86	Clarksville, TN-KY	2.0
NA	Cleveland-Elyria-Mentor, OH**	NA
NA	Cleveland, TN**	NA
276	Coeur d'Alene, ID	(12.5)
235	College Station-Bryan, TX	(7.3)
223	Colorado Springs, CO	(6.5)
132	Columbia, MO	(0.6)
172	Columbia, SC	(3.4)
82	Columbus, GA-AL	2.3
44	Columbus, IN	6.2
165	Columbus, OH	(2.7)
227	Corpus Christi, TX	(6.7)
16	Cumberland, MD-WV	9.4
217	Dallas (greater), TX	(6.2)
219	Dallas-Plano-Irving, TX M.D.	(6.3)
NA	Dalton, GA**	NA
128	Danville, VA	(0.3)
35	Daytona Beach, FL	7.5
128	Dayton, OH	(0.3)
49	Decatur, AL	5.5
288	Denver-Aurora, CO	(16.1)
NA	Des Moines-West Des Moines, IA**	NA
NA	Detroit (greater), MI**	NA
30	Detroit-Livonia-Dearborn, MI M.D.	7.8
238	Dothan, AL	(7.5)
77	Dover, DE	2.7
199	Dubuque, IA	(5.3)
NA	Duluth, MN-WI**	NA
NA	Durham, NC**	NA
21	Eau Claire, WI	9.1
89	Edison, NJ M.D.	1.8
151	El Centro, CA	(1.9)
92	El Paso, TX	1.5
235	Elizabethtown, KY	(7.3)
151	Elkhart-Goshen, IN	(1.9)
250	Elmira, NY	(8.8)
67	Erie, PA	3.7
290	Eugene-Springfield, OR	(17.3)
109	Evansville, IN-KY	0.8
NA	Fairbanks, AK**	NA
NA	Fargo, ND-MN**	NA
NA	Farmington, NM**	NA
77	Fayetteville, AR-MO	2.7
30	Fayetteville, NC	7.8
NA	Flagstaff, AZ**	NA
70	Flint, MI	3.0
153	Florence, SC	(2.0)
57	Fond du Lac, WI	5.0
90	Fort Collins-Loveland, CO	1.7
150	Fort Lauderdale, FL M.D.	(1.8)
143	Fort Smith, AR-OK	(1.4)
86	Fort Walton Beach, FL	2.0
NA	Fort Wayne, IN**	NA
212	Fort Worth-Arlington, TX M.D.	(6.0)
244	Fresno, CA	(8.0)
19	Gadsden, AL	9.2
7	Gainesville, FL	11.9
287	Gainesville, GA	(16.0)
NA	Glens Falls, NY**	NA
118	Goldsboro, NC	0.3
NA	Grand Forks, ND-MN**	NA
280	Grand Junction, CO	(13.5)
70	Grand Rapids-Wyoming, MI	3.0
298	Great Falls, MT	(19.8)
299	Greeley, CO	(20.2)
132	Green Bay, WI	(0.6)
122	Greensboro-High Point, NC	0.1
32	Greenville, NC	7.7
184	Greenville, SC	(4.2)
4	Hagerstown-Martinsburg, MD-WV	13.0
250	Hanford-Corcoran, CA	(8.8)
238	Harrisburg-Carlisle, PA	(7.5)
24	Harrisonburg, VA	8.4
139	Hartford, CT	(1.2)
NA	Hattiesburg, MS**	NA
61	Holland-Grand Haven, MI	4.6
254	Honolulu, HI	(9.1)
153	Hot Springs, AR	(2.0)
51	Houma, LA	5.4
156	Houston, TX	(2.1)
26	Huntington-Ashland, WV-KY-OH	8.3
175	Huntsville, AL	(3.6)
32	Idaho Falls, ID	7.7
148	Indianapolis, IN	(1.6)
135	Iowa City, IA	(0.8)
NA	Ithaca, NY**	NA
NA	Jacksonville, FL**	NA
NA	Jacksonville, NC**	NA
47	Jackson, MI	5.7
35	Jackson, MS	7.5
247	Jackson, TN	(8.4)
104	Janesville, WI	1.0
227	Jefferson City, MO	(6.7)
269	Johnson City, TN	(11.7)
NA	Johnstown, PA**	NA
158	Jonesboro, AR	(2.4)
262	Joplin, MO	(9.9)
6	Kalamazoo-Portage, MI	12.0
NA	Kansas City, MO-KS**	NA
267	Kennewick-Richland-Pasco, WA	(11.3)
NA	Killeen-Temple-Fort Hood, TX**	NA
112	Kingsport, TN-VA	0.7
223	Kingston, NY	(6.5)
175	Knoxville, TN	(3.6)
201	Kokomo, IN	(5.4)
NA	La Crosse, WI-MN**	NA
103	Lafayette, IN	1.1
22	Lake Charles, LA	8.9
NA	Lake Havasu City-Kingman, AZ**	NA
191	Lakeland, FL	(4.6)
42	Lancaster, PA	6.3
208	Lansing-East Lansing, MI	(5.8)
149	Laredo, TX	(1.7)
137	Las Cruces, NM	(1.0)
94	Las Vegas-Paradise, NV	1.4

Note: All listings are for Metropolitan Statistical Areas (M.S.A.s) except for those ending with "M.D." Listings with "M.D." are Metropolitan Divisions which are smaller parts of eleven large M.S.A.s. See explanatory note at beginning of metropolitan area section on page 23.

RANK	METROPOLITAN AREA	% CHANGE
1	Lawrence, KS	39.9
80	Lawton, OK	2.5
180	Lebanon, PA	(3.8)
167	Lewiston-Auburn, ME	(3.1)
265	Lewiston, ID-WA	(10.5)
NA	Lexington-Fayette, KY**	NA
241	Lima, OH	(7.8)
184	Lincoln, NE	(4.2)
142	Little Rock, AR	(1.3)
264	Logan, UT-ID	(10.3)
182	Longview, TX	(4.1)
275	Longview, WA	(12.3)
199	Los Angeles County, CA M.D.	(5.3)
204	Los Angeles (greater), CA	(5.5)
64	Louisville, KY-IN	4.2
208	Lubbock, TX	(5.8)
115	Lynchburg, VA	0.4
138	Macon, GA	(1.1)
284	Madera, CA	(14.8)
109	Madison, WI	0.8
104	Manchester-Nashua, NH	1.0
19	Mansfield, OH	9.2
282	McAllen-Edinburg-Mission, TX	(14.4)
300	Medford, OR	(20.6)
126	Memphis, TN-MS-AR	(0.1)
196	Merced, CA	(5.2)
161	Miami (greater), FL	(2.5)
178	Miami-Dade County, FL M.D.	(3.7)
14	Michigan City-La Porte, IN	9.9
145	Midland, TX	(1.5)
3	Milwaukee, WI	13.2
NA	Minneapolis-St. Paul, MN-WI**	NA
292	Missoula, MT	(17.5)
24	Mobile, AL	8.4
246	Modesto, CA	(8.1)
65	Monroe, LA	4.1
69	Monroe, MI	3.3
186	Montgomery, AL	(4.3)
98	Morgantown, WV	1.3
130	Morristown, TN	(0.4)
301	Mount Vernon-Anacortes, WA	(21.4)
9	Muncie, IN	11.4
100	Muskegon-Norton Shores, MI	1.2
167	Myrtle Beach, SC	(3.1)
153	Napa, CA	(2.0)
195	Naples-Marco Island, FL	(5.0)
225	Nashville-Davidson, TN	(6.6)
91	Nassau-Suffolk, NY M.D.	1.6
NA	New Orleans, LA**	NA
173	New York (greater), NY-NJ-PA	(3.5)
193	New York-W. Plains NY-NJ M.D.	(4.8)
215	Newark-Union, NJ-PA M.D.	(6.1)
88	Niles-Benton Harbor, MI	1.9
76	Oakland-Fremont, CA M.D.	2.8
215	Ocala, FL	(6.1)
37	Ocean City, NJ	7.2
222	Odessa, TX	(6.4)
201	Ogden-Clearfield, UT	(5.4)
277	Oklahoma City, OK	(12.7)
266	Olympia, WA	(10.6)

RANK	METROPOLITAN AREA	% CHANGE
158	Omaha-Council Bluffs, NE-IA	(2.4)
98	Orlando, FL	1.3
23	Oshkosh-Neenah, WI	8.8
123	Oxnard-Thousand Oaks, CA	0.0
46	Palm Bay-Melbourne, FL	5.8
NA	Palm Coast, FL**	NA
156	Panama City-Lynn Haven, FL	(2.1)
2	Pascagoula, MS	13.4
27	Pensacola, FL	8.1
45	Philadelphia (greater) PA-NJ-DE	6.0
48	Philadelphia, PA M.D.	5.6
219	Phoenix-Mesa-Scottsdale, AZ	(6.3)
259	Pine Bluff, AR	(9.8)
175	Pittsburgh, PA	(3.6)
10	Pittsfield, MA	11.0
256	Pocatello, ID	(9.3)
40	Port St. Lucie, FL	6.6
289	Portland-Vancouver, OR-WA	(16.2)
38	Portland, ME	6.9
92	Poughkeepsie, NY	1.5
257	Prescott, AZ	(9.5)
295	Provo-Orem, UT	(18.7)
259	Pueblo, CO	(9.8)
18	Punta Gorda, FL	9.3
126	Racine, WI	(0.1)
94	Raleigh-Cary, NC	1.4
296	Rapid City, SD	(19.1)
212	Reading, PA	(6.0)
297	Redding, CA	(19.2)
158	Reno-Sparks, NV	(2.4)
NA	Richmond, VA**	NA
210	Riverside-San Bernardino, CA	(5.9)
272	Roanoke, VA	(11.9)
NA	Rochester, MN**	NA
100	Rochester, NY	1.2
12	Rocky Mount, NC	10.6
271	Rome, GA	(11.8)
145	Sacramento, CA	(1.5)
108	Saginaw, MI	0.9
278	Salem, OR	(13.4)
241	Salinas, CA	(7.8)
42	Salisbury, MD	6.3
238	Salt Lake City, UT	(7.5)
278	San Angelo, TX	(13.4)
190	San Antonio, TX	(4.5)
189	San Diego, CA	(4.4)
70	San Francisco (greater), CA	3.0
68	San Francisco-S. Mateo, CA M.D.	3.4
81	San Jose, CA	2.4
70	San Luis Obispo, CA	3.0
115	Sandusky, OH	0.4
210	Santa Ana-Anaheim, CA M.D.	(5.9)
194	Santa Barbara-Santa Maria, CA	(4.9)
171	Santa Cruz-Watsonville, CA	(3.3)
196	Santa Fe, NM	(5.2)
286	Santa Rosa-Petaluma, CA	(15.2)
82	Sarasota-Bradenton-Venice, FL	2.3
NA	Savannah, GA**	NA
123	Scranton--Wilkes-Barre, PA	0.0
207	Seattle (greater), WA	(5.7)

RANK	METROPOLITAN AREA	% CHANGE
217	Seattle-Bellevue, WA M.D.	(6.2)
257	Sebastian-Vero Beach, FL	(9.5)
5	Sheboygan, WI	12.1
272	Sherman-Denison, TX	(11.9)
59	Shreveport-Bossier City, LA	4.8
167	Sioux City, IA-NE-SD	(3.1)
283	Sioux Falls, SD	(14.7)
28	South Bend-Mishawaka, IN-MI	8.0
52	Spartanburg, SC	5.3
204	Spokane, WA	(5.5)
NA	Springfield, MA**	NA
65	Springfield, MO	4.1
114	Springfield, OH	0.6
104	State College, PA	1.0
166	Stockton, CA	(2.9)
NA	St. Cloud, MN**	NA
186	St. Joseph, MO-KS	(4.3)
79	St. Louis, MO-IL	2.6
104	Sumter, SC	1.0
100	Syracuse, NY	1.2
182	Tacoma, WA M.D.	(4.1)
192	Tallahassee, FL	(4.7)
115	Tampa-St Petersburg, FL	0.4
243	Texarkana, TX-Texarkana, AR	(7.9)
70	Toledo, OH	3.0
212	Topeka, KS	(6.0)
274	Trenton-Ewing, NJ	(12.2)
NA	Tucson, AZ**	NA
235	Tulsa, OK	(7.3)
NA	Tuscaloosa, AL**	NA
259	Tyler, TX	(9.8)
94	Utica-Rome, NY	1.4
269	Valdosta, GA	(11.7)
NA	Vallejo-Fairfield, CA**	NA
285	Victoria, TX	(15.1)
121	Vineland, NJ	0.2
232	Virginia Beach-Norfolk, VA-NC	(6.9)
NA	Visalia-Porterville, CA**	NA
281	Waco, TX	(13.8)
248	Warner Robins, GA	(8.5)
NA	Warren-Farmington Hills, MI M.D.**	NA
NA	Washington (greater) DC-VA-MD**	NA
NA	Washington, DC-VA-MD-WV M.D.**	NA
112	Waterloo-Cedar Falls, IA	0.7
82	Wausau, WI	2.3
248	Wenatchee, WA	(8.5)
130	West Palm Beach, FL M.D.	(0.4)
206	Wheeling, WV-OH	(5.6)
294	Wichita Falls, TX	(18.6)
NA	Wichita, KS**	NA
8	Williamsport, PA	11.5
13	Wilmington, DE-MD-NJ M.D.	10.1
161	Wilmington, NC	(2.5)
29	Winchester, VA-WV	7.9
58	Winston-Salem, NC	4.9
NA	Worcester, MA**	NA
254	Yakima, WA	(9.1)
267	Yuba City, CA	(11.3)
135	Yuma, AZ	(0.8)

Source: CQ Press using data from Federal Bureau of Investigation "Crime in the United States 2006" (Uniform Crime Reports, September 24, 2007)

**Includes murder, rape, robbery, aggravated assault, burglary, larceny-theft, and motor vehicle theft.*

***Not available.*

3. Percent Change in Crime Rate: 2005 to 2006 (continued)

National Percent Change = 2.4% Decrease*

RANK	METROPOLITAN AREA	% CHANGE
1	Lawrence, KS	39.9
2	Pascagoula, MS	13.4
3	Milwaukee, WI	13.2
4	Hagerstown-Martinsburg, MD-WV	13.0
5	Sheboygan, WI	12.1
6	Kalamazoo-Portage, MI	12.0
7	Gainesville, FL	11.9
8	Williamsport, PA	11.5
9	Muncie, IN	11.4
10	Bloomington, IN	11.0
10	Pittsfield, MA	11.0
12	Rocky Mount, NC	10.6
13	Wilmington, DE-MD-NJ M.D.	10.1
14	Michigan City-La Porte, IN	9.9
15	Bangor, ME	9.7
16	Alexandria, LA	9.4
16	Cumberland, MD-WV	9.4
18	Punta Gorda, FL	9.3
19	Gadsden, AL	9.2
19	Mansfield, OH	9.2
21	Eau Claire, WI	9.1
22	Lake Charles, LA	8.9
23	Oshkosh-Neenah, WI	8.8
24	Harrisonburg, VA	8.4
24	Mobile, AL	8.4
26	Huntington-Ashland, WV-KY-OH	8.3
27	Pensacola, FL	8.1
28	South Bend-Mishawaka, IN-MI	8.0
29	Winchester, VA-WV	7.9
30	Detroit-Livonia-Dearborn, MI M.D.	7.8
30	Fayetteville, NC	7.8
32	Charlottesville, VA	7.7
32	Greenville, NC	7.7
32	Idaho Falls, ID	7.7
35	Daytona Beach, FL	7.5
35	Jackson, MS	7.5
37	Ocean City, NJ	7.2
38	Appleton, WI	6.9
38	Portland, ME	6.9
40	Port St. Lucie, FL	6.6
41	Baton Rouge, LA	6.5
42	Lancaster, PA	6.3
42	Salisbury, MD	6.3
44	Columbus, IN	6.2
45	Philadelphia (greater) PA-NJ-DE	6.0
46	Palm Bay-Melbourne, FL	5.8
47	Jackson, MI	5.7
48	Philadelphia, PA M.D.	5.6
49	Bethesda-Frederick, MD M.D.	5.5
49	Decatur, AL	5.5
51	Houma, LA	5.4
52	Albany, GA	5.3
52	Anchorage, AK	5.3
52	Spartanburg, SC	5.3
55	Bismarck, ND	5.2
56	Athens-Clarke County, GA	5.1
57	Fond du Lac, WI	5.0
58	Winston-Salem, NC	4.9
59	Camden, NJ M.D.	4.8
59	Shreveport-Bossier City, LA	4.8
61	Binghamton, NY	4.6
61	Holland-Grand Haven, MI	4.6
63	Altoona, PA	4.4
64	Louisville, KY-IN	4.2
65	Monroe, LA	4.1
65	Springfield, MO	4.1
67	Erie, PA	3.7
68	San Francisco-S. Mateo, CA M.D.	3.4
69	Monroe, MI	3.3
70	Flint, MI	3.0
70	Grand Rapids-Wyoming, MI	3.0
70	San Francisco (greater), CA	3.0
70	San Luis Obispo, CA	3.0
70	Toledo, OH	3.0
75	Albany-Schenectady-Troy, NY	2.9
76	Oakland-Fremont, CA M.D.	2.8
77	Dover, DE	2.7
77	Fayetteville, AR-MO	2.7
79	St. Louis, MO-IL	2.6
80	Lawton, OK	2.5
81	San Jose, CA	2.4
82	Columbus, GA-AL	2.3
82	Sarasota-Bradenton-Venice, FL	2.3
82	Wausau, WI	2.3
85	Cape Coral-Fort Myers, FL	2.1
86	Clarksville, TN-KY	2.0
86	Fort Walton Beach, FL	2.0
88	Niles-Benton Harbor, MI	1.9
89	Edison, NJ M.D.	1.8
90	Fort Collins-Loveland, CO	1.7
91	Nassau-Suffolk, NY M.D.	1.6
92	El Paso, TX	1.5
92	Poughkeepsie, NY	1.5
94	Burlington, NC	1.4
94	Las Vegas-Paradise, NV	1.4
94	Raleigh-Cary, NC	1.4
94	Utica-Rome, NY	1.4
98	Morgantown, WV	1.3
98	Orlando, FL	1.3
100	Muskegon-Norton Shores, MI	1.2
100	Rochester, NY	1.2
100	Syracuse, NY	1.2
103	Lafayette, IN	1.1
104	Janesville, WI	1.0
104	Manchester-Nashua, NH	1.0
104	State College, PA	1.0
104	Sumter, SC	1.0
108	Saginaw, MI	0.9
109	Battle Creek, MI	0.8
109	Evansville, IN-KY	0.8
109	Madison, WI	0.8
112	Kingsport, TN-VA	0.7
112	Waterloo-Cedar Falls, IA	0.7
114	Springfield, OH	0.6
115	Lynchburg, VA	0.4
115	Sandusky, OH	0.4
115	Tampa-St Petersburg, FL	0.4
118	Augusta, GA-SC	0.3
118	Cincinnati-Middletown, OH-KY-IN	0.3
118	Goldsboro, NC	0.3
121	Vineland, NJ	0.2
122	Greensboro-High Point, NC	0.1
123	Baltimore-Towson, MD	0.0
123	Oxnard-Thousand Oaks, CA	0.0
123	Scranton--Wilkes-Barre, PA	0.0
126	Memphis, TN-MS-AR	(0.1)
126	Racine, WI	(0.1)
128	Danville, VA	(0.3)
128	Dayton, OH	(0.3)
130	Morristown, TN	(0.4)
130	West Palm Beach, FL M.D.	(0.4)
132	Columbia, MO	(0.6)
132	Green Bay, WI	(0.6)
134	Ames, IA	(0.7)
135	Iowa City, IA	(0.8)
135	Yuma, AZ	(0.8)
137	Las Cruces, NM	(1.0)
138	Macon, GA	(1.1)
139	Brunswick, GA	(1.2)
139	Charleston-North Charleston, SC	(1.2)
139	Hartford, CT	(1.2)
142	Little Rock, AR	(1.3)
143	Blacksburg, VA	(1.4)
143	Fort Smith, AR-OK	(1.4)
145	Atlantic City, NJ	(1.5)
145	Midland, TX	(1.5)
145	Sacramento, CA	(1.5)
148	Indianapolis, IN	(1.6)
149	Laredo, TX	(1.7)
150	Fort Lauderdale, FL M.D.	(1.8)
151	El Centro, CA	(1.9)
151	Elkhart-Goshen, IN	(1.9)
153	Florence, SC	(2.0)
153	Hot Springs, AR	(2.0)
153	Napa, CA	(2.0)
156	Houston, TX	(2.1)
156	Panama City-Lynn Haven, FL	(2.1)
158	Jonesboro, AR	(2.4)
158	Omaha-Council Bluffs, NE-IA	(2.4)
158	Reno-Sparks, NV	(2.4)
161	Buffalo-Niagara Falls, NY	(2.5)
161	Miami (greater), FL	(2.5)
161	Wilmington, NC	(2.5)
164	Albuquerque, NM	(2.6)
165	Columbus, OH	(2.7)
166	Stockton, CA	(2.9)
167	Lewiston-Auburn, ME	(3.1)
167	Myrtle Beach, SC	(3.1)
167	Sioux City, IA-NE-SD	(3.1)
170	Chico, CA	(3.2)
171	Santa Cruz-Watsonville, CA	(3.3)

Note: All listings are for Metropolitan Statistical Areas (M.S.A.s) except for those ending with "M.D." Listings with "M.D." are Metropolitan Divisions which are smaller parts of eleven large M.S.A.s. See explanatory note at beginning of metropolitan area section on page 23.

RANK	METROPOLITAN AREA	% CHANGE
172	Columbia, SC	(3.4)
173	Bowling Green, KY	(3.5)
173	New York (greater), NY-NJ-PA	(3.5)
175	Huntsville, AL	(3.6)
175	Knoxville, TN	(3.6)
175	Pittsburgh, PA	(3.6)
178	Bakersfield, CA	(3.7)
178	Miami-Dade County, FL M.D.	(3.7)
180	Lebanon, PA	(3.8)
181	Bay City, MI	(3.9)
182	Longview, TX	(4.1)
182	Tacoma, WA M.D.	(4.1)
184	Greenville, SC	(4.2)
184	Lincoln, NE	(4.2)
186	Austin-Round Rock, TX	(4.3)
186	Montgomery, AL	(4.3)
186	St. Joseph, MO-KS	(4.3)
189	San Diego, CA	(4.4)
190	San Antonio, TX	(4.5)
191	Lakeland, FL	(4.6)
192	Tallahassee, FL	(4.7)
193	New York-W. Plains NY-NJ M.D.	(4.8)
194	Santa Barbara-Santa Maria, CA	(4.9)
195	Naples-Marco Island, FL	(5.0)
196	Casper, WY	(5.2)
196	Merced, CA	(5.2)
196	Santa Fe, NM	(5.2)
199	Dubuque, IA	(5.3)
199	Los Angeles County, CA M.D.	(5.3)
201	Cedar Rapids, IA	(5.4)
201	Kokomo, IN	(5.4)
201	Ogden-Clearfield, UT	(5.4)
204	Los Angeles (greater), CA	(5.5)
204	Spokane, WA	(5.5)
206	Wheeling, WV-OH	(5.6)
207	Seattle (greater), WA	(5.7)
208	Lansing-East Lansing, MI	(5.8)
208	Lubbock, TX	(5.8)
210	Riverside-San Bernardino, CA	(5.9)
210	Santa Ana-Anaheim, CA M.D.	(5.9)
212	Fort Worth-Arlington, TX M.D.	(6.0)
212	Reading, PA	(6.0)
212	Topeka, KS	(6.0)
215	Newark-Union, NJ-PA M.D.	(6.1)
215	Ocala, FL	(6.1)
217	Dallas (greater), TX	(6.2)
217	Seattle-Bellevue, WA M.D.	(6.2)
219	Anderson, SC	(6.3)
219	Dallas-Plano-Irving, TX M.D.	(6.3)
219	Phoenix-Mesa-Scottsdale, AZ	(6.3)
222	Odessa, TX	(6.4)
223	Colorado Springs, CO	(6.5)
223	Kingston, NY	(6.5)
225	Cheyenne, WY	(6.6)
225	Nashville-Davidson, TN	(6.6)
227	Bremerton-Silverdale, WA	(6.7)
227	Corpus Christi, TX	(6.7)
227	Jefferson City, MO	(6.7)
230	Ann Arbor, MI	(6.8)
230	Brownsville-Harlingen, TX	(6.8)

RANK	METROPOLITAN AREA	% CHANGE
232	Virginia Beach-Norfolk, VA-NC	(6.9)
233	Chattanooga, TN-GA	(7.0)
234	Asheville, NC	(7.2)
235	College Station-Bryan, TX	(7.3)
235	Elizabethtown, KY	(7.3)
235	Tulsa, OK	(7.3)
238	Dothan, AL	(7.5)
238	Harrisburg-Carlisle, PA	(7.5)
238	Salt Lake City, UT	(7.5)
241	Lima, OH	(7.8)
241	Salinas, CA	(7.8)
243	Texarkana, TX-Texarkana, AR	(7.9)
244	Amarillo, TX	(8.0)
244	Fresno, CA	(8.0)
246	Modesto, CA	(8.1)
247	Jackson, TN	(8.4)
248	Warner Robins, GA	(8.5)
248	Wenatchee, WA	(8.5)
250	Bellingham, WA	(8.8)
250	Elmira, NY	(8.8)
250	Hanford-Corcoran, CA	(8.8)
253	Charleston, WV	(9.0)
254	Honolulu, HI	(9.1)
254	Yakima, WA	(9.1)
256	Pocatello, ID	(9.3)
257	Prescott, AZ	(9.5)
257	Sebastian-Vero Beach, FL	(9.5)
259	Pine Bluff, AR	(9.8)
259	Pueblo, CO	(9.8)
259	Tyler, TX	(9.8)
262	Joplin, MO	(9.9)
263	Beaumont-Port Arthur, TX	(10.0)
264	Logan, UT-ID	(10.3)
265	Lewiston, ID-WA	(10.5)
266	Olympia, WA	(10.6)
267	Kennewick-Richland-Pasco, WA	(11.3)
267	Yuba City, CA	(11.3)
269	Johnson City, TN	(11.7)
269	Valdosta, GA	(11.7)
271	Rome, GA	(11.8)
272	Roanoke, VA	(11.9)
272	Sherman-Denison, TX	(11.9)
274	Trenton-Ewing, NJ	(12.2)
275	Longview, WA	(12.3)
276	Coeur d'Alene, ID	(12.5)
277	Oklahoma City, OK	(12.7)
278	Salem, OR	(13.4)
278	San Angelo, TX	(13.4)
280	Grand Junction, CO	(13.5)
281	Waco, TX	(13.8)
282	McAllen-Edinburg-Mission, TX	(14.4)
283	Sioux Falls, SD	(14.7)
284	Madera, CA	(14.8)
285	Victoria, TX	(15.1)
286	Santa Rosa-Petaluma, CA	(15.2)
287	Gainesville, GA	(16.0)
288	Denver-Aurora, CO	(16.1)
289	Portland-Vancouver, OR-WA	(16.2)
290	Carson City, NV	(17.3)
290	Eugene-Springfield, OR	(17.3)

RANK	METROPOLITAN AREA	% CHANGE
292	Missoula, MT	(17.5)
293	Bend, OR	(17.9)
294	Wichita Falls, TX	(18.6)
295	Provo-Orem, UT	(18.7)
296	Rapid City, SD	(19.1)
297	Redding, CA	(19.2)
298	Great Falls, MT	(19.8)
299	Greeley, CO	(20.2)
300	Medford, OR	(20.6)
301	Mount Vernon-Anacortes, WA	(21.4)
302	Billings, MT	(21.5)
NA	Abilene, TX**	NA
NA	Atlanta, GA**	NA
NA	Barnstable Town, MA**	NA
NA	Birmingham-Hoover, AL**	NA
NA	Boise City-Nampa, ID**	NA
NA	Charlotte-Gastonia, NC-SC**	NA
NA	Chicago, IL**	NA
NA	Cleveland-Elyria-Mentor, OH**	NA
NA	Cleveland, TN**	NA
NA	Dalton, GA**	NA
NA	Des Moines-West Des Moines, IA**	NA
NA	Detroit (greater), MI**	NA
NA	Duluth, MN-WI**	NA
NA	Durham, NC**	NA
NA	Fairbanks, AK**	NA
NA	Fargo, ND-MN**	NA
NA	Farmington, NM**	NA
NA	Flagstaff, AZ**	NA
NA	Fort Wayne, IN**	NA
NA	Glens Falls, NY**	NA
NA	Grand Forks, ND-MN**	NA
NA	Hattiesburg, MS**	NA
NA	Ithaca, NY**	NA
NA	Jacksonville, FL**	NA
NA	Jacksonville, NC**	NA
NA	Johnstown, PA**	NA
NA	Kansas City, MO-KS**	NA
NA	Killeen-Temple-Fort Hood, TX**	NA
NA	La Crosse, WI-MN**	NA
NA	Lake Havasu City-Kingman, AZ**	NA
NA	Lexington-Fayette, KY**	NA
NA	Minneapolis-St. Paul, MN-WI**	NA
NA	New Orleans, LA**	NA
NA	Palm Coast, FL**	NA
NA	Richmond, VA**	NA
NA	Rochester, MN**	NA
NA	Savannah, GA**	NA
NA	Springfield, MA**	NA
NA	St. Cloud, MN**	NA
NA	Tucson, AZ**	NA
NA	Tuscaloosa, AL**	NA
NA	Vallejo-Fairfield, CA**	NA
NA	Visalia-Porterville, CA**	NA
NA	Warren-Farmington Hills, MI M.D.**	NA
NA	Washington (greater) DC-VA-MD**	NA
NA	Washington, DC-VA-MD-WV M.D.**	NA
NA	Wichita, KS**	NA
NA	Worcester, MA**	NA

Source: CQ Press using data from Federal Bureau of Investigation "Crime in the United States 2006" (Uniform Crime Reports, September 24, 2007)

**Includes murder, rape, robbery, aggravated assault, burglary, larceny-theft, and motor vehicle theft.*

***Not available.*

4. Percent Change in Crime Rate: 2002 to 2006

National Percent Change = 7.7% Decrease*

RANK	METROPOLITAN AREA	% CHANGE
NA	Abilene, TX**	NA
NA	Albany-Schenectady-Troy, NY**	NA
117	Albany, GA	(12.0)
100	Albuquerque, NM	(9.1)
74	Alexandria, LA	(5.6)
49	Altoona, PA	(1.2)
130	Amarillo, TX	(13.5)
NA	Ames, IA**	NA
33	Anchorage, AK	3.6
NA	Anderson, SC**	NA
NA	Ann Arbor, MI**	NA
NA	Appleton, WI**	NA
104	Asheville, NC	(9.4)
120	Athens-Clarke County, GA	(12.2)
NA	Atlanta, GA**	NA
NA	Atlantic City, NJ**	NA
11	Augusta, GA-SC	11.8
107	Austin-Round Rock, TX	(9.9)
5	Bakersfield, CA	16.0
147	Baltimore-Towson, MD	(16.0)
NA	Bangor, ME**	NA
NA	Barnstable Town, MA**	NA
126	Baton Rouge, LA	(13.2)
NA	Battle Creek, MI**	NA
NA	Bay City, MI**	NA
137	Beaumont-Port Arthur, TX	(14.8)
71	Bellingham, WA	(5.1)
NA	Bend, OR**	NA
NA	Bethesda-Frederick, MD M.D.**	NA
155	Billings, MT	(18.1)
24	Binghamton, NY	6.1
31	Birmingham-Hoover, AL	4.0
75	Bismarck, ND	(5.8)
NA	Blacksburg, VA**	NA
90	Bloomington, IN	(7.6)
189	Boise City-Nampa, ID	(27.1)
NA	Bowling Green, KY**	NA
161	Bremerton-Silverdale, WA	(19.6)
165	Brownsville-Harlingen, TX	(20.6)
NA	Brunswick, GA**	NA
53	Buffalo-Niagara Falls, NY	(2.0)
NA	Burlington, NC**	NA
NA	Camden, NJ M.D.**	NA
111	Cape Coral-Fort Myers, FL	(10.3)
NA	Carson City, NV**	NA
69	Casper, WY	(4.9)
187	Cedar Rapids, IA	(26.7)
114	Charleston-North Charleston, SC	(10.8)
36	Charleston, WV	3.0
NA	Charlotte-Gastonia, NC-SC**	NA
NA	Charlottesville, VA**	NA
116	Chattanooga, TN-GA	(11.9)
106	Cheyenne, WY	(9.7)
NA	Chicago, IL**	NA
91	Chico, CA	(7.7)
113	Cincinnati-Middletown, OH-KY-IN	(10.7)
185	Clarksville, TN-KY	(25.8)
NA	Cleveland-Elyria-Mentor, OH**	NA
NA	Cleveland, TN**	NA
NA	Coeur d'Alene, ID**	NA
NA	College Station-Bryan, TX**	NA
100	Colorado Springs, CO	(9.1)
115	Columbia, MO	(11.3)
177	Columbia, SC	(23.2)
3	Columbus, GA-AL	19.6
NA	Columbus, IN**	NA
154	Columbus, OH	(17.8)
45	Corpus Christi, TX	0.8
14	Cumberland, MD-WV	10.1
NA	Dallas (greater), TX**	NA
143	Dallas-Plano-Irving, TX M.D.	(15.4)
NA	Dalton, GA**	NA
10	Danville, VA	12.1
69	Daytona Beach, FL	(4.9)
NA	Dayton, OH**	NA
9	Decatur, AL	12.4
135	Denver-Aurora, CO	(14.7)
NA	Des Moines-West Des Moines, IA**	NA
43	Detroit (greater), MI	1.2
NA	Detroit-Livonia-Dearborn, MI M.D.**	NA
NA	Dothan, AL**	NA
68	Dover, DE	(4.5)
75	Dubuque, IA	(5.8)
NA	Duluth, MN-WI**	NA
NA	Durham, NC**	NA
128	Eau Claire, WI	(13.4)
NA	Edison, NJ M.D.**	NA
NA	El Centro, CA**	NA
146	El Paso, TX	(15.7)
NA	Elizabethtown, KY**	NA
98	Elkhart-Goshen, IN	(8.9)
NA	Elmira, NY**	NA
81	Erie, PA	(6.3)
72	Eugene-Springfield, OR	(5.2)
NA	Evansville, IN-KY**	NA
NA	Fairbanks, AK**	NA
NA	Fargo, ND-MN**	NA
NA	Farmington, NM**	NA
NA	Fayetteville, AR-MO**	NA
23	Fayetteville, NC	6.5
NA	Flagstaff, AZ**	NA
32	Flint, MI	3.8
33	Florence, SC	3.6
NA	Fond du Lac, WI**	NA
118	Fort Collins-Loveland, CO	(12.1)
58	Fort Lauderdale, FL M.D.	(3.3)
160	Fort Smith, AR-OK	(19.4)
19	Fort Walton Beach, FL	7.3
NA	Fort Wayne, IN**	NA
135	Fort Worth-Arlington, TX M.D.	(14.7)
124	Fresno, CA	(12.8)
35	Gadsden, AL	3.5
52	Gainesville, FL	(1.8)
NA	Gainesville, GA**	NA
95	Glens Falls, NY	(8.4)
63	Goldsboro, NC	(4.1)
NA	Grand Forks, ND-MN**	NA
18	Grand Junction, CO	7.6
NA	Grand Rapids-Wyoming, MI**	NA
197	Great Falls, MT	(36.2)
162	Greeley, CO	(19.9)
124	Green Bay, WI	(12.8)
NA	Greensboro-High Point, NC**	NA
118	Greenville, NC	(12.1)
NA	Greenville, SC**	NA
NA	Hagerstown-Martinsburg, MD-WV**	NA
NA	Hanford-Corcoran, CA**	NA
NA	Harrisburg-Carlisle, PA**	NA
NA	Harrisonburg, VA**	NA
44	Hartford, CT	1.1
NA	Hattiesburg, MS**	NA
NA	Holland-Grand Haven, MI**	NA
192	Honolulu, HI	(29.3)
NA	Hot Springs, AR**	NA
63	Houma, LA	(4.1)
122	Houston, TX	(12.3)
NA	Huntington-Ashland, WV-KY-OH**	NA
2	Huntsville, AL	21.0
NA	Idaho Falls, ID**	NA
NA	Indianapolis, IN**	NA
193	Iowa City, IA	(30.9)
NA	Ithaca, NY**	NA
NA	Jacksonville, FL**	NA
NA	Jacksonville, NC**	NA
86	Jackson, MI	(7.3)
179	Jackson, MS	(24.0)
15	Jackson, TN	9.6
107	Janesville, WI	(9.9)
NA	Jefferson City, MO**	NA
NA	Johnson City, TN**	NA
NA	Johnstown, PA**	NA
6	Jonesboro, AR	15.7
41	Joplin, MO	1.8
NA	Kalamazoo-Portage, MI**	NA
NA	Kansas City, MO-KS**	NA
78	Kennewick-Richland-Pasco, WA	(5.9)
NA	Killeen-Temple-Fort Hood, TX**	NA
NA	Kingsport, TN-VA**	NA
NA	Kingston, NY**	NA
85	Knoxville, TN	(6.9)
25	Kokomo, IN	5.6
NA	La Crosse, WI-MN**	NA
78	Lafayette, IN	(5.9)
103	Lake Charles, LA	(9.2)
NA	Lake Havasu City-Kingman, AZ**	NA
142	Lakeland, FL	(15.2)
97	Lancaster, PA	(8.6)
107	Lansing-East Lansing, MI	(9.9)
91	Laredo, TX	(7.7)
NA	Las Cruces, NM**	NA
12	Las Vegas-Paradise, NV	11.4

Note: All listings are for Metropolitan Statistical Areas (M.S.A.s) except for those ending with "M.D." Listings with "M.D." are Metropolitan Divisions which are smaller parts of eleven large M.S.A.s. See explanatory note at beginning of metropolitan area section on page 23.

RANK	METROPOLITAN AREA	% CHANGE
1	Lawrence, KS	31.6
37	Lawton, OK	2.9
NA	Lebanon, PA**	NA
155	Lewiston-Auburn, ME	(18.1)
NA	Lewiston, ID-WA**	NA
NA	Lexington-Fayette, KY**	NA
NA	Lima, OH**	NA
157	Lincoln, NE	(18.2)
61	Little Rock, AR	(3.8)
NA	Logan, UT-ID**	NA
48	Longview, TX	(0.3)
NA	Longview, WA**	NA
151	Los Angeles County, CA M.D.	(16.6)
NA	Los Angeles (greater), CA**	NA
128	Louisville, KY-IN	(13.4)
66	Lubbock, TX	(4.3)
94	Lynchburg, VA	(8.1)
NA	Macon, GA**	NA
NA	Madera, CA**	NA
111	Madison, WI	(10.3)
NA	Manchester-Nashua, NH**	NA
NA	Mansfield, OH**	NA
139	McAllen-Edinburg-Mission, TX	(14.9)
184	Medford, OR	(25.7)
NA	Memphis, TN-MS-AR**	NA
137	Merced, CA	(14.8)
NA	Miami (greater), FL**	NA
148	Miami-Dade County, FL M.D.	(16.1)
NA	Michigan City-La Porte, IN**	NA
NA	Midland, TX**	NA
NA	Milwaukee, WI**	NA
NA	Minneapolis-St. Paul, MN-WI**	NA
NA	Missoula, MT**	NA
NA	Mobile, AL**	NA
93	Modesto, CA	(8.0)
NA	Monroe, LA**	NA
NA	Monroe, MI**	NA
179	Montgomery, AL	(24.0)
NA	Morgantown, WV**	NA
NA	Morristown, TN**	NA
NA	Mount Vernon-Anacortes, WA**	NA
20	Muncie, IN	7.2
NA	Muskegon-Norton Shores, MI**	NA
88	Myrtle Beach, SC	(7.4)
NA	Napa, CA**	NA
196	Naples-Marco Island, FL	(34.5)
144	Nashville-Davidson, TN	(15.5)
NA	Nassau-Suffolk, NY M.D.**	NA
182	New Orleans, LA	(24.9)
NA	New York (greater), NY-NJ-PA**	NA
158	New York-W. Plains NY-NJ M.D.	(18.5)
167	Newark-Union, NJ-PA M.D.	(21.0)
NA	Niles-Benton Harbor, MI**	NA
51	Oakland-Fremont, CA M.D.	(1.5)
144	Ocala, FL	(15.5)
NA	Ocean City, NJ**	NA
NA	Odessa, TX**	NA
NA	Ogden-Clearfield, UT**	NA
166	Oklahoma City, OK	(20.7)
133	Olympia, WA	(13.8)

RANK	METROPOLITAN AREA	% CHANGE
178	Omaha-Council Bluffs, NE-IA	(23.7)
98	Orlando, FL	(8.9)
NA	Oshkosh-Neenah, WI**	NA
NA	Oxnard-Thousand Oaks, CA**	NA
126	Palm Bay-Melbourne, FL	(13.2)
NA	Palm Coast, FL**	NA
181	Panama City-Lynn Haven, FL	(24.1)
NA	Pascagoula, MS**	NA
60	Pensacola, FL	(3.5)
26	Philadelphia (greater) PA-NJ-DE	5.1
NA	Philadelphia, PA M.D.**	NA
168	Phoenix-Mesa-Scottsdale, AZ	(21.3)
159	Pine Bluff, AR	(19.2)
56	Pittsburgh, PA	(2.8)
NA	Pittsfield, MA**	NA
39	Pocatello, ID	2.3
140	Port St. Lucie, FL	(15.0)
172	Portland-Vancouver, OR-WA	(22.1)
NA	Portland, ME**	NA
NA	Poughkeepsie, NY**	NA
NA	Prescott, AZ**	NA
191	Provo-Orem, UT	(28.0)
13	Pueblo, CO	11.1
4	Punta Gorda, FL	18.3
46	Racine, WI	0.0
NA	Raleigh-Cary, NC**	NA
199	Rapid City, SD	(45.1)
78	Reading, PA	(5.9)
86	Redding, CA	(7.3)
67	Reno-Sparks, NV	(4.4)
186	Richmond, VA	(26.4)
89	Riverside-San Bernardino, CA	(7.5)
NA	Roanoke, VA**	NA
NA	Rochester, MN**	NA
54	Rochester, NY	(2.6)
28	Rocky Mount, NC	5.0
NA	Rome, GA**	NA
73	Sacramento, CA	(5.5)
NA	Saginaw, MI**	NA
194	Salem, OR	(32.7)
26	Salinas, CA	5.1
NA	Salisbury, MD**	NA
NA	Salt Lake City, UT**	NA
123	San Angelo, TX	(12.7)
153	San Antonio, TX	(17.3)
46	San Diego, CA	0.0
NA	San Francisco (greater), CA**	NA
16	San Francisco-S. Mateo, CA M.D.	8.9
7	San Jose, CA	14.7
56	San Luis Obispo, CA	(2.8)
NA	Sandusky, OH**	NA
105	Santa Ana-Anaheim, CA M.D.	(9.6)
NA	Santa Barbara-Santa Maria, CA**	NA
8	Santa Cruz-Watsonville, CA	14.4
81	Santa Fe, NM	(6.3)
176	Santa Rosa-Petaluma, CA	(23.0)
75	Sarasota-Bradenton-Venice, FL	(5.8)
NA	Savannah, GA**	NA
22	Scranton--Wilkes-Barre, PA	6.6
NA	Seattle (greater), WA**	NA

RANK	METROPOLITAN AREA	% CHANGE
38	Seattle-Bellevue, WA M.D.	2.8
NA	Sebastian-Vero Beach, FL**	NA
50	Sheboygan, WI	(1.4)
149	Sherman-Denison, TX	(16.3)
40	Shreveport-Bossier City, LA	2.1
198	Sioux City, IA-NE-SD	(42.1)
175	Sioux Falls, SD	(22.8)
133	South Bend-Mishawaka, IN-MI	(13.8)
NA	Spartanburg, SC**	NA
170	Spokane, WA	(21.6)
NA	Springfield, MA**	NA
41	Springfield, MO	1.8
NA	Springfield, OH**	NA
30	State College, PA	4.4
55	Stockton, CA	(2.7)
NA	St. Cloud, MN**	NA
151	St. Joseph, MO-KS	(16.6)
NA	St. Louis, MO-IL**	NA
110	Sumter, SC	(10.1)
NA	Syracuse, NY**	NA
100	Tacoma, WA M.D.	(9.1)
174	Tallahassee, FL	(22.5)
150	Tampa-St Petersburg, FL	(16.4)
59	Texarkana, TX-Texarkana, AR	(3.4)
96	Toledo, OH	(8.5)
183	Topeka, KS	(25.0)
190	Trenton-Ewing, NJ	(27.3)
NA	Tucson, AZ**	NA
120	Tulsa, OK	(12.2)
84	Tuscaloosa, AL	(6.7)
163	Tyler, TX	(20.0)
141	Utica-Rome, NY	(15.1)
NA	Valdosta, GA**	NA
NA	Vallejo-Fairfield, CA**	NA
187	Victoria, TX	(26.7)
62	Vineland, NJ	(3.9)
132	Virginia Beach-Norfolk, VA-NC	(13.7)
17	Visalia-Porterville, CA	7.8
169	Waco, TX	(21.5)
NA	Warner Robins, GA**	NA
NA	Warren-Farmington Hills, MI M.D.**	NA
NA	Washington (greater) DC-VA-MD**	NA
NA	Washington, DC-VA-MD-WV M.D.**	NA
195	Waterloo-Cedar Falls, IA	(33.1)
65	Wausau, WI	(4.2)
NA	Wenatchee, WA**	NA
172	West Palm Beach, FL M.D.	(22.1)
NA	Wheeling, WV-OH**	NA
164	Wichita Falls, TX	(20.1)
81	Wichita, KS	(6.3)
29	Williamsport, PA	4.8
NA	Wilmington, DE-MD-NJ M.D.**	NA
170	Wilmington, NC	(21.6)
NA	Winchester, VA-WV**	NA
NA	Winston-Salem, NC**	NA
NA	Worcester, MA**	NA
21	Yakima, WA	6.9
130	Yuba City, CA	(13.5)
NA	Yuma, AZ**	NA

Source: CQ Press using data from Federal Bureau of Investigation "Crime in the United States 2006" (Uniform Crime Reports, September 24, 2007)

**Includes murder, rape, robbery, aggravated assault, burglary, larceny-theft, and motor vehicle theft.*

***Not available.*

4. Percent Change in Crime Rate: 2002 to 2006 (continued)

National Percent Change = 7.7% Decrease*

RANK	METROPOLITAN AREA	% CHANGE	RANK	METROPOLITAN AREA	% CHANGE	RANK	METROPOLITAN AREA	% CHANGE
1	Lawrence, KS	31.6	58	Fort Lauderdale, FL M.D.	(3.3)	115	Columbia, MO	(11.3)
2	Huntsville, AL	21.0	59	Texarkana, TX-Texarkana, AR	(3.4)	116	Chattanooga, TN-GA	(11.9)
3	Columbus, GA-AL	19.6	60	Pensacola, FL	(3.5)	117	Albany, GA	(12.0)
4	Punta Gorda, FL	18.3	61	Little Rock, AR	(3.8)	118	Fort Collins-Loveland, CO	(12.1)
5	Bakersfield, CA	16.0	62	Vineland, NJ	(3.9)	118	Greenville, NC	(12.1)
6	Jonesboro, AR	15.7	63	Goldsboro, NC	(4.1)	120	Athens-Clarke County, GA	(12.2)
7	San Jose, CA	14.7	63	Houma, LA	(4.1)	120	Tulsa, OK	(12.2)
8	Santa Cruz-Watsonville, CA	14.4	65	Wausau, WI	(4.2)	122	Houston, TX	(12.3)
9	Decatur, AL	12.4	66	Lubbock, TX	(4.3)	123	San Angelo, TX	(12.7)
10	Danville, VA	12.1	67	Reno-Sparks, NV	(4.4)	124	Fresno, CA	(12.8)
11	Augusta, GA-SC	11.8	68	Dover, DE	(4.5)	124	Green Bay, WI	(12.8)
12	Las Vegas-Paradise, NV	11.4	69	Casper, WY	(4.9)	126	Baton Rouge, LA	(13.2)
13	Pueblo, CO	11.1	69	Daytona Beach, FL	(4.9)	126	Palm Bay-Melbourne, FL	(13.2)
14	Cumberland, MD-WV	10.1	71	Bellingham, WA	(5.1)	128	Eau Claire, WI	(13.4)
15	Jackson, TN	9.6	72	Eugene-Springfield, OR	(5.2)	128	Louisville, KY-IN	(13.4)
16	San Francisco-S. Mateo, CA M.D.	8.9	73	Sacramento, CA	(5.5)	130	Amarillo, TX	(13.5)
17	Visalia-Porterville, CA	7.8	74	Alexandria, LA	(5.6)	130	Yuba City, CA	(13.5)
18	Grand Junction, CO	7.6	75	Bismarck, ND	(5.8)	132	Virginia Beach-Norfolk, VA-NC	(13.7)
19	Fort Walton Beach, FL	7.3	75	Dubuque, IA	(5.8)	133	Olympia, WA	(13.8)
20	Muncie, IN	7.2	75	Sarasota-Bradenton-Venice, FL	(5.8)	133	South Bend-Mishawaka, IN-MI	(13.8)
21	Yakima, WA	6.9	78	Kennewick-Richland-Pasco, WA	(5.9)	135	Denver-Aurora, CO	(14.7)
22	Scranton--Wilkes-Barre, PA	6.6	78	Lafayette, IN	(5.9)	135	Fort Worth-Arlington, TX M.D.	(14.7)
23	Fayetteville, NC	6.5	78	Reading, PA	(5.9)	137	Beaumont-Port Arthur, TX	(14.8)
24	Binghamton, NY	6.1	81	Erie, PA	(6.3)	137	Merced, CA	(14.8)
25	Kokomo, IN	5.6	81	Santa Fe, NM	(6.3)	139	McAllen-Edinburg-Mission, TX	(14.9)
26	Philadelphia (greater) PA-NJ-DE	5.1	81	Wichita, KS	(6.3)	140	Port St. Lucie, FL	(15.0)
26	Salinas, CA	5.1	84	Tuscaloosa, AL	(6.7)	141	Utica-Rome, NY	(15.1)
28	Rocky Mount, NC	5.0	85	Knoxville, TN	(6.9)	142	Lakeland, FL	(15.2)
29	Williamsport, PA	4.8	86	Jackson, MI	(7.3)	143	Dallas-Plano-Irving, TX M.D.	(15.4)
30	State College, PA	4.4	86	Redding, CA	(7.3)	144	Nashville-Davidson, TN	(15.5)
31	Birmingham-Hoover, AL	4.0	88	Myrtle Beach, SC	(7.4)	144	Ocala, FL	(15.5)
32	Flint, MI	3.8	89	Riverside-San Bernardino, CA	(7.5)	146	El Paso, TX	(15.7)
33	Anchorage, AK	3.6	90	Bloomington, IN	(7.6)	147	Baltimore-Towson, MD	(16.0)
33	Florence, SC	3.6	91	Chico, CA	(7.7)	148	Miami-Dade County, FL M.D.	(16.1)
35	Gadsden, AL	3.5	91	Laredo, TX	(7.7)	149	Sherman-Denison, TX	(16.3)
36	Charleston, WV	3.0	93	Modesto, CA	(8.0)	150	Tampa-St Petersburg, FL	(16.4)
37	Lawton, OK	2.9	94	Lynchburg, VA	(8.1)	151	Los Angeles County, CA M.D.	(16.6)
38	Seattle-Bellevue, WA M.D.	2.8	95	Glens Falls, NY	(8.4)	151	St. Joseph, MO-KS	(16.6)
39	Pocatello, ID	2.3	96	Toledo, OH	(8.5)	153	San Antonio, TX	(17.3)
40	Shreveport-Bossier City, LA	2.1	97	Lancaster, PA	(8.6)	154	Columbus, OH	(17.8)
41	Joplin, MO	1.8	98	Elkhart-Goshen, IN	(8.9)	155	Billings, MT	(18.1)
41	Springfield, MO	1.8	98	Orlando, FL	(8.9)	155	Lewiston-Auburn, ME	(18.1)
43	Detroit (greater), MI	1.2	100	Albuquerque, NM	(9.1)	157	Lincoln, NE	(18.2)
44	Hartford, CT	1.1	100	Colorado Springs, CO	(9.1)	158	New York-W. Plains NY-NJ M.D.	(18.5)
45	Corpus Christi, TX	0.8	100	Tacoma, WA M.D.	(9.1)	159	Pine Bluff, AR	(19.2)
46	Racine, WI	0.0	103	Lake Charles, LA	(9.2)	160	Fort Smith, AR-OK	(19.4)
46	San Diego, CA	0.0	104	Asheville, NC	(9.4)	161	Bremerton-Silverdale, WA	(19.6)
48	Longview, TX	(0.3)	105	Santa Ana-Anaheim, CA M.D.	(9.6)	162	Greeley, CO	(19.9)
49	Altoona, PA	(1.2)	106	Cheyenne, WY	(9.7)	163	Tyler, TX	(20.0)
50	Sheboygan, WI	(1.4)	107	Austin-Round Rock, TX	(9.9)	164	Wichita Falls, TX	(20.1)
51	Oakland-Fremont, CA M.D.	(1.5)	107	Janesville, WI	(9.9)	165	Brownsville-Harlingen, TX	(20.6)
52	Gainesville, FL	(1.8)	107	Lansing-East Lansing, MI	(9.9)	166	Oklahoma City, OK	(20.7)
53	Buffalo-Niagara Falls, NY	(2.0)	110	Sumter, SC	(10.1)	167	Newark-Union, NJ-PA M.D.	(21.0)
54	Rochester, NY	(2.6)	111	Cape Coral-Fort Myers, FL	(10.3)	168	Phoenix-Mesa-Scottsdale, AZ	(21.3)
55	Stockton, CA	(2.7)	111	Madison, WI	(10.3)	169	Waco, TX	(21.5)
56	Pittsburgh, PA	(2.8)	113	Cincinnati-Middletown, OH-KY-IN	(10.7)	170	Spokane, WA	(21.6)
56	San Luis Obispo, CA	(2.8)	114	Charleston-North Charleston, SC	(10.8)	170	Wilmington, NC	(21.6)

Note: All listings are for Metropolitan Statistical Areas (M.S.A.s) except for those ending with "M.D." Listings with "M.D." are Metropolitan Divisions which are smaller parts of eleven large M.S.A.s. See explanatory note at beginning of metropolitan area section on page 23.

RANK	METROPOLITAN AREA	% CHANGE
172	Portland-Vancouver, OR-WA	(22.1)
172	West Palm Beach, FL M.D.	(22.1)
174	Tallahassee, FL	(22.5)
175	Sioux Falls, SD	(22.8)
176	Santa Rosa-Petaluma, CA	(23.0)
177	Columbia, SC	(23.2)
178	Omaha-Council Bluffs, NE-IA	(23.7)
179	Jackson, MS	(24.0)
179	Montgomery, AL	(24.0)
181	Panama City-Lynn Haven, FL	(24.1)
182	New Orleans, LA	(24.9)
183	Topeka, KS	(25.0)
184	Medford, OR	(25.7)
185	Clarksville, TN-KY	(25.8)
186	Richmond, VA	(26.4)
187	Cedar Rapids, IA	(26.7)
187	Victoria, TX	(26.7)
189	Boise City-Nampa, ID	(27.1)
190	Trenton-Ewing, NJ	(27.3)
191	Provo-Orem, UT	(28.0)
192	Honolulu, HI	(29.3)
193	Iowa City, IA	(30.9)
194	Salem, OR	(32.7)
195	Waterloo-Cedar Falls, IA	(33.1)
196	Naples-Marco Island, FL	(34.5)
197	Great Falls, MT	(36.2)
198	Sioux City, IA-NE-SD	(42.1)
199	Rapid City, SD	(45.1)
NA	Abilene, TX**	NA
NA	Albany-Schenectady-Troy, NY**	NA
NA	Ames, IA**	NA
NA	Anderson, SC**	NA
NA	Ann Arbor, MI**	NA
NA	Appleton, WI**	NA
NA	Atlanta, GA**	NA
NA	Atlantic City, NJ**	NA
NA	Bangor, ME**	NA
NA	Barnstable Town, MA**	NA
NA	Battle Creek, MI**	NA
NA	Bay City, MI**	NA
NA	Bend, OR**	NA
NA	Bethesda-Frederick, MD M.D.**	NA
NA	Blacksburg, VA**	NA
NA	Bowling Green, KY**	NA
NA	Brunswick, GA**	NA
NA	Burlington, NC**	NA
NA	Camden, NJ M.D.**	NA
NA	Carson City, NV**	NA
NA	Charlotte-Gastonia, NC-SC**	NA
NA	Charlottesville, VA**	NA
NA	Chicago, IL**	NA
NA	Cleveland-Elyria-Mentor, OH**	NA
NA	Cleveland, TN**	NA
NA	Coeur d'Alene, ID**	NA
NA	College Station-Bryan, TX**	NA
NA	Columbus, IN**	NA
NA	Dallas (greater), TX**	NA
NA	Dalton, GA**	NA
NA	Dayton, OH**	NA
NA	Des Moines-West Des Moines, IA**	NA
NA	Detroit-Livonia-Dearborn, MI M.D.**	NA
NA	Dothan, AL**	NA
NA	Duluth, MN-WI**	NA
NA	Durham, NC**	NA
NA	Edison, NJ M.D.**	NA
NA	El Centro, CA**	NA
NA	Elizabethtown, KY**	NA
NA	Elmira, NY**	NA
NA	Evansville, IN-KY**	NA
NA	Fairbanks, AK**	NA
NA	Fargo, ND-MN**	NA
NA	Farmington, NM**	NA
NA	Fayetteville, AR-MO**	NA
NA	Flagstaff, AZ**	NA
NA	Fond du Lac, WI**	NA
NA	Fort Wayne, IN**	NA
NA	Gainesville, GA**	NA
NA	Grand Forks, ND-MN**	NA
NA	Grand Rapids-Wyoming, MI**	NA
NA	Greensboro-High Point, NC**	NA
NA	Greenville, SC**	NA
NA	Hagerstown-Martinsburg, MD-WV**	NA
NA	Hanford-Corcoran, CA**	NA
NA	Harrisburg-Carlisle, PA**	NA
NA	Harrisonburg, VA**	NA
NA	Hattiesburg, MS**	NA
NA	Holland-Grand Haven, MI**	NA
NA	Hot Springs, AR**	NA
NA	Huntington-Ashland, WV-KY-OH**	NA
NA	Idaho Falls, ID**	NA
NA	Indianapolis, IN**	NA
NA	Ithaca, NY**	NA
NA	Jacksonville, FL**	NA
NA	Jacksonville, NC**	NA
NA	Jefferson City, MO**	NA
NA	Johnson City, TN**	NA
NA	Johnstown, PA**	NA
NA	Kalamazoo-Portage, MI**	NA
NA	Kansas City, MO-KS**	NA
NA	Killeen-Temple-Fort Hood, TX**	NA
NA	Kingsport, TN-VA**	NA
NA	Kingston, NY**	NA
NA	La Crosse, WI-MN**	NA
NA	Lake Havasu City-Kingman, AZ**	NA
NA	Las Cruces, NM**	NA
NA	Lebanon, PA**	NA
NA	Lewiston, ID-WA**	NA
NA	Lexington-Fayette, KY**	NA
NA	Lima, OH**	NA
NA	Logan, UT-ID**	NA
NA	Longview, WA**	NA
NA	Los Angeles (greater), CA**	NA
NA	Macon, GA**	NA
NA	Madera, CA**	NA
NA	Manchester-Nashua, NH**	NA
NA	Mansfield, OH**	NA
NA	Memphis, TN-MS-AR**	NA
NA	Miami (greater), FL**	NA
NA	Michigan City-La Porte, IN**	NA
NA	Midland, TX**	NA
NA	Milwaukee, WI**	NA
NA	Minneapolis-St. Paul, MN-WI**	NA
NA	Missoula, MT**	NA
NA	Mobile, AL**	NA
NA	Monroe, LA**	NA
NA	Monroe, MI**	NA
NA	Morgantown, WV**	NA
NA	Morristown, TN**	NA
NA	Mount Vernon-Anacortes, WA**	NA
NA	Muskegon-Norton Shores, MI**	NA
NA	Napa, CA**	NA
NA	Nassau-Suffolk, NY M.D.**	NA
NA	New York (greater), NY-NJ-PA**	NA
NA	Niles-Benton Harbor, MI**	NA
NA	Ocean City, NJ**	NA
NA	Odessa, TX**	NA
NA	Ogden-Clearfield, UT**	NA
NA	Oshkosh-Neenah, WI**	NA
NA	Oxnard-Thousand Oaks, CA**	NA
NA	Palm Coast, FL**	NA
NA	Pascagoula, MS**	NA
NA	Philadelphia, PA M.D.**	NA
NA	Pittsfield, MA**	NA
NA	Portland, ME**	NA
NA	Poughkeepsie, NY**	NA
NA	Prescott, AZ**	NA
NA	Raleigh-Cary, NC**	NA
NA	Roanoke, VA**	NA
NA	Rochester, MN**	NA
NA	Rome, GA**	NA
NA	Saginaw, MI**	NA
NA	Salisbury, MD**	NA
NA	Salt Lake City, UT**	NA
NA	San Francisco (greater), CA**	NA
NA	Sandusky, OH**	NA
NA	Santa Barbara-Santa Maria, CA**	NA
NA	Savannah, GA**	NA
NA	Seattle (greater), WA**	NA
NA	Sebastian-Vero Beach, FL**	NA
NA	Spartanburg, SC**	NA
NA	Springfield, MA**	NA
NA	Springfield, OH**	NA
NA	St. Cloud, MN**	NA
NA	St. Louis, MO-IL**	NA
NA	Syracuse, NY**	NA
NA	Tucson, AZ**	NA
NA	Valdosta, GA**	NA
NA	Vallejo-Fairfield, CA**	NA
NA	Warner Robins, GA**	NA
NA	Warren-Farmington Hills, MI M.D.**	NA
NA	Washington (greater) DC-VA-MD**	NA
NA	Washington, DC-VA-MD-WV M.D.**	NA
NA	Wenatchee, WA**	NA
NA	Wheeling, WV-OH**	NA
NA	Wilmington, DE-MD-NJ M.D.**	NA
NA	Winchester, VA-WV**	NA
NA	Winston-Salem, NC**	NA
NA	Worcester, MA**	NA
NA	Yuma, AZ**	NA

Source: CQ Press using data from Federal Bureau of Investigation "Crime in the United States 2006" (Uniform Crime Reports, September 24, 2007)

**Includes murder, rape, robbery, aggravated assault, burglary, larceny-theft, and motor vehicle theft.*

***Not available.*

5. Violent Crimes in 2006

National Total = 1,417,745 Violent Crimes*

RANK	METROPOLITAN AREA	CRIMES
227	Abilene, TX	638
88	Albany-Schenectady-Troy, NY	3,165
219	Albany, GA	676
51	Albuquerque, NM	6,291
145	Alexandria, LA	1,497
280	Altoona, PA	386
135	Amarillo, TX	1,722
314	Ames, IA	205
99	Anchorage, AK	2,749
166	Anderson, SC	1,163
175	Ann Arbor, MI	1,060
303	Appleton, WI	273
168	Asheville, NC	1,146
234	Athens-Clarke County, GA	596
11	Atlanta, GA	26,762
142	Atlantic City, NJ	1,519
121	Augusta, GA-SC	2,041
62	Austin-Round Rock, TX	5,157
74	Bakersfield, CA	4,189
18	Baltimore-Towson, MD	21,937
333	Bangor, ME	111
NA	Barnstable Town, MA**	NA
58	Baton Rouge, LA	5,711
170	Battle Creek, MI	1,104
300	Bay City, MI	280
114	Beaumont-Port Arthur, TX	2,228
269	Bellingham, WA	432
293	Bend, OR	313
93	Bethesda-Frederick, MD M.D.	3,055
304	Billings, MT	272
250	Binghamton, NY	529
52	Birmingham-Hoover, AL	6,187
321	Bismarck, ND	191
291	Blacksburg, VA	324
270	Bloomington, IN	425
139	Boise City-Nampa, ID	1,610
278	Bowling Green, KY	393
178	Bremerton-Silverdale, WA	1,014
136	Brownsville-Harlingen, TX	1,678
200	Brunswick, GA	803
56	Buffalo-Niagara Falls, NY	5,899
205	Burlington, NC	759
70	Camden, NJ M.D.	4,387
90	Cape Coral-Fort Myers, FL	3,157
319	Carson City, NV	195
326	Casper, WY	169
249	Cedar Rapids, IA	531
64	Charleston-North Charleston, SC	5,017
163	Charleston, WV	1,220
NA	Charlotte-Gastonia, NC-SC**	NA
243	Charlottesville, VA	539
94	Chattanooga, TN-GA	3,004
327	Cheyenne, WY	168
NA	Chicago, IL**	NA
201	Chico, CA	787
47	Cincinnati-Middletown, OH-KY-IN	7,572
150	Clarksville, TN-KY	1,392
34	Cleveland-Elyria-Mentor, OH	9,786
215	Cleveland, TN	694
264	Coeur d'Alene, ID	451
182	College Station-Bryan, TX	950
86	Colorado Springs, CO	3,298
217	Columbia, MO	679
63	Columbia, SC	5,092
147	Columbus, GA-AL	1,435
329	Columbus, IN	152
48	Columbus, OH	7,292
106	Corpus Christi, TX	2,449
282	Cumberland, MD-WV	373
9	Dallas (greater), TX	31,976
16	Dallas-Plano-Irving, TX M.D.	22,400
266	Dalton, GA	440
305	Danville, VA	270
102	Daytona Beach, FL	2,716
100	Dayton, OH	2,747
274	Decatur, AL	412
33	Denver-Aurora, CO	10,285
130	Des Moines-West Des Moines, IA	1,829
8	Detroit (greater), MI	33,894
13	Detroit-Livonia-Dearborn, MI M.D.	25,459
254	Dothan, AL	508
190	Dover, DE	881
275	Dubuque, IA	403
NA	Duluth, MN-WI**	NA
95	Durham, NC	2,824
317	Eau Claire, WI	201
72	Edison, NJ M.D.	4,252
222	El Centro, CA	663
97	El Paso, TX	2,804
324	Elizabethtown, KY	175
273	Elkhart-Goshen, IN	420
320	Elmira, NY	193
198	Erie, PA	824
185	Eugene-Springfield, OR	910
184	Evansville, IN-KY	912
302	Fairbanks, AK	274
NA	Fargo, ND-MN**	NA
204	Farmington, NM	763
155	Fayetteville, AR-MO	1,308
117	Fayetteville, NC	2,139
216	Flagstaff, AZ	690
75	Flint, MI	4,116
109	Florence, SC	2,339
323	Fond du Lac, WI	188
211	Fort Collins-Loveland, CO	718
32	Fort Lauderdale, FL M.D.	10,764
143	Fort Smith, AR-OK	1,505
213	Fort Walton Beach, FL	710
191	Fort Wayne, IN	877
36	Fort Worth-Arlington, TX M.D.	9,576
66	Fresno, CA	4,895
256	Gadsden, AL	499
112	Gainesville, FL	2,282
268	Gainesville, GA	433
314	Glens Falls, NY	205
233	Goldsboro, NC	602
NA	Grand Forks, ND-MN**	NA
284	Grand Junction, CO	368
87	Grand Rapids-Wyoming, MI	3,293
312	Great Falls, MT	216
196	Greeley, CO	832
218	Green Bay, WI	678
83	Greensboro-High Point, NC	3,472
169	Greenville, NC	1,137
76	Greenville, SC	4,024
195	Hagerstown-Martinsburg, MD-WV	845
244	Hanford-Corcoran, CA	535
133	Harrisburg-Carlisle, PA	1,768
325	Harrisonburg, VA	173
89	Hartford, CT	3,160
287	Hattiesburg, MS	346
252	Holland-Grand Haven, MI	521
101	Honolulu, HI	2,745
232	Hot Springs, AR	615
177	Houma, LA	1,035
7	Houston, TX	38,398
223	Huntington-Ashland, WV-KY-OH	657
123	Huntsville, AL	2,005
297	Idaho Falls, ID	295
40	Indianapolis, IN	9,032
277	Iowa City, IA	394
328	Ithaca, NY	154
NA	Jacksonville, FL**	NA
239	Jacksonville, NC	557
224	Jackson, MI	654
108	Jackson, MS	2,375
179	Jackson, TN	987
283	Janesville, WI	372
245	Jefferson City, MO	533
210	Johnson City, TN	731
285	Johnstown, PA	363
228	Jonesboro, AR	637
214	Joplin, MO	702
148	Kalamazoo-Portage, MI	1,434
31	Kansas City, MO-KS	11,690
225	Kennewick-Richland-Pasco, WA	651
NA	Killeen-Temple-Fort Hood, TX**	NA
151	Kingsport, TN-VA	1,378
253	Kingston, NY	513
84	Knoxville, TN	3,408
295	Kokomo, IN	304
NA	La Crosse, WI-MN**	NA
270	Lafayette, IN	425
153	Lake Charles, LA	1,373
237	Lake Havasu City-Kingman, AZ	589
91	Lakeland, FL	3,078
174	Lancaster, PA	1,062
126	Lansing-East Lansing, MI	1,947
159	Laredo, TX	1,261
188	Las Cruces, NM	893
26	Las Vegas-Paradise, NV	15,506

Note: All listings are for Metropolitan Statistical Areas (M.S.A.s) except for those ending with "M.D." Listings with "M.D." are Metropolitan Divisions which are smaller parts of eleven large M.S.A.s. See explanatory note at beginning of metropolitan area section on page 23.

Alpha Order - Metro Area (continued)

RANK	METROPOLITAN AREA	CRIMES
240	Lawrence, KS	556
180	Lawton, OK	975
281	Lebanon, PA	380
330	Lewiston-Auburn, ME	146
335	Lewiston, ID-WA	72
124	Lexington-Fayette, KY	1,966
262	Lima, OH	455
158	Lincoln, NE	1,281
57	Little Rock, AR	5,891
334	Logan, UT-ID	86
167	Longview, TX	1,161
298	Longview, WA	291
3	Los Angeles County, CA M.D.	65,044
2	Los Angeles (greater), CA	73,407
65	Louisville, KY-IN	4,922
111	Lubbock, TX	2,316
241	Lynchburg, VA	555
160	Macon, GA	1,248
202	Madera, CA	777
149	Madison, WI	1,411
230	Manchester-Nashua, NH	634
294	Mansfield, OH	307
103	McAllen-Edinburg-Mission, TX	2,640
257	Medford, OR	491
24	Memphis, TN-MS-AR	16,080
138	Merced, CA	1,616
5	Miami (greater), FL	43,556
15	Miami-Dade County, FL M.D.	23,520
311	Michigan City-La Porte, IN	250
265	Midland, TX	443
42	Milwaukee, WI	8,800
NA	Minneapolis-St. Paul, MN-WI**	NA
306	Missoula, MT	269
140	Mobile, AL	1,594
92	Modesto, CA	3,056
194	Monroe, LA	846
286	Monroe, MI	347
141	Montgomery, AL	1,561
301	Morgantown, WV	275
238	Morristown, TN	571
309	Mount Vernon-Anacortes, WA	259
275	Muncie, IN	403
181	Muskegon-Norton Shores, MI	961
125	Myrtle Beach, SC	1,958
261	Napa, CA	463
152	Naples-Marco Island, FL	1,377
30	Nashville-Davidson, TN	12,357
59	Nassau-Suffolk, NY M.D.	5,682
49	New Orleans, LA	6,953
1	New York (greater), NY-NJ-PA	82,359
4	New York-W. Plains NY-NJ M.D.	63,477
41	Newark-Union, NJ-PA M.D.	8,948
203	Niles-Benton Harbor, MI	774
23	Oakland-Fremont, CA M.D.	17,208
110	Ocala, FL	2,326
288	Ocean City, NJ	344
221	Odessa, TX	673
193	Ogden-Clearfield, UT	861
55	Oklahoma City, OK	6,015
234	Olympia, WA	596

RANK	METROPOLITAN AREA	CRIMES
85	Omaha-Council Bluffs, NE-IA	3,403
22	Orlando, FL	17,284
290	Oshkosh-Neenah, WI	329
115	Oxnard-Thousand Oaks, CA	2,223
81	Palm Bay-Melbourne, FL	3,622
321	Palm Coast, FL	191
156	Panama City-Lynn Haven, FL	1,300
279	Pascagoula, MS	388
96	Pensacola, FL	2,808
6	Philadelphia (greater) PA-NJ-DE	38,459
10	Philadelphia, PA M.D.	29,460
19	Phoenix-Mesa-Scottsdale, AZ	20,461
183	Pine Bluff, AR	919
43	Pittsburgh, PA	8,594
236	Pittsfield, MA	595
299	Pocatello, ID	283
119	Port St. Lucie, FL	2,098
50	Portland-Vancouver, OR-WA	6,898
212	Portland, ME	714
128	Poughkeepsie, NY	1,847
189	Prescott, AZ	882
267	Provo-Orem, UT	437
220	Pueblo, CO	674
208	Punta Gorda, FL	739
245	Racine, WI	533
82	Raleigh-Cary, NC	3,485
292	Rapid City, SD	321
144	Reading, PA	1,504
226	Redding, CA	648
120	Reno-Sparks, NV	2,075
69	Richmond, VA	4,489
20	Riverside-San Bernardino, CA	19,301
161	Roanoke, VA	1,243
NA	Rochester, MN**	NA
78	Rochester, NY	3,764
199	Rocky Mount, NC	821
251	Rome, GA	527
29	Sacramento, CA	13,098
113	Saginaw, MI	2,265
172	Salem, OR	1,074
122	Salinas, CA	2,014
176	Salisbury, MD	1,058
80	Salt Lake City, UT	3,690
272	San Angelo, TX	423
35	San Antonio, TX	9,659
27	San Diego, CA	13,578
12	San Francisco (greater), CA	26,646
37	San Francisco-S. Mateo, CA M.D.	9,438
61	San Jose, CA	5,607
209	San Luis Obispo, CA	736
308	Sandusky, OH	266
45	Santa Ana-Anaheim, CA M.D.	8,363
134	Santa Barbara-Santa Maria, CA	1,752
171	Santa Cruz-Watsonville, CA	1,083
229	Santa Fe, NM	636
116	Santa Rosa-Petaluma, CA	2,163
67	Sarasota-Bradenton-Venice, FL	4,624
NA	Savannah, GA**	NA
137	Scranton--Wilkes-Barre, PA	1,668
28	Seattle (greater), WA	13,552

RANK	METROPOLITAN AREA	CRIMES
38	Seattle-Bellevue, WA M.D.	9,343
259	Sebastian-Vero Beach, FL	479
332	Sheboygan, WI	134
296	Sherman-Denison, TX	300
71	Shreveport-Bossier City, LA	4,315
260	Sioux City, IA-NE-SD	473
258	Sioux Falls, SD	481
164	South Bend-Mishawaka, IN-MI	1,203
129	Spartanburg, SC	1,830
131	Spokane, WA	1,799
NA	Springfield, MA**	NA
126	Springfield, MO	1,947
231	Springfield, OH	620
331	State College, PA	144
54	Stockton, CA	6,079
NA	St. Cloud, MN**	NA
289	St. Joseph, MO-KS	335
25	St. Louis, MO-IL	15,846
154	Sumter, SC	1,333
118	Syracuse, NY	2,110
73	Tacoma, WA M.D.	4,209
98	Tallahassee, FL	2,789
21	Tampa-St Petersburg, FL	19,095
165	Texarkana, TX-Texarkana, AR	1,179
78	Toledo, OH	3,764
187	Topeka, KS	905
132	Trenton-Ewing, NJ	1,781
59	Tucson, AZ	5,682
53	Tulsa, OK	6,158
173	Tuscaloosa, AL	1,073
185	Tyler, TX	910
197	Utica-Rome, NY	829
242	Valdosta, GA	543
104	Vallejo-Fairfield, CA	2,531
263	Victoria, TX	454
161	Vineland, NJ	1,243
46	Virginia Beach-Norfolk, VA-NC	7,693
107	Visalia-Porterville, CA	2,442
157	Waco, TX	1,283
255	Warner Robins, GA	505
44	Warren-Farmington Hills, MI M.D.	8,435
14	Washington (greater) DC-VA-MD	25,229
17	Washington, DC-VA-MD-WV M.D.	22,174
245	Waterloo-Cedar Falls, IA	533
314	Wausau, WI	205
313	Wenatchee, WA	214
39	West Palm Beach, FL M.D.	9,272
310	Wheeling, WV-OH	251
245	Wichita Falls, TX	533
77	Wichita, KS	3,964
318	Williamsport, PA	198
68	Wilmington, DE-MD-NJ M.D.	4,612
146	Wilmington, NC	1,480
307	Winchester, VA-WV	267
105	Winston-Salem, NC	2,471
NA	Worcester, MA**	NA
206	Yakima, WA	756
207	Yuba City, CA	748
192	Yuma, AZ	873

Source: Federal Bureau of Investigation
"Crime in the United States 2006" (Uniform Crime Reports, September 24, 2007)
**Violent crimes are offenses of murder, forcible rape, robbery, and aggravated assault.*
***Not available.*

5. Violent Crimes in 2006 (continued)

National Total = 1,417,745 Violent Crimes*

RANK	METROPOLITAN AREA	CRIMES
1	New York (greater), NY-NJ-PA	82,359
2	Los Angeles (greater), CA	73,407
3	Los Angeles County, CA M.D.	65,044
4	New York-W. Plains NY-NJ M.D.	63,477
5	Miami (greater), FL	43,556
6	Philadelphia (greater) PA-NJ-DE	38,459
7	Houston, TX	38,398
8	Detroit (greater), MI	33,894
9	Dallas (greater), TX	31,976
10	Philadelphia, PA M.D.	29,460
11	Atlanta, GA	26,762
12	San Francisco (greater), CA	26,646
13	Detroit-Livonia-Dearborn, MI M.D.	25,459
14	Washington (greater) DC-VA-MD	25,229
15	Miami-Dade County, FL M.D.	23,520
16	Dallas-Plano-Irving, TX M.D.	22,400
17	Washington, DC-VA-MD-WV M.D.	22,174
18	Baltimore-Towson, MD	21,937
19	Phoenix-Mesa-Scottsdale, AZ	20,461
20	Riverside-San Bernardino, CA	19,301
21	Tampa-St Petersburg, FL	19,095
22	Orlando, FL	17,284
23	Oakland-Fremont, CA M.D.	17,208
24	Memphis, TN-MS-AR	16,080
25	St. Louis, MO-IL	15,846
26	Las Vegas-Paradise, NV	15,506
27	San Diego, CA	13,578
28	Seattle (greater), WA	13,552
29	Sacramento, CA	13,098
30	Nashville-Davidson, TN	12,357
31	Kansas City, MO-KS	11,690
32	Fort Lauderdale, FL M.D.	10,764
33	Denver-Aurora, CO	10,285
34	Cleveland-Elyria-Mentor, OH	9,786
35	San Antonio, TX	9,659
36	Fort Worth-Arlington, TX M.D.	9,576
37	San Francisco-S. Mateo, CA M.D.	9,438
38	Seattle-Bellevue, WA M.D.	9,343
39	West Palm Beach, FL M.D.	9,272
40	Indianapolis, IN	9,032
41	Newark-Union, NJ-PA M.D.	8,948
42	Milwaukee, WI	8,800
43	Pittsburgh, PA	8,594
44	Warren-Farmington Hills, MI M.D.	8,435
45	Santa Ana-Anaheim, CA M.D.	8,363
46	Virginia Beach-Norfolk, VA-NC	7,693
47	Cincinnati-Middletown, OH-KY-IN	7,572
48	Columbus, OH	7,292
49	New Orleans, LA	6,953
50	Portland-Vancouver, OR-WA	6,898
51	Albuquerque, NM	6,291
52	Birmingham-Hoover, AL	6,187
53	Tulsa, OK	6,158
54	Stockton, CA	6,079
55	Oklahoma City, OK	6,015
56	Buffalo-Niagara Falls, NY	5,899
57	Little Rock, AR	5,891
58	Baton Rouge, LA	5,711
59	Nassau-Suffolk, NY M.D.	5,682
59	Tucson, AZ	5,682
61	San Jose, CA	5,607
62	Austin-Round Rock, TX	5,157
63	Columbia, SC	5,092
64	Charleston-North Charleston, SC	5,017
65	Louisville, KY-IN	4,922
66	Fresno, CA	4,895
67	Sarasota-Bradenton-Venice, FL	4,624
68	Wilmington, DE-MD-NJ M.D.	4,612
69	Richmond, VA	4,489
70	Camden, NJ M.D.	4,387
71	Shreveport-Bossier City, LA	4,315
72	Edison, NJ M.D.	4,252
73	Tacoma, WA M.D.	4,209
74	Bakersfield, CA	4,189
75	Flint, MI	4,116
76	Greenville, SC	4,024
77	Wichita, KS	3,964
78	Rochester, NY	3,764
78	Toledo, OH	3,764
80	Salt Lake City, UT	3,690
81	Palm Bay-Melbourne, FL	3,622
82	Raleigh-Cary, NC	3,485
83	Greensboro-High Point, NC	3,472
84	Knoxville, TN	3,408
85	Omaha-Council Bluffs, NE-IA	3,403
86	Colorado Springs, CO	3,298
87	Grand Rapids-Wyoming, MI	3,293
88	Albany-Schenectady-Troy, NY	3,165
89	Hartford, CT	3,160
90	Cape Coral-Fort Myers, FL	3,157
91	Lakeland, FL	3,078
92	Modesto, CA	3,056
93	Bethesda-Frederick, MD M.D.	3,055
94	Chattanooga, TN-GA	3,004
95	Durham, NC	2,824
96	Pensacola, FL	2,808
97	El Paso, TX	2,804
98	Tallahassee, FL	2,789
99	Anchorage, AK	2,749
100	Dayton, OH	2,747
101	Honolulu, HI	2,745
102	Daytona Beach, FL	2,716
103	McAllen-Edinburg-Mission, TX	2,640
104	Vallejo-Fairfield, CA	2,531
105	Winston-Salem, NC	2,471
106	Corpus Christi, TX	2,449
107	Visalia-Porterville, CA	2,442
108	Jackson, MS	2,375
109	Florence, SC	2,339
110	Ocala, FL	2,326
111	Lubbock, TX	2,316
112	Gainesville, FL	2,282
113	Saginaw, MI	2,265
114	Beaumont-Port Arthur, TX	2,228
115	Oxnard-Thousand Oaks, CA	2,223
116	Santa Rosa-Petaluma, CA	2,163
117	Fayetteville, NC	2,139
118	Syracuse, NY	2,110
119	Port St. Lucie, FL	2,098
120	Reno-Sparks, NV	2,075
121	Augusta, GA-SC	2,041
122	Salinas, CA	2,014
123	Huntsville, AL	2,005
124	Lexington-Fayette, KY	1,966
125	Myrtle Beach, SC	1,958
126	Lansing-East Lansing, MI	1,947
126	Springfield, MO	1,947
128	Poughkeepsie, NY	1,847
129	Spartanburg, SC	1,830
130	Des Moines-West Des Moines, IA	1,829
131	Spokane, WA	1,799
132	Trenton-Ewing, NJ	1,781
133	Harrisburg-Carlisle, PA	1,768
134	Santa Barbara-Santa Maria, CA	1,752
135	Amarillo, TX	1,722
136	Brownsville-Harlingen, TX	1,678
137	Scranton--Wilkes-Barre, PA	1,668
138	Merced, CA	1,616
139	Boise City-Nampa, ID	1,610
140	Mobile, AL	1,594
141	Montgomery, AL	1,561
142	Atlantic City, NJ	1,519
143	Fort Smith, AR-OK	1,505
144	Reading, PA	1,504
145	Alexandria, LA	1,497
146	Wilmington, NC	1,480
147	Columbus, GA-AL	1,435
148	Kalamazoo-Portage, MI	1,434
149	Madison, WI	1,411
150	Clarksville, TN-KY	1,392
151	Kingsport, TN-VA	1,378
152	Naples-Marco Island, FL	1,377
153	Lake Charles, LA	1,373
154	Sumter, SC	1,333
155	Fayetteville, AR-MO	1,308
156	Panama City-Lynn Haven, FL	1,300
157	Waco, TX	1,283
158	Lincoln, NE	1,281
159	Laredo, TX	1,261
160	Macon, GA	1,248
161	Roanoke, VA	1,243
161	Vineland, NJ	1,243
163	Charleston, WV	1,220
164	South Bend-Mishawaka, IN-MI	1,203
165	Texarkana, TX-Texarkana, AR	1,179
166	Anderson, SC	1,163
167	Longview, TX	1,161
168	Asheville, NC	1,146
169	Greenville, NC	1,137
170	Battle Creek, MI	1,104
171	Santa Cruz-Watsonville, CA	1,083

Note: All listings are for Metropolitan Statistical Areas (M.S.A.s) except for those ending with "M.D." Listings with "M.D." are Metropolitan Divisions which are smaller parts of eleven large M.S.A.s. See explanatory note at beginning of metropolitan area section on page 23.

RANK	METROPOLITAN AREA	CRIMES
172	Salem, OR	1,074
173	Tuscaloosa, AL	1,073
174	Lancaster, PA	1,062
175	Ann Arbor, MI	1,060
176	Salisbury, MD	1,058
177	Houma, LA	1,035
178	Bremerton-Silverdale, WA	1,014
179	Jackson, TN	987
180	Lawton, OK	975
181	Muskegon-Norton Shores, MI	961
182	College Station-Bryan, TX	950
183	Pine Bluff, AR	919
184	Evansville, IN-KY	912
185	Eugene-Springfield, OR	910
185	Tyler, TX	910
187	Topeka, KS	905
188	Las Cruces, NM	893
189	Prescott, AZ	882
190	Dover, DE	881
191	Fort Wayne, IN	877
192	Yuma, AZ	873
193	Ogden-Clearfield, UT	861
194	Monroe, LA	846
195	Hagerstown-Martinsburg, MD-WV	845
196	Greeley, CO	832
197	Utica-Rome, NY	829
198	Erie, PA	824
199	Rocky Mount, NC	821
200	Brunswick, GA	803
201	Chico, CA	787
202	Madera, CA	777
203	Niles-Benton Harbor, MI	774
204	Farmington, NM	763
205	Burlington, NC	759
206	Yakima, WA	756
207	Yuba City, CA	748
208	Punta Gorda, FL	739
209	San Luis Obispo, CA	736
210	Johnson City, TN	731
211	Fort Collins-Loveland, CO	718
212	Portland, ME	714
213	Fort Walton Beach, FL	710
214	Joplin, MO	702
215	Cleveland, TN	694
216	Flagstaff, AZ	690
217	Columbia, MO	679
218	Green Bay, WI	678
219	Albany, GA	676
220	Pueblo, CO	674
221	Odessa, TX	673
222	El Centro, CA	663
223	Huntington-Ashland, WV-KY-OH	657
224	Jackson, MI	654
225	Kennewick-Richland-Pasco, WA	651
226	Redding, CA	648
227	Abilene, TX	638
228	Jonesboro, AR	637
229	Santa Fe, NM	636
230	Manchester-Nashua, NH	634
231	Springfield, OH	620

RANK	METROPOLITAN AREA	CRIMES
232	Hot Springs, AR	615
233	Goldsboro, NC	602
234	Athens-Clarke County, GA	596
234	Olympia, WA	596
236	Pittsfield, MA	595
237	Lake Havasu City-Kingman, AZ	589
238	Morristown, TN	571
239	Jacksonville, NC	557
240	Lawrence, KS	556
241	Lynchburg, VA	555
242	Valdosta, GA	543
243	Charlottesville, VA	539
244	Hanford-Corcoran, CA	535
245	Jefferson City, MO	533
245	Racine, WI	533
245	Waterloo-Cedar Falls, IA	533
245	Wichita Falls, TX	533
249	Cedar Rapids, IA	531
250	Binghamton, NY	529
251	Rome, GA	527
252	Holland-Grand Haven, MI	521
253	Kingston, NY	513
254	Dothan, AL	508
255	Warner Robins, GA	505
256	Gadsden, AL	499
257	Medford, OR	491
258	Sioux Falls, SD	481
259	Sebastian-Vero Beach, FL	479
260	Sioux City, IA-NE-SD	473
261	Napa, CA	463
262	Lima, OH	455
263	Victoria, TX	454
264	Coeur d'Alene, ID	451
265	Midland, TX	443
266	Dalton, GA	440
267	Provo-Orem, UT	437
268	Gainesville, GA	433
269	Bellingham, WA	432
270	Bloomington, IN	425
270	Lafayette, IN	425
272	San Angelo, TX	423
273	Elkhart-Goshen, IN	420
274	Decatur, AL	412
275	Dubuque, IA	403
275	Muncie, IN	403
277	Iowa City, IA	394
278	Bowling Green, KY	393
279	Pascagoula, MS	388
280	Altoona, PA	386
281	Lebanon, PA	380
282	Cumberland, MD-WV	373
283	Janesville, WI	372
284	Grand Junction, CO	368
285	Johnstown, PA	363
286	Monroe, MI	347
287	Hattiesburg, MS	346
288	Ocean City, NJ	344
289	St. Joseph, MO-KS	335
290	Oshkosh-Neenah, WI	329
291	Blacksburg, VA	324

RANK	METROPOLITAN AREA	CRIMES
292	Rapid City, SD	321
293	Bend, OR	313
294	Mansfield, OH	307
295	Kokomo, IN	304
296	Sherman-Denison, TX	300
297	Idaho Falls, ID	295
298	Longview, WA	291
299	Pocatello, ID	283
300	Bay City, MI	280
301	Morgantown, WV	275
302	Fairbanks, AK	274
303	Appleton, WI	273
304	Billings, MT	272
305	Danville, VA	270
306	Missoula, MT	269
307	Winchester, VA-WV	267
308	Sandusky, OH	266
309	Mount Vernon-Anacortes, WA	259
310	Wheeling, WV-OH	251
311	Michigan City-La Porte, IN	250
312	Great Falls, MT	216
313	Wenatchee, WA	214
314	Ames, IA	205
314	Glens Falls, NY	205
314	Wausau, WI	205
317	Eau Claire, WI	201
318	Williamsport, PA	198
319	Carson City, NV	195
320	Elmira, NY	193
321	Bismarck, ND	191
321	Palm Coast, FL	191
323	Fond du Lac, WI	188
324	Elizabethtown, KY	175
325	Harrisonburg, VA	173
326	Casper, WY	169
327	Cheyenne, WY	168
328	Ithaca, NY	154
329	Columbus, IN	152
330	Lewiston-Auburn, ME	146
331	State College, PA	144
332	Sheboygan, WI	134
333	Bangor, ME	111
334	Logan, UT-ID	86
335	Lewiston, ID-WA	72
NA	Barnstable Town, MA**	NA
NA	Charlotte-Gastonia, NC-SC**	NA
NA	Chicago, IL**	NA
NA	Duluth, MN-WI**	NA
NA	Fargo, ND-MN**	NA
NA	Grand Forks, ND-MN**	NA
NA	Jacksonville, FL**	NA
NA	Killeen-Temple-Fort Hood, TX**	NA
NA	La Crosse, WI-MN**	NA
NA	Minneapolis-St. Paul, MN-WI**	NA
NA	Rochester, MN**	NA
NA	Savannah, GA**	NA
NA	Springfield, MA**	NA
NA	St. Cloud, MN**	NA
NA	Worcester, MA**	NA

Source: Federal Bureau of Investigation
"Crime in the United States 2006" (Uniform Crime Reports, September 24, 2007)
**Violent crimes are offenses of murder, forcible rape, robbery, and aggravated assault.*
***Not available.*

6. Violent Crime Rate in 2006

National Rate = 473.5 Violent Crimes per 100,000 Population*

RANK	METROPOLITAN AREA	RATE
183	Abilene, TX	391.9
196	Albany-Schenectady-Troy, NY	371.8
177	Albany, GA	402.2
33	Albuquerque, NM	777.8
7	Alexandria, LA	1,067.4
239	Altoona, PA	304.2
42	Amarillo, TX	701.6
274	Ames, IA	255.0
10	Anchorage, AK	932.3
54	Anderson, SC	652.5
238	Ann Arbor, MI	310.9
328	Appleton, WI	126.4
249	Asheville, NC	286.0
227	Athens-Clarke County, GA	329.8
112	Atlanta, GA	527.3
83	Atlantic City, NJ	560.1
188	Augusta, GA-SC	382.1
218	Austin-Round Rock, TX	345.3
95	Bakersfield, CA	548.6
25	Baltimore-Towson, MD	823.8
333	Bangor, ME	75.5
NA	Barnstable Town, MA**	NA
26	Baton Rouge, LA	821.1
29	Battle Creek, MI	795.1
272	Bay City, MI	257.5
78	Beaumont-Port Arthur, TX	564.9
289	Bellingham, WA	231.5
298	Bend, OR	217.8
267	Bethesda-Frederick, MD M.D.	265.3
315	Billings, MT	183.8
304	Binghamton, NY	212.4
80	Birmingham-Hoover, AL	562.5
312	Bismarck, ND	192.5
304	Blacksburg, VA	212.4
286	Bloomington, IN	237.6
248	Boise City-Nampa, ID	288.3
213	Bowling Green, KY	351.3
175	Bremerton-Silverdale, WA	414.2
160	Brownsville-Harlingen, TX	431.3
31	Brunswick, GA	790.4
119	Buffalo-Niagara Falls, NY	512.6
110	Burlington, NC	529.5
212	Camden, NJ M.D.	351.8
75	Cape Coral-Fort Myers, FL	569.9
224	Carson City, NV	336.6
285	Casper, WY	239.4
302	Cedar Rapids, IA	214.4
24	Charleston-North Charleston, SC	830.4
180	Charleston, WV	397.8
NA	Charlotte-Gastonia, NC-SC**	NA
251	Charlottesville, VA	283.2
65	Chattanooga, TN-GA	599.5
311	Cheyenne, WY	195.1
NA	Chicago, IL**	NA
203	Chico, CA	364.2
202	Cincinnati-Middletown, OH-KY-IN	364.7
77	Clarksville, TN-KY	565.0
141	Cleveland-Elyria-Mentor, OH	459.7
59	Cleveland, TN	634.3
219	Coeur d'Alene, ID	344.3
126	College Station-Bryan, TX	486.9
92	Colorado Springs, CO	550.9
152	Columbia, MO	439.8
38	Columbia, SC	726.8
124	Columbus, GA-AL	490.9
307	Columbus, IN	205.3
167	Columbus, OH	426.3
73	Corpus Christi, TX	575.9
197	Cumberland, MD-WV	369.7
109	Dallas (greater), TX	534.3
84	Dallas-Plano-Irving, TX M.D.	559.5
231	Dalton, GA	323.7
279	Danville, VA	247.5
99	Daytona Beach, FL	545.0
229	Dayton, OH	325.2
260	Decatur, AL	275.2
165	Denver-Aurora, CO	427.7
214	Des Moines-West Des Moines, IA	348.2
34	Detroit (greater), MI	757.0
1	Detroit-Livonia-Dearborn, MI M.D.	1,277.3
199	Dothan, AL	368.6
64	Dover, DE	604.8
154	Dubuque, IA	437.5
NA	Duluth, MN-WI**	NA
62	Durham, NC	606.9
327	Eau Claire, WI	130.0
314	Edison, NJ M.D.	184.4
169	El Centro, CA	421.7
193	El Paso, TX	377.9
322	Elizabethtown, KY	156.9
303	Elkhart-Goshen, IN	213.6
301	Elmira, NY	215.0
246	Erie, PA	293.6
265	Eugene-Springfield, OR	267.1
270	Evansville, IN-KY	259.1
NA	Fairbanks, AK**	NA
NA	Fargo, ND-MN**	NA
67	Farmington, NM	596.4
235	Fayetteville, AR-MO	319.3
62	Fayetteville, NC	606.9
107	Flagstaff, AZ	536.5
11	Flint, MI	929.6
5	Florence, SC	1,160.6
313	Fond du Lac, WI	188.6
270	Fort Collins-Loveland, CO	259.1
69	Fort Lauderdale, FL M.D.	595.5
113	Fort Smith, AR-OK	522.5
187	Fort Walton Beach, FL	383.3
300	Fort Wayne, IN	215.4
130	Fort Worth-Arlington, TX M.D.	483.4
90	Fresno, CA	552.8
131	Gadsden, AL	479.2
9	Gainesville, FL	934.1
276	Gainesville, GA	253.1
319	Glens Falls, NY	159.0
116	Goldsboro, NC	515.7
NA	Grand Forks, ND-MN**	NA
255	Grand Junction, CO	278.1
163	Grand Rapids-Wyoming, MI	428.1
264	Great Falls, MT	268.9
209	Greeley, CO	356.7
294	Green Bay, WI	227.1
122	Greensboro-High Point, NC	504.7
45	Greenville, NC	685.6
50	Greenville, SC	670.2
225	Hagerstown-Martinsburg, MD-WV	335.6
197	Hanford-Corcoran, CA	369.7
222	Harrisburg-Carlisle, PA	338.5
324	Harrisonburg, VA	153.4
237	Hartford, CT	315.4
268	Hattiesburg, MS	263.3
308	Holland-Grand Haven, MI	204.5
243	Honolulu, HI	300.8
55	Hot Springs, AR	650.0
96	Houma, LA	546.9
41	Houston, TX	707.2
292	Huntington-Ashland, WV-KY-OH	229.0
105	Huntsville, AL	539.0
275	Idaho Falls, ID	253.4
96	Indianapolis, IN	546.9
252	Iowa City, IA	282.9
323	Ithaca, NY	153.6
NA	Jacksonville, FL**	NA
207	Jacksonville, NC	358.2
179	Jackson, MI	400.7
144	Jackson, MS	456.1
15	Jackson, TN	879.2
287	Janesville, WI	235.3
200	Jefferson City, MO	367.8
189	Johnson City, TN	382.0
282	Johnstown, PA	244.9
81	Jonesboro, AR	561.9
171	Joplin, MO	419.4
148	Kalamazoo-Portage, MI	450.2
68	Kansas City, MO-KS	595.9
247	Kennewick-Richland-Pasco, WA	289.6
NA	Killeen-Temple-Fort Hood, TX**	NA
147	Kingsport, TN-VA	452.0
254	Kingston, NY	280.0
118	Knoxville, TN	513.5
244	Kokomo, IN	297.9
NA	La Crosse, WI-MN**	NA
290	Lafayette, IN	230.3
37	Lake Charles, LA	742.9
240	Lake Havasu City-Kingman, AZ	303.1
85	Lakeland, FL	557.5
299	Lancaster, PA	216.3
162	Lansing-East Lansing, MI	428.7
98	Laredo, TX	545.7
135	Las Cruces, NM	465.1
17	Las Vegas-Paradise, NV	877.2

Note: All listings are for Metropolitan Statistical Areas (M.S.A.s) except for those ending with "M.D." Listings with "M.D." are Metropolitan Divisions which are smaller parts of eleven large M.S.A.s. See explanatory note at beginning of metropolitan area section on page 23.

RANK	METROPOLITAN AREA	RATE
107	Lawrence, KS	536.5
21	Lawton, OK	859.6
242	Lebanon, PA	302.3
326	Lewiston-Auburn, ME	135.1
329	Lewiston, ID-WA	119.1
145	Lexington-Fayette, KY	453.8
164	Lima, OH	427.8
146	Lincoln, NE	452.5
14	Little Rock, AR	905.5
333	Logan, UT-ID	75.5
82	Longview, TX	560.3
245	Longview, WA	293.9
56	Los Angeles County, CA M.D.	648.8
79	Los Angeles (greater), CA	562.9
176	Louisville, KY-IN	404.2
18	Lubbock, TX	869.7
288	Lynchburg, VA	232.0
111	Macon, GA	528.7
104	Madera, CA	539.3
269	Madison, WI	261.8
321	Manchester-Nashua, NH	157.4
284	Mansfield, OH	239.6
191	McAllen-Edinburg-Mission, TX	378.5
280	Medford, OR	247.3
2	Memphis, TN-MS-AR	1,262.7
52	Merced, CA	662.6
32	Miami (greater), FL	790.0
8	Miami-Dade County, FL M.D.	973.5
297	Michigan City-La Porte, IN	224.7
210	Midland, TX	354.9
72	Milwaukee, WI	579.6
NA	Minneapolis-St. Paul, MN-WI**	NA
266	Missoula, MT	266.2
181	Mobile, AL	393.5
66	Modesto, CA	599.1
115	Monroe, LA	521.5
295	Monroe, MI	226.0
158	Montgomery, AL	433.0
283	Morgantown, WV	240.0
159	Morristown, TN	431.8
296	Mount Vernon-Anacortes, WA	225.0
220	Muncie, IN	344.1
94	Muskegon-Norton Shores, MI	548.8
23	Myrtle Beach, SC	849.4
216	Napa, CA	345.6
151	Naples-Marco Island, FL	440.7
22	Nashville-Davidson, TN	857.7
309	Nassau-Suffolk, NY M.D.	201.8
86	New Orleans, LA	556.0
153	New York (greater), NY-NJ-PA	438.4
91	New York-W. Plains NY-NJ M.D.	551.5
174	Newark-Union, NJ-PA M.D.	415.3
133	Niles-Benton Harbor, MI	477.2
43	Oakland-Fremont, CA M.D.	691.4
36	Ocala, FL	753.8
215	Ocean City, NJ	346.2
114	Odessa, TX	522.1
316	Ogden-Clearfield, UT	171.3
117	Oklahoma City, OK	515.4
273	Olympia, WA	256.0

RANK	METROPOLITAN AREA	RATE
172	Omaha-Council Bluffs, NE-IA	416.2
15	Orlando, FL	879.2
306	Oshkosh-Neenah, WI	205.5
258	Oxnard-Thousand Oaks, CA	276.7
48	Palm Bay-Melbourne, FL	670.5
281	Palm Coast, FL	245.8
30	Panama City-Lynn Haven, FL	791.3
278	Pascagoula, MS	247.7
60	Pensacola, FL	627.8
53	Philadelphia (greater) PA-NJ-DE	659.2
35	Philadelphia, PA M.D.	756.6
120	Phoenix-Mesa-Scottsdale, AZ	509.9
19	Pine Bluff, AR	866.5
205	Pittsburgh, PA	359.9
149	Pittsfield, MA	448.5
233	Pocatello, ID	321.0
101	Port St. Lucie, FL	541.5
230	Portland-Vancouver, OR-WA	323.8
325	Portland, ME	138.8
259	Poughkeepsie, NY	275.9
166	Prescott, AZ	427.5
332	Provo-Orem, UT	93.5
155	Pueblo, CO	437.1
139	Punta Gorda, FL	461.3
262	Racine, WI	271.3
206	Raleigh-Cary, NC	359.8
263	Rapid City, SD	269.5
190	Reading, PA	379.2
208	Redding, CA	357.0
121	Reno-Sparks, NV	509.7
192	Richmond, VA	378.1
125	Riverside-San Bernardino, CA	489.2
170	Roanoke, VA	420.1
NA	Rochester, MN**	NA
204	Rochester, NY	361.3
89	Rocky Mount, NC	553.2
100	Rome, GA	542.1
58	Sacramento, CA	635.6
6	Saginaw, MI	1,089.8
253	Salem, OR	281.4
129	Salinas, CA	484.4
12	Salisbury, MD	907.6
217	Salt Lake City, UT	345.4
184	San Angelo, TX	390.4
123	San Antonio, TX	497.0
143	San Diego, CA	458.7
57	San Francisco (greater), CA	635.9
88	San Francisco-S. Mateo, CA M.D.	554.8
236	San Jose, CA	316.6
250	San Luis Obispo, CA	285.5
223	Sandusky, OH	337.7
257	Santa Ana-Anaheim, CA M.D.	277.4
157	Santa Barbara-Santa Maria, CA	433.3
161	Santa Cruz-Watsonville, CA	429.9
150	Santa Fe, NM	445.5
142	Santa Rosa-Petaluma, CA	459.5
46	Sarasota-Bradenton-Venice, FL	675.6
NA	Savannah, GA**	NA
241	Scranton--Wilkes-Barre, PA	302.7
173	Seattle (greater), WA	415.9

RANK	METROPOLITAN AREA	RATE
195	Seattle-Bellevue, WA M.D.	375.0
201	Sebastian-Vero Beach, FL	366.3
330	Sheboygan, WI	116.5
277	Sherman-Denison, TX	249.7
4	Shreveport-Bossier City, LA	1,187.9
226	Sioux City, IA-NE-SD	329.9
291	Sioux Falls, SD	229.6
194	South Bend-Mishawaka, IN-MI	376.2
47	Spartanburg, SC	675.4
178	Spokane, WA	401.3
NA	Springfield, MA**	NA
128	Springfield, MO	485.5
156	Springfield, OH	434.9
331	State College, PA	102.4
13	Stockton, CA	907.2
NA	St. Cloud, MN**	NA
261	St. Joseph, MO-KS	272.7
76	St. Louis, MO-IL	566.1
3	Sumter, SC	1,244.0
232	Syracuse, NY	322.9
93	Tacoma, WA M.D.	548.9
27	Tallahassee, FL	819.0
40	Tampa-St Petersburg, FL	709.2
20	Texarkana, TX-Texarkana, AR	861.4
74	Toledo, OH	572.5
182	Topeka, KS	392.3
127	Trenton-Ewing, NJ	485.9
70	Tucson, AZ	591.8
44	Tulsa, OK	687.6
102	Tuscaloosa, AL	540.1
136	Tyler, TX	464.3
256	Utica-Rome, NY	277.6
168	Valdosta, GA	424.9
61	Vallejo-Fairfield, CA	609.4
185	Victoria, TX	389.5
28	Vineland, NJ	810.5
138	Virginia Beach-Norfolk, VA-NC	462.3
71	Visalia-Porterville, CA	589.0
87	Waco, TX	555.3
186	Warner Robins, GA	387.8
221	Warren-Farmington Hills, MI M.D.	339.6
132	Washington (greater) DC-VA-MD	478.2
106	Washington, DC-VA-MD-WV M.D.	537.7
228	Waterloo-Cedar Falls, IA	327.5
320	Wausau, WI	158.4
310	Wenatchee, WA	200.8
39	West Palm Beach, FL M.D.	718.8
317	Wheeling, WV-OH	168.6
211	Wichita Falls, TX	354.3
48	Wichita, KS	670.5
318	Williamsport, PA	167.1
51	Wilmington, DE-MD-NJ M.D.	664.9
140	Wilmington, NC	460.4
293	Winchester, VA-WV	227.8
103	Winston-Salem, NC	540.0
NA	Worcester, MA**	NA
234	Yakima, WA	320.9
134	Yuba City, CA	475.1
137	Yuma, AZ	463.9

Source: Federal Bureau of Investigation
"Crime in the United States 2006" (Uniform Crime Reports, September 24, 2007)
**Violent crimes are offenses of murder, forcible rape, robbery, and aggravated assault.*
***Not available.*

6. Violent Crime Rate in 2006 (continued)

National Rate = 473.5 Violent Crimes per 100,000 Population*

RANK	METROPOLITAN AREA	RATE
1	Detroit-Livonia-Dearborn, MI M.D.	1,277.3
2	Memphis, TN-MS-AR	1,262.7
3	Sumter, SC	1,244.0
4	Shreveport-Bossier City, LA	1,187.9
5	Florence, SC	1,160.6
6	Saginaw, MI	1,089.8
7	Alexandria, LA	1,067.4
8	Miami-Dade County, FL M.D.	973.5
9	Gainesville, FL	934.1
10	Anchorage, AK	932.3
11	Flint, MI	929.6
12	Salisbury, MD	907.6
13	Stockton, CA	907.2
14	Little Rock, AR	905.5
15	Jackson, TN	879.2
15	Orlando, FL	879.2
17	Las Vegas-Paradise, NV	877.2
18	Lubbock, TX	869.7
19	Pine Bluff, AR	866.5
20	Texarkana, TX-Texarkana, AR	861.4
21	Lawton, OK	859.6
22	Nashville-Davidson, TN	857.7
23	Myrtle Beach, SC	849.4
24	Charleston-North Charleston, SC	830.4
25	Baltimore-Towson, MD	823.8
26	Baton Rouge, LA	821.1
27	Tallahassee, FL	819.0
28	Vineland, NJ	810.5
29	Battle Creek, MI	795.1
30	Panama City-Lynn Haven, FL	791.3
31	Brunswick, GA	790.4
32	Miami (greater), FL	790.0
33	Albuquerque, NM	777.8
34	Detroit (greater), MI	757.0
35	Philadelphia, PA M.D.	756.6
36	Ocala, FL	753.8
37	Lake Charles, LA	742.9
38	Columbia, SC	726.8
39	West Palm Beach, FL M.D.	718.8
40	Tampa-St Petersburg, FL	709.2
41	Houston, TX	707.2
42	Amarillo, TX	701.6
43	Oakland-Fremont, CA M.D.	691.4
44	Tulsa, OK	687.6
45	Greenville, NC	685.6
46	Sarasota-Bradenton-Venice, FL	675.6
47	Spartanburg, SC	675.4
48	Palm Bay-Melbourne, FL	670.5
48	Wichita, KS	670.5
50	Greenville, SC	670.2
51	Wilmington, DE-MD-NJ M.D.	664.9
52	Merced, CA	662.6
53	Philadelphia (greater) PA-NJ-DE	659.2
54	Anderson, SC	652.5
55	Hot Springs, AR	650.0
56	Los Angeles County, CA M.D.	648.8
57	San Francisco (greater), CA	635.9
58	Sacramento, CA	635.6
59	Cleveland, TN	634.3
60	Pensacola, FL	627.8
61	Vallejo-Fairfield, CA	609.4
62	Durham, NC	606.9
62	Fayetteville, NC	606.9
64	Dover, DE	604.8
65	Chattanooga, TN-GA	599.5
66	Modesto, CA	599.1
67	Farmington, NM	596.4
68	Kansas City, MO-KS	595.9
69	Fort Lauderdale, FL M.D.	595.5
70	Tucson, AZ	591.8
71	Visalia-Porterville, CA	589.0
72	Milwaukee, WI	579.6
73	Corpus Christi, TX	575.9
74	Toledo, OH	572.5
75	Cape Coral-Fort Myers, FL	569.9
76	St. Louis, MO-IL	566.1
77	Clarksville, TN-KY	565.0
78	Beaumont-Port Arthur, TX	564.9
79	Los Angeles (greater), CA	562.9
80	Birmingham-Hoover, AL	562.5
81	Jonesboro, AR	561.9
82	Longview, TX	560.3
83	Atlantic City, NJ	560.1
84	Dallas-Plano-Irving, TX M.D.	559.5
85	Lakeland, FL	557.5
86	New Orleans, LA	556.0
87	Waco, TX	555.3
88	San Francisco-S. Mateo, CA M.D.	554.8
89	Rocky Mount, NC	553.2
90	Fresno, CA	552.8
91	New York-W. Plains NY-NJ M.D.	551.5
92	Colorado Springs, CO	550.9
93	Tacoma, WA M.D.	548.9
94	Muskegon-Norton Shores, MI	548.8
95	Bakersfield, CA	548.6
96	Houma, LA	546.9
96	Indianapolis, IN	546.9
98	Laredo, TX	545.7
99	Daytona Beach, FL	545.0
100	Rome, GA	542.1
101	Port St. Lucie, FL	541.5
102	Tuscaloosa, AL	540.1
103	Winston-Salem, NC	540.0
104	Madera, CA	539.3
105	Huntsville, AL	539.0
106	Washington, DC-VA-MD-WV M.D.	537.7
107	Flagstaff, AZ	536.5
107	Lawrence, KS	536.5
109	Dallas (greater), TX	534.3
110	Burlington, NC	529.5
111	Macon, GA	528.7
112	Atlanta, GA	527.3
113	Fort Smith, AR-OK	522.5
114	Odessa, TX	522.1
115	Monroe, LA	521.5
116	Goldsboro, NC	515.7
117	Oklahoma City, OK	515.4
118	Knoxville, TN	513.5
119	Buffalo-Niagara Falls, NY	512.6
120	Phoenix-Mesa-Scottsdale, AZ	509.9
121	Reno-Sparks, NV	509.7
122	Greensboro-High Point, NC	504.7
123	San Antonio, TX	497.0
124	Columbus, GA-AL	490.9
125	Riverside-San Bernardino, CA	489.2
126	College Station-Bryan, TX	486.9
127	Trenton-Ewing, NJ	485.9
128	Springfield, MO	485.5
129	Salinas, CA	484.4
130	Fort Worth-Arlington, TX M.D.	483.4
131	Gadsden, AL	479.2
132	Washington (greater) DC-VA-MD	478.2
133	Niles-Benton Harbor, MI	477.2
134	Yuba City, CA	475.1
135	Las Cruces, NM	465.1
136	Tyler, TX	464.3
137	Yuma, AZ	463.9
138	Virginia Beach-Norfolk, VA-NC	462.3
139	Punta Gorda, FL	461.3
140	Wilmington, NC	460.4
141	Cleveland-Elyria-Mentor, OH	459.7
142	Santa Rosa-Petaluma, CA	459.5
143	San Diego, CA	458.7
144	Jackson, MS	456.1
145	Lexington-Fayette, KY	453.8
146	Lincoln, NE	452.5
147	Kingsport, TN-VA	452.0
148	Kalamazoo-Portage, MI	450.2
149	Pittsfield, MA	448.5
150	Santa Fe, NM	445.5
151	Naples-Marco Island, FL	440.7
152	Columbia, MO	439.8
153	New York (greater), NY-NJ-PA	438.4
154	Dubuque, IA	437.5
155	Pueblo, CO	437.1
156	Springfield, OH	434.9
157	Santa Barbara-Santa Maria, CA	433.3
158	Montgomery, AL	433.0
159	Morristown, TN	431.8
160	Brownsville-Harlingen, TX	431.3
161	Santa Cruz-Watsonville, CA	429.9
162	Lansing-East Lansing, MI	428.7
163	Grand Rapids-Wyoming, MI	428.1
164	Lima, OH	427.8
165	Denver-Aurora, CO	427.7
166	Prescott, AZ	427.5
167	Columbus, OH	426.3
168	Valdosta, GA	424.9
169	El Centro, CA	421.7
170	Roanoke, VA	420.1
171	Joplin, MO	419.4

Note: All listings are for Metropolitan Statistical Areas (M.S.A.s) except for those ending with "M.D." Listings with "M.D." are Metropolitan Divisions which are smaller parts of eleven large M.S.A.s. See explanatory note at beginning of metropolitan area section on page 23.

RANK	METROPOLITAN AREA	RATE
172	Omaha-Council Bluffs, NE-IA	416.2
173	Seattle (greater), WA	415.9
174	Newark-Union, NJ-PA M.D.	415.3
175	Bremerton-Silverdale, WA	414.2
176	Louisville, KY-IN	404.2
177	Albany, GA	402.2
178	Spokane, WA	401.3
179	Jackson, MI	400.7
180	Charleston, WV	397.8
181	Mobile, AL	393.5
182	Topeka, KS	392.3
183	Abilene, TX	391.9
184	San Angelo, TX	390.4
185	Victoria, TX	389.5
186	Warner Robins, GA	387.8
187	Fort Walton Beach, FL	383.3
188	Augusta, GA-SC	382.1
189	Johnson City, TN	382.0
190	Reading, PA	379.2
191	McAllen-Edinburg-Mission, TX	378.5
192	Richmond, VA	378.1
193	El Paso, TX	377.9
194	South Bend-Mishawaka, IN-MI	376.2
195	Seattle-Bellevue, WA M.D.	375.0
196	Albany-Schenectady-Troy, NY	371.8
197	Cumberland, MD-WV	369.7
197	Hanford-Corcoran, CA	369.7
199	Dothan, AL	368.6
200	Jefferson City, MO	367.8
201	Sebastian-Vero Beach, FL	366.3
202	Cincinnati-Middletown, OH-KY-IN	364.7
203	Chico, CA	364.2
204	Rochester, NY	361.3
205	Pittsburgh, PA	359.9
206	Raleigh-Cary, NC	359.8
207	Jacksonville, NC	358.2
208	Redding, CA	357.0
209	Greeley, CO	356.7
210	Midland, TX	354.9
211	Wichita Falls, TX	354.3
212	Camden, NJ M.D.	351.8
213	Bowling Green, KY	351.3
214	Des Moines-West Des Moines, IA	348.2
215	Ocean City, NJ	346.2
216	Napa, CA	345.6
217	Salt Lake City, UT	345.4
218	Austin-Round Rock, TX	345.3
219	Coeur d'Alene, ID	344.3
220	Muncie, IN	344.1
221	Warren-Farmington Hills, MI M.D.	339.6
222	Harrisburg-Carlisle, PA	338.5
223	Sandusky, OH	337.7
224	Carson City, NV	336.6
225	Hagerstown-Martinsburg, MD-WV	335.6
226	Sioux City, IA-NE-SD	329.9
227	Athens-Clarke County, GA	329.8
228	Waterloo-Cedar Falls, IA	327.5
229	Dayton, OH	325.2
230	Portland-Vancouver, OR-WA	323.8
231	Dalton, GA	323.7

RANK	METROPOLITAN AREA	RATE
232	Syracuse, NY	322.9
233	Pocatello, ID	321.0
234	Yakima, WA	320.9
235	Fayetteville, AR-MO	319.3
236	San Jose, CA	316.6
237	Hartford, CT	315.4
238	Ann Arbor, MI	310.9
239	Altoona, PA	304.2
240	Lake Havasu City-Kingman, AZ	303.1
241	Scranton--Wilkes-Barre, PA	302.7
242	Lebanon, PA	302.3
243	Honolulu, HI	300.8
244	Kokomo, IN	297.9
245	Longview, WA	293.9
246	Erie, PA	293.6
247	Kennewick-Richland-Pasco, WA	289.6
248	Boise City-Nampa, ID	288.3
249	Asheville, NC	286.0
250	San Luis Obispo, CA	285.5
251	Charlottesville, VA	283.2
252	Iowa City, IA	282.9
253	Salem, OR	281.4
254	Kingston, NY	280.0
255	Grand Junction, CO	278.1
256	Utica-Rome, NY	277.6
257	Santa Ana-Anaheim, CA M.D.	277.4
258	Oxnard-Thousand Oaks, CA	276.7
259	Poughkeepsie, NY	275.9
260	Decatur, AL	275.2
261	St. Joseph, MO-KS	272.7
262	Racine, WI	271.3
263	Rapid City, SD	269.5
264	Great Falls, MT	268.9
265	Eugene-Springfield, OR	267.1
266	Missoula, MT	266.2
267	Bethesda-Frederick, MD M.D.	265.3
268	Hattiesburg, MS	263.3
269	Madison, WI	261.8
270	Evansville, IN-KY	259.1
270	Fort Collins-Loveland, CO	259.1
272	Bay City, MI	257.5
273	Olympia, WA	256.0
274	Ames, IA	255.0
275	Idaho Falls, ID	253.4
276	Gainesville, GA	253.1
277	Sherman-Denison, TX	249.7
278	Pascagoula, MS	247.7
279	Danville, VA	247.5
280	Medford, OR	247.3
281	Palm Coast, FL	245.8
282	Johnstown, PA	244.9
283	Morgantown, WV	240.0
284	Mansfield, OH	239.6
285	Casper, WY	239.4
286	Bloomington, IN	237.6
287	Janesville, WI	235.3
288	Lynchburg, VA	232.0
289	Bellingham, WA	231.5
290	Lafayette, IN	230.3
291	Sioux Falls, SD	229.6

RANK	METROPOLITAN AREA	RATE
292	Huntington-Ashland, WV-KY-OH	229.0
293	Winchester, VA-WV	227.8
294	Green Bay, WI	227.1
295	Monroe, MI	226.0
296	Mount Vernon-Anacortes, WA	225.0
297	Michigan City-La Porte, IN	224.7
298	Bend, OR	217.8
299	Lancaster, PA	216.3
300	Fort Wayne, IN	215.4
301	Elmira, NY	215.0
302	Cedar Rapids, IA	214.4
303	Elkhart-Goshen, IN	213.6
304	Binghamton, NY	212.4
304	Blacksburg, VA	212.4
306	Oshkosh-Neenah, WI	205.5
307	Columbus, IN	205.3
308	Holland-Grand Haven, MI	204.5
309	Nassau-Suffolk, NY M.D.	201.8
310	Wenatchee, WA	200.8
311	Cheyenne, WY	195.1
312	Bismarck, ND	192.5
313	Fond du Lac, WI	188.6
314	Edison, NJ M.D.	184.4
315	Billings, MT	183.8
316	Ogden-Clearfield, UT	171.3
317	Wheeling, WV-OH	168.6
318	Williamsport, PA	167.1
319	Glens Falls, NY	159.0
320	Wausau, WI	158.4
321	Manchester-Nashua, NH	157.4
322	Elizabethtown, KY	156.9
323	Ithaca, NY	153.6
324	Harrisonburg, VA	153.4
325	Portland, ME	138.8
326	Lewiston-Auburn, ME	135.1
327	Eau Claire, WI	130.0
328	Appleton, WI	126.4
329	Lewiston, ID-WA	119.1
330	Sheboygan, WI	116.5
331	State College, PA	102.4
332	Provo-Orem, UT	93.5
333	Bangor, ME	75.5
333	Logan, UT-ID	75.5
NA	Barnstable Town, MA**	NA
NA	Charlotte-Gastonia, NC-SC**	NA
NA	Chicago, IL**	NA
NA	Duluth, MN-WI**	NA
NA	Fairbanks, AK**	NA
NA	Fargo, ND-MN**	NA
NA	Grand Forks, ND-MN**	NA
NA	Jacksonville, FL**	NA
NA	Killeen-Temple-Fort Hood, TX**	NA
NA	La Crosse, WI-MN**	NA
NA	Minneapolis-St. Paul, MN-WI**	NA
NA	Rochester, MN**	NA
NA	Savannah, GA**	NA
NA	Springfield, MA**	NA
NA	St. Cloud, MN**	NA
NA	Worcester, MA**	NA

Source: Federal Bureau of Investigation
"Crime in the United States 2006" (Uniform Crime Reports, September 24, 2007)
**Violent crimes are offenses of murder, forcible rape, robbery, and aggravated assault.*
***Not available.*

7. Percent Change in Violent Crime Rate: 2005 to 2006

National Percent Change = 1.0% Increase*

RANK	METROPOLITAN AREA	% CHANGE
NA	Abilene, TX**	NA
161	Albany-Schenectady-Troy, NY	1.7
92	Albany, GA	7.3
264	Albuquerque, NM	(7.3)
76	Alexandria, LA	8.6
40	Altoona, PA	14.6
140	Amarillo, TX	3.7
7	Ames, IA	36.3
20	Anchorage, AK	23.7
119	Anderson, SC	5.0
274	Ann Arbor, MI	(9.7)
47	Appleton, WI	13.3
58	Asheville, NC	11.2
32	Athens-Clarke County, GA	17.8
95	Atlanta, GA	7.2
78	Atlantic City, NJ	8.5
222	Augusta, GA-SC	(2.6)
189	Austin-Round Rock, TX	(0.3)
131	Bakersfield, CA	4.1
203	Baltimore-Towson, MD	(1.6)
269	Bangor, ME	(8.7)
NA	Barnstable Town, MA**	NA
44	Baton Rouge, LA	14.2
142	Battle Creek, MI	3.6
268	Bay City, MI	(8.1)
144	Beaumont-Port Arthur, TX	3.3
172	Bellingham, WA	0.9
158	Bend, OR	2.0
136	Bethesda-Frederick, MD M.D.	3.9
298	Billings, MT	(16.0)
21	Binghamton, NY	22.7
NA	Birmingham-Hoover, AL**	NA
1	Bismarck, ND	75.2
74	Blacksburg, VA	8.7
14	Bloomington, IN	28.2
NA	Boise City-Nampa, ID**	NA
54	Bowling Green, KY	11.8
202	Bremerton-Silverdale, WA	(1.5)
279	Brownsville-Harlingen, TX	(10.1)
51	Brunswick, GA	12.5
194	Buffalo-Niagara Falls, NY	(0.6)
125	Burlington, NC	4.8
179	Camden, NJ M.D.	0.1
178	Cape Coral-Fort Myers, FL	0.4
308	Carson City, NV	(33.7)
159	Casper, WY	1.9
264	Cedar Rapids, IA	(7.3)
203	Charleston-North Charleston, SC	(1.6)
136	Charleston, WV	3.9
NA	Charlotte-Gastonia, NC-SC**	NA
208	Charlottesville, VA	(1.8)
161	Chattanooga, TN-GA	1.7
68	Cheyenne, WY	9.4
NA	Chicago, IL**	NA
139	Chico, CA	3.8
194	Cincinnati-Middletown, OH-KY-IN	(0.6)
80	Clarksville, TN-KY	8.3
NA	Cleveland-Elyria-Mentor, OH**	NA
NA	Cleveland, TN**	NA
109	Coeur d'Alene, ID	6.2
241	College Station-Bryan, TX	(4.2)
37	Colorado Springs, CO	15.4
129	Columbia, MO	4.3
179	Columbia, SC	0.1
36	Columbus, GA-AL	16.3
5	Columbus, IN	42.2
230	Columbus, OH	(3.4)
244	Corpus Christi, TX	(4.3)
70	Cumberland, MD-WV	9.2
224	Dallas (greater), TX	(3.0)
253	Dallas-Plano-Irving, TX M.D.	(5.3)
NA	Dalton, GA**	NA
293	Danville, VA	(15.2)
239	Daytona Beach, FL	(4.1)
105	Dayton, OH	6.6
11	Decatur, AL	31.9
235	Denver-Aurora, CO	(3.7)
NA	Des Moines-West Des Moines, IA**	NA
151	Detroit (greater), MI	2.8
157	Detroit-Livonia-Dearborn, MI M.D.	2.1
189	Dothan, AL	(0.3)
184	Dover, DE	(0.1)
87	Dubuque, IA	7.7
NA	Duluth, MN-WI**	NA
NA	Durham, NC**	NA
140	Eau Claire, WI	3.7
98	Edison, NJ M.D.	7.0
300	El Centro, CA	(17.6)
267	El Paso, TX	(7.6)
214	Elizabethtown, KY	(2.2)
27	Elkhart-Goshen, IN	20.1
264	Elmira, NY	(7.3)
50	Erie, PA	12.7
84	Eugene-Springfield, OR	8.0
56	Evansville, IN-KY	11.4
NA	Fairbanks, AK**	NA
NA	Fargo, ND-MN**	NA
NA	Farmington, NM**	NA
72	Fayetteville, AR-MO	9.0
129	Fayetteville, NC	4.3
270	Flagstaff, AZ	(8.8)
82	Flint, MI	8.2
276	Florence, SC	(9.8)
4	Fond du Lac, WI	49.6
92	Fort Collins-Loveland, CO	7.3
173	Fort Lauderdale, FL M.D.	0.8
251	Fort Smith, AR-OK	(5.2)
25	Fort Walton Beach, FL	20.8
NA	Fort Wayne, IN**	NA
150	Fort Worth-Arlington, TX M.D.	2.9
289	Fresno, CA	(13.5)
38	Gadsden, AL	14.7
87	Gainesville, FL	7.7
142	Gainesville, GA	3.6
NA	Glens Falls, NY**	NA
45	Goldsboro, NC	14.1
NA	Grand Forks, ND-MN**	NA
154	Grand Junction, CO	2.5
241	Grand Rapids-Wyoming, MI	(4.2)
126	Great Falls, MT	4.7
304	Greeley, CO	(19.0)
43	Green Bay, WI	14.3
119	Greensboro-High Point, NC	5.0
22	Greenville, NC	22.6
250	Greenville, SC	(5.0)
59	Hagerstown-Martinsburg, MD-WV	10.9
224	Hanford-Corcoran, CA	(3.0)
232	Harrisburg-Carlisle, PA	(3.5)
12	Harrisonburg, VA	30.2
98	Hartford, CT	7.0
NA	Hattiesburg, MS**	NA
114	Holland-Grand Haven, MI	5.2
107	Honolulu, HI	6.3
210	Hot Springs, AR	(2.0)
30	Houma, LA	19.1
197	Houston, TX	(0.8)
66	Huntington-Ashland, WV-KY-OH	10.0
64	Huntsville, AL	10.3
29	Idaho Falls, ID	19.6
247	Indianapolis, IN	(4.8)
35	Iowa City, IA	16.9
NA	Ithaca, NY**	NA
NA	Jacksonville, FL**	NA
NA	Jacksonville, NC**	NA
152	Jackson, MI	2.6
16	Jackson, MS	25.7
283	Jackson, TN	(11.1)
294	Janesville, WI	(15.3)
92	Jefferson City, MO	7.3
285	Johnson City, TN	(11.5)
NA	Johnstown, PA**	NA
263	Jonesboro, AR	(7.1)
84	Joplin, MO	8.0
62	Kalamazoo-Portage, MI	10.6
NA	Kansas City, MO-KS**	NA
23	Kennewick-Richland-Pasco, WA	21.6
NA	Killeen-Temple-Fort Hood, TX**	NA
168	Kingsport, TN-VA	1.0
282	Kingston, NY	(10.6)
107	Knoxville, TN	6.3
167	Kokomo, IN	1.1
NA	La Crosse, WI-MN**	NA
70	Lafayette, IN	9.2
18	Lake Charles, LA	25.5
NA	Lake Havasu City-Kingman, AZ**	NA
48	Lakeland, FL	13.0
17	Lancaster, PA	25.6
279	Lansing-East Lansing, MI	(10.1)
76	Laredo, TX	8.6
69	Las Cruces, NM	9.3
13	Las Vegas-Paradise, NV	30.0

Note: All listings are for Metropolitan Statistical Areas (M.S.A.s) except for those ending with "M.D." Listings with "M.D." are Metropolitan Divisions which are smaller parts of eleven large M.S.A.s. See explanatory note at beginning of metropolitan area section on page 23.

Alpha Order - Metro Area (continued)

RANK	METROPOLITAN AREA	% CHANGE
2	Lawrence, KS	72.9
9	Lawton, OK	32.7
271	Lebanon, PA	(8.9)
60	Lewiston-Auburn, ME	10.7
303	Lewiston, ID-WA	(18.9)
NA	Lexington-Fayette, KY**	NA
292	Lima, OH	(14.7)
274	Lincoln, NE	(9.7)
123	Little Rock, AR	4.9
51	Logan, UT-ID	12.5
295	Longview, TX	(15.5)
262	Longview, WA	(7.0)
214	Los Angeles County, CA M.D.	(2.2)
214	Los Angeles (greater), CA	(2.2)
210	Louisville, KY-IN	(2.0)
238	Lubbock, TX	(3.8)
38	Lynchburg, VA	14.7
113	Macon, GA	5.4
146	Madera, CA	3.2
45	Madison, WI	14.1
155	Manchester-Nashua, NH	2.3
8	Mansfield, OH	32.9
302	McAllen-Edinburg-Mission, TX	(18.4)
301	Medford, OR	(18.3)
112	Memphis, TN-MS-AR	5.5
110	Merced, CA	5.7
174	Miami (greater), FL	0.7
203	Miami-Dade County, FL M.D.	(1.6)
60	Michigan City-La Porte, IN	10.7
235	Midland, TX	(3.7)
15	Milwaukee, WI	26.6
NA	Minneapolis-St. Paul, MN-WI**	NA
299	Missoula, MT	(17.1)
198	Mobile, AL	(0.9)
220	Modesto, CA	(2.4)
288	Monroe, LA	(13.4)
103	Monroe, MI	6.8
305	Montgomery, AL	(23.4)
254	Morgantown, WV	(5.4)
148	Morristown, TN	3.1
117	Mount Vernon-Anacortes, WA	5.1
32	Muncie, IN	17.8
221	Muskegon-Norton Shores, MI	(2.5)
200	Myrtle Beach, SC	(1.3)
232	Napa, CA	(3.5)
192	Naples-Marco Island, FL	(0.5)
239	Nashville-Davidson, TN	(4.1)
183	Nassau-Suffolk, NY M.D.	0.0
NA	New Orleans, LA**	NA
228	New York (greater), NY-NJ-PA	(3.3)
244	New York-W. Plains NY-NJ M.D.	(4.3)
226	Newark-Union, NJ-PA M.D.	(3.1)
210	Niles-Benton Harbor, MI	(2.0)
26	Oakland-Fremont, CA M.D.	20.3
97	Ocala, FL	7.1
49	Ocean City, NJ	12.8
127	Odessa, TX	4.5
206	Ogden-Clearfield, UT	(1.7)
227	Oklahoma City, OK	(3.2)
214	Olympia, WA	(2.2)

RANK	METROPOLITAN AREA	% CHANGE
228	Omaha-Council Bluffs, NE-IA	(3.3)
98	Orlando, FL	7.0
89	Oshkosh-Neenah, WI	7.6
104	Oxnard-Thousand Oaks, CA	6.7
89	Palm Bay-Melbourne, FL	7.6
NA	Palm Coast, FL**	NA
28	Panama City-Lynn Haven, FL	19.7
161	Pascagoula, MS	1.7
148	Pensacola, FL	3.1
114	Philadelphia (greater) PA-NJ-DE	5.2
119	Philadelphia, PA M.D.	5.0
194	Phoenix-Mesa-Scottsdale, AZ	(0.6)
80	Pine Bluff, AR	8.3
186	Pittsburgh, PA	(0.2)
131	Pittsfield, MA	4.1
110	Pocatello, ID	5.7
174	Port St. Lucie, FL	0.7
199	Portland-Vancouver, OR-WA	(1.1)
192	Portland, ME	(0.5)
176	Poughkeepsie, NY	0.6
24	Prescott, AZ	21.1
295	Provo-Orem, UT	(15.5)
273	Pueblo, CO	(9.6)
168	Punta Gorda, FL	1.0
31	Racine, WI	18.2
74	Raleigh-Cary, NC	8.7
297	Rapid City, SD	(15.7)
123	Reading, PA	4.9
306	Redding, CA	(24.9)
241	Reno-Sparks, NV	(4.2)
261	Richmond, VA	(6.9)
165	Riverside-San Bernardino, CA	1.5
191	Roanoke, VA	(0.4)
NA	Rochester, MN**	NA
19	Rochester, NY	25.4
95	Rocky Mount, NC	7.2
3	Rome, GA	52.2
56	Sacramento, CA	11.4
119	Saginaw, MI	5.0
287	Salem, OR	(12.3)
73	Salinas, CA	8.8
179	Salisbury, MD	0.1
136	Salt Lake City, UT	3.9
128	San Angelo, TX	4.4
230	San Antonio, TX	(3.4)
219	San Diego, CA	(2.3)
42	San Francisco (greater), CA	14.5
114	San Francisco-S. Mateo, CA M.D.	5.2
179	San Jose, CA	0.1
235	San Luis Obispo, CA	(3.7)
40	Sandusky, OH	14.6
214	Santa Ana-Anaheim, CA M.D.	(2.2)
117	Santa Barbara-Santa Maria, CA	5.1
257	Santa Cruz-Watsonville, CA	(6.1)
309	Santa Fe, NM	(37.0)
278	Santa Rosa-Petaluma, CA	(10.0)
101	Sarasota-Bradenton-Venice, FL	6.9
NA	Savannah, GA**	NA
259	Scranton--Wilkes-Barre, PA	(6.4)
152	Seattle (greater), WA	2.6

RANK	METROPOLITAN AREA	% CHANGE
144	Seattle-Bellevue, WA M.D.	3.3
133	Sebastian-Vero Beach, FL	4.0
78	Sheboygan, WI	8.5
284	Sherman-Denison, TX	(11.4)
65	Shreveport-Bossier City, LA	10.1
168	Sioux City, IA-NE-SD	1.0
286	Sioux Falls, SD	(12.2)
146	South Bend-Mishawaka, IN-MI	3.2
133	Spartanburg, SC	4.0
186	Spokane, WA	(0.2)
NA	Springfield, MA**	NA
6	Springfield, MO	36.5
201	Springfield, OH	(1.4)
251	State College, PA	(5.2)
186	Stockton, CA	(0.2)
NA	St. Cloud, MN**	NA
55	St. Joseph, MO-KS	11.6
133	St. Louis, MO-IL	4.0
10	Sumter, SC	32.4
257	Syracuse, NY	(6.1)
168	Tacoma, WA M.D.	1.0
184	Tallahassee, FL	(0.1)
254	Tampa-St Petersburg, FL	(5.4)
164	Texarkana, TX-Texarkana, AR	1.6
248	Toledo, OH	(4.9)
209	Topeka, KS	(1.9)
281	Trenton-Ewing, NJ	(10.5)
271	Tucson, AZ	(8.9)
210	Tulsa, OK	(2.0)
NA	Tuscaloosa, AL**	NA
260	Tyler, TX	(6.5)
82	Utica-Rome, NY	8.2
256	Valdosta, GA	(5.7)
NA	Vallejo-Fairfield, CA**	NA
63	Victoria, TX	10.4
277	Vineland, NJ	(9.9)
206	Virginia Beach-Norfolk, VA-NC	(1.7)
291	Visalia-Porterville, CA	(13.8)
176	Waco, TX	0.6
34	Warner Robins, GA	17.4
101	Warren-Farmington Hills, MI M.D.	6.9
NA	Washington (greater) DC-VA-MD**	NA
NA	Washington, DC-VA-MD-WV M.D.**	NA
160	Waterloo-Cedar Falls, IA	1.8
106	Wausau, WI	6.5
232	Wenatchee, WA	(3.5)
91	West Palm Beach, FL M.D.	7.4
246	Wheeling, WV-OH	(4.5)
307	Wichita Falls, TX	(32.4)
NA	Wichita, KS**	NA
290	Williamsport, PA	(13.7)
53	Wilmington, DE-MD-NJ M.D.	12.2
156	Wilmington, NC	2.2
67	Winchester, VA-WV	9.8
166	Winston-Salem, NC	1.4
NA	Worcester, MA**	NA
222	Yakima, WA	(2.6)
86	Yuba City, CA	7.9
248	Yuma, AZ	(4.9)

Source: CQ Press using data from Federal Bureau of Investigation "Crime in the United States 2006" (Uniform Crime Reports, September 24, 2007)

**Violent crimes are offenses of murder, forcible rape, robbery, and aggravated assault.*

***Not available.*

7. Percent Change in Violent Crime Rate: 2005 to 2006 (continued)

National Percent Change = 1.0% Increase*

RANK	METROPOLITAN AREA	% CHANGE
1	Bismarck, ND	75.2
2	Lawrence, KS	72.9
3	Rome, GA	52.2
4	Fond du Lac, WI	49.6
5	Columbus, IN	42.2
6	Springfield, MO	36.5
7	Ames, IA	36.3
8	Mansfield, OH	32.9
9	Lawton, OK	32.7
10	Sumter, SC	32.4
11	Decatur, AL	31.9
12	Harrisonburg, VA	30.2
13	Las Vegas-Paradise, NV	30.0
14	Bloomington, IN	28.2
15	Milwaukee, WI	26.6
16	Jackson, MS	25.7
17	Lancaster, PA	25.6
18	Lake Charles, LA	25.5
19	Rochester, NY	25.4
20	Anchorage, AK	23.7
21	Binghamton, NY	22.7
22	Greenville, NC	22.6
23	Kennewick-Richland-Pasco, WA	21.6
24	Prescott, AZ	21.1
25	Fort Walton Beach, FL	20.8
26	Oakland-Fremont, CA M.D.	20.3
27	Elkhart-Goshen, IN	20.1
28	Panama City-Lynn Haven, FL	19.7
29	Idaho Falls, ID	19.6
30	Houma, LA	19.1
31	Racine, WI	18.2
32	Athens-Clarke County, GA	17.8
32	Muncie, IN	17.8
34	Warner Robins, GA	17.4
35	Iowa City, IA	16.9
36	Columbus, GA-AL	16.3
37	Colorado Springs, CO	15.4
38	Gadsden, AL	14.7
38	Lynchburg, VA	14.7
40	Altoona, PA	14.6
40	Sandusky, OH	14.6
42	San Francisco (greater), CA	14.5
43	Green Bay, WI	14.3
44	Baton Rouge, LA	14.2
45	Goldsboro, NC	14.1
45	Madison, WI	14.1
47	Appleton, WI	13.3
48	Lakeland, FL	13.0
49	Ocean City, NJ	12.8
50	Erie, PA	12.7
51	Brunswick, GA	12.5
51	Logan, UT-ID	12.5
53	Wilmington, DE-MD-NJ M.D.	12.2
54	Bowling Green, KY	11.8
55	St. Joseph, MO-KS	11.6
56	Evansville, IN-KY	11.4
56	Sacramento, CA	11.4
58	Asheville, NC	11.2
59	Hagerstown-Martinsburg, MD-WV	10.9
60	Lewiston-Auburn, ME	10.7
60	Michigan City-La Porte, IN	10.7
62	Kalamazoo-Portage, MI	10.6
63	Victoria, TX	10.4
64	Huntsville, AL	10.3
65	Shreveport-Bossier City, LA	10.1
66	Huntington-Ashland, WV-KY-OH	10.0
67	Winchester, VA-WV	9.8
68	Cheyenne, WY	9.4
69	Las Cruces, NM	9.3
70	Cumberland, MD-WV	9.2
70	Lafayette, IN	9.2
72	Fayetteville, AR-MO	9.0
73	Salinas, CA	8.8
74	Blacksburg, VA	8.7
74	Raleigh-Cary, NC	8.7
76	Alexandria, LA	8.6
76	Laredo, TX	8.6
78	Atlantic City, NJ	8.5
78	Sheboygan, WI	8.5
80	Clarksville, TN-KY	8.3
80	Pine Bluff, AR	8.3
82	Flint, MI	8.2
82	Utica-Rome, NY	8.2
84	Eugene-Springfield, OR	8.0
84	Joplin, MO	8.0
86	Yuba City, CA	7.9
87	Dubuque, IA	7.7
87	Gainesville, FL	7.7
89	Oshkosh-Neenah, WI	7.6
89	Palm Bay-Melbourne, FL	7.6
91	West Palm Beach, FL M.D.	7.4
92	Albany, GA	7.3
92	Fort Collins-Loveland, CO	7.3
92	Jefferson City, MO	7.3
95	Atlanta, GA	7.2
95	Rocky Mount, NC	7.2
97	Ocala, FL	7.1
98	Edison, NJ M.D.	7.0
98	Hartford, CT	7.0
98	Orlando, FL	7.0
101	Sarasota-Bradenton-Venice, FL	6.9
101	Warren-Farmington Hills, MI M.D.	6.9
103	Monroe, MI	6.8
104	Oxnard-Thousand Oaks, CA	6.7
105	Dayton, OH	6.6
106	Wausau, WI	6.5
107	Honolulu, HI	6.3
107	Knoxville, TN	6.3
109	Coeur d'Alene, ID	6.2
110	Merced, CA	5.7
110	Pocatello, ID	5.7
112	Memphis, TN-MS-AR	5.5
113	Macon, GA	5.4
114	Holland-Grand Haven, MI	5.2
114	Philadelphia (greater) PA-NJ-DE	5.2
114	San Francisco-S. Mateo, CA M.D.	5.2
117	Mount Vernon-Anacortes, WA	5.1
117	Santa Barbara-Santa Maria, CA	5.1
119	Anderson, SC	5.0
119	Greensboro-High Point, NC	5.0
119	Philadelphia, PA M.D.	5.0
119	Saginaw, MI	5.0
123	Little Rock, AR	4.9
123	Reading, PA	4.9
125	Burlington, NC	4.8
126	Great Falls, MT	4.7
127	Odessa, TX	4.5
128	San Angelo, TX	4.4
129	Columbia, MO	4.3
129	Fayetteville, NC	4.3
131	Bakersfield, CA	4.1
131	Pittsfield, MA	4.1
133	Sebastian-Vero Beach, FL	4.0
133	Spartanburg, SC	4.0
133	St. Louis, MO-IL	4.0
136	Bethesda-Frederick, MD M.D.	3.9
136	Charleston, WV	3.9
136	Salt Lake City, UT	3.9
139	Chico, CA	3.8
140	Amarillo, TX	3.7
140	Eau Claire, WI	3.7
142	Battle Creek, MI	3.6
142	Gainesville, GA	3.6
144	Beaumont-Port Arthur, TX	3.3
144	Seattle-Bellevue, WA M.D.	3.3
146	Madera, CA	3.2
146	South Bend-Mishawaka, IN-MI	3.2
148	Morristown, TN	3.1
148	Pensacola, FL	3.1
150	Fort Worth-Arlington, TX M.D.	2.9
151	Detroit (greater), MI	2.8
152	Jackson, MI	2.6
152	Seattle (greater), WA	2.6
154	Grand Junction, CO	2.5
155	Manchester-Nashua, NH	2.3
156	Wilmington, NC	2.2
157	Detroit-Livonia-Dearborn, MI M.D.	2.1
158	Bend, OR	2.0
159	Casper, WY	1.9
160	Waterloo-Cedar Falls, IA	1.8
161	Albany-Schenectady-Troy, NY	1.7
161	Chattanooga, TN-GA	1.7
161	Pascagoula, MS	1.7
164	Texarkana, TX-Texarkana, AR	1.6
165	Riverside-San Bernardino, CA	1.5
166	Winston-Salem, NC	1.4
167	Kokomo, IN	1.1
168	Kingsport, TN-VA	1.0
168	Punta Gorda, FL	1.0
168	Sioux City, IA-NE-SD	1.0
168	Tacoma, WA M.D.	1.0

Note: All listings are for Metropolitan Statistical Areas (M.S.A.s) except for those ending with "M.D." Listings with "M.D." are Metropolitan Divisions which are smaller parts of eleven large M.S.A.s. See explanatory note at beginning of metropolitan area section on page 23.

RANK	METROPOLITAN AREA	% CHANGE
172	Bellingham, WA	0.9
173	Fort Lauderdale, FL M.D.	0.8
174	Miami (greater), FL	0.7
174	Port St. Lucie, FL	0.7
176	Poughkeepsie, NY	0.6
176	Waco, TX	0.6
178	Cape Coral-Fort Myers, FL	0.4
179	Camden, NJ M.D.	0.1
179	Columbia, SC	0.1
179	Salisbury, MD	0.1
179	San Jose, CA	0.1
183	Nassau-Suffolk, NY M.D.	0.0
184	Dover, DE	(0.1)
184	Tallahassee, FL	(0.1)
186	Pittsburgh, PA	(0.2)
186	Spokane, WA	(0.2)
186	Stockton, CA	(0.2)
189	Austin-Round Rock, TX	(0.3)
189	Dothan, AL	(0.3)
191	Roanoke, VA	(0.4)
192	Naples-Marco Island, FL	(0.5)
192	Portland, ME	(0.5)
194	Buffalo-Niagara Falls, NY	(0.6)
194	Cincinnati-Middletown, OH-KY-IN	(0.6)
194	Phoenix-Mesa-Scottsdale, AZ	(0.6)
197	Houston, TX	(0.8)
198	Mobile, AL	(0.9)
199	Portland-Vancouver, OR-WA	(1.1)
200	Myrtle Beach, SC	(1.3)
201	Springfield, OH	(1.4)
202	Bremerton-Silverdale, WA	(1.5)
203	Baltimore-Towson, MD	(1.6)
203	Charleston-North Charleston, SC	(1.6)
203	Miami-Dade County, FL M.D.	(1.6)
206	Ogden-Clearfield, UT	(1.7)
206	Virginia Beach-Norfolk, VA-NC	(1.7)
208	Charlottesville, VA	(1.8)
209	Topeka, KS	(1.9)
210	Hot Springs, AR	(2.0)
210	Louisville, KY-IN	(2.0)
210	Niles-Benton Harbor, MI	(2.0)
210	Tulsa, OK	(2.0)
214	Elizabethtown, KY	(2.2)
214	Los Angeles County, CA M.D.	(2.2)
214	Los Angeles (greater), CA	(2.2)
214	Olympia, WA	(2.2)
214	Santa Ana-Anaheim, CA M.D.	(2.2)
219	San Diego, CA	(2.3)
220	Modesto, CA	(2.4)
221	Muskegon-Norton Shores, MI	(2.5)
222	Augusta, GA-SC	(2.6)
222	Yakima, WA	(2.6)
224	Dallas (greater), TX	(3.0)
224	Hanford-Corcoran, CA	(3.0)
226	Newark-Union, NJ-PA M.D.	(3.1)
227	Oklahoma City, OK	(3.2)
228	New York (greater), NY-NJ-PA	(3.3)
228	Omaha-Council Bluffs, NE-IA	(3.3)
230	Columbus, OH	(3.4)
230	San Antonio, TX	(3.4)
232	Harrisburg-Carlisle, PA	(3.5)
232	Napa, CA	(3.5)
232	Wenatchee, WA	(3.5)
235	Denver-Aurora, CO	(3.7)
235	Midland, TX	(3.7)
235	San Luis Obispo, CA	(3.7)
238	Lubbock, TX	(3.8)
239	Daytona Beach, FL	(4.1)
239	Nashville-Davidson, TN	(4.1)
241	College Station-Bryan, TX	(4.2)
241	Grand Rapids-Wyoming, MI	(4.2)
241	Reno-Sparks, NV	(4.2)
244	Corpus Christi, TX	(4.3)
244	New York-W. Plains NY-NJ M.D.	(4.3)
246	Wheeling, WV-OH	(4.5)
247	Indianapolis, IN	(4.8)
248	Toledo, OH	(4.9)
248	Yuma, AZ	(4.9)
250	Greenville, SC	(5.0)
251	Fort Smith, AR-OK	(5.2)
251	State College, PA	(5.2)
253	Dallas-Plano-Irving, TX M.D.	(5.3)
254	Morgantown, WV	(5.4)
254	Tampa-St Petersburg, FL	(5.4)
256	Valdosta, GA	(5.7)
257	Santa Cruz-Watsonville, CA	(6.1)
257	Syracuse, NY	(6.1)
259	Scranton--Wilkes-Barre, PA	(6.4)
260	Tyler, TX	(6.5)
261	Richmond, VA	(6.9)
262	Longview, WA	(7.0)
263	Jonesboro, AR	(7.1)
264	Albuquerque, NM	(7.3)
264	Cedar Rapids, IA	(7.3)
264	Elmira, NY	(7.3)
267	El Paso, TX	(7.6)
268	Bay City, MI	(8.1)
269	Bangor, ME	(8.7)
270	Flagstaff, AZ	(8.8)
271	Lebanon, PA	(8.9)
271	Tucson, AZ	(8.9)
273	Pueblo, CO	(9.6)
274	Ann Arbor, MI	(9.7)
274	Lincoln, NE	(9.7)
276	Florence, SC	(9.8)
277	Vineland, NJ	(9.9)
278	Santa Rosa-Petaluma, CA	(10.0)
279	Brownsville-Harlingen, TX	(10.1)
279	Lansing-East Lansing, MI	(10.1)
281	Trenton-Ewing, NJ	(10.5)
282	Kingston, NY	(10.6)
283	Jackson, TN	(11.1)
284	Sherman-Denison, TX	(11.4)
285	Johnson City, TN	(11.5)
286	Sioux Falls, SD	(12.2)
287	Salem, OR	(12.3)
288	Monroe, LA	(13.4)
289	Fresno, CA	(13.5)
290	Williamsport, PA	(13.7)
291	Visalia-Porterville, CA	(13.8)
292	Lima, OH	(14.7)
293	Danville, VA	(15.2)
294	Janesville, WI	(15.3)
295	Longview, TX	(15.5)
295	Provo-Orem, UT	(15.5)
297	Rapid City, SD	(15.7)
298	Billings, MT	(16.0)
299	Missoula, MT	(17.1)
300	El Centro, CA	(17.6)
301	Medford, OR	(18.3)
302	McAllen-Edinburg-Mission, TX	(18.4)
303	Lewiston, ID-WA	(18.9)
304	Greeley, CO	(19.0)
305	Montgomery, AL	(23.4)
306	Redding, CA	(24.9)
307	Wichita Falls, TX	(32.4)
308	Carson City, NV	(33.7)
309	Santa Fe, NM	(37.0)
NA	Abilene, TX**	NA
NA	Barnstable Town, MA**	NA
NA	Birmingham-Hoover, AL**	NA
NA	Boise City-Nampa, ID**	NA
NA	Charlotte-Gastonia, NC-SC**	NA
NA	Chicago, IL**	NA
NA	Cleveland-Elyria-Mentor, OH**	NA
NA	Cleveland, TN**	NA
NA	Dalton, GA**	NA
NA	Des Moines-West Des Moines, IA**	NA
NA	Duluth, MN-WI**	NA
NA	Durham, NC**	NA
NA	Fairbanks, AK**	NA
NA	Fargo, ND-MN**	NA
NA	Farmington, NM**	NA
NA	Fort Wayne, IN**	NA
NA	Glens Falls, NY**	NA
NA	Grand Forks, ND-MN**	NA
NA	Hattiesburg, MS**	NA
NA	Ithaca, NY**	NA
NA	Jacksonville, FL**	NA
NA	Jacksonville, NC**	NA
NA	Johnstown, PA**	NA
NA	Kansas City, MO-KS**	NA
NA	Killeen-Temple-Fort Hood, TX**	NA
NA	La Crosse, WI-MN**	NA
NA	Lake Havasu City-Kingman, AZ**	NA
NA	Lexington-Fayette, KY**	NA
NA	Minneapolis-St. Paul, MN-WI**	NA
NA	New Orleans, LA**	NA
NA	Palm Coast, FL**	NA
NA	Rochester, MN**	NA
NA	Savannah, GA**	NA
NA	Springfield, MA**	NA
NA	St. Cloud, MN**	NA
NA	Tuscaloosa, AL**	NA
NA	Vallejo-Fairfield, CA**	NA
NA	Washington (greater) DC-VA-MD**	NA
NA	Washington, DC-VA-MD-WV M.D.**	NA
NA	Wichita, KS**	NA
NA	Worcester, MA**	NA

Source: CQ Press using data from Federal Bureau of Investigation "Crime in the United States 2006" (Uniform Crime Reports, September 24, 2007)

**Violent crimes are offenses of murder, forcible rape, robbery, and aggravated assault.*

***Not available.*

8. Percent Change in Violent Crime Rate: 2002 to 2006

National Percent Change = 4.2% Decrease*

RANK	METROPOLITAN AREA	% CHANGE
NA	Abilene, TX**	NA
NA	Albany-Schenectady-Troy, NY**	NA
134	Albany, GA	(9.1)
158	Albuquerque, NM	(14.9)
68	Alexandria, LA	4.9
54	Altoona, PA	9.0
79	Amarillo, TX	2.6
NA	Ames, IA**	NA
9	Anchorage, AK	44.8
NA	Anderson, SC**	NA
NA	Ann Arbor, MI**	NA
NA	Appleton, WI**	NA
166	Asheville, NC	(16.1)
85	Athens-Clarke County, GA	1.6
88	Atlanta, GA	0.4
NA	Atlantic City, NJ**	NA
31	Augusta, GA-SC	21.0
127	Austin-Round Rock, TX	(6.8)
47	Bakersfield, CA	11.6
169	Baltimore-Towson, MD	(16.8)
NA	Bangor, ME**	NA
NA	Barnstable Town, MA**	NA
43	Baton Rouge, LA	13.4
NA	Battle Creek, MI**	NA
NA	Bay City, MI**	NA
103	Beaumont-Port Arthur, TX	(1.9)
121	Bellingham, WA	(5.8)
NA	Bend, OR**	NA
NA	Bethesda-Frederick, MD M.D.**	NA
189	Billings, MT	(25.6)
83	Binghamton, NY	2.3
68	Birmingham-Hoover, AL	4.9
1	Bismarck, ND	117.0
NA	Blacksburg, VA**	NA
45	Bloomington, IN	12.4
138	Boise City-Nampa, ID	(10.0)
NA	Bowling Green, KY**	NA
63	Bremerton-Silverdale, WA	7.1
89	Brownsville-Harlingen, TX	0.1
NA	Brunswick, GA**	NA
61	Buffalo-Niagara Falls, NY	7.4
NA	Burlington, NC**	NA
NA	Camden, NJ M.D.**	NA
146	Cape Coral-Fort Myers, FL	(11.7)
NA	Carson City, NV**	NA
152	Casper, WY	(12.6)
167	Cedar Rapids, IA	(16.3)
99	Charleston-North Charleston, SC	(1.2)
87	Charleston, WV	1.1
NA	Charlotte-Gastonia, NC-SC**	NA
NA	Charlottesville, VA**	NA
164	Chattanooga, TN-GA	(15.5)
147	Cheyenne, WY	(12.1)
NA	Chicago, IL**	NA
42	Chico, CA	13.6
164	Cincinnati-Middletown, OH-KY-IN	(15.5)
28	Clarksville, TN-KY	23.0
NA	Cleveland-Elyria-Mentor, OH**	NA
NA	Cleveland, TN**	NA
NA	Coeur d'Alene, ID**	NA
NA	College Station-Bryan, TX**	NA
25	Colorado Springs, CO	24.2
26	Columbia, MO	23.7
171	Columbia, SC	(17.3)
14	Columbus, GA-AL	38.0
NA	Columbus, IN**	NA
167	Columbus, OH	(16.3)
122	Corpus Christi, TX	(6.2)
20	Cumberland, MD-WV	30.6
NA	Dallas (greater), TX**	NA
174	Dallas-Plano-Irving, TX M.D.	(18.0)
NA	Dalton, GA**	NA
192	Danville, VA	(27.8)
157	Daytona Beach, FL	(13.7)
NA	Dayton, OH**	NA
17	Decatur, AL	34.1
51	Denver-Aurora, CO	10.7
NA	Des Moines-West Des Moines, IA**	NA
61	Detroit (greater), MI	7.4
NA	Detroit-Livonia-Dearborn, MI M.D.**	NA
NA	Dothan, AL**	NA
117	Dover, DE	(4.7)
2	Dubuque, IA	95.7
NA	Duluth, MN-WI**	NA
NA	Durham, NC**	NA
112	Eau Claire, WI	(4.1)
NA	Edison, NJ M.D.**	NA
NA	El Centro, CA**	NA
197	El Paso, TX	(37.6)
NA	Elizabethtown, KY**	NA
186	Elkhart-Goshen, IN	(22.3)
NA	Elmira, NY**	NA
56	Erie, PA	8.5
55	Eugene-Springfield, OR	8.7
NA	Evansville, IN-KY**	NA
NA	Fairbanks, AK**	NA
NA	Fargo, ND-MN**	NA
NA	Farmington, NM**	NA
NA	Fayetteville, AR-MO**	NA
118	Fayetteville, NC	(4.9)
112	Flagstaff, AZ	(4.1)
6	Flint, MI	48.4
19	Florence, SC	32.1
NA	Fond du Lac, WI**	NA
115	Fort Collins-Loveland, CO	(4.4)
53	Fort Lauderdale, FL M.D.	9.3
104	Fort Smith, AR-OK	(2.2)
50	Fort Walton Beach, FL	10.9
NA	Fort Wayne, IN**	NA
91	Fort Worth-Arlington, TX M.D.	(0.1)
137	Fresno, CA	(9.7)
198	Gadsden, AL	(37.9)
40	Gainesville, FL	14.3
NA	Gainesville, GA**	NA
199	Glens Falls, NY	(38.8)
38	Goldsboro, NC	16.4
NA	Grand Forks, ND-MN**	NA
18	Grand Junction, CO	33.9
NA	Grand Rapids-Wyoming, MI**	NA
194	Great Falls, MT	(31.1)
86	Greeley, CO	1.2
41	Green Bay, WI	13.8
NA	Greensboro-High Point, NC**	NA
64	Greenville, NC	6.7
NA	Greenville, SC**	NA
NA	Hagerstown-Martinsburg, MD-WV**	NA
NA	Hanford-Corcoran, CA**	NA
NA	Harrisburg-Carlisle, PA**	NA
NA	Harrisonburg, VA**	NA
96	Hartford, CT	(0.6)
NA	Hattiesburg, MS**	NA
NA	Holland-Grand Haven, MI**	NA
73	Honolulu, HI	4.1
NA	Hot Springs, AR**	NA
65	Houma, LA	6.5
156	Houston, TX	(13.1)
NA	Huntington-Ashland, WV-KY-OH**	NA
6	Huntsville, AL	48.4
NA	Idaho Falls, ID**	NA
NA	Indianapolis, IN**	NA
196	Iowa City, IA	(33.9)
NA	Ithaca, NY**	NA
NA	Jacksonville, FL**	NA
NA	Jacksonville, NC**	NA
177	Jackson, MI	(19.1)
159	Jackson, MS	(15.0)
60	Jackson, TN	7.5
101	Janesville, WI	(1.5)
NA	Jefferson City, MO**	NA
NA	Johnson City, TN**	NA
NA	Johnstown, PA**	NA
3	Jonesboro, AR	63.6
185	Joplin, MO	(21.9)
NA	Kalamazoo-Portage, MI**	NA
NA	Kansas City, MO-KS**	NA
44	Kennewick-Richland-Pasco, WA	13.3
NA	Killeen-Temple-Fort Hood, TX**	NA
NA	Kingsport, TN-VA**	NA
NA	Kingston, NY**	NA
108	Knoxville, TN	(3.7)
170	Kokomo, IN	(17.0)
NA	La Crosse, WI-MN**	NA
81	Lafayette, IN	2.5
59	Lake Charles, LA	7.6
NA	Lake Havasu City-Kingman, AZ**	NA
102	Lakeland, FL	(1.6)
93	Lancaster, PA	(0.2)
126	Lansing-East Lansing, MI	(6.6)
128	Laredo, TX	(7.2)
NA	Las Cruces, NM**	NA
21	Las Vegas-Paradise, NV	29.2

Note: All listings are for Metropolitan Statistical Areas (M.S.A.s) except for those ending with "M.D." Listings with "M.D." are Metropolitan Divisions which are smaller parts of eleven large M.S.A.s. See explanatory note at beginning of metropolitan area section on page 23.

RANK	METROPOLITAN AREA	% CHANGE
10	Lawrence, KS	44.1
16	Lawton, OK	34.8
NA	Lebanon, PA**	NA
77	Lewiston-Auburn, ME	3.0
NA	Lewiston, ID-WA**	NA
NA	Lexington-Fayette, KY**	NA
NA	Lima, OH**	NA
147	Lincoln, NE	(12.1)
15	Little Rock, AR	37.8
NA	Logan, UT-ID**	NA
24	Longview, TX	26.4
NA	Longview, WA**	NA
193	Los Angeles County, CA M.D.	(28.1)
NA	Los Angeles (greater), CA**	NA
183	Louisville, KY-IN	(20.9)
171	Lubbock, TX	(17.3)
110	Lynchburg, VA	(3.8)
NA	Macon, GA**	NA
NA	Madera, CA**	NA
49	Madison, WI	11.3
NA	Manchester-Nashua, NH**	NA
NA	Mansfield, OH**	NA
186	McAllen-Edinburg-Mission, TX	(22.3)
124	Medford, OR	(6.4)
NA	Memphis, TN-MS-AR**	NA
79	Merced, CA	2.6
NA	Miami (greater), FL**	NA
154	Miami-Dade County, FL M.D.	(12.8)
NA	Michigan City-La Porte, IN**	NA
NA	Midland, TX**	NA
NA	Milwaukee, WI**	NA
NA	Minneapolis-St. Paul, MN-WI**	NA
NA	Missoula, MT**	NA
NA	Mobile, AL**	NA
48	Modesto, CA	11.4
NA	Monroe, LA**	NA
NA	Monroe, MI**	NA
184	Montgomery, AL	(21.8)
NA	Morgantown, WV**	NA
NA	Morristown, TN**	NA
NA	Mount Vernon-Anacortes, WA**	NA
33	Muncie, IN	17.3
NA	Muskegon-Norton Shores, MI**	NA
139	Myrtle Beach, SC	(10.2)
NA	Napa, CA**	NA
175	Naples-Marco Island, FL	(18.1)
130	Nashville-Davidson, TN	(7.5)
NA	Nassau-Suffolk, NY M.D.**	NA
180	New Orleans, LA	(19.7)
NA	New York (greater), NY-NJ-PA**	NA
188	New York-W. Plains NY-NJ M.D.	(23.1)
181	Newark-Union, NJ-PA M.D.	(19.8)
NA	Niles-Benton Harbor, MI**	NA
27	Oakland-Fremont, CA M.D.	23.1
111	Ocala, FL	(4.0)
NA	Ocean City, NJ**	NA
NA	Odessa, TX**	NA
NA	Ogden-Clearfield, UT**	NA
119	Oklahoma City, OK	(5.2)
153	Olympia, WA	(12.7)
177	Omaha-Council Bluffs, NE-IA	(19.1)
58	Orlando, FL	7.7
NA	Oshkosh-Neenah, WI**	NA
NA	Oxnard-Thousand Oaks, CA**	NA
176	Palm Bay-Melbourne, FL	(18.3)
NA	Palm Coast, FL**	NA
67	Panama City-Lynn Haven, FL	5.7
NA	Pascagoula, MS**	NA
68	Pensacola, FL	4.9
46	Philadelphia (greater) PA-NJ-DE	12.0
NA	Philadelphia, PA M.D.**	NA
143	Phoenix-Mesa-Scottsdale, AZ	(10.9)
133	Pine Bluff, AR	(8.6)
105	Pittsburgh, PA	(3.0)
NA	Pittsfield, MA**	NA
84	Pocatello, ID	1.8
151	Port St. Lucie, FL	(12.4)
155	Portland-Vancouver, OR-WA	(13.0)
NA	Portland, ME**	NA
NA	Poughkeepsie, NY**	NA
NA	Prescott, AZ**	NA
144	Provo-Orem, UT	(11.1)
161	Pueblo, CO	(15.2)
13	Punta Gorda, FL	39.4
52	Racine, WI	9.9
NA	Raleigh-Cary, NC**	NA
179	Rapid City, SD	(19.5)
125	Reading, PA	(6.5)
191	Redding, CA	(26.8)
131	Reno-Sparks, NV	(8.0)
160	Richmond, VA	(15.1)
162	Riverside-San Bernardino, CA	(15.3)
NA	Roanoke, VA**	NA
NA	Rochester, MN**	NA
12	Rochester, NY	43.0
29	Rocky Mount, NC	22.6
NA	Rome, GA**	NA
33	Sacramento, CA	17.3
NA	Saginaw, MI**	NA
37	Salem, OR	17.0
76	Salinas, CA	3.3
NA	Salisbury, MD**	NA
NA	Salt Lake City, UT**	NA
72	San Angelo, TX	4.2
190	San Antonio, TX	(26.6)
116	San Diego, CA	(4.6)
NA	San Francisco (greater), CA**	NA
39	San Francisco-S. Mateo, CA M.D.	14.9
145	San Jose, CA	(11.4)
71	San Luis Obispo, CA	4.5
NA	Sandusky, OH**	NA
95	Santa Ana-Anaheim, CA M.D.	(0.3)
NA	Santa Barbara-Santa Maria, CA**	NA
75	Santa Cruz-Watsonville, CA	3.7
120	Santa Fe, NM	(5.4)
6	Santa Rosa-Petaluma, CA	48.4
57	Sarasota-Bradenton-Venice, FL	8.1
NA	Savannah, GA**	NA
35	Scranton--Wilkes-Barre, PA	17.2
NA	Seattle (greater), WA**	NA
66	Seattle-Bellevue, WA M.D.	6.1
NA	Sebastian-Vero Beach, FL**	NA
89	Sheboygan, WI	0.1
135	Sherman-Denison, TX	(9.3)
4	Shreveport-Bossier City, LA	58.6
195	Sioux City, IA-NE-SD	(33.3)
147	Sioux Falls, SD	(12.1)
129	South Bend-Mishawaka, IN-MI	(7.3)
NA	Spartanburg, SC**	NA
107	Spokane, WA	(3.4)
NA	Springfield, MA**	NA
74	Springfield, MO	4.0
NA	Springfield, OH**	NA
150	State College, PA	(12.2)
106	Stockton, CA	(3.2)
NA	St. Cloud, MN**	NA
23	St. Joseph, MO-KS	27.1
NA	St. Louis, MO-IL**	NA
30	Sumter, SC	22.5
NA	Syracuse, NY**	NA
100	Tacoma, WA M.D.	(1.4)
96	Tallahassee, FL	(0.6)
182	Tampa-St Petersburg, FL	(20.2)
5	Texarkana, TX-Texarkana, AR	58.0
98	Toledo, OH	(0.8)
200	Topeka, KS	(39.3)
142	Trenton-Ewing, NJ	(10.8)
123	Tucson, AZ	(6.3)
81	Tulsa, OK	2.5
78	Tuscaloosa, AL	2.8
131	Tyler, TX	(8.0)
163	Utica-Rome, NY	(15.4)
NA	Valdosta, GA**	NA
NA	Vallejo-Fairfield, CA**	NA
201	Victoria, TX	(41.8)
35	Vineland, NJ	17.2
93	Virginia Beach-Norfolk, VA-NC	(0.2)
140	Visalia-Porterville, CA	(10.5)
114	Waco, TX	(4.3)
NA	Warner Robins, GA**	NA
NA	Warren-Farmington Hills, MI M.D.**	NA
NA	Washington (greater) DC-VA-MD**	NA
NA	Washington, DC-VA-MD-WV M.D.**	NA
136	Waterloo-Cedar Falls, IA	(9.5)
11	Wausau, WI	43.3
NA	Wenatchee, WA**	NA
108	West Palm Beach, FL M.D.	(3.7)
NA	Wheeling, WV-OH**	NA
202	Wichita Falls, TX	(51.8)
22	Wichita, KS	28.2
140	Williamsport, PA	(10.5)
NA	Wilmington, DE-MD-NJ M.D.**	NA
171	Wilmington, NC	(17.3)
NA	Winchester, VA-WV**	NA
NA	Winston-Salem, NC**	NA
NA	Worcester, MA**	NA
32	Yakima, WA	18.4
91	Yuba City, CA	(0.1)
NA	Yuma, AZ**	NA

Source: CQ Press using data from Federal Bureau of Investigation "Crime in the United States 2006" (Uniform Crime Reports, September 24, 2007)

**Violent crimes are offenses of murder, forcible rape, robbery, and aggravated assault.*

***Not available.*

8. Percent Change in Violent Crime Rate: 2002 to 2006 (continued)

National Percent Change = 4.2% Decrease*

RANK	METROPOLITAN AREA	% CHANGE
1	Bismarck, ND	117.0
2	Dubuque, IA	95.7
3	Jonesboro, AR	63.6
4	Shreveport-Bossier City, LA	58.6
5	Texarkana, TX-Texarkana, AR	58.0
6	Flint, MI	48.4
6	Huntsville, AL	48.4
6	Santa Rosa-Petaluma, CA	48.4
9	Anchorage, AK	44.8
10	Lawrence, KS	44.1
11	Wausau, WI	43.3
12	Rochester, NY	43.0
13	Punta Gorda, FL	39.4
14	Columbus, GA-AL	38.0
15	Little Rock, AR	37.8
16	Lawton, OK	34.8
17	Decatur, AL	34.1
18	Grand Junction, CO	33.9
19	Florence, SC	32.1
20	Cumberland, MD-WV	30.6
21	Las Vegas-Paradise, NV	29.2
22	Wichita, KS	28.2
23	St. Joseph, MO-KS	27.1
24	Longview, TX	26.4
25	Colorado Springs, CO	24.2
26	Columbia, MO	23.7
27	Oakland-Fremont, CA M.D.	23.1
28	Clarksville, TN-KY	23.0
29	Rocky Mount, NC	22.6
30	Sumter, SC	22.5
31	Augusta, GA-SC	21.0
32	Yakima, WA	18.4
33	Muncie, IN	17.3
33	Sacramento, CA	17.3
35	Scranton--Wilkes-Barre, PA	17.2
35	Vineland, NJ	17.2
37	Salem, OR	17.0
38	Goldsboro, NC	16.4
39	San Francisco-S. Mateo, CA M.D.	14.9
40	Gainesville, FL	14.3
41	Green Bay, WI	13.8
42	Chico, CA	13.6
43	Baton Rouge, LA	13.4
44	Kennewick-Richland-Pasco, WA	13.3
45	Bloomington, IN	12.4
46	Philadelphia (greater) PA-NJ-DE	12.0
47	Bakersfield, CA	11.6
48	Modesto, CA	11.4
49	Madison, WI	11.3
50	Fort Walton Beach, FL	10.9
51	Denver-Aurora, CO	10.7
52	Racine, WI	9.9
53	Fort Lauderdale, FL M.D.	9.3
54	Altoona, PA	9.0
55	Eugene-Springfield, OR	8.7
56	Erie, PA	8.5
57	Sarasota-Bradenton-Venice, FL	8.1
58	Orlando, FL	7.7
59	Lake Charles, LA	7.6
60	Jackson, TN	7.5
61	Buffalo-Niagara Falls, NY	7.4
61	Detroit (greater), MI	7.4
63	Bremerton-Silverdale, WA	7.1
64	Greenville, NC	6.7
65	Houma, LA	6.5
66	Seattle-Bellevue, WA M.D.	6.1
67	Panama City-Lynn Haven, FL	5.7
68	Alexandria, LA	4.9
68	Birmingham-Hoover, AL	4.9
68	Pensacola, FL	4.9
71	San Luis Obispo, CA	4.5
72	San Angelo, TX	4.2
73	Honolulu, HI	4.1
74	Springfield, MO	4.0
75	Santa Cruz-Watsonville, CA	3.7
76	Salinas, CA	3.3
77	Lewiston-Auburn, ME	3.0
78	Tuscaloosa, AL	2.8
79	Amarillo, TX	2.6
79	Merced, CA	2.6
81	Lafayette, IN	2.5
81	Tulsa, OK	2.5
83	Binghamton, NY	2.3
84	Pocatello, ID	1.8
85	Athens-Clarke County, GA	1.6
86	Greeley, CO	1.2
87	Charleston, WV	1.1
88	Atlanta, GA	0.4
89	Brownsville-Harlingen, TX	0.1
89	Sheboygan, WI	0.1
91	Fort Worth-Arlington, TX M.D.	(0.1)
91	Yuba City, CA	(0.1)
93	Lancaster, PA	(0.2)
93	Virginia Beach-Norfolk, VA-NC	(0.2)
95	Santa Ana-Anaheim, CA M.D.	(0.3)
96	Hartford, CT	(0.6)
96	Tallahassee, FL	(0.6)
98	Toledo, OH	(0.8)
99	Charleston-North Charleston, SC	(1.2)
100	Tacoma, WA M.D.	(1.4)
101	Janesville, WI	(1.5)
102	Lakeland, FL	(1.6)
103	Beaumont-Port Arthur, TX	(1.9)
104	Fort Smith, AR-OK	(2.2)
105	Pittsburgh, PA	(3.0)
106	Stockton, CA	(3.2)
107	Spokane, WA	(3.4)
108	Knoxville, TN	(3.7)
108	West Palm Beach, FL M.D.	(3.7)
110	Lynchburg, VA	(3.8)
111	Ocala, FL	(4.0)
112	Eau Claire, WI	(4.1)
112	Flagstaff, AZ	(4.1)
114	Waco, TX	(4.3)
115	Fort Collins-Loveland, CO	(4.4)
116	San Diego, CA	(4.6)
117	Dover, DE	(4.7)
118	Fayetteville, NC	(4.9)
119	Oklahoma City, OK	(5.2)
120	Santa Fe, NM	(5.4)
121	Bellingham, WA	(5.8)
122	Corpus Christi, TX	(6.2)
123	Tucson, AZ	(6.3)
124	Medford, OR	(6.4)
125	Reading, PA	(6.5)
126	Lansing-East Lansing, MI	(6.6)
127	Austin-Round Rock, TX	(6.8)
128	Laredo, TX	(7.2)
129	South Bend-Mishawaka, IN-MI	(7.3)
130	Nashville-Davidson, TN	(7.5)
131	Reno-Sparks, NV	(8.0)
131	Tyler, TX	(8.0)
133	Pine Bluff, AR	(8.6)
134	Albany, GA	(9.1)
135	Sherman-Denison, TX	(9.3)
136	Waterloo-Cedar Falls, IA	(9.5)
137	Fresno, CA	(9.7)
138	Boise City-Nampa, ID	(10.0)
139	Myrtle Beach, SC	(10.2)
140	Visalia-Porterville, CA	(10.5)
140	Williamsport, PA	(10.5)
142	Trenton-Ewing, NJ	(10.8)
143	Phoenix-Mesa-Scottsdale, AZ	(10.9)
144	Provo-Orem, UT	(11.1)
145	San Jose, CA	(11.4)
146	Cape Coral-Fort Myers, FL	(11.7)
147	Cheyenne, WY	(12.1)
147	Lincoln, NE	(12.1)
147	Sioux Falls, SD	(12.1)
150	State College, PA	(12.2)
151	Port St. Lucie, FL	(12.4)
152	Casper, WY	(12.6)
153	Olympia, WA	(12.7)
154	Miami-Dade County, FL M.D.	(12.8)
155	Portland-Vancouver, OR-WA	(13.0)
156	Houston, TX	(13.1)
157	Daytona Beach, FL	(13.7)
158	Albuquerque, NM	(14.9)
159	Jackson, MS	(15.0)
160	Richmond, VA	(15.1)
161	Pueblo, CO	(15.2)
162	Riverside-San Bernardino, CA	(15.3)
163	Utica-Rome, NY	(15.4)
164	Chattanooga, TN-GA	(15.5)
164	Cincinnati-Middletown, OH-KY-IN	(15.5)
166	Asheville, NC	(16.1)
167	Cedar Rapids, IA	(16.3)
167	Columbus, OH	(16.3)
169	Baltimore-Towson, MD	(16.8)
170	Kokomo, IN	(17.0)
171	Columbia, SC	(17.3)

Note: All listings are for Metropolitan Statistical Areas (M.S.A.s) except for those ending with "M.D." Listings with "M.D." are Metropolitan Divisions which are smaller parts of eleven large M.S.A.s. See explanatory note at beginning of metropolitan area section on page 23.

RANK	METROPOLITAN AREA	% CHANGE
171	Lubbock, TX	(17.3)
171	Wilmington, NC	(17.3)
174	Dallas-Plano-Irving, TX M.D.	(18.0)
175	Naples-Marco Island, FL	(18.1)
176	Palm Bay-Melbourne, FL	(18.3)
177	Jackson, MI	(19.1)
177	Omaha-Council Bluffs, NE-IA	(19.1)
179	Rapid City, SD	(19.5)
180	New Orleans, LA	(19.7)
181	Newark-Union, NJ-PA M.D.	(19.8)
182	Tampa-St Petersburg, FL	(20.2)
183	Louisville, KY-IN	(20.9)
184	Montgomery, AL	(21.8)
185	Joplin, MO	(21.9)
186	Elkhart-Goshen, IN	(22.3)
186	McAllen-Edinburg-Mission, TX	(22.3)
188	New York-W. Plains NY-NJ M.D.	(23.1)
189	Billings, MT	(25.6)
190	San Antonio, TX	(26.6)
191	Redding, CA	(26.8)
192	Danville, VA	(27.8)
193	Los Angeles County, CA M.D.	(28.1)
194	Great Falls, MT	(31.1)
195	Sioux City, IA-NE-SD	(33.3)
196	Iowa City, IA	(33.9)
197	El Paso, TX	(37.6)
198	Gadsden, AL	(37.9)
199	Glens Falls, NY	(38.8)
200	Topeka, KS	(39.3)
201	Victoria, TX	(41.8)
202	Wichita Falls, TX	(51.8)
NA	Abilene, TX**	NA
NA	Albany-Schenectady-Troy, NY**	NA
NA	Ames, IA**	NA
NA	Anderson, SC**	NA
NA	Ann Arbor, MI**	NA
NA	Appleton, WI**	NA
NA	Atlantic City, NJ**	NA
NA	Bangor, ME**	NA
NA	Barnstable Town, MA**	NA
NA	Battle Creek, MI**	NA
NA	Bay City, MI**	NA
NA	Bend, OR**	NA
NA	Bethesda-Frederick, MD M.D.**	NA
NA	Blacksburg, VA**	NA
NA	Bowling Green, KY**	NA
NA	Brunswick, GA**	NA
NA	Burlington, NC**	NA
NA	Camden, NJ M.D.**	NA
NA	Carson City, NV**	NA
NA	Charlotte-Gastonia, NC-SC**	NA
NA	Charlottesville, VA**	NA
NA	Chicago, IL**	NA
NA	Cleveland-Elyria-Mentor, OH**	NA
NA	Cleveland, TN**	NA
NA	Coeur d'Alene, ID**	NA
NA	College Station-Bryan, TX**	NA
NA	Columbus, IN**	NA
NA	Dallas (greater), TX**	NA
NA	Dalton, GA**	NA
NA	Dayton, OH**	NA
NA	Des Moines-West Des Moines, IA**	NA
NA	Detroit-Livonia-Dearborn, MI M.D.**	NA
NA	Dothan, AL**	NA
NA	Duluth, MN-WI**	NA
NA	Durham, NC**	NA
NA	Edison, NJ M.D.**	NA
NA	El Centro, CA**	NA
NA	Elizabethtown, KY**	NA
NA	Elmira, NY**	NA
NA	Evansville, IN-KY**	NA
NA	Fairbanks, AK**	NA
NA	Fargo, ND-MN**	NA
NA	Farmington, NM**	NA
NA	Fayetteville, AR-MO**	NA
NA	Fond du Lac, WI**	NA
NA	Fort Wayne, IN**	NA
NA	Gainesville, GA**	NA
NA	Grand Forks, ND-MN**	NA
NA	Grand Rapids-Wyoming, MI**	NA
NA	Greensboro-High Point, NC**	NA
NA	Greenville, SC**	NA
NA	Hagerstown-Martinsburg, MD-WV**	NA
NA	Hanford-Corcoran, CA**	NA
NA	Harrisburg-Carlisle, PA**	NA
NA	Harrisonburg, VA**	NA
NA	Hattiesburg, MS**	NA
NA	Holland-Grand Haven, MI**	NA
NA	Hot Springs, AR**	NA
NA	Huntington-Ashland, WV-KY-OH**	NA
NA	Idaho Falls, ID**	NA
NA	Indianapolis, IN**	NA
NA	Ithaca, NY**	NA
NA	Jacksonville, FL**	NA
NA	Jacksonville, NC**	NA
NA	Jefferson City, MO**	NA
NA	Johnson City, TN**	NA
NA	Johnstown, PA**	NA
NA	Kalamazoo-Portage, MI**	NA
NA	Kansas City, MO-KS**	NA
NA	Killeen-Temple-Fort Hood, TX**	NA
NA	Kingsport, TN-VA**	NA
NA	Kingston, NY**	NA
NA	La Crosse, WI-MN**	NA
NA	Lake Havasu City-Kingman, AZ**	NA
NA	Las Cruces, NM**	NA
NA	Lebanon, PA**	NA
NA	Lewiston, ID-WA**	NA
NA	Lexington-Fayette, KY**	NA
NA	Lima, OH**	NA
NA	Logan, UT-ID**	NA
NA	Longview, WA**	NA
NA	Los Angeles (greater), CA**	NA
NA	Macon, GA**	NA
NA	Madera, CA**	NA
NA	Manchester-Nashua, NH**	NA
NA	Mansfield, OH**	NA
NA	Memphis, TN-MS-AR**	NA
NA	Miami (greater), FL**	NA
NA	Michigan City-La Porte, IN**	NA
NA	Midland, TX**	NA
NA	Milwaukee, WI**	NA
NA	Minneapolis-St. Paul, MN-WI**	NA
NA	Missoula, MT**	NA
NA	Mobile, AL**	NA
NA	Monroe, LA**	NA
NA	Monroe, MI**	NA
NA	Morgantown, WV**	NA
NA	Morristown, TN**	NA
NA	Mount Vernon-Anacortes, WA**	NA
NA	Muskegon-Norton Shores, MI**	NA
NA	Napa, CA**	NA
NA	Nassau-Suffolk, NY M.D.**	NA
NA	New York (greater), NY-NJ-PA**	NA
NA	Niles-Benton Harbor, MI**	NA
NA	Ocean City, NJ**	NA
NA	Odessa, TX**	NA
NA	Ogden-Clearfield, UT**	NA
NA	Oshkosh-Neenah, WI**	NA
NA	Oxnard-Thousand Oaks, CA**	NA
NA	Palm Coast, FL**	NA
NA	Pascagoula, MS**	NA
NA	Philadelphia, PA M.D.**	NA
NA	Pittsfield, MA**	NA
NA	Portland, ME**	NA
NA	Poughkeepsie, NY**	NA
NA	Prescott, AZ**	NA
NA	Raleigh-Cary, NC**	NA
NA	Roanoke, VA**	NA
NA	Rochester, MN**	NA
NA	Rome, GA**	NA
NA	Saginaw, MI**	NA
NA	Salisbury, MD**	NA
NA	Salt Lake City, UT**	NA
NA	San Francisco (greater), CA**	NA
NA	Sandusky, OH**	NA
NA	Santa Barbara-Santa Maria, CA**	NA
NA	Savannah, GA**	NA
NA	Seattle (greater), WA**	NA
NA	Sebastian-Vero Beach, FL**	NA
NA	Spartanburg, SC**	NA
NA	Springfield, MA**	NA
NA	Springfield, OH**	NA
NA	St. Cloud, MN**	NA
NA	St. Louis, MO-IL**	NA
NA	Syracuse, NY**	NA
NA	Valdosta, GA**	NA
NA	Vallejo-Fairfield, CA**	NA
NA	Warner Robins, GA**	NA
NA	Warren-Farmington Hills, MI M.D.**	NA
NA	Washington (greater) DC-VA-MD**	NA
NA	Washington, DC-VA-MD-WV M.D.**	NA
NA	Wenatchee, WA**	NA
NA	Wheeling, WV-OH**	NA
NA	Wilmington, DE-MD-NJ M.D.**	NA
NA	Winchester, VA-WV**	NA
NA	Winston-Salem, NC**	NA
NA	Worcester, MA**	NA
NA	Yuma, AZ**	NA

Source: CQ Press using data from Federal Bureau of Investigation "Crime in the United States 2006" (Uniform Crime Reports, September 24, 2007)

**Violent crimes are offenses of murder, forcible rape, robbery, and aggravated assault.*

***Not available.*

9. Murders in 2006

National Total = 17,034 Murders*

RANK	METROPOLITAN AREA	MURDERS
224	Abilene, TX	6
128	Albany-Schenectady-Troy, NY	18
171	Albany, GA	11
60	Albuquerque, NM	72
180	Alexandria, LA	10
321	Altoona, PA	1
210	Amarillo, TX	7
340	Ames, IA	0
135	Anchorage, AK	17
128	Anderson, SC	18
189	Ann Arbor, MI	9
295	Appleton, WI	2
171	Asheville, NC	11
189	Athens-Clarke County, GA	9
12	Atlanta, GA	377
94	Atlantic City, NJ	30
91	Augusta, GA-SC	32
98	Austin-Round Rock, TX	29
64	Bakersfield, CA	65
15	Baltimore-Towson, MD	355
276	Bangor, ME	3
255	Barnstable Town, MA	4
48	Baton Rouge, LA	100
171	Battle Creek, MI	11
295	Bay City, MI	2
128	Beaumont-Port Arthur, TX	18
321	Bellingham, WA	1
295	Bend, OR	2
103	Bethesda-Frederick, MD M.D.	27
276	Billings, MT	3
224	Binghamton, NY	6
30	Birmingham-Hoover, AL	138
295	Bismarck, ND	2
198	Blacksburg, VA	8
255	Bloomington, IN	4
145	Boise City-Nampa, ID	15
239	Bowling Green, KY	5
276	Bremerton-Silverdale, WA	3
163	Brownsville-Harlingen, TX	12
239	Brunswick, GA	5
53	Buffalo-Niagara Falls, NY	86
224	Burlington, NC	6
67	Camden, NJ M.D.	58
73	Cape Coral-Fort Myers, FL	48
295	Carson City, NV	2
295	Casper, WY	2
210	Cedar Rapids, IA	7
58	Charleston-North Charleston, SC	76
110	Charleston, WV	23
34	Charlotte-Gastonia, NC-SC	128
255	Charlottesville, VA	4
104	Chattanooga, TN-GA	26
295	Cheyenne, WY	2
NA	Chicago, IL**	NA
171	Chico, CA	11
36	Cincinnati-Middletown, OH-KY-IN	122
163	Clarksville, TN-KY	12
49	Cleveland-Elyria-Mentor, OH	99
321	Cleveland, TN	1
321	Coeur d'Alene, ID	1
198	College Station-Bryan, TX	8
128	Colorado Springs, CO	18
276	Columbia, MO	3
65	Columbia, SC	59
122	Columbus, GA-AL	20
276	Columbus, IN	3
40	Columbus, OH	113
106	Corpus Christi, TX	25
321	Cumberland, MD-WV	1
17	Dallas (greater), TX	336
21	Dallas-Plano-Irving, TX M.D.	255
295	Dalton, GA	2
239	Danville, VA	5
118	Daytona Beach, FL	21
79	Dayton, OH	45
210	Decatur, AL	7
45	Denver-Aurora, CO	106
198	Des Moines-West Des Moines, IA	8
7	Detroit (greater), MI	507
8	Detroit-Livonia-Dearborn, MI M.D.	459
198	Dothan, AL	8
198	Dover, DE	8
340	Dubuque, IA	0
255	Duluth, MN-WI	4
113	Durham, NC	22
340	Eau Claire, WI	0
77	Edison, NJ M.D.	47
276	El Centro, CA	3
113	El Paso, TX	22
340	Elizabethtown, KY	0
145	Elkhart-Goshen, IN	15
295	Elmira, NY	2
255	Erie, PA	4
198	Eugene-Springfield, OR	8
180	Evansville, IN-KY	10
321	Fairbanks, AK	1
295	Fargo, ND-MN	2
255	Farmington, NM	4
189	Fayetteville, AR-MO	9
94	Fayetteville, NC	30
276	Flagstaff, AZ	3
62	Flint, MI	68
163	Florence, SC	12
321	Fond du Lac, WI	1
239	Fort Collins-Loveland, CO	5
52	Fort Lauderdale, FL M.D.	87
135	Fort Smith, AR-OK	17
239	Fort Walton Beach, FL	5
124	Fort Wayne, IN	19
56	Fort Worth-Arlington, TX M.D.	81
59	Fresno, CA	74
224	Gadsden, AL	6
152	Gainesville, FL	14
276	Gainesville, GA	3
295	Glens Falls, NY	2
210	Goldsboro, NC	7
295	Grand Forks, ND-MN	2
224	Grand Junction, CO	6
104	Grand Rapids-Wyoming, MI	26
295	Great Falls, MT	2
255	Greeley, CO	4
295	Green Bay, WI	2
73	Greensboro-High Point, NC	48
163	Greenville, NC	12
81	Greenville, SC	40
224	Hagerstown-Martinsburg, MD-WV	6
255	Hanford-Corcoran, CA	4
141	Harrisburg-Carlisle, PA	16
239	Harrisonburg, VA	5
84	Hartford, CT	38
161	Hattiesburg, MS	13
340	Holland-Grand Haven, MI	0
135	Honolulu, HI	17
239	Hot Springs, AR	5
189	Houma, LA	9
6	Houston, TX	519
276	Huntington-Ashland, WV-KY-OH	3
122	Huntsville, AL	20
295	Idaho Falls, ID	2
29	Indianapolis, IN	156
340	Iowa City, IA	0
321	Ithaca, NY	1
32	Jacksonville, FL	134
198	Jacksonville, NC	8
255	Jackson, MI	4
67	Jackson, MS	58
152	Jackson, TN	14
255	Janesville, WI	4
255	Jefferson City, MO	4
171	Johnson City, TN	11
224	Johnstown, PA	6
224	Jonesboro, AR	6
224	Joplin, MO	6
198	Kalamazoo-Portage, MI	8
27	Kansas City, MO-KS	174
224	Kennewick-Richland-Pasco, WA	6
171	Killeen-Temple-Fort Hood, TX	11
163	Kingsport, TN-VA	12
239	Kingston, NY	5
89	Knoxville, TN	34
239	Kokomo, IN	5
340	La Crosse, WI-MN	0
295	Lafayette, IN	2
163	Lake Charles, LA	12
135	Lake Havasu City-Kingman, AZ	17
118	Lakeland, FL	21
113	Lancaster, PA	22
171	Lansing-East Lansing, MI	11
108	Laredo, TX	24
239	Las Cruces, NM	5
25	Las Vegas-Paradise, NV	181

Note: All listings are for Metropolitan Statistical Areas (M.S.A.s) except for those ending with "M.D." Listings with "M.D." are Metropolitan Divisions which are smaller parts of eleven large M.S.A.s. See explanatory note at beginning of metropolitan area section on page 23.

RANK	METROPOLITAN AREA	MURDERS
239	Lawrence, KS	5
198	Lawton, OK	8
255	Lebanon, PA	4
321	Lewiston-Auburn, ME	1
321	Lewiston, ID-WA	1
180	Lexington-Fayette, KY	10
180	Lima, OH	10
239	Lincoln, NE	5
50	Little Rock, AR	93
295	Logan, UT-ID	2
141	Longview, TX	16
210	Longview, WA	7
2	Los Angeles County, CA M.D.	1,012
1	Los Angeles (greater), CA	1,092
69	Louisville, KY-IN	57
152	Lubbock, TX	14
210	Lynchburg, VA	7
128	Macon, GA	18
295	Madera, CA	2
255	Madison, WI	4
239	Manchester-Nashua, NH	5
276	Mansfield, OH	3
91	McAllen-Edinburg-Mission, TX	32
276	Medford, OR	3
26	Memphis, TN-MS-AR	175
113	Merced, CA	22
10	Miami (greater), FL	419
22	Miami-Dade County, FL M.D.	240
276	Michigan City-La Porte, IN	3
239	Midland, TX	5
41	Milwaukee, WI	112
43	Minneapolis-St. Paul, MN-WI	110
340	Missoula, MT	0
77	Mobile, AL	47
98	Modesto, CA	29
152	Monroe, LA	14
321	Monroe, MI	1
90	Montgomery, AL	33
255	Morgantown, WV	4
295	Morristown, TN	2
295	Mount Vernon-Anacortes, WA	2
255	Muncie, IN	4
255	Muskegon-Norton Shores, MI	4
106	Myrtle Beach, SC	25
295	Napa, CA	2
210	Naples-Marco Island, FL	7
47	Nashville-Davidson, TN	104
65	Nassau-Suffolk, NY M.D.	59
18	New Orleans, LA	272
3	New York (greater), NY-NJ-PA	978
4	New York-W. Plains NY-NJ M.D.	684
23	Newark-Union, NJ-PA M.D.	188
198	Niles-Benton Harbor, MI	8
20	Oakland-Fremont, CA M.D.	265
145	Ocala, FL	15
321	Ocean City, NJ	1
276	Odessa, TX	3
189	Ogden-Clearfield, UT	9
54	Oklahoma City, OK	82
255	Olympia, WA	4
83	Omaha-Council Bluffs, NE-IA	39
28	Orlando, FL	160
255	Oshkosh-Neenah, WI	4
98	Oxnard-Thousand Oaks, CA	29
113	Palm Bay-Melbourne, FL	22
255	Palm Coast, FL	4
239	Panama City-Lynn Haven, FL	5
189	Pascagoula, MS	9
152	Pensacola, FL	14
5	Philadelphia (greater) PA-NJ-DE	554
9	Philadelphia, PA M.D.	458
16	Phoenix-Mesa-Scottsdale, AZ	349
145	Pine Bluff, AR	15
45	Pittsburgh, PA	106
295	Pittsfield, MA	2
321	Pocatello, ID	1
124	Port St. Lucie, FL	19
73	Portland-Vancouver, OR-WA	48
239	Portland, ME	5
141	Poughkeepsie, NY	16
180	Prescott, AZ	10
276	Provo-Orem, UT	3
224	Pueblo, CO	6
295	Punta Gorda, FL	2
198	Racine, WI	8
86	Raleigh-Cary, NC	37
340	Rapid City, SD	0
163	Reading, PA	12
198	Redding, CA	8
94	Reno-Sparks, NV	30
38	Richmond, VA	117
19	Riverside-San Bernardino, CA	271
152	Roanoke, VA	14
295	Rochester, MN	2
71	Rochester, NY	56
128	Rocky Mount, NC	18
255	Rome, GA	4
41	Sacramento, CA	112
102	Saginaw, MI	28
152	Salem, OR	14
145	Salinas, CA	15
180	Salisbury, MD	10
110	Salt Lake City, UT	23
276	San Angelo, TX	3
31	San Antonio, TX	137
35	San Diego, CA	126
13	San Francisco (greater), CA	375
43	San Francisco-S. Mateo, CA M.D.	110
81	San Jose, CA	40
224	San Luis Obispo, CA	6
340	Sandusky, OH	0
57	Santa Ana-Anaheim, CA M.D.	80
161	Santa Barbara-Santa Maria, CA	13
141	Santa Cruz-Watsonville, CA	16
189	Santa Fe, NM	9
171	Santa Rosa-Petaluma, CA	11
94	Sarasota-Bradenton-Venice, FL	30
91	Savannah, GA	32
124	Scranton--Wilkes-Barre, PA	19
38	Seattle (greater), WA	117
54	Seattle-Bellevue, WA M.D.	82
210	Sebastian-Vero Beach, FL	7
321	Sheboygan, WI	1
321	Sherman-Denison, TX	1
80	Shreveport-Bossier City, LA	41
321	Sioux City, IA-NE-SD	1
210	Sioux Falls, SD	7
135	South Bend-Mishawaka, IN-MI	17
124	Spartanburg, SC	19
135	Spokane, WA	17
118	Springfield, MA	21
210	Springfield, MO	7
224	Springfield, OH	6
276	State College, PA	3
69	Stockton, CA	57
321	St. Cloud, MN	1
295	St. Joseph, MO-KS	2
24	St. Louis, MO-IL	185
180	Sumter, SC	10
128	Syracuse, NY	18
88	Tacoma, WA M.D.	35
171	Tallahassee, FL	11
33	Tampa-St Petersburg, FL	133
152	Texarkana, TX-Texarkana, AR	14
86	Toledo, OH	37
163	Topeka, KS	12
118	Trenton-Ewing, NJ	21
60	Tucson, AZ	72
63	Tulsa, OK	67
110	Tuscaloosa, AL	23
224	Tyler, TX	6
210	Utica-Rome, NY	7
276	Valdosta, GA	3
152	Vallejo-Fairfield, CA	14
210	Victoria, TX	7
145	Vineland, NJ	15
37	Virginia Beach-Norfolk, VA-NC	121
72	Visalia-Porterville, CA	49
180	Waco, TX	10
276	Warner Robins, GA	3
73	Warren-Farmington Hills, MI M.D.	48
11	Washington (greater) DC-VA-MD	390
14	Washington, DC-VA-MD-WV M.D.	363
276	Waterloo-Cedar Falls, IA	3
255	Wausau, WI	4
295	Wenatchee, WA	2
51	West Palm Beach, FL M.D.	92
321	Wheeling, WV-OH	1
189	Wichita Falls, TX	9
98	Wichita, KS	29
321	Williamsport, PA	1
84	Wilmington, DE-MD-NJ M.D.	38
145	Wilmington, NC	15
224	Winchester, VA-WV	6
108	Winston-Salem, NC	24
189	Worcester, MA	9
180	Yakima, WA	10
210	Yuba City, CA	7
210	Yuma, AZ	7

Source: Federal Bureau of Investigation
"Crime in the United States 2006" (Uniform Crime Reports, September 24, 2007)
**Includes nonnegligent manslaughter.*
***Not available.*

9. Murders in 2006 (continued)

National Total = 17,034 Murders*

RANK	METROPOLITAN AREA	MURDERS
1	Los Angeles (greater), CA	1,092
2	Los Angeles County, CA M.D.	1,012
3	New York (greater), NY-NJ-PA	978
4	New York-W. Plains NY-NJ M.D.	684
5	Philadelphia (greater) PA-NJ-DE	554
6	Houston, TX	519
7	Detroit (greater), MI	507
8	Detroit-Livonia-Dearborn, MI M.D.	459
9	Philadelphia, PA M.D.	458
10	Miami (greater), FL	419
11	Washington (greater) DC-VA-MD	390
12	Atlanta, GA	377
13	San Francisco (greater), CA	375
14	Washington, DC-VA-MD-WV M.D.	363
15	Baltimore-Towson, MD	355
16	Phoenix-Mesa-Scottsdale, AZ	349
17	Dallas (greater), TX	336
18	New Orleans, LA	272
19	Riverside-San Bernardino, CA	271
20	Oakland-Fremont, CA M.D.	265
21	Dallas-Plano-Irving, TX M.D.	255
22	Miami-Dade County, FL M.D.	240
23	Newark-Union, NJ-PA M.D.	188
24	St. Louis, MO-IL	185
25	Las Vegas-Paradise, NV	181
26	Memphis, TN-MS-AR	175
27	Kansas City, MO-KS	174
28	Orlando, FL	160
29	Indianapolis, IN	156
30	Birmingham-Hoover, AL	138
31	San Antonio, TX	137
32	Jacksonville, FL	134
33	Tampa-St Petersburg, FL	133
34	Charlotte-Gastonia, NC-SC	128
35	San Diego, CA	126
36	Cincinnati-Middletown, OH-KY-IN	122
37	Virginia Beach-Norfolk, VA-NC	121
38	Richmond, VA	117
38	Seattle (greater), WA	117
40	Columbus, OH	113
41	Milwaukee, WI	112
41	Sacramento, CA	112
43	Minneapolis-St. Paul, MN-WI	110
43	San Francisco-S. Mateo, CA M.D.	110
45	Denver-Aurora, CO	106
45	Pittsburgh, PA	106
47	Nashville-Davidson, TN	104
48	Baton Rouge, LA	100
49	Cleveland-Elyria-Mentor, OH	99
50	Little Rock, AR	93
51	West Palm Beach, FL M.D.	92
52	Fort Lauderdale, FL M.D.	87
53	Buffalo-Niagara Falls, NY	86
54	Oklahoma City, OK	82
54	Seattle-Bellevue, WA M.D.	82
56	Fort Worth-Arlington, TX M.D.	81
57	Santa Ana-Anaheim, CA M.D.	80
58	Charleston-North Charleston, SC	76
59	Fresno, CA	74
60	Albuquerque, NM	72
60	Tucson, AZ	72
62	Flint, MI	68
63	Tulsa, OK	67
64	Bakersfield, CA	65
65	Columbia, SC	59
65	Nassau-Suffolk, NY M.D.	59
67	Camden, NJ M.D.	58
67	Jackson, MS	58
69	Louisville, KY-IN	57
69	Stockton, CA	57
71	Rochester, NY	56
72	Visalia-Porterville, CA	49
73	Cape Coral-Fort Myers, FL	48
73	Greensboro-High Point, NC	48
73	Portland-Vancouver, OR-WA	48
73	Warren-Farmington Hills, MI M.D.	48
77	Edison, NJ M.D.	47
77	Mobile, AL	47
79	Dayton, OH	45
80	Shreveport-Bossier City, LA	41
81	Greenville, SC	40
81	San Jose, CA	40
83	Omaha-Council Bluffs, NE-IA	39
84	Hartford, CT	38
84	Wilmington, DE-MD-NJ M.D.	38
86	Raleigh-Cary, NC	37
86	Toledo, OH	37
88	Tacoma, WA M.D.	35
89	Knoxville, TN	34
90	Montgomery, AL	33
91	Augusta, GA-SC	32
91	McAllen-Edinburg-Mission, TX	32
91	Savannah, GA	32
94	Atlantic City, NJ	30
94	Fayetteville, NC	30
94	Reno-Sparks, NV	30
94	Sarasota-Bradenton-Venice, FL	30
98	Austin-Round Rock, TX	29
98	Modesto, CA	29
98	Oxnard-Thousand Oaks, CA	29
98	Wichita, KS	29
102	Saginaw, MI	28
103	Bethesda-Frederick, MD M.D.	27
104	Chattanooga, TN-GA	26
104	Grand Rapids-Wyoming, MI	26
106	Corpus Christi, TX	25
106	Myrtle Beach, SC	25
108	Laredo, TX	24
108	Winston-Salem, NC	24
110	Charleston, WV	23
110	Salt Lake City, UT	23
110	Tuscaloosa, AL	23
113	Durham, NC	22
113	El Paso, TX	22
113	Lancaster, PA	22
113	Merced, CA	22
113	Palm Bay-Melbourne, FL	22
118	Daytona Beach, FL	21
118	Lakeland, FL	21
118	Springfield, MA	21
118	Trenton-Ewing, NJ	21
122	Columbus, GA-AL	20
122	Huntsville, AL	20
124	Fort Wayne, IN	19
124	Port St. Lucie, FL	19
124	Scranton--Wilkes-Barre, PA	19
124	Spartanburg, SC	19
128	Albany-Schenectady-Troy, NY	18
128	Anderson, SC	18
128	Beaumont-Port Arthur, TX	18
128	Colorado Springs, CO	18
128	Macon, GA	18
128	Rocky Mount, NC	18
128	Syracuse, NY	18
135	Anchorage, AK	17
135	Fort Smith, AR-OK	17
135	Honolulu, HI	17
135	Lake Havasu City-Kingman, AZ	17
135	South Bend-Mishawaka, IN-MI	17
135	Spokane, WA	17
141	Harrisburg-Carlisle, PA	16
141	Longview, TX	16
141	Poughkeepsie, NY	16
141	Santa Cruz-Watsonville, CA	16
145	Boise City-Nampa, ID	15
145	Elkhart-Goshen, IN	15
145	Ocala, FL	15
145	Pine Bluff, AR	15
145	Salinas, CA	15
145	Vineland, NJ	15
145	Wilmington, NC	15
152	Gainesville, FL	14
152	Jackson, TN	14
152	Lubbock, TX	14
152	Monroe, LA	14
152	Pensacola, FL	14
152	Roanoke, VA	14
152	Salem, OR	14
152	Texarkana, TX-Texarkana, AR	14
152	Vallejo-Fairfield, CA	14
161	Hattiesburg, MS	13
161	Santa Barbara-Santa Maria, CA	13
163	Brownsville-Harlingen, TX	12
163	Clarksville, TN-KY	12
163	Florence, SC	12
163	Greenville, NC	12
163	Kingsport, TN-VA	12
163	Lake Charles, LA	12
163	Reading, PA	12
163	Topeka, KS	12
171	Albany, GA	11

Note: All listings are for Metropolitan Statistical Areas (M.S.A.s) except for those ending with "M.D." Listings with "M.D." are Metropolitan Divisions which are smaller parts of eleven large M.S.A.s. See explanatory note at beginning of metropolitan area section on page 23.

Rank Order - Metro Area (continued)

RANK	METROPOLITAN AREA	MURDERS
171	Asheville, NC	11
171	Battle Creek, MI	11
171	Chico, CA	11
171	Johnson City, TN	11
171	Killeen-Temple-Fort Hood, TX	11
171	Lansing-East Lansing, MI	11
171	Santa Rosa-Petaluma, CA	11
171	Tallahassee, FL	11
180	Alexandria, LA	10
180	Evansville, IN-KY	10
180	Lexington-Fayette, KY	10
180	Lima, OH	10
180	Prescott, AZ	10
180	Salisbury, MD	10
180	Sumter, SC	10
180	Waco, TX	10
180	Yakima, WA	10
189	Ann Arbor, MI	9
189	Athens-Clarke County, GA	9
189	Fayetteville, AR-MO	9
189	Houma, LA	9
189	Ogden-Clearfield, UT	9
189	Pascagoula, MS	9
189	Santa Fe, NM	9
189	Wichita Falls, TX	9
189	Worcester, MA	9
198	Blacksburg, VA	8
198	College Station-Bryan, TX	8
198	Des Moines-West Des Moines, IA	8
198	Dothan, AL	8
198	Dover, DE	8
198	Eugene-Springfield, OR	8
198	Jacksonville, NC	8
198	Kalamazoo-Portage, MI	8
198	Lawton, OK	8
198	Niles-Benton Harbor, MI	8
198	Racine, WI	8
198	Redding, CA	8
210	Amarillo, TX	7
210	Cedar Rapids, IA	7
210	Decatur, AL	7
210	Goldsboro, NC	7
210	Longview, WA	7
210	Lynchburg, VA	7
210	Naples-Marco Island, FL	7
210	Sebastian-Vero Beach, FL	7
210	Sioux Falls, SD	7
210	Springfield, MO	7
210	Utica-Rome, NY	7
210	Victoria, TX	7
210	Yuba City, CA	7
210	Yuma, AZ	7
224	Abilene, TX	6
224	Binghamton, NY	6
224	Burlington, NC	6
224	Gadsden, AL	6
224	Grand Junction, CO	6
224	Hagerstown-Martinsburg, MD-WV	6
224	Johnstown, PA	6
224	Jonesboro, AR	6
224	Joplin, MO	6
224	Kennewick-Richland-Pasco, WA	6
224	Pueblo, CO	6
224	San Luis Obispo, CA	6
224	Springfield, OH	6
224	Tyler, TX	6
224	Winchester, VA-WV	6
239	Bowling Green, KY	5
239	Brunswick, GA	5
239	Danville, VA	5
239	Fort Collins-Loveland, CO	5
239	Fort Walton Beach, FL	5
239	Harrisonburg, VA	5
239	Hot Springs, AR	5
239	Kingston, NY	5
239	Kokomo, IN	5
239	Las Cruces, NM	5
239	Lawrence, KS	5
239	Lincoln, NE	5
239	Manchester-Nashua, NH	5
239	Midland, TX	5
239	Panama City-Lynn Haven, FL	5
239	Portland, ME	5
255	Barnstable Town, MA	4
255	Bloomington, IN	4
255	Charlottesville, VA	4
255	Duluth, MN-WI	4
255	Erie, PA	4
255	Farmington, NM	4
255	Greeley, CO	4
255	Hanford-Corcoran, CA	4
255	Jackson, MI	4
255	Janesville, WI	4
255	Jefferson City, MO	4
255	Lebanon, PA	4
255	Madison, WI	4
255	Morgantown, WV	4
255	Muncie, IN	4
255	Muskegon-Norton Shores, MI	4
255	Olympia, WA	4
255	Oshkosh-Neenah, WI	4
255	Palm Coast, FL	4
255	Rome, GA	4
255	Wausau, WI	4
276	Bangor, ME	3
276	Billings, MT	3
276	Bremerton-Silverdale, WA	3
276	Columbia, MO	3
276	Columbus, IN	3
276	El Centro, CA	3
276	Flagstaff, AZ	3
276	Gainesville, GA	3
276	Huntington-Ashland, WV-KY-OH	3
276	Mansfield, OH	3
276	Medford, OR	3
276	Michigan City-La Porte, IN	3
276	Odessa, TX	3
276	Provo-Orem, UT	3
276	San Angelo, TX	3
276	State College, PA	3
276	Valdosta, GA	3
276	Warner Robins, GA	3
276	Waterloo-Cedar Falls, IA	3
295	Appleton, WI	2
295	Bay City, MI	2
295	Bend, OR	2
295	Bismarck, ND	2
295	Carson City, NV	2
295	Casper, WY	2
295	Cheyenne, WY	2
295	Dalton, GA	2
295	Elmira, NY	2
295	Fargo, ND-MN	2
295	Glens Falls, NY	2
295	Grand Forks, ND-MN	2
295	Great Falls, MT	2
295	Green Bay, WI	2
295	Idaho Falls, ID	2
295	Lafayette, IN	2
295	Logan, UT-ID	2
295	Madera, CA	2
295	Morristown, TN	2
295	Mount Vernon-Anacortes, WA	2
295	Napa, CA	2
295	Pittsfield, MA	2
295	Punta Gorda, FL	2
295	Rochester, MN	2
295	St. Joseph, MO-KS	2
295	Wenatchee, WA	2
321	Altoona, PA	1
321	Bellingham, WA	1
321	Cleveland, TN	1
321	Coeur d'Alene, ID	1
321	Cumberland, MD-WV	1
321	Fairbanks, AK	1
321	Fond du Lac, WI	1
321	Ithaca, NY	1
321	Lewiston-Auburn, ME	1
321	Lewiston, ID-WA	1
321	Monroe, MI	1
321	Ocean City, NJ	1
321	Pocatello, ID	1
321	Sheboygan, WI	1
321	Sherman-Denison, TX	1
321	Sioux City, IA-NE-SD	1
321	St. Cloud, MN	1
321	Wheeling, WV-OH	1
321	Williamsport, PA	1
340	Ames, IA	0
340	Dubuque, IA	0
340	Eau Claire, WI	0
340	Elizabethtown, KY	0
340	Holland-Grand Haven, MI	0
340	Iowa City, IA	0
340	La Crosse, WI-MN	0
340	Missoula, MT	0
340	Rapid City, SD	0
340	Sandusky, OH	0
NA	Chicago, IL**	NA

Source: Federal Bureau of Investigation
"Crime in the United States 2006" (Uniform Crime Reports, September 24, 2007)
**Includes nonnegligent manslaughter.*
***Not available.*

10. Murder Rate in 2006

National Rate = 5.7 Murders per 100,000 Population*

RANK	METROPOLITAN AREA	RATE
190	Abilene, TX	3.7
268	Albany-Schenectady-Troy, NY	2.1
89	Albany, GA	6.5
42	Albuquerque, NM	8.9
76	Alexandria, LA	7.1
327	Altoona, PA	0.8
221	Amarillo, TX	2.9
339	Ames, IA	0.0
104	Anchorage, AK	5.8
28	Anderson, SC	10.1
237	Ann Arbor, MI	2.6
323	Appleton, WI	0.9
230	Asheville, NC	2.7
135	Athens-Clarke County, GA	5.0
69	Atlanta, GA	7.4
20	Atlantic City, NJ	11.1
95	Augusta, GA-SC	6.0
277	Austin-Round Rock, TX	1.9
52	Bakersfield, CA	8.5
9	Baltimore-Towson, MD	13.3
273	Bangor, ME	2.0
283	Barnstable Town, MA	1.8
4	Baton Rouge, LA	14.4
60	Battle Creek, MI	7.9
283	Bay City, MI	1.8
157	Beaumont-Port Arthur, TX	4.6
337	Bellingham, WA	0.5
305	Bend, OR	1.4
248	Bethesda-Frederick, MD M.D.	2.3
273	Billings, MT	2.0
244	Binghamton, NY	2.4
11	Birmingham-Hoover, AL	12.5
273	Bismarck, ND	2.0
125	Blacksburg, VA	5.2
263	Bloomington, IN	2.2
230	Boise City-Nampa, ID	2.7
161	Bowling Green, KY	4.5
309	Bremerton-Silverdale, WA	1.2
209	Brownsville-Harlingen, TX	3.1
136	Brunswick, GA	4.9
65	Buffalo-Niagara Falls, NY	7.5
172	Burlington, NC	4.2
149	Camden, NJ M.D.	4.7
46	Cape Coral-Fort Myers, FL	8.7
197	Carson City, NV	3.5
223	Casper, WY	2.8
223	Cedar Rapids, IA	2.8
10	Charleston-North Charleston, SC	12.6
65	Charleston, WV	7.5
58	Charlotte-Gastonia, NC-SC	8.3
268	Charlottesville, VA	2.1
125	Chattanooga, TN-GA	5.2
248	Cheyenne, WY	2.3
NA	Chicago, IL**	NA
130	Chico, CA	5.1
100	Cincinnati-Middletown, OH-KY-IN	5.9
136	Clarksville, TN-KY	4.9
149	Cleveland-Elyria-Mentor, OH	4.7
323	Cleveland, TN	0.9
327	Coeur d'Alene, ID	0.8
176	College Station-Bryan, TX	4.1
215	Colorado Springs, CO	3.0
277	Columbia, MO	1.9
55	Columbia, SC	8.4
85	Columbus, GA-AL	6.8
176	Columbus, IN	4.1
87	Columbus, OH	6.6
100	Corpus Christi, TX	5.9
317	Cumberland, MD-WV	1.0
112	Dallas (greater), TX	5.6
92	Dallas-Plano-Irving, TX M.D.	6.4
299	Dalton, GA	1.5
157	Danville, VA	4.6
172	Daytona Beach, FL	4.2
120	Dayton, OH	5.3
149	Decatur, AL	4.7
164	Denver-Aurora, CO	4.4
299	Des Moines-West Des Moines, IA	1.5
18	Detroit (greater), MI	11.3
1	Detroit-Livonia-Dearborn, MI M.D.	23.0
104	Dothan, AL	5.8
114	Dover, DE	5.5
339	Dubuque, IA	0.0
305	Duluth, MN-WI	1.4
149	Durham, NC	4.7
339	Eau Claire, WI	0.0
273	Edison, NJ M.D.	2.0
277	El Centro, CA	1.9
215	El Paso, TX	3.0
339	Elizabethtown, KY	0.0
62	Elkhart-Goshen, IN	7.6
263	Elmira, NY	2.2
305	Erie, PA	1.4
248	Eugene-Springfield, OR	2.3
223	Evansville, IN-KY	2.8
NA	Fairbanks, AK**	NA
312	Fargo, ND-MN	1.1
209	Farmington, NM	3.1
263	Fayetteville, AR-MO	2.2
52	Fayetteville, NC	8.5
248	Flagstaff, AZ	2.3
3	Flint, MI	15.4
95	Florence, SC	6.0
317	Fond du Lac, WI	1.0
283	Fort Collins-Loveland, CO	1.8
144	Fort Lauderdale, FL M.D.	4.8
100	Fort Smith, AR-OK	5.9
230	Fort Walton Beach, FL	2.7
149	Fort Wayne, IN	4.7
176	Fort Worth-Arlington, TX M.D.	4.1
55	Fresno, CA	8.4
104	Gadsden, AL	5.8
107	Gainesville, FL	5.7
283	Gainesville, GA	1.8
297	Glens Falls, NY	1.6
95	Goldsboro, NC	6.0
268	Grand Forks, ND-MN	2.1
161	Grand Junction, CO	4.5
200	Grand Rapids-Wyoming, MI	3.4
239	Great Falls, MT	2.5
291	Greeley, CO	1.7
331	Green Bay, WI	0.7
80	Greensboro-High Point, NC	7.0
74	Greenville, NC	7.2
86	Greenville, SC	6.7
244	Hagerstown-Martinsburg, MD-WV	2.4
223	Hanford-Corcoran, CA	2.8
209	Harrisburg-Carlisle, PA	3.1
164	Harrisonburg, VA	4.4
186	Hartford, CT	3.8
30	Hattiesburg, MS	9.9
339	Holland-Grand Haven, MI	0.0
277	Honolulu, HI	1.9
120	Hot Springs, AR	5.3
144	Houma, LA	4.8
35	Houston, TX	9.6
317	Huntington-Ashland, WV-KY-OH	1.0
116	Huntsville, AL	5.4
291	Idaho Falls, ID	1.7
37	Indianapolis, IN	9.4
339	Iowa City, IA	0.0
317	Ithaca, NY	1.0
23	Jacksonville, FL	10.6
130	Jacksonville, NC	5.1
239	Jackson, MI	2.5
20	Jackson, MS	11.1
11	Jackson, TN	12.5
239	Janesville, WI	2.5
223	Jefferson City, MO	2.8
107	Johnson City, TN	5.7
182	Johnstown, PA	4.0
120	Jonesboro, AR	5.3
193	Joplin, MO	3.6
239	Kalamazoo-Portage, MI	2.5
42	Kansas City, MO-KS	8.9
230	Kennewick-Richland-Pasco, WA	2.7
215	Killeen-Temple-Fort Hood, TX	3.0
184	Kingsport, TN-VA	3.9
230	Kingston, NY	2.7
130	Knoxville, TN	5.1
136	Kokomo, IN	4.9
339	La Crosse, WI-MN	0.0
312	Lafayette, IN	1.1
89	Lake Charles, LA	6.5
46	Lake Havasu City-Kingman, AZ	8.7
186	Lakeland, FL	3.8
161	Lancaster, PA	4.5
244	Lansing-East Lansing, MI	2.4
25	Laredo, TX	10.4
237	Las Cruces, NM	2.6
26	Las Vegas-Paradise, NV	10.2

Note: All listings are for Metropolitan Statistical Areas (M.S.A.s) except for those ending with "M.D." Listings with "M.D." are Metropolitan Divisions which are smaller parts of eleven large M.S.A.s. See explanatory note at beginning of metropolitan area section on page 23.

RANK	METROPOLITAN AREA	RATE
144	Lawrence, KS	4.8
76	Lawton, OK	7.1
206	Lebanon, PA	3.2
323	Lewiston-Auburn, ME	0.9
291	Lewiston, ID-WA	1.7
248	Lexington-Fayette, KY	2.3
37	Lima, OH	9.4
283	Lincoln, NE	1.8
5	Little Rock, AR	14.3
283	Logan, UT-ID	1.8
61	Longview, TX	7.7
76	Longview, WA	7.1
28	Los Angeles County, CA M.D.	10.1
55	Los Angeles (greater), CA	8.4
149	Louisville, KY-IN	4.7
120	Lubbock, TX	5.3
221	Lynchburg, VA	2.9
62	Macon, GA	7.6
305	Madera, CA	1.4
331	Madison, WI	0.7
309	Manchester-Nashua, NH	1.2
248	Mansfield, OH	2.3
157	McAllen-Edinburg-Mission, TX	4.6
299	Medford, OR	1.5
7	Memphis, TN-MS-AR	13.7
41	Merced, CA	9.0
62	Miami (greater), FL	7.6
30	Miami-Dade County, FL M.D.	9.9
230	Michigan City-La Porte, IN	2.7
182	Midland, TX	4.0
69	Milwaukee, WI	7.4
197	Minneapolis-St. Paul, MN-WI	3.5
339	Missoula, MT	0.0
16	Mobile, AL	11.6
107	Modesto, CA	5.7
50	Monroe, LA	8.6
331	Monroe, MI	0.7
40	Montgomery, AL	9.2
197	Morgantown, WV	3.5
299	Morristown, TN	1.5
291	Mount Vernon-Anacortes, WA	1.7
200	Muncie, IN	3.4
248	Muskegon-Norton Shores, MI	2.3
22	Myrtle Beach, SC	10.8
299	Napa, CA	1.5
263	Naples-Marco Island, FL	2.2
74	Nashville-Davidson, TN	7.2
268	Nassau-Suffolk, NY M.D.	2.1
2	New Orleans, LA	21.7
125	New York (greater), NY-NJ-PA	5.2
100	New York-W. Plains NY-NJ M.D.	5.9
46	Newark-Union, NJ-PA M.D.	8.7
136	Niles-Benton Harbor, MI	4.9
23	Oakland-Fremont, CA M.D.	10.6
136	Ocala, FL	4.9
317	Ocean City, NJ	1.0
248	Odessa, TX	2.3
283	Ogden-Clearfield, UT	1.8
80	Oklahoma City, OK	7.0
291	Olympia, WA	1.7
144	Omaha-Council Bluffs, NE-IA	4.8
59	Orlando, FL	8.1
239	Oshkosh-Neenah, WI	2.5
193	Oxnard-Thousand Oaks, CA	3.6
176	Palm Bay-Melbourne, FL	4.1
130	Palm Coast, FL	5.1
215	Panama City-Lynn Haven, FL	3.0
107	Pascagoula, MS	5.7
209	Pensacola, FL	3.1
36	Philadelphia (greater) PA-NJ-DE	9.5
14	Philadelphia, PA M.D.	11.8
46	Phoenix-Mesa-Scottsdale, AZ	8.7
6	Pine Bluff, AR	14.1
164	Pittsburgh, PA	4.4
299	Pittsfield, MA	1.5
312	Pocatello, ID	1.1
136	Port St. Lucie, FL	4.9
248	Portland-Vancouver, OR-WA	2.3
317	Portland, ME	1.0
244	Poughkeepsie, NY	2.4
144	Prescott, AZ	4.8
336	Provo-Orem, UT	0.6
184	Pueblo, CO	3.9
309	Punta Gorda, FL	1.2
176	Racine, WI	4.1
186	Raleigh-Cary, NC	3.8
339	Rapid City, SD	0.0
215	Reading, PA	3.0
164	Redding, CA	4.4
69	Reno-Sparks, NV	7.4
30	Richmond, VA	9.9
84	Riverside-San Bernardino, CA	6.9
149	Roanoke, VA	4.7
312	Rochester, MN	1.1
116	Rochester, NY	5.4
13	Rocky Mount, NC	12.1
176	Rome, GA	4.1
116	Sacramento, CA	5.4
8	Saginaw, MI	13.5
190	Salem, OR	3.7
193	Salinas, CA	3.6
50	Salisbury, MD	8.6
263	Salt Lake City, UT	2.2
223	San Angelo, TX	2.8
80	San Antonio, TX	7.0
170	San Diego, CA	4.3
42	San Francisco (greater), CA	8.9
89	San Francisco-S. Mateo, CA M.D.	6.5
248	San Jose, CA	2.3
248	San Luis Obispo, CA	2.3
339	Sandusky, OH	0.0
230	Santa Ana-Anaheim, CA M.D.	2.7
206	Santa Barbara-Santa Maria, CA	3.2
92	Santa Cruz-Watsonville, CA	6.4
94	Santa Fe, NM	6.3
248	Santa Rosa-Petaluma, CA	2.3
164	Sarasota-Bradenton-Venice, FL	4.4
30	Savannah, GA	9.9
200	Scranton--Wilkes-Barre, PA	3.4
193	Seattle (greater), WA	3.6
204	Seattle-Bellevue, WA M.D.	3.3
116	Sebastian-Vero Beach, FL	5.4
323	Sheboygan, WI	0.9
327	Sherman-Denison, TX	0.8
18	Shreveport-Bossier City, LA	11.3
331	Sioux City, IA-NE-SD	0.7
204	Sioux Falls, SD	3.3
120	South Bend-Mishawaka, IN-MI	5.3
80	Spartanburg, SC	7.0
186	Spokane, WA	3.8
215	Springfield, MA	3.0
291	Springfield, MO	1.7
172	Springfield, OH	4.2
268	State College, PA	2.1
52	Stockton, CA	8.5
337	St. Cloud, MN	0.5
297	St. Joseph, MO-KS	1.6
87	St. Louis, MO-IL	6.6
39	Sumter, SC	9.3
223	Syracuse, NY	2.8
157	Tacoma, WA M.D.	4.6
206	Tallahassee, FL	3.2
136	Tampa-St Petersburg, FL	4.9
26	Texarkana, TX-Texarkana, AR	10.2
112	Toledo, OH	5.6
125	Topeka, KS	5.2
107	Trenton-Ewing, NJ	5.7
65	Tucson, AZ	7.5
65	Tulsa, OK	7.5
16	Tuscaloosa, AL	11.6
209	Tyler, TX	3.1
248	Utica-Rome, NY	2.3
248	Valdosta, GA	2.3
200	Vallejo-Fairfield, CA	3.4
95	Victoria, TX	6.0
34	Vineland, NJ	9.8
73	Virginia Beach-Norfolk, VA-NC	7.3
14	Visalia-Porterville, CA	11.8
170	Waco, TX	4.3
248	Warner Robins, GA	2.3
277	Warren-Farmington Hills, MI M.D.	1.9
69	Washington (greater) DC-VA-MD	7.4
45	Washington, DC-VA-MD-WV M.D.	8.8
283	Waterloo-Cedar Falls, IA	1.8
209	Wausau, WI	3.1
277	Wenatchee, WA	1.9
76	West Palm Beach, FL M.D.	7.1
331	Wheeling, WV-OH	0.7
95	Wichita Falls, TX	6.0
136	Wichita, KS	4.9
327	Williamsport, PA	0.8
114	Wilmington, DE-MD-NJ M.D.	5.5
149	Wilmington, NC	4.7
130	Winchester, VA-WV	5.1
125	Winston-Salem, NC	5.2
312	Worcester, MA	1.1
172	Yakima, WA	4.2
164	Yuba City, CA	4.4
190	Yuma, AZ	3.7

Source: Federal Bureau of Investigation
"Crime in the United States 2006" (Uniform Crime Reports, September 24, 2007)
**Includes nonnegligent manslaughter.*
***Not available.*

10. Murder Rate in 2006 (continued)

National Rate = 5.7 Murders per 100,000 Population*

RANK	METROPOLITAN AREA	RATE
1	Detroit-Livonia-Dearborn, MI M.D.	23.0
2	New Orleans, LA	21.7
3	Flint, MI	15.4
4	Baton Rouge, LA	14.4
5	Little Rock, AR	14.3
6	Pine Bluff, AR	14.1
7	Memphis, TN-MS-AR	13.7
8	Saginaw, MI	13.5
9	Baltimore-Towson, MD	13.3
10	Charleston-North Charleston, SC	12.6
11	Birmingham-Hoover, AL	12.5
11	Jackson, TN	12.5
13	Rocky Mount, NC	12.1
14	Philadelphia, PA M.D.	11.8
14	Visalia-Porterville, CA	11.8
16	Mobile, AL	11.6
16	Tuscaloosa, AL	11.6
18	Detroit (greater), MI	11.3
18	Shreveport-Bossier City, LA	11.3
20	Atlantic City, NJ	11.1
20	Jackson, MS	11.1
22	Myrtle Beach, SC	10.8
23	Jacksonville, FL	10.6
23	Oakland-Fremont, CA M.D.	10.6
25	Laredo, TX	10.4
26	Las Vegas-Paradise, NV	10.2
26	Texarkana, TX-Texarkana, AR	10.2
28	Anderson, SC	10.1
28	Los Angeles County, CA M.D.	10.1
30	Hattiesburg, MS	9.9
30	Miami-Dade County, FL M.D.	9.9
30	Richmond, VA	9.9
30	Savannah, GA	9.9
34	Vineland, NJ	9.8
35	Houston, TX	9.6
36	Philadelphia (greater) PA-NJ-DE	9.5
37	Indianapolis, IN	9.4
37	Lima, OH	9.4
39	Sumter, SC	9.3
40	Montgomery, AL	9.2
41	Merced, CA	9.0
42	Albuquerque, NM	8.9
42	Kansas City, MO-KS	8.9
42	San Francisco (greater), CA	8.9
45	Washington, DC-VA-MD-WV M.D.	8.8
46	Cape Coral-Fort Myers, FL	8.7
46	Lake Havasu City-Kingman, AZ	8.7
46	Newark-Union, NJ-PA M.D.	8.7
46	Phoenix-Mesa-Scottsdale, AZ	8.7
50	Monroe, LA	8.6
50	Salisbury, MD	8.6
52	Bakersfield, CA	8.5
52	Fayetteville, NC	8.5
52	Stockton, CA	8.5
55	Columbia, SC	8.4
55	Fresno, CA	8.4
55	Los Angeles (greater), CA	8.4
58	Charlotte-Gastonia, NC-SC	8.3
59	Orlando, FL	8.1
60	Battle Creek, MI	7.9
61	Longview, TX	7.7
62	Elkhart-Goshen, IN	7.6
62	Macon, GA	7.6
62	Miami (greater), FL	7.6
65	Buffalo-Niagara Falls, NY	7.5
65	Charleston, WV	7.5
65	Tucson, AZ	7.5
65	Tulsa, OK	7.5
69	Atlanta, GA	7.4
69	Milwaukee, WI	7.4
69	Reno-Sparks, NV	7.4
69	Washington (greater) DC-VA-MD	7.4
73	Virginia Beach-Norfolk, VA-NC	7.3
74	Greenville, NC	7.2
74	Nashville-Davidson, TN	7.2
76	Alexandria, LA	7.1
76	Lawton, OK	7.1
76	Longview, WA	7.1
76	West Palm Beach, FL M.D.	7.1
80	Greensboro-High Point, NC	7.0
80	Oklahoma City, OK	7.0
80	San Antonio, TX	7.0
80	Spartanburg, SC	7.0
84	Riverside-San Bernardino, CA	6.9
85	Columbus, GA-AL	6.8
86	Greenville, SC	6.7
87	Columbus, OH	6.6
87	St. Louis, MO-IL	6.6
89	Albany, GA	6.5
89	Lake Charles, LA	6.5
89	San Francisco-S. Mateo, CA M.D.	6.5
92	Dallas-Plano-Irving, TX M.D.	6.4
92	Santa Cruz-Watsonville, CA	6.4
94	Santa Fe, NM	6.3
95	Augusta, GA-SC	6.0
95	Florence, SC	6.0
95	Goldsboro, NC	6.0
95	Victoria, TX	6.0
95	Wichita Falls, TX	6.0
100	Cincinnati-Middletown, OH-KY-IN	5.9
100	Corpus Christi, TX	5.9
100	Fort Smith, AR-OK	5.9
100	New York-W. Plains NY-NJ M.D.	5.9
104	Anchorage, AK	5.8
104	Dothan, AL	5.8
104	Gadsden, AL	5.8
107	Gainesville, FL	5.7
107	Johnson City, TN	5.7
107	Modesto, CA	5.7
107	Pascagoula, MS	5.7
107	Trenton-Ewing, NJ	5.7
112	Dallas (greater), TX	5.6
112	Toledo, OH	5.6
114	Dover, DE	5.5
114	Wilmington, DE-MD-NJ M.D.	5.5
116	Huntsville, AL	5.4
116	Rochester, NY	5.4
116	Sacramento, CA	5.4
116	Sebastian-Vero Beach, FL	5.4
120	Dayton, OH	5.3
120	Hot Springs, AR	5.3
120	Jonesboro, AR	5.3
120	Lubbock, TX	5.3
120	South Bend-Mishawaka, IN-MI	5.3
125	Blacksburg, VA	5.2
125	Chattanooga, TN-GA	5.2
125	New York (greater), NY-NJ-PA	5.2
125	Topeka, KS	5.2
125	Winston-Salem, NC	5.2
130	Chico, CA	5.1
130	Jacksonville, NC	5.1
130	Knoxville, TN	5.1
130	Palm Coast, FL	5.1
130	Winchester, VA-WV	5.1
135	Athens-Clarke County, GA	5.0
136	Brunswick, GA	4.9
136	Clarksville, TN-KY	4.9
136	Kokomo, IN	4.9
136	Niles-Benton Harbor, MI	4.9
136	Ocala, FL	4.9
136	Port St. Lucie, FL	4.9
136	Tampa-St Petersburg, FL	4.9
136	Wichita, KS	4.9
144	Fort Lauderdale, FL M.D.	4.8
144	Houma, LA	4.8
144	Lawrence, KS	4.8
144	Omaha-Council Bluffs, NE-IA	4.8
144	Prescott, AZ	4.8
149	Camden, NJ M.D.	4.7
149	Cleveland-Elyria-Mentor, OH	4.7
149	Decatur, AL	4.7
149	Durham, NC	4.7
149	Fort Wayne, IN	4.7
149	Louisville, KY-IN	4.7
149	Roanoke, VA	4.7
149	Wilmington, NC	4.7
157	Beaumont-Port Arthur, TX	4.6
157	Danville, VA	4.6
157	McAllen-Edinburg-Mission, TX	4.6
157	Tacoma, WA M.D.	4.6
161	Bowling Green, KY	4.5
161	Grand Junction, CO	4.5
161	Lancaster, PA	4.5
164	Denver-Aurora, CO	4.4
164	Harrisonburg, VA	4.4
164	Pittsburgh, PA	4.4
164	Redding, CA	4.4
164	Sarasota-Bradenton-Venice, FL	4.4
164	Yuba City, CA	4.4
170	San Diego, CA	4.3
170	Waco, TX	4.3

Note: All listings are for Metropolitan Statistical Areas (M.S.A.s) except for those ending with "M.D." Listings with "M.D." are Metropolitan Divisions which are smaller parts of eleven large M.S.A.s. See explanatory note at beginning of metropolitan area section on page 23.

RANK	METROPOLITAN AREA	RATE
172	Burlington, NC	4.2
172	Daytona Beach, FL	4.2
172	Springfield, OH	4.2
172	Yakima, WA	4.2
176	College Station-Bryan, TX	4.1
176	Columbus, IN	4.1
176	Fort Worth-Arlington, TX M.D.	4.1
176	Palm Bay-Melbourne, FL	4.1
176	Racine, WI	4.1
176	Rome, GA	4.1
182	Johnstown, PA	4.0
182	Midland, TX	4.0
184	Kingsport, TN-VA	3.9
184	Pueblo, CO	3.9
186	Hartford, CT	3.8
186	Lakeland, FL	3.8
186	Raleigh-Cary, NC	3.8
186	Spokane, WA	3.8
190	Abilene, TX	3.7
190	Salem, OR	3.7
190	Yuma, AZ	3.7
193	Joplin, MO	3.6
193	Oxnard-Thousand Oaks, CA	3.6
193	Salinas, CA	3.6
193	Seattle (greater), WA	3.6
197	Carson City, NV	3.5
197	Minneapolis-St. Paul, MN-WI	3.5
197	Morgantown, WV	3.5
200	Grand Rapids-Wyoming, MI	3.4
200	Muncie, IN	3.4
200	Scranton--Wilkes-Barre, PA	3.4
200	Vallejo-Fairfield, CA	3.4
204	Seattle-Bellevue, WA M.D.	3.3
204	Sioux Falls, SD	3.3
206	Lebanon, PA	3.2
206	Santa Barbara-Santa Maria, CA	3.2
206	Tallahassee, FL	3.2
209	Brownsville-Harlingen, TX	3.1
209	Farmington, NM	3.1
209	Harrisburg-Carlisle, PA	3.1
209	Pensacola, FL	3.1
209	Tyler, TX	3.1
209	Wausau, WI	3.1
215	Colorado Springs, CO	3.0
215	El Paso, TX	3.0
215	Killeen-Temple-Fort Hood, TX	3.0
215	Panama City-Lynn Haven, FL	3.0
215	Reading, PA	3.0
215	Springfield, MA	3.0
221	Amarillo, TX	2.9
221	Lynchburg, VA	2.9
223	Casper, WY	2.8
223	Cedar Rapids, IA	2.8
223	Evansville, IN-KY	2.8
223	Hanford-Corcoran, CA	2.8
223	Jefferson City, MO	2.8
223	San Angelo, TX	2.8
223	Syracuse, NY	2.8
230	Asheville, NC	2.7
230	Boise City-Nampa, ID	2.7
230	Fort Walton Beach, FL	2.7
230	Kennewick-Richland-Pasco, WA	2.7
230	Kingston, NY	2.7
230	Michigan City-La Porte, IN	2.7
230	Santa Ana-Anaheim, CA M.D.	2.7
237	Ann Arbor, MI	2.6
237	Las Cruces, NM	2.6
239	Great Falls, MT	2.5
239	Jackson, MI	2.5
239	Janesville, WI	2.5
239	Kalamazoo-Portage, MI	2.5
239	Oshkosh-Neenah, WI	2.5
244	Binghamton, NY	2.4
244	Hagerstown-Martinsburg, MD-WV	2.4
244	Lansing-East Lansing, MI	2.4
244	Poughkeepsie, NY	2.4
248	Bethesda-Frederick, MD M.D.	2.3
248	Cheyenne, WY	2.3
248	Eugene-Springfield, OR	2.3
248	Flagstaff, AZ	2.3
248	Lexington-Fayette, KY	2.3
248	Mansfield, OH	2.3
248	Muskegon-Norton Shores, MI	2.3
248	Odessa, TX	2.3
248	Portland-Vancouver, OR-WA	2.3
248	San Jose, CA	2.3
248	San Luis Obispo, CA	2.3
248	Santa Rosa-Petaluma, CA	2.3
248	Utica-Rome, NY	2.3
248	Valdosta, GA	2.3
248	Warner Robins, GA	2.3
263	Bloomington, IN	2.2
263	Elmira, NY	2.2
263	Fayetteville, AR-MO	2.2
263	Naples-Marco Island, FL	2.2
263	Salt Lake City, UT	2.2
268	Albany-Schenectady-Troy, NY	2.1
268	Charlottesville, VA	2.1
268	Grand Forks, ND-MN	2.1
268	Nassau-Suffolk, NY M.D.	2.1
268	State College, PA	2.1
273	Bangor, ME	2.0
273	Billings, MT	2.0
273	Bismarck, ND	2.0
273	Edison, NJ M.D.	2.0
277	Austin-Round Rock, TX	1.9
277	Columbia, MO	1.9
277	El Centro, CA	1.9
277	Honolulu, HI	1.9
277	Warren-Farmington Hills, MI M.D.	1.9
277	Wenatchee, WA	1.9
283	Barnstable Town, MA	1.8
283	Bay City, MI	1.8
283	Fort Collins-Loveland, CO	1.8
283	Gainesville, GA	1.8
283	Lincoln, NE	1.8
283	Logan, UT-ID	1.8
283	Ogden-Clearfield, UT	1.8
283	Waterloo-Cedar Falls, IA	1.8
291	Greeley, CO	1.7
291	Idaho Falls, ID	1.7
291	Lewiston, ID-WA	1.7
291	Mount Vernon-Anacortes, WA	1.7
291	Olympia, WA	1.7
291	Springfield, MO	1.7
297	Glens Falls, NY	1.6
297	St. Joseph, MO-KS	1.6
299	Dalton, GA	1.5
299	Des Moines-West Des Moines, IA	1.5
299	Medford, OR	1.5
299	Morristown, TN	1.5
299	Napa, CA	1.5
299	Pittsfield, MA	1.5
305	Bend, OR	1.4
305	Duluth, MN-WI	1.4
305	Erie, PA	1.4
305	Madera, CA	1.4
309	Bremerton-Silverdale, WA	1.2
309	Manchester-Nashua, NH	1.2
309	Punta Gorda, FL	1.2
312	Fargo, ND-MN	1.1
312	Lafayette, IN	1.1
312	Pocatello, ID	1.1
312	Rochester, MN	1.1
312	Worcester, MA	1.1
317	Cumberland, MD-WV	1.0
317	Fond du Lac, WI	1.0
317	Huntington-Ashland, WV-KY-OH	1.0
317	Ithaca, NY	1.0
317	Ocean City, NJ	1.0
317	Portland, ME	1.0
323	Appleton, WI	0.9
323	Cleveland, TN	0.9
323	Lewiston-Auburn, ME	0.9
323	Sheboygan, WI	0.9
327	Altoona, PA	0.8
327	Coeur d'Alene, ID	0.8
327	Sherman-Denison, TX	0.8
327	Williamsport, PA	0.8
331	Green Bay, WI	0.7
331	Madison, WI	0.7
331	Monroe, MI	0.7
331	Sioux City, IA-NE-SD	0.7
331	Wheeling, WV-OH	0.7
336	Provo-Orem, UT	0.6
337	Bellingham, WA	0.5
337	St. Cloud, MN	0.5
339	Ames, IA	0.0
339	Dubuque, IA	0.0
339	Eau Claire, WI	0.0
339	Elizabethtown, KY	0.0
339	Holland-Grand Haven, MI	0.0
339	Iowa City, IA	0.0
339	La Crosse, WI-MN	0.0
339	Missoula, MT	0.0
339	Rapid City, SD	0.0
339	Sandusky, OH	0.0
NA	Chicago, IL**	NA
NA	Fairbanks, AK**	NA

Source: Federal Bureau of Investigation

"Crime in the United States 2006" (Uniform Crime Reports, September 24, 2007)

**Includes nonnegligent manslaughter.*

***Not available.*

11. Percent Change in Murder Rate: 2005 to 2006

National Percent Change = 0.8% Increase*

RANK	METROPOLITAN AREA	% CHANGE
NA	Abilene, TX**	NA
237	Albany-Schenectady-Troy, NY	(30.0)
66	Albany, GA	35.4
170	Albuquerque, NM	(4.3)
174	Alexandria, LA	(5.3)
303	Altoona, PA	(85.5)
256	Amarillo, TX	(37.0)
142	Ames, IA	0.0
126	Anchorage, AK	5.5
113	Anderson, SC	11.0
118	Ann Arbor, MI	8.3
142	Appleton, WI	0.0
223	Asheville, NC	(25.0)
40	Athens-Clarke County, GA	78.6
121	Atlanta, GA	7.2
35	Atlantic City, NJ	88.1
97	Augusta, GA-SC	17.6
251	Austin-Round Rock, TX	(34.5)
185	Bakersfield, CA	(8.6)
132	Baltimore-Towson, MD	4.7
NA	Bangor, ME***	NA
61	Barnstable Town, MA	38.5
86	Baton Rouge, LA	21.0
51	Battle Creek, MI	58.0
25	Bay City, MI	100.0
263	Beaumont-Port Arthur, TX	(40.3)
300	Bellingham, WA	(81.5)
283	Bend, OR	(51.7)
85	Bethesda-Frederick, MD M.D.	21.1
264	Billings, MT	(41.2)
223	Binghamton, NY	(25.0)
NA	Birmingham-Hoover, AL**	NA
NA	Bismarck, ND***	NA
4	Blacksburg, VA	300.0
73	Bloomington, IN	29.4
NA	Boise City-Nampa, ID**	NA
47	Bowling Green, KY	66.7
289	Bremerton-Silverdale, WA	(58.6)
186	Brownsville-Harlingen, TX	(8.8)
48	Brunswick, GA	63.3
68	Buffalo-Niagara Falls, NY	31.6
229	Burlington, NC	(26.3)
88	Camden, NJ M.D.	20.5
63	Cape Coral-Fort Myers, FL	38.1
142	Carson City, NV	0.0
166	Casper, WY	(3.4)
1	Cedar Rapids, IA	600.0
37	Charleston-North Charleston, SC	85.3
100	Charleston, WV	15.4
129	Charlotte-Gastonia, NC-SC	5.1
255	Charlottesville, VA	(36.4)
213	Chattanooga, TN-GA	(16.1)
290	Cheyenne, WY	(60.3)
NA	Chicago, IL**	NA
117	Chico, CA	8.5
128	Cincinnati-Middletown, OH-KY-IN	5.4
53	Clarksville, TN-KY	48.5
NA	Cleveland-Elyria-Mentor, OH**	NA
NA	Cleveland, TN**	NA
298	Coeur d'Alene, ID	(80.0)
204	College Station-Bryan, TX	(12.8)
137	Colorado Springs, CO	3.4
292	Columbia, MO	(67.8)
94	Columbia, SC	18.3
233	Columbus, GA-AL	(27.7)
NA	Columbus, IN***	NA
142	Columbus, OH	0.0
24	Corpus Christi, TX	103.4
142	Cumberland, MD-WV	0.0
216	Dallas (greater), TX	(17.6)
199	Dallas-Plano-Irving, TX M.D.	(12.3)
NA	Dalton, GA**	NA
284	Danville, VA	(54.0)
229	Daytona Beach, FL	(26.3)
114	Dayton, OH	10.4
7	Decatur, AL	261.5
197	Denver-Aurora, CO	(12.0)
NA	Des Moines-West Des Moines, IA**	NA
101	Detroit (greater), MI	15.3
96	Detroit-Livonia-Dearborn, MI M.D.	17.9
218	Dothan, AL	(20.5)
31	Dover, DE	96.4
304	Dubuque, IA	(100.0)
NA	Duluth, MN-WI**	NA
NA	Durham, NC**	NA
304	Eau Claire, WI	(100.0)
39	Edison, NJ M.D.	81.8
NA	El Centro, CA***	NA
91	El Paso, TX	20.0
304	Elizabethtown, KY	(100.0)
16	Elkhart-Goshen, IN	145.2
274	Elmira, NY	(50.0)
274	Erie, PA	(50.0)
169	Eugene-Springfield, OR	(4.2)
166	Evansville, IN-KY	(3.4)
NA	Fairbanks, AK**	NA
242	Fargo, ND-MN	(31.3)
164	Farmington, NM	(3.1)
219	Fayetteville, AR-MO	(21.4)
71	Fayetteville, NC	30.8
13	Flagstaff, AZ	187.5
90	Flint, MI	20.3
223	Florence, SC	(25.0)
NA	Fond du Lac, WI***	NA
142	Fort Collins-Loveland, CO	0.0
64	Fort Lauderdale, FL M.D.	37.1
59	Fort Smith, AR-OK	40.5
45	Fort Walton Beach, FL	68.8
NA	Fort Wayne, IN**	NA
232	Fort Worth-Arlington, TX M.D.	(26.8)
171	Fresno, CA	(4.5)
206	Gadsden, AL	(13.4)
30	Gainesville, FL	96.6
274	Gainesville, GA	(50.0)
NA	Glens Falls, NY**	NA
270	Goldsboro, NC	(46.4)
245	Grand Forks, ND-MN	(32.3)
NA	Grand Junction, CO***	NA
20	Grand Rapids-Wyoming, MI	112.5
142	Great Falls, MT	0.0
267	Greeley, CO	(45.2)
297	Green Bay, WI	(79.4)
200	Greensboro-High Point, NC	(12.5)
220	Greenville, NC	(21.7)
122	Greenville, SC	6.3
208	Hagerstown-Martinsburg, MD-WV	(14.3)
142	Hanford-Corcoran, CA	0.0
214	Harrisburg-Carlisle, PA	(16.2)
17	Harrisonburg, VA	144.4
178	Hartford, CT	(7.3)
NA	Hattiesburg, MS**	NA
304	Holland-Grand Haven, MI	(100.0)
111	Honolulu, HI	11.8
259	Hot Springs, AR	(38.4)
203	Houma, LA	(12.7)
126	Houston, TX	5.5
301	Huntington-Ashland, WV-KY-OH	(82.1)
260	Huntsville, AL	(38.6)
NA	Idaho Falls, ID***	NA
80	Indianapolis, IN	25.3
304	Iowa City, IA	(100.0)
NA	Ithaca, NY**	NA
76	Jacksonville, FL	27.7
NA	Jacksonville, NC**	NA
246	Jackson, MI	(32.4)
132	Jackson, MS	4.7
42	Jackson, TN	73.6
142	Janesville, WI	0.0
291	Jefferson City, MO	(63.6)
120	Johnson City, TN	7.5
NA	Johnstown, PA**	NA
12	Jonesboro, AR	194.4
223	Joplin, MO	(25.0)
192	Kalamazoo-Portage, MI	(10.7)
NA	Kansas City, MO-KS**	NA
212	Kennewick-Richland-Pasco, WA	(15.6)
247	Killeen-Temple-Fort Hood, TX	(33.3)
187	Kingsport, TN-VA	(9.3)
45	Kingston, NY	68.8
210	Knoxville, TN	(15.0)
288	Kokomo, IN	(58.5)
304	La Crosse, WI-MN	(100.0)
274	Lafayette, IN	(50.0)
131	Lake Charles, LA	4.8
NA	Lake Havasu City-Kingman, AZ**	NA
116	Lakeland, FL	8.6
6	Lancaster, PA	275.0
244	Lansing-East Lansing, MI	(31.4)
140	Laredo, TX	1.0
258	Las Cruces, NM	(38.1)
160	Las Vegas-Paradise, NV	(1.0)

Note: All listings are for Metropolitan Statistical Areas (M.S.A.s) except for those ending with "M.D." Listings with "M.D." are Metropolitan Divisions which are smaller parts of eleven large M.S.A.s. See explanatory note at beginning of metropolitan area section on page 23.

RANK	METROPOLITAN AREA	% CHANGE
15	Lawrence, KS	152.6
69	Lawton, OK	31.5
4	Lebanon, PA	300.0
293	Lewiston-Auburn, ME	(67.9)
272	Lewiston, ID-WA	(48.5)
NA	Lexington-Fayette, KY**	NA
25	Lima, OH	100.0
75	Lincoln, NE	28.6
49	Little Rock, AR	60.7
142	Logan, UT-ID	0.0
200	Longview, TX	(12.5)
19	Longview, WA	129.0
175	Los Angeles County, CA M.D.	(5.6)
171	Los Angeles (greater), CA	(4.5)
205	Louisville, KY-IN	(13.0)
142	Lubbock, TX	0.0
241	Lynchburg, VA	(31.0)
253	Macon, GA	(36.1)
299	Madera, CA	(80.3)
41	Madison, WI	75.0
236	Manchester-Nashua, NH	(29.4)
56	Mansfield, OH	43.8
215	McAllen-Edinburg-Mission, TX	(16.4)
265	Medford, OR	(42.3)
162	Memphis, TN-MS-AR	(1.4)
163	Merced, CA	(2.2)
62	Miami (greater), FL	38.2
60	Miami-Dade County, FL M.D.	39.4
287	Michigan City-La Porte, IN	(57.1)
2	Midland, TX	400.0
207	Milwaukee, WI	(14.0)
NA	Minneapolis-St. Paul, MN-WI**	NA
304	Missoula, MT	(100.0)
176	Mobile, AL	(6.5)
173	Modesto, CA	(5.0)
22	Monroe, LA	109.8
269	Monroe, MI	(46.2)
142	Montgomery, AL	0.0
33	Morgantown, WV	94.4
142	Morristown, TN	0.0
256	Mount Vernon-Anacortes, WA	(37.0)
25	Muncie, IN	100.0
142	Muskegon-Norton Shores, MI	0.0
216	Myrtle Beach, SC	(17.6)
36	Napa, CA	87.5
231	Naples-Marco Island, FL	(26.7)
193	Nashville-Davidson, TN	(11.1)
130	Nassau-Suffolk, NY M.D.	5.0
NA	New Orleans, LA**	NA
134	New York (greater), NY-NJ-PA	4.0
136	New York-W. Plains NY-NJ M.D.	3.5
165	Newark-Union, NJ-PA M.D.	(3.3)
50	Niles-Benton Harbor, MI	58.1
76	Oakland-Fremont, CA M.D.	27.7
187	Ocala, FL	(9.3)
274	Ocean City, NJ	(50.0)
282	Odessa, TX	(51.1)
190	Ogden-Clearfield, UT	(10.0)
81	Oklahoma City, OK	25.0
34	Olympia, WA	88.9

RANK	METROPOLITAN AREA	% CHANGE
98	Omaha-Council Bluffs, NE-IA	17.1
52	Orlando, FL	50.0
3	Oshkosh-Neenah, WI	316.7
190	Oxnard-Thousand Oaks, CA	(10.0)
87	Palm Bay-Melbourne, FL	20.6
NA	Palm Coast, FL**	NA
91	Panama City-Lynn Haven, FL	20.0
223	Pascagoula, MS	(25.0)
103	Pensacola, FL	14.8
138	Philadelphia (greater) PA-NJ-DE	3.3
141	Philadelphia, PA M.D.	0.9
135	Phoenix-Mesa-Scottsdale, AZ	3.6
234	Pine Bluff, AR	(28.1)
181	Pittsburgh, PA	(8.3)
252	Pittsfield, MA	(34.8)
181	Pocatello, ID	(8.3)
74	Port St. Lucie, FL	28.9
194	Portland-Vancouver, OR-WA	(11.5)
235	Portland, ME	(28.6)
91	Poughkeepsie, NY	20.0
18	Prescott, AZ	140.0
274	Provo-Orem, UT	(50.0)
285	Pueblo, CO	(54.1)
142	Punta Gorda, FL	0.0
274	Racine, WI	(50.0)
102	Raleigh-Cary, NC	15.2
304	Rapid City, SD	(100.0)
273	Reading, PA	(49.2)
25	Redding, CA	100.0
21	Reno-Sparks, NV	111.4
211	Richmond, VA	(15.4)
177	Riverside-San Bernardino, CA	(6.8)
240	Roanoke, VA	(30.9)
NA	Rochester, MN***	NA
184	Rochester, NY	(8.5)
78	Rocky Mount, NC	27.4
32	Rome, GA	95.2
194	Sacramento, CA	(11.5)
67	Saginaw, MI	35.0
65	Salem, OR	37.0
123	Salinas, CA	5.9
25	Salisbury, MD	100.0
242	Salt Lake City, UT	(31.3)
222	San Angelo, TX	(24.3)
84	San Antonio, TX	22.8
72	San Diego, CA	30.3
112	San Francisco (greater), CA	11.2
209	San Francisco-S. Mateo, CA M.D.	(14.5)
180	San Jose, CA	(8.0)
56	San Luis Obispo, CA	43.8
304	Sandusky, OH	(100.0)
119	Santa Ana-Anaheim, CA M.D.	8.0
55	Santa Barbara-Santa Maria, CA	45.5
9	Santa Cruz-Watsonville, CA	220.0
54	Santa Fe, NM	46.5
23	Santa Rosa-Petaluma, CA	109.1
79	Sarasota-Bradenton-Venice, FL	25.7
168	Savannah, GA	(3.9)
115	Scranton--Wilkes-Barre, PA	9.7
99	Seattle (greater), WA	16.1

RANK	METROPOLITAN AREA	% CHANGE
107	Seattle-Bellevue, WA M.D.	13.8
8	Sebastian-Vero Beach, FL	237.5
NA	Sheboygan, WI***	NA
294	Sherman-Denison, TX	(68.0)
124	Shreveport-Bossier City, LA	5.6
274	Sioux City, IA-NE-SD	(50.0)
107	Sioux Falls, SD	13.8
88	South Bend-Mishawaka, IN-MI	20.5
247	Spartanburg, SC	(33.3)
124	Spokane, WA	5.6
254	Springfield, MA	(36.2)
228	Springfield, MO	(26.1)
247	Springfield, OH	(33.3)
10	State College, PA	200.0
161	Stockton, CA	(1.2)
301	St. Cloud, MN	(82.1)
247	St. Joseph, MO-KS	(33.3)
197	St. Louis, MO-IL	(12.0)
83	Sumter, SC	24.0
200	Syracuse, NY	(12.5)
82	Tacoma, WA M.D.	24.3
268	Tallahassee, FL	(45.8)
106	Tampa-St Petersburg, FL	14.0
43	Texarkana, TX-Texarkana, AR	72.9
105	Toledo, OH	14.3
95	Topeka, KS	18.2
261	Trenton-Ewing, NJ	(38.7)
189	Tucson, AZ	(9.6)
179	Tulsa, OK	(7.4)
NA	Tuscaloosa, AL**	NA
271	Tyler, TX	(46.6)
238	Utica-Rome, NY	(30.3)
295	Valdosta, GA	(70.9)
NA	Vallejo-Fairfield, CA**	NA
44	Victoria, TX	71.4
38	Vineland, NJ	84.9
221	Virginia Beach-Norfolk, VA-NC	(23.2)
196	Visalia-Porterville, CA	(11.9)
239	Waco, TX	(30.6)
56	Warner Robins, GA	43.8
142	Warren-Farmington Hills, MI M.D.	0.0
NA	Washington (greater) DC-VA-MD**	NA
NA	Washington, DC-VA-MD-WV M.D.**	NA
10	Waterloo-Cedar Falls, IA	200.0
NA	Wausau, WI***	NA
142	Wenatchee, WA	0.0
69	West Palm Beach, FL M.D.	31.5
142	Wheeling, WV-OH	0.0
109	Wichita Falls, TX	13.2
NA	Wichita, KS**	NA
296	Williamsport, PA	(76.5)
104	Wilmington, DE-MD-NJ M.D.	14.6
110	Wilmington, NC	11.9
14	Winchester, VA-WV	183.3
139	Winston-Salem, NC	2.0
181	Worcester, MA	(8.3)
286	Yakima, WA	(55.8)
262	Yuba City, CA	(38.9)
266	Yuma, AZ	(43.9)

Source: CQ Press using data from Federal Bureau of Investigation "Crime in the United States 2006" (Uniform Crime Reports, September 24, 2007)

**Includes nonnegligent manslaughter. **Not available. ***These metro areas had murder rates of 0 in 2005 but had at least one murder in 2006. Calculating percent increase from zero results in an infinite number. This is shown as "NA."*

11. Percent Change in Murder Rate: 2005 to 2006 (continued)

National Percent Change = 0.8% Increase*

RANK	METROPOLITAN AREA	% CHANGE
1	Cedar Rapids, IA	600.0
2	Midland, TX	400.0
3	Oshkosh-Neenah, WI	316.7
4	Blacksburg, VA	300.0
4	Lebanon, PA	300.0
6	Lancaster, PA	275.0
7	Decatur, AL	261.5
8	Sebastian-Vero Beach, FL	237.5
9	Santa Cruz-Watsonville, CA	220.0
10	State College, PA	200.0
10	Waterloo-Cedar Falls, IA	200.0
12	Jonesboro, AR	194.4
13	Flagstaff, AZ	187.5
14	Winchester, VA-WV	183.3
15	Lawrence, KS	152.6
16	Elkhart-Goshen, IN	145.2
17	Harrisonburg, VA	144.4
18	Prescott, AZ	140.0
19	Longview, WA	129.0
20	Grand Rapids-Wyoming, MI	112.5
21	Reno-Sparks, NV	111.4
22	Monroe, LA	109.8
23	Santa Rosa-Petaluma, CA	109.1
24	Corpus Christi, TX	103.4
25	Bay City, MI	100.0
25	Lima, OH	100.0
25	Muncie, IN	100.0
25	Redding, CA	100.0
25	Salisbury, MD	100.0
30	Gainesville, FL	96.6
31	Dover, DE	96.4
32	Rome, GA	95.2
33	Morgantown, WV	94.4
34	Olympia, WA	88.9
35	Atlantic City, NJ	88.1
36	Napa, CA	87.5
37	Charleston-North Charleston, SC	85.3
38	Vineland, NJ	84.9
39	Edison, NJ M.D.	81.8
40	Athens-Clarke County, GA	78.6
41	Madison, WI	75.0
42	Jackson, TN	73.6
43	Texarkana, TX-Texarkana, AR	72.9
44	Victoria, TX	71.4
45	Fort Walton Beach, FL	68.8
45	Kingston, NY	68.8
47	Bowling Green, KY	66.7
48	Brunswick, GA	63.3
49	Little Rock, AR	60.7
50	Niles-Benton Harbor, MI	58.1
51	Battle Creek, MI	58.0
52	Orlando, FL	50.0
53	Clarksville, TN-KY	48.5
54	Santa Fe, NM	46.5
55	Santa Barbara-Santa Maria, CA	45.5
56	Mansfield, OH	43.8
56	San Luis Obispo, CA	43.8
56	Warner Robins, GA	43.8
59	Fort Smith, AR-OK	40.5
60	Miami-Dade County, FL M.D.	39.4
61	Barnstable Town, MA	38.5
62	Miami (greater), FL	38.2
63	Cape Coral-Fort Myers, FL	38.1
64	Fort Lauderdale, FL M.D.	37.1
65	Salem, OR	37.0
66	Albany, GA	35.4
67	Saginaw, MI	35.0
68	Buffalo-Niagara Falls, NY	31.6
69	Lawton, OK	31.5
69	West Palm Beach, FL M.D.	31.5
71	Fayetteville, NC	30.8
72	San Diego, CA	30.3
73	Bloomington, IN	29.4
74	Port St. Lucie, FL	28.9
75	Lincoln, NE	28.6
76	Jacksonville, FL	27.7
76	Oakland-Fremont, CA M.D.	27.7
78	Rocky Mount, NC	27.4
79	Sarasota-Bradenton-Venice, FL	25.7
80	Indianapolis, IN	25.3
81	Oklahoma City, OK	25.0
82	Tacoma, WA M.D.	24.3
83	Sumter, SC	24.0
84	San Antonio, TX	22.8
85	Bethesda-Frederick, MD M.D.	21.1
86	Baton Rouge, LA	21.0
87	Palm Bay-Melbourne, FL	20.6
88	Camden, NJ M.D.	20.5
88	South Bend-Mishawaka, IN-MI	20.5
90	Flint, MI	20.3
91	El Paso, TX	20.0
91	Panama City-Lynn Haven, FL	20.0
91	Poughkeepsie, NY	20.0
94	Columbia, SC	18.3
95	Topeka, KS	18.2
96	Detroit-Livonia-Dearborn, MI M.D.	17.9
97	Augusta, GA-SC	17.6
98	Omaha-Council Bluffs, NE-IA	17.1
99	Seattle (greater), WA	16.1
100	Charleston, WV	15.4
101	Detroit (greater), MI	15.3
102	Raleigh-Cary, NC	15.2
103	Pensacola, FL	14.8
104	Wilmington, DE-MD-NJ M.D.	14.6
105	Toledo, OH	14.3
106	Tampa-St Petersburg, FL	14.0
107	Seattle-Bellevue, WA M.D.	13.8
107	Sioux Falls, SD	13.8
109	Wichita Falls, TX	13.2
110	Wilmington, NC	11.9
111	Honolulu, HI	11.8
112	San Francisco (greater), CA	11.2
113	Anderson, SC	11.0
114	Dayton, OH	10.4
115	Scranton--Wilkes-Barre, PA	9.7
116	Lakeland, FL	8.6
117	Chico, CA	8.5
118	Ann Arbor, MI	8.3
119	Santa Ana-Anaheim, CA M.D.	8.0
120	Johnson City, TN	7.5
121	Atlanta, GA	7.2
122	Greenville, SC	6.3
123	Salinas, CA	5.9
124	Shreveport-Bossier City, LA	5.6
124	Spokane, WA	5.6
126	Anchorage, AK	5.5
126	Houston, TX	5.5
128	Cincinnati-Middletown, OH-KY-IN	5.4
129	Charlotte-Gastonia, NC-SC	5.1
130	Nassau-Suffolk, NY M.D.	5.0
131	Lake Charles, LA	4.8
132	Baltimore-Towson, MD	4.7
132	Jackson, MS	4.7
134	New York (greater), NY-NJ-PA	4.0
135	Phoenix-Mesa-Scottsdale, AZ	3.6
136	New York-W. Plains NY-NJ M.D.	3.5
137	Colorado Springs, CO	3.4
138	Philadelphia (greater) PA-NJ-DE	3.3
139	Winston-Salem, NC	2.0
140	Laredo, TX	1.0
141	Philadelphia, PA M.D.	0.9
142	Ames, IA	0.0
142	Appleton, WI	0.0
142	Carson City, NV	0.0
142	Columbus, OH	0.0
142	Cumberland, MD-WV	0.0
142	Fort Collins-Loveland, CO	0.0
142	Great Falls, MT	0.0
142	Hanford-Corcoran, CA	0.0
142	Janesville, WI	0.0
142	Logan, UT-ID	0.0
142	Lubbock, TX	0.0
142	Montgomery, AL	0.0
142	Morristown, TN	0.0
142	Muskegon-Norton Shores, MI	0.0
142	Punta Gorda, FL	0.0
142	Warren-Farmington Hills, MI M.D.	0.0
142	Wenatchee, WA	0.0
142	Wheeling, WV-OH	0.0
160	Las Vegas-Paradise, NV	(1.0)
161	Stockton, CA	(1.2)
162	Memphis, TN-MS-AR	(1.4)
163	Merced, CA	(2.2)
164	Farmington, NM	(3.1)
165	Newark-Union, NJ-PA M.D.	(3.3)
166	Casper, WY	(3.4)
166	Evansville, IN-KY	(3.4)
168	Savannah, GA	(3.9)
169	Eugene-Springfield, OR	(4.2)
170	Albuquerque, NM	(4.3)
171	Fresno, CA	(4.5)

Note: All listings are for Metropolitan Statistical Areas (M.S.A.s) except for those ending with "M.D." Listings with "M.D." are Metropolitan Divisions which are smaller parts of eleven large M.S.A.s. See explanatory note at beginning of metropolitan area section on page 23.

RANK	METROPOLITAN AREA	% CHANGE
171	Los Angeles (greater), CA	(4.5)
173	Modesto, CA	(5.0)
174	Alexandria, LA	(5.3)
175	Los Angeles County, CA M.D.	(5.6)
176	Mobile, AL	(6.5)
177	Riverside-San Bernardino, CA	(6.8)
178	Hartford, CT	(7.3)
179	Tulsa, OK	(7.4)
180	San Jose, CA	(8.0)
181	Pittsburgh, PA	(8.3)
181	Pocatello, ID	(8.3)
181	Worcester, MA	(8.3)
184	Rochester, NY	(8.5)
185	Bakersfield, CA	(8.6)
186	Brownsville-Harlingen, TX	(8.8)
187	Kingsport, TN-VA	(9.3)
187	Ocala, FL	(9.3)
189	Tucson, AZ	(9.6)
190	Ogden-Clearfield, UT	(10.0)
190	Oxnard-Thousand Oaks, CA	(10.0)
192	Kalamazoo-Portage, MI	(10.7)
193	Nashville-Davidson, TN	(11.1)
194	Portland-Vancouver, OR-WA	(11.5)
194	Sacramento, CA	(11.5)
196	Visalia-Porterville, CA	(11.9)
197	Denver-Aurora, CO	(12.0)
197	St. Louis, MO-IL	(12.0)
199	Dallas-Plano-Irving, TX M.D.	(12.3)
200	Greensboro-High Point, NC	(12.5)
200	Longview, TX	(12.5)
200	Syracuse, NY	(12.5)
203	Houma, LA	(12.7)
204	College Station-Bryan, TX	(12.8)
205	Louisville, KY-IN	(13.0)
206	Gadsden, AL	(13.4)
207	Milwaukee, WI	(14.0)
208	Hagerstown-Martinsburg, MD-WV	(14.3)
209	San Francisco-S. Mateo, CA M.D.	(14.5)
210	Knoxville, TN	(15.0)
211	Richmond, VA	(15.4)
212	Kennewick-Richland-Pasco, WA	(15.6)
213	Chattanooga, TN-GA	(16.1)
214	Harrisburg-Carlisle, PA	(16.2)
215	McAllen-Edinburg-Mission, TX	(16.4)
216	Dallas (greater), TX	(17.6)
216	Myrtle Beach, SC	(17.6)
218	Dothan, AL	(20.5)
219	Fayetteville, AR-MO	(21.4)
220	Greenville, NC	(21.7)
221	Virginia Beach-Norfolk, VA-NC	(23.2)
222	San Angelo, TX	(24.3)
223	Asheville, NC	(25.0)
223	Binghamton, NY	(25.0)
223	Florence, SC	(25.0)
223	Joplin, MO	(25.0)
223	Pascagoula, MS	(25.0)
228	Springfield, MO	(26.1)
229	Burlington, NC	(26.3)
229	Daytona Beach, FL	(26.3)
231	Naples-Marco Island, FL	(26.7)
232	Fort Worth-Arlington, TX M.D.	(26.8)
233	Columbus, GA-AL	(27.7)
234	Pine Bluff, AR	(28.1)
235	Portland, ME	(28.6)
236	Manchester-Nashua, NH	(29.4)
237	Albany-Schenectady-Troy, NY	(30.0)
238	Utica-Rome, NY	(30.3)
239	Waco, TX	(30.6)
240	Roanoke, VA	(30.9)
241	Lynchburg, VA	(31.0)
242	Fargo, ND-MN	(31.3)
242	Salt Lake City, UT	(31.3)
244	Lansing-East Lansing, MI	(31.4)
245	Grand Forks, ND-MN	(32.3)
246	Jackson, MI	(32.4)
247	Killeen-Temple-Fort Hood, TX	(33.3)
247	Spartanburg, SC	(33.3)
247	Springfield, OH	(33.3)
247	St. Joseph, MO-KS	(33.3)
251	Austin-Round Rock, TX	(34.5)
252	Pittsfield, MA	(34.8)
253	Macon, GA	(36.1)
254	Springfield, MA	(36.2)
255	Charlottesville, VA	(36.4)
256	Amarillo, TX	(37.0)
256	Mount Vernon-Anacortes, WA	(37.0)
258	Las Cruces, NM	(38.1)
259	Hot Springs, AR	(38.4)
260	Huntsville, AL	(38.6)
261	Trenton-Ewing, NJ	(38.7)
262	Yuba City, CA	(38.9)
263	Beaumont-Port Arthur, TX	(40.3)
264	Billings, MT	(41.2)
265	Medford, OR	(42.3)
266	Yuma, AZ	(43.9)
267	Greeley, CO	(45.2)
268	Tallahassee, FL	(45.8)
269	Monroe, MI	(46.2)
270	Goldsboro, NC	(46.4)
271	Tyler, TX	(46.6)
272	Lewiston, ID-WA	(48.5)
273	Reading, PA	(49.2)
274	Elmira, NY	(50.0)
274	Erie, PA	(50.0)
274	Gainesville, GA	(50.0)
274	Lafayette, IN	(50.0)
274	Ocean City, NJ	(50.0)
274	Provo-Orem, UT	(50.0)
274	Racine, WI	(50.0)
274	Sioux City, IA-NE-SD	(50.0)
282	Odessa, TX	(51.1)
283	Bend, OR	(51.7)
284	Danville, VA	(54.0)
285	Pueblo, CO	(54.1)
286	Yakima, WA	(55.8)
287	Michigan City-La Porte, IN	(57.1)
288	Kokomo, IN	(58.5)
289	Bremerton-Silverdale, WA	(58.6)
290	Cheyenne, WY	(60.3)
291	Jefferson City, MO	(63.6)
292	Columbia, MO	(67.8)
293	Lewiston-Auburn, ME	(67.9)
294	Sherman-Denison, TX	(68.0)
295	Valdosta, GA	(70.9)
296	Williamsport, PA	(76.5)
297	Green Bay, WI	(79.4)
298	Coeur d'Alene, ID	(80.0)
299	Madera, CA	(80.3)
300	Bellingham, WA	(81.5)
301	Huntington-Ashland, WV-KY-OH	(82.1)
301	St. Cloud, MN	(82.1)
303	Altoona, PA	(85.5)
304	Dubuque, IA	(100.0)
304	Eau Claire, WI	(100.0)
304	Elizabethtown, KY	(100.0)
304	Holland-Grand Haven, MI	(100.0)
304	Iowa City, IA	(100.0)
304	La Crosse, WI-MN	(100.0)
304	Missoula, MT	(100.0)
304	Rapid City, SD	(100.0)
304	Sandusky, OH	(100.0)
NA	Abilene, TX**	NA
NA	Bangor, ME***	NA
NA	Birmingham-Hoover, AL**	NA
NA	Bismarck, ND***	NA
NA	Boise City-Nampa, ID**	NA
NA	Chicago, IL**	NA
NA	Cleveland-Elyria-Mentor, OH**	NA
NA	Cleveland, TN**	NA
NA	Columbus, IN***	NA
NA	Dalton, GA**	NA
NA	Des Moines-West Des Moines, IA**	NA
NA	Duluth, MN-WI**	NA
NA	Durham, NC**	NA
NA	El Centro, CA***	NA
NA	Fairbanks, AK**	NA
NA	Fond du Lac, WI***	NA
NA	Fort Wayne, IN**	NA
NA	Glens Falls, NY**	NA
NA	Grand Junction, CO***	NA
NA	Hattiesburg, MS**	NA
NA	Idaho Falls, ID***	NA
NA	Ithaca, NY**	NA
NA	Jacksonville, NC**	NA
NA	Johnstown, PA**	NA
NA	Kansas City, MO-KS**	NA
NA	Lake Havasu City-Kingman, AZ**	NA
NA	Lexington-Fayette, KY**	NA
NA	Minneapolis-St. Paul, MN-WI**	NA
NA	New Orleans, LA**	NA
NA	Palm Coast, FL**	NA
NA	Rochester, MN***	NA
NA	Sheboygan, WI***	NA
NA	Tuscaloosa, AL**	NA
NA	Vallejo-Fairfield, CA**	NA
NA	Washington (greater) DC-VA-MD**	NA
NA	Washington, DC-VA-MD-WV M.D.**	NA
NA	Wausau, WI***	NA
NA	Wichita, KS**	NA

Source: CQ Press using data from Federal Bureau of Investigation "Crime in the United States 2006" (Uniform Crime Reports, September 24, 2007)

**Includes nonnegligent manslaughter. **Not available. ***These metro areas had murder rates of 0 in 2005 but had at least one murder in 2006. Calculating percent increase from zero results in an infinite number. This is shown as "NA."*

12. Percent Change in Murder Rate: 2002 to 2006

National Percent Change = 1.0% Increase*

RANK	METROPOLITAN AREA	% CHANGE	RANK	METROPOLITAN AREA	% CHANGE	RANK	METROPOLITAN AREA	% CHANGE
NA	Abilene, TX**	NA	NA	Cleveland-Elyria-Mentor, OH**	NA	172	Glens Falls, NY	(33.3)
NA	Albany-Schenectady-Troy, NY**	NA	NA	Cleveland, TN**	NA	158	Goldsboro, NC	(22.1)
69	Albany, GA	18.2	NA	Coeur d'Alene, ID**	NA	NA	Grand Forks, ND-MN***	NA
123	Albuquerque, NM	(7.3)	NA	College Station-Bryan, TX**	NA	1	Grand Junction, CO	462.5
187	Alexandria, LA	(50.0)	192	Colorado Springs, CO	(58.3)	NA	Grand Rapids-Wyoming, MI**	NA
197	Altoona, PA	(65.2)	141	Columbia, MO	(13.6)	185	Great Falls, MT	(49.0)
122	Amarillo, TX	(6.5)	80	Columbia, SC	12.0	195	Greeley, CO	(63.8)
NA	Ames, IA**	NA	159	Columbus, GA-AL	(22.7)	193	Green Bay, WI	(58.8)
140	Anchorage, AK	(13.4)	NA	Columbus, IN**	NA	NA	Greensboro-High Point, NC**	NA
NA	Anderson, SC**	NA	101	Columbus, OH	0.0	150	Greenville, NC	(17.2)
NA	Ann Arbor, MI**	NA	99	Corpus Christi, TX	1.7	NA	Greenville, SC**	NA
NA	Appleton, WI**	NA	101	Cumberland, MD-WV	0.0	NA	Hagerstown-Martinsburg, MD-WV**	NA
200	Asheville, NC	(70.0)	NA	Dallas (greater), TX**	NA	NA	Hanford-Corcoran, CA**	NA
133	Athens-Clarke County, GA	(10.7)	152	Dallas-Plano-Irving, TX M.D.	(17.9)	NA	Harrisburg-Carlisle, PA**	NA
134	Atlanta, GA	(10.8)	NA	Dalton, GA**	NA	NA	Harrisonburg, VA**	NA
NA	Atlantic City, NJ**	NA	174	Danville, VA	(34.3)	57	Hartford, CT	26.7
54	Augusta, GA-SC	30.4	169	Daytona Beach, FL	(32.3)	NA	Hattiesburg, MS**	NA
178	Austin-Round Rock, TX	(36.7)	NA	Dayton, OH**	NA	NA	Holland-Grand Haven, MI**	NA
74	Bakersfield, CA	14.9	75	Decatur, AL	14.6	118	Honolulu, HI	(5.0)
81	Baltimore-Towson, MD	10.8	113	Denver-Aurora, CO	(4.3)	NA	Hot Springs, AR**	NA
NA	Bangor, ME**	NA	NA	Des Moines-West Des Moines, IA**	NA	38	Houma, LA	54.8
NA	Barnstable Town, MA**	NA	93	Detroit (greater), MI	3.7	76	Houston, TX	14.3
100	Baton Rouge, LA	1.4	NA	Detroit-Livonia-Dearborn, MI M.D.**	NA	NA	Huntington-Ashland, WV-KY-OH**	NA
NA	Battle Creek, MI**	NA	NA	Dothan, AL**	NA	53	Huntsville, AL	31.7
NA	Bay City, MI**	NA	14	Dover, DE	139.1	NA	Idaho Falls, ID**	NA
108	Beaumont-Port Arthur, TX	(2.1)	203	Dubuque, IA	(100.0)	NA	Indianapolis, IN**	NA
202	Bellingham, WA	(78.3)	139	Duluth, MN-WI	(12.5)	101	Iowa City, IA	0.0
NA	Bend, OR**	NA	NA	Durham, NC**	NA	NA	Ithaca, NY**	NA
NA	Bethesda-Frederick, MD M.D.**	NA	203	Eau Claire, WI	(100.0)	68	Jacksonville, FL	19.1
NA	Billings, MT***	NA	NA	Edison, NJ M.D.**	NA	NA	Jacksonville, NC**	NA
167	Binghamton, NY	(31.4)	NA	El Centro, CA**	NA	187	Jackson, MI	(50.0)
49	Birmingham-Hoover, AL	37.4	58	El Paso, TX	25.0	160	Jackson, MS	(22.9)
116	Bismarck, ND	(4.8)	NA	Elizabethtown, KY**	NA	17	Jackson, TN	127.3
NA	Blacksburg, VA**	NA	31	Elkhart-Goshen, IN	76.7	3	Janesville, WI	316.7
194	Bloomington, IN	(61.4)	NA	Elmira, NY**	NA	NA	Jefferson City, MO**	NA
101	Boise City-Nampa, ID	0.0	183	Erie, PA	(44.0)	NA	Johnson City, TN**	NA
NA	Bowling Green, KY**	NA	56	Eugene-Springfield, OR	27.8	NA	Johnstown, PA**	NA
5	Bremerton-Silverdale, WA	200.0	NA	Evansville, IN-KY**	NA	42	Jonesboro, AR	47.2
101	Brownsville-Harlingen, TX	0.0	NA	Fairbanks, AK**	NA	9	Joplin, MO	176.9
NA	Brunswick, GA**	NA	NA	Fargo, ND-MN***	NA	NA	Kalamazoo-Portage, MI**	NA
34	Buffalo-Niagara Falls, NY	70.5	NA	Farmington, NM**	NA	NA	Kansas City, MO-KS**	NA
NA	Burlington, NC**	NA	NA	Fayetteville, AR-MO**	NA	130	Kennewick-Richland-Pasco, WA	(10.0)
NA	Camden, NJ M.D.**	NA	173	Fayetteville, NC	(33.6)	45	Killeen-Temple-Fort Hood, TX	42.9
114	Cape Coral-Fort Myers, FL	(4.4)	39	Flagstaff, AZ	53.3	NA	Kingsport, TN-VA**	NA
NA	Carson City, NV**	NA	32	Flint, MI	75.0	NA	Kingston, NY**	NA
179	Casper, WY	(37.8)	23	Florence, SC	93.5	98	Knoxville, TN	2.0
7	Cedar Rapids, IA	180.0	NA	Fond du Lac, WI**	NA	101	Kokomo, IN	0.0
51	Charleston-North Charleston, SC	35.5	NA	Fort Collins-Loveland, CO***	NA	101	La Crosse, WI-MN	0.0
11	Charleston, WV	167.9	129	Fort Lauderdale, FL M.D.	(9.4)	198	Lafayette, IN	(65.6)
NA	Charlotte-Gastonia, NC-SC**	NA	116	Fort Smith, AR-OK	(4.8)	128	Lake Charles, LA	(8.5)
NA	Charlottesville, VA**	NA	61	Fort Walton Beach, FL	22.7	NA	Lake Havasu City-Kingman, AZ**	NA
175	Chattanooga, TN-GA	(35.0)	NA	Fort Wayne, IN**	NA	165	Lakeland, FL	(28.3)
112	Cheyenne, WY	(4.2)	153	Fort Worth-Arlington, TX M.D.	(18.0)	20	Lancaster, PA	114.3
NA	Chicago, IL**	NA	71	Fresno, CA	16.7	135	Lansing-East Lansing, MI	(11.1)
10	Chico, CA	168.4	65	Gadsden, AL	20.8	12	Laredo, TX	160.0
66	Cincinnati-Middletown, OH-KY-IN	20.4	26	Gainesville, FL	83.9	NA	Las Cruces, NM**	NA
97	Clarksville, TN-KY	2.1	NA	Gainesville, GA**	NA	94	Las Vegas-Paradise, NV	3.0

Note: All listings are for Metropolitan Statistical Areas (M.S.A.s) except for those ending with "M.D." Listings with "M.D." are Metropolitan Divisions which are smaller parts of eleven large M.S.A.s. See explanatory note at beginning of metropolitan area section on page 23.

RANK	METROPOLITAN AREA	% CHANGE
13	Lawrence, KS	140.0
96	Lawton, OK	2.9
NA	Lebanon, PA**	NA
191	Lewiston-Auburn, ME	(55.0)
NA	Lewiston, ID-WA**	NA
NA	Lexington-Fayette, KY**	NA
NA	Lima, OH**	NA
161	Lincoln, NE	(25.0)
47	Little Rock, AR	38.8
NA	Logan, UT-ID**	NA
46	Longview, TX	40.0
NA	Longview, WA**	NA
144	Los Angeles County, CA M.D.	(14.4)
NA	Los Angeles (greater), CA**	NA
157	Louisville, KY-IN	(21.7)
60	Lubbock, TX	23.3
189	Lynchburg, VA	(50.8)
NA	Macon, GA**	NA
NA	Madera, CA**	NA
181	Madison, WI	(41.7)
NA	Manchester-Nashua, NH**	NA
NA	Mansfield, OH**	NA
180	McAllen-Edinburg-Mission, TX	(40.3)
5	Medford, OR	200.0
NA	Memphis, TN-MS-AR**	NA
84	Merced, CA	9.8
NA	Miami (greater), FL**	NA
77	Miami-Dade County, FL M.D.	13.8
NA	Michigan City-La Porte, IN**	NA
NA	Midland, TX**	NA
NA	Milwaukee, WI**	NA
71	Minneapolis-St. Paul, MN-WI	16.7
NA	Missoula, MT**	NA
NA	Mobile, AL**	NA
29	Modesto, CA	78.1
NA	Monroe, LA**	NA
NA	Monroe, MI**	NA
121	Montgomery, AL	(6.1)
NA	Morgantown, WV**	NA
NA	Morristown, TN**	NA
NA	Mount Vernon-Anacortes, WA**	NA
22	Muncie, IN	100.0
NA	Muskegon-Norton Shores, MI**	NA
55	Myrtle Beach, SC	28.6
NA	Napa, CA**	NA
154	Naples-Marco Island, FL	(18.5)
79	Nashville-Davidson, TN	12.5
NA	Nassau-Suffolk, NY M.D.**	NA
135	New Orleans, LA	(11.1)
NA	New York (greater), NY-NJ-PA**	NA
132	New York-W. Plains NY-NJ M.D.	(10.6)
52	Newark-Union, NJ-PA M.D.	33.8
NA	Niles-Benton Harbor, MI**	NA
50	Oakland-Fremont, CA M.D.	35.9
148	Ocala, FL	(16.9)
NA	Ocean City, NJ**	NA
NA	Odessa, TX**	NA
NA	Ogden-Clearfield, UT**	NA
40	Oklahoma City, OK	52.2
25	Olympia, WA	88.9
89	Omaha-Council Bluffs, NE-IA	4.3
28	Orlando, FL	80.0
NA	Oshkosh-Neenah, WI**	NA
NA	Oxnard-Thousand Oaks, CA**	NA
33	Palm Bay-Melbourne, FL	70.8
NA	Palm Coast, FL**	NA
182	Panama City-Lynn Haven, FL	(42.3)
NA	Pascagoula, MS**	NA
171	Pensacola, FL	(32.6)
63	Philadelphia (greater) PA-NJ-DE	21.8
NA	Philadelphia, PA M.D.**	NA
88	Phoenix-Mesa-Scottsdale, AZ	6.1
142	Pine Bluff, AR	(14.0)
127	Pittsburgh, PA	(8.3)
NA	Pittsfield, MA**	NA
145	Pocatello, ID	(15.4)
110	Port St. Lucie, FL	(3.9)
86	Portland-Vancouver, OR-WA	9.5
NA	Portland, ME**	NA
NA	Poughkeepsie, NY**	NA
NA	Prescott, AZ**	NA
161	Provo-Orem, UT	(25.0)
149	Pueblo, CO	(17.0)
143	Punta Gorda, FL	(14.3)
4	Racine, WI	310.0
NA	Raleigh-Cary, NC**	NA
203	Rapid City, SD	(100.0)
186	Reading, PA	(49.2)
43	Redding, CA	46.7
16	Reno-Sparks, NV	131.3
138	Richmond, VA	(11.6)
126	Riverside-San Bernardino, CA	(8.0)
NA	Roanoke, VA**	NA
48	Rochester, MN	37.5
70	Rochester, NY	17.4
30	Rocky Mount, NC	77.9
NA	Rome, GA**	NA
91	Sacramento, CA	3.8
NA	Saginaw, MI**	NA
36	Salem, OR	68.2
184	Salinas, CA	(46.3)
NA	Salisbury, MD**	NA
NA	Salt Lake City, UT**	NA
NA	San Angelo, TX***	NA
111	San Antonio, TX	(4.1)
44	San Diego, CA	43.3
NA	San Francisco (greater), CA**	NA
58	San Francisco-S. Mateo, CA M.D.	25.0
86	San Jose, CA	9.5
24	San Luis Obispo, CA	91.7
NA	Sandusky, OH**	NA
91	Santa Ana-Anaheim, CA M.D.	3.8
NA	Santa Barbara-Santa Maria, CA**	NA
8	Santa Cruz-Watsonville, CA	178.3
64	Santa Fe, NM	21.2
170	Santa Rosa-Petaluma, CA	(32.4)
62	Sarasota-Bradenton-Venice, FL	22.2
164	Savannah, GA	(27.7)
94	Scranton--Wilkes-Barre, PA	3.0
NA	Seattle (greater), WA**	NA
77	Seattle-Bellevue, WA M.D.	13.8
NA	Sebastian-Vero Beach, FL**	NA
NA	Sheboygan, WI***	NA
199	Sherman-Denison, TX	(69.2)
155	Shreveport-Bossier City, LA	(19.3)
201	Sioux City, IA-NE-SD	(70.8)
2	Sioux Falls, SD	450.0
176	South Bend-Mishawaka, IN-MI	(35.4)
NA	Spartanburg, SC**	NA
151	Spokane, WA	(17.4)
NA	Springfield, MA**	NA
119	Springfield, MO	(5.6)
NA	Springfield, OH**	NA
163	State College, PA	(27.6)
146	Stockton, CA	(15.8)
147	St. Cloud, MN	(16.7)
NA	St. Joseph, MO-KS***	NA
NA	St. Louis, MO-IL**	NA
82	Sumter, SC	10.7
NA	Syracuse, NY**	NA
73	Tacoma, WA M.D.	15.0
168	Tallahassee, FL	(31.9)
125	Tampa-St Petersburg, FL	(7.5)
35	Texarkana, TX-Texarkana, AR	70.0
84	Toledo, OH	9.8
83	Topeka, KS	10.6
109	Trenton-Ewing, NJ	(3.4)
124	Tucson, AZ	(7.4)
41	Tulsa, OK	50.0
19	Tuscaloosa, AL	114.8
166	Tyler, TX	(29.5)
137	Utica-Rome, NY	(11.5)
NA	Valdosta, GA**	NA
NA	Vallejo-Fairfield, CA**	NA
196	Victoria, TX	(64.9)
27	Vineland, NJ	81.5
67	Virginia Beach-Norfolk, VA-NC	19.7
37	Visalia-Porterville, CA	55.3
177	Waco, TX	(35.8)
NA	Warner Robins, GA**	NA
NA	Warren-Farmington Hills, MI M.D.**	NA
NA	Washington (greater) DC-VA-MD**	NA
NA	Washington, DC-VA-MD-WV M.D.**	NA
18	Waterloo-Cedar Falls, IA	125.0
NA	Wausau, WI***	NA
NA	Wenatchee, WA**	NA
15	West Palm Beach, FL M.D.	136.7
NA	Wheeling, WV-OH**	NA
156	Wichita Falls, TX	(20.0)
89	Wichita, KS	4.3
190	Williamsport, PA	(52.9)
NA	Wilmington, DE-MD-NJ M.D.**	NA
120	Wilmington, NC	(6.0)
NA	Winchester, VA-WV**	NA
NA	Winston-Salem, NC**	NA
NA	Worcester, MA**	NA
115	Yakima, WA	(4.5)
131	Yuba City, CA	(10.2)
21	Yuma, AZ	105.6

Source: CQ Press using data from Federal Bureau of Investigation "Crime in the United States 2006" (Uniform Crime Reports, September 24, 2007)

**Includes nonnegligent manslaughter. **Not available. ***These metro areas had murder rates of 0 in 2002 but had at least one murder in 2006. Calculating percent increase from zero results in an infinite number. This is shown as "NA."*

12. Percent Change in Murder Rate: 2002 to 2006 (continued)

National Percent Change = 1.0% Increase*

RANK	METROPOLITAN AREA	% CHANGE
1	Grand Junction, CO	462.5
2	Sioux Falls, SD	450.0
3	Janesville, WI	316.7
4	Racine, WI	310.0
5	Bremerton-Silverdale, WA	200.0
5	Medford, OR	200.0
7	Cedar Rapids, IA	180.0
8	Santa Cruz-Watsonville, CA	178.3
9	Joplin, MO	176.9
10	Chico, CA	168.4
11	Charleston, WV	167.9
12	Laredo, TX	160.0
13	Lawrence, KS	140.0
14	Dover, DE	139.1
15	West Palm Beach, FL M.D.	136.7
16	Reno-Sparks, NV	131.3
17	Jackson, TN	127.3
18	Waterloo-Cedar Falls, IA	125.0
19	Tuscaloosa, AL	114.8
20	Lancaster, PA	114.3
21	Yuma, AZ	105.6
22	Muncie, IN	100.0
23	Florence, SC	93.5
24	San Luis Obispo, CA	91.7
25	Olympia, WA	88.9
26	Gainesville, FL	83.9
27	Vineland, NJ	81.5
28	Orlando, FL	80.0
29	Modesto, CA	78.1
30	Rocky Mount, NC	77.9
31	Elkhart-Goshen, IN	76.7
32	Flint, MI	75.0
33	Palm Bay-Melbourne, FL	70.8
34	Buffalo-Niagara Falls, NY	70.5
35	Texarkana, TX-Texarkana, AR	70.0
36	Salem, OR	68.2
37	Visalia-Porterville, CA	55.3
38	Houma, LA	54.8
39	Flagstaff, AZ	53.3
40	Oklahoma City, OK	52.2
41	Tulsa, OK	50.0
42	Jonesboro, AR	47.2
43	Redding, CA	46.7
44	San Diego, CA	43.3
45	Killeen-Temple-Fort Hood, TX	42.9
46	Longview, TX	40.0
47	Little Rock, AR	38.8
48	Rochester, MN	37.5
49	Birmingham-Hoover, AL	37.4
50	Oakland-Fremont, CA M.D.	35.9
51	Charleston-North Charleston, SC	35.5
52	Newark-Union, NJ-PA M.D.	33.8
53	Huntsville, AL	31.7
54	Augusta, GA-SC	30.4
55	Myrtle Beach, SC	28.6
56	Eugene-Springfield, OR	27.8
57	Hartford, CT	26.7
58	El Paso, TX	25.0
58	San Francisco-S. Mateo, CA M.D.	25.0
60	Lubbock, TX	23.3
61	Fort Walton Beach, FL	22.7
62	Sarasota-Bradenton-Venice, FL	22.2
63	Philadelphia (greater) PA-NJ-DE	21.8
64	Santa Fe, NM	21.2
65	Gadsden, AL	20.8
66	Cincinnati-Middletown, OH-KY-IN	20.4
67	Virginia Beach-Norfolk, VA-NC	19.7
68	Jacksonville, FL	19.1
69	Albany, GA	18.2
70	Rochester, NY	17.4
71	Fresno, CA	16.7
71	Minneapolis-St. Paul, MN-WI	16.7
73	Tacoma, WA M.D.	15.0
74	Bakersfield, CA	14.9
75	Decatur, AL	14.6
76	Houston, TX	14.3
77	Miami-Dade County, FL M.D.	13.8
77	Seattle-Bellevue, WA M.D.	13.8
79	Nashville-Davidson, TN	12.5
80	Columbia, SC	12.0
81	Baltimore-Towson, MD	10.8
82	Sumter, SC	10.7
83	Topeka, KS	10.6
84	Merced, CA	9.8
84	Toledo, OH	9.8
86	Portland-Vancouver, OR-WA	9.5
86	San Jose, CA	9.5
88	Phoenix-Mesa-Scottsdale, AZ	6.1
89	Omaha-Council Bluffs, NE-IA	4.3
89	Wichita, KS	4.3
91	Sacramento, CA	3.8
91	Santa Ana-Anaheim, CA M.D.	3.8
93	Detroit (greater), MI	3.7
94	Las Vegas-Paradise, NV	3.0
94	Scranton--Wilkes-Barre, PA	3.0
96	Lawton, OK	2.9
97	Clarksville, TN-KY	2.1
98	Knoxville, TN	2.0
99	Corpus Christi, TX	1.7
100	Baton Rouge, LA	1.4
101	Boise City-Nampa, ID	0.0
101	Brownsville-Harlingen, TX	0.0
101	Columbus, OH	0.0
101	Cumberland, MD-WV	0.0
101	Iowa City, IA	0.0
101	Kokomo, IN	0.0
101	La Crosse, WI-MN	0.0
108	Beaumont-Port Arthur, TX	(2.1)
109	Trenton-Ewing, NJ	(3.4)
110	Port St. Lucie, FL	(3.9)
111	San Antonio, TX	(4.1)
112	Cheyenne, WY	(4.2)
113	Denver-Aurora, CO	(4.3)
114	Cape Coral-Fort Myers, FL	(4.4)
115	Yakima, WA	(4.5)
116	Bismarck, ND	(4.8)
116	Fort Smith, AR-OK	(4.8)
118	Honolulu, HI	(5.0)
119	Springfield, MO	(5.6)
120	Wilmington, NC	(6.0)
121	Montgomery, AL	(6.1)
122	Amarillo, TX	(6.5)
123	Albuquerque, NM	(7.3)
124	Tucson, AZ	(7.4)
125	Tampa-St Petersburg, FL	(7.5)
126	Riverside-San Bernardino, CA	(8.0)
127	Pittsburgh, PA	(8.3)
128	Lake Charles, LA	(8.5)
129	Fort Lauderdale, FL M.D.	(9.4)
130	Kennewick-Richland-Pasco, WA	(10.0)
131	Yuba City, CA	(10.2)
132	New York-W. Plains NY-NJ M.D.	(10.6)
133	Athens-Clarke County, GA	(10.7)
134	Atlanta, GA	(10.8)
135	Lansing-East Lansing, MI	(11.1)
135	New Orleans, LA	(11.1)
137	Utica-Rome, NY	(11.5)
138	Richmond, VA	(11.6)
139	Duluth, MN-WI	(12.5)
140	Anchorage, AK	(13.4)
141	Columbia, MO	(13.6)
142	Pine Bluff, AR	(14.0)
143	Punta Gorda, FL	(14.3)
144	Los Angeles County, CA M.D.	(14.4)
145	Pocatello, ID	(15.4)
146	Stockton, CA	(15.8)
147	St. Cloud, MN	(16.7)
148	Ocala, FL	(16.9)
149	Pueblo, CO	(17.0)
150	Greenville, NC	(17.2)
151	Spokane, WA	(17.4)
152	Dallas-Plano-Irving, TX M.D.	(17.9)
153	Fort Worth-Arlington, TX M.D.	(18.0)
154	Naples-Marco Island, FL	(18.5)
155	Shreveport-Bossier City, LA	(19.3)
156	Wichita Falls, TX	(20.0)
157	Louisville, KY-IN	(21.7)
158	Goldsboro, NC	(22.1)
159	Columbus, GA-AL	(22.7)
160	Jackson, MS	(22.9)
161	Lincoln, NE	(25.0)
161	Provo-Orem, UT	(25.0)
163	State College, PA	(27.6)
164	Savannah, GA	(27.7)
165	Lakeland, FL	(28.3)
166	Tyler, TX	(29.5)
167	Binghamton, NY	(31.4)
168	Tallahassee, FL	(31.9)
169	Daytona Beach, FL	(32.3)
170	Santa Rosa-Petaluma, CA	(32.4)
171	Pensacola, FL	(32.6)

Note: All listings are for Metropolitan Statistical Areas (M.S.A.s) except for those ending with "M.D." Listings with "M.D." are Metropolitan Divisions which are smaller parts of eleven large M.S.A.s. See explanatory note at beginning of metropolitan area section on page 23.

RANK	METROPOLITAN AREA	% CHANGE
172	Glens Falls, NY	(33.3)
173	Fayetteville, NC	(33.6)
174	Danville, VA	(34.3)
175	Chattanooga, TN-GA	(35.0)
176	South Bend-Mishawaka, IN-MI	(35.4)
177	Waco, TX	(35.8)
178	Austin-Round Rock, TX	(36.7)
179	Casper, WY	(37.8)
180	McAllen-Edinburg-Mission, TX	(40.3)
181	Madison, WI	(41.7)
182	Panama City-Lynn Haven, FL	(42.3)
183	Erie, PA	(44.0)
184	Salinas, CA	(46.3)
185	Great Falls, MT	(49.0)
186	Reading, PA	(49.2)
187	Alexandria, LA	(50.0)
187	Jackson, MI	(50.0)
189	Lynchburg, VA	(50.8)
190	Williamsport, PA	(52.9)
191	Lewiston-Auburn, ME	(55.0)
192	Colorado Springs, CO	(58.3)
193	Green Bay, WI	(58.8)
194	Bloomington, IN	(61.4)
195	Greeley, CO	(63.8)
196	Victoria, TX	(64.9)
197	Altoona, PA	(65.2)
198	Lafayette, IN	(65.6)
199	Sherman-Denison, TX	(69.2)
200	Asheville, NC	(70.0)
201	Sioux City, IA-NE-SD	(70.8)
202	Bellingham, WA	(78.3)
203	Dubuque, IA	(100.0)
203	Eau Claire, WI	(100.0)
203	Rapid City, SD	(100.0)
NA	Abilene, TX**	NA
NA	Albany-Schenectady-Troy, NY**	NA
NA	Ames, IA**	NA
NA	Anderson, SC**	NA
NA	Ann Arbor, MI**	NA
NA	Appleton, WI**	NA
NA	Atlantic City, NJ**	NA
NA	Bangor, ME**	NA
NA	Barnstable Town, MA**	NA
NA	Battle Creek, MI**	NA
NA	Bay City, MI**	NA
NA	Bend, OR**	NA
NA	Bethesda-Frederick, MD M.D.**	NA
NA	Billings, MT***	NA
NA	Blacksburg, VA**	NA
NA	Bowling Green, KY**	NA
NA	Brunswick, GA**	NA
NA	Burlington, NC**	NA
NA	Camden, NJ M.D.**	NA
NA	Carson City, NV**	NA
NA	Charlotte-Gastonia, NC-SC**	NA
NA	Charlottesville, VA**	NA
NA	Chicago, IL**	NA
NA	Cleveland-Elyria-Mentor, OH**	NA
NA	Cleveland, TN**	NA
NA	Coeur d'Alene, ID**	NA
NA	College Station-Bryan, TX**	NA
NA	Columbus, IN**	NA
NA	Dallas (greater), TX**	NA
NA	Dalton, GA**	NA
NA	Dayton, OH**	NA
NA	Des Moines-West Des Moines, IA**	NA
NA	Detroit-Livonia-Dearborn, MI M.D.**	NA
NA	Dothan, AL**	NA
NA	Durham, NC**	NA
NA	Edison, NJ M.D.**	NA
NA	El Centro, CA**	NA
NA	Elizabethtown, KY**	NA
NA	Elmira, NY**	NA
NA	Evansville, IN-KY**	NA
NA	Fairbanks, AK**	NA
NA	Fargo, ND-MN***	NA
NA	Farmington, NM**	NA
NA	Fayetteville, AR-MO**	NA
NA	Fond du Lac, WI**	NA
NA	Fort Collins-Loveland, CO***	NA
NA	Fort Wayne, IN**	NA
NA	Gainesville, GA**	NA
NA	Grand Forks, ND-MN***	NA
NA	Grand Rapids-Wyoming, MI**	NA
NA	Greensboro-High Point, NC**	NA
NA	Greenville, SC**	NA
NA	Hagerstown-Martinsburg, MD-WV**	NA
NA	Hanford-Corcoran, CA**	NA
NA	Harrisburg-Carlisle, PA**	NA
NA	Harrisonburg, VA**	NA
NA	Hattiesburg, MS**	NA
NA	Holland-Grand Haven, MI**	NA
NA	Hot Springs, AR**	NA
NA	Huntington-Ashland, WV-KY-OH**	NA
NA	Idaho Falls, ID**	NA
NA	Indianapolis, IN**	NA
NA	Ithaca, NY**	NA
NA	Jacksonville, NC**	NA
NA	Jefferson City, MO**	NA
NA	Johnson City, TN**	NA
NA	Johnstown, PA**	NA
NA	Kalamazoo-Portage, MI**	NA
NA	Kansas City, MO-KS**	NA
NA	Kingsport, TN-VA**	NA
NA	Kingston, NY**	NA
NA	Lake Havasu City-Kingman, AZ**	NA
NA	Las Cruces, NM**	NA
NA	Lebanon, PA**	NA
NA	Lewiston, ID-WA**	NA
NA	Lexington-Fayette, KY**	NA
NA	Lima, OH**	NA
NA	Logan, UT-ID**	NA
NA	Longview, WA**	NA
NA	Los Angeles (greater), CA**	NA
NA	Macon, GA**	NA
NA	Madera, CA**	NA
NA	Manchester-Nashua, NH**	NA
NA	Mansfield, OH**	NA
NA	Memphis, TN-MS-AR**	NA
NA	Miami (greater), FL**	NA
NA	Michigan City-La Porte, IN**	NA
NA	Midland, TX**	NA
NA	Milwaukee, WI**	NA
NA	Missoula, MT**	NA
NA	Mobile, AL**	NA
NA	Monroe, LA**	NA
NA	Monroe, MI**	NA
NA	Morgantown, WV**	NA
NA	Morristown, TN**	NA
NA	Mount Vernon-Anacortes, WA**	NA
NA	Muskegon-Norton Shores, MI**	NA
NA	Napa, CA**	NA
NA	Nassau-Suffolk, NY M.D.**	NA
NA	New York (greater), NY-NJ-PA**	NA
NA	Niles-Benton Harbor, MI**	NA
NA	Ocean City, NJ**	NA
NA	Odessa, TX**	NA
NA	Ogden-Clearfield, UT**	NA
NA	Oshkosh-Neenah, WI**	NA
NA	Oxnard-Thousand Oaks, CA**	NA
NA	Palm Coast, FL**	NA
NA	Pascagoula, MS**	NA
NA	Philadelphia, PA M.D.**	NA
NA	Pittsfield, MA**	NA
NA	Portland, ME**	NA
NA	Poughkeepsie, NY**	NA
NA	Prescott, AZ**	NA
NA	Raleigh-Cary, NC**	NA
NA	Roanoke, VA**	NA
NA	Rome, GA**	NA
NA	Saginaw, MI**	NA
NA	Salisbury, MD**	NA
NA	Salt Lake City, UT**	NA
NA	San Angelo, TX***	NA
NA	San Francisco (greater), CA**	NA
NA	Sandusky, OH**	NA
NA	Santa Barbara-Santa Maria, CA**	NA
NA	Seattle (greater), WA**	NA
NA	Sebastian-Vero Beach, FL**	NA
NA	Sheboygan, WI***	NA
NA	Spartanburg, SC**	NA
NA	Springfield, MA**	NA
NA	Springfield, OH**	NA
NA	St. Joseph, MO-KS***	NA
NA	St. Louis, MO-IL**	NA
NA	Syracuse, NY**	NA
NA	Valdosta, GA**	NA
NA	Vallejo-Fairfield, CA**	NA
NA	Warner Robins, GA**	NA
NA	Warren-Farmington Hills, MI M.D.**	NA
NA	Washington (greater) DC-VA-MD**	NA
NA	Washington, DC-VA-MD-WV M.D.**	NA
NA	Wausau, WI***	NA
NA	Wenatchee, WA**	NA
NA	Wheeling, WV-OH**	NA
NA	Wilmington, DE-MD-NJ M.D.**	NA
NA	Winchester, VA-WV**	NA
NA	Winston-Salem, NC**	NA
NA	Worcester, MA**	NA

Source: CQ Press using data from Federal Bureau of Investigation "Crime in the United States 2006" (Uniform Crime Reports, September 24, 2007)

**Includes nonnegligent manslaughter. **Not available. ***These metro areas had murder rates of 0 in 2002 but had at least one murder in 2006. Calculating percent increase from zero results in an infinite number. This is shown as "NA."*

13. Rapes in 2006

National Total = 92,455 Rapes*

RANK	METROPOLITAN AREA	RAPES
209	Abilene, TX	75
97	Albany-Schenectady-Troy, NY	207
294	Albany, GA	37
52	Albuquerque, NM	420
213	Alexandria, LA	73
263	Altoona, PA	49
168	Amarillo, TX	103
299	Ames, IA	35
80	Anchorage, AK	256
188	Anderson, SC	90
154	Ann Arbor, MI	114
257	Appleton, WI	54
165	Asheville, NC	105
221	Athens-Clarke County, GA	68
15	Atlanta, GA	1,098
198	Atlantic City, NJ	79
91	Augusta, GA-SC	226
44	Austin-Round Rock, TX	523
100	Bakersfield, CA	201
45	Baltimore-Towson, MD	501
334	Bangor, ME	14
239	Barnstable Town, MA	62
86	Baton Rouge, LA	236
168	Battle Creek, MI	103
235	Bay City, MI	64
118	Beaumont-Port Arthur, TX	162
206	Bellingham, WA	76
272	Bend, OR	43
108	Bethesda-Frederick, MD M.D.	180
285	Billings, MT	38
221	Binghamton, NY	68
46	Birmingham-Hoover, AL	487
312	Bismarck, ND	29
235	Blacksburg, VA	64
267	Bloomington, IN	47
78	Boise City-Nampa, ID	260
242	Bowling Green, KY	60
89	Bremerton-Silverdale, WA	231
146	Brownsville-Harlingen, TX	125
302	Brunswick, GA	34
62	Buffalo-Niagara Falls, NY	331
305	Burlington, NC	31
68	Camden, NJ M.D.	305
103	Cape Coral-Fort Myers, FL	196
341	Carson City, NV	2
323	Casper, WY	21
244	Cedar Rapids, IA	59
72	Charleston-North Charleston, SC	291
195	Charleston, WV	82
41	Charlotte-Gastonia, NC-SC	569
241	Charlottesville, VA	61
106	Chattanooga, TN-GA	187
285	Cheyenne, WY	38
NA	Chicago, IL**	NA
156	Chico, CA	113
22	Cincinnati-Middletown, OH-KY-IN	907
180	Clarksville, TN-KY	95

RANK	METROPOLITAN AREA	RAPES
32	Cleveland-Elyria-Mentor, OH	766
281	Cleveland, TN	39
205	Coeur d'Alene, ID	77
188	College Station-Bryan, TX	90
63	Colorado Springs, CO	326
303	Columbia, MO	33
81	Columbia, SC	250
295	Columbus, GA-AL	36
332	Columbus, IN	16
23	Columbus, OH	874
82	Corpus Christi, TX	247
285	Cumberland, MD-WV	38
4	Dallas (greater), TX	2,036
11	Dallas-Plano-Irving, TX M.D.	1,313
305	Dalton, GA	31
327	Danville, VA	19
118	Daytona Beach, FL	162
57	Dayton, OH	367
269	Decatur, AL	46
14	Denver-Aurora, CO	1,153
147	Des Moines-West Des Moines, IA	122
7	Detroit (greater), MI	1,822
20	Detroit-Livonia-Dearborn, MI M.D.	964
237	Dothan, AL	63
186	Dover, DE	92
320	Dubuque, IA	23
NA	Duluth, MN-WI**	NA
124	Durham, NC	157
329	Eau Claire, WI	18
88	Edison, NJ M.D.	233
329	El Centro, CA	18
64	El Paso, TX	322
315	Elizabethtown, KY	27
245	Elkhart-Goshen, IN	58
326	Elmira, NY	20
156	Erie, PA	113
180	Eugene-Springfield, OR	95
172	Evansville, IN-KY	100
221	Fairbanks, AK	68
NA	Fargo, ND-MN**	NA
172	Farmington, NM	100
78	Fayetteville, AR-MO	260
165	Fayetteville, NC	105
232	Flagstaff, AZ	65
66	Flint, MI	310
198	Florence, SC	79
277	Fond du Lac, WI	41
156	Fort Collins-Loveland, CO	113
47	Fort Lauderdale, FL M.D.	477
122	Fort Smith, AR-OK	159
247	Fort Walton Beach, FL	57
170	Fort Wayne, IN	102
33	Fort Worth-Arlington, TX M.D.	723
95	Fresno, CA	214
251	Gadsden, AL	55
107	Gainesville, FL	181
295	Gainesville, GA	36

RANK	METROPOLITAN AREA	RAPES
285	Glens Falls, NY	38
338	Goldsboro, NC	9
NA	Grand Forks, ND-MN**	NA
272	Grand Junction, CO	43
55	Grand Rapids-Wyoming, MI	396
337	Great Falls, MT	11
185	Greeley, CO	93
203	Green Bay, WI	78
118	Greensboro-High Point, NC	162
221	Greenville, NC	68
95	Greenville, SC	214
274	Hagerstown-Martinsburg, MD-WV	42
305	Hanford-Corcoran, CA	31
126	Harrisburg-Carlisle, PA	148
309	Harrisonburg, VA	30
108	Hartford, CT	180
266	Hattiesburg, MS	48
121	Holland-Grand Haven, MI	160
90	Honolulu, HI	229
285	Hot Springs, AR	38
203	Houma, LA	78
6	Houston, TX	1,881
192	Huntington-Ashland, WV-KY-OH	87
129	Huntsville, AL	146
218	Idaho Falls, ID	69
36	Indianapolis, IN	678
229	Iowa City, IA	66
309	Ithaca, NY	30
60	Jacksonville, FL	340
232	Jacksonville, NC	65
159	Jackson, MI	112
74	Jackson, MS	282
278	Jackson, TN	40
227	Janesville, WI	67
281	Jefferson City, MO	39
299	Johnson City, TN	35
319	Johnstown, PA	24
251	Jonesboro, AR	55
198	Joplin, MO	79
113	Kalamazoo-Portage, MI	172
24	Kansas City, MO-KS	858
218	Kennewick-Richland-Pasco, WA	69
NA	Killeen-Temple-Fort Hood, TX**	NA
165	Kingsport, TN-VA	105
259	Kingston, NY	50
104	Knoxville, TN	192
314	Kokomo, IN	28
NA	La Crosse, WI-MN**	NA
209	Lafayette, IN	75
128	Lake Charles, LA	147
315	Lake Havasu City-Kingman, AZ	27
83	Lakeland, FL	245
188	Lancaster, PA	90
76	Lansing-East Lansing, MI	275
175	Laredo, TX	96
137	Las Cruces, NM	133
26	Las Vegas-Paradise, NV	845

Note: All listings are for Metropolitan Statistical Areas (M.S.A.s) except for those ending with "M.D." Listings with "M.D." are Metropolitan Divisions which are smaller parts of eleven large M.S.A.s. See explanatory note at beginning of metropolitan area section on page 23.

RANK	METROPOLITAN AREA	RAPES
247	Lawrence, KS	57
193	Lawton, OK	86
258	Lebanon, PA	53
285	Lewiston-Auburn, ME	38
338	Lewiston, ID-WA	9
115	Lexington-Fayette, KY	167
212	Lima, OH	74
164	Lincoln, NE	108
56	Little Rock, AR	377
320	Logan, UT-ID	23
162	Longview, TX	109
198	Longview, WA	79
2	Los Angeles County, CA M.D.	2,342
1	Los Angeles (greater), CA	2,817
77	Louisville, KY-IN	267
152	Lubbock, TX	115
218	Lynchburg, VA	69
186	Macon, GA	92
251	Madera, CA	55
134	Madison, WI	139
182	Manchester-Nashua, NH	94
213	Mansfield, OH	73
110	McAllen-Edinburg-Mission, TX	179
251	Medford, OR	55
40	Memphis, TN-MS-AR	589
197	Merced, CA	81
8	Miami (greater), FL	1,759
29	Miami-Dade County, FL M.D.	822
281	Michigan City-La Porte, IN	39
221	Midland, TX	68
94	Milwaukee, WI	216
NA	Minneapolis-St. Paul, MN-WI**	NA
259	Missoula, MT	50
149	Mobile, AL	120
125	Modesto, CA	151
232	Monroe, LA	65
249	Monroe, MI	56
150	Montgomery, AL	117
274	Morgantown, WV	42
303	Morristown, TN	33
216	Mount Vernon-Anacortes, WA	71
229	Muncie, IN	66
130	Muskegon-Norton Shores, MI	145
117	Myrtle Beach, SC	164
295	Napa, CA	36
195	Naples-Marco Island, FL	82
39	Nashville-Davidson, TN	593
101	Nassau-Suffolk, NY M.D.	200
70	New Orleans, LA	299
3	New York (greater), NY-NJ-PA	2,106
9	New York-W. Plains NY-NJ M.D.	1,376
71	Newark-Union, NJ-PA M.D.	297
161	Niles-Benton Harbor, MI	110
33	Oakland-Fremont, CA M.D.	723
111	Ocala, FL	177
312	Ocean City, NJ	29
334	Odessa, TX	14
126	Ogden-Clearfield, UT	148
43	Oklahoma City, OK	543
209	Olympia, WA	75

RANK	METROPOLITAN AREA	RAPES
67	Omaha-Council Bluffs, NE-IA	307
30	Orlando, FL	792
320	Oshkosh-Neenah, WI	23
142	Oxnard-Thousand Oaks, CA	128
92	Palm Bay-Melbourne, FL	223
340	Palm Coast, FL	8
174	Panama City-Lynn Haven, FL	97
251	Pascagoula, MS	55
101	Pensacola, FL	200
5	Philadelphia (greater) PA-NJ-DE	1,890
10	Philadelphia, PA M.D.	1,364
13	Phoenix-Mesa-Scottsdale, AZ	1,269
263	Pine Bluff, AR	49
51	Pittsburgh, PA	452
217	Pittsfield, MA	70
274	Pocatello, ID	42
154	Port St. Lucie, FL	114
26	Portland-Vancouver, OR-WA	845
132	Portland, ME	141
171	Poughkeepsie, NY	101
267	Prescott, AZ	47
162	Provo-Orem, UT	109
259	Pueblo, CO	50
333	Punta Gorda, FL	15
323	Racine, WI	21
99	Raleigh-Cary, NC	203
175	Rapid City, SD	96
194	Reading, PA	83
182	Redding, CA	94
132	Reno-Sparks, NV	141
75	Richmond, VA	280
17	Riverside-San Bernardino, CA	1,054
175	Roanoke, VA	96
NA	Rochester, MN**	NA
84	Rochester, NY	239
299	Rocky Mount, NC	35
295	Rome, GA	36
37	Sacramento, CA	653
123	Saginaw, MI	158
142	Salem, OR	128
151	Salinas, CA	116
263	Salisbury, MD	49
49	Salt Lake City, UT	473
249	San Angelo, TX	56
35	San Antonio, TX	714
31	San Diego, CA	777
16	San Francisco (greater), CA	1,079
58	San Francisco-S. Mateo, CA M.D.	356
61	San Jose, CA	338
198	San Luis Obispo, CA	79
334	Sandusky, OH	14
48	Santa Ana-Anaheim, CA M.D.	475
138	Santa Barbara-Santa Maria, CA	131
175	Santa Cruz-Watsonville, CA	96
221	Santa Fe, NM	68
112	Santa Rosa-Petaluma, CA	173
105	Sarasota-Bradenton-Venice, FL	188
188	Savannah, GA	90
134	Scranton--Wilkes-Barre, PA	139
12	Seattle (greater), WA	1,285

RANK	METROPOLITAN AREA	RAPES
21	Seattle-Bellevue, WA M.D.	932
285	Sebastian-Vero Beach, FL	38
269	Sheboygan, WI	46
317	Sherman-Denison, TX	25
97	Shreveport-Bossier City, LA	207
242	Sioux City, IA-NE-SD	60
144	Sioux Falls, SD	126
159	South Bend-Mishawaka, IN-MI	112
206	Spartanburg, SC	76
140	Spokane, WA	129
72	Springfield, MA	291
152	Springfield, MO	115
213	Springfield, OH	73
317	State College, PA	25
116	Stockton, CA	165
NA	St. Cloud, MN**	NA
323	St. Joseph, MO-KS	21
38	St. Louis, MO-IL	639
278	Sumter, SC	40
130	Syracuse, NY	145
59	Tacoma, WA M.D.	353
84	Tallahassee, FL	239
18	Tampa-St Petersburg, FL	1,025
227	Texarkana, TX-Texarkana, AR	67
87	Toledo, OH	234
175	Topeka, KS	96
229	Trenton-Ewing, NJ	66
54	Tucson, AZ	400
53	Tulsa, OK	408
182	Tuscaloosa, AL	94
206	Tyler, TX	76
251	Utica-Rome, NY	55
285	Valdosta, GA	38
140	Vallejo-Fairfield, CA	129
245	Victoria, TX	58
259	Vineland, NJ	50
42	Virginia Beach-Norfolk, VA-NC	547
139	Visalia-Porterville, CA	130
147	Waco, TX	122
305	Warner Robins, GA	31
24	Warren-Farmington Hills, MI M.D.	858
19	Washington (greater) DC-VA-MD	1,004
28	Washington, DC-VA-MD-WV M.D.	824
237	Waterloo-Cedar Falls, IA	63
329	Wausau, WI	18
309	Wenatchee, WA	30
50	West Palm Beach, FL M.D.	460
285	Wheeling, WV-OH	38
278	Wichita Falls, TX	40
65	Wichita, KS	314
327	Williamsport, PA	19
93	Wilmington, DE-MD-NJ M.D.	221
136	Wilmington, NC	134
281	Winchester, VA-WV	39
114	Winston-Salem, NC	171
68	Worcester, MA	305
144	Yakima, WA	126
239	Yuba City, CA	62
269	Yuma, AZ	46

Source: Federal Bureau of Investigation
"Crime in the United States 2006" (Uniform Crime Reports, September 24, 2007)
**Forcible rape is the carnal knowledge of a female forcibly and against her will. Assaults or attempts to commit rape by force or threat of force are included. However, statutory rape without force and other sex offenses are excluded. **Not available*

13. Rapes in 2006 (continued)

National Total = 92,455 Rapes*

RANK	METROPOLITAN AREA	RAPES
1	Los Angeles (greater), CA	2,817
2	Los Angeles County, CA M.D.	2,342
3	New York (greater), NY-NJ-PA	2,106
4	Dallas (greater), TX	2,036
5	Philadelphia (greater) PA-NJ-DE	1,890
6	Houston, TX	1,881
7	Detroit (greater), MI	1,822
8	Miami (greater), FL	1,759
9	New York-W. Plains NY-NJ M.D.	1,376
10	Philadelphia, PA M.D.	1,364
11	Dallas-Plano-Irving, TX M.D.	1,313
12	Seattle (greater), WA	1,285
13	Phoenix-Mesa-Scottsdale, AZ	1,269
14	Denver-Aurora, CO	1,153
15	Atlanta, GA	1,098
16	San Francisco (greater), CA	1,079
17	Riverside-San Bernardino, CA	1,054
18	Tampa-St Petersburg, FL	1,025
19	Washington (greater) DC-VA-MD	1,004
20	Detroit-Livonia-Dearborn, MI M.D.	964
21	Seattle-Bellevue, WA M.D.	932
22	Cincinnati-Middletown, OH-KY-IN	907
23	Columbus, OH	874
24	Kansas City, MO-KS	858
24	Warren-Farmington Hills, MI M.D.	858
26	Las Vegas-Paradise, NV	845
26	Portland-Vancouver, OR-WA	845
28	Washington, DC-VA-MD-WV M.D.	824
29	Miami-Dade County, FL M.D.	822
30	Orlando, FL	792
31	San Diego, CA	777
32	Cleveland-Elyria-Mentor, OH	766
33	Fort Worth-Arlington, TX M.D.	723
33	Oakland-Fremont, CA M.D.	723
35	San Antonio, TX	714
36	Indianapolis, IN	678
37	Sacramento, CA	653
38	St. Louis, MO-IL	639
39	Nashville-Davidson, TN	593
40	Memphis, TN-MS-AR	589
41	Charlotte-Gastonia, NC-SC	569
42	Virginia Beach-Norfolk, VA-NC	547
43	Oklahoma City, OK	543
44	Austin-Round Rock, TX	523
45	Baltimore-Towson, MD	501
46	Birmingham-Hoover, AL	487
47	Fort Lauderdale, FL M.D.	477
48	Santa Ana-Anaheim, CA M.D.	475
49	Salt Lake City, UT	473
50	West Palm Beach, FL M.D.	460
51	Pittsburgh, PA	452
52	Albuquerque, NM	420
53	Tulsa, OK	408
54	Tucson, AZ	400
55	Grand Rapids-Wyoming, MI	396
56	Little Rock, AR	377
57	Dayton, OH	367
58	San Francisco-S. Mateo, CA M.D.	356
59	Tacoma, WA M.D.	353
60	Jacksonville, FL	340
61	San Jose, CA	338
62	Buffalo-Niagara Falls, NY	331
63	Colorado Springs, CO	326
64	El Paso, TX	322
65	Wichita, KS	314
66	Flint, MI	310
67	Omaha-Council Bluffs, NE-IA	307
68	Camden, NJ M.D.	305
68	Worcester, MA	305
70	New Orleans, LA	299
71	Newark-Union, NJ-PA M.D.	297
72	Charleston-North Charleston, SC	291
72	Springfield, MA	291
74	Jackson, MS	282
75	Richmond, VA	280
76	Lansing-East Lansing, MI	275
77	Louisville, KY-IN	267
78	Boise City-Nampa, ID	260
78	Fayetteville, AR-MO	260
80	Anchorage, AK	256
81	Columbia, SC	250
82	Corpus Christi, TX	247
83	Lakeland, FL	245
84	Rochester, NY	239
84	Tallahassee, FL	239
86	Baton Rouge, LA	236
87	Toledo, OH	234
88	Edison, NJ M.D.	233
89	Bremerton-Silverdale, WA	231
90	Honolulu, HI	229
91	Augusta, GA-SC	226
92	Palm Bay-Melbourne, FL	223
93	Wilmington, DE-MD-NJ M.D.	221
94	Milwaukee, WI	216
95	Fresno, CA	214
95	Greenville, SC	214
97	Albany-Schenectady-Troy, NY	207
97	Shreveport-Bossier City, LA	207
99	Raleigh-Cary, NC	203
100	Bakersfield, CA	201
101	Nassau-Suffolk, NY M.D.	200
101	Pensacola, FL	200
103	Cape Coral-Fort Myers, FL	196
104	Knoxville, TN	192
105	Sarasota-Bradenton-Venice, FL	188
106	Chattanooga, TN-GA	187
107	Gainesville, FL	181
108	Bethesda-Frederick, MD M.D.	180
108	Hartford, CT	180
110	McAllen-Edinburg-Mission, TX	179
111	Ocala, FL	177
112	Santa Rosa-Petaluma, CA	173
113	Kalamazoo-Portage, MI	172
114	Winston-Salem, NC	171
115	Lexington-Fayette, KY	167
116	Stockton, CA	165
117	Myrtle Beach, SC	164
118	Beaumont-Port Arthur, TX	162
118	Daytona Beach, FL	162
118	Greensboro-High Point, NC	162
121	Holland-Grand Haven, MI	160
122	Fort Smith, AR-OK	159
123	Saginaw, MI	158
124	Durham, NC	157
125	Modesto, CA	151
126	Harrisburg-Carlisle, PA	148
126	Ogden-Clearfield, UT	148
128	Lake Charles, LA	147
129	Huntsville, AL	146
130	Muskegon-Norton Shores, MI	145
130	Syracuse, NY	145
132	Portland, ME	141
132	Reno-Sparks, NV	141
134	Madison, WI	139
134	Scranton--Wilkes-Barre, PA	139
136	Wilmington, NC	134
137	Las Cruces, NM	133
138	Santa Barbara-Santa Maria, CA	131
139	Visalia-Porterville, CA	130
140	Spokane, WA	129
140	Vallejo-Fairfield, CA	129
142	Oxnard-Thousand Oaks, CA	128
142	Salem, OR	128
144	Sioux Falls, SD	126
144	Yakima, WA	126
146	Brownsville-Harlingen, TX	125
147	Des Moines-West Des Moines, IA	122
147	Waco, TX	122
149	Mobile, AL	120
150	Montgomery, AL	117
151	Salinas, CA	116
152	Lubbock, TX	115
152	Springfield, MO	115
154	Ann Arbor, MI	114
154	Port St. Lucie, FL	114
156	Chico, CA	113
156	Erie, PA	113
156	Fort Collins-Loveland, CO	113
159	Jackson, MI	112
159	South Bend-Mishawaka, IN-MI	112
161	Niles-Benton Harbor, MI	110
162	Longview, TX	109
162	Provo-Orem, UT	109
164	Lincoln, NE	108
165	Asheville, NC	105
165	Fayetteville, NC	105
165	Kingsport, TN-VA	105
168	Amarillo, TX	103
168	Battle Creek, MI	103
170	Fort Wayne, IN	102
171	Poughkeepsie, NY	101

Note: All listings are for Metropolitan Statistical Areas (M.S.A.s) except for those ending with "M.D." Listings with "M.D." are Metropolitan Divisions which are smaller parts of eleven large M.S.A.s. See explanatory note at beginning of metropolitan area section on page 23.

Rank Order - Metro Area (continued)

RANK	METROPOLITAN AREA	RAPES
172	Evansville, IN-KY	100
172	Farmington, NM	100
174	Panama City-Lynn Haven, FL	97
175	Laredo, TX	96
175	Rapid City, SD	96
175	Roanoke, VA	96
175	Santa Cruz-Watsonville, CA	96
175	Topeka, KS	96
180	Clarksville, TN-KY	95
180	Eugene-Springfield, OR	95
182	Manchester-Nashua, NH	94
182	Redding, CA	94
182	Tuscaloosa, AL	94
185	Greeley, CO	93
186	Dover, DE	92
186	Macon, GA	92
188	Anderson, SC	90
188	College Station-Bryan, TX	90
188	Lancaster, PA	90
188	Savannah, GA	90
192	Huntington-Ashland, WV-KY-OH	87
193	Lawton, OK	86
194	Reading, PA	83
195	Charleston, WV	82
195	Naples-Marco Island, FL	82
197	Merced, CA	81
198	Atlantic City, NJ	79
198	Florence, SC	79
198	Joplin, MO	79
198	Longview, WA	79
198	San Luis Obispo, CA	79
203	Green Bay, WI	78
203	Houma, LA	78
205	Coeur d'Alene, ID	77
206	Bellingham, WA	76
206	Spartanburg, SC	76
206	Tyler, TX	76
209	Abilene, TX	75
209	Lafayette, IN	75
209	Olympia, WA	75
212	Lima, OH	74
213	Alexandria, LA	73
213	Mansfield, OH	73
213	Springfield, OH	73
216	Mount Vernon-Anacortes, WA	71
217	Pittsfield, MA	70
218	Idaho Falls, ID	69
218	Kennewick-Richland-Pasco, WA	69
218	Lynchburg, VA	69
221	Athens-Clarke County, GA	68
221	Binghamton, NY	68
221	Fairbanks, AK	68
221	Greenville, NC	68
221	Midland, TX	68
221	Santa Fe, NM	68
227	Janesville, WI	67
227	Texarkana, TX-Texarkana, AR	67
229	Iowa City, IA	66
229	Muncie, IN	66
229	Trenton-Ewing, NJ	66
232	Flagstaff, AZ	65
232	Jacksonville, NC	65
232	Monroe, LA	65
235	Bay City, MI	64
235	Blacksburg, VA	64
237	Dothan, AL	63
237	Waterloo-Cedar Falls, IA	63
239	Barnstable Town, MA	62
239	Yuba City, CA	62
241	Charlottesville, VA	61
242	Bowling Green, KY	60
242	Sioux City, IA-NE-SD	60
244	Cedar Rapids, IA	59
245	Elkhart-Goshen, IN	58
245	Victoria, TX	58
247	Fort Walton Beach, FL	57
247	Lawrence, KS	57
249	Monroe, MI	56
249	San Angelo, TX	56
251	Gadsden, AL	55
251	Jonesboro, AR	55
251	Madera, CA	55
251	Medford, OR	55
251	Pascagoula, MS	55
251	Utica-Rome, NY	55
257	Appleton, WI	54
258	Lebanon, PA	53
259	Kingston, NY	50
259	Missoula, MT	50
259	Pueblo, CO	50
259	Vineland, NJ	50
263	Altoona, PA	49
263	Pine Bluff, AR	49
263	Salisbury, MD	49
266	Hattiesburg, MS	48
267	Bloomington, IN	47
267	Prescott, AZ	47
269	Decatur, AL	46
269	Sheboygan, WI	46
269	Yuma, AZ	46
272	Bend, OR	43
272	Grand Junction, CO	43
274	Hagerstown-Martinsburg, MD-WV	42
274	Morgantown, WV	42
274	Pocatello, ID	42
277	Fond du Lac, WI	41
278	Jackson, TN	40
278	Sumter, SC	40
278	Wichita Falls, TX	40
281	Cleveland, TN	39
281	Jefferson City, MO	39
281	Michigan City-La Porte, IN	39
281	Winchester, VA-WV	39
285	Billings, MT	38
285	Cheyenne, WY	38
285	Cumberland, MD-WV	38
285	Glens Falls, NY	38
285	Hot Springs, AR	38
285	Lewiston-Auburn, ME	38
285	Sebastian-Vero Beach, FL	38
285	Valdosta, GA	38
285	Wheeling, WV-OH	38
294	Albany, GA	37
295	Columbus, GA-AL	36
295	Gainesville, GA	36
295	Napa, CA	36
295	Rome, GA	36
299	Ames, IA	35
299	Johnson City, TN	35
299	Rocky Mount, NC	35
302	Brunswick, GA	34
303	Columbia, MO	33
303	Morristown, TN	33
305	Burlington, NC	31
305	Dalton, GA	31
305	Hanford-Corcoran, CA	31
305	Warner Robins, GA	31
309	Harrisonburg, VA	30
309	Ithaca, NY	30
309	Wenatchee, WA	30
312	Bismarck, ND	29
312	Ocean City, NJ	29
314	Kokomo, IN	28
315	Elizabethtown, KY	27
315	Lake Havasu City-Kingman, AZ	27
317	Sherman-Denison, TX	25
317	State College, PA	25
319	Johnstown, PA	24
320	Dubuque, IA	23
320	Logan, UT-ID	23
320	Oshkosh-Neenah, WI	23
323	Casper, WY	21
323	Racine, WI	21
323	St. Joseph, MO-KS	21
326	Elmira, NY	20
327	Danville, VA	19
327	Williamsport, PA	19
329	Eau Claire, WI	18
329	El Centro, CA	18
329	Wausau, WI	18
332	Columbus, IN	16
333	Punta Gorda, FL	15
334	Bangor, ME	14
334	Odessa, TX	14
334	Sandusky, OH	14
337	Great Falls, MT	11
338	Goldsboro, NC	9
338	Lewiston, ID-WA	9
340	Palm Coast, FL	8
341	Carson City, NV	2
NA	Chicago, IL**	NA
NA	Duluth, MN-WI**	NA
NA	Fargo, ND-MN**	NA
NA	Grand Forks, ND-MN**	NA
NA	Killeen-Temple-Fort Hood, TX**	NA
NA	La Crosse, WI-MN**	NA
NA	Minneapolis-St. Paul, MN-WI**	NA
NA	Rochester, MN**	NA
NA	St. Cloud, MN**	NA

Source: Federal Bureau of Investigation
"Crime in the United States 2006" (Uniform Crime Reports, September 24, 2007)
**Forcible rape is the carnal knowledge of a female forcibly and against her will. Assaults or attempts to commit rape by force or threat of force are included. However, statutory rape without force and other sex offenses are excluded. **Not available*

14. Rape Rate in 2006

National Rate = 30.9 Rapes per 100,000 Population*

RANK	METROPOLITAN AREA	RATE
75	Abilene, TX	46.1
266	Albany-Schenectady-Troy, NY	24.3
285	Albany, GA	22.0
50	Albuquerque, NM	51.9
49	Alexandria, LA	52.0
130	Altoona, PA	38.6
95	Amarillo, TX	42.0
87	Ames, IA	43.5
2	Anchorage, AK	86.8
56	Anderson, SC	50.5
176	Ann Arbor, MI	33.4
260	Appleton, WI	25.0
249	Asheville, NC	26.2
138	Athens-Clarke County, GA	37.6
287	Atlanta, GA	21.6
216	Atlantic City, NJ	29.1
92	Augusta, GA-SC	42.3
163	Austin-Round Rock, TX	35.0
246	Bakersfield, CA	26.3
303	Baltimore-Towson, MD	18.8
336	Bangor, ME	9.5
237	Barnstable Town, MA	27.2
172	Baton Rouge, LA	33.9
10	Battle Creek, MI	74.2
27	Bay City, MI	58.8
107	Beaumont-Port Arthur, TX	41.1
112	Bellingham, WA	40.7
203	Bend, OR	29.9
318	Bethesda-Frederick, MD M.D.	15.6
254	Billings, MT	25.7
235	Binghamton, NY	27.3
82	Birmingham-Hoover, AL	44.3
214	Bismarck, ND	29.2
95	Blacksburg, VA	42.0
246	Bloomington, IN	26.3
71	Boise City-Nampa, ID	46.6
41	Bowling Green, KY	53.6
1	Bremerton-Silverdale, WA	94.4
190	Brownsville-Harlingen, TX	32.1
174	Brunswick, GA	33.5
220	Buffalo-Niagara Falls, NY	28.8
287	Burlington, NC	21.6
264	Camden, NJ M.D.	24.5
159	Cape Coral-Fort Myers, FL	35.4
340	Carson City, NV	3.5
205	Casper, WY	29.8
270	Cedar Rapids, IA	23.8
63	Charleston-North Charleston, SC	48.2
241	Charleston, WV	26.7
146	Charlotte-Gastonia, NC-SC	36.7
190	Charlottesville, VA	32.1
142	Chattanooga, TN-GA	37.3
84	Cheyenne, WY	44.1
NA	Chicago, IL**	NA
48	Chico, CA	52.3
85	Cincinnati-Middletown, OH-KY-IN	43.7
130	Clarksville, TN-KY	38.6
152	Cleveland-Elyria-Mentor, OH	36.0
155	Cleveland, TN	35.6
27	Coeur d'Alene, ID	58.8
75	College Station-Bryan, TX	46.1
37	Colorado Springs, CO	54.5
291	Columbia, MO	21.4
153	Columbia, SC	35.7
327	Columbus, GA-AL	12.3
287	Columbus, IN	21.6
55	Columbus, OH	51.1
29	Corpus Christi, TX	58.1
137	Cumberland, MD-WV	37.7
170	Dallas (greater), TX	34.0
180	Dallas-Plano-Irving, TX M.D.	32.8
280	Dalton, GA	22.8
311	Danville, VA	17.4
182	Daytona Beach, FL	32.5
87	Dayton, OH	43.5
199	Decatur, AL	30.7
64	Denver-Aurora, CO	47.9
278	Des Moines-West Des Moines, IA	23.2
112	Detroit (greater), MI	40.7
62	Detroit-Livonia-Dearborn, MI M.D.	48.4
78	Dothan, AL	45.7
20	Dover, DE	63.2
260	Dubuque, IA	25.0
NA	Duluth, MN-WI**	NA
173	Durham, NC	33.7
329	Eau Claire, WI	11.6
335	Edison, NJ M.D.	10.1
330	El Centro, CA	11.4
89	El Paso, TX	43.4
267	Elizabethtown, KY	24.2
210	Elkhart-Goshen, IN	29.5
283	Elmira, NY	22.3
115	Erie, PA	40.3
228	Eugene-Springfield, OR	27.9
224	Evansville, IN-KY	28.4
NA	Fairbanks, AK**	NA
NA	Fargo, ND-MN**	NA
7	Farmington, NM	78.2
19	Fayetteville, AR-MO	63.5
205	Fayetteville, NC	29.8
56	Flagstaff, AZ	50.5
14	Flint, MI	70.0
124	Florence, SC	39.2
107	Fond du Lac, WI	41.1
111	Fort Collins-Loveland, CO	40.8
245	Fort Lauderdale, FL M.D.	26.4
35	Fort Smith, AR-OK	55.2
198	Fort Walton Beach, FL	30.8
258	Fort Wayne, IN	25.1
149	Fort Worth-Arlington, TX M.D.	36.5
267	Fresno, CA	24.2
44	Gadsden, AL	52.8
11	Gainesville, FL	74.1
293	Gainesville, GA	21.0
210	Glens Falls, NY	29.5
338	Goldsboro, NC	7.7
NA	Grand Forks, ND-MN**	NA
182	Grand Junction, CO	32.5
53	Grand Rapids-Wyoming, MI	51.5
326	Great Falls, MT	13.7
120	Greeley, CO	39.9
251	Green Bay, WI	26.1
274	Greensboro-High Point, NC	23.5
110	Greenville, NC	41.0
155	Greenville, SC	35.6
313	Hagerstown-Martinsburg, MD-WV	16.7
291	Hanford-Corcoran, CA	21.4
225	Harrisburg-Carlisle, PA	28.3
243	Harrisonburg, VA	26.6
307	Hartford, CT	18.0
149	Hattiesburg, MS	36.5
21	Holland-Grand Haven, MI	62.8
258	Honolulu, HI	25.1
117	Hot Springs, AR	40.2
105	Houma, LA	41.2
166	Houston, TX	34.6
202	Huntington-Ashland, WV-KY-OH	30.3
124	Huntsville, AL	39.2
25	Idaho Falls, ID	59.3
107	Indianapolis, IN	41.1
68	Iowa City, IA	47.4
203	Ithaca, NY	29.9
240	Jacksonville, FL	26.8
99	Jacksonville, NC	41.8
17	Jackson, MI	68.6
39	Jackson, MS	54.2
155	Jackson, TN	35.6
91	Janesville, WI	42.4
238	Jefferson City, MO	26.9
305	Johnson City, TN	18.3
314	Johnstown, PA	16.2
61	Jonesboro, AR	48.5
70	Joplin, MO	47.2
40	Kalamazoo-Portage, MI	54.0
85	Kansas City, MO-KS	43.7
199	Kennewick-Richland-Pasco, WA	30.7
NA	Killeen-Temple-Fort Hood, TX**	NA
169	Kingsport, TN-VA	34.4
235	Kingston, NY	27.3
219	Knoxville, TN	28.9
233	Kokomo, IN	27.4
NA	La Crosse, WI-MN**	NA
114	Lafayette, IN	40.6
6	Lake Charles, LA	79.5
323	Lake Havasu City-Kingman, AZ	13.9
81	Lakeland, FL	44.4
305	Lancaster, PA	18.3
23	Lansing-East Lansing, MI	60.5
103	Laredo, TX	41.5
16	Las Cruces, NM	69.3
65	Las Vegas-Paradise, NV	47.8

Note: All listings are for Metropolitan Statistical Areas (M.S.A.s) except for those ending with "M.D." Listings with "M.D." are Metropolitan Divisions which are smaller parts of eleven large M.S.A.s. See explanatory note at beginning of metropolitan area section on page 23.

RANK	METROPOLITAN AREA	RATE
36	Lawrence, KS	55.0
9	Lawton, OK	75.8
93	Lebanon, PA	42.2
160	Lewiston-Auburn, ME	35.2
320	Lewiston, ID-WA	14.9
132	Lexington-Fayette, KY	38.5
15	Lima, OH	69.6
133	Lincoln, NE	38.2
30	Little Rock, AR	57.9
298	Logan, UT-ID	20.2
47	Longview, TX	52.6
5	Longview, WA	79.8
275	Los Angeles County, CA M.D.	23.4
287	Los Angeles (greater), CA	21.6
286	Louisville, KY-IN	21.9
90	Lubbock, TX	43.2
220	Lynchburg, VA	28.8
126	Macon, GA	39.0
133	Madera, CA	38.2
252	Madison, WI	25.8
276	Manchester-Nashua, NH	23.3
32	Mansfield, OH	57.0
254	McAllen-Edinburg-Mission, TX	25.7
231	Medford, OR	27.7
73	Memphis, TN-MS-AR	46.3
178	Merced, CA	33.2
192	Miami (greater), FL	31.9
170	Miami-Dade County, FL M.D.	34.0
161	Michigan City-La Porte, IN	35.1
37	Midland, TX	54.5
322	Milwaukee, WI	14.2
NA	Minneapolis-St. Paul, MN-WI**	NA
59	Missoula, MT	49.5
208	Mobile, AL	29.6
208	Modesto, CA	29.6
118	Monroe, LA	40.1
149	Monroe, MI	36.5
182	Montgomery, AL	32.5
148	Morgantown, WV	36.6
260	Morristown, TN	25.0
22	Mount Vernon-Anacortes, WA	61.7
34	Muncie, IN	56.3
3	Muskegon-Norton Shores, MI	82.8
12	Myrtle Beach, SC	71.1
238	Napa, CA	26.9
249	Naples-Marco Island, FL	26.2
105	Nashville-Davidson, TN	41.2
339	Nassau-Suffolk, NY M.D.	7.1
269	New Orleans, LA	23.9
331	New York (greater), NY-NJ-PA	11.2
328	New York-W. Plains NY-NJ M.D.	12.0
325	Newark-Union, NJ-PA M.D.	13.8
18	Niles-Benton Harbor, MI	67.8
218	Oakland-Fremont, CA M.D.	29.0
31	Ocala, FL	57.4
214	Ocean City, NJ	29.2
332	Odessa, TX	10.9
212	Ogden-Clearfield, UT	29.4
72	Oklahoma City, OK	46.5
189	Olympia, WA	32.2

RANK	METROPOLITAN AREA	RATE
138	Omaha-Council Bluffs, NE-IA	37.6
115	Orlando, FL	40.3
321	Oshkosh-Neenah, WI	14.4
316	Oxnard-Thousand Oaks, CA	15.9
104	Palm Bay-Melbourne, FL	41.3
334	Palm Coast, FL	10.3
26	Panama City-Lynn Haven, FL	59.0
161	Pascagoula, MS	35.1
80	Pensacola, FL	44.7
185	Philadelphia (greater) PA-NJ-DE	32.4
163	Philadelphia, PA M.D.	35.0
195	Phoenix-Mesa-Scottsdale, AZ	31.6
74	Pine Bluff, AR	46.2
302	Pittsburgh, PA	18.9
44	Pittsfield, MA	52.8
66	Pocatello, ID	47.6
212	Port St. Lucie, FL	29.4
121	Portland-Vancouver, OR-WA	39.7
233	Portland, ME	27.4
319	Poughkeepsie, NY	15.1
280	Prescott, AZ	22.8
276	Provo-Orem, UT	23.3
185	Pueblo, CO	32.4
337	Punta Gorda, FL	9.4
333	Racine, WI	10.7
293	Raleigh-Cary, NC	21.0
4	Rapid City, SD	80.6
295	Reading, PA	20.9
51	Redding, CA	51.8
166	Reno-Sparks, NV	34.6
272	Richmond, VA	23.6
241	Riverside-San Bernardino, CA	26.7
185	Roanoke, VA	32.4
NA	Rochester, MN**	NA
279	Rochester, NY	22.9
272	Rocky Mount, NC	23.6
144	Rome, GA	37.0
194	Sacramento, CA	31.7
8	Saginaw, MI	76.0
174	Salem, OR	33.5
228	Salinas, CA	27.9
95	Salisbury, MD	42.0
82	Salt Lake City, UT	44.3
52	San Angelo, TX	51.7
146	San Antonio, TX	36.7
246	San Diego, CA	26.3
252	San Francisco (greater), CA	25.8
295	San Francisco-S. Mateo, CA M.D.	20.9
300	San Jose, CA	19.1
201	San Luis Obispo, CA	30.6
309	Sandusky, OH	17.8
317	Santa Ana-Anaheim, CA M.D.	15.8
185	Santa Barbara-Santa Maria, CA	32.4
135	Santa Cruz-Watsonville, CA	38.1
66	Santa Fe, NM	47.6
145	Santa Rosa-Petaluma, CA	36.8
232	Sarasota-Bradenton-Venice, FL	27.5
230	Savannah, GA	27.8
257	Scranton--Wilkes-Barre, PA	25.2
122	Seattle (greater), WA	39.4

RANK	METROPOLITAN AREA	RATE
140	Seattle-Bellevue, WA M.D.	37.4
216	Sebastian-Vero Beach, FL	29.1
119	Sheboygan, WI	40.0
297	Sherman-Denison, TX	20.8
32	Shreveport-Bossier City, LA	57.0
98	Sioux City, IA-NE-SD	41.9
24	Sioux Falls, SD	60.1
163	South Bend-Mishawaka, IN-MI	35.0
227	Spartanburg, SC	28.0
220	Spokane, WA	28.8
94	Springfield, MA	42.1
223	Springfield, MO	28.7
54	Springfield, OH	51.2
309	State College, PA	17.8
263	Stockton, CA	24.6
NA	St. Cloud, MN**	NA
312	St. Joseph, MO-KS	17.1
280	St. Louis, MO-IL	22.8
142	Sumter, SC	37.3
284	Syracuse, NY	22.2
77	Tacoma, WA M.D.	46.0
13	Tallahassee, FL	70.2
135	Tampa-St Petersburg, FL	38.1
60	Texarkana, TX-Texarkana, AR	49.0
155	Toledo, OH	35.6
102	Topeka, KS	41.6
307	Trenton-Ewing, NJ	18.0
100	Tucson, AZ	41.7
79	Tulsa, OK	45.6
69	Tuscaloosa, AL	47.3
127	Tyler, TX	38.8
304	Utica-Rome, NY	18.4
207	Valdosta, GA	29.7
197	Vallejo-Fairfield, CA	31.1
58	Victoria, TX	49.8
181	Vineland, NJ	32.6
179	Virginia Beach-Norfolk, VA-NC	32.9
196	Visalia-Porterville, CA	31.4
44	Waco, TX	52.8
270	Warner Robins, GA	23.8
168	Warren-Farmington Hills, MI M.D.	34.5
301	Washington (greater) DC-VA-MD	19.0
299	Washington, DC-VA-MD-WV M.D.	20.0
128	Waterloo-Cedar Falls, IA	38.7
323	Wausau, WI	13.9
226	Wenatchee, WA	28.2
153	West Palm Beach, FL M.D.	35.7
256	Wheeling, WV-OH	25.5
243	Wichita Falls, TX	26.6
43	Wichita, KS	53.1
315	Williamsport, PA	16.0
192	Wilmington, DE-MD-NJ M.D.	31.9
100	Wilmington, NC	41.7
177	Winchester, VA-WV	33.3
140	Winston-Salem, NC	37.4
128	Worcester, MA	38.7
42	Yakima, WA	53.5
122	Yuba City, CA	39.4
265	Yuma, AZ	24.4

Source: Federal Bureau of Investigation

"Crime in the United States 2006" (Uniform Crime Reports, September 24, 2007)

**Forcible rape is the carnal knowledge of a female forcibly and against her will. Assaults or attempts to commit rape by force or threat of force are included. However, statutory rape without force and other sex offenses are excluded. **Not available.*

14. Rape Rate in 2006 (continued)

National Rate = 30.9 Rapes per 100,000 Population*

RANK	METROPOLITAN AREA	RATE
1	Bremerton-Silverdale, WA	94.4
2	Anchorage, AK	86.8
3	Muskegon-Norton Shores, MI	82.8
4	Rapid City, SD	80.6
5	Longview, WA	79.8
6	Lake Charles, LA	79.5
7	Farmington, NM	78.2
8	Saginaw, MI	76.0
9	Lawton, OK	75.8
10	Battle Creek, MI	74.2
11	Gainesville, FL	74.1
12	Myrtle Beach, SC	71.1
13	Tallahassee, FL	70.2
14	Flint, MI	70.0
15	Lima, OH	69.6
16	Las Cruces, NM	69.3
17	Jackson, MI	68.6
18	Niles-Benton Harbor, MI	67.8
19	Fayetteville, AR-MO	63.5
20	Dover, DE	63.2
21	Holland-Grand Haven, MI	62.8
22	Mount Vernon-Anacortes, WA	61.7
23	Lansing-East Lansing, MI	60.5
24	Sioux Falls, SD	60.1
25	Idaho Falls, ID	59.3
26	Panama City-Lynn Haven, FL	59.0
27	Bay City, MI	58.8
27	Coeur d'Alene, ID	58.8
29	Corpus Christi, TX	58.1
30	Little Rock, AR	57.9
31	Ocala, FL	57.4
32	Mansfield, OH	57.0
32	Shreveport-Bossier City, LA	57.0
34	Muncie, IN	56.3
35	Fort Smith, AR-OK	55.2
36	Lawrence, KS	55.0
37	Colorado Springs, CO	54.5
37	Midland, TX	54.5
39	Jackson, MS	54.2
40	Kalamazoo-Portage, MI	54.0
41	Bowling Green, KY	53.6
42	Yakima, WA	53.5
43	Wichita, KS	53.1
44	Gadsden, AL	52.8
44	Pittsfield, MA	52.8
44	Waco, TX	52.8
47	Longview, TX	52.6
48	Chico, CA	52.3
49	Alexandria, LA	52.0
50	Albuquerque, NM	51.9
51	Redding, CA	51.8
52	San Angelo, TX	51.7
53	Grand Rapids-Wyoming, MI	51.5
54	Springfield, OH	51.2
55	Columbus, OH	51.1
56	Anderson, SC	50.5
56	Flagstaff, AZ	50.5
58	Victoria, TX	49.8
59	Missoula, MT	49.5
60	Texarkana, TX-Texarkana, AR	49.0
61	Jonesboro, AR	48.5
62	Detroit-Livonia-Dearborn, MI M.D.	48.4
63	Charleston-North Charleston, SC	48.2
64	Denver-Aurora, CO	47.9
65	Las Vegas-Paradise, NV	47.8
66	Pocatello, ID	47.6
66	Santa Fe, NM	47.6
68	Iowa City, IA	47.4
69	Tuscaloosa, AL	47.3
70	Joplin, MO	47.2
71	Boise City-Nampa, ID	46.6
72	Oklahoma City, OK	46.5
73	Memphis, TN-MS-AR	46.3
74	Pine Bluff, AR	46.2
75	Abilene, TX	46.1
75	College Station-Bryan, TX	46.1
77	Tacoma, WA M.D.	46.0
78	Dothan, AL	45.7
79	Tulsa, OK	45.6
80	Pensacola, FL	44.7
81	Lakeland, FL	44.4
82	Birmingham-Hoover, AL	44.3
82	Salt Lake City, UT	44.3
84	Cheyenne, WY	44.1
85	Cincinnati-Middletown, OH-KY-IN	43.7
85	Kansas City, MO-KS	43.7
87	Ames, IA	43.5
87	Dayton, OH	43.5
89	El Paso, TX	43.4
90	Lubbock, TX	43.2
91	Janesville, WI	42.4
92	Augusta, GA-SC	42.3
93	Lebanon, PA	42.2
94	Springfield, MA	42.1
95	Amarillo, TX	42.0
95	Blacksburg, VA	42.0
95	Salisbury, MD	42.0
98	Sioux City, IA-NE-SD	41.9
99	Jacksonville, NC	41.8
100	Tucson, AZ	41.7
100	Wilmington, NC	41.7
102	Topeka, KS	41.6
103	Laredo, TX	41.5
104	Palm Bay-Melbourne, FL	41.3
105	Houma, LA	41.2
105	Nashville-Davidson, TN	41.2
107	Beaumont-Port Arthur, TX	41.1
107	Fond du Lac, WI	41.1
107	Indianapolis, IN	41.1
110	Greenville, NC	41.0
111	Fort Collins-Loveland, CO	40.8
112	Bellingham, WA	40.7
112	Detroit (greater), MI	40.7
114	Lafayette, IN	40.6
115	Erie, PA	40.3
115	Orlando, FL	40.3
117	Hot Springs, AR	40.2
118	Monroe, LA	40.1
119	Sheboygan, WI	40.0
120	Greeley, CO	39.9
121	Portland-Vancouver, OR-WA	39.7
122	Seattle (greater), WA	39.4
122	Yuba City, CA	39.4
124	Florence, SC	39.2
124	Huntsville, AL	39.2
126	Macon, GA	39.0
127	Tyler, TX	38.8
128	Waterloo-Cedar Falls, IA	38.7
128	Worcester, MA	38.7
130	Altoona, PA	38.6
130	Clarksville, TN-KY	38.6
132	Lexington-Fayette, KY	38.5
133	Lincoln, NE	38.2
133	Madera, CA	38.2
135	Santa Cruz-Watsonville, CA	38.1
135	Tampa-St Petersburg, FL	38.1
137	Cumberland, MD-WV	37.7
138	Athens-Clarke County, GA	37.6
138	Omaha-Council Bluffs, NE-IA	37.6
140	Seattle-Bellevue, WA M.D.	37.4
140	Winston-Salem, NC	37.4
142	Chattanooga, TN-GA	37.3
142	Sumter, SC	37.3
144	Rome, GA	37.0
145	Santa Rosa-Petaluma, CA	36.8
146	Charlotte-Gastonia, NC-SC	36.7
146	San Antonio, TX	36.7
148	Morgantown, WV	36.6
149	Fort Worth-Arlington, TX M.D.	36.5
149	Hattiesburg, MS	36.5
149	Monroe, MI	36.5
152	Cleveland-Elyria-Mentor, OH	36.0
153	Columbia, SC	35.7
153	West Palm Beach, FL M.D.	35.7
155	Cleveland, TN	35.6
155	Greenville, SC	35.6
155	Jackson, TN	35.6
155	Toledo, OH	35.6
159	Cape Coral-Fort Myers, FL	35.4
160	Lewiston-Auburn, ME	35.2
161	Michigan City-La Porte, IN	35.1
161	Pascagoula, MS	35.1
163	Austin-Round Rock, TX	35.0
163	Philadelphia, PA M.D.	35.0
163	South Bend-Mishawaka, IN-MI	35.0
166	Houston, TX	34.6
166	Reno-Sparks, NV	34.6
168	Warren-Farmington Hills, MI M.D.	34.5
169	Kingsport, TN-VA	34.4
170	Dallas (greater), TX	34.0
170	Miami-Dade County, FL M.D.	34.0

Note: All listings are for Metropolitan Statistical Areas (M.S.A.s) except for those ending with "M.D." Listings with "M.D." are Metropolitan Divisions which are smaller parts of eleven large M.S.A.s. See explanatory note at beginning of metropolitan area section on page 23.

RANK	METROPOLITAN AREA	RATE
172	Baton Rouge, LA	33.9
173	Durham, NC	33.7
174	Brunswick, GA	33.5
174	Salem, OR	33.5
176	Ann Arbor, MI	33.4
177	Winchester, VA-WV	33.3
178	Merced, CA	33.2
179	Virginia Beach-Norfolk, VA-NC	32.9
180	Dallas-Plano-Irving, TX M.D.	32.8
181	Vineland, NJ	32.6
182	Daytona Beach, FL	32.5
182	Grand Junction, CO	32.5
182	Montgomery, AL	32.5
185	Philadelphia (greater) PA-NJ-DE	32.4
185	Pueblo, CO	32.4
185	Roanoke, VA	32.4
185	Santa Barbara-Santa Maria, CA	32.4
189	Olympia, WA	32.2
190	Brownsville-Harlingen, TX	32.1
190	Charlottesville, VA	32.1
192	Miami (greater), FL	31.9
192	Wilmington, DE-MD-NJ M.D.	31.9
194	Sacramento, CA	31.7
195	Phoenix-Mesa-Scottsdale, AZ	31.6
196	Visalia-Porterville, CA	31.4
197	Vallejo-Fairfield, CA	31.1
198	Fort Walton Beach, FL	30.8
199	Decatur, AL	30.7
199	Kennewick-Richland-Pasco, WA	30.7
201	San Luis Obispo, CA	30.6
202	Huntington-Ashland, WV-KY-OH	30.3
203	Bend, OR	29.9
203	Ithaca, NY	29.9
205	Casper, WY	29.8
205	Fayetteville, NC	29.8
207	Valdosta, GA	29.7
208	Mobile, AL	29.6
208	Modesto, CA	29.6
210	Elkhart-Goshen, IN	29.5
210	Glens Falls, NY	29.5
212	Ogden-Clearfield, UT	29.4
212	Port St. Lucie, FL	29.4
214	Bismarck, ND	29.2
214	Ocean City, NJ	29.2
216	Atlantic City, NJ	29.1
216	Sebastian-Vero Beach, FL	29.1
218	Oakland-Fremont, CA M.D.	29.0
219	Knoxville, TN	28.9
220	Buffalo-Niagara Falls, NY	28.8
220	Lynchburg, VA	28.8
220	Spokane, WA	28.8
223	Springfield, MO	28.7
224	Evansville, IN-KY	28.4
225	Harrisburg-Carlisle, PA	28.3
226	Wenatchee, WA	28.2
227	Spartanburg, SC	28.0
228	Eugene-Springfield, OR	27.9
228	Salinas, CA	27.9
230	Savannah, GA	27.8
231	Medford, OR	27.7
232	Sarasota-Bradenton-Venice, FL	27.5
233	Kokomo, IN	27.4
233	Portland, ME	27.4
235	Binghamton, NY	27.3
235	Kingston, NY	27.3
237	Barnstable Town, MA	27.2
238	Jefferson City, MO	26.9
238	Napa, CA	26.9
240	Jacksonville, FL	26.8
241	Charleston, WV	26.7
241	Riverside-San Bernardino, CA	26.7
243	Harrisonburg, VA	26.6
243	Wichita Falls, TX	26.6
245	Fort Lauderdale, FL M.D.	26.4
246	Bakersfield, CA	26.3
246	Bloomington, IN	26.3
246	San Diego, CA	26.3
249	Asheville, NC	26.2
249	Naples-Marco Island, FL	26.2
251	Green Bay, WI	26.1
252	Madison, WI	25.8
252	San Francisco (greater), CA	25.8
254	Billings, MT	25.7
254	McAllen-Edinburg-Mission, TX	25.7
256	Wheeling, WV-OH	25.5
257	Scranton--Wilkes-Barre, PA	25.2
258	Fort Wayne, IN	25.1
258	Honolulu, HI	25.1
260	Appleton, WI	25.0
260	Dubuque, IA	25.0
260	Morristown, TN	25.0
263	Stockton, CA	24.6
264	Camden, NJ M.D.	24.5
265	Yuma, AZ	24.4
266	Albany-Schenectady-Troy, NY	24.3
267	Elizabethtown, KY	24.2
267	Fresno, CA	24.2
269	New Orleans, LA	23.9
270	Cedar Rapids, IA	23.8
270	Warner Robins, GA	23.8
272	Richmond, VA	23.6
272	Rocky Mount, NC	23.6
274	Greensboro-High Point, NC	23.5
275	Los Angeles County, CA M.D.	23.4
276	Manchester-Nashua, NH	23.3
276	Provo-Orem, UT	23.3
278	Des Moines-West Des Moines, IA	23.2
279	Rochester, NY	22.9
280	Dalton, GA	22.8
280	Prescott, AZ	22.8
280	St. Louis, MO-IL	22.8
283	Elmira, NY	22.3
284	Syracuse, NY	22.2
285	Albany, GA	22.0
286	Louisville, KY-IN	21.9
287	Atlanta, GA	21.6
287	Burlington, NC	21.6
287	Columbus, IN	21.6
287	Los Angeles (greater), CA	21.6
291	Columbia, MO	21.4
291	Hanford-Corcoran, CA	21.4
293	Gainesville, GA	21.0
293	Raleigh-Cary, NC	21.0
295	Reading, PA	20.9
295	San Francisco-S. Mateo, CA M.D.	20.9
297	Sherman-Denison, TX	20.8
298	Logan, UT-ID	20.2
299	Washington, DC-VA-MD-WV M.D.	20.0
300	San Jose, CA	19.1
301	Washington (greater) DC-VA-MD	19.0
302	Pittsburgh, PA	18.9
303	Baltimore-Towson, MD	18.8
304	Utica-Rome, NY	18.4
305	Johnson City, TN	18.3
305	Lancaster, PA	18.3
307	Hartford, CT	18.0
307	Trenton-Ewing, NJ	18.0
309	Sandusky, OH	17.8
309	State College, PA	17.8
311	Danville, VA	17.4
312	St. Joseph, MO-KS	17.1
313	Hagerstown-Martinsburg, MD-WV	16.7
314	Johnstown, PA	16.2
315	Williamsport, PA	16.0
316	Oxnard-Thousand Oaks, CA	15.9
317	Santa Ana-Anaheim, CA M.D.	15.8
318	Bethesda-Frederick, MD M.D.	15.6
319	Poughkeepsie, NY	15.1
320	Lewiston, ID-WA	14.9
321	Oshkosh-Neenah, WI	14.4
322	Milwaukee, WI	14.2
323	Lake Havasu City-Kingman, AZ	13.9
323	Wausau, WI	13.9
325	Newark-Union, NJ-PA M.D.	13.8
326	Great Falls, MT	13.7
327	Columbus, GA-AL	12.3
328	New York-W. Plains NY-NJ M.D.	12.0
329	Eau Claire, WI	11.6
330	El Centro, CA	11.4
331	New York (greater), NY-NJ-PA	11.2
332	Odessa, TX	10.9
333	Racine, WI	10.7
334	Palm Coast, FL	10.3
335	Edison, NJ M.D.	10.1
336	Bangor, ME	9.5
337	Punta Gorda, FL	9.4
338	Goldsboro, NC	7.7
339	Nassau-Suffolk, NY M.D.	7.1
340	Carson City, NV	3.5
NA	Chicago, IL**	NA
NA	Duluth, MN-WI**	NA
NA	Fairbanks, AK**	NA
NA	Fargo, ND-MN**	NA
NA	Grand Forks, ND-MN**	NA
NA	Killeen-Temple-Fort Hood, TX**	NA
NA	La Crosse, WI-MN**	NA
NA	Minneapolis-St. Paul, MN-WI**	NA
NA	Rochester, MN**	NA
NA	St. Cloud, MN**	NA

Source: Federal Bureau of Investigation
"Crime in the United States 2006" (Uniform Crime Reports, September 24, 2007)
**Forcible rape is the carnal knowledge of a female forcibly and against her will. Assaults or attempts to commit rape by force or threat of force are included. However, statutory rape without force and other sex offenses are excluded. **Not available.*

15. Percent Change in Rape Rate: 2005 to 2006

National Percent Change = 3.0% Decrease*

RANK	METROPOLITAN AREA	% CHANGE
NA	Abilene, TX**	NA
223	Albany-Schenectady-Troy, NY	(8.6)
296	Albany, GA	(27.9)
93	Albuquerque, NM	9.0
24	Alexandria, LA	44.4
52	Altoona, PA	20.2
111	Amarillo, TX	5.0
60	Ames, IA	16.9
88	Anchorage, AK	11.0
35	Anderson, SC	30.5
279	Ann Arbor, MI	(21.8)
27	Appleton, WI	41.2
37	Asheville, NC	29.1
23	Athens-Clarke County, GA	45.7
173	Atlanta, GA	(2.7)
208	Atlantic City, NJ	(6.7)
234	Augusta, GA-SC	(11.1)
150	Austin-Round Rock, TX	0.0
199	Bakersfield, CA	(5.1)
221	Baltimore-Towson, MD	(8.3)
205	Bangor, ME	(5.9)
260	Barnstable Town, MA	(16.0)
85	Baton Rouge, LA	11.5
163	Battle Creek, MI	(1.6)
248	Bay City, MI	(14.2)
225	Beaumont-Port Arthur, TX	(9.1)
124	Bellingham, WA	3.3
284	Bend, OR	(23.1)
191	Bethesda-Frederick, MD M.D.	(4.3)
243	Billings, MT	(12.9)
48	Binghamton, NY	21.9
NA	Birmingham-Hoover, AL**	NA
20	Bismarck, ND	51.3
38	Blacksburg, VA	28.4
272	Bloomington, IN	(17.6)
NA	Boise City-Nampa, ID**	NA
44	Bowling Green, KY	25.2
97	Bremerton-Silverdale, WA	8.4
252	Brownsville-Harlingen, TX	(15.1)
207	Brunswick, GA	(6.2)
167	Buffalo-Niagara Falls, NY	(2.0)
137	Burlington, NC	1.4
62	Camden, NJ M.D.	16.7
157	Cape Coral-Fort Myers, FL	(0.6)
150	Carson City, NV	0.0
2	Casper, WY	195.0
231	Cedar Rapids, IA	(10.2)
167	Charleston-North Charleston, SC	(2.0)
22	Charleston, WV	46.7
166	Charlotte-Gastonia, NC-SC	(1.9)
288	Charlottesville, VA	(24.5)
142	Chattanooga, TN-GA	0.8
28	Cheyenne, WY	40.0
NA	Chicago, IL**	NA
69	Chico, CA	14.4
159	Cincinnati-Middletown, OH-KY-IN	(0.9)
206	Clarksville, TN-KY	(6.1)
NA	Cleveland-Elyria-Mentor, OH**	NA
NA	Cleveland, TN**	NA
82	Coeur d'Alene, ID	11.8
262	College Station-Bryan, TX	(16.2)
148	Colorado Springs, CO	0.4
78	Columbia, MO	12.6
245	Columbia, SC	(13.3)
228	Columbus, GA-AL	(9.6)
16	Columbus, IN	58.8
107	Columbus, OH	5.6
254	Corpus Christi, TX	(15.4)
64	Cumberland, MD-WV	16.0
157	Dallas (greater), TX	(0.6)
127	Dallas-Plano-Irving, TX M.D.	3.1
NA	Dalton, GA**	NA
287	Danville, VA	(23.7)
258	Daytona Beach, FL	(15.8)
160	Dayton, OH	(1.1)
12	Decatur, AL	62.4
114	Denver-Aurora, CO	4.8
NA	Des Moines-West Des Moines, IA**	NA
124	Detroit (greater), MI	3.3
161	Detroit-Livonia-Dearborn, MI M.D.	(1.4)
260	Dothan, AL	(16.0)
47	Dover, DE	22.0
119	Dubuque, IA	3.7
NA	Duluth, MN-WI**	NA
NA	Durham, NC**	NA
85	Eau Claire, WI	11.5
196	Edison, NJ M.D.	(4.7)
315	El Centro, CA	(52.7)
208	El Paso, TX	(6.7)
218	Elizabethtown, KY	(8.0)
199	Elkhart-Goshen, IN	(5.1)
298	Elmira, NY	(28.3)
173	Erie, PA	(2.7)
232	Eugene-Springfield, OR	(10.9)
101	Evansville, IN-KY	7.2
NA	Fairbanks, AK**	NA
NA	Fargo, ND-MN**	NA
266	Farmington, NM	(16.6)
70	Fayetteville, AR-MO	13.8
60	Fayetteville, NC	16.9
257	Flagstaff, AZ	(15.7)
149	Flint, MI	0.3
284	Florence, SC	(23.1)
1	Fond du Lac, WI	351.6
303	Fort Collins-Loveland, CO	(32.6)
239	Fort Lauderdale, FL M.D.	(12.3)
80	Fort Smith, AR-OK	12.2
41	Fort Walton Beach, FL	26.7
NA	Fort Wayne, IN**	NA
210	Fort Worth-Arlington, TX M.D.	(6.9)
270	Fresno, CA	(17.1)
100	Gadsden, AL	7.5
131	Gainesville, FL	2.3
299	Gainesville, GA	(29.1)
NA	Glens Falls, NY**	NA
84	Goldsboro, NC	11.6
NA	Grand Forks, ND-MN**	NA
13	Grand Junction, CO	60.9
121	Grand Rapids-Wyoming, MI	3.6
313	Great Falls, MT	(44.8)
56	Greeley, CO	18.4
216	Green Bay, WI	(7.8)
104	Greensboro-High Point, NC	6.3
11	Greenville, NC	63.3
247	Greenville, SC	(14.0)
7	Hagerstown-Martinsburg, MD-WV	87.6
300	Hanford-Corcoran, CA	(30.3)
277	Harrisburg-Carlisle, PA	(20.5)
51	Harrisonburg, VA	20.4
163	Hartford, CT	(1.6)
NA	Hattiesburg, MS**	NA
276	Holland-Grand Haven, MI	(20.3)
173	Honolulu, HI	(2.7)
297	Hot Springs, AR	(28.1)
59	Houma, LA	17.0
183	Houston, TX	(3.4)
29	Huntington-Ashland, WV-KY-OH	38.4
119	Huntsville, AL	3.7
19	Idaho Falls, ID	52.8
122	Indianapolis, IN	3.5
75	Iowa City, IA	12.9
NA	Ithaca, NY**	NA
103	Jacksonville, FL	6.8
NA	Jacksonville, NC**	NA
184	Jackson, MI	(3.5)
75	Jackson, MS	12.9
311	Jackson, TN	(42.6)
92	Janesville, WI	9.3
71	Jefferson City, MO	13.5
245	Johnson City, TN	(13.3)
NA	Johnstown, PA**	NA
111	Jonesboro, AR	5.0
72	Joplin, MO	13.2
170	Kalamazoo-Portage, MI	(2.5)
NA	Kansas City, MO-KS**	NA
180	Kennewick-Richland-Pasco, WA	(2.8)
NA	Killeen-Temple-Fort Hood, TX**	NA
263	Kingsport, TN-VA	(16.3)
290	Kingston, NY	(24.8)
173	Knoxville, TN	(2.7)
254	Kokomo, IN	(15.4)
NA	La Crosse, WI-MN**	NA
31	Lafayette, IN	34.9
33	Lake Charles, LA	31.4
NA	Lake Havasu City-Kingman, AZ**	NA
53	Lakeland, FL	19.7
110	Lancaster, PA	5.2
118	Lansing-East Lansing, MI	3.8
35	Laredo, TX	30.5
243	Las Cruces, NM	(12.9)
77	Las Vegas-Paradise, NV	12.7

Note: All listings are for Metropolitan Statistical Areas (M.S.A.s) except for those ending with "M.D." Listings with "M.D." are Metropolitan Divisions which are smaller parts of eleven large M.S.A.s. See explanatory note at beginning of metropolitan area section on page 23.

RANK	METROPOLITAN AREA	% CHANGE
6	Lawrence, KS	89.0
7	Lawton, OK	87.6
10	Lebanon, PA	64.2
42	Lewiston-Auburn, ME	26.2
310	Lewiston, ID-WA	(40.4)
NA	Lexington-Fayette, KY**	NA
302	Lima, OH	(31.1)
265	Lincoln, NE	(16.4)
49	Little Rock, AR	21.6
304	Logan, UT-ID	(32.7)
98	Longview, TX	8.2
57	Longview, WA	17.9
165	Los Angeles County, CA M.D.	(1.7)
156	Los Angeles (greater), CA	(0.5)
250	Louisville, KY-IN	(14.8)
226	Lubbock, TX	(9.4)
39	Lynchburg, VA	28.0
54	Macon, GA	18.9
50	Madera, CA	21.3
134	Madison, WI	2.0
286	Manchester-Nashua, NH	(23.4)
25	Mansfield, OH	43.2
292	McAllen-Edinburg-Mission, TX	(25.9)
269	Medford, OR	(16.8)
132	Memphis, TN-MS-AR	2.2
184	Merced, CA	(3.5)
173	Miami (greater), FL	(2.7)
107	Miami-Dade County, FL M.D.	5.6
18	Michigan City-La Porte, IN	54.6
268	Midland, TX	(16.7)
301	Milwaukee, WI	(30.4)
NA	Minneapolis-St. Paul, MN-WI**	NA
229	Missoula, MT	(10.0)
79	Mobile, AL	12.5
68	Modesto, CA	15.2
87	Monroe, LA	11.1
230	Monroe, MI	(10.1)
293	Montgomery, AL	(26.0)
21	Morgantown, WV	48.8
111	Morristown, TN	5.0
65	Mount Vernon-Anacortes, WA	15.8
256	Muncie, IN	(15.6)
129	Muskegon-Norton Shores, MI	2.5
30	Myrtle Beach, SC	35.2
155	Napa, CA	(0.4)
263	Naples-Marco Island, FL	(16.3)
218	Nashville-Davidson, TN	(8.0)
188	Nassau-Suffolk, NY M.D.	(4.1)
NA	New Orleans, LA**	NA
258	New York (greater), NY-NJ-PA	(15.8)
277	New York-W. Plains NY-NJ M.D.	(20.5)
169	Newark-Union, NJ-PA M.D.	(2.1)
144	Niles-Benton Harbor, MI	0.6
173	Oakland-Fremont, CA M.D.	(2.7)
89	Ocala, FL	10.4
4	Ocean City, NJ	110.1
222	Odessa, TX	(8.4)
238	Ogden-Clearfield, UT	(12.0)
173	Oklahoma City, OK	(2.7)
74	Olympia, WA	13.0
216	Omaha-Council Bluffs, NE-IA	(7.8)
198	Orlando, FL	(5.0)
273	Oshkosh-Neenah, WI	(17.7)
241	Oxnard-Thousand Oaks, CA	(12.6)
143	Palm Bay-Melbourne, FL	0.7
NA	Palm Coast, FL**	NA
130	Panama City-Lynn Haven, FL	2.4
291	Pascagoula, MS	(25.5)
102	Pensacola, FL	6.9
144	Philadelphia (greater) PA-NJ-DE	0.6
170	Philadelphia, PA M.D.	(2.5)
201	Phoenix-Mesa-Scottsdale, AZ	(5.4)
210	Pine Bluff, AR	(6.9)
139	Pittsburgh, PA	1.1
40	Pittsfield, MA	26.9
202	Pocatello, ID	(5.6)
67	Port St. Lucie, FL	15.3
220	Portland-Vancouver, OR-WA	(8.1)
186	Portland, ME	(3.9)
308	Poughkeepsie, NY	(34.3)
132	Prescott, AZ	2.2
295	Provo-Orem, UT	(27.4)
5	Pueblo, CO	105.1
316	Punta Gorda, FL	(65.7)
314	Racine, WI	(49.0)
146	Raleigh-Cary, NC	0.5
232	Rapid City, SD	(10.9)
195	Reading, PA	(4.6)
282	Redding, CA	(22.1)
280	Reno-Sparks, NV	(21.9)
117	Richmond, VA	4.4
204	Riverside-San Bernardino, CA	(5.7)
135	Roanoke, VA	1.9
NA	Rochester, MN**	NA
126	Rochester, NY	3.2
250	Rocky Mount, NC	(14.8)
3	Rome, GA	110.2
63	Sacramento, CA	16.5
26	Saginaw, MI	43.1
104	Salem, OR	6.3
161	Salinas, CA	(1.4)
34	Salisbury, MD	31.3
172	Salt Lake City, UT	(2.6)
213	San Angelo, TX	(7.5)
241	San Antonio, TX	(12.6)
196	San Diego, CA	(4.7)
188	San Francisco (greater), CA	(4.1)
213	San Francisco-S. Mateo, CA M.D.	(7.5)
275	San Jose, CA	(19.4)
128	San Luis Obispo, CA	3.0
237	Sandusky, OH	(11.9)
98	Santa Ana-Anaheim, CA M.D.	8.2
90	Santa Barbara-Santa Maria, CA	10.2
248	Santa Cruz-Watsonville, CA	(14.2)
154	Santa Fe, NM	(0.2)
123	Santa Rosa-Petaluma, CA	3.4
224	Sarasota-Bradenton-Venice, FL	(8.9)
226	Savannah, GA	(9.4)
294	Scranton--Wilkes-Barre, PA	(26.7)
136	Seattle (greater), WA	1.5
146	Seattle-Bellevue, WA M.D.	0.5
81	Sebastian-Vero Beach, FL	11.9
17	Sheboygan, WI	58.1
9	Sherman-Denison, TX	74.8
150	Shreveport-Bossier City, LA	0.0
106	Sioux City, IA-NE-SD	5.8
283	Sioux Falls, SD	(22.7)
270	South Bend-Mishawaka, IN-MI	(17.1)
236	Spartanburg, SC	(11.7)
191	Spokane, WA	(4.3)
193	Springfield, MA	(4.5)
116	Springfield, MO	4.7
252	Springfield, OH	(15.1)
43	State College, PA	25.4
235	Stockton, CA	(11.2)
NA	St. Cloud, MN**	NA
289	St. Joseph, MO-KS	(24.7)
66	St. Louis, MO-IL	15.7
14	Sumter, SC	60.1
239	Syracuse, NY	(12.3)
114	Tacoma, WA M.D.	4.8
82	Tallahassee, FL	11.8
215	Tampa-St Petersburg, FL	(7.7)
45	Texarkana, TX-Texarkana, AR	24.4
139	Toledo, OH	1.1
46	Topeka, KS	23.4
58	Trenton-Ewing, NJ	17.6
274	Tucson, AZ	(18.2)
150	Tulsa, OK	0.0
NA	Tuscaloosa, AL**	NA
306	Tyler, TX	(33.2)
307	Utica-Rome, NY	(33.6)
281	Valdosta, GA	(22.0)
NA	Vallejo-Fairfield, CA**	NA
32	Victoria, TX	33.5
182	Vineland, NJ	(3.3)
96	Virginia Beach-Norfolk, VA-NC	8.6
95	Visalia-Porterville, CA	8.7
139	Waco, TX	1.1
15	Warner Robins, GA	59.7
91	Warren-Farmington Hills, MI M.D.	9.5
NA	Washington (greater) DC-VA-MD**	NA
NA	Washington, DC-VA-MD-WV M.D.**	NA
212	Waterloo-Cedar Falls, IA	(7.4)
311	Wausau, WI	(42.6)
305	Wenatchee, WA	(32.9)
202	West Palm Beach, FL M.D.	(5.6)
93	Wheeling, WV-OH	9.0
266	Wichita Falls, TX	(16.6)
NA	Wichita, KS**	NA
309	Williamsport, PA	(34.4)
138	Wilmington, DE-MD-NJ M.D.	1.3
188	Wilmington, NC	(4.1)
54	Winchester, VA-WV	18.9
181	Winston-Salem, NC	(2.9)
187	Worcester, MA	(4.0)
193	Yakima, WA	(4.5)
72	Yuba City, CA	13.2
107	Yuma, AZ	5.6

Source: CQ Press using data from Federal Bureau of Investigation "Crime in the United States 2006" (Uniform Crime Reports, September 24, 2007)

**Forcible rape is the carnal knowledge of a female forcibly and against her will. Assaults or attempts to commit rape by force or threat of force are included. However, statutory rape without force and other sex offenses are excluded. **Not available.*

15. Percent Change in Rape Rate: 2005 to 2006 (continued)

National Percent Change = 3.0% Decrease*

RANK	METROPOLITAN AREA	% CHANGE
1	Fond du Lac, WI	351.6
2	Casper, WY	195.0
3	Rome, GA	110.2
4	Ocean City, NJ	110.1
5	Pueblo, CO	105.1
6	Lawrence, KS	89.0
7	Hagerstown-Martinsburg, MD-WV	87.6
7	Lawton, OK	87.6
9	Sherman-Denison, TX	74.8
10	Lebanon, PA	64.2
11	Greenville, NC	63.3
12	Decatur, AL	62.4
13	Grand Junction, CO	60.9
14	Sumter, SC	60.1
15	Warner Robins, GA	59.7
16	Columbus, IN	58.8
17	Sheboygan, WI	58.1
18	Michigan City-La Porte, IN	54.6
19	Idaho Falls, ID	52.8
20	Bismarck, ND	51.3
21	Morgantown, WV	48.8
22	Charleston, WV	46.7
23	Athens-Clarke County, GA	45.7
24	Alexandria, LA	44.4
25	Mansfield, OH	43.2
26	Saginaw, MI	43.1
27	Appleton, WI	41.2
28	Cheyenne, WY	40.0
29	Huntington-Ashland, WV-KY-OH	38.4
30	Myrtle Beach, SC	35.2
31	Lafayette, IN	34.9
32	Victoria, TX	33.5
33	Lake Charles, LA	31.4
34	Salisbury, MD	31.3
35	Anderson, SC	30.5
35	Laredo, TX	30.5
37	Asheville, NC	29.1
38	Blacksburg, VA	28.4
39	Lynchburg, VA	28.0
40	Pittsfield, MA	26.9
41	Fort Walton Beach, FL	26.7
42	Lewiston-Auburn, ME	26.2
43	State College, PA	25.4
44	Bowling Green, KY	25.2
45	Texarkana, TX-Texarkana, AR	24.4
46	Topeka, KS	23.4
47	Dover, DE	22.0
48	Binghamton, NY	21.9
49	Little Rock, AR	21.6
50	Madera, CA	21.3
51	Harrisonburg, VA	20.4
52	Altoona, PA	20.2
53	Lakeland, FL	19.7
54	Macon, GA	18.9
54	Winchester, VA-WV	18.9
56	Greeley, CO	18.4
57	Longview, WA	17.9
58	Trenton-Ewing, NJ	17.6
59	Houma, LA	17.0
60	Ames, IA	16.9
60	Fayetteville, NC	16.9
62	Camden, NJ M.D.	16.7
63	Sacramento, CA	16.5
64	Cumberland, MD-WV	16.0
65	Mount Vernon-Anacortes, WA	15.8
66	St. Louis, MO-IL	15.7
67	Port St. Lucie, FL	15.3
68	Modesto, CA	15.2
69	Chico, CA	14.4
70	Fayetteville, AR-MO	13.8
71	Jefferson City, MO	13.5
72	Joplin, MO	13.2
72	Yuba City, CA	13.2
74	Olympia, WA	13.0
75	Iowa City, IA	12.9
75	Jackson, MS	12.9
77	Las Vegas-Paradise, NV	12.7
78	Columbia, MO	12.6
79	Mobile, AL	12.5
80	Fort Smith, AR-OK	12.2
81	Sebastian-Vero Beach, FL	11.9
82	Coeur d'Alene, ID	11.8
82	Tallahassee, FL	11.8
84	Goldsboro, NC	11.6
85	Baton Rouge, LA	11.5
85	Eau Claire, WI	11.5
87	Monroe, LA	11.1
88	Anchorage, AK	11.0
89	Ocala, FL	10.4
90	Santa Barbara-Santa Maria, CA	10.2
91	Warren-Farmington Hills, MI M.D.	9.5
92	Janesville, WI	9.3
93	Albuquerque, NM	9.0
93	Wheeling, WV-OH	9.0
95	Visalia-Porterville, CA	8.7
96	Virginia Beach-Norfolk, VA-NC	8.6
97	Bremerton-Silverdale, WA	8.4
98	Longview, TX	8.2
98	Santa Ana-Anaheim, CA M.D.	8.2
100	Gadsden, AL	7.5
101	Evansville, IN-KY	7.2
102	Pensacola, FL	6.9
103	Jacksonville, FL	6.8
104	Greensboro-High Point, NC	6.3
104	Salem, OR	6.3
106	Sioux City, IA-NE-SD	5.8
107	Columbus, OH	5.6
107	Miami-Dade County, FL M.D.	5.6
107	Yuma, AZ	5.6
110	Lancaster, PA	5.2
111	Amarillo, TX	5.0
111	Jonesboro, AR	5.0
111	Morristown, TN	5.0
114	Denver-Aurora, CO	4.8
114	Tacoma, WA M.D.	4.8
116	Springfield, MO	4.7
117	Richmond, VA	4.4
118	Lansing-East Lansing, MI	3.8
119	Dubuque, IA	3.7
119	Huntsville, AL	3.7
121	Grand Rapids-Wyoming, MI	3.6
122	Indianapolis, IN	3.5
123	Santa Rosa-Petaluma, CA	3.4
124	Bellingham, WA	3.3
124	Detroit (greater), MI	3.3
126	Rochester, NY	3.2
127	Dallas-Plano-Irving, TX M.D.	3.1
128	San Luis Obispo, CA	3.0
129	Muskegon-Norton Shores, MI	2.5
130	Panama City-Lynn Haven, FL	2.4
131	Gainesville, FL	2.3
132	Memphis, TN-MS-AR	2.2
132	Prescott, AZ	2.2
134	Madison, WI	2.0
135	Roanoke, VA	1.9
136	Seattle (greater), WA	1.5
137	Burlington, NC	1.4
138	Wilmington, DE-MD-NJ M.D.	1.3
139	Pittsburgh, PA	1.1
139	Toledo, OH	1.1
139	Waco, TX	1.1
142	Chattanooga, TN-GA	0.8
143	Palm Bay-Melbourne, FL	0.7
144	Niles-Benton Harbor, MI	0.6
144	Philadelphia (greater) PA-NJ-DE	0.6
146	Raleigh-Cary, NC	0.5
146	Seattle-Bellevue, WA M.D.	0.5
148	Colorado Springs, CO	0.4
149	Flint, MI	0.3
150	Austin-Round Rock, TX	0.0
150	Carson City, NV	0.0
150	Shreveport-Bossier City, LA	0.0
150	Tulsa, OK	0.0
154	Santa Fe, NM	(0.2)
155	Napa, CA	(0.4)
156	Los Angeles (greater), CA	(0.5)
157	Cape Coral-Fort Myers, FL	(0.6)
157	Dallas (greater), TX	(0.6)
159	Cincinnati-Middletown, OH-KY-IN	(0.9)
160	Dayton, OH	(1.1)
161	Detroit-Livonia-Dearborn, MI M.D.	(1.4)
161	Salinas, CA	(1.4)
163	Battle Creek, MI	(1.6)
163	Hartford, CT	(1.6)
165	Los Angeles County, CA M.D.	(1.7)
166	Charlotte-Gastonia, NC-SC	(1.9)
167	Buffalo-Niagara Falls, NY	(2.0)
167	Charleston-North Charleston, SC	(2.0)
169	Newark-Union, NJ-PA M.D.	(2.1)
170	Kalamazoo-Portage, MI	(2.5)
170	Philadelphia, PA M.D.	(2.5)

Note: All listings are for Metropolitan Statistical Areas (M.S.A.s) except for those ending with "M.D." Listings with "M.D." are Metropolitan Divisions which are smaller parts of eleven large M.S.A.s. See explanatory note at beginning of metropolitan area section on page 23.

Rank Order - Metro Area (continued)

RANK	METROPOLITAN AREA	% CHANGE
172	Salt Lake City, UT	(2.6)
173	Atlanta, GA	(2.7)
173	Erie, PA	(2.7)
173	Honolulu, HI	(2.7)
173	Knoxville, TN	(2.7)
173	Miami (greater), FL	(2.7)
173	Oakland-Fremont, CA M.D.	(2.7)
173	Oklahoma City, OK	(2.7)
180	Kennewick-Richland-Pasco, WA	(2.8)
181	Winston-Salem, NC	(2.9)
182	Vineland, NJ	(3.3)
183	Houston, TX	(3.4)
184	Jackson, MI	(3.5)
184	Merced, CA	(3.5)
186	Portland, ME	(3.9)
187	Worcester, MA	(4.0)
188	Nassau-Suffolk, NY M.D.	(4.1)
188	San Francisco (greater), CA	(4.1)
188	Wilmington, NC	(4.1)
191	Bethesda-Frederick, MD M.D.	(4.3)
191	Spokane, WA	(4.3)
193	Springfield, MA	(4.5)
193	Yakima, WA	(4.5)
195	Reading, PA	(4.6)
196	Edison, NJ M.D.	(4.7)
196	San Diego, CA	(4.7)
198	Orlando, FL	(5.0)
199	Bakersfield, CA	(5.1)
199	Elkhart-Goshen, IN	(5.1)
201	Phoenix-Mesa-Scottsdale, AZ	(5.4)
202	Pocatello, ID	(5.6)
202	West Palm Beach, FL M.D.	(5.6)
204	Riverside-San Bernardino, CA	(5.7)
205	Bangor, ME	(5.9)
206	Clarksville, TN-KY	(6.1)
207	Brunswick, GA	(6.2)
208	Atlantic City, NJ	(6.7)
208	El Paso, TX	(6.7)
210	Fort Worth-Arlington, TX M.D.	(6.9)
210	Pine Bluff, AR	(6.9)
212	Waterloo-Cedar Falls, IA	(7.4)
213	San Angelo, TX	(7.5)
213	San Francisco-S. Mateo, CA M.D.	(7.5)
215	Tampa-St Petersburg, FL	(7.7)
216	Green Bay, WI	(7.8)
216	Omaha-Council Bluffs, NE-IA	(7.8)
218	Elizabethtown, KY	(8.0)
218	Nashville-Davidson, TN	(8.0)
220	Portland-Vancouver, OR-WA	(8.1)
221	Baltimore-Towson, MD	(8.3)
222	Odessa, TX	(8.4)
223	Albany-Schenectady-Troy, NY	(8.6)
224	Sarasota-Bradenton-Venice, FL	(8.9)
225	Beaumont-Port Arthur, TX	(9.1)
226	Lubbock, TX	(9.4)
226	Savannah, GA	(9.4)
228	Columbus, GA-AL	(9.6)
229	Missoula, MT	(10.0)
230	Monroe, MI	(10.1)
231	Cedar Rapids, IA	(10.2)
232	Eugene-Springfield, OR	(10.9)
232	Rapid City, SD	(10.9)
234	Augusta, GA-SC	(11.1)
235	Stockton, CA	(11.2)
236	Spartanburg, SC	(11.7)
237	Sandusky, OH	(11.9)
238	Ogden-Clearfield, UT	(12.0)
239	Fort Lauderdale, FL M.D.	(12.3)
239	Syracuse, NY	(12.3)
241	Oxnard-Thousand Oaks, CA	(12.6)
241	San Antonio, TX	(12.6)
243	Billings, MT	(12.9)
243	Las Cruces, NM	(12.9)
245	Columbia, SC	(13.3)
245	Johnson City, TN	(13.3)
247	Greenville, SC	(14.0)
248	Bay City, MI	(14.2)
248	Santa Cruz-Watsonville, CA	(14.2)
250	Louisville, KY-IN	(14.8)
250	Rocky Mount, NC	(14.8)
252	Brownsville-Harlingen, TX	(15.1)
252	Springfield, OH	(15.1)
254	Corpus Christi, TX	(15.4)
254	Kokomo, IN	(15.4)
256	Muncie, IN	(15.6)
257	Flagstaff, AZ	(15.7)
258	Daytona Beach, FL	(15.8)
258	New York (greater), NY-NJ-PA	(15.8)
260	Barnstable Town, MA	(16.0)
260	Dothan, AL	(16.0)
262	College Station-Bryan, TX	(16.2)
263	Kingsport, TN-VA	(16.3)
263	Naples-Marco Island, FL	(16.3)
265	Lincoln, NE	(16.4)
266	Farmington, NM	(16.6)
266	Wichita Falls, TX	(16.6)
268	Midland, TX	(16.7)
269	Medford, OR	(16.8)
270	Fresno, CA	(17.1)
270	South Bend-Mishawaka, IN-MI	(17.1)
272	Bloomington, IN	(17.6)
273	Oshkosh-Neenah, WI	(17.7)
274	Tucson, AZ	(18.2)
275	San Jose, CA	(19.4)
276	Holland-Grand Haven, MI	(20.3)
277	Harrisburg-Carlisle, PA	(20.5)
277	New York-W. Plains NY-NJ M.D.	(20.5)
279	Ann Arbor, MI	(21.8)
280	Reno-Sparks, NV	(21.9)
281	Valdosta, GA	(22.0)
282	Redding, CA	(22.1)
283	Sioux Falls, SD	(22.7)
284	Bend, OR	(23.1)
284	Florence, SC	(23.1)
286	Manchester-Nashua, NH	(23.4)
287	Danville, VA	(23.7)
288	Charlottesville, VA	(24.5)
289	St. Joseph, MO-KS	(24.7)
290	Kingston, NY	(24.8)
291	Pascagoula, MS	(25.5)
292	McAllen-Edinburg-Mission, TX	(25.9)
293	Montgomery, AL	(26.0)
294	Scranton--Wilkes-Barre, PA	(26.7)
295	Provo-Orem, UT	(27.4)
296	Albany, GA	(27.9)
297	Hot Springs, AR	(28.1)
298	Elmira, NY	(28.3)
299	Gainesville, GA	(29.1)
300	Hanford-Corcoran, CA	(30.3)
301	Milwaukee, WI	(30.4)
302	Lima, OH	(31.1)
303	Fort Collins-Loveland, CO	(32.6)
304	Logan, UT-ID	(32.7)
305	Wenatchee, WA	(32.9)
306	Tyler, TX	(33.2)
307	Utica-Rome, NY	(33.6)
308	Poughkeepsie, NY	(34.3)
309	Williamsport, PA	(34.4)
310	Lewiston, ID-WA	(40.4)
311	Jackson, TN	(42.6)
311	Wausau, WI	(42.6)
313	Great Falls, MT	(44.8)
314	Racine, WI	(49.0)
315	El Centro, CA	(52.7)
316	Punta Gorda, FL	(65.7)
NA	Abilene, TX**	NA
NA	Birmingham-Hoover, AL**	NA
NA	Boise City-Nampa, ID**	NA
NA	Chicago, IL**	NA
NA	Cleveland-Elyria-Mentor, OH**	NA
NA	Cleveland, TN**	NA
NA	Dalton, GA**	NA
NA	Des Moines-West Des Moines, IA**	NA
NA	Duluth, MN-WI**	NA
NA	Durham, NC**	NA
NA	Fairbanks, AK**	NA
NA	Fargo, ND-MN**	NA
NA	Fort Wayne, IN**	NA
NA	Glens Falls, NY**	NA
NA	Grand Forks, ND-MN**	NA
NA	Hattiesburg, MS**	NA
NA	Ithaca, NY**	NA
NA	Jacksonville, NC**	NA
NA	Johnstown, PA**	NA
NA	Kansas City, MO-KS**	NA
NA	Killeen-Temple-Fort Hood, TX**	NA
NA	La Crosse, WI-MN**	NA
NA	Lake Havasu City-Kingman, AZ**	NA
NA	Lexington-Fayette, KY**	NA
NA	Minneapolis-St. Paul, MN-WI**	NA
NA	New Orleans, LA**	NA
NA	Palm Coast, FL**	NA
NA	Rochester, MN**	NA
NA	St. Cloud, MN**	NA
NA	Tuscaloosa, AL**	NA
NA	Vallejo-Fairfield, CA**	NA
NA	Washington (greater) DC-VA-MD**	NA
NA	Washington, DC-VA-MD-WV M.D.**	NA
NA	Wichita, KS**	NA

Source: CQ Press using data from Federal Bureau of Investigation "Crime in the United States 2006" (Uniform Crime Reports, September 24, 2007)

**Forcible rape is the carnal knowledge of a female forcibly and against her will. Assaults or attempts to commit rape by force or threat of force are included. However, statutory rape without force and other sex offenses are excluded. **Not available.*

16. Percent Change in Rape Rate: 2002 to 2006

National Percent Change = 6.6% Decrease*

RANK	METROPOLITAN AREA	% CHANGE
NA	Abilene, TX**	NA
NA	Albany-Schenectady-Troy, NY**	NA
199	Albany, GA	(44.4)
105	Albuquerque, NM	(8.5)
4	Alexandria, LA	83.1
33	Altoona, PA	16.3
140	Amarillo, TX	(17.6)
NA	Ames, IA**	NA
106	Anchorage, AK	(8.6)
NA	Anderson, SC**	NA
NA	Ann Arbor, MI**	NA
NA	Appleton, WI**	NA
56	Asheville, NC	5.6
55	Athens-Clarke County, GA	5.9
122	Atlanta, GA	(11.8)
NA	Atlantic City, NJ**	NA
121	Augusta, GA-SC	(11.1)
109	Austin-Round Rock, TX	(8.9)
144	Bakersfield, CA	(18.1)
159	Baltimore-Towson, MD	(21.7)
NA	Bangor, ME**	NA
NA	Barnstable Town, MA**	NA
158	Baton Rouge, LA	(21.5)
NA	Battle Creek, MI**	NA
NA	Bay City, MI**	NA
202	Beaumont-Port Arthur, TX	(47.0)
186	Bellingham, WA	(32.2)
NA	Bend, OR**	NA
NA	Bethesda-Frederick, MD M.D.**	NA
2	Billings, MT	108.9
30	Binghamton, NY	21.9
68	Birmingham-Hoover, AL	1.6
24	Bismarck, ND	29.8
NA	Blacksburg, VA**	NA
196	Bloomington, IN	(38.3)
125	Boise City-Nampa, ID	(12.6)
NA	Bowling Green, KY**	NA
31	Bremerton-Silverdale, WA	21.8
61	Brownsville-Harlingen, TX	4.2
NA	Brunswick, GA**	NA
60	Buffalo-Niagara Falls, NY	4.3
NA	Burlington, NC**	NA
NA	Camden, NJ M.D.**	NA
76	Cape Coral-Fort Myers, FL	(1.1)
NA	Carson City, NV**	NA
16	Casper, WY	43.3
181	Cedar Rapids, IA	(30.6)
79	Charleston-North Charleston, SC	(2.8)
35	Charleston, WV	15.6
NA	Charlotte-Gastonia, NC-SC**	NA
NA	Charlottesville, VA**	NA
52	Chattanooga, TN-GA	6.0
111	Cheyenne, WY	(9.1)
NA	Chicago, IL**	NA
13	Chico, CA	49.0
96	Cincinnati-Middletown, OH-KY-IN	(5.6)
82	Clarksville, TN-KY	(3.3)
NA	Cleveland-Elyria-Mentor, OH**	NA
NA	Cleveland, TN**	NA
NA	Coeur d'Alene, ID**	NA
NA	College Station-Bryan, TX**	NA
80	Colorado Springs, CO	(2.9)
154	Columbia, MO	(20.4)
179	Columbia, SC	(27.9)
52	Columbus, GA-AL	6.0
NA	Columbus, IN**	NA
141	Columbus, OH	(17.7)
151	Corpus Christi, TX	(19.8)
19	Cumberland, MD-WV	40.1
NA	Dallas (greater), TX**	NA
124	Dallas-Plano-Irving, TX M.D.	(12.3)
NA	Dalton, GA**	NA
169	Danville, VA	(24.0)
187	Daytona Beach, FL	(33.3)
NA	Dayton, OH**	NA
3	Decatur, AL	88.3
67	Denver-Aurora, CO	1.7
NA	Des Moines-West Des Moines, IA**	NA
89	Detroit (greater), MI	(4.7)
NA	Detroit-Livonia-Dearborn, MI M.D.**	NA
NA	Dothan, AL**	NA
28	Dover, DE	24.9
42	Dubuque, IA	11.6
NA	Duluth, MN-WI**	NA
NA	Durham, NC**	NA
194	Eau Claire, WI	(37.6)
NA	Edison, NJ M.D.**	NA
NA	El Centro, CA**	NA
40	El Paso, TX	13.3
NA	Elizabethtown, KY**	NA
15	Elkhart-Goshen, IN	43.9
NA	Elmira, NY**	NA
71	Erie, PA	0.5
88	Eugene-Springfield, OR	(4.5)
NA	Evansville, IN-KY**	NA
NA	Fairbanks, AK**	NA
NA	Fargo, ND-MN**	NA
NA	Farmington, NM**	NA
NA	Fayetteville, AR-MO**	NA
92	Fayetteville, NC	(4.8)
108	Flagstaff, AZ	(8.8)
27	Flint, MI	28.2
156	Florence, SC	(21.1)
NA	Fond du Lac, WI**	NA
189	Fort Collins-Loveland, CO	(34.8)
87	Fort Lauderdale, FL M.D.	(4.3)
7	Fort Smith, AR-OK	59.1
93	Fort Walton Beach, FL	(5.2)
NA	Fort Wayne, IN**	NA
110	Fort Worth-Arlington, TX M.D.	(9.0)
176	Fresno, CA	(26.2)
11	Gadsden, AL	49.2
56	Gainesville, FL	5.6
NA	Gainesville, GA**	NA
78	Glens Falls, NY	(2.6)
25	Goldsboro, NC	28.3
NA	Grand Forks, ND-MN**	NA
5	Grand Junction, CO	65.0
NA	Grand Rapids-Wyoming, MI**	NA
203	Great Falls, MT	(47.1)
195	Greeley, CO	(38.0)
173	Green Bay, WI	(25.9)
NA	Greensboro-High Point, NC**	NA
12	Greenville, NC	49.1
NA	Greenville, SC**	NA
NA	Hagerstown-Martinsburg, MD-WV**	NA
NA	Hanford-Corcoran, CA**	NA
NA	Harrisburg-Carlisle, PA**	NA
NA	Harrisonburg, VA**	NA
106	Hartford, CT	(8.6)
NA	Hattiesburg, MS**	NA
NA	Holland-Grand Haven, MI**	NA
172	Honolulu, HI	(25.7)
NA	Hot Springs, AR**	NA
71	Houma, LA	0.5
89	Houston, TX	(4.7)
NA	Huntington-Ashland, WV-KY-OH**	NA
35	Huntsville, AL	15.6
NA	Idaho Falls, ID**	NA
NA	Indianapolis, IN**	NA
75	Iowa City, IA	(0.4)
NA	Ithaca, NY**	NA
170	Jacksonville, FL	(24.7)
NA	Jacksonville, NC**	NA
93	Jackson, MI	(5.2)
155	Jackson, MS	(20.6)
182	Jackson, TN	(31.7)
6	Janesville, WI	63.7
NA	Jefferson City, MO**	NA
NA	Johnson City, TN**	NA
NA	Johnstown, PA**	NA
1	Jonesboro, AR	349.1
17	Joplin, MO	42.2
NA	Kalamazoo-Portage, MI**	NA
NA	Kansas City, MO-KS**	NA
64	Kennewick-Richland-Pasco, WA	2.7
NA	Killeen-Temple-Fort Hood, TX**	NA
NA	Kingsport, TN-VA**	NA
NA	Kingston, NY**	NA
100	Knoxville, TN	(6.8)
49	Kokomo, IN	8.3
NA	La Crosse, WI-MN**	NA
115	Lafayette, IN	(9.4)
21	Lake Charles, LA	33.2
NA	Lake Havasu City-Kingman, AZ**	NA
45	Lakeland, FL	10.2
132	Lancaster, PA	(13.7)
165	Lansing-East Lansing, MI	(23.2)
18	Laredo, TX	42.1
NA	Las Cruces, NM**	NA
32	Las Vegas-Paradise, NV	19.2

Note: All listings are for Metropolitan Statistical Areas (M.S.A.s) except for those ending with "M.D." Listings with "M.D." are Metropolitan Divisions which are smaller parts of eleven large M.S.A.s. See explanatory note at beginning of metropolitan area section on page 23.

RANK	METROPOLITAN AREA	% CHANGE
10	Lawrence, KS	50.3
14	Lawton, OK	45.8
NA	Lebanon, PA**	NA
177	Lewiston-Auburn, ME	(26.7)
NA	Lewiston, ID-WA**	NA
NA	Lexington-Fayette, KY**	NA
NA	Lima, OH**	NA
93	Lincoln, NE	(5.2)
20	Little Rock, AR	33.4
NA	Logan, UT-ID**	NA
192	Longview, TX	(36.6)
NA	Longview, WA**	NA
152	Los Angeles County, CA M.D.	(20.1)
NA	Los Angeles (greater), CA**	NA
34	Louisville, KY-IN	15.9
180	Lubbock, TX	(28.0)
136	Lynchburg, VA	(17.2)
NA	Macon, GA**	NA
NA	Madera, CA**	NA
119	Madison, WI	(10.7)
NA	Manchester-Nashua, NH**	NA
NA	Mansfield, OH**	NA
131	McAllen-Edinburg-Mission, TX	(13.2)
50	Medford, OR	7.8
NA	Memphis, TN-MS-AR**	NA
98	Merced, CA	(5.9)
NA	Miami (greater), FL**	NA
86	Miami-Dade County, FL M.D.	(4.2)
NA	Michigan City-La Porte, IN**	NA
NA	Midland, TX**	NA
NA	Milwaukee, WI**	NA
NA	Minneapolis-St. Paul, MN-WI**	NA
NA	Missoula, MT**	NA
NA	Mobile, AL**	NA
156	Modesto, CA	(21.1)
NA	Monroe, LA**	NA
NA	Monroe, MI**	NA
188	Montgomery, AL	(34.2)
NA	Morgantown, WV**	NA
NA	Morristown, TN**	NA
NA	Mount Vernon-Anacortes, WA**	NA
116	Muncie, IN	(9.6)
NA	Muskegon-Norton Shores, MI**	NA
44	Myrtle Beach, SC	10.9
NA	Napa, CA**	NA
164	Naples-Marco Island, FL	(22.7)
153	Nashville-Davidson, TN	(20.2)
NA	Nassau-Suffolk, NY M.D.**	NA
145	New Orleans, LA	(18.4)
NA	New York (greater), NY-NJ-PA**	NA
193	New York-W. Plains NY-NJ M.D.	(37.5)
178	Newark-Union, NJ-PA M.D.	(27.4)
NA	Niles-Benton Harbor, MI**	NA
58	Oakland-Fremont, CA M.D.	5.5
51	Ocala, FL	7.1
NA	Ocean City, NJ**	NA
NA	Odessa, TX**	NA
NA	Ogden-Clearfield, UT**	NA
162	Oklahoma City, OK	(22.2)
201	Olympia, WA	(45.9)

RANK	METROPOLITAN AREA	% CHANGE
85	Omaha-Council Bluffs, NE-IA	(4.1)
69	Orlando, FL	1.3
NA	Oshkosh-Neenah, WI**	NA
NA	Oxnard-Thousand Oaks, CA**	NA
135	Palm Bay-Melbourne, FL	(16.7)
NA	Palm Coast, FL**	NA
146	Panama City-Lynn Haven, FL	(19.1)
NA	Pascagoula, MS**	NA
128	Pensacola, FL	(12.9)
81	Philadelphia (greater) PA-NJ-DE	(3.0)
NA	Philadelphia, PA M.D.**	NA
37	Phoenix-Mesa-Scottsdale, AZ	14.9
148	Pine Bluff, AR	(19.5)
165	Pittsburgh, PA	(23.2)
NA	Pittsfield, MA**	NA
22	Pocatello, ID	33.0
165	Port St. Lucie, FL	(23.2)
103	Portland-Vancouver, OR-WA	(8.3)
NA	Portland, ME**	NA
NA	Poughkeepsie, NY**	NA
NA	Prescott, AZ**	NA
43	Provo-Orem, UT	11.5
8	Pueblo, CO	55.0
205	Punta Gorda, FL	(59.1)
204	Racine, WI	(50.0)
NA	Raleigh-Cary, NC**	NA
159	Rapid City, SD	(21.7)
71	Reading, PA	0.5
149	Redding, CA	(19.6)
185	Reno-Sparks, NV	(32.0)
125	Richmond, VA	(12.6)
123	Riverside-San Bernardino, CA	(11.9)
NA	Roanoke, VA**	NA
NA	Rochester, MN**	NA
48	Rochester, NY	8.5
9	Rocky Mount, NC	51.3
NA	Rome, GA**	NA
117	Sacramento, CA	(10.2)
NA	Saginaw, MI**	NA
112	Salem, OR	(9.2)
141	Salinas, CA	(17.7)
NA	Salisbury, MD**	NA
NA	Salt Lake City, UT**	NA
120	San Angelo, TX	(10.9)
74	San Antonio, TX	0.0
84	San Diego, CA	(4.0)
NA	San Francisco (greater), CA**	NA
103	San Francisco-S. Mateo, CA M.D.	(8.3)
197	San Jose, CA	(38.6)
138	San Luis Obispo, CA	(17.5)
NA	Sandusky, OH**	NA
62	Santa Ana-Anaheim, CA M.D.	3.9
NA	Santa Barbara-Santa Maria, CA**	NA
102	Santa Cruz-Watsonville, CA	(7.3)
58	Santa Fe, NM	5.5
100	Santa Rosa-Petaluma, CA	(6.8)
168	Sarasota-Bradenton-Venice, FL	(23.8)
76	Savannah, GA	(1.1)
83	Scranton--Wilkes-Barre, PA	(3.4)
NA	Seattle (greater), WA**	NA

RANK	METROPOLITAN AREA	% CHANGE
63	Seattle-Bellevue, WA M.D.	3.6
NA	Sebastian-Vero Beach, FL**	NA
38	Sheboygan, WI	14.3
46	Sherman-Denison, TX	9.5
29	Shreveport-Bossier City, LA	24.7
66	Sioux City, IA-NE-SD	2.4
161	Sioux Falls, SD	(22.0)
170	South Bend-Mishawaka, IN-MI	(24.7)
NA	Spartanburg, SC**	NA
138	Spokane, WA	(17.5)
NA	Springfield, MA**	NA
149	Springfield, MO	(19.6)
NA	Springfield, OH**	NA
190	State College, PA	(36.2)
183	Stockton, CA	(31.9)
NA	St. Cloud, MN**	NA
147	St. Joseph, MO-KS	(19.3)
NA	St. Louis, MO-IL**	NA
130	Sumter, SC	(13.1)
NA	Syracuse, NY**	NA
143	Tacoma, WA M.D.	(18.0)
112	Tallahassee, FL	(9.2)
134	Tampa-St Petersburg, FL	(15.9)
23	Texarkana, TX-Texarkana, AR	31.7
112	Toledo, OH	(9.2)
129	Topeka, KS	(13.0)
190	Trenton-Ewing, NJ	(36.2)
133	Tucson, AZ	(14.4)
65	Tulsa, OK	2.5
99	Tuscaloosa, AL	(6.3)
200	Tyler, TX	(44.7)
198	Utica-Rome, NY	(38.9)
NA	Valdosta, GA**	NA
NA	Vallejo-Fairfield, CA**	NA
173	Victoria, TX	(25.9)
25	Vineland, NJ	28.3
97	Virginia Beach-Norfolk, VA-NC	(5.7)
137	Visalia-Porterville, CA	(17.4)
38	Waco, TX	14.3
NA	Warner Robins, GA**	NA
NA	Warren-Farmington Hills, MI M.D.**	NA
NA	Washington (greater) DC-VA-MD**	NA
NA	Washington, DC-VA-MD-WV M.D.**	NA
163	Waterloo-Cedar Falls, IA	(22.3)
183	Wausau, WI	(31.9)
NA	Wenatchee, WA**	NA
118	West Palm Beach, FL M.D.	(10.3)
NA	Wheeling, WV-OH**	NA
89	Wichita Falls, TX	(4.7)
52	Wichita, KS	6.0
173	Williamsport, PA	(25.9)
NA	Wilmington, DE-MD-NJ M.D.**	NA
41	Wilmington, NC	11.8
NA	Winchester, VA-WV**	NA
NA	Winston-Salem, NC**	NA
NA	Worcester, MA**	NA
69	Yakima, WA	1.3
125	Yuba City, CA	(12.6)
47	Yuma, AZ	9.4

Source: CQ Press using data from Federal Bureau of Investigation "Crime in the United States 2006" (Uniform Crime Reports, September 24, 2007)

**Forcible rape is the carnal knowledge of a female forcibly and against her will. Assaults or attempts to commit rape by force or threat of force are included. However, statutory rape without force and other sex offenses are excluded. **Not available.*

16. Percent Change in Rape Rate: 2002 to 2006 (continued)

National Percent Change = 6.6% Decrease*

RANK	METROPOLITAN AREA	% CHANGE
1	Jonesboro, AR	349.1
2	Billings, MT	108.9
3	Decatur, AL	88.3
4	Alexandria, LA	83.1
5	Grand Junction, CO	65.0
6	Janesville, WI	63.7
7	Fort Smith, AR-OK	59.1
8	Pueblo, CO	55.0
9	Rocky Mount, NC	51.3
10	Lawrence, KS	50.3
11	Gadsden, AL	49.2
12	Greenville, NC	49.1
13	Chico, CA	49.0
14	Lawton, OK	45.8
15	Elkhart-Goshen, IN	43.9
16	Casper, WY	43.3
17	Joplin, MO	42.2
18	Laredo, TX	42.1
19	Cumberland, MD-WV	40.1
20	Little Rock, AR	33.4
21	Lake Charles, LA	33.2
22	Pocatello, ID	33.0
23	Texarkana, TX-Texarkana, AR	31.7
24	Bismarck, ND	29.8
25	Goldsboro, NC	28.3
25	Vineland, NJ	28.3
27	Flint, MI	28.2
28	Dover, DE	24.9
29	Shreveport-Bossier City, LA	24.7
30	Binghamton, NY	21.9
31	Bremerton-Silverdale, WA	21.8
32	Las Vegas-Paradise, NV	19.2
33	Altoona, PA	16.3
34	Louisville, KY-IN	15.9
35	Charleston, WV	15.6
35	Huntsville, AL	15.6
37	Phoenix-Mesa-Scottsdale, AZ	14.9
38	Sheboygan, WI	14.3
38	Waco, TX	14.3
40	El Paso, TX	13.3
41	Wilmington, NC	11.8
42	Dubuque, IA	11.6
43	Provo-Orem, UT	11.5
44	Myrtle Beach, SC	10.9
45	Lakeland, FL	10.2
46	Sherman-Denison, TX	9.5
47	Yuma, AZ	9.4
48	Rochester, NY	8.5
49	Kokomo, IN	8.3
50	Medford, OR	7.8
51	Ocala, FL	7.1
52	Chattanooga, TN-GA	6.0
52	Columbus, GA-AL	6.0
52	Wichita, KS	6.0
55	Athens-Clarke County, GA	5.9
56	Asheville, NC	5.6
56	Gainesville, FL	5.6
58	Oakland-Fremont, CA M.D.	5.5
58	Santa Fe, NM	5.5
60	Buffalo-Niagara Falls, NY	4.3
61	Brownsville-Harlingen, TX	4.2
62	Santa Ana-Anaheim, CA M.D.	3.9
63	Seattle-Bellevue, WA M.D.	3.6
64	Kennewick-Richland-Pasco, WA	2.7
65	Tulsa, OK	2.5
66	Sioux City, IA-NE-SD	2.4
67	Denver-Aurora, CO	1.7
68	Birmingham-Hoover, AL	1.6
69	Orlando, FL	1.3
69	Yakima, WA	1.3
71	Erie, PA	0.5
71	Houma, LA	0.5
71	Reading, PA	0.5
74	San Antonio, TX	0.0
75	Iowa City, IA	(0.4)
76	Cape Coral-Fort Myers, FL	(1.1)
76	Savannah, GA	(1.1)
78	Glens Falls, NY	(2.6)
79	Charleston-North Charleston, SC	(2.8)
80	Colorado Springs, CO	(2.9)
81	Philadelphia (greater) PA-NJ-DE	(3.0)
82	Clarksville, TN-KY	(3.3)
83	Scranton--Wilkes-Barre, PA	(3.4)
84	San Diego, CA	(4.0)
85	Omaha-Council Bluffs, NE-IA	(4.1)
86	Miami-Dade County, FL M.D.	(4.2)
87	Fort Lauderdale, FL M.D.	(4.3)
88	Eugene-Springfield, OR	(4.5)
89	Detroit (greater), MI	(4.7)
89	Houston, TX	(4.7)
89	Wichita Falls, TX	(4.7)
92	Fayetteville, NC	(4.8)
93	Fort Walton Beach, FL	(5.2)
93	Jackson, MI	(5.2)
93	Lincoln, NE	(5.2)
96	Cincinnati-Middletown, OH-KY-IN	(5.6)
97	Virginia Beach-Norfolk, VA-NC	(5.7)
98	Merced, CA	(5.9)
99	Tuscaloosa, AL	(6.3)
100	Knoxville, TN	(6.8)
100	Santa Rosa-Petaluma, CA	(6.8)
102	Santa Cruz-Watsonville, CA	(7.3)
103	Portland-Vancouver, OR-WA	(8.3)
103	San Francisco-S. Mateo, CA M.D.	(8.3)
105	Albuquerque, NM	(8.5)
106	Anchorage, AK	(8.6)
106	Hartford, CT	(8.6)
108	Flagstaff, AZ	(8.8)
109	Austin-Round Rock, TX	(8.9)
110	Fort Worth-Arlington, TX M.D.	(9.0)
111	Cheyenne, WY	(9.1)
112	Salem, OR	(9.2)
112	Tallahassee, FL	(9.2)
112	Toledo, OH	(9.2)
115	Lafayette, IN	(9.4)
116	Muncie, IN	(9.6)
117	Sacramento, CA	(10.2)
118	West Palm Beach, FL M.D.	(10.3)
119	Madison, WI	(10.7)
120	San Angelo, TX	(10.9)
121	Augusta, GA-SC	(11.1)
122	Atlanta, GA	(11.8)
123	Riverside-San Bernardino, CA	(11.9)
124	Dallas-Plano-Irving, TX M.D.	(12.3)
125	Boise City-Nampa, ID	(12.6)
125	Richmond, VA	(12.6)
125	Yuba City, CA	(12.6)
128	Pensacola, FL	(12.9)
129	Topeka, KS	(13.0)
130	Sumter, SC	(13.1)
131	McAllen-Edinburg-Mission, TX	(13.2)
132	Lancaster, PA	(13.7)
133	Tucson, AZ	(14.4)
134	Tampa-St Petersburg, FL	(15.9)
135	Palm Bay-Melbourne, FL	(16.7)
136	Lynchburg, VA	(17.2)
137	Visalia-Porterville, CA	(17.4)
138	San Luis Obispo, CA	(17.5)
138	Spokane, WA	(17.5)
140	Amarillo, TX	(17.6)
141	Columbus, OH	(17.7)
141	Salinas, CA	(17.7)
143	Tacoma, WA M.D.	(18.0)
144	Bakersfield, CA	(18.1)
145	New Orleans, LA	(18.4)
146	Panama City-Lynn Haven, FL	(19.1)
147	St. Joseph, MO-KS	(19.3)
148	Pine Bluff, AR	(19.5)
149	Redding, CA	(19.6)
149	Springfield, MO	(19.6)
151	Corpus Christi, TX	(19.8)
152	Los Angeles County, CA M.D.	(20.1)
153	Nashville-Davidson, TN	(20.2)
154	Columbia, MO	(20.4)
155	Jackson, MS	(20.6)
156	Florence, SC	(21.1)
156	Modesto, CA	(21.1)
158	Baton Rouge, LA	(21.5)
159	Baltimore-Towson, MD	(21.7)
159	Rapid City, SD	(21.7)
161	Sioux Falls, SD	(22.0)
162	Oklahoma City, OK	(22.2)
163	Waterloo-Cedar Falls, IA	(22.3)
164	Naples-Marco Island, FL	(22.7)
165	Lansing-East Lansing, MI	(23.2)
165	Pittsburgh, PA	(23.2)
165	Port St. Lucie, FL	(23.2)
168	Sarasota-Bradenton-Venice, FL	(23.8)
169	Danville, VA	(24.0)
170	Jacksonville, FL	(24.7)
170	South Bend-Mishawaka, IN-MI	(24.7)

Note: All listings are for Metropolitan Statistical Areas (M.S.A.s) except for those ending with "M.D." Listings with "M.D." are Metropolitan Divisions which are smaller parts of eleven large M.S.A.s. See explanatory note at beginning of metropolitan area section on page 23.

Rank Order - Metro Area (continued)

RANK	METROPOLITAN AREA	% CHANGE
172	Honolulu, HI	(25.7)
173	Green Bay, WI	(25.9)
173	Victoria, TX	(25.9)
173	Williamsport, PA	(25.9)
176	Fresno, CA	(26.2)
177	Lewiston-Auburn, ME	(26.7)
178	Newark-Union, NJ-PA M.D.	(27.4)
179	Columbia, SC	(27.9)
180	Lubbock, TX	(28.0)
181	Cedar Rapids, IA	(30.6)
182	Jackson, TN	(31.7)
183	Stockton, CA	(31.9)
183	Wausau, WI	(31.9)
185	Reno-Sparks, NV	(32.0)
186	Bellingham, WA	(32.2)
187	Daytona Beach, FL	(33.3)
188	Montgomery, AL	(34.2)
189	Fort Collins-Loveland, CO	(34.8)
190	State College, PA	(36.2)
190	Trenton-Ewing, NJ	(36.2)
192	Longview, TX	(36.6)
193	New York-W. Plains NY-NJ M.D.	(37.5)
194	Eau Claire, WI	(37.6)
195	Greeley, CO	(38.0)
196	Bloomington, IN	(38.3)
197	San Jose, CA	(38.6)
198	Utica-Rome, NY	(38.9)
199	Albany, GA	(44.4)
200	Tyler, TX	(44.7)
201	Olympia, WA	(45.9)
202	Beaumont-Port Arthur, TX	(47.0)
203	Great Falls, MT	(47.1)
204	Racine, WI	(50.0)
205	Punta Gorda, FL	(59.1)
NA	Abilene, TX**	NA
NA	Albany-Schenectady-Troy, NY**	NA
NA	Ames, IA**	NA
NA	Anderson, SC**	NA
NA	Ann Arbor, MI**	NA
NA	Appleton, WI**	NA
NA	Atlantic City, NJ**	NA
NA	Bangor, ME**	NA
NA	Barnstable Town, MA**	NA
NA	Battle Creek, MI**	NA
NA	Bay City, MI**	NA
NA	Bend, OR**	NA
NA	Bethesda-Frederick, MD M.D.**	NA
NA	Blacksburg, VA**	NA
NA	Bowling Green, KY**	NA
NA	Brunswick, GA**	NA
NA	Burlington, NC**	NA
NA	Camden, NJ M.D.**	NA
NA	Carson City, NV**	NA
NA	Charlotte-Gastonia, NC-SC**	NA
NA	Charlottesville, VA**	NA
NA	Chicago, IL**	NA
NA	Cleveland-Elyria-Mentor, OH**	NA
NA	Cleveland, TN**	NA
NA	Coeur d'Alene, ID**	NA
NA	College Station-Bryan, TX**	NA
NA	Columbus, IN**	NA
NA	Dallas (greater), TX**	NA
NA	Dalton, GA**	NA
NA	Dayton, OH**	NA
NA	Des Moines-West Des Moines, IA**	NA
NA	Detroit-Livonia-Dearborn, MI M.D.**	NA
NA	Dothan, AL**	NA
NA	Duluth, MN-WI**	NA
NA	Durham, NC**	NA
NA	Edison, NJ M.D.**	NA
NA	El Centro, CA**	NA
NA	Elizabethtown, KY**	NA
NA	Elmira, NY**	NA
NA	Evansville, IN-KY**	NA
NA	Fairbanks, AK**	NA
NA	Fargo, ND-MN**	NA
NA	Farmington, NM**	NA
NA	Fayetteville, AR-MO**	NA
NA	Fond du Lac, WI**	NA
NA	Fort Wayne, IN**	NA
NA	Gainesville, GA**	NA
NA	Grand Forks, ND-MN**	NA
NA	Grand Rapids-Wyoming, MI**	NA
NA	Greensboro-High Point, NC**	NA
NA	Greenville, SC**	NA
NA	Hagerstown-Martinsburg, MD-WV**	NA
NA	Hanford-Corcoran, CA**	NA
NA	Harrisburg-Carlisle, PA**	NA
NA	Harrisonburg, VA**	NA
NA	Hattiesburg, MS**	NA
NA	Holland-Grand Haven, MI**	NA
NA	Hot Springs, AR**	NA
NA	Huntington-Ashland, WV-KY-OH**	NA
NA	Idaho Falls, ID**	NA
NA	Indianapolis, IN**	NA
NA	Ithaca, NY**	NA
NA	Jacksonville, NC**	NA
NA	Jefferson City, MO**	NA
NA	Johnson City, TN**	NA
NA	Johnstown, PA**	NA
NA	Kalamazoo-Portage, MI**	NA
NA	Kansas City, MO-KS**	NA
NA	Killeen-Temple-Fort Hood, TX**	NA
NA	Kingsport, TN-VA**	NA
NA	Kingston, NY**	NA
NA	La Crosse, WI-MN**	NA
NA	Lake Havasu City-Kingman, AZ**	NA
NA	Las Cruces, NM**	NA
NA	Lebanon, PA**	NA
NA	Lewiston, ID-WA**	NA
NA	Lexington-Fayette, KY**	NA
NA	Lima, OH**	NA
NA	Logan, UT-ID**	NA
NA	Longview, WA**	NA
NA	Los Angeles (greater), CA**	NA
NA	Macon, GA**	NA
NA	Madera, CA**	NA
NA	Manchester-Nashua, NH**	NA
NA	Mansfield, OH**	NA
NA	Memphis, TN-MS-AR**	NA
NA	Miami (greater), FL**	NA
NA	Michigan City-La Porte, IN**	NA
NA	Midland, TX**	NA
NA	Milwaukee, WI**	NA
NA	Minneapolis-St. Paul, MN-WI**	NA
NA	Missoula, MT**	NA
NA	Mobile, AL**	NA
NA	Monroe, LA**	NA
NA	Monroe, MI**	NA
NA	Morgantown, WV**	NA
NA	Morristown, TN**	NA
NA	Mount Vernon-Anacortes, WA**	NA
NA	Muskegon-Norton Shores, MI**	NA
NA	Napa, CA**	NA
NA	Nassau-Suffolk, NY M.D.**	NA
NA	New York (greater), NY-NJ-PA**	NA
NA	Niles-Benton Harbor, MI**	NA
NA	Ocean City, NJ**	NA
NA	Odessa, TX**	NA
NA	Ogden-Clearfield, UT**	NA
NA	Oshkosh-Neenah, WI**	NA
NA	Oxnard-Thousand Oaks, CA**	NA
NA	Palm Coast, FL**	NA
NA	Pascagoula, MS**	NA
NA	Philadelphia, PA M.D.**	NA
NA	Pittsfield, MA**	NA
NA	Portland, ME**	NA
NA	Poughkeepsie, NY**	NA
NA	Prescott, AZ**	NA
NA	Raleigh-Cary, NC**	NA
NA	Roanoke, VA**	NA
NA	Rochester, MN**	NA
NA	Rome, GA**	NA
NA	Saginaw, MI**	NA
NA	Salisbury, MD**	NA
NA	Salt Lake City, UT**	NA
NA	San Francisco (greater), CA**	NA
NA	Sandusky, OH**	NA
NA	Santa Barbara-Santa Maria, CA**	NA
NA	Seattle (greater), WA**	NA
NA	Sebastian-Vero Beach, FL**	NA
NA	Spartanburg, SC**	NA
NA	Springfield, MA**	NA
NA	Springfield, OH**	NA
NA	St. Cloud, MN**	NA
NA	St. Louis, MO-IL**	NA
NA	Syracuse, NY**	NA
NA	Valdosta, GA**	NA
NA	Vallejo-Fairfield, CA**	NA
NA	Warner Robins, GA**	NA
NA	Warren-Farmington Hills, MI M.D.**	NA
NA	Washington (greater) DC-VA-MD**	NA
NA	Washington, DC-VA-MD-WV M.D.**	NA
NA	Wenatchee, WA**	NA
NA	Wheeling, WV-OH**	NA
NA	Wilmington, DE-MD-NJ M.D.**	NA
NA	Winchester, VA-WV**	NA
NA	Winston-Salem, NC**	NA
NA	Worcester, MA**	NA

Source: CQ Press using data from Federal Bureau of Investigation
"Crime in the United States 2006" (Uniform Crime Reports, September 24, 2007)
**Forcible rape is the carnal knowledge of a female forcibly and against her will. Assaults or attempts to commit rape by force or threat of force are included. However, statutory rape without force and other sex offenses are excluded. **Not available.*

17. Robberies in 2006

National Total = 447,403 Robberies*

RANK	METROPOLITAN AREA	ROBBERY
248	Abilene, TX	109
87	Albany-Schenectady-Troy, NY	964
174	Albany, GA	265
72	Albuquerque, NM	1,410
188	Alexandria, LA	216
245	Altoona, PA	112
144	Amarillo, TX	406
338	Ames, IA	19
133	Anchorage, AK	490
206	Anderson, SC	159
172	Ann Arbor, MI	268
318	Appleton, WI	39
156	Asheville, NC	316
200	Athens-Clarke County, GA	172
12	Atlanta, GA	10,620
120	Atlantic City, NJ	599
92	Augusta, GA-SC	866
66	Austin-Round Rock, TX	1,566
83	Bakersfield, CA	1,059
18	Baltimore-Towson, MD	7,842
323	Bangor, ME	33
265	Barnstable Town, MA	89
68	Baton Rouge, LA	1,509
211	Battle Creek, MI	153
306	Bay City, MI	50
117	Beaumont-Port Arthur, TX	618
256	Bellingham, WA	98
308	Bend, OR	48
70	Bethesda-Frederick, MD M.D.	1,442
308	Billings, MT	48
238	Binghamton, NY	117
50	Birmingham-Hoover, AL	2,572
347	Bismarck, ND	11
305	Blacksburg, VA	51
269	Bloomington, IN	87
193	Boise City-Nampa, ID	186
250	Bowling Green, KY	108
234	Bremerton-Silverdale, WA	125
168	Brownsville-Harlingen, TX	277
197	Brunswick, GA	176
53	Buffalo-Niagara Falls, NY	2,249
214	Burlington, NC	147
61	Camden, NJ M.D.	1,674
92	Cape Coral-Fort Myers, FL	866
334	Carson City, NV	22
341	Casper, WY	16
220	Cedar Rapids, IA	141
76	Charleston-North Charleston, SC	1,226
187	Charleston, WV	218
35	Charlotte-Gastonia, NC-SC	4,180
231	Charlottesville, VA	129
114	Chattanooga, TN-GA	646
327	Cheyenne, WY	29
NA	Chicago, IL**	NA
216	Chico, CA	144
39	Cincinnati-Middletown, OH-KY-IN	3,627
173	Clarksville, TN-KY	267
24	Cleveland-Elyria-Mentor, OH	5,461
319	Cleveland, TN	38
331	Coeur d'Alene, ID	27
216	College Station-Bryan, TX	144
112	Colorado Springs, CO	665
226	Columbia, MO	134
90	Columbia, SC	942
113	Columbus, GA-AL	651
339	Columbus, IN	17
34	Columbus, OH	4,215
132	Corpus Christi, TX	508
313	Cumberland, MD-WV	46
10	Dallas (greater), TX	11,622
15	Dallas-Plano-Irving, TX M.D.	8,790
315	Dalton, GA	45
265	Danville, VA	89
115	Daytona Beach, FL	636
80	Dayton, OH	1,153
240	Decatur, AL	115
48	Denver-Aurora, CO	2,628
140	Des Moines-West Des Moines, IA	435
13	Detroit (greater), MI	10,196
16	Detroit-Livonia-Dearborn, MI M.D.	8,499
185	Dothan, AL	219
221	Dover, DE	140
341	Dubuque, IA	16
208	Duluth, MN-WI	156
78	Durham, NC	1,185
335	Eau Claire, WI	21
65	Edison, NJ M.D.	1,597
223	El Centro, CA	139
127	El Paso, TX	546
297	Elizabethtown, KY	56
167	Elkhart-Goshen, IN	281
297	Elmira, NY	56
157	Erie, PA	309
185	Eugene-Springfield, OR	219
178	Evansville, IN-KY	248
308	Fairbanks, AK	48
326	Fargo, ND-MN	30
313	Farmington, NM	46
242	Fayetteville, AR-MO	114
109	Fayetteville, NC	696
248	Flagstaff, AZ	109
94	Flint, MI	864
145	Florence, SC	395
339	Fond du Lac, WI	17
290	Fort Collins-Loveland, CO	61
37	Fort Lauderdale, FL M.D.	3,685
205	Fort Smith, AR-OK	160
251	Fort Walton Beach, FL	107
138	Fort Wayne, IN	442
47	Fort Worth-Arlington, TX M.D.	2,832
63	Fresno, CA	1,621
180	Gadsden, AL	244
148	Gainesville, FL	382
259	Gainesville, GA	95
345	Glens Falls, NY	14
216	Goldsboro, NC	144
344	Grand Forks, ND-MN	15
308	Grand Junction, CO	48
95	Grand Rapids-Wyoming, MI	860
327	Great Falls, MT	29
281	Greeley, CO	73
242	Green Bay, WI	114
74	Greensboro-High Point, NC	1,336
154	Greenville, NC	321
106	Greenville, SC	717
184	Hagerstown-Martinsburg, MD-WV	223
275	Hanford-Corcoran, CA	83
108	Harrisburg-Carlisle, PA	704
323	Harrisonburg, VA	33
70	Hartford, CT	1,442
212	Hattiesburg, MS	150
307	Holland-Grand Haven, MI	49
88	Honolulu, HI	956
215	Hot Springs, AR	146
209	Houma, LA	155
6	Houston, TX	15,181
177	Huntington-Ashland, WV-KY-OH	258
102	Huntsville, AL	769
336	Idaho Falls, ID	20
38	Indianapolis, IN	3,633
293	Iowa City, IA	58
321	Ithaca, NY	34
49	Jacksonville, FL	2,627
242	Jacksonville, NC	114
247	Jackson, MI	110
77	Jackson, MS	1,193
191	Jackson, TN	204
228	Janesville, WI	132
293	Jefferson City, MO	58
269	Johnson City, TN	87
277	Johnstown, PA	79
253	Jonesboro, AR	106
235	Joplin, MO	122
152	Kalamazoo-Portage, MI	347
42	Kansas City, MO-KS	3,119
265	Kennewick-Richland-Pasco, WA	89
150	Killeen-Temple-Fort Hood, TX	364
207	Kingsport, TN-VA	158
280	Kingston, NY	77
104	Knoxville, TN	744
282	Kokomo, IN	72
327	La Crosse, WI-MN	29
259	Lafayette, IN	95
162	Lake Charles, LA	291
254	Lake Havasu City-Kingman, AZ	102
105	Lakeland, FL	736
143	Lancaster, PA	410
145	Lansing-East Lansing, MI	395
171	Laredo, TX	270
240	Las Cruces, NM	115
22	Las Vegas-Paradise, NV	6,293

Note: All listings are for Metropolitan Statistical Areas (M.S.A.s) except for those ending with "M.D." Listings with "M.D." are Metropolitan Divisions which are smaller parts of eleven large M.S.A.s. See explanatory note at beginning of metropolitan area section on page 23.

RANK	METROPOLITAN AREA	ROBBERY
277	Lawrence, KS	79
199	Lawton, OK	173
269	Lebanon, PA	87
301	Lewiston-Auburn, ME	54
349	Lewiston, ID-WA	4
124	Lexington-Fayette, KY	572
221	Lima, OH	140
204	Lincoln, NE	163
73	Little Rock, AR	1,362
348	Logan, UT-ID	7
202	Longview, TX	168
285	Longview, WA	68
4	Los Angeles County, CA M.D.	27,731
2	Los Angeles (greater), CA	30,798
54	Louisville, KY-IN	2,130
149	Lubbock, TX	378
236	Lynchburg, VA	121
142	Macon, GA	414
231	Madera, CA	129
129	Madison, WI	542
182	Manchester-Nashua, NH	231
233	Mansfield, OH	126
128	McAllen-Edinburg-Mission, TX	545
286	Medford, OR	66
23	Memphis, TN-MS-AR	5,839
164	Merced, CA	286
7	Miami (greater), FL	14,131
19	Miami-Dade County, FL M.D.	7,538
257	Michigan City-La Porte, IN	97
276	Midland, TX	81
36	Milwaukee, WI	4,052
26	Minneapolis-St. Paul, MN-WI	4,984
325	Missoula, MT	32
97	Mobile, AL	833
103	Modesto, CA	767
230	Monroe, LA	130
312	Monroe, MI	47
99	Montgomery, AL	790
297	Morgantown, WV	56
293	Morristown, TN	58
292	Mount Vernon-Anacortes, WA	60
255	Muncie, IN	100
192	Muskegon-Norton Shores, MI	194
137	Myrtle Beach, SC	444
273	Napa, CA	84
162	Naples-Marco Island, FL	291
45	Nashville-Davidson, TN	2,947
52	Nassau-Suffolk, NY M.D.	2,409
59	New Orleans, LA	1,727
1	New York (greater), NY-NJ-PA	37,129
3	New York-W. Plains NY-NJ M.D.	28,852
33	Newark-Union, NJ-PA M.D.	4,271
251	Niles-Benton Harbor, MI	107
17	Oakland-Fremont, CA M.D.	8,123
168	Ocala, FL	277
277	Ocean City, NJ	79
258	Odessa, TX	96
195	Ogden-Clearfield, UT	183
69	Oklahoma City, OK	1,452
245	Olympia, WA	112
86	Omaha-Council Bluffs, NE-IA	965
25	Orlando, FL	5,179
336	Oshkosh-Neenah, WI	20
98	Oxnard-Thousand Oaks, CA	802
116	Palm Bay-Melbourne, FL	635
327	Palm Coast, FL	29
194	Panama City-Lynn Haven, FL	184
209	Pascagoula, MS	155
119	Pensacola, FL	613
5	Philadelphia (greater) PA-NJ-DE	16,240
8	Philadelphia, PA M.D.	12,959
20	Phoenix-Mesa-Scottsdale, AZ	6,719
189	Pine Bluff, AR	212
43	Pittsburgh, PA	3,114
315	Pittsfield, MA	45
341	Pocatello, ID	16
136	Port St. Lucie, FL	462
55	Portland-Vancouver, OR-WA	2,099
179	Portland, ME	245
118	Poughkeepsie, NY	614
297	Prescott, AZ	56
288	Provo-Orem, UT	63
196	Pueblo, CO	178
259	Punta Gorda, FL	95
174	Racine, WI	265
82	Raleigh-Cary, NC	1,079
319	Rapid City, SD	38
125	Reading, PA	570
272	Redding, CA	85
111	Reno-Sparks, NV	671
57	Richmond, VA	1,959
21	Riverside-San Bernardino, CA	6,601
176	Roanoke, VA	263
268	Rochester, MN	88
62	Rochester, NY	1,626
166	Rocky Mount, NC	283
287	Rome, GA	64
31	Sacramento, CA	4,377
151	Saginaw, MI	351
190	Salem, OR	205
120	Salinas, CA	599
165	Salisbury, MD	284
89	Salt Lake City, UT	944
289	San Angelo, TX	62
51	San Antonio, TX	2,559
32	San Diego, CA	4,313
9	San Francisco (greater), CA	12,942
27	San Francisco-S. Mateo, CA M.D.	4,819
67	San Jose, CA	1,555
259	San Luis Obispo, CA	95
301	Sandusky, OH	54
44	Santa Ana-Anaheim, CA M.D.	3,067
160	Santa Barbara-Santa Maria, CA	299
183	Santa Cruz-Watsonville, CA	227
239	Santa Fe, NM	116
159	Santa Rosa-Petaluma, CA	300
84	Sarasota-Bradenton-Venice, FL	997
100	Savannah, GA	789
147	Scranton--Wilkes-Barre, PA	389
28	Seattle (greater), WA	4,688
40	Seattle-Bellevue, WA M.D.	3,512
236	Sebastian-Vero Beach, FL	121
346	Sheboygan, WI	13
303	Sherman-Denison, TX	53
107	Shreveport-Bossier City, LA	706
293	Sioux City, IA-NE-SD	58
321	Sioux Falls, SD	34
130	South Bend-Mishawaka, IN-MI	535
139	Spartanburg, SC	441
134	Spokane, WA	468
85	Springfield, MA	969
170	Springfield, MO	275
153	Springfield, OH	339
332	State College, PA	26
58	Stockton, CA	1,916
290	St. Cloud, MN	61
284	St. Joseph, MO-KS	69
29	St. Louis, MO-IL	4,676
219	Sumter, SC	142
110	Syracuse, NY	687
79	Tacoma, WA M.D.	1,176
123	Tallahassee, FL	583
30	Tampa-St Petersburg, FL	4,511
203	Texarkana, TX-Texarkana, AR	167
75	Toledo, OH	1,327
154	Topeka, KS	321
91	Trenton-Ewing, NJ	867
56	Tucson, AZ	1,975
81	Tulsa, OK	1,113
158	Tuscaloosa, AL	303
225	Tyler, TX	137
198	Utica-Rome, NY	175
228	Valdosta, GA	132
96	Vallejo-Fairfield, CA	849
263	Victoria, TX	92
141	Vineland, NJ	434
41	Virginia Beach-Norfolk, VA-NC	3,180
135	Visalia-Porterville, CA	466
161	Waco, TX	292
213	Warner Robins, GA	148
60	Warren-Farmington Hills, MI M.D.	1,697
11	Washington (greater) DC-VA-MD	11,079
14	Washington, DC-VA-MD-WV M.D.	9,637
264	Waterloo-Cedar Falls, IA	90
333	Wausau, WI	25
317	Wenatchee, WA	40
46	West Palm Beach, FL M.D.	2,908
303	Wheeling, WV-OH	53
200	Wichita Falls, TX	172
126	Wichita, KS	547
273	Williamsport, PA	84
64	Wilmington, DE-MD-NJ M.D.	1,607
131	Wilmington, NC	517
283	Winchester, VA-WV	71
101	Winston-Salem, NC	781
122	Worcester, MA	589
181	Yakima, WA	233
226	Yuba City, CA	134
224	Yuma, AZ	138

Source: Federal Bureau of Investigation

"Crime in the United States 2006" (Uniform Crime Reports, September 24, 2007)

**Robbery is the taking of anything of value by force or threat of force. Attempts are included.*

***Not available.*

17. Robberies in 2006 (continued)

National Total = 447,403 Robberies*

RANK	METROPOLITAN AREA	ROBBERY
1	New York (greater), NY-NJ-PA	37,129
2	Los Angeles (greater), CA	30,798
3	New York-W. Plains NY-NJ M.D.	28,852
4	Los Angeles County, CA M.D.	27,731
5	Philadelphia (greater) PA-NJ-DE	16,240
6	Houston, TX	15,181
7	Miami (greater), FL	14,131
8	Philadelphia, PA M.D.	12,959
9	San Francisco (greater), CA	12,942
10	Dallas (greater), TX	11,622
11	Washington (greater) DC-VA-MD	11,079
12	Atlanta, GA	10,620
13	Detroit (greater), MI	10,196
14	Washington, DC-VA-MD-WV M.D.	9,637
15	Dallas-Plano-Irving, TX M.D.	8,790
16	Detroit-Livonia-Dearborn, MI M.D.	8,499
17	Oakland-Fremont, CA M.D.	8,123
18	Baltimore-Towson, MD	7,842
19	Miami-Dade County, FL M.D.	7,538
20	Phoenix-Mesa-Scottsdale, AZ	6,719
21	Riverside-San Bernardino, CA	6,601
22	Las Vegas-Paradise, NV	6,293
23	Memphis, TN-MS-AR	5,839
24	Cleveland-Elyria-Mentor, OH	5,461
25	Orlando, FL	5,179
26	Minneapolis-St. Paul, MN-WI	4,984
27	San Francisco-S. Mateo, CA M.D.	4,819
28	Seattle (greater), WA	4,688
29	St. Louis, MO-IL	4,676
30	Tampa-St Petersburg, FL	4,511
31	Sacramento, CA	4,377
32	San Diego, CA	4,313
33	Newark-Union, NJ-PA M.D.	4,271
34	Columbus, OH	4,215
35	Charlotte-Gastonia, NC-SC	4,180
36	Milwaukee, WI	4,052
37	Fort Lauderdale, FL M.D.	3,685
38	Indianapolis, IN	3,633
39	Cincinnati-Middletown, OH-KY-IN	3,627
40	Seattle-Bellevue, WA M.D.	3,512
41	Virginia Beach-Norfolk, VA-NC	3,180
42	Kansas City, MO-KS	3,119
43	Pittsburgh, PA	3,114
44	Santa Ana-Anaheim, CA M.D.	3,067
45	Nashville-Davidson, TN	2,947
46	West Palm Beach, FL M.D.	2,908
47	Fort Worth-Arlington, TX M.D.	2,832
48	Denver-Aurora, CO	2,628
49	Jacksonville, FL	2,627
50	Birmingham-Hoover, AL	2,572
51	San Antonio, TX	2,559
52	Nassau-Suffolk, NY M.D.	2,409
53	Buffalo-Niagara Falls, NY	2,249
54	Louisville, KY-IN	2,130
55	Portland-Vancouver, OR-WA	2,099
56	Tucson, AZ	1,975
57	Richmond, VA	1,959

RANK	METROPOLITAN AREA	ROBBERY
58	Stockton, CA	1,916
59	New Orleans, LA	1,727
60	Warren-Farmington Hills, MI M.D.	1,697
61	Camden, NJ M.D.	1,674
62	Rochester, NY	1,626
63	Fresno, CA	1,621
64	Wilmington, DE-MD-NJ M.D.	1,607
65	Edison, NJ M.D.	1,597
66	Austin-Round Rock, TX	1,566
67	San Jose, CA	1,555
68	Baton Rouge, LA	1,509
69	Oklahoma City, OK	1,452
70	Bethesda-Frederick, MD M.D.	1,442
70	Hartford, CT	1,442
72	Albuquerque, NM	1,410
73	Little Rock, AR	1,362
74	Greensboro-High Point, NC	1,336
75	Toledo, OH	1,327
76	Charleston-North Charleston, SC	1,226
77	Jackson, MS	1,193
78	Durham, NC	1,185
79	Tacoma, WA M.D.	1,176
80	Dayton, OH	1,153
81	Tulsa, OK	1,113
82	Raleigh-Cary, NC	1,079
83	Bakersfield, CA	1,059
84	Sarasota-Bradenton-Venice, FL	997
85	Springfield, MA	969
86	Omaha-Council Bluffs, NE-IA	965
87	Albany-Schenectady-Troy, NY	964
88	Honolulu, HI	956
89	Salt Lake City, UT	944
90	Columbia, SC	942
91	Trenton-Ewing, NJ	867
92	Augusta, GA-SC	866
92	Cape Coral-Fort Myers, FL	866
94	Flint, MI	864
95	Grand Rapids-Wyoming, MI	860
96	Vallejo-Fairfield, CA	849
97	Mobile, AL	833
98	Oxnard-Thousand Oaks, CA	802
99	Montgomery, AL	790
100	Savannah, GA	789
101	Winston-Salem, NC	781
102	Huntsville, AL	769
103	Modesto, CA	767
104	Knoxville, TN	744
105	Lakeland, FL	736
106	Greenville, SC	717
107	Shreveport-Bossier City, LA	706
108	Harrisburg-Carlisle, PA	704
109	Fayetteville, NC	696
110	Syracuse, NY	687
111	Reno-Sparks, NV	671
112	Colorado Springs, CO	665
113	Columbus, GA-AL	651
114	Chattanooga, TN-GA	646

RANK	METROPOLITAN AREA	ROBBERY
115	Daytona Beach, FL	636
116	Palm Bay-Melbourne, FL	635
117	Beaumont-Port Arthur, TX	618
118	Poughkeepsie, NY	614
119	Pensacola, FL	613
120	Atlantic City, NJ	599
120	Salinas, CA	599
122	Worcester, MA	589
123	Tallahassee, FL	583
124	Lexington-Fayette, KY	572
125	Reading, PA	570
126	Wichita, KS	547
127	El Paso, TX	546
128	McAllen-Edinburg-Mission, TX	545
129	Madison, WI	542
130	South Bend-Mishawaka, IN-MI	535
131	Wilmington, NC	517
132	Corpus Christi, TX	508
133	Anchorage, AK	490
134	Spokane, WA	468
135	Visalia-Porterville, CA	466
136	Port St. Lucie, FL	462
137	Myrtle Beach, SC	444
138	Fort Wayne, IN	442
139	Spartanburg, SC	441
140	Des Moines-West Des Moines, IA	435
141	Vineland, NJ	434
142	Macon, GA	414
143	Lancaster, PA	410
144	Amarillo, TX	406
145	Florence, SC	395
145	Lansing-East Lansing, MI	395
147	Scranton--Wilkes-Barre, PA	389
148	Gainesville, FL	382
149	Lubbock, TX	378
150	Killeen-Temple-Fort Hood, TX	364
151	Saginaw, MI	351
152	Kalamazoo-Portage, MI	347
153	Springfield, OH	339
154	Greenville, NC	321
154	Topeka, KS	321
156	Asheville, NC	316
157	Erie, PA	309
158	Tuscaloosa, AL	303
159	Santa Rosa-Petaluma, CA	300
160	Santa Barbara-Santa Maria, CA	299
161	Waco, TX	292
162	Lake Charles, LA	291
162	Naples-Marco Island, FL	291
164	Merced, CA	286
165	Salisbury, MD	284
166	Rocky Mount, NC	283
167	Elkhart-Goshen, IN	281
168	Brownsville-Harlingen, TX	277
168	Ocala, FL	277
170	Springfield, MO	275
171	Laredo, TX	270

Note: All listings are for Metropolitan Statistical Areas (M.S.A.s) except for those ending with "M.D." Listings with "M.D." are Metropolitan Divisions which are smaller parts of eleven large M.S.A.s. See explanatory note at beginning of metropolitan area section on page 23.

RANK	METROPOLITAN AREA	ROBBERY
172	Ann Arbor, MI	268
173	Clarksville, TN-KY	267
174	Albany, GA	265
174	Racine, WI	265
176	Roanoke, VA	263
177	Huntington-Ashland, WV-KY-OH	258
178	Evansville, IN-KY	248
179	Portland, ME	245
180	Gadsden, AL	244
181	Yakima, WA	233
182	Manchester-Nashua, NH	231
183	Santa Cruz-Watsonville, CA	227
184	Hagerstown-Martinsburg, MD-WV	223
185	Dothan, AL	219
185	Eugene-Springfield, OR	219
187	Charleston, WV	218
188	Alexandria, LA	216
189	Pine Bluff, AR	212
190	Salem, OR	205
191	Jackson, TN	204
192	Muskegon-Norton Shores, MI	194
193	Boise City-Nampa, ID	186
194	Panama City-Lynn Haven, FL	184
195	Ogden-Clearfield, UT	183
196	Pueblo, CO	178
197	Brunswick, GA	176
198	Utica-Rome, NY	175
199	Lawton, OK	173
200	Athens-Clarke County, GA	172
200	Wichita Falls, TX	172
202	Longview, TX	168
203	Texarkana, TX-Texarkana, AR	167
204	Lincoln, NE	163
205	Fort Smith, AR-OK	160
206	Anderson, SC	159
207	Kingsport, TN-VA	158
208	Duluth, MN-WI	156
209	Houma, LA	155
209	Pascagoula, MS	155
211	Battle Creek, MI	153
212	Hattiesburg, MS	150
213	Warner Robins, GA	148
214	Burlington, NC	147
215	Hot Springs, AR	146
216	Chico, CA	144
216	College Station-Bryan, TX	144
216	Goldsboro, NC	144
219	Sumter, SC	142
220	Cedar Rapids, IA	141
221	Dover, DE	140
221	Lima, OH	140
223	El Centro, CA	139
224	Yuma, AZ	138
225	Tyler, TX	137
226	Columbia, MO	134
226	Yuba City, CA	134
228	Janesville, WI	132
228	Valdosta, GA	132
230	Monroe, LA	130
231	Charlottesville, VA	129
231	Madera, CA	129
233	Mansfield, OH	126
234	Bremerton-Silverdale, WA	125
235	Joplin, MO	122
236	Lynchburg, VA	121
236	Sebastian-Vero Beach, FL	121
238	Binghamton, NY	117
239	Santa Fe, NM	116
240	Decatur, AL	115
240	Las Cruces, NM	115
242	Fayetteville, AR-MO	114
242	Green Bay, WI	114
242	Jacksonville, NC	114
245	Altoona, PA	112
245	Olympia, WA	112
247	Jackson, MI	110
248	Abilene, TX	109
248	Flagstaff, AZ	109
250	Bowling Green, KY	108
251	Fort Walton Beach, FL	107
251	Niles-Benton Harbor, MI	107
253	Jonesboro, AR	106
254	Lake Havasu City-Kingman, AZ	102
255	Muncie, IN	100
256	Bellingham, WA	98
257	Michigan City-La Porte, IN	97
258	Odessa, TX	96
259	Gainesville, GA	95
259	Lafayette, IN	95
259	Punta Gorda, FL	95
259	San Luis Obispo, CA	95
263	Victoria, TX	92
264	Waterloo-Cedar Falls, IA	90
265	Barnstable Town, MA	89
265	Danville, VA	89
265	Kennewick-Richland-Pasco, WA	89
268	Rochester, MN	88
269	Bloomington, IN	87
269	Johnson City, TN	87
269	Lebanon, PA	87
272	Redding, CA	85
273	Napa, CA	84
273	Williamsport, PA	84
275	Hanford-Corcoran, CA	83
276	Midland, TX	81
277	Johnstown, PA	79
277	Lawrence, KS	79
277	Ocean City, NJ	79
280	Kingston, NY	77
281	Greeley, CO	73
282	Kokomo, IN	72
283	Winchester, VA-WV	71
284	St. Joseph, MO-KS	69
285	Longview, WA	68
286	Medford, OR	66
287	Rome, GA	64
288	Provo-Orem, UT	63
289	San Angelo, TX	62
290	Fort Collins-Loveland, CO	61
290	St. Cloud, MN	61
292	Mount Vernon-Anacortes, WA	60
293	Iowa City, IA	58
293	Jefferson City, MO	58
293	Morristown, TN	58
293	Sioux City, IA-NE-SD	58
297	Elizabethtown, KY	56
297	Elmira, NY	56
297	Morgantown, WV	56
297	Prescott, AZ	56
301	Lewiston-Auburn, ME	54
301	Sandusky, OH	54
303	Sherman-Denison, TX	53
303	Wheeling, WV-OH	53
305	Blacksburg, VA	51
306	Bay City, MI	50
307	Holland-Grand Haven, MI	49
308	Bend, OR	48
308	Billings, MT	48
308	Fairbanks, AK	48
308	Grand Junction, CO	48
312	Monroe, MI	47
313	Cumberland, MD-WV	46
313	Farmington, NM	46
315	Dalton, GA	45
315	Pittsfield, MA	45
317	Wenatchee, WA	40
318	Appleton, WI	39
319	Cleveland, TN	38
319	Rapid City, SD	38
321	Ithaca, NY	34
321	Sioux Falls, SD	34
323	Bangor, ME	33
323	Harrisonburg, VA	33
325	Missoula, MT	32
326	Fargo, ND-MN	30
327	Cheyenne, WY	29
327	Great Falls, MT	29
327	La Crosse, WI-MN	29
327	Palm Coast, FL	29
331	Coeur d'Alene, ID	27
332	State College, PA	26
333	Wausau, WI	25
334	Carson City, NV	22
335	Eau Claire, WI	21
336	Idaho Falls, ID	20
336	Oshkosh-Neenah, WI	20
338	Ames, IA	19
339	Columbus, IN	17
339	Fond du Lac, WI	17
341	Casper, WY	16
341	Dubuque, IA	16
341	Pocatello, ID	16
344	Grand Forks, ND-MN	15
345	Glens Falls, NY	14
346	Sheboygan, WI	13
347	Bismarck, ND	11
348	Logan, UT-ID	7
349	Lewiston, ID-WA	4
NA	Chicago, IL**	NA

Source: Federal Bureau of Investigation
"Crime in the United States 2006" (Uniform Crime Reports, September 24, 2007)
**Robbery is the taking of anything of value by force or threat of force. Attempts are included.*
***Not available.*

18. Robbery Rate in 2006

National Rate = 149.4 Robberies per 100,000 Population*

RANK	METROPOLITAN AREA	RATE
242	Abilene, TX	67.0
150	Albany-Schenectady-Troy, NY	113.3
92	Albany, GA	157.7
73	Albuquerque, NM	174.3
100	Alexandria, LA	154.0
195	Altoona, PA	88.3
84	Amarillo, TX	165.4
323	Ames, IA	23.6
83	Anchorage, AK	166.2
190	Anderson, SC	89.2
215	Ann Arbor, MI	78.6
333	Appleton, WI	18.1
213	Asheville, NC	78.9
180	Athens-Clarke County, GA	95.2
44	Atlanta, GA	209.2
36	Atlantic City, NJ	220.9
88	Augusta, GA-SC	162.1
165	Austin-Round Rock, TX	104.8
117	Bakersfield, CA	138.7
8	Baltimore-Towson, MD	294.5
326	Bangor, ME	22.4
294	Barnstable Town, MA	39.1
40	Baton Rouge, LA	217.0
158	Battle Creek, MI	110.2
284	Bay City, MI	46.0
95	Beaumont-Port Arthur, TX	156.7
268	Bellingham, WA	52.5
309	Bend, OR	33.4
134	Bethesda-Frederick, MD M.D.	125.2
315	Billings, MT	32.4
282	Binghamton, NY	47.0
29	Birmingham-Hoover, AL	233.8
345	Bismarck, ND	11.1
309	Blacksburg, VA	33.4
279	Bloomington, IN	48.6
312	Boise City-Nampa, ID	33.3
178	Bowling Green, KY	96.6
273	Bremerton-Silverdale, WA	51.1
227	Brownsville-Harlingen, TX	71.2
74	Brunswick, GA	173.2
59	Buffalo-Niagara Falls, NY	195.4
169	Burlington, NC	102.6
124	Camden, NJ M.D.	134.3
97	Cape Coral-Fort Myers, FL	156.3
296	Carson City, NV	38.0
325	Casper, WY	22.7
260	Cedar Rapids, IA	56.9
52	Charleston-North Charleston, SC	202.9
228	Charleston, WV	71.1
15	Charlotte-Gastonia, NC-SC	269.5
240	Charlottesville, VA	67.8
131	Chattanooga, TN-GA	128.9
308	Cheyenne, WY	33.7
NA	Chicago, IL**	NA
243	Chico, CA	66.6
72	Cincinnati-Middletown, OH-KY-IN	174.7
163	Clarksville, TN-KY	108.4
18	Cleveland-Elyria-Mentor, OH	256.5
305	Cleveland, TN	34.7
329	Coeur d'Alene, ID	20.6
222	College Station-Bryan, TX	73.8
156	Colorado Springs, CO	111.1
199	Columbia, MO	86.8
123	Columbia, SC	134.5
35	Columbus, GA-AL	222.7
324	Columbus, IN	23.0
22	Columbus, OH	246.4
139	Corpus Christi, TX	119.5
285	Cumberland, MD-WV	45.6
62	Dallas (greater), TX	194.2
38	Dallas-Plano-Irving, TX M.D.	219.6
314	Dalton, GA	33.1
208	Danville, VA	81.6
132	Daytona Beach, FL	127.6
120	Dayton, OH	136.5
217	Decatur, AL	76.8
160	Denver-Aurora, CO	109.3
206	Des Moines-West Des Moines, IA	82.8
33	Detroit (greater), MI	227.7
2	Detroit-Livonia-Dearborn, MI M.D.	426.4
91	Dothan, AL	158.9
179	Dover, DE	96.1
335	Dubuque, IA	17.4
261	Duluth, MN-WI	56.3
20	Durham, NC	254.7
341	Eau Claire, WI	13.6
234	Edison, NJ M.D.	69.3
193	El Centro, CA	88.4
223	El Paso, TX	73.6
275	Elizabethtown, KY	50.2
112	Elkhart-Goshen, IN	142.9
250	Elmira, NY	62.4
159	Erie, PA	110.1
247	Eugene-Springfield, OR	64.3
232	Evansville, IN-KY	70.5
NA	Fairbanks, AK**	NA
338	Fargo, ND-MN	16.2
303	Farmington, NM	36.0
321	Fayetteville, AR-MO	27.8
57	Fayetteville, NC	197.5
203	Flagstaff, AZ	84.8
60	Flint, MI	195.1
58	Florence, SC	196.0
337	Fond du Lac, WI	17.1
328	Fort Collins-Loveland, CO	22.0
51	Fort Lauderdale, FL M.D.	203.9
263	Fort Smith, AR-OK	55.6
255	Fort Walton Beach, FL	57.8
162	Fort Wayne, IN	108.6
111	Fort Worth-Arlington, TX M.D.	143.0
68	Fresno, CA	183.1
28	Gadsden, AL	234.3
96	Gainesville, FL	156.4
264	Gainesville, GA	55.5
346	Glens Falls, NY	10.9
137	Goldsboro, NC	123.4
340	Grand Forks, ND-MN	15.4
301	Grand Junction, CO	36.3
154	Grand Rapids-Wyoming, MI	111.8
302	Great Falls, MT	36.1
318	Greeley, CO	31.3
295	Green Bay, WI	38.2
62	Greensboro-High Point, NC	194.2
64	Greenville, NC	193.6
140	Greenville, SC	119.4
192	Hagerstown-Martinsburg, MD-WV	88.6
257	Hanford-Corcoran, CA	57.4
122	Harrisburg-Carlisle, PA	134.8
320	Harrisonburg, VA	29.3
108	Hartford, CT	143.9
148	Hattiesburg, MS	114.2
331	Holland-Grand Haven, MI	19.2
166	Honolulu, HI	104.7
99	Hot Springs, AR	154.3
207	Houma, LA	81.9
12	Houston, TX	279.6
187	Huntington-Ashland, WV-KY-OH	89.9
46	Huntsville, AL	206.7
336	Idaho Falls, ID	17.2
37	Indianapolis, IN	220.0
290	Iowa City, IA	41.6
306	Ithaca, NY	33.9
45	Jacksonville, FL	206.9
224	Jacksonville, NC	73.3
241	Jackson, MI	67.4
32	Jackson, MS	229.1
69	Jackson, TN	181.7
204	Janesville, WI	83.5
292	Jefferson City, MO	40.0
286	Johnson City, TN	45.5
267	Johnstown, PA	53.3
181	Jonesboro, AR	93.5
226	Joplin, MO	72.9
161	Kalamazoo-Portage, MI	108.9
90	Kansas City, MO-KS	159.0
293	Kennewick-Richland-Pasco, WA	39.6
171	Killeen-Temple-Fort Hood, TX	100.7
271	Kingsport, TN-VA	51.8
289	Kingston, NY	42.0
152	Knoxville, TN	112.1
230	Kokomo, IN	70.6
326	La Crosse, WI-MN	22.4
272	Lafayette, IN	51.5
94	Lake Charles, LA	157.5
268	Lake Havasu City-Kingman, AZ	52.5
125	Lakeland, FL	133.3
204	Lancaster, PA	83.5
198	Lansing-East Lansing, MI	87.0
145	Laredo, TX	116.9
252	Las Cruces, NM	59.9
3	Las Vegas-Paradise, NV	356.0

Note: All listings are for Metropolitan Statistical Areas (M.S.A.s) except for those ending with "M.D." Listings with "M.D." are Metropolitan Divisions which are smaller parts of eleven large M.S.A.s. See explanatory note at beginning of metropolitan area section on page 23.

RANK	METROPOLITAN AREA	RATE
218	Lawrence, KS	76.2
102	Lawton, OK	152.5
235	Lebanon, PA	69.2
276	Lewiston-Auburn, ME	50.0
347	Lewiston, ID-WA	6.6
127	Lexington-Fayette, KY	132.0
129	Lima, OH	131.6
256	Lincoln, NE	57.6
43	Little Rock, AR	209.3
348	Logan, UT-ID	6.1
210	Longview, TX	81.1
236	Longview, WA	68.7
14	Los Angeles County, CA M.D.	276.6
27	Los Angeles (greater), CA	236.2
71	Louisville, KY-IN	174.9
113	Lubbock, TX	141.9
274	Lynchburg, VA	50.6
70	Macon, GA	175.4
189	Madera, CA	89.5
172	Madison, WI	100.6
258	Manchester-Nashua, NH	57.3
177	Mansfield, OH	98.4
216	McAllen-Edinburg-Mission, TX	78.1
313	Medford, OR	33.2
1	Memphis, TN-MS-AR	458.5
144	Merced, CA	117.3
19	Miami (greater), FL	256.3
6	Miami-Dade County, FL M.D.	312.0
197	Michigan City-La Porte, IN	87.2
246	Midland, TX	64.9
16	Milwaukee, WI	266.9
93	Minneapolis-St. Paul, MN-WI	157.6
317	Missoula, MT	31.7
48	Mobile, AL	205.6
104	Modesto, CA	150.4
211	Monroe, LA	80.1
319	Monroe, MI	30.6
39	Montgomery, AL	219.2
278	Morgantown, WV	48.9
288	Morristown, TN	43.9
270	Mount Vernon-Anacortes, WA	52.1
201	Muncie, IN	85.4
157	Muskegon-Norton Shores, MI	110.8
65	Myrtle Beach, SC	192.6
249	Napa, CA	62.7
182	Naples-Marco Island, FL	93.1
49	Nashville-Davidson, TN	204.6
200	Nassau-Suffolk, NY M.D.	85.6
118	New Orleans, LA	138.1
56	New York (greater), NY-NJ-PA	197.7
21	New York-W. Plains NY-NJ M.D.	250.7
55	Newark-Union, NJ-PA M.D.	198.2
244	Niles-Benton Harbor, MI	66.0
5	Oakland-Fremont, CA M.D.	326.4
188	Ocala, FL	89.8
212	Ocean City, NJ	79.5
220	Odessa, TX	74.5
300	Ogden-Clearfield, UT	36.4
135	Oklahoma City, OK	124.4
280	Olympia, WA	48.1

RANK	METROPOLITAN AREA	RATE
142	Omaha-Council Bluffs, NE-IA	118.0
17	Orlando, FL	263.4
343	Oshkosh-Neenah, WI	12.5
173	Oxnard-Thousand Oaks, CA	99.8
143	Palm Bay-Melbourne, FL	117.5
298	Palm Coast, FL	37.3
153	Panama City-Lynn Haven, FL	112.0
174	Pascagoula, MS	99.0
119	Pensacola, FL	137.0
13	Philadelphia (greater) PA-NJ-DE	278.4
4	Philadelphia, PA M.D.	332.8
79	Phoenix-Mesa-Scottsdale, AZ	167.4
54	Pine Bluff, AR	199.9
130	Pittsburgh, PA	130.4
306	Pittsfield, MA	33.9
333	Pocatello, ID	18.1
141	Port St. Lucie, FL	119.2
176	Portland-Vancouver, OR-WA	98.5
281	Portland, ME	47.6
185	Poughkeepsie, NY	91.7
322	Prescott, AZ	27.1
342	Provo-Orem, UT	13.5
146	Pueblo, CO	115.4
253	Punta Gorda, FL	59.3
121	Racine, WI	134.9
155	Raleigh-Cary, NC	111.4
316	Rapid City, SD	31.9
110	Reading, PA	143.7
283	Redding, CA	46.8
86	Reno-Sparks, NV	164.8
85	Richmond, VA	165.0
80	Riverside-San Bernardino, CA	167.3
191	Roanoke, VA	88.9
277	Rochester, MN	49.4
98	Rochester, NY	156.1
67	Rocky Mount, NC	190.7
245	Rome, GA	65.8
41	Sacramento, CA	212.4
77	Saginaw, MI	168.9
266	Salem, OR	53.7
107	Salinas, CA	144.1
23	Salisbury, MD	243.6
193	Salt Lake City, UT	88.4
259	San Angelo, TX	57.2
128	San Antonio, TX	131.7
105	San Diego, CA	145.7
7	San Francisco (greater), CA	308.9
10	San Francisco-S. Mateo, CA M.D.	283.3
196	San Jose, CA	87.8
299	San Luis Obispo, CA	36.9
237	Sandusky, OH	68.6
170	Santa Ana-Anaheim, CA M.D.	101.7
221	Santa Barbara-Santa Maria, CA	73.9
186	Santa Cruz-Watsonville, CA	90.1
209	Santa Fe, NM	81.2
248	Santa Rosa-Petaluma, CA	63.7
105	Sarasota-Bradenton-Venice, FL	145.7
24	Savannah, GA	243.5
230	Scranton--Wilkes-Barre, PA	70.6
108	Seattle (greater), WA	143.9

RANK	METROPOLITAN AREA	RATE
114	Seattle-Bellevue, WA M.D.	141.0
183	Sebastian-Vero Beach, FL	92.5
344	Sheboygan, WI	11.3
287	Sherman-Denison, TX	44.1
61	Shreveport-Bossier City, LA	194.4
291	Sioux City, IA-NE-SD	40.5
338	Sioux Falls, SD	16.2
80	South Bend-Mishawaka, IN-MI	167.3
87	Spartanburg, SC	162.8
167	Spokane, WA	104.4
115	Springfield, MA	140.2
237	Springfield, MO	68.6
25	Springfield, OH	237.8
332	State College, PA	18.5
9	Stockton, CA	285.9
309	St. Cloud, MN	33.4
262	St. Joseph, MO-KS	56.2
82	St. Louis, MO-IL	167.1
126	Sumter, SC	132.5
164	Syracuse, NY	105.1
101	Tacoma, WA M.D.	153.4
75	Tallahassee, FL	171.2
78	Tampa-St Petersburg, FL	167.6
138	Texarkana, TX-Texarkana, AR	122.0
53	Toledo, OH	201.8
116	Topeka, KS	139.1
26	Trenton-Ewing, NJ	236.5
47	Tucson, AZ	205.7
136	Tulsa, OK	124.3
102	Tuscaloosa, AL	152.5
233	Tyler, TX	69.9
254	Utica-Rome, NY	58.6
168	Valdosta, GA	103.3
50	Vallejo-Fairfield, CA	204.4
213	Victoria, TX	78.9
11	Vineland, NJ	283.0
66	Virginia Beach-Norfolk, VA-NC	191.1
151	Visalia-Porterville, CA	112.4
133	Waco, TX	126.4
149	Warner Robins, GA	113.7
239	Warren-Farmington Hills, MI M.D.	68.3
42	Washington (greater) DC-VA-MD	210.0
30	Washington, DC-VA-MD-WV M.D.	233.7
265	Waterloo-Cedar Falls, IA	55.3
330	Wausau, WI	19.3
297	Wenatchee, WA	37.5
34	West Palm Beach, FL M.D.	225.4
304	Wheeling, WV-OH	35.6
147	Wichita Falls, TX	114.3
183	Wichita, KS	92.5
229	Williamsport, PA	70.9
31	Wilmington, DE-MD-NJ M.D.	231.7
89	Wilmington, NC	160.8
251	Winchester, VA-WV	60.6
76	Winston-Salem, NC	170.7
219	Worcester, MA	74.7
175	Yakima, WA	98.9
202	Yuba City, CA	85.1
224	Yuma, AZ	73.3

Source: Federal Bureau of Investigation
"Crime in the United States 2006" (Uniform Crime Reports, September 24, 2007)
**Robbery is the taking of anything of value by force or threat of force. Attempts are included.*
***Not available.*

18. Robbery Rate in 2006 (continued)

National Rate = 149.4 Robberies per 100,000 Population*

RANK	METROPOLITAN AREA	RATE
1	Memphis, TN-MS-AR	458.5
2	Detroit-Livonia-Dearborn, MI M.D.	426.4
3	Las Vegas-Paradise, NV	356.0
4	Philadelphia, PA M.D.	332.8
5	Oakland-Fremont, CA M.D.	326.4
6	Miami-Dade County, FL M.D.	312.0
7	San Francisco (greater), CA	308.9
8	Baltimore-Towson, MD	294.5
9	Stockton, CA	285.9
10	San Francisco-S. Mateo, CA M.D.	283.3
11	Vineland, NJ	283.0
12	Houston, TX	279.6
13	Philadelphia (greater) PA-NJ-DE	278.4
14	Los Angeles County, CA M.D.	276.6
15	Charlotte-Gastonia, NC-SC	269.5
16	Milwaukee, WI	266.9
17	Orlando, FL	263.4
18	Cleveland-Elyria-Mentor, OH	256.5
19	Miami (greater), FL	256.3
20	Durham, NC	254.7
21	New York-W. Plains NY-NJ M.D.	250.7
22	Columbus, OH	246.4
23	Salisbury, MD	243.6
24	Savannah, GA	243.5
25	Springfield, OH	237.8
26	Trenton-Ewing, NJ	236.5
27	Los Angeles (greater), CA	236.2
28	Gadsden, AL	234.3
29	Birmingham-Hoover, AL	233.8
30	Washington, DC-VA-MD-WV M.D.	233.7
31	Wilmington, DE-MD-NJ M.D.	231.7
32	Jackson, MS	229.1
33	Detroit (greater), MI	227.7
34	West Palm Beach, FL M.D.	225.4
35	Columbus, GA-AL	222.7
36	Atlantic City, NJ	220.9
37	Indianapolis, IN	220.0
38	Dallas-Plano-Irving, TX M.D.	219.6
39	Montgomery, AL	219.2
40	Baton Rouge, LA	217.0
41	Sacramento, CA	212.4
42	Washington (greater) DC-VA-MD	210.0
43	Little Rock, AR	209.3
44	Atlanta, GA	209.2
45	Jacksonville, FL	206.9
46	Huntsville, AL	206.7
47	Tucson, AZ	205.7
48	Mobile, AL	205.6
49	Nashville-Davidson, TN	204.6
50	Vallejo-Fairfield, CA	204.4
51	Fort Lauderdale, FL M.D.	203.9
52	Charleston-North Charleston, SC	202.9
53	Toledo, OH	201.8
54	Pine Bluff, AR	199.9
55	Newark-Union, NJ-PA M.D.	198.2
56	New York (greater), NY-NJ-PA	197.7
57	Fayetteville, NC	197.5
58	Florence, SC	196.0
59	Buffalo-Niagara Falls, NY	195.4
60	Flint, MI	195.1
61	Shreveport-Bossier City, LA	194.4
62	Dallas (greater), TX	194.2
62	Greensboro-High Point, NC	194.2
64	Greenville, NC	193.6
65	Myrtle Beach, SC	192.6
66	Virginia Beach-Norfolk, VA-NC	191.1
67	Rocky Mount, NC	190.7
68	Fresno, CA	183.1
69	Jackson, TN	181.7
70	Macon, GA	175.4
71	Louisville, KY-IN	174.9
72	Cincinnati-Middletown, OH-KY-IN	174.7
73	Albuquerque, NM	174.3
74	Brunswick, GA	173.2
75	Tallahassee, FL	171.2
76	Winston-Salem, NC	170.7
77	Saginaw, MI	168.9
78	Tampa-St Petersburg, FL	167.6
79	Phoenix-Mesa-Scottsdale, AZ	167.4
80	Riverside-San Bernardino, CA	167.3
80	South Bend-Mishawaka, IN-MI	167.3
82	St. Louis, MO-IL	167.1
83	Anchorage, AK	166.2
84	Amarillo, TX	165.4
85	Richmond, VA	165.0
86	Reno-Sparks, NV	164.8
87	Spartanburg, SC	162.8
88	Augusta, GA-SC	162.1
89	Wilmington, NC	160.8
90	Kansas City, MO-KS	159.0
91	Dothan, AL	158.9
92	Albany, GA	157.7
93	Minneapolis-St. Paul, MN-WI	157.6
94	Lake Charles, LA	157.5
95	Beaumont-Port Arthur, TX	156.7
96	Gainesville, FL	156.4
97	Cape Coral-Fort Myers, FL	156.3
98	Rochester, NY	156.1
99	Hot Springs, AR	154.3
100	Alexandria, LA	154.0
101	Tacoma, WA M.D.	153.4
102	Lawton, OK	152.5
102	Tuscaloosa, AL	152.5
104	Modesto, CA	150.4
105	San Diego, CA	145.7
105	Sarasota-Bradenton-Venice, FL	145.7
107	Salinas, CA	144.1
108	Hartford, CT	143.9
108	Seattle (greater), WA	143.9
110	Reading, PA	143.7
111	Fort Worth-Arlington, TX M.D.	143.0
112	Elkhart-Goshen, IN	142.9
113	Lubbock, TX	141.9
114	Seattle-Bellevue, WA M.D.	141.0
115	Springfield, MA	140.2
116	Topeka, KS	139.1
117	Bakersfield, CA	138.7
118	New Orleans, LA	138.1
119	Pensacola, FL	137.0
120	Dayton, OH	136.5
121	Racine, WI	134.9
122	Harrisburg-Carlisle, PA	134.8
123	Columbia, SC	134.5
124	Camden, NJ M.D.	134.3
125	Lakeland, FL	133.3
126	Sumter, SC	132.5
127	Lexington-Fayette, KY	132.0
128	San Antonio, TX	131.7
129	Lima, OH	131.6
130	Pittsburgh, PA	130.4
131	Chattanooga, TN-GA	128.9
132	Daytona Beach, FL	127.6
133	Waco, TX	126.4
134	Bethesda-Frederick, MD M.D.	125.2
135	Oklahoma City, OK	124.4
136	Tulsa, OK	124.3
137	Goldsboro, NC	123.4
138	Texarkana, TX-Texarkana, AR	122.0
139	Corpus Christi, TX	119.5
140	Greenville, SC	119.4
141	Port St. Lucie, FL	119.2
142	Omaha-Council Bluffs, NE-IA	118.0
143	Palm Bay-Melbourne, FL	117.5
144	Merced, CA	117.3
145	Laredo, TX	116.9
146	Pueblo, CO	115.4
147	Wichita Falls, TX	114.3
148	Hattiesburg, MS	114.2
149	Warner Robins, GA	113.7
150	Albany-Schenectady-Troy, NY	113.3
151	Visalia-Porterville, CA	112.4
152	Knoxville, TN	112.1
153	Panama City-Lynn Haven, FL	112.0
154	Grand Rapids-Wyoming, MI	111.8
155	Raleigh-Cary, NC	111.4
156	Colorado Springs, CO	111.1
157	Muskegon-Norton Shores, MI	110.8
158	Battle Creek, MI	110.2
159	Erie, PA	110.1
160	Denver-Aurora, CO	109.3
161	Kalamazoo-Portage, MI	108.9
162	Fort Wayne, IN	108.6
163	Clarksville, TN-KY	108.4
164	Syracuse, NY	105.1
165	Austin-Round Rock, TX	104.8
166	Honolulu, HI	104.7
167	Spokane, WA	104.4
168	Valdosta, GA	103.3
169	Burlington, NC	102.6
170	Santa Ana-Anaheim, CA M.D.	101.7
171	Killeen-Temple-Fort Hood, TX	100.7

Note: All listings are for Metropolitan Statistical Areas (M.S.A.s) except for those ending with "M.D." Listings with "M.D." are Metropolitan Divisions which are smaller parts of eleven large M.S.A.s. See explanatory note at beginning of metropolitan area section on page 23.

Rank Order - Metro Area (continued)

RANK	METROPOLITAN AREA	RATE
172	Madison, WI	100.6
173	Oxnard-Thousand Oaks, CA	99.8
174	Pascagoula, MS	99.0
175	Yakima, WA	98.9
176	Portland-Vancouver, OR-WA	98.5
177	Mansfield, OH	98.4
178	Bowling Green, KY	96.6
179	Dover, DE	96.1
180	Athens-Clarke County, GA	95.2
181	Jonesboro, AR	93.5
182	Naples-Marco Island, FL	93.1
183	Sebastian-Vero Beach, FL	92.5
183	Wichita, KS	92.5
185	Poughkeepsie, NY	91.7
186	Santa Cruz-Watsonville, CA	90.1
187	Huntington-Ashland, WV-KY-OH	89.9
188	Ocala, FL	89.8
189	Madera, CA	89.5
190	Anderson, SC	89.2
191	Roanoke, VA	88.9
192	Hagerstown-Martinsburg, MD-WV	88.6
193	El Centro, CA	88.4
193	Salt Lake City, UT	88.4
195	Altoona, PA	88.3
196	San Jose, CA	87.8
197	Michigan City-La Porte, IN	87.2
198	Lansing-East Lansing, MI	87.0
199	Columbia, MO	86.8
200	Nassau-Suffolk, NY M.D.	85.6
201	Muncie, IN	85.4
202	Yuba City, CA	85.1
203	Flagstaff, AZ	84.8
204	Janesville, WI	83.5
204	Lancaster, PA	83.5
206	Des Moines-West Des Moines, IA	82.8
207	Houma, LA	81.9
208	Danville, VA	81.6
209	Santa Fe, NM	81.2
210	Longview, TX	81.1
211	Monroe, LA	80.1
212	Ocean City, NJ	79.5
213	Asheville, NC	78.9
213	Victoria, TX	78.9
215	Ann Arbor, MI	78.6
216	McAllen-Edinburg-Mission, TX	78.1
217	Decatur, AL	76.8
218	Lawrence, KS	76.2
219	Worcester, MA	74.7
220	Odessa, TX	74.5
221	Santa Barbara-Santa Maria, CA	73.9
222	College Station-Bryan, TX	73.8
223	El Paso, TX	73.6
224	Jacksonville, NC	73.3
224	Yuma, AZ	73.3
226	Joplin, MO	72.9
227	Brownsville-Harlingen, TX	71.2
228	Charleston, WV	71.1
229	Williamsport, PA	70.9
230	Kokomo, IN	70.6
230	Scranton--Wilkes-Barre, PA	70.6
232	Evansville, IN-KY	70.5
233	Tyler, TX	69.9
234	Edison, NJ M.D.	69.3
235	Lebanon, PA	69.2
236	Longview, WA	68.7
237	Sandusky, OH	68.6
237	Springfield, MO	68.6
239	Warren-Farmington Hills, MI M.D.	68.3
240	Charlottesville, VA	67.8
241	Jackson, MI	67.4
242	Abilene, TX	67.0
243	Chico, CA	66.6
244	Niles-Benton Harbor, MI	66.0
245	Rome, GA	65.8
246	Midland, TX	64.9
247	Eugene-Springfield, OR	64.3
248	Santa Rosa-Petaluma, CA	63.7
249	Napa, CA	62.7
250	Elmira, NY	62.4
251	Winchester, VA-WV	60.6
252	Las Cruces, NM	59.9
253	Punta Gorda, FL	59.3
254	Utica-Rome, NY	58.6
255	Fort Walton Beach, FL	57.8
256	Lincoln, NE	57.6
257	Hanford-Corcoran, CA	57.4
258	Manchester-Nashua, NH	57.3
259	San Angelo, TX	57.2
260	Cedar Rapids, IA	56.9
261	Duluth, MN-WI	56.3
262	St. Joseph, MO-KS	56.2
263	Fort Smith, AR-OK	55.6
264	Gainesville, GA	55.5
265	Waterloo-Cedar Falls, IA	55.3
266	Salem, OR	53.7
267	Johnstown, PA	53.3
268	Bellingham, WA	52.5
268	Lake Havasu City-Kingman, AZ	52.5
270	Mount Vernon-Anacortes, WA	52.1
271	Kingsport, TN-VA	51.8
272	Lafayette, IN	51.5
273	Bremerton-Silverdale, WA	51.1
274	Lynchburg, VA	50.6
275	Elizabethtown, KY	50.2
276	Lewiston-Auburn, ME	50.0
277	Rochester, MN	49.4
278	Morgantown, WV	48.9
279	Bloomington, IN	48.6
280	Olympia, WA	48.1
281	Portland, ME	47.6
282	Binghamton, NY	47.0
283	Redding, CA	46.8
284	Bay City, MI	46.0
285	Cumberland, MD-WV	45.6
286	Johnson City, TN	45.5
287	Sherman-Denison, TX	44.1
288	Morristown, TN	43.9
289	Kingston, NY	42.0
290	Iowa City, IA	41.6
291	Sioux City, IA-NE-SD	40.5
292	Jefferson City, MO	40.0
293	Kennewick-Richland-Pasco, WA	39.6
294	Barnstable Town, MA	39.1
295	Green Bay, WI	38.2
296	Carson City, NV	38.0
297	Wenatchee, WA	37.5
298	Palm Coast, FL	37.3
299	San Luis Obispo, CA	36.9
300	Ogden-Clearfield, UT	36.4
301	Grand Junction, CO	36.3
302	Great Falls, MT	36.1
303	Farmington, NM	36.0
304	Wheeling, WV-OH	35.6
305	Cleveland, TN	34.7
306	Ithaca, NY	33.9
306	Pittsfield, MA	33.9
308	Cheyenne, WY	33.7
309	Bend, OR	33.4
309	Blacksburg, VA	33.4
309	St. Cloud, MN	33.4
312	Boise City-Nampa, ID	33.3
313	Medford, OR	33.2
314	Dalton, GA	33.1
315	Billings, MT	32.4
316	Rapid City, SD	31.9
317	Missoula, MT	31.7
318	Greeley, CO	31.3
319	Monroe, MI	30.6
320	Harrisonburg, VA	29.3
321	Fayetteville, AR-MO	27.8
322	Prescott, AZ	27.1
323	Ames, IA	23.6
324	Columbus, IN	23.0
325	Casper, WY	22.7
326	Bangor, ME	22.4
326	La Crosse, WI-MN	22.4
328	Fort Collins-Loveland, CO	22.0
329	Coeur d'Alene, ID	20.6
330	Wausau, WI	19.3
331	Holland-Grand Haven, MI	19.2
332	State College, PA	18.5
333	Appleton, WI	18.1
333	Pocatello, ID	18.1
335	Dubuque, IA	17.4
336	Idaho Falls, ID	17.2
337	Fond du Lac, WI	17.1
338	Fargo, ND-MN	16.2
338	Sioux Falls, SD	16.2
340	Grand Forks, ND-MN	15.4
341	Eau Claire, WI	13.6
342	Provo-Orem, UT	13.5
343	Oshkosh-Neenah, WI	12.5
344	Sheboygan, WI	11.3
345	Bismarck, ND	11.1
346	Glens Falls, NY	10.9
347	Lewiston, ID-WA	6.6
348	Logan, UT-ID	6.1
NA	Chicago, IL**	NA
NA	Fairbanks, AK**	NA

Source: Federal Bureau of Investigation

"Crime in the United States 2006" (Uniform Crime Reports, September 24, 2007)

**Robbery is the taking of anything of value by force or threat of force. Attempts are included.*

***Not available.*

19. Percent Change in Robbery Rate: 2005 to 2006

National Percent Change = 6.1% Increase*

RANK	METROPOLITAN AREA	% CHANGE
NA	Abilene, TX**	NA
182	Albany-Schenectady-Troy, NY	5.9
120	Albany, GA	13.2
210	Albuquerque, NM	3.2
36	Alexandria, LA	34.4
94	Altoona, PA	17.4
125	Amarillo, TX	12.7
183	Ames, IA	5.8
73	Anchorage, AK	22.1
253	Anderson, SC	(2.0)
256	Ann Arbor, MI	(2.2)
3	Appleton, WI	84.7
267	Asheville, NC	(3.5)
142	Athens-Clarke County, GA	11.1
175	Atlanta, GA	6.8
183	Atlantic City, NJ	5.8
173	Augusta, GA-SC	6.9
160	Austin-Round Rock, TX	8.5
166	Bakersfield, CA	7.8
148	Baltimore-Towson, MD	10.7
225	Bangor, ME	0.9
55	Barnstable Town, MA	27.4
127	Baton Rouge, LA	12.4
170	Battle Creek, MI	7.3
225	Bay City, MI	0.9
158	Beaumont-Port Arthur, TX	8.9
98	Bellingham, WA	16.9
39	Bend, OR	33.6
114	Bethesda-Frederick, MD M.D.	14.3
299	Billings, MT	(12.4)
86	Binghamton, NY	19.6
NA	Birmingham-Hoover, AL**	NA
240	Bismarck, ND	(0.9)
267	Blacksburg, VA	(3.5)
94	Bloomington, IN	17.4
NA	Boise City-Nampa, ID**	NA
90	Bowling Green, KY	17.8
204	Bremerton-Silverdale, WA	4.1
213	Brownsville-Harlingen, TX	3.0
22	Brunswick, GA	44.2
237	Buffalo-Niagara Falls, NY	(0.6)
132	Burlington, NC	12.0
169	Camden, NJ M.D.	7.5
232	Cape Coral-Fort Myers, FL	(0.1)
311	Carson City, NV	(18.5)
248	Casper, WY	(1.7)
136	Cedar Rapids, IA	11.8
225	Charleston-North Charleston, SC	0.9
142	Charleston, WV	11.1
294	Charlotte-Gastonia, NC-SC	(10.4)
68	Charlottesville, VA	23.3
89	Chattanooga, TN-GA	18.0
42	Cheyenne, WY	31.1
NA	Chicago, IL**	NA
303	Chico, CA	(14.0)
243	Cincinnati-Middletown, OH-KY-IN	(1.4)
82	Clarksville, TN-KY	20.4
NA	Cleveland-Elyria-Mentor, OH**	NA
NA	Cleveland, TN**	NA
273	Coeur d'Alene, ID	(4.2)
261	College Station-Bryan, TX	(2.6)
34	Colorado Springs, CO	36.7
208	Columbia, MO	3.5
279	Columbia, SC	(4.8)
62	Columbus, GA-AL	25.7
297	Columbus, IN	(11.2)
271	Columbus, OH	(3.9)
288	Corpus Christi, TX	(7.7)
4	Cumberland, MD-WV	78.1
235	Dallas (greater), TX	(0.5)
254	Dallas-Plano-Irving, TX M.D.	(2.1)
NA	Dalton, GA**	NA
302	Danville, VA	(13.9)
230	Daytona Beach, FL	0.2
256	Dayton, OH	(2.2)
21	Decatur, AL	44.4
296	Denver-Aurora, CO	(11.1)
NA	Des Moines-West Des Moines, IA**	NA
181	Detroit (greater), MI	6.0
178	Detroit-Livonia-Dearborn, MI M.D.	6.3
73	Dothan, AL	22.1
30	Dover, DE	39.7
8	Dubuque, IA	59.6
NA	Duluth, MN-WI**	NA
NA	Durham, NC**	NA
319	Eau Claire, WI	(30.3)
108	Edison, NJ M.D.	15.1
72	El Centro, CA	22.3
133	El Paso, TX	11.9
146	Elizabethtown, KY	10.8
9	Elkhart-Goshen, IN	58.4
71	Elmira, NY	22.4
59	Erie, PA	26.1
119	Eugene-Springfield, OR	13.6
139	Evansville, IN-KY	11.4
NA	Fairbanks, AK**	NA
18	Fargo, ND-MN	47.3
282	Farmington, NM	(5.8)
77	Fayetteville, AR-MO	21.9
170	Fayetteville, NC	7.3
19	Flagstaff, AZ	45.5
131	Flint, MI	12.1
298	Florence, SC	(11.9)
11	Fond du Lac, WI	54.1
315	Fort Collins-Loveland, CO	(27.6)
160	Fort Lauderdale, FL M.D.	8.5
178	Fort Smith, AR-OK	6.3
224	Fort Walton Beach, FL	1.2
NA	Fort Wayne, IN**	NA
195	Fort Worth-Arlington, TX M.D.	4.9
235	Fresno, CA	(0.5)
25	Gadsden, AL	42.3
46	Gainesville, FL	30.1
23	Gainesville, GA	43.4
NA	Glens Falls, NY**	NA
250	Goldsboro, NC	(1.8)
35	Grand Forks, ND-MN	35.1
115	Grand Junction, CO	14.2
264	Grand Rapids-Wyoming, MI	(3.0)
100	Great Falls, MT	16.5
313	Greeley, CO	(22.7)
12	Green Bay, WI	53.4
133	Greensboro-High Point, NC	11.9
37	Greenville, NC	34.1
218	Greenville, SC	2.4
33	Hagerstown-Martinsburg, MD-WV	37.2
251	Hanford-Corcoran, CA	(1.9)
287	Harrisburg-Carlisle, PA	(7.6)
301	Harrisonburg, VA	(13.1)
156	Hartford, CT	9.2
NA	Hattiesburg, MS**	NA
51	Holland-Grand Haven, MI	28.0
121	Honolulu, HI	13.1
32	Hot Springs, AR	38.0
111	Houma, LA	14.9
228	Houston, TX	0.7
126	Huntington-Ashland, WV-KY-OH	12.5
103	Huntsville, AL	16.0
15	Idaho Falls, ID	49.6
234	Indianapolis, IN	(0.4)
53	Iowa City, IA	27.6
NA	Ithaca, NY**	NA
216	Jacksonville, FL	2.8
NA	Jacksonville, NC**	NA
145	Jackson, MI	11.0
10	Jackson, MS	57.9
203	Jackson, TN	4.2
102	Janesville, WI	16.3
197	Jefferson City, MO	4.4
281	Johnson City, TN	(5.4)
NA	Johnstown, PA**	NA
266	Jonesboro, AR	(3.4)
123	Joplin, MO	12.8
54	Kalamazoo-Portage, MI	27.5
NA	Kansas City, MO-KS**	NA
189	Kennewick-Richland-Pasco, WA	5.6
193	Killeen-Temple-Fort Hood, TX	5.1
152	Kingsport, TN-VA	10.2
316	Kingston, NY	(29.2)
229	Knoxville, TN	0.3
293	Kokomo, IN	(10.2)
231	La Crosse, WI-MN	0.0
210	Lafayette, IN	3.2
64	Lake Charles, LA	24.8
NA	Lake Havasu City-Kingman, AZ**	NA
37	Lakeland, FL	34.1
50	Lancaster, PA	28.3
197	Lansing-East Lansing, MI	4.4
212	Laredo, TX	3.1
285	Las Cruces, NM	(6.7)
16	Las Vegas-Paradise, NV	49.2

Note: All listings are for Metropolitan Statistical Areas (M.S.A.s) except for those ending with "M.D." Listings with "M.D." are Metropolitan Divisions which are smaller parts of eleven large M.S.A.s. See explanatory note at beginning of metropolitan area section on page 23.

RANK	METROPOLITAN AREA	% CHANGE
1	Lawrence, KS	91.5
69	Lawton, OK	23.0
273	Lebanon, PA	(4.2)
76	Lewiston-Auburn, ME	22.0
322	Lewiston, ID-WA	(64.1)
NA	Lexington-Fayette, KY**	NA
286	Lima, OH	(6.8)
316	Lincoln, NE	(29.2)
180	Little Rock, AR	6.1
247	Logan, UT-ID	(1.6)
271	Longview, TX	(3.9)
78	Longview, WA	21.8
207	Los Angeles County, CA M.D.	3.7
197	Los Angeles (greater), CA	4.4
261	Louisville, KY-IN	(2.6)
108	Lubbock, TX	15.1
138	Lynchburg, VA	11.5
191	Macon, GA	5.5
146	Madera, CA	10.8
48	Madison, WI	29.0
108	Manchester-Nashua, NH	15.1
159	Mansfield, OH	8.7
223	McAllen-Edinburg-Mission, TX	1.3
307	Medford, OR	(14.7)
93	Memphis, TN-MS-AR	17.6
127	Merced, CA	12.4
177	Miami (greater), FL	6.4
220	Miami-Dade County, FL M.D.	2.1
186	Michigan City-La Porte, IN	5.7
27	Midland, TX	41.7
66	Milwaukee, WI	23.7
NA	Minneapolis-St. Paul, MN-WI**	NA
312	Missoula, MT	(20.8)
97	Mobile, AL	17.0
117	Modesto, CA	13.8
70	Monroe, LA	22.7
278	Monroe, MI	(4.7)
310	Montgomery, AL	(16.9)
192	Morgantown, WV	5.2
290	Morristown, TN	(9.1)
123	Mount Vernon-Anacortes, WA	12.8
25	Muncie, IN	42.3
117	Muskegon-Norton Shores, MI	13.8
215	Myrtle Beach, SC	2.9
2	Napa, CA	90.0
47	Naples-Marco Island, FL	29.5
221	Nashville-Davidson, TN	1.9
219	Nassau-Suffolk, NY M.D.	2.3
NA	New Orleans, LA**	NA
263	New York (greater), NY-NJ-PA	(2.7)
270	New York-W. Plains NY-NJ M.D.	(3.8)
269	Newark-Union, NJ-PA M.D.	(3.7)
41	Niles-Benton Harbor, MI	31.5
49	Oakland-Fremont, CA M.D.	28.8
176	Ocala, FL	6.5
189	Ocean City, NJ	5.6
65	Odessa, TX	24.0
295	Ogden-Clearfield, UT	(11.0)
241	Oklahoma City, OK	(1.1)
163	Olympia, WA	8.3
101	Omaha-Council Bluffs, NE-IA	16.4
58	Orlando, FL	26.8
276	Oshkosh-Neenah, WI	(4.6)
154	Oxnard-Thousand Oaks, CA	9.9
63	Palm Bay-Melbourne, FL	25.0
NA	Palm Coast, FL**	NA
151	Panama City-Lynn Haven, FL	10.3
43	Pascagoula, MS	30.8
52	Pensacola, FL	27.8
152	Philadelphia (greater) PA-NJ-DE	10.2
160	Philadelphia, PA M.D.	8.5
216	Phoenix-Mesa-Scottsdale, AZ	2.8
265	Pine Bluff, AR	(3.3)
167	Pittsburgh, PA	7.7
303	Pittsfield, MA	(14.0)
5	Pocatello, ID	70.8
140	Port St. Lucie, FL	11.2
172	Portland-Vancouver, OR-WA	7.2
45	Portland, ME	30.4
165	Poughkeepsie, NY	7.9
57	Prescott, AZ	27.2
148	Provo-Orem, UT	10.7
196	Pueblo, CO	4.6
17	Punta Gorda, FL	49.0
243	Racine, WI	(1.4)
237	Raleigh-Cary, NC	(0.6)
292	Rapid City, SD	(10.1)
91	Reading, PA	17.7
300	Redding, CA	(12.7)
79	Reno-Sparks, NV	21.6
276	Richmond, VA	(4.6)
106	Riverside-San Bernardino, CA	15.9
242	Roanoke, VA	(1.3)
103	Rochester, MN	16.0
61	Rochester, NY	25.9
113	Rocky Mount, NC	14.6
314	Rome, GA	(26.1)
88	Sacramento, CA	18.4
83	Saginaw, MI	20.2
275	Salem, OR	(4.3)
186	Salinas, CA	5.7
91	Salisbury, MD	17.7
96	Salt Lake City, UT	17.1
12	San Angelo, TX	53.4
206	San Antonio, TX	4.0
157	San Diego, CA	9.1
60	San Francisco (greater), CA	26.0
80	San Francisco-S. Mateo, CA M.D.	21.5
112	San Jose, CA	14.8
193	San Luis Obispo, CA	5.1
280	Sandusky, OH	(4.9)
142	Santa Ana-Anaheim, CA M.D.	11.1
87	Santa Barbara-Santa Maria, CA	18.6
254	Santa Cruz-Watsonville, CA	(2.1)
28	Santa Fe, NM	41.0
201	Santa Rosa-Petaluma, CA	4.3
83	Sarasota-Bradenton-Venice, FL	20.2
256	Savannah, GA	(2.2)
251	Scranton--Wilkes-Barre, PA	(1.9)
155	Seattle (greater), WA	9.4
137	Seattle-Bellevue, WA M.D.	11.7
31	Sebastian-Vero Beach, FL	38.1
168	Sheboygan, WI	7.6
222	Sherman-Denison, TX	1.8
245	Shreveport-Bossier City, LA	(1.5)
204	Sioux City, IA-NE-SD	4.1
321	Sioux Falls, SD	(55.2)
73	South Bend-Mishawaka, IN-MI	22.1
24	Spartanburg, SC	42.4
56	Spokane, WA	27.3
289	Springfield, MA	(7.9)
85	Springfield, MO	19.7
130	Springfield, OH	12.3
14	State College, PA	52.9
173	Stockton, CA	6.9
7	St. Cloud, MN	62.9
209	St. Joseph, MO-KS	3.3
183	St. Louis, MO-IL	5.8
309	Sumter, SC	(16.8)
239	Syracuse, NY	(0.7)
213	Tacoma, WA M.D.	3.0
150	Tallahassee, FL	10.4
140	Tampa-St Petersburg, FL	11.2
40	Texarkana, TX-Texarkana, AR	32.5
283	Toledo, OH	(6.0)
116	Topeka, KS	13.9
305	Trenton-Ewing, NJ	(14.2)
248	Tucson, AZ	(1.7)
291	Tulsa, OK	(9.9)
NA	Tuscaloosa, AL**	NA
320	Tyler, TX	(34.4)
284	Utica-Rome, NY	(6.2)
308	Valdosta, GA	(14.9)
NA	Vallejo-Fairfield, CA**	NA
20	Victoria, TX	44.5
201	Vineland, NJ	4.3
233	Virginia Beach-Norfolk, VA-NC	(0.3)
260	Visalia-Porterville, CA	(2.3)
245	Waco, TX	(1.5)
107	Warner Robins, GA	15.7
164	Warren-Farmington Hills, MI M.D.	8.1
NA	Washington (greater) DC-VA-MD**	NA
NA	Washington, DC-VA-MD-WV M.D.**	NA
186	Waterloo-Cedar Falls, IA	5.7
306	Wausau, WI	(14.6)
29	Wenatchee, WA	40.4
99	West Palm Beach, FL M.D.	16.8
103	Wheeling, WV-OH	16.0
318	Wichita Falls, TX	(30.2)
NA	Wichita, KS**	NA
127	Williamsport, PA	12.4
43	Wilmington, DE-MD-NJ M.D.	30.8
67	Wilmington, NC	23.6
6	Winchester, VA-WV	64.7
133	Winston-Salem, NC	11.9
256	Worcester, MA	(2.2)
197	Yakima, WA	4.4
81	Yuba City, CA	21.2
121	Yuma, AZ	13.1

Source: CQ Press using data from Federal Bureau of Investigation "Crime in the United States 2006" (Uniform Crime Reports, September 24, 2007)

**Robbery is the taking of anything of value by force or threat of force. Attempts are included.*

***Not available.*

19. Percent Change in Robbery Rate: 2005 to 2006 (continued)

National Percent Change = 6.1% Increase*

RANK	METROPOLITAN AREA	% CHANGE
1	Lawrence, KS	91.5
2	Napa, CA	90.0
3	Appleton, WI	84.7
4	Cumberland, MD-WV	78.1
5	Pocatello, ID	70.8
6	Winchester, VA-WV	64.7
7	St. Cloud, MN	62.9
8	Dubuque, IA	59.6
9	Elkhart-Goshen, IN	58.4
10	Jackson, MS	57.9
11	Fond du Lac, WI	54.1
12	Green Bay, WI	53.4
12	San Angelo, TX	53.4
14	State College, PA	52.9
15	Idaho Falls, ID	49.6
16	Las Vegas-Paradise, NV	49.2
17	Punta Gorda, FL	49.0
18	Fargo, ND-MN	47.3
19	Flagstaff, AZ	45.5
20	Victoria, TX	44.5
21	Decatur, AL	44.4
22	Brunswick, GA	44.2
23	Gainesville, GA	43.4
24	Spartanburg, SC	42.4
25	Gadsden, AL	42.3
25	Muncie, IN	42.3
27	Midland, TX	41.7
28	Santa Fe, NM	41.0
29	Wenatchee, WA	40.4
30	Dover, DE	39.7
31	Sebastian-Vero Beach, FL	38.1
32	Hot Springs, AR	38.0
33	Hagerstown-Martinsburg, MD-WV	37.2
34	Colorado Springs, CO	36.7
35	Grand Forks, ND-MN	35.1
36	Alexandria, LA	34.4
37	Greenville, NC	34.1
37	Lakeland, FL	34.1
39	Bend, OR	33.6
40	Texarkana, TX-Texarkana, AR	32.5
41	Niles-Benton Harbor, MI	31.5
42	Cheyenne, WY	31.1
43	Pascagoula, MS	30.8
43	Wilmington, DE-MD-NJ M.D.	30.8
45	Portland, ME	30.4
46	Gainesville, FL	30.1
47	Naples-Marco Island, FL	29.5
48	Madison, WI	29.0
49	Oakland-Fremont, CA M.D.	28.8
50	Lancaster, PA	28.3
51	Holland-Grand Haven, MI	28.0
52	Pensacola, FL	27.8
53	Iowa City, IA	27.6
54	Kalamazoo-Portage, MI	27.5
55	Barnstable Town, MA	27.4
56	Spokane, WA	27.3
57	Prescott, AZ	27.2
58	Orlando, FL	26.8
59	Erie, PA	26.1
60	San Francisco (greater), CA	26.0
61	Rochester, NY	25.9
62	Columbus, GA-AL	25.7
63	Palm Bay-Melbourne, FL	25.0
64	Lake Charles, LA	24.8
65	Odessa, TX	24.0
66	Milwaukee, WI	23.7
67	Wilmington, NC	23.6
68	Charlottesville, VA	23.3
69	Lawton, OK	23.0
70	Monroe, LA	22.7
71	Elmira, NY	22.4
72	El Centro, CA	22.3
73	Anchorage, AK	22.1
73	Dothan, AL	22.1
73	South Bend-Mishawaka, IN-MI	22.1
76	Lewiston-Auburn, ME	22.0
77	Fayetteville, AR-MO	21.9
78	Longview, WA	21.8
79	Reno-Sparks, NV	21.6
80	San Francisco-S. Mateo, CA M.D.	21.5
81	Yuba City, CA	21.2
82	Clarksville, TN-KY	20.4
83	Saginaw, MI	20.2
83	Sarasota-Bradenton-Venice, FL	20.2
85	Springfield, MO	19.7
86	Binghamton, NY	19.6
87	Santa Barbara-Santa Maria, CA	18.6
88	Sacramento, CA	18.4
89	Chattanooga, TN-GA	18.0
90	Bowling Green, KY	17.8
91	Reading, PA	17.7
91	Salisbury, MD	17.7
93	Memphis, TN-MS-AR	17.6
94	Altoona, PA	17.4
94	Bloomington, IN	17.4
96	Salt Lake City, UT	17.1
97	Mobile, AL	17.0
98	Bellingham, WA	16.9
99	West Palm Beach, FL M.D.	16.8
100	Great Falls, MT	16.5
101	Omaha-Council Bluffs, NE-IA	16.4
102	Janesville, WI	16.3
103	Huntsville, AL	16.0
103	Rochester, MN	16.0
103	Wheeling, WV-OH	16.0
106	Riverside-San Bernardino, CA	15.9
107	Warner Robins, GA	15.7
108	Edison, NJ M.D.	15.1
108	Lubbock, TX	15.1
108	Manchester-Nashua, NH	15.1
111	Houma, LA	14.9
112	San Jose, CA	14.8
113	Rocky Mount, NC	14.6
114	Bethesda-Frederick, MD M.D.	14.3
115	Grand Junction, CO	14.2
116	Topeka, KS	13.9
117	Modesto, CA	13.8
117	Muskegon-Norton Shores, MI	13.8
119	Eugene-Springfield, OR	13.6
120	Albany, GA	13.2
121	Honolulu, HI	13.1
121	Yuma, AZ	13.1
123	Joplin, MO	12.8
123	Mount Vernon-Anacortes, WA	12.8
125	Amarillo, TX	12.7
126	Huntington-Ashland, WV-KY-OH	12.5
127	Baton Rouge, LA	12.4
127	Merced, CA	12.4
127	Williamsport, PA	12.4
130	Springfield, OH	12.3
131	Flint, MI	12.1
132	Burlington, NC	12.0
133	El Paso, TX	11.9
133	Greensboro-High Point, NC	11.9
133	Winston-Salem, NC	11.9
136	Cedar Rapids, IA	11.8
137	Seattle-Bellevue, WA M.D.	11.7
138	Lynchburg, VA	11.5
139	Evansville, IN-KY	11.4
140	Port St. Lucie, FL	11.2
140	Tampa-St Petersburg, FL	11.2
142	Athens-Clarke County, GA	11.1
142	Charleston, WV	11.1
142	Santa Ana-Anaheim, CA M.D.	11.1
145	Jackson, MI	11.0
146	Elizabethtown, KY	10.8
146	Madera, CA	10.8
148	Baltimore-Towson, MD	10.7
148	Provo-Orem, UT	10.7
150	Tallahassee, FL	10.4
151	Panama City-Lynn Haven, FL	10.3
152	Kingsport, TN-VA	10.2
152	Philadelphia (greater) PA-NJ-DE	10.2
154	Oxnard-Thousand Oaks, CA	9.9
155	Seattle (greater), WA	9.4
156	Hartford, CT	9.2
157	San Diego, CA	9.1
158	Beaumont-Port Arthur, TX	8.9
159	Mansfield, OH	8.7
160	Austin-Round Rock, TX	8.5
160	Fort Lauderdale, FL M.D.	8.5
160	Philadelphia, PA M.D.	8.5
163	Olympia, WA	8.3
164	Warren-Farmington Hills, MI M.D.	8.1
165	Poughkeepsie, NY	7.9
166	Bakersfield, CA	7.8
167	Pittsburgh, PA	7.7
168	Sheboygan, WI	7.6
169	Camden, NJ M.D.	7.5
170	Battle Creek, MI	7.3
170	Fayetteville, NC	7.3

Note: All listings are for Metropolitan Statistical Areas (M.S.A.s) except for those ending with "M.D." Listings with "M.D." are Metropolitan Divisions which are smaller parts of eleven large M.S.A.s. See explanatory note at beginning of metropolitan area section on page 23.

RANK	METROPOLITAN AREA	% CHANGE
172	Portland-Vancouver, OR-WA	7.2
173	Augusta, GA-SC	6.9
173	Stockton, CA	6.9
175	Atlanta, GA	6.8
176	Ocala, FL	6.5
177	Miami (greater), FL	6.4
178	Detroit-Livonia-Dearborn, MI M.D.	6.3
178	Fort Smith, AR-OK	6.3
180	Little Rock, AR	6.1
181	Detroit (greater), MI	6.0
182	Albany-Schenectady-Troy, NY	5.9
183	Ames, IA	5.8
183	Atlantic City, NJ	5.8
183	St. Louis, MO-IL	5.8
186	Michigan City-La Porte, IN	5.7
186	Salinas, CA	5.7
186	Waterloo-Cedar Falls, IA	5.7
189	Kennewick-Richland-Pasco, WA	5.6
189	Ocean City, NJ	5.6
191	Macon, GA	5.5
192	Morgantown, WV	5.2
193	Killeen-Temple-Fort Hood, TX	5.1
193	San Luis Obispo, CA	5.1
195	Fort Worth-Arlington, TX M.D.	4.9
196	Pueblo, CO	4.6
197	Jefferson City, MO	4.4
197	Lansing-East Lansing, MI	4.4
197	Los Angeles (greater), CA	4.4
197	Yakima, WA	4.4
201	Santa Rosa-Petaluma, CA	4.3
201	Vineland, NJ	4.3
203	Jackson, TN	4.2
204	Bremerton-Silverdale, WA	4.1
204	Sioux City, IA-NE-SD	4.1
206	San Antonio, TX	4.0
207	Los Angeles County, CA M.D.	3.7
208	Columbia, MO	3.5
209	St. Joseph, MO-KS	3.3
210	Albuquerque, NM	3.2
210	Lafayette, IN	3.2
212	Laredo, TX	3.1
213	Brownsville-Harlingen, TX	3.0
213	Tacoma, WA M.D.	3.0
215	Myrtle Beach, SC	2.9
216	Jacksonville, FL	2.8
216	Phoenix-Mesa-Scottsdale, AZ	2.8
218	Greenville, SC	2.4
219	Nassau-Suffolk, NY M.D.	2.3
220	Miami-Dade County, FL M.D.	2.1
221	Nashville-Davidson, TN	1.9
222	Sherman-Denison, TX	1.8
223	McAllen-Edinburg-Mission, TX	1.3
224	Fort Walton Beach, FL	1.2
225	Bangor, ME	0.9
225	Bay City, MI	0.9
225	Charleston-North Charleston, SC	0.9
228	Houston, TX	0.7
229	Knoxville, TN	0.3
230	Daytona Beach, FL	0.2
231	La Crosse, WI-MN	0.0

RANK	METROPOLITAN AREA	% CHANGE
232	Cape Coral-Fort Myers, FL	(0.1)
233	Virginia Beach-Norfolk, VA-NC	(0.3)
234	Indianapolis, IN	(0.4)
235	Dallas (greater), TX	(0.5)
235	Fresno, CA	(0.5)
237	Buffalo-Niagara Falls, NY	(0.6)
237	Raleigh-Cary, NC	(0.6)
239	Syracuse, NY	(0.7)
240	Bismarck, ND	(0.9)
241	Oklahoma City, OK	(1.1)
242	Roanoke, VA	(1.3)
243	Cincinnati-Middletown, OH-KY-IN	(1.4)
243	Racine, WI	(1.4)
245	Shreveport-Bossier City, LA	(1.5)
245	Waco, TX	(1.5)
247	Logan, UT-ID	(1.6)
248	Casper, WY	(1.7)
248	Tucson, AZ	(1.7)
250	Goldsboro, NC	(1.8)
251	Hanford-Corcoran, CA	(1.9)
251	Scranton--Wilkes-Barre, PA	(1.9)
253	Anderson, SC	(2.0)
254	Dallas-Plano-Irving, TX M.D.	(2.1)
254	Santa Cruz-Watsonville, CA	(2.1)
256	Ann Arbor, MI	(2.2)
256	Dayton, OH	(2.2)
256	Savannah, GA	(2.2)
256	Worcester, MA	(2.2)
260	Visalia-Porterville, CA	(2.3)
261	College Station-Bryan, TX	(2.6)
261	Louisville, KY-IN	(2.6)
263	New York (greater), NY-NJ-PA	(2.7)
264	Grand Rapids-Wyoming, MI	(3.0)
265	Pine Bluff, AR	(3.3)
266	Jonesboro, AR	(3.4)
267	Asheville, NC	(3.5)
267	Blacksburg, VA	(3.5)
269	Newark-Union, NJ-PA M.D.	(3.7)
270	New York-W. Plains NY-NJ M.D.	(3.8)
271	Columbus, OH	(3.9)
271	Longview, TX	(3.9)
273	Coeur d'Alene, ID	(4.2)
273	Lebanon, PA	(4.2)
275	Salem, OR	(4.3)
276	Oshkosh-Neenah, WI	(4.6)
276	Richmond, VA	(4.6)
278	Monroe, MI	(4.7)
279	Columbia, SC	(4.8)
280	Sandusky, OH	(4.9)
281	Johnson City, TN	(5.4)
282	Farmington, NM	(5.8)
283	Toledo, OH	(6.0)
284	Utica-Rome, NY	(6.2)
285	Las Cruces, NM	(6.7)
286	Lima, OH	(6.8)
287	Harrisburg-Carlisle, PA	(7.6)
288	Corpus Christi, TX	(7.7)
289	Springfield, MA	(7.9)
290	Morristown, TN	(9.1)
291	Tulsa, OK	(9.9)

RANK	METROPOLITAN AREA	% CHANGE
292	Rapid City, SD	(10.1)
293	Kokomo, IN	(10.2)
294	Charlotte-Gastonia, NC-SC	(10.4)
295	Ogden-Clearfield, UT	(11.0)
296	Denver-Aurora, CO	(11.1)
297	Columbus, IN	(11.2)
298	Florence, SC	(11.9)
299	Billings, MT	(12.4)
300	Redding, CA	(12.7)
301	Harrisonburg, VA	(13.1)
302	Danville, VA	(13.9)
303	Chico, CA	(14.0)
303	Pittsfield, MA	(14.0)
305	Trenton-Ewing, NJ	(14.2)
306	Wausau, WI	(14.6)
307	Medford, OR	(14.7)
308	Valdosta, GA	(14.9)
309	Sumter, SC	(16.8)
310	Montgomery, AL	(16.9)
311	Carson City, NV	(18.5)
312	Missoula, MT	(20.8)
313	Greeley, CO	(22.7)
314	Rome, GA	(26.1)
315	Fort Collins-Loveland, CO	(27.6)
316	Kingston, NY	(29.2)
316	Lincoln, NE	(29.2)
318	Wichita Falls, TX	(30.2)
319	Eau Claire, WI	(30.3)
320	Tyler, TX	(34.4)
321	Sioux Falls, SD	(55.2)
322	Lewiston, ID-WA	(64.1)
NA	Abilene, TX**	NA
NA	Birmingham-Hoover, AL**	NA
NA	Boise City-Nampa, ID**	NA
NA	Chicago, IL**	NA
NA	Cleveland-Elyria-Mentor, OH**	NA
NA	Cleveland, TN**	NA
NA	Dalton, GA**	NA
NA	Des Moines-West Des Moines, IA**	NA
NA	Duluth, MN-WI**	NA
NA	Durham, NC**	NA
NA	Fairbanks, AK**	NA
NA	Fort Wayne, IN**	NA
NA	Glens Falls, NY**	NA
NA	Hattiesburg, MS**	NA
NA	Ithaca, NY**	NA
NA	Jacksonville, NC**	NA
NA	Johnstown, PA**	NA
NA	Kansas City, MO-KS**	NA
NA	Lake Havasu City-Kingman, AZ**	NA
NA	Lexington-Fayette, KY**	NA
NA	Minneapolis-St. Paul, MN-WI**	NA
NA	New Orleans, LA**	NA
NA	Palm Coast, FL**	NA
NA	Tuscaloosa, AL**	NA
NA	Vallejo-Fairfield, CA**	NA
NA	Washington (greater) DC-VA-MD**	NA
NA	Washington, DC-VA-MD-WV M.D.**	NA
NA	Wichita, KS**	NA

Source: CQ Press using data from Federal Bureau of Investigation "Crime in the United States 2006" (Uniform Crime Reports, September 24, 2007)

**Robbery is the taking of anything of value by force or threat of force. Attempts are included.*

***Not available.*

20. Percent Change in Robbery Rate: 2002 to 2006

National Percent Change = 2.3% Increase*

RANK	METROPOLITAN AREA	% CHANGE
NA	Abilene, TX**	NA
NA	Albany-Schenectady-Troy, NY**	NA
168	Albany, GA	(14.1)
176	Albuquerque, NM	(15.6)
166	Alexandria, LA	(14.0)
108	Altoona, PA	0.5
64	Amarillo, TX	12.7
NA	Ames, IA**	NA
51	Anchorage, AK	16.3
NA	Anderson, SC**	NA
NA	Ann Arbor, MI**	NA
NA	Appleton, WI**	NA
185	Asheville, NC	(20.2)
159	Athens-Clarke County, GA	(11.7)
119	Atlanta, GA	(2.5)
NA	Atlantic City, NJ**	NA
34	Augusta, GA-SC	26.7
119	Austin-Round Rock, TX	(2.5)
41	Bakersfield, CA	22.1
112	Baltimore-Towson, MD	0.1
NA	Bangor, ME**	NA
NA	Barnstable Town, MA**	NA
136	Baton Rouge, LA	(6.8)
NA	Battle Creek, MI**	NA
NA	Bay City, MI**	NA
153	Beaumont-Port Arthur, TX	(10.1)
111	Bellingham, WA	0.2
NA	Bend, OR**	NA
NA	Bethesda-Frederick, MD M.D.**	NA
207	Billings, MT	(38.8)
181	Binghamton, NY	(17.4)
49	Birmingham-Hoover, AL	18.0
212	Bismarck, ND	(45.3)
NA	Blacksburg, VA**	NA
16	Bloomington, IN	41.3
98	Boise City-Nampa, ID	2.8
NA	Bowling Green, KY**	NA
86	Bremerton-Silverdale, WA	5.1
155	Brownsville-Harlingen, TX	(10.7)
NA	Brunswick, GA**	NA
79	Buffalo-Niagara Falls, NY	7.1
NA	Burlington, NC**	NA
NA	Camden, NJ M.D.**	NA
148	Cape Coral-Fort Myers, FL	(9.2)
NA	Carson City, NV**	NA
172	Casper, WY	(15.3)
117	Cedar Rapids, IA	(1.4)
80	Charleston-North Charleston, SC	6.5
178	Charleston, WV	(16.3)
NA	Charlotte-Gastonia, NC-SC**	NA
NA	Charlottesville, VA**	NA
173	Chattanooga, TN-GA	(15.4)
177	Cheyenne, WY	(15.8)
NA	Chicago, IL**	NA
131	Chico, CA	(5.3)
153	Cincinnati-Middletown, OH-KY-IN	(10.1)
22	Clarksville, TN-KY	36.7
NA	Cleveland-Elyria-Mentor, OH**	NA
NA	Cleveland, TN**	NA
NA	Coeur d'Alene, ID**	NA
NA	College Station-Bryan, TX**	NA
73	Colorado Springs, CO	8.6
61	Columbia, MO	13.5
205	Columbia, SC	(36.1)
10	Columbus, GA-AL	55.7
NA	Columbus, IN**	NA
137	Columbus, OH	(7.1)
171	Corpus Christi, TX	(14.9)
2	Cumberland, MD-WV	98.3
NA	Dallas (greater), TX**	NA
184	Dallas-Plano-Irving, TX M.D.	(19.4)
NA	Dalton, GA**	NA
56	Danville, VA	15.7
144	Daytona Beach, FL	(8.7)
NA	Dayton, OH**	NA
141	Decatur, AL	(8.1)
115	Denver-Aurora, CO	(0.8)
NA	Des Moines-West Des Moines, IA**	NA
43	Detroit (greater), MI	19.2
NA	Detroit-Livonia-Dearborn, MI M.D.**	NA
NA	Dothan, AL**	NA
53	Dover, DE	16.2
3	Dubuque, IA	95.5
59	Duluth, MN-WI	14.7
NA	Durham, NC**	NA
157	Eau Claire, WI	(11.1)
NA	Edison, NJ M.D.**	NA
NA	El Centro, CA**	NA
164	El Paso, TX	(13.1)
NA	Elizabethtown, KY**	NA
13	Elkhart-Goshen, IN	45.4
NA	Elmira, NY**	NA
30	Erie, PA	30.0
123	Eugene-Springfield, OR	(3.3)
NA	Evansville, IN-KY**	NA
NA	Fairbanks, AK**	NA
17	Fargo, ND-MN	40.9
NA	Farmington, NM**	NA
NA	Fayetteville, AR-MO**	NA
145	Fayetteville, NC	(8.8)
12	Flagstaff, AZ	50.9
30	Flint, MI	30.0
97	Florence, SC	3.0
NA	Fond du Lac, WI**	NA
170	Fort Collins-Loveland, CO	(14.7)
53	Fort Lauderdale, FL M.D.	16.2
197	Fort Smith, AR-OK	(28.4)
128	Fort Walton Beach, FL	(4.6)
NA	Fort Wayne, IN**	NA
157	Fort Worth-Arlington, TX M.D.	(11.1)
146	Fresno, CA	(8.9)
1	Gadsden, AL	135.2
81	Gainesville, FL	6.4
NA	Gainesville, GA**	NA
61	Glens Falls, NY	13.5
47	Goldsboro, NC	18.5
57	Grand Forks, ND-MN	14.9
11	Grand Junction, CO	52.5
NA	Grand Rapids-Wyoming, MI**	NA
187	Great Falls, MT	(21.0)
200	Greeley, CO	(30.1)
102	Green Bay, WI	2.1
NA	Greensboro-High Point, NC**	NA
116	Greenville, NC	(1.2)
NA	Greenville, SC**	NA
NA	Hagerstown-Martinsburg, MD-WV**	NA
NA	Hanford-Corcoran, CA**	NA
NA	Harrisburg-Carlisle, PA**	NA
NA	Harrisonburg, VA**	NA
126	Hartford, CT	(3.6)
NA	Hattiesburg, MS**	NA
NA	Holland-Grand Haven, MI**	NA
160	Honolulu, HI	(12.1)
NA	Hot Springs, AR**	NA
91	Houma, LA	4.5
165	Houston, TX	(13.2)
NA	Huntington-Ashland, WV-KY-OH**	NA
4	Huntsville, AL	85.9
NA	Idaho Falls, ID**	NA
NA	Indianapolis, IN**	NA
185	Iowa City, IA	(20.2)
NA	Ithaca, NY**	NA
107	Jacksonville, FL	0.8
NA	Jacksonville, NC**	NA
71	Jackson, MI	9.1
183	Jackson, MS	(17.6)
92	Jackson, TN	4.1
63	Janesville, WI	13.1
NA	Jefferson City, MO**	NA
NA	Johnson City, TN**	NA
NA	Johnstown, PA**	NA
101	Jonesboro, AR	2.4
14	Joplin, MO	43.5
NA	Kalamazoo-Portage, MI**	NA
NA	Kansas City, MO-KS**	NA
152	Kennewick-Richland-Pasco, WA	(10.0)
45	Killeen-Temple-Fort Hood, TX	18.9
NA	Kingsport, TN-VA**	NA
NA	Kingston, NY**	NA
100	Knoxville, TN	2.5
15	Kokomo, IN	42.3
94	La Crosse, WI-MN	3.2
8	Lafayette, IN	70.5
156	Lake Charles, LA	(11.0)
NA	Lake Havasu City-Kingman, AZ**	NA
104	Lakeland, FL	1.4
114	Lancaster, PA	(0.6)
86	Lansing-East Lansing, MI	5.1
53	Laredo, TX	16.2
NA	Las Cruces, NM**	NA
25	Las Vegas-Paradise, NV	33.4

Note: All listings are for Metropolitan Statistical Areas (M.S.A.s) except for those ending with "M.D." Listings with "M.D." are Metropolitan Divisions which are smaller parts of eleven large M.S.A.s. See explanatory note at beginning of metropolitan area section on page 23.

RANK	METROPOLITAN AREA	% CHANGE
7	Lawrence, KS	70.9
65	Lawton, OK	12.0
NA	Lebanon, PA**	NA
20	Lewiston-Auburn, ME	38.1
NA	Lewiston, ID-WA**	NA
NA	Lexington-Fayette, KY**	NA
NA	Lima, OH**	NA
188	Lincoln, NE	(21.2)
93	Little Rock, AR	3.6
NA	Logan, UT-ID**	NA
194	Longview, TX	(25.4)
NA	Longview, WA**	NA
147	Los Angeles County, CA M.D.	(9.0)
NA	Los Angeles (greater), CA**	NA
38	Louisville, KY-IN	22.8
48	Lubbock, TX	18.3
105	Lynchburg, VA	1.0
NA	Macon, GA**	NA
NA	Madera, CA**	NA
28	Madison, WI	30.6
NA	Manchester-Nashua, NH**	NA
NA	Mansfield, OH**	NA
191	McAllen-Edinburg-Mission, TX	(24.1)
179	Medford, OR	(16.4)
NA	Memphis, TN-MS-AR**	NA
26	Merced, CA	32.7
NA	Miami (greater), FL**	NA
163	Miami-Dade County, FL M.D.	(12.8)
NA	Michigan City-La Porte, IN**	NA
NA	Midland, TX**	NA
NA	Milwaukee, WI**	NA
27	Minneapolis-St. Paul, MN-WI	31.7
NA	Missoula, MT**	NA
NA	Mobile, AL**	NA
70	Modesto, CA	9.2
NA	Monroe, LA**	NA
NA	Monroe, MI**	NA
141	Montgomery, AL	(8.1)
NA	Morgantown, WV**	NA
NA	Morristown, TN**	NA
NA	Mount Vernon-Anacortes, WA**	NA
37	Muncie, IN	23.8
NA	Muskegon-Norton Shores, MI**	NA
68	Myrtle Beach, SC	9.8
NA	Napa, CA**	NA
162	Naples-Marco Island, FL	(12.6)
76	Nashville-Davidson, TN	8.3
NA	Nassau-Suffolk, NY M.D.**	NA
208	New Orleans, LA	(39.6)
NA	New York (greater), NY-NJ-PA**	NA
181	New York-W. Plains NY-NJ M.D.	(17.4)
190	Newark-Union, NJ-PA M.D.	(21.7)
NA	Niles-Benton Harbor, MI**	NA
18	Oakland-Fremont, CA M.D.	40.4
84	Ocala, FL	5.8
NA	Ocean City, NJ**	NA
NA	Odessa, TX**	NA
NA	Ogden-Clearfield, UT**	NA
124	Oklahoma City, OK	(3.5)
143	Olympia, WA	(8.4)
193	Omaha-Council Bluffs, NE-IA	(24.9)
24	Orlando, FL	34.7
NA	Oshkosh-Neenah, WI**	NA
NA	Oxnard-Thousand Oaks, CA**	NA
139	Palm Bay-Melbourne, FL	(8.0)
NA	Palm Coast, FL**	NA
124	Panama City-Lynn Haven, FL	(3.5)
NA	Pascagoula, MS**	NA
69	Pensacola, FL	9.3
44	Philadelphia (greater) PA-NJ-DE	19.0
NA	Philadelphia, PA M.D.**	NA
133	Phoenix-Mesa-Scottsdale, AZ	(5.5)
196	Pine Bluff, AR	(26.7)
72	Pittsburgh, PA	8.9
NA	Pittsfield, MA**	NA
6	Pocatello, ID	77.5
139	Port St. Lucie, FL	(8.0)
149	Portland-Vancouver, OR-WA	(9.3)
NA	Portland, ME**	NA
NA	Poughkeepsie, NY**	NA
NA	Prescott, AZ**	NA
135	Provo-Orem, UT	(6.3)
118	Pueblo, CO	(1.7)
9	Punta Gorda, FL	62.5
105	Racine, WI	1.0
NA	Raleigh-Cary, NC**	NA
129	Rapid City, SD	(5.1)
166	Reading, PA	(14.0)
189	Redding, CA	(21.6)
82	Reno-Sparks, NV	6.2
169	Richmond, VA	(14.6)
85	Riverside-San Bernardino, CA	5.4
NA	Roanoke, VA**	NA
23	Rochester, MN	36.1
21	Rochester, NY	37.4
39	Rocky Mount, NC	22.6
NA	Rome, GA**	NA
60	Sacramento, CA	13.8
NA	Saginaw, MI**	NA
173	Salem, OR	(15.4)
90	Salinas, CA	4.6
NA	Salisbury, MD**	NA
NA	Salt Lake City, UT**	NA
36	San Angelo, TX	24.3
134	San Antonio, TX	(5.7)
33	San Diego, CA	27.1
NA	San Francisco (greater), CA**	NA
35	San Francisco-S. Mateo, CA M.D.	25.3
49	San Jose, CA	18.0
42	San Luis Obispo, CA	21.0
NA	Sandusky, OH**	NA
77	Santa Ana-Anaheim, CA M.D.	7.6
NA	Santa Barbara-Santa Maria, CA**	NA
109	Santa Cruz-Watsonville, CA	0.3
66	Santa Fe, NM	11.5
99	Santa Rosa-Petaluma, CA	2.7
86	Sarasota-Bradenton-Venice, FL	5.1
151	Savannah, GA	(9.7)
103	Scranton--Wilkes-Barre, PA	1.6
NA	Seattle (greater), WA**	NA
51	Seattle-Bellevue, WA M.D.	16.3
NA	Sebastian-Vero Beach, FL**	NA
192	Sheboygan, WI	(24.2)
206	Sherman-Denison, TX	(37.1)
127	Shreveport-Bossier City, LA	(4.1)
203	Sioux City, IA-NE-SD	(35.2)
213	Sioux Falls, SD	(47.9)
94	South Bend-Mishawaka, IN-MI	3.2
NA	Spartanburg, SC**	NA
138	Spokane, WA	(7.9)
NA	Springfield, MA**	NA
130	Springfield, MO	(5.2)
NA	Springfield, OH**	NA
57	State College, PA	14.9
74	Stockton, CA	8.5
19	St. Cloud, MN	39.2
173	St. Joseph, MO-KS	(15.4)
NA	St. Louis, MO-IL**	NA
201	Sumter, SC	(31.1)
NA	Syracuse, NY**	NA
109	Tacoma, WA M.D.	0.3
122	Tallahassee, FL	(3.2)
195	Tampa-St Petersburg, FL	(25.5)
75	Texarkana, TX-Texarkana, AR	8.4
180	Toledo, OH	(17.0)
211	Topeka, KS	(44.4)
132	Trenton-Ewing, NJ	(5.4)
46	Tucson, AZ	18.6
113	Tulsa, OK	(0.4)
96	Tuscaloosa, AL	3.1
199	Tyler, TX	(29.5)
204	Utica-Rome, NY	(35.5)
NA	Valdosta, GA**	NA
NA	Vallejo-Fairfield, CA**	NA
209	Victoria, TX	(39.7)
89	Vineland, NJ	4.7
67	Virginia Beach-Norfolk, VA-NC	10.4
39	Visalia-Porterville, CA	22.6
149	Waco, TX	(9.3)
NA	Warner Robins, GA**	NA
NA	Warren-Farmington Hills, MI M.D.**	NA
NA	Washington (greater) DC-VA-MD**	NA
NA	Washington, DC-VA-MD-WV M.D.**	NA
198	Waterloo-Cedar Falls, IA	(28.9)
78	Wausau, WI	7.2
NA	Wenatchee, WA**	NA
83	West Palm Beach, FL M.D.	6.1
NA	Wheeling, WV-OH**	NA
202	Wichita Falls, TX	(34.5)
210	Wichita, KS	(40.0)
121	Williamsport, PA	(2.9)
NA	Wilmington, DE-MD-NJ M.D.**	NA
161	Wilmington, NC	(12.2)
NA	Winchester, VA-WV**	NA
NA	Winston-Salem, NC**	NA
NA	Worcester, MA**	NA
32	Yakima, WA	29.5
29	Yuba City, CA	30.5
5	Yuma, AZ	81.0

Source: CQ Press using data from Federal Bureau of Investigation "Crime in the United States 2006" (Uniform Crime Reports, September 24, 2007)

**Robbery is the taking of anything of value by force or threat of force. Attempts are included.*

***Not available.*

20. Percent Change in Robbery Rate: 2002 to 2006 (continued)

National Percent Change = 2.3% Increase*

RANK	METROPOLITAN AREA	% CHANGE
1	Gadsden, AL	135.2
2	Cumberland, MD-WV	98.3
3	Dubuque, IA	95.5
4	Huntsville, AL	85.9
5	Yuma, AZ	81.0
6	Pocatello, ID	77.5
7	Lawrence, KS	70.9
8	Lafayette, IN	70.5
9	Punta Gorda, FL	62.5
10	Columbus, GA-AL	55.7
11	Grand Junction, CO	52.5
12	Flagstaff, AZ	50.9
13	Elkhart-Goshen, IN	45.4
14	Joplin, MO	43.5
15	Kokomo, IN	42.3
16	Bloomington, IN	41.3
17	Fargo, ND-MN	40.9
18	Oakland-Fremont, CA M.D.	40.4
19	St. Cloud, MN	39.2
20	Lewiston-Auburn, ME	38.1
21	Rochester, NY	37.4
22	Clarksville, TN-KY	36.7
23	Rochester, MN	36.1
24	Orlando, FL	34.7
25	Las Vegas-Paradise, NV	33.4
26	Merced, CA	32.7
27	Minneapolis-St. Paul, MN-WI	31.7
28	Madison, WI	30.6
29	Yuba City, CA	30.5
30	Erie, PA	30.0
30	Flint, MI	30.0
32	Yakima, WA	29.5
33	San Diego, CA	27.1
34	Augusta, GA-SC	26.7
35	San Francisco-S. Mateo, CA M.D.	25.3
36	San Angelo, TX	24.3
37	Muncie, IN	23.8
38	Louisville, KY-IN	22.8
39	Rocky Mount, NC	22.6
39	Visalia-Porterville, CA	22.6
41	Bakersfield, CA	22.1
42	San Luis Obispo, CA	21.0
43	Detroit (greater), MI	19.2
44	Philadelphia (greater) PA-NJ-DE	19.0
45	Killeen-Temple-Fort Hood, TX	18.9
46	Tucson, AZ	18.6
47	Goldsboro, NC	18.5
48	Lubbock, TX	18.3
49	Birmingham-Hoover, AL	18.0
49	San Jose, CA	18.0
51	Anchorage, AK	16.3
51	Seattle-Bellevue, WA M.D.	16.3
53	Dover, DE	16.2
53	Fort Lauderdale, FL M.D.	16.2
53	Laredo, TX	16.2
56	Danville, VA	15.7
57	Grand Forks, ND-MN	14.9
57	State College, PA	14.9
59	Duluth, MN-WI	14.7
60	Sacramento, CA	13.8
61	Columbia, MO	13.5
61	Glens Falls, NY	13.5
63	Janesville, WI	13.1
64	Amarillo, TX	12.7
65	Lawton, OK	12.0
66	Santa Fe, NM	11.5
67	Virginia Beach-Norfolk, VA-NC	10.4
68	Myrtle Beach, SC	9.8
69	Pensacola, FL	9.3
70	Modesto, CA	9.2
71	Jackson, MI	9.1
72	Pittsburgh, PA	8.9
73	Colorado Springs, CO	8.6
74	Stockton, CA	8.5
75	Texarkana, TX-Texarkana, AR	8.4
76	Nashville-Davidson, TN	8.3
77	Santa Ana-Anaheim, CA M.D.	7.6
78	Wausau, WI	7.2
79	Buffalo-Niagara Falls, NY	7.1
80	Charleston-North Charleston, SC	6.5
81	Gainesville, FL	6.4
82	Reno-Sparks, NV	6.2
83	West Palm Beach, FL M.D.	6.1
84	Ocala, FL	5.8
85	Riverside-San Bernardino, CA	5.4
86	Bremerton-Silverdale, WA	5.1
86	Lansing-East Lansing, MI	5.1
86	Sarasota-Bradenton-Venice, FL	5.1
89	Vineland, NJ	4.7
90	Salinas, CA	4.6
91	Houma, LA	4.5
92	Jackson, TN	4.1
93	Little Rock, AR	3.6
94	La Crosse, WI-MN	3.2
94	South Bend-Mishawaka, IN-MI	3.2
96	Tuscaloosa, AL	3.1
97	Florence, SC	3.0
98	Boise City-Nampa, ID	2.8
99	Santa Rosa-Petaluma, CA	2.7
100	Knoxville, TN	2.5
101	Jonesboro, AR	2.4
102	Green Bay, WI	2.1
103	Scranton--Wilkes-Barre, PA	1.6
104	Lakeland, FL	1.4
105	Lynchburg, VA	1.0
105	Racine, WI	1.0
107	Jacksonville, FL	0.8
108	Altoona, PA	0.5
109	Santa Cruz-Watsonville, CA	0.3
109	Tacoma, WA M.D.	0.3
111	Bellingham, WA	0.2
112	Baltimore-Towson, MD	0.1
113	Tulsa, OK	(0.4)
114	Lancaster, PA	(0.6)
115	Denver-Aurora, CO	(0.8)
116	Greenville, NC	(1.2)
117	Cedar Rapids, IA	(1.4)
118	Pueblo, CO	(1.7)
119	Atlanta, GA	(2.5)
119	Austin-Round Rock, TX	(2.5)
121	Williamsport, PA	(2.9)
122	Tallahassee, FL	(3.2)
123	Eugene-Springfield, OR	(3.3)
124	Oklahoma City, OK	(3.5)
124	Panama City-Lynn Haven, FL	(3.5)
126	Hartford, CT	(3.6)
127	Shreveport-Bossier City, LA	(4.1)
128	Fort Walton Beach, FL	(4.6)
129	Rapid City, SD	(5.1)
130	Springfield, MO	(5.2)
131	Chico, CA	(5.3)
132	Trenton-Ewing, NJ	(5.4)
133	Phoenix-Mesa-Scottsdale, AZ	(5.5)
134	San Antonio, TX	(5.7)
135	Provo-Orem, UT	(6.3)
136	Baton Rouge, LA	(6.8)
137	Columbus, OH	(7.1)
138	Spokane, WA	(7.9)
139	Palm Bay-Melbourne, FL	(8.0)
139	Port St. Lucie, FL	(8.0)
141	Decatur, AL	(8.1)
141	Montgomery, AL	(8.1)
143	Olympia, WA	(8.4)
144	Daytona Beach, FL	(8.7)
145	Fayetteville, NC	(8.8)
146	Fresno, CA	(8.9)
147	Los Angeles County, CA M.D.	(9.0)
148	Cape Coral-Fort Myers, FL	(9.2)
149	Portland-Vancouver, OR-WA	(9.3)
149	Waco, TX	(9.3)
151	Savannah, GA	(9.7)
152	Kennewick-Richland-Pasco, WA	(10.0)
153	Beaumont-Port Arthur, TX	(10.1)
153	Cincinnati-Middletown, OH-KY-IN	(10.1)
155	Brownsville-Harlingen, TX	(10.7)
156	Lake Charles, LA	(11.0)
157	Eau Claire, WI	(11.1)
157	Fort Worth-Arlington, TX M.D.	(11.1)
159	Athens-Clarke County, GA	(11.7)
160	Honolulu, HI	(12.1)
161	Wilmington, NC	(12.2)
162	Naples-Marco Island, FL	(12.6)
163	Miami-Dade County, FL M.D.	(12.8)
164	El Paso, TX	(13.1)
165	Houston, TX	(13.2)
166	Alexandria, LA	(14.0)
166	Reading, PA	(14.0)
168	Albany, GA	(14.1)
169	Richmond, VA	(14.6)
170	Fort Collins-Loveland, CO	(14.7)
171	Corpus Christi, TX	(14.9)

Note: All listings are for Metropolitan Statistical Areas (M.S.A.s) except for those ending with "M.D." Listings with "M.D." are Metropolitan Divisions which are smaller parts of eleven large M.S.A.s. See explanatory note at beginning of metropolitan area section on page 23.

Rank Order - Metro Area (continued)

RANK	METROPOLITAN AREA	% CHANGE
172	Casper, WY	(15.3)
173	Chattanooga, TN-GA	(15.4)
173	Salem, OR	(15.4)
173	St. Joseph, MO-KS	(15.4)
176	Albuquerque, NM	(15.6)
177	Cheyenne, WY	(15.8)
178	Charleston, WV	(16.3)
179	Medford, OR	(16.4)
180	Toledo, OH	(17.0)
181	Binghamton, NY	(17.4)
181	New York-W. Plains NY-NJ M.D.	(17.4)
183	Jackson, MS	(17.6)
184	Dallas-Plano-Irving, TX M.D.	(19.4)
185	Asheville, NC	(20.2)
185	Iowa City, IA	(20.2)
187	Great Falls, MT	(21.0)
188	Lincoln, NE	(21.2)
189	Redding, CA	(21.6)
190	Newark-Union, NJ-PA M.D.	(21.7)
191	McAllen-Edinburg-Mission, TX	(24.1)
192	Sheboygan, WI	(24.2)
193	Omaha-Council Bluffs, NE-IA	(24.9)
194	Longview, TX	(25.4)
195	Tampa-St Petersburg, FL	(25.5)
196	Pine Bluff, AR	(26.7)
197	Fort Smith, AR-OK	(28.4)
198	Waterloo-Cedar Falls, IA	(28.9)
199	Tyler, TX	(29.5)
200	Greeley, CO	(30.1)
201	Sumter, SC	(31.1)
202	Wichita Falls, TX	(34.5)
203	Sioux City, IA-NE-SD	(35.2)
204	Utica-Rome, NY	(35.5)
205	Columbia, SC	(36.1)
206	Sherman-Denison, TX	(37.1)
207	Billings, MT	(38.8)
208	New Orleans, LA	(39.6)
209	Victoria, TX	(39.7)
210	Wichita, KS	(40.0)
211	Topeka, KS	(44.4)
212	Bismarck, ND	(45.3)
213	Sioux Falls, SD	(47.9)
NA	Abilene, TX**	NA
NA	Albany-Schenectady-Troy, NY**	NA
NA	Ames, IA**	NA
NA	Anderson, SC**	NA
NA	Ann Arbor, MI**	NA
NA	Appleton, WI**	NA
NA	Atlantic City, NJ**	NA
NA	Bangor, ME**	NA
NA	Barnstable Town, MA**	NA
NA	Battle Creek, MI**	NA
NA	Bay City, MI**	NA
NA	Bend, OR**	NA
NA	Bethesda-Frederick, MD M.D.**	NA
NA	Blacksburg, VA**	NA
NA	Bowling Green, KY**	NA
NA	Brunswick, GA**	NA
NA	Burlington, NC**	NA
NA	Camden, NJ M.D.**	NA

RANK	METROPOLITAN AREA	% CHANGE
NA	Carson City, NV**	NA
NA	Charlotte-Gastonia, NC-SC**	NA
NA	Charlottesville, VA**	NA
NA	Chicago, IL**	NA
NA	Cleveland-Elyria-Mentor, OH**	NA
NA	Cleveland, TN**	NA
NA	Coeur d'Alene, ID**	NA
NA	College Station-Bryan, TX**	NA
NA	Columbus, IN**	NA
NA	Dallas (greater), TX**	NA
NA	Dalton, GA**	NA
NA	Dayton, OH**	NA
NA	Des Moines-West Des Moines, IA**	NA
NA	Detroit-Livonia-Dearborn, MI M.D.**	NA
NA	Dothan, AL**	NA
NA	Durham, NC**	NA
NA	Edison, NJ M.D.**	NA
NA	El Centro, CA**	NA
NA	Elizabethtown, KY**	NA
NA	Elmira, NY**	NA
NA	Evansville, IN-KY**	NA
NA	Fairbanks, AK**	NA
NA	Farmington, NM**	NA
NA	Fayetteville, AR-MO**	NA
NA	Fond du Lac, WI**	NA
NA	Fort Wayne, IN**	NA
NA	Gainesville, GA**	NA
NA	Grand Rapids-Wyoming, MI**	NA
NA	Greensboro-High Point, NC**	NA
NA	Greenville, SC**	NA
NA	Hagerstown-Martinsburg, MD-WV**	NA
NA	Hanford-Corcoran, CA**	NA
NA	Harrisburg-Carlisle, PA**	NA
NA	Harrisonburg, VA**	NA
NA	Hattiesburg, MS**	NA
NA	Holland-Grand Haven, MI**	NA
NA	Hot Springs, AR**	NA
NA	Huntington-Ashland, WV-KY-OH**	NA
NA	Idaho Falls, ID**	NA
NA	Indianapolis, IN**	NA
NA	Ithaca, NY**	NA
NA	Jacksonville, NC**	NA
NA	Jefferson City, MO**	NA
NA	Johnson City, TN**	NA
NA	Johnstown, PA**	NA
NA	Kalamazoo-Portage, MI**	NA
NA	Kansas City, MO-KS**	NA
NA	Kingsport, TN-VA**	NA
NA	Kingston, NY**	NA
NA	Lake Havasu City-Kingman, AZ**	NA
NA	Las Cruces, NM**	NA
NA	Lebanon, PA**	NA
NA	Lewiston, ID-WA**	NA
NA	Lexington-Fayette, KY**	NA
NA	Lima, OH**	NA
NA	Logan, UT-ID**	NA
NA	Longview, WA**	NA
NA	Los Angeles (greater), CA**	NA
NA	Macon, GA**	NA
NA	Madera, CA**	NA

RANK	METROPOLITAN AREA	% CHANGE
NA	Manchester-Nashua, NH**	NA
NA	Mansfield, OH**	NA
NA	Memphis, TN-MS-AR**	NA
NA	Miami (greater), FL**	NA
NA	Michigan City-La Porte, IN**	NA
NA	Midland, TX**	NA
NA	Milwaukee, WI**	NA
NA	Missoula, MT**	NA
NA	Mobile, AL**	NA
NA	Monroe, LA**	NA
NA	Monroe, MI**	NA
NA	Morgantown, WV**	NA
NA	Morristown, TN**	NA
NA	Mount Vernon-Anacortes, WA**	NA
NA	Muskegon-Norton Shores, MI**	NA
NA	Napa, CA**	NA
NA	Nassau-Suffolk, NY M.D.**	NA
NA	New York (greater), NY-NJ-PA**	NA
NA	Niles-Benton Harbor, MI**	NA
NA	Ocean City, NJ**	NA
NA	Odessa, TX**	NA
NA	Ogden-Clearfield, UT**	NA
NA	Oshkosh-Neenah, WI**	NA
NA	Oxnard-Thousand Oaks, CA**	NA
NA	Palm Coast, FL**	NA
NA	Pascagoula, MS**	NA
NA	Philadelphia, PA M.D.**	NA
NA	Pittsfield, MA**	NA
NA	Portland, ME**	NA
NA	Poughkeepsie, NY**	NA
NA	Prescott, AZ**	NA
NA	Raleigh-Cary, NC**	NA
NA	Roanoke, VA**	NA
NA	Rome, GA**	NA
NA	Saginaw, MI**	NA
NA	Salisbury, MD**	NA
NA	Salt Lake City, UT**	NA
NA	San Francisco (greater), CA**	NA
NA	Sandusky, OH**	NA
NA	Santa Barbara-Santa Maria, CA**	NA
NA	Seattle (greater), WA**	NA
NA	Sebastian-Vero Beach, FL**	NA
NA	Spartanburg, SC**	NA
NA	Springfield, MA**	NA
NA	Springfield, OH**	NA
NA	St. Louis, MO-IL**	NA
NA	Syracuse, NY**	NA
NA	Valdosta, GA**	NA
NA	Vallejo-Fairfield, CA**	NA
NA	Warner Robins, GA**	NA
NA	Warren-Farmington Hills, MI M.D.**	NA
NA	Washington (greater) DC-VA-MD**	NA
NA	Washington, DC-VA-MD-WV M.D.**	NA
NA	Wenatchee, WA**	NA
NA	Wheeling, WV-OH**	NA
NA	Wilmington, DE-MD-NJ M.D.**	NA
NA	Winchester, VA-WV**	NA
NA	Winston-Salem, NC**	NA
NA	Worcester, MA**	NA

Source: CQ Press using data from Federal Bureau of Investigation "Crime in the United States 2006" (Uniform Crime Reports, September 24, 2007)

**Robbery is the taking of anything of value by force or threat of force. Attempts are included.*

***Not available.*

21. Aggravated Assaults in 2006

National Total = 860,853 Aggravated Assaults*

RANK	METROPOLITAN AREA	ASSAULTS
224	Abilene, TX	448
93	Albany-Schenectady-Troy, NY	1,976
245	Albany, GA	363
46	Albuquerque, NM	4,389
131	Alexandria, LA	1,198
286	Altoona, PA	224
130	Amarillo, TX	1,206
316	Ames, IA	151
91	Anchorage, AK	1,986
152	Anderson, SC	896
180	Ann Arbor, MI	669
304	Appleton, WI	178
175	Asheville, NC	714
249	Athens-Clarke County, GA	347
13	Atlanta, GA	14,667
162	Atlantic City, NJ	811
148	Augusta, GA-SC	917
65	Austin-Round Rock, TX	3,039
71	Bakersfield, CA	2,864
15	Baltimore-Towson, MD	13,239
340	Bangor, ME	61
NA	Barnstable Town, MA**	NA
53	Baton Rouge, LA	3,866
159	Battle Creek, MI	837
310	Bay City, MI	164
115	Beaumont-Port Arthur, TX	1,430
274	Bellingham, WA	257
289	Bend, OR	220
116	Bethesda-Frederick, MD M.D.	1,406
302	Billings, MT	183
253	Binghamton, NY	338
67	Birmingham-Hoover, AL	2,990
320	Bismarck, ND	149
295	Blacksburg, VA	201
269	Bloomington, IN	287
135	Boise City-Nampa, ID	1,149
289	Bowling Green, KY	220
182	Bremerton-Silverdale, WA	655
123	Brownsville-Harlingen, TX	1,264
197	Brunswick, GA	588
62	Buffalo-Niagara Falls, NY	3,233
199	Burlington, NC	575
78	Camden, NJ M.D.	2,350
89	Cape Coral-Fort Myers, FL	2,047
307	Carson City, NV	169
324	Casper, WY	130
254	Cedar Rapids, IA	324
58	Charleston-North Charleston, SC	3,424
151	Charleston, WV	897
NA	Charlotte-Gastonia, NC-SC**	NA
251	Charlottesville, VA	345
83	Chattanooga, TN-GA	2,145
333	Cheyenne, WY	99
NA	Chicago, IL**	NA
211	Chico, CA	519
69	Cincinnati-Middletown, OH-KY-IN	2,916
141	Clarksville, TN-KY	1,018
57	Cleveland-Elyria-Mentor, OH	3,460
191	Cleveland, TN	616
250	Coeur d'Alene, ID	346
176	College Station-Bryan, TX	708
79	Colorado Springs, CO	2,289
213	Columbia, MO	509
55	Columbia, SC	3,841
170	Columbus, GA-AL	728
327	Columbus, IN	116
87	Columbus, OH	2,090
107	Corpus Christi, TX	1,669
268	Cumberland, MD-WV	288
9	Dallas (greater), TX	17,982
19	Dallas-Plano-Irving, TX M.D.	12,042
246	Dalton, GA	362
314	Danville, VA	157
97	Daytona Beach, FL	1,897
133	Dayton, OH	1,182
277	Decatur, AL	244
34	Denver-Aurora, CO	6,398
123	Des Moines-West Des Moines, IA	1,264
6	Detroit (greater), MI	21,369
10	Detroit-Livonia-Dearborn, MI M.D.	15,537
291	Dothan, AL	218
185	Dover, DE	641
244	Dubuque, IA	364
229	Duluth, MN-WI	438
114	Durham, NC	1,460
311	Eau Claire, WI	162
77	Edison, NJ M.D.	2,375
214	El Centro, CA	503
96	El Paso, TX	1,914
335	Elizabethtown, KY	92
339	Elkhart-Goshen, IN	66
328	Elmira, NY	115
237	Erie, PA	398
197	Eugene-Springfield, OR	588
203	Evansville, IN-KY	554
314	Fairbanks, AK	157
292	Fargo, ND-MN	215
192	Farmington, NM	613
146	Fayetteville, AR-MO	925
119	Fayetteville, NC	1,308
212	Flagstaff, AZ	513
70	Flint, MI	2,874
100	Florence, SC	1,853
325	Fond du Lac, WI	129
208	Fort Collins-Loveland, CO	539
33	Fort Lauderdale, FL M.D.	6,515
134	Fort Smith, AR-OK	1,169
206	Fort Walton Beach, FL	541
257	Fort Wayne, IN	314
36	Fort Worth-Arlington, TX M.D.	5,940
68	Fresno, CA	2,986
298	Gadsden, AL	194
105	Gainesville, FL	1,705
265	Gainesville, GA	299
316	Glens Falls, NY	151
227	Goldsboro, NC	442
329	Grand Forks, ND-MN	113
271	Grand Junction, CO	271
90	Grand Rapids-Wyoming, MI	2,011
305	Great Falls, MT	174
181	Greeley, CO	662
218	Green Bay, WI	484
95	Greensboro-High Point, NC	1,926
168	Greenville, NC	736
64	Greenville, SC	3,053
200	Hagerstown-Martinsburg, MD-WV	574
234	Hanford-Corcoran, CA	417
150	Harrisburg-Carlisle, PA	900
331	Harrisonburg, VA	105
112	Hartford, CT	1,500
323	Hattiesburg, MS	135
260	Holland-Grand Haven, MI	312
109	Honolulu, HI	1,543
232	Hot Springs, AR	426
163	Houma, LA	793
7	Houston, TX	20,817
262	Huntington-Ashland, WV-KY-OH	309
140	Huntsville, AL	1,070
293	Idaho Falls, ID	204
44	Indianapolis, IN	4,565
272	Iowa City, IA	270
337	Ithaca, NY	89
NA	Jacksonville, FL**	NA
241	Jacksonville, NC	370
231	Jackson, MI	428
157	Jackson, MS	842
169	Jackson, TN	729
307	Janesville, WI	169
230	Jefferson City, MO	432
193	Johnson City, TN	598
275	Johnstown, PA	254
222	Jonesboro, AR	470
215	Joplin, MO	495
149	Kalamazoo-Portage, MI	907
30	Kansas City, MO-KS	7,539
216	Kennewick-Richland-Pasco, WA	487
165	Killeen-Temple-Fort Hood, TX	747
139	Kingsport, TN-VA	1,103
239	Kingston, NY	381
76	Knoxville, TN	2,438
296	Kokomo, IN	199
303	La Crosse, WI-MN	179
276	Lafayette, IN	253
147	Lake Charles, LA	923
225	Lake Havasu City-Kingman, AZ	443
88	Lakeland, FL	2,076
207	Lancaster, PA	540
122	Lansing-East Lansing, MI	1,266
153	Laredo, TX	871
186	Las Cruces, NM	640
27	Las Vegas-Paradise, NV	8,187

Note: All listings are for Metropolitan Statistical Areas (M.S.A.s) except for those ending with "M.D." Listings with "M.D." are Metropolitan Divisions which are smaller parts of eleven large M.S.A.s. See explanatory note at beginning of metropolitan area section on page 23.

Alpha Order - Metro Area (continued)

RANK	METROPOLITAN AREA	ASSAULTS
235	Lawrence, KS	415
176	Lawton, OK	708
281	Lebanon, PA	236
343	Lewiston-Auburn, ME	53
341	Lewiston, ID-WA	58
129	Lexington-Fayette, KY	1,217
284	Lima, OH	231
143	Lincoln, NE	1,005
49	Little Rock, AR	4,059
342	Logan, UT-ID	54
155	Longview, TX	868
322	Longview, WA	137
3	Los Angeles County, CA M.D.	33,959
2	Los Angeles (greater), CA	38,700
75	Louisville, KY-IN	2,468
102	Lubbock, TX	1,809
247	Lynchburg, VA	358
173	Macon, GA	724
196	Madera, CA	591
172	Madison, WI	726
263	Manchester-Nashua, NH	304
331	Mansfield, OH	105
98	McAllen-Edinburg-Mission, TX	1,884
243	Medford, OR	367
24	Memphis, TN-MS-AR	9,477
128	Merced, CA	1,227
5	Miami (greater), FL	27,247
11	Miami-Dade County, FL M.D.	14,920
330	Michigan City-La Porte, IN	111
267	Midland, TX	289
45	Milwaukee, WI	4,420
32	Minneapolis-St. Paul, MN-WI	6,546
299	Missoula, MT	187
194	Mobile, AL	594
85	Modesto, CA	2,109
187	Monroe, LA	637
278	Monroe, MI	243
189	Montgomery, AL	621
306	Morgantown, WV	173
219	Morristown, TN	478
326	Mount Vernon-Anacortes, WA	126
283	Muncie, IN	233
190	Muskegon-Norton Shores, MI	618
117	Myrtle Beach, SC	1,325
252	Napa, CA	341
144	Naples-Marco Island, FL	997
25	Nashville-Davidson, TN	8,713
66	Nassau-Suffolk, NY M.D.	3,014
42	New Orleans, LA	4,655
1	New York (greater), NY-NJ-PA	42,146
4	New York-W. Plains NY-NJ M.D.	32,565
47	Newark-Union, NJ-PA M.D.	4,192
204	Niles-Benton Harbor, MI	549
28	Oakland-Fremont, CA M.D.	8,097
99	Ocala, FL	1,857
282	Ocean City, NJ	235
201	Odessa, TX	560
210	Ogden-Clearfield, UT	521
51	Oklahoma City, OK	3,938
236	Olympia, WA	405

RANK	METROPOLITAN AREA	ASSAULTS
86	Omaha-Council Bluffs, NE-IA	2,092
22	Orlando, FL	11,153
270	Oshkosh-Neenah, WI	282
123	Oxnard-Thousand Oaks, CA	1,264
73	Palm Bay-Melbourne, FL	2,742
319	Palm Coast, FL	150
142	Panama City-Lynn Haven, FL	1,014
307	Pascagoula, MS	169
92	Pensacola, FL	1,981
8	Philadelphia (greater) PA-NJ-DE	19,775
12	Philadelphia, PA M.D.	14,679
18	Phoenix-Mesa-Scottsdale, AZ	12,124
184	Pine Bluff, AR	643
39	Pittsburgh, PA	4,922
219	Pittsfield, MA	478
286	Pocatello, ID	224
111	Port St. Lucie, FL	1,503
52	Portland-Vancouver, OR-WA	3,906
255	Portland, ME	323
138	Poughkeepsie, NY	1,116
164	Prescott, AZ	769
273	Provo-Orem, UT	262
228	Pueblo, CO	440
188	Punta Gorda, FL	627
280	Racine, WI	239
81	Raleigh-Cary, NC	2,166
299	Rapid City, SD	187
158	Reading, PA	839
223	Redding, CA	461
127	Reno-Sparks, NV	1,233
84	Richmond, VA	2,133
20	Riverside-San Bernardino, CA	11,375
154	Roanoke, VA	870
299	Rochester, MN	187
101	Rochester, NY	1,843
217	Rocky Mount, NC	485
233	Rome, GA	423
29	Sacramento, CA	7,956
104	Saginaw, MI	1,728
171	Salem, OR	727
121	Salinas, CA	1,284
174	Salisbury, MD	715
80	Salt Lake City, UT	2,250
264	San Angelo, TX	302
35	San Antonio, TX	6,249
26	San Diego, CA	8,362
17	San Francisco (greater), CA	12,250
48	San Francisco-S. Mateo, CA M.D.	4,153
56	San Jose, CA	3,674
202	San Luis Obispo, CA	556
297	Sandusky, OH	198
41	Santa Ana-Anaheim, CA M.D.	4,741
118	Santa Barbara-Santa Maria, CA	1,309
166	Santa Cruz-Watsonville, CA	744
225	Santa Fe, NM	443
106	Santa Rosa-Petaluma, CA	1,679
59	Sarasota-Bradenton-Venice, FL	3,409
NA	Savannah, GA**	NA
137	Scranton--Wilkes-Barre, PA	1,121
31	Seattle (greater), WA	7,462

RANK	METROPOLITAN AREA	ASSAULTS
40	Seattle-Bellevue, WA M.D.	4,817
259	Sebastian-Vero Beach, FL	313
338	Sheboygan, WI	74
288	Sherman-Denison, TX	221
60	Shreveport-Bossier City, LA	3,361
248	Sioux City, IA-NE-SD	354
257	Sioux Falls, SD	314
208	South Bend-Mishawaka, IN-MI	539
120	Spartanburg, SC	1,294
132	Spokane, WA	1,185
NA	Springfield, MA**	NA
108	Springfield, MO	1,550
294	Springfield, OH	202
336	State College, PA	90
50	Stockton, CA	3,941
285	St. Cloud, MN	227
278	St. Joseph, MO-KS	243
23	St. Louis, MO-IL	10,346
136	Sumter, SC	1,141
126	Syracuse, NY	1,260
74	Tacoma, WA M.D.	2,645
94	Tallahassee, FL	1,956
14	Tampa-St Petersburg, FL	13,426
145	Texarkana, TX-Texarkana, AR	931
81	Toledo, OH	2,166
221	Topeka, KS	476
160	Trenton-Ewing, NJ	827
61	Tucson, AZ	3,235
43	Tulsa, OK	4,570
183	Tuscaloosa, AL	653
178	Tyler, TX	691
195	Utica-Rome, NY	592
241	Valdosta, GA	370
110	Vallejo-Fairfield, CA	1,539
266	Victoria, TX	297
166	Vineland, NJ	744
54	Virginia Beach-Norfolk, VA-NC	3,845
103	Visalia-Porterville, CA	1,797
156	Waco, TX	859
255	Warner Robins, GA	323
37	Warren-Farmington Hills, MI M.D.	5,832
16	Washington (greater) DC-VA-MD	12,756
21	Washington, DC-VA-MD-WV M.D.	11,350
240	Waterloo-Cedar Falls, IA	377
313	Wausau, WI	158
321	Wenatchee, WA	142
38	West Palm Beach, FL M.D.	5,812
312	Wheeling, WV-OH	159
260	Wichita Falls, TX	312
63	Wichita, KS	3,074
334	Williamsport, PA	94
72	Wilmington, DE-MD-NJ M.D.	2,746
161	Wilmington, NC	814
316	Winchester, VA-WV	151
113	Winston-Salem, NC	1,495
NA	Worcester, MA**	NA
238	Yakima, WA	387
205	Yuba City, CA	545
179	Yuma, AZ	682

Source: Federal Bureau of Investigation
"Crime in the United States 2006" (Uniform Crime Reports, September 24, 2007)
Aggravated assault is an attack for the purpose of inflicting severe bodily injury.
**Not available.*

21. Aggravated Assaults in 2006 (continued)

National Total = 860,853 Aggravated Assaults*

RANK	METROPOLITAN AREA	ASSAULTS
1	New York (greater), NY-NJ-PA	42,146
2	Los Angeles (greater), CA	38,700
3	Los Angeles County, CA M.D.	33,959
4	New York-W. Plains NY-NJ M.D.	32,565
5	Miami (greater), FL	27,247
6	Detroit (greater), MI	21,369
7	Houston, TX	20,817
8	Philadelphia (greater) PA-NJ-DE	19,775
9	Dallas (greater), TX	17,982
10	Detroit-Livonia-Dearborn, MI M.D.	15,537
11	Miami-Dade County, FL M.D.	14,920
12	Philadelphia, PA M.D.	14,679
13	Atlanta, GA	14,667
14	Tampa-St Petersburg, FL	13,426
15	Baltimore-Towson, MD	13,239
16	Washington (greater) DC-VA-MD	12,756
17	San Francisco (greater), CA	12,250
18	Phoenix-Mesa-Scottsdale, AZ	12,124
19	Dallas-Plano-Irving, TX M.D.	12,042
20	Riverside-San Bernardino, CA	11,375
21	Washington, DC-VA-MD-WV M.D.	11,350
22	Orlando, FL	11,153
23	St. Louis, MO-IL	10,346
24	Memphis, TN-MS-AR	9,477
25	Nashville-Davidson, TN	8,713
26	San Diego, CA	8,362
27	Las Vegas-Paradise, NV	8,187
28	Oakland-Fremont, CA M.D.	8,097
29	Sacramento, CA	7,956
30	Kansas City, MO-KS	7,539
31	Seattle (greater), WA	7,462
32	Minneapolis-St. Paul, MN-WI	6,546
33	Fort Lauderdale, FL M.D.	6,515
34	Denver-Aurora, CO	6,398
35	San Antonio, TX	6,249
36	Fort Worth-Arlington, TX M.D.	5,940
37	Warren-Farmington Hills, MI M.D.	5,832
38	West Palm Beach, FL M.D.	5,812
39	Pittsburgh, PA	4,922
40	Seattle-Bellevue, WA M.D.	4,817
41	Santa Ana-Anaheim, CA M.D.	4,741
42	New Orleans, LA	4,655
43	Tulsa, OK	4,570
44	Indianapolis, IN	4,565
45	Milwaukee, WI	4,420
46	Albuquerque, NM	4,389
47	Newark-Union, NJ-PA M.D.	4,192
48	San Francisco-S. Mateo, CA M.D.	4,153
49	Little Rock, AR	4,059
50	Stockton, CA	3,941
51	Oklahoma City, OK	3,938
52	Portland-Vancouver, OR-WA	3,906
53	Baton Rouge, LA	3,866
54	Virginia Beach-Norfolk, VA-NC	3,845
55	Columbia, SC	3,841
56	San Jose, CA	3,674
57	Cleveland-Elyria-Mentor, OH	3,460
58	Charleston-North Charleston, SC	3,424
59	Sarasota-Bradenton-Venice, FL	3,409
60	Shreveport-Bossier City, LA	3,361
61	Tucson, AZ	3,235
62	Buffalo-Niagara Falls, NY	3,233
63	Wichita, KS	3,074
64	Greenville, SC	3,053
65	Austin-Round Rock, TX	3,039
66	Nassau-Suffolk, NY M.D.	3,014
67	Birmingham-Hoover, AL	2,990
68	Fresno, CA	2,986
69	Cincinnati-Middletown, OH-KY-IN	2,916
70	Flint, MI	2,874
71	Bakersfield, CA	2,864
72	Wilmington, DE-MD-NJ M.D.	2,746
73	Palm Bay-Melbourne, FL	2,742
74	Tacoma, WA M.D.	2,645
75	Louisville, KY-IN	2,468
76	Knoxville, TN	2,438
77	Edison, NJ M.D.	2,375
78	Camden, NJ M.D.	2,350
79	Colorado Springs, CO	2,289
80	Salt Lake City, UT	2,250
81	Raleigh-Cary, NC	2,166
81	Toledo, OH	2,166
83	Chattanooga, TN-GA	2,145
84	Richmond, VA	2,133
85	Modesto, CA	2,109
86	Omaha-Council Bluffs, NE-IA	2,092
87	Columbus, OH	2,090
88	Lakeland, FL	2,076
89	Cape Coral-Fort Myers, FL	2,047
90	Grand Rapids-Wyoming, MI	2,011
91	Anchorage, AK	1,986
92	Pensacola, FL	1,981
93	Albany-Schenectady-Troy, NY	1,976
94	Tallahassee, FL	1,956
95	Greensboro-High Point, NC	1,926
96	El Paso, TX	1,914
97	Daytona Beach, FL	1,897
98	McAllen-Edinburg-Mission, TX	1,884
99	Ocala, FL	1,857
100	Florence, SC	1,853
101	Rochester, NY	1,843
102	Lubbock, TX	1,809
103	Visalia-Porterville, CA	1,797
104	Saginaw, MI	1,728
105	Gainesville, FL	1,705
106	Santa Rosa-Petaluma, CA	1,679
107	Corpus Christi, TX	1,669
108	Springfield, MO	1,550
109	Honolulu, HI	1,543
110	Vallejo-Fairfield, CA	1,539
111	Port St. Lucie, FL	1,503
112	Hartford, CT	1,500
113	Winston-Salem, NC	1,495
114	Durham, NC	1,460
115	Beaumont-Port Arthur, TX	1,430
116	Bethesda-Frederick, MD M.D.	1,406
117	Myrtle Beach, SC	1,325
118	Santa Barbara-Santa Maria, CA	1,309
119	Fayetteville, NC	1,308
120	Spartanburg, SC	1,294
121	Salinas, CA	1,284
122	Lansing-East Lansing, MI	1,266
123	Brownsville-Harlingen, TX	1,264
123	Des Moines-West Des Moines, IA	1,264
123	Oxnard-Thousand Oaks, CA	1,264
126	Syracuse, NY	1,260
127	Reno-Sparks, NV	1,233
128	Merced, CA	1,227
129	Lexington-Fayette, KY	1,217
130	Amarillo, TX	1,206
131	Alexandria, LA	1,198
132	Spokane, WA	1,185
133	Dayton, OH	1,182
134	Fort Smith, AR-OK	1,169
135	Boise City-Nampa, ID	1,149
136	Sumter, SC	1,141
137	Scranton--Wilkes-Barre, PA	1,121
138	Poughkeepsie, NY	1,116
139	Kingsport, TN-VA	1,103
140	Huntsville, AL	1,070
141	Clarksville, TN-KY	1,018
142	Panama City-Lynn Haven, FL	1,014
143	Lincoln, NE	1,005
144	Naples-Marco Island, FL	997
145	Texarkana, TX-Texarkana, AR	931
146	Fayetteville, AR-MO	925
147	Lake Charles, LA	923
148	Augusta, GA-SC	917
149	Kalamazoo-Portage, MI	907
150	Harrisburg-Carlisle, PA	900
151	Charleston, WV	897
152	Anderson, SC	896
153	Laredo, TX	871
154	Roanoke, VA	870
155	Longview, TX	868
156	Waco, TX	859
157	Jackson, MS	842
158	Reading, PA	839
159	Battle Creek, MI	837
160	Trenton-Ewing, NJ	827
161	Wilmington, NC	814
162	Atlantic City, NJ	811
163	Houma, LA	793
164	Prescott, AZ	769
165	Killeen-Temple-Fort Hood, TX	747
166	Santa Cruz-Watsonville, CA	744
166	Vineland, NJ	744
168	Greenville, NC	736
169	Jackson, TN	729
170	Columbus, GA-AL	728
171	Salem, OR	727

Note: All listings are for Metropolitan Statistical Areas (M.S.A.s) except for those ending with "M.D." Listings with "M.D." are Metropolitan Divisions which are smaller parts of eleven large M.S.A.s. See explanatory note at beginning of metropolitan area section on page 23.

RANK	METROPOLITAN AREA	ASSAULTS
172	Madison, WI	726
173	Macon, GA	724
174	Salisbury, MD	715
175	Asheville, NC	714
176	College Station-Bryan, TX	708
176	Lawton, OK	708
178	Tyler, TX	691
179	Yuma, AZ	682
180	Ann Arbor, MI	669
181	Greeley, CO	662
182	Bremerton-Silverdale, WA	655
183	Tuscaloosa, AL	653
184	Pine Bluff, AR	643
185	Dover, DE	641
186	Las Cruces, NM	640
187	Monroe, LA	637
188	Punta Gorda, FL	627
189	Montgomery, AL	621
190	Muskegon-Norton Shores, MI	618
191	Cleveland, TN	616
192	Farmington, NM	613
193	Johnson City, TN	598
194	Mobile, AL	594
195	Utica-Rome, NY	592
196	Madera, CA	591
197	Brunswick, GA	588
197	Eugene-Springfield, OR	588
199	Burlington, NC	575
200	Hagerstown-Martinsburg, MD-WV	574
201	Odessa, TX	560
202	San Luis Obispo, CA	556
203	Evansville, IN-KY	554
204	Niles-Benton Harbor, MI	549
205	Yuba City, CA	545
206	Fort Walton Beach, FL	541
207	Lancaster, PA	540
208	Fort Collins-Loveland, CO	539
208	South Bend-Mishawaka, IN-MI	539
210	Ogden-Clearfield, UT	521
211	Chico, CA	519
212	Flagstaff, AZ	513
213	Columbia, MO	509
214	El Centro, CA	503
215	Joplin, MO	495
216	Kennewick-Richland-Pasco, WA	487
217	Rocky Mount, NC	485
218	Green Bay, WI	484
219	Morristown, TN	478
219	Pittsfield, MA	478
221	Topeka, KS	476
222	Jonesboro, AR	470
223	Redding, CA	461
224	Abilene, TX	448
225	Lake Havasu City-Kingman, AZ	443
225	Santa Fe, NM	443
227	Goldsboro, NC	442
228	Pueblo, CO	440
229	Duluth, MN-WI	438
230	Jefferson City, MO	432
231	Jackson, MI	428
232	Hot Springs, AR	426
233	Rome, GA	423
234	Hanford-Corcoran, CA	417
235	Lawrence, KS	415
236	Olympia, WA	405
237	Erie, PA	398
238	Yakima, WA	387
239	Kingston, NY	381
240	Waterloo-Cedar Falls, IA	377
241	Jacksonville, NC	370
241	Valdosta, GA	370
243	Medford, OR	367
244	Dubuque, IA	364
245	Albany, GA	363
246	Dalton, GA	362
247	Lynchburg, VA	358
248	Sioux City, IA-NE-SD	354
249	Athens-Clarke County, GA	347
250	Coeur d'Alene, ID	346
251	Charlottesville, VA	345
252	Napa, CA	341
253	Binghamton, NY	338
254	Cedar Rapids, IA	324
255	Portland, ME	323
255	Warner Robins, GA	323
257	Fort Wayne, IN	314
257	Sioux Falls, SD	314
259	Sebastian-Vero Beach, FL	313
260	Holland-Grand Haven, MI	312
260	Wichita Falls, TX	312
262	Huntington-Ashland, WV-KY-OH	309
263	Manchester-Nashua, NH	304
264	San Angelo, TX	302
265	Gainesville, GA	299
266	Victoria, TX	297
267	Midland, TX	289
268	Cumberland, MD-WV	288
269	Bloomington, IN	287
270	Oshkosh-Neenah, WI	282
271	Grand Junction, CO	271
272	Iowa City, IA	270
273	Provo-Orem, UT	262
274	Bellingham, WA	257
275	Johnstown, PA	254
276	Lafayette, IN	253
277	Decatur, AL	244
278	Monroe, MI	243
278	St. Joseph, MO-KS	243
280	Racine, WI	239
281	Lebanon, PA	236
282	Ocean City, NJ	235
283	Muncie, IN	233
284	Lima, OH	231
285	St. Cloud, MN	227
286	Altoona, PA	224
286	Pocatello, ID	224
288	Sherman-Denison, TX	221
289	Bend, OR	220
289	Bowling Green, KY	220
291	Dothan, AL	218
292	Fargo, ND-MN	215
293	Idaho Falls, ID	204
294	Springfield, OH	202
295	Blacksburg, VA	201
296	Kokomo, IN	199
297	Sandusky, OH	198
298	Gadsden, AL	194
299	Missoula, MT	187
299	Rapid City, SD	187
299	Rochester, MN	187
302	Billings, MT	183
303	La Crosse, WI-MN	179
304	Appleton, WI	178
305	Great Falls, MT	174
306	Morgantown, WV	173
307	Carson City, NV	169
307	Janesville, WI	169
307	Pascagoula, MS	169
310	Bay City, MI	164
311	Eau Claire, WI	162
312	Wheeling, WV-OH	159
313	Wausau, WI	158
314	Danville, VA	157
314	Fairbanks, AK	157
316	Ames, IA	151
316	Glens Falls, NY	151
316	Winchester, VA-WV	151
319	Palm Coast, FL	150
320	Bismarck, ND	149
321	Wenatchee, WA	142
322	Longview, WA	137
323	Hattiesburg, MS	135
324	Casper, WY	130
325	Fond du Lac, WI	129
326	Mount Vernon-Anacortes, WA	126
327	Columbus, IN	116
328	Elmira, NY	115
329	Grand Forks, ND-MN	113
330	Michigan City-La Porte, IN	111
331	Harrisonburg, VA	105
331	Mansfield, OH	105
333	Cheyenne, WY	99
334	Williamsport, PA	94
335	Elizabethtown, KY	92
336	State College, PA	90
337	Ithaca, NY	89
338	Sheboygan, WI	74
339	Elkhart-Goshen, IN	66
340	Bangor, ME	61
341	Lewiston, ID-WA	58
342	Logan, UT-ID	54
343	Lewiston-Auburn, ME	53
NA	Barnstable Town, MA**	NA
NA	Charlotte-Gastonia, NC-SC**	NA
NA	Chicago, IL**	NA
NA	Jacksonville, FL**	NA
NA	Savannah, GA**	NA
NA	Springfield, MA**	NA
NA	Worcester, MA**	NA

Source: Federal Bureau of Investigation
"Crime in the United States 2006" (Uniform Crime Reports, September 24, 2007)
**Aggravated assault is an attack for the purpose of inflicting severe bodily injury.*
***Not available.*

22. Aggravated Assault Rate in 2006

National Rate = 287.5 Aggravated Assaults per 100,000 Population*

RANK	METROPOLITAN AREA	RATE
163	Abilene, TX	275.2
193	Albany-Schenectady-Troy, NY	232.2
207	Albany, GA	216.0
32	Albuquerque, NM	542.7
4	Alexandria, LA	854.2
250	Altoona, PA	176.5
44	Amarillo, TX	491.4
238	Ames, IA	187.9
11	Anchorage, AK	673.5
38	Anderson, SC	502.7
227	Ann Arbor, MI	196.2
330	Appleton, WI	82.4
248	Asheville, NC	178.2
235	Athens-Clarke County, GA	192.0
147	Atlanta, GA	289.0
135	Atlantic City, NJ	299.0
258	Augusta, GA-SC	171.7
220	Austin-Round Rock, TX	203.5
85	Bakersfield, CA	375.0
42	Baltimore-Towson, MD	497.2
341	Bangor, ME	41.5
NA	Barnstable Town, MA**	NA
30	Baton Rouge, LA	555.8
21	Battle Creek, MI	602.8
279	Bay City, MI	150.8
95	Beaumont-Port Arthur, TX	362.6
292	Bellingham, WA	137.7
277	Bend, OR	153.1
306	Bethesda-Frederick, MD M.D.	122.1
303	Billings, MT	123.7
294	Binghamton, NY	135.7
165	Birmingham-Hoover, AL	271.8
280	Bismarck, ND	150.2
297	Blacksburg, VA	131.7
268	Bloomington, IN	160.4
218	Boise City-Nampa, ID	205.8
226	Bowling Green, KY	196.7
167	Bremerton-Silverdale, WA	267.6
120	Brownsville-Harlingen, TX	324.9
24	Brunswick, GA	578.8
157	Buffalo-Niagara Falls, NY	280.9
66	Burlington, NC	401.2
237	Camden, NJ M.D.	188.5
92	Cape Coral-Fort Myers, FL	369.5
144	Carson City, NV	291.7
243	Casper, WY	184.2
298	Cedar Rapids, IA	130.8
28	Charleston-North Charleston, SC	566.7
141	Charleston, WV	292.5
NA	Charlotte-Gastonia, NC-SC**	NA
246	Charlottesville, VA	181.3
58	Chattanooga, TN-GA	428.0
312	Cheyenne, WY	115.0
NA	Chicago, IL**	NA
188	Chico, CA	240.2
288	Cincinnati-Middletown, OH-KY-IN	140.5
63	Clarksville, TN-KY	413.2
265	Cleveland-Elyria-Mentor, OH	162.5
29	Cleveland, TN	563.0
171	Coeur d'Alene, ID	264.1
94	College Station-Bryan, TX	362.9
79	Colorado Springs, CO	382.4
114	Columbia, MO	329.7
31	Columbia, SC	548.2
182	Columbus, GA-AL	249.1
276	Columbus, IN	156.7
305	Columbus, OH	122.2
72	Corpus Christi, TX	392.5
151	Cumberland, MD-WV	285.5
133	Dallas (greater), TX	300.5
132	Dallas-Plano-Irving, TX M.D.	300.8
168	Dalton, GA	266.3
285	Danville, VA	143.9
80	Daytona Beach, FL	380.7
289	Dayton, OH	139.9
264	Decatur, AL	163.0
169	Denver-Aurora, CO	266.1
187	Des Moines-West Des Moines, IA	240.7
48	Detroit (greater), MI	477.3
6	Detroit-Livonia-Dearborn, MI M.D.	779.5
270	Dothan, AL	158.2
54	Dover, DE	440.0
70	Dubuque, IA	395.1
271	Duluth, MN-WI	158.1
125	Durham, NC	313.8
321	Eau Claire, WI	104.8
323	Edison, NJ M.D.	103.0
123	El Centro, CA	319.9
174	El Paso, TX	257.9
329	Elizabethtown, KY	82.5
342	Elkhart-Goshen, IN	33.6
301	Elmira, NY	128.1
286	Erie, PA	141.8
255	Eugene-Springfield, OR	172.6
272	Evansville, IN-KY	157.4
NA	Fairbanks, AK**	NA
311	Fargo, ND-MN	116.2
46	Farmington, NM	479.2
200	Fayetteville, AR-MO	225.8
89	Fayetteville, NC	371.1
68	Flagstaff, AZ	398.9
13	Flint, MI	649.1
3	Florence, SC	919.5
299	Fond du Lac, WI	129.4
230	Fort Collins-Loveland, CO	194.5
99	Fort Lauderdale, FL M.D.	360.4
65	Fort Smith, AR-OK	405.9
143	Fort Walton Beach, FL	292.0
333	Fort Wayne, IN	77.1
134	Fort Worth-Arlington, TX M.D.	299.9
111	Fresno, CA	337.2
240	Gadsden, AL	186.3
8	Gainesville, FL	697.9
253	Gainesville, GA	174.8
309	Glens Falls, NY	117.1
81	Goldsboro, NC	378.6
310	Grand Forks, ND-MN	116.3
219	Grand Junction, CO	204.8
173	Grand Rapids-Wyoming, MI	261.4
206	Great Falls, MT	216.6
154	Greeley, CO	283.8
266	Green Bay, WI	162.1
159	Greensboro-High Point, NC	280.0
52	Greenville, NC	443.8
35	Greenville, SC	508.5
198	Hagerstown-Martinsburg, MD-WV	228.0
149	Hanford-Corcoran, CA	288.2
256	Harrisburg-Carlisle, PA	172.3
327	Harrisonburg, VA	93.1
282	Hartford, CT	149.7
324	Hattiesburg, MS	102.7
304	Holland-Grand Haven, MI	122.5
260	Honolulu, HI	169.1
51	Hot Springs, AR	450.2
59	Houma, LA	419.0
78	Houston, TX	383.4
316	Huntington-Ashland, WV-KY-OH	107.7
150	Huntsville, AL	287.6
252	Idaho Falls, ID	175.3
162	Indianapolis, IN	276.4
231	Iowa City, IA	193.9
328	Ithaca, NY	88.7
NA	Jacksonville, FL**	NA
190	Jacksonville, NC	238.0
172	Jackson, MI	262.2
267	Jackson, MS	161.7
12	Jackson, TN	649.3
318	Janesville, WI	106.9
136	Jefferson City, MO	298.1
126	Johnson City, TN	312.5
259	Johnstown, PA	171.4
61	Jonesboro, AR	414.6
138	Joplin, MO	295.7
153	Kalamazoo-Portage, MI	284.7
77	Kansas City, MO-KS	384.3
205	Kennewick-Richland-Pasco, WA	216.7
215	Killeen-Temple-Fort Hood, TX	206.6
97	Kingsport, TN-VA	361.8
211	Kingston, NY	208.0
93	Knoxville, TN	367.3
228	Kokomo, IN	195.0
291	La Crosse, WI-MN	138.3
293	Lafayette, IN	137.1
39	Lake Charles, LA	499.4
199	Lake Havasu City-Kingman, AZ	227.9
84	Lakeland, FL	376.0
313	Lancaster, PA	110.0
160	Lansing-East Lansing, MI	278.7
82	Laredo, TX	377.0
113	Las Cruces, NM	333.3
49	Las Vegas-Paradise, NV	463.1

Note: All listings are for Metropolitan Statistical Areas (M.S.A.s) except for those ending with "M.D." Listings with "M.D." are Metropolitan Divisions which are smaller parts of eleven large M.S.A.s. See explanatory note at beginning of metropolitan area section on page 23.

RANK	METROPOLITAN AREA	RATE
67	Lawrence, KS	400.4
14	Lawton, OK	624.2
239	Lebanon, PA	187.8
339	Lewiston-Auburn, ME	49.1
326	Lewiston, ID-WA	95.9
157	Lexington-Fayette, KY	280.9
204	Lima, OH	217.2
102	Lincoln, NE	355.0
15	Little Rock, AR	623.9
340	Logan, UT-ID	47.4
60	Longview, TX	418.9
290	Longview, WA	138.4
108	Los Angeles County, CA M.D.	338.7
137	Los Angeles (greater), CA	296.8
222	Louisville, KY-IN	202.7
10	Lubbock, TX	679.3
283	Lynchburg, VA	149.6
129	Macon, GA	306.7
64	Madera, CA	410.2
295	Madison, WI	134.7
334	Manchester-Nashua, NH	75.5
331	Mansfield, OH	82.0
166	McAllen-Edinburg-Mission, TX	270.1
242	Medford, OR	184.9
7	Memphis, TN-MS-AR	744.2
37	Merced, CA	503.1
43	Miami (greater), FL	494.2
16	Miami-Dade County, FL M.D.	617.5
325	Michigan City-La Porte, IN	99.8
194	Midland, TX	231.6
145	Milwaukee, WI	291.1
214	Minneapolis-St. Paul, MN-WI	206.9
241	Missoula, MT	185.1
284	Mobile, AL	146.6
62	Modesto, CA	413.5
71	Monroe, LA	392.7
269	Monroe, MI	158.3
256	Montgomery, AL	172.3
278	Morgantown, WV	151.0
98	Morristown, TN	361.5
314	Mount Vernon-Anacortes, WA	109.5
223	Muncie, IN	198.9
103	Muskegon-Norton Shores, MI	352.9
25	Myrtle Beach, SC	574.8
177	Napa, CA	254.6
124	Naples-Marco Island, FL	319.1
20	Nashville-Davidson, TN	604.8
317	Nassau-Suffolk, NY M.D.	107.0
87	New Orleans, LA	372.2
202	New York (greater), NY-NJ-PA	224.4
155	New York-W. Plains NY-NJ M.D.	282.9
229	Newark-Union, NJ-PA M.D.	194.6
109	Niles-Benton Harbor, MI	338.5
119	Oakland-Fremont, CA M.D.	325.3
22	Ocala, FL	601.8
191	Ocean City, NJ	236.5
56	Odessa, TX	434.5
322	Ogden-Clearfield, UT	103.6
110	Oklahoma City, OK	337.4
254	Olympia, WA	174.0
175	Omaha-Council Bluffs, NE-IA	255.9
27	Orlando, FL	567.3
251	Oshkosh-Neenah, WI	176.2
272	Oxnard-Thousand Oaks, CA	157.4
36	Palm Bay-Melbourne, FL	507.6
233	Palm Coast, FL	193.1
17	Panama City-Lynn Haven, FL	617.2
315	Pascagoula, MS	107.9
53	Pensacola, FL	442.9
107	Philadelphia (greater) PA-NJ-DE	339.0
82	Philadelphia, PA M.D.	377.0
131	Phoenix-Mesa-Scottsdale, AZ	302.1
19	Pine Bluff, AR	606.2
217	Pittsburgh, PA	206.1
100	Pittsfield, MA	360.3
178	Pocatello, ID	254.1
74	Port St. Lucie, FL	387.9
245	Portland-Vancouver, OR-WA	183.3
337	Portland, ME	62.8
262	Poughkeepsie, NY	166.7
86	Prescott, AZ	372.8
338	Provo-Orem, UT	56.0
152	Pueblo, CO	285.4
73	Punta Gorda, FL	391.4
308	Racine, WI	121.7
203	Raleigh-Cary, NC	223.6
275	Rapid City, SD	157.0
209	Reading, PA	211.5
179	Redding, CA	254.0
130	Reno-Sparks, NV	302.9
247	Richmond, VA	179.6
148	Riverside-San Bernardino, CA	288.3
140	Roanoke, VA	294.0
320	Rochester, MN	105.0
249	Rochester, NY	176.9
117	Rocky Mount, NC	326.8
55	Rome, GA	435.1
76	Sacramento, CA	386.1
5	Saginaw, MI	831.4
236	Salem, OR	190.5
128	Salinas, CA	308.8
18	Salisbury, MD	613.4
210	Salt Lake City, UT	210.6
160	San Angelo, TX	278.7
122	San Antonio, TX	321.6
156	San Diego, CA	282.5
142	San Francisco (greater), CA	292.4
185	San Francisco-S. Mateo, CA M.D.	244.1
212	San Jose, CA	207.5
208	San Luis Obispo, CA	215.7
181	Sandusky, OH	251.4
274	Santa Ana-Anaheim, CA M.D.	157.2
121	Santa Barbara-Santa Maria, CA	323.7
139	Santa Cruz-Watsonville, CA	295.3
127	Santa Fe, NM	310.3
101	Santa Rosa-Petaluma, CA	356.7
41	Sarasota-Bradenton-Venice, FL	498.1
NA	Savannah, GA**	NA
221	Scranton--Wilkes-Barre, PA	203.4
197	Seattle (greater), WA	229.0
232	Seattle-Bellevue, WA M.D.	193.3
189	Sebastian-Vero Beach, FL	239.4
335	Sheboygan, WI	64.3
244	Sherman-Denison, TX	183.9
2	Shreveport-Bossier City, LA	925.3
184	Sioux City, IA-NE-SD	246.9
281	Sioux Falls, SD	149.9
261	South Bend-Mishawaka, IN-MI	168.5
47	Spartanburg, SC	477.6
170	Spokane, WA	264.3
NA	Springfield, MA**	NA
75	Springfield, MO	386.5
287	Springfield, OH	141.7
336	State College, PA	64.0
23	Stockton, CA	588.1
302	St. Cloud, MN	124.5
225	St. Joseph, MO-KS	197.8
91	St. Louis, MO-IL	369.6
1	Sumter, SC	1,064.8
234	Syracuse, NY	192.8
106	Tacoma, WA M.D.	345.0
26	Tallahassee, FL	574.4
40	Tampa-St Petersburg, FL	498.7
9	Texarkana, TX-Texarkana, AR	680.2
115	Toledo, OH	329.4
216	Topeka, KS	206.3
201	Trenton-Ewing, NJ	225.6
112	Tucson, AZ	336.9
34	Tulsa, OK	510.3
116	Tuscaloosa, AL	328.7
104	Tyler, TX	352.6
224	Utica-Rome, NY	198.2
146	Valdosta, GA	289.5
90	Vallejo-Fairfield, CA	370.6
176	Victoria, TX	254.8
45	Vineland, NJ	485.1
196	Virginia Beach-Norfolk, VA-NC	231.1
57	Visalia-Porterville, CA	433.5
88	Waco, TX	371.8
183	Warner Robins, GA	248.1
192	Warren-Farmington Hills, MI M.D.	234.8
186	Washington (greater) DC-VA-MD	241.8
163	Washington, DC-VA-MD-WV M.D.	275.2
194	Waterloo-Cedar Falls, IA	231.6
306	Wausau, WI	122.1
296	Wenatchee, WA	133.2
50	West Palm Beach, FL M.D.	450.6
319	Wheeling, WV-OH	106.8
213	Wichita Falls, TX	207.4
33	Wichita, KS	520.0
332	Williamsport, PA	79.3
69	Wilmington, DE-MD-NJ M.D.	395.9
180	Wilmington, NC	253.2
300	Winchester, VA-WV	128.8
118	Winston-Salem, NC	326.7
NA	Worcester, MA**	NA
263	Yakima, WA	164.3
105	Yuba City, CA	346.2
96	Yuma, AZ	362.4

Source: Federal Bureau of Investigation
"Crime in the United States 2006" (Uniform Crime Reports, September 24, 2007)
**Aggravated assault is an attack for the purpose of inflicting severe bodily injury.*
***Not available.*

22. Aggravated Assault Rate in 2006 (continued)

National Rate = 287.5 Aggravated Assaults per 100,000 Population*

RANK	METROPOLITAN AREA	RATE
1	Sumter, SC	1,064.8
2	Shreveport-Bossier City, LA	925.3
3	Florence, SC	919.5
4	Alexandria, LA	854.2
5	Saginaw, MI	831.4
6	Detroit-Livonia-Dearborn, MI M.D.	779.5
7	Memphis, TN-MS-AR	744.2
8	Gainesville, FL	697.9
9	Texarkana, TX-Texarkana, AR	680.2
10	Lubbock, TX	679.3
11	Anchorage, AK	673.5
12	Jackson, TN	649.3
13	Flint, MI	649.1
14	Lawton, OK	624.2
15	Little Rock, AR	623.9
16	Miami-Dade County, FL M.D.	617.5
17	Panama City-Lynn Haven, FL	617.2
18	Salisbury, MD	613.4
19	Pine Bluff, AR	606.2
20	Nashville-Davidson, TN	604.8
21	Battle Creek, MI	602.8
22	Ocala, FL	601.8
23	Stockton, CA	588.1
24	Brunswick, GA	578.8
25	Myrtle Beach, SC	574.8
26	Tallahassee, FL	574.4
27	Orlando, FL	567.3
28	Charleston-North Charleston, SC	566.7
29	Cleveland, TN	563.0
30	Baton Rouge, LA	555.8
31	Columbia, SC	548.2
32	Albuquerque, NM	542.7
33	Wichita, KS	520.0
34	Tulsa, OK	510.3
35	Greenville, SC	508.5
36	Palm Bay-Melbourne, FL	507.6
37	Merced, CA	503.1
38	Anderson, SC	502.7
39	Lake Charles, LA	499.4
40	Tampa-St Petersburg, FL	498.7
41	Sarasota-Bradenton-Venice, FL	498.1
42	Baltimore-Towson, MD	497.2
43	Miami (greater), FL	494.2
44	Amarillo, TX	491.4
45	Vineland, NJ	485.1
46	Farmington, NM	479.2
47	Spartanburg, SC	477.6
48	Detroit (greater), MI	477.3
49	Las Vegas-Paradise, NV	463.1
50	West Palm Beach, FL M.D.	450.6
51	Hot Springs, AR	450.2
52	Greenville, NC	443.8
53	Pensacola, FL	442.9
54	Dover, DE	440.0
55	Rome, GA	435.1
56	Odessa, TX	434.5
57	Visalia-Porterville, CA	433.5
58	Chattanooga, TN-GA	428.0
59	Houma, LA	419.0
60	Longview, TX	418.9
61	Jonesboro, AR	414.6
62	Modesto, CA	413.5
63	Clarksville, TN-KY	413.2
64	Madera, CA	410.2
65	Fort Smith, AR-OK	405.9
66	Burlington, NC	401.2
67	Lawrence, KS	400.4
68	Flagstaff, AZ	398.9
69	Wilmington, DE-MD-NJ M.D.	395.9
70	Dubuque, IA	395.1
71	Monroe, LA	392.7
72	Corpus Christi, TX	392.5
73	Punta Gorda, FL	391.4
74	Port St. Lucie, FL	387.9
75	Springfield, MO	386.5
76	Sacramento, CA	386.1
77	Kansas City, MO-KS	384.3
78	Houston, TX	383.4
79	Colorado Springs, CO	382.4
80	Daytona Beach, FL	380.7
81	Goldsboro, NC	378.6
82	Laredo, TX	377.0
82	Philadelphia, PA M.D.	377.0
84	Lakeland, FL	376.0
85	Bakersfield, CA	375.0
86	Prescott, AZ	372.8
87	New Orleans, LA	372.2
88	Waco, TX	371.8
89	Fayetteville, NC	371.1
90	Vallejo-Fairfield, CA	370.6
91	St. Louis, MO-IL	369.6
92	Cape Coral-Fort Myers, FL	369.5
93	Knoxville, TN	367.3
94	College Station-Bryan, TX	362.9
95	Beaumont-Port Arthur, TX	362.6
96	Yuma, AZ	362.4
97	Kingsport, TN-VA	361.8
98	Morristown, TN	361.5
99	Fort Lauderdale, FL M.D.	360.4
100	Pittsfield, MA	360.3
101	Santa Rosa-Petaluma, CA	356.7
102	Lincoln, NE	355.0
103	Muskegon-Norton Shores, MI	352.9
104	Tyler, TX	352.6
105	Yuba City, CA	346.2
106	Tacoma, WA M.D.	345.0
107	Philadelphia (greater) PA-NJ-DE	339.0
108	Los Angeles County, CA M.D.	338.7
109	Niles-Benton Harbor, MI	338.5
110	Oklahoma City, OK	337.4
111	Fresno, CA	337.2
112	Tucson, AZ	336.9
113	Las Cruces, NM	333.3
114	Columbia, MO	329.7
115	Toledo, OH	329.4
116	Tuscaloosa, AL	328.7
117	Rocky Mount, NC	326.8
118	Winston-Salem, NC	326.7
119	Oakland-Fremont, CA M.D.	325.3
120	Brownsville-Harlingen, TX	324.9
121	Santa Barbara-Santa Maria, CA	323.7
122	San Antonio, TX	321.6
123	El Centro, CA	319.9
124	Naples-Marco Island, FL	319.1
125	Durham, NC	313.8
126	Johnson City, TN	312.5
127	Santa Fe, NM	310.3
128	Salinas, CA	308.8
129	Macon, GA	306.7
130	Reno-Sparks, NV	302.9
131	Phoenix-Mesa-Scottsdale, AZ	302.1
132	Dallas-Plano-Irving, TX M.D.	300.8
133	Dallas (greater), TX	300.5
134	Fort Worth-Arlington, TX M.D.	299.9
135	Atlantic City, NJ	299.0
136	Jefferson City, MO	298.1
137	Los Angeles (greater), CA	296.8
138	Joplin, MO	295.7
139	Santa Cruz-Watsonville, CA	295.3
140	Roanoke, VA	294.0
141	Charleston, WV	292.5
142	San Francisco (greater), CA	292.4
143	Fort Walton Beach, FL	292.0
144	Carson City, NV	291.7
145	Milwaukee, WI	291.1
146	Valdosta, GA	289.5
147	Atlanta, GA	289.0
148	Riverside-San Bernardino, CA	288.3
149	Hanford-Corcoran, CA	288.2
150	Huntsville, AL	287.6
151	Cumberland, MD-WV	285.5
152	Pueblo, CO	285.4
153	Kalamazoo-Portage, MI	284.7
154	Greeley, CO	283.8
155	New York-W. Plains NY-NJ M.D.	282.9
156	San Diego, CA	282.5
157	Buffalo-Niagara Falls, NY	280.9
157	Lexington-Fayette, KY	280.9
159	Greensboro-High Point, NC	280.0
160	Lansing-East Lansing, MI	278.7
160	San Angelo, TX	278.7
162	Indianapolis, IN	276.4
163	Abilene, TX	275.2
163	Washington, DC-VA-MD-WV M.D.	275.2
165	Birmingham-Hoover, AL	271.8
166	McAllen-Edinburg-Mission, TX	270.1
167	Bremerton-Silverdale, WA	267.6
168	Dalton, GA	266.3
169	Denver-Aurora, CO	266.1
170	Spokane, WA	264.3
171	Coeur d'Alene, ID	264.1

Note: All listings are for Metropolitan Statistical Areas (M.S.A.s) except for those ending with "M.D." Listings with "M.D." are Metropolitan Divisions which are smaller parts of eleven large M.S.A.s. See explanatory note at beginning of metropolitan area section on page 23.

RANK	METROPOLITAN AREA	RATE
172	Jackson, MI	262.2
173	Grand Rapids-Wyoming, MI	261.4
174	El Paso, TX	257.9
175	Omaha-Council Bluffs, NE-IA	255.9
176	Victoria, TX	254.8
177	Napa, CA	254.6
178	Pocatello, ID	254.1
179	Redding, CA	254.0
180	Wilmington, NC	253.2
181	Sandusky, OH	251.4
182	Columbus, GA-AL	249.1
183	Warner Robins, GA	248.1
184	Sioux City, IA-NE-SD	246.9
185	San Francisco-S. Mateo, CA M.D.	244.1
186	Washington (greater) DC-VA-MD	241.8
187	Des Moines-West Des Moines, IA	240.7
188	Chico, CA	240.2
189	Sebastian-Vero Beach, FL	239.4
190	Jacksonville, NC	238.0
191	Ocean City, NJ	236.5
192	Warren-Farmington Hills, MI M.D.	234.8
193	Albany-Schenectady-Troy, NY	232.2
194	Midland, TX	231.6
194	Waterloo-Cedar Falls, IA	231.6
196	Virginia Beach-Norfolk, VA-NC	231.1
197	Seattle (greater), WA	229.0
198	Hagerstown-Martinsburg, MD-WV	228.0
199	Lake Havasu City-Kingman, AZ	227.9
200	Fayetteville, AR-MO	225.8
201	Trenton-Ewing, NJ	225.6
202	New York (greater), NY-NJ-PA	224.4
203	Raleigh-Cary, NC	223.6
204	Lima, OH	217.2
205	Kennewick-Richland-Pasco, WA	216.7
206	Great Falls, MT	216.6
207	Albany, GA	216.0
208	San Luis Obispo, CA	215.7
209	Reading, PA	211.5
210	Salt Lake City, UT	210.6
211	Kingston, NY	208.0
212	San Jose, CA	207.5
213	Wichita Falls, TX	207.4
214	Minneapolis-St. Paul, MN-WI	206.9
215	Killeen-Temple-Fort Hood, TX	206.6
216	Topeka, KS	206.3
217	Pittsburgh, PA	206.1
218	Boise City-Nampa, ID	205.8
219	Grand Junction, CO	204.8
220	Austin-Round Rock, TX	203.5
221	Scranton--Wilkes-Barre, PA	203.4
222	Louisville, KY-IN	202.7
223	Muncie, IN	198.9
224	Utica-Rome, NY	198.2
225	St. Joseph, MO-KS	197.8
226	Bowling Green, KY	196.7
227	Ann Arbor, MI	196.2
228	Kokomo, IN	195.0
229	Newark-Union, NJ-PA M.D.	194.6
230	Fort Collins-Loveland, CO	194.5
231	Iowa City, IA	193.9
232	Seattle-Bellevue, WA M.D.	193.3
233	Palm Coast, FL	193.1
234	Syracuse, NY	192.8
235	Athens-Clarke County, GA	192.0
236	Salem, OR	190.5
237	Camden, NJ M.D.	188.5
238	Ames, IA	187.9
239	Lebanon, PA	187.8
240	Gadsden, AL	186.3
241	Missoula, MT	185.1
242	Medford, OR	184.9
243	Casper, WY	184.2
244	Sherman-Denison, TX	183.9
245	Portland-Vancouver, OR-WA	183.3
246	Charlottesville, VA	181.3
247	Richmond, VA	179.6
248	Asheville, NC	178.2
249	Rochester, NY	176.9
250	Altoona, PA	176.5
251	Oshkosh-Neenah, WI	176.2
252	Idaho Falls, ID	175.3
253	Gainesville, GA	174.8
254	Olympia, WA	174.0
255	Eugene-Springfield, OR	172.6
256	Harrisburg-Carlisle, PA	172.3
256	Montgomery, AL	172.3
258	Augusta, GA-SC	171.7
259	Johnstown, PA	171.4
260	Honolulu, HI	169.1
261	South Bend-Mishawaka, IN-MI	168.5
262	Poughkeepsie, NY	166.7
263	Yakima, WA	164.3
264	Decatur, AL	163.0
265	Cleveland-Elyria-Mentor, OH	162.5
266	Green Bay, WI	162.1
267	Jackson, MS	161.7
268	Bloomington, IN	160.4
269	Monroe, MI	158.3
270	Dothan, AL	158.2
271	Duluth, MN-WI	158.1
272	Evansville, IN-KY	157.4
272	Oxnard-Thousand Oaks, CA	157.4
274	Santa Ana-Anaheim, CA M.D.	157.2
275	Rapid City, SD	157.0
276	Columbus, IN	156.7
277	Bend, OR	153.1
278	Morgantown, WV	151.0
279	Bay City, MI	150.8
280	Bismarck, ND	150.2
281	Sioux Falls, SD	149.9
282	Hartford, CT	149.7
283	Lynchburg, VA	149.6
284	Mobile, AL	146.6
285	Danville, VA	143.9
286	Erie, PA	141.8
287	Springfield, OH	141.7
288	Cincinnati-Middletown, OH-KY-IN	140.5
289	Dayton, OH	139.9
290	Longview, WA	138.4
291	La Crosse, WI-MN	138.3
292	Bellingham, WA	137.7
293	Lafayette, IN	137.1
294	Binghamton, NY	135.7
295	Madison, WI	134.7
296	Wenatchee, WA	133.2
297	Blacksburg, VA	131.7
298	Cedar Rapids, IA	130.8
299	Fond du Lac, WI	129.4
300	Winchester, VA-WV	128.8
301	Elmira, NY	128.1
302	St. Cloud, MN	124.5
303	Billings, MT	123.7
304	Holland-Grand Haven, MI	122.5
305	Columbus, OH	122.2
306	Bethesda-Frederick, MD M.D.	122.1
306	Wausau, WI	122.1
308	Racine, WI	121.7
309	Glens Falls, NY	117.1
310	Grand Forks, ND-MN	116.3
311	Fargo, ND-MN	116.2
312	Cheyenne, WY	115.0
313	Lancaster, PA	110.0
314	Mount Vernon-Anacortes, WA	109.5
315	Pascagoula, MS	107.9
316	Huntington-Ashland, WV-KY-OH	107.7
317	Nassau-Suffolk, NY M.D.	107.0
318	Janesville, WI	106.9
319	Wheeling, WV-OH	106.8
320	Rochester, MN	105.0
321	Eau Claire, WI	104.8
322	Ogden-Clearfield, UT	103.6
323	Edison, NJ M.D.	103.0
324	Hattiesburg, MS	102.7
325	Michigan City-La Porte, IN	99.8
326	Lewiston, ID-WA	95.9
327	Harrisonburg, VA	93.1
328	Ithaca, NY	88.7
329	Elizabethtown, KY	82.5
330	Appleton, WI	82.4
331	Mansfield, OH	82.0
332	Williamsport, PA	79.3
333	Fort Wayne, IN	77.1
334	Manchester-Nashua, NH	75.5
335	Sheboygan, WI	64.3
336	State College, PA	64.0
337	Portland, ME	62.8
338	Provo-Orem, UT	56.0
339	Lewiston-Auburn, ME	49.1
340	Logan, UT-ID	47.4
341	Bangor, ME	41.5
342	Elkhart-Goshen, IN	33.6
NA	Barnstable Town, MA**	NA
NA	Charlotte-Gastonia, NC-SC**	NA
NA	Chicago, IL**	NA
NA	Fairbanks, AK**	NA
NA	Jacksonville, FL**	NA
NA	Savannah, GA**	NA
NA	Springfield, MA**	NA
NA	Worcester, MA**	NA

Source: Federal Bureau of Investigation
"Crime in the United States 2006" (Uniform Crime Reports, September 24, 2007)
**Aggravated assault is an attack for the purpose of inflicting severe bodily injury.*
***Not available.*

23. Percent Change in Aggravated Assault Rate: 2005 to 2006

National Percent Change = 1.1% Decrease*

RANK	METROPOLITAN AREA	% CHANGE
NA	Abilene, TX**	NA
144	Albany-Schenectady-Troy, NY	1.3
77	Albany, GA	7.8
267	Albuquerque, NM	(11.5)
121	Alexandria, LA	3.6
45	Altoona, PA	15.6
144	Amarillo, TX	1.3
10	Ames, IA	47.3
20	Anchorage, AK	26.1
110	Anderson, SC	4.2
264	Ann Arbor, MI	(10.4)
167	Appleton, WI	(0.8)
40	Asheville, NC	17.7
43	Athens-Clarke County, GA	15.8
73	Atlanta, GA	8.2
60	Atlantic City, NJ	10.6
252	Augusta, GA-SC	(8.7)
200	Austin-Round Rock, TX	(3.8)
116	Bakersfield, CA	3.8
238	Baltimore-Towson, MD	(7.5)
292	Bangor, ME	(17.7)
NA	Barnstable Town, MA**	NA
49	Baton Rouge, LA	14.9
123	Battle Creek, MI	3.2
252	Bay City, MI	(8.7)
122	Beaumont-Port Arthur, TX	3.5
192	Bellingham, WA	(3.3)
109	Bend, OR	4.3
206	Bethesda-Frederick, MD M.D.	(4.4)
288	Billings, MT	(16.9)
21	Binghamton, NY	25.4
NA	Birmingham-Hoover, AL**	NA
2	Bismarck, ND	89.2
113	Blacksburg, VA	3.9
11	Bloomington, IN	45.4
NA	Boise City-Nampa, ID**	NA
98	Bowling Green, KY	5.4
213	Bremerton-Silverdale, WA	(4.9)
270	Brownsville-Harlingen, TX	(12.0)
90	Brunswick, GA	6.4
168	Buffalo-Niagara Falls, NY	(1.1)
116	Burlington, NC	3.8
226	Camden, NJ M.D.	(6.5)
158	Cape Coral-Fort Myers, FL	0.0
313	Carson City, NV	(35.8)
236	Casper, WY	(7.4)
284	Cedar Rapids, IA	(14.8)
197	Charleston-North Charleston, SC	(3.4)
164	Charleston, WV	(0.5)
NA	Charlotte-Gastonia, NC-SC**	NA
192	Charlottesville, VA	(3.3)
175	Chattanooga, TN-GA	(2.0)
161	Cheyenne, WY	(0.3)
NA	Chicago, IL**	NA
78	Chico, CA	7.7
154	Cincinnati-Middletown, OH-KY-IN	0.2
86	Clarksville, TN-KY	6.7
NA	Cleveland-Elyria-Mentor, OH**	NA
NA	Cleveland, TN**	NA
81	Coeur d'Alene, ID	7.3
182	College Station-Bryan, TX	(2.7)
55	Colorado Springs, CO	12.8
98	Columbia, MO	5.4
130	Columbia, SC	2.2
57	Columbus, GA-AL	12.3
9	Columbus, IN	49.4
221	Columbus, OH	(6.1)
175	Corpus Christi, TX	(2.0)
132	Cumberland, MD-WV	2.1
208	Dallas (greater), TX	(4.5)
249	Dallas-Plano-Irving, TX M.D.	(8.2)
NA	Dalton, GA**	NA
272	Danville, VA	(12.3)
201	Daytona Beach, FL	(4.0)
38	Dayton, OH	19.9
35	Decatur, AL	20.5
172	Denver-Aurora, CO	(1.7)
NA	Des Moines-West Des Moines, IA**	NA
148	Detroit (greater), MI	1.0
160	Detroit-Livonia-Dearborn, MI M.D.	(0.2)
266	Dothan, AL	(11.0)
252	Dover, DE	(8.7)
84	Dubuque, IA	6.8
NA	Duluth, MN-WI**	NA
NA	Durham, NC**	NA
61	Eau Claire, WI	10.4
128	Edison, NJ M.D.	2.5
307	El Centro, CA	(22.9)
272	El Paso, TX	(12.3)
223	Elizabethtown, KY	(6.3)
314	Elkhart-Goshen, IN	(37.1)
269	Elmira, NY	(11.9)
63	Erie, PA	9.9
64	Eugene-Springfield, OR	9.8
56	Evansville, IN-KY	12.6
NA	Fairbanks, AK**	NA
6	Fargo, ND-MN	66.7
NA	Farmington, NM**	NA
86	Fayetteville, AR-MO	6.7
139	Fayetteville, NC	1.5
285	Flagstaff, AZ	(15.0)
78	Flint, MI	7.7
250	Florence, SC	(8.5)
29	Fond du Lac, WI	22.2
16	Fort Collins-Loveland, CO	30.9
180	Fort Lauderdale, FL M.D.	(2.3)
255	Fort Smith, AR-OK	(8.8)
24	Fort Walton Beach, FL	24.6
NA	Fort Wayne, IN**	NA
113	Fort Worth-Arlington, TX M.D.	3.9
298	Fresno, CA	(19.1)
219	Gadsden, AL	(5.6)
113	Gainesville, FL	3.9
143	Gainesville, GA	1.4
NA	Glens Falls, NY**	NA
27	Goldsboro, NC	22.8
58	Grand Forks, ND-MN	12.2
227	Grand Junction, CO	(6.7)
229	Grand Rapids-Wyoming, MI	(6.8)
68	Great Falls, MT	9.1
304	Greeley, CO	(21.8)
52	Green Bay, WI	14.1
147	Greensboro-High Point, NC	1.1
41	Greenville, NC	16.6
221	Greenville, SC	(6.1)
149	Hagerstown-Martinsburg, MD-WV	0.8
161	Hanford-Corcoran, CA	(0.3)
111	Harrisburg-Carlisle, PA	4.1
8	Harrisonburg, VA	54.7
89	Hartford, CT	6.5
NA	Hattiesburg, MS**	NA
28	Holland-Grand Haven, MI	22.7
116	Honolulu, HI	3.8
238	Hot Springs, AR	(7.5)
33	Houma, LA	20.7
172	Houston, TX	(1.7)
84	Huntington-Ashland, WV-KY-OH	6.8
70	Huntsville, AL	9.0
72	Idaho Falls, ID	8.5
257	Indianapolis, IN	(9.8)
42	Iowa City, IA	16.3
NA	Ithaca, NY**	NA
NA	Jacksonville, FL**	NA
NA	Jacksonville, NC**	NA
125	Jackson, MI	2.8
139	Jackson, MS	1.5
275	Jackson, TN	(12.9)
311	Janesville, WI	(35.1)
67	Jefferson City, MO	9.2
274	Johnson City, TN	(12.5)
NA	Johnstown, PA**	NA
259	Jonesboro, AR	(9.9)
88	Joplin, MO	6.6
75	Kalamazoo-Portage, MI	8.0
NA	Kansas City, MO-KS**	NA
17	Kennewick-Richland-Pasco, WA	30.7
265	Killeen-Temple-Fort Hood, TX	(10.9)
135	Kingsport, TN-VA	1.9
199	Kingston, NY	(3.7)
65	Knoxville, TN	9.5
54	Kokomo, IN	13.4
15	La Crosse, WI-MN	31.5
90	Lafayette, IN	6.4
22	Lake Charles, LA	25.2
NA	Lake Havasu City-Kingman, AZ**	NA
90	Lakeland, FL	6.4
25	Lancaster, PA	24.3
286	Lansing-East Lansing, MI	(16.0)
71	Laredo, TX	8.6
36	Las Cruces, NM	20.2
33	Las Vegas-Paradise, NV	20.7

Note: All listings are for Metropolitan Statistical Areas (M.S.A.s) except for those ending with "M.D." Listings with "M.D." are Metropolitan Divisions which are smaller parts of eleven large M.S.A.s. See explanatory note at beginning of metropolitan area section on page 23.

Alpha Order - Metro Area (continued)

RANK	METROPOLITAN AREA	% CHANGE
5	Lawrence, KS	67.2
18	Lawton, OK	30.6
299	Lebanon, PA	(19.5)
181	Lewiston-Auburn, ME	(2.4)
205	Lewiston, ID-WA	(4.3)
NA	Lexington-Fayette, KY**	NA
283	Lima, OH	(14.6)
211	Lincoln, NE	(4.7)
129	Little Rock, AR	2.3
7	Logan, UT-ID	62.9
300	Longview, TX	(19.6)
308	Longview, WA	(26.7)
225	Los Angeles County, CA M.D.	(6.4)
230	Los Angeles (greater), CA	(6.9)
153	Louisville, KY-IN	0.3
227	Lubbock, TX	(6.7)
48	Lynchburg, VA	15.0
96	Macon, GA	5.6
137	Madera, CA	1.7
82	Madison, WI	7.1
101	Manchester-Nashua, NH	5.0
4	Mansfield, OH	69.4
305	McAllen-Edinburg-Mission, TX	(22.0)
297	Medford, OR	(18.9)
164	Memphis, TN-MS-AR	(0.5)
101	Merced, CA	5.0
179	Miami (greater), FL	(2.2)
203	Miami-Dade County, FL M.D.	(4.2)
68	Michigan City-La Porte, IN	9.1
257	Midland, TX	(9.8)
14	Milwaukee, WI	36.5
NA	Minneapolis-St. Paul, MN-WI**	NA
289	Missoula, MT	(17.0)
301	Mobile, AL	(19.7)
248	Modesto, CA	(8.1)
302	Monroe, LA	(20.9)
46	Monroe, MI	15.1
310	Montgomery, AL	(30.5)
287	Morgantown, WV	(16.5)
104	Morristown, TN	4.7
178	Mount Vernon-Anacortes, WA	(2.1)
31	Muncie, IN	21.4
241	Muskegon-Norton Shores, MI	(7.6)
217	Myrtle Beach, SC	(5.4)
282	Napa, CA	(14.4)
215	Naples-Marco Island, FL	(5.2)
219	Nashville-Davidson, TN	(5.6)
171	Nassau-Suffolk, NY M.D.	(1.5)
NA	New Orleans, LA**	NA
192	New York (greater), NY-NJ-PA	(3.3)
201	New York-W. Plains NY-NJ M.D.	(4.0)
182	Newark-Union, NJ-PA M.D.	(2.7)
241	Niles-Benton Harbor, MI	(7.6)
51	Oakland-Fremont, CA M.D.	14.8
83	Ocala, FL	7.0
65	Ocean City, NJ	9.5
125	Odessa, TX	2.8
95	Ogden-Clearfield, UT	5.8
210	Oklahoma City, OK	(4.6)
236	Olympia, WA	(7.4)
259	Omaha-Council Bluffs, NE-IA	(9.9)
154	Orlando, FL	0.2
61	Oshkosh-Neenah, WI	10.4
80	Oxnard-Thousand Oaks, CA	7.4
104	Palm Bay-Melbourne, FL	4.7
NA	Palm Coast, FL**	NA
26	Panama City-Lynn Haven, FL	23.5
211	Pascagoula, MS	(4.7)
190	Pensacola, FL	(3.2)
133	Philadelphia (greater) PA-NJ-DE	2.0
124	Philadelphia, PA M.D.	3.0
175	Phoenix-Mesa-Scottsdale, AZ	(2.0)
44	Pine Bluff, AR	15.7
208	Pittsburgh, PA	(4.5)
119	Pittsfield, MA	3.7
100	Pocatello, ID	5.2
192	Port St. Lucie, FL	(3.3)
192	Portland-Vancouver, OR-WA	(3.3)
281	Portland, ME	(14.2)
139	Poughkeepsie, NY	1.5
32	Prescott, AZ	21.3
280	Provo-Orem, UT	(14.1)
296	Pueblo, CO	(18.2)
149	Punta Gorda, FL	0.8
1	Racine, WI	91.7
49	Raleigh-Cary, NC	14.9
294	Rapid City, SD	(17.8)
158	Reading, PA	0.0
309	Redding, CA	(28.1)
277	Reno-Sparks, NV	(13.2)
256	Richmond, VA	(9.6)
206	Riverside-San Bernardino, CA	(4.4)
152	Roanoke, VA	0.4
139	Rochester, MN	1.5
19	Rochester, NY	30.0
106	Rocky Mount, NC	4.6
3	Rome, GA	75.9
75	Sacramento, CA	8.0
161	Saginaw, MI	(0.3)
290	Salem, OR	(17.4)
59	Salinas, CA	11.4
238	Salisbury, MD	(7.5)
146	Salt Lake City, UT	1.2
151	San Angelo, TX	0.7
218	San Antonio, TX	(5.5)
235	San Diego, CA	(7.3)
94	San Francisco (greater), CA	6.1
241	San Francisco-S. Mateo, CA M.D.	(7.6)
184	San Jose, CA	(2.8)
223	San Luis Obispo, CA	(6.3)
23	Sandusky, OH	25.0
262	Santa Ana-Anaheim, CA M.D.	(10.2)
137	Santa Barbara-Santa Maria, CA	1.7
241	Santa Cruz-Watsonville, CA	(7.6)
315	Santa Fe, NM	(48.0)
278	Santa Rosa-Petaluma, CA	(13.6)
108	Sarasota-Bradenton-Venice, FL	4.4
NA	Savannah, GA**	NA
213	Scranton--Wilkes-Barre, PA	(4.9)
170	Seattle (greater), WA	(1.3)
174	Seattle-Bellevue, WA M.D.	(1.8)
232	Sebastian-Vero Beach, FL	(7.1)
262	Sheboygan, WI	(10.2)
295	Sherman-Denison, TX	(17.9)
53	Shreveport-Bossier City, LA	13.8
156	Sioux City, IA-NE-SD	0.1
119	Sioux Falls, SD	3.7
231	South Bend-Mishawaka, IN-MI	(7.0)
188	Spartanburg, SC	(3.1)
245	Spokane, WA	(7.7)
NA	Springfield, MA**	NA
12	Springfield, MO	43.8
275	Springfield, OH	(12.9)
303	State College, PA	(21.0)
186	Stockton, CA	(2.9)
103	St. Cloud, MN	4.9
37	St. Joseph, MO-KS	20.0
125	St. Louis, MO-IL	2.8
13	Sumter, SC	42.0
247	Syracuse, NY	(7.9)
164	Tacoma, WA M.D.	(0.5)
198	Tallahassee, FL	(3.6)
259	Tampa-St Petersburg, FL	(9.9)
203	Texarkana, TX-Texarkana, AR	(4.2)
215	Toledo, OH	(5.2)
279	Topeka, KS	(13.9)
232	Trenton-Ewing, NJ	(7.1)
268	Tucson, AZ	(11.6)
156	Tulsa, OK	0.1
NA	Tuscaloosa, AL**	NA
74	Tyler, TX	8.1
30	Utica-Rome, NY	21.5
130	Valdosta, GA	2.2
NA	Vallejo-Fairfield, CA**	NA
168	Victoria, TX	(1.1)
292	Vineland, NJ	(17.7)
190	Virginia Beach-Norfolk, VA-NC	(3.2)
291	Visalia-Porterville, CA	(17.5)
136	Waco, TX	1.8
46	Warner Robins, GA	15.1
93	Warren-Farmington Hills, MI M.D.	6.2
NA	Washington (greater) DC-VA-MD**	NA
NA	Washington, DC-VA-MD-WV M.D.**	NA
133	Waterloo-Cedar Falls, IA	2.0
39	Wausau, WI	19.6
188	Wenatchee, WA	(3.1)
112	West Palm Beach, FL M.D.	4.0
271	Wheeling, WV-OH	(12.2)
312	Wichita Falls, TX	(35.7)
NA	Wichita, KS**	NA
306	Williamsport, PA	(22.8)
107	Wilmington, DE-MD-NJ M.D.	4.5
234	Wilmington, NC	(7.2)
251	Winchester, VA-WV	(8.6)
184	Winston-Salem, NC	(2.8)
NA	Worcester, MA**	NA
187	Yakima, WA	(3.0)
97	Yuba City, CA	5.5
246	Yuma, AZ	(7.8)

Source: CQ Press using data from Federal Bureau of Investigation "Crime in the United States 2006" (Uniform Crime Reports, September 24, 2007)

**Aggravated assault is an attack for the purpose of inflicting severe bodily injury.*

***Not available.*

23. Percent Change in Aggravated Assault Rate: 2005 to 2006 (continued)

National Percent Change = 1.1% Decrease*

RANK	METROPOLITAN AREA	% CHANGE
1	Racine, WI	91.7
2	Bismarck, ND	89.2
3	Rome, GA	75.9
4	Mansfield, OH	69.4
5	Lawrence, KS	67.2
6	Fargo, ND-MN	66.7
7	Logan, UT-ID	62.9
8	Harrisonburg, VA	54.7
9	Columbus, IN	49.4
10	Ames, IA	47.3
11	Bloomington, IN	45.4
12	Springfield, MO	43.8
13	Sumter, SC	42.0
14	Milwaukee, WI	36.5
15	La Crosse, WI-MN	31.5
16	Fort Collins-Loveland, CO	30.9
17	Kennewick-Richland-Pasco, WA	30.7
18	Lawton, OK	30.6
19	Rochester, NY	30.0
20	Anchorage, AK	26.1
21	Binghamton, NY	25.4
22	Lake Charles, LA	25.2
23	Sandusky, OH	25.0
24	Fort Walton Beach, FL	24.6
25	Lancaster, PA	24.3
26	Panama City-Lynn Haven, FL	23.5
27	Goldsboro, NC	22.8
28	Holland-Grand Haven, MI	22.7
29	Fond du Lac, WI	22.2
30	Utica-Rome, NY	21.5
31	Muncie, IN	21.4
32	Prescott, AZ	21.3
33	Houma, LA	20.7
33	Las Vegas-Paradise, NV	20.7
35	Decatur, AL	20.5
36	Las Cruces, NM	20.2
37	St. Joseph, MO-KS	20.0
38	Dayton, OH	19.9
39	Wausau, WI	19.6
40	Asheville, NC	17.7
41	Greenville, NC	16.6
42	Iowa City, IA	16.3
43	Athens-Clarke County, GA	15.8
44	Pine Bluff, AR	15.7
45	Altoona, PA	15.6
46	Monroe, MI	15.1
46	Warner Robins, GA	15.1
48	Lynchburg, VA	15.0
49	Baton Rouge, LA	14.9
49	Raleigh-Cary, NC	14.9
51	Oakland-Fremont, CA M.D.	14.8
52	Green Bay, WI	14.1
53	Shreveport-Bossier City, LA	13.8
54	Kokomo, IN	13.4
55	Colorado Springs, CO	12.8
56	Evansville, IN-KY	12.6
57	Columbus, GA-AL	12.3
58	Grand Forks, ND-MN	12.2
59	Salinas, CA	11.4
60	Atlantic City, NJ	10.6
61	Eau Claire, WI	10.4
61	Oshkosh-Neenah, WI	10.4
63	Erie, PA	9.9
64	Eugene-Springfield, OR	9.8
65	Knoxville, TN	9.5
65	Ocean City, NJ	9.5
67	Jefferson City, MO	9.2
68	Great Falls, MT	9.1
68	Michigan City-La Porte, IN	9.1
70	Huntsville, AL	9.0
71	Laredo, TX	8.6
72	Idaho Falls, ID	8.5
73	Atlanta, GA	8.2
74	Tyler, TX	8.1
75	Kalamazoo-Portage, MI	8.0
75	Sacramento, CA	8.0
77	Albany, GA	7.8
78	Chico, CA	7.7
78	Flint, MI	7.7
80	Oxnard-Thousand Oaks, CA	7.4
81	Coeur d'Alene, ID	7.3
82	Madison, WI	7.1
83	Ocala, FL	7.0
84	Dubuque, IA	6.8
84	Huntington-Ashland, WV-KY-OH	6.8
86	Clarksville, TN-KY	6.7
86	Fayetteville, AR-MO	6.7
88	Joplin, MO	6.6
89	Hartford, CT	6.5
90	Brunswick, GA	6.4
90	Lafayette, IN	6.4
90	Lakeland, FL	6.4
93	Warren-Farmington Hills, MI M.D.	6.2
94	San Francisco (greater), CA	6.1
95	Ogden-Clearfield, UT	5.8
96	Macon, GA	5.6
97	Yuba City, CA	5.5
98	Bowling Green, KY	5.4
98	Columbia, MO	5.4
100	Pocatello, ID	5.2
101	Manchester-Nashua, NH	5.0
101	Merced, CA	5.0
103	St. Cloud, MN	4.9
104	Morristown, TN	4.7
104	Palm Bay-Melbourne, FL	4.7
106	Rocky Mount, NC	4.6
107	Wilmington, DE-MD-NJ M.D.	4.5
108	Sarasota-Bradenton-Venice, FL	4.4
109	Bend, OR	4.3
110	Anderson, SC	4.2
111	Harrisburg-Carlisle, PA	4.1
112	West Palm Beach, FL M.D.	4.0
113	Blacksburg, VA	3.9
113	Fort Worth-Arlington, TX M.D.	3.9
113	Gainesville, FL	3.9
116	Bakersfield, CA	3.8
116	Burlington, NC	3.8
116	Honolulu, HI	3.8
119	Pittsfield, MA	3.7
119	Sioux Falls, SD	3.7
121	Alexandria, LA	3.6
122	Beaumont-Port Arthur, TX	3.5
123	Battle Creek, MI	3.2
124	Philadelphia, PA M.D.	3.0
125	Jackson, MI	2.8
125	Odessa, TX	2.8
125	St. Louis, MO-IL	2.8
128	Edison, NJ M.D.	2.5
129	Little Rock, AR	2.3
130	Columbia, SC	2.2
130	Valdosta, GA	2.2
132	Cumberland, MD-WV	2.1
133	Philadelphia (greater) PA-NJ-DE	2.0
133	Waterloo-Cedar Falls, IA	2.0
135	Kingsport, TN-VA	1.9
136	Waco, TX	1.8
137	Madera, CA	1.7
137	Santa Barbara-Santa Maria, CA	1.7
139	Fayetteville, NC	1.5
139	Jackson, MS	1.5
139	Poughkeepsie, NY	1.5
139	Rochester, MN	1.5
143	Gainesville, GA	1.4
144	Albany-Schenectady-Troy, NY	1.3
144	Amarillo, TX	1.3
146	Salt Lake City, UT	1.2
147	Greensboro-High Point, NC	1.1
148	Detroit (greater), MI	1.0
149	Hagerstown-Martinsburg, MD-WV	0.8
149	Punta Gorda, FL	0.8
151	San Angelo, TX	0.7
152	Roanoke, VA	0.4
153	Louisville, KY-IN	0.3
154	Cincinnati-Middletown, OH-KY-IN	0.2
154	Orlando, FL	0.2
156	Sioux City, IA-NE-SD	0.1
156	Tulsa, OK	0.1
158	Cape Coral-Fort Myers, FL	0.0
158	Reading, PA	0.0
160	Detroit-Livonia-Dearborn, MI M.D.	(0.2)
161	Cheyenne, WY	(0.3)
161	Hanford-Corcoran, CA	(0.3)
161	Saginaw, MI	(0.3)
164	Charleston, WV	(0.5)
164	Memphis, TN-MS-AR	(0.5)
164	Tacoma, WA M.D.	(0.5)
167	Appleton, WI	(0.8)
168	Buffalo-Niagara Falls, NY	(1.1)
168	Victoria, TX	(1.1)
170	Seattle (greater), WA	(1.3)
171	Nassau-Suffolk, NY M.D.	(1.5)

Note: All listings are for Metropolitan Statistical Areas (M.S.A.s) except for those ending with "M.D." Listings with "M.D." are Metropolitan Divisions which are smaller parts of eleven large M.S.A.s. See explanatory note at beginning of metropolitan area section on page 23.

Rank Order - Metro Area (continued)

RANK	METROPOLITAN AREA	% CHANGE	RANK	METROPOLITAN AREA	% CHANGE	RANK	METROPOLITAN AREA	% CHANGE
172	Denver-Aurora, CO	(1.7)	232	Sebastian-Vero Beach, FL	(7.1)	292	Bangor, ME	(17.7)
172	Houston, TX	(1.7)	232	Trenton-Ewing, NJ	(7.1)	292	Vineland, NJ	(17.7)
174	Seattle-Bellevue, WA M.D.	(1.8)	234	Wilmington, NC	(7.2)	294	Rapid City, SD	(17.8)
175	Chattanooga, TN-GA	(2.0)	235	San Diego, CA	(7.3)	295	Sherman-Denison, TX	(17.9)
175	Corpus Christi, TX	(2.0)	236	Casper, WY	(7.4)	296	Pueblo, CO	(18.2)
175	Phoenix-Mesa-Scottsdale, AZ	(2.0)	236	Olympia, WA	(7.4)	297	Medford, OR	(18.9)
178	Mount Vernon-Anacortes, WA	(2.1)	238	Baltimore-Towson, MD	(7.5)	298	Fresno, CA	(19.1)
179	Miami (greater), FL	(2.2)	238	Hot Springs, AR	(7.5)	299	Lebanon, PA	(19.5)
180	Fort Lauderdale, FL M.D.	(2.3)	238	Salisbury, MD	(7.5)	300	Longview, TX	(19.6)
181	Lewiston-Auburn, ME	(2.4)	241	Muskegon-Norton Shores, MI	(7.6)	301	Mobile, AL	(19.7)
182	College Station-Bryan, TX	(2.7)	241	Niles-Benton Harbor, MI	(7.6)	302	Monroe, LA	(20.9)
182	Newark-Union, NJ-PA M.D.	(2.7)	241	San Francisco-S. Mateo, CA M.D.	(7.6)	303	State College, PA	(21.0)
184	San Jose, CA	(2.8)	241	Santa Cruz-Watsonville, CA	(7.6)	304	Greeley, CO	(21.8)
184	Winston-Salem, NC	(2.8)	245	Spokane, WA	(7.7)	305	McAllen-Edinburg-Mission, TX	(22.0)
186	Stockton, CA	(2.9)	246	Yuma, AZ	(7.8)	306	Williamsport, PA	(22.8)
187	Yakima, WA	(3.0)	247	Syracuse, NY	(7.9)	307	El Centro, CA	(22.9)
188	Spartanburg, SC	(3.1)	248	Modesto, CA	(8.1)	308	Longview, WA	(26.7)
188	Wenatchee, WA	(3.1)	249	Dallas-Plano-Irving, TX M.D.	(8.2)	309	Redding, CA	(28.1)
190	Pensacola, FL	(3.2)	250	Florence, SC	(8.5)	310	Montgomery, AL	(30.5)
190	Virginia Beach-Norfolk, VA-NC	(3.2)	251	Winchester, VA-WV	(8.6)	311	Janesville, WI	(35.1)
192	Bellingham, WA	(3.3)	252	Augusta, GA-SC	(8.7)	312	Wichita Falls, TX	(35.7)
192	Charlottesville, VA	(3.3)	252	Bay City, MI	(8.7)	313	Carson City, NV	(35.8)
192	New York (greater), NY-NJ-PA	(3.3)	252	Dover, DE	(8.7)	314	Elkhart-Goshen, IN	(37.1)
192	Port St. Lucie, FL	(3.3)	255	Fort Smith, AR-OK	(8.8)	315	Santa Fe, NM	(48.0)
192	Portland-Vancouver, OR-WA	(3.3)	256	Richmond, VA	(9.6)	NA	Abilene, TX**	NA
197	Charleston-North Charleston, SC	(3.4)	257	Indianapolis, IN	(9.8)	NA	Barnstable Town, MA**	NA
198	Tallahassee, FL	(3.6)	257	Midland, TX	(9.8)	NA	Birmingham-Hoover, AL**	NA
199	Kingston, NY	(3.7)	259	Jonesboro, AR	(9.9)	NA	Boise City-Nampa, ID**	NA
200	Austin-Round Rock, TX	(3.8)	259	Omaha-Council Bluffs, NE-IA	(9.9)	NA	Charlotte-Gastonia, NC-SC**	NA
201	Daytona Beach, FL	(4.0)	259	Tampa-St Petersburg, FL	(9.9)	NA	Chicago, IL**	NA
201	New York-W. Plains NY-NJ M.D.	(4.0)	262	Santa Ana-Anaheim, CA M.D.	(10.2)	NA	Cleveland-Elyria-Mentor, OH**	NA
203	Miami-Dade County, FL M.D.	(4.2)	262	Sheboygan, WI	(10.2)	NA	Cleveland, TN**	NA
203	Texarkana, TX-Texarkana, AR	(4.2)	264	Ann Arbor, MI	(10.4)	NA	Dalton, GA**	NA
205	Lewiston, ID-WA	(4.3)	265	Killeen-Temple-Fort Hood, TX	(10.9)	NA	Des Moines-West Des Moines, IA**	NA
206	Bethesda-Frederick, MD M.D.	(4.4)	266	Dothan, AL	(11.0)	NA	Duluth, MN-WI**	NA
206	Riverside-San Bernardino, CA	(4.4)	267	Albuquerque, NM	(11.5)	NA	Durham, NC**	NA
208	Dallas (greater), TX	(4.5)	268	Tucson, AZ	(11.6)	NA	Fairbanks, AK**	NA
208	Pittsburgh, PA	(4.5)	269	Elmira, NY	(11.9)	NA	Farmington, NM**	NA
210	Oklahoma City, OK	(4.6)	270	Brownsville-Harlingen, TX	(12.0)	NA	Fort Wayne, IN**	NA
211	Lincoln, NE	(4.7)	271	Wheeling, WV-OH	(12.2)	NA	Glens Falls, NY**	NA
211	Pascagoula, MS	(4.7)	272	Danville, VA	(12.3)	NA	Hattiesburg, MS**	NA
213	Bremerton-Silverdale, WA	(4.9)	272	El Paso, TX	(12.3)	NA	Ithaca, NY**	NA
213	Scranton--Wilkes-Barre, PA	(4.9)	274	Johnson City, TN	(12.5)	NA	Jacksonville, FL**	NA
215	Naples-Marco Island, FL	(5.2)	275	Jackson, TN	(12.9)	NA	Jacksonville, NC**	NA
215	Toledo, OH	(5.2)	275	Springfield, OH	(12.9)	NA	Johnstown, PA**	NA
217	Myrtle Beach, SC	(5.4)	277	Reno-Sparks, NV	(13.2)	NA	Kansas City, MO-KS**	NA
218	San Antonio, TX	(5.5)	278	Santa Rosa-Petaluma, CA	(13.6)	NA	Lake Havasu City-Kingman, AZ**	NA
219	Gadsden, AL	(5.6)	279	Topeka, KS	(13.9)	NA	Lexington-Fayette, KY**	NA
219	Nashville-Davidson, TN	(5.6)	280	Provo-Orem, UT	(14.1)	NA	Minneapolis-St. Paul, MN-WI**	NA
221	Columbus, OH	(6.1)	281	Portland, ME	(14.2)	NA	New Orleans, LA**	NA
221	Greenville, SC	(6.1)	282	Napa, CA	(14.4)	NA	Palm Coast, FL**	NA
223	Elizabethtown, KY	(6.3)	283	Lima, OH	(14.6)	NA	Savannah, GA**	NA
223	San Luis Obispo, CA	(6.3)	284	Cedar Rapids, IA	(14.8)	NA	Springfield, MA**	NA
225	Los Angeles County, CA M.D.	(6.4)	285	Flagstaff, AZ	(15.0)	NA	Tuscaloosa, AL**	NA
226	Camden, NJ M.D.	(6.5)	286	Lansing-East Lansing, MI	(16.0)	NA	Vallejo-Fairfield, CA**	NA
227	Grand Junction, CO	(6.7)	287	Morgantown, WV	(16.5)	NA	Washington (greater) DC-VA-MD**	NA
227	Lubbock, TX	(6.7)	288	Billings, MT	(16.9)	NA	Washington, DC-VA-MD-WV M.D.**	NA
229	Grand Rapids-Wyoming, MI	(6.8)	289	Missoula, MT	(17.0)	NA	Wichita, KS**	NA
230	Los Angeles (greater), CA	(6.9)	290	Salem, OR	(17.4)	NA	Worcester, MA**	NA
231	South Bend-Mishawaka, IN-MI	(7.0)	291	Visalia-Porterville, CA	(17.5)			

Source: CQ Press using data from Federal Bureau of Investigation
"Crime in the United States 2006" (Uniform Crime Reports, September 24, 2007)
**Aggravated assault is an attack for the purpose of inflicting severe bodily injury.*
***Not available.*

24. Percent Change in Aggravated Assault Rate: 2002 to 2006

National Percent Change = 7.1% Decrease*

RANK	METROPOLITAN AREA	% CHANGE
NA	Abilene, TX**	NA
NA	Albany-Schenectady-Troy, NY**	NA
98	Albany, GA	1.1
158	Albuquerque, NM	(15.4)
72	Alexandria, LA	7.3
57	Altoona, PA	13.4
96	Amarillo, TX	1.7
NA	Ames, IA**	NA
9	Anchorage, AK	68.7
NA	Anderson, SC**	NA
NA	Ann Arbor, MI**	NA
NA	Appleton, WI**	NA
157	Asheville, NC	(14.4)
65	Athens-Clarke County, GA	9.2
86	Atlanta, GA	4.1
NA	Atlantic City, NJ**	NA
34	Augusta, GA-SC	26.6
136	Austin-Round Rock, TX	(8.3)
62	Bakersfield, CA	10.8
187	Baltimore-Towson, MD	(24.6)
NA	Bangor, ME**	NA
NA	Barnstable Town, MA**	NA
31	Baton Rouge, LA	28.2
NA	Battle Creek, MI**	NA
NA	Bay City, MI**	NA
56	Beaumont-Port Arthur, TX	13.6
83	Bellingham, WA	5.1
NA	Bend, OR**	NA
NA	Bethesda-Frederick, MD M.D.**	NA
195	Billings, MT	(32.0)
67	Binghamton, NY	8.7
123	Birmingham-Hoover, AL	(4.8)
1	Bismarck, ND	242.9
NA	Blacksburg, VA**	NA
37	Bloomington, IN	24.7
146	Boise City-Nampa, ID	(11.3)
NA	Bowling Green, KY**	NA
92	Bremerton-Silverdale, WA	2.8
94	Brownsville-Harlingen, TX	2.5
NA	Brunswick, GA**	NA
75	Buffalo-Niagara Falls, NY	6.8
NA	Burlington, NC**	NA
NA	Camden, NJ M.D.**	NA
155	Cape Coral-Fort Myers, FL	(13.8)
NA	Carson City, NV**	NA
166	Casper, WY	(16.9)
177	Cedar Rapids, IA	(19.9)
121	Charleston-North Charleston, SC	(4.1)
89	Charleston, WV	3.5
NA	Charlotte-Gastonia, NC-SC**	NA
NA	Charlottesville, VA**	NA
164	Chattanooga, TN-GA	(16.8)
149	Cheyenne, WY	(12.2)
NA	Chicago, IL**	NA
58	Chico, CA	12.7
186	Cincinnati-Middletown, OH-KY-IN	(24.5)
41	Clarksville, TN-KY	23.2
NA	Cleveland-Elyria-Mentor, OH**	NA
NA	Cleveland, TN**	NA
NA	Coeur d'Alene, ID**	NA
NA	College Station-Bryan, TX**	NA
24	Colorado Springs, CO	37.6
28	Columbia, MO	32.0
140	Columbia, SC	(10.4)
29	Columbus, GA-AL	29.5
NA	Columbus, IN**	NA
193	Columbus, OH	(30.3)
107	Corpus Christi, TX	(0.7)
42	Cumberland, MD-WV	22.9
NA	Dallas (greater), TX**	NA
169	Dallas-Plano-Irving, TX M.D.	(17.5)
NA	Dalton, GA**	NA
202	Danville, VA	(40.6)
152	Daytona Beach, FL	(12.9)
NA	Dayton, OH**	NA
11	Decatur, AL	60.9
49	Denver-Aurora, CO	18.7
NA	Des Moines-West Des Moines, IA**	NA
88	Detroit (greater), MI	3.7
NA	Detroit-Livonia-Dearborn, MI M.D.**	NA
NA	Dothan, AL**	NA
147	Dover, DE	(11.8)
2	Dubuque, IA	106.8
82	Duluth, MN-WI	5.3
NA	Durham, NC**	NA
87	Eau Claire, WI	3.8
NA	Edison, NJ M.D.**	NA
NA	El Centro, CA**	NA
207	El Paso, TX	(46.3)
NA	Elizabethtown, KY**	NA
210	Elkhart-Goshen, IN	(77.9)
NA	Elmira, NY**	NA
109	Erie, PA	(1.0)
52	Eugene-Springfield, OR	16.4
NA	Evansville, IN-KY**	NA
NA	Fairbanks, AK**	NA
25	Fargo, ND-MN	34.6
NA	Farmington, NM**	NA
NA	Fayetteville, AR-MO**	NA
111	Fayetteville, NC	(1.7)
141	Flagstaff, AZ	(10.6)
12	Flint, MI	57.2
17	Florence, SC	44.7
NA	Fond du Lac, WI**	NA
77	Fort Collins-Loveland, CO	6.6
73	Fort Lauderdale, FL M.D.	7.1
114	Fort Smith, AR-OK	(2.3)
51	Fort Walton Beach, FL	16.8
NA	Fort Wayne, IN**	NA
71	Fort Worth-Arlington, TX M.D.	7.8
138	Fresno, CA	(9.2)
209	Gadsden, AL	(70.5)
50	Gainesville, FL	16.9
NA	Gainesville, GA**	NA
206	Glens Falls, NY	(46.2)
52	Goldsboro, NC	16.4
18	Grand Forks, ND-MN	43.2
36	Grand Junction, CO	25.3
NA	Grand Rapids-Wyoming, MI**	NA
194	Great Falls, MT	(30.9)
48	Greeley, CO	19.0
29	Green Bay, WI	29.5
NA	Greensboro-High Point, NC**	NA
70	Greenville, NC	8.1
NA	Greenville, SC**	NA
NA	Hagerstown-Martinsburg, MD-WV**	NA
NA	Hanford-Corcoran, CA**	NA
NA	Harrisburg-Carlisle, PA**	NA
NA	Harrisonburg, VA**	NA
91	Hartford, CT	2.9
NA	Hattiesburg, MS**	NA
NA	Holland-Grand Haven, MI**	NA
35	Honolulu, HI	26.2
NA	Hot Springs, AR**	NA
73	Houma, LA	7.1
156	Houston, TX	(14.3)
NA	Huntington-Ashland, WV-KY-OH**	NA
26	Huntsville, AL	34.3
NA	Idaho Falls, ID**	NA
NA	Indianapolis, IN**	NA
203	Iowa City, IA	(41.0)
NA	Ithaca, NY**	NA
NA	Jacksonville, FL**	NA
NA	Jacksonville, NC**	NA
188	Jackson, MI	(26.3)
134	Jackson, MS	(8.1)
62	Jackson, TN	10.8
182	Janesville, WI	(22.8)
NA	Jefferson City, MO**	NA
NA	Johnson City, TN**	NA
NA	Johnstown, PA**	NA
5	Jonesboro, AR	74.3
197	Joplin, MO	(34.5)
NA	Kalamazoo-Portage, MI**	NA
NA	Kansas City, MO-KS**	NA
45	Kennewick-Richland-Pasco, WA	21.3
190	Killeen-Temple-Fort Hood, TX	(28.7)
NA	Kingsport, TN-VA**	NA
NA	Kingston, NY**	NA
126	Knoxville, TN	(5.3)
192	Kokomo, IN	(30.1)
19	La Crosse, WI-MN	41.4
130	Lafayette, IN	(6.3)
59	Lake Charles, LA	11.9
NA	Lake Havasu City-Kingman, AZ**	NA
117	Lakeland, FL	(3.4)
101	Lancaster, PA	0.4
127	Lansing-East Lansing, MI	(5.5)
168	Laredo, TX	(17.0)
NA	Las Cruces, NM**	NA
32	Las Vegas-Paradise, NV	27.9

Note: All listings are for Metropolitan Statistical Areas (M.S.A.s) except for those ending with "M.D." Listings with "M.D." are Metropolitan Divisions which are smaller parts of eleven large M.S.A.s. See explanatory note at beginning of metropolitan area section on page 23.

RANK	METROPOLITAN AREA	% CHANGE
21	Lawrence, KS	38.5
20	Lawton, OK	41.0
NA	Lebanon, PA**	NA
66	Lewiston-Auburn, ME	8.9
NA	Lewiston, ID-WA**	NA
NA	Lexington-Fayette, KY**	NA
NA	Lima, OH**	NA
144	Lincoln, NE	(11.0)
15	Little Rock, AR	55.4
NA	Logan, UT-ID**	NA
7	Longview, TX	70.1
NA	Longview, WA**	NA
200	Los Angeles County, CA M.D.	(39.2)
NA	Los Angeles (greater), CA**	NA
203	Louisville, KY-IN	(41.0)
180	Lubbock, TX	(21.7)
106	Lynchburg, VA	(0.5)
NA	Macon, GA**	NA
NA	Madera, CA**	NA
84	Madison, WI	5.0
NA	Manchester-Nashua, NH**	NA
NA	Mansfield, OH**	NA
181	McAllen-Edinburg-Mission, TX	(22.1)
131	Medford, OR	(6.8)
NA	Memphis, TN-MS-AR**	NA
113	Merced, CA	(2.0)
NA	Miami (greater), FL**	NA
153	Miami-Dade County, FL M.D.	(13.5)
NA	Michigan City-La Porte, IN**	NA
NA	Midland, TX**	NA
NA	Milwaukee, WI**	NA
40	Minneapolis-St. Paul, MN-WI	23.7
NA	Missoula, MT**	NA
NA	Mobile, AL**	NA
54	Modesto, CA	15.0
NA	Monroe, LA**	NA
NA	Monroe, MI**	NA
196	Montgomery, AL	(32.7)
NA	Morgantown, WV**	NA
NA	Morristown, TN**	NA
NA	Mount Vernon-Anacortes, WA**	NA
39	Muncie, IN	24.0
NA	Muskegon-Norton Shores, MI**	NA
170	Myrtle Beach, SC	(17.7)
NA	Napa, CA**	NA
176	Naples-Marco Island, FL	(19.3)
145	Nashville-Davidson, TN	(11.1)
NA	Nassau-Suffolk, NY M.D.**	NA
138	New Orleans, LA	(9.2)
NA	New York (greater), NY-NJ-PA**	NA
189	New York-W. Plains NY-NJ M.D.	(27.1)
174	Newark-Union, NJ-PA M.D.	(18.7)
NA	Niles-Benton Harbor, MI**	NA
64	Oakland-Fremont, CA M.D.	10.7
128	Ocala, FL	(6.1)
NA	Ocean City, NJ**	NA
NA	Odessa, TX**	NA
NA	Ogden-Clearfield, UT**	NA
119	Oklahoma City, OK	(3.6)
118	Olympia, WA	(3.5)
172	Omaha-Council Bluffs, NE-IA	(18.3)
111	Orlando, FL	(1.7)
NA	Oshkosh-Neenah, WI**	NA
NA	Oxnard-Thousand Oaks, CA**	NA
179	Palm Bay-Melbourne, FL	(20.8)
NA	Palm Coast, FL**	NA
61	Panama City-Lynn Haven, FL	11.4
NA	Pascagoula, MS**	NA
80	Pensacola, FL	6.1
69	Philadelphia (greater) PA-NJ-DE	8.2
NA	Philadelphia, PA M.D.**	NA
159	Phoenix-Mesa-Scottsdale, AZ	(15.9)
99	Pine Bluff, AR	0.8
132	Pittsburgh, PA	(7.1)
NA	Pittsfield, MA**	NA
124	Pocatello, ID	(5.2)
151	Port St. Lucie, FL	(12.8)
161	Portland-Vancouver, OR-WA	(16.0)
NA	Portland, ME**	NA
NA	Poughkeepsie, NY**	NA
NA	Prescott, AZ**	NA
175	Provo-Orem, UT	(19.0)
183	Pueblo, CO	(23.4)
16	Punta Gorda, FL	44.9
27	Racine, WI	34.0
NA	Raleigh-Cary, NC**	NA
177	Rapid City, SD	(19.9)
105	Reading, PA	(0.1)
191	Redding, CA	(29.5)
148	Reno-Sparks, NV	(12.1)
163	Richmond, VA	(16.1)
185	Riverside-San Bernardino, CA	(24.4)
NA	Roanoke, VA**	NA
171	Rochester, MN	(17.8)
13	Rochester, NY	55.9
46	Rocky Mount, NC	19.6
NA	Rome, GA**	NA
43	Sacramento, CA	22.7
NA	Saginaw, MI**	NA
22	Salem, OR	38.0
79	Salinas, CA	6.3
NA	Salisbury, MD**	NA
NA	Salt Lake City, UT**	NA
90	San Angelo, TX	3.0
198	San Antonio, TX	(34.8)
159	San Diego, CA	(15.9)
NA	San Francisco (greater), CA**	NA
76	San Francisco-S. Mateo, CA M.D.	6.7
166	San Jose, CA	(16.9)
81	San Luis Obispo, CA	5.5
NA	Sandusky, OH**	NA
124	Santa Ana-Anaheim, CA M.D.	(5.2)
NA	Santa Barbara-Santa Maria, CA**	NA
85	Santa Cruz-Watsonville, CA	4.9
142	Santa Fe, NM	(10.8)
5	Santa Rosa-Petaluma, CA	74.3
60	Sarasota-Bradenton-Venice, FL	11.6
NA	Savannah, GA**	NA
33	Scranton--Wilkes-Barre, PA	27.8
NA	Seattle (greater), WA**	NA
104	Seattle-Bellevue, WA M.D.	0.1
NA	Sebastian-Vero Beach, FL**	NA
116	Sheboygan, WI	(3.3)
103	Sherman-Denison, TX	0.2
3	Shreveport-Bossier City, LA	90.2
199	Sioux City, IA-NE-SD	(36.5)
110	Sioux Falls, SD	(1.6)
143	South Bend-Mishawaka, IN-MI	(10.9)
NA	Spartanburg, SC**	NA
100	Spokane, WA	0.6
NA	Springfield, MA**	NA
68	Springfield, MO	8.3
NA	Springfield, OH**	NA
135	State College, PA	(8.2)
129	Stockton, CA	(6.2)
44	St. Cloud, MN	22.2
14	St. Joseph, MO-KS	55.7
NA	St. Louis, MO-IL**	NA
23	Sumter, SC	37.9
NA	Syracuse, NY**	NA
101	Tacoma, WA M.D.	0.4
97	Tallahassee, FL	1.6
173	Tampa-St Petersburg, FL	(18.6)
4	Texarkana, TX-Texarkana, AR	74.6
55	Toledo, OH	13.7
201	Topeka, KS	(40.1)
153	Trenton-Ewing, NJ	(13.5)
161	Tucson, AZ	(16.0)
93	Tulsa, OK	2.7
95	Tuscaloosa, AL	2.2
78	Tyler, TX	6.5
115	Utica-Rome, NY	(3.1)
NA	Valdosta, GA**	NA
NA	Vallejo-Fairfield, CA**	NA
205	Victoria, TX	(43.9)
38	Vineland, NJ	24.2
133	Virginia Beach-Norfolk, VA-NC	(7.2)
164	Visalia-Porterville, CA	(16.8)
122	Waco, TX	(4.2)
NA	Warner Robins, GA**	NA
NA	Warren-Farmington Hills, MI M.D.**	NA
NA	Washington (greater) DC-VA-MD**	NA
NA	Washington, DC-VA-MD-WV M.D.**	NA
108	Waterloo-Cedar Falls, IA	(0.8)
8	Wausau, WI	69.3
NA	Wenatchee, WA**	NA
136	West Palm Beach, FL M.D.	(8.3)
NA	Wheeling, WV-OH**	NA
208	Wichita Falls, TX	(60.5)
10	Wichita, KS	65.6
150	Williamsport, PA	(12.3)
NA	Wilmington, DE-MD-NJ M.D.**	NA
184	Wilmington, NC	(23.5)
NA	Winchester, VA-WV**	NA
NA	Winston-Salem, NC**	NA
NA	Worcester, MA**	NA
46	Yakima, WA	19.6
120	Yuba City, CA	(4.0)
NA	Yuma, AZ**	NA

Source: CQ Press using data from Federal Bureau of Investigation "Crime in the United States 2006" (Uniform Crime Reports, September 24, 2007)

**Aggravated assault is an attack for the purpose of inflicting severe bodily injury.*

***Not available.*

24. Percent Change in Aggravated Assault Rate: 2002 to 2006 (continued)

National Percent Change = 7.1% Decrease*

RANK	METROPOLITAN AREA	% CHANGE
1	Bismarck, ND	242.9
2	Dubuque, IA	106.8
3	Shreveport-Bossier City, LA	90.2
4	Texarkana, TX-Texarkana, AR	74.6
5	Jonesboro, AR	74.3
5	Santa Rosa-Petaluma, CA	74.3
7	Longview, TX	70.1
8	Wausau, WI	69.3
9	Anchorage, AK	68.7
10	Wichita, KS	65.6
11	Decatur, AL	60.9
12	Flint, MI	57.2
13	Rochester, NY	55.9
14	St. Joseph, MO-KS	55.7
15	Little Rock, AR	55.4
16	Punta Gorda, FL	44.9
17	Florence, SC	44.7
18	Grand Forks, ND-MN	43.2
19	La Crosse, WI-MN	41.4
20	Lawton, OK	41.0
21	Lawrence, KS	38.5
22	Salem, OR	38.0
23	Sumter, SC	37.9
24	Colorado Springs, CO	37.6
25	Fargo, ND-MN	34.6
26	Huntsville, AL	34.3
27	Racine, WI	34.0
28	Columbia, MO	32.0
29	Columbus, GA-AL	29.5
29	Green Bay, WI	29.5
31	Baton Rouge, LA	28.2
32	Las Vegas-Paradise, NV	27.9
33	Scranton--Wilkes-Barre, PA	27.8
34	Augusta, GA-SC	26.6
35	Honolulu, HI	26.2
36	Grand Junction, CO	25.3
37	Bloomington, IN	24.7
38	Vineland, NJ	24.2
39	Muncie, IN	24.0
40	Minneapolis-St. Paul, MN-WI	23.7
41	Clarksville, TN-KY	23.2
42	Cumberland, MD-WV	22.9
43	Sacramento, CA	22.7
44	St. Cloud, MN	22.2
45	Kennewick-Richland-Pasco, WA	21.3
46	Rocky Mount, NC	19.6
46	Yakima, WA	19.6
48	Greeley, CO	19.0
49	Denver-Aurora, CO	18.7
50	Gainesville, FL	16.9
51	Fort Walton Beach, FL	16.8
52	Eugene-Springfield, OR	16.4
52	Goldsboro, NC	16.4
54	Modesto, CA	15.0
55	Toledo, OH	13.7
56	Beaumont-Port Arthur, TX	13.6
57	Altoona, PA	13.4
58	Chico, CA	12.7
59	Lake Charles, LA	11.9
60	Sarasota-Bradenton-Venice, FL	11.6
61	Panama City-Lynn Haven, FL	11.4
62	Bakersfield, CA	10.8
62	Jackson, TN	10.8
64	Oakland-Fremont, CA M.D.	10.7
65	Athens-Clarke County, GA	9.2
66	Lewiston-Auburn, ME	8.9
67	Binghamton, NY	8.7
68	Springfield, MO	8.3
69	Philadelphia (greater) PA-NJ-DE	8.2
70	Greenville, NC	8.1
71	Fort Worth-Arlington, TX M.D.	7.8
72	Alexandria, LA	7.3
73	Fort Lauderdale, FL M.D.	7.1
73	Houma, LA	7.1
75	Buffalo-Niagara Falls, NY	6.8
76	San Francisco-S. Mateo, CA M.D.	6.7
77	Fort Collins-Loveland, CO	6.6
78	Tyler, TX	6.5
79	Salinas, CA	6.3
80	Pensacola, FL	6.1
81	San Luis Obispo, CA	5.5
82	Duluth, MN-WI	5.3
83	Bellingham, WA	5.1
84	Madison, WI	5.0
85	Santa Cruz-Watsonville, CA	4.9
86	Atlanta, GA	4.1
87	Eau Claire, WI	3.8
88	Detroit (greater), MI	3.7
89	Charleston, WV	3.5
90	San Angelo, TX	3.0
91	Hartford, CT	2.9
92	Bremerton-Silverdale, WA	2.8
93	Tulsa, OK	2.7
94	Brownsville-Harlingen, TX	2.5
95	Tuscaloosa, AL	2.2
96	Amarillo, TX	1.7
97	Tallahassee, FL	1.6
98	Albany, GA	1.1
99	Pine Bluff, AR	0.8
100	Spokane, WA	0.6
101	Lancaster, PA	0.4
101	Tacoma, WA M.D.	0.4
103	Sherman-Denison, TX	0.2
104	Seattle-Bellevue, WA M.D.	0.1
105	Reading, PA	(0.1)
106	Lynchburg, VA	(0.5)
107	Corpus Christi, TX	(0.7)
108	Waterloo-Cedar Falls, IA	(0.8)
109	Erie, PA	(1.0)
110	Sioux Falls, SD	(1.6)
111	Fayetteville, NC	(1.7)
111	Orlando, FL	(1.7)
113	Merced, CA	(2.0)
114	Fort Smith, AR-OK	(2.3)
115	Utica-Rome, NY	(3.1)
116	Sheboygan, WI	(3.3)
117	Lakeland, FL	(3.4)
118	Olympia, WA	(3.5)
119	Oklahoma City, OK	(3.6)
120	Yuba City, CA	(4.0)
121	Charleston-North Charleston, SC	(4.1)
122	Waco, TX	(4.2)
123	Birmingham-Hoover, AL	(4.8)
124	Pocatello, ID	(5.2)
124	Santa Ana-Anaheim, CA M.D.	(5.2)
126	Knoxville, TN	(5.3)
127	Lansing-East Lansing, MI	(5.5)
128	Ocala, FL	(6.1)
129	Stockton, CA	(6.2)
130	Lafayette, IN	(6.3)
131	Medford, OR	(6.8)
132	Pittsburgh, PA	(7.1)
133	Virginia Beach-Norfolk, VA-NC	(7.2)
134	Jackson, MS	(8.1)
135	State College, PA	(8.2)
136	Austin-Round Rock, TX	(8.3)
136	West Palm Beach, FL M.D.	(8.3)
138	Fresno, CA	(9.2)
138	New Orleans, LA	(9.2)
140	Columbia, SC	(10.4)
141	Flagstaff, AZ	(10.6)
142	Santa Fe, NM	(10.8)
143	South Bend-Mishawaka, IN-MI	(10.9)
144	Lincoln, NE	(11.0)
145	Nashville-Davidson, TN	(11.1)
146	Boise City-Nampa, ID	(11.3)
147	Dover, DE	(11.8)
148	Reno-Sparks, NV	(12.1)
149	Cheyenne, WY	(12.2)
150	Williamsport, PA	(12.3)
151	Port St. Lucie, FL	(12.8)
152	Daytona Beach, FL	(12.9)
153	Miami-Dade County, FL M.D.	(13.5)
153	Trenton-Ewing, NJ	(13.5)
155	Cape Coral-Fort Myers, FL	(13.8)
156	Houston, TX	(14.3)
157	Asheville, NC	(14.4)
158	Albuquerque, NM	(15.4)
159	Phoenix-Mesa-Scottsdale, AZ	(15.9)
159	San Diego, CA	(15.9)
161	Portland-Vancouver, OR-WA	(16.0)
161	Tucson, AZ	(16.0)
163	Richmond, VA	(16.1)
164	Chattanooga, TN-GA	(16.8)
164	Visalia-Porterville, CA	(16.8)
166	Casper, WY	(16.9)
166	San Jose, CA	(16.9)
168	Laredo, TX	(17.0)
169	Dallas-Plano-Irving, TX M.D.	(17.5)
170	Myrtle Beach, SC	(17.7)
171	Rochester, MN	(17.8)

Note: All listings are for Metropolitan Statistical Areas (M.S.A.s) except for those ending with "M.D." Listings with "M.D." are Metropolitan Divisions which are smaller parts of eleven large M.S.A.s. See explanatory note at beginning of metropolitan area section on page 23.

RANK	METROPOLITAN AREA	% CHANGE
172	Omaha-Council Bluffs, NE-IA	(18.3)
173	Tampa-St Petersburg, FL	(18.6)
174	Newark-Union, NJ-PA M.D.	(18.7)
175	Provo-Orem, UT	(19.0)
176	Naples-Marco Island, FL	(19.3)
177	Cedar Rapids, IA	(19.9)
177	Rapid City, SD	(19.9)
179	Palm Bay-Melbourne, FL	(20.8)
180	Lubbock, TX	(21.7)
181	McAllen-Edinburg-Mission, TX	(22.1)
182	Janesville, WI	(22.8)
183	Pueblo, CO	(23.4)
184	Wilmington, NC	(23.5)
185	Riverside-San Bernardino, CA	(24.4)
186	Cincinnati-Middletown, OH-KY-IN	(24.5)
187	Baltimore-Towson, MD	(24.6)
188	Jackson, MI	(26.3)
189	New York-W. Plains NY-NJ M.D.	(27.1)
190	Killeen-Temple-Fort Hood, TX	(28.7)
191	Redding, CA	(29.5)
192	Kokomo, IN	(30.1)
193	Columbus, OH	(30.3)
194	Great Falls, MT	(30.9)
195	Billings, MT	(32.0)
196	Montgomery, AL	(32.7)
197	Joplin, MO	(34.5)
198	San Antonio, TX	(34.8)
199	Sioux City, IA-NE-SD	(36.5)
200	Los Angeles County, CA M.D.	(39.2)
201	Topeka, KS	(40.1)
202	Danville, VA	(40.6)
203	Iowa City, IA	(41.0)
203	Louisville, KY-IN	(41.0)
205	Victoria, TX	(43.9)
206	Glens Falls, NY	(46.2)
207	El Paso, TX	(46.3)
208	Wichita Falls, TX	(60.5)
209	Gadsden, AL	(70.5)
210	Elkhart-Goshen, IN	(77.9)
NA	Abilene, TX**	NA
NA	Albany-Schenectady-Troy, NY**	NA
NA	Ames, IA**	NA
NA	Anderson, SC**	NA
NA	Ann Arbor, MI**	NA
NA	Appleton, WI**	NA
NA	Atlantic City, NJ**	NA
NA	Bangor, ME**	NA
NA	Barnstable Town, MA**	NA
NA	Battle Creek, MI**	NA
NA	Bay City, MI**	NA
NA	Bend, OR**	NA
NA	Bethesda-Frederick, MD M.D.**	NA
NA	Blacksburg, VA**	NA
NA	Bowling Green, KY**	NA
NA	Brunswick, GA**	NA
NA	Burlington, NC**	NA
NA	Camden, NJ M.D.**	NA
NA	Carson City, NV**	NA
NA	Charlotte-Gastonia, NC-SC**	NA
NA	Charlottesville, VA**	NA
NA	Chicago, IL**	NA
NA	Cleveland-Elyria-Mentor, OH**	NA
NA	Cleveland, TN**	NA
NA	Coeur d'Alene, ID**	NA
NA	College Station-Bryan, TX**	NA
NA	Columbus, IN**	NA
NA	Dallas (greater), TX**	NA
NA	Dalton, GA**	NA
NA	Dayton, OH**	NA
NA	Des Moines-West Des Moines, IA**	NA
NA	Detroit-Livonia-Dearborn, MI M.D.**	NA
NA	Dothan, AL**	NA
NA	Durham, NC**	NA
NA	Edison, NJ M.D.**	NA
NA	El Centro, CA**	NA
NA	Elizabethtown, KY**	NA
NA	Elmira, NY**	NA
NA	Evansville, IN-KY**	NA
NA	Fairbanks, AK**	NA
NA	Farmington, NM**	NA
NA	Fayetteville, AR-MO**	NA
NA	Fond du Lac, WI**	NA
NA	Fort Wayne, IN**	NA
NA	Gainesville, GA**	NA
NA	Grand Rapids-Wyoming, MI**	NA
NA	Greensboro-High Point, NC**	NA
NA	Greenville, SC**	NA
NA	Hagerstown-Martinsburg, MD-WV**	NA
NA	Hanford-Corcoran, CA**	NA
NA	Harrisburg-Carlisle, PA**	NA
NA	Harrisonburg, VA**	NA
NA	Hattiesburg, MS**	NA
NA	Holland-Grand Haven, MI**	NA
NA	Hot Springs, AR**	NA
NA	Huntington-Ashland, WV-KY-OH**	NA
NA	Idaho Falls, ID**	NA
NA	Indianapolis, IN**	NA
NA	Ithaca, NY**	NA
NA	Jacksonville, FL**	NA
NA	Jacksonville, NC**	NA
NA	Jefferson City, MO**	NA
NA	Johnson City, TN**	NA
NA	Johnstown, PA**	NA
NA	Kalamazoo-Portage, MI**	NA
NA	Kansas City, MO-KS**	NA
NA	Kingsport, TN-VA**	NA
NA	Kingston, NY**	NA
NA	Lake Havasu City-Kingman, AZ**	NA
NA	Las Cruces, NM**	NA
NA	Lebanon, PA**	NA
NA	Lewiston, ID-WA**	NA
NA	Lexington-Fayette, KY**	NA
NA	Lima, OH**	NA
NA	Logan, UT-ID**	NA
NA	Longview, WA**	NA
NA	Los Angeles (greater), CA**	NA
NA	Macon, GA**	NA
NA	Madera, CA**	NA
NA	Manchester-Nashua, NH**	NA
NA	Mansfield, OH**	NA
NA	Memphis, TN-MS-AR**	NA
NA	Miami (greater), FL**	NA
NA	Michigan City-La Porte, IN**	NA
NA	Midland, TX**	NA
NA	Milwaukee, WI**	NA
NA	Missoula, MT**	NA
NA	Mobile, AL**	NA
NA	Monroe, LA**	NA
NA	Monroe, MI**	NA
NA	Morgantown, WV**	NA
NA	Morristown, TN**	NA
NA	Mount Vernon-Anacortes, WA**	NA
NA	Muskegon-Norton Shores, MI**	NA
NA	Napa, CA**	NA
NA	Nassau-Suffolk, NY M.D.**	NA
NA	New York (greater), NY-NJ-PA**	NA
NA	Niles-Benton Harbor, MI**	NA
NA	Ocean City, NJ**	NA
NA	Odessa, TX**	NA
NA	Ogden-Clearfield, UT**	NA
NA	Oshkosh-Neenah, WI**	NA
NA	Oxnard-Thousand Oaks, CA**	NA
NA	Palm Coast, FL**	NA
NA	Pascagoula, MS**	NA
NA	Philadelphia, PA M.D.**	NA
NA	Pittsfield, MA**	NA
NA	Portland, ME**	NA
NA	Poughkeepsie, NY**	NA
NA	Prescott, AZ**	NA
NA	Raleigh-Cary, NC**	NA
NA	Roanoke, VA**	NA
NA	Rome, GA**	NA
NA	Saginaw, MI**	NA
NA	Salisbury, MD**	NA
NA	Salt Lake City, UT**	NA
NA	San Francisco (greater), CA**	NA
NA	Sandusky, OH**	NA
NA	Santa Barbara-Santa Maria, CA**	NA
NA	Savannah, GA**	NA
NA	Seattle (greater), WA**	NA
NA	Sebastian-Vero Beach, FL**	NA
NA	Spartanburg, SC**	NA
NA	Springfield, MA**	NA
NA	Springfield, OH**	NA
NA	St. Louis, MO-IL**	NA
NA	Syracuse, NY**	NA
NA	Valdosta, GA**	NA
NA	Vallejo-Fairfield, CA**	NA
NA	Warner Robins, GA**	NA
NA	Warren-Farmington Hills, MI M.D.**	NA
NA	Washington (greater) DC-VA-MD**	NA
NA	Washington, DC-VA-MD-WV M.D.**	NA
NA	Wenatchee, WA**	NA
NA	Wheeling, WV-OH**	NA
NA	Wilmington, DE-MD-NJ M.D.**	NA
NA	Winchester, VA-WV**	NA
NA	Winston-Salem, NC**	NA
NA	Worcester, MA**	NA
NA	Yuma, AZ**	NA

Source: CQ Press using data from Federal Bureau of Investigation "Crime in the United States 2006" (Uniform Crime Reports, September 24, 2007)

**Aggravated assault is an attack for the purpose of inflicting severe bodily injury.*

***Not available.*

25. Property Crimes in 2006

National Total = 9,983,568 Property Crimes*

RANK	METROPOLITAN AREA	CRIMES
233	Abilene, TX	5,741
93	Albany-Schenectady-Troy, NY	23,349
201	Albany, GA	7,171
62	Albuquerque, NM	39,023
197	Alexandria, LA	7,358
311	Altoona, PA	3,192
153	Amarillo, TX	11,879
337	Ames, IA	2,140
145	Anchorage, AK	12,875
187	Anderson, SC	8,213
170	Ann Arbor, MI	9,542
262	Appleton, WI	4,928
152	Asheville, NC	11,962
192	Athens-Clarke County, GA	7,856
NA	Atlanta, GA**	NA
163	Atlantic City, NJ	10,534
89	Augusta, GA-SC	24,274
46	Austin-Round Rock, TX	58,892
71	Bakersfield, CA	33,464
27	Baltimore-Towson, MD	92,748
274	Bangor, ME	4,626
224	Barnstable Town, MA	6,116
68	Baton Rouge, LA	34,601
234	Battle Creek, MI	5,707
324	Bay City, MI	2,819
120	Beaumont-Port Arthur, TX	15,678
178	Bellingham, WA	8,840
253	Bend, OR	5,111
82	Bethesda-Frederick, MD M.D.	28,016
244	Billings, MT	5,327
218	Binghamton, NY	6,438
57	Birmingham-Hoover, AL	47,475
336	Bismarck, ND	2,224
290	Blacksburg, VA	3,997
246	Bloomington, IN	5,293
127	Boise City-Nampa, ID	15,193
300	Bowling Green, KY	3,655
215	Bremerton-Silverdale, WA	6,521
111	Brownsville-Harlingen, TX	18,292
279	Brunswick, GA	4,435
70	Buffalo-Niagara Falls, NY	33,709
231	Burlington, NC	5,778
73	Camden, NJ M.D.	33,126
105	Cape Coral-Fort Myers, FL	20,043
346	Carson City, NV	1,247
312	Casper, WY	3,186
196	Cedar Rapids, IA	7,441
85	Charleston-North Charleston, SC	26,263
160	Charleston, WV	11,336
32	Charlotte-Gastonia, NC-SC	81,387
237	Charlottesville, VA	5,517
96	Chattanooga, TN-GA	21,287
319	Cheyenne, WY	2,914
NA	Chicago, IL**	NA
204	Chico, CA	7,107
37	Cincinnati-Middletown, OH-KY-IN	76,619
195	Clarksville, TN-KY	7,653
41	Cleveland-Elyria-Mentor, OH	66,651
304	Cleveland, TN	3,456
296	Coeur d'Alene, ID	3,801
184	College Station-Bryan, TX	8,284
95	Colorado Springs, CO	22,359
273	Columbia, MO	4,632
83	Columbia, SC	26,993
118	Columbus, GA-AL	16,186
314	Columbus, IN	3,068
34	Columbus, OH	80,395
88	Corpus Christi, TX	24,932
328	Cumberland, MD-WV	2,727
4	Dallas (greater), TX	264,451
9	Dallas-Plano-Irving, TX M.D.	176,682
277	Dalton, GA	4,440
327	Danville, VA	2,772
107	Daytona Beach, FL	19,139
76	Dayton, OH	31,625
235	Decatur, AL	5,662
28	Denver-Aurora, CO	88,575
99	Des Moines-West Des Moines, IA	21,169
13	Detroit (greater), MI	160,892
25	Detroit-Livonia-Dearborn, MI M.D.	98,374
264	Dothan, AL	4,898
275	Dover, DE	4,523
340	Dubuque, IA	1,945
174	Duluth, MN-WI	9,138
101	Durham, NC	21,041
295	Eau Claire, WI	3,854
59	Edison, NJ M.D.	43,830
219	El Centro, CA	6,388
92	El Paso, TX	23,656
342	Elizabethtown, KY	1,913
202	Elkhart-Goshen, IN	7,144
335	Elmira, NY	2,387
230	Erie, PA	5,795
124	Eugene-Springfield, OR	15,287
166	Evansville, IN-KY	10,043
341	Fairbanks, AK	1,929
280	Fargo, ND-MN	4,369
316	Farmington, NM	2,948
144	Fayetteville, AR-MO	12,918
98	Fayetteville, NC	21,198
236	Flagstaff, AZ	5,660
110	Flint, MI	18,367
157	Florence, SC	11,518
345	Fond du Lac, WI	1,853
183	Fort Collins-Loveland, CO	8,433
42	Fort Lauderdale, FL M.D.	64,550
168	Fort Smith, AR-OK	9,762
241	Fort Walton Beach, FL	5,364
138	Fort Wayne, IN	13,337
29	Fort Worth-Arlington, TX M.D.	87,769
61	Fresno, CA	39,437
254	Gadsden, AL	5,096
159	Gainesville, FL	11,359
256	Gainesville, GA	5,088
329	Glens Falls, NY	2,666
260	Goldsboro, NC	4,946
NA	Grand Forks, ND-MN**	NA
271	Grand Junction, CO	4,654
87	Grand Rapids-Wyoming, MI	25,013
315	Great Falls, MT	2,973
186	Greeley, CO	8,238
209	Green Bay, WI	6,856
75	Greensboro-High Point, NC	31,632
194	Greenville, NC	7,774
94	Greenville, SC	23,304
217	Hagerstown-Martinsburg, MD-WV	6,455
301	Hanford-Corcoran, CA	3,623
156	Harrisburg-Carlisle, PA	11,623
344	Harrisonburg, VA	1,877
77	Hartford, CT	31,551
278	Hattiesburg, MS	4,438
257	Holland-Grand Haven, MI	5,080
64	Honolulu, HI	38,310
206	Hot Springs, AR	7,046
199	Houma, LA	7,202
6	Houston, TX	223,846
171	Huntington-Ashland, WV-KY-OH	9,332
114	Huntsville, AL	17,101
307	Idaho Falls, ID	3,258
39	Indianapolis, IN	68,963
318	Iowa City, IA	2,933
332	Ithaca, NY	2,570
47	Jacksonville, FL	57,465
261	Jacksonville, NC	4,932
255	Jackson, MI	5,089
97	Jackson, MS	21,199
229	Jackson, TN	5,796
227	Janesville, WI	5,891
302	Jefferson City, MO	3,519
220	Johnson City, TN	6,336
308	Johnstown, PA	3,256
239	Jonesboro, AR	5,446
200	Joplin, MO	7,194
142	Kalamazoo-Portage, MI	12,992
31	Kansas City, MO-KS	81,922
198	Kennewick-Richland-Pasco, WA	7,253
148	Killeen-Temple-Fort Hood, TX	12,798
162	Kingsport, TN-VA	10,710
305	Kingston, NY	3,405
90	Knoxville, TN	24,028
286	Kokomo, IN	4,046
309	La Crosse, WI-MN	3,234
228	Lafayette, IN	5,804
173	Lake Charles, LA	9,170
176	Lake Havasu City-Kingman, AZ	9,045
103	Lakeland, FL	20,953
158	Lancaster, PA	11,440
146	Lansing-East Lansing, MI	12,831
143	Laredo, TX	12,981
226	Las Cruces, NM	6,008
35	Las Vegas-Paradise, NV	79,277

Note: All listings are for Metropolitan Statistical Areas (M.S.A.s) except for those ending with "M.D." Listings with "M.D." are Metropolitan Divisions which are smaller parts of eleven large M.S.A.s. *See explanatory note at beginning of metropolitan area section on page 23.*

Alpha Order - Metro Area (continued)

RANK	METROPOLITAN AREA	CRIMES
232	Lawrence, KS	5,751
259	Lawton, OK	4,979
330	Lebanon, PA	2,587
325	Lewiston-Auburn, ME	2,792
338	Lewiston, ID-WA	1,977
121	Lexington-Fayette, KY	15,631
282	Lima, OH	4,289
139	Lincoln, NE	13,328
65	Little Rock, AR	36,705
343	Logan, UT-ID	1,879
169	Longview, TX	9,620
248	Longview, WA	5,268
3	Los Angeles County, CA M.D.	269,334
2	Los Angeles (greater), CA	336,940
58	Louisville, KY-IN	44,585
135	Lubbock, TX	13,779
266	Lynchburg, VA	4,739
133	Macon, GA	14,359
303	Madera, CA	3,478
125	Madison, WI	15,283
185	Manchester-Nashua, NH	8,276
221	Mansfield, OH	6,256
78	McAllen-Edinburg-Mission, TX	31,477
225	Medford, OR	6,109
38	Memphis, TN-MS-AR	76,570
177	Merced, CA	8,995
5	Miami (greater), FL	240,839
18	Miami-Dade County, FL M.D.	121,826
267	Michigan City-La Porte, IN	4,728
283	Midland, TX	4,256
45	Milwaukee, WI	59,620
21	Minneapolis-St. Paul, MN-WI	111,819
297	Missoula, MT	3,792
104	Mobile, AL	20,591
86	Modesto, CA	25,230
179	Monroe, LA	8,696
298	Monroe, MI	3,744
115	Montgomery, AL	16,978
326	Morgantown, WV	2,783
276	Morristown, TN	4,461
213	Mount Vernon-Anacortes, WA	6,689
285	Muncie, IN	4,108
181	Muskegon-Norton Shores, MI	8,520
123	Myrtle Beach, SC	15,298
310	Napa, CA	3,233
222	Naples-Marco Island, FL	6,199
50	Nashville-Davidson, TN	55,350
55	Nassau-Suffolk, NY M.D.	48,162
60	New Orleans, LA	41,679
1	New York (greater), NY-NJ-PA	357,850
7	New York-W. Plains NY-NJ M.D.	215,351
54	Newark-Union, NJ-PA M.D.	50,507
247	Niles-Benton Harbor, MI	5,273
23	Oakland-Fremont, CA M.D.	102,843
189	Ocala, FL	8,064
269	Ocean City, NJ	4,709
268	Odessa, TX	4,721
131	Ogden-Clearfield, UT	14,851
52	Oklahoma City, OK	53,838
193	Olympia, WA	7,796
72	Omaha-Council Bluffs, NE-IA	33,351
30	Orlando, FL	84,945
299	Oshkosh-Neenah, WI	3,698
116	Oxnard-Thousand Oaks, CA	16,590
112	Palm Bay-Melbourne, FL	18,282
339	Palm Coast, FL	1,946
216	Panama City-Lynn Haven, FL	6,485
214	Pascagoula, MS	6,611
122	Pensacola, FL	15,447
10	Philadelphia (greater) PA-NJ-DE	169,390
20	Philadelphia, PA M.D.	112,566
8	Phoenix-Mesa-Scottsdale, AZ	195,751
252	Pine Bluff, AR	5,122
49	Pittsburgh, PA	55,754
317	Pittsfield, MA	2,939
334	Pocatello, ID	2,441
151	Port St. Lucie, FL	12,311
36	Portland-Vancouver, OR-WA	77,650
136	Portland, ME	13,495
149	Poughkeepsie, NY	12,791
242	Prescott, AZ	5,352
155	Provo-Orem, UT	11,680
191	Pueblo, CO	7,888
238	Punta Gorda, FL	5,454
210	Racine, WI	6,809
80	Raleigh-Cary, NC	28,434
320	Rapid City, SD	2,905
164	Reading, PA	10,341
258	Redding, CA	4,986
117	Reno-Sparks, NV	16,337
67	Richmond, VA	35,264
15	Riverside-San Bernardino, CA	135,378
182	Roanoke, VA	8,450
294	Rochester, MN	3,879
79	Rochester, NY	31,094
190	Rocky Mount, NC	7,908
288	Rome, GA	4,018
33	Sacramento, CA	80,995
205	Saginaw, MI	7,075
126	Salem, OR	15,210
141	Salinas, CA	13,118
245	Salisbury, MD	5,298
53	Salt Lake City, UT	51,806
262	San Angelo, TX	4,928
24	San Antonio, TX	99,173
26	San Diego, CA	93,354
11	San Francisco (greater), CA	164,668
44	San Francisco-S. Mateo, CA M.D.	61,825
56	San Jose, CA	48,117
212	San Luis Obispo, CA	6,711
321	Sandusky, OH	2,881
40	Santa Ana-Anaheim, CA M.D.	67,606
175	Santa Barbara-Santa Maria, CA	9,092
167	Santa Cruz-Watsonville, CA	9,936
243	Santa Fe, NM	5,335
165	Santa Rosa-Petaluma, CA	10,083
81	Sarasota-Bradenton-Venice, FL	28,197
137	Savannah, GA	13,421
140	Scranton--Wilkes-Barre, PA	13,249
12	Seattle (greater), WA	163,199
17	Seattle-Bellevue, WA M.D.	124,339
293	Sebastian-Vero Beach, FL	3,943
306	Sheboygan, WI	3,334
291	Sherman-Denison, TX	3,954
108	Shreveport-Bossier City, LA	18,432
286	Sioux City, IA-NE-SD	4,046
284	Sioux Falls, SD	4,200
134	South Bend-Mishawaka, IN-MI	14,257
147	Spartanburg, SC	12,829
109	Spokane, WA	18,427
100	Springfield, MA	21,117
113	Springfield, MO	18,027
180	Springfield, OH	8,658
323	State College, PA	2,852
66	Stockton, CA	36,202
251	St. Cloud, MN	5,158
265	St. Joseph, MO-KS	4,825
22	St. Louis, MO-IL	104,435
272	Sumter, SC	4,641
119	Syracuse, NY	16,048
63	Tacoma, WA M.D.	38,860
150	Tallahassee, FL	12,749
19	Tampa-St Petersburg, FL	113,752
250	Texarkana, TX-Texarkana, AR	5,230
74	Toledo, OH	32,581
154	Topeka, KS	11,821
188	Trenton-Ewing, NJ	8,086
NA	Tucson, AZ**	NA
69	Tulsa, OK	34,196
172	Tuscaloosa, AL	9,322
207	Tyler, TX	6,959
211	Utica-Rome, NY	6,746
240	Valdosta, GA	5,386
128	Vallejo-Fairfield, CA	15,129
289	Victoria, TX	4,005
223	Vineland, NJ	6,197
48	Virginia Beach-Norfolk, VA-NC	56,616
106	Visalia-Porterville, CA	19,326
161	Waco, TX	10,819
281	Warner Robins, GA	4,316
43	Warren-Farmington Hills, MI M.D.	62,518
14	Washington (greater) DC-VA-MD	152,388
16	Washington, DC-VA-MD-WV M.D.	124,372
270	Waterloo-Cedar Falls, IA	4,658
333	Wausau, WI	2,482
292	Wenatchee, WA	3,946
51	West Palm Beach, FL M.D.	54,463
331	Wheeling, WV-OH	2,579
203	Wichita Falls, TX	7,120
84	Wichita, KS	26,288
322	Williamsport, PA	2,876
91	Wilmington, DE-MD-NJ M.D.	23,698
129	Wilmington, NC	15,078
313	Winchester, VA-WV	3,164
102	Winston-Salem, NC	20,961
132	Worcester, MA	14,737
130	Yakima, WA	14,974
249	Yuba City, CA	5,253
208	Yuma, AZ	6,889

Source: Federal Bureau of Investigation
"Crime in the United States 2006" (Uniform Crime Reports, September 24, 2007)
**Property crimes are offenses of burglary, larceny-theft, and motor vehicle theft. Attempts are included.*
***Not available.*

25. Property Crimes in 2006 (continued)

National Total = 9,983,568 Property Crimes*

RANK	METROPOLITAN AREA	CRIMES
1	New York (greater), NY-NJ-PA	357,850
2	Los Angeles (greater), CA	336,940
3	Los Angeles County, CA M.D.	269,334
4	Dallas (greater), TX	264,451
5	Miami (greater), FL	240,839
6	Houston, TX	223,846
7	New York-W. Plains NY-NJ M.D.	215,351
8	Phoenix-Mesa-Scottsdale, AZ	195,751
9	Dallas-Plano-Irving, TX M.D.	176,682
10	Philadelphia (greater) PA-NJ-DE	169,390
11	San Francisco (greater), CA	164,668
12	Seattle (greater), WA	163,199
13	Detroit (greater), MI	160,892
14	Washington (greater) DC-VA-MD	152,388
15	Riverside-San Bernardino, CA	135,378
16	Washington, DC-VA-MD-WV M.D.	124,372
17	Seattle-Bellevue, WA M.D.	124,339
18	Miami-Dade County, FL M.D.	121,826
19	Tampa-St Petersburg, FL	113,752
20	Philadelphia, PA M.D.	112,566
21	Minneapolis-St. Paul, MN-WI	111,819
22	St. Louis, MO-IL	104,435
23	Oakland-Fremont, CA M.D.	102,843
24	San Antonio, TX	99,173
25	Detroit-Livonia-Dearborn, MI M.D.	98,374
26	San Diego, CA	93,354
27	Baltimore-Towson, MD	92,748
28	Denver-Aurora, CO	88,575
29	Fort Worth-Arlington, TX M.D.	87,769
30	Orlando, FL	84,945
31	Kansas City, MO-KS	81,922
32	Charlotte-Gastonia, NC-SC	81,387
33	Sacramento, CA	80,995
34	Columbus, OH	80,395
35	Las Vegas-Paradise, NV	79,277
36	Portland-Vancouver, OR-WA	77,650
37	Cincinnati-Middletown, OH-KY-IN	76,619
38	Memphis, TN-MS-AR	76,570
39	Indianapolis, IN	68,963
40	Santa Ana-Anaheim, CA M.D.	67,606
41	Cleveland-Elyria-Mentor, OH	66,651
42	Fort Lauderdale, FL M.D.	64,550
43	Warren-Farmington Hills, MI M.D.	62,518
44	San Francisco-S. Mateo, CA M.D.	61,825
45	Milwaukee, WI	59,620
46	Austin-Round Rock, TX	58,892
47	Jacksonville, FL	57,465
48	Virginia Beach-Norfolk, VA-NC	56,616
49	Pittsburgh, PA	55,754
50	Nashville-Davidson, TN	55,350
51	West Palm Beach, FL M.D.	54,463
52	Oklahoma City, OK	53,838
53	Salt Lake City, UT	51,806
54	Newark-Union, NJ-PA M.D.	50,507
55	Nassau-Suffolk, NY M.D.	48,162
56	San Jose, CA	48,117
57	Birmingham-Hoover, AL	47,475
58	Louisville, KY-IN	44,585
59	Edison, NJ M.D.	43,830
60	New Orleans, LA	41,679
61	Fresno, CA	39,437
62	Albuquerque, NM	39,023
63	Tacoma, WA M.D.	38,860
64	Honolulu, HI	38,310
65	Little Rock, AR	36,705
66	Stockton, CA	36,202
67	Richmond, VA	35,264
68	Baton Rouge, LA	34,601
69	Tulsa, OK	34,196
70	Buffalo-Niagara Falls, NY	33,709
71	Bakersfield, CA	33,464
72	Omaha-Council Bluffs, NE-IA	33,351
73	Camden, NJ M.D.	33,126
74	Toledo, OH	32,581
75	Greensboro-High Point, NC	31,632
76	Dayton, OH	31,625
77	Hartford, CT	31,551
78	McAllen-Edinburg-Mission, TX	31,477
79	Rochester, NY	31,094
80	Raleigh-Cary, NC	28,434
81	Sarasota-Bradenton-Venice, FL	28,197
82	Bethesda-Frederick, MD M.D.	28,016
83	Columbia, SC	26,993
84	Wichita, KS	26,288
85	Charleston-North Charleston, SC	26,263
86	Modesto, CA	25,230
87	Grand Rapids-Wyoming, MI	25,013
88	Corpus Christi, TX	24,932
89	Augusta, GA-SC	24,274
90	Knoxville, TN	24,028
91	Wilmington, DE-MD-NJ M.D.	23,698
92	El Paso, TX	23,656
93	Albany-Schenectady-Troy, NY	23,349
94	Greenville, SC	23,304
95	Colorado Springs, CO	22,359
96	Chattanooga, TN-GA	21,287
97	Jackson, MS	21,199
98	Fayetteville, NC	21,198
99	Des Moines-West Des Moines, IA	21,169
100	Springfield, MA	21,117
101	Durham, NC	21,041
102	Winston-Salem, NC	20,961
103	Lakeland, FL	20,953
104	Mobile, AL	20,591
105	Cape Coral-Fort Myers, FL	20,043
106	Visalia-Porterville, CA	19,326
107	Daytona Beach, FL	19,139
108	Shreveport-Bossier City, LA	18,432
109	Spokane, WA	18,427
110	Flint, MI	18,367
111	Brownsville-Harlingen, TX	18,292
112	Palm Bay-Melbourne, FL	18,282
113	Springfield, MO	18,027
114	Huntsville, AL	17,101
115	Montgomery, AL	16,978
116	Oxnard-Thousand Oaks, CA	16,590
117	Reno-Sparks, NV	16,337
118	Columbus, GA-AL	16,186
119	Syracuse, NY	16,048
120	Beaumont-Port Arthur, TX	15,678
121	Lexington-Fayette, KY	15,631
122	Pensacola, FL	15,447
123	Myrtle Beach, SC	15,298
124	Eugene-Springfield, OR	15,287
125	Madison, WI	15,283
126	Salem, OR	15,210
127	Boise City-Nampa, ID	15,193
128	Vallejo-Fairfield, CA	15,129
129	Wilmington, NC	15,078
130	Yakima, WA	14,974
131	Ogden-Clearfield, UT	14,851
132	Worcester, MA	14,737
133	Macon, GA	14,359
134	South Bend-Mishawaka, IN-MI	14,257
135	Lubbock, TX	13,779
136	Portland, ME	13,495
137	Savannah, GA	13,421
138	Fort Wayne, IN	13,337
139	Lincoln, NE	13,328
140	Scranton--Wilkes-Barre, PA	13,249
141	Salinas, CA	13,118
142	Kalamazoo-Portage, MI	12,992
143	Laredo, TX	12,981
144	Fayetteville, AR-MO	12,918
145	Anchorage, AK	12,875
146	Lansing-East Lansing, MI	12,831
147	Spartanburg, SC	12,829
148	Killeen-Temple-Fort Hood, TX	12,798
149	Poughkeepsie, NY	12,791
150	Tallahassee, FL	12,749
151	Port St. Lucie, FL	12,311
152	Asheville, NC	11,962
153	Amarillo, TX	11,879
154	Topeka, KS	11,821
155	Provo-Orem, UT	11,680
156	Harrisburg-Carlisle, PA	11,623
157	Florence, SC	11,518
158	Lancaster, PA	11,440
159	Gainesville, FL	11,359
160	Charleston, WV	11,336
161	Waco, TX	10,819
162	Kingsport, TN-VA	10,710
163	Atlantic City, NJ	10,534
164	Reading, PA	10,341
165	Santa Rosa-Petaluma, CA	10,083
166	Evansville, IN-KY	10,043
167	Santa Cruz-Watsonville, CA	9,936
168	Fort Smith, AR-OK	9,762
169	Longview, TX	9,620
170	Ann Arbor, MI	9,542
171	Huntington-Ashland, WV-KY-OH	9,332

Note: All listings are for Metropolitan Statistical Areas (M.S.A.s) except for those ending with "M.D." Listings with "M.D." are Metropolitan Divisions which are smaller parts of eleven large M.S.A.s. See explanatory note at beginning of metropolitan area section on page 23.

RANK	METROPOLITAN AREA	CRIMES
172	Tuscaloosa, AL	9,322
173	Lake Charles, LA	9,170
174	Duluth, MN-WI	9,138
175	Santa Barbara-Santa Maria, CA	9,092
176	Lake Havasu City-Kingman, AZ	9,045
177	Merced, CA	8,995
178	Bellingham, WA	8,840
179	Monroe, LA	8,696
180	Springfield, OH	8,658
181	Muskegon-Norton Shores, MI	8,520
182	Roanoke, VA	8,450
183	Fort Collins-Loveland, CO	8,433
184	College Station-Bryan, TX	8,284
185	Manchester-Nashua, NH	8,276
186	Greeley, CO	8,238
187	Anderson, SC	8,213
188	Trenton-Ewing, NJ	8,086
189	Ocala, FL	8,064
190	Rocky Mount, NC	7,908
191	Pueblo, CO	7,888
192	Athens-Clarke County, GA	7,856
193	Olympia, WA	7,796
194	Greenville, NC	7,774
195	Clarksville, TN-KY	7,653
196	Cedar Rapids, IA	7,441
197	Alexandria, LA	7,358
198	Kennewick-Richland-Pasco, WA	7,253
199	Houma, LA	7,202
200	Joplin, MO	7,194
201	Albany, GA	7,171
202	Elkhart-Goshen, IN	7,144
203	Wichita Falls, TX	7,120
204	Chico, CA	7,107
205	Saginaw, MI	7,075
206	Hot Springs, AR	7,046
207	Tyler, TX	6,959
208	Yuma, AZ	6,889
209	Green Bay, WI	6,856
210	Racine, WI	6,809
211	Utica-Rome, NY	6,746
212	San Luis Obispo, CA	6,711
213	Mount Vernon-Anacortes, WA	6,689
214	Pascagoula, MS	6,611
215	Bremerton-Silverdale, WA	6,521
216	Panama City-Lynn Haven, FL	6,485
217	Hagerstown-Martinsburg, MD-WV	6,455
218	Binghamton, NY	6,438
219	El Centro, CA	6,388
220	Johnson City, TN	6,336
221	Mansfield, OH	6,256
222	Naples-Marco Island, FL	6,199
223	Vineland, NJ	6,197
224	Barnstable Town, MA	6,116
225	Medford, OR	6,109
226	Las Cruces, NM	6,008
227	Janesville, WI	5,891
228	Lafayette, IN	5,804
229	Jackson, TN	5,796
230	Erie, PA	5,795
231	Burlington, NC	5,778
232	Lawrence, KS	5,751
233	Abilene, TX	5,741
234	Battle Creek, MI	5,707
235	Decatur, AL	5,662
236	Flagstaff, AZ	5,660
237	Charlottesville, VA	5,517
238	Punta Gorda, FL	5,454
239	Jonesboro, AR	5,446
240	Valdosta, GA	5,386
241	Fort Walton Beach, FL	5,364
242	Prescott, AZ	5,352
243	Santa Fe, NM	5,335
244	Billings, MT	5,327
245	Salisbury, MD	5,298
246	Bloomington, IN	5,293
247	Niles-Benton Harbor, MI	5,273
248	Longview, WA	5,268
249	Yuba City, CA	5,253
250	Texarkana, TX-Texarkana, AR	5,230
251	St. Cloud, MN	5,158
252	Pine Bluff, AR	5,122
253	Bend, OR	5,111
254	Gadsden, AL	5,096
255	Jackson, MI	5,089
256	Gainesville, GA	5,088
257	Holland-Grand Haven, MI	5,080
258	Redding, CA	4,986
259	Lawton, OK	4,979
260	Goldsboro, NC	4,946
261	Jacksonville, NC	4,932
262	Appleton, WI	4,928
262	San Angelo, TX	4,928
264	Dothan, AL	4,898
265	St. Joseph, MO-KS	4,825
266	Lynchburg, VA	4,739
267	Michigan City-La Porte, IN	4,728
268	Odessa, TX	4,721
269	Ocean City, NJ	4,709
270	Waterloo-Cedar Falls, IA	4,658
271	Grand Junction, CO	4,654
272	Sumter, SC	4,641
273	Columbia, MO	4,632
274	Bangor, ME	4,626
275	Dover, DE	4,523
276	Morristown, TN	4,461
277	Dalton, GA	4,440
278	Hattiesburg, MS	4,438
279	Brunswick, GA	4,435
280	Fargo, ND-MN	4,369
281	Warner Robins, GA	4,316
282	Lima, OH	4,289
283	Midland, TX	4,256
284	Sioux Falls, SD	4,200
285	Muncie, IN	4,108
286	Kokomo, IN	4,046
286	Sioux City, IA-NE-SD	4,046
288	Rome, GA	4,018
289	Victoria, TX	4,005
290	Blacksburg, VA	3,997
291	Sherman-Denison, TX	3,954
292	Wenatchee, WA	3,946
293	Sebastian-Vero Beach, FL	3,943
294	Rochester, MN	3,879
295	Eau Claire, WI	3,854
296	Coeur d'Alene, ID	3,801
297	Missoula, MT	3,792
298	Monroe, MI	3,744
299	Oshkosh-Neenah, WI	3,698
300	Bowling Green, KY	3,655
301	Hanford-Corcoran, CA	3,623
302	Jefferson City, MO	3,519
303	Madera, CA	3,478
304	Cleveland, TN	3,456
305	Kingston, NY	3,405
306	Sheboygan, WI	3,334
307	Idaho Falls, ID	3,258
308	Johnstown, PA	3,256
309	La Crosse, WI-MN	3,234
310	Napa, CA	3,233
311	Altoona, PA	3,192
312	Casper, WY	3,186
313	Winchester, VA-WV	3,164
314	Columbus, IN	3,068
315	Great Falls, MT	2,973
316	Farmington, NM	2,948
317	Pittsfield, MA	2,939
318	Iowa City, IA	2,933
319	Cheyenne, WY	2,914
320	Rapid City, SD	2,905
321	Sandusky, OH	2,881
322	Williamsport, PA	2,876
323	State College, PA	2,852
324	Bay City, MI	2,819
325	Lewiston-Auburn, ME	2,792
326	Morgantown, WV	2,783
327	Danville, VA	2,772
328	Cumberland, MD-WV	2,727
329	Glens Falls, NY	2,666
330	Lebanon, PA	2,587
331	Wheeling, WV-OH	2,579
332	Ithaca, NY	2,570
333	Wausau, WI	2,482
334	Pocatello, ID	2,441
335	Elmira, NY	2,387
336	Bismarck, ND	2,224
337	Ames, IA	2,140
338	Lewiston, ID-WA	1,977
339	Palm Coast, FL	1,946
340	Dubuque, IA	1,945
341	Fairbanks, AK	1,929
342	Elizabethtown, KY	1,913
343	Logan, UT-ID	1,879
344	Harrisonburg, VA	1,877
345	Fond du Lac, WI	1,853
346	Carson City, NV	1,247
NA	Atlanta, GA**	NA
NA	Chicago, IL**	NA
NA	Grand Forks, ND-MN**	NA
NA	Tucson, AZ**	NA

Source: Federal Bureau of Investigation

"Crime in the United States 2006" (Uniform Crime Reports, September 24, 2007)

**Property crimes are offenses of burglary, larceny-theft, and motor vehicle theft. Attempts are included.*

***Not available.*

26. Property Crime Rate in 2006

National Rate = 3,334.5 Property Crimes per 100,000 Population*

RANK	METROPOLITAN AREA	RATE
178	Abilene, TX	3,526.9
261	Albany-Schenectady-Troy, NY	2,743.2
95	Albany, GA	4,266.6
44	Albuquerque, NM	4,824.9
20	Alexandria, LA	5,246.3
286	Altoona, PA	2,515.2
42	Amarillo, TX	4,840.1
269	Ames, IA	2,662.5
87	Anchorage, AK	4,366.4
63	Anderson, SC	4,607.8
258	Ann Arbor, MI	2,798.3
309	Appleton, WI	2,282.2
235	Asheville, NC	2,985.5
89	Athens-Clarke County, GA	4,347.4
NA	Atlanta, GA**	NA
135	Atlantic City, NJ	3,883.9
69	Augusta, GA-SC	4,544.6
130	Austin-Round Rock, TX	3,942.7
85	Bakersfield, CA	4,382.2
182	Baltimore-Towson, MD	3,482.9
221	Bangor, ME	3,145.3
267	Barnstable Town, MA	2,683.9
32	Baton Rouge, LA	4,974.7
115	Battle Creek, MI	4,110.4
278	Bay City, MI	2,592.0
126	Beaumont-Port Arthur, TX	3,975.2
47	Bellingham, WA	4,736.8
172	Bend, OR	3,556.7
295	Bethesda-Frederick, MD M.D.	2,433.2
169	Billings, MT	3,599.4
279	Binghamton, NY	2,584.6
93	Birmingham-Hoover, AL	4,316.0
313	Bismarck, ND	2,241.5
273	Blacksburg, VA	2,619.9
239	Bloomington, IN	2,958.9
262	Boise City-Nampa, ID	2,720.7
207	Bowling Green, KY	3,267.5
268	Bremerton-Silverdale, WA	2,663.9
52	Brownsville-Harlingen, TX	4,701.9
88	Brunswick, GA	4,365.5
242	Buffalo-Niagara Falls, NY	2,929.2
122	Burlington, NC	4,031.1
271	Camden, NJ M.D.	2,656.8
167	Cape Coral-Fort Myers, FL	3,618.2
319	Carson City, NV	2,152.4
72	Casper, WY	4,513.9
233	Cedar Rapids, IA	3,003.8
90	Charleston-North Charleston, SC	4,347.1
154	Charleston, WV	3,696.0
19	Charlotte-Gastonia, NC-SC	5,248.1
245	Charlottesville, VA	2,899.1
97	Chattanooga, TN-GA	4,247.9
194	Cheyenne, WY	3,383.8
NA	Chicago, IL**	NA
204	Chico, CA	3,288.5
155	Cincinnati-Middletown, OH-KY-IN	3,690.6
226	Clarksville, TN-KY	3,106.5
223	Cleveland-Elyria-Mentor, OH	3,130.8
216	Cleveland, TN	3,158.8
244	Coeur d'Alene, ID	2,901.4
98	College Station-Bryan, TX	4,245.8
149	Colorado Springs, CO	3,735.2
234	Columbia, MO	2,999.9
137	Columbia, SC	3,852.8
14	Columbus, GA-AL	5,537.6
108	Columbus, IN	4,144.4
53	Columbus, OH	4,699.5
8	Corpus Christi, TX	5,862.6
264	Cumberland, MD-WV	2,702.9
81	Dallas (greater), TX	4,419.0
82	Dallas-Plano-Irving, TX M.D.	4,413.2
208	Dalton, GA	3,266.4
284	Danville, VA	2,541.4
139	Daytona Beach, FL	3,840.7
146	Dayton, OH	3,744.4
144	Decatur, AL	3,782.6
157	Denver-Aurora, CO	3,683.5
123	Des Moines-West Des Moines, IA	4,030.5
170	Detroit (greater), MI	3,593.6
36	Detroit-Livonia-Dearborn, MI M.D.	4,935.4
173	Dothan, AL	3,553.7
227	Dover, DE	3,105.0
321	Dubuque, IA	2,111.4
202	Duluth, MN-WI	3,297.5
71	Durham, NC	4,522.1
291	Eau Claire, WI	2,492.8
336	Edison, NJ M.D.	1,901.1
119	El Centro, CA	4,062.9
213	El Paso, TX	3,187.9
342	Elizabethtown, KY	1,715.5
165	Elkhart-Goshen, IN	3,632.7
270	Elmira, NY	2,659.6
325	Erie, PA	2,064.5
75	Eugene-Springfield, OR	4,487.3
252	Evansville, IN-KY	2,853.7
NA	Fairbanks, AK**	NA
302	Fargo, ND-MN	2,361.0
307	Farmington, NM	2,304.5
219	Fayetteville, AR-MO	3,153.6
6	Fayetteville, NC	6,014.8
83	Flagstaff, AZ	4,401.2
107	Flint, MI	4,148.1
10	Florence, SC	5,715.3
340	Fond du Lac, WI	1,858.6
230	Fort Collins-Loveland, CO	3,043.7
171	Fort Lauderdale, FL M.D.	3,571.0
192	Fort Smith, AR-OK	3,389.4
247	Fort Walton Beach, FL	2,895.6
205	Fort Wayne, IN	3,276.2
80	Fort Worth-Arlington, TX M.D.	4,430.7
78	Fresno, CA	4,453.7
37	Gadsden, AL	4,894.3
60	Gainesville, FL	4,649.5
237	Gainesville, GA	2,973.8
323	Glens Falls, NY	2,068.0
99	Goldsboro, NC	4,237.1
NA	Grand Forks, ND-MN**	NA
179	Grand Junction, CO	3,517.0
210	Grand Rapids-Wyoming, MI	3,251.6
153	Great Falls, MT	3,700.9
177	Greeley, CO	3,531.5
308	Green Bay, WI	2,296.2
64	Greensboro-High Point, NC	4,597.9
56	Greenville, NC	4,687.6
136	Greenville, SC	3,881.1
282	Hagerstown-Martinsburg, MD-WV	2,563.6
288	Hanford-Corcoran, CA	2,503.6
314	Harrisburg-Carlisle, PA	2,225.5
344	Harrisonburg, VA	1,664.0
220	Hartford, CT	3,149.1
195	Hattiesburg, MS	3,377.6
330	Holland-Grand Haven, MI	1,994.0
104	Honolulu, HI	4,197.5
1	Hot Springs, AR	7,446.7
142	Houma, LA	3,805.4
112	Houston, TX	4,122.6
209	Huntington-Ashland, WV-KY-OH	3,252.8
65	Huntsville, AL	4,597.1
257	Idaho Falls, ID	2,798.9
106	Indianapolis, IN	4,175.9
322	Iowa City, IA	2,106.1
283	Ithaca, NY	2,562.7
70	Jacksonville, FL	4,526.9
215	Jacksonville, NC	3,172.1
225	Jackson, MI	3,117.9
118	Jackson, MS	4,071.3
22	Jackson, TN	5,162.7
151	Janesville, WI	3,725.7
297	Jefferson City, MO	2,428.3
201	Johnson City, TN	3,311.2
317	Johnstown, PA	2,197.0
45	Jonesboro, AR	4,804.0
94	Joplin, MO	4,297.7
117	Kalamazoo-Portage, MI	4,078.4
105	Kansas City, MO-KS	4,176.0
212	Kennewick-Richland-Pasco, WA	3,227.0
175	Killeen-Temple-Fort Hood, TX	3,540.4
180	Kingsport, TN-VA	3,512.9
339	Kingston, NY	1,858.8
166	Knoxville, TN	3,620.1
127	Kokomo, IN	3,965.3
289	La Crosse, WI-MN	2,498.6
222	Lafayette, IN	3,144.9
33	Lake Charles, LA	4,961.8
59	Lake Havasu City-Kingman, AZ	4,653.8
143	Lakeland, FL	3,795.4
305	Lancaster, PA	2,330.0
255	Lansing-East Lansing, MI	2,825.1
12	Laredo, TX	5,618.0
224	Las Cruces, NM	3,128.9
76	Las Vegas-Paradise, NV	4,484.7

Note: All listings are for Metropolitan Statistical Areas (M.S.A.s) except for those ending with "M.D." Listings with "M.D." are Metropolitan Divisions which are smaller parts of eleven large M.S.A.s. See explanatory note at beginning of metropolitan area section on page 23.

RANK	METROPOLITAN AREA	RATE	RANK	METROPOLITAN AREA	RATE	RANK	METROPOLITAN AREA	RATE
13	Lawrence, KS	5,549.0	116	Omaha-Council Bluffs, NE-IA	4,079.3	31	Seattle-Bellevue, WA M.D.	4,990.3
84	Lawton, OK	4,389.8	92	Orlando, FL	4,321.0	232	Sebastian-Vero Beach, FL	3,015.4
326	Lebanon, PA	2,058.3	306	Oshkosh-Neenah, WI	2,310.3	246	Sheboygan, WI	2,898.4
280	Lewiston-Auburn, ME	2,584.1	324	Oxnard-Thousand Oaks, CA	2,065.3	203	Sherman-Denison, TX	3,291.0
206	Lewiston, ID-WA	3,269.7	193	Palm Bay-Melbourne, FL	3,384.2	27	Shreveport-Bossier City, LA	5,074.2
168	Lexington-Fayette, KY	3,607.8	287	Palm Coast, FL	2,504.5	256	Sioux City, IA-NE-SD	2,822.2
121	Lima, OH	4,032.4	128	Panama City-Lynn Haven, FL	3,947.5	329	Sioux Falls, SD	2,004.6
51	Lincoln, NE	4,708.2	102	Pascagoula, MS	4,220.7	77	South Bend-Mishawaka, IN-MI	4,458.3
11	Little Rock, AR	5,641.6	184	Pensacola, FL	3,453.4	48	Spartanburg, SC	4,734.7
345	Logan, UT-ID	1,649.1	243	Philadelphia (greater) PA-NJ-DE	2,903.4	114	Spokane, WA	4,110.6
61	Longview, TX	4,642.6	248	Philadelphia, PA M.D.	2,891.0	229	Springfield, MA	3,054.3
18	Longview, WA	5,321.4	39	Phoenix-Mesa-Scottsdale, AZ	4,878.1	74	Springfield, MO	4,495.1
266	Los Angeles County, CA M.D.	2,686.6	43	Pine Bluff, AR	4,829.3	5	Springfield, OH	6,073.7
281	Los Angeles (greater), CA	2,583.9	304	Pittsburgh, PA	2,334.6	328	State College, PA	2,027.2
159	Louisville, KY-IN	3,661.6	315	Pittsfield, MA	2,215.4	15	Stockton, CA	5,402.5
21	Lubbock, TX	5,174.1	259	Pocatello, ID	2,769.0	254	St. Cloud, MN	2,828.3
332	Lynchburg, VA	1,980.6	214	Port St. Lucie, FL	3,177.4	133	St. Joseph, MO-KS	3,927.5
4	Macon, GA	6,082.9	162	Portland-Vancouver, OR-WA	3,644.6	150	St. Louis, MO-IL	3,731.2
299	Madera, CA	2,414.0	272	Portland, ME	2,624.2	91	Sumter, SC	4,331.0
253	Madison, WI	2,835.4	334	Poughkeepsie, NY	1,910.4	292	Syracuse, NY	2,455.7
327	Manchester-Nashua, NH	2,054.6	277	Prescott, AZ	2,594.3	28	Tacoma, WA M.D.	5,068.2
38	Mansfield, OH	4,883.5	290	Provo-Orem, UT	2,497.8	147	Tallahassee, FL	3,743.8
73	McAllen-Edinburg-Mission, TX	4,512.9	24	Pueblo, CO	5,116.0	100	Tampa-St Petersburg, FL	4,225.1
228	Medford, OR	3,077.2	189	Punta Gorda, FL	3,404.6	140	Texarkana, TX-Texarkana, AR	3,821.2
7	Memphis, TN-MS-AR	6,012.8	183	Racine, WI	3,466.4	34	Toledo, OH	4,955.3
156	Merced, CA	3,688.2	241	Raleigh-Cary, NC	2,935.5	23	Topeka, KS	5,124.1
86	Miami (greater), FL	4,368.1	293	Rapid City, SD	2,438.8	316	Trenton-Ewing, NJ	2,206.1
29	Miami-Dade County, FL M.D.	5,042.3	275	Reading, PA	2,607.0	NA	Tucson, AZ**	NA
96	Michigan City-La Porte, IN	4,250.1	260	Redding, CA	2,746.7	141	Tulsa, OK	3,818.4
188	Midland, TX	3,410.0	124	Reno-Sparks, NV	4,012.9	54	Tuscaloosa, AL	4,692.3
134	Milwaukee, WI	3,926.5	238	Richmond, VA	2,969.9	174	Tyler, TX	3,550.6
176	Minneapolis-St. Paul, MN-WI	3,534.7	186	Riverside-San Bernardino, CA	3,431.5	310	Utica-Rome, NY	2,258.6
145	Missoula, MT	3,752.8	251	Roanoke, VA	2,855.7	103	Valdosta, GA	4,214.8
26	Mobile, AL	5,083.5	318	Rochester, MN	2,177.2	163	Vallejo-Fairfield, CA	3,642.9
35	Modesto, CA	4,946.5	236	Rochester, NY	2,984.6	185	Victoria, TX	3,435.8
16	Monroe, LA	5,360.8	17	Rocky Mount, NC	5,328.5	120	Vineland, NJ	4,040.6
294	Monroe, MI	2,438.3	110	Rome, GA	4,132.8	191	Virginia Beach-Norfolk, VA-NC	3,402.4
50	Montgomery, AL	4,709.9	131	Sacramento, CA	3,930.5	58	Visalia-Porterville, CA	4,661.7
296	Morgantown, WV	2,428.4	190	Saginaw, MI	3,404.1	57	Waco, TX	4,682.8
196	Morristown, TN	3,373.5	125	Salem, OR	3,984.6	200	Warner Robins, GA	3,314.5
9	Mount Vernon-Anacortes, WA	5,810.7	217	Salinas, CA	3,154.8	285	Warren-Farmington Hills, MI M.D.	2,516.9
181	Muncie, IN	3,507.1	68	Salisbury, MD	4,545.1	249	Washington (greater) DC-VA-MD	2,888.5
40	Muskegon-Norton Shores, MI	4,865.3	41	Salt Lake City, UT	4,849.9	231	Washington, DC-VA-MD-WV M.D.	3,015.6
2	Myrtle Beach, SC	6,636.2	67	San Angelo, TX	4,548.1	250	Waterloo-Cedar Falls, IA	2,862.0
300	Napa, CA	2,413.4	25	San Antonio, TX	5,103.2	333	Wausau, WI	1,917.9
331	Naples-Marco Island, FL	1,984.2	218	San Diego, CA	3,154.0	152	Wenatchee, WA	3,702.8
138	Nashville-Davidson, TN	3,842.0	132	San Francisco (greater), CA	3,929.9	101	West Palm Beach, FL M.D.	4,222.1
343	Nassau-Suffolk, NY M.D.	1,710.6	164	San Francisco-S. Mateo, CA M.D.	3,634.2	341	Wheeling, WV-OH	1,732.8
199	New Orleans, LA	3,332.8	263	San Jose, CA	2,717.3	49	Wichita Falls, TX	4,733.4
335	New York (greater), NY-NJ-PA	1,905.0	276	San Luis Obispo, CA	2,603.4	79	Wichita, KS	4,446.5
337	New York-W. Plains NY-NJ M.D.	1,871.1	161	Sandusky, OH	3,657.9	298	Williamsport, PA	2,427.0
303	Newark-Union, NJ-PA M.D.	2,344.1	312	Santa Ana-Anaheim, CA M.D.	2,242.3	187	Wilmington, DE-MD-NJ M.D.	3,416.5
211	Niles-Benton Harbor, MI	3,250.8	311	Santa Barbara-Santa Maria, CA	2,248.4	55	Wilmington, NC	4,690.9
111	Oakland-Fremont, CA M.D.	4,132.1	129	Santa Cruz-Watsonville, CA	3,944.2	265	Winchester, VA-WV	2,699.1
274	Ocala, FL	2,613.4	148	Santa Fe, NM	3,736.8	66	Winston-Salem, NC	4,580.8
46	Ocean City, NJ	4,739.2	320	Santa Rosa-Petaluma, CA	2,142.2	338	Worcester, MA	1,870.3
158	Odessa, TX	3,662.8	113	Sarasota-Bradenton-Venice, FL	4,120.0	3	Yakima, WA	6,356.6
240	Ogden-Clearfield, UT	2,954.2	109	Savannah, GA	4,142.7	198	Yuba City, CA	3,336.6
62	Oklahoma City, OK	4,613.3	301	Scranton--Wilkes-Barre, PA	2,404.4	160	Yuma, AZ	3,660.4
197	Olympia, WA	3,348.8	30	Seattle (greater), WA	5,008.6			

Source: Federal Bureau of Investigation
"Crime in the United States 2006" (Uniform Crime Reports, September 24, 2007)
**Property crimes are offenses of burglary, larceny-theft, and motor vehicle theft. Attempts are included.*
***Not available.*

26. Property Crime Rate in 2006 (continued)

National Rate = 3,334.5 Property Crimes per 100,000 Population*

RANK	METROPOLITAN AREA	RATE
1	Hot Springs, AR	7,446.7
2	Myrtle Beach, SC	6,636.2
3	Yakima, WA	6,356.6
4	Macon, GA	6,082.9
5	Springfield, OH	6,073.7
6	Fayetteville, NC	6,014.8
7	Memphis, TN-MS-AR	6,012.8
8	Corpus Christi, TX	5,862.6
9	Mount Vernon-Anacortes, WA	5,810.7
10	Florence, SC	5,715.3
11	Little Rock, AR	5,641.6
12	Laredo, TX	5,618.0
13	Lawrence, KS	5,549.0
14	Columbus, GA-AL	5,537.6
15	Stockton, CA	5,402.5
16	Monroe, LA	5,360.8
17	Rocky Mount, NC	5,328.5
18	Longview, WA	5,321.4
19	Charlotte-Gastonia, NC-SC	5,248.1
20	Alexandria, LA	5,246.3
21	Lubbock, TX	5,174.1
22	Jackson, TN	5,162.7
23	Topeka, KS	5,124.1
24	Pueblo, CO	5,116.0
25	San Antonio, TX	5,103.2
26	Mobile, AL	5,083.5
27	Shreveport-Bossier City, LA	5,074.2
28	Tacoma, WA M.D.	5,068.2
29	Miami-Dade County, FL M.D.	5,042.3
30	Seattle (greater), WA	5,008.6
31	Seattle-Bellevue, WA M.D.	4,990.3
32	Baton Rouge, LA	4,974.7
33	Lake Charles, LA	4,961.8
34	Toledo, OH	4,955.3
35	Modesto, CA	4,946.5
36	Detroit-Livonia-Dearborn, MI M.D.	4,935.4
37	Gadsden, AL	4,894.3
38	Mansfield, OH	4,883.5
39	Phoenix-Mesa-Scottsdale, AZ	4,878.1
40	Muskegon-Norton Shores, MI	4,865.3
41	Salt Lake City, UT	4,849.9
42	Amarillo, TX	4,840.1
43	Pine Bluff, AR	4,829.3
44	Albuquerque, NM	4,824.9
45	Jonesboro, AR	4,804.0
46	Ocean City, NJ	4,739.2
47	Bellingham, WA	4,736.8
48	Spartanburg, SC	4,734.7
49	Wichita Falls, TX	4,733.4
50	Montgomery, AL	4,709.9
51	Lincoln, NE	4,708.2
52	Brownsville-Harlingen, TX	4,701.9
53	Columbus, OH	4,699.5
54	Tuscaloosa, AL	4,692.3
55	Wilmington, NC	4,690.9
56	Greenville, NC	4,687.6
57	Waco, TX	4,682.8
58	Visalia-Porterville, CA	4,661.7
59	Lake Havasu City-Kingman, AZ	4,653.8
60	Gainesville, FL	4,649.5
61	Longview, TX	4,642.6
62	Oklahoma City, OK	4,613.3
63	Anderson, SC	4,607.8
64	Greensboro-High Point, NC	4,597.9
65	Huntsville, AL	4,597.1
66	Winston-Salem, NC	4,580.8
67	San Angelo, TX	4,548.1
68	Salisbury, MD	4,545.1
69	Augusta, GA-SC	4,544.6
70	Jacksonville, FL	4,526.9
71	Durham, NC	4,522.1
72	Casper, WY	4,513.9
73	McAllen-Edinburg-Mission, TX	4,512.9
74	Springfield, MO	4,495.1
75	Eugene-Springfield, OR	4,487.3
76	Las Vegas-Paradise, NV	4,484.7
77	South Bend-Mishawaka, IN-MI	4,458.3
78	Fresno, CA	4,453.7
79	Wichita, KS	4,446.5
80	Fort Worth-Arlington, TX M.D.	4,430.7
81	Dallas (greater), TX	4,419.0
82	Dallas-Plano-Irving, TX M.D.	4,413.2
83	Flagstaff, AZ	4,401.2
84	Lawton, OK	4,389.8
85	Bakersfield, CA	4,382.2
86	Miami (greater), FL	4,368.1
87	Anchorage, AK	4,366.4
88	Brunswick, GA	4,365.5
89	Athens-Clarke County, GA	4,347.4
90	Charleston-North Charleston, SC	4,347.1
91	Sumter, SC	4,331.0
92	Orlando, FL	4,321.0
93	Birmingham-Hoover, AL	4,316.0
94	Joplin, MO	4,297.7
95	Albany, GA	4,266.6
96	Michigan City-La Porte, IN	4,250.1
97	Chattanooga, TN-GA	4,247.9
98	College Station-Bryan, TX	4,245.8
99	Goldsboro, NC	4,237.1
100	Tampa-St Petersburg, FL	4,225.1
101	West Palm Beach, FL M.D.	4,222.1
102	Pascagoula, MS	4,220.7
103	Valdosta, GA	4,214.8
104	Honolulu, HI	4,197.5
105	Kansas City, MO-KS	4,176.0
106	Indianapolis, IN	4,175.9
107	Flint, MI	4,148.1
108	Columbus, IN	4,144.4
109	Savannah, GA	4,142.7
110	Rome, GA	4,132.8
111	Oakland-Fremont, CA M.D.	4,132.1
112	Houston, TX	4,122.6
113	Sarasota-Bradenton-Venice, FL	4,120.0
114	Spokane, WA	4,110.6
115	Battle Creek, MI	4,110.4
116	Omaha-Council Bluffs, NE-IA	4,079.3
117	Kalamazoo-Portage, MI	4,078.4
118	Jackson, MS	4,071.3
119	El Centro, CA	4,062.9
120	Vineland, NJ	4,040.6
121	Lima, OH	4,032.4
122	Burlington, NC	4,031.1
123	Des Moines-West Des Moines, IA	4,030.5
124	Reno-Sparks, NV	4,012.9
125	Salem, OR	3,984.6
126	Beaumont-Port Arthur, TX	3,975.2
127	Kokomo, IN	3,965.3
128	Panama City-Lynn Haven, FL	3,947.5
129	Santa Cruz-Watsonville, CA	3,944.2
130	Austin-Round Rock, TX	3,942.7
131	Sacramento, CA	3,930.5
132	San Francisco (greater), CA	3,929.9
133	St. Joseph, MO-KS	3,927.5
134	Milwaukee, WI	3,926.5
135	Atlantic City, NJ	3,883.9
136	Greenville, SC	3,881.1
137	Columbia, SC	3,852.8
138	Nashville-Davidson, TN	3,842.0
139	Daytona Beach, FL	3,840.7
140	Texarkana, TX-Texarkana, AR	3,821.2
141	Tulsa, OK	3,818.4
142	Houma, LA	3,805.4
143	Lakeland, FL	3,795.4
144	Decatur, AL	3,782.6
145	Missoula, MT	3,752.8
146	Dayton, OH	3,744.4
147	Tallahassee, FL	3,743.8
148	Santa Fe, NM	3,736.8
149	Colorado Springs, CO	3,735.2
150	St. Louis, MO-IL	3,731.2
151	Janesville, WI	3,725.7
152	Wenatchee, WA	3,702.8
153	Great Falls, MT	3,700.9
154	Charleston, WV	3,696.0
155	Cincinnati-Middletown, OH-KY-IN	3,690.6
156	Merced, CA	3,688.2
157	Denver-Aurora, CO	3,683.5
158	Odessa, TX	3,662.8
159	Louisville, KY-IN	3,661.6
160	Yuma, AZ	3,660.4
161	Sandusky, OH	3,657.9
162	Portland-Vancouver, OR-WA	3,644.6
163	Vallejo-Fairfield, CA	3,642.9
164	San Francisco-S. Mateo, CA M.D.	3,634.2
165	Elkhart-Goshen, IN	3,632.7
166	Knoxville, TN	3,620.1
167	Cape Coral-Fort Myers, FL	3,618.2
168	Lexington-Fayette, KY	3,607.8
169	Billings, MT	3,599.4
170	Detroit (greater), MI	3,593.6
171	Fort Lauderdale, FL M.D.	3,571.0

Note: All listings are for Metropolitan Statistical Areas (M.S.A.s) except for those ending with "M.D." Listings with "M.D." are Metropolitan Divisions which are smaller parts of eleven large M.S.A.s. See explanatory note at beginning of metropolitan area section on page 23.

RANK	METROPOLITAN AREA	RATE
172	Bend, OR	3,556.7
173	Dothan, AL	3,553.7
174	Tyler, TX	3,550.6
175	Killeen-Temple-Fort Hood, TX	3,540.4
176	Minneapolis-St. Paul, MN-WI	3,534.7
177	Greeley, CO	3,531.5
178	Abilene, TX	3,526.9
179	Grand Junction, CO	3,517.0
180	Kingsport, TN-VA	3,512.9
181	Muncie, IN	3,507.1
182	Baltimore-Towson, MD	3,482.9
183	Racine, WI	3,466.4
184	Pensacola, FL	3,453.4
185	Victoria, TX	3,435.8
186	Riverside-San Bernardino, CA	3,431.5
187	Wilmington, DE-MD-NJ M.D.	3,416.5
188	Midland, TX	3,410.0
189	Punta Gorda, FL	3,404.6
190	Saginaw, MI	3,404.1
191	Virginia Beach-Norfolk, VA-NC	3,402.4
192	Fort Smith, AR-OK	3,389.4
193	Palm Bay-Melbourne, FL	3,384.2
194	Cheyenne, WY	3,383.8
195	Hattiesburg, MS	3,377.6
196	Morristown, TN	3,373.5
197	Olympia, WA	3,348.8
198	Yuba City, CA	3,336.6
199	New Orleans, LA	3,332.8
200	Warner Robins, GA	3,314.5
201	Johnson City, TN	3,311.2
202	Duluth, MN-WI	3,297.5
203	Sherman-Denison, TX	3,291.0
204	Chico, CA	3,288.5
205	Fort Wayne, IN	3,276.2
206	Lewiston, ID-WA	3,269.7
207	Bowling Green, KY	3,267.5
208	Dalton, GA	3,266.4
209	Huntington-Ashland, WV-KY-OH	3,252.8
210	Grand Rapids-Wyoming, MI	3,251.6
211	Niles-Benton Harbor, MI	3,250.8
212	Kennewick-Richland-Pasco, WA	3,227.0
213	El Paso, TX	3,187.9
214	Port St. Lucie, FL	3,177.4
215	Jacksonville, NC	3,172.1
216	Cleveland, TN	3,158.8
217	Salinas, CA	3,154.8
218	San Diego, CA	3,154.0
219	Fayetteville, AR-MO	3,153.6
220	Hartford, CT	3,149.1
221	Bangor, ME	3,145.3
222	Lafayette, IN	3,144.9
223	Cleveland-Elyria-Mentor, OH	3,130.8
224	Las Cruces, NM	3,128.9
225	Jackson, MI	3,117.9
226	Clarksville, TN-KY	3,106.5
227	Dover, DE	3,105.0
228	Medford, OR	3,077.2
229	Springfield, MA	3,054.3
230	Fort Collins-Loveland, CO	3,043.7
231	Washington, DC-VA-MD-WV M.D.	3,015.6
232	Sebastian-Vero Beach, FL	3,015.4
233	Cedar Rapids, IA	3,003.8
234	Columbia, MO	2,999.9
235	Asheville, NC	2,985.5
236	Rochester, NY	2,984.6
237	Gainesville, GA	2,973.8
238	Richmond, VA	2,969.9
239	Bloomington, IN	2,958.9
240	Ogden-Clearfield, UT	2,954.2
241	Raleigh-Cary, NC	2,935.5
242	Buffalo-Niagara Falls, NY	2,929.2
243	Philadelphia (greater) PA-NJ-DE	2,903.4
244	Coeur d'Alene, ID	2,901.4
245	Charlottesville, VA	2,899.1
246	Sheboygan, WI	2,898.4
247	Fort Walton Beach, FL	2,895.6
248	Philadelphia, PA M.D.	2,891.0
249	Washington (greater) DC-VA-MD	2,888.5
250	Waterloo-Cedar Falls, IA	2,862.0
251	Roanoke, VA	2,855.7
252	Evansville, IN-KY	2,853.7
253	Madison, WI	2,835.4
254	St. Cloud, MN	2,828.3
255	Lansing-East Lansing, MI	2,825.1
256	Sioux City, IA-NE-SD	2,822.2
257	Idaho Falls, ID	2,798.9
258	Ann Arbor, MI	2,798.3
259	Pocatello, ID	2,769.0
260	Redding, CA	2,746.7
261	Albany-Schenectady-Troy, NY	2,743.2
262	Boise City-Nampa, ID	2,720.7
263	San Jose, CA	2,717.3
264	Cumberland, MD-WV	2,702.9
265	Winchester, VA-WV	2,699.1
266	Los Angeles County, CA M.D.	2,686.6
267	Barnstable Town, MA	2,683.9
268	Bremerton-Silverdale, WA	2,663.9
269	Ames, IA	2,662.5
270	Elmira, NY	2,659.6
271	Camden, NJ M.D.	2,656.8
272	Portland, ME	2,624.2
273	Blacksburg, VA	2,619.9
274	Ocala, FL	2,613.4
275	Reading, PA	2,607.0
276	San Luis Obispo, CA	2,603.4
277	Prescott, AZ	2,594.3
278	Bay City, MI	2,592.0
279	Binghamton, NY	2,584.6
280	Lewiston-Auburn, ME	2,584.1
281	Los Angeles (greater), CA	2,583.9
282	Hagerstown-Martinsburg, MD-WV	2,563.6
283	Ithaca, NY	2,562.7
284	Danville, VA	2,541.4
285	Warren-Farmington Hills, MI M.D.	2,516.9
286	Altoona, PA	2,515.2
287	Palm Coast, FL	2,504.5
288	Hanford-Corcoran, CA	2,503.6
289	La Crosse, WI-MN	2,498.6
290	Provo-Orem, UT	2,497.8
291	Eau Claire, WI	2,492.8
292	Syracuse, NY	2,455.7
293	Rapid City, SD	2,438.8
294	Monroe, MI	2,438.3
295	Bethesda-Frederick, MD M.D.	2,433.2
296	Morgantown, WV	2,428.4
297	Jefferson City, MO	2,428.3
298	Williamsport, PA	2,427.0
299	Madera, CA	2,414.0
300	Napa, CA	2,413.4
301	Scranton--Wilkes-Barre, PA	2,404.4
302	Fargo, ND-MN	2,361.0
303	Newark-Union, NJ-PA M.D.	2,344.1
304	Pittsburgh, PA	2,334.6
305	Lancaster, PA	2,330.0
306	Oshkosh-Neenah, WI	2,310.3
307	Farmington, NM	2,304.5
308	Green Bay, WI	2,296.2
309	Appleton, WI	2,282.2
310	Utica-Rome, NY	2,258.6
311	Santa Barbara-Santa Maria, CA	2,248.4
312	Santa Ana-Anaheim, CA M.D.	2,242.3
313	Bismarck, ND	2,241.5
314	Harrisburg-Carlisle, PA	2,225.5
315	Pittsfield, MA	2,215.4
316	Trenton-Ewing, NJ	2,206.1
317	Johnstown, PA	2,197.0
318	Rochester, MN	2,177.2
319	Carson City, NV	2,152.4
320	Santa Rosa-Petaluma, CA	2,142.2
321	Dubuque, IA	2,111.4
322	Iowa City, IA	2,106.1
323	Glens Falls, NY	2,068.0
324	Oxnard-Thousand Oaks, CA	2,065.3
325	Erie, PA	2,064.5
326	Lebanon, PA	2,058.3
327	Manchester-Nashua, NH	2,054.6
328	State College, PA	2,027.2
329	Sioux Falls, SD	2,004.6
330	Holland-Grand Haven, MI	1,994.0
331	Naples-Marco Island, FL	1,984.2
332	Lynchburg, VA	1,980.6
333	Wausau, WI	1,917.9
334	Poughkeepsie, NY	1,910.4
335	New York (greater), NY-NJ-PA	1,905.0
336	Edison, NJ M.D.	1,901.1
337	New York-W. Plains NY-NJ M.D.	1,871.1
338	Worcester, MA	1,870.3
339	Kingston, NY	1,858.8
340	Fond du Lac, WI	1,858.6
341	Wheeling, WV-OH	1,732.8
342	Elizabethtown, KY	1,715.5
343	Nassau-Suffolk, NY M.D.	1,710.6
344	Harrisonburg, VA	1,664.0
345	Logan, UT-ID	1,649.1
NA	Atlanta, GA**	NA
NA	Chicago, IL**	NA
NA	Fairbanks, AK**	NA
NA	Grand Forks, ND-MN**	NA
NA	Tucson, AZ**	NA

Source: Federal Bureau of Investigation
"Crime in the United States 2006" (Uniform Crime Reports, September 24, 2007)
**Property crimes are offenses of burglary, larceny-theft, and motor vehicle theft. Attempts are included.*
***Not available.*

27. Percent Change in Property Crime Rate: 2005 to 2006

National Percent Change = 2.8% Decrease*

RANK	METROPOLITAN AREA	% CHANGE
NA	Abilene, TX**	NA
73	Albany-Schenectady-Troy, NY	3.0
57	Albany, GA	5.2
148	Albuquerque, NM	(1.8)
20	Alexandria, LA	9.6
70	Altoona, PA	3.3
260	Amarillo, TX	(9.5)
174	Ames, IA	(3.2)
84	Anchorage, AK	2.1
241	Anderson, SC	(7.7)
219	Ann Arbor, MI	(6.5)
43	Appleton, WI	6.5
252	Asheville, NC	(8.7)
62	Athens-Clarke County, GA	4.2
NA	Atlanta, GA**	NA
166	Atlantic City, NJ	(2.8)
112	Augusta, GA-SC	0.6
190	Austin-Round Rock, TX	(4.6)
190	Bakersfield, CA	(4.6)
116	Baltimore-Towson, MD	0.4
16	Bangor, ME	10.2
2	Barnstable Town, MA	14.6
55	Baton Rouge, LA	5.3
118	Battle Creek, MI	0.3
179	Bay City, MI	(3.5)
275	Beaumont-Port Arthur, TX	(11.6)
257	Bellingham, WA	(9.2)
308	Bend, OR	(18.9)
49	Bethesda-Frederick, MD M.D.	5.7
314	Billings, MT	(21.8)
69	Binghamton, NY	3.4
NA	Birmingham-Hoover, AL**	NA
90	Bismarck, ND	1.8
154	Blacksburg, VA	(2.1)
18	Bloomington, IN	9.8
NA	Boise City-Nampa, ID**	NA
195	Bowling Green, KY	(4.9)
236	Bremerton-Silverdale, WA	(7.5)
219	Brownsville-Harlingen, TX	(6.5)
175	Brunswick, GA	(3.3)
166	Buffalo-Niagara Falls, NY	(2.8)
105	Burlington, NC	0.9
54	Camden, NJ M.D.	5.4
80	Cape Coral-Fort Myers, FL	2.4
290	Carson City, NV	(14.0)
203	Casper, WY	(5.5)
201	Cedar Rapids, IA	(5.3)
136	Charleston-North Charleston, SC	(1.1)
267	Charleston, WV	(10.2)
95	Charlotte-Gastonia, NC-SC	1.5
28	Charlottesville, VA	8.8
246	Chattanooga, TN-GA	(8.1)
235	Cheyenne, WY	(7.4)
NA	Chicago, IL**	NA
185	Chico, CA	(3.9)
116	Cincinnati-Middletown, OH-KY-IN	0.4
104	Clarksville, TN-KY	1.0
NA	Cleveland-Elyria-Mentor, OH**	NA
NA	Cleveland, TN**	NA
292	Coeur d'Alene, ID	(14.3)
238	College Station-Bryan, TX	(7.6)
256	Colorado Springs, CO	(9.0)
143	Columbia, MO	(1.3)
186	Columbia, SC	(4.0)
101	Columbus, GA-AL	1.3
58	Columbus, IN	4.9
163	Columbus, OH	(2.6)
229	Corpus Christi, TX	(6.9)
21	Cumberland, MD-WV	9.5
219	Dallas (greater), TX	(6.5)
218	Dallas-Plano-Irving, TX M.D.	(6.4)
NA	Dalton, GA**	NA
98	Danville, VA	1.4
23	Daytona Beach, FL	9.3
133	Dayton, OH	(0.9)
64	Decatur, AL	4.0
303	Denver-Aurora, CO	(17.4)
NA	Des Moines-West Des Moines, IA**	NA
NA	Detroit (greater), MI**	NA
23	Detroit-Livonia-Dearborn, MI M.D.	9.3
248	Dothan, AL	(8.2)
71	Dover, DE	3.2
241	Dubuque, IA	(7.7)
NA	Duluth, MN-WI**	NA
NA	Durham, NC**	NA
22	Eau Claire, WI	9.4
98	Edison, NJ M.D.	1.4
122	El Centro, CA	0.1
75	El Paso, TX	2.8
244	Elizabethtown, KY	(7.8)
169	Elkhart-Goshen, IN	(2.9)
255	Elmira, NY	(8.9)
77	Erie, PA	2.5
306	Eugene-Springfield, OR	(18.4)
123	Evansville, IN-KY	(0.1)
NA	Fairbanks, AK**	NA
49	Fargo, ND-MN	5.7
283	Farmington, NM	(13.0)
84	Fayetteville, AR-MO	2.1
32	Fayetteville, NC	8.2
238	Flagstaff, AZ	(7.6)
88	Flint, MI	1.9
125	Florence, SC	(0.3)
88	Fond du Lac, WI	1.9
103	Fort Collins-Loveland, CO	1.2
156	Fort Lauderdale, FL M.D.	(2.2)
131	Fort Smith, AR-OK	(0.8)
123	Fort Walton Beach, FL	(0.1)
NA	Fort Wayne, IN**	NA
226	Fort Worth-Arlington, TX M.D.	(6.8)
234	Fresno, CA	(7.2)
29	Gadsden, AL	8.7
6	Gainesville, FL	12.8
300	Gainesville, GA	(17.3)
NA	Glens Falls, NY**	NA
139	Goldsboro, NC	(1.2)
NA	Grand Forks, ND-MN**	NA
293	Grand Junction, CO	(14.6)
63	Grand Rapids-Wyoming, MI	4.1
313	Great Falls, MT	(21.1)
311	Greeley, CO	(20.3)
151	Green Bay, WI	(1.9)
128	Greensboro-High Point, NC	(0.4)
47	Greenville, NC	5.8
186	Greenville, SC	(4.0)
5	Hagerstown-Martinsburg, MD-WV	13.3
261	Hanford-Corcoran, CA	(9.6)
246	Harrisburg-Carlisle, PA	(8.1)
42	Harrisonburg, VA	6.7
152	Hartford, CT	(2.0)
NA	Hattiesburg, MS**	NA
61	Holland-Grand Haven, MI	4.6
265	Honolulu, HI	(10.0)
152	Hot Springs, AR	(2.0)
67	Houma, LA	3.7
159	Houston, TX	(2.3)
33	Huntington-Ashland, WV-KY-OH	8.1
198	Huntsville, AL	(5.0)
39	Idaho Falls, ID	6.8
139	Indianapolis, IN	(1.2)
165	Iowa City, IA	(2.7)
NA	Ithaca, NY**	NA
118	Jacksonville, FL	0.3
NA	Jacksonville, NC**	NA
46	Jackson, MI	6.1
47	Jackson, MS	5.8
245	Jackson, TN	(7.9)
82	Janesville, WI	2.3
251	Jefferson City, MO	(8.5)
276	Johnson City, TN	(11.8)
NA	Johnstown, PA**	NA
148	Jonesboro, AR	(1.8)
274	Joplin, MO	(11.3)
9	Kalamazoo-Portage, MI	12.1
NA	Kansas City, MO-KS**	NA
285	Kennewick-Richland-Pasco, WA	(13.4)
184	Killeen-Temple-Fort Hood, TX	(3.8)
109	Kingsport, TN-VA	0.7
209	Kingston, NY	(5.9)
195	Knoxville, TN	(4.9)
208	Kokomo, IN	(5.8)
37	La Crosse, WI-MN	7.5
112	Lafayette, IN	0.6
39	Lake Charles, LA	6.8
NA	Lake Havasu City-Kingman, AZ**	NA
224	Lakeland, FL	(6.7)
60	Lancaster, PA	4.8
199	Lansing-East Lansing, MI	(5.1)
163	Laredo, TX	(2.6)
161	Las Cruces, NM	(2.4)
166	Las Vegas-Paradise, NV	(2.8)

Note: All listings are for Metropolitan Statistical Areas (M.S.A.s) except for those ending with "M.D." Listings with "M.D." are Metropolitan Divisions which are smaller parts of eleven large M.S.A.s. See explanatory note at beginning of metropolitan area section on page 23.

RANK	METROPOLITAN AREA	% CHANGE
1	Lawrence, KS	37.3
148	Lawton, OK	(1.8)
172	Lebanon, PA	(3.1)
182	Lewiston-Auburn, ME	(3.7)
266	Lewiston, ID-WA	(10.1)
NA	Lexington-Fayette, KY**	NA
232	Lima, OH	(7.0)
182	Lincoln, NE	(3.7)
156	Little Rock, AR	(2.2)
272	Logan, UT-ID	(11.1)
162	Longview, TX	(2.5)
280	Longview, WA	(12.6)
212	Los Angeles County, CA M.D.	(6.1)
212	Los Angeles (greater), CA	(6.1)
58	Louisville, KY-IN	4.9
212	Lubbock, TX	(6.1)
136	Lynchburg, VA	(1.1)
145	Macon, GA	(1.6)
305	Madera, CA	(18.0)
125	Madison, WI	(0.3)
105	Manchester-Nashua, NH	0.9
31	Mansfield, OH	8.3
291	McAllen-Edinburg-Mission, TX	(14.1)
312	Medford, OR	(20.8)
139	Memphis, TN-MS-AR	(1.2)
229	Merced, CA	(6.9)
172	Miami (greater), FL	(3.1)
188	Miami-Dade County, FL M.D.	(4.1)
17	Michigan City-La Porte, IN	9.9
139	Midland, TX	(1.2)
10	Milwaukee, WI	11.5
NA	Minneapolis-St. Paul, MN-WI**	NA
304	Missoula, MT	(17.5)
25	Mobile, AL	9.2
252	Modesto, CA	(8.7)
44	Monroe, LA	6.2
73	Monroe, MI	3.0
154	Montgomery, AL	(2.1)
86	Morgantown, WV	2.0
131	Morristown, TN	(0.8)
315	Mount Vernon-Anacortes, WA	(22.2)
12	Muncie, IN	10.8
92	Muskegon-Norton Shores, MI	1.7
175	Myrtle Beach, SC	(3.3)
147	Napa, CA	(1.7)
210	Naples-Marco Island, FL	(6.0)
233	Nashville-Davidson, TN	(7.1)
90	Nassau-Suffolk, NY M.D.	1.8
NA	New Orleans, LA**	NA
180	New York (greater), NY-NJ-PA	(3.6)
195	New York-W. Plains NY-NJ M.D.	(4.9)
222	Newark-Union, NJ-PA M.D.	(6.6)
77	Niles-Benton Harbor, MI	2.5
118	Oakland-Fremont, CA M.D.	0.3
258	Ocala, FL	(9.3)
39	Ocean City, NJ	6.8
241	Odessa, TX	(7.7)
204	Ogden-Clearfield, UT	(5.6)
289	Oklahoma City, OK	(13.7)
273	Olympia, WA	(11.2)
159	Omaha-Council Bluffs, NE-IA	(2.3)
121	Orlando, FL	0.2
27	Oshkosh-Neenah, WI	8.9
133	Oxnard-Thousand Oaks, CA	(0.9)
52	Palm Bay-Melbourne, FL	5.5
NA	Palm Coast, FL**	NA
204	Panama City-Lynn Haven, FL	(5.6)
3	Pascagoula, MS	14.2
26	Pensacola, FL	9.0
44	Philadelphia (greater) PA-NJ-DE	6.2
49	Philadelphia, PA M.D.	5.7
226	Phoenix-Mesa-Scottsdale, AZ	(6.8)
279	Pine Bluff, AR	(12.5)
188	Pittsburgh, PA	(4.1)
7	Pittsfield, MA	12.5
269	Pocatello, ID	(10.7)
34	Port St. Lucie, FL	7.7
300	Portland-Vancouver, OR-WA	(17.3)
38	Portland, ME	7.3
93	Poughkeepsie, NY	1.6
284	Prescott, AZ	(13.1)
308	Provo-Orem, UT	(18.9)
262	Pueblo, CO	(9.8)
15	Punta Gorda, FL	10.5
143	Racine, WI	(1.3)
112	Raleigh-Cary, NC	0.6
310	Rapid City, SD	(19.5)
236	Reading, PA	(7.5)
306	Redding, CA	(18.4)
156	Reno-Sparks, NV	(2.2)
NA	Richmond, VA**	NA
226	Riverside-San Bernardino, CA	(6.8)
285	Roanoke, VA	(13.4)
13	Rochester, MN	10.7
136	Rochester, NY	(1.1)
11	Rocky Mount, NC	11.0
298	Rome, GA	(16.4)
175	Sacramento, CA	(3.3)
128	Saginaw, MI	(0.4)
287	Salem, OR	(13.5)
264	Salinas, CA	(9.9)
36	Salisbury, MD	7.6
250	Salt Lake City, UT	(8.3)
293	San Angelo, TX	(14.6)
190	San Antonio, TX	(4.6)
194	San Diego, CA	(4.7)
98	San Francisco (greater), CA	1.4
72	San Francisco-S. Mateo, CA M.D.	3.1
76	San Jose, CA	2.6
66	San Luis Obispo, CA	3.8
130	Sandusky, OH	(0.7)
215	Santa Ana-Anaheim, CA M.D.	(6.3)
222	Santa Barbara-Santa Maria, CA	(6.6)
170	Santa Cruz-Watsonville, CA	(3.0)
105	Santa Fe, NM	0.9
297	Santa Rosa-Petaluma, CA	(16.3)
93	Sarasota-Bradenton-Venice, FL	1.6
280	Savannah, GA	(12.6)
105	Scranton--Wilkes-Barre, PA	0.9
215	Seattle (greater), WA	(6.3)
229	Seattle-Bellevue, WA M.D.	(6.9)
271	Sebastian-Vero Beach, FL	(10.9)
8	Sheboygan, WI	12.2
277	Sherman-Denison, TX	(11.9)
67	Shreveport-Bossier City, LA	3.7
180	Sioux City, IA-NE-SD	(3.6)
295	Sioux Falls, SD	(15.0)
30	South Bend-Mishawaka, IN-MI	8.4
52	Spartanburg, SC	5.5
210	Spokane, WA	(6.0)
133	Springfield, MA	(0.9)
95	Springfield, MO	1.5
109	Springfield, OH	0.7
101	State College, PA	1.3
175	Stockton, CA	(3.3)
13	St. Cloud, MN	10.7
200	St. Joseph, MO-KS	(5.2)
80	St. Louis, MO-IL	2.4
202	Sumter, SC	(5.4)
83	Syracuse, NY	2.2
190	Tacoma, WA M.D.	(4.6)
206	Tallahassee, FL	(5.7)
95	Tampa-St Petersburg, FL	1.5
262	Texarkana, TX-Texarkana, AR	(9.8)
64	Toledo, OH	4.0
215	Topeka, KS	(6.3)
280	Trenton-Ewing, NJ	(12.6)
NA	Tucson, AZ**	NA
248	Tulsa, OK	(8.2)
NA	Tuscaloosa, AL**	NA
267	Tyler, TX	(10.2)
109	Utica-Rome, NY	0.7
278	Valdosta, GA	(12.2)
NA	Vallejo-Fairfield, CA**	NA
299	Victoria, TX	(17.2)
77	Vineland, NJ	2.5
238	Virginia Beach-Norfolk, VA-NC	(7.6)
NA	Visalia-Porterville, CA**	NA
296	Waco, TX	(15.2)
270	Warner Robins, GA	(10.8)
NA	Warren-Farmington Hills, MI M.D.**	NA
NA	Washington (greater) DC-VA-MD**	NA
NA	Washington, DC-VA-MD-WV M.D.**	NA
112	Waterloo-Cedar Falls, IA	0.6
86	Wausau, WI	2.0
254	Wenatchee, WA	(8.8)
145	West Palm Beach, FL M.D.	(1.6)
206	Wheeling, WV-OH	(5.7)
300	Wichita Falls, TX	(17.3)
NA	Wichita, KS**	NA
4	Williamsport, PA	13.8
19	Wilmington, DE-MD-NJ M.D.	9.7
170	Wilmington, NC	(3.0)
34	Winchester, VA-WV	7.7
55	Winston-Salem, NC	5.3
224	Worcester, MA	(6.7)
259	Yakima, WA	(9.4)
287	Yuba City, CA	(13.5)
125	Yuma, AZ	(0.3)

Source: CQ Press using data from Federal Bureau of Investigation
"Crime in the United States 2006" (Uniform Crime Reports, September 24, 2007)
**Property crimes are offenses of burglary, larceny-theft, and motor vehicle theft. Attempts are included.*
***Not available.*

27. Percent Change in Property Crime Rate: 2005 to 2006 (continued)

National Percent Change = 2.8% Decrease*

RANK	METROPOLITAN AREA	% CHANGE
1	Lawrence, KS	37.3
2	Barnstable Town, MA	14.6
3	Pascagoula, MS	14.2
4	Williamsport, PA	13.8
5	Hagerstown-Martinsburg, MD-WV	13.3
6	Gainesville, FL	12.8
7	Pittsfield, MA	12.5
8	Sheboygan, WI	12.2
9	Kalamazoo-Portage, MI	12.1
10	Milwaukee, WI	11.5
11	Rocky Mount, NC	11.0
12	Muncie, IN	10.8
13	Rochester, MN	10.7
13	St. Cloud, MN	10.7
15	Punta Gorda, FL	10.5
16	Bangor, ME	10.2
17	Michigan City-La Porte, IN	9.9
18	Bloomington, IN	9.8
19	Wilmington, DE-MD-NJ M.D.	9.7
20	Alexandria, LA	9.6
21	Cumberland, MD-WV	9.5
22	Eau Claire, WI	9.4
23	Daytona Beach, FL	9.3
23	Detroit-Livonia-Dearborn, MI M.D.	9.3
25	Mobile, AL	9.2
26	Pensacola, FL	9.0
27	Oshkosh-Neenah, WI	8.9
28	Charlottesville, VA	8.8
29	Gadsden, AL	8.7
30	South Bend-Mishawaka, IN-MI	8.4
31	Mansfield, OH	8.3
32	Fayetteville, NC	8.2
33	Huntington-Ashland, WV-KY-OH	8.1
34	Port St. Lucie, FL	7.7
34	Winchester, VA-WV	7.7
36	Salisbury, MD	7.6
37	La Crosse, WI-MN	7.5
38	Portland, ME	7.3
39	Idaho Falls, ID	6.8
39	Lake Charles, LA	6.8
39	Ocean City, NJ	6.8
42	Harrisonburg, VA	6.7
43	Appleton, WI	6.5
44	Monroe, LA	6.2
44	Philadelphia (greater) PA-NJ-DE	6.2
46	Jackson, MI	6.1
47	Greenville, NC	5.8
47	Jackson, MS	5.8
49	Bethesda-Frederick, MD M.D.	5.7
49	Fargo, ND-MN	5.7
49	Philadelphia, PA M.D.	5.7
52	Palm Bay-Melbourne, FL	5.5
52	Spartanburg, SC	5.5
54	Camden, NJ M.D.	5.4
55	Baton Rouge, LA	5.3
55	Winston-Salem, NC	5.3
57	Albany, GA	5.2
58	Columbus, IN	4.9
58	Louisville, KY-IN	4.9
60	Lancaster, PA	4.8
61	Holland-Grand Haven, MI	4.6
62	Athens-Clarke County, GA	4.2
63	Grand Rapids-Wyoming, MI	4.1
64	Decatur, AL	4.0
64	Toledo, OH	4.0
66	San Luis Obispo, CA	3.8
67	Houma, LA	3.7
67	Shreveport-Bossier City, LA	3.7
69	Binghamton, NY	3.4
70	Altoona, PA	3.3
71	Dover, DE	3.2
72	San Francisco-S. Mateo, CA M.D.	3.1
73	Albany-Schenectady-Troy, NY	3.0
73	Monroe, MI	3.0
75	El Paso, TX	2.8
76	San Jose, CA	2.6
77	Erie, PA	2.5
77	Niles-Benton Harbor, MI	2.5
77	Vineland, NJ	2.5
80	Cape Coral-Fort Myers, FL	2.4
80	St. Louis, MO-IL	2.4
82	Janesville, WI	2.3
83	Syracuse, NY	2.2
84	Anchorage, AK	2.1
84	Fayetteville, AR-MO	2.1
86	Morgantown, WV	2.0
86	Wausau, WI	2.0
88	Flint, MI	1.9
88	Fond du Lac, WI	1.9
90	Bismarck, ND	1.8
90	Nassau-Suffolk, NY M.D.	1.8
92	Muskegon-Norton Shores, MI	1.7
93	Poughkeepsie, NY	1.6
93	Sarasota-Bradenton-Venice, FL	1.6
95	Charlotte-Gastonia, NC-SC	1.5
95	Springfield, MO	1.5
95	Tampa-St Petersburg, FL	1.5
98	Danville, VA	1.4
98	Edison, NJ M.D.	1.4
98	San Francisco (greater), CA	1.4
101	Columbus, GA-AL	1.3
101	State College, PA	1.3
103	Fort Collins-Loveland, CO	1.2
104	Clarksville, TN-KY	1.0
105	Burlington, NC	0.9
105	Manchester-Nashua, NH	0.9
105	Santa Fe, NM	0.9
105	Scranton--Wilkes-Barre, PA	0.9
109	Kingsport, TN-VA	0.7
109	Springfield, OH	0.7
109	Utica-Rome, NY	0.7
112	Augusta, GA-SC	0.6
112	Lafayette, IN	0.6
112	Raleigh-Cary, NC	0.6
112	Waterloo-Cedar Falls, IA	0.6
116	Baltimore-Towson, MD	0.4
116	Cincinnati-Middletown, OH-KY-IN	0.4
118	Battle Creek, MI	0.3
118	Jacksonville, FL	0.3
118	Oakland-Fremont, CA M.D.	0.3
121	Orlando, FL	0.2
122	El Centro, CA	0.1
123	Evansville, IN-KY	(0.1)
123	Fort Walton Beach, FL	(0.1)
125	Florence, SC	(0.3)
125	Madison, WI	(0.3)
125	Yuma, AZ	(0.3)
128	Greensboro-High Point, NC	(0.4)
128	Saginaw, MI	(0.4)
130	Sandusky, OH	(0.7)
131	Fort Smith, AR-OK	(0.8)
131	Morristown, TN	(0.8)
133	Dayton, OH	(0.9)
133	Oxnard-Thousand Oaks, CA	(0.9)
133	Springfield, MA	(0.9)
136	Charleston-North Charleston, SC	(1.1)
136	Lynchburg, VA	(1.1)
136	Rochester, NY	(1.1)
139	Goldsboro, NC	(1.2)
139	Indianapolis, IN	(1.2)
139	Memphis, TN-MS-AR	(1.2)
139	Midland, TX	(1.2)
143	Columbia, MO	(1.3)
143	Racine, WI	(1.3)
145	Macon, GA	(1.6)
145	West Palm Beach, FL M.D.	(1.6)
147	Napa, CA	(1.7)
148	Albuquerque, NM	(1.8)
148	Jonesboro, AR	(1.8)
148	Lawton, OK	(1.8)
151	Green Bay, WI	(1.9)
152	Hartford, CT	(2.0)
152	Hot Springs, AR	(2.0)
154	Blacksburg, VA	(2.1)
154	Montgomery, AL	(2.1)
156	Fort Lauderdale, FL M.D.	(2.2)
156	Little Rock, AR	(2.2)
156	Reno-Sparks, NV	(2.2)
159	Houston, TX	(2.3)
159	Omaha-Council Bluffs, NE-IA	(2.3)
161	Las Cruces, NM	(2.4)
162	Longview, TX	(2.5)
163	Columbus, OH	(2.6)
163	Laredo, TX	(2.6)
165	Iowa City, IA	(2.7)
166	Atlantic City, NJ	(2.8)
166	Buffalo-Niagara Falls, NY	(2.8)
166	Las Vegas-Paradise, NV	(2.8)
169	Elkhart-Goshen, IN	(2.9)
170	Santa Cruz-Watsonville, CA	(3.0)
170	Wilmington, NC	(3.0)

Note: All listings are for Metropolitan Statistical Areas (M.S.A.s) except for those ending with "M.D." Listings with "M.D." are Metropolitan Divisions which are smaller parts of eleven large M.S.A.s. See explanatory note at beginning of metropolitan area section on page 23.

RANK	METROPOLITAN AREA	% CHANGE
172	Lebanon, PA	(3.1)
172	Miami (greater), FL	(3.1)
174	Ames, IA	(3.2)
175	Brunswick, GA	(3.3)
175	Myrtle Beach, SC	(3.3)
175	Sacramento, CA	(3.3)
175	Stockton, CA	(3.3)
179	Bay City, MI	(3.5)
180	New York (greater), NY-NJ-PA	(3.6)
180	Sioux City, IA-NE-SD	(3.6)
182	Lewiston-Auburn, ME	(3.7)
182	Lincoln, NE	(3.7)
184	Killeen-Temple-Fort Hood, TX	(3.8)
185	Chico, CA	(3.9)
186	Columbia, SC	(4.0)
186	Greenville, SC	(4.0)
188	Miami-Dade County, FL M.D.	(4.1)
188	Pittsburgh, PA	(4.1)
190	Austin-Round Rock, TX	(4.6)
190	Bakersfield, CA	(4.6)
190	San Antonio, TX	(4.6)
190	Tacoma, WA M.D.	(4.6)
194	San Diego, CA	(4.7)
195	Bowling Green, KY	(4.9)
195	Knoxville, TN	(4.9)
195	New York-W. Plains NY-NJ M.D.	(4.9)
198	Huntsville, AL	(5.0)
199	Lansing-East Lansing, MI	(5.1)
200	St. Joseph, MO-KS	(5.2)
201	Cedar Rapids, IA	(5.3)
202	Sumter, SC	(5.4)
203	Casper, WY	(5.5)
204	Ogden-Clearfield, UT	(5.6)
204	Panama City-Lynn Haven, FL	(5.6)
206	Tallahassee, FL	(5.7)
206	Wheeling, WV-OH	(5.7)
208	Kokomo, IN	(5.8)
209	Kingston, NY	(5.9)
210	Naples-Marco Island, FL	(6.0)
210	Spokane, WA	(6.0)
212	Los Angeles County, CA M.D.	(6.1)
212	Los Angeles (greater), CA	(6.1)
212	Lubbock, TX	(6.1)
215	Santa Ana-Anaheim, CA M.D.	(6.3)
215	Seattle (greater), WA	(6.3)
215	Topeka, KS	(6.3)
218	Dallas-Plano-Irving, TX M.D.	(6.4)
219	Ann Arbor, MI	(6.5)
219	Brownsville-Harlingen, TX	(6.5)
219	Dallas (greater), TX	(6.5)
222	Newark-Union, NJ-PA M.D.	(6.6)
222	Santa Barbara-Santa Maria, CA	(6.6)
224	Lakeland, FL	(6.7)
224	Worcester, MA	(6.7)
226	Fort Worth-Arlington, TX M.D.	(6.8)
226	Phoenix-Mesa-Scottsdale, AZ	(6.8)
226	Riverside-San Bernardino, CA	(6.8)
229	Corpus Christi, TX	(6.9)
229	Merced, CA	(6.9)
229	Seattle-Bellevue, WA M.D.	(6.9)
232	Lima, OH	(7.0)
233	Nashville-Davidson, TN	(7.1)
234	Fresno, CA	(7.2)
235	Cheyenne, WY	(7.4)
236	Bremerton-Silverdale, WA	(7.5)
236	Reading, PA	(7.5)
238	College Station-Bryan, TX	(7.6)
238	Flagstaff, AZ	(7.6)
238	Virginia Beach-Norfolk, VA-NC	(7.6)
241	Anderson, SC	(7.7)
241	Dubuque, IA	(7.7)
241	Odessa, TX	(7.7)
244	Elizabethtown, KY	(7.8)
245	Jackson, TN	(7.9)
246	Chattanooga, TN-GA	(8.1)
246	Harrisburg-Carlisle, PA	(8.1)
248	Dothan, AL	(8.2)
248	Tulsa, OK	(8.2)
250	Salt Lake City, UT	(8.3)
251	Jefferson City, MO	(8.5)
252	Asheville, NC	(8.7)
252	Modesto, CA	(8.7)
254	Wenatchee, WA	(8.8)
255	Elmira, NY	(8.9)
256	Colorado Springs, CO	(9.0)
257	Bellingham, WA	(9.2)
258	Ocala, FL	(9.3)
259	Yakima, WA	(9.4)
260	Amarillo, TX	(9.5)
261	Hanford-Corcoran, CA	(9.6)
262	Pueblo, CO	(9.8)
262	Texarkana, TX-Texarkana, AR	(9.8)
264	Salinas, CA	(9.9)
265	Honolulu, HI	(10.0)
266	Lewiston, ID-WA	(10.1)
267	Charleston, WV	(10.2)
267	Tyler, TX	(10.2)
269	Pocatello, ID	(10.7)
270	Warner Robins, GA	(10.8)
271	Sebastian-Vero Beach, FL	(10.9)
272	Logan, UT-ID	(11.1)
273	Olympia, WA	(11.2)
274	Joplin, MO	(11.3)
275	Beaumont-Port Arthur, TX	(11.6)
276	Johnson City, TN	(11.8)
277	Sherman-Denison, TX	(11.9)
278	Valdosta, GA	(12.2)
279	Pine Bluff, AR	(12.5)
280	Longview, WA	(12.6)
280	Savannah, GA	(12.6)
280	Trenton-Ewing, NJ	(12.6)
283	Farmington, NM	(13.0)
284	Prescott, AZ	(13.1)
285	Kennewick-Richland-Pasco, WA	(13.4)
285	Roanoke, VA	(13.4)
287	Salem, OR	(13.5)
287	Yuba City, CA	(13.5)
289	Oklahoma City, OK	(13.7)
290	Carson City, NV	(14.0)
291	McAllen-Edinburg-Mission, TX	(14.1)
292	Coeur d'Alene, ID	(14.3)
293	Grand Junction, CO	(14.6)
293	San Angelo, TX	(14.6)
295	Sioux Falls, SD	(15.0)
296	Waco, TX	(15.2)
297	Santa Rosa-Petaluma, CA	(16.3)
298	Rome, GA	(16.4)
299	Victoria, TX	(17.2)
300	Gainesville, GA	(17.3)
300	Portland-Vancouver, OR-WA	(17.3)
300	Wichita Falls, TX	(17.3)
303	Denver-Aurora, CO	(17.4)
304	Missoula, MT	(17.5)
305	Madera, CA	(18.0)
306	Eugene-Springfield, OR	(18.4)
306	Redding, CA	(18.4)
308	Bend, OR	(18.9)
308	Provo-Orem, UT	(18.9)
310	Rapid City, SD	(19.5)
311	Greeley, CO	(20.3)
312	Medford, OR	(20.8)
313	Great Falls, MT	(21.1)
314	Billings, MT	(21.8)
315	Mount Vernon-Anacortes, WA	(22.2)
NA	Abilene, TX**	NA
NA	Atlanta, GA**	NA
NA	Birmingham-Hoover, AL**	NA
NA	Boise City-Nampa, ID**	NA
NA	Chicago, IL**	NA
NA	Cleveland-Elyria-Mentor, OH**	NA
NA	Cleveland, TN**	NA
NA	Dalton, GA**	NA
NA	Des Moines-West Des Moines, IA**	NA
NA	Detroit (greater), MI**	NA
NA	Duluth, MN-WI**	NA
NA	Durham, NC**	NA
NA	Fairbanks, AK**	NA
NA	Fort Wayne, IN**	NA
NA	Glens Falls, NY**	NA
NA	Grand Forks, ND-MN**	NA
NA	Hattiesburg, MS**	NA
NA	Ithaca, NY**	NA
NA	Jacksonville, NC**	NA
NA	Johnstown, PA**	NA
NA	Kansas City, MO-KS**	NA
NA	Lake Havasu City-Kingman, AZ**	NA
NA	Lexington-Fayette, KY**	NA
NA	Minneapolis-St. Paul, MN-WI**	NA
NA	New Orleans, LA**	NA
NA	Palm Coast, FL**	NA
NA	Richmond, VA**	NA
NA	Tucson, AZ**	NA
NA	Tuscaloosa, AL**	NA
NA	Vallejo-Fairfield, CA**	NA
NA	Visalia-Porterville, CA**	NA
NA	Warren-Farmington Hills, MI M.D.**	NA
NA	Washington (greater) DC-VA-MD**	NA
NA	Washington, DC-VA-MD-WV M.D.**	NA
NA	Wichita, KS**	NA

Source: CQ Press using data from Federal Bureau of Investigation "Crime in the United States 2006" (Uniform Crime Reports, September 24, 2007)

**Property crimes are offenses of burglary, larceny-theft, and motor vehicle theft. Attempts are included.*

***Not available.*

28. Percent Change in Property Crime Rate: 2002 to 2006

National Percent Change = 8.2% Decrease*

RANK	METROPOLITAN AREA	% CHANGE	RANK	METROPOLITAN AREA	% CHANGE	RANK	METROPOLITAN AREA	% CHANGE
NA	Abilene, TX**	NA	NA	Cleveland-Elyria-Mentor, OH**	NA	65	Glens Falls, NY	(4.8)
NA	Albany-Schenectady-Troy, NY**	NA	NA	Cleveland, TN**	NA	74	Goldsboro, NC	(6.1)
121	Albany, GA	(12.3)	NA	Coeur d'Alene, ID**	NA	NA	Grand Forks, ND-MN**	NA
90	Albuquerque, NM	(8.1)	NA	College Station-Bryan, TX**	NA	27	Grand Junction, CO	5.9
85	Alexandria, LA	(7.5)	123	Colorado Springs, CO	(12.5)	NA	Grand Rapids-Wyoming, MI**	NA
49	Altoona, PA	(2.3)	138	Columbia, MO	(14.8)	207	Great Falls, MT	(36.6)
144	Amarillo, TX	(15.4)	187	Columbia, SC	(24.2)	172	Greeley, CO	(21.6)
NA	Ames, IA**	NA	5	Columbus, GA-AL	18.2	137	Green Bay, WI	(14.7)
49	Anchorage, AK	(2.3)	NA	Columbus, IN**	NA	NA	Greensboro-High Point, NC**	NA
NA	Anderson, SC**	NA	163	Columbus, OH	(17.9)	134	Greenville, NC	(14.3)
NA	Ann Arbor, MI**	NA	38	Corpus Christi, TX	1.6	NA	Greenville, SC**	NA
NA	Appleton, WI**	NA	21	Cumberland, MD-WV	7.7	NA	Hagerstown-Martinsburg, MD-WV**	NA
95	Asheville, NC	(8.7)	NA	Dallas (greater), TX**	NA	NA	Hanford-Corcoran, CA**	NA
126	Athens-Clarke County, GA	(13.0)	140	Dallas-Plano-Irving, TX M.D.	(15.1)	NA	Harrisburg-Carlisle, PA**	NA
NA	Atlanta, GA**	NA	NA	Dalton, GA**	NA	NA	Harrisonburg, VA**	NA
NA	Atlantic City, NJ**	NA	4	Danville, VA	18.4	40	Hartford, CT	1.3
11	Augusta, GA-SC	11.1	55	Daytona Beach, FL	(3.5)	NA	Hattiesburg, MS**	NA
108	Austin-Round Rock, TX	(10.2)	NA	Dayton, OH**	NA	NA	Holland-Grand Haven, MI**	NA
6	Bakersfield, CA	16.6	11	Decatur, AL	11.1	204	Honolulu, HI	(30.9)
147	Baltimore-Towson, MD	(15.8)	156	Denver-Aurora, CO	(16.9)	NA	Hot Springs, AR**	NA
NA	Bangor, ME**	NA	NA	Des Moines-West Des Moines, IA**	NA	69	Houma, LA	(5.5)
NA	Barnstable Town, MA**	NA	42	Detroit (greater), MI	0.0	119	Houston, TX	(12.1)
152	Baton Rouge, LA	(16.5)	NA	Detroit-Livonia-Dearborn, MI M.D.**	NA	NA	Huntington-Ashland, WV-KY-OH**	NA
NA	Battle Creek, MI**	NA	NA	Dothan, AL**	NA	3	Huntsville, AL	18.5
NA	Bay City, MI**	NA	61	Dover, DE	(4.4)	NA	Idaho Falls, ID**	NA
151	Beaumont-Port Arthur, TX	(16.4)	139	Dubuque, IA	(14.9)	NA	Indianapolis, IN**	NA
67	Bellingham, WA	(5.1)	161	Duluth, MN-WI	(17.4)	202	Iowa City, IA	(30.5)
NA	Bend, OR**	NA	NA	Durham, NC**	NA	NA	Ithaca, NY**	NA
NA	Bethesda-Frederick, MD M.D.**	NA	130	Eau Claire, WI	(13.8)	97	Jacksonville, FL	(9.2)
162	Billings, MT	(17.6)	NA	Edison, NJ M.D.**	NA	NA	Jacksonville, NC**	NA
23	Binghamton, NY	6.4	NA	El Centro, CA**	NA	70	Jackson, MI	(5.6)
32	Birmingham-Hoover, AL	3.9	118	El Paso, TX	(12.0)	191	Jackson, MS	(24.9)
107	Bismarck, ND	(10.1)	NA	Elizabethtown, KY**	NA	16	Jackson, TN	9.9
NA	Blacksburg, VA**	NA	89	Elkhart-Goshen, IN	(8.0)	110	Janesville, WI	(10.4)
96	Bloomington, IN	(8.9)	NA	Elmira, NY**	NA	NA	Jefferson City, MO**	NA
198	Boise City-Nampa, ID	(28.5)	90	Erie, PA	(8.1)	NA	Johnson City, TN**	NA
NA	Bowling Green, KY**	NA	73	Eugene-Springfield, OR	(5.9)	NA	Johnstown, PA**	NA
179	Bremerton-Silverdale, WA	(22.6)	NA	Evansville, IN-KY**	NA	10	Jonesboro, AR	11.9
174	Brownsville-Harlingen, TX	(22.0)	NA	Fairbanks, AK**	NA	31	Joplin, MO	4.8
NA	Brunswick, GA**	NA	184	Fargo, ND-MN	(23.7)	NA	Kalamazoo-Portage, MI**	NA
55	Buffalo-Niagara Falls, NY	(3.5)	NA	Farmington, NM**	NA	NA	Kansas City, MO-KS**	NA
NA	Burlington, NC**	NA	NA	Fayetteville, AR-MO**	NA	81	Kennewick-Richland-Pasco, WA	(7.3)
NA	Camden, NJ M.D.**	NA	19	Fayetteville, NC	7.8	97	Killeen-Temple-Fort Hood, TX	(9.2)
106	Cape Coral-Fort Myers, FL	(10.0)	168	Flagstaff, AZ	(19.7)	NA	Kingsport, TN-VA**	NA
NA	Carson City, NV**	NA	52	Flint, MI	(2.7)	NA	Kingston, NY**	NA
62	Casper, WY	(4.5)	43	Florence, SC	(0.7)	81	Knoxville, TN	(7.3)
195	Cedar Rapids, IA	(27.3)	NA	Fond du Lac, WI**	NA	19	Kokomo, IN	7.8
122	Charleston-North Charleston, SC	(12.4)	125	Fort Collins-Loveland, CO	(12.7)	46	La Crosse, WI-MN	(1.6)
35	Charleston, WV	3.3	67	Fort Lauderdale, FL M.D.	(5.1)	77	Lafayette, IN	(6.4)
NA	Charlotte-Gastonia, NC-SC**	NA	172	Fort Smith, AR-OK	(21.6)	114	Lake Charles, LA	(11.3)
NA	Charlottesville, VA**	NA	22	Fort Walton Beach, FL	6.8	NA	Lake Havasu City-Kingman, AZ**	NA
115	Chattanooga, TN-GA	(11.4)	NA	Fort Wayne, IN**	NA	156	Lakeland, FL	(16.9)
101	Cheyenne, WY	(9.5)	149	Fort Worth-Arlington, TX M.D.	(16.1)	99	Lancaster, PA	(9.3)
NA	Chicago, IL**	NA	127	Fresno, CA	(13.1)	110	Lansing-East Lansing, MI	(10.4)
102	Chico, CA	(9.6)	13	Gadsden, AL	10.7	86	Laredo, TX	(7.7)
108	Cincinnati-Middletown, OH-KY-IN	(10.2)	62	Gainesville, FL	(4.5)	NA	Las Cruces, NM**	NA
203	Clarksville, TN-KY	(30.7)	NA	Gainesville, GA**	NA	17	Las Vegas-Paradise, NV	8.5

Note: All listings are for Metropolitan Statistical Areas (M.S.A.s) except for those ending with "M.D." Listings with "M.D." are Metropolitan Divisions which are smaller parts of eleven large M.S.A.s. See explanatory note at beginning of metropolitan area section on page 23.

RANK	METROPOLITAN AREA	% CHANGE
1	Lawrence, KS	30.6
47	Lawton, OK	(1.7)
NA	Lebanon, PA**	NA
167	Lewiston-Auburn, ME	(19.0)
NA	Lewiston, ID-WA**	NA
NA	Lexington-Fayette, KY**	NA
NA	Lima, OH**	NA
166	Lincoln, NE	(18.7)
92	Little Rock, AR	(8.3)
NA	Logan, UT-ID**	NA
53	Longview, TX	(2.8)
NA	Longview, WA**	NA
128	Los Angeles County, CA M.D.	(13.2)
NA	Los Angeles (greater), CA**	NA
123	Louisville, KY-IN	(12.5)
47	Lubbock, TX	(1.7)
94	Lynchburg, VA	(8.6)
NA	Macon, GA**	NA
NA	Madera, CA**	NA
117	Madison, WI	(11.9)
NA	Manchester-Nashua, NH**	NA
NA	Mansfield, OH**	NA
133	McAllen-Edinburg-Mission, TX	(14.2)
194	Medford, OR	(26.9)
NA	Memphis, TN-MS-AR**	NA
160	Merced, CA	(17.3)
NA	Miami (greater), FL**	NA
154	Miami-Dade County, FL M.D.	(16.7)
NA	Michigan City-La Porte, IN**	NA
NA	Midland, TX**	NA
NA	Milwaukee, WI**	NA
60	Minneapolis-St. Paul, MN-WI	(4.3)
NA	Missoula, MT**	NA
NA	Mobile, AL**	NA
103	Modesto, CA	(9.9)
NA	Monroe, LA**	NA
NA	Monroe, MI**	NA
187	Montgomery, AL	(24.2)
NA	Morgantown, WV**	NA
NA	Morristown, TN**	NA
NA	Mount Vernon-Anacortes, WA**	NA
23	Muncie, IN	6.4
NA	Muskegon-Norton Shores, MI**	NA
80	Myrtle Beach, SC	(7.0)
NA	Napa, CA**	NA
208	Naples-Marco Island, FL	(37.3)
158	Nashville-Davidson, TN	(17.1)
NA	Nassau-Suffolk, NY M.D.**	NA
192	New Orleans, LA	(25.7)
NA	New York (greater), NY-NJ-PA**	NA
158	New York-W. Plains NY-NJ M.D.	(17.1)
170	Newark-Union, NJ-PA M.D.	(21.2)
NA	Niles-Benton Harbor, MI**	NA
64	Oakland-Fremont, CA M.D.	(4.7)
164	Ocala, FL	(18.3)
NA	Ocean City, NJ**	NA
NA	Odessa, TX**	NA
NA	Ogden-Clearfield, UT**	NA
176	Oklahoma City, OK	(22.1)
131	Olympia, WA	(13.9)
186	Omaha-Council Bluffs, NE-IA	(24.1)
116	Orlando, FL	(11.7)
NA	Oshkosh-Neenah, WI**	NA
NA	Oxnard-Thousand Oaks, CA**	NA
120	Palm Bay-Melbourne, FL	(12.2)
NA	Palm Coast, FL**	NA
197	Panama City-Lynn Haven, FL	(28.1)
NA	Pascagoula, MS**	NA
66	Pensacola, FL	(4.9)
33	Philadelphia (greater) PA-NJ-DE	3.7
NA	Philadelphia, PA M.D.**	NA
177	Phoenix-Mesa-Scottsdale, AZ	(22.3)
169	Pine Bluff, AR	(20.8)
53	Pittsburgh, PA	(2.8)
NA	Pittsfield, MA**	NA
37	Pocatello, ID	2.4
145	Port St. Lucie, FL	(15.5)
180	Portland-Vancouver, OR-WA	(22.8)
NA	Portland, ME**	NA
NA	Poughkeepsie, NY**	NA
NA	Prescott, AZ**	NA
198	Provo-Orem, UT	(28.5)
9	Pueblo, CO	14.1
7	Punta Gorda, FL	15.9
43	Racine, WI	(0.7)
NA	Raleigh-Cary, NC**	NA
210	Rapid City, SD	(47.0)
71	Reading, PA	(5.8)
58	Redding, CA	(4.0)
58	Reno-Sparks, NV	(4.0)
196	Richmond, VA	(27.6)
75	Riverside-San Bernardino, CA	(6.2)
NA	Roanoke, VA**	NA
128	Rochester, MN	(13.2)
75	Rochester, NY	(6.2)
34	Rocky Mount, NC	3.5
NA	Rome, GA**	NA
92	Sacramento, CA	(8.3)
NA	Saginaw, MI**	NA
205	Salem, OR	(34.7)
29	Salinas, CA	5.3
NA	Salisbury, MD**	NA
NA	Salt Lake City, UT**	NA
131	San Angelo, TX	(13.9)
150	San Antonio, TX	(16.3)
41	San Diego, CA	0.7
NA	San Francisco (greater), CA**	NA
18	San Francisco-S. Mateo, CA M.D.	8.0
2	San Jose, CA	18.8
57	San Luis Obispo, CA	(3.6)
NA	Sandusky, OH**	NA
112	Santa Ana-Anaheim, CA M.D.	(10.7)
NA	Santa Barbara-Santa Maria, CA**	NA
8	Santa Cruz-Watsonville, CA	15.7
77	Santa Fe, NM	(6.4)
201	Santa Rosa-Petaluma, CA	(30.2)
86	Sarasota-Bradenton-Venice, FL	(7.7)
178	Savannah, GA	(22.4)
29	Scranton--Wilkes-Barre, PA	5.3
NA	Seattle (greater), WA**	NA
36	Seattle-Bellevue, WA M.D.	2.6
NA	Sebastian-Vero Beach, FL**	NA
45	Sheboygan, WI	(1.5)
155	Sherman-Denison, TX	(16.8)
71	Shreveport-Bossier City, LA	(5.8)
209	Sioux City, IA-NE-SD	(43.0)
185	Sioux Falls, SD	(23.9)
134	South Bend-Mishawaka, IN-MI	(14.3)
NA	Spartanburg, SC**	NA
181	Spokane, WA	(23.1)
NA	Springfield, MA**	NA
39	Springfield, MO	1.5
NA	Springfield, OH**	NA
28	State College, PA	5.4
51	Stockton, CA	(2.6)
84	St. Cloud, MN	(7.4)
165	St. Joseph, MO-KS	(18.5)
NA	St. Louis, MO-IL**	NA
152	Sumter, SC	(16.5)
NA	Syracuse, NY**	NA
103	Tacoma, WA M.D.	(9.9)
193	Tallahassee, FL	(26.0)
146	Tampa-St Petersburg, FL	(15.7)
113	Texarkana, TX-Texarkana, AR	(11.2)
99	Toledo, OH	(9.3)
183	Topeka, KS	(23.6)
200	Trenton-Ewing, NJ	(30.1)
NA	Tucson, AZ**	NA
136	Tulsa, OK	(14.4)
86	Tuscaloosa, AL	(7.7)
171	Tyler, TX	(21.3)
140	Utica-Rome, NY	(15.1)
NA	Valdosta, GA**	NA
NA	Vallejo-Fairfield, CA**	NA
189	Victoria, TX	(24.5)
81	Vineland, NJ	(7.3)
143	Virginia Beach-Norfolk, VA-NC	(15.3)
15	Visalia-Porterville, CA	10.6
181	Waco, TX	(23.1)
NA	Warner Robins, GA**	NA
NA	Warren-Farmington Hills, MI M.D.**	NA
NA	Washington (greater) DC-VA-MD**	NA
NA	Washington, DC-VA-MD-WV M.D.**	NA
206	Waterloo-Cedar Falls, IA	(35.0)
79	Wausau, WI	(6.8)
NA	Wenatchee, WA**	NA
190	West Palm Beach, FL M.D.	(24.6)
NA	Wheeling, WV-OH**	NA
148	Wichita Falls, TX	(16.0)
103	Wichita, KS	(9.9)
26	Williamsport, PA	6.0
NA	Wilmington, DE-MD-NJ M.D.**	NA
174	Wilmington, NC	(22.0)
NA	Winchester, VA-WV**	NA
NA	Winston-Salem, NC**	NA
NA	Worcester, MA**	NA
23	Yakima, WA	6.4
140	Yuba City, CA	(15.1)
13	Yuma, AZ	10.7

Source: CQ Press using data from Federal Bureau of Investigation "Crime in the United States 2006" (Uniform Crime Reports, September 24, 2007)

**Property crimes are offenses of burglary, larceny-theft, and motor vehicle theft. Attempts are included.*

***Not available.*

28. Percent Change in Property Crime Rate: 2002 to 2006 (continued)

National Percent Change = 8.2% Decrease*

RANK	METROPOLITAN AREA	% CHANGE
1	Lawrence, KS	30.6
2	San Jose, CA	18.8
3	Huntsville, AL	18.5
4	Danville, VA	18.4
5	Columbus, GA-AL	18.2
6	Bakersfield, CA	16.6
7	Punta Gorda, FL	15.9
8	Santa Cruz-Watsonville, CA	15.7
9	Pueblo, CO	14.1
10	Jonesboro, AR	11.9
11	Augusta, GA-SC	11.1
11	Decatur, AL	11.1
13	Gadsden, AL	10.7
13	Yuma, AZ	10.7
15	Visalia-Porterville, CA	10.6
16	Jackson, TN	9.9
17	Las Vegas-Paradise, NV	8.5
18	San Francisco-S. Mateo, CA M.D.	8.0
19	Fayetteville, NC	7.8
19	Kokomo, IN	7.8
21	Cumberland, MD-WV	7.7
22	Fort Walton Beach, FL	6.8
23	Binghamton, NY	6.4
23	Muncie, IN	6.4
23	Yakima, WA	6.4
26	Williamsport, PA	6.0
27	Grand Junction, CO	5.9
28	State College, PA	5.4
29	Salinas, CA	5.3
29	Scranton--Wilkes-Barre, PA	5.3
31	Joplin, MO	4.8
32	Birmingham-Hoover, AL	3.9
33	Philadelphia (greater) PA-NJ-DE	3.7
34	Rocky Mount, NC	3.5
35	Charleston, WV	3.3
36	Seattle-Bellevue, WA M.D.	2.6
37	Pocatello, ID	2.4
38	Corpus Christi, TX	1.6
39	Springfield, MO	1.5
40	Hartford, CT	1.3
41	San Diego, CA	0.7
42	Detroit (greater), MI	0.0
43	Florence, SC	(0.7)
43	Racine, WI	(0.7)
45	Sheboygan, WI	(1.5)
46	La Crosse, WI-MN	(1.6)
47	Lawton, OK	(1.7)
47	Lubbock, TX	(1.7)
49	Altoona, PA	(2.3)
49	Anchorage, AK	(2.3)
51	Stockton, CA	(2.6)
52	Flint, MI	(2.7)
53	Longview, TX	(2.8)
53	Pittsburgh, PA	(2.8)
55	Buffalo-Niagara Falls, NY	(3.5)
55	Daytona Beach, FL	(3.5)
57	San Luis Obispo, CA	(3.6)
58	Redding, CA	(4.0)
58	Reno-Sparks, NV	(4.0)
60	Minneapolis-St. Paul, MN-WI	(4.3)
61	Dover, DE	(4.4)
62	Casper, WY	(4.5)
62	Gainesville, FL	(4.5)
64	Oakland-Fremont, CA M.D.	(4.7)
65	Glens Falls, NY	(4.8)
66	Pensacola, FL	(4.9)
67	Bellingham, WA	(5.1)
67	Fort Lauderdale, FL M.D.	(5.1)
69	Houma, LA	(5.5)
70	Jackson, MI	(5.6)
71	Reading, PA	(5.8)
71	Shreveport-Bossier City, LA	(5.8)
73	Eugene-Springfield, OR	(5.9)
74	Goldsboro, NC	(6.1)
75	Riverside-San Bernardino, CA	(6.2)
75	Rochester, NY	(6.2)
77	Lafayette, IN	(6.4)
77	Santa Fe, NM	(6.4)
79	Wausau, WI	(6.8)
80	Myrtle Beach, SC	(7.0)
81	Kennewick-Richland-Pasco, WA	(7.3)
81	Knoxville, TN	(7.3)
81	Vineland, NJ	(7.3)
84	St. Cloud, MN	(7.4)
85	Alexandria, LA	(7.5)
86	Laredo, TX	(7.7)
86	Sarasota-Bradenton-Venice, FL	(7.7)
86	Tuscaloosa, AL	(7.7)
89	Elkhart-Goshen, IN	(8.0)
90	Albuquerque, NM	(8.1)
90	Erie, PA	(8.1)
92	Little Rock, AR	(8.3)
92	Sacramento, CA	(8.3)
94	Lynchburg, VA	(8.6)
95	Asheville, NC	(8.7)
96	Bloomington, IN	(8.9)
97	Jacksonville, FL	(9.2)
97	Killeen-Temple-Fort Hood, TX	(9.2)
99	Lancaster, PA	(9.3)
99	Toledo, OH	(9.3)
101	Cheyenne, WY	(9.5)
102	Chico, CA	(9.6)
103	Modesto, CA	(9.9)
103	Tacoma, WA M.D.	(9.9)
103	Wichita, KS	(9.9)
106	Cape Coral-Fort Myers, FL	(10.0)
107	Bismarck, ND	(10.1)
108	Austin-Round Rock, TX	(10.2)
108	Cincinnati-Middletown, OH-KY-IN	(10.2)
110	Janesville, WI	(10.4)
110	Lansing-East Lansing, MI	(10.4)
112	Santa Ana-Anaheim, CA M.D.	(10.7)
113	Texarkana, TX-Texarkana, AR	(11.2)
114	Lake Charles, LA	(11.3)
115	Chattanooga, TN-GA	(11.4)
116	Orlando, FL	(11.7)
117	Madison, WI	(11.9)
118	El Paso, TX	(12.0)
119	Houston, TX	(12.1)
120	Palm Bay-Melbourne, FL	(12.2)
121	Albany, GA	(12.3)
122	Charleston-North Charleston, SC	(12.4)
123	Colorado Springs, CO	(12.5)
123	Louisville, KY-IN	(12.5)
125	Fort Collins-Loveland, CO	(12.7)
126	Athens-Clarke County, GA	(13.0)
127	Fresno, CA	(13.1)
128	Los Angeles County, CA M.D.	(13.2)
128	Rochester, MN	(13.2)
130	Eau Claire, WI	(13.8)
131	Olympia, WA	(13.9)
131	San Angelo, TX	(13.9)
133	McAllen-Edinburg-Mission, TX	(14.2)
134	Greenville, NC	(14.3)
134	South Bend-Mishawaka, IN-MI	(14.3)
136	Tulsa, OK	(14.4)
137	Green Bay, WI	(14.7)
138	Columbia, MO	(14.8)
139	Dubuque, IA	(14.9)
140	Dallas-Plano-Irving, TX M.D.	(15.1)
140	Utica-Rome, NY	(15.1)
140	Yuba City, CA	(15.1)
143	Virginia Beach-Norfolk, VA-NC	(15.3)
144	Amarillo, TX	(15.4)
145	Port St. Lucie, FL	(15.5)
146	Tampa-St Petersburg, FL	(15.7)
147	Baltimore-Towson, MD	(15.8)
148	Wichita Falls, TX	(16.0)
149	Fort Worth-Arlington, TX M.D.	(16.1)
150	San Antonio, TX	(16.3)
151	Beaumont-Port Arthur, TX	(16.4)
152	Baton Rouge, LA	(16.5)
152	Sumter, SC	(16.5)
154	Miami-Dade County, FL M.D.	(16.7)
155	Sherman-Denison, TX	(16.8)
156	Denver-Aurora, CO	(16.9)
156	Lakeland, FL	(16.9)
158	Nashville-Davidson, TN	(17.1)
158	New York-W. Plains NY-NJ M.D.	(17.1)
160	Merced, CA	(17.3)
161	Duluth, MN-WI	(17.4)
162	Billings, MT	(17.6)
163	Columbus, OH	(17.9)
164	Ocala, FL	(18.3)
165	St. Joseph, MO-KS	(18.5)
166	Lincoln, NE	(18.7)
167	Lewiston-Auburn, ME	(19.0)
168	Flagstaff, AZ	(19.7)
169	Pine Bluff, AR	(20.8)
170	Newark-Union, NJ-PA M.D.	(21.2)
171	Tyler, TX	(21.3)

Note: All listings are for Metropolitan Statistical Areas (M.S.A.s) except for those ending with "M.D." Listings with "M.D." are Metropolitan Divisions which are smaller parts of eleven large M.S.A.s. See explanatory note at beginning of metropolitan area section on page 23.

RANK	METROPOLITAN AREA	% CHANGE
172	Fort Smith, AR-OK	(21.6)
172	Greeley, CO	(21.6)
174	Brownsville-Harlingen, TX	(22.0)
174	Wilmington, NC	(22.0)
176	Oklahoma City, OK	(22.1)
177	Phoenix-Mesa-Scottsdale, AZ	(22.3)
178	Savannah, GA	(22.4)
179	Bremerton-Silverdale, WA	(22.6)
180	Portland-Vancouver, OR-WA	(22.8)
181	Spokane, WA	(23.1)
181	Waco, TX	(23.1)
183	Topeka, KS	(23.6)
184	Fargo, ND-MN	(23.7)
185	Sioux Falls, SD	(23.9)
186	Omaha-Council Bluffs, NE-IA	(24.1)
187	Columbia, SC	(24.2)
187	Montgomery, AL	(24.2)
189	Victoria, TX	(24.5)
190	West Palm Beach, FL M.D.	(24.6)
191	Jackson, MS	(24.9)
192	New Orleans, LA	(25.7)
193	Tallahassee, FL	(26.0)
194	Medford, OR	(26.9)
195	Cedar Rapids, IA	(27.3)
196	Richmond, VA	(27.6)
197	Panama City-Lynn Haven, FL	(28.1)
198	Boise City-Nampa, ID	(28.5)
198	Provo-Orem, UT	(28.5)
200	Trenton-Ewing, NJ	(30.1)
201	Santa Rosa-Petaluma, CA	(30.2)
202	Iowa City, IA	(30.5)
203	Clarksville, TN-KY	(30.7)
204	Honolulu, HI	(30.9)
205	Salem, OR	(34.7)
206	Waterloo-Cedar Falls, IA	(35.0)
207	Great Falls, MT	(36.6)
208	Naples-Marco Island, FL	(37.3)
209	Sioux City, IA-NE-SD	(43.0)
210	Rapid City, SD	(47.0)
NA	Abilene, TX**	NA
NA	Albany-Schenectady-Troy, NY**	NA
NA	Ames, IA**	NA
NA	Anderson, SC**	NA
NA	Ann Arbor, MI**	NA
NA	Appleton, WI**	NA
NA	Atlanta, GA**	NA
NA	Atlantic City, NJ**	NA
NA	Bangor, ME**	NA
NA	Barnstable Town, MA**	NA
NA	Battle Creek, MI**	NA
NA	Bay City, MI**	NA
NA	Bend, OR**	NA
NA	Bethesda-Frederick, MD M.D.**	NA
NA	Blacksburg, VA**	NA
NA	Bowling Green, KY**	NA
NA	Brunswick, GA**	NA
NA	Burlington, NC**	NA
NA	Camden, NJ M.D.**	NA
NA	Carson City, NV**	NA
NA	Charlotte-Gastonia, NC-SC**	NA
NA	Charlottesville, VA**	NA
NA	Chicago, IL**	NA
NA	Cleveland-Elyria-Mentor, OH**	NA
NA	Cleveland, TN**	NA
NA	Coeur d'Alene, ID**	NA
NA	College Station-Bryan, TX**	NA
NA	Columbus, IN**	NA
NA	Dallas (greater), TX**	NA
NA	Dalton, GA**	NA
NA	Dayton, OH**	NA
NA	Des Moines-West Des Moines, IA**	NA
NA	Detroit-Livonia-Dearborn, MI M.D.**	NA
NA	Dothan, AL**	NA
NA	Durham, NC**	NA
NA	Edison, NJ M.D.**	NA
NA	El Centro, CA**	NA
NA	Elizabethtown, KY**	NA
NA	Elmira, NY**	NA
NA	Evansville, IN-KY**	NA
NA	Fairbanks, AK**	NA
NA	Farmington, NM**	NA
NA	Fayetteville, AR-MO**	NA
NA	Fond du Lac, WI**	NA
NA	Fort Wayne, IN**	NA
NA	Gainesville, GA**	NA
NA	Grand Forks, ND-MN**	NA
NA	Grand Rapids-Wyoming, MI**	NA
NA	Greensboro-High Point, NC**	NA
NA	Greenville, SC**	NA
NA	Hagerstown-Martinsburg, MD-WV**	NA
NA	Hanford-Corcoran, CA**	NA
NA	Harrisburg-Carlisle, PA**	NA
NA	Harrisonburg, VA**	NA
NA	Hattiesburg, MS**	NA
NA	Holland-Grand Haven, MI**	NA
NA	Hot Springs, AR**	NA
NA	Huntington-Ashland, WV-KY-OH**	NA
NA	Idaho Falls, ID**	NA
NA	Indianapolis, IN**	NA
NA	Ithaca, NY**	NA
NA	Jacksonville, NC**	NA
NA	Jefferson City, MO**	NA
NA	Johnson City, TN**	NA
NA	Johnstown, PA**	NA
NA	Kalamazoo-Portage, MI**	NA
NA	Kansas City, MO-KS**	NA
NA	Kingsport, TN-VA**	NA
NA	Kingston, NY**	NA
NA	Lake Havasu City-Kingman, AZ**	NA
NA	Las Cruces, NM**	NA
NA	Lebanon, PA**	NA
NA	Lewiston, ID-WA**	NA
NA	Lexington-Fayette, KY**	NA
NA	Lima, OH**	NA
NA	Logan, UT-ID**	NA
NA	Longview, WA**	NA
NA	Los Angeles (greater), CA**	NA
NA	Macon, GA**	NA
NA	Madera, CA**	NA
NA	Manchester-Nashua, NH**	NA
NA	Mansfield, OH**	NA
NA	Memphis, TN-MS-AR**	NA
NA	Miami (greater), FL**	NA
NA	Michigan City-La Porte, IN**	NA
NA	Midland, TX**	NA
NA	Milwaukee, WI**	NA
NA	Missoula, MT**	NA
NA	Mobile, AL**	NA
NA	Monroe, LA**	NA
NA	Monroe, MI**	NA
NA	Morgantown, WV**	NA
NA	Morristown, TN**	NA
NA	Mount Vernon-Anacortes, WA**	NA
NA	Muskegon-Norton Shores, MI**	NA
NA	Napa, CA**	NA
NA	Nassau-Suffolk, NY M.D.**	NA
NA	New York (greater), NY-NJ-PA**	NA
NA	Niles-Benton Harbor, MI**	NA
NA	Ocean City, NJ**	NA
NA	Odessa, TX**	NA
NA	Ogden-Clearfield, UT**	NA
NA	Oshkosh-Neenah, WI**	NA
NA	Oxnard-Thousand Oaks, CA**	NA
NA	Palm Coast, FL**	NA
NA	Pascagoula, MS**	NA
NA	Philadelphia, PA M.D.**	NA
NA	Pittsfield, MA**	NA
NA	Portland, ME**	NA
NA	Poughkeepsie, NY**	NA
NA	Prescott, AZ**	NA
NA	Raleigh-Cary, NC**	NA
NA	Roanoke, VA**	NA
NA	Rome, GA**	NA
NA	Saginaw, MI**	NA
NA	Salisbury, MD**	NA
NA	Salt Lake City, UT**	NA
NA	San Francisco (greater), CA**	NA
NA	Sandusky, OH**	NA
NA	Santa Barbara-Santa Maria, CA**	NA
NA	Seattle (greater), WA**	NA
NA	Sebastian-Vero Beach, FL**	NA
NA	Spartanburg, SC**	NA
NA	Springfield, MA**	NA
NA	Springfield, OH**	NA
NA	St. Louis, MO-IL**	NA
NA	Syracuse, NY**	NA
NA	Tucson, AZ**	NA
NA	Valdosta, GA**	NA
NA	Vallejo-Fairfield, CA**	NA
NA	Warner Robins, GA**	NA
NA	Warren-Farmington Hills, MI M.D.**	NA
NA	Washington (greater) DC-VA-MD**	NA
NA	Washington, DC-VA-MD-WV M.D.**	NA
NA	Wenatchee, WA**	NA
NA	Wheeling, WV-OH**	NA
NA	Wilmington, DE-MD-NJ M.D.**	NA
NA	Winchester, VA-WV**	NA
NA	Winston-Salem, NC**	NA
NA	Worcester, MA**	NA

Source: CQ Press using data from Federal Bureau of Investigation "Crime in the United States 2006" (Uniform Crime Reports, September 24, 2007)

**Property crimes are offenses of burglary, larceny-theft, and motor vehicle theft. Attempts are included.*

***Not available.*

29. Burglaries in 2006

National Total = 2,183,746 Burglaries*

RANK	METROPOLITAN AREA	BURGLARY	RANK	METROPOLITAN AREA	BURGLARY	RANK	METROPOLITAN AREA	BURGLARY
214	Abilene, TX	1,531	33	Cleveland-Elyria-Mentor, OH	18,242	322	Glens Falls, NY	576
102	Albany-Schenectady-Troy, NY	4,849	287	Cleveland, TN	845	210	Goldsboro, NC	1,561
175	Albany, GA	2,162	279	Coeur d'Alene, ID	874	NA	Grand Forks, ND-MN**	NA
59	Albuquerque, NM	8,972	193	College Station-Bryan, TX	1,944	284	Grand Junction, CO	852
176	Alexandria, LA	2,151	108	Colorado Springs, CO	4,469	84	Grand Rapids-Wyoming, MI	5,813
295	Altoona, PA	783	285	Columbia, MO	847	347	Great Falls, MT	233
152	Amarillo, TX	2,591	90	Columbia, SC	5,483	197	Greeley, CO	1,833
326	Ames, IA	512	128	Columbus, GA-AL	3,340	232	Green Bay, WI	1,390
196	Anchorage, AK	1,835	339	Columbus, IN	382	58	Greensboro-High Point, NC	9,047
192	Anderson, SC	1,952	23	Columbus, OH	21,420	166	Greenville, NC	2,294
185	Ann Arbor, MI	2,061	110	Corpus Christi, TX	4,352	80	Greenville, SC	6,096
304	Appleton, WI	696	305	Cumberland, MD-WV	694	231	Hagerstown-Martinsburg, MD-WV	1,392
125	Asheville, NC	3,510	2	Dallas (greater), TX	60,538	308	Hanford-Corcoran, CA	682
212	Athens-Clarke County, GA	1,536	7	Dallas-Plano-Irving, TX M.D.	41,037	181	Harrisburg-Carlisle, PA	2,105
NA	Atlanta, GA**	NA	267	Dalton, GA	988	336	Harrisonburg, VA	421
188	Atlantic City, NJ	1,985	310	Danville, VA	673	96	Hartford, CT	5,119
97	Augusta, GA-SC	5,117	92	Daytona Beach, FL	5,407	238	Hattiesburg, MS	1,352
48	Austin-Round Rock, TX	11,429	72	Dayton, OH	7,323	260	Holland-Grand Haven, MI	1,031
62	Bakersfield, CA	8,712	244	Decatur, AL	1,275	91	Honolulu, HI	5,482
30	Baltimore-Towson, MD	19,052	34	Denver-Aurora, CO	17,924	178	Hot Springs, AR	2,145
294	Bangor, ME	784	120	Des Moines-West Des Moines, IA	3,549	226	Houma, LA	1,412
169	Barnstable Town, MA	2,213	9	Detroit (greater), MI	36,513	5	Houston, TX	52,392
64	Baton Rouge, LA	8,443	17	Detroit-Livonia-Dearborn, MI M.D.	24,507	158	Huntington-Ashland, WV-KY-OH	2,442
237	Battle Creek, MI	1,366	243	Dothan, AL	1,291	116	Huntsville, AL	3,886
312	Bay City, MI	662	275	Dover, DE	901	306	Idaho Falls, ID	693
107	Beaumont-Port Arthur, TX	4,531	325	Dubuque, IA	533	39	Indianapolis, IN	15,085
198	Bellingham, WA	1,818	202	Duluth, MN-WI	1,738	323	Iowa City, IA	560
271	Bend, OR	964	89	Durham, NC	5,567	342	Ithaca, NY	334
103	Bethesda-Frederick, MD M.D.	4,804	301	Eau Claire, WI	708	44	Jacksonville, FL	12,821
318	Billings, MT	609	65	Edison, NJ M.D.	8,432	236	Jacksonville, NC	1,374
268	Binghamton, NY	983	171	El Centro, CA	2,192	262	Jackson, MI	1,007
47	Birmingham-Hoover, AL	11,565	144	El Paso, TX	2,771	82	Jackson, MS	5,951
337	Bismarck, ND	412	333	Elizabethtown, KY	434	215	Jackson, TN	1,527
298	Blacksburg, VA	747	211	Elkhart-Goshen, IN	1,538	252	Janesville, WI	1,167
241	Bloomington, IN	1,334	335	Elmira, NY	422	299	Jefferson City, MO	723
130	Boise City-Nampa, ID	3,292	227	Erie, PA	1,411	208	Johnson City, TN	1,585
295	Bowling Green, KY	783	131	Eugene-Springfield, OR	3,280	310	Johnstown, PA	673
201	Bremerton-Silverdale, WA	1,742	190	Evansville, IN-KY	1,970	171	Jonesboro, AR	2,192
117	Brownsville-Harlingen, TX	3,882	341	Fairbanks, AK	337	219	Joplin, MO	1,495
257	Brunswick, GA	1,069	290	Fargo, ND-MN	818	132	Kalamazoo-Portage, MI	3,228
68	Buffalo-Niagara Falls, NY	8,261	300	Farmington, NM	709	37	Kansas City, MO-KS	16,681
224	Burlington, NC	1,451	147	Fayetteville, AR-MO	2,731	220	Kennewick-Richland-Pasco, WA	1,490
77	Camden, NJ M.D.	6,618	78	Fayetteville, NC	6,362	114	Killeen-Temple-Fort Hood, TX	3,979
85	Cape Coral-Fort Myers, FL	5,736	293	Flagstaff, AZ	786	163	Kingsport, TN-VA	2,374
345	Carson City, NV	291	88	Flint, MI	5,575	303	Kingston, NY	698
319	Casper, WY	592	157	Florence, SC	2,447	86	Knoxville, TN	5,638
222	Cedar Rapids, IA	1,484	346	Fond du Lac, WI	290	266	Kokomo, IN	995
93	Charleston-North Charleston, SC	5,390	233	Fort Collins-Loveland, CO	1,386	334	La Crosse, WI-MN	428
151	Charleston, WV	2,627	41	Fort Lauderdale, FL M.D.	13,218	245	Lafayette, IN	1,259
19	Charlotte-Gastonia, NC-SC	21,797	160	Fort Smith, AR-OK	2,435	138	Lake Charles, LA	3,056
283	Charlottesville, VA	853	258	Fort Walton Beach, FL	1,044	161	Lake Havasu City-Kingman, AZ	2,426
111	Chattanooga, TN-GA	4,307	149	Fort Wayne, IN	2,707	81	Lakeland, FL	5,979
338	Cheyenne, WY	401	26	Fort Worth-Arlington, TX M.D.	19,501	179	Lancaster, PA	2,118
NA	Chicago, IL**	NA	70	Fresno, CA	7,761	143	Lansing-East Lansing, MI	2,804
184	Chico, CA	2,085	242	Gadsden, AL	1,306	200	Laredo, TX	1,778
38	Cincinnati-Middletown, OH-KY-IN	16,008	142	Gainesville, FL	2,880	239	Las Cruces, NM	1,343
167	Clarksville, TN-KY	2,254	270	Gainesville, GA	965	27	Las Vegas-Paradise, NV	19,476

Note: All listings are for Metropolitan Statistical Areas (M.S.A.s) except for those ending with "M.D." Listings with "M.D." are Metropolitan Divisions which are smaller parts of eleven large M.S.A.s. See explanatory note at beginning of metropolitan area section on page 23.

RANK	METROPOLITAN AREA	BURGLARY
291	Lawrence, KS	794
206	Lawton, OK	1,632
332	Lebanon, PA	437
324	Lewiston-Auburn, ME	545
340	Lewiston, ID-WA	368
129	Lexington-Fayette, KY	3,322
249	Lima, OH	1,219
182	Lincoln, NE	2,099
56	Little Rock, AR	9,280
344	Logan, UT-ID	298
168	Longview, TX	2,228
248	Longview, WA	1,223
4	Los Angeles County, CA M.D.	55,499
1	Los Angeles (greater), CA	68,227
52	Louisville, KY-IN	11,048
126	Lubbock, TX	3,447
278	Lynchburg, VA	879
127	Macon, GA	3,378
256	Madera, CA	1,074
145	Madison, WI	2,753
217	Manchester-Nashua, NH	1,516
216	Mansfield, OH	1,526
83	McAllen-Edinburg-Mission, TX	5,933
272	Medford, OR	960
21	Memphis, TN-MS-AR	21,653
154	Merced, CA	2,526
6	Miami (greater), FL	50,611
16	Miami-Dade County, FL M.D.	24,525
297	Michigan City-La Porte, IN	766
264	Midland, TX	1,005
61	Milwaukee, WI	8,856
24	Minneapolis-St. Paul, MN-WI	20,704
328	Missoula, MT	466
101	Mobile, AL	4,959
100	Modesto, CA	5,002
162	Monroe, LA	2,384
281	Monroe, MI	867
109	Montgomery, AL	4,399
307	Morgantown, WV	689
288	Morristown, TN	834
253	Mount Vernon-Anacortes, WA	1,150
285	Muncie, IN	847
235	Muskegon-Norton Shores, MI	1,378
136	Myrtle Beach, SC	3,130
301	Napa, CA	708
223	Naples-Marco Island, FL	1,456
50	Nashville-Davidson, TN	11,413
74	Nassau-Suffolk, NY M.D.	6,983
49	New Orleans, LA	11,415
3	New York (greater), NY-NJ-PA	58,230
10	New York-W. Plains NY-NJ M.D.	33,287
55	Newark-Union, NJ-PA M.D.	9,528
259	Niles-Benton Harbor, MI	1,040
25	Oakland-Fremont, CA M.D.	19,988
179	Ocala, FL	2,118
276	Ocean City, NJ	888
265	Odessa, TX	1,004
158	Ogden-Clearfield, UT	2,442
40	Oklahoma City, OK	14,169
203	Olympia, WA	1,686
95	Omaha-Council Bluffs, NE-IA	5,256
22	Orlando, FL	21,602
316	Oshkosh-Neenah, WI	627
124	Oxnard-Thousand Oaks, CA	3,516
104	Palm Bay-Melbourne, FL	4,735
330	Palm Coast, FL	460
233	Panama City-Lynn Haven, FL	1,386
186	Pascagoula, MS	2,040
113	Pensacola, FL	3,994
14	Philadelphia (greater) PA-NJ-DE	30,658
32	Philadelphia, PA M.D.	18,951
8	Phoenix-Mesa-Scottsdale, AZ	39,272
187	Pine Bluff, AR	2,039
51	Pittsburgh, PA	11,241
280	Pittsfield, MA	871
343	Pocatello, ID	325
133	Port St. Lucie, FL	3,222
42	Portland-Vancouver, OR-WA	13,190
150	Portland, ME	2,693
177	Poughkeepsie, NY	2,149
254	Prescott, AZ	1,116
174	Provo-Orem, UT	2,175
199	Pueblo, CO	1,791
239	Punta Gorda, FL	1,343
230	Racine, WI	1,399
71	Raleigh-Cary, NC	7,527
320	Rapid City, SD	590
189	Reading, PA	1,981
251	Redding, CA	1,202
119	Reno-Sparks, NV	3,621
76	Richmond, VA	6,781
11	Riverside-San Bernardino, CA	33,166
218	Roanoke, VA	1,515
289	Rochester, MN	820
87	Rochester, NY	5,584
156	Rocky Mount, NC	2,492
292	Rome, GA	788
29	Sacramento, CA	19,181
165	Saginaw, MI	2,348
171	Salem, OR	2,192
148	Salinas, CA	2,712
229	Salisbury, MD	1,400
69	Salt Lake City, UT	7,946
255	San Angelo, TX	1,075
28	San Antonio, TX	19,367
35	San Diego, CA	17,855
13	San Francisco (greater), CA	30,914
53	San Francisco-S. Mateo, CA M.D.	10,926
57	San Jose, CA	9,165
221	San Luis Obispo, CA	1,486
320	Sandusky, OH	590
45	Santa Ana-Anaheim, CA M.D.	12,728
194	Santa Barbara-Santa Maria, CA	1,927
191	Santa Cruz-Watsonville, CA	1,961
139	Santa Fe, NM	2,976
170	Santa Rosa-Petaluma, CA	2,209
75	Sarasota-Bradenton-Venice, FL	6,838
146	Savannah, GA	2,736
155	Scranton--Wilkes-Barre, PA	2,497
12	Seattle (greater), WA	31,676
18	Seattle-Bellevue, WA M.D.	23,246
276	Sebastian-Vero Beach, FL	888
331	Sheboygan, WI	454
263	Sherman-Denison, TX	1,006
112	Shreveport-Bossier City, LA	4,091
282	Sioux City, IA-NE-SD	858
269	Sioux Falls, SD	972
137	South Bend-Mishawaka, IN-MI	3,063
134	Spartanburg, SC	3,182
121	Spokane, WA	3,547
94	Springfield, MA	5,353
135	Springfield, MO	3,135
153	Springfield, OH	2,553
329	State College, PA	461
73	Stockton, CA	7,234
309	St. Cloud, MN	677
261	St. Joseph, MO-KS	1,027
31	St. Louis, MO-IL	18,997
228	Sumter, SC	1,407
118	Syracuse, NY	3,774
66	Tacoma, WA M.D.	8,430
115	Tallahassee, FL	3,891
15	Tampa-St Petersburg, FL	26,017
246	Texarkana, TX-Texarkana, AR	1,247
63	Toledo, OH	8,593
183	Topeka, KS	2,097
195	Trenton-Ewing, NJ	1,860
67	Tucson, AZ	8,365
59	Tulsa, OK	8,972
164	Tuscaloosa, AL	2,352
204	Tyler, TX	1,658
207	Utica-Rome, NY	1,620
250	Valdosta, GA	1,214
141	Vallejo-Fairfield, CA	2,884
273	Victoria, TX	958
213	Vineland, NJ	1,532
54	Virginia Beach-Norfolk, VA-NC	9,877
106	Visalia-Porterville, CA	4,611
140	Waco, TX	2,960
274	Warner Robins, GA	916
46	Warren-Farmington Hills, MI M.D.	12,006
20	Washington (greater) DC-VA-MD	21,759
36	Washington, DC-VA-MD-WV M.D.	16,955
247	Waterloo-Cedar Falls, IA	1,241
327	Wausau, WI	480
315	Wenatchee, WA	629
43	West Palm Beach, FL M.D.	12,868
317	Wheeling, WV-OH	622
209	Wichita Falls, TX	1,583
98	Wichita, KS	5,106
313	Williamsport, PA	656
99	Wilmington, DE-MD-NJ M.D.	5,089
105	Wilmington, NC	4,658
314	Winchester, VA-WV	650
79	Winston-Salem, NC	6,356
122	Worcester, MA	3,535
123	Yakima, WA	3,518
205	Yuba City, CA	1,637
225	Yuma, AZ	1,426

Source: Federal Bureau of Investigation

"Crime in the United States 2006" (Uniform Crime Reports, September 24, 2007)

**Burglary is the unlawful entry of a structure to commit a felony or theft. Attempts are included.*

***Not available.*

29. Burglaries in 2006 (continued)

National Total = 2,183,746 Burglaries*

RANK	METROPOLITAN AREA	BURGLARY
1	Los Angeles (greater), CA	68,227
2	Dallas (greater), TX	60,538
3	New York (greater), NY-NJ-PA	58,230
4	Los Angeles County, CA M.D.	55,499
5	Houston, TX	52,392
6	Miami (greater), FL	50,611
7	Dallas-Plano-Irving, TX M.D.	41,037
8	Phoenix-Mesa-Scottsdale, AZ	39,272
9	Detroit (greater), MI	36,513
10	New York-W. Plains NY-NJ M.D.	33,287
11	Riverside-San Bernardino, CA	33,166
12	Seattle (greater), WA	31,676
13	San Francisco (greater), CA	30,914
14	Philadelphia (greater) PA-NJ-DE	30,658
15	Tampa-St Petersburg, FL	26,017
16	Miami-Dade County, FL M.D.	24,525
17	Detroit-Livonia-Dearborn, MI M.D.	24,507
18	Seattle-Bellevue, WA M.D.	23,246
19	Charlotte-Gastonia, NC-SC	21,797
20	Washington (greater) DC-VA-MD	21,759
21	Memphis, TN-MS-AR	21,653
22	Orlando, FL	21,602
23	Columbus, OH	21,420
24	Minneapolis-St. Paul, MN-WI	20,704
25	Oakland-Fremont, CA M.D.	19,988
26	Fort Worth-Arlington, TX M.D.	19,501
27	Las Vegas-Paradise, NV	19,476
28	San Antonio, TX	19,367
29	Sacramento, CA	19,181
30	Baltimore-Towson, MD	19,052
31	St. Louis, MO-IL	18,997
32	Philadelphia, PA M.D.	18,951
33	Cleveland-Elyria-Mentor, OH	18,242
34	Denver-Aurora, CO	17,924
35	San Diego, CA	17,855
36	Washington, DC-VA-MD-WV M.D.	16,955
37	Kansas City, MO-KS	16,681
38	Cincinnati-Middletown, OH-KY-IN	16,008
39	Indianapolis, IN	15,085
40	Oklahoma City, OK	14,169
41	Fort Lauderdale, FL M.D.	13,218
42	Portland-Vancouver, OR-WA	13,190
43	West Palm Beach, FL M.D.	12,868
44	Jacksonville, FL	12,821
45	Santa Ana-Anaheim, CA M.D.	12,728
46	Warren-Farmington Hills, MI M.D.	12,006
47	Birmingham-Hoover, AL	11,565
48	Austin-Round Rock, TX	11,429
49	New Orleans, LA	11,415
50	Nashville-Davidson, TN	11,413
51	Pittsburgh, PA	11,241
52	Louisville, KY-IN	11,048
53	San Francisco-S. Mateo, CA M.D.	10,926
54	Virginia Beach-Norfolk, VA-NC	9,877
55	Newark-Union, NJ-PA M.D.	9,528
56	Little Rock, AR	9,280
57	San Jose, CA	9,165
58	Greensboro-High Point, NC	9,047
59	Albuquerque, NM	8,972
59	Tulsa, OK	8,972
61	Milwaukee, WI	8,856
62	Bakersfield, CA	8,712
63	Toledo, OH	8,593
64	Baton Rouge, LA	8,443
65	Edison, NJ M.D.	8,432
66	Tacoma, WA M.D.	8,430
67	Tucson, AZ	8,365
68	Buffalo-Niagara Falls, NY	8,261
69	Salt Lake City, UT	7,946
70	Fresno, CA	7,761
71	Raleigh-Cary, NC	7,527
72	Dayton, OH	7,323
73	Stockton, CA	7,234
74	Nassau-Suffolk, NY M.D.	6,983
75	Sarasota-Bradenton-Venice, FL	6,838
76	Richmond, VA	6,781
77	Camden, NJ M.D.	6,618
78	Fayetteville, NC	6,362
79	Winston-Salem, NC	6,356
80	Greenville, SC	6,096
81	Lakeland, FL	5,979
82	Jackson, MS	5,951
83	McAllen-Edinburg-Mission, TX	5,933
84	Grand Rapids-Wyoming, MI	5,813
85	Cape Coral-Fort Myers, FL	5,736
86	Knoxville, TN	5,638
87	Rochester, NY	5,584
88	Flint, MI	5,575
89	Durham, NC	5,567
90	Columbia, SC	5,483
91	Honolulu, HI	5,482
92	Daytona Beach, FL	5,407
93	Charleston-North Charleston, SC	5,390
94	Springfield, MA	5,353
95	Omaha-Council Bluffs, NE-IA	5,256
96	Hartford, CT	5,119
97	Augusta, GA-SC	5,117
98	Wichita, KS	5,106
99	Wilmington, DE-MD-NJ M.D.	5,089
100	Modesto, CA	5,002
101	Mobile, AL	4,959
102	Albany-Schenectady-Troy, NY	4,849
103	Bethesda-Frederick, MD M.D.	4,804
104	Palm Bay-Melbourne, FL	4,735
105	Wilmington, NC	4,658
106	Visalia-Porterville, CA	4,611
107	Beaumont-Port Arthur, TX	4,531
108	Colorado Springs, CO	4,469
109	Montgomery, AL	4,399
110	Corpus Christi, TX	4,352
111	Chattanooga, TN-GA	4,307
112	Shreveport-Bossier City, LA	4,091
113	Pensacola, FL	3,994
114	Killeen-Temple-Fort Hood, TX	3,979
115	Tallahassee, FL	3,891
116	Huntsville, AL	3,886
117	Brownsville-Harlingen, TX	3,882
118	Syracuse, NY	3,774
119	Reno-Sparks, NV	3,621
120	Des Moines-West Des Moines, IA	3,549
121	Spokane, WA	3,547
122	Worcester, MA	3,535
123	Yakima, WA	3,518
124	Oxnard-Thousand Oaks, CA	3,516
125	Asheville, NC	3,510
126	Lubbock, TX	3,447
127	Macon, GA	3,378
128	Columbus, GA-AL	3,340
129	Lexington-Fayette, KY	3,322
130	Boise City-Nampa, ID	3,292
131	Eugene-Springfield, OR	3,280
132	Kalamazoo-Portage, MI	3,228
133	Port St. Lucie, FL	3,222
134	Spartanburg, SC	3,182
135	Springfield, MO	3,135
136	Myrtle Beach, SC	3,130
137	South Bend-Mishawaka, IN-MI	3,063
138	Lake Charles, LA	3,056
139	Santa Fe, NM	2,976
140	Waco, TX	2,960
141	Vallejo-Fairfield, CA	2,884
142	Gainesville, FL	2,880
143	Lansing-East Lansing, MI	2,804
144	El Paso, TX	2,771
145	Madison, WI	2,753
146	Savannah, GA	2,736
147	Fayetteville, AR-MO	2,731
148	Salinas, CA	2,712
149	Fort Wayne, IN	2,707
150	Portland, ME	2,693
151	Charleston, WV	2,627
152	Amarillo, TX	2,591
153	Springfield, OH	2,553
154	Merced, CA	2,526
155	Scranton--Wilkes-Barre, PA	2,497
156	Rocky Mount, NC	2,492
157	Florence, SC	2,447
158	Huntington-Ashland, WV-KY-OH	2,442
158	Ogden-Clearfield, UT	2,442
160	Fort Smith, AR-OK	2,435
161	Lake Havasu City-Kingman, AZ	2,426
162	Monroe, LA	2,384
163	Kingsport, TN-VA	2,374
164	Tuscaloosa, AL	2,352
165	Saginaw, MI	2,348
166	Greenville, NC	2,294
167	Clarksville, TN-KY	2,254
168	Longview, TX	2,228
169	Barnstable Town, MA	2,213
170	Santa Rosa-Petaluma, CA	2,209
171	El Centro, CA	2,192

Note: All listings are for Metropolitan Statistical Areas (M.S.A.s) except for those ending with "M.D." Listings with "M.D." are Metropolitan Divisions which are smaller parts of eleven large M.S.A.s. See explanatory note at beginning of metropolitan area section on page 23.

RANK	METROPOLITAN AREA	BURGLARY
171	Jonesboro, AR	2,192
171	Salem, OR	2,192
174	Provo-Orem, UT	2,175
175	Albany, GA	2,162
176	Alexandria, LA	2,151
177	Poughkeepsie, NY	2,149
178	Hot Springs, AR	2,145
179	Lancaster, PA	2,118
179	Ocala, FL	2,118
181	Harrisburg-Carlisle, PA	2,105
182	Lincoln, NE	2,099
183	Topeka, KS	2,097
184	Chico, CA	2,085
185	Ann Arbor, MI	2,061
186	Pascagoula, MS	2,040
187	Pine Bluff, AR	2,039
188	Atlantic City, NJ	1,985
189	Reading, PA	1,981
190	Evansville, IN-KY	1,970
191	Santa Cruz-Watsonville, CA	1,961
192	Anderson, SC	1,952
193	College Station-Bryan, TX	1,944
194	Santa Barbara-Santa Maria, CA	1,927
195	Trenton-Ewing, NJ	1,860
196	Anchorage, AK	1,835
197	Greeley, CO	1,833
198	Bellingham, WA	1,818
199	Pueblo, CO	1,791
200	Laredo, TX	1,778
201	Bremerton-Silverdale, WA	1,742
202	Duluth, MN-WI	1,738
203	Olympia, WA	1,686
204	Tyler, TX	1,658
205	Yuba City, CA	1,637
206	Lawton, OK	1,632
207	Utica-Rome, NY	1,620
208	Johnson City, TN	1,585
209	Wichita Falls, TX	1,583
210	Goldsboro, NC	1,561
211	Elkhart-Goshen, IN	1,538
212	Athens-Clarke County, GA	1,536
213	Vineland, NJ	1,532
214	Abilene, TX	1,531
215	Jackson, TN	1,527
216	Mansfield, OH	1,526
217	Manchester-Nashua, NH	1,516
218	Roanoke, VA	1,515
219	Joplin, MO	1,495
220	Kennewick-Richland-Pasco, WA	1,490
221	San Luis Obispo, CA	1,486
222	Cedar Rapids, IA	1,484
223	Naples-Marco Island, FL	1,456
224	Burlington, NC	1,451
225	Yuma, AZ	1,426
226	Houma, LA	1,412
227	Erie, PA	1,411
228	Sumter, SC	1,407
229	Salisbury, MD	1,400
230	Racine, WI	1,399
231	Hagerstown-Martinsburg, MD-WV	1,392
232	Green Bay, WI	1,390
233	Fort Collins-Loveland, CO	1,386
233	Panama City-Lynn Haven, FL	1,386
235	Muskegon-Norton Shores, MI	1,378
236	Jacksonville, NC	1,374
237	Battle Creek, MI	1,366
238	Hattiesburg, MS	1,352
239	Las Cruces, NM	1,343
239	Punta Gorda, FL	1,343
241	Bloomington, IN	1,334
242	Gadsden, AL	1,306
243	Dothan, AL	1,291
244	Decatur, AL	1,275
245	Lafayette, IN	1,259
246	Texarkana, TX-Texarkana, AR	1,247
247	Waterloo-Cedar Falls, IA	1,241
248	Longview, WA	1,223
249	Lima, OH	1,219
250	Valdosta, GA	1,214
251	Redding, CA	1,202
252	Janesville, WI	1,167
253	Mount Vernon-Anacortes, WA	1,150
254	Prescott, AZ	1,116
255	San Angelo, TX	1,075
256	Madera, CA	1,074
257	Brunswick, GA	1,069
258	Fort Walton Beach, FL	1,044
259	Niles-Benton Harbor, MI	1,040
260	Holland-Grand Haven, MI	1,031
261	St. Joseph, MO-KS	1,027
262	Jackson, MI	1,007
263	Sherman-Denison, TX	1,006
264	Midland, TX	1,005
265	Odessa, TX	1,004
266	Kokomo, IN	995
267	Dalton, GA	988
268	Binghamton, NY	983
269	Sioux Falls, SD	972
270	Gainesville, GA	965
271	Bend, OR	964
272	Medford, OR	960
273	Victoria, TX	958
274	Warner Robins, GA	916
275	Dover, DE	901
276	Ocean City, NJ	888
276	Sebastian-Vero Beach, FL	888
278	Lynchburg, VA	879
279	Coeur d'Alene, ID	874
280	Pittsfield, MA	871
281	Monroe, MI	867
282	Sioux City, IA-NE-SD	858
283	Charlottesville, VA	853
284	Grand Junction, CO	852
285	Columbia, MO	847
285	Muncie, IN	847
287	Cleveland, TN	845
288	Morristown, TN	834
289	Rochester, MN	820
290	Fargo, ND-MN	818
291	Lawrence, KS	794
292	Rome, GA	788
293	Flagstaff, AZ	786
294	Bangor, ME	784
295	Altoona, PA	783
295	Bowling Green, KY	783
297	Michigan City-La Porte, IN	766
298	Blacksburg, VA	747
299	Jefferson City, MO	723
300	Farmington, NM	709
301	Eau Claire, WI	708
301	Napa, CA	708
303	Kingston, NY	698
304	Appleton, WI	696
305	Cumberland, MD-WV	694
306	Idaho Falls, ID	693
307	Morgantown, WV	689
308	Hanford-Corcoran, CA	682
309	St. Cloud, MN	677
310	Danville, VA	673
310	Johnstown, PA	673
312	Bay City, MI	662
313	Williamsport, PA	656
314	Winchester, VA-WV	650
315	Wenatchee, WA	629
316	Oshkosh-Neenah, WI	627
317	Wheeling, WV-OH	622
318	Billings, MT	609
319	Casper, WY	592
320	Rapid City, SD	590
320	Sandusky, OH	590
322	Glens Falls, NY	576
323	Iowa City, IA	560
324	Lewiston-Auburn, ME	545
325	Dubuque, IA	533
326	Ames, IA	512
327	Wausau, WI	480
328	Missoula, MT	466
329	State College, PA	461
330	Palm Coast, FL	460
331	Sheboygan, WI	454
332	Lebanon, PA	437
333	Elizabethtown, KY	434
334	La Crosse, WI-MN	428
335	Elmira, NY	422
336	Harrisonburg, VA	421
337	Bismarck, ND	412
338	Cheyenne, WY	401
339	Columbus, IN	382
340	Lewiston, ID-WA	368
341	Fairbanks, AK	337
342	Ithaca, NY	334
343	Pocatello, ID	325
344	Logan, UT-ID	298
345	Carson City, NV	291
346	Fond du Lac, WI	290
347	Great Falls, MT	233
NA	Atlanta, GA**	NA
NA	Chicago, IL**	NA
NA	Grand Forks, ND-MN**	NA

Source: Federal Bureau of Investigation
"Crime in the United States 2006" (Uniform Crime Reports, September 24, 2007)
**Burglary is the unlawful entry of a structure to commit a felony or theft. Attempts are included.*
***Not available.*

30. Burglary Rate in 2006

National Rate = 729.4 Burglaries per 100,000 Population*

RANK	METROPOLITAN AREA	RATE
109	Abilene, TX	940.6
252	Albany-Schenectady-Troy, NY	569.7
29	Albany, GA	1,286.4
58	Albuquerque, NM	1,109.3
10	Alexandria, LA	1,533.7
229	Altoona, PA	617.0
68	Amarillo, TX	1,055.7
222	Ames, IA	637.0
225	Anchorage, AK	622.3
63	Anderson, SC	1,095.1
235	Ann Arbor, MI	604.4
339	Appleton, WI	322.3
128	Asheville, NC	876.0
139	Athens-Clarke County, GA	850.0
NA	Atlanta, GA**	NA
189	Atlantic City, NJ	731.9
106	Augusta, GA-SC	958.0
174	Austin-Round Rock, TX	765.2
54	Bakersfield, CA	1,140.9
195	Baltimore-Towson, MD	715.4
266	Bangor, ME	533.1
101	Barnstable Town, MA	971.1
41	Baton Rouge, LA	1,213.9
95	Battle Creek, MI	983.8
233	Bay City, MI	608.7
49	Beaumont-Port Arthur, TX	1,148.8
99	Bellingham, WA	974.2
209	Bend, OR	670.8
314	Bethesda-Frederick, MD M.D.	417.2
317	Billings, MT	411.5
323	Binghamton, NY	394.6
71	Birmingham-Hoover, AL	1,051.4
315	Bismarck, ND	415.2
285	Blacksburg, VA	489.6
181	Bloomington, IN	745.7
245	Boise City-Nampa, ID	589.5
199	Bowling Green, KY	700.0
197	Bremerton-Silverdale, WA	711.6
89	Brownsville-Harlingen, TX	997.9
70	Brunswick, GA	1,052.2
194	Buffalo-Niagara Falls, NY	717.9
82	Burlington, NC	1,012.3
267	Camden, NJ M.D.	530.8
75	Cape Coral-Fort Myers, FL	1,035.5
280	Carson City, NV	502.3
146	Casper, WY	838.7
239	Cedar Rapids, IA	599.1
123	Charleston-North Charleston, SC	892.2
134	Charleston, WV	856.5
17	Charlotte-Gastonia, NC-SC	1,405.5
306	Charlottesville, VA	448.2
132	Chattanooga, TN-GA	859.5
296	Cheyenne, WY	465.6
NA	Chicago, IL**	NA
104	Chico, CA	964.8
170	Cincinnati-Middletown, OH-KY-IN	771.1
114	Clarksville, TN-KY	914.9
133	Cleveland-Elyria-Mentor, OH	856.9
169	Cleveland, TN	772.3
210	Coeur d'Alene, ID	667.1
92	College Station-Bryan, TX	996.4
179	Colorado Springs, CO	746.6
262	Columbia, MO	548.6
161	Columbia, SC	782.6
52	Columbus, GA-AL	1,142.7
273	Columbus, IN	516.0
33	Columbus, OH	1,252.1
78	Corpus Christi, TX	1,023.3
203	Cumberland, MD-WV	687.9
83	Dallas (greater), TX	1,011.6
77	Dallas-Plano-Irving, TX M.D.	1,025.0
191	Dalton, GA	726.8
229	Danville, VA	617.0
64	Daytona Beach, FL	1,085.0
130	Dayton, OH	867.0
135	Decatur, AL	851.8
183	Denver-Aurora, CO	745.4
208	Des Moines-West Des Moines, IA	675.7
153	Detroit (greater), MI	815.5
36	Detroit-Livonia-Dearborn, MI M.D.	1,229.5
110	Dothan, AL	936.7
227	Dover, DE	618.5
247	Dubuque, IA	578.6
224	Duluth, MN-WI	627.2
43	Durham, NC	1,196.5
302	Eau Claire, WI	457.9
334	Edison, NJ M.D.	365.7
18	El Centro, CA	1,394.2
328	El Paso, TX	373.4
325	Elizabethtown, KY	389.2
162	Elkhart-Goshen, IN	782.1
293	Elmira, NY	470.2
279	Erie, PA	502.7
105	Eugene-Springfield, OR	962.8
256	Evansville, IN-KY	559.8
NA	Fairbanks, AK**	NA
309	Fargo, ND-MN	442.0
258	Farmington, NM	554.2
211	Fayetteville, AR-MO	666.7
5	Fayetteville, NC	1,805.2
232	Flagstaff, AZ	611.2
31	Flint, MI	1,259.1
39	Florence, SC	1,214.2
342	Fond du Lac, WI	290.9
281	Fort Collins-Loveland, CO	500.2
190	Fort Lauderdale, FL M.D.	731.2
142	Fort Smith, AR-OK	845.4
255	Fort Walton Beach, FL	563.6
212	Fort Wayne, IN	665.0
94	Fort Worth-Arlington, TX M.D.	984.4
126	Fresno, CA	876.5
32	Gadsden, AL	1,254.3
46	Gainesville, FL	1,178.8
254	Gainesville, GA	564.0
307	Glens Falls, NY	446.8
23	Goldsboro, NC	1,337.3
NA	Grand Forks, ND-MN**	NA
218	Grand Junction, CO	643.9
177	Grand Rapids-Wyoming, MI	755.7
343	Great Falls, MT	290.0
160	Greeley, CO	785.8
297	Green Bay, WI	465.5
24	Greensboro-High Point, NC	1,315.0
20	Greenville, NC	1,383.3
79	Greenville, SC	1,015.2
261	Hagerstown-Martinsburg, MD-WV	552.8
291	Hanford-Corcoran, CA	471.3
320	Harrisburg-Carlisle, PA	403.0
329	Harrisonburg, VA	373.2
275	Hartford, CT	510.9
76	Hattiesburg, MS	1,029.0
319	Holland-Grand Haven, MI	404.7
238	Honolulu, HI	600.6
1	Hot Springs, AR	2,267.0
180	Houma, LA	746.1
103	Houston, TX	964.9
136	Huntington-Ashland, WV-KY-OH	851.2
72	Huntsville, AL	1,044.6
241	Idaho Falls, ID	595.4
115	Indianapolis, IN	913.4
321	Iowa City, IA	402.1
336	Ithaca, NY	333.0
84	Jacksonville, FL	1,010.0
125	Jacksonville, NC	883.7
229	Jackson, MI	617.0
51	Jackson, MS	1,142.9
21	Jackson, TN	1,360.2
186	Janesville, WI	738.1
283	Jefferson City, MO	498.9
151	Johnson City, TN	828.3
303	Johnstown, PA	454.1
3	Jonesboro, AR	1,933.6
121	Joplin, MO	893.1
81	Kalamazoo-Portage, MI	1,013.3
138	Kansas City, MO-KS	850.3
213	Kennewick-Richland-Pasco, WA	662.9
60	Killeen-Temple-Fort Hood, TX	1,100.7
165	Kingsport, TN-VA	778.7
326	Kingston, NY	381.0
140	Knoxville, TN	849.4
98	Kokomo, IN	975.2
337	La Crosse, WI-MN	330.7
205	Lafayette, IN	682.2
9	Lake Charles, LA	1,653.6
34	Lake Havasu City-Kingman, AZ	1,248.2
65	Lakeland, FL	1,083.0
311	Lancaster, PA	431.4
228	Lansing-East Lansing, MI	617.4
171	Laredo, TX	769.5
200	Las Cruces, NM	699.4
59	Las Vegas-Paradise, NV	1,101.8

Note: All listings are for Metropolitan Statistical Areas (M.S.A.s) except for those ending with "M.D." Listings with "M.D." are Metropolitan Divisions which are smaller parts of eleven large M.S.A.s. See explanatory note at beginning of metropolitan area section on page 23.

RANK	METROPOLITAN AREA	RATE
173	Lawrence, KS	766.1
14	Lawton, OK	1,438.9
335	Lebanon, PA	347.7
278	Lewiston-Auburn, ME	504.4
234	Lewiston, ID-WA	608.6
172	Lexington-Fayette, KY	766.8
50	Lima, OH	1,146.1
185	Lincoln, NE	741.5
16	Little Rock, AR	1,426.3
345	Logan, UT-ID	261.5
67	Longview, TX	1,075.2
35	Longview, WA	1,235.4
259	Los Angeles County, CA M.D.	553.6
271	Los Angeles (greater), CA	523.2
119	Louisville, KY-IN	907.3
28	Lubbock, TX	1,294.4
333	Lynchburg, VA	367.4
15	Macon, GA	1,431.0
182	Madera, CA	745.5
276	Madison, WI	510.8
327	Manchester-Nashua, NH	376.4
44	Mansfield, OH	1,191.2
137	McAllen-Edinburg-Mission, TX	850.6
288	Medford, OR	483.6
7	Memphis, TN-MS-AR	1,700.3
74	Merced, CA	1,035.7
113	Miami (greater), FL	917.9
80	Miami-Dade County, FL M.D.	1,015.1
202	Michigan City-La Porte, IN	688.6
155	Midland, TX	805.2
246	Milwaukee, WI	583.2
216	Minneapolis-St. Paul, MN-WI	654.5
300	Missoula, MT	461.2
37	Mobile, AL	1,224.3
96	Modesto, CA	980.7
12	Monroe, LA	1,469.7
253	Monroe, MI	564.6
38	Montgomery, AL	1,220.3
237	Morgantown, WV	601.2
223	Morristown, TN	630.7
87	Mount Vernon-Anacortes, WA	999.0
193	Muncie, IN	723.1
159	Muskegon-Norton Shores, MI	786.9
22	Myrtle Beach, SC	1,357.8
268	Napa, CA	528.5
295	Naples-Marco Island, FL	466.0
157	Nashville-Davidson, TN	792.2
346	Nassau-Suffolk, NY M.D.	248.0
116	New Orleans, LA	912.8
341	New York (greater), NY-NJ-PA	310.0
344	New York-W. Plains NY-NJ M.D.	289.2
308	Newark-Union, NJ-PA M.D.	442.2
221	Niles-Benton Harbor, MI	641.2
156	Oakland-Fremont, CA M.D.	803.1
204	Ocala, FL	686.4
120	Ocean City, NJ	893.7
164	Odessa, TX	779.0
287	Ogden-Clearfield, UT	485.8
40	Oklahoma City, OK	1,214.1
192	Olympia, WA	724.2
219	Omaha-Council Bluffs, NE-IA	642.9
62	Orlando, FL	1,098.9
324	Oshkosh-Neenah, WI	391.7
310	Oxnard-Thousand Oaks, CA	437.7
126	Palm Bay-Melbourne, FL	876.5
243	Palm Coast, FL	592.0
144	Panama City-Lynn Haven, FL	843.7
27	Pascagoula, MS	1,302.4
122	Pensacola, FL	892.9
269	Philadelphia (greater) PA-NJ-DE	525.5
286	Philadelphia, PA M.D.	486.7
97	Phoenix-Mesa-Scottsdale, AZ	978.7
4	Pine Bluff, AR	1,922.5
292	Pittsburgh, PA	470.7
215	Pittsfield, MA	656.6
332	Pocatello, ID	368.7
150	Port St. Lucie, FL	831.6
226	Portland-Vancouver, OR-WA	619.1
270	Portland, ME	523.7
340	Poughkeepsie, NY	321.0
264	Prescott, AZ	541.0
298	Provo-Orem, UT	465.1
48	Pueblo, CO	1,161.6
147	Punta Gorda, FL	838.4
196	Racine, WI	712.2
167	Raleigh-Cary, NC	777.1
284	Rapid City, SD	495.3
282	Reading, PA	499.4
214	Redding, CA	662.2
124	Reno-Sparks, NV	889.4
251	Richmond, VA	571.1
145	Riverside-San Bernardino, CA	840.7
274	Roanoke, VA	512.0
301	Rochester, MN	460.2
265	Rochester, NY	536.0
8	Rocky Mount, NC	1,679.1
154	Rome, GA	810.5
112	Sacramento, CA	930.8
55	Saginaw, MI	1,129.7
250	Salem, OR	574.2
217	Salinas, CA	652.2
42	Salisbury, MD	1,201.0
184	Salt Lake City, UT	743.9
93	San Angelo, TX	992.1
91	San Antonio, TX	996.6
236	San Diego, CA	603.2
187	San Francisco (greater), CA	737.8
220	San Francisco-S. Mateo, CA M.D.	642.3
272	San Jose, CA	517.6
249	San Luis Obispo, CA	576.5
178	Sandusky, OH	749.1
312	Santa Ana-Anaheim, CA M.D.	422.2
290	Santa Barbara-Santa Maria, CA	476.5
166	Santa Cruz-Watsonville, CA	778.4
2	Santa Fe, NM	2,084.5
294	Santa Rosa-Petaluma, CA	469.3
86	Sarasota-Bradenton-Venice, FL	999.1
143	Savannah, GA	844.5
304	Scranton--Wilkes-Barre, PA	453.1
100	Seattle (greater), WA	972.1
111	Seattle-Bellevue, WA M.D.	933.0
206	Sebastian-Vero Beach, FL	679.1
322	Sheboygan, WI	394.7
148	Sherman-Denison, TX	837.3
56	Shreveport-Bossier City, LA	1,126.2
240	Sioux City, IA-NE-SD	598.5
299	Sioux Falls, SD	463.9
107	South Bend-Mishawaka, IN-MI	957.8
47	Spartanburg, SC	1,174.4
158	Spokane, WA	791.3
168	Springfield, MA	774.2
163	Springfield, MO	781.7
6	Springfield, OH	1,791.0
338	State College, PA	327.7
66	Stockton, CA	1,079.5
330	St. Cloud, MN	371.2
149	St. Joseph, MO-KS	836.0
207	St. Louis, MO-IL	678.7
25	Sumter, SC	1,313.0
248	Syracuse, NY	577.5
61	Tacoma, WA M.D.	1,099.5
53	Tallahassee, FL	1,142.6
102	Tampa-St Petersburg, FL	966.3
117	Texarkana, TX-Texarkana, AR	911.1
26	Toledo, OH	1,306.9
118	Topeka, KS	909.0
277	Trenton-Ewing, NJ	507.5
129	Tucson, AZ	871.2
85	Tulsa, OK	1,001.8
45	Tuscaloosa, AL	1,183.9
141	Tyler, TX	845.9
263	Utica-Rome, NY	542.4
108	Valdosta, GA	950.0
201	Vallejo-Fairfield, CA	694.4
152	Victoria, TX	821.8
88	Vineland, NJ	998.9
242	Virginia Beach-Norfolk, VA-NC	593.6
57	Visalia-Porterville, CA	1,112.2
30	Waco, TX	1,281.2
198	Warner Robins, GA	703.5
289	Warren-Farmington Hills, MI M.D.	483.4
316	Washington (greater) DC-VA-MD	412.4
318	Washington, DC-VA-MD-WV M.D.	411.1
175	Waterloo-Cedar Falls, IA	762.5
331	Wausau, WI	370.9
244	Wenatchee, WA	590.2
90	West Palm Beach, FL M.D.	997.6
313	Wheeling, WV-OH	417.9
69	Wichita Falls, TX	1,052.4
131	Wichita, KS	863.7
259	Williamsport, PA	553.6
188	Wilmington, DE-MD-NJ M.D.	733.7
13	Wilmington, NC	1,449.1
257	Winchester, VA-WV	554.5
19	Winston-Salem, NC	1,389.0
305	Worcester, MA	448.6
11	Yakima, WA	1,493.4
73	Yuba City, CA	1,039.8
176	Yuma, AZ	757.7

Source: CQ Press using data from Federal Bureau of Investigation "Crime in the United States 2006" (Uniform Crime Reports, September 24, 2007)
**Burglary is the unlawful entry of a structure to commit a felony or theft. Attempts are included.*
***Not available.*

30. Burglary Rate in 2006 (continued)

National Rate = 729.4 Burglaries per 100,000 Population*

RANK	METROPOLITAN AREA	RATE
1	Hot Springs, AR	2,267.0
2	Santa Fe, NM	2,084.5
3	Jonesboro, AR	1,933.6
4	Pine Bluff, AR	1,922.5
5	Fayetteville, NC	1,805.2
6	Springfield, OH	1,791.0
7	Memphis, TN-MS-AR	1,700.3
8	Rocky Mount, NC	1,679.1
9	Lake Charles, LA	1,653.6
10	Alexandria, LA	1,533.7
11	Yakima, WA	1,493.4
12	Monroe, LA	1,469.7
13	Wilmington, NC	1,449.1
14	Lawton, OK	1,438.9
15	Macon, GA	1,431.0
16	Little Rock, AR	1,426.3
17	Charlotte-Gastonia, NC-SC	1,405.5
18	El Centro, CA	1,394.2
19	Winston-Salem, NC	1,389.0
20	Greenville, NC	1,383.3
21	Jackson, TN	1,360.2
22	Myrtle Beach, SC	1,357.8
23	Goldsboro, NC	1,337.3
24	Greensboro-High Point, NC	1,315.0
25	Sumter, SC	1,313.0
26	Toledo, OH	1,306.9
27	Pascagoula, MS	1,302.4
28	Lubbock, TX	1,294.4
29	Albany, GA	1,286.4
30	Waco, TX	1,281.2
31	Flint, MI	1,259.1
32	Gadsden, AL	1,254.3
33	Columbus, OH	1,252.1
34	Lake Havasu City-Kingman, AZ	1,248.2
35	Longview, WA	1,235.4
36	Detroit-Livonia-Dearborn, MI M.D.	1,229.5
37	Mobile, AL	1,224.3
38	Montgomery, AL	1,220.3
39	Florence, SC	1,214.2
40	Oklahoma City, OK	1,214.1
41	Baton Rouge, LA	1,213.9
42	Salisbury, MD	1,201.0
43	Durham, NC	1,196.5
44	Mansfield, OH	1,191.2
45	Tuscaloosa, AL	1,183.9
46	Gainesville, FL	1,178.8
47	Spartanburg, SC	1,174.4
48	Pueblo, CO	1,161.6
49	Beaumont-Port Arthur, TX	1,148.8
50	Lima, OH	1,146.1
51	Jackson, MS	1,142.9
52	Columbus, GA-AL	1,142.7
53	Tallahassee, FL	1,142.6
54	Bakersfield, CA	1,140.9
55	Saginaw, MI	1,129.7
56	Shreveport-Bossier City, LA	1,126.2
57	Visalia-Porterville, CA	1,112.2
58	Albuquerque, NM	1,109.3
59	Las Vegas-Paradise, NV	1,101.8
60	Killeen-Temple-Fort Hood, TX	1,100.7
61	Tacoma, WA M.D.	1,099.5
62	Orlando, FL	1,098.9
63	Anderson, SC	1,095.1
64	Daytona Beach, FL	1,085.0
65	Lakeland, FL	1,083.0
66	Stockton, CA	1,079.5
67	Longview, TX	1,075.2
68	Amarillo, TX	1,055.7
69	Wichita Falls, TX	1,052.4
70	Brunswick, GA	1,052.2
71	Birmingham-Hoover, AL	1,051.4
72	Huntsville, AL	1,044.6
73	Yuba City, CA	1,039.8
74	Merced, CA	1,035.7
75	Cape Coral-Fort Myers, FL	1,035.5
76	Hattiesburg, MS	1,029.0
77	Dallas-Plano-Irving, TX M.D.	1,025.0
78	Corpus Christi, TX	1,023.3
79	Greenville, SC	1,015.2
80	Miami-Dade County, FL M.D.	1,015.1
81	Kalamazoo-Portage, MI	1,013.3
82	Burlington, NC	1,012.3
83	Dallas (greater), TX	1,011.6
84	Jacksonville, FL	1,010.0
85	Tulsa, OK	1,001.8
86	Sarasota-Bradenton-Venice, FL	999.1
87	Mount Vernon-Anacortes, WA	999.0
88	Vineland, NJ	998.9
89	Brownsville-Harlingen, TX	997.9
90	West Palm Beach, FL M.D.	997.6
91	San Antonio, TX	996.6
92	College Station-Bryan, TX	996.4
93	San Angelo, TX	992.1
94	Fort Worth-Arlington, TX M.D.	984.4
95	Battle Creek, MI	983.8
96	Modesto, CA	980.7
97	Phoenix-Mesa-Scottsdale, AZ	978.7
98	Kokomo, IN	975.2
99	Bellingham, WA	974.2
100	Seattle (greater), WA	972.1
101	Barnstable Town, MA	971.1
102	Tampa-St Petersburg, FL	966.3
103	Houston, TX	964.9
104	Chico, CA	964.8
105	Eugene-Springfield, OR	962.8
106	Augusta, GA-SC	958.0
107	South Bend-Mishawaka, IN-MI	957.8
108	Valdosta, GA	950.0
109	Abilene, TX	940.6
110	Dothan, AL	936.7
111	Seattle-Bellevue, WA M.D.	933.0
112	Sacramento, CA	930.8
113	Miami (greater), FL	917.9
114	Clarksville, TN-KY	914.9
115	Indianapolis, IN	913.4
116	New Orleans, LA	912.8
117	Texarkana, TX-Texarkana, AR	911.1
118	Topeka, KS	909.0
119	Louisville, KY-IN	907.3
120	Ocean City, NJ	893.7
121	Joplin, MO	893.1
122	Pensacola, FL	892.9
123	Charleston-North Charleston, SC	892.2
124	Reno-Sparks, NV	889.4
125	Jacksonville, NC	883.7
126	Fresno, CA	876.5
126	Palm Bay-Melbourne, FL	876.5
128	Asheville, NC	876.0
129	Tucson, AZ	871.2
130	Dayton, OH	867.0
131	Wichita, KS	863.7
132	Chattanooga, TN-GA	859.5
133	Cleveland-Elyria-Mentor, OH	856.9
134	Charleston, WV	856.5
135	Decatur, AL	851.8
136	Huntington-Ashland, WV-KY-OH	851.2
137	McAllen-Edinburg-Mission, TX	850.6
138	Kansas City, MO-KS	850.3
139	Athens-Clarke County, GA	850.0
140	Knoxville, TN	849.4
141	Tyler, TX	845.9
142	Fort Smith, AR-OK	845.4
143	Savannah, GA	844.5
144	Panama City-Lynn Haven, FL	843.7
145	Riverside-San Bernardino, CA	840.7
146	Casper, WY	838.7
147	Punta Gorda, FL	838.4
148	Sherman-Denison, TX	837.3
149	St. Joseph, MO-KS	836.0
150	Port St. Lucie, FL	831.6
151	Johnson City, TN	828.3
152	Victoria, TX	821.8
153	Detroit (greater), MI	815.5
154	Rome, GA	810.5
155	Midland, TX	805.2
156	Oakland-Fremont, CA M.D.	803.1
157	Nashville-Davidson, TN	792.2
158	Spokane, WA	791.3
159	Muskegon-Norton Shores, MI	786.9
160	Greeley, CO	785.8
161	Columbia, SC	782.6
162	Elkhart-Goshen, IN	782.1
163	Springfield, MO	781.7
164	Odessa, TX	779.0
165	Kingsport, TN-VA	778.7
166	Santa Cruz-Watsonville, CA	778.4
167	Raleigh-Cary, NC	777.1
168	Springfield, MA	774.2
169	Cleveland, TN	772.3
170	Cincinnati-Middletown, OH-KY-IN	771.1
171	Laredo, TX	769.5

Note: All listings are for Metropolitan Statistical Areas (M.S.A.s) except for those ending with "M.D." Listings with "M.D." are Metropolitan Divisions which are smaller parts of eleven large M.S.A.s. See explanatory note at beginning of metropolitan area section on page 23.

RANK	METROPOLITAN AREA	RATE
172	Lexington-Fayette, KY	766.8
173	Lawrence, KS	766.1
174	Austin-Round Rock, TX	765.2
175	Waterloo-Cedar Falls, IA	762.5
176	Yuma, AZ	757.7
177	Grand Rapids-Wyoming, MI	755.7
178	Sandusky, OH	749.1
179	Colorado Springs, CO	746.6
180	Houma, LA	746.1
181	Bloomington, IN	745.7
182	Madera, CA	745.5
183	Denver-Aurora, CO	745.4
184	Salt Lake City, UT	743.9
185	Lincoln, NE	741.5
186	Janesville, WI	738.1
187	San Francisco (greater), CA	737.8
188	Wilmington, DE-MD-NJ M.D.	733.7
189	Atlantic City, NJ	731.9
190	Fort Lauderdale, FL M.D.	731.2
191	Dalton, GA	726.8
192	Olympia, WA	724.2
193	Muncie, IN	723.1
194	Buffalo-Niagara Falls, NY	717.9
195	Baltimore-Towson, MD	715.4
196	Racine, WI	712.2
197	Bremerton-Silverdale, WA	711.6
198	Warner Robins, GA	703.5
199	Bowling Green, KY	700.0
200	Las Cruces, NM	699.4
201	Vallejo-Fairfield, CA	694.4
202	Michigan City-La Porte, IN	688.6
203	Cumberland, MD-WV	687.9
204	Ocala, FL	686.4
205	Lafayette, IN	682.2
206	Sebastian-Vero Beach, FL	679.1
207	St. Louis, MO-IL	678.7
208	Des Moines-West Des Moines, IA	675.7
209	Bend, OR	670.8
210	Coeur d'Alene, ID	667.1
211	Fayetteville, AR-MO	666.7
212	Fort Wayne, IN	665.0
213	Kennewick-Richland-Pasco, WA	662.9
214	Redding, CA	662.2
215	Pittsfield, MA	656.6
216	Minneapolis-St. Paul, MN-WI	654.5
217	Salinas, CA	652.2
218	Grand Junction, CO	643.9
219	Omaha-Council Bluffs, NE-IA	642.9
220	San Francisco-S. Mateo, CA M.D.	642.3
221	Niles-Benton Harbor, MI	641.2
222	Ames, IA	637.0
223	Morristown, TN	630.7
224	Duluth, MN-WI	627.2
225	Anchorage, AK	622.3
226	Portland-Vancouver, OR-WA	619.1
227	Dover, DE	618.5
228	Lansing-East Lansing, MI	617.4
229	Altoona, PA	617.0
229	Danville, VA	617.0
229	Jackson, MI	617.0

RANK	METROPOLITAN AREA	RATE
232	Flagstaff, AZ	611.2
233	Bay City, MI	608.7
234	Lewiston, ID-WA	608.6
235	Ann Arbor, MI	604.4
236	San Diego, CA	603.2
237	Morgantown, WV	601.2
238	Honolulu, HI	600.6
239	Cedar Rapids, IA	599.1
240	Sioux City, IA-NE-SD	598.5
241	Idaho Falls, ID	595.4
242	Virginia Beach-Norfolk, VA-NC	593.6
243	Palm Coast, FL	592.0
244	Wenatchee, WA	590.2
245	Boise City-Nampa, ID	589.5
246	Milwaukee, WI	583.2
247	Dubuque, IA	578.6
248	Syracuse, NY	577.5
249	San Luis Obispo, CA	576.5
250	Salem, OR	574.2
251	Richmond, VA	571.1
252	Albany-Schenectady-Troy, NY	569.7
253	Monroe, MI	564.6
254	Gainesville, GA	564.0
255	Fort Walton Beach, FL	563.6
256	Evansville, IN-KY	559.8
257	Winchester, VA-WV	554.5
258	Farmington, NM	554.2
259	Los Angeles County, CA M.D.	553.6
259	Williamsport, PA	553.6
261	Hagerstown-Martinsburg, MD-WV	552.8
262	Columbia, MO	548.6
263	Utica-Rome, NY	542.4
264	Prescott, AZ	541.0
265	Rochester, NY	536.0
266	Bangor, ME	533.1
267	Camden, NJ M.D.	530.8
268	Napa, CA	528.5
269	Philadelphia (greater) PA-NJ-DE	525.5
270	Portland, ME	523.7
271	Los Angeles (greater), CA	523.2
272	San Jose, CA	517.6
273	Columbus, IN	516.0
274	Roanoke, VA	512.0
275	Hartford, CT	510.9
276	Madison, WI	510.8
277	Trenton-Ewing, NJ	507.5
278	Lewiston-Auburn, ME	504.4
279	Erie, PA	502.7
280	Carson City, NV	502.3
281	Fort Collins-Loveland, CO	500.2
282	Reading, PA	499.4
283	Jefferson City, MO	498.9
284	Rapid City, SD	495.3
285	Blacksburg, VA	489.6
286	Philadelphia, PA M.D.	486.7
287	Ogden-Clearfield, UT	485.8
288	Medford, OR	483.6
289	Warren-Farmington Hills, MI M.D.	483.4
290	Santa Barbara-Santa Maria, CA	476.5
291	Hanford-Corcoran, CA	471.3

RANK	METROPOLITAN AREA	RATE
292	Pittsburgh, PA	470.7
293	Elmira, NY	470.2
294	Santa Rosa-Petaluma, CA	469.3
295	Naples-Marco Island, FL	466.0
296	Cheyenne, WY	465.6
297	Green Bay, WI	465.5
298	Provo-Orem, UT	465.1
299	Sioux Falls, SD	463.9
300	Missoula, MT	461.2
301	Rochester, MN	460.2
302	Eau Claire, WI	457.9
303	Johnstown, PA	454.1
304	Scranton--Wilkes-Barre, PA	453.1
305	Worcester, MA	448.6
306	Charlottesville, VA	448.2
307	Glens Falls, NY	446.8
308	Newark-Union, NJ-PA M.D.	442.2
309	Fargo, ND-MN	442.0
310	Oxnard-Thousand Oaks, CA	437.7
311	Lancaster, PA	431.4
312	Santa Ana-Anaheim, CA M.D.	422.2
313	Wheeling, WV-OH	417.9
314	Bethesda-Frederick, MD M.D.	417.2
315	Bismarck, ND	415.2
316	Washington (greater) DC-VA-MD	412.4
317	Billings, MT	411.5
318	Washington, DC-VA-MD-WV M.D.	411.1
319	Holland-Grand Haven, MI	404.7
320	Harrisburg-Carlisle, PA	403.0
321	Iowa City, IA	402.1
322	Sheboygan, WI	394.7
323	Binghamton, NY	394.6
324	Oshkosh-Neenah, WI	391.7
325	Elizabethtown, KY	389.2
326	Kingston, NY	381.0
327	Manchester-Nashua, NH	376.4
328	El Paso, TX	373.4
329	Harrisonburg, VA	373.2
330	St. Cloud, MN	371.2
331	Wausau, WI	370.9
332	Pocatello, ID	368.7
333	Lynchburg, VA	367.4
334	Edison, NJ M.D.	365.7
335	Lebanon, PA	347.7
336	Ithaca, NY	333.0
337	La Crosse, WI-MN	330.7
338	State College, PA	327.7
339	Appleton, WI	322.3
340	Poughkeepsie, NY	321.0
341	New York (greater), NY-NJ-PA	310.0
342	Fond du Lac, WI	290.9
343	Great Falls, MT	290.0
344	New York-W. Plains NY-NJ M.D.	289.2
345	Logan, UT-ID	261.5
346	Nassau-Suffolk, NY M.D.	248.0
NA	Atlanta, GA**	NA
NA	Chicago, IL**	NA
NA	Fairbanks, AK**	NA
NA	Grand Forks, ND-MN**	NA

Source: CQ Press using data from Federal Bureau of Investigation "Crime in the United States 2006" (Uniform Crime Reports, September 24, 2007)

**Burglary is the unlawful entry of a structure to commit a felony or theft. Attempts are included.*

***Not available.*

31. Percent Change in Burglary Rate: 2005 to 2006

National Percent Change = 0.3% Increase*

RANK	METROPOLITAN AREA	% CHANGE
NA	Abilene, TX**	NA
88	Albany-Schenectady-Troy, NY	6.9
195	Albany, GA	(1.6)
156	Albuquerque, NM	1.0
19	Alexandria, LA	20.7
127	Altoona, PA	3.1
272	Amarillo, TX	(9.9)
304	Ames, IA	(18.9)
219	Anchorage, AK	(3.6)
255	Anderson, SC	(7.5)
277	Ann Arbor, MI	(11.2)
182	Appleton, WI	(0.6)
139	Asheville, NC	1.8
38	Athens-Clarke County, GA	14.4
NA	Atlanta, GA**	NA
76	Atlantic City, NJ	8.2
99	Augusta, GA-SC	5.9
205	Austin-Round Rock, TX	(2.3)
177	Bakersfield, CA	(0.4)
106	Baltimore-Towson, MD	5.3
145	Bangor, ME	1.6
23	Barnstable Town, MA	19.3
31	Baton Rouge, LA	16.6
22	Battle Creek, MI	19.5
137	Bay City, MI	2.0
259	Beaumont-Port Arthur, TX	(7.6)
147	Bellingham, WA	1.4
301	Bend, OR	(17.8)
73	Bethesda-Frederick, MD M.D.	8.8
317	Billings, MT	(25.0)
41	Binghamton, NY	13.3
NA	Birmingham-Hoover, AL**	NA
1	Bismarck, ND	48.4
166	Blacksburg, VA	0.6
7	Bloomington, IN	29.0
NA	Boise City-Nampa, ID**	NA
139	Bowling Green, KY	1.8
233	Bremerton-Silverdale, WA	(5.2)
161	Brownsville-Harlingen, TX	0.8
161	Brunswick, GA	0.8
68	Buffalo-Niagara Falls, NY	9.9
210	Burlington, NC	(2.9)
113	Camden, NJ M.D.	4.3
54	Cape Coral-Fort Myers, FL	11.7
315	Carson City, NV	(24.7)
291	Casper, WY	(15.3)
113	Cedar Rapids, IA	4.3
187	Charleston-North Charleston, SC	(1.1)
278	Charleston, WV	(11.4)
118	Charlotte-Gastonia, NC-SC	3.9
16	Charlottesville, VA	22.4
230	Chattanooga, TN-GA	(4.5)
99	Cheyenne, WY	5.9
NA	Chicago, IL**	NA
255	Chico, CA	(7.5)
112	Cincinnati-Middletown, OH-KY-IN	4.4
40	Clarksville, TN-KY	13.5
NA	Cleveland-Elyria-Mentor, OH**	NA
NA	Cleveland, TN**	NA
238	Coeur d'Alene, ID	(5.6)
291	College Station-Bryan, TX	(15.3)
244	Colorado Springs, CO	(6.2)
158	Columbia, MO	0.9
208	Columbia, SC	(2.6)
166	Columbus, GA-AL	0.6
47	Columbus, IN	13.0
161	Columbus, OH	0.8
279	Corpus Christi, TX	(11.5)
17	Cumberland, MD-WV	21.3
221	Dallas (greater), TX	(3.8)
224	Dallas-Plano-Irving, TX M.D.	(4.1)
NA	Dalton, GA**	NA
3	Danville, VA	40.4
13	Daytona Beach, FL	23.0
128	Dayton, OH	2.9
90	Decatur, AL	6.8
261	Denver-Aurora, CO	(7.9)
NA	Des Moines-West Des Moines, IA**	NA
59	Detroit (greater), MI	11.0
48	Detroit-Livonia-Dearborn, MI M.D.	12.5
92	Dothan, AL	6.7
48	Dover, DE	12.5
90	Dubuque, IA	6.8
NA	Duluth, MN-WI**	NA
NA	Durham, NC**	NA
24	Eau Claire, WI	19.2
72	Edison, NJ M.D.	8.9
218	El Centro, CA	(3.5)
124	El Paso, TX	3.4
63	Elizabethtown, KY	10.6
69	Elkhart-Goshen, IN	9.2
190	Elmira, NY	(1.2)
39	Erie, PA	13.6
269	Eugene-Springfield, OR	(9.2)
117	Evansville, IN-KY	4.0
NA	Fairbanks, AK**	NA
28	Fargo, ND-MN	17.5
268	Farmington, NM	(9.0)
6	Fayetteville, AR-MO	31.6
103	Fayetteville, NC	5.8
286	Flagstaff, AZ	(13.3)
56	Flint, MI	11.4
289	Florence, SC	(13.6)
34	Fond du Lac, WI	16.3
177	Fort Collins-Loveland, CO	(0.4)
202	Fort Lauderdale, FL M.D.	(2.2)
105	Fort Smith, AR-OK	5.6
215	Fort Walton Beach, FL	(3.3)
NA	Fort Wayne, IN**	NA
212	Fort Worth-Arlington, TX M.D.	(3.1)
161	Fresno, CA	0.8
4	Gadsden, AL	37.7
46	Gainesville, FL	13.1
296	Gainesville, GA	(17.3)
NA	Glens Falls, NY**	NA
35	Goldsboro, NC	16.1
NA	Grand Forks, ND-MN**	NA
296	Grand Junction, CO	(17.3)
60	Grand Rapids-Wyoming, MI	10.9
314	Great Falls, MT	(23.6)
312	Greeley, CO	(23.5)
86	Green Bay, WI	7.0
198	Greensboro-High Point, NC	(1.8)
231	Greenville, NC	(4.9)
156	Greenville, SC	1.0
9	Hagerstown-Martinsburg, MD-WV	26.1
305	Hanford-Corcoran, CA	(19.0)
252	Harrisburg-Carlisle, PA	(7.4)
18	Harrisonburg, VA	21.1
182	Hartford, CT	(0.6)
NA	Hattiesburg, MS**	NA
151	Holland-Grand Haven, MI	1.2
281	Honolulu, HI	(12.1)
29	Hot Springs, AR	16.9
124	Houma, LA	3.4
222	Houston, TX	(3.9)
27	Huntington-Ashland, WV-KY-OH	17.8
246	Huntsville, AL	(6.3)
20	Idaho Falls, ID	20.2
166	Indianapolis, IN	0.6
249	Iowa City, IA	(6.9)
NA	Ithaca, NY**	NA
99	Jacksonville, FL	5.9
NA	Jacksonville, NC**	NA
255	Jackson, MI	(7.5)
37	Jackson, MS	15.4
252	Jackson, TN	(7.4)
75	Janesville, WI	8.3
293	Jefferson City, MO	(16.3)
187	Johnson City, TN	(1.1)
NA	Johnstown, PA**	NA
97	Jonesboro, AR	6.4
118	Joplin, MO	3.9
14	Kalamazoo-Portage, MI	22.5
NA	Kansas City, MO-KS**	NA
232	Kennewick-Richland-Pasco, WA	(5.1)
133	Killeen-Temple-Fort Hood, TX	2.4
77	Kingsport, TN-VA	8.1
21	Kingston, NY	20.0
261	Knoxville, TN	(7.9)
274	Kokomo, IN	(10.5)
173	La Crosse, WI-MN	0.2
79	Lafayette, IN	7.7
81	Lake Charles, LA	7.2
NA	Lake Havasu City-Kingman, AZ**	NA
50	Lakeland, FL	12.3
150	Lancaster, PA	1.3
131	Lansing-East Lansing, MI	2.5
124	Laredo, TX	3.4
242	Las Cruces, NM	(6.0)
129	Las Vegas-Paradise, NV	2.8

Note: All listings are for Metropolitan Statistical Areas (M.S.A.s) except for those ending with "M.D." Listings with "M.D." are Metropolitan Divisions which are smaller parts of eleven large M.S.A.s. See explanatory note at beginning of metropolitan area section on page 23.

RANK	METROPOLITAN AREA	% CHANGE
56	Lawrence, KS	11.4
65	Lawton, OK	10.3
270	Lebanon, PA	(9.3)
86	Lewiston-Auburn, ME	7.0
130	Lewiston, ID-WA	2.7
NA	Lexington-Fayette, KY**	NA
134	Lima, OH	2.3
182	Lincoln, NE	(0.6)
103	Little Rock, AR	5.8
283	Logan, UT-ID	(12.4)
166	Longview, TX	0.6
300	Longview, WA	(17.7)
240	Los Angeles County, CA M.D.	(5.9)
239	Los Angeles (greater), CA	(5.8)
99	Louisville, KY-IN	5.9
113	Lubbock, TX	4.3
109	Lynchburg, VA	5.1
123	Macon, GA	3.5
263	Madera, CA	(8.0)
53	Madison, WI	11.9
94	Manchester-Nashua, NH	6.6
67	Mansfield, OH	10.0
294	McAllen-Edinburg-Mission, TX	(16.6)
312	Medford, OR	(23.5)
151	Memphis, TN-MS-AR	1.2
83	Merced, CA	7.1
209	Miami (greater), FL	(2.8)
224	Miami-Dade County, FL M.D.	(4.1)
5	Michigan City-La Porte, IN	36.4
65	Midland, TX	10.3
26	Milwaukee, WI	17.9
NA	Minneapolis-St. Paul, MN-WI**	NA
282	Missoula, MT	(12.2)
215	Mobile, AL	(3.3)
142	Modesto, CA	1.7
11	Monroe, LA	24.1
122	Monroe, MI	3.7
244	Montgomery, AL	(6.2)
154	Morgantown, WV	1.1
194	Morristown, TN	(1.5)
318	Mount Vernon-Anacortes, WA	(29.4)
14	Muncie, IN	22.5
202	Muskegon-Norton Shores, MI	(2.2)
172	Myrtle Beach, SC	0.3
78	Napa, CA	8.0
174	Naples-Marco Island, FL	0.0
135	Nashville-Davidson, TN	2.2
200	Nassau-Suffolk, NY M.D.	(1.9)
NA	New Orleans, LA**	NA
205	New York (greater), NY-NJ-PA	(2.3)
229	New York-W. Plains NY-NJ M.D.	(4.4)
222	Newark-Union, NJ-PA M.D.	(3.9)
36	Niles-Benton Harbor, MI	15.6
220	Oakland-Fremont, CA M.D.	(3.7)
302	Ocala, FL	(18.2)
171	Ocean City, NJ	0.4
142	Odessa, TX	1.7
193	Ogden-Clearfield, UT	(1.4)
116	Oklahoma City, OK	4.2
263	Olympia, WA	(8.0)

RANK	METROPOLITAN AREA	% CHANGE
224	Omaha-Council Bluffs, NE-IA	(4.1)
158	Orlando, FL	0.9
202	Oshkosh-Neenah, WI	(2.2)
249	Oxnard-Thousand Oaks, CA	(6.9)
83	Palm Bay-Melbourne, FL	7.1
NA	Palm Coast, FL**	NA
186	Panama City-Lynn Haven, FL	(0.8)
52	Pascagoula, MS	12.0
25	Pensacola, FL	18.7
107	Philadelphia (greater) PA-NJ-DE	5.2
96	Philadelphia, PA M.D.	6.5
224	Phoenix-Mesa-Scottsdale, AZ	(4.1)
236	Pine Bluff, AR	(5.5)
88	Pittsburgh, PA	6.9
32	Pittsfield, MA	16.4
320	Pocatello, ID	(35.6)
83	Port St. Lucie, FL	7.1
287	Portland-Vancouver, OR-WA	(13.4)
41	Portland, ME	13.3
107	Poughkeepsie, NY	5.2
306	Prescott, AZ	(19.1)
290	Provo-Orem, UT	(15.0)
252	Pueblo, CO	(7.4)
50	Punta Gorda, FL	12.3
158	Racine, WI	0.9
176	Raleigh-Cary, NC	(0.2)
288	Rapid City, SD	(13.5)
307	Reading, PA	(19.3)
316	Redding, CA	(24.9)
71	Reno-Sparks, NV	9.0
251	Richmond, VA	(7.3)
196	Riverside-San Bernardino, CA	(1.7)
190	Roanoke, VA	(1.2)
10	Rochester, MN	24.2
180	Rochester, NY	(0.5)
30	Rocky Mount, NC	16.7
319	Rome, GA	(32.9)
138	Sacramento, CA	1.9
80	Saginaw, MI	7.5
311	Salem, OR	(22.7)
212	Salinas, CA	(3.1)
94	Salisbury, MD	6.6
201	Salt Lake City, UT	(2.1)
285	San Angelo, TX	(13.1)
175	San Antonio, TX	(0.1)
161	San Diego, CA	0.8
211	San Francisco (greater), CA	(3.0)
198	San Francisco-S. Mateo, CA M.D.	(1.8)
74	San Jose, CA	8.4
166	San Luis Obispo, CA	0.6
180	Sandusky, OH	(0.5)
234	Santa Ana-Anaheim, CA M.D.	(5.3)
255	Santa Barbara-Santa Maria, CA	(7.5)
151	Santa Cruz-Watsonville, CA	1.2
32	Santa Fe, NM	16.4
235	Santa Rosa-Petaluma, CA	(5.4)
92	Sarasota-Bradenton-Venice, FL	6.7
298	Savannah, GA	(17.4)
224	Scranton--Wilkes-Barre, PA	(4.1)
146	Seattle (greater), WA	1.5

RANK	METROPOLITAN AREA	% CHANGE
131	Seattle-Bellevue, WA M.D.	2.5
284	Sebastian-Vero Beach, FL	(12.6)
12	Sheboygan, WI	23.5
247	Sherman-Denison, TX	(6.7)
109	Shreveport-Bossier City, LA	5.1
273	Sioux City, IA-NE-SD	(10.4)
64	Sioux Falls, SD	10.4
44	South Bend-Mishawaka, IN-MI	13.2
55	Spartanburg, SC	11.6
280	Spokane, WA	(11.6)
187	Springfield, MA	(1.1)
62	Springfield, MO	10.8
81	Springfield, OH	7.2
118	State College, PA	3.9
177	Stockton, CA	(0.4)
260	St. Cloud, MN	(7.7)
111	St. Joseph, MO-KS	4.8
58	St. Louis, MO-IL	11.2
298	Sumter, SC	(17.4)
98	Syracuse, NY	6.2
190	Tacoma, WA M.D.	(1.2)
266	Tallahassee, FL	(8.5)
147	Tampa-St Petersburg, FL	1.4
207	Texarkana, TX-Texarkana, AR	(2.4)
121	Toledo, OH	3.8
274	Topeka, KS	(10.5)
243	Trenton-Ewing, NJ	(6.1)
154	Tucson, AZ	1.1
248	Tulsa, OK	(6.8)
NA	Tuscaloosa, AL**	NA
308	Tyler, TX	(19.7)
44	Utica-Rome, NY	13.2
142	Valdosta, GA	1.7
NA	Vallejo-Fairfield, CA**	NA
295	Victoria, TX	(16.8)
41	Vineland, NJ	13.3
196	Virginia Beach-Norfolk, VA-NC	(1.7)
217	Visalia-Porterville, CA	(3.4)
267	Waco, TX	(8.9)
310	Warner Robins, GA	(21.7)
70	Warren-Farmington Hills, MI M.D.	9.1
NA	Washington (greater) DC-VA-MD**	NA
NA	Washington, DC-VA-MD-WV M.D.**	NA
60	Waterloo-Cedar Falls, IA	10.9
214	Wausau, WI	(3.2)
303	Wenatchee, WA	(18.8)
185	West Palm Beach, FL M.D.	(0.7)
265	Wheeling, WV-OH	(8.3)
309	Wichita Falls, TX	(21.2)
NA	Wichita, KS**	NA
8	Williamsport, PA	28.2
147	Wilmington, DE-MD-NJ M.D.	1.4
240	Wilmington, NC	(5.9)
2	Winchester, VA-WV	47.7
139	Winston-Salem, NC	1.8
236	Worcester, MA	(5.5)
271	Yakima, WA	(9.8)
135	Yuba City, CA	2.2
276	Yuma, AZ	(10.6)

Source: CQ Press using data from Federal Bureau of Investigation "Crime in the United States 2006" (Uniform Crime Reports, September 24, 2007)

**Burglary is the unlawful entry of a structure to commit a felony or theft. Attempts are included.*

***Not available.*

31. Percent Change in Burglary Rate: 2005 to 2006 (continued)

National Percent Change = 0.3% Increase*

RANK	METROPOLITAN AREA	% CHANGE
1	Bismarck, ND	48.4
2	Winchester, VA-WV	47.7
3	Danville, VA	40.4
4	Gadsden, AL	37.7
5	Michigan City-La Porte, IN	36.4
6	Fayetteville, AR-MO	31.6
7	Bloomington, IN	29.0
8	Williamsport, PA	28.2
9	Hagerstown-Martinsburg, MD-WV	26.1
10	Rochester, MN	24.2
11	Monroe, LA	24.1
12	Sheboygan, WI	23.5
13	Daytona Beach, FL	23.0
14	Kalamazoo-Portage, MI	22.5
14	Muncie, IN	22.5
16	Charlottesville, VA	22.4
17	Cumberland, MD-WV	21.3
18	Harrisonburg, VA	21.1
19	Alexandria, LA	20.7
20	Idaho Falls, ID	20.2
21	Kingston, NY	20.0
22	Battle Creek, MI	19.5
23	Barnstable Town, MA	19.3
24	Eau Claire, WI	19.2
25	Pensacola, FL	18.7
26	Milwaukee, WI	17.9
27	Huntington-Ashland, WV-KY-OH	17.8
28	Fargo, ND-MN	17.5
29	Hot Springs, AR	16.9
30	Rocky Mount, NC	16.7
31	Baton Rouge, LA	16.6
32	Pittsfield, MA	16.4
32	Santa Fe, NM	16.4
34	Fond du Lac, WI	16.3
35	Goldsboro, NC	16.1
36	Niles-Benton Harbor, MI	15.6
37	Jackson, MS	15.4
38	Athens-Clarke County, GA	14.4
39	Erie, PA	13.6
40	Clarksville, TN-KY	13.5
41	Binghamton, NY	13.3
41	Portland, ME	13.3
41	Vineland, NJ	13.3
44	South Bend-Mishawaka, IN-MI	13.2
44	Utica-Rome, NY	13.2
46	Gainesville, FL	13.1
47	Columbus, IN	13.0
48	Detroit-Livonia-Dearborn, MI M.D.	12.5
48	Dover, DE	12.5
50	Lakeland, FL	12.3
50	Punta Gorda, FL	12.3
52	Pascagoula, MS	12.0
53	Madison, WI	11.9
54	Cape Coral-Fort Myers, FL	11.7
55	Spartanburg, SC	11.6
56	Flint, MI	11.4
56	Lawrence, KS	11.4
58	St. Louis, MO-IL	11.2
59	Detroit (greater), MI	11.0
60	Grand Rapids-Wyoming, MI	10.9
60	Waterloo-Cedar Falls, IA	10.9
62	Springfield, MO	10.8
63	Elizabethtown, KY	10.6
64	Sioux Falls, SD	10.4
65	Lawton, OK	10.3
65	Midland, TX	10.3
67	Mansfield, OH	10.0
68	Buffalo-Niagara Falls, NY	9.9
69	Elkhart-Goshen, IN	9.2
70	Warren-Farmington Hills, MI M.D.	9.1
71	Reno-Sparks, NV	9.0
72	Edison, NJ M.D.	8.9
73	Bethesda-Frederick, MD M.D.	8.8
74	San Jose, CA	8.4
75	Janesville, WI	8.3
76	Atlantic City, NJ	8.2
77	Kingsport, TN-VA	8.1
78	Napa, CA	8.0
79	Lafayette, IN	7.7
80	Saginaw, MI	7.5
81	Lake Charles, LA	7.2
81	Springfield, OH	7.2
83	Merced, CA	7.1
83	Palm Bay-Melbourne, FL	7.1
83	Port St. Lucie, FL	7.1
86	Green Bay, WI	7.0
86	Lewiston-Auburn, ME	7.0
88	Albany-Schenectady-Troy, NY	6.9
88	Pittsburgh, PA	6.9
90	Decatur, AL	6.8
90	Dubuque, IA	6.8
92	Dothan, AL	6.7
92	Sarasota-Bradenton-Venice, FL	6.7
94	Manchester-Nashua, NH	6.6
94	Salisbury, MD	6.6
96	Philadelphia, PA M.D.	6.5
97	Jonesboro, AR	6.4
98	Syracuse, NY	6.2
99	Augusta, GA-SC	5.9
99	Cheyenne, WY	5.9
99	Jacksonville, FL	5.9
99	Louisville, KY-IN	5.9
103	Fayetteville, NC	5.8
103	Little Rock, AR	5.8
105	Fort Smith, AR-OK	5.6
106	Baltimore-Towson, MD	5.3
107	Philadelphia (greater) PA-NJ-DE	5.2
107	Poughkeepsie, NY	5.2
109	Lynchburg, VA	5.1
109	Shreveport-Bossier City, LA	5.1
111	St. Joseph, MO-KS	4.8
112	Cincinnati-Middletown, OH-KY-IN	4.4
113	Camden, NJ M.D.	4.3
113	Cedar Rapids, IA	4.3
113	Lubbock, TX	4.3
116	Oklahoma City, OK	4.2
117	Evansville, IN-KY	4.0
118	Charlotte-Gastonia, NC-SC	3.9
118	Joplin, MO	3.9
118	State College, PA	3.9
121	Toledo, OH	3.8
122	Monroe, MI	3.7
123	Macon, GA	3.5
124	El Paso, TX	3.4
124	Houma, LA	3.4
124	Laredo, TX	3.4
127	Altoona, PA	3.1
128	Dayton, OH	2.9
129	Las Vegas-Paradise, NV	2.8
130	Lewiston, ID-WA	2.7
131	Lansing-East Lansing, MI	2.5
131	Seattle-Bellevue, WA M.D.	2.5
133	Killeen-Temple-Fort Hood, TX	2.4
134	Lima, OH	2.3
135	Nashville-Davidson, TN	2.2
135	Yuba City, CA	2.2
137	Bay City, MI	2.0
138	Sacramento, CA	1.9
139	Asheville, NC	1.8
139	Bowling Green, KY	1.8
139	Winston-Salem, NC	1.8
142	Modesto, CA	1.7
142	Odessa, TX	1.7
142	Valdosta, GA	1.7
145	Bangor, ME	1.6
146	Seattle (greater), WA	1.5
147	Bellingham, WA	1.4
147	Tampa-St Petersburg, FL	1.4
147	Wilmington, DE-MD-NJ M.D.	1.4
150	Lancaster, PA	1.3
151	Holland-Grand Haven, MI	1.2
151	Memphis, TN-MS-AR	1.2
151	Santa Cruz-Watsonville, CA	1.2
154	Morgantown, WV	1.1
154	Tucson, AZ	1.1
156	Albuquerque, NM	1.0
156	Greenville, SC	1.0
158	Columbia, MO	0.9
158	Orlando, FL	0.9
158	Racine, WI	0.9
161	Brownsville-Harlingen, TX	0.8
161	Brunswick, GA	0.8
161	Columbus, OH	0.8
161	Fresno, CA	0.8
161	San Diego, CA	0.8
166	Blacksburg, VA	0.6
166	Columbus, GA-AL	0.6
166	Indianapolis, IN	0.6
166	Longview, TX	0.6
166	San Luis Obispo, CA	0.6
171	Ocean City, NJ	0.4

Note: All listings are for Metropolitan Statistical Areas (M.S.A.s) except for those ending with "M.D." Listings with "M.D." are Metropolitan Divisions which are smaller parts of eleven large M.S.A.s. See explanatory note at beginning of metropolitan area section on page 23.

Rank Order - Metro Area (continued)

RANK	METROPOLITAN AREA	% CHANGE
172	Myrtle Beach, SC	0.3
173	La Crosse, WI-MN	0.2
174	Naples-Marco Island, FL	0.0
175	San Antonio, TX	(0.1)
176	Raleigh-Cary, NC	(0.2)
177	Bakersfield, CA	(0.4)
177	Fort Collins-Loveland, CO	(0.4)
177	Stockton, CA	(0.4)
180	Rochester, NY	(0.5)
180	Sandusky, OH	(0.5)
182	Appleton, WI	(0.6)
182	Hartford, CT	(0.6)
182	Lincoln, NE	(0.6)
185	West Palm Beach, FL M.D.	(0.7)
186	Panama City-Lynn Haven, FL	(0.8)
187	Charleston-North Charleston, SC	(1.1)
187	Johnson City, TN	(1.1)
187	Springfield, MA	(1.1)
190	Elmira, NY	(1.2)
190	Roanoke, VA	(1.2)
190	Tacoma, WA M.D.	(1.2)
193	Ogden-Clearfield, UT	(1.4)
194	Morristown, TN	(1.5)
195	Albany, GA	(1.6)
196	Riverside-San Bernardino, CA	(1.7)
196	Virginia Beach-Norfolk, VA-NC	(1.7)
198	Greensboro-High Point, NC	(1.8)
198	San Francisco-S. Mateo, CA M.D.	(1.8)
200	Nassau-Suffolk, NY M.D.	(1.9)
201	Salt Lake City, UT	(2.1)
202	Fort Lauderdale, FL M.D.	(2.2)
202	Muskegon-Norton Shores, MI	(2.2)
202	Oshkosh-Neenah, WI	(2.2)
205	Austin-Round Rock, TX	(2.3)
205	New York (greater), NY-NJ-PA	(2.3)
207	Texarkana, TX-Texarkana, AR	(2.4)
208	Columbia, SC	(2.6)
209	Miami (greater), FL	(2.8)
210	Burlington, NC	(2.9)
211	San Francisco (greater), CA	(3.0)
212	Fort Worth-Arlington, TX M.D.	(3.1)
212	Salinas, CA	(3.1)
214	Wausau, WI	(3.2)
215	Fort Walton Beach, FL	(3.3)
215	Mobile, AL	(3.3)
217	Visalia-Porterville, CA	(3.4)
218	El Centro, CA	(3.5)
219	Anchorage, AK	(3.6)
220	Oakland-Fremont, CA M.D.	(3.7)
221	Dallas (greater), TX	(3.8)
222	Houston, TX	(3.9)
222	Newark-Union, NJ-PA M.D.	(3.9)
224	Dallas-Plano-Irving, TX M.D.	(4.1)
224	Miami-Dade County, FL M.D.	(4.1)
224	Omaha-Council Bluffs, NE-IA	(4.1)
224	Phoenix-Mesa-Scottsdale, AZ	(4.1)
224	Scranton--Wilkes-Barre, PA	(4.1)
229	New York-W. Plains NY-NJ M.D.	(4.4)
230	Chattanooga, TN-GA	(4.5)
231	Greenville, NC	(4.9)
232	Kennewick-Richland-Pasco, WA	(5.1)
233	Bremerton-Silverdale, WA	(5.2)
234	Santa Ana-Anaheim, CA M.D.	(5.3)
235	Santa Rosa-Petaluma, CA	(5.4)
236	Pine Bluff, AR	(5.5)
236	Worcester, MA	(5.5)
238	Coeur d'Alene, ID	(5.6)
239	Los Angeles (greater), CA	(5.8)
240	Los Angeles County, CA M.D.	(5.9)
240	Wilmington, NC	(5.9)
242	Las Cruces, NM	(6.0)
243	Trenton-Ewing, NJ	(6.1)
244	Colorado Springs, CO	(6.2)
244	Montgomery, AL	(6.2)
246	Huntsville, AL	(6.3)
247	Sherman-Denison, TX	(6.7)
248	Tulsa, OK	(6.8)
249	Iowa City, IA	(6.9)
249	Oxnard-Thousand Oaks, CA	(6.9)
251	Richmond, VA	(7.3)
252	Harrisburg-Carlisle, PA	(7.4)
252	Jackson, TN	(7.4)
252	Pueblo, CO	(7.4)
255	Anderson, SC	(7.5)
255	Chico, CA	(7.5)
255	Jackson, MI	(7.5)
255	Santa Barbara-Santa Maria, CA	(7.5)
259	Beaumont-Port Arthur, TX	(7.6)
260	St. Cloud, MN	(7.7)
261	Denver-Aurora, CO	(7.9)
261	Knoxville, TN	(7.9)
263	Madera, CA	(8.0)
263	Olympia, WA	(8.0)
265	Wheeling, WV-OH	(8.3)
266	Tallahassee, FL	(8.5)
267	Waco, TX	(8.9)
268	Farmington, NM	(9.0)
269	Eugene-Springfield, OR	(9.2)
270	Lebanon, PA	(9.3)
271	Yakima, WA	(9.8)
272	Amarillo, TX	(9.9)
273	Sioux City, IA-NE-SD	(10.4)
274	Kokomo, IN	(10.5)
274	Topeka, KS	(10.5)
276	Yuma, AZ	(10.6)
277	Ann Arbor, MI	(11.2)
278	Charleston, WV	(11.4)
279	Corpus Christi, TX	(11.5)
280	Spokane, WA	(11.6)
281	Honolulu, HI	(12.1)
282	Missoula, MT	(12.2)
283	Logan, UT-ID	(12.4)
284	Sebastian-Vero Beach, FL	(12.6)
285	San Angelo, TX	(13.1)
286	Flagstaff, AZ	(13.3)
287	Portland-Vancouver, OR-WA	(13.4)
288	Rapid City, SD	(13.5)
289	Florence, SC	(13.6)
290	Provo-Orem, UT	(15.0)
291	Casper, WY	(15.3)
291	College Station-Bryan, TX	(15.3)
293	Jefferson City, MO	(16.3)
294	McAllen-Edinburg-Mission, TX	(16.6)
295	Victoria, TX	(16.8)
296	Gainesville, GA	(17.3)
296	Grand Junction, CO	(17.3)
298	Savannah, GA	(17.4)
298	Sumter, SC	(17.4)
300	Longview, WA	(17.7)
301	Bend, OR	(17.8)
302	Ocala, FL	(18.2)
303	Wenatchee, WA	(18.8)
304	Ames, IA	(18.9)
305	Hanford-Corcoran, CA	(19.0)
306	Prescott, AZ	(19.1)
307	Reading, PA	(19.3)
308	Tyler, TX	(19.7)
309	Wichita Falls, TX	(21.2)
310	Warner Robins, GA	(21.7)
311	Salem, OR	(22.7)
312	Greeley, CO	(23.5)
312	Medford, OR	(23.5)
314	Great Falls, MT	(23.6)
315	Carson City, NV	(24.7)
316	Redding, CA	(24.9)
317	Billings, MT	(25.0)
318	Mount Vernon-Anacortes, WA	(29.4)
319	Rome, GA	(32.9)
320	Pocatello, ID	(35.6)
NA	Abilene, TX**	NA
NA	Atlanta, GA**	NA
NA	Birmingham-Hoover, AL**	NA
NA	Boise City-Nampa, ID**	NA
NA	Chicago, IL**	NA
NA	Cleveland-Elyria-Mentor, OH**	NA
NA	Cleveland, TN**	NA
NA	Dalton, GA**	NA
NA	Des Moines-West Des Moines, IA**	NA
NA	Duluth, MN-WI**	NA
NA	Durham, NC**	NA
NA	Fairbanks, AK**	NA
NA	Fort Wayne, IN**	NA
NA	Glens Falls, NY**	NA
NA	Grand Forks, ND-MN**	NA
NA	Hattiesburg, MS**	NA
NA	Ithaca, NY**	NA
NA	Jacksonville, NC**	NA
NA	Johnstown, PA**	NA
NA	Kansas City, MO-KS**	NA
NA	Lake Havasu City-Kingman, AZ**	NA
NA	Lexington-Fayette, KY**	NA
NA	Minneapolis-St. Paul, MN-WI**	NA
NA	New Orleans, LA**	NA
NA	Palm Coast, FL**	NA
NA	Tuscaloosa, AL**	NA
NA	Vallejo-Fairfield, CA**	NA
NA	Washington (greater) DC-VA-MD**	NA
NA	Washington, DC-VA-MD-WV M.D.**	NA
NA	Wichita, KS**	NA

Source: CQ Press using data from Federal Bureau of Investigation "Crime in the United States 2006" (Uniform Crime Reports, September 24, 2007)

**Burglary is the unlawful entry of a structure to commit a felony or theft. Attempts are included.*

***Not available.*

32. Percent Change in Burglary Rate: 2002 to 2006

National Percent Change = 2.4% Decrease*

RANK	METROPOLITAN AREA	% CHANGE
NA	Abilene, TX**	NA
NA	Albany-Schenectady-Troy, NY**	NA
74	Albany, GA	3.1
42	Albuquerque, NM	10.9
126	Alexandria, LA	(7.0)
159	Altoona, PA	(13.4)
156	Amarillo, TX	(12.8)
NA	Ames, IA**	NA
50	Anchorage, AK	9.3
NA	Anderson, SC**	NA
NA	Ann Arbor, MI**	NA
NA	Appleton, WI**	NA
39	Asheville, NC	11.6
83	Athens-Clarke County, GA	1.0
NA	Atlanta, GA**	NA
NA	Atlantic City, NJ**	NA
30	Augusta, GA-SC	14.3
138	Austin-Round Rock, TX	(9.1)
20	Bakersfield, CA	20.1
144	Baltimore-Towson, MD	(9.9)
NA	Bangor, ME**	NA
NA	Barnstable Town, MA**	NA
153	Baton Rouge, LA	(12.4)
NA	Battle Creek, MI**	NA
NA	Bay City, MI**	NA
60	Beaumont-Port Arthur, TX	6.4
92	Bellingham, WA	(0.7)
NA	Bend, OR**	NA
NA	Bethesda-Frederick, MD M.D.**	NA
72	Billings, MT	3.2
57	Binghamton, NY	7.1
32	Birmingham-Hoover, AL	13.2
10	Bismarck, ND	31.2
NA	Blacksburg, VA**	NA
8	Bloomington, IN	34.7
171	Boise City-Nampa, ID	(15.3)
NA	Bowling Green, KY**	NA
174	Bremerton-Silverdale, WA	(16.6)
43	Brownsville-Harlingen, TX	10.6
NA	Brunswick, GA**	NA
27	Buffalo-Niagara Falls, NY	15.6
NA	Burlington, NC**	NA
NA	Camden, NJ M.D.**	NA
88	Cape Coral-Fort Myers, FL	0.0
NA	Carson City, NV**	NA
172	Casper, WY	(15.5)
180	Cedar Rapids, IA	(18.2)
141	Charleston-North Charleston, SC	(9.5)
34	Charleston, WV	12.9
NA	Charlotte-Gastonia, NC-SC**	NA
NA	Charlottesville, VA**	NA
161	Chattanooga, TN-GA	(13.8)
22	Cheyenne, WY	19.5
NA	Chicago, IL**	NA
100	Chico, CA	(2.2)
110	Cincinnati-Middletown, OH-KY-IN	(4.8)
57	Clarksville, TN-KY	7.1
NA	Cleveland-Elyria-Mentor, OH**	NA
NA	Cleveland, TN**	NA
NA	Coeur d'Alene, ID**	NA
NA	College Station-Bryan, TX**	NA
177	Colorado Springs, CO	(17.6)
31	Columbia, MO	13.6
205	Columbia, SC	(31.1)
7	Columbus, GA-AL	35.1
NA	Columbus, IN**	NA
160	Columbus, OH	(13.6)
139	Corpus Christi, TX	(9.2)
24	Cumberland, MD-WV	17.9
NA	Dallas (greater), TX**	NA
121	Dallas-Plano-Irving, TX M.D.	(6.3)
NA	Dalton, GA**	NA
3	Danville, VA	45.0
91	Daytona Beach, FL	(0.6)
NA	Dayton, OH**	NA
59	Decatur, AL	6.6
90	Denver-Aurora, CO	(0.5)
NA	Des Moines-West Des Moines, IA**	NA
28	Detroit (greater), MI	15.5
NA	Detroit-Livonia-Dearborn, MI M.D.**	NA
NA	Dothan, AL**	NA
64	Dover, DE	5.4
54	Dubuque, IA	7.4
193	Duluth, MN-WI	(22.8)
NA	Durham, NC**	NA
111	Eau Claire, WI	(5.1)
NA	Edison, NJ M.D.**	NA
NA	El Centro, CA**	NA
100	El Paso, TX	(2.2)
NA	Elizabethtown, KY**	NA
157	Elkhart-Goshen, IN	(12.9)
NA	Elmira, NY**	NA
104	Erie, PA	(2.5)
12	Eugene-Springfield, OR	28.7
NA	Evansville, IN-KY**	NA
NA	Fairbanks, AK**	NA
85	Fargo, ND-MN	0.3
NA	Farmington, NM**	NA
NA	Fayetteville, AR-MO**	NA
41	Fayetteville, NC	11.2
204	Flagstaff, AZ	(30.4)
19	Flint, MI	20.4
81	Florence, SC	1.2
NA	Fond du Lac, WI**	NA
123	Fort Collins-Loveland, CO	(6.4)
102	Fort Lauderdale, FL M.D.	(2.4)
78	Fort Smith, AR-OK	1.8
46	Fort Walton Beach, FL	10.3
NA	Fort Wayne, IN**	NA
150	Fort Worth-Arlington, TX M.D.	(11.6)
108	Fresno, CA	(4.7)
18	Gadsden, AL	22.2
105	Gainesville, FL	(2.9)
NA	Gainesville, GA**	NA
38	Glens Falls, NY	11.7
77	Goldsboro, NC	2.2
NA	Grand Forks, ND-MN**	NA
49	Grand Junction, CO	9.5
NA	Grand Rapids-Wyoming, MI**	NA
208	Great Falls, MT	(37.0)
94	Greeley, CO	(1.2)
87	Green Bay, WI	0.1
NA	Greensboro-High Point, NC**	NA
113	Greenville, NC	(5.6)
NA	Greenville, SC**	NA
NA	Hagerstown-Martinsburg, MD-WV**	NA
NA	Hanford-Corcoran, CA**	NA
NA	Harrisburg-Carlisle, PA**	NA
NA	Harrisonburg, VA**	NA
79	Hartford, CT	1.5
NA	Hattiesburg, MS**	NA
NA	Holland-Grand Haven, MI**	NA
209	Honolulu, HI	(39.5)
NA	Hot Springs, AR**	NA
188	Houma, LA	(20.7)
129	Houston, TX	(7.4)
NA	Huntington-Ashland, WV-KY-OH**	NA
9	Huntsville, AL	32.4
NA	Idaho Falls, ID**	NA
NA	Indianapolis, IN**	NA
187	Iowa City, IA	(20.3)
NA	Ithaca, NY**	NA
108	Jacksonville, FL	(4.7)
NA	Jacksonville, NC**	NA
124	Jackson, MI	(6.7)
183	Jackson, MS	(19.0)
11	Jackson, TN	29.3
52	Janesville, WI	8.6
NA	Jefferson City, MO**	NA
NA	Johnson City, TN**	NA
NA	Johnstown, PA**	NA
1	Jonesboro, AR	147.0
37	Joplin, MO	12.0
NA	Kalamazoo-Portage, MI**	NA
NA	Kansas City, MO-KS**	NA
83	Kennewick-Richland-Pasco, WA	1.0
64	Killeen-Temple-Fort Hood, TX	5.4
NA	Kingsport, TN-VA**	NA
NA	Kingston, NY**	NA
151	Knoxville, TN	(11.7)
13	Kokomo, IN	27.9
75	La Crosse, WI-MN	2.9
70	Lafayette, IN	3.5
133	Lake Charles, LA	(7.8)
NA	Lake Havasu City-Kingman, AZ**	NA
115	Lakeland, FL	(5.7)
140	Lancaster, PA	(9.4)
80	Lansing-East Lansing, MI	1.4
199	Laredo, TX	(25.2)
NA	Las Cruces, NM**	NA
48	Las Vegas-Paradise, NV	9.8

Note: All listings are for Metropolitan Statistical Areas (M.S.A.s) except for those ending with "M.D." Listings with "M.D." are Metropolitan Divisions which are smaller parts of eleven large M.S.A.s. See explanatory note at beginning of metropolitan area section on page 23.

RANK	METROPOLITAN AREA	% CHANGE
137	Lawrence, KS	(8.8)
17	Lawton, OK	22.4
NA	Lebanon, PA**	NA
185	Lewiston-Auburn, ME	(19.7)
NA	Lewiston, ID-WA**	NA
NA	Lexington-Fayette, KY**	NA
NA	Lima, OH**	NA
167	Lincoln, NE	(15.1)
62	Little Rock, AR	6.1
NA	Logan, UT-ID**	NA
113	Longview, TX	(5.6)
NA	Longview, WA**	NA
152	Los Angeles County, CA M.D.	(12.0)
NA	Los Angeles (greater), CA**	NA
112	Louisville, KY-IN	(5.2)
88	Lubbock, TX	0.0
131	Lynchburg, VA	(7.5)
NA	Macon, GA**	NA
NA	Madera, CA**	NA
116	Madison, WI	(6.0)
NA	Manchester-Nashua, NH**	NA
NA	Mansfield, OH**	NA
191	McAllen-Edinburg-Mission, TX	(22.0)
200	Medford, OR	(26.8)
NA	Memphis, TN-MS-AR**	NA
173	Merced, CA	(16.3)
NA	Miami (greater), FL**	NA
136	Miami-Dade County, FL M.D.	(8.4)
NA	Michigan City-La Porte, IN**	NA
NA	Midland, TX**	NA
NA	Milwaukee, WI**	NA
44	Minneapolis-St. Paul, MN-WI	10.5
NA	Missoula, MT**	NA
NA	Mobile, AL**	NA
116	Modesto, CA	(6.0)
NA	Monroe, LA**	NA
NA	Monroe, MI**	NA
164	Montgomery, AL	(14.9)
NA	Morgantown, WV**	NA
NA	Morristown, TN**	NA
NA	Mount Vernon-Anacortes, WA**	NA
15	Muncie, IN	23.2
NA	Muskegon-Norton Shores, MI**	NA
134	Myrtle Beach, SC	(8.1)
NA	Napa, CA**	NA
210	Naples-Marco Island, FL	(46.8)
163	Nashville-Davidson, TN	(14.6)
NA	Nassau-Suffolk, NY M.D.**	NA
32	New Orleans, LA	13.2
NA	New York (greater), NY-NJ-PA**	NA
186	New York-W. Plains NY-NJ M.D.	(19.9)
180	Newark-Union, NJ-PA M.D.	(18.2)
NA	Niles-Benton Harbor, MI**	NA
45	Oakland-Fremont, CA M.D.	10.4
202	Ocala, FL	(28.9)
NA	Ocean City, NJ**	NA
NA	Odessa, TX**	NA
NA	Ogden-Clearfield, UT**	NA
92	Oklahoma City, OK	(0.7)
157	Olympia, WA	(12.9)
147	Omaha-Council Bluffs, NE-IA	(10.5)
121	Orlando, FL	(6.3)
NA	Oshkosh-Neenah, WI**	NA
NA	Oxnard-Thousand Oaks, CA**	NA
143	Palm Bay-Melbourne, FL	(9.6)
NA	Palm Coast, FL**	NA
197	Panama City-Lynn Haven, FL	(24.1)
NA	Pascagoula, MS**	NA
145	Pensacola, FL	(10.0)
56	Philadelphia (greater) PA-NJ-DE	7.2
NA	Philadelphia, PA M.D.**	NA
176	Phoenix-Mesa-Scottsdale, AZ	(16.9)
4	Pine Bluff, AR	43.2
67	Pittsburgh, PA	4.7
NA	Pittsfield, MA**	NA
148	Pocatello, ID	(10.9)
182	Port St. Lucie, FL	(18.3)
167	Portland-Vancouver, OR-WA	(15.1)
NA	Portland, ME**	NA
NA	Poughkeepsie, NY**	NA
NA	Prescott, AZ**	NA
162	Provo-Orem, UT	(14.4)
25	Pueblo, CO	17.8
29	Punta Gorda, FL	14.9
61	Racine, WI	6.3
NA	Raleigh-Cary, NC**	NA
207	Rapid City, SD	(31.5)
175	Reading, PA	(16.8)
194	Redding, CA	(23.2)
6	Reno-Sparks, NV	35.2
166	Richmond, VA	(15.0)
107	Riverside-San Bernardino, CA	(4.2)
NA	Roanoke, VA**	NA
69	Rochester, MN	4.0
36	Rochester, NY	12.4
14	Rocky Mount, NC	25.3
NA	Rome, GA**	NA
66	Sacramento, CA	4.9
NA	Saginaw, MI**	NA
203	Salem, OR	(29.8)
53	Salinas, CA	7.5
NA	Salisbury, MD**	NA
NA	Salt Lake City, UT**	NA
125	San Angelo, TX	(6.8)
96	San Antonio, TX	(1.3)
106	San Diego, CA	(3.3)
NA	San Francisco (greater), CA**	NA
26	San Francisco-S. Mateo, CA M.D.	15.8
2	San Jose, CA	48.2
96	San Luis Obispo, CA	(1.3)
NA	Sandusky, OH**	NA
116	Santa Ana-Anaheim, CA M.D.	(6.0)
NA	Santa Barbara-Santa Maria, CA**	NA
16	Santa Cruz-Watsonville, CA	23.1
21	Santa Fe, NM	19.8
201	Santa Rosa-Petaluma, CA	(28.2)
129	Sarasota-Bradenton-Venice, FL	(7.4)
196	Savannah, GA	(23.9)
40	Scranton--Wilkes-Barre, PA	11.3
NA	Seattle (greater), WA**	NA
35	Seattle-Bellevue, WA M.D.	12.5
NA	Sebastian-Vero Beach, FL**	NA
51	Sheboygan, WI	8.7
76	Sherman-Denison, TX	2.6
135	Shreveport-Bossier City, LA	(8.3)
211	Sioux City, IA-NE-SD	(47.0)
132	Sioux Falls, SD	(7.6)
149	South Bend-Mishawaka, IN-MI	(11.3)
NA	Spartanburg, SC**	NA
192	Spokane, WA	(22.7)
NA	Springfield, MA**	NA
116	Springfield, MO	(6.0)
NA	Springfield, OH**	NA
5	State College, PA	39.2
72	Stockton, CA	3.2
82	St. Cloud, MN	1.1
47	St. Joseph, MO-KS	10.2
NA	St. Louis, MO-IL**	NA
128	Sumter, SC	(7.3)
NA	Syracuse, NY**	NA
67	Tacoma, WA M.D.	4.7
146	Tallahassee, FL	(10.2)
164	Tampa-St Petersburg, FL	(14.9)
102	Texarkana, TX-Texarkana, AR	(2.4)
55	Toledo, OH	7.3
198	Topeka, KS	(25.0)
195	Trenton-Ewing, NJ	(23.5)
177	Tucson, AZ	(17.6)
127	Tulsa, OK	(7.1)
63	Tuscaloosa, AL	5.5
179	Tyler, TX	(17.9)
153	Utica-Rome, NY	(12.4)
NA	Valdosta, GA**	NA
NA	Vallejo-Fairfield, CA**	NA
155	Victoria, TX	(12.5)
169	Vineland, NJ	(15.2)
141	Virginia Beach-Norfolk, VA-NC	(9.5)
98	Visalia-Porterville, CA	(1.7)
120	Waco, TX	(6.1)
NA	Warner Robins, GA**	NA
NA	Warren-Farmington Hills, MI M.D.**	NA
NA	Washington (greater) DC-VA-MD**	NA
NA	Washington, DC-VA-MD-WV M.D.**	NA
206	Waterloo-Cedar Falls, IA	(31.4)
85	Wausau, WI	0.3
NA	Wenatchee, WA**	NA
190	West Palm Beach, FL M.D.	(21.8)
NA	Wheeling, WV-OH**	NA
189	Wichita Falls, TX	(20.9)
169	Wichita, KS	(15.2)
23	Williamsport, PA	18.8
NA	Wilmington, DE-MD-NJ M.D.**	NA
184	Wilmington, NC	(19.1)
NA	Winchester, VA-WV**	NA
NA	Winston-Salem, NC**	NA
NA	Worcester, MA**	NA
99	Yakima, WA	(1.8)
71	Yuba City, CA	3.4
94	Yuma, AZ	(1.2)

Source: CQ Press using data from Federal Bureau of Investigation "Crime in the United States 2006" (Uniform Crime Reports, September 24, 2007)

**Burglary is the unlawful entry of a structure to commit a felony or theft. Attempts are included.*

***Not available.*

32. Percent Change in Burglary Rate: 2002 to 2006 (continued)

National Percent Change = 2.4% Decrease*

RANK	METROPOLITAN AREA	% CHANGE
1	Jonesboro, AR	147.0
2	San Jose, CA	48.2
3	Danville, VA	45.0
4	Pine Bluff, AR	43.2
5	State College, PA	39.2
6	Reno-Sparks, NV	35.2
7	Columbus, GA-AL	35.1
8	Bloomington, IN	34.7
9	Huntsville, AL	32.4
10	Bismarck, ND	31.2
11	Jackson, TN	29.3
12	Eugene-Springfield, OR	28.7
13	Kokomo, IN	27.9
14	Rocky Mount, NC	25.3
15	Muncie, IN	23.2
16	Santa Cruz-Watsonville, CA	23.1
17	Lawton, OK	22.4
18	Gadsden, AL	22.2
19	Flint, MI	20.4
20	Bakersfield, CA	20.1
21	Santa Fe, NM	19.8
22	Cheyenne, WY	19.5
23	Williamsport, PA	18.8
24	Cumberland, MD-WV	17.9
25	Pueblo, CO	17.8
26	San Francisco-S. Mateo, CA M.D.	15.8
27	Buffalo-Niagara Falls, NY	15.6
28	Detroit (greater), MI	15.5
29	Punta Gorda, FL	14.9
30	Augusta, GA-SC	14.3
31	Columbia, MO	13.6
32	Birmingham-Hoover, AL	13.2
32	New Orleans, LA	13.2
34	Charleston, WV	12.9
35	Seattle-Bellevue, WA M.D.	12.5
36	Rochester, NY	12.4
37	Joplin, MO	12.0
38	Glens Falls, NY	11.7
39	Asheville, NC	11.6
40	Scranton--Wilkes-Barre, PA	11.3
41	Fayetteville, NC	11.2
42	Albuquerque, NM	10.9
43	Brownsville-Harlingen, TX	10.6
44	Minneapolis-St. Paul, MN-WI	10.5
45	Oakland-Fremont, CA M.D.	10.4
46	Fort Walton Beach, FL	10.3
47	St. Joseph, MO-KS	10.2
48	Las Vegas-Paradise, NV	9.8
49	Grand Junction, CO	9.5
50	Anchorage, AK	9.3
51	Sheboygan, WI	8.7
52	Janesville, WI	8.6
53	Salinas, CA	7.5
54	Dubuque, IA	7.4
55	Toledo, OH	7.3
56	Philadelphia (greater) PA-NJ-DE	7.2
57	Binghamton, NY	7.1
57	Clarksville, TN-KY	7.1
59	Decatur, AL	6.6
60	Beaumont-Port Arthur, TX	6.4
61	Racine, WI	6.3
62	Little Rock, AR	6.1
63	Tuscaloosa, AL	5.5
64	Dover, DE	5.4
64	Killeen-Temple-Fort Hood, TX	5.4
66	Sacramento, CA	4.9
67	Pittsburgh, PA	4.7
67	Tacoma, WA M.D.	4.7
69	Rochester, MN	4.0
70	Lafayette, IN	3.5
71	Yuba City, CA	3.4
72	Billings, MT	3.2
72	Stockton, CA	3.2
74	Albany, GA	3.1
75	La Crosse, WI-MN	2.9
76	Sherman-Denison, TX	2.6
77	Goldsboro, NC	2.2
78	Fort Smith, AR-OK	1.8
79	Hartford, CT	1.5
80	Lansing-East Lansing, MI	1.4
81	Florence, SC	1.2
82	St. Cloud, MN	1.1
83	Athens-Clarke County, GA	1.0
83	Kennewick-Richland-Pasco, WA	1.0
85	Fargo, ND-MN	0.3
85	Wausau, WI	0.3
87	Green Bay, WI	0.1
88	Cape Coral-Fort Myers, FL	0.0
88	Lubbock, TX	0.0
90	Denver-Aurora, CO	(0.5)
91	Daytona Beach, FL	(0.6)
92	Bellingham, WA	(0.7)
92	Oklahoma City, OK	(0.7)
94	Greeley, CO	(1.2)
94	Yuma, AZ	(1.2)
96	San Antonio, TX	(1.3)
96	San Luis Obispo, CA	(1.3)
98	Visalia-Porterville, CA	(1.7)
99	Yakima, WA	(1.8)
100	Chico, CA	(2.2)
100	El Paso, TX	(2.2)
102	Fort Lauderdale, FL M.D.	(2.4)
102	Texarkana, TX-Texarkana, AR	(2.4)
104	Erie, PA	(2.5)
105	Gainesville, FL	(2.9)
106	San Diego, CA	(3.3)
107	Riverside-San Bernardino, CA	(4.2)
108	Fresno, CA	(4.7)
108	Jacksonville, FL	(4.7)
110	Cincinnati-Middletown, OH-KY-IN	(4.8)
111	Eau Claire, WI	(5.1)
112	Louisville, KY-IN	(5.2)
113	Greenville, NC	(5.6)
113	Longview, TX	(5.6)
115	Lakeland, FL	(5.7)
116	Madison, WI	(6.0)
116	Modesto, CA	(6.0)
116	Santa Ana-Anaheim, CA M.D.	(6.0)
116	Springfield, MO	(6.0)
120	Waco, TX	(6.1)
121	Dallas-Plano-Irving, TX M.D.	(6.3)
121	Orlando, FL	(6.3)
123	Fort Collins-Loveland, CO	(6.4)
124	Jackson, MI	(6.7)
125	San Angelo, TX	(6.8)
126	Alexandria, LA	(7.0)
127	Tulsa, OK	(7.1)
128	Sumter, SC	(7.3)
129	Houston, TX	(7.4)
129	Sarasota-Bradenton-Venice, FL	(7.4)
131	Lynchburg, VA	(7.5)
132	Sioux Falls, SD	(7.6)
133	Lake Charles, LA	(7.8)
134	Myrtle Beach, SC	(8.1)
135	Shreveport-Bossier City, LA	(8.3)
136	Miami-Dade County, FL M.D.	(8.4)
137	Lawrence, KS	(8.8)
138	Austin-Round Rock, TX	(9.1)
139	Corpus Christi, TX	(9.2)
140	Lancaster, PA	(9.4)
141	Charleston-North Charleston, SC	(9.5)
141	Virginia Beach-Norfolk, VA-NC	(9.5)
143	Palm Bay-Melbourne, FL	(9.6)
144	Baltimore-Towson, MD	(9.9)
145	Pensacola, FL	(10.0)
146	Tallahassee, FL	(10.2)
147	Omaha-Council Bluffs, NE-IA	(10.5)
148	Pocatello, ID	(10.9)
149	South Bend-Mishawaka, IN-MI	(11.3)
150	Fort Worth-Arlington, TX M.D.	(11.6)
151	Knoxville, TN	(11.7)
152	Los Angeles County, CA M.D.	(12.0)
153	Baton Rouge, LA	(12.4)
153	Utica-Rome, NY	(12.4)
155	Victoria, TX	(12.5)
156	Amarillo, TX	(12.8)
157	Elkhart-Goshen, IN	(12.9)
157	Olympia, WA	(12.9)
159	Altoona, PA	(13.4)
160	Columbus, OH	(13.6)
161	Chattanooga, TN-GA	(13.8)
162	Provo-Orem, UT	(14.4)
163	Nashville-Davidson, TN	(14.6)
164	Montgomery, AL	(14.9)
164	Tampa-St Petersburg, FL	(14.9)
166	Richmond, VA	(15.0)
167	Lincoln, NE	(15.1)
167	Portland-Vancouver, OR-WA	(15.1)
169	Vineland, NJ	(15.2)
169	Wichita, KS	(15.2)
171	Boise City-Nampa, ID	(15.3)

Note: All listings are for Metropolitan Statistical Areas (M.S.A.s) except for those ending with "M.D." Listings with "M.D." are Metropolitan Divisions which are smaller parts of eleven large M.S.A.s. See explanatory note at beginning of metropolitan area section on page 23.

RANK	METROPOLITAN AREA	% CHANGE
172	Casper, WY	(15.5)
173	Merced, CA	(16.3)
174	Bremerton-Silverdale, WA	(16.6)
175	Reading, PA	(16.8)
176	Phoenix-Mesa-Scottsdale, AZ	(16.9)
177	Colorado Springs, CO	(17.6)
177	Tucson, AZ	(17.6)
179	Tyler, TX	(17.9)
180	Cedar Rapids, IA	(18.2)
180	Newark-Union, NJ-PA M.D.	(18.2)
182	Port St. Lucie, FL	(18.3)
183	Jackson, MS	(19.0)
184	Wilmington, NC	(19.1)
185	Lewiston-Auburn, ME	(19.7)
186	New York-W. Plains NY-NJ M.D.	(19.9)
187	Iowa City, IA	(20.3)
188	Houma, LA	(20.7)
189	Wichita Falls, TX	(20.9)
190	West Palm Beach, FL M.D.	(21.8)
191	McAllen-Edinburg-Mission, TX	(22.0)
192	Spokane, WA	(22.7)
193	Duluth, MN-WI	(22.8)
194	Redding, CA	(23.2)
195	Trenton-Ewing, NJ	(23.5)
196	Savannah, GA	(23.9)
197	Panama City-Lynn Haven, FL	(24.1)
198	Topeka, KS	(25.0)
199	Laredo, TX	(25.2)
200	Medford, OR	(26.8)
201	Santa Rosa-Petaluma, CA	(28.2)
202	Ocala, FL	(28.9)
203	Salem, OR	(29.8)
204	Flagstaff, AZ	(30.4)
205	Columbia, SC	(31.1)
206	Waterloo-Cedar Falls, IA	(31.4)
207	Rapid City, SD	(31.5)
208	Great Falls, MT	(37.0)
209	Honolulu, HI	(39.5)
210	Naples-Marco Island, FL	(46.8)
211	Sioux City, IA-NE-SD	(47.0)
NA	Abilene, TX**	NA
NA	Albany-Schenectady-Troy, NY**	NA
NA	Ames, IA**	NA
NA	Anderson, SC**	NA
NA	Ann Arbor, MI**	NA
NA	Appleton, WI**	NA
NA	Atlanta, GA**	NA
NA	Atlantic City, NJ**	NA
NA	Bangor, ME**	NA
NA	Barnstable Town, MA**	NA
NA	Battle Creek, MI**	NA
NA	Bay City, MI**	NA
NA	Bend, OR**	NA
NA	Bethesda-Frederick, MD M.D.**	NA
NA	Blacksburg, VA**	NA
NA	Bowling Green, KY**	NA
NA	Brunswick, GA**	NA
NA	Burlington, NC**	NA
NA	Camden, NJ M.D.**	NA
NA	Carson City, NV**	NA
NA	Charlotte-Gastonia, NC-SC**	NA
NA	Charlottesville, VA**	NA
NA	Chicago, IL**	NA
NA	Cleveland-Elyria-Mentor, OH**	NA
NA	Cleveland, TN**	NA
NA	Coeur d'Alene, ID**	NA
NA	College Station-Bryan, TX**	NA
NA	Columbus, IN**	NA
NA	Dallas (greater), TX**	NA
NA	Dalton, GA**	NA
NA	Dayton, OH**	NA
NA	Des Moines-West Des Moines, IA**	NA
NA	Detroit-Livonia-Dearborn, MI M.D.**	NA
NA	Dothan, AL**	NA
NA	Durham, NC**	NA
NA	Edison, NJ M.D.**	NA
NA	El Centro, CA**	NA
NA	Elizabethtown, KY**	NA
NA	Elmira, NY**	NA
NA	Evansville, IN-KY**	NA
NA	Fairbanks, AK**	NA
NA	Farmington, NM**	NA
NA	Fayetteville, AR-MO**	NA
NA	Fond du Lac, WI**	NA
NA	Fort Wayne, IN**	NA
NA	Gainesville, GA**	NA
NA	Grand Forks, ND-MN**	NA
NA	Grand Rapids-Wyoming, MI**	NA
NA	Greensboro-High Point, NC**	NA
NA	Greenville, SC**	NA
NA	Hagerstown-Martinsburg, MD-WV**	NA
NA	Hanford-Corcoran, CA**	NA
NA	Harrisburg-Carlisle, PA**	NA
NA	Harrisonburg, VA**	NA
NA	Hattiesburg, MS**	NA
NA	Holland-Grand Haven, MI**	NA
NA	Hot Springs, AR**	NA
NA	Huntington-Ashland, WV-KY-OH**	NA
NA	Idaho Falls, ID**	NA
NA	Indianapolis, IN**	NA
NA	Ithaca, NY**	NA
NA	Jacksonville, NC**	NA
NA	Jefferson City, MO**	NA
NA	Johnson City, TN**	NA
NA	Johnstown, PA**	NA
NA	Kalamazoo-Portage, MI**	NA
NA	Kansas City, MO-KS**	NA
NA	Kingsport, TN-VA**	NA
NA	Kingston, NY**	NA
NA	Lake Havasu City-Kingman, AZ**	NA
NA	Las Cruces, NM**	NA
NA	Lebanon, PA**	NA
NA	Lewiston, ID-WA**	NA
NA	Lexington-Fayette, KY**	NA
NA	Lima, OH**	NA
NA	Logan, UT-ID**	NA
NA	Longview, WA**	NA
NA	Los Angeles (greater), CA**	NA
NA	Macon, GA**	NA
NA	Madera, CA**	NA
NA	Manchester-Nashua, NH**	NA
NA	Mansfield, OH**	NA
NA	Memphis, TN-MS-AR**	NA
NA	Miami (greater), FL**	NA
NA	Michigan City-La Porte, IN**	NA
NA	Midland, TX**	NA
NA	Milwaukee, WI**	NA
NA	Missoula, MT**	NA
NA	Mobile, AL**	NA
NA	Monroe, LA**	NA
NA	Monroe, MI**	NA
NA	Morgantown, WV**	NA
NA	Morristown, TN**	NA
NA	Mount Vernon-Anacortes, WA**	NA
NA	Muskegon-Norton Shores, MI**	NA
NA	Napa, CA**	NA
NA	Nassau-Suffolk, NY M.D.**	NA
NA	New York (greater), NY-NJ-PA**	NA
NA	Niles-Benton Harbor, MI**	NA
NA	Ocean City, NJ**	NA
NA	Odessa, TX**	NA
NA	Ogden-Clearfield, UT**	NA
NA	Oshkosh-Neenah, WI**	NA
NA	Oxnard-Thousand Oaks, CA**	NA
NA	Palm Coast, FL**	NA
NA	Pascagoula, MS**	NA
NA	Philadelphia, PA M.D.**	NA
NA	Pittsfield, MA**	NA
NA	Portland, ME**	NA
NA	Poughkeepsie, NY**	NA
NA	Prescott, AZ**	NA
NA	Raleigh-Cary, NC**	NA
NA	Roanoke, VA**	NA
NA	Rome, GA**	NA
NA	Saginaw, MI**	NA
NA	Salisbury, MD**	NA
NA	Salt Lake City, UT**	NA
NA	San Francisco (greater), CA**	NA
NA	Sandusky, OH**	NA
NA	Santa Barbara-Santa Maria, CA**	NA
NA	Seattle (greater), WA**	NA
NA	Sebastian-Vero Beach, FL**	NA
NA	Spartanburg, SC**	NA
NA	Springfield, MA**	NA
NA	Springfield, OH**	NA
NA	St. Louis, MO-IL**	NA
NA	Syracuse, NY**	NA
NA	Valdosta, GA**	NA
NA	Vallejo-Fairfield, CA**	NA
NA	Warner Robins, GA**	NA
NA	Warren-Farmington Hills, MI M.D.**	NA
NA	Washington (greater) DC-VA-MD**	NA
NA	Washington, DC-VA-MD-WV M.D.**	NA
NA	Wenatchee, WA**	NA
NA	Wheeling, WV-OH**	NA
NA	Wilmington, DE-MD-NJ M.D.**	NA
NA	Winchester, VA-WV**	NA
NA	Winston-Salem, NC**	NA
NA	Worcester, MA**	NA

Source: CQ Press using data from Federal Bureau of Investigation "Crime in the United States 2006" (Uniform Crime Reports, September 24, 2007)

**Burglary is the unlawful entry of a structure to commit a felony or theft. Attempts are included.*

***Not available.*

33. Larcenies and Thefts in 2006

National Total = 6,607,013 Larcenies and Thefts*

RANK	METROPOLITAN AREA	THEFTS
240	Abilene, TX	3,852
89	Albany-Schenectady-Troy, NY	17,314
217	Albany, GA	4,494
68	Albuquerque, NM	23,336
213	Alexandria, LA	4,669
315	Altoona, PA	2,237
157	Amarillo, TX	8,182
339	Ames, IA	1,559
138	Anchorage, AK	9,524
188	Anderson, SC	5,486
169	Ann Arbor, MI	6,691
232	Appleton, WI	4,067
164	Asheville, NC	7,275
183	Athens-Clarke County, GA	5,731
8	Atlanta, GA	118,849
158	Atlantic City, NJ	8,072
91	Augusta, GA-SC	16,399
40	Austin-Round Rock, TX	44,089
84	Bakersfield, CA	18,991
25	Baltimore-Towson, MD	60,997
247	Bangor, ME	3,699
255	Barnstable Town, MA	3,569
70	Baton Rouge, LA	23,173
234	Battle Creek, MI	4,011
329	Bay City, MI	1,940
135	Beaumont-Port Arthur, TX	9,750
175	Bellingham, WA	6,504
244	Bend, OR	3,771
79	Bethesda-Frederick, MD M.D.	20,348
223	Billings, MT	4,324
194	Binghamton, NY	5,307
57	Birmingham-Hoover, AL	31,463
338	Bismarck, ND	1,678
279	Blacksburg, VA	3,033
249	Bloomington, IN	3,694
124	Boise City-Nampa, ID	10,704
297	Bowling Green, KY	2,679
228	Bremerton-Silverdale, WA	4,178
103	Brownsville-Harlingen, TX	13,316
274	Brunswick, GA	3,081
74	Buffalo-Niagara Falls, NY	22,475
237	Burlington, NC	3,961
67	Camden, NJ M.D.	23,515
110	Cape Coral-Fort Myers, FL	11,998
348	Carson City, NV	819
307	Casper, WY	2,451
187	Cedar Rapids, IA	5,571
87	Charleston-North Charleston, SC	17,713
161	Charleston, WV	7,653
35	Charlotte-Gastonia, NC-SC	49,944
226	Charlottesville, VA	4,230
97	Chattanooga, TN-GA	15,132
309	Cheyenne, WY	2,356
NA	Chicago, IL**	NA
233	Chico, CA	4,012
28	Cincinnati-Middletown, OH-KY-IN	54,862
206	Clarksville, TN-KY	4,859
49	Cleveland-Elyria-Mentor, OH	39,190
310	Cleveland, TN	2,343
298	Coeur d'Alene, ID	2,673
182	College Station-Bryan, TX	5,941
95	Colorado Springs, CO	15,642
259	Columbia, MO	3,447
83	Columbia, SC	19,134
122	Columbus, GA-AL	10,816
305	Columbus, IN	2,556
34	Columbus, OH	51,149
81	Corpus Christi, TX	19,508
331	Cumberland, MD-WV	1,915
3	Dallas (greater), TX	173,946
11	Dallas-Plano-Irving, TX M.D.	113,204
275	Dalton, GA	3,062
330	Danville, VA	1,920
111	Daytona Beach, FL	11,877
78	Dayton, OH	20,775
236	Decatur, AL	3,964
27	Denver-Aurora, CO	55,872
92	Des Moines-West Des Moines, IA	16,249
15	Detroit (greater), MI	85,864
39	Detroit-Livonia-Dearborn, MI M.D.	44,184
266	Dothan, AL	3,265
264	Dover, DE	3,289
347	Dubuque, IA	1,305
168	Duluth, MN-WI	6,890
99	Durham, NC	13,859
283	Eau Claire, WI	2,975
56	Edison, NJ M.D.	32,482
276	El Centro, CA	3,054
90	El Paso, TX	17,096
344	Elizabethtown, KY	1,383
199	Elkhart-Goshen, IN	5,136
332	Elmira, NY	1,902
231	Erie, PA	4,080
133	Eugene-Springfield, OR	9,952
163	Evansville, IN-KY	7,528
343	Fairbanks, AK	1,419
269	Fargo, ND-MN	3,206
326	Farmington, NM	2,001
140	Fayetteville, AR-MO	9,403
104	Fayetteville, NC	13,281
214	Flagstaff, AZ	4,623
128	Flint, MI	10,210
156	Florence, SC	8,200
342	Fond du Lac, WI	1,487
173	Fort Collins-Loveland, CO	6,532
38	Fort Lauderdale, FL M.D.	44,240
170	Fort Smith, AR-OK	6,690
239	Fort Walton Beach, FL	3,884
136	Fort Wayne, IN	9,688
26	Fort Worth-Arlington, TX M.D.	60,742
65	Fresno, CA	23,728
262	Gadsden, AL	3,400
160	Gainesville, FL	7,655
258	Gainesville, GA	3,467
324	Glens Falls, NY	2,018
273	Goldsboro, NC	3,092
328	Grand Forks, ND-MN	1,976
263	Grand Junction, CO	3,379
88	Grand Rapids-Wyoming, MI	17,662
301	Great Falls, MT	2,592
184	Greeley, CO	5,660
200	Green Bay, WI	5,074
80	Greensboro-High Point, NC	20,110
202	Greenville, NC	5,044
98	Greenville, SC	14,916
216	Hagerstown-Martinsburg, MD-WV	4,504
314	Hanford-Corcoran, CA	2,253
147	Harrisburg-Carlisle, PA	8,966
345	Harrisonburg, VA	1,345
73	Hartford, CT	22,665
300	Hattiesburg, MS	2,665
241	Holland-Grand Haven, MI	3,828
61	Honolulu, HI	26,540
219	Hot Springs, AR	4,462
195	Houma, LA	5,266
7	Houston, TX	139,587
180	Huntington-Ashland, WV-KY-OH	6,221
116	Huntsville, AL	11,383
311	Idaho Falls, ID	2,327
41	Indianapolis, IN	43,426
316	Iowa City, IA	2,220
319	Ithaca, NY	2,162
48	Jacksonville, FL	39,352
268	Jacksonville, NC	3,220
243	Jackson, MI	3,778
107	Jackson, MS	12,759
246	Jackson, TN	3,719
218	Janesville, WI	4,473
302	Jefferson City, MO	2,585
220	Johnson City, TN	4,381
308	Johnstown, PA	2,415
278	Jonesboro, AR	3,036
198	Joplin, MO	5,158
149	Kalamazoo-Portage, MI	8,915
31	Kansas City, MO-KS	53,770
197	Kennewick-Richland-Pasco, WA	5,211
154	Killeen-Temple-Fort Hood, TX	8,214
162	Kingsport, TN-VA	7,597
306	Kingston, NY	2,553
93	Knoxville, TN	16,187
289	Kokomo, IN	2,869
299	La Crosse, WI-MN	2,671
227	Lafayette, IN	4,208
193	Lake Charles, LA	5,338
185	Lake Havasu City-Kingman, AZ	5,656
102	Lakeland, FL	13,403
152	Lancaster, PA	8,485
146	Lansing-East Lansing, MI	9,061
132	Laredo, TX	9,956
229	Las Cruces, NM	4,162
53	Las Vegas-Paradise, NV	35,849

Note: All listings are for Metropolitan Statistical Areas (M.S.A.s) except for those ending with "M.D." Listings with "M.D." are Metropolitan Divisions which are smaller parts of eleven large M.S.A.s. See explanatory note at beginning of metropolitan area section on page 23.

Alpha Order - Metro Area (continued)

RANK	METROPOLITAN AREA	THEFTS
212	Lawrence, KS	4,718
277	Lawton, OK	3,038
327	Lebanon, PA	1,991
321	Lewiston-Auburn, ME	2,140
341	Lewiston, ID-WA	1,510
117	Lexington-Fayette, KY	11,317
290	Lima, OH	2,856
123	Lincoln, NE	10,757
63	Little Rock, AR	24,409
340	Logan, UT-ID	1,527
174	Longview, TX	6,507
257	Longview, WA	3,519
6	Los Angeles County, CA M.D.	149,138
2	Los Angeles (greater), CA	193,468
60	Louisville, KY-IN	28,531
139	Lubbock, TX	9,508
255	Lynchburg, VA	3,569
144	Macon, GA	9,161
336	Madera, CA	1,791
112	Madison, WI	11,717
179	Manchester-Nashua, NH	6,236
215	Mansfield, OH	4,571
71	McAllen-Edinburg-Mission, TX	22,935
209	Medford, OR	4,810
36	Memphis, TN-MS-AR	46,447
196	Merced, CA	5,250
4	Miami (greater), FL	160,079
18	Miami-Dade County, FL M.D.	80,282
253	Michigan City-La Porte, IN	3,593
281	Midland, TX	2,997
45	Milwaukee, WI	41,360
17	Minneapolis-St. Paul, MN-WI	80,415
272	Missoula, MT	3,126
100	Mobile, AL	13,762
96	Modesto, CA	15,586
181	Monroe, LA	5,981
303	Monroe, MI	2,582
120	Montgomery, AL	11,248
333	Morgantown, WV	1,898
265	Morristown, TN	3,277
203	Mount Vernon-Anacortes, WA	5,010
280	Muncie, IN	3,011
171	Muskegon-Norton Shores, MI	6,671
125	Myrtle Beach, SC	10,541
317	Napa, CA	2,169
221	Naples-Marco Island, FL	4,379
50	Nashville-Davidson, TN	39,143
52	Nassau-Suffolk, NY M.D.	37,111
64	New Orleans, LA	24,145
1	New York (greater), NY-NJ-PA	258,495
5	New York-W. Plains NY-NJ M.D.	159,082
58	Newark-Union, NJ-PA M.D.	29,820
235	Niles-Benton Harbor, MI	3,970
30	Oakland-Fremont, CA M.D.	54,401
192	Ocala, FL	5,376
248	Ocean City, NJ	3,696
261	Odessa, TX	3,405
115	Ogden-Clearfield, UT	11,501
55	Oklahoma City, OK	33,305
190	Olympia, WA	5,426
66	Omaha-Council Bluffs, NE-IA	23,550
32	Orlando, FL	52,944
286	Oshkosh-Neenah, WI	2,922
118	Oxnard-Thousand Oaks, CA	11,314
109	Palm Bay-Melbourne, FL	12,270
346	Palm Coast, FL	1,332
211	Panama City-Lynn Haven, FL	4,720
254	Pascagoula, MS	3,570
127	Pensacola, FL	10,272
9	Philadelphia (greater) PA-NJ-DE	117,710
19	Philadelphia, PA M.D.	78,194
10	Phoenix-Mesa-Scottsdale, AZ	115,375
304	Pine Bluff, AR	2,576
47	Pittsburgh, PA	39,650
335	Pittsfield, MA	1,886
325	Pocatello, ID	2,012
153	Port St. Lucie, FL	8,257
29	Portland-Vancouver, OR-WA	54,858
129	Portland, ME	10,179
131	Poughkeepsie, NY	10,074
242	Prescott, AZ	3,816
150	Provo-Orem, UT	8,867
186	Pueblo, CO	5,580
245	Punta Gorda, FL	3,754
204	Racine, WI	4,945
85	Raleigh-Cary, NC	18,860
318	Rapid City, SD	2,168
172	Reading, PA	6,569
284	Redding, CA	2,964
126	Reno-Sparks, NV	10,395
62	Richmond, VA	25,308
22	Riverside-San Bernardino, CA	73,633
177	Roanoke, VA	6,319
293	Rochester, MN	2,814
75	Rochester, NY	22,251
208	Rocky Mount, NC	4,834
288	Rome, GA	2,908
42	Sacramento, CA	43,274
230	Saginaw, MI	4,099
114	Salem, OR	11,525
155	Salinas, CA	8,204
252	Salisbury, MD	3,603
51	Salt Lake City, UT	37,767
251	San Angelo, TX	3,617
23	San Antonio, TX	72,134
33	San Diego, CA	51,454
14	San Francisco (greater), CA	95,040
46	San Francisco-S. Mateo, CA M.D.	40,639
59	San Jose, CA	28,751
210	San Luis Obispo, CA	4,737
320	Sandusky, OH	2,161
37	Santa Ana-Anaheim, CA M.D.	44,330
178	Santa Barbara-Santa Maria, CA	6,268
166	Santa Cruz-Watsonville, CA	7,118
322	Santa Fe, NM	2,132
167	Santa Rosa-Petaluma, CA	6,903
82	Sarasota-Bradenton-Venice, FL	19,358
145	Savannah, GA	9,155
134	Scranton--Wilkes-Barre, PA	9,868
13	Seattle (greater), WA	98,622
20	Seattle-Bellevue, WA M.D.	75,295
291	Sebastian-Vero Beach, FL	2,852
295	Sheboygan, WI	2,775
296	Sherman-Denison, TX	2,726
108	Shreveport-Bossier City, LA	12,576
285	Sioux City, IA-NE-SD	2,958
282	Sioux Falls, SD	2,976
130	South Bend-Mishawaka, IN-MI	10,166
151	Spartanburg, SC	8,691
113	Spokane, WA	11,590
106	Springfield, MA	12,882
101	Springfield, MO	13,744
189	Springfield, OH	5,461
312	State College, PA	2,309
72	Stockton, CA	22,705
225	St. Cloud, MN	4,257
260	St. Joseph, MO-KS	3,409
24	St. Louis, MO-IL	71,794
287	Sumter, SC	2,912
119	Syracuse, NY	11,262
69	Tacoma, WA M.D.	23,327
159	Tallahassee, FL	7,912
21	Tampa-St Petersburg, FL	74,405
250	Texarkana, TX-Texarkana, AR	3,639
77	Toledo, OH	20,960
148	Topeka, KS	8,935
191	Trenton-Ewing, NJ	5,403
NA	Tucson, AZ**	NA
76	Tulsa, OK	21,106
176	Tuscaloosa, AL	6,327
205	Tyler, TX	4,901
207	Utica-Rome, NY	4,853
238	Valdosta, GA	3,915
141	Vallejo-Fairfield, CA	9,329
294	Victoria, TX	2,797
222	Vineland, NJ	4,329
43	Virginia Beach-Norfolk, VA-NC	42,653
121	Visalia-Porterville, CA	10,858
165	Waco, TX	7,222
270	Warner Robins, GA	3,149
44	Warren-Farmington Hills, MI M.D.	41,680
12	Washington (greater) DC-VA-MD	102,905
16	Washington, DC-VA-MD-WV M.D.	82,557
267	Waterloo-Cedar Falls, IA	3,234
333	Wausau, WI	1,898
271	Wenatchee, WA	3,130
54	West Palm Beach, FL M.D.	35,557
337	Wheeling, WV-OH	1,754
201	Wichita Falls, TX	5,062
86	Wichita, KS	18,838
323	Williamsport, PA	2,075
94	Wilmington, DE-MD-NJ M.D.	16,001
143	Wilmington, NC	9,210
313	Winchester, VA-WV	2,270
105	Winston-Salem, NC	13,122
137	Worcester, MA	9,526
142	Yakima, WA	9,280
292	Yuba City, CA	2,840
224	Yuma, AZ	4,312

Source: Federal Bureau of Investigation

"Crime in the United States 2006" (Uniform Crime Reports, September 24, 2007)

**Larceny and theft is the unlawful taking of property. Attempts are included.*

***Not available.*

33. Larcenies and Thefts in 2006 (continued)

National Total = 6,607,013 Larcenies and Thefts*

RANK	METROPOLITAN AREA	THEFTS
1	New York (greater), NY-NJ-PA	258,495
2	Los Angeles (greater), CA	193,468
3	Dallas (greater), TX	173,946
4	Miami (greater), FL	160,079
5	New York-W. Plains NY-NJ M.D.	159,082
6	Los Angeles County, CA M.D.	149,138
7	Houston, TX	139,587
8	Atlanta, GA	118,849
9	Philadelphia (greater) PA-NJ-DE	117,710
10	Phoenix-Mesa-Scottsdale, AZ	115,375
11	Dallas-Plano-Irving, TX M.D.	113,204
12	Washington (greater) DC-VA-MD	102,905
13	Seattle (greater), WA	98,622
14	San Francisco (greater), CA	95,040
15	Detroit (greater), MI	85,864
16	Washington, DC-VA-MD-WV M.D.	82,557
17	Minneapolis-St. Paul, MN-WI	80,415
18	Miami-Dade County, FL M.D.	80,282
19	Philadelphia, PA M.D.	78,194
20	Seattle-Bellevue, WA M.D.	75,295
21	Tampa-St Petersburg, FL	74,405
22	Riverside-San Bernardino, CA	73,633
23	San Antonio, TX	72,134
24	St. Louis, MO-IL	71,794
25	Baltimore-Towson, MD	60,997
26	Fort Worth-Arlington, TX M.D.	60,742
27	Denver-Aurora, CO	55,872
28	Cincinnati-Middletown, OH-KY-IN	54,862
29	Portland-Vancouver, OR-WA	54,858
30	Oakland-Fremont, CA M.D.	54,401
31	Kansas City, MO-KS	53,770
32	Orlando, FL	52,944
33	San Diego, CA	51,454
34	Columbus, OH	51,149
35	Charlotte-Gastonia, NC-SC	49,944
36	Memphis, TN-MS-AR	46,447
37	Santa Ana-Anaheim, CA M.D.	44,330
38	Fort Lauderdale, FL M.D.	44,240
39	Detroit-Livonia-Dearborn, MI M.D.	44,184
40	Austin-Round Rock, TX	44,089
41	Indianapolis, IN	43,426
42	Sacramento, CA	43,274
43	Virginia Beach-Norfolk, VA-NC	42,653
44	Warren-Farmington Hills, MI M.D.	41,680
45	Milwaukee, WI	41,360
46	San Francisco-S. Mateo, CA M.D.	40,639
47	Pittsburgh, PA	39,650
48	Jacksonville, FL	39,352
49	Cleveland-Elyria-Mentor, OH	39,190
50	Nashville-Davidson, TN	39,143
51	Salt Lake City, UT	37,767
52	Nassau-Suffolk, NY M.D.	37,111
53	Las Vegas-Paradise, NV	35,849
54	West Palm Beach, FL M.D.	35,557
55	Oklahoma City, OK	33,305
56	Edison, NJ M.D.	32,482
57	Birmingham-Hoover, AL	31,463
58	Newark-Union, NJ-PA M.D.	29,820
59	San Jose, CA	28,751
60	Louisville, KY-IN	28,531
61	Honolulu, HI	26,540
62	Richmond, VA	25,308
63	Little Rock, AR	24,409
64	New Orleans, LA	24,145
65	Fresno, CA	23,728
66	Omaha-Council Bluffs, NE-IA	23,550
67	Camden, NJ M.D.	23,515
68	Albuquerque, NM	23,336
69	Tacoma, WA M.D.	23,327
70	Baton Rouge, LA	23,173
71	McAllen-Edinburg-Mission, TX	22,935
72	Stockton, CA	22,705
73	Hartford, CT	22,665
74	Buffalo-Niagara Falls, NY	22,475
75	Rochester, NY	22,251
76	Tulsa, OK	21,106
77	Toledo, OH	20,960
78	Dayton, OH	20,775
79	Bethesda-Frederick, MD M.D.	20,348
80	Greensboro-High Point, NC	20,110
81	Corpus Christi, TX	19,508
82	Sarasota-Bradenton-Venice, FL	19,358
83	Columbia, SC	19,134
84	Bakersfield, CA	18,991
85	Raleigh-Cary, NC	18,860
86	Wichita, KS	18,838
87	Charleston-North Charleston, SC	17,713
88	Grand Rapids-Wyoming, MI	17,662
89	Albany-Schenectady-Troy, NY	17,314
90	El Paso, TX	17,096
91	Augusta, GA-SC	16,399
92	Des Moines-West Des Moines, IA	16,249
93	Knoxville, TN	16,187
94	Wilmington, DE-MD-NJ M.D.	16,001
95	Colorado Springs, CO	15,642
96	Modesto, CA	15,586
97	Chattanooga, TN-GA	15,132
98	Greenville, SC	14,916
99	Durham, NC	13,859
100	Mobile, AL	13,762
101	Springfield, MO	13,744
102	Lakeland, FL	13,403
103	Brownsville-Harlingen, TX	13,316
104	Fayetteville, NC	13,281
105	Winston-Salem, NC	13,122
106	Springfield, MA	12,882
107	Jackson, MS	12,759
108	Shreveport-Bossier City, LA	12,576
109	Palm Bay-Melbourne, FL	12,270
110	Cape Coral-Fort Myers, FL	11,998
111	Daytona Beach, FL	11,877
112	Madison, WI	11,717
113	Spokane, WA	11,590
114	Salem, OR	11,525
115	Ogden-Clearfield, UT	11,501
116	Huntsville, AL	11,383
117	Lexington-Fayette, KY	11,317
118	Oxnard-Thousand Oaks, CA	11,314
119	Syracuse, NY	11,262
120	Montgomery, AL	11,248
121	Visalia-Porterville, CA	10,858
122	Columbus, GA-AL	10,816
123	Lincoln, NE	10,757
124	Boise City-Nampa, ID	10,704
125	Myrtle Beach, SC	10,541
126	Reno-Sparks, NV	10,395
127	Pensacola, FL	10,272
128	Flint, MI	10,210
129	Portland, ME	10,179
130	South Bend-Mishawaka, IN-MI	10,166
131	Poughkeepsie, NY	10,074
132	Laredo, TX	9,956
133	Eugene-Springfield, OR	9,952
134	Scranton--Wilkes-Barre, PA	9,868
135	Beaumont-Port Arthur, TX	9,750
136	Fort Wayne, IN	9,688
137	Worcester, MA	9,526
138	Anchorage, AK	9,524
139	Lubbock, TX	9,508
140	Fayetteville, AR-MO	9,403
141	Vallejo-Fairfield, CA	9,329
142	Yakima, WA	9,280
143	Wilmington, NC	9,210
144	Macon, GA	9,161
145	Savannah, GA	9,155
146	Lansing-East Lansing, MI	9,061
147	Harrisburg-Carlisle, PA	8,966
148	Topeka, KS	8,935
149	Kalamazoo-Portage, MI	8,915
150	Provo-Orem, UT	8,867
151	Spartanburg, SC	8,691
152	Lancaster, PA	8,485
153	Port St. Lucie, FL	8,257
154	Killeen-Temple-Fort Hood, TX	8,214
155	Salinas, CA	8,204
156	Florence, SC	8,200
157	Amarillo, TX	8,182
158	Atlantic City, NJ	8,072
159	Tallahassee, FL	7,912
160	Gainesville, FL	7,655
161	Charleston, WV	7,653
162	Kingsport, TN-VA	7,597
163	Evansville, IN-KY	7,528
164	Asheville, NC	7,275
165	Waco, TX	7,222
166	Santa Cruz-Watsonville, CA	7,118
167	Santa Rosa-Petaluma, CA	6,903
168	Duluth, MN-WI	6,890
169	Ann Arbor, MI	6,691
170	Fort Smith, AR-OK	6,690
171	Muskegon-Norton Shores, MI	6,671

Note: All listings are for Metropolitan Statistical Areas (M.S.A.s) except for those ending with "M.D." Listings with "M.D." are Metropolitan Divisions which are smaller parts of eleven large M.S.A.s. See explanatory note at beginning of metropolitan area section on page 23.

RANK	METROPOLITAN AREA	THEFTS
172	Reading, PA	6,569
173	Fort Collins-Loveland, CO	6,532
174	Longview, TX	6,507
175	Bellingham, WA	6,504
176	Tuscaloosa, AL	6,327
177	Roanoke, VA	6,319
178	Santa Barbara-Santa Maria, CA	6,268
179	Manchester-Nashua, NH	6,236
180	Huntington-Ashland, WV-KY-OH	6,221
181	Monroe, LA	5,981
182	College Station-Bryan, TX	5,941
183	Athens-Clarke County, GA	5,731
184	Greeley, CO	5,660
185	Lake Havasu City-Kingman, AZ	5,656
186	Pueblo, CO	5,580
187	Cedar Rapids, IA	5,571
188	Anderson, SC	5,486
189	Springfield, OH	5,461
190	Olympia, WA	5,426
191	Trenton-Ewing, NJ	5,403
192	Ocala, FL	5,376
193	Lake Charles, LA	5,338
194	Binghamton, NY	5,307
195	Houma, LA	5,266
196	Merced, CA	5,250
197	Kennewick-Richland-Pasco, WA	5,211
198	Joplin, MO	5,158
199	Elkhart-Goshen, IN	5,136
200	Green Bay, WI	5,074
201	Wichita Falls, TX	5,062
202	Greenville, NC	5,044
203	Mount Vernon-Anacortes, WA	5,010
204	Racine, WI	4,945
205	Tyler, TX	4,901
206	Clarksville, TN-KY	4,859
207	Utica-Rome, NY	4,853
208	Rocky Mount, NC	4,834
209	Medford, OR	4,810
210	San Luis Obispo, CA	4,737
211	Panama City-Lynn Haven, FL	4,720
212	Lawrence, KS	4,718
213	Alexandria, LA	4,669
214	Flagstaff, AZ	4,623
215	Mansfield, OH	4,571
216	Hagerstown-Martinsburg, MD-WV	4,504
217	Albany, GA	4,494
218	Janesville, WI	4,473
219	Hot Springs, AR	4,462
220	Johnson City, TN	4,381
221	Naples-Marco Island, FL	4,379
222	Vineland, NJ	4,329
223	Billings, MT	4,324
224	Yuma, AZ	4,312
225	St. Cloud, MN	4,257
226	Charlottesville, VA	4,230
227	Lafayette, IN	4,208
228	Bremerton-Silverdale, WA	4,178
229	Las Cruces, NM	4,162
230	Saginaw, MI	4,099
231	Erie, PA	4,080
232	Appleton, WI	4,067
233	Chico, CA	4,012
234	Battle Creek, MI	4,011
235	Niles-Benton Harbor, MI	3,970
236	Decatur, AL	3,964
237	Burlington, NC	3,961
238	Valdosta, GA	3,915
239	Fort Walton Beach, FL	3,884
240	Abilene, TX	3,852
241	Holland-Grand Haven, MI	3,828
242	Prescott, AZ	3,816
243	Jackson, MI	3,778
244	Bend, OR	3,771
245	Punta Gorda, FL	3,754
246	Jackson, TN	3,719
247	Bangor, ME	3,699
248	Ocean City, NJ	3,696
249	Bloomington, IN	3,694
250	Texarkana, TX-Texarkana, AR	3,639
251	San Angelo, TX	3,617
252	Salisbury, MD	3,603
253	Michigan City-La Porte, IN	3,593
254	Pascagoula, MS	3,570
255	Barnstable Town, MA	3,569
255	Lynchburg, VA	3,569
257	Longview, WA	3,519
258	Gainesville, GA	3,467
259	Columbia, MO	3,447
260	St. Joseph, MO-KS	3,409
261	Odessa, TX	3,405
262	Gadsden, AL	3,400
263	Grand Junction, CO	3,379
264	Dover, DE	3,289
265	Morristown, TN	3,277
266	Dothan, AL	3,265
267	Waterloo-Cedar Falls, IA	3,234
268	Jacksonville, NC	3,220
269	Fargo, ND-MN	3,206
270	Warner Robins, GA	3,149
271	Wenatchee, WA	3,130
272	Missoula, MT	3,126
273	Goldsboro, NC	3,092
274	Brunswick, GA	3,081
275	Dalton, GA	3,062
276	El Centro, CA	3,054
277	Lawton, OK	3,038
278	Jonesboro, AR	3,036
279	Blacksburg, VA	3,033
280	Muncie, IN	3,011
281	Midland, TX	2,997
282	Sioux Falls, SD	2,976
283	Eau Claire, WI	2,975
284	Redding, CA	2,964
285	Sioux City, IA-NE-SD	2,958
286	Oshkosh-Neenah, WI	2,922
287	Sumter, SC	2,912
288	Rome, GA	2,908
289	Kokomo, IN	2,869
290	Lima, OH	2,856
291	Sebastian-Vero Beach, FL	2,852
292	Yuba City, CA	2,840
293	Rochester, MN	2,814
294	Victoria, TX	2,797
295	Sheboygan, WI	2,775
296	Sherman-Denison, TX	2,726
297	Bowling Green, KY	2,679
298	Coeur d'Alene, ID	2,673
299	La Crosse, WI-MN	2,671
300	Hattiesburg, MS	2,665
301	Great Falls, MT	2,592
302	Jefferson City, MO	2,585
303	Monroe, MI	2,582
304	Pine Bluff, AR	2,576
305	Columbus, IN	2,556
306	Kingston, NY	2,553
307	Casper, WY	2,451
308	Johnstown, PA	2,415
309	Cheyenne, WY	2,356
310	Cleveland, TN	2,343
311	Idaho Falls, ID	2,327
312	State College, PA	2,309
313	Winchester, VA-WV	2,270
314	Hanford-Corcoran, CA	2,253
315	Altoona, PA	2,237
316	Iowa City, IA	2,220
317	Napa, CA	2,169
318	Rapid City, SD	2,168
319	Ithaca, NY	2,162
320	Sandusky, OH	2,161
321	Lewiston-Auburn, ME	2,140
322	Santa Fe, NM	2,132
323	Williamsport, PA	2,075
324	Glens Falls, NY	2,018
325	Pocatello, ID	2,012
326	Farmington, NM	2,001
327	Lebanon, PA	1,991
328	Grand Forks, ND-MN	1,976
329	Bay City, MI	1,940
330	Danville, VA	1,920
331	Cumberland, MD-WV	1,915
332	Elmira, NY	1,902
333	Morgantown, WV	1,898
333	Wausau, WI	1,898
335	Pittsfield, MA	1,886
336	Madera, CA	1,791
337	Wheeling, WV-OH	1,754
338	Bismarck, ND	1,678
339	Ames, IA	1,559
340	Logan, UT-ID	1,527
341	Lewiston, ID-WA	1,510
342	Fond du Lac, WI	1,487
343	Fairbanks, AK	1,419
344	Elizabethtown, KY	1,383
345	Harrisonburg, VA	1,345
346	Palm Coast, FL	1,332
347	Dubuque, IA	1,305
348	Carson City, NV	819
NA	Chicago, IL**	NA
NA	Tucson, AZ**	NA

Source: Federal Bureau of Investigation
"Crime in the United States 2006" (Uniform Crime Reports, September 24, 2007)
**Larceny and theft is the unlawful taking of property. Attempts are included.*
***Not available.*

34. Larceny and Theft Rate in 2006

National Rate = 2,206.8 Larcenies and Thefts per 100,000 Population*

RANK	METROPOLITAN AREA	RATE
177	Abilene, TX	2,366.4
238	Albany-Schenectady-Troy, NY	2,034.2
127	Albany, GA	2,673.9
94	Albuquerque, NM	2,885.3
39	Alexandria, LA	3,329.1
285	Altoona, PA	1,762.7
37	Amarillo, TX	3,333.8
260	Ames, IA	1,939.6
45	Anchorage, AK	3,230.0
64	Anderson, SC	3,077.8
255	Ann Arbor, MI	1,962.2
269	Appleton, WI	1,883.5
278	Asheville, NC	1,815.7
54	Athens-Clarke County, GA	3,171.4
182	Atlanta, GA	2,341.6
81	Atlantic City, NJ	2,976.2
65	Augusta, GA-SC	3,070.2
82	Austin-Round Rock, TX	2,951.7
154	Bakersfield, CA	2,486.9
197	Baltimore-Towson, MD	2,290.6
149	Bangor, ME	2,515.0
312	Barnstable Town, MA	1,566.2
38	Baton Rouge, LA	3,331.7
92	Battle Creek, MI	2,888.9
282	Bay City, MI	1,783.8
158	Beaumont-Port Arthur, TX	2,472.1
27	Bellingham, WA	3,485.1
134	Bend, OR	2,624.2
284	Bethesda-Frederick, MD M.D.	1,767.2
86	Billings, MT	2,921.7
229	Binghamton, NY	2,130.6
100	Birmingham-Hoover, AL	2,860.3
297	Bismarck, ND	1,691.2
248	Blacksburg, VA	1,988.0
234	Bloomington, IN	2,065.0
265	Boise City-Nampa, ID	1,916.8
172	Bowling Green, KY	2,395.0
295	Bremerton-Silverdale, WA	1,706.7
32	Brownsville-Harlingen, TX	3,422.9
73	Brunswick, GA	3,032.7
256	Buffalo-Niagara Falls, NY	1,953.0
113	Burlington, NC	2,763.4
268	Camden, NJ M.D.	1,886.0
220	Cape Coral-Fort Myers, FL	2,165.9
333	Carson City, NV	1,413.6
28	Casper, WY	3,472.6
210	Cedar Rapids, IA	2,248.9
84	Charleston-North Charleston, SC	2,931.9
152	Charleston, WV	2,495.2
48	Charlotte-Gastonia, NC-SC	3,220.5
213	Charlottesville, VA	2,222.8
76	Chattanooga, TN-GA	3,019.7
117	Cheyenne, WY	2,735.8
NA	Chicago, IL**	NA
272	Chico, CA	1,856.4
131	Cincinnati-Middletown, OH-KY-IN	2,642.6
253	Clarksville, TN-KY	1,972.4
274	Cleveland-Elyria-Mentor, OH	1,840.9
223	Cleveland, TN	2,141.5
237	Coeur d'Alene, ID	2,040.4
70	College Station-Bryan, TX	3,044.9
136	Colorado Springs, CO	2,613.1
212	Columbia, MO	2,232.5
118	Columbia, SC	2,731.1
18	Columbus, GA-AL	3,700.4
30	Columbus, IN	3,452.8
79	Columbus, OH	2,989.9
2	Corpus Christi, TX	4,587.2
266	Cumberland, MD-WV	1,898.1
90	Dallas (greater), TX	2,906.7
104	Dallas-Plano-Irving, TX M.D.	2,827.7
209	Dalton, GA	2,252.6
286	Danville, VA	1,760.3
174	Daytona Beach, FL	2,383.4
159	Dayton, OH	2,459.7
130	Decatur, AL	2,648.2
185	Denver-Aurora, CO	2,323.5
60	Des Moines-West Des Moines, IA	3,093.7
264	Detroit (greater), MI	1,917.8
214	Detroit-Livonia-Dearborn, MI M.D.	2,216.7
176	Dothan, AL	2,368.9
208	Dover, DE	2,257.9
332	Dubuque, IA	1,416.7
155	Duluth, MN-WI	2,486.3
80	Durham, NC	2,978.6
263	Eau Claire, WI	1,924.3
334	Edison, NJ M.D.	1,408.9
259	El Centro, CA	1,942.4
192	El Paso, TX	2,303.9
344	Elizabethtown, KY	1,240.2
138	Elkhart-Goshen, IN	2,611.7
230	Elmira, NY	2,119.2
329	Erie, PA	1,453.5
87	Eugene-Springfield, OR	2,921.3
224	Evansville, IN-KY	2,139.1
NA	Fairbanks, AK**	NA
290	Fargo, ND-MN	1,732.5
314	Farmington, NM	1,564.2
195	Fayetteville, AR-MO	2,295.5
14	Fayetteville, NC	3,768.4
22	Flagstaff, AZ	3,594.8
191	Flint, MI	2,305.9
7	Florence, SC	4,068.9
322	Fond du Lac, WI	1,491.5
178	Fort Collins-Loveland, CO	2,357.5
162	Fort Lauderdale, FL M.D.	2,447.4
187	Fort Smith, AR-OK	2,322.8
232	Fort Walton Beach, FL	2,096.7
175	Fort Wayne, IN	2,379.8
66	Fort Worth-Arlington, TX M.D.	3,066.3
124	Fresno, CA	2,679.7
43	Gadsden, AL	3,265.4
56	Gainesville, FL	3,133.4
242	Gainesville, GA	2,026.4
313	Glens Falls, NY	1,565.3
129	Goldsboro, NC	2,648.8
239	Grand Forks, ND-MN	2,033.0
145	Grand Junction, CO	2,553.5
194	Grand Rapids-Wyoming, MI	2,296.0
47	Great Falls, MT	3,226.6
166	Greeley, CO	2,426.4
296	Green Bay, WI	1,699.4
85	Greensboro-High Point, NC	2,923.1
72	Greenville, NC	3,041.5
156	Greenville, SC	2,484.2
281	Hagerstown-Martinsburg, MD-WV	1,788.7
315	Hanford-Corcoran, CA	1,556.9
293	Harrisburg-Carlisle, PA	1,716.7
346	Harrisonburg, VA	1,192.4
207	Hartford, CT	2,262.2
240	Hattiesburg, MS	2,028.2
319	Holland-Grand Haven, MI	1,502.5
89	Honolulu, HI	2,907.9
1	Hot Springs, AR	4,715.8
110	Houma, LA	2,782.4
141	Houston, TX	2,570.8
218	Huntington-Ashland, WV-KY-OH	2,168.4
68	Huntsville, AL	3,060.0
246	Idaho Falls, ID	1,999.1
133	Indianapolis, IN	2,629.6
309	Iowa City, IA	1,594.1
221	Ithaca, NY	2,155.8
59	Jacksonville, FL	3,100.0
233	Jacksonville, NC	2,071.0
189	Jackson, MI	2,314.7
160	Jackson, MS	2,450.4
41	Jackson, TN	3,312.6
102	Janesville, WI	2,828.9
282	Jefferson City, MO	1,783.8
198	Johnson City, TN	2,289.5
305	Johnstown, PA	1,629.5
126	Jonesboro, AR	2,678.1
63	Joplin, MO	3,081.4
109	Kalamazoo-Portage, MI	2,798.6
116	Kansas City, MO-KS	2,740.9
188	Kennewick-Richland-Pasco, WA	2,318.5
203	Killeen-Temple-Fort Hood, TX	2,272.3
153	Kingsport, TN-VA	2,491.9
337	Kingston, NY	1,393.7
163	Knoxville, TN	2,438.8
108	Kokomo, IN	2,811.8
235	La Crosse, WI-MN	2,063.6
201	Lafayette, IN	2,280.1
93	Lake Charles, LA	2,888.4
88	Lake Havasu City-Kingman, AZ	2,910.1
165	Lakeland, FL	2,427.8
291	Lancaster, PA	1,728.1
247	Lansing-East Lansing, MI	1,995.0
6	Laredo, TX	4,308.8
219	Las Cruces, NM	2,167.5
241	Las Vegas-Paradise, NV	2,028.0

Note: All listings are for Metropolitan Statistical Areas (M.S.A.s) except for those ending with "M.D." Listings with "M.D." are Metropolitan Divisions which are smaller parts of eleven large M.S.A.s. See explanatory note at beginning of metropolitan area section on page 23.

RANK	METROPOLITAN AREA	RATE
4	Lawrence, KS	4,552.3
125	Lawton, OK	2,678.5
310	Lebanon, PA	1,584.1
250	Lewiston-Auburn, ME	1,980.7
151	Lewiston, ID-WA	2,497.3
137	Lexington-Fayette, KY	2,612.1
123	Lima, OH	2,685.1
13	Lincoln, NE	3,800.0
15	Little Rock, AR	3,751.7
341	Logan, UT-ID	1,340.1
55	Longview, TX	3,140.3
25	Longview, WA	3,554.7
323	Los Angeles County, CA M.D.	1,487.7
324	Los Angeles (greater), CA	1,483.7
181	Louisville, KY-IN	2,343.2
23	Lubbock, TX	3,570.3
321	Lynchburg, VA	1,491.6
9	Macon, GA	3,880.8
343	Madera, CA	1,243.1
217	Madison, WI	2,173.8
317	Manchester-Nashua, NH	1,548.1
24	Mansfield, OH	3,568.2
42	McAllen-Edinburg-Mission, TX	3,288.2
167	Medford, OR	2,422.9
20	Memphis, TN-MS-AR	3,647.3
222	Merced, CA	2,152.7
91	Miami (greater), FL	2,903.3
40	Miami-Dade County, FL M.D.	3,322.8
46	Michigan City-La Porte, IN	3,229.8
170	Midland, TX	2,401.2
119	Milwaukee, WI	2,723.9
147	Minneapolis-St. Paul, MN-WI	2,542.0
60	Missoula, MT	3,093.7
33	Mobile, AL	3,397.5
69	Modesto, CA	3,055.7
19	Monroe, LA	3,687.1
298	Monroe, MI	1,681.5
58	Montgomery, AL	3,120.3
301	Morgantown, WV	1,656.2
157	Morristown, TN	2,478.1
5	Mount Vernon-Anacortes, WA	4,352.1
142	Muncie, IN	2,570.6
12	Muskegon-Norton Shores, MI	3,809.5
3	Myrtle Beach, SC	4,572.7
308	Napa, CA	1,619.1
336	Naples-Marco Island, FL	1,401.6
121	Nashville-Davidson, TN	2,717.1
342	Nassau-Suffolk, NY M.D.	1,318.1
262	New Orleans, LA	1,930.7
340	New York (greater), NY-NJ-PA	1,376.1
339	New York-W. Plains NY-NJ M.D.	1,382.2
338	Newark-Union, NJ-PA M.D.	1,384.0
161	Niles-Benton Harbor, MI	2,447.5
215	Oakland-Fremont, CA M.D.	2,185.7
288	Ocala, FL	1,742.3
16	Ocean City, NJ	3,719.7
132	Odessa, TX	2,641.8
199	Ogden-Clearfield, UT	2,287.8
101	Oklahoma City, OK	2,853.8
184	Olympia, WA	2,330.8
95	Omaha-Council Bluffs, NE-IA	2,880.5
122	Orlando, FL	2,693.2
276	Oshkosh-Neenah, WI	1,825.5
335	Oxnard-Thousand Oaks, CA	1,408.5
204	Palm Bay-Melbourne, FL	2,271.3
294	Palm Coast, FL	1,714.3
97	Panama City-Lynn Haven, FL	2,873.1
202	Pascagoula, MS	2,279.2
193	Pensacola, FL	2,296.5
243	Philadelphia (greater) PA-NJ-DE	2,017.6
244	Philadelphia, PA M.D.	2,008.3
96	Phoenix-Mesa-Scottsdale, AZ	2,875.2
164	Pine Bluff, AR	2,428.8
300	Pittsburgh, PA	1,660.3
330	Pittsfield, MA	1,421.7
200	Pocatello, ID	2,282.3
228	Port St. Lucie, FL	2,131.1
140	Portland-Vancouver, OR-WA	2,574.8
251	Portland, ME	1,979.4
318	Poughkeepsie, NY	1,504.6
273	Prescott, AZ	1,849.8
267	Provo-Orem, UT	1,896.2
21	Pueblo, CO	3,619.1
180	Punta Gorda, FL	2,343.4
148	Racine, WI	2,517.5
258	Raleigh-Cary, NC	1,947.1
277	Rapid City, SD	1,820.1
302	Reading, PA	1,656.1
304	Redding, CA	1,632.8
146	Reno-Sparks, NV	2,553.3
227	Richmond, VA	2,131.4
270	Riverside-San Bernardino, CA	1,866.4
226	Roanoke, VA	2,135.5
311	Rochester, MN	1,579.4
225	Rochester, NY	2,135.8
44	Rocky Mount, NC	3,257.2
78	Rome, GA	2,991.1
231	Sacramento, CA	2,100.0
254	Saginaw, MI	1,972.2
77	Salem, OR	3,019.2
252	Salinas, CA	1,973.0
62	Salisbury, MD	3,091.0
26	Salt Lake City, UT	3,535.6
36	San Angelo, TX	3,338.2
17	San Antonio, TX	3,711.8
289	San Diego, CA	1,738.4
206	San Francisco (greater), CA	2,268.2
173	San Francisco-S. Mateo, CA M.D.	2,388.9
307	San Jose, CA	1,623.6
275	San Luis Obispo, CA	1,837.6
115	Sandusky, OH	2,743.7
326	Santa Ana-Anaheim, CA M.D.	1,470.3
316	Santa Barbara-Santa Maria, CA	1,550.1
106	Santa Cruz-Watsonville, CA	2,825.6
320	Santa Fe, NM	1,493.3
327	Santa Rosa-Petaluma, CA	1,466.6
103	Sarasota-Bradenton-Venice, FL	2,828.5
105	Savannah, GA	2,825.9
280	Scranton--Wilkes-Barre, PA	1,790.8
74	Seattle (greater), WA	3,026.7
75	Seattle-Bellevue, WA M.D.	3,021.9
216	Sebastian-Vero Beach, FL	2,181.0
169	Sheboygan, WI	2,412.4
205	Sherman-Denison, TX	2,268.9
29	Shreveport-Bossier City, LA	3,462.1
236	Sioux City, IA-NE-SD	2,063.3
331	Sioux Falls, SD	1,420.4
53	South Bend-Mishawaka, IN-MI	3,179.0
49	Spartanburg, SC	3,207.5
139	Spokane, WA	2,585.4
271	Springfield, MA	1,863.2
31	Springfield, MO	3,427.1
11	Springfield, OH	3,831.0
303	State College, PA	1,641.3
34	Stockton, CA	3,388.3
183	St. Cloud, MN	2,334.3
111	St. Joseph, MO-KS	2,774.9
143	St. Louis, MO-IL	2,565.0
120	Sumter, SC	2,717.5
292	Syracuse, NY	1,723.3
71	Tacoma, WA M.D.	3,042.4
186	Tallahassee, FL	2,323.4
112	Tampa-St Petersburg, FL	2,763.6
128	Texarkana, TX-Texarkana, AR	2,658.8
50	Toledo, OH	3,187.9
10	Topeka, KS	3,873.1
325	Trenton-Ewing, NJ	1,474.1
NA	Tucson, AZ**	NA
179	Tulsa, OK	2,356.8
52	Tuscaloosa, AL	3,184.7
150	Tyler, TX	2,500.6
306	Utica-Rome, NY	1,624.8
67	Valdosta, GA	3,063.7
211	Vallejo-Fairfield, CA	2,246.3
171	Victoria, TX	2,399.5
107	Vineland, NJ	2,822.6
144	Virginia Beach-Norfolk, VA-NC	2,563.3
135	Visalia-Porterville, CA	2,619.1
57	Waco, TX	3,125.9
168	Warner Robins, GA	2,418.3
299	Warren-Farmington Hills, MI M.D.	1,678.0
257	Washington (greater) DC-VA-MD	1,950.6
245	Washington, DC-VA-MD-WV M.D.	2,001.8
249	Waterloo-Cedar Falls, IA	1,987.0
327	Wausau, WI	1,466.6
83	Wenatchee, WA	2,937.1
114	West Palm Beach, FL M.D.	2,756.5
347	Wheeling, WV-OH	1,178.5
35	Wichita Falls, TX	3,365.2
51	Wichita, KS	3,186.4
287	Williamsport, PA	1,751.1
190	Wilmington, DE-MD-NJ M.D.	2,306.8
99	Wilmington, NC	2,865.3
261	Winchester, VA-WV	1,936.4
98	Winston-Salem, NC	2,867.7
345	Worcester, MA	1,208.9
8	Yakima, WA	3,939.5
279	Yuba City, CA	1,803.9
196	Yuma, AZ	2,291.1

Source: Federal Bureau of Investigation

"Crime in the United States 2006" (Uniform Crime Reports, September 24, 2007)

**Larceny and theft is the unlawful taking of property. Attempts are included.*

***Not available.*

34. Larceny and Theft Rate in 2006 (continued)

National Rate = 2,206.8 Larcenies and Thefts per 100,000 Population*

RANK	METROPOLITAN AREA	RATE	RANK	METROPOLITAN AREA	RATE	RANK	METROPOLITAN AREA	RATE
1	Hot Springs, AR	4,715.8	58	Montgomery, AL	3,120.3	115	Sandusky, OH	2,743.7
2	Corpus Christi, TX	4,587.2	59	Jacksonville, FL	3,100.0	116	Kansas City, MO-KS	2,740.9
3	Myrtle Beach, SC	4,572.7	60	Des Moines-West Des Moines, IA	3,093.7	117	Cheyenne, WY	2,735.8
4	Lawrence, KS	4,552.3	60	Missoula, MT	3,093.7	118	Columbia, SC	2,731.1
5	Mount Vernon-Anacortes, WA	4,352.1	62	Salisbury, MD	3,091.0	119	Milwaukee, WI	2,723.9
6	Laredo, TX	4,308.8	63	Joplin, MO	3,081.4	120	Sumter, SC	2,717.5
7	Florence, SC	4,068.9	64	Anderson, SC	3,077.8	121	Nashville-Davidson, TN	2,717.1
8	Yakima, WA	3,939.5	65	Augusta, GA-SC	3,070.2	122	Orlando, FL	2,693.2
9	Macon, GA	3,880.8	66	Fort Worth-Arlington, TX M.D.	3,066.3	123	Lima, OH	2,685.1
10	Topeka, KS	3,873.1	67	Valdosta, GA	3,063.7	124	Fresno, CA	2,679.7
11	Springfield, OH	3,831.0	68	Huntsville, AL	3,060.0	125	Lawton, OK	2,678.5
12	Muskegon-Norton Shores, MI	3,809.5	69	Modesto, CA	3,055.7	126	Jonesboro, AR	2,678.1
13	Lincoln, NE	3,800.0	70	College Station-Bryan, TX	3,044.9	127	Albany, GA	2,673.9
14	Fayetteville, NC	3,768.4	71	Tacoma, WA M.D.	3,042.4	128	Texarkana, TX-Texarkana, AR	2,658.8
15	Little Rock, AR	3,751.7	72	Greenville, NC	3,041.5	129	Goldsboro, NC	2,648.8
16	Ocean City, NJ	3,719.7	73	Brunswick, GA	3,032.7	130	Decatur, AL	2,648.2
17	San Antonio, TX	3,711.8	74	Seattle (greater), WA	3,026.7	131	Cincinnati-Middletown, OH-KY-IN	2,642.6
18	Columbus, GA-AL	3,700.4	75	Seattle-Bellevue, WA M.D.	3,021.9	132	Odessa, TX	2,641.8
19	Monroe, LA	3,687.1	76	Chattanooga, TN-GA	3,019.7	133	Indianapolis, IN	2,629.6
20	Memphis, TN-MS-AR	3,647.3	77	Salem, OR	3,019.2	134	Bend, OR	2,624.2
21	Pueblo, CO	3,619.1	78	Rome, GA	2,991.1	135	Visalia-Porterville, CA	2,619.1
22	Flagstaff, AZ	3,594.8	79	Columbus, OH	2,989.9	136	Colorado Springs, CO	2,613.1
23	Lubbock, TX	3,570.3	80	Durham, NC	2,978.6	137	Lexington-Fayette, KY	2,612.1
24	Mansfield, OH	3,568.2	81	Atlantic City, NJ	2,976.2	138	Elkhart-Goshen, IN	2,611.7
25	Longview, WA	3,554.7	82	Austin-Round Rock, TX	2,951.7	139	Spokane, WA	2,585.4
26	Salt Lake City, UT	3,535.6	83	Wenatchee, WA	2,937.1	140	Portland-Vancouver, OR-WA	2,574.8
27	Bellingham, WA	3,485.1	84	Charleston-North Charleston, SC	2,931.9	141	Houston, TX	2,570.8
28	Casper, WY	3,472.6	85	Greensboro-High Point, NC	2,923.1	142	Muncie, IN	2,570.6
29	Shreveport-Bossier City, LA	3,462.1	86	Billings, MT	2,921.7	143	St. Louis, MO-IL	2,565.0
30	Columbus, IN	3,452.8	87	Eugene-Springfield, OR	2,921.3	144	Virginia Beach-Norfolk, VA-NC	2,563.3
31	Springfield, MO	3,427.1	88	Lake Havasu City-Kingman, AZ	2,910.1	145	Grand Junction, CO	2,553.5
32	Brownsville-Harlingen, TX	3,422.9	89	Honolulu, HI	2,907.9	146	Reno-Sparks, NV	2,553.3
33	Mobile, AL	3,397.5	90	Dallas (greater), TX	2,906.7	147	Minneapolis-St. Paul, MN-WI	2,542.0
34	Stockton, CA	3,388.3	91	Miami (greater), FL	2,903.3	148	Racine, WI	2,517.5
35	Wichita Falls, TX	3,365.2	92	Battle Creek, MI	2,888.9	149	Bangor, ME	2,515.0
36	San Angelo, TX	3,338.2	93	Lake Charles, LA	2,888.4	150	Tyler, TX	2,500.6
37	Amarillo, TX	3,333.8	94	Albuquerque, NM	2,885.3	151	Lewiston, ID-WA	2,497.3
38	Baton Rouge, LA	3,331.7	95	Omaha-Council Bluffs, NE-IA	2,880.5	152	Charleston, WV	2,495.2
39	Alexandria, LA	3,329.1	96	Phoenix-Mesa-Scottsdale, AZ	2,875.2	153	Kingsport, TN-VA	2,491.9
40	Miami-Dade County, FL M.D.	3,322.8	97	Panama City-Lynn Haven, FL	2,873.1	154	Bakersfield, CA	2,486.9
41	Jackson, TN	3,312.6	98	Winston-Salem, NC	2,867.7	155	Duluth, MN-WI	2,486.3
42	McAllen-Edinburg-Mission, TX	3,288.2	99	Wilmington, NC	2,865.3	156	Greenville, SC	2,484.2
43	Gadsden, AL	3,265.4	100	Birmingham-Hoover, AL	2,860.3	157	Morristown, TN	2,478.1
44	Rocky Mount, NC	3,257.2	101	Oklahoma City, OK	2,853.8	158	Beaumont-Port Arthur, TX	2,472.1
45	Anchorage, AK	3,230.0	102	Janesville, WI	2,828.9	159	Dayton, OH	2,459.7
46	Michigan City-La Porte, IN	3,229.8	103	Sarasota-Bradenton-Venice, FL	2,828.5	160	Jackson, MS	2,450.4
47	Great Falls, MT	3,226.6	104	Dallas-Plano-Irving, TX M.D.	2,827.7	161	Niles-Benton Harbor, MI	2,447.5
48	Charlotte-Gastonia, NC-SC	3,220.5	105	Savannah, GA	2,825.9	162	Fort Lauderdale, FL M.D.	2,447.4
49	Spartanburg, SC	3,207.5	106	Santa Cruz-Watsonville, CA	2,825.6	163	Knoxville, TN	2,438.8
50	Toledo, OH	3,187.9	107	Vineland, NJ	2,822.6	164	Pine Bluff, AR	2,428.8
51	Wichita, KS	3,186.4	108	Kokomo, IN	2,811.8	165	Lakeland, FL	2,427.8
52	Tuscaloosa, AL	3,184.7	109	Kalamazoo-Portage, MI	2,798.6	166	Greeley, CO	2,426.4
53	South Bend-Mishawaka, IN-MI	3,179.0	110	Houma, LA	2,782.4	167	Medford, OR	2,422.9
54	Athens-Clarke County, GA	3,171.4	111	St. Joseph, MO-KS	2,774.9	168	Warner Robins, GA	2,418.3
55	Longview, TX	3,140.3	112	Tampa-St Petersburg, FL	2,763.6	169	Sheboygan, WI	2,412.4
56	Gainesville, FL	3,133.4	113	Burlington, NC	2,763.4	170	Midland, TX	2,401.2
57	Waco, TX	3,125.9	114	West Palm Beach, FL M.D.	2,756.5	171	Victoria, TX	2,399.5

Note: All listings are for Metropolitan Statistical Areas (M.S.A.s) except for those ending with "M.D." Listings with "M.D." are Metropolitan Divisions which are smaller parts of eleven large M.S.A.s. See explanatory note at beginning of metropolitan area section on page 23.

RANK	METROPOLITAN AREA	RATE
172	Bowling Green, KY	2,395.0
173	San Francisco-S. Mateo, CA M.D.	2,388.9
174	Daytona Beach, FL	2,383.4
175	Fort Wayne, IN	2,379.8
176	Dothan, AL	2,368.9
177	Abilene, TX	2,366.4
178	Fort Collins-Loveland, CO	2,357.5
179	Tulsa, OK	2,356.8
180	Punta Gorda, FL	2,343.4
181	Louisville, KY-IN	2,343.2
182	Atlanta, GA	2,341.6
183	St. Cloud, MN	2,334.3
184	Olympia, WA	2,330.8
185	Denver-Aurora, CO	2,323.5
186	Tallahassee, FL	2,323.4
187	Fort Smith, AR-OK	2,322.8
188	Kennewick-Richland-Pasco, WA	2,318.5
189	Jackson, MI	2,314.7
190	Wilmington, DE-MD-NJ M.D.	2,306.8
191	Flint, MI	2,305.9
192	El Paso, TX	2,303.9
193	Pensacola, FL	2,296.5
194	Grand Rapids-Wyoming, MI	2,296.0
195	Fayetteville, AR-MO	2,295.5
196	Yuma, AZ	2,291.1
197	Baltimore-Towson, MD	2,290.6
198	Johnson City, TN	2,289.5
199	Ogden-Clearfield, UT	2,287.8
200	Pocatello, ID	2,282.3
201	Lafayette, IN	2,280.1
202	Pascagoula, MS	2,279.2
203	Killeen-Temple-Fort Hood, TX	2,272.3
204	Palm Bay-Melbourne, FL	2,271.3
205	Sherman-Denison, TX	2,268.9
206	San Francisco (greater), CA	2,268.2
207	Hartford, CT	2,262.2
208	Dover, DE	2,257.9
209	Dalton, GA	2,252.6
210	Cedar Rapids, IA	2,248.9
211	Vallejo-Fairfield, CA	2,246.3
212	Columbia, MO	2,232.5
213	Charlottesville, VA	2,222.8
214	Detroit-Livonia-Dearborn, MI M.D.	2,216.7
215	Oakland-Fremont, CA M.D.	2,185.7
216	Sebastian-Vero Beach, FL	2,181.0
217	Madison, WI	2,173.8
218	Huntington-Ashland, WV-KY-OH	2,168.4
219	Las Cruces, NM	2,167.5
220	Cape Coral-Fort Myers, FL	2,165.9
221	Ithaca, NY	2,155.8
222	Merced, CA	2,152.7
223	Cleveland, TN	2,141.5
224	Evansville, IN-KY	2,139.1
225	Rochester, NY	2,135.8
226	Roanoke, VA	2,135.5
227	Richmond, VA	2,131.4
228	Port St. Lucie, FL	2,131.1
229	Binghamton, NY	2,130.6
230	Elmira, NY	2,119.2
231	Sacramento, CA	2,100.0
232	Fort Walton Beach, FL	2,096.7
233	Jacksonville, NC	2,071.0
234	Bloomington, IN	2,065.0
235	La Crosse, WI-MN	2,063.6
236	Sioux City, IA-NE-SD	2,063.3
237	Coeur d'Alene, ID	2,040.4
238	Albany-Schenectady-Troy, NY	2,034.2
239	Grand Forks, ND-MN	2,033.0
240	Hattiesburg, MS	2,028.2
241	Las Vegas-Paradise, NV	2,028.0
242	Gainesville, GA	2,026.4
243	Philadelphia (greater) PA-NJ-DE	2,017.6
244	Philadelphia, PA M.D.	2,008.3
245	Washington, DC-VA-MD-WV M.D.	2,001.8
246	Idaho Falls, ID	1,999.1
247	Lansing-East Lansing, MI	1,995.0
248	Blacksburg, VA	1,988.0
249	Waterloo-Cedar Falls, IA	1,987.0
250	Lewiston-Auburn, ME	1,980.7
251	Portland, ME	1,979.4
252	Salinas, CA	1,973.0
253	Clarksville, TN-KY	1,972.4
254	Saginaw, MI	1,972.2
255	Ann Arbor, MI	1,962.2
256	Buffalo-Niagara Falls, NY	1,953.0
257	Washington (greater) DC-VA-MD	1,950.6
258	Raleigh-Cary, NC	1,947.1
259	El Centro, CA	1,942.4
260	Ames, IA	1,939.6
261	Winchester, VA-WV	1,936.4
262	New Orleans, LA	1,930.7
263	Eau Claire, WI	1,924.3
264	Detroit (greater), MI	1,917.8
265	Boise City-Nampa, ID	1,916.8
266	Cumberland, MD-WV	1,898.1
267	Provo-Orem, UT	1,896.2
268	Camden, NJ M.D.	1,886.0
269	Appleton, WI	1,883.5
270	Riverside-San Bernardino, CA	1,866.4
271	Springfield, MA	1,863.2
272	Chico, CA	1,856.4
273	Prescott, AZ	1,849.8
274	Cleveland-Elyria-Mentor, OH	1,840.9
275	San Luis Obispo, CA	1,837.6
276	Oshkosh-Neenah, WI	1,825.5
277	Rapid City, SD	1,820.1
278	Asheville, NC	1,815.7
279	Yuba City, CA	1,803.9
280	Scranton--Wilkes-Barre, PA	1,790.8
281	Hagerstown-Martinsburg, MD-WV	1,788.7
282	Bay City, MI	1,783.8
282	Jefferson City, MO	1,783.8
284	Bethesda-Frederick, MD M.D.	1,767.2
285	Altoona, PA	1,762.7
286	Danville, VA	1,760.3
287	Williamsport, PA	1,751.1
288	Ocala, FL	1,742.3
289	San Diego, CA	1,738.4
290	Fargo, ND-MN	1,732.5
291	Lancaster, PA	1,728.1
292	Syracuse, NY	1,723.3
293	Harrisburg-Carlisle, PA	1,716.7
294	Palm Coast, FL	1,714.3
295	Bremerton-Silverdale, WA	1,706.7
296	Green Bay, WI	1,699.4
297	Bismarck, ND	1,691.2
298	Monroe, MI	1,681.5
299	Warren-Farmington Hills, MI M.D.	1,678.0
300	Pittsburgh, PA	1,660.3
301	Morgantown, WV	1,656.2
302	Reading, PA	1,656.1
303	State College, PA	1,641.3
304	Redding, CA	1,632.8
305	Johnstown, PA	1,629.5
306	Utica-Rome, NY	1,624.8
307	San Jose, CA	1,623.6
308	Napa, CA	1,619.1
309	Iowa City, IA	1,594.1
310	Lebanon, PA	1,584.1
311	Rochester, MN	1,579.4
312	Barnstable Town, MA	1,566.2
313	Glens Falls, NY	1,565.3
314	Farmington, NM	1,564.2
315	Hanford-Corcoran, CA	1,556.9
316	Santa Barbara-Santa Maria, CA	1,550.1
317	Manchester-Nashua, NH	1,548.1
318	Poughkeepsie, NY	1,504.6
319	Holland-Grand Haven, MI	1,502.5
320	Santa Fe, NM	1,493.3
321	Lynchburg, VA	1,491.6
322	Fond du Lac, WI	1,491.5
323	Los Angeles County, CA M.D.	1,487.7
324	Los Angeles (greater), CA	1,483.7
325	Trenton-Ewing, NJ	1,474.1
326	Santa Ana-Anaheim, CA M.D.	1,470.3
327	Santa Rosa-Petaluma, CA	1,466.6
327	Wausau, WI	1,466.6
329	Erie, PA	1,453.5
330	Pittsfield, MA	1,421.7
331	Sioux Falls, SD	1,420.4
332	Dubuque, IA	1,416.7
333	Carson City, NV	1,413.6
334	Edison, NJ M.D.	1,408.9
335	Oxnard-Thousand Oaks, CA	1,408.5
336	Naples-Marco Island, FL	1,401.6
337	Kingston, NY	1,393.7
338	Newark-Union, NJ-PA M.D.	1,384.0
339	New York-W. Plains NY-NJ M.D.	1,382.2
340	New York (greater), NY-NJ-PA	1,376.1
341	Logan, UT-ID	1,340.1
342	Nassau-Suffolk, NY M.D.	1,318.1
343	Madera, CA	1,243.1
344	Elizabethtown, KY	1,240.2
345	Worcester, MA	1,208.9
346	Harrisonburg, VA	1,192.4
347	Wheeling, WV-OH	1,178.5
NA	Chicago, IL**	NA
NA	Fairbanks, AK**	NA
NA	Tucson, AZ**	NA

Source: Federal Bureau of Investigation
"Crime in the United States 2006" (Uniform Crime Reports, September 24, 2007)
**Larceny and theft is the unlawful taking of property. Attempts are included.*
***Not available.*

35. Percent Change in Larceny and Theft Rate: 2005 to 2006

National Percent Change = 3.5% Decrease*

RANK	METROPOLITAN AREA	% CHANGE
NA	Abilene, TX**	NA
63	Albany-Schenectady-Troy, NY	3.2
31	Albany, GA	6.9
242	Albuquerque, NM	(9.0)
49	Alexandria, LA	4.9
74	Altoona, PA	2.5
253	Amarillo, TX	(10.0)
71	Ames, IA	3.0
72	Anchorage, AK	2.8
235	Anderson, SC	(8.1)
163	Ann Arbor, MI	(3.6)
26	Appleton, WI	7.6
281	Asheville, NC	(12.9)
94	Athens-Clarke County, GA	0.6
239	Atlanta, GA	(8.9)
186	Atlantic City, NJ	(5.4)
126	Augusta, GA-SC	(1.4)
180	Austin-Round Rock, TX	(5.1)
206	Bakersfield, CA	(6.2)
140	Baltimore-Towson, MD	(2.0)
7	Bangor, ME	12.4
6	Barnstable Town, MA	12.5
88	Baton Rouge, LA	1.0
190	Battle Creek, MI	(5.5)
213	Bay City, MI	(6.8)
296	Beaumont-Port Arthur, TX	(15.5)
271	Bellingham, WA	(11.3)
306	Bend, OR	(18.5)
42	Bethesda-Frederick, MD M.D.	5.9
320	Billings, MT	(22.3)
82	Binghamton, NY	1.4
NA	Birmingham-Hoover, AL**	NA
141	Bismarck, ND	(2.1)
165	Blacksburg, VA	(3.7)
39	Bloomington, IN	6.1
NA	Boise City-Nampa, ID**	NA
211	Bowling Green, KY	(6.6)
248	Bremerton-Silverdale, WA	(9.5)
248	Brownsville-Harlingen, TX	(9.5)
194	Brunswick, GA	(5.6)
194	Buffalo-Niagara Falls, NY	(5.6)
102	Burlington, NC	0.3
43	Camden, NJ M.D.	5.6
98	Cape Coral-Fort Myers, FL	0.4
285	Carson City, NV	(13.7)
159	Casper, WY	(3.5)
229	Cedar Rapids, IA	(7.8)
133	Charleston-North Charleston, SC	(1.8)
250	Charleston, WV	(9.7)
87	Charlotte-Gastonia, NC-SC	1.2
53	Charlottesville, VA	4.7
244	Chattanooga, TN-GA	(9.1)
259	Cheyenne, WY	(10.6)
NA	Chicago, IL**	NA
41	Chico, CA	6.0
88	Cincinnati-Middletown, OH-KY-IN	1.0
194	Clarksville, TN-KY	(5.6)
NA	Cleveland-Elyria-Mentor, OH**	NA
NA	Cleveland, TN**	NA
292	Coeur d'Alene, ID	(15.0)
194	College Station-Bryan, TX	(5.6)
266	Colorado Springs, CO	(10.8)
165	Columbia, MO	(3.7)
167	Columbia, SC	(3.8)
94	Columbus, GA-AL	0.6
57	Columbus, IN	4.1
126	Columbus, OH	(1.4)
190	Corpus Christi, TX	(5.5)
51	Cumberland, MD-WV	4.8
220	Dallas (greater), TX	(7.3)
220	Dallas-Plano-Irving, TX M.D.	(7.3)
NA	Dalton, GA**	NA
229	Danville, VA	(7.8)
44	Daytona Beach, FL	5.5
133	Dayton, OH	(1.8)
104	Decatur, AL	0.2
303	Denver-Aurora, CO	(17.9)
NA	Des Moines-West Des Moines, IA**	NA
48	Detroit (greater), MI	5.3
15	Detroit-Livonia-Dearborn, MI M.D.	10.0
291	Dothan, AL	(14.8)
105	Dover, DE	0.0
282	Dubuque, IA	(13.0)
NA	Duluth, MN-WI**	NA
NA	Durham, NC**	NA
28	Eau Claire, WI	7.4
108	Edison, NJ M.D.	(0.1)
85	El Centro, CA	1.3
138	El Paso, TX	(1.9)
276	Elizabethtown, KY	(12.2)
186	Elkhart-Goshen, IN	(5.4)
262	Elmira, NY	(10.7)
126	Erie, PA	(1.4)
301	Eugene-Springfield, OR	(17.3)
133	Evansville, IN-KY	(1.8)
NA	Fairbanks, AK**	NA
63	Fargo, ND-MN	3.2
266	Farmington, NM	(10.8)
167	Fayetteville, AR-MO	(3.8)
24	Fayetteville, NC	8.0
209	Flagstaff, AZ	(6.4)
122	Flint, MI	(1.1)
58	Florence, SC	4.0
124	Fond du Lac, WI	(1.3)
55	Fort Collins-Loveland, CO	4.2
143	Fort Lauderdale, FL M.D.	(2.2)
159	Fort Smith, AR-OK	(3.5)
112	Fort Walton Beach, FL	(0.5)
NA	Fort Wayne, IN**	NA
223	Fort Worth-Arlington, TX M.D.	(7.4)
259	Fresno, CA	(10.6)
111	Gadsden, AL	(0.4)
3	Gainesville, FL	13.7
310	Gainesville, GA	(19.1)
NA	Glens Falls, NY**	NA
244	Goldsboro, NC	(9.1)
321	Grand Forks, ND-MN	(22.5)
292	Grand Junction, CO	(15.0)
76	Grand Rapids-Wyoming, MI	2.1
316	Great Falls, MT	(20.6)
304	Greeley, CO	(18.1)
169	Green Bay, WI	(3.9)
113	Greensboro-High Point, NC	(0.6)
15	Greenville, NC	10.0
217	Greenville, SC	(7.1)
21	Hagerstown-Martinsburg, MD-WV	8.4
269	Hanford-Corcoran, CA	(10.9)
233	Harrisburg-Carlisle, PA	(8.0)
73	Harrisonburg, VA	2.6
143	Hartford, CT	(2.2)
NA	Hattiesburg, MS**	NA
44	Holland-Grand Haven, MI	5.5
254	Honolulu, HI	(10.1)
231	Hot Springs, AR	(7.9)
92	Houma, LA	0.7
151	Houston, TX	(2.8)
47	Huntington-Ashland, WV-KY-OH	5.4
220	Huntsville, AL	(7.3)
75	Idaho Falls, ID	2.3
141	Indianapolis, IN	(2.1)
153	Iowa City, IA	(3.1)
NA	Ithaca, NY**	NA
98	Jacksonville, FL	0.4
NA	Jacksonville, NC**	NA
5	Jackson, MI	12.7
67	Jackson, MS	3.1
226	Jackson, TN	(7.5)
79	Janesville, WI	1.8
213	Jefferson City, MO	(6.8)
295	Johnson City, TN	(15.4)
NA	Johnstown, PA**	NA
208	Jonesboro, AR	(6.3)
288	Joplin, MO	(14.4)
22	Kalamazoo-Portage, MI	8.3
NA	Kansas City, MO-KS**	NA
288	Kennewick-Richland-Pasco, WA	(14.4)
231	Killeen-Temple-Fort Hood, TX	(7.9)
138	Kingsport, TN-VA	(1.9)
262	Kingston, NY	(10.7)
157	Knoxville, TN	(3.4)
159	Kokomo, IN	(3.5)
20	La Crosse, WI-MN	8.6
119	Lafayette, IN	(0.9)
62	Lake Charles, LA	3.4
NA	Lake Havasu City-Kingman, AZ**	NA
276	Lakeland, FL	(12.2)
60	Lancaster, PA	3.6
239	Lansing-East Lansing, MI	(8.9)
201	Laredo, TX	(5.9)
149	Las Cruces, NM	(2.6)
176	Las Vegas-Paradise, NV	(4.9)

Note: All listings are for Metropolitan Statistical Areas (M.S.A.s) except for those ending with "M.D." Listings with "M.D." are Metropolitan Divisions which are smaller parts of eleven large M.S.A.s. See explanatory note at beginning of metropolitan area section on page 23.

RANK	METROPOLITAN AREA	% CHANGE
1	Lawrence, KS	43.3
242	Lawton, OK	(9.0)
113	Lebanon, PA	(0.6)
180	Lewiston-Auburn, ME	(5.1)
275	Lewiston, ID-WA	(12.0)
NA	Lexington-Fayette, KY**	NA
256	Lima, OH	(10.4)
173	Lincoln, NE	(4.5)
210	Little Rock, AR	(6.5)
255	Logan, UT-ID	(10.2)
155	Longview, TX	(3.3)
258	Longview, WA	(10.5)
178	Los Angeles County, CA M.D.	(5.0)
173	Los Angeles (greater), CA	(4.5)
63	Louisville, KY-IN	3.2
239	Lubbock, TX	(8.9)
130	Lynchburg, VA	(1.6)
190	Macon, GA	(5.5)
313	Madera, CA	(19.9)
145	Madison, WI	(2.3)
110	Manchester-Nashua, NH	(0.3)
9	Mansfield, OH	11.5
292	McAllen-Edinburg-Mission, TX	(15.0)
311	Medford, OR	(19.4)
82	Memphis, TN-MS-AR	1.4
256	Merced, CA	(10.4)
157	Miami (greater), FL	(3.4)
175	Miami-Dade County, FL M.D.	(4.7)
53	Michigan City-La Porte, IN	4.7
203	Midland, TX	(6.0)
22	Milwaukee, WI	8.3
NA	Minneapolis-St. Paul, MN-WI**	NA
304	Missoula, MT	(18.1)
4	Mobile, AL	13.2
171	Modesto, CA	(4.1)
109	Monroe, LA	(0.2)
44	Monroe, MI	5.5
119	Montgomery, AL	(0.9)
129	Morgantown, WV	(1.5)
80	Morristown, TN	1.7
318	Mount Vernon-Anacortes, WA	(21.4)
25	Muncie, IN	7.9
55	Muskegon-Norton Shores, MI	4.2
200	Myrtle Beach, SC	(5.8)
180	Napa, CA	(5.1)
216	Naples-Marco Island, FL	(6.9)
247	Nashville-Davidson, TN	(9.2)
60	Nassau-Suffolk, NY M.D.	3.6
NA	New Orleans, LA**	NA
145	New York (greater), NY-NJ-PA	(2.3)
169	New York-W. Plains NY-NJ M.D.	(3.9)
153	Newark-Union, NJ-PA M.D.	(3.1)
94	Niles-Benton Harbor, MI	0.6
123	Oakland-Fremont, CA M.D.	(1.2)
180	Ocala, FL	(5.1)
19	Ocean City, NJ	9.5
279	Odessa, TX	(12.4)
199	Ogden-Clearfield, UT	(5.7)
319	Oklahoma City, OK	(21.8)
271	Olympia, WA	(11.3)
105	Omaha-Council Bluffs, NE-IA	0.0
132	Orlando, FL	(1.7)
10	Oshkosh-Neenah, WI	11.2
67	Oxnard-Thousand Oaks, CA	3.1
49	Palm Bay-Melbourne, FL	4.9
NA	Palm Coast, FL**	NA
219	Panama City-Lynn Haven, FL	(7.2)
27	Pascagoula, MS	7.5
34	Pensacola, FL	6.7
32	Philadelphia (greater) PA-NJ-DE	6.8
37	Philadelphia, PA M.D.	6.3
223	Phoenix-Mesa-Scottsdale, AZ	(7.4)
314	Pine Bluff, AR	(20.2)
205	Pittsburgh, PA	(6.1)
14	Pittsfield, MA	10.5
186	Pocatello, ID	(5.4)
8	Port St. Lucie, FL	12.1
300	Portland-Vancouver, OR-WA	(16.9)
39	Portland, ME	6.1
78	Poughkeepsie, NY	2.0
274	Prescott, AZ	(11.6)
312	Provo-Orem, UT	(19.6)
269	Pueblo, CO	(10.9)
18	Punta Gorda, FL	9.6
133	Racine, WI	(1.8)
92	Raleigh-Cary, NC	0.7
317	Rapid City, SD	(21.3)
233	Reading, PA	(8.0)
307	Redding, CA	(18.6)
206	Reno-Sparks, NV	(6.2)
286	Richmond, VA	(14.3)
227	Riverside-San Bernardino, CA	(7.6)
299	Roanoke, VA	(16.4)
36	Rochester, MN	6.5
145	Rochester, NY	(2.3)
51	Rocky Mount, NC	4.8
276	Rome, GA	(12.2)
194	Sacramento, CA	(5.6)
155	Saginaw, MI	(3.3)
244	Salem, OR	(9.1)
284	Salinas, CA	(13.2)
34	Salisbury, MD	6.7
262	Salt Lake City, UT	(10.7)
290	San Angelo, TX	(14.7)
212	San Antonio, TX	(6.7)
186	San Diego, CA	(5.4)
63	San Francisco (greater), CA	3.2
17	San Francisco-S. Mateo, CA M.D.	9.8
176	San Jose, CA	(4.9)
38	San Luis Obispo, CA	6.2
148	Sandusky, OH	(2.5)
152	Santa Ana-Anaheim, CA M.D.	(2.9)
171	Santa Barbara-Santa Maria, CA	(4.1)
133	Santa Cruz-Watsonville, CA	(1.8)
262	Santa Fe, NM	(10.7)
302	Santa Rosa-Petaluma, CA	(17.8)
102	Sarasota-Bradenton-Venice, FL	0.3
259	Savannah, GA	(10.6)
76	Scranton--Wilkes-Barre, PA	2.1
227	Seattle (greater), WA	(7.6)
236	Seattle-Bellevue, WA M.D.	(8.3)
238	Sebastian-Vero Beach, FL	(8.8)
10	Sheboygan, WI	11.2
283	Sherman-Denison, TX	(13.1)
88	Shreveport-Bossier City, LA	1.0
113	Sioux City, IA-NE-SD	(0.6)
308	Sioux Falls, SD	(19.0)
29	South Bend-Mishawaka, IN-MI	7.1
59	Spartanburg, SC	3.9
251	Spokane, WA	(9.8)
118	Springfield, MA	(0.7)
98	Springfield, MO	0.4
150	Springfield, OH	(2.7)
81	State College, PA	1.5
113	Stockton, CA	(0.6)
2	St. Cloud, MN	15.1
223	St. Joseph, MO-KS	(7.4)
94	St. Louis, MO-IL	0.6
82	Sumter, SC	1.4
67	Syracuse, NY	3.1
184	Tacoma, WA M.D.	(5.2)
163	Tallahassee, FL	(3.6)
105	Tampa-St Petersburg, FL	0.0
271	Texarkana, TX-Texarkana, AR	(11.3)
32	Toledo, OH	6.8
178	Topeka, KS	(5.0)
280	Trenton-Ewing, NJ	(12.7)
NA	Tucson, AZ**	NA
217	Tulsa, OK	(7.1)
NA	Tuscaloosa, AL**	NA
213	Tyler, TX	(6.8)
159	Utica-Rome, NY	(3.5)
286	Valdosta, GA	(14.3)
NA	Vallejo-Fairfield, CA**	NA
308	Victoria, TX	(19.0)
98	Vineland, NJ	0.4
237	Virginia Beach-Norfolk, VA-NC	(8.4)
251	Visalia-Porterville, CA	(9.8)
298	Waco, TX	(15.8)
203	Warner Robins, GA	(6.0)
91	Warren-Farmington Hills, MI M.D.	0.8
NA	Washington (greater) DC-VA-MD**	NA
NA	Washington, DC-VA-MD-WV M.D.**	NA
119	Waterloo-Cedar Falls, IA	(0.9)
67	Wausau, WI	3.1
190	Wenatchee, WA	(5.5)
130	West Palm Beach, FL M.D.	(1.6)
184	Wheeling, WV-OH	(5.2)
296	Wichita Falls, TX	(15.5)
NA	Wichita, KS**	NA
12	Williamsport, PA	11.1
12	Wilmington, DE-MD-NJ M.D.	11.1
124	Wilmington, NC	(1.3)
113	Winchester, VA-WV	(0.6)
29	Winston-Salem, NC	7.1
201	Worcester, MA	(5.9)
266	Yakima, WA	(10.8)
315	Yuba City, CA	(20.4)
85	Yuma, AZ	1.3

Source: CQ Press using data from Federal Bureau of Investigation "Crime in the United States 2006" (Uniform Crime Reports, September 24, 2007)

**Larceny and theft is the unlawful taking of property. Attempts are included.*

***Not available.*

35. Percent Change in Larceny and Theft Rate: 2005 to 2006 (continued)

National Percent Change = 3.5% Decrease*

RANK	METROPOLITAN AREA	% CHANGE
1	Lawrence, KS	43.3
2	St. Cloud, MN	15.1
3	Gainesville, FL	13.7
4	Mobile, AL	13.2
5	Jackson, MI	12.7
6	Barnstable Town, MA	12.5
7	Bangor, ME	12.4
8	Port St. Lucie, FL	12.1
9	Mansfield, OH	11.5
10	Oshkosh-Neenah, WI	11.2
10	Sheboygan, WI	11.2
12	Williamsport, PA	11.1
12	Wilmington, DE-MD-NJ M.D.	11.1
14	Pittsfield, MA	10.5
15	Detroit-Livonia-Dearborn, MI M.D.	10.0
15	Greenville, NC	10.0
17	San Francisco-S. Mateo, CA M.D.	9.8
18	Punta Gorda, FL	9.6
19	Ocean City, NJ	9.5
20	La Crosse, WI-MN	8.6
21	Hagerstown-Martinsburg, MD-WV	8.4
22	Kalamazoo-Portage, MI	8.3
22	Milwaukee, WI	8.3
24	Fayetteville, NC	8.0
25	Muncie, IN	7.9
26	Appleton, WI	7.6
27	Pascagoula, MS	7.5
28	Eau Claire, WI	7.4
29	South Bend-Mishawaka, IN-MI	7.1
29	Winston-Salem, NC	7.1
31	Albany, GA	6.9
32	Philadelphia (greater) PA-NJ-DE	6.8
32	Toledo, OH	6.8
34	Pensacola, FL	6.7
34	Salisbury, MD	6.7
36	Rochester, MN	6.5
37	Philadelphia, PA M.D.	6.3
38	San Luis Obispo, CA	6.2
39	Bloomington, IN	6.1
39	Portland, ME	6.1
41	Chico, CA	6.0
42	Bethesda-Frederick, MD M.D.	5.9
43	Camden, NJ M.D.	5.6
44	Daytona Beach, FL	5.5
44	Holland-Grand Haven, MI	5.5
44	Monroe, MI	5.5
47	Huntington-Ashland, WV-KY-OH	5.4
48	Detroit (greater), MI	5.3
49	Alexandria, LA	4.9
49	Palm Bay-Melbourne, FL	4.9
51	Cumberland, MD-WV	4.8
51	Rocky Mount, NC	4.8
53	Charlottesville, VA	4.7
53	Michigan City-La Porte, IN	4.7
55	Fort Collins-Loveland, CO	4.2
55	Muskegon-Norton Shores, MI	4.2
57	Columbus, IN	4.1
58	Florence, SC	4.0
59	Spartanburg, SC	3.9
60	Lancaster, PA	3.6
60	Nassau-Suffolk, NY M.D.	3.6
62	Lake Charles, LA	3.4
63	Albany-Schenectady-Troy, NY	3.2
63	Fargo, ND-MN	3.2
63	Louisville, KY-IN	3.2
63	San Francisco (greater), CA	3.2
67	Jackson, MS	3.1
67	Oxnard-Thousand Oaks, CA	3.1
67	Syracuse, NY	3.1
67	Wausau, WI	3.1
71	Ames, IA	3.0
72	Anchorage, AK	2.8
73	Harrisonburg, VA	2.6
74	Altoona, PA	2.5
75	Idaho Falls, ID	2.3
76	Grand Rapids-Wyoming, MI	2.1
76	Scranton--Wilkes-Barre, PA	2.1
78	Poughkeepsie, NY	2.0
79	Janesville, WI	1.8
80	Morristown, TN	1.7
81	State College, PA	1.5
82	Binghamton, NY	1.4
82	Memphis, TN-MS-AR	1.4
82	Sumter, SC	1.4
85	El Centro, CA	1.3
85	Yuma, AZ	1.3
87	Charlotte-Gastonia, NC-SC	1.2
88	Baton Rouge, LA	1.0
88	Cincinnati-Middletown, OH-KY-IN	1.0
88	Shreveport-Bossier City, LA	1.0
91	Warren-Farmington Hills, MI M.D.	0.8
92	Houma, LA	0.7
92	Raleigh-Cary, NC	0.7
94	Athens-Clarke County, GA	0.6
94	Columbus, GA-AL	0.6
94	Niles-Benton Harbor, MI	0.6
94	St. Louis, MO-IL	0.6
98	Cape Coral-Fort Myers, FL	0.4
98	Jacksonville, FL	0.4
98	Springfield, MO	0.4
98	Vineland, NJ	0.4
102	Burlington, NC	0.3
102	Sarasota-Bradenton-Venice, FL	0.3
104	Decatur, AL	0.2
105	Dover, DE	0.0
105	Omaha-Council Bluffs, NE-IA	0.0
105	Tampa-St Petersburg, FL	0.0
108	Edison, NJ M.D.	(0.1)
109	Monroe, LA	(0.2)
110	Manchester-Nashua, NH	(0.3)
111	Gadsden, AL	(0.4)
112	Fort Walton Beach, FL	(0.5)
113	Greensboro-High Point, NC	(0.6)
113	Lebanon, PA	(0.6)
113	Sioux City, IA-NE-SD	(0.6)
113	Stockton, CA	(0.6)
113	Winchester, VA-WV	(0.6)
118	Springfield, MA	(0.7)
119	Lafayette, IN	(0.9)
119	Montgomery, AL	(0.9)
119	Waterloo-Cedar Falls, IA	(0.9)
122	Flint, MI	(1.1)
123	Oakland-Fremont, CA M.D.	(1.2)
124	Fond du Lac, WI	(1.3)
124	Wilmington, NC	(1.3)
126	Augusta, GA-SC	(1.4)
126	Columbus, OH	(1.4)
126	Erie, PA	(1.4)
129	Morgantown, WV	(1.5)
130	Lynchburg, VA	(1.6)
130	West Palm Beach, FL M.D.	(1.6)
132	Orlando, FL	(1.7)
133	Charleston-North Charleston, SC	(1.8)
133	Dayton, OH	(1.8)
133	Evansville, IN-KY	(1.8)
133	Racine, WI	(1.8)
133	Santa Cruz-Watsonville, CA	(1.8)
138	El Paso, TX	(1.9)
138	Kingsport, TN-VA	(1.9)
140	Baltimore-Towson, MD	(2.0)
141	Bismarck, ND	(2.1)
141	Indianapolis, IN	(2.1)
143	Fort Lauderdale, FL M.D.	(2.2)
143	Hartford, CT	(2.2)
145	Madison, WI	(2.3)
145	New York (greater), NY-NJ-PA	(2.3)
145	Rochester, NY	(2.3)
148	Sandusky, OH	(2.5)
149	Las Cruces, NM	(2.6)
150	Springfield, OH	(2.7)
151	Houston, TX	(2.8)
152	Santa Ana-Anaheim, CA M.D.	(2.9)
153	Iowa City, IA	(3.1)
153	Newark-Union, NJ-PA M.D.	(3.1)
155	Longview, TX	(3.3)
155	Saginaw, MI	(3.3)
157	Knoxville, TN	(3.4)
157	Miami (greater), FL	(3.4)
159	Casper, WY	(3.5)
159	Fort Smith, AR-OK	(3.5)
159	Kokomo, IN	(3.5)
159	Utica-Rome, NY	(3.5)
163	Ann Arbor, MI	(3.6)
163	Tallahassee, FL	(3.6)
165	Blacksburg, VA	(3.7)
165	Columbia, MO	(3.7)
167	Columbia, SC	(3.8)
167	Fayetteville, AR-MO	(3.8)
169	Green Bay, WI	(3.9)
169	New York-W. Plains NY-NJ M.D.	(3.9)
171	Modesto, CA	(4.1)

Note: All listings are for Metropolitan Statistical Areas (M.S.A.s) except for those ending with "M.D." Listings with "M.D." are Metropolitan Divisions which are smaller parts of eleven large M.S.A.s. See explanatory note at beginning of metropolitan area section on page 23.

RANK	METROPOLITAN AREA	% CHANGE
171	Santa Barbara-Santa Maria, CA	(4.1)
173	Lincoln, NE	(4.5)
173	Los Angeles (greater), CA	(4.5)
175	Miami-Dade County, FL M.D.	(4.7)
176	Las Vegas-Paradise, NV	(4.9)
176	San Jose, CA	(4.9)
178	Los Angeles County, CA M.D.	(5.0)
178	Topeka, KS	(5.0)
180	Austin-Round Rock, TX	(5.1)
180	Lewiston-Auburn, ME	(5.1)
180	Napa, CA	(5.1)
180	Ocala, FL	(5.1)
184	Tacoma, WA M.D.	(5.2)
184	Wheeling, WV-OH	(5.2)
186	Atlantic City, NJ	(5.4)
186	Elkhart-Goshen, IN	(5.4)
186	Pocatello, ID	(5.4)
186	San Diego, CA	(5.4)
190	Battle Creek, MI	(5.5)
190	Corpus Christi, TX	(5.5)
190	Macon, GA	(5.5)
190	Wenatchee, WA	(5.5)
194	Brunswick, GA	(5.6)
194	Buffalo-Niagara Falls, NY	(5.6)
194	Clarksville, TN-KY	(5.6)
194	College Station-Bryan, TX	(5.6)
194	Sacramento, CA	(5.6)
199	Ogden-Clearfield, UT	(5.7)
200	Myrtle Beach, SC	(5.8)
201	Laredo, TX	(5.9)
201	Worcester, MA	(5.9)
203	Midland, TX	(6.0)
203	Warner Robins, GA	(6.0)
205	Pittsburgh, PA	(6.1)
206	Bakersfield, CA	(6.2)
206	Reno-Sparks, NV	(6.2)
208	Jonesboro, AR	(6.3)
209	Flagstaff, AZ	(6.4)
210	Little Rock, AR	(6.5)
211	Bowling Green, KY	(6.6)
212	San Antonio, TX	(6.7)
213	Bay City, MI	(6.8)
213	Jefferson City, MO	(6.8)
213	Tyler, TX	(6.8)
216	Naples-Marco Island, FL	(6.9)
217	Greenville, SC	(7.1)
217	Tulsa, OK	(7.1)
219	Panama City-Lynn Haven, FL	(7.2)
220	Dallas (greater), TX	(7.3)
220	Dallas-Plano-Irving, TX M.D.	(7.3)
220	Huntsville, AL	(7.3)
223	Fort Worth-Arlington, TX M.D.	(7.4)
223	Phoenix-Mesa-Scottsdale, AZ	(7.4)
223	St. Joseph, MO-KS	(7.4)
226	Jackson, TN	(7.5)
227	Riverside-San Bernardino, CA	(7.6)
227	Seattle (greater), WA	(7.6)
229	Cedar Rapids, IA	(7.8)
229	Danville, VA	(7.8)
231	Hot Springs, AR	(7.9)
231	Killeen-Temple-Fort Hood, TX	(7.9)
233	Harrisburg-Carlisle, PA	(8.0)
233	Reading, PA	(8.0)
235	Anderson, SC	(8.1)
236	Seattle-Bellevue, WA M.D.	(8.3)
237	Virginia Beach-Norfolk, VA-NC	(8.4)
238	Sebastian-Vero Beach, FL	(8.8)
239	Atlanta, GA	(8.9)
239	Lansing-East Lansing, MI	(8.9)
239	Lubbock, TX	(8.9)
242	Albuquerque, NM	(9.0)
242	Lawton, OK	(9.0)
244	Chattanooga, TN-GA	(9.1)
244	Goldsboro, NC	(9.1)
244	Salem, OR	(9.1)
247	Nashville-Davidson, TN	(9.2)
248	Bremerton-Silverdale, WA	(9.5)
248	Brownsville-Harlingen, TX	(9.5)
250	Charleston, WV	(9.7)
251	Spokane, WA	(9.8)
251	Visalia-Porterville, CA	(9.8)
253	Amarillo, TX	(10.0)
254	Honolulu, HI	(10.1)
255	Logan, UT-ID	(10.2)
256	Lima, OH	(10.4)
256	Merced, CA	(10.4)
258	Longview, WA	(10.5)
259	Cheyenne, WY	(10.6)
259	Fresno, CA	(10.6)
259	Savannah, GA	(10.6)
262	Elmira, NY	(10.7)
262	Kingston, NY	(10.7)
262	Salt Lake City, UT	(10.7)
262	Santa Fe, NM	(10.7)
266	Colorado Springs, CO	(10.8)
266	Farmington, NM	(10.8)
266	Yakima, WA	(10.8)
269	Hanford-Corcoran, CA	(10.9)
269	Pueblo, CO	(10.9)
271	Bellingham, WA	(11.3)
271	Olympia, WA	(11.3)
271	Texarkana, TX-Texarkana, AR	(11.3)
274	Prescott, AZ	(11.6)
275	Lewiston, ID-WA	(12.0)
276	Elizabethtown, KY	(12.2)
276	Lakeland, FL	(12.2)
276	Rome, GA	(12.2)
279	Odessa, TX	(12.4)
280	Trenton-Ewing, NJ	(12.7)
281	Asheville, NC	(12.9)
282	Dubuque, IA	(13.0)
283	Sherman-Denison, TX	(13.1)
284	Salinas, CA	(13.2)
285	Carson City, NV	(13.7)
286	Richmond, VA	(14.3)
286	Valdosta, GA	(14.3)
288	Joplin, MO	(14.4)
288	Kennewick-Richland-Pasco, WA	(14.4)
290	San Angelo, TX	(14.7)
291	Dothan, AL	(14.8)
292	Coeur d'Alene, ID	(15.0)
292	Grand Junction, CO	(15.0)
292	McAllen-Edinburg-Mission, TX	(15.0)
295	Johnson City, TN	(15.4)
296	Beaumont-Port Arthur, TX	(15.5)
296	Wichita Falls, TX	(15.5)
298	Waco, TX	(15.8)
299	Roanoke, VA	(16.4)
300	Portland-Vancouver, OR-WA	(16.9)
301	Eugene-Springfield, OR	(17.3)
302	Santa Rosa-Petaluma, CA	(17.8)
303	Denver-Aurora, CO	(17.9)
304	Greeley, CO	(18.1)
304	Missoula, MT	(18.1)
306	Bend, OR	(18.5)
307	Redding, CA	(18.6)
308	Sioux Falls, SD	(19.0)
308	Victoria, TX	(19.0)
310	Gainesville, GA	(19.1)
311	Medford, OR	(19.4)
312	Provo-Orem, UT	(19.6)
313	Madera, CA	(19.9)
314	Pine Bluff, AR	(20.2)
315	Yuba City, CA	(20.4)
316	Great Falls, MT	(20.6)
317	Rapid City, SD	(21.3)
318	Mount Vernon-Anacortes, WA	(21.4)
319	Oklahoma City, OK	(21.8)
320	Billings, MT	(22.3)
321	Grand Forks, ND-MN	(22.5)
NA	Abilene, TX**	NA
NA	Birmingham-Hoover, AL**	NA
NA	Boise City-Nampa, ID**	NA
NA	Chicago, IL**	NA
NA	Cleveland-Elyria-Mentor, OH**	NA
NA	Cleveland, TN**	NA
NA	Dalton, GA**	NA
NA	Des Moines-West Des Moines, IA**	NA
NA	Duluth, MN-WI**	NA
NA	Durham, NC**	NA
NA	Fairbanks, AK**	NA
NA	Fort Wayne, IN**	NA
NA	Glens Falls, NY**	NA
NA	Hattiesburg, MS**	NA
NA	Ithaca, NY**	NA
NA	Jacksonville, NC**	NA
NA	Johnstown, PA**	NA
NA	Kansas City, MO-KS**	NA
NA	Lake Havasu City-Kingman, AZ**	NA
NA	Lexington-Fayette, KY**	NA
NA	Minneapolis-St. Paul, MN-WI**	NA
NA	New Orleans, LA**	NA
NA	Palm Coast, FL**	NA
NA	Tucson, AZ**	NA
NA	Tuscaloosa, AL**	NA
NA	Vallejo-Fairfield, CA**	NA
NA	Washington (greater) DC-VA-MD**	NA
NA	Washington, DC-VA-MD-WV M.D.**	NA
NA	Wichita, KS**	NA

Source: CQ Press using data from Federal Bureau of Investigation "Crime in the United States 2006" (Uniform Crime Reports, September 24, 2007)

**Larceny and theft is the unlawful taking of property. Attempts are included.*

***Not available.*

36. Percent Change in Larceny and Theft Rate: 2002 to 2006

National Percent Change = 10.0% Decrease*

RANK	METROPOLITAN AREA	% CHANGE
NA	Abilene, TX**	NA
NA	Albany-Schenectady-Troy, NY**	NA
157	Albany, GA	(19.6)
154	Albuquerque, NM	(19.3)
90	Alexandria, LA	(10.5)
24	Altoona, PA	3.6
147	Amarillo, TX	(17.8)
NA	Ames, IA**	NA
65	Anchorage, AK	(6.7)
NA	Anderson, SC**	NA
NA	Ann Arbor, MI**	NA
NA	Appleton, WI**	NA
130	Asheville, NC	(15.8)
136	Athens-Clarke County, GA	(16.4)
96	Atlanta, GA	(12.1)
NA	Atlantic City, NJ**	NA
15	Augusta, GA-SC	6.1
78	Austin-Round Rock, TX	(8.8)
11	Bakersfield, CA	7.7
157	Baltimore-Towson, MD	(19.6)
NA	Bangor, ME**	NA
NA	Barnstable Town, MA**	NA
159	Baton Rouge, LA	(19.8)
NA	Battle Creek, MI**	NA
NA	Bay City, MI**	NA
177	Beaumont-Port Arthur, TX	(25.4)
61	Bellingham, WA	(5.7)
NA	Bend, OR**	NA
NA	Bethesda-Frederick, MD M.D.**	NA
166	Billings, MT	(21.1)
10	Binghamton, NY	7.8
34	Birmingham-Hoover, AL	1.4
120	Bismarck, ND	(15.1)
NA	Blacksburg, VA**	NA
145	Bloomington, IN	(17.7)
201	Boise City-Nampa, ID	(32.3)
NA	Bowling Green, KY**	NA
178	Bremerton-Silverdale, WA	(25.6)
191	Brownsville-Harlingen, TX	(29.5)
NA	Brunswick, GA**	NA
65	Buffalo-Niagara Falls, NY	(6.7)
NA	Burlington, NC**	NA
NA	Camden, NJ M.D.**	NA
99	Cape Coral-Fort Myers, FL	(12.8)
NA	Carson City, NV**	NA
35	Casper, WY	0.7
194	Cedar Rapids, IA	(29.8)
93	Charleston-North Charleston, SC	(11.6)
30	Charleston, WV	2.2
NA	Charlotte-Gastonia, NC-SC**	NA
NA	Charlottesville, VA**	NA
86	Chattanooga, TN-GA	(9.9)
118	Cheyenne, WY	(14.6)
NA	Chicago, IL**	NA
58	Chico, CA	(5.3)
74	Cincinnati-Middletown, OH-KY-IN	(8.5)
210	Clarksville, TN-KY	(41.8)
NA	Cleveland-Elyria-Mentor, OH**	NA
NA	Cleveland, TN**	NA
NA	Coeur d'Alene, ID**	NA
NA	College Station-Bryan, TX**	NA
106	Colorado Springs, CO	(13.5)
168	Columbia, MO	(21.6)
162	Columbia, SC	(20.3)
8	Columbus, GA-AL	8.2
NA	Columbus, IN**	NA
150	Columbus, OH	(18.3)
7	Corpus Christi, TX	8.3
20	Cumberland, MD-WV	4.9
NA	Dallas (greater), TX**	NA
126	Dallas-Plano-Irving, TX M.D.	(15.6)
NA	Dalton, GA**	NA
4	Danville, VA	10.6
57	Daytona Beach, FL	(5.1)
NA	Dayton, OH**	NA
13	Decatur, AL	7.6
156	Denver-Aurora, CO	(19.4)
NA	Des Moines-West Des Moines, IA**	NA
68	Detroit (greater), MI	(7.2)
NA	Detroit-Livonia-Dearborn, MI M.D.**	NA
NA	Dothan, AL**	NA
80	Dover, DE	(9.1)
160	Dubuque, IA	(20.0)
122	Duluth, MN-WI	(15.2)
NA	Durham, NC**	NA
119	Eau Claire, WI	(14.7)
NA	Edison, NJ M.D.**	NA
NA	El Centro, CA**	NA
167	El Paso, TX	(21.2)
NA	Elizabethtown, KY**	NA
62	Elkhart-Goshen, IN	(6.1)
NA	Elmira, NY**	NA
85	Erie, PA	(9.8)
149	Eugene-Springfield, OR	(18.1)
NA	Evansville, IN-KY**	NA
NA	Fairbanks, AK**	NA
192	Fargo, ND-MN	(29.6)
NA	Farmington, NM**	NA
NA	Fayetteville, AR-MO**	NA
19	Fayetteville, NC	5.2
134	Flagstaff, AZ	(16.1)
109	Flint, MI	(13.8)
38	Florence, SC	(1.2)
NA	Fond du Lac, WI**	NA
130	Fort Collins-Loveland, CO	(15.8)
48	Fort Lauderdale, FL M.D.	(3.0)
187	Fort Smith, AR-OK	(28.8)
27	Fort Walton Beach, FL	2.6
NA	Fort Wayne, IN**	NA
139	Fort Worth-Arlington, TX M.D.	(17.1)
114	Fresno, CA	(14.2)
14	Gadsden, AL	7.2
52	Gainesville, FL	(3.9)
NA	Gainesville, GA**	NA
79	Glens Falls, NY	(8.9)
84	Goldsboro, NC	(9.6)
195	Grand Forks, ND-MN	(30.2)
29	Grand Junction, CO	2.5
NA	Grand Rapids-Wyoming, MI**	NA
208	Great Falls, MT	(37.2)
182	Greeley, CO	(26.7)
143	Green Bay, WI	(17.5)
NA	Greensboro-High Point, NC**	NA
151	Greenville, NC	(18.4)
NA	Greenville, SC**	NA
NA	Hagerstown-Martinsburg, MD-WV**	NA
NA	Hanford-Corcoran, CA**	NA
NA	Harrisburg-Carlisle, PA**	NA
NA	Harrisonburg, VA**	NA
18	Hartford, CT	5.3
NA	Hattiesburg, MS**	NA
NA	Holland-Grand Haven, MI**	NA
193	Honolulu, HI	(29.7)
NA	Hot Springs, AR**	NA
49	Houma, LA	(3.3)
92	Houston, TX	(11.3)
NA	Huntington-Ashland, WV-KY-OH**	NA
5	Huntsville, AL	10.2
NA	Idaho Falls, ID**	NA
NA	Indianapolis, IN**	NA
205	Iowa City, IA	(33.7)
NA	Ithaca, NY**	NA
69	Jacksonville, FL	(7.6)
NA	Jacksonville, NC**	NA
39	Jackson, MI	(1.6)
175	Jackson, MS	(24.8)
27	Jackson, TN	2.6
106	Janesville, WI	(13.5)
NA	Jefferson City, MO**	NA
NA	Johnson City, TN**	NA
NA	Johnstown, PA**	NA
140	Jonesboro, AR	(17.2)
32	Joplin, MO	2.1
NA	Kalamazoo-Portage, MI**	NA
NA	Kansas City, MO-KS**	NA
75	Kennewick-Richland-Pasco, WA	(8.6)
101	Killeen-Temple-Fort Hood, TX	(13.2)
NA	Kingsport, TN-VA**	NA
NA	Kingston, NY**	NA
60	Knoxville, TN	(5.6)
24	Kokomo, IN	3.6
47	La Crosse, WI-MN	(2.7)
91	Lafayette, IN	(10.9)
128	Lake Charles, LA	(15.7)
NA	Lake Havasu City-Kingman, AZ**	NA
161	Lakeland, FL	(20.1)
83	Lancaster, PA	(9.5)
125	Lansing-East Lansing, MI	(15.5)
63	Laredo, TX	(6.4)
NA	Las Cruces, NM**	NA
67	Las Vegas-Paradise, NV	(7.0)

Note: All listings are for Metropolitan Statistical Areas (M.S.A.s) except for those ending with "M.D." Listings with "M.D." are Metropolitan Divisions which are smaller parts of eleven large M.S.A.s. See explanatory note at beginning of metropolitan area section on page 23.

RANK	METROPOLITAN AREA	% CHANGE
1	Lawrence, KS	41.5
87	Lawton, OK	(10.0)
NA	Lebanon, PA**	NA
152	Lewiston-Auburn, ME	(18.7)
NA	Lewiston, ID-WA**	NA
NA	Lexington-Fayette, KY**	NA
NA	Lima, OH**	NA
153	Lincoln, NE	(19.1)
109	Little Rock, AR	(13.8)
NA	Logan, UT-ID**	NA
51	Longview, TX	(3.8)
NA	Longview, WA**	NA
116	Los Angeles County, CA M.D.	(14.4)
NA	Los Angeles (greater), CA**	NA
132	Louisville, KY-IN	(15.9)
50	Lubbock, TX	(3.6)
64	Lynchburg, VA	(6.5)
NA	Macon, GA**	NA
NA	Madera, CA**	NA
95	Madison, WI	(12.0)
NA	Manchester-Nashua, NH**	NA
NA	Mansfield, OH**	NA
101	McAllen-Edinburg-Mission, TX	(13.2)
183	Medford, OR	(26.9)
NA	Memphis, TN-MS-AR**	NA
145	Merced, CA	(17.7)
NA	Miami (greater), FL**	NA
148	Miami-Dade County, FL M.D.	(17.9)
NA	Michigan City-La Porte, IN**	NA
NA	Midland, TX**	NA
NA	Milwaukee, WI**	NA
72	Minneapolis-St. Paul, MN-WI	(7.8)
NA	Missoula, MT**	NA
NA	Mobile, AL**	NA
103	Modesto, CA	(13.4)
NA	Monroe, LA**	NA
NA	Monroe, MI**	NA
180	Montgomery, AL	(25.8)
NA	Morgantown, WV**	NA
NA	Morristown, TN**	NA
NA	Mount Vernon-Anacortes, WA**	NA
30	Muncie, IN	2.2
NA	Muskegon-Norton Shores, MI**	NA
77	Myrtle Beach, SC	(8.7)
NA	Napa, CA**	NA
204	Naples-Marco Island, FL	(33.2)
123	Nashville-Davidson, TN	(15.3)
NA	Nassau-Suffolk, NY M.D.**	NA
202	New Orleans, LA	(32.4)
NA	New York (greater), NY-NJ-PA**	NA
98	New York-W. Plains NY-NJ M.D.	(12.6)
124	Newark-Union, NJ-PA M.D.	(15.4)
NA	Niles-Benton Harbor, MI**	NA
154	Oakland-Fremont, CA M.D.	(19.3)
113	Ocala, FL	(14.1)
NA	Ocean City, NJ**	NA
NA	Odessa, TX**	NA
NA	Ogden-Clearfield, UT**	NA
203	Oklahoma City, OK	(32.8)
128	Olympia, WA	(15.7)

RANK	METROPOLITAN AREA	% CHANGE
178	Omaha-Council Bluffs, NE-IA	(25.6)
116	Orlando, FL	(14.4)
NA	Oshkosh-Neenah, WI**	NA
NA	Oxnard-Thousand Oaks, CA**	NA
103	Palm Bay-Melbourne, FL	(13.4)
NA	Palm Coast, FL**	NA
197	Panama City-Lynn Haven, FL	(30.3)
NA	Pascagoula, MS**	NA
59	Pensacola, FL	(5.5)
15	Philadelphia (greater) PA-NJ-DE	6.1
NA	Philadelphia, PA M.D.**	NA
172	Phoenix-Mesa-Scottsdale, AZ	(23.9)
211	Pine Bluff, AR	(42.0)
45	Pittsburgh, PA	(2.5)
NA	Pittsfield, MA**	NA
21	Pocatello, ID	4.6
103	Port St. Lucie, FL	(13.4)
176	Portland-Vancouver, OR-WA	(24.9)
NA	Portland, ME**	NA
NA	Poughkeepsie, NY**	NA
NA	Prescott, AZ**	NA
199	Provo-Orem, UT	(31.6)
3	Pueblo, CO	12.8
2	Punta Gorda, FL	15.2
42	Racine, WI	(2.2)
NA	Raleigh-Cary, NC**	NA
212	Rapid City, SD	(50.6)
87	Reading, PA	(10.0)
37	Redding, CA	(0.7)
140	Reno-Sparks, NV	(17.2)
189	Richmond, VA	(29.0)
82	Riverside-San Bernardino, CA	(9.4)
NA	Roanoke, VA**	NA
138	Rochester, MN	(16.8)
81	Rochester, NY	(9.3)
71	Rocky Mount, NC	(7.7)
NA	Rome, GA**	NA
142	Sacramento, CA	(17.4)
NA	Saginaw, MI**	NA
206	Salem, OR	(33.9)
53	Salinas, CA	(4.0)
NA	Salisbury, MD**	NA
NA	Salt Lake City, UT**	NA
135	San Angelo, TX	(16.3)
165	San Antonio, TX	(20.8)
56	San Diego, CA	(4.8)
NA	San Francisco (greater), CA**	NA
23	San Francisco-S. Mateo, CA M.D.	4.1
39	San Jose, CA	(1.6)
55	San Luis Obispo, CA	(4.3)
NA	Sandusky, OH**	NA
100	Santa Ana-Anaheim, CA M.D.	(13.1)
NA	Santa Barbara-Santa Maria, CA**	NA
6	Santa Cruz-Watsonville, CA	9.4
184	Santa Fe, NM	(27.1)
195	Santa Rosa-Petaluma, CA	(30.2)
75	Sarasota-Bradenton-Venice, FL	(8.6)
163	Savannah, GA	(20.4)
17	Scranton--Wilkes-Barre, PA	5.8
NA	Seattle (greater), WA**	NA

RANK	METROPOLITAN AREA	% CHANGE
43	Seattle-Bellevue, WA M.D.	(2.3)
NA	Sebastian-Vero Beach, FL**	NA
44	Sheboygan, WI	(2.4)
169	Sherman-Denison, TX	(21.9)
54	Shreveport-Bossier City, LA	(4.1)
209	Sioux City, IA-NE-SD	(40.8)
188	Sioux Falls, SD	(28.9)
120	South Bend-Mishawaka, IN-MI	(15.1)
NA	Spartanburg, SC**	NA
198	Spokane, WA	(30.8)
NA	Springfield, MA**	NA
22	Springfield, MO	4.5
NA	Springfield, OH**	NA
36	State College, PA	0.2
46	Stockton, CA	(2.6)
69	St. Cloud, MN	(7.6)
185	St. Joseph, MO-KS	(27.6)
NA	St. Louis, MO-IL**	NA
126	Sumter, SC	(15.6)
NA	Syracuse, NY**	NA
143	Tacoma, WA M.D.	(17.5)
200	Tallahassee, FL	(32.0)
108	Tampa-St Petersburg, FL	(13.6)
112	Texarkana, TX-Texarkana, AR	(13.9)
97	Toledo, OH	(12.2)
171	Topeka, KS	(23.5)
181	Trenton-Ewing, NJ	(26.3)
NA	Tucson, AZ**	NA
137	Tulsa, OK	(16.6)
94	Tuscaloosa, AL	(11.9)
164	Tyler, TX	(20.6)
133	Utica-Rome, NY	(16.0)
NA	Valdosta, GA**	NA
NA	Vallejo-Fairfield, CA**	NA
190	Victoria, TX	(29.4)
41	Vineland, NJ	(2.0)
109	Virginia Beach-Norfolk, VA-NC	(13.8)
11	Visalia-Porterville, CA	7.7
186	Waco, TX	(27.9)
NA	Warner Robins, GA**	NA
NA	Warren-Farmington Hills, MI M.D.**	NA
NA	Washington (greater) DC-VA-MD**	NA
NA	Washington, DC-VA-MD-WV M.D.**	NA
207	Waterloo-Cedar Falls, IA	(34.6)
73	Wausau, WI	(8.0)
NA	Wenatchee, WA**	NA
174	West Palm Beach, FL M.D.	(24.7)
NA	Wheeling, WV-OH**	NA
115	Wichita Falls, TX	(14.3)
87	Wichita, KS	(10.0)
26	Williamsport, PA	2.8
NA	Wilmington, DE-MD-NJ M.D.**	NA
172	Wilmington, NC	(23.9)
NA	Winchester, VA-WV**	NA
NA	Winston-Salem, NC**	NA
NA	Worcester, MA**	NA
32	Yakima, WA	2.1
169	Yuba City, CA	(21.9)
9	Yuma, AZ	7.9

Source: CQ Press using data from Federal Bureau of Investigation
"Crime in the United States 2006" (Uniform Crime Reports, September 24, 2007)
**Larceny and theft is the unlawful taking of property. Attempts are included.*
***Not available.*

36. Percent Change in Larceny and Theft Rate: 2002 to 2006 (continued)

National Percent Change = 10.0% Decrease*

RANK	METROPOLITAN AREA	% CHANGE
1	Lawrence, KS	41.5
2	Punta Gorda, FL	15.2
3	Pueblo, CO	12.8
4	Danville, VA	10.6
5	Huntsville, AL	10.2
6	Santa Cruz-Watsonville, CA	9.4
7	Corpus Christi, TX	8.3
8	Columbus, GA-AL	8.2
9	Yuma, AZ	7.9
10	Binghamton, NY	7.8
11	Bakersfield, CA	7.7
11	Visalia-Porterville, CA	7.7
13	Decatur, AL	7.6
14	Gadsden, AL	7.2
15	Augusta, GA-SC	6.1
15	Philadelphia (greater) PA-NJ-DE	6.1
17	Scranton--Wilkes-Barre, PA	5.8
18	Hartford, CT	5.3
19	Fayetteville, NC	5.2
20	Cumberland, MD-WV	4.9
21	Pocatello, ID	4.6
22	Springfield, MO	4.5
23	San Francisco-S. Mateo, CA M.D.	4.1
24	Altoona, PA	3.6
24	Kokomo, IN	3.6
26	Williamsport, PA	2.8
27	Fort Walton Beach, FL	2.6
27	Jackson, TN	2.6
29	Grand Junction, CO	2.5
30	Charleston, WV	2.2
30	Muncie, IN	2.2
32	Joplin, MO	2.1
32	Yakima, WA	2.1
34	Birmingham-Hoover, AL	1.4
35	Casper, WY	0.7
36	State College, PA	0.2
37	Redding, CA	(0.7)
38	Florence, SC	(1.2)
39	Jackson, MI	(1.6)
39	San Jose, CA	(1.6)
41	Vineland, NJ	(2.0)
42	Racine, WI	(2.2)
43	Seattle-Bellevue, WA M.D.	(2.3)
44	Sheboygan, WI	(2.4)
45	Pittsburgh, PA	(2.5)
46	Stockton, CA	(2.6)
47	La Crosse, WI-MN	(2.7)
48	Fort Lauderdale, FL M.D.	(3.0)
49	Houma, LA	(3.3)
50	Lubbock, TX	(3.6)
51	Longview, TX	(3.8)
52	Gainesville, FL	(3.9)
53	Salinas, CA	(4.0)
54	Shreveport-Bossier City, LA	(4.1)
55	San Luis Obispo, CA	(4.3)
56	San Diego, CA	(4.8)
57	Daytona Beach, FL	(5.1)
58	Chico, CA	(5.3)
59	Pensacola, FL	(5.5)
60	Knoxville, TN	(5.6)
61	Bellingham, WA	(5.7)
62	Elkhart-Goshen, IN	(6.1)
63	Laredo, TX	(6.4)
64	Lynchburg, VA	(6.5)
65	Anchorage, AK	(6.7)
65	Buffalo-Niagara Falls, NY	(6.7)
67	Las Vegas-Paradise, NV	(7.0)
68	Detroit (greater), MI	(7.2)
69	Jacksonville, FL	(7.6)
69	St. Cloud, MN	(7.6)
71	Rocky Mount, NC	(7.7)
72	Minneapolis-St. Paul, MN-WI	(7.8)
73	Wausau, WI	(8.0)
74	Cincinnati-Middletown, OH-KY-IN	(8.5)
75	Kennewick-Richland-Pasco, WA	(8.6)
75	Sarasota-Bradenton-Venice, FL	(8.6)
77	Myrtle Beach, SC	(8.7)
78	Austin-Round Rock, TX	(8.8)
79	Glens Falls, NY	(8.9)
80	Dover, DE	(9.1)
81	Rochester, NY	(9.3)
82	Riverside-San Bernardino, CA	(9.4)
83	Lancaster, PA	(9.5)
84	Goldsboro, NC	(9.6)
85	Erie, PA	(9.8)
86	Chattanooga, TN-GA	(9.9)
87	Lawton, OK	(10.0)
87	Reading, PA	(10.0)
87	Wichita, KS	(10.0)
90	Alexandria, LA	(10.5)
91	Lafayette, IN	(10.9)
92	Houston, TX	(11.3)
93	Charleston-North Charleston, SC	(11.6)
94	Tuscaloosa, AL	(11.9)
95	Madison, WI	(12.0)
96	Atlanta, GA	(12.1)
97	Toledo, OH	(12.2)
98	New York-W. Plains NY-NJ M.D.	(12.6)
99	Cape Coral-Fort Myers, FL	(12.8)
100	Santa Ana-Anaheim, CA M.D.	(13.1)
101	Killeen-Temple-Fort Hood, TX	(13.2)
101	McAllen-Edinburg-Mission, TX	(13.2)
103	Modesto, CA	(13.4)
103	Palm Bay-Melbourne, FL	(13.4)
103	Port St. Lucie, FL	(13.4)
106	Colorado Springs, CO	(13.5)
106	Janesville, WI	(13.5)
108	Tampa-St Petersburg, FL	(13.6)
109	Flint, MI	(13.8)
109	Little Rock, AR	(13.8)
109	Virginia Beach-Norfolk, VA-NC	(13.8)
112	Texarkana, TX-Texarkana, AR	(13.9)
113	Ocala, FL	(14.1)
114	Fresno, CA	(14.2)
115	Wichita Falls, TX	(14.3)
116	Los Angeles County, CA M.D.	(14.4)
116	Orlando, FL	(14.4)
118	Cheyenne, WY	(14.6)
119	Eau Claire, WI	(14.7)
120	Bismarck, ND	(15.1)
120	South Bend-Mishawaka, IN-MI	(15.1)
122	Duluth, MN-WI	(15.2)
123	Nashville-Davidson, TN	(15.3)
124	Newark-Union, NJ-PA M.D.	(15.4)
125	Lansing-East Lansing, MI	(15.5)
126	Dallas-Plano-Irving, TX M.D.	(15.6)
126	Sumter, SC	(15.6)
128	Lake Charles, LA	(15.7)
128	Olympia, WA	(15.7)
130	Asheville, NC	(15.8)
130	Fort Collins-Loveland, CO	(15.8)
132	Louisville, KY-IN	(15.9)
133	Utica-Rome, NY	(16.0)
134	Flagstaff, AZ	(16.1)
135	San Angelo, TX	(16.3)
136	Athens-Clarke County, GA	(16.4)
137	Tulsa, OK	(16.6)
138	Rochester, MN	(16.8)
139	Fort Worth-Arlington, TX M.D.	(17.1)
140	Jonesboro, AR	(17.2)
140	Reno-Sparks, NV	(17.2)
142	Sacramento, CA	(17.4)
143	Green Bay, WI	(17.5)
143	Tacoma, WA M.D.	(17.5)
145	Bloomington, IN	(17.7)
145	Merced, CA	(17.7)
147	Amarillo, TX	(17.8)
148	Miami-Dade County, FL M.D.	(17.9)
149	Eugene-Springfield, OR	(18.1)
150	Columbus, OH	(18.3)
151	Greenville, NC	(18.4)
152	Lewiston-Auburn, ME	(18.7)
153	Lincoln, NE	(19.1)
154	Albuquerque, NM	(19.3)
154	Oakland-Fremont, CA M.D.	(19.3)
156	Denver-Aurora, CO	(19.4)
157	Albany, GA	(19.6)
157	Baltimore-Towson, MD	(19.6)
159	Baton Rouge, LA	(19.8)
160	Dubuque, IA	(20.0)
161	Lakeland, FL	(20.1)
162	Columbia, SC	(20.3)
163	Savannah, GA	(20.4)
164	Tyler, TX	(20.6)
165	San Antonio, TX	(20.8)
166	Billings, MT	(21.1)
167	El Paso, TX	(21.2)
168	Columbia, MO	(21.6)
169	Sherman-Denison, TX	(21.9)
169	Yuba City, CA	(21.9)
171	Topeka, KS	(23.5)

Note: All listings are for Metropolitan Statistical Areas (M.S.A.s) except for those ending with "M.D." Listings with "M.D." are Metropolitan Divisions which are smaller parts of eleven large M.S.A.s. See explanatory note at beginning of metropolitan area section on page 23.

RANK	METROPOLITAN AREA	% CHANGE
172	Phoenix-Mesa-Scottsdale, AZ	(23.9)
172	Wilmington, NC	(23.9)
174	West Palm Beach, FL M.D.	(24.7)
175	Jackson, MS	(24.8)
176	Portland-Vancouver, OR-WA	(24.9)
177	Beaumont-Port Arthur, TX	(25.4)
178	Bremerton-Silverdale, WA	(25.6)
178	Omaha-Council Bluffs, NE-IA	(25.6)
180	Montgomery, AL	(25.8)
181	Trenton-Ewing, NJ	(26.3)
182	Greeley, CO	(26.7)
183	Medford, OR	(26.9)
184	Santa Fe, NM	(27.1)
185	St. Joseph, MO-KS	(27.6)
186	Waco, TX	(27.9)
187	Fort Smith, AR-OK	(28.8)
188	Sioux Falls, SD	(28.9)
189	Richmond, VA	(29.0)
190	Victoria, TX	(29.4)
191	Brownsville-Harlingen, TX	(29.5)
192	Fargo, ND-MN	(29.6)
193	Honolulu, HI	(29.7)
194	Cedar Rapids, IA	(29.8)
195	Grand Forks, ND-MN	(30.2)
195	Santa Rosa-Petaluma, CA	(30.2)
197	Panama City-Lynn Haven, FL	(30.3)
198	Spokane, WA	(30.8)
199	Provo-Orem, UT	(31.6)
200	Tallahassee, FL	(32.0)
201	Boise City-Nampa, ID	(32.3)
202	New Orleans, LA	(32.4)
203	Oklahoma City, OK	(32.8)
204	Naples-Marco Island, FL	(33.2)
205	Iowa City, IA	(33.7)
206	Salem, OR	(33.9)
207	Waterloo-Cedar Falls, IA	(34.6)
208	Great Falls, MT	(37.2)
209	Sioux City, IA-NE-SD	(40.8)
210	Clarksville, TN-KY	(41.8)
211	Pine Bluff, AR	(42.0)
212	Rapid City, SD	(50.6)
NA	Abilene, TX**	NA
NA	Albany-Schenectady-Troy, NY**	NA
NA	Ames, IA**	NA
NA	Anderson, SC**	NA
NA	Ann Arbor, MI**	NA
NA	Appleton, WI**	NA
NA	Atlantic City, NJ**	NA
NA	Bangor, ME**	NA
NA	Barnstable Town, MA**	NA
NA	Battle Creek, MI**	NA
NA	Bay City, MI**	NA
NA	Bend, OR**	NA
NA	Bethesda-Frederick, MD M.D.**	NA
NA	Blacksburg, VA**	NA
NA	Bowling Green, KY**	NA
NA	Brunswick, GA**	NA
NA	Burlington, NC**	NA
NA	Camden, NJ M.D.**	NA
NA	Carson City, NV**	NA
NA	Charlotte-Gastonia, NC-SC**	NA
NA	Charlottesville, VA**	NA
NA	Chicago, IL**	NA
NA	Cleveland-Elyria-Mentor, OH**	NA
NA	Cleveland, TN**	NA
NA	Coeur d'Alene, ID**	NA
NA	College Station-Bryan, TX**	NA
NA	Columbus, IN**	NA
NA	Dallas (greater), TX**	NA
NA	Dalton, GA**	NA
NA	Dayton, OH**	NA
NA	Des Moines-West Des Moines, IA**	NA
NA	Detroit-Livonia-Dearborn, MI M.D.**	NA
NA	Dothan, AL**	NA
NA	Durham, NC**	NA
NA	Edison, NJ M.D.**	NA
NA	El Centro, CA**	NA
NA	Elizabethtown, KY**	NA
NA	Elmira, NY**	NA
NA	Evansville, IN-KY**	NA
NA	Fairbanks, AK**	NA
NA	Farmington, NM**	NA
NA	Fayetteville, AR-MO**	NA
NA	Fond du Lac, WI**	NA
NA	Fort Wayne, IN**	NA
NA	Gainesville, GA**	NA
NA	Grand Rapids-Wyoming, MI**	NA
NA	Greensboro-High Point, NC**	NA
NA	Greenville, SC**	NA
NA	Hagerstown-Martinsburg, MD-WV**	NA
NA	Hanford-Corcoran, CA**	NA
NA	Harrisburg-Carlisle, PA**	NA
NA	Harrisonburg, VA**	NA
NA	Hattiesburg, MS**	NA
NA	Holland-Grand Haven, MI**	NA
NA	Hot Springs, AR**	NA
NA	Huntington-Ashland, WV-KY-OH**	NA
NA	Idaho Falls, ID**	NA
NA	Indianapolis, IN**	NA
NA	Ithaca, NY**	NA
NA	Jacksonville, NC**	NA
NA	Jefferson City, MO**	NA
NA	Johnson City, TN**	NA
NA	Johnstown, PA**	NA
NA	Kalamazoo-Portage, MI**	NA
NA	Kansas City, MO-KS**	NA
NA	Kingsport, TN-VA**	NA
NA	Kingston, NY**	NA
NA	Lake Havasu City-Kingman, AZ**	NA
NA	Las Cruces, NM**	NA
NA	Lebanon, PA**	NA
NA	Lewiston, ID-WA**	NA
NA	Lexington-Fayette, KY**	NA
NA	Lima, OH**	NA
NA	Logan, UT-ID**	NA
NA	Longview, WA**	NA
NA	Los Angeles (greater), CA**	NA
NA	Macon, GA**	NA
NA	Madera, CA**	NA
NA	Manchester-Nashua, NH**	NA
NA	Mansfield, OH**	NA
NA	Memphis, TN-MS-AR**	NA
NA	Miami (greater), FL**	NA
NA	Michigan City-La Porte, IN**	NA
NA	Midland, TX**	NA
NA	Milwaukee, WI**	NA
NA	Missoula, MT**	NA
NA	Mobile, AL**	NA
NA	Monroe, LA**	NA
NA	Monroe, MI**	NA
NA	Morgantown, WV**	NA
NA	Morristown, TN**	NA
NA	Mount Vernon-Anacortes, WA**	NA
NA	Muskegon-Norton Shores, MI**	NA
NA	Napa, CA**	NA
NA	Nassau-Suffolk, NY M.D.**	NA
NA	New York (greater), NY-NJ-PA**	NA
NA	Niles-Benton Harbor, MI**	NA
NA	Ocean City, NJ**	NA
NA	Odessa, TX**	NA
NA	Ogden-Clearfield, UT**	NA
NA	Oshkosh-Neenah, WI**	NA
NA	Oxnard-Thousand Oaks, CA**	NA
NA	Palm Coast, FL**	NA
NA	Pascagoula, MS**	NA
NA	Philadelphia, PA M.D.**	NA
NA	Pittsfield, MA**	NA
NA	Portland, ME**	NA
NA	Poughkeepsie, NY**	NA
NA	Prescott, AZ**	NA
NA	Raleigh-Cary, NC**	NA
NA	Roanoke, VA**	NA
NA	Rome, GA**	NA
NA	Saginaw, MI**	NA
NA	Salisbury, MD**	NA
NA	Salt Lake City, UT**	NA
NA	San Francisco (greater), CA**	NA
NA	Sandusky, OH**	NA
NA	Santa Barbara-Santa Maria, CA**	NA
NA	Seattle (greater), WA**	NA
NA	Sebastian-Vero Beach, FL**	NA
NA	Spartanburg, SC**	NA
NA	Springfield, MA**	NA
NA	Springfield, OH**	NA
NA	St. Louis, MO-IL**	NA
NA	Syracuse, NY**	NA
NA	Tucson, AZ**	NA
NA	Valdosta, GA**	NA
NA	Vallejo-Fairfield, CA**	NA
NA	Warner Robins, GA**	NA
NA	Warren-Farmington Hills, MI M.D.**	NA
NA	Washington (greater) DC-VA-MD**	NA
NA	Washington, DC-VA-MD-WV M.D.**	NA
NA	Wenatchee, WA**	NA
NA	Wheeling, WV-OH**	NA
NA	Wilmington, DE-MD-NJ M.D.**	NA
NA	Winchester, VA-WV**	NA
NA	Winston-Salem, NC**	NA
NA	Worcester, MA**	NA

Source: CQ Press using data from Federal Bureau of Investigation "Crime in the United States 2006" (Uniform Crime Reports, September 24, 2007)

**Larceny and theft is the unlawful taking of property. Attempts are included.*

***Not available.*

37. Motor Vehicle Thefts in 2006

National Total = 1,192,809 Motor Vehicle Thefts*

RANK	METROPOLITAN AREA	THEFTS
243	Abilene, TX	358
133	Albany-Schenectady-Troy, NY	1,186
209	Albany, GA	515
51	Albuquerque, NM	6,715
202	Alexandria, LA	538
311	Altoona, PA	172
139	Amarillo, TX	1,106
347	Ames, IA	69
122	Anchorage, AK	1,516
173	Anderson, SC	775
168	Ann Arbor, MI	790
314	Appleton, WI	165
135	Asheville, NC	1,177
191	Athens-Clarke County, GA	589
12	Atlanta, GA	28,594
215	Atlantic City, NJ	477
88	Augusta, GA-SC	2,758
74	Austin-Round Rock, TX	3,374
58	Bakersfield, CA	5,761
29	Baltimore-Towson, MD	12,699
326	Bangor, ME	143
255	Barnstable Town, MA	334
82	Baton Rouge, LA	2,985
258	Battle Creek, MI	330
295	Bay City, MI	217
125	Beaumont-Port Arthur, TX	1,397
207	Bellingham, WA	518
238	Bend, OR	376
87	Bethesda-Frederick, MD M.D.	2,864
231	Billings, MT	394
322	Binghamton, NY	148
66	Birmingham-Hoover, AL	4,447
330	Bismarck, ND	134
295	Blacksburg, VA	217
272	Bloomington, IN	265
132	Boise City-Nampa, ID	1,197
304	Bowling Green, KY	193
190	Bremerton-Silverdale, WA	601
140	Brownsville-Harlingen, TX	1,094
269	Brunswick, GA	285
83	Buffalo-Niagara Falls, NY	2,973
241	Burlington, NC	366
81	Camden, NJ M.D.	2,993
97	Cape Coral-Fort Myers, FL	2,309
328	Carson City, NV	137
326	Casper, WY	143
236	Cedar Rapids, IA	386
78	Charleston-North Charleston, SC	3,160
142	Charleston, WV	1,056
38	Charlotte-Gastonia, NC-SC	9,646
224	Charlottesville, VA	434
109	Chattanooga, TN-GA	1,848
317	Cheyenne, WY	157
NA	Chicago, IL**	NA
145	Chico, CA	1,010
59	Cincinnati-Middletown, OH-KY-IN	5,749
201	Clarksville, TN-KY	540
42	Cleveland-Elyria-Mentor, OH	9,219
271	Cleveland, TN	268
275	Coeur d'Alene, ID	254
230	College Station-Bryan, TX	399
99	Colorado Springs, CO	2,248
251	Columbia, MO	338
94	Columbia, SC	2,376
105	Columbus, GA-AL	2,030
331	Columbus, IN	130
46	Columbus, OH	7,826
141	Corpus Christi, TX	1,072
334	Cumberland, MD-WV	118
10	Dallas (greater), TX	29,967
21	Dallas-Plano-Irving, TX M.D.	22,441
233	Dalton, GA	390
309	Danville, VA	179
108	Daytona Beach, FL	1,855
73	Dayton, OH	3,527
225	Decatur, AL	423
26	Denver-Aurora, CO	14,779
126	Des Moines-West Des Moines, IA	1,371
6	Detroit (greater), MI	38,515
11	Detroit-Livonia-Dearborn, MI M.D.	29,683
249	Dothan, AL	342
256	Dover, DE	333
336	Dubuque, IA	107
211	Duluth, MN-WI	510
117	Durham, NC	1,615
312	Eau Claire, WI	171
84	Edison, NJ M.D.	2,916
138	El Centro, CA	1,142
71	El Paso, TX	3,789
342	Elizabethtown, KY	96
219	Elkhart-Goshen, IN	470
348	Elmira, NY	63
263	Erie, PA	304
103	Eugene-Springfield, OR	2,055
199	Evansville, IN-KY	545
310	Fairbanks, AK	173
247	Fargo, ND-MN	345
286	Farmington, NM	238
170	Fayetteville, AR-MO	784
119	Fayetteville, NC	1,555
278	Flagstaff, AZ	251
91	Flint, MI	2,582
158	Florence, SC	871
344	Fond du Lac, WI	76
209	Fort Collins-Loveland, CO	515
50	Fort Lauderdale, FL M.D.	7,092
183	Fort Smith, AR-OK	637
222	Fort Walton Beach, FL	436
153	Fort Wayne, IN	942
48	Fort Worth-Arlington, TX M.D.	7,526
45	Fresno, CA	7,948
233	Gadsden, AL	390
163	Gainesville, FL	824
179	Gainesville, GA	656
346	Glens Falls, NY	72
267	Goldsboro, NC	293
298	Grand Forks, ND-MN	211
225	Grand Junction, CO	423
120	Grand Rapids-Wyoming, MI	1,538
322	Great Falls, MT	148
174	Greeley, CO	745
232	Green Bay, WI	392
93	Greensboro-High Point, NC	2,475
222	Greenville, NC	436
98	Greenville, SC	2,292
195	Hagerstown-Martinsburg, MD-WV	559
176	Hanford-Corcoran, CA	688
196	Harrisburg-Carlisle, PA	552
335	Harrisonburg, VA	111
72	Hartford, CT	3,767
227	Hattiesburg, MS	421
293	Holland-Grand Haven, MI	221
53	Honolulu, HI	6,288
221	Hot Springs, AR	439
205	Houma, LA	524
8	Houston, TX	31,867
178	Huntington-Ashland, WV-KY-OH	669
110	Huntsville, AL	1,832
286	Idaho Falls, ID	238
34	Indianapolis, IN	10,452
320	Iowa City, IA	153
345	Ithaca, NY	74
60	Jacksonville, FL	5,292
251	Jacksonville, NC	338
263	Jackson, MI	304
92	Jackson, MS	2,489
198	Jackson, TN	550
278	Janesville, WI	251
298	Jefferson City, MO	211
239	Johnson City, TN	370
313	Johnstown, PA	168
294	Jonesboro, AR	218
200	Joplin, MO	541
160	Kalamazoo-Portage, MI	849
30	Kansas City, MO-KS	11,471
196	Kennewick-Richland-Pasco, WA	552
189	Killeen-Temple-Fort Hood, TX	605
175	Kingsport, TN-VA	739
318	Kingston, NY	154
100	Knoxville, TN	2,203
307	Kokomo, IN	182
329	La Crosse, WI-MN	135
253	Lafayette, IN	337
171	Lake Charles, LA	776
150	Lake Havasu City-Kingman, AZ	963
118	Lakeland, FL	1,571
161	Lancaster, PA	837
149	Lansing-East Lansing, MI	966
129	Laredo, TX	1,247
213	Las Cruces, NM	503
19	Las Vegas-Paradise, NV	23,952

Note: All listings are for Metropolitan Statistical Areas (M.S.A.s) except for those ending with "M.D." Listings with "M.D." are Metropolitan Divisions which are smaller parts of eleven large M.S.A.s. See explanatory note at beginning of metropolitan area section on page 23.

RANK	METROPOLITAN AREA	THEFTS
285	Lawrence, KS	239
262	Lawton, OK	309
315	Lebanon, PA	159
336	Lewiston-Auburn, ME	107
341	Lewiston, ID-WA	99
147	Lexington-Fayette, KY	992
297	Lima, OH	214
217	Lincoln, NE	472
80	Little Rock, AR	3,016
349	Logan, UT-ID	54
156	Longview, TX	885
204	Longview, WA	526
2	Los Angeles County, CA M.D.	64,697
1	Los Angeles (greater), CA	75,245
61	Louisville, KY-IN	5,006
163	Lubbock, TX	824
268	Lynchburg, VA	291
111	Macon, GA	1,820
188	Madera, CA	613
167	Madison, WI	813
205	Manchester-Nashua, NH	524
315	Mansfield, OH	159
89	McAllen-Edinburg-Mission, TX	2,609
250	Medford, OR	339
44	Memphis, TN-MS-AR	8,470
130	Merced, CA	1,219
9	Miami (greater), FL	30,149
24	Miami-Dade County, FL M.D.	17,019
240	Michigan City-La Porte, IN	369
275	Midland, TX	254
41	Milwaukee, WI	9,404
32	Minneapolis-St. Paul, MN-WI	10,700
302	Missoula, MT	200
107	Mobile, AL	1,870
64	Modesto, CA	4,642
257	Monroe, LA	331
265	Monroe, MI	295
127	Montgomery, AL	1,331
303	Morgantown, WV	196
246	Morristown, TN	350
203	Mount Vernon-Anacortes, WA	529
281	Muncie, IN	250
218	Muskegon-Norton Shores, MI	471
116	Myrtle Beach, SC	1,627
245	Napa, CA	356
242	Naples-Marco Island, FL	364
63	Nashville-Davidson, TN	4,794
69	Nassau-Suffolk, NY M.D.	4,068
55	New Orleans, LA	6,119
3	New York (greater), NY-NJ-PA	41,125
20	New York-W. Plains NY-NJ M.D.	22,982
31	Newark-Union, NJ-PA M.D.	11,159
273	Niles-Benton Harbor, MI	263
14	Oakland-Fremont, CA M.D.	28,454
193	Ocala, FL	570
333	Ocean City, NJ	125
261	Odessa, TX	312
154	Ogden-Clearfield, UT	908
52	Oklahoma City, OK	6,364
177	Olympia, WA	684

RANK	METROPOLITAN AREA	THEFTS
65	Omaha-Council Bluffs, NE-IA	4,545
35	Orlando, FL	10,399
321	Oshkosh-Neenah, WI	149
114	Oxnard-Thousand Oaks, CA	1,760
128	Palm Bay-Melbourne, FL	1,277
318	Palm Coast, FL	154
237	Panama City-Lynn Haven, FL	379
146	Pascagoula, MS	1,001
134	Pensacola, FL	1,181
22	Philadelphia (greater) PA-NJ-DE	21,022
25	Philadelphia, PA M.D.	15,421
4	Phoenix-Mesa-Scottsdale, AZ	41,104
212	Pine Bluff, AR	507
62	Pittsburgh, PA	4,863
307	Pittsfield, MA	182
339	Pocatello, ID	104
162	Port St. Lucie, FL	832
39	Portland-Vancouver, OR-WA	9,602
186	Portland, ME	623
194	Poughkeepsie, NY	568
228	Prescott, AZ	420
182	Provo-Orem, UT	638
208	Pueblo, CO	517
244	Punta Gorda, FL	357
220	Racine, WI	465
104	Raleigh-Cary, NC	2,047
324	Rapid City, SD	147
112	Reading, PA	1,791
166	Redding, CA	820
96	Reno-Sparks, NV	2,321
77	Richmond, VA	3,175
13	Riverside-San Bernardino, CA	28,579
187	Roanoke, VA	616
283	Rochester, MN	245
76	Rochester, NY	3,259
192	Rocky Mount, NC	582
259	Rome, GA	322
23	Sacramento, CA	18,540
185	Saginaw, MI	628
123	Salem, OR	1,493
101	Salinas, CA	2,202
265	Salisbury, MD	295
56	Salt Lake City, UT	6,093
288	San Angelo, TX	236
47	San Antonio, TX	7,672
18	San Diego, CA	24,045
5	San Francisco (greater), CA	38,714
36	San Francisco-S. Mateo, CA M.D.	10,260
37	San Jose, CA	10,201
214	San Luis Obispo, CA	488
331	Sandusky, OH	130
33	Santa Ana-Anaheim, CA M.D.	10,548
155	Santa Barbara-Santa Maria, CA	897
159	Santa Cruz-Watsonville, CA	857
290	Santa Fe, NM	227
148	Santa Rosa-Petaluma, CA	971
106	Sarasota-Bradenton-Venice, FL	2,001
121	Savannah, GA	1,530
157	Scranton--Wilkes-Barre, PA	884
7	Seattle (greater), WA	32,901

RANK	METROPOLITAN AREA	THEFTS
16	Seattle-Bellevue, WA M.D.	25,798
300	Sebastian-Vero Beach, FL	203
338	Sheboygan, WI	105
292	Sherman-Denison, TX	222
113	Shreveport-Bossier City, LA	1,765
289	Sioux City, IA-NE-SD	230
277	Sioux Falls, SD	252
143	South Bend-Mishawaka, IN-MI	1,028
151	Spartanburg, SC	956
75	Spokane, WA	3,290
86	Springfield, MA	2,882
137	Springfield, MO	1,148
180	Springfield, OH	644
343	State College, PA	82
54	Stockton, CA	6,263
291	St. Cloud, MN	224
235	St. Joseph, MO-KS	389
27	St. Louis, MO-IL	13,644
259	Sumter, SC	322
144	Syracuse, NY	1,012
49	Tacoma, WA M.D.	7,103
152	Tallahassee, FL	946
28	Tampa-St Petersburg, FL	13,330
248	Texarkana, TX-Texarkana, AR	344
79	Toledo, OH	3,028
169	Topeka, KS	789
165	Trenton-Ewing, NJ	823
40	Tucson, AZ	9,592
67	Tulsa, OK	4,118
181	Tuscaloosa, AL	643
229	Tyler, TX	400
270	Utica-Rome, NY	273
274	Valdosta, GA	257
84	Vallejo-Fairfield, CA	2,916
281	Victoria, TX	250
254	Vineland, NJ	336
68	Virginia Beach-Norfolk, VA-NC	4,086
70	Visalia-Porterville, CA	3,857
183	Waco, TX	637
278	Warner Robins, GA	251
43	Warren-Farmington Hills, MI M.D.	8,832
15	Washington (greater) DC-VA-MD	27,724
17	Washington, DC-VA-MD-WV M.D.	24,860
306	Waterloo-Cedar Falls, IA	183
339	Wausau, WI	104
305	Wenatchee, WA	187
57	West Palm Beach, FL M.D.	6,038
300	Wheeling, WV-OH	203
216	Wichita Falls, TX	475
95	Wichita, KS	2,344
325	Williamsport, PA	145
90	Wilmington, DE-MD-NJ M.D.	2,608
131	Wilmington, NC	1,210
284	Winchester, VA-WV	244
124	Winston-Salem, NC	1,483
115	Worcester, MA	1,676
102	Yakima, WA	2,176
171	Yuba City, CA	776
136	Yuma, AZ	1,151

Source: Federal Bureau of Investigation
"Crime in the United States 2006" (Uniform Crime Reports, September 24, 2007)
**Motor vehicle theft includes the theft or attempted theft of a self-propelled vehicle. Excludes motorboats, construction equipment, airplanes, and farming equipment. **Not available.*

37. Motor Vehicle Thefts in 2006 (continued)

National Total = 1,192,809 Motor Vehicle Thefts*

RANK	METROPOLITAN AREA	THEFTS
1	Los Angeles (greater), CA	75,245
2	Los Angeles County, CA M.D.	64,697
3	New York (greater), NY-NJ-PA	41,125
4	Phoenix-Mesa-Scottsdale, AZ	41,104
5	San Francisco (greater), CA	38,714
6	Detroit (greater), MI	38,515
7	Seattle (greater), WA	32,901
8	Houston, TX	31,867
9	Miami (greater), FL	30,149
10	Dallas (greater), TX	29,967
11	Detroit-Livonia-Dearborn, MI M.D.	29,683
12	Atlanta, GA	28,594
13	Riverside-San Bernardino, CA	28,579
14	Oakland-Fremont, CA M.D.	28,454
15	Washington (greater) DC-VA-MD	27,724
16	Seattle-Bellevue, WA M.D.	25,798
17	Washington, DC-VA-MD-WV M.D.	24,860
18	San Diego, CA	24,045
19	Las Vegas-Paradise, NV	23,952
20	New York-W. Plains NY-NJ M.D.	22,982
21	Dallas-Plano-Irving, TX M.D.	22,441
22	Philadelphia (greater) PA-NJ-DE	21,022
23	Sacramento, CA	18,540
24	Miami-Dade County, FL M.D.	17,019
25	Philadelphia, PA M.D.	15,421
26	Denver-Aurora, CO	14,779
27	St. Louis, MO-IL	13,644
28	Tampa-St Petersburg, FL	13,330
29	Baltimore-Towson, MD	12,699
30	Kansas City, MO-KS	11,471
31	Newark-Union, NJ-PA M.D.	11,159
32	Minneapolis-St. Paul, MN-WI	10,700
33	Santa Ana-Anaheim, CA M.D.	10,548
34	Indianapolis, IN	10,452
35	Orlando, FL	10,399
36	San Francisco-S. Mateo, CA M.D.	10,260
37	San Jose, CA	10,201
38	Charlotte-Gastonia, NC-SC	9,646
39	Portland-Vancouver, OR-WA	9,602
40	Tucson, AZ	9,592
41	Milwaukee, WI	9,404
42	Cleveland-Elyria-Mentor, OH	9,219
43	Warren-Farmington Hills, MI M.D.	8,832
44	Memphis, TN-MS-AR	8,470
45	Fresno, CA	7,948
46	Columbus, OH	7,826
47	San Antonio, TX	7,672
48	Fort Worth-Arlington, TX M.D.	7,526
49	Tacoma, WA M.D.	7,103
50	Fort Lauderdale, FL M.D.	7,092
51	Albuquerque, NM	6,715
52	Oklahoma City, OK	6,364
53	Honolulu, HI	6,288
54	Stockton, CA	6,263
55	New Orleans, LA	6,119
56	Salt Lake City, UT	6,093
57	West Palm Beach, FL M.D.	6,038
58	Bakersfield, CA	5,761
59	Cincinnati-Middletown, OH-KY-IN	5,749
60	Jacksonville, FL	5,292
61	Louisville, KY-IN	5,006
62	Pittsburgh, PA	4,863
63	Nashville-Davidson, TN	4,794
64	Modesto, CA	4,642
65	Omaha-Council Bluffs, NE-IA	4,545
66	Birmingham-Hoover, AL	4,447
67	Tulsa, OK	4,118
68	Virginia Beach-Norfolk, VA-NC	4,086
69	Nassau-Suffolk, NY M.D.	4,068
70	Visalia-Porterville, CA	3,857
71	El Paso, TX	3,789
72	Hartford, CT	3,767
73	Dayton, OH	3,527
74	Austin-Round Rock, TX	3,374
75	Spokane, WA	3,290
76	Rochester, NY	3,259
77	Richmond, VA	3,175
78	Charleston-North Charleston, SC	3,160
79	Toledo, OH	3,028
80	Little Rock, AR	3,016
81	Camden, NJ M.D.	2,993
82	Baton Rouge, LA	2,985
83	Buffalo-Niagara Falls, NY	2,973
84	Edison, NJ M.D.	2,916
84	Vallejo-Fairfield, CA	2,916
86	Springfield, MA	2,882
87	Bethesda-Frederick, MD M.D.	2,864
88	Augusta, GA-SC	2,758
89	McAllen-Edinburg-Mission, TX	2,609
90	Wilmington, DE-MD-NJ M.D.	2,608
91	Flint, MI	2,582
92	Jackson, MS	2,489
93	Greensboro-High Point, NC	2,475
94	Columbia, SC	2,376
95	Wichita, KS	2,344
96	Reno-Sparks, NV	2,321
97	Cape Coral-Fort Myers, FL	2,309
98	Greenville, SC	2,292
99	Colorado Springs, CO	2,248
100	Knoxville, TN	2,203
101	Salinas, CA	2,202
102	Yakima, WA	2,176
103	Eugene-Springfield, OR	2,055
104	Raleigh-Cary, NC	2,047
105	Columbus, GA-AL	2,030
106	Sarasota-Bradenton-Venice, FL	2,001
107	Mobile, AL	1,870
108	Daytona Beach, FL	1,855
109	Chattanooga, TN-GA	1,848
110	Huntsville, AL	1,832
111	Macon, GA	1,820
112	Reading, PA	1,791
113	Shreveport-Bossier City, LA	1,765
114	Oxnard-Thousand Oaks, CA	1,760
115	Worcester, MA	1,676
116	Myrtle Beach, SC	1,627
117	Durham, NC	1,615
118	Lakeland, FL	1,571
119	Fayetteville, NC	1,555
120	Grand Rapids-Wyoming, MI	1,538
121	Savannah, GA	1,530
122	Anchorage, AK	1,516
123	Salem, OR	1,493
124	Winston-Salem, NC	1,483
125	Beaumont-Port Arthur, TX	1,397
126	Des Moines-West Des Moines, IA	1,371
127	Montgomery, AL	1,331
128	Palm Bay-Melbourne, FL	1,277
129	Laredo, TX	1,247
130	Merced, CA	1,219
131	Wilmington, NC	1,210
132	Boise City-Nampa, ID	1,197
133	Albany-Schenectady-Troy, NY	1,186
134	Pensacola, FL	1,181
135	Asheville, NC	1,177
136	Yuma, AZ	1,151
137	Springfield, MO	1,148
138	El Centro, CA	1,142
139	Amarillo, TX	1,106
140	Brownsville-Harlingen, TX	1,094
141	Corpus Christi, TX	1,072
142	Charleston, WV	1,056
143	South Bend-Mishawaka, IN-MI	1,028
144	Syracuse, NY	1,012
145	Chico, CA	1,010
146	Pascagoula, MS	1,001
147	Lexington-Fayette, KY	992
148	Santa Rosa-Petaluma, CA	971
149	Lansing-East Lansing, MI	966
150	Lake Havasu City-Kingman, AZ	963
151	Spartanburg, SC	956
152	Tallahassee, FL	946
153	Fort Wayne, IN	942
154	Ogden-Clearfield, UT	908
155	Santa Barbara-Santa Maria, CA	897
156	Longview, TX	885
157	Scranton--Wilkes-Barre, PA	884
158	Florence, SC	871
159	Santa Cruz-Watsonville, CA	857
160	Kalamazoo-Portage, MI	849
161	Lancaster, PA	837
162	Port St. Lucie, FL	832
163	Gainesville, FL	824
163	Lubbock, TX	824
165	Trenton-Ewing, NJ	823
166	Redding, CA	820
167	Madison, WI	813
168	Ann Arbor, MI	790
169	Topeka, KS	789
170	Fayetteville, AR-MO	784
171	Lake Charles, LA	776

Note: All listings are for Metropolitan Statistical Areas (M.S.A.s) except for those ending with "M.D." Listings with "M.D." are Metropolitan Divisions which are smaller parts of eleven large M.S.A.s. See explanatory note at beginning of metropolitan area section on page 23.

RANK	METROPOLITAN AREA	THEFTS
171	Yuba City, CA	776
173	Anderson, SC	775
174	Greeley, CO	745
175	Kingsport, TN-VA	739
176	Hanford-Corcoran, CA	688
177	Olympia, WA	684
178	Huntington-Ashland, WV-KY-OH	669
179	Gainesville, GA	656
180	Springfield, OH	644
181	Tuscaloosa, AL	643
182	Provo-Orem, UT	638
183	Fort Smith, AR-OK	637
183	Waco, TX	637
185	Saginaw, MI	628
186	Portland, ME	623
187	Roanoke, VA	616
188	Madera, CA	613
189	Killeen-Temple-Fort Hood, TX	605
190	Bremerton-Silverdale, WA	601
191	Athens-Clarke County, GA	589
192	Rocky Mount, NC	582
193	Ocala, FL	570
194	Poughkeepsie, NY	568
195	Hagerstown-Martinsburg, MD-WV	559
196	Harrisburg-Carlisle, PA	552
196	Kennewick-Richland-Pasco, WA	552
198	Jackson, TN	550
199	Evansville, IN-KY	545
200	Joplin, MO	541
201	Clarksville, TN-KY	540
202	Alexandria, LA	538
203	Mount Vernon-Anacortes, WA	529
204	Longview, WA	526
205	Houma, LA	524
205	Manchester-Nashua, NH	524
207	Bellingham, WA	518
208	Pueblo, CO	517
209	Albany, GA	515
209	Fort Collins-Loveland, CO	515
211	Duluth, MN-WI	510
212	Pine Bluff, AR	507
213	Las Cruces, NM	503
214	San Luis Obispo, CA	488
215	Atlantic City, NJ	477
216	Wichita Falls, TX	475
217	Lincoln, NE	472
218	Muskegon-Norton Shores, MI	471
219	Elkhart-Goshen, IN	470
220	Racine, WI	465
221	Hot Springs, AR	439
222	Fort Walton Beach, FL	436
222	Greenville, NC	436
224	Charlottesville, VA	434
225	Decatur, AL	423
225	Grand Junction, CO	423
227	Hattiesburg, MS	421
228	Prescott, AZ	420
229	Tyler, TX	400
230	College Station-Bryan, TX	399
231	Billings, MT	394
232	Green Bay, WI	392
233	Dalton, GA	390
233	Gadsden, AL	390
235	St. Joseph, MO-KS	389
236	Cedar Rapids, IA	386
237	Panama City-Lynn Haven, FL	379
238	Bend, OR	376
239	Johnson City, TN	370
240	Michigan City-La Porte, IN	369
241	Burlington, NC	366
242	Naples-Marco Island, FL	364
243	Abilene, TX	358
244	Punta Gorda, FL	357
245	Napa, CA	356
246	Morristown, TN	350
247	Fargo, ND-MN	345
248	Texarkana, TX-Texarkana, AR	344
249	Dothan, AL	342
250	Medford, OR	339
251	Columbia, MO	338
251	Jacksonville, NC	338
253	Lafayette, IN	337
254	Vineland, NJ	336
255	Barnstable Town, MA	334
256	Dover, DE	333
257	Monroe, LA	331
258	Battle Creek, MI	330
259	Rome, GA	322
259	Sumter, SC	322
261	Odessa, TX	312
262	Lawton, OK	309
263	Erie, PA	304
263	Jackson, MI	304
265	Monroe, MI	295
265	Salisbury, MD	295
267	Goldsboro, NC	293
268	Lynchburg, VA	291
269	Brunswick, GA	285
270	Utica-Rome, NY	273
271	Cleveland, TN	268
272	Bloomington, IN	265
273	Niles-Benton Harbor, MI	263
274	Valdosta, GA	257
275	Coeur d'Alene, ID	254
275	Midland, TX	254
277	Sioux Falls, SD	252
278	Flagstaff, AZ	251
278	Janesville, WI	251
278	Warner Robins, GA	251
281	Muncie, IN	250
281	Victoria, TX	250
283	Rochester, MN	245
284	Winchester, VA-WV	244
285	Lawrence, KS	239
286	Farmington, NM	238
286	Idaho Falls, ID	238
288	San Angelo, TX	236
289	Sioux City, IA-NE-SD	230
290	Santa Fe, NM	227
291	St. Cloud, MN	224
292	Sherman-Denison, TX	222
293	Holland-Grand Haven, MI	221
294	Jonesboro, AR	218
295	Bay City, MI	217
295	Blacksburg, VA	217
297	Lima, OH	214
298	Grand Forks, ND-MN	211
298	Jefferson City, MO	211
300	Sebastian-Vero Beach, FL	203
300	Wheeling, WV-OH	203
302	Missoula, MT	200
303	Morgantown, WV	196
304	Bowling Green, KY	193
305	Wenatchee, WA	187
306	Waterloo-Cedar Falls, IA	183
307	Kokomo, IN	182
307	Pittsfield, MA	182
309	Danville, VA	179
310	Fairbanks, AK	173
311	Altoona, PA	172
312	Eau Claire, WI	171
313	Johnstown, PA	168
314	Appleton, WI	165
315	Lebanon, PA	159
315	Mansfield, OH	159
317	Cheyenne, WY	157
318	Kingston, NY	154
318	Palm Coast, FL	154
320	Iowa City, IA	153
321	Oshkosh-Neenah, WI	149
322	Binghamton, NY	148
322	Great Falls, MT	148
324	Rapid City, SD	147
325	Williamsport, PA	145
326	Bangor, ME	143
326	Casper, WY	143
328	Carson City, NV	137
329	La Crosse, WI-MN	135
330	Bismarck, ND	134
331	Columbus, IN	130
331	Sandusky, OH	130
333	Ocean City, NJ	125
334	Cumberland, MD-WV	118
335	Harrisonburg, VA	111
336	Dubuque, IA	107
336	Lewiston-Auburn, ME	107
338	Sheboygan, WI	105
339	Pocatello, ID	104
339	Wausau, WI	104
341	Lewiston, ID-WA	99
342	Elizabethtown, KY	96
343	State College, PA	82
344	Fond du Lac, WI	76
345	Ithaca, NY	74
346	Glens Falls, NY	72
347	Ames, IA	69
348	Elmira, NY	63
349	Logan, UT-ID	54
NA	Chicago, IL**	NA

Source: Federal Bureau of Investigation
"Crime in the United States 2006" (Uniform Crime Reports, September 24, 2007)
**Motor vehicle theft includes the theft or attempted theft of a self-propelled vehicle. Excludes motorboats, construction equipment, airplanes, and farming equipment. **Not available.*

38. Motor Vehicle Theft Rate in 2006

National Rate = 398.4 Motor Vehicle Thefts per 100,000 Population*

RANK	METROPOLITAN AREA	RATE
218	Abilene, TX	219.9
299	Albany-Schenectady-Troy, NY	139.3
154	Albany, GA	306.4
17	Albuquerque, NM	830.3
111	Alexandria, LA	383.6
304	Altoona, PA	135.5
90	Amarillo, TX	450.6
337	Ames, IA	85.8
60	Anchorage, AK	514.1
92	Anderson, SC	434.8
205	Ann Arbor, MI	231.7
341	Appleton, WI	76.4
157	Asheville, NC	293.8
142	Athens-Clarke County, GA	325.9
47	Atlanta, GA	563.4
272	Atlantic City, NJ	175.9
59	Augusta, GA-SC	516.4
212	Austin-Round Rock, TX	225.9
20	Bakersfield, CA	754.4
74	Baltimore-Towson, MD	476.9
331	Bangor, ME	97.2
295	Barnstable Town, MA	146.6
95	Baton Rouge, LA	429.2
199	Battle Creek, MI	237.7
249	Bay City, MI	199.5
127	Beaumont-Port Arthur, TX	354.2
167	Bellingham, WA	277.6
181	Bend, OR	261.7
189	Bethesda-Frederick, MD M.D.	248.7
175	Billings, MT	266.2
345	Binghamton, NY	59.4
104	Birmingham-Hoover, AL	404.3
305	Bismarck, ND	135.1
298	Blacksburg, VA	142.2
294	Bloomington, IN	148.1
229	Boise City-Nampa, ID	214.4
275	Bowling Green, KY	172.5
193	Bremerton-Silverdale, WA	245.5
164	Brownsville-Harlingen, TX	281.2
165	Brunswick, GA	280.5
183	Buffalo-Niagara Falls, NY	258.3
184	Burlington, NC	255.3
197	Camden, NJ M.D.	240.0
101	Cape Coral-Fort Myers, FL	416.8
201	Carson City, NV	236.5
244	Casper, WY	202.6
289	Cedar Rapids, IA	155.8
57	Charleston-North Charleston, SC	523.0
131	Charleston, WV	344.3
33	Charlotte-Gastonia, NC-SC	622.0
211	Charlottesville, VA	228.1
123	Chattanooga, TN-GA	368.8
269	Cheyenne, WY	182.3
NA	Chicago, IL**	NA
78	Chico, CA	467.3
168	Cincinnati-Middletown, OH-KY-IN	276.9
219	Clarksville, TN-KY	219.2
93	Cleveland-Elyria-Mentor, OH	433.0
194	Cleveland, TN	245.0
253	Coeur d'Alene, ID	193.9
237	College Station-Bryan, TX	204.5
118	Colorado Springs, CO	375.5
222	Columbia, MO	218.9
134	Columbia, SC	339.1
27	Columbus, GA-AL	694.5
273	Columbus, IN	175.6
85	Columbus, OH	457.5
186	Corpus Christi, TX	252.1
319	Cumberland, MD-WV	117.0
62	Dallas (greater), TX	500.8
48	Dallas-Plano-Irving, TX M.D.	560.5
160	Dalton, GA	286.9
282	Danville, VA	164.1
121	Daytona Beach, FL	372.3
99	Dayton, OH	417.6
163	Decatur, AL	282.6
35	Denver-Aurora, CO	614.6
182	Des Moines-West Des Moines, IA	261.0
16	Detroit (greater), MI	860.3
1	Detroit-Livonia-Dearborn, MI M.D.	1,489.2
190	Dothan, AL	248.1
210	Dover, DE	228.6
321	Dubuque, IA	116.2
267	Duluth, MN-WI	184.0
130	Durham, NC	347.1
324	Eau Claire, WI	110.6
308	Edison, NJ M.D.	126.5
22	El Centro, CA	726.3
61	El Paso, TX	510.6
336	Elizabethtown, KY	86.1
198	Elkhart-Goshen, IN	239.0
344	Elmira, NY	70.2
326	Erie, PA	108.3
37	Eugene-Springfield, OR	603.2
291	Evansville, IN-KY	154.9
NA	Fairbanks, AK**	NA
260	Fargo, ND-MN	186.4
262	Farmington, NM	186.0
258	Fayetteville, AR-MO	191.4
91	Fayetteville, NC	441.2
252	Flagstaff, AZ	195.2
42	Flint, MI	583.1
94	Florence, SC	432.2
342	Fond du Lac, WI	76.2
263	Fort Collins-Loveland, CO	185.9
108	Fort Lauderdale, FL M.D.	392.3
217	Fort Smith, AR-OK	221.2
203	Fort Walton Beach, FL	235.4
206	Fort Wayne, IN	231.4
114	Fort Worth-Arlington, TX M.D.	379.9
15	Fresno, CA	897.6
119	Gadsden, AL	374.6
136	Gainesville, FL	337.3
112	Gainesville, GA	383.4
347	Glens Falls, NY	55.8
188	Goldsboro, NC	251.0
226	Grand Forks, ND-MN	217.1
148	Grand Junction, CO	319.7
247	Grand Rapids-Wyoming, MI	199.9
266	Great Falls, MT	184.2
149	Greeley, CO	319.4
306	Green Bay, WI	131.3
125	Greensboro-High Point, NC	359.8
179	Greenville, NC	262.9
113	Greenville, SC	381.7
215	Hagerstown-Martinsburg, MD-WV	222.0
75	Hanford-Corcoran, CA	475.4
327	Harrisburg-Carlisle, PA	105.7
330	Harrisonburg, VA	98.4
116	Hartford, CT	376.0
147	Hattiesburg, MS	320.4
335	Holland-Grand Haven, MI	86.7
28	Honolulu, HI	689.0
79	Hot Springs, AR	464.0
168	Houma, LA	276.9
40	Houston, TX	586.9
204	Huntington-Ashland, WV-KY-OH	233.2
67	Huntsville, AL	492.5
237	Idaho Falls, ID	204.5
32	Indianapolis, IN	632.9
325	Iowa City, IA	109.9
343	Ithaca, NY	73.8
100	Jacksonville, FL	416.9
225	Jacksonville, NC	217.4
261	Jackson, MI	186.3
72	Jackson, MS	478.0
68	Jackson, TN	489.9
288	Janesville, WI	158.7
296	Jefferson City, MO	145.6
254	Johnson City, TN	193.4
322	Johnstown, PA	113.4
256	Jonesboro, AR	192.3
145	Joplin, MO	323.2
174	Kalamazoo-Portage, MI	266.5
41	Kansas City, MO-KS	584.7
191	Kennewick-Richland-Pasco, WA	245.6
279	Killeen-Temple-Fort Hood, TX	167.4
195	Kingsport, TN-VA	242.4
339	Kingston, NY	84.1
139	Knoxville, TN	331.9
271	Kokomo, IN	178.4
328	La Crosse, WI-MN	104.3
268	Lafayette, IN	182.6
98	Lake Charles, LA	419.9
64	Lake Havasu City-Kingman, AZ	495.5
162	Lakeland, FL	284.6
278	Lancaster, PA	170.5
231	Lansing-East Lansing, MI	212.7
52	Laredo, TX	539.7
180	Las Cruces, NM	262.0
2	Las Vegas-Paradise, NV	1,355.0

Note: All listings are for Metropolitan Statistical Areas (M.S.A.s) except for those ending with "M.D." Listings with "M.D." are Metropolitan Divisions which are smaller parts of eleven large M.S.A.s. See explanatory note at beginning of metropolitan area section on page 23.

RANK	METROPOLITAN AREA	RATE
208	Lawrence, KS	230.6
171	Lawton, OK	272.4
308	Lebanon, PA	126.5
329	Lewiston-Auburn, ME	99.0
283	Lewiston, ID-WA	163.7
209	Lexington-Fayette, KY	229.0
245	Lima, OH	201.2
280	Lincoln, NE	166.7
80	Little Rock, AR	463.6
348	Logan, UT-ID	47.4
96	Longview, TX	427.1
53	Longview, WA	531.3
30	Los Angeles County, CA M.D.	645.4
43	Los Angeles (greater), CA	577.0
103	Louisville, KY-IN	411.1
153	Lubbock, TX	309.4
315	Lynchburg, VA	121.6
19	Macon, GA	771.0
97	Madera, CA	425.5
293	Madison, WI	150.8
307	Manchester-Nashua, NH	130.1
311	Mansfield, OH	124.1
120	McAllen-Edinburg-Mission, TX	374.1
277	Medford, OR	170.8
29	Memphis, TN-MS-AR	665.1
63	Merced, CA	499.8
50	Miami (greater), FL	546.8
25	Miami-Dade County, FL M.D.	704.4
140	Michigan City-La Porte, IN	331.7
243	Midland, TX	203.5
34	Milwaukee, WI	619.3
135	Minneapolis-St. Paul, MN-WI	338.2
251	Missoula, MT	197.9
81	Mobile, AL	461.7
13	Modesto, CA	910.1
239	Monroe, LA	204.1
257	Monroe, MI	192.1
122	Montgomery, AL	369.2
276	Morgantown, WV	171.0
177	Morristown, TN	264.7
84	Mount Vernon-Anacortes, WA	459.5
230	Muncie, IN	213.4
172	Muskegon-Norton Shores, MI	269.0
24	Myrtle Beach, SC	705.8
176	Napa, CA	265.8
320	Naples-Marco Island, FL	116.5
138	Nashville-Davidson, TN	332.8
297	Nassau-Suffolk, NY M.D.	144.5
69	New Orleans, LA	489.3
222	New York (greater), NY-NJ-PA	218.9
248	New York-W. Plains NY-NJ M.D.	199.7
58	Newark-Union, NJ-PA M.D.	517.9
284	Niles-Benton Harbor, MI	162.1
3	Oakland-Fremont, CA M.D.	1,143.2
265	Ocala, FL	184.7
310	Ocean City, NJ	125.8
196	Odessa, TX	242.1
270	Ogden-Clearfield, UT	180.6
51	Oklahoma City, OK	545.3
157	Olympia, WA	293.8

RANK	METROPOLITAN AREA	RATE
49	Omaha-Council Bluffs, NE-IA	555.9
55	Orlando, FL	529.0
332	Oshkosh-Neenah, WI	93.1
220	Oxnard-Thousand Oaks, CA	219.1
202	Palm Bay-Melbourne, FL	236.4
250	Palm Coast, FL	198.2
207	Panama City-Lynn Haven, FL	230.7
31	Pascagoula, MS	639.1
178	Pensacola, FL	264.0
124	Philadelphia (greater) PA-NJ-DE	360.3
106	Philadelphia, PA M.D.	396.1
5	Phoenix-Mesa-Scottsdale, AZ	1,024.3
72	Pine Bluff, AR	478.0
241	Pittsburgh, PA	203.6
301	Pittsfield, MA	137.2
318	Pocatello, ID	118.0
227	Port St. Lucie, FL	214.7
89	Portland-Vancouver, OR-WA	450.7
316	Portland, ME	121.1
338	Poughkeepsie, NY	84.8
241	Prescott, AZ	203.6
302	Provo-Orem, UT	136.4
137	Pueblo, CO	335.3
214	Punta Gorda, FL	222.9
200	Racine, WI	236.7
233	Raleigh-Cary, NC	211.3
312	Rapid City, SD	123.4
88	Reading, PA	451.5
87	Redding, CA	451.7
46	Reno-Sparks, NV	570.1
173	Richmond, VA	267.4
23	Riverside-San Bernardino, CA	724.4
234	Roanoke, VA	208.2
300	Rochester, MN	137.5
152	Rochester, NY	312.8
109	Rocky Mount, NC	392.2
141	Rome, GA	331.2
14	Sacramento, CA	899.7
155	Saginaw, MI	302.2
110	Salem, OR	391.1
54	Salinas, CA	529.6
185	Salisbury, MD	253.1
45	Salt Lake City, UT	570.4
224	San Angelo, TX	217.8
107	San Antonio, TX	394.8
18	San Diego, CA	812.4
11	San Francisco (greater), CA	923.9
38	San Francisco-S. Mateo, CA M.D.	603.1
44	San Jose, CA	576.1
259	San Luis Obispo, CA	189.3
281	Sandusky, OH	165.1
129	Santa Ana-Anaheim, CA M.D.	349.9
216	Santa Barbara-Santa Maria, CA	221.8
133	Santa Cruz-Watsonville, CA	340.2
287	Santa Fe, NM	159.0
236	Santa Rosa-Petaluma, CA	206.3
159	Sarasota-Bradenton-Venice, FL	292.4
76	Savannah, GA	472.3
285	Scranton--Wilkes-Barre, PA	160.4
6	Seattle (greater), WA	1,009.7

RANK	METROPOLITAN AREA	RATE
4	Seattle-Bellevue, WA M.D.	1,035.4
290	Sebastian-Vero Beach, FL	155.2
334	Sheboygan, WI	91.3
264	Sherman-Denison, TX	184.8
71	Shreveport-Bossier City, LA	485.9
285	Sioux City, IA-NE-SD	160.4
317	Sioux Falls, SD	120.3
146	South Bend-Mishawaka, IN-MI	321.5
128	Spartanburg, SC	352.8
21	Spokane, WA	733.9
101	Springfield, MA	416.8
161	Springfield, MO	286.3
86	Springfield, OH	451.8
346	State College, PA	58.3
8	Stockton, CA	934.6
313	St. Cloud, MN	122.8
150	St. Joseph, MO-KS	316.6
70	St. Louis, MO-IL	487.5
156	Sumter, SC	300.5
291	Syracuse, NY	154.9
10	Tacoma, WA M.D.	926.4
166	Tallahassee, FL	277.8
65	Tampa-St Petersburg, FL	495.1
187	Texarkana, TX-Texarkana, AR	251.3
82	Toledo, OH	460.5
132	Topeka, KS	342.0
213	Trenton-Ewing, NJ	224.5
7	Tucson, AZ	999.0
83	Tulsa, OK	459.8
144	Tuscaloosa, AL	323.7
239	Tyler, TX	204.1
333	Utica-Rome, NY	91.4
246	Valdosta, GA	201.1
26	Vallejo-Fairfield, CA	702.1
228	Victoria, TX	214.5
220	Vineland, NJ	219.1
191	Virginia Beach-Norfolk, VA-NC	245.6
9	Visalia-Porterville, CA	930.4
170	Waco, TX	275.7
255	Warner Robins, GA	192.8
126	Warren-Farmington Hills, MI M.D.	355.6
56	Washington (greater) DC-VA-MD	525.5
39	Washington, DC-VA-MD-WV M.D.	602.8
323	Waterloo-Cedar Falls, IA	112.4
340	Wausau, WI	80.4
274	Wenatchee, WA	175.5
77	West Palm Beach, FL M.D.	468.1
302	Wheeling, WV-OH	136.4
151	Wichita Falls, TX	315.8
105	Wichita, KS	396.5
314	Williamsport, PA	122.4
116	Wilmington, DE-MD-NJ M.D.	376.0
115	Wilmington, NC	376.4
235	Winchester, VA-WV	208.1
143	Winston-Salem, NC	324.1
231	Worcester, MA	212.7
12	Yakima, WA	923.7
66	Yuba City, CA	492.9
36	Yuma, AZ	611.6

Source: Federal Bureau of Investigation
"Crime in the United States 2006" (Uniform Crime Reports, September 24, 2007)

**Motor vehicle theft includes the theft or attempted theft of a self-propelled vehicle. Excludes motorboats, construction equipment, airplanes, and farming equipment. **Not available.*

38. Motor Vehicle Theft Rate in 2006 (continued)

National Rate = 398.4 Motor Vehicle Thefts per 100,000 Population*

RANK	METROPOLITAN AREA	RATE
1	Detroit-Livonia-Dearborn, MI M.D.	1,489.2
2	Las Vegas-Paradise, NV	1,355.0
3	Oakland-Fremont, CA M.D.	1,143.2
4	Seattle-Bellevue, WA M.D.	1,035.4
5	Phoenix-Mesa-Scottsdale, AZ	1,024.3
6	Seattle (greater), WA	1,009.7
7	Tucson, AZ	999.0
8	Stockton, CA	934.6
9	Visalia-Porterville, CA	930.4
10	Tacoma, WA M.D.	926.4
11	San Francisco (greater), CA	923.9
12	Yakima, WA	923.7
13	Modesto, CA	910.1
14	Sacramento, CA	899.7
15	Fresno, CA	897.6
16	Detroit (greater), MI	860.3
17	Albuquerque, NM	830.3
18	San Diego, CA	812.4
19	Macon, GA	771.0
20	Bakersfield, CA	754.4
21	Spokane, WA	733.9
22	El Centro, CA	726.3
23	Riverside-San Bernardino, CA	724.4
24	Myrtle Beach, SC	705.8
25	Miami-Dade County, FL M.D.	704.4
26	Vallejo-Fairfield, CA	702.1
27	Columbus, GA-AL	694.5
28	Honolulu, HI	689.0
29	Memphis, TN-MS-AR	665.1
30	Los Angeles County, CA M.D.	645.4
31	Pascagoula, MS	639.1
32	Indianapolis, IN	632.9
33	Charlotte-Gastonia, NC-SC	622.0
34	Milwaukee, WI	619.3
35	Denver-Aurora, CO	614.6
36	Yuma, AZ	611.6
37	Eugene-Springfield, OR	603.2
38	San Francisco-S. Mateo, CA M.D.	603.1
39	Washington, DC-VA-MD-WV M.D.	602.8
40	Houston, TX	586.9
41	Kansas City, MO-KS	584.7
42	Flint, MI	583.1
43	Los Angeles (greater), CA	577.0
44	San Jose, CA	576.1
45	Salt Lake City, UT	570.4
46	Reno-Sparks, NV	570.1
47	Atlanta, GA	563.4
48	Dallas-Plano-Irving, TX M.D.	560.5
49	Omaha-Council Bluffs, NE-IA	555.9
50	Miami (greater), FL	546.8
51	Oklahoma City, OK	545.3
52	Laredo, TX	539.7
53	Longview, WA	531.3
54	Salinas, CA	529.6
55	Orlando, FL	529.0
56	Washington (greater) DC-VA-MD	525.5
57	Charleston-North Charleston, SC	523.0
58	Newark-Union, NJ-PA M.D.	517.9
59	Augusta, GA-SC	516.4
60	Anchorage, AK	514.1
61	El Paso, TX	510.6
62	Dallas (greater), TX	500.8
63	Merced, CA	499.8
64	Lake Havasu City-Kingman, AZ	495.5
65	Tampa-St Petersburg, FL	495.1
66	Yuba City, CA	492.9
67	Huntsville, AL	492.5
68	Jackson, TN	489.9
69	New Orleans, LA	489.3
70	St. Louis, MO-IL	487.5
71	Shreveport-Bossier City, LA	485.9
72	Jackson, MS	478.0
72	Pine Bluff, AR	478.0
74	Baltimore-Towson, MD	476.9
75	Hanford-Corcoran, CA	475.4
76	Savannah, GA	472.3
77	West Palm Beach, FL M.D.	468.1
78	Chico, CA	467.3
79	Hot Springs, AR	464.0
80	Little Rock, AR	463.6
81	Mobile, AL	461.7
82	Toledo, OH	460.5
83	Tulsa, OK	459.8
84	Mount Vernon-Anacortes, WA	459.5
85	Columbus, OH	457.5
86	Springfield, OH	451.8
87	Redding, CA	451.7
88	Reading, PA	451.5
89	Portland-Vancouver, OR-WA	450.7
90	Amarillo, TX	450.6
91	Fayetteville, NC	441.2
92	Anderson, SC	434.8
93	Cleveland-Elyria-Mentor, OH	433.0
94	Florence, SC	432.2
95	Baton Rouge, LA	429.2
96	Longview, TX	427.1
97	Madera, CA	425.5
98	Lake Charles, LA	419.9
99	Dayton, OH	417.6
100	Jacksonville, FL	416.9
101	Cape Coral-Fort Myers, FL	416.8
101	Springfield, MA	416.8
103	Louisville, KY-IN	411.1
104	Birmingham-Hoover, AL	404.3
105	Wichita, KS	396.5
106	Philadelphia, PA M.D.	396.1
107	San Antonio, TX	394.8
108	Fort Lauderdale, FL M.D.	392.3
109	Rocky Mount, NC	392.2
110	Salem, OR	391.1
111	Alexandria, LA	383.6
112	Gainesville, GA	383.4
113	Greenville, SC	381.7
114	Fort Worth-Arlington, TX M.D.	379.9
115	Wilmington, NC	376.4
116	Hartford, CT	376.0
116	Wilmington, DE-MD-NJ M.D.	376.0
118	Colorado Springs, CO	375.5
119	Gadsden, AL	374.6
120	McAllen-Edinburg-Mission, TX	374.1
121	Daytona Beach, FL	372.3
122	Montgomery, AL	369.2
123	Chattanooga, TN-GA	368.8
124	Philadelphia (greater) PA-NJ-DE	360.3
125	Greensboro-High Point, NC	359.8
126	Warren-Farmington Hills, MI M.D.	355.6
127	Beaumont-Port Arthur, TX	354.2
128	Spartanburg, SC	352.8
129	Santa Ana-Anaheim, CA M.D.	349.9
130	Durham, NC	347.1
131	Charleston, WV	344.3
132	Topeka, KS	342.0
133	Santa Cruz-Watsonville, CA	340.2
134	Columbia, SC	339.1
135	Minneapolis-St. Paul, MN-WI	338.2
136	Gainesville, FL	337.3
137	Pueblo, CO	335.3
138	Nashville-Davidson, TN	332.8
139	Knoxville, TN	331.9
140	Michigan City-La Porte, IN	331.7
141	Rome, GA	331.2
142	Athens-Clarke County, GA	325.9
143	Winston-Salem, NC	324.1
144	Tuscaloosa, AL	323.7
145	Joplin, MO	323.2
146	South Bend-Mishawaka, IN-MI	321.5
147	Hattiesburg, MS	320.4
148	Grand Junction, CO	319.7
149	Greeley, CO	319.4
150	St. Joseph, MO-KS	316.6
151	Wichita Falls, TX	315.8
152	Rochester, NY	312.8
153	Lubbock, TX	309.4
154	Albany, GA	306.4
155	Saginaw, MI	302.2
156	Sumter, SC	300.5
157	Asheville, NC	293.8
157	Olympia, WA	293.8
159	Sarasota-Bradenton-Venice, FL	292.4
160	Dalton, GA	286.9
161	Springfield, MO	286.3
162	Lakeland, FL	284.6
163	Decatur, AL	282.6
164	Brownsville-Harlingen, TX	281.2
165	Brunswick, GA	280.5
166	Tallahassee, FL	277.8
167	Bellingham, WA	277.6
168	Cincinnati-Middletown, OH-KY-IN	276.9
168	Houma, LA	276.9
170	Waco, TX	275.7
171	Lawton, OK	272.4

Note: All listings are for Metropolitan Statistical Areas (M.S.A.s) except for those ending with "M.D." Listings with "M.D." are Metropolitan Divisions which are smaller parts of eleven large M.S.A.s. See explanatory note at beginning of metropolitan area section on page 23.

RANK	METROPOLITAN AREA	RATE
172	Muskegon-Norton Shores, MI	269.0
173	Richmond, VA	267.4
174	Kalamazoo-Portage, MI	266.5
175	Billings, MT	266.2
176	Napa, CA	265.8
177	Morristown, TN	264.7
178	Pensacola, FL	264.0
179	Greenville, NC	262.9
180	Las Cruces, NM	262.0
181	Bend, OR	261.7
182	Des Moines-West Des Moines, IA	261.0
183	Buffalo-Niagara Falls, NY	258.3
184	Burlington, NC	255.3
185	Salisbury, MD	253.1
186	Corpus Christi, TX	252.1
187	Texarkana, TX-Texarkana, AR	251.3
188	Goldsboro, NC	251.0
189	Bethesda-Frederick, MD M.D.	248.7
190	Dothan, AL	248.1
191	Kennewick-Richland-Pasco, WA	245.6
191	Virginia Beach-Norfolk, VA-NC	245.6
193	Bremerton-Silverdale, WA	245.5
194	Cleveland, TN	245.0
195	Kingsport, TN-VA	242.4
196	Odessa, TX	242.1
197	Camden, NJ M.D.	240.0
198	Elkhart-Goshen, IN	239.0
199	Battle Creek, MI	237.7
200	Racine, WI	236.7
201	Carson City, NV	236.5
202	Palm Bay-Melbourne, FL	236.4
203	Fort Walton Beach, FL	235.4
204	Huntington-Ashland, WV-KY-OH	233.2
205	Ann Arbor, MI	231.7
206	Fort Wayne, IN	231.4
207	Panama City-Lynn Haven, FL	230.7
208	Lawrence, KS	230.6
209	Lexington-Fayette, KY	229.0
210	Dover, DE	228.6
211	Charlottesville, VA	228.1
212	Austin-Round Rock, TX	225.9
213	Trenton-Ewing, NJ	224.5
214	Punta Gorda, FL	222.9
215	Hagerstown-Martinsburg, MD-WV	222.0
216	Santa Barbara-Santa Maria, CA	221.8
217	Fort Smith, AR-OK	221.2
218	Abilene, TX	219.9
219	Clarksville, TN-KY	219.2
220	Oxnard-Thousand Oaks, CA	219.1
220	Vineland, NJ	219.1
222	Columbia, MO	218.9
222	New York (greater), NY-NJ-PA	218.9
224	San Angelo, TX	217.8
225	Jacksonville, NC	217.4
226	Grand Forks, ND-MN	217.1
227	Port St. Lucie, FL	214.7
228	Victoria, TX	214.5
229	Boise City-Nampa, ID	214.4
230	Muncie, IN	213.4
231	Lansing-East Lansing, MI	212.7

RANK	METROPOLITAN AREA	RATE
231	Worcester, MA	212.7
233	Raleigh-Cary, NC	211.3
234	Roanoke, VA	208.2
235	Winchester, VA-WV	208.1
236	Santa Rosa-Petaluma, CA	206.3
237	College Station-Bryan, TX	204.5
237	Idaho Falls, ID	204.5
239	Monroe, LA	204.1
239	Tyler, TX	204.1
241	Pittsburgh, PA	203.6
241	Prescott, AZ	203.6
243	Midland, TX	203.5
244	Casper, WY	202.6
245	Lima, OH	201.2
246	Valdosta, GA	201.1
247	Grand Rapids-Wyoming, MI	199.9
248	New York-W. Plains NY-NJ M.D.	199.7
249	Bay City, MI	199.5
250	Palm Coast, FL	198.2
251	Missoula, MT	197.9
252	Flagstaff, AZ	195.2
253	Coeur d'Alene, ID	193.9
254	Johnson City, TN	193.4
255	Warner Robins, GA	192.8
256	Jonesboro, AR	192.3
257	Monroe, MI	192.1
258	Fayetteville, AR-MO	191.4
259	San Luis Obispo, CA	189.3
260	Fargo, ND-MN	186.4
261	Jackson, MI	186.3
262	Farmington, NM	186.0
263	Fort Collins-Loveland, CO	185.9
264	Sherman-Denison, TX	184.8
265	Ocala, FL	184.7
266	Great Falls, MT	184.2
267	Duluth, MN-WI	184.0
268	Lafayette, IN	182.6
269	Cheyenne, WY	182.3
270	Ogden-Clearfield, UT	180.6
271	Kokomo, IN	178.4
272	Atlantic City, NJ	175.9
273	Columbus, IN	175.6
274	Wenatchee, WA	175.5
275	Bowling Green, KY	172.5
276	Morgantown, WV	171.0
277	Medford, OR	170.8
278	Lancaster, PA	170.5
279	Killeen-Temple-Fort Hood, TX	167.4
280	Lincoln, NE	166.7
281	Sandusky, OH	165.1
282	Danville, VA	164.1
283	Lewiston, ID-WA	163.7
284	Niles-Benton Harbor, MI	162.1
285	Scranton--Wilkes-Barre, PA	160.4
285	Sioux City, IA-NE-SD	160.4
287	Santa Fe, NM	159.0
288	Janesville, WI	158.7
289	Cedar Rapids, IA	155.8
290	Sebastian-Vero Beach, FL	155.2
291	Evansville, IN-KY	154.9

RANK	METROPOLITAN AREA	RATE
291	Syracuse, NY	154.9
293	Madison, WI	150.8
294	Bloomington, IN	148.1
295	Barnstable Town, MA	146.6
296	Jefferson City, MO	145.6
297	Nassau-Suffolk, NY M.D.	144.5
298	Blacksburg, VA	142.2
299	Albany-Schenectady-Troy, NY	139.3
300	Rochester, MN	137.5
301	Pittsfield, MA	137.2
302	Provo-Orem, UT	136.4
302	Wheeling, WV-OH	136.4
304	Altoona, PA	135.5
305	Bismarck, ND	135.1
306	Green Bay, WI	131.3
307	Manchester-Nashua, NH	130.1
308	Edison, NJ M.D.	126.5
308	Lebanon, PA	126.5
310	Ocean City, NJ	125.8
311	Mansfield, OH	124.1
312	Rapid City, SD	123.4
313	St. Cloud, MN	122.8
314	Williamsport, PA	122.4
315	Lynchburg, VA	121.6
316	Portland, ME	121.1
317	Sioux Falls, SD	120.3
318	Pocatello, ID	118.0
319	Cumberland, MD-WV	117.0
320	Naples-Marco Island, FL	116.5
321	Dubuque, IA	116.2
322	Johnstown, PA	113.4
323	Waterloo-Cedar Falls, IA	112.4
324	Eau Claire, WI	110.6
325	Iowa City, IA	109.9
326	Erie, PA	108.3
327	Harrisburg-Carlisle, PA	105.7
328	La Crosse, WI-MN	104.3
329	Lewiston-Auburn, ME	99.0
330	Harrisonburg, VA	98.4
331	Bangor, ME	97.2
332	Oshkosh-Neenah, WI	93.1
333	Utica-Rome, NY	91.4
334	Sheboygan, WI	91.3
335	Holland-Grand Haven, MI	86.7
336	Elizabethtown, KY	86.1
337	Ames, IA	85.8
338	Poughkeepsie, NY	84.8
339	Kingston, NY	84.1
340	Wausau, WI	80.4
341	Appleton, WI	76.4
342	Fond du Lac, WI	76.2
343	Ithaca, NY	73.8
344	Elmira, NY	70.2
345	Binghamton, NY	59.4
346	State College, PA	58.3
347	Glens Falls, NY	55.8
348	Logan, UT-ID	47.4
NA	Chicago, IL**	NA
NA	Fairbanks, AK**	NA

Source: Federal Bureau of Investigation
"Crime in the United States 2006" (Uniform Crime Reports, September 24, 2007)
**Motor vehicle theft includes the theft or attempted theft of a self-propelled vehicle. Excludes motorboats, construction equipment, airplanes, and farming equipment. **Not available.*

39. Percent Change in Motor Vehicle Theft Rate: 2005 to 2006

National Percent Change = 4.4% Decrease*

RANK	METROPOLITAN AREA	% CHANGE
NA	Abilene, TX**	NA
228	Albany-Schenectady-Troy, NY	(11.3)
21	Albany, GA	23.5
14	Albuquerque, NM	28.3
63	Alexandria, LA	12.4
48	Altoona, PA	15.3
175	Amarillo, TX	(4.6)
102	Ames, IA	4.9
101	Anchorage, AK	5.3
182	Anderson, SC	(5.9)
265	Ann Arbor, MI	(16.0)
57	Appleton, WI	13.7
206	Asheville, NC	(8.8)
41	Athens-Clarke County, GA	18.5
194	Atlanta, GA	(7.3)
125	Atlantic City, NJ	2.3
116	Augusta, GA-SC	3.1
184	Austin-Round Rock, TX	(6.1)
179	Bakersfield, CA	(5.3)
97	Baltimore-Towson, MD	5.9
106	Bangor, ME	4.7
87	Barnstable Town, MA	6.8
65	Baton Rouge, LA	12.2
79	Battle Creek, MI	8.1
50	Bay City, MI	15.1
83	Beaumont-Port Arthur, TX	7.6
262	Bellingham, WA	(15.0)
297	Bend, OR	(24.9)
144	Bethesda-Frederick, MD M.D.	(0.4)
208	Billings, MT	(9.1)
43	Binghamton, NY	16.7
NA	Birmingham-Hoover, AL**	NA
310	Bismarck, ND	(31.2)
53	Blacksburg, VA	14.6
242	Bloomington, IN	(12.4)
NA	Boise City-Nampa, ID**	NA
177	Bowling Green, KY	(4.8)
129	Bremerton-Silverdale, WA	1.5
70	Brownsville-Harlingen, TX	10.9
81	Brunswick, GA	7.8
226	Buffalo-Niagara Falls, NY	(10.9)
11	Burlington, NC	29.3
91	Camden, NJ M.D.	6.5
193	Cape Coral-Fort Myers, FL	(7.2)
37	Carson City, NV	19.1
85	Casper, WY	7.3
155	Cedar Rapids, IA	(1.9)
115	Charleston-North Charleston, SC	3.2
221	Charleston, WV	(10.4)
157	Charlotte-Gastonia, NC-SC	(2.1)
13	Charlottesville, VA	28.8
203	Chattanooga, TN-GA	(8.2)
43	Cheyenne, WY	16.7
NA	Chicago, IL**	NA
301	Chico, CA	(25.5)
253	Cincinnati-Middletown, OH-KY-IN	(13.4)
27	Clarksville, TN-KY	21.5
NA	Cleveland-Elyria-Mentor, OH**	NA
NA	Cleveland, TN**	NA
309	Coeur d'Alene, ID	(30.5)
104	College Station-Bryan, TX	4.8
150	Colorado Springs, CO	(1.2)
22	Columbia, MO	22.7
207	Columbia, SC	(9.0)
96	Columbus, GA-AL	6.0
153	Columbus, IN	(1.6)
273	Columbus, OH	(17.3)
225	Corpus Christi, TX	(10.8)
12	Cumberland, MD-WV	29.1
196	Dallas (greater), TX	(7.4)
183	Dallas-Plano-Irving, TX M.D.	(6.0)
NA	Dalton, GA**	NA
114	Danville, VA	3.5
140	Daytona Beach, FL	(0.1)
164	Dayton, OH	(2.7)
5	Decatur, AL	42.3
297	Denver-Aurora, CO	(24.9)
NA	Des Moines-West Des Moines, IA**	NA
NA	Detroit (greater), MI**	NA
97	Detroit-Livonia-Dearborn, MI M.D.	5.9
49	Dothan, AL	15.2
54	Dover, DE	13.8
138	Dubuque, IA	0.2
NA	Duluth, MN-WI**	NA
NA	Durham, NC**	NA
92	Eau Claire, WI	6.3
164	Edison, NJ M.D.	(2.7)
110	El Centro, CA	4.4
10	El Paso, TX	30.3
221	Elizabethtown, KY	(10.4)
214	Elkhart-Goshen, IN	(9.6)
148	Elmira, NY	(1.1)
68	Erie, PA	11.0
314	Eugene-Springfield, OR	(33.7)
68	Evansville, IN-KY	11.0
NA	Fairbanks, AK**	NA
112	Fargo, ND-MN	3.9
317	Farmington, NM	(35.0)
147	Fayetteville, AR-MO	(1.0)
30	Fayetteville, NC	21.1
216	Flagstaff, AZ	(9.9)
172	Flint, MI	(4.1)
108	Florence, SC	4.5
32	Fond du Lac, WI	20.0
294	Fort Collins-Loveland, CO	(23.1)
162	Fort Lauderdale, FL M.D.	(2.4)
89	Fort Smith, AR-OK	6.6
62	Fort Walton Beach, FL	12.6
NA	Fort Wayne, IN**	NA
231	Fort Worth-Arlington, TX M.D.	(11.6)
170	Fresno, CA	(3.7)
34	Gadsden, AL	19.7
108	Gainesville, FL	4.5
186	Gainesville, GA	(6.6)
NA	Glens Falls, NY**	NA
60	Goldsboro, NC	13.4
217	Grand Forks, ND-MN	(10.1)
178	Grand Junction, CO	(5.0)
117	Grand Rapids-Wyoming, MI	3.0
299	Great Falls, MT	(25.0)
308	Greeley, CO	(28.4)
174	Green Bay, WI	(4.4)
88	Greensboro-High Point, NC	6.7
18	Greenville, NC	24.6
102	Greenville, SC	4.9
16	Hagerstown-Martinsburg, MD-WV	26.7
81	Hanford-Corcoran, CA	7.8
228	Harrisburg-Carlisle, PA	(11.3)
67	Harrisonburg, VA	11.1
162	Hartford, CT	(2.4)
NA	Hattiesburg, MS**	NA
106	Holland-Grand Haven, MI	4.7
201	Honolulu, HI	(7.9)
259	Hot Springs, AR	(14.7)
4	Houma, LA	49.8
118	Houston, TX	2.9
120	Huntington-Ashland, WV-KY-OH	2.6
45	Huntsville, AL	16.3
40	Idaho Falls, ID	18.8
139	Indianapolis, IN	0.1
19	Iowa City, IA	24.3
NA	Ithaca, NY**	NA
231	Jacksonville, FL	(11.6)
NA	Jacksonville, NC**	NA
257	Jackson, MI	(14.4)
145	Jackson, MS	(0.5)
235	Jackson, TN	(11.9)
251	Janesville, WI	(13.3)
132	Jefferson City, MO	1.0
191	Johnson City, TN	(7.1)
NA	Johnstown, PA**	NA
237	Jonesboro, AR	(12.0)
270	Joplin, MO	(16.5)
42	Kalamazoo-Portage, MI	17.9
NA	Kansas City, MO-KS**	NA
292	Kennewick-Richland-Pasco, WA	(22.5)
33	Killeen-Temple-Fort Hood, TX	19.9
97	Kingsport, TN-VA	5.9
237	Kingston, NY	(12.0)
196	Knoxville, TN	(7.4)
248	Kokomo, IN	(13.1)
63	La Crosse, WI-MN	12.4
179	Lafayette, IN	(5.3)
7	Lake Charles, LA	36.7
NA	Lake Havasu City-Kingman, AZ**	NA
268	Lakeland, FL	(16.3)
8	Lancaster, PA	31.3
51	Lansing-East Lansing, MI	14.8
25	Laredo, TX	22.0
73	Las Cruces, NM	10.5
171	Las Vegas-Paradise, NV	(3.9)

Note: All listings are for Metropolitan Statistical Areas (M.S.A.s) except for those ending with "M.D." Listings with "M.D." are Metropolitan Divisions which are smaller parts of eleven large M.S.A.s. See explanatory note at beginning of metropolitan area section on page 23.

RANK	METROPOLITAN AREA	% CHANGE
9	Lawrence, KS	30.7
24	Lawton, OK	22.2
251	Lebanon, PA	(13.3)
288	Lewiston-Auburn, ME	(21.2)
290	Lewiston, ID-WA	(21.5)
NA	Lexington-Fayette, KY**	NA
204	Lima, OH	(8.5)
124	Lincoln, NE	2.4
54	Little Rock, AR	13.8
303	Logan, UT-ID	(26.5)
172	Longview, TX	(4.1)
253	Longview, WA	(13.4)
205	Los Angeles County, CA M.D.	(8.6)
218	Los Angeles (greater), CA	(10.3)
58	Louisville, KY-IN	13.6
231	Lubbock, TX	(11.6)
234	Lynchburg, VA	(11.8)
66	Macon, GA	11.7
304	Madera, CA	(26.8)
199	Madison, WI	(7.5)
141	Manchester-Nashua, NH	(0.2)
318	Mansfield, OH	(45.4)
113	McAllen-Edinburg-Mission, TX	3.7
311	Medford, OR	(31.3)
276	Memphis, TN-MS-AR	(17.7)
264	Merced, CA	(15.6)
157	Miami (greater), FL	(2.1)
152	Miami-Dade County, FL M.D.	(1.4)
36	Michigan City-La Porte, IN	19.2
28	Midland, TX	21.4
29	Milwaukee, WI	21.3
NA	Minneapolis-St. Paul, MN-WI**	NA
284	Missoula, MT	(19.6)
38	Mobile, AL	19.0
307	Modesto, CA	(28.2)
35	Monroe, LA	19.5
265	Monroe, MI	(16.0)
121	Montgomery, AL	2.5
1	Morgantown, WV	63.6
278	Morristown, TN	(18.2)
235	Mount Vernon-Anacortes, WA	(11.9)
74	Muncie, IN	10.3
273	Muskegon-Norton Shores, MI	(17.3)
78	Myrtle Beach, SC	8.3
127	Napa, CA	1.8
267	Naples-Marco Island, FL	(16.2)
212	Nashville-Davidson, TN	(9.5)
191	Nassau-Suffolk, NY M.D.	(7.1)
NA	New Orleans, LA**	NA
245	New York (greater), NY-NJ-PA	(12.6)
242	New York-W. Plains NY-NJ M.D.	(12.4)
271	Newark-Union, NJ-PA M.D.	(16.7)
242	Niles-Benton Harbor, MI	(12.4)
89	Oakland-Fremont, CA M.D.	6.6
218	Ocala, FL	(10.3)
275	Ocean City, NJ	(17.5)
15	Odessa, TX	28.2
256	Ogden-Clearfield, UT	(14.0)
121	Oklahoma City, OK	2.5
277	Olympia, WA	(17.8)
227	Omaha-Council Bluffs, NE-IA	(11.2)
75	Orlando, FL	9.2
46	Oshkosh-Neenah, WI	16.2
230	Oxnard-Thousand Oaks, CA	(11.5)
100	Palm Bay-Melbourne, FL	5.7
NA	Palm Coast, FL**	NA
156	Panama City-Lynn Haven, FL	(2.0)
2	Pascagoula, MS	54.1
133	Pensacola, FL	0.7
111	Philadelphia (greater) PA-NJ-DE	4.3
127	Philadelphia, PA M.D.	1.8
200	Phoenix-Mesa-Scottsdale, AZ	(7.8)
77	Pine Bluff, AR	8.7
214	Pittsburgh, PA	(9.6)
47	Pittsfield, MA	15.5
143	Pocatello, ID	(0.3)
291	Port St. Lucie, FL	(21.6)
296	Portland-Vancouver, OR-WA	(24.1)
121	Portland, ME	2.5
261	Poughkeepsie, NY	(14.9)
210	Prescott, AZ	(9.2)
285	Provo-Orem, UT	(20.7)
187	Pueblo, CO	(6.7)
51	Punta Gorda, FL	14.8
154	Racine, WI	(1.7)
119	Raleigh-Cary, NC	2.7
249	Rapid City, SD	(13.2)
61	Reading, PA	13.3
181	Redding, CA	(5.7)
131	Reno-Sparks, NV	1.1
NA	Richmond, VA**	NA
221	Riverside-San Bernardino, CA	(10.4)
189	Roanoke, VA	(6.8)
26	Rochester, MN	21.6
93	Rochester, NY	6.2
3	Rocky Mount, NC	53.4
137	Rome, GA	0.3
167	Sacramento, CA	(2.9)
202	Saginaw, MI	(8.0)
306	Salem, OR	(27.9)
176	Salinas, CA	(4.7)
17	Salisbury, MD	26.0
135	Salt Lake City, UT	0.5
286	San Angelo, TX	(20.8)
86	San Antonio, TX	6.9
190	San Diego, CA	(6.9)
134	San Francisco (greater), CA	0.6
247	San Francisco-S. Mateo, CA M.D.	(13.0)
20	San Jose, CA	24.2
196	San Luis Obispo, CA	(7.4)
6	Sandusky, OH	40.3
283	Santa Ana-Anaheim, CA M.D.	(19.5)
282	Santa Barbara-Santa Maria, CA	(19.3)
281	Santa Cruz-Watsonville, CA	(18.9)
314	Santa Fe, NM	(33.7)
302	Santa Rosa-Petaluma, CA	(25.7)
159	Sarasota-Bradenton-Venice, FL	(2.2)
263	Savannah, GA	(15.1)
126	Scranton--Wilkes-Barre, PA	2.1
211	Seattle (greater), WA	(9.4)
218	Seattle-Bellevue, WA M.D.	(10.3)
305	Sebastian-Vero Beach, FL	(27.6)
159	Sheboygan, WI	(2.2)
280	Sherman-Denison, TX	(18.4)
23	Shreveport-Bossier City, LA	22.3
240	Sioux City, IA-NE-SD	(12.3)
316	Sioux Falls, SD	(34.3)
79	South Bend-Mishawaka, IN-MI	8.1
135	Spartanburg, SC	0.5
31	Spokane, WA	20.2
150	Springfield, MA	(1.2)
187	Springfield, MO	(6.7)
93	Springfield, OH	6.2
258	State College, PA	(14.5)
259	Stockton, CA	(14.7)
141	St. Cloud, MN	(0.2)
212	St. Joseph, MO-KS	(9.5)
130	St. Louis, MO-IL	1.2
166	Sumter, SC	(2.8)
272	Syracuse, NY	(17.2)
185	Tacoma, WA M.D.	(6.3)
221	Tallahassee, FL	(10.4)
72	Tampa-St Petersburg, FL	10.7
279	Texarkana, TX-Texarkana, AR	(18.3)
237	Toledo, OH	(12.0)
208	Topeka, KS	(9.1)
295	Trenton-Ewing, NJ	(23.6)
70	Tucson, AZ	10.9
268	Tulsa, OK	(16.3)
NA	Tuscaloosa, AL**	NA
194	Tyler, TX	(7.3)
59	Utica-Rome, NY	13.5
311	Valdosta, GA	(31.3)
NA	Vallejo-Fairfield, CA**	NA
95	Victoria, TX	6.1
245	Vineland, NJ	(12.6)
240	Virginia Beach-Norfolk, VA-NC	(12.3)
NA	Visalia-Porterville, CA**	NA
313	Waco, TX	(31.8)
287	Warner Robins, GA	(20.9)
NA	Warren-Farmington Hills, MI M.D.**	NA
NA	Washington (greater) DC-VA-MD**	NA
NA	Washington, DC-VA-MD-WV M.D.**	NA
300	Waterloo-Cedar Falls, IA	(25.4)
84	Wausau, WI	7.5
289	Wenatchee, WA	(21.4)
168	West Palm Beach, FL M.D.	(3.2)
146	Wheeling, WV-OH	(0.9)
292	Wichita Falls, TX	(22.5)
NA	Wichita, KS**	NA
148	Williamsport, PA	(1.1)
39	Wilmington, DE-MD-NJ M.D.	18.9
169	Wilmington, NC	(3.5)
54	Winchester, VA-WV	13.8
104	Winston-Salem, NC	4.8
249	Worcester, MA	(13.2)
161	Yakima, WA	(2.3)
255	Yuba City, CA	(13.9)
76	Yuma, AZ	8.8

Source: CQ Press using data from Federal Bureau of Investigation "Crime in the United States 2006" (Uniform Crime Reports, September 24, 2007)

**Motor vehicle theft includes the theft or attempted theft of a self-propelled vehicle. Excludes motorboats, construction equipment, airplanes, and farming equipment. **Not available.*

39. Percent Change in Motor Vehicle Theft Rate: 2005 to 2006 (continued)

National Percent Change = 4.4% Decrease*

RANK	METROPOLITAN AREA	% CHANGE
1	Morgantown, WV	63.6
2	Pascagoula, MS	54.1
3	Rocky Mount, NC	53.4
4	Houma, LA	49.8
5	Decatur, AL	42.3
6	Sandusky, OH	40.3
7	Lake Charles, LA	36.7
8	Lancaster, PA	31.3
9	Lawrence, KS	30.7
10	El Paso, TX	30.3
11	Burlington, NC	29.3
12	Cumberland, MD-WV	29.1
13	Charlottesville, VA	28.8
14	Albuquerque, NM	28.3
15	Odessa, TX	28.2
16	Hagerstown-Martinsburg, MD-WV	26.7
17	Salisbury, MD	26.0
18	Greenville, NC	24.6
19	Iowa City, IA	24.3
20	San Jose, CA	24.2
21	Albany, GA	23.5
22	Columbia, MO	22.7
23	Shreveport-Bossier City, LA	22.3
24	Lawton, OK	22.2
25	Laredo, TX	22.0
26	Rochester, MN	21.6
27	Clarksville, TN-KY	21.5
28	Midland, TX	21.4
29	Milwaukee, WI	21.3
30	Fayetteville, NC	21.1
31	Spokane, WA	20.2
32	Fond du Lac, WI	20.0
33	Killeen-Temple-Fort Hood, TX	19.9
34	Gadsden, AL	19.7
35	Monroe, LA	19.5
36	Michigan City-La Porte, IN	19.2
37	Carson City, NV	19.1
38	Mobile, AL	19.0
39	Wilmington, DE-MD-NJ M.D.	18.9
40	Idaho Falls, ID	18.8
41	Athens-Clarke County, GA	18.5
42	Kalamazoo-Portage, MI	17.9
43	Binghamton, NY	16.7
43	Cheyenne, WY	16.7
45	Huntsville, AL	16.3
46	Oshkosh-Neenah, WI	16.2
47	Pittsfield, MA	15.5
48	Altoona, PA	15.3
49	Dothan, AL	15.2
50	Bay City, MI	15.1
51	Lansing-East Lansing, MI	14.8
51	Punta Gorda, FL	14.8
53	Blacksburg, VA	14.6
54	Dover, DE	13.8
54	Little Rock, AR	13.8
54	Winchester, VA-WV	13.8
57	Appleton, WI	13.7
58	Louisville, KY-IN	13.6
59	Utica-Rome, NY	13.5
60	Goldsboro, NC	13.4
61	Reading, PA	13.3
62	Fort Walton Beach, FL	12.6
63	Alexandria, LA	12.4
63	La Crosse, WI-MN	12.4
65	Baton Rouge, LA	12.2
66	Macon, GA	11.7
67	Harrisonburg, VA	11.1
68	Erie, PA	11.0
68	Evansville, IN-KY	11.0
70	Brownsville-Harlingen, TX	10.9
70	Tucson, AZ	10.9
72	Tampa-St Petersburg, FL	10.7
73	Las Cruces, NM	10.5
74	Muncie, IN	10.3
75	Orlando, FL	9.2
76	Yuma, AZ	8.8
77	Pine Bluff, AR	8.7
78	Myrtle Beach, SC	8.3
79	Battle Creek, MI	8.1
79	South Bend-Mishawaka, IN-MI	8.1
81	Brunswick, GA	7.8
81	Hanford-Corcoran, CA	7.8
83	Beaumont-Port Arthur, TX	7.6
84	Wausau, WI	7.5
85	Casper, WY	7.3
86	San Antonio, TX	6.9
87	Barnstable Town, MA	6.8
88	Greensboro-High Point, NC	6.7
89	Fort Smith, AR-OK	6.6
89	Oakland-Fremont, CA M.D.	6.6
91	Camden, NJ M.D.	6.5
92	Eau Claire, WI	6.3
93	Rochester, NY	6.2
93	Springfield, OH	6.2
95	Victoria, TX	6.1
96	Columbus, GA-AL	6.0
97	Baltimore-Towson, MD	5.9
97	Detroit-Livonia-Dearborn, MI M.D.	5.9
97	Kingsport, TN-VA	5.9
100	Palm Bay-Melbourne, FL	5.7
101	Anchorage, AK	5.3
102	Ames, IA	4.9
102	Greenville, SC	4.9
104	College Station-Bryan, TX	4.8
104	Winston-Salem, NC	4.8
106	Bangor, ME	4.7
106	Holland-Grand Haven, MI	4.7
108	Florence, SC	4.5
108	Gainesville, FL	4.5
110	El Centro, CA	4.4
111	Philadelphia (greater) PA-NJ-DE	4.3
112	Fargo, ND-MN	3.9
113	McAllen-Edinburg-Mission, TX	3.7
114	Danville, VA	3.5
115	Charleston-North Charleston, SC	3.2
116	Augusta, GA-SC	3.1
117	Grand Rapids-Wyoming, MI	3.0
118	Houston, TX	2.9
119	Raleigh-Cary, NC	2.7
120	Huntington-Ashland, WV-KY-OH	2.6
121	Montgomery, AL	2.5
121	Oklahoma City, OK	2.5
121	Portland, ME	2.5
124	Lincoln, NE	2.4
125	Atlantic City, NJ	2.3
126	Scranton--Wilkes-Barre, PA	2.1
127	Napa, CA	1.8
127	Philadelphia, PA M.D.	1.8
129	Bremerton-Silverdale, WA	1.5
130	St. Louis, MO-IL	1.2
131	Reno-Sparks, NV	1.1
132	Jefferson City, MO	1.0
133	Pensacola, FL	0.7
134	San Francisco (greater), CA	0.6
135	Salt Lake City, UT	0.5
135	Spartanburg, SC	0.5
137	Rome, GA	0.3
138	Dubuque, IA	0.2
139	Indianapolis, IN	0.1
140	Daytona Beach, FL	(0.1)
141	Manchester-Nashua, NH	(0.2)
141	St. Cloud, MN	(0.2)
143	Pocatello, ID	(0.3)
144	Bethesda-Frederick, MD M.D.	(0.4)
145	Jackson, MS	(0.5)
146	Wheeling, WV-OH	(0.9)
147	Fayetteville, AR-MO	(1.0)
148	Elmira, NY	(1.1)
148	Williamsport, PA	(1.1)
150	Colorado Springs, CO	(1.2)
150	Springfield, MA	(1.2)
152	Miami-Dade County, FL M.D.	(1.4)
153	Columbus, IN	(1.6)
154	Racine, WI	(1.7)
155	Cedar Rapids, IA	(1.9)
156	Panama City-Lynn Haven, FL	(2.0)
157	Charlotte-Gastonia, NC-SC	(2.1)
157	Miami (greater), FL	(2.1)
159	Sarasota-Bradenton-Venice, FL	(2.2)
159	Sheboygan, WI	(2.2)
161	Yakima, WA	(2.3)
162	Fort Lauderdale, FL M.D.	(2.4)
162	Hartford, CT	(2.4)
164	Dayton, OH	(2.7)
164	Edison, NJ M.D.	(2.7)
166	Sumter, SC	(2.8)
167	Sacramento, CA	(2.9)
168	West Palm Beach, FL M.D.	(3.2)
169	Wilmington, NC	(3.5)
170	Fresno, CA	(3.7)
171	Las Vegas-Paradise, NV	(3.9)

Note: All listings are for Metropolitan Statistical Areas (M.S.A.s) except for those ending with "M.D." Listings with "M.D." are Metropolitan Divisions which are smaller parts of eleven large M.S.A.s. See explanatory note at beginning of metropolitan area section on page 23.

RANK	METROPOLITAN AREA	% CHANGE
172	Flint, MI	(4.1)
172	Longview, TX	(4.1)
174	Green Bay, WI	(4.4)
175	Amarillo, TX	(4.6)
176	Salinas, CA	(4.7)
177	Bowling Green, KY	(4.8)
178	Grand Junction, CO	(5.0)
179	Bakersfield, CA	(5.3)
179	Lafayette, IN	(5.3)
181	Redding, CA	(5.7)
182	Anderson, SC	(5.9)
183	Dallas-Plano-Irving, TX M.D.	(6.0)
184	Austin-Round Rock, TX	(6.1)
185	Tacoma, WA M.D.	(6.3)
186	Gainesville, GA	(6.6)
187	Pueblo, CO	(6.7)
187	Springfield, MO	(6.7)
189	Roanoke, VA	(6.8)
190	San Diego, CA	(6.9)
191	Johnson City, TN	(7.1)
191	Nassau-Suffolk, NY M.D.	(7.1)
193	Cape Coral-Fort Myers, FL	(7.2)
194	Atlanta, GA	(7.3)
194	Tyler, TX	(7.3)
196	Dallas (greater), TX	(7.4)
196	Knoxville, TN	(7.4)
196	San Luis Obispo, CA	(7.4)
199	Madison, WI	(7.5)
200	Phoenix-Mesa-Scottsdale, AZ	(7.8)
201	Honolulu, HI	(7.9)
202	Saginaw, MI	(8.0)
203	Chattanooga, TN-GA	(8.2)
204	Lima, OH	(8.5)
205	Los Angeles County, CA M.D.	(8.6)
206	Asheville, NC	(8.8)
207	Columbia, SC	(9.0)
208	Billings, MT	(9.1)
208	Topeka, KS	(9.1)
210	Prescott, AZ	(9.2)
211	Seattle (greater), WA	(9.4)
212	Nashville-Davidson, TN	(9.5)
212	St. Joseph, MO-KS	(9.5)
214	Elkhart-Goshen, IN	(9.6)
214	Pittsburgh, PA	(9.6)
216	Flagstaff, AZ	(9.9)
217	Grand Forks, ND-MN	(10.1)
218	Los Angeles (greater), CA	(10.3)
218	Ocala, FL	(10.3)
218	Seattle-Bellevue, WA M.D.	(10.3)
221	Charleston, WV	(10.4)
221	Elizabethtown, KY	(10.4)
221	Riverside-San Bernardino, CA	(10.4)
221	Tallahassee, FL	(10.4)
225	Corpus Christi, TX	(10.8)
226	Buffalo-Niagara Falls, NY	(10.9)
227	Omaha-Council Bluffs, NE-IA	(11.2)
228	Albany-Schenectady-Troy, NY	(11.3)
228	Harrisburg-Carlisle, PA	(11.3)
230	Oxnard-Thousand Oaks, CA	(11.5)
231	Fort Worth-Arlington, TX M.D.	(11.6)

RANK	METROPOLITAN AREA	% CHANGE
231	Jacksonville, FL	(11.6)
231	Lubbock, TX	(11.6)
234	Lynchburg, VA	(11.8)
235	Jackson, TN	(11.9)
235	Mount Vernon-Anacortes, WA	(11.9)
237	Jonesboro, AR	(12.0)
237	Kingston, NY	(12.0)
237	Toledo, OH	(12.0)
240	Sioux City, IA-NE-SD	(12.3)
240	Virginia Beach-Norfolk, VA-NC	(12.3)
242	Bloomington, IN	(12.4)
242	New York-W. Plains NY-NJ M.D.	(12.4)
242	Niles-Benton Harbor, MI	(12.4)
245	New York (greater), NY-NJ-PA	(12.6)
245	Vineland, NJ	(12.6)
247	San Francisco-S. Mateo, CA M.D.	(13.0)
248	Kokomo, IN	(13.1)
249	Rapid City, SD	(13.2)
249	Worcester, MA	(13.2)
251	Janesville, WI	(13.3)
251	Lebanon, PA	(13.3)
253	Cincinnati-Middletown, OH-KY-IN	(13.4)
253	Longview, WA	(13.4)
255	Yuba City, CA	(13.9)
256	Ogden-Clearfield, UT	(14.0)
257	Jackson, MI	(14.4)
258	State College, PA	(14.5)
259	Hot Springs, AR	(14.7)
259	Stockton, CA	(14.7)
261	Poughkeepsie, NY	(14.9)
262	Bellingham, WA	(15.0)
263	Savannah, GA	(15.1)
264	Merced, CA	(15.6)
265	Ann Arbor, MI	(16.0)
265	Monroe, MI	(16.0)
267	Naples-Marco Island, FL	(16.2)
268	Lakeland, FL	(16.3)
268	Tulsa, OK	(16.3)
270	Joplin, MO	(16.5)
271	Newark-Union, NJ-PA M.D.	(16.7)
272	Syracuse, NY	(17.2)
273	Columbus, OH	(17.3)
273	Muskegon-Norton Shores, MI	(17.3)
275	Ocean City, NJ	(17.5)
276	Memphis, TN-MS-AR	(17.7)
277	Olympia, WA	(17.8)
278	Morristown, TN	(18.2)
279	Texarkana, TX-Texarkana, AR	(18.3)
280	Sherman-Denison, TX	(18.4)
281	Santa Cruz-Watsonville, CA	(18.9)
282	Santa Barbara-Santa Maria, CA	(19.3)
283	Santa Ana-Anaheim, CA M.D.	(19.5)
284	Missoula, MT	(19.6)
285	Provo-Orem, UT	(20.7)
286	San Angelo, TX	(20.8)
287	Warner Robins, GA	(20.9)
288	Lewiston-Auburn, ME	(21.2)
289	Wenatchee, WA	(21.4)
290	Lewiston, ID-WA	(21.5)
291	Port St. Lucie, FL	(21.6)

RANK	METROPOLITAN AREA	% CHANGE
292	Kennewick-Richland-Pasco, WA	(22.5)
292	Wichita Falls, TX	(22.5)
294	Fort Collins-Loveland, CO	(23.1)
295	Trenton-Ewing, NJ	(23.6)
296	Portland-Vancouver, OR-WA	(24.1)
297	Bend, OR	(24.9)
297	Denver-Aurora, CO	(24.9)
299	Great Falls, MT	(25.0)
300	Waterloo-Cedar Falls, IA	(25.4)
301	Chico, CA	(25.5)
302	Santa Rosa-Petaluma, CA	(25.7)
303	Logan, UT-ID	(26.5)
304	Madera, CA	(26.8)
305	Sebastian-Vero Beach, FL	(27.6)
306	Salem, OR	(27.9)
307	Modesto, CA	(28.2)
308	Greeley, CO	(28.4)
309	Coeur d'Alene, ID	(30.5)
310	Bismarck, ND	(31.2)
311	Medford, OR	(31.3)
311	Valdosta, GA	(31.3)
313	Waco, TX	(31.8)
314	Eugene-Springfield, OR	(33.7)
314	Santa Fe, NM	(33.7)
316	Sioux Falls, SD	(34.3)
317	Farmington, NM	(35.0)
318	Mansfield, OH	(45.4)
NA	Abilene, TX**	NA
NA	Birmingham-Hoover, AL**	NA
NA	Boise City-Nampa, ID**	NA
NA	Chicago, IL**	NA
NA	Cleveland-Elyria-Mentor, OH**	NA
NA	Cleveland, TN**	NA
NA	Dalton, GA**	NA
NA	Des Moines-West Des Moines, IA**	NA
NA	Detroit (greater), MI**	NA
NA	Duluth, MN-WI**	NA
NA	Durham, NC**	NA
NA	Fairbanks, AK**	NA
NA	Fort Wayne, IN**	NA
NA	Glens Falls, NY**	NA
NA	Hattiesburg, MS**	NA
NA	Ithaca, NY**	NA
NA	Jacksonville, NC**	NA
NA	Johnstown, PA**	NA
NA	Kansas City, MO-KS**	NA
NA	Lake Havasu City-Kingman, AZ**	NA
NA	Lexington-Fayette, KY**	NA
NA	Minneapolis-St. Paul, MN-WI**	NA
NA	New Orleans, LA**	NA
NA	Palm Coast, FL**	NA
NA	Richmond, VA**	NA
NA	Tuscaloosa, AL**	NA
NA	Vallejo-Fairfield, CA**	NA
NA	Visalia-Porterville, CA**	NA
NA	Warren-Farmington Hills, MI M.D.**	NA
NA	Washington (greater) DC-VA-MD**	NA
NA	Washington, DC-VA-MD-WV M.D.**	NA
NA	Wichita, KS**	NA

Source: CQ Press using data from Federal Bureau of Investigation "Crime in the United States 2006" (Uniform Crime Reports, September 24, 2007)

**Motor vehicle theft includes the theft or attempted theft of a self-propelled vehicle. Excludes motorboats, construction equipment, airplanes, and farming equipment. **Not available.*

40. Percent Change in Motor Vehicle Theft Rate: 2002 to 2006

National Percent Change = 8.0% Decrease*

RANK	METROPOLITAN AREA	% CHANGE
NA	Abilene, TX**	NA
NA	Albany-Schenectady-Troy, NY**	NA
59	Albany, GA	5.2
32	Albuquerque, NM	23.1
25	Alexandria, LA	27.3
129	Altoona, PA	(15.9)
75	Amarillo, TX	(0.4)
NA	Ames, IA**	NA
42	Anchorage, AK	17.1
NA	Anderson, SC**	NA
NA	Ann Arbor, MI**	NA
NA	Appleton, WI**	NA
110	Asheville, NC	(10.6)
108	Athens-Clarke County, GA	(10.3)
83	Atlanta, GA	(1.8)
NA	Atlantic City, NJ**	NA
12	Augusta, GA-SC	44.2
179	Austin-Round Rock, TX	(28.0)
9	Bakersfield, CA	51.3
87	Baltimore-Towson, MD	(3.1)
NA	Bangor, ME**	NA
NA	Barnstable Town, MA**	NA
64	Baton Rouge, LA	3.4
NA	Battle Creek, MI**	NA
NA	Bay City, MI**	NA
79	Beaumont-Port Arthur, TX	(1.3)
115	Bellingham, WA	(11.5)
NA	Bend, OR**	NA
NA	Bethesda-Frederick, MD M.D.**	NA
76	Billings, MT	(0.6)
186	Binghamton, NY	(30.0)
74	Birmingham-Hoover, AL	(0.1)
178	Bismarck, ND	(27.8)
NA	Blacksburg, VA**	NA
149	Bloomington, IN	(20.7)
162	Boise City-Nampa, ID	(23.7)
NA	Bowling Green, KY**	NA
132	Bremerton-Silverdale, WA	(17.2)
65	Brownsville-Harlingen, TX	3.1
NA	Brunswick, GA**	NA
144	Buffalo-Niagara Falls, NY	(19.8)
NA	Burlington, NC**	NA
NA	Camden, NJ M.D.**	NA
130	Cape Coral-Fort Myers, FL	(16.9)
NA	Carson City, NV**	NA
181	Casper, WY	(29.1)
147	Cedar Rapids, IA	(20.5)
148	Charleston-North Charleston, SC	(20.6)
103	Charleston, WV	(9.2)
NA	Charlotte-Gastonia, NC-SC**	NA
NA	Charlottesville, VA**	NA
133	Chattanooga, TN-GA	(17.3)
31	Cheyenne, WY	23.2
NA	Chicago, IL**	NA
190	Chico, CA	(32.4)
192	Cincinnati-Middletown, OH-KY-IN	(32.6)
102	Clarksville, TN-KY	(9.0)
NA	Cleveland-Elyria-Mentor, OH**	NA
NA	Cleveland, TN**	NA
NA	Coeur d'Alene, ID**	NA
NA	College Station-Bryan, TX**	NA
51	Colorado Springs, CO	9.2
48	Columbia, MO	13.4
196	Columbia, SC	(34.7)
4	Columbus, GA-AL	65.1
NA	Columbus, IN**	NA
168	Columbus, OH	(25.3)
204	Corpus Christi, TX	(38.3)
70	Cumberland, MD-WV	1.6
NA	Dallas (greater), TX**	NA
170	Dallas-Plano-Irving, TX M.D.	(25.5)
NA	Dalton, GA**	NA
28	Danville, VA	26.7
76	Daytona Beach, FL	(0.6)
NA	Dayton, OH**	NA
2	Decatur, AL	96.1
160	Denver-Aurora, CO	(23.3)
NA	Des Moines-West Des Moines, IA**	NA
61	Detroit (greater), MI	4.8
NA	Detroit-Livonia-Dearborn, MI M.D.**	NA
NA	Dothan, AL**	NA
24	Dover, DE	27.5
191	Dubuque, IA	(32.5)
166	Duluth, MN-WI	(25.0)
NA	Durham, NC**	NA
180	Eau Claire, WI	(28.6)
NA	Edison, NJ M.D.**	NA
NA	El Centro, CA**	NA
5	El Paso, TX	61.3
NA	Elizabethtown, KY**	NA
114	Elkhart-Goshen, IN	(11.3)
NA	Elmira, NY**	NA
100	Erie, PA	(8.5)
18	Eugene-Springfield, OR	33.1
NA	Evansville, IN-KY**	NA
NA	Fairbanks, AK**	NA
90	Fargo, ND-MN	(4.4)
NA	Farmington, NM**	NA
NA	Fayetteville, AR-MO**	NA
37	Fayetteville, NC	18.8
205	Flagstaff, AZ	(38.7)
56	Flint, MI	7.4
79	Florence, SC	(1.3)
NA	Fond du Lac, WI**	NA
33	Fort Collins-Loveland, CO	21.3
145	Fort Lauderdale, FL M.D.	(19.9)
86	Fort Smith, AR-OK	(3.0)
10	Fort Walton Beach, FL	51.0
NA	Fort Wayne, IN**	NA
141	Fort Worth-Arlington, TX M.D.	(18.6)
131	Fresno, CA	(17.1)
57	Gadsden, AL	6.5
122	Gainesville, FL	(14.1)
NA	Gainesville, GA**	NA
62	Glens Falls, NY	4.5
96	Goldsboro, NC	(7.8)
134	Grand Forks, ND-MN	(17.5)
20	Grand Junction, CO	32.4
NA	Grand Rapids-Wyoming, MI**	NA
157	Great Falls, MT	(22.7)
142	Greeley, CO	(19.6)
152	Green Bay, WI	(21.6)
NA	Greensboro-High Point, NC**	NA
91	Greenville, NC	(4.6)
NA	Greenville, SC**	NA
NA	Hagerstown-Martinsburg, MD-WV**	NA
NA	Hanford-Corcoran, CA**	NA
NA	Harrisburg-Carlisle, PA**	NA
NA	Harrisonburg, VA**	NA
138	Hartford, CT	(17.9)
NA	Hattiesburg, MS**	NA
NA	Holland-Grand Haven, MI**	NA
175	Honolulu, HI	(26.9)
NA	Hot Springs, AR**	NA
18	Houma, LA	33.1
154	Houston, TX	(21.9)
NA	Huntington-Ashland, WV-KY-OH**	NA
7	Huntsville, AL	56.2
NA	Idaho Falls, ID**	NA
NA	Indianapolis, IN**	NA
106	Iowa City, IA	(10.0)
NA	Ithaca, NY**	NA
175	Jacksonville, FL	(26.9)
NA	Jacksonville, NC**	NA
197	Jackson, MI	(35.0)
201	Jackson, MS	(36.4)
39	Jackson, TN	17.5
157	Janesville, WI	(22.7)
NA	Jefferson City, MO**	NA
NA	Johnson City, TN**	NA
NA	Johnstown, PA**	NA
187	Jonesboro, AR	(30.4)
47	Joplin, MO	14.0
NA	Kalamazoo-Portage, MI**	NA
NA	Kansas City, MO-KS**	NA
124	Kennewick-Richland-Pasco, WA	(14.9)
183	Killeen-Temple-Fort Hood, TX	(29.3)
NA	Kingsport, TN-VA**	NA
NA	Kingston, NY**	NA
98	Knoxville, TN	(8.3)
118	Kokomo, IN	(12.2)
55	La Crosse, WI-MN	8.3
23	Lafayette, IN	28.6
49	Lake Charles, LA	13.0
NA	Lake Havasu City-Kingman, AZ**	NA
171	Lakeland, FL	(25.6)
94	Lancaster, PA	(6.8)
43	Lansing-East Lansing, MI	16.7
38	Laredo, TX	18.3
NA	Las Cruces, NM**	NA
13	Las Vegas-Paradise, NV	43.1

Note: All listings are for Metropolitan Statistical Areas (M.S.A.s) except for those ending with "M.D." Listings with "M.D." are Metropolitan Divisions which are smaller parts of eleven large M.S.A.s. See explanatory note at beginning of metropolitan area section on page 23.

RANK	METROPOLITAN AREA	% CHANGE
35	Lawrence, KS	19.4
120	Lawton, OK	(12.7)
NA	Lebanon, PA**	NA
155	Lewiston-Auburn, ME	(22.2)
NA	Lewiston, ID-WA**	NA
NA	Lexington-Fayette, KY**	NA
NA	Lima, OH**	NA
165	Lincoln, NE	(24.6)
68	Little Rock, AR	1.9
NA	Logan, UT-ID**	NA
46	Longview, TX	14.7
NA	Longview, WA**	NA
115	Los Angeles County, CA M.D.	(11.5)
NA	Los Angeles (greater), CA**	NA
95	Louisville, KY-IN	(7.2)
40	Lubbock, TX	17.4
187	Lynchburg, VA	(30.4)
NA	Macon, GA**	NA
NA	Madera, CA**	NA
172	Madison, WI	(26.7)
NA	Manchester-Nashua, NH**	NA
NA	Mansfield, OH**	NA
84	McAllen-Edinburg-Mission, TX	(2.1)
175	Medford, OR	(26.9)
NA	Memphis, TN-MS-AR**	NA
134	Merced, CA	(17.5)
NA	Miami (greater), FL**	NA
153	Miami-Dade County, FL M.D.	(21.7)
NA	Michigan City-La Porte, IN**	NA
NA	Midland, TX**	NA
NA	Milwaukee, WI**	NA
82	Minneapolis-St. Paul, MN-WI	(1.7)
NA	Missoula, MT**	NA
NA	Mobile, AL**	NA
76	Modesto, CA	(0.6)
NA	Monroe, LA**	NA
NA	Monroe, MI**	NA
199	Montgomery, AL	(36.2)
NA	Morgantown, WV**	NA
NA	Morristown, TN**	NA
NA	Mount Vernon-Anacortes, WA**	NA
52	Muncie, IN	8.8
NA	Muskegon-Norton Shores, MI**	NA
54	Myrtle Beach, SC	8.5
NA	Napa, CA**	NA
207	Naples-Marco Island, FL	(39.4)
193	Nashville-Davidson, TN	(33.4)
NA	Nassau-Suffolk, NY M.D.**	NA
208	New Orleans, LA	(40.7)
NA	New York (greater), NY-NJ-PA**	NA
199	New York-W. Plains NY-NJ M.D.	(36.2)
198	Newark-Union, NJ-PA M.D.	(35.1)
NA	Niles-Benton Harbor, MI**	NA
25	Oakland-Fremont, CA M.D.	27.3
104	Ocala, FL	(9.5)
NA	Ocean City, NJ**	NA
NA	Odessa, TX**	NA
NA	Ogden-Clearfield, UT**	NA
34	Oklahoma City, OK	19.6
73	Olympia, WA	0.4

RANK	METROPOLITAN AREA	% CHANGE
183	Omaha-Council Bluffs, NE-IA	(29.3)
97	Orlando, FL	(8.2)
NA	Oshkosh-Neenah, WI**	NA
NA	Oxnard-Thousand Oaks, CA**	NA
105	Palm Bay-Melbourne, FL	(9.7)
NA	Palm Coast, FL**	NA
109	Panama City-Lynn Haven, FL	(10.4)
NA	Pascagoula, MS**	NA
29	Pensacola, FL	26.3
117	Philadelphia (greater) PA-NJ-DE	(12.0)
NA	Philadelphia, PA M.D.**	NA
156	Phoenix-Mesa-Scottsdale, AZ	(22.4)
127	Pine Bluff, AR	(15.6)
139	Pittsburgh, PA	(18.1)
NA	Pittsfield, MA**	NA
52	Pocatello, ID	8.8
163	Port St. Lucie, FL	(23.9)
146	Portland-Vancouver, OR-WA	(20.1)
NA	Portland, ME**	NA
NA	Poughkeepsie, NY**	NA
NA	Prescott, AZ**	NA
163	Provo-Orem, UT	(23.9)
44	Pueblo, CO	15.6
22	Punta Gorda, FL	29.4
88	Racine, WI	(3.3)
NA	Raleigh-Cary, NC**	NA
194	Rapid City, SD	(34.4)
16	Reading, PA	38.8
27	Redding, CA	27.0
21	Reno-Sparks, NV	29.9
203	Richmond, VA	(37.8)
72	Riverside-San Bernardino, CA	0.6
NA	Roanoke, VA**	NA
137	Rochester, MN	(17.8)
111	Rochester, NY	(10.7)
15	Rocky Mount, NC	39.7
NA	Rome, GA**	NA
60	Sacramento, CA	4.9
NA	Saginaw, MI**	NA
209	Salem, OR	(45.2)
6	Salinas, CA	58.8
NA	Salisbury, MD**	NA
NA	Salt Lake City, UT**	NA
89	San Angelo, TX	(3.4)
81	San Antonio, TX	(1.4)
36	San Diego, CA	19.2
NA	San Francisco (greater), CA**	NA
41	San Francisco-S. Mateo, CA M.D.	17.2
1	San Jose, CA	99.9
85	San Luis Obispo, CA	(2.8)
NA	Sandusky, OH**	NA
92	Santa Ana-Anaheim, CA M.D.	(5.0)
NA	Santa Barbara-Santa Maria, CA**	NA
3	Santa Cruz-Watsonville, CA	74.4
159	Santa Fe, NM	(22.9)
195	Santa Rosa-Petaluma, CA	(34.5)
71	Sarasota-Bradenton-Venice, FL	1.1
187	Savannah, GA	(30.4)
119	Scranton--Wilkes-Barre, PA	(12.5)
NA	Seattle (greater), WA**	NA

RANK	METROPOLITAN AREA	% CHANGE
50	Seattle-Bellevue, WA M.D.	9.6
NA	Sebastian-Vero Beach, FL**	NA
125	Sheboygan, WI	(15.1)
151	Sherman-Denison, TX	(21.2)
113	Shreveport-Bossier City, LA	(11.2)
211	Sioux City, IA-NE-SD	(51.6)
112	Sioux Falls, SD	(11.0)
123	South Bend-Mishawaka, IN-MI	(14.2)
NA	Spartanburg, SC**	NA
30	Spokane, WA	25.6
NA	Springfield, MA**	NA
101	Springfield, MO	(8.9)
NA	Springfield, OH**	NA
45	State College, PA	15.2
99	Stockton, CA	(8.4)
161	St. Cloud, MN	(23.4)
17	St. Joseph, MO-KS	38.2
NA	St. Louis, MO-IL**	NA
210	Sumter, SC	(45.3)
NA	Syracuse, NY**	NA
63	Tacoma, WA M.D.	4.3
168	Tallahassee, FL	(25.3)
172	Tampa-St Petersburg, FL	(26.7)
107	Texarkana, TX-Texarkana, AR	(10.2)
167	Toledo, OH	(25.1)
150	Topeka, KS	(21.0)
212	Trenton-Ewing, NJ	(54.5)
66	Tucson, AZ	3.0
134	Tulsa, OK	(17.5)
93	Tuscaloosa, AL	(6.7)
205	Tyler, TX	(38.7)
125	Utica-Rome, NY	(15.1)
NA	Valdosta, GA**	NA
NA	Vallejo-Fairfield, CA**	NA
68	Victoria, TX	1.9
172	Vineland, NJ	(26.7)
202	Virginia Beach-Norfolk, VA-NC	(36.6)
14	Visalia-Porterville, CA	43.0
185	Waco, TX	(29.8)
NA	Warner Robins, GA**	NA
NA	Warren-Farmington Hills, MI M.D.**	NA
NA	Washington (greater) DC-VA-MD**	NA
NA	Washington, DC-VA-MD-WV M.D.**	NA
213	Waterloo-Cedar Falls, IA	(55.8)
121	Wausau, WI	(13.0)
NA	Wenatchee, WA**	NA
181	West Palm Beach, FL M.D.	(29.1)
NA	Wheeling, WV-OH**	NA
128	Wichita Falls, TX	(15.7)
58	Wichita, KS	5.3
67	Williamsport, PA	2.5
NA	Wilmington, DE-MD-NJ M.D.**	NA
140	Wilmington, NC	(18.2)
NA	Winchester, VA-WV**	NA
NA	Winston-Salem, NC**	NA
NA	Worcester, MA**	NA
8	Yakima, WA	55.2
143	Yuba City, CA	(19.7)
11	Yuma, AZ	46.6

Source: CQ Press using data from Federal Bureau of Investigation "Crime in the United States 2006" (Uniform Crime Reports, September 24, 2007)

**Motor vehicle theft includes the theft or attempted theft of a self-propelled vehicle. Excludes motorboats, construction equipment, airplanes, and farming equipment. **Not available.*

40. Percent Change in Motor Vehicle Theft Rate: 2002 to 2006 (continued)

National Percent Change = 8.0% Decrease*

RANK	METROPOLITAN AREA	% CHANGE
1	San Jose, CA	99.9
2	Decatur, AL	96.1
3	Santa Cruz-Watsonville, CA	74.4
4	Columbus, GA-AL	65.1
5	El Paso, TX	61.3
6	Salinas, CA	58.8
7	Huntsville, AL	56.2
8	Yakima, WA	55.2
9	Bakersfield, CA	51.3
10	Fort Walton Beach, FL	51.0
11	Yuma, AZ	46.6
12	Augusta, GA-SC	44.2
13	Las Vegas-Paradise, NV	43.1
14	Visalia-Porterville, CA	43.0
15	Rocky Mount, NC	39.7
16	Reading, PA	38.8
17	St. Joseph, MO-KS	38.2
18	Eugene-Springfield, OR	33.1
18	Houma, LA	33.1
20	Grand Junction, CO	32.4
21	Reno-Sparks, NV	29.9
22	Punta Gorda, FL	29.4
23	Lafayette, IN	28.6
24	Dover, DE	27.5
25	Alexandria, LA	27.3
25	Oakland-Fremont, CA M.D.	27.3
27	Redding, CA	27.0
28	Danville, VA	26.7
29	Pensacola, FL	26.3
30	Spokane, WA	25.6
31	Cheyenne, WY	23.2
32	Albuquerque, NM	23.1
33	Fort Collins-Loveland, CO	21.3
34	Oklahoma City, OK	19.6
35	Lawrence, KS	19.4
36	San Diego, CA	19.2
37	Fayetteville, NC	18.8
38	Laredo, TX	18.3
39	Jackson, TN	17.5
40	Lubbock, TX	17.4
41	San Francisco-S. Mateo, CA M.D.	17.2
42	Anchorage, AK	17.1
43	Lansing-East Lansing, MI	16.7
44	Pueblo, CO	15.6
45	State College, PA	15.2
46	Longview, TX	14.7
47	Joplin, MO	14.0
48	Columbia, MO	13.4
49	Lake Charles, LA	13.0
50	Seattle-Bellevue, WA M.D.	9.6
51	Colorado Springs, CO	9.2
52	Muncie, IN	8.8
52	Pocatello, ID	8.8
54	Myrtle Beach, SC	8.5
55	La Crosse, WI-MN	8.3
56	Flint, MI	7.4
57	Gadsden, AL	6.5
58	Wichita, KS	5.3
59	Albany, GA	5.2
60	Sacramento, CA	4.9
61	Detroit (greater), MI	4.8
62	Glens Falls, NY	4.5
63	Tacoma, WA M.D.	4.3
64	Baton Rouge, LA	3.4
65	Brownsville-Harlingen, TX	3.1
66	Tucson, AZ	3.0
67	Williamsport, PA	2.5
68	Little Rock, AR	1.9
68	Victoria, TX	1.9
70	Cumberland, MD-WV	1.6
71	Sarasota-Bradenton-Venice, FL	1.1
72	Riverside-San Bernardino, CA	0.6
73	Olympia, WA	0.4
74	Birmingham-Hoover, AL	(0.1)
75	Amarillo, TX	(0.4)
76	Billings, MT	(0.6)
76	Daytona Beach, FL	(0.6)
76	Modesto, CA	(0.6)
79	Beaumont-Port Arthur, TX	(1.3)
79	Florence, SC	(1.3)
81	San Antonio, TX	(1.4)
82	Minneapolis-St. Paul, MN-WI	(1.7)
83	Atlanta, GA	(1.8)
84	McAllen-Edinburg-Mission, TX	(2.1)
85	San Luis Obispo, CA	(2.8)
86	Fort Smith, AR-OK	(3.0)
87	Baltimore-Towson, MD	(3.1)
88	Racine, WI	(3.3)
89	San Angelo, TX	(3.4)
90	Fargo, ND-MN	(4.4)
91	Greenville, NC	(4.6)
92	Santa Ana-Anaheim, CA M.D.	(5.0)
93	Tuscaloosa, AL	(6.7)
94	Lancaster, PA	(6.8)
95	Louisville, KY-IN	(7.2)
96	Goldsboro, NC	(7.8)
97	Orlando, FL	(8.2)
98	Knoxville, TN	(8.3)
99	Stockton, CA	(8.4)
100	Erie, PA	(8.5)
101	Springfield, MO	(8.9)
102	Clarksville, TN-KY	(9.0)
103	Charleston, WV	(9.2)
104	Ocala, FL	(9.5)
105	Palm Bay-Melbourne, FL	(9.7)
106	Iowa City, IA	(10.0)
107	Texarkana, TX-Texarkana, AR	(10.2)
108	Athens-Clarke County, GA	(10.3)
109	Panama City-Lynn Haven, FL	(10.4)
110	Asheville, NC	(10.6)
111	Rochester, NY	(10.7)
112	Sioux Falls, SD	(11.0)
113	Shreveport-Bossier City, LA	(11.2)
114	Elkhart-Goshen, IN	(11.3)
115	Bellingham, WA	(11.5)
115	Los Angeles County, CA M.D.	(11.5)
117	Philadelphia (greater) PA-NJ-DE	(12.0)
118	Kokomo, IN	(12.2)
119	Scranton--Wilkes-Barre, PA	(12.5)
120	Lawton, OK	(12.7)
121	Wausau, WI	(13.0)
122	Gainesville, FL	(14.1)
123	South Bend-Mishawaka, IN-MI	(14.2)
124	Kennewick-Richland-Pasco, WA	(14.9)
125	Sheboygan, WI	(15.1)
125	Utica-Rome, NY	(15.1)
127	Pine Bluff, AR	(15.6)
128	Wichita Falls, TX	(15.7)
129	Altoona, PA	(15.9)
130	Cape Coral-Fort Myers, FL	(16.9)
131	Fresno, CA	(17.1)
132	Bremerton-Silverdale, WA	(17.2)
133	Chattanooga, TN-GA	(17.3)
134	Grand Forks, ND-MN	(17.5)
134	Merced, CA	(17.5)
134	Tulsa, OK	(17.5)
137	Rochester, MN	(17.8)
138	Hartford, CT	(17.9)
139	Pittsburgh, PA	(18.1)
140	Wilmington, NC	(18.2)
141	Fort Worth-Arlington, TX M.D.	(18.6)
142	Greeley, CO	(19.6)
143	Yuba City, CA	(19.7)
144	Buffalo-Niagara Falls, NY	(19.8)
145	Fort Lauderdale, FL M.D.	(19.9)
146	Portland-Vancouver, OR-WA	(20.1)
147	Cedar Rapids, IA	(20.5)
148	Charleston-North Charleston, SC	(20.6)
149	Bloomington, IN	(20.7)
150	Topeka, KS	(21.0)
151	Sherman-Denison, TX	(21.2)
152	Green Bay, WI	(21.6)
153	Miami-Dade County, FL M.D.	(21.7)
154	Houston, TX	(21.9)
155	Lewiston-Auburn, ME	(22.2)
156	Phoenix-Mesa-Scottsdale, AZ	(22.4)
157	Great Falls, MT	(22.7)
157	Janesville, WI	(22.7)
159	Santa Fe, NM	(22.9)
160	Denver-Aurora, CO	(23.3)
161	St. Cloud, MN	(23.4)
162	Boise City-Nampa, ID	(23.7)
163	Port St. Lucie, FL	(23.9)
163	Provo-Orem, UT	(23.9)
165	Lincoln, NE	(24.6)
166	Duluth, MN-WI	(25.0)
167	Toledo, OH	(25.1)
168	Columbus, OH	(25.3)
168	Tallahassee, FL	(25.3)
170	Dallas-Plano-Irving, TX M.D.	(25.5)
171	Lakeland, FL	(25.6)

Note: All listings are for Metropolitan Statistical Areas (M.S.A.s) except for those ending with "M.D." Listings with "M.D." are Metropolitan Divisions which are smaller parts of eleven large M.S.A.s. See explanatory note at beginning of metropolitan area section on page 23.

RANK	METROPOLITAN AREA	% CHANGE
172	Madison, WI	(26.7)
172	Tampa-St Petersburg, FL	(26.7)
172	Vineland, NJ	(26.7)
175	Honolulu, HI	(26.9)
175	Jacksonville, FL	(26.9)
175	Medford, OR	(26.9)
178	Bismarck, ND	(27.8)
179	Austin-Round Rock, TX	(28.0)
180	Eau Claire, WI	(28.6)
181	Casper, WY	(29.1)
181	West Palm Beach, FL M.D.	(29.1)
183	Killeen-Temple-Fort Hood, TX	(29.3)
183	Omaha-Council Bluffs, NE-IA	(29.3)
185	Waco, TX	(29.8)
186	Binghamton, NY	(30.0)
187	Jonesboro, AR	(30.4)
187	Lynchburg, VA	(30.4)
187	Savannah, GA	(30.4)
190	Chico, CA	(32.4)
191	Dubuque, IA	(32.5)
192	Cincinnati-Middletown, OH-KY-IN	(32.6)
193	Nashville-Davidson, TN	(33.4)
194	Rapid City, SD	(34.4)
195	Santa Rosa-Petaluma, CA	(34.5)
196	Columbia, SC	(34.7)
197	Jackson, MI	(35.0)
198	Newark-Union, NJ-PA M.D.	(35.1)
199	Montgomery, AL	(36.2)
199	New York-W. Plains NY-NJ M.D.	(36.2)
201	Jackson, MS	(36.4)
202	Virginia Beach-Norfolk, VA-NC	(36.6)
203	Richmond, VA	(37.8)
204	Corpus Christi, TX	(38.3)
205	Flagstaff, AZ	(38.7)
205	Tyler, TX	(38.7)
207	Naples-Marco Island, FL	(39.4)
208	New Orleans, LA	(40.7)
209	Salem, OR	(45.2)
210	Sumter, SC	(45.3)
211	Sioux City, IA-NE-SD	(51.6)
212	Trenton-Ewing, NJ	(54.5)
213	Waterloo-Cedar Falls, IA	(55.8)
NA	Abilene, TX**	NA
NA	Albany-Schenectady-Troy, NY**	NA
NA	Ames, IA**	NA
NA	Anderson, SC**	NA
NA	Ann Arbor, MI**	NA
NA	Appleton, WI**	NA
NA	Atlantic City, NJ**	NA
NA	Bangor, ME**	NA
NA	Barnstable Town, MA**	NA
NA	Battle Creek, MI**	NA
NA	Bay City, MI**	NA
NA	Bend, OR**	NA
NA	Bethesda-Frederick, MD M.D.**	NA
NA	Blacksburg, VA**	NA
NA	Bowling Green, KY**	NA
NA	Brunswick, GA**	NA
NA	Burlington, NC**	NA
NA	Camden, NJ M.D.**	NA

RANK	METROPOLITAN AREA	% CHANGE
NA	Carson City, NV**	NA
NA	Charlotte-Gastonia, NC-SC**	NA
NA	Charlottesville, VA**	NA
NA	Chicago, IL**	NA
NA	Cleveland-Elyria-Mentor, OH**	NA
NA	Cleveland, TN**	NA
NA	Coeur d'Alene, ID**	NA
NA	College Station-Bryan, TX**	NA
NA	Columbus, IN**	NA
NA	Dallas (greater), TX**	NA
NA	Dalton, GA**	NA
NA	Dayton, OH**	NA
NA	Des Moines-West Des Moines, IA**	NA
NA	Detroit-Livonia-Dearborn, MI M.D.**	NA
NA	Dothan, AL**	NA
NA	Durham, NC**	NA
NA	Edison, NJ M.D.**	NA
NA	El Centro, CA**	NA
NA	Elizabethtown, KY**	NA
NA	Elmira, NY**	NA
NA	Evansville, IN-KY**	NA
NA	Fairbanks, AK**	NA
NA	Farmington, NM**	NA
NA	Fayetteville, AR-MO**	NA
NA	Fond du Lac, WI**	NA
NA	Fort Wayne, IN**	NA
NA	Gainesville, GA**	NA
NA	Grand Rapids-Wyoming, MI**	NA
NA	Greensboro-High Point, NC**	NA
NA	Greenville, SC**	NA
NA	Hagerstown-Martinsburg, MD-WV**	NA
NA	Hanford-Corcoran, CA**	NA
NA	Harrisburg-Carlisle, PA**	NA
NA	Harrisonburg, VA**	NA
NA	Hattiesburg, MS**	NA
NA	Holland-Grand Haven, MI**	NA
NA	Hot Springs, AR**	NA
NA	Huntington-Ashland, WV-KY-OH**	NA
NA	Idaho Falls, ID**	NA
NA	Indianapolis, IN**	NA
NA	Ithaca, NY**	NA
NA	Jacksonville, NC**	NA
NA	Jefferson City, MO**	NA
NA	Johnson City, TN**	NA
NA	Johnstown, PA**	NA
NA	Kalamazoo-Portage, MI**	NA
NA	Kansas City, MO-KS**	NA
NA	Kingsport, TN-VA**	NA
NA	Kingston, NY**	NA
NA	Lake Havasu City-Kingman, AZ**	NA
NA	Las Cruces, NM**	NA
NA	Lebanon, PA**	NA
NA	Lewiston, ID-WA**	NA
NA	Lexington-Fayette, KY**	NA
NA	Lima, OH**	NA
NA	Logan, UT-ID**	NA
NA	Longview, WA**	NA
NA	Los Angeles (greater), CA**	NA
NA	Macon, GA**	NA
NA	Madera, CA**	NA

RANK	METROPOLITAN AREA	% CHANGE
NA	Manchester-Nashua, NH**	NA
NA	Mansfield, OH**	NA
NA	Memphis, TN-MS-AR**	NA
NA	Miami (greater), FL**	NA
NA	Michigan City-La Porte, IN**	NA
NA	Midland, TX**	NA
NA	Milwaukee, WI**	NA
NA	Missoula, MT**	NA
NA	Mobile, AL**	NA
NA	Monroe, LA**	NA
NA	Monroe, MI**	NA
NA	Morgantown, WV**	NA
NA	Morristown, TN**	NA
NA	Mount Vernon-Anacortes, WA**	NA
NA	Muskegon-Norton Shores, MI**	NA
NA	Napa, CA**	NA
NA	Nassau-Suffolk, NY M.D.**	NA
NA	New York (greater), NY-NJ-PA**	NA
NA	Niles-Benton Harbor, MI**	NA
NA	Ocean City, NJ**	NA
NA	Odessa, TX**	NA
NA	Ogden-Clearfield, UT**	NA
NA	Oshkosh-Neenah, WI**	NA
NA	Oxnard-Thousand Oaks, CA**	NA
NA	Palm Coast, FL**	NA
NA	Pascagoula, MS**	NA
NA	Philadelphia, PA M.D.**	NA
NA	Pittsfield, MA**	NA
NA	Portland, ME**	NA
NA	Poughkeepsie, NY**	NA
NA	Prescott, AZ**	NA
NA	Raleigh-Cary, NC**	NA
NA	Roanoke, VA**	NA
NA	Rome, GA**	NA
NA	Saginaw, MI**	NA
NA	Salisbury, MD**	NA
NA	Salt Lake City, UT**	NA
NA	San Francisco (greater), CA**	NA
NA	Sandusky, OH**	NA
NA	Santa Barbara-Santa Maria, CA**	NA
NA	Seattle (greater), WA**	NA
NA	Sebastian-Vero Beach, FL**	NA
NA	Spartanburg, SC**	NA
NA	Springfield, MA**	NA
NA	Springfield, OH**	NA
NA	St. Louis, MO-IL**	NA
NA	Syracuse, NY**	NA
NA	Valdosta, GA**	NA
NA	Vallejo-Fairfield, CA**	NA
NA	Warner Robins, GA**	NA
NA	Warren-Farmington Hills, MI M.D.**	NA
NA	Washington (greater) DC-VA-MD**	NA
NA	Washington, DC-VA-MD-WV M.D.**	NA
NA	Wenatchee, WA**	NA
NA	Wheeling, WV-OH**	NA
NA	Wilmington, DE-MD-NJ M.D.**	NA
NA	Winchester, VA-WV**	NA
NA	Winston-Salem, NC**	NA
NA	Worcester, MA**	NA

Source: CQ Press using data from Federal Bureau of Investigation "Crime in the United States 2006" (Uniform Crime Reports, September 24, 2007)

**Motor vehicle theft includes the theft or attempted theft of a self-propelled vehicle. Excludes motorboats, construction equipment, airplanes, and farming equipment. **Not available.*

CITY CRIME STATISTICS

(cities with populations of 75,000 or more)

41. Crimes in 2006

National Total = 11,401,313 Crimes*

RANK	CITY	CRIMES	RANK	CITY	CRIMES	RANK	CITY	CRIMES
199	Abilene, TX	5,599	332	Chino, CA	2,618	227	Garden Grove, CA	4,860
189	Albany, GA	5,832	139	Chula Vista, CA	7,981	132	Garland, TX	8,460
178	Albany, NY	6,037	42	Cincinnati, OH	25,873	174	Gary, IN	6,271
28	Albuquerque, NM	36,307	372	Clarkstown, NY	1,668	213	Gilbert, AZ	5,189
277	Alexandria, VA	3,642	209	Clarksville, TN	5,265	86	Glendale, AZ	13,633
324	Alhambra, CA	2,769	194	Clearwater, FL	5,699	244	Glendale, CA	4,303
155	Allentown, PA	7,140	30	Cleveland, OH	35,224	140	Grand Prairie, TX	7,969
95	Amarillo, TX	12,703	354	Clifton, NJ	2,090	99	Grand Rapids, MI	12,026
360	Amherst, NY	2,004	322	Clinton Twnshp, MI	2,789	342	Greece, NY	2,418
111	Anaheim, CA	10,341	292	Clovis, CA	3,302	231	Greeley, CO	4,791
76	Anchorage, AK	14,313	312	Colonie, NY	2,984	287	Green Bay, WI	3,432
295	Ann Arbor, MI	3,267	53	Colorado Springs, CO	20,221	63	Greensboro, NC	16,398
285	Antioch, CA	3,501	279	Columbia, MO	3,565	236	Gresham, OR	4,588
50	Arlington, TX	22,394	134	Columbia, SC	8,284	356	Hamilton Twnshp, NJ	2,079
289	Arvada, CO	3,395	67	Columbus, GA	15,012	229	Hammond, IN	4,806
181	Athens-Clarke, GA	6,007	11	Columbus, OH	58,046	204	Hampton, VA	5,432
25	Atlanta, GA	39,779	252	Compton, CA	4,083	110	Hartford, CT	10,414
72	Aurora, CO	14,663	183	Concord, CA	5,906	325	Hawthorne, CA	2,724
NA	Aurora, IL**	NA	299	Coral Springs, FL	3,241	165	Hayward, CA	6,512
18	Austin, TX	45,231	242	Corona, CA	4,370	151	Henderson, NV	7,262
60	Bakersfield, CA	17,490	52	Corpus Christi, TX	21,208	348	Hesperia, CA	2,281
345	Baldwin Park, CA	2,369	275	Costa Mesa, CA	3,686	114	Hialeah, FL	9,937
21	Baltimore, MD	43,137	360	Cranston, RI	2,004	171	High Point, NC	6,351
59	Baton Rouge, LA	17,638	5	Dallas, TX	100,650	315	Hillsboro, OR	2,944
138	Beaumont, TX	8,117	330	Daly City, CA	2,633	159	Hollywood, FL	6,992
343	Beaverton, OR	2,413	369	Danbury, CT	1,733	23	Honolulu, HI	41,055
240	Bellevue, WA	4,429	303	Davie, FL	3,160	2	Houston, TX	145,303
326	Bellflower, CA	2,693	89	Dayton, OH	13,480	225	Huntington Beach, CA	4,875
200	Bellingham, WA	5,530	206	Dearborn, MI	5,403	94	Huntsville, AL	12,934
140	Berkeley, CA	7,969	305	Deerfield Beach, FL	3,152	133	Independence, MO	8,421
237	Billings, MT	4,513	286	Denton, TX	3,497	12	Indianapolis, IN	57,288
51	Birmingham, AL	22,182	36	Denver, CO	30,591	257	Inglewood, CA	3,977
NA	Bloomington, MN**	NA	71	Des Moines, IA	14,811	303	Irvine, CA	3,160
300	Boca Raton, FL	3,189	8	Detroit, MI	83,732	108	Irving, TX	10,494
147	Boise, ID	7,388	253	Downey, CA	4,067	15	Jacksonville, FL	49,766
33	Boston, MA	32,627	NA	Duluth, MN**	NA	68	Jackson, MS	14,944
298	Boulder, CO	3,245	83	Durham, NC	13,823	109	Jersey City, NJ	10,480
373	Brick Twnshp, NJ	1,546	333	Edison Twnshp, NJ	2,615	NA	Joliet, IL**	NA
128	Bridgeport, CT	8,496	359	Edmond, OK	2,052	102	Kansas City, KS	11,526
NA	Brockton, MA**	NA	250	El Cajon, CA	4,085	27	Kansas City, MO	37,571
364	Broken Arrow, OK	1,851	264	El Monte, CA	3,827	297	Kenosha, WI	3,256
121	Brownsville, TX	9,252	46	El Paso, TX	22,989	162	Kent, WA	6,815
351	Buena Park, CA	2,234	195	Elizabeth, NJ	5,668	175	Killeen, TX	6,258
55	Buffalo, NY	19,393	281	Erie, PA	3,541	93	Knoxville, TN	12,957
313	Burbank, CA	2,973	214	Escondido, CA	5,120	146	Lafayette, LA	7,535
274	Cambridge, MA	3,741	129	Eugene, OR	8,483	376	Lake Forest, CA	1,201
167	Camden, NJ	6,480	186	Evansville, IN	5,847	192	Lakeland, FL	5,751
367	Canton Twnshp, MI	1,810	116	Everett, WA	9,665	328	Lakewood, CA	2,662
158	Canton, OH	7,035	220	Fairfield, CA	5,017	144	Lakewood, CO	7,697
208	Cape Coral, FL	5,314	317	Fargo, ND	2,910	172	Lancaster, CA	6,301
323	Carlsbad, CA	2,784	371	Farmington Hills, MI	1,687	190	Lansing, MI	5,829
256	Carrollton, TX	4,011	75	Fayetteville, NC	14,390	84	Laredo, TX	13,709
280	Carson, CA	3,561	201	Federal Way, WA	5,513	301	Largo, FL	3,172
347	Cary, NC	2,320	104	Flint, MI	11,187	241	Las Cruces, NM	4,421
173	Cedar Rapids, IA	6,273	249	Fontana, CA	4,172	9	Las Vegas, NV	74,336
368	Centennial, CO	1,798	218	Fort Collins, CO	5,063	205	Lawrence, KS	5,414
115	Chandler, AZ	9,683	101	Fort Lauderdale, FL	11,620	196	Lawton, OK	5,656
207	Charleston, SC	5,318	169	Fort Smith, AR	6,367	340	Lee's Summit, MO	2,440
13	Charlotte, NC	56,418	103	Fort Wayne, IN	11,475	296	Lewisville, TX	3,259
80	Chattanooga, TN	14,210	24	Fort Worth, TX	40,682	97	Lexington, KY	12,149
329	Cheektowaga, NY	2,640	185	Fremont, CA	5,867	88	Lincoln, NE	13,493
143	Chesapeake, VA	7,851	39	Fresno, CA	26,931	56	Little Rock, AR	19,113
NA	Chicago, IL**	NA	229	Fullerton, CA	4,806	365	Livermore, CA	1,850
375	Chino Hills, CA	1,341	161	Gainesville, FL	6,853	337	Livonia, MI	2,485

Alpha Order- City (continued)

RANK	CITY	CRIMES	RANK	CITY	CRIMES	RANK	CITY	CRIMES
64	Long Beach, CA	16,198	179	Peoria, AZ	6,036	265	Spokane Valley, WA	3,823
198	Longview, TX	5,621	NA	Peoria, IL**	NA	92	Spokane, WA	13,001
3	Los Angeles, CA	135,985	7	Philadelphia, PA	85,495	NA	Springfield, IL**	NA
32	Louisville, KY	32,972	4	Phoenix, AZ	101,244	106	Springfield, MA	11,007
246	Lowell, MA	4,272	57	Pittsburgh, PA	18,709	81	Springfield, MO	14,162
73	Lubbock, TX	14,542	119	Plano, TX	9,361	276	Sterling Heights, MI	3,671
261	Lynn, MA	3,852	258	Plantation, FL	3,937	44	Stockton, CA	24,007
112	Macon, GA	10,339	166	Pomona, CA	6,482	16	St. Louis, MO	49,356
130	Madison, WI	8,471	170	Pompano Beach, FL	6,352	NA	St. Paul, MN**	NA
271	Manchester, NH	3,767	260	Port St. Lucie, FL	3,903	54	St. Petersburg, FL	20,162
150	McAllen, TX	7,309	29	Portland, OR	35,868	317	Suffolk, VA	2,910
338	McKinney, TX	2,481	182	Portsmouth, VA	5,915	370	Sugar Land, TX	1,710
223	Melbourne, FL	4,894	117	Providence, RI	9,557	320	Sunnyvale, CA	2,816
10	Memphis, TN	70,449	311	Provo, UT	3,028	270	Sunrise, FL	3,769
45	Mesa, AZ	23,307	160	Pueblo, CO	6,945	346	Surprise, AZ	2,359
184	Mesquite, TX	5,870	362	Quincy, MA	1,989	136	Syracuse, NY	8,192
126	Miami Beach, FL	8,697	217	Racine, WI	5,069	58	Tacoma, WA	18,616
137	Miami Gardens, FL	8,149	70	Raleigh, NC	14,873	120	Tallahassee, FL	9,324
40	Miami, FL	26,219	243	Rancho Cucamon., CA	4,328	48	Tampa, FL	22,628
250	Midland, TX	4,085	197	Reading, PA	5,638	308	Temecula, CA	3,097
17	Milwaukee, WI	45,931	268	Redding, CA	3,777	85	Tempe, AZ	13,683
NA	Minneapolis, MN**	NA	96	Reno, NV	12,275	216	Thornton, CO	5,077
269	Miramar, FL	3,774	288	Rialto, CA	3,416	363	Thousand Oaks, CA	1,976
374	Mission Viejo, CA	1,469	290	Richardson, TX	3,352	41	Toledo, OH	26,172
61	Mobile, AL	17,016	164	Richmond, CA	6,719	358	Toms River Twnshp, NJ	2,070
90	Modesto, CA	13,222	98	Richmond, VA	12,133	118	Topeka, KS	9,417
79	Montgomery, AL	14,270	78	Riverside, CA	14,281	283	Torrance, CA	3,525
142	Moreno Valley, CA	7,867	177	Roanoke, VA	6,248	314	Tracy, CA	2,959
219	Murfreesboro, TN	5,030	NA	Rochester, MN**	NA	272	Trenton, NJ	3,751
355	Murrieta, CA	2,087	65	Rochester, NY	15,665	353	Troy, MI	2,111
336	Napa, CA	2,500	91	Rockford, IL	13,081	NA	Tucson, AZ**	NA
NA	Naperville, IL**	NA	248	Roseville, CA	4,262	37	Tulsa, OK	28,827
341	Nashua, NH	2,431	344	Roswell, GA	2,396	188	Tuscaloosa, AL	5,838
22	Nashville, TN	41,190	357	Round Rock, TX	2,072	224	Tyler, TX	4,876
245	New Bedford, MA	4,283	35	Sacramento, CA	31,668	339	Upper Darby Twnshp, PA	2,468
74	New Orleans, LA	14,433	123	Salem, OR	8,958	327	Vacaville, CA	2,664
1	New York, NY	205,522	154	Salinas, CA	7,141	152	Vallejo, CA	7,177
77	Newark, NJ	14,295	62	Salt Lake City, UT	16,914	156	Vancouver, WA	7,125
335	Newport Beach, CA	2,561	222	San Angelo, TX	4,953	255	Ventura, CA	4,021
122	Newport News, VA	9,000	6	San Antonio, TX	86,598	232	Victorville, CA	4,717
377	Newton, MA	1,198	100	San Bernardino, CA	11,777	82	Virginia Beach, VA	14,111
87	Norfolk, VA	13,527	14	San Diego, CA	51,600	149	Visalia, CA	7,337
266	Norman, OK	3,793	20	San Francisco, CA	43,525	293	Vista, CA	3,284
124	North Charleston, SC	8,951	38	San Jose, CA	27,801	131	Waco, TX	8,464
113	North Las Vegas, NV	10,312	228	San Leandro, CA	4,846	193	Warren, MI	5,725
302	Norwalk, CA	3,169	321	San Mateo, CA	2,813	351	Warwick, RI	2,234
34	Oakland, CA	31,943	291	Sandy, UT	3,312	31	Washington, DC	34,423
191	Oceanside, CA	5,809	107	Santa Ana, CA	10,628	168	Waterbury, CT	6,447
247	Odessa, TX	4,268	316	Santa Barbara, CA	2,941	239	West Covina, CA	4,449
203	Ogden, UT	5,444	282	Santa Clara, CA	3,534	284	West Jordan, UT	3,502
26	Oklahoma City, OK	38,593	262	Santa Clarita, CA	3,836	127	West Palm Beach, FL	8,506
334	Olathe, KS	2,565	305	Santa Maria, CA	3,152	176	West Valley, UT	6,256
43	Omaha, NE	24,292	259	Santa Monica, CA	3,904	307	Westland, MI	3,125
148	Ontario, CA	7,348	215	Santa Rosa, CA	5,103	319	Westminster, CA	2,908
278	Orange, CA	3,589	105	Savannah, GA	11,108	233	Westminster, CO	4,651
331	Orem, UT	2,624	125	Scottsdale, AZ	8,820	309	Whittier, CA	3,073
49	Orlando, FL	22,618	19	Seattle, WA	43,684	163	Wichita Falls, TX	6,776
226	Overland Park, KS	4,873	69	Shreveport, LA	14,942	47	Wichita, KS	22,881
211	Oxnard, CA	5,217	350	Simi Valley, CA	2,259	157	Wilmington, NC	7,064
273	Palm Bay, FL	3,742	267	Sioux City, IA	3,782	66	Winston-Salem, NC	15,103
212	Palmdale, CA	5,201	254	Sioux Falls, SD	4,022	310	Woodbridge Twnshp, NJ	3,064
366	Parma, OH	1,812	349	Somerville, MA	2,276	153	Worcester, MA	7,167
221	Pasadena, CA	5,009	135	South Bend, IN	8,216	145	Yakima, WA	7,608
202	Pasadena, TX	5,468	294	South Gate, CA	3,270	238	Yonkers, NY	4,480
180	Paterson, NJ	6,032	234	Southfield, MI	4,645	186	Youngstown, OH	5,847
210	Pembroke Pines, FL	5,249	263	Sparks, NV	3,832	235	Yuma, AZ	4,608

Source: CQ Press using data from F.B.I. "Crime in the United States 2006"

**Includes murder, rape, robbery, aggravated assault, burglary, larceny-theft, and motor vehicle theft.*

***Not available.*

41. Crimes in 2006 (continued)

National Total = 11,401,313 Crimes*

RANK	CITY	CRIMES
1	New York, NY	205,522
2	Houston, TX	145,303
3	Los Angeles, CA	135,985
4	Phoenix, AZ	101,244
5	Dallas, TX	100,650
6	San Antonio, TX	86,598
7	Philadelphia, PA	85,495
8	Detroit, MI	83,732
9	Las Vegas, NV	74,336
10	Memphis, TN	70,449
11	Columbus, OH	58,046
12	Indianapolis, IN	57,288
13	Charlotte, NC	56,418
14	San Diego, CA	51,600
15	Jacksonville, FL	49,766
16	St. Louis, MO	49,356
17	Milwaukee, WI	45,931
18	Austin, TX	45,231
19	Seattle, WA	43,684
20	San Francisco, CA	43,525
21	Baltimore, MD	43,137
22	Nashville, TN	41,190
23	Honolulu, HI	41,055
24	Fort Worth, TX	40,682
25	Atlanta, GA	39,779
26	Oklahoma City, OK	38,593
27	Kansas City, MO	37,571
28	Albuquerque, NM	36,307
29	Portland, OR	35,868
30	Cleveland, OH	35,224
31	Washington, DC	34,423
32	Louisville, KY	32,972
33	Boston, MA	32,627
34	Oakland, CA	31,943
35	Sacramento, CA	31,668
36	Denver, CO	30,591
37	Tulsa, OK	28,827
38	San Jose, CA	27,801
39	Fresno, CA	26,931
40	Miami, FL	26,219
41	Toledo, OH	26,172
42	Cincinnati, OH	25,873
43	Omaha, NE	24,292
44	Stockton, CA	24,007
45	Mesa, AZ	23,307
46	El Paso, TX	22,989
47	Wichita, KS	22,881
48	Tampa, FL	22,628
49	Orlando, FL	22,618
50	Arlington, TX	22,394
51	Birmingham, AL	22,182
52	Corpus Christi, TX	21,208
53	Colorado Springs, CO	20,221
54	St. Petersburg, FL	20,162
55	Buffalo, NY	19,393
56	Little Rock, AR	19,113
57	Pittsburgh, PA	18,709
58	Tacoma, WA	18,616
59	Baton Rouge, LA	17,638
60	Bakersfield, CA	17,490
61	Mobile, AL	17,016
62	Salt Lake City, UT	16,914
63	Greensboro, NC	16,398
64	Long Beach, CA	16,198
65	Rochester, NY	15,665
66	Winston-Salem, NC	15,103
67	Columbus, GA	15,012
68	Jackson, MS	14,944
69	Shreveport, LA	14,942
70	Raleigh, NC	14,873
71	Des Moines, IA	14,811
72	Aurora, CO	14,663
73	Lubbock, TX	14,542
74	New Orleans, LA	14,433
75	Fayetteville, NC	14,390
76	Anchorage, AK	14,313
77	Newark, NJ	14,295
78	Riverside, CA	14,281
79	Montgomery, AL	14,270
80	Chattanooga, TN	14,210
81	Springfield, MO	14,162
82	Virginia Beach, VA	14,111
83	Durham, NC	13,823
84	Laredo, TX	13,709
85	Tempe, AZ	13,683
86	Glendale, AZ	13,633
87	Norfolk, VA	13,527
88	Lincoln, NE	13,493
89	Dayton, OH	13,480
90	Modesto, CA	13,222
91	Rockford, IL	13,081
92	Spokane, WA	13,001
93	Knoxville, TN	12,957
94	Huntsville, AL	12,934
95	Amarillo, TX	12,703
96	Reno, NV	12,275
97	Lexington, KY	12,149
98	Richmond, VA	12,133
99	Grand Rapids, MI	12,026
100	San Bernardino, CA	11,777
101	Fort Lauderdale, FL	11,620
102	Kansas City, KS	11,526
103	Fort Wayne, IN	11,475
104	Flint, MI	11,187
105	Savannah, GA	11,108
106	Springfield, MA	11,007
107	Santa Ana, CA	10,628
108	Irving, TX	10,494
109	Jersey City, NJ	10,480
110	Hartford, CT	10,414
111	Anaheim, CA	10,341
112	Macon, GA	10,339
113	North Las Vegas, NV	10,312
114	Hialeah, FL	9,937
115	Chandler, AZ	9,683
116	Everett, WA	9,665
117	Providence, RI	9,557
118	Topeka, KS	9,417
119	Plano, TX	9,361
120	Tallahassee, FL	9,324
121	Brownsville, TX	9,252
122	Newport News, VA	9,000
123	Salem, OR	8,958
124	North Charleston, SC	8,951
125	Scottsdale, AZ	8,820
126	Miami Beach, FL	8,697
127	West Palm Beach, FL	8,506
128	Bridgeport, CT	8,496
129	Eugene, OR	8,483
130	Madison, WI	8,471
131	Waco, TX	8,464
132	Garland, TX	8,460
133	Independence, MO	8,421
134	Columbia, SC	8,284
135	South Bend, IN	8,216
136	Syracuse, NY	8,192
137	Miami Gardens, FL	8,149
138	Beaumont, TX	8,117
139	Chula Vista, CA	7,981
140	Berkeley, CA	7,969
140	Grand Prairie, TX	7,969
142	Moreno Valley, CA	7,867
143	Chesapeake, VA	7,851
144	Lakewood, CO	7,697
145	Yakima, WA	7,608
146	Lafayette, LA	7,535
147	Boise, ID	7,388
148	Ontario, CA	7,348
149	Visalia, CA	7,337
150	McAllen, TX	7,309
151	Henderson, NV	7,262
152	Vallejo, CA	7,177
153	Worcester, MA	7,167
154	Salinas, CA	7,141
155	Allentown, PA	7,140
156	Vancouver, WA	7,125
157	Wilmington, NC	7,064
158	Canton, OH	7,035
159	Hollywood, FL	6,992
160	Pueblo, CO	6,945
161	Gainesville, FL	6,853
162	Kent, WA	6,815
163	Wichita Falls, TX	6,776
164	Richmond, CA	6,719
165	Hayward, CA	6,512
166	Pomona, CA	6,482
167	Camden, NJ	6,480
168	Waterbury, CT	6,447
169	Fort Smith, AR	6,367
170	Pompano Beach, FL	6,352
171	High Point, NC	6,351
172	Lancaster, CA	6,301
173	Cedar Rapids, IA	6,273
174	Gary, IN	6,271
175	Killeen, TX	6,258
176	West Valley, UT	6,256
177	Roanoke, VA	6,248
178	Albany, NY	6,037
179	Peoria, AZ	6,036
180	Paterson, NJ	6,032
181	Athens-Clarke, GA	6,007
182	Portsmouth, VA	5,915
183	Concord, CA	5,906
184	Mesquite, TX	5,870
185	Fremont, CA	5,867
186	Evansville, IN	5,847
186	Youngstown, OH	5,847
188	Tuscaloosa, AL	5,838
189	Albany, GA	5,832
190	Lansing, MI	5,829
191	Oceanside, CA	5,809
192	Lakeland, FL	5,751

RANK	CITY	CRIMES
193	Warren, MI	5,725
194	Clearwater, FL	5,699
195	Elizabeth, NJ	5,668
196	Lawton, OK	5,656
197	Reading, PA	5,638
198	Longview, TX	5,621
199	Abilene, TX	5,599
200	Bellingham, WA	5,530
201	Federal Way, WA	5,513
202	Pasadena, TX	5,468
203	Ogden, UT	5,444
204	Hampton, VA	5,432
205	Lawrence, KS	5,414
206	Dearborn, MI	5,403
207	Charleston, SC	5,318
208	Cape Coral, FL	5,314
209	Clarksville, TN	5,265
210	Pembroke Pines, FL	5,249
211	Oxnard, CA	5,217
212	Palmdale, CA	5,201
213	Gilbert, AZ	5,189
214	Escondido, CA	5,120
215	Santa Rosa, CA	5,103
216	Thornton, CO	5,077
217	Racine, WI	5,069
218	Fort Collins, CO	5,063
219	Murfreesboro, TN	5,030
220	Fairfield, CA	5,017
221	Pasadena, CA	5,009
222	San Angelo, TX	4,953
223	Melbourne, FL	4,894
224	Tyler, TX	4,876
225	Huntington Beach, CA	4,875
226	Overland Park, KS	4,873
227	Garden Grove, CA	4,860
228	San Leandro, CA	4,846
229	Fullerton, CA	4,806
229	Hammond, IN	4,806
231	Greeley, CO	4,791
232	Victorville, CA	4,717
233	Westminster, CO	4,651
234	Southfield, MI	4,645
235	Yuma, AZ	4,608
236	Gresham, OR	4,588
237	Billings, MT	4,513
238	Yonkers, NY	4,480
239	West Covina, CA	4,449
240	Bellevue, WA	4,429
241	Las Cruces, NM	4,421
242	Corona, CA	4,370
243	Rancho Cucamon., CA	4,328
244	Glendale, CA	4,303
245	New Bedford, MA	4,283
246	Lowell, MA	4,272
247	Odessa, TX	4,268
248	Roseville, CA	4,262
249	Fontana, CA	4,172
250	El Cajon, CA	4,085
250	Midland, TX	4,085
252	Compton, CA	4,083
253	Downey, CA	4,067
254	Sioux Falls, SD	4,022
255	Ventura, CA	4,021
256	Carrollton, TX	4,011
257	Inglewood, CA	3,977
258	Plantation, FL	3,937
259	Santa Monica, CA	3,904
260	Port St. Lucie, FL	3,903
261	Lynn, MA	3,852
262	Santa Clarita, CA	3,836
263	Sparks, NV	3,832
264	El Monte, CA	3,827
265	Spokane Valley, WA	3,823
266	Norman, OK	3,793
267	Sioux City, IA	3,782
268	Redding, CA	3,777
269	Miramar, FL	3,774
270	Sunrise, FL	3,769
271	Manchester, NH	3,767
272	Trenton, NJ	3,751
273	Palm Bay, FL	3,742
274	Cambridge, MA	3,741
275	Costa Mesa, CA	3,686
276	Sterling Heights, MI	3,671
277	Alexandria, VA	3,642
278	Orange, CA	3,589
279	Columbia, MO	3,565
280	Carson, CA	3,561
281	Erie, PA	3,541
282	Santa Clara, CA	3,534
283	Torrance, CA	3,525
284	West Jordan, UT	3,502
285	Antioch, CA	3,501
286	Denton, TX	3,497
287	Green Bay, WI	3,432
288	Rialto, CA	3,416
289	Arvada, CO	3,395
290	Richardson, TX	3,352
291	Sandy, UT	3,312
292	Clovis, CA	3,302
293	Vista, CA	3,284
294	South Gate, CA	3,270
295	Ann Arbor, MI	3,267
296	Lewisville, TX	3,259
297	Kenosha, WI	3,256
298	Boulder, CO	3,245
299	Coral Springs, FL	3,241
300	Boca Raton, FL	3,189
301	Largo, FL	3,172
302	Norwalk, CA	3,169
303	Davie, FL	3,160
303	Irvine, CA	3,160
305	Deerfield Beach, FL	3,152
305	Santa Maria, CA	3,152
307	Westland, MI	3,125
308	Temecula, CA	3,097
309	Whittier, CA	3,073
310	Woodbridge Twnshp, NJ	3,064
311	Provo, UT	3,028
312	Colonie, NY	2,984
313	Burbank, CA	2,973
314	Tracy, CA	2,959
315	Hillsboro, OR	2,944
316	Santa Barbara, CA	2,941
317	Fargo, ND	2,910
317	Suffolk, VA	2,910
319	Westminster, CA	2,908
320	Sunnyvale, CA	2,816
321	San Mateo, CA	2,813
322	Clinton Twnshp, MI	2,789
323	Carlsbad, CA	2,784
324	Alhambra, CA	2,769
325	Hawthorne, CA	2,724
326	Bellflower, CA	2,693
327	Vacaville, CA	2,664
328	Lakewood, CA	2,662
329	Cheektowaga, NY	2,640
330	Daly City, CA	2,633
331	Orem, UT	2,624
332	Chino, CA	2,618
333	Edison Twnshp, NJ	2,615
334	Olathe, KS	2,565
335	Newport Beach, CA	2,561
336	Napa, CA	2,500
337	Livonia, MI	2,485
338	McKinney, TX	2,481
339	Upper Darby Twnshp, PA	2,468
340	Lee's Summit, MO	2,440
341	Nashua, NH	2,431
342	Greece, NY	2,418
343	Beaverton, OR	2,413
344	Roswell, GA	2,396
345	Baldwin Park, CA	2,369
346	Surprise, AZ	2,359
347	Cary, NC	2,320
348	Hesperia, CA	2,281
349	Somerville, MA	2,276
350	Simi Valley, CA	2,259
351	Buena Park, CA	2,234
351	Warwick, RI	2,234
353	Troy, MI	2,111
354	Clifton, NJ	2,090
355	Murrieta, CA	2,087
356	Hamilton Twnshp, NJ	2,079
357	Round Rock, TX	2,072
358	Toms River Twnshp, NJ	2,070
359	Edmond, OK	2,052
360	Amherst, NY	2,004
360	Cranston, RI	2,004
362	Quincy, MA	1,989
363	Thousand Oaks, CA	1,976
364	Broken Arrow, OK	1,851
365	Livermore, CA	1,850
366	Parma, OH	1,812
367	Canton Twnshp, MI	1,810
368	Centennial, CO	1,798
369	Danbury, CT	1,733
370	Sugar Land, TX	1,710
371	Farmington Hills, MI	1,687
372	Clarkstown, NY	1,668
373	Brick Twnshp, NJ	1,546
374	Mission Viejo, CA	1,469
375	Chino Hills, CA	1,341
376	Lake Forest, CA	1,201
377	Newton, MA	1,198
NA	Aurora, IL**	NA
NA	Bloomington, MN**	NA
NA	Brockton, MA**	NA
NA	Chicago, IL**	NA
NA	Duluth, MN**	NA
NA	Joliet, IL**	NA
NA	Minneapolis, MN**	NA
NA	Naperville, IL**	NA
NA	Peoria, IL**	NA
NA	Rochester, MN**	NA
NA	Springfield, IL**	NA
NA	St. Paul, MN**	NA
NA	Tucson, AZ**	NA

Source: CQ Press using data from F.B.I. "Crime in the United States 2006"

**Includes murder, rape, robbery, aggravated assault, burglary, larceny-theft, and motor vehicle theft.*

***Not available.*

42. Crime Rate in 2006

National Rate = 3,808.0 Crimes per 100,000 Population*

RANK	CITY	RATE
179	Abilene, TX	4,744.6
52	Albany, GA	7,494.7
100	Albany, NY	6,437.9
60	Albuquerque, NM	7,247.6
331	Alexandria, VA	2,664.5
296	Alhambra, CA	3,139.6
90	Allentown, PA	6,667.5
82	Amarillo, TX	6,749.4
371	Amherst, NY	1,784.8
300	Anaheim, CA	3,088.8
164	Anchorage, AK	5,154.3
317	Ann Arbor, MI	2,891.4
267	Antioch, CA	3,448.0
121	Arlington, TX	6,002.4
291	Arvada, CO	3,204.9
145	Athens-Clarke, GA	5,629.8
30	Atlanta, GA	8,188.3
175	Aurora, CO	4,841.6
NA	Aurora, IL**	NA
104	Austin, TX	6,372.2
127	Bakersfield, CA	5,865.2
309	Baldwin Park, CA	2,977.2
81	Baltimore, MD	6,766.0
26	Baton Rouge, LA	8,379.7
69	Beaumont, TX	7,060.3
328	Beaverton, OR	2,767.8
240	Bellevue, WA	3,717.2
257	Bellflower, CA	3,579.1
57	Bellingham, WA	7,292.8
43	Berkeley, CA	7,839.6
188	Billings, MT	4,528.1
10	Birmingham, AL	9,496.7
NA	Bloomington, MN**	NA
253	Boca Raton, FL	3,620.0
239	Boise, ID	3,727.3
133	Boston, MA	5,801.5
264	Boulder, CO	3,473.6
368	Brick Twnshp, NJ	1,976.6
116	Bridgeport, CT	6,121.4
NA	Brockton, MA**	NA
364	Broken Arrow, OK	2,127.9
151	Brownsville, TX	5,371.6
326	Buena Park, CA	2,796.4
75	Buffalo, NY	6,913.9
324	Burbank, CA	2,830.2
241	Cambridge, MA	3,713.6
32	Camden, NJ	8,092.8
367	Canton Twnshp, MI	2,108.0
18	Canton, OH	8,840.7
238	Cape Coral, FL	3,732.5
304	Carlsbad, CA	3,039.6
285	Carrollton, TX	3,281.3
236	Carson, CA	3,756.3
362	Cary, NC	2,137.0
169	Cedar Rapids, IA	5,068.1
370	Centennial, CO	1,796.2
223	Chandler, AZ	3,969.8
173	Charleston, SC	4,907.2
33	Charlotte, NC	8,066.7
17	Chattanooga, TN	9,066.5
289	Cheektowaga, NY	3,259.5
260	Chesapeake, VA	3,550.1
NA	Chicago, IL**	NA
372	Chino Hills, CA	1,755.1
279	Chino, CA	3,344.5
235	Chula Vista, CA	3,757.7
27	Cincinnati, OH	8,370.3
365	Clarkstown, NY	2,121.0
185	Clarksville, TN	4,605.7
163	Clearwater, FL	5,156.5
44	Cleveland, OH	7,779.9
333	Clifton, NJ	2,613.1
318	Clinton Twnshp, MI	2,887.6
233	Clovis, CA	3,782.1
226	Colonie, NY	3,857.4
155	Colorado Springs, CO	5,366.4
227	Columbia, MO	3,854.7
73	Columbia, SC	6,966.7
42	Columbus, GA	7,850.6
39	Columbus, OH	7,934.7
208	Compton, CA	4,230.2
178	Concord, CA	4,749.0
348	Coral Springs, FL	2,474.5
315	Corona, CA	2,899.2
58	Corpus Christi, TX	7,275.3
280	Costa Mesa, CA	3,326.1
347	Cranston, RI	2,475.2
34	Dallas, TX	8,063.5
335	Daly City, CA	2,600.7
357	Danbury, CT	2,204.5
247	Davie, FL	3,690.6
22	Dayton, OH	8,474.4
140	Dearborn, MI	5,756.7
218	Deerfield Beach, FL	4,060.0
288	Denton, TX	3,265.0
150	Denver, CO	5,381.3
50	Des Moines, IA	7,587.8
11	Detroit, MI	9,467.0
248	Downey, CA	3,673.7
NA	Duluth, MN**	NA
91	Durham, NC	6,616.0
336	Edison Twnshp, NJ	2,600.0
329	Edmond, OK	2,716.4
201	El Cajon, CA	4,377.4
298	El Monte, CA	3,095.9
237	El Paso, TX	3,734.7
192	Elizabeth, NJ	4,501.8
268	Erie, PA	3,447.8
232	Escondido, CA	3,784.4
136	Eugene, OR	5,775.3
171	Evansville, IN	5,010.9
8	Everett, WA	9,835.7
177	Fairfield, CA	4,759.2
292	Fargo, ND	3,204.2
366	Farmington Hills, MI	2,108.1
2	Fayetteville, NC	10,858.7
97	Federal Way, WA	6,523.0
12	Flint, MI	9,460.0
342	Fontana, CA	2,523.3
225	Fort Collins, CO	3,881.3
78	Fort Lauderdale, FL	6,827.1
49	Fort Smith, AR	7,632.3
166	Fort Wayne, IN	5,104.1
106	Fort Worth, TX	6,339.2
313	Fremont, CA	2,900.5
134	Fresno, CA	5,788.3
256	Fullerton, CA	3,587.0
111	Gainesville, FL	6,229.5
314	Garden Grove, CA	2,900.3
231	Garland, TX	3,802.6
108	Gary, IN	6,310.8
320	Gilbert, AZ	2,872.6
147	Glendale, AZ	5,484.2
363	Glendale, CA	2,131.6
153	Grand Prairie, TX	5,369.0
112	Grand Rapids, MI	6,221.5
339	Greece, NY	2,566.0
154	Greeley, CO	5,367.9
277	Green Bay, WI	3,378.8
74	Greensboro, NC	6,930.9
182	Gresham, OR	4,698.6
352	Hamilton Twnshp, NJ	2,308.4
120	Hammond, IN	6,026.9
246	Hampton, VA	3,694.5
24	Hartford, CT	8,384.7
295	Hawthorne, CA	3,150.3
186	Hayward, CA	4,600.3
305	Henderson, NV	3,027.0
316	Hesperia, CA	2,898.9
197	Hialeah, FL	4,432.1
96	High Point, NC	6,548.6
271	Hillsboro, OR	3,426.5
181	Hollywood, FL	4,721.6
193	Honolulu, HI	4,498.2
71	Houston, TX	7,006.8
346	Huntington Beach, CA	2,484.6
46	Huntsville, AL	7,707.2
51	Independence, MO	7,585.5
64	Indianapolis, IN	7,152.3
269	Inglewood, CA	3,443.3
373	Irvine, CA	1,676.1
158	Irving, TX	5,269.7
110	Jacksonville, FL	6,253.4
23	Jackson, MS	8,427.0
203	Jersey City, NJ	4,370.4
NA	Joliet, IL**	NA
38	Kansas City, KS	7,936.4
25	Kansas City, MO	8,382.3
273	Kenosha, WI	3,406.2
29	Kent, WA	8,190.5
117	Killeen, TX	6,071.4
66	Knoxville, TN	7,102.8
67	Lafayette, LA	7,095.8
375	Lake Forest, CA	1,557.7
103	Lakeland, FL	6,375.2
286	Lakewood, CA	3,278.6
152	Lakewood, CO	5,370.1
183	Lancaster, CA	4,659.2
170	Lansing, MI	5,058.6
102	Laredo, TX	6,386.1
211	Largo, FL	4,188.6
157	Las Cruces, NM	5,276.0
143	Las Vegas, NV	5,650.2
95	Lawrence, KS	6,570.9
113	Lawton, OK	6,213.3
308	Lee's Summit, MO	3,015.1
261	Lewisville, TX	3,507.8
194	Lexington, KY	4,496.6
146	Lincoln, NE	5,610.1
6	Little Rock, AR	10,238.9
350	Livermore, CA	2,338.4
340	Livonia, MI	2,542.6

RANK	CITY	RATE
276	Long Beach, CA	3,386.7
61	Longview, TX	7,229.4
262	Los Angeles, CA	3,505.3
159	Louisville, KY	5,266.9
214	Lowell, MA	4,118.4
83	Lubbock, TX	6,742.4
205	Lynn, MA	4,312.5
3	Macon, GA	10,621.0
230	Madison, WI	3,809.5
272	Manchester, NH	3,421.2
141	McAllen, TX	5,749.5
345	McKinney, TX	2,498.0
109	Melbourne, FL	6,279.3
5	Memphis, TN	10,347.5
168	Mesa, AZ	5,070.0
200	Mesquite, TX	4,394.3
9	Miami Beach, FL	9,727.3
35	Miami Gardens, FL	8,059.1
88	Miami, FL	6,672.6
221	Midland, TX	4,003.4
41	Milwaukee, WI	7,905.4
NA	Minneapolis, MN**	NA
263	Miramar, FL	3,480.9
376	Mission Viejo, CA	1,532.8
80	Mobile, AL	6,802.3
107	Modesto, CA	6,330.1
68	Montgomery, AL	7,066.6
202	Moreno Valley, CA	4,371.2
142	Murfreesboro, TN	5,722.6
344	Murrieta, CA	2,498.7
282	Napa, CA	3,313.2
NA	Naperville, IL**	NA
327	Nashua, NH	2,773.5
56	Nashville, TN	7,344.7
187	New Bedford, MA	4,572.9
278	New Orleans, LA	3,347.5
343	New York, NY	2,517.1
167	Newark, NJ	5,089.4
294	Newport Beach, CA	3,179.3
172	Newport News, VA	4,953.4
377	Newton, MA	1,432.0
137	Norfolk, VA	5,774.2
245	Norman, OK	3,696.3
7	North Charleston, SC	10,211.6
144	North Las Vegas, NV	5,649.2
310	Norwalk, CA	2,967.6
36	Oakland, CA	8,009.1
265	Oceanside, CA	3,465.9
196	Odessa, TX	4,436.7
84	Ogden, UT	6,732.5
63	Oklahoma City, OK	7,200.0
353	Olathe, KS	2,287.7
132	Omaha, NE	5,828.6
209	Ontario, CA	4,217.3
332	Orange, CA	2,635.8
323	Orem, UT	2,832.6
4	Orlando, FL	10,431.7
311	Overland Park, KS	2,936.0
325	Oxnard, CA	2,815.7
224	Palm Bay, FL	3,964.0
229	Palmdale, CA	3,830.4
356	Parma, OH	2,221.5
266	Pasadena, CA	3,453.9
244	Pasadena, TX	3,696.4
220	Paterson, NJ	4,022.5
270	Pembroke Pines, FL	3,432.6
210	Peoria, AZ	4,206.8
NA	Peoria, IL**	NA
129	Philadelphia, PA	5,837.5
89	Phoenix, AZ	6,672.0
139	Pittsburgh, PA	5,763.6
252	Plano, TX	3,639.8
191	Plantation, FL	4,502.6
212	Pomona, CA	4,177.3
122	Pompano Beach, FL	5,996.1
312	Port St. Lucie, FL	2,914.6
92	Portland, OR	6,615.6
128	Portsmouth, VA	5,846.8
149	Providence, RI	5,447.1
337	Provo, UT	2,584.6
94	Pueblo, CO	6,585.9
359	Quincy, MA	2,190.7
105	Racine, WI	6,361.5
206	Raleigh, NC	4,269.6
341	Rancho Cucamon., CA	2,532.8
72	Reading, PA	6,966.8
213	Redding, CA	4,175.9
130	Reno, NV	5,835.4
274	Rialto, CA	3,402.1
284	Richardson, TX	3,286.3
98	Richmond, CA	6,516.6
114	Richmond, VA	6,199.5
174	Riverside, CA	4,879.1
87	Roanoke, VA	6,678.5
NA	Rochester, MN**	NA
55	Rochester, NY	7,401.2
21	Rockford, IL	8,508.6
222	Roseville, CA	3,987.1
330	Roswell, GA	2,701.9
351	Round Rock, TX	2,334.3
76	Sacramento, CA	6,876.1
124	Salem, OR	5,925.0
176	Salinas, CA	4,833.2
16	Salt Lake City, UT	9,197.3
148	San Angelo, TX	5,472.4
85	San Antonio, TX	6,702.0
126	San Bernardino, CA	5,878.6
217	San Diego, CA	4,073.1
131	San Francisco, CA	5,833.8
306	San Jose, CA	3,020.0
115	San Leandro, CA	6,143.4
301	San Mateo, CA	3,060.9
259	Sandy, UT	3,577.2
299	Santa Ana, CA	3,094.6
275	Santa Barbara, CA	3,393.2
281	Santa Clara, CA	3,323.0
355	Santa Clarita, CA	2,259.6
243	Santa Maria, CA	3,703.6
199	Santa Monica, CA	4,406.8
283	Santa Rosa, CA	3,302.1
161	Savannah, GA	5,203.1
234	Scottsdale, AZ	3,758.8
53	Seattle, WA	7,483.1
40	Shreveport, LA	7,926.6
369	Simi Valley, CA	1,886.3
189	Sioux City, IA	4,524.5
321	Sioux Falls, SD	2,860.7
307	Somerville, MA	3,018.0
45	South Bend, IN	7,753.9
287	South Gate, CA	3,276.9
118	Southfield, MI	6,061.8
190	Sparks, NV	4,519.2
184	Spokane Valley, WA	4,618.4
99	Spokane, WA	6,494.0
NA	Springfield, IL**	NA
62	Springfield, MA	7,210.9
13	Springfield, MO	9,354.2
319	Sterling Heights, MI	2,874.4
28	Stockton, CA	8,292.3
1	St. Louis, MO	14,228.6
NA	St. Paul, MN**	NA
37	St. Petersburg, FL	7,960.4
251	Suffolk, VA	3,647.5
358	Sugar Land, TX	2,195.1
361	Sunnyvale, CA	2,165.1
215	Sunrise, FL	4,091.5
302	Surprise, AZ	3,053.5
138	Syracuse, NY	5,766.5
14	Tacoma, WA	9,342.4
135	Tallahassee, FL	5,785.1
79	Tampa, FL	6,826.2
258	Temecula, CA	3,577.4
31	Tempe, AZ	8,178.6
180	Thornton, CO	4,737.3
374	Thousand Oaks, CA	1,574.8
19	Toledo, OH	8,676.2
360	Toms River Twnshp, NJ	2,185.1
47	Topeka, KS	7,668.1
349	Torrance, CA	2,453.6
249	Tracy, CA	3,667.4
198	Trenton, NJ	4,428.4
334	Troy, MI	2,607.3
NA	Tucson, AZ**	NA
54	Tulsa, OK	7,471.3
65	Tuscaloosa, AL	7,111.4
162	Tyler, TX	5,157.6
297	Upper Darby Twnshp, PA	3,097.0
322	Vacaville, CA	2,839.4
119	Vallejo, CA	6,054.4
195	Vancouver, WA	4,447.6
228	Ventura, CA	3,831.2
165	Victorville, CA	5,122.4
293	Virginia Beach, VA	3,186.9
86	Visalia, CA	6,691.4
255	Vista, CA	3,600.2
77	Waco, TX	6,832.5
207	Warren, MI	4,241.6
338	Warwick, RI	2,581.5
125	Washington, DC	5,919.4
123	Waterbury, CT	5,984.2
216	West Covina, CA	4,075.7
242	West Jordan, UT	3,708.8
20	West Palm Beach, FL	8,579.6
156	West Valley, UT	5,347.4
250	Westland, MI	3,658.8
290	Westminster, CA	3,219.3
204	Westminster, CO	4,343.8
254	Whittier, CA	3,605.4
93	Wichita Falls, TX	6,599.5
101	Wichita, KS	6,402.6
59	Wilmington, NC	7,254.0
48	Winston-Salem, NC	7,642.4
303	Woodbridge Twnshp, NJ	3,044.1
219	Worcester, MA	4,050.2
15	Yakima, WA	9,209.7
354	Yonkers, NY	2,274.7
70	Youngstown, OH	7,049.8
160	Yuma, AZ	5,240.8

Source: CQ Press using data from F.B.I. "Crime in the United States 2006"

**Includes murder, rape, robbery, aggravated assault, burglary, larceny-theft, and motor vehicle theft.*

***Not available.*

42. Crime Rate in 2006 (continued)

National Rate = 3,808.0 Crimes per 100,000 Population*

RANK	CITY	RATE
1	St. Louis, MO	14,228.6
2	Fayetteville, NC	10,858.7
3	Macon, GA	10,621.0
4	Orlando, FL	10,431.7
5	Memphis, TN	10,347.5
6	Little Rock, AR	10,238.9
7	North Charleston, SC	10,211.6
8	Everett, WA	9,835.7
9	Miami Beach, FL	9,727.3
10	Birmingham, AL	9,496.7
11	Detroit, MI	9,467.0
12	Flint, MI	9,460.0
13	Springfield, MO	9,354.2
14	Tacoma, WA	9,342.4
15	Yakima, WA	9,209.7
16	Salt Lake City, UT	9,197.3
17	Chattanooga, TN	9,066.5
18	Canton, OH	8,840.7
19	Toledo, OH	8,676.2
20	West Palm Beach, FL	8,579.6
21	Rockford, IL	8,508.6
22	Dayton, OH	8,474.4
23	Jackson, MS	8,427.0
24	Hartford, CT	8,384.7
25	Kansas City, MO	8,382.3
26	Baton Rouge, LA	8,379.7
27	Cincinnati, OH	8,370.3
28	Stockton, CA	8,292.3
29	Kent, WA	8,190.5
30	Atlanta, GA	8,188.3
31	Tempe, AZ	8,178.6
32	Camden, NJ	8,092.8
33	Charlotte, NC	8,066.7
34	Dallas, TX	8,063.5
35	Miami Gardens, FL	8,059.1
36	Oakland, CA	8,009.1
37	St. Petersburg, FL	7,960.4
38	Kansas City, KS	7,936.4
39	Columbus, OH	7,934.7
40	Shreveport, LA	7,926.6
41	Milwaukee, WI	7,905.4
42	Columbus, GA	7,850.6
43	Berkeley, CA	7,839.6
44	Cleveland, OH	7,779.9
45	South Bend, IN	7,753.9
46	Huntsville, AL	7,707.2
47	Topeka, KS	7,668.1
48	Winston-Salem, NC	7,642.4
49	Fort Smith, AR	7,632.3
50	Des Moines, IA	7,587.8
51	Independence, MO	7,585.5
52	Albany, GA	7,494.7
53	Seattle, WA	7,483.1
54	Tulsa, OK	7,471.3
55	Rochester, NY	7,401.2
56	Nashville, TN	7,344.7
57	Bellingham, WA	7,292.8
58	Corpus Christi, TX	7,275.3
59	Wilmington, NC	7,254.0
60	Albuquerque, NM	7,247.6
61	Longview, TX	7,229.4
62	Springfield, MA	7,210.9
63	Oklahoma City, OK	7,200.0
64	Indianapolis, IN	7,152.3

RANK	CITY	RATE
65	Tuscaloosa, AL	7,111.4
66	Knoxville, TN	7,102.8
67	Lafayette, LA	7,095.8
68	Montgomery, AL	7,066.6
69	Beaumont, TX	7,060.3
70	Youngstown, OH	7,049.8
71	Houston, TX	7,006.8
72	Reading, PA	6,966.8
73	Columbia, SC	6,966.7
74	Greensboro, NC	6,930.9
75	Buffalo, NY	6,913.9
76	Sacramento, CA	6,876.1
77	Waco, TX	6,832.5
78	Fort Lauderdale, FL	6,827.1
79	Tampa, FL	6,826.2
80	Mobile, AL	6,802.3
81	Baltimore, MD	6,766.0
82	Amarillo, TX	6,749.4
83	Lubbock, TX	6,742.4
84	Ogden, UT	6,732.5
85	San Antonio, TX	6,702.0
86	Visalia, CA	6,691.4
87	Roanoke, VA	6,678.5
88	Miami, FL	6,672.6
89	Phoenix, AZ	6,672.0
90	Allentown, PA	6,667.5
91	Durham, NC	6,616.0
92	Portland, OR	6,615.6
93	Wichita Falls, TX	6,599.5
94	Pueblo, CO	6,585.9
95	Lawrence, KS	6,570.9
96	High Point, NC	6,548.6
97	Federal Way, WA	6,523.0
98	Richmond, CA	6,516.6
99	Spokane, WA	6,494.0
100	Albany, NY	6,437.9
101	Wichita, KS	6,402.6
102	Laredo, TX	6,386.1
103	Lakeland, FL	6,375.2
104	Austin, TX	6,372.2
105	Racine, WI	6,361.5
106	Fort Worth, TX	6,339.2
107	Modesto, CA	6,330.1
108	Gary, IN	6,310.8
109	Melbourne, FL	6,279.3
110	Jacksonville, FL	6,253.4
111	Gainesville, FL	6,229.5
112	Grand Rapids, MI	6,221.5
113	Lawton, OK	6,213.3
114	Richmond, VA	6,199.5
115	San Leandro, CA	6,143.4
116	Bridgeport, CT	6,121.4
117	Killeen, TX	6,071.4
118	Southfield, MI	6,061.8
119	Vallejo, CA	6,054.4
120	Hammond, IN	6,026.9
121	Arlington, TX	6,002.4
122	Pompano Beach, FL	5,996.1
123	Waterbury, CT	5,984.2
124	Salem, OR	5,925.0
125	Washington, DC	5,919.4
126	San Bernardino, CA	5,878.6
127	Bakersfield, CA	5,865.2
128	Portsmouth, VA	5,846.8

RANK	CITY	RATE
129	Philadelphia, PA	5,837.5
130	Reno, NV	5,835.4
131	San Francisco, CA	5,833.8
132	Omaha, NE	5,828.6
133	Boston, MA	5,801.5
134	Fresno, CA	5,788.3
135	Tallahassee, FL	5,785.1
136	Eugene, OR	5,775.3
137	Norfolk, VA	5,774.2
138	Syracuse, NY	5,766.5
139	Pittsburgh, PA	5,763.6
140	Dearborn, MI	5,756.7
141	McAllen, TX	5,749.5
142	Murfreesboro, TN	5,722.6
143	Las Vegas, NV	5,650.2
144	North Las Vegas, NV	5,649.2
145	Athens-Clarke, GA	5,629.8
146	Lincoln, NE	5,610.1
147	Glendale, AZ	5,484.2
148	San Angelo, TX	5,472.4
149	Providence, RI	5,447.1
150	Denver, CO	5,381.3
151	Brownsville, TX	5,371.6
152	Lakewood, CO	5,370.1
153	Grand Prairie, TX	5,369.0
154	Greeley, CO	5,367.9
155	Colorado Springs, CO	5,366.4
156	West Valley, UT	5,347.4
157	Las Cruces, NM	5,276.0
158	Irving, TX	5,269.7
159	Louisville, KY	5,266.9
160	Yuma, AZ	5,240.8
161	Savannah, GA	5,203.1
162	Tyler, TX	5,157.6
163	Clearwater, FL	5,156.5
164	Anchorage, AK	5,154.3
165	Victorville, CA	5,122.4
166	Fort Wayne, IN	5,104.1
167	Newark, NJ	5,089.4
168	Mesa, AZ	5,070.0
169	Cedar Rapids, IA	5,068.1
170	Lansing, MI	5,058.6
171	Evansville, IN	5,010.9
172	Newport News, VA	4,953.4
173	Charleston, SC	4,907.2
174	Riverside, CA	4,879.1
175	Aurora, CO	4,841.6
176	Salinas, CA	4,833.2
177	Fairfield, CA	4,759.2
178	Concord, CA	4,749.0
179	Abilene, TX	4,744.6
180	Thornton, CO	4,737.3
181	Hollywood, FL	4,721.6
182	Gresham, OR	4,698.6
183	Lancaster, CA	4,659.2
184	Spokane Valley, WA	4,618.4
185	Clarksville, TN	4,605.7
186	Hayward, CA	4,600.3
187	New Bedford, MA	4,572.9
188	Billings, MT	4,528.1
189	Sioux City, IA	4,524.5
190	Sparks, NV	4,519.2
191	Plantation, FL	4,502.6
192	Elizabeth, NJ	4,501.8

RANK	CITY	RATE
193	Honolulu, HI	4,498.2
194	Lexington, KY	4,496.6
195	Vancouver, WA	4,447.6
196	Odessa, TX	4,436.7
197	Hialeah, FL	4,432.1
198	Trenton, NJ	4,428.4
199	Santa Monica, CA	4,406.8
200	Mesquite, TX	4,394.3
201	El Cajon, CA	4,377.4
202	Moreno Valley, CA	4,371.2
203	Jersey City, NJ	4,370.4
204	Westminster, CO	4,343.8
205	Lynn, MA	4,312.5
206	Raleigh, NC	4,269.6
207	Warren, MI	4,241.6
208	Compton, CA	4,230.2
209	Ontario, CA	4,217.3
210	Peoria, AZ	4,206.8
211	Largo, FL	4,188.6
212	Pomona, CA	4,177.3
213	Redding, CA	4,175.9
214	Lowell, MA	4,118.4
215	Sunrise, FL	4,091.5
216	West Covina, CA	4,075.7
217	San Diego, CA	4,073.1
218	Deerfield Beach, FL	4,060.0
219	Worcester, MA	4,050.2
220	Paterson, NJ	4,022.5
221	Midland, TX	4,003.4
222	Roseville, CA	3,987.1
223	Chandler, AZ	3,969.8
224	Palm Bay, FL	3,964.0
225	Fort Collins, CO	3,881.3
226	Colonie, NY	3,857.4
227	Columbia, MO	3,854.7
228	Ventura, CA	3,831.2
229	Palmdale, CA	3,830.4
230	Madison, WI	3,809.5
231	Garland, TX	3,802.6
232	Escondido, CA	3,784.4
233	Clovis, CA	3,782.1
234	Scottsdale, AZ	3,758.8
235	Chula Vista, CA	3,757.7
236	Carson, CA	3,756.3
237	El Paso, TX	3,734.7
238	Cape Coral, FL	3,732.5
239	Boise, ID	3,727.3
240	Bellevue, WA	3,717.2
241	Cambridge, MA	3,713.6
242	West Jordan, UT	3,708.8
243	Santa Maria, CA	3,703.6
244	Pasadena, TX	3,696.4
245	Norman, OK	3,696.3
246	Hampton, VA	3,694.5
247	Davie, FL	3,690.6
248	Downey, CA	3,673.7
249	Tracy, CA	3,667.4
250	Westland, MI	3,658.8
251	Suffolk, VA	3,647.5
252	Plano, TX	3,639.8
253	Boca Raton, FL	3,620.0
254	Whittier, CA	3,605.4
255	Vista, CA	3,600.2
256	Fullerton, CA	3,587.0
257	Bellflower, CA	3,579.1
258	Temecula, CA	3,577.4
259	Sandy, UT	3,577.2
260	Chesapeake, VA	3,550.1
261	Lewisville, TX	3,507.8
262	Los Angeles, CA	3,505.3
263	Miramar, FL	3,480.9
264	Boulder, CO	3,473.6
265	Oceanside, CA	3,465.9
266	Pasadena, CA	3,453.9
267	Antioch, CA	3,448.0
268	Erie, PA	3,447.8
269	Inglewood, CA	3,443.3
270	Pembroke Pines, FL	3,432.6
271	Hillsboro, OR	3,426.5
272	Manchester, NH	3,421.2
273	Kenosha, WI	3,406.2
274	Rialto, CA	3,402.1
275	Santa Barbara, CA	3,393.2
276	Long Beach, CA	3,386.7
277	Green Bay, WI	3,378.8
278	New Orleans, LA	3,347.5
279	Chino, CA	3,344.5
280	Costa Mesa, CA	3,326.1
281	Santa Clara, CA	3,323.0
282	Napa, CA	3,313.2
283	Santa Rosa, CA	3,302.1
284	Richardson, TX	3,286.3
285	Carrollton, TX	3,281.3
286	Lakewood, CA	3,278.6
287	South Gate, CA	3,276.9
288	Denton, TX	3,265.0
289	Cheektowaga, NY	3,259.5
290	Westminster, CA	3,219.3
291	Arvada, CO	3,204.9
292	Fargo, ND	3,204.2
293	Virginia Beach, VA	3,186.9
294	Newport Beach, CA	3,179.3
295	Hawthorne, CA	3,150.3
296	Alhambra, CA	3,139.6
297	Upper Darby Twnshp, PA	3,097.0
298	El Monte, CA	3,095.9
299	Santa Ana, CA	3,094.6
300	Anaheim, CA	3,088.8
301	San Mateo, CA	3,060.9
302	Surprise, AZ	3,053.5
303	Woodbridge Twnshp, NJ	3,044.1
304	Carlsbad, CA	3,039.6
305	Henderson, NV	3,027.0
306	San Jose, CA	3,020.0
307	Somerville, MA	3,018.0
308	Lee's Summit, MO	3,015.1
309	Baldwin Park, CA	2,977.2
310	Norwalk, CA	2,967.6
311	Overland Park, KS	2,936.0
312	Port St. Lucie, FL	2,914.6
313	Fremont, CA	2,900.5
314	Garden Grove, CA	2,900.3
315	Corona, CA	2,899.2
316	Hesperia, CA	2,898.9
317	Ann Arbor, MI	2,891.4
318	Clinton Twnshp, MI	2,887.6
319	Sterling Heights, MI	2,874.4
320	Gilbert, AZ	2,872.6
321	Sioux Falls, SD	2,860.7
322	Vacaville, CA	2,839.4
323	Orem, UT	2,832.6
324	Burbank, CA	2,830.2
325	Oxnard, CA	2,815.7
326	Buena Park, CA	2,796.4
327	Nashua, NH	2,773.5
328	Beaverton, OR	2,767.8
329	Edmond, OK	2,716.4
330	Roswell, GA	2,701.9
331	Alexandria, VA	2,664.5
332	Orange, CA	2,635.8
333	Clifton, NJ	2,613.1
334	Troy, MI	2,607.3
335	Daly City, CA	2,600.7
336	Edison Twnshp, NJ	2,600.0
337	Provo, UT	2,584.6
338	Warwick, RI	2,581.5
339	Greece, NY	2,566.0
340	Livonia, MI	2,542.6
341	Rancho Cucamon., CA	2,532.8
342	Fontana, CA	2,523.3
343	New York, NY	2,517.1
344	Murrieta, CA	2,498.7
345	McKinney, TX	2,498.0
346	Huntington Beach, CA	2,484.6
347	Cranston, RI	2,475.2
348	Coral Springs, FL	2,474.5
349	Torrance, CA	2,453.6
350	Livermore, CA	2,338.4
351	Round Rock, TX	2,334.3
352	Hamilton Twnshp, NJ	2,308.4
353	Olathe, KS	2,287.7
354	Yonkers, NY	2,274.7
355	Santa Clarita, CA	2,259.6
356	Parma, OH	2,221.5
357	Danbury, CT	2,204.5
358	Sugar Land, TX	2,195.1
359	Quincy, MA	2,190.7
360	Toms River Twnshp, NJ	2,185.1
361	Sunnyvale, CA	2,165.1
362	Cary, NC	2,137.0
363	Glendale, CA	2,131.6
364	Broken Arrow, OK	2,127.9
365	Clarkstown, NY	2,121.0
366	Farmington Hills, MI	2,108.1
367	Canton Twnshp, MI	2,108.0
368	Brick Twnshp, NJ	1,976.6
369	Simi Valley, CA	1,886.3
370	Centennial, CO	1,796.2
371	Amherst, NY	1,784.8
372	Chino Hills, CA	1,755.1
373	Irvine, CA	1,676.1
374	Thousand Oaks, CA	1,574.8
375	Lake Forest, CA	1,557.7
376	Mission Viejo, CA	1,532.8
377	Newton, MA	1,432.0
NA	Aurora, IL**	NA
NA	Bloomington, MN**	NA
NA	Brockton, MA**	NA
NA	Chicago, IL**	NA
NA	Duluth, MN**	NA
NA	Joliet, IL**	NA
NA	Minneapolis, MN**	NA
NA	Naperville, IL**	NA
NA	Peoria, IL**	NA
NA	Rochester, MN**	NA
NA	Springfield, IL**	NA
NA	St. Paul, MN**	NA
NA	Tucson, AZ**	NA

Source: CQ Press using data from F.B.I. "Crime in the United States 2006"

**Includes murder, rape, robbery, aggravated assault, burglary, larceny-theft, and motor vehicle theft.*

***Not available.*

43. Percent Change in Crime Rate: 2005 to 2006

National Percent Change = 2.4% Decrease*

RANK	CITY	% CHANGE
276	Abilene, TX	(8.9)
45	Albany, GA	6.6
144	Albany, NY	(1.3)
92	Albuquerque, NM	1.9
267	Alexandria, VA	(8.6)
221	Alhambra, CA	(5.0)
39	Allentown, PA	7.5
256	Amarillo, TX	(7.3)
151	Amherst, NY	(1.6)
253	Anaheim, CA	(6.7)
47	Anchorage, AK	6.2
314	Ann Arbor, MI	(12.1)
104	Antioch, CA	0.9
196	Arlington, TX	(3.7)
343	Arvada, CO	(18.2)
121	Athens-Clarke, GA	0.0
271	Atlanta, GA	(8.7)
317	Aurora, CO	(13.5)
NA	Aurora, IL**	NA
162	Austin, TX	(2.0)
257	Bakersfield, CA	(7.6)
196	Baldwin Park, CA	(3.7)
172	Baltimore, MD	(2.5)
25	Baton Rouge, LA	10.2
325	Beaumont, TX	(14.7)
361	Beaverton, OR	(26.1)
276	Bellevue, WA	(8.9)
302	Bellflower, CA	(11.1)
243	Bellingham, WA	(6.1)
245	Berkeley, CA	(6.3)
356	Billings, MT	(22.5)
130	Birmingham, AL	(0.4)
NA	Bloomington, MN**	NA
245	Boca Raton, FL	(6.3)
307	Boise, ID	(11.7)
106	Boston, MA	0.7
331	Boulder, CO	(15.4)
16	Brick Twnshp, NJ	12.6
133	Bridgeport, CT	(0.5)
NA	Brockton, MA**	NA
348	Broken Arrow, OK	(19.9)
215	Brownsville, TX	(4.5)
117	Buena Park, CA	0.1
228	Buffalo, NY	(5.2)
154	Burbank, CA	(1.7)
159	Cambridge, MA	(1.9)
34	Camden, NJ	8.3
86	Canton Twnshp, MI	2.1
54	Canton, OH	5.2
13	Cape Coral, FL	14.6
84	Carlsbad, CA	2.2
298	Carrollton, TX	(10.5)
11	Carson, CA	16.3
57	Cary, NC	5.0
271	Cedar Rapids, IA	(8.7)
351	Centennial, CO	(20.1)
110	Chandler, AZ	0.5
286	Charleston, SC	(9.4)
115	Charlotte, NC	0.2
142	Chattanooga, TN	(1.2)
185	Cheektowaga, NY	(3.3)
321	Chesapeake, VA	(14.0)
NA	Chicago, IL**	NA
17	Chino Hills, CA	12.1
254	Chino, CA	(6.9)
259	Chula Vista, CA	(7.9)
106	Cincinnati, OH	0.7
NA	Clarkstown, NY**	NA
98	Clarksville, TN	1.2
238	Clearwater, FL	(5.7)
86	Cleveland, OH	2.1
94	Clifton, NJ	1.7
51	Clinton Twnshp, MI	5.6
275	Clovis, CA	(8.8)
124	Colonie, NY	(0.1)
243	Colorado Springs, CO	(6.1)
154	Columbia, MO	(1.7)
271	Columbia, SC	(8.7)
61	Columbus, GA	4.5
201	Columbus, OH	(3.8)
238	Compton, CA	(5.7)
310	Concord, CA	(12.0)
15	Coral Springs, FL	13.3
301	Corona, CA	(11.0)
245	Corpus Christi, TX	(6.3)
299	Costa Mesa, CA	(10.9)
267	Cranston, RI	(8.6)
221	Dallas, TX	(5.0)
38	Daly City, CA	7.8
95	Danbury, CT	1.3
293	Davie, FL	(9.9)
61	Dayton, OH	4.5
117	Dearborn, MI	0.1
305	Deerfield Beach, FL	(11.6)
363	Denton, TX	(27.3)
354	Denver, CO	(20.9)
NA	Des Moines, IA**	NA
14	Detroit, MI	13.4
82	Downey, CA	2.5
NA	Duluth, MN**	NA
NA	Durham, NC**	NA
177	Edison Twnshp, NJ	(2.9)
154	Edmond, OK	(1.7)
283	El Cajon, CA	(9.2)
285	El Monte, CA	(9.3)
NA	El Paso, TX**	NA
185	Elizabeth, NJ	(3.3)
39	Erie, PA	7.5
259	Escondido, CA	(7.9)
344	Eugene, OR	(18.4)
280	Evansville, IN	(9.0)
8	Everett, WA	17.7
144	Fairfield, CA	(1.3)
2	Fargo, ND	19.4
245	Farmington Hills, MI	(6.3)
7	Fayetteville, NC	18.1
335	Federal Way, WA	(16.9)
30	Flint, MI	8.8
271	Fontana, CA	(8.7)
82	Fort Collins, CO	2.5
290	Fort Lauderdale, FL	(9.7)
128	Fort Smith, AR	(0.3)
NA	Fort Wayne, IN**	NA
235	Fort Worth, TX	(5.5)
23	Fremont, CA	11.0
286	Fresno, CA	(9.4)
182	Fullerton, CA	(3.1)
4	Gainesville, FL	18.7
254	Garden Grove, CA	(6.9)
231	Garland, TX	(5.3)
58	Gary, IN	4.8
126	Gilbert, AZ	(0.2)
185	Glendale, AZ	(3.3)
64	Glendale, CA	4.3
185	Grand Prairie, TX	(3.3)
71	Grand Rapids, MI	3.6
6	Greece, NY	18.2
357	Greeley, CO	(23.5)
115	Green Bay, WI	0.2
117	Greensboro, NC	0.1
355	Gresham, OR	(22.4)
17	Hamilton Twnshp, NJ	12.1
262	Hammond, IN	(8.0)
267	Hampton, VA	(8.6)
212	Hartford, CT	(4.3)
106	Hawthorne, CA	0.7
45	Hayward, CA	6.6
135	Henderson, NV	(0.7)
221	Hesperia, CA	(5.0)
110	Hialeah, FL	0.5
240	High Point, NC	(5.9)
359	Hillsboro, OR	(25.4)
206	Hollywood, FL	(4.0)
282	Honolulu, HI	(9.1)
135	Houston, TX	(0.7)
44	Huntington Beach, CA	6.9
121	Huntsville, AL	0.0
235	Independence, MO	(5.5)
148	Indianapolis, IN	(1.4)
192	Inglewood, CA	(3.6)
299	Irvine, CA	(10.9)
130	Irving, TX	(0.4)
137	Jacksonville, FL	(0.8)
12	Jackson, MS	14.9
307	Jersey City, NJ	(11.7)
NA	Joliet, IL**	NA
172	Kansas City, KS	(2.5)
NA	Kansas City, MO**	NA
89	Kenosha, WI	2.0
84	Kent, WA	2.2
297	Killeen, TX	(10.3)
121	Knoxville, TN	0.0
32	Lafayette, LA	8.5
24	Lake Forest, CA	10.6
56	Lakeland, FL	5.1
330	Lakewood, CA	(15.3)
322	Lakewood, CO	(14.5)
79	Lancaster, CA	2.6
201	Lansing, MI	(3.8)
169	Laredo, TX	(2.4)
48	Largo, FL	5.7
196	Las Cruces, NM	(3.7)
98	Las Vegas, NV	1.2
1	Lawrence, KS	43.2
70	Lawton, OK	3.7
105	Lee's Summit, MO	0.8
349	Lewisville, TX	(20.0)
NA	Lexington, KY**	NA
228	Lincoln, NE	(5.2)
180	Little Rock, AR	(3.0)
89	Livermore, CA	2.0
92	Livonia, MI	1.9

RANK	CITY	% CHANGE	RANK	CITY	% CHANGE	RANK	CITY	% CHANGE
203	Long Beach, CA	(3.9)	264	Peoria, AZ	(8.1)	296	Spokane Valley, WA	(10.2)
209	Longview, TX	(4.1)	NA	Peoria, IL**	NA	174	Spokane, WA	(2.6)
280	Los Angeles, CA	(9.0)	58	Philadelphia, PA	4.8	NA	Springfield, IL**	NA
58	Louisville, KY	4.8	240	Phoenix, AZ	(5.9)	206	Springfield, MA	(4.0)
141	Lowell, MA	(1.1)	112	Pittsburgh, PA	0.3	63	Springfield, MO	4.4
225	Lubbock, TX	(5.1)	189	Plano, TX	(3.4)	10	Sterling Heights, MI	17.5
196	Lynn, MA	(3.7)	52	Plantation, FL	5.4	95	Stockton, CA	1.3
76	Macon, GA	3.3	124	Pomona, CA	(0.1)	48	St. Louis, MO	5.7
151	Madison, WI	(1.6)	339	Pompano Beach, FL	(17.8)	NA	St. Paul, MN**	NA
149	Manchester, NH	(1.5)	5	Port St. Lucie, FL	18.3	117	St. Petersburg, FL	0.1
340	McAllen, TX	(18.0)	319	Portland, OR	(13.9)	307	Suffolk, VA	(11.7)
157	McKinney, TX	(1.8)	177	Portsmouth, VA	(2.9)	332	Sugar Land, TX	(15.5)
20	Melbourne, FL	11.5	250	Providence, RI	(6.5)	192	Sunnyvale, CA	(3.6)
98	Memphis, TN	1.2	357	Provo, UT	(23.5)	43	Sunrise, FL	7.0
315	Mesa, AZ	(13.0)	292	Pueblo, CO	(9.8)	151	Surprise, AZ	(1.6)
209	Mesquite, TX	(4.1)	20	Quincy, MA	11.5	79	Syracuse, NY	2.6
217	Miami Beach, FL	(4.6)	73	Racine, WI	3.5	144	Tacoma, WA	(1.3)
164	Miami Gardens, FL	(2.3)	176	Raleigh, NC	(2.7)	276	Tallahassee, FL	(8.9)
310	Miami, FL	(12.0)	325	Rancho Cucamon., CA	(14.7)	295	Tampa, FL	(10.1)
214	Midland, TX	(4.4)	250	Reading, PA	(6.5)	203	Temecula, CA	(3.9)
2	Milwaukee, WI	19.4	349	Redding, CA	(20.0)	103	Tempe, AZ	1.0
NA	Minneapolis, MN**	NA	215	Reno, NV	(4.5)	237	Thornton, CO	(5.6)
164	Miramar, FL	(2.3)	352	Rialto, CA	(20.5)	98	Thousand Oaks, CA	1.2
32	Mission Viejo, CA	8.5	303	Richardson, TX	(11.3)	183	Toledo, OH	(3.2)
27	Mobile, AL	9.5	203	Richmond, CA	(3.9)	67	Toms River Twnshp, NJ	4.2
265	Modesto, CA	(8.3)	353	Richmond, VA	(20.8)	286	Topeka, KS	(9.4)
169	Montgomery, AL	(2.4)	259	Riverside, CA	(7.9)	164	Torrance, CA	(2.3)
64	Moreno Valley, CA	4.3	319	Roanoke, VA	(13.9)	338	Tracy, CA	(17.7)
102	Murfreesboro, TN	1.1	NA	Rochester, MN**	NA	360	Trenton, NJ	(25.5)
183	Murrieta, CA	(3.2)	128	Rochester, NY	(0.3)	77	Troy, MI	3.0
86	Napa, CA	2.1	NA	Rockford, IL**	NA	NA	Tucson, AZ**	NA
NA	Naperville, IL**	NA	346	Roseville, CA	(18.7)	212	Tulsa, OK	(4.3)
26	Nashua, NH	9.8	221	Roswell, GA	(5.0)	71	Tuscaloosa, AL	3.6
267	Nashville, TN	(8.6)	334	Round Rock, TX	(16.3)	304	Tyler, TX	(11.5)
73	New Bedford, MA	3.5	112	Sacramento, CA	0.3	41	Upper Darby Twnshp, PA	7.3
NA	New Orleans, LA**	NA	290	Salem, OR	(9.7)	180	Vacaville, CA	(3.0)
240	New York, NY	(5.9)	258	Salinas, CA	(7.7)	NA	Vallejo, CA**	NA
262	Newark, NJ	(8.0)	138	Salt Lake City, UT	(0.9)	344	Vancouver, WA	(18.4)
164	Newport Beach, CA	(2.3)	322	San Angelo, TX	(14.5)	217	Ventura, CA	(4.6)
231	Newport News, VA	(5.3)	233	San Antonio, TX	(5.4)	266	Victorville, CA	(8.5)
144	Newton, MA	(1.3)	322	San Bernardino, CA	(14.5)	157	Virginia Beach, VA	(1.8)
250	Norfolk, VA	(6.5)	159	San Diego, CA	(1.9)	293	Visalia, CA	(9.9)
29	Norman, OK	9.1	31	San Francisco, CA	8.6	228	Vista, CA	(5.2)
138	North Charleston, SC	(0.9)	68	San Jose, CA	4.1	333	Waco, TX	(15.8)
69	North Las Vegas, NV	3.8	37	San Leandro, CA	8.0	NA	Warren, MI**	NA
190	Norwalk, CA	(3.5)	305	San Mateo, CA	(11.6)	337	Warwick, RI	(17.6)
19	Oakland, CA	11.7	163	Sandy, UT	(2.2)	140	Washington, DC	(1.0)
310	Oceanside, CA	(12.0)	310	Santa Ana, CA	(12.0)	109	Waterbury, CT	0.6
177	Odessa, TX	(2.9)	327	Santa Barbara, CA	(14.8)	95	West Covina, CA	1.3
78	Ogden, UT	2.8	192	Santa Clara, CA	(3.6)	NA	West Jordan, UT**	NA
340	Oklahoma City, OK	(18.0)	192	Santa Clarita, CA	(3.6)	133	West Palm Beach, FL	(0.5)
364	Olathe, KS	(32.1)	48	Santa Maria, CA	5.7	342	West Valley, UT	(18.1)
149	Omaha, NE	(1.5)	196	Santa Monica, CA	(3.7)	35	Westland, MI	8.2
225	Ontario, CA	(5.1)	318	Santa Rosa, CA	(13.7)	289	Westminster, CA	(9.5)
174	Orange, CA	(2.6)	328	Savannah, GA	(14.9)	329	Westminster, CO	(15.0)
362	Orem, UT	(26.9)	54	Scottsdale, AZ	5.2	42	Whittier, CA	7.1
130	Orlando, FL	(0.4)	276	Seattle, WA	(8.9)	347	Wichita Falls, TX	(19.2)
225	Overland Park, KS	(5.1)	64	Shreveport, LA	4.3	NA	Wichita, KS**	NA
126	Oxnard, CA	(0.2)	283	Simi Valley, CA	(9.2)	249	Wilmington, NC	(6.4)
209	Palm Bay, FL	(4.1)	219	Sioux City, IA	(4.7)	35	Winston-Salem, NC	8.2
159	Palmdale, CA	(1.9)	335	Sioux Falls, SD	(16.9)	142	Woodbridge Twnshp, NJ	(1.2)
315	Parma, OH	(13.0)	9	Somerville, MA	17.6	220	Worcester, MA	(4.8)
190	Pasadena, CA	(3.5)	22	South Bend, IN	11.1	233	Yakima, WA	(5.4)
164	Pasadena, TX	(2.3)	206	South Gate, CA	(4.0)	79	Yonkers, NY	2.6
73	Paterson, NJ	3.5	112	Southfield, MI	0.3	169	Youngstown, OH	(2.4)
28	Pembroke Pines, FL	9.2	52	Sparks, NV	5.4	89	Yuma, AZ	2.0

Source: CQ Press using data from F.B.I. "Crime in the United States 2006"

**Includes murder, rape, robbery, aggravated assault, burglary, larceny-theft, and motor vehicle theft.*

***Not available.*

43. Percent Change in Crime Rate: 2005 to 2006 (continued)

National Percent Change = 2.4% Decrease*

RANK	CITY	% CHANGE
1	Lawrence, KS	43.2
2	Fargo, ND	19.4
2	Milwaukee, WI	19.4
4	Gainesville, FL	18.7
5	Port St. Lucie, FL	18.3
6	Greece, NY	18.2
7	Fayetteville, NC	18.1
8	Everett, WA	17.7
9	Somerville, MA	17.6
10	Sterling Heights, MI	17.5
11	Carson, CA	16.3
12	Jackson, MS	14.9
13	Cape Coral, FL	14.6
14	Detroit, MI	13.4
15	Coral Springs, FL	13.3
16	Brick Twnshp, NJ	12.6
17	Chino Hills, CA	12.1
17	Hamilton Twnshp, NJ	12.1
19	Oakland, CA	11.7
20	Melbourne, FL	11.5
20	Quincy, MA	11.5
22	South Bend, IN	11.1
23	Fremont, CA	11.0
24	Lake Forest, CA	10.6
25	Baton Rouge, LA	10.2
26	Nashua, NH	9.8
27	Mobile, AL	9.5
28	Pembroke Pines, FL	9.2
29	Norman, OK	9.1
30	Flint, MI	8.8
31	San Francisco, CA	8.6
32	Lafayette, LA	8.5
32	Mission Viejo, CA	8.5
34	Camden, NJ	8.3
35	Westland, MI	8.2
35	Winston-Salem, NC	8.2
37	San Leandro, CA	8.0
38	Daly City, CA	7.8
39	Allentown, PA	7.5
39	Erie, PA	7.5
41	Upper Darby Twnshp, PA	7.3
42	Whittier, CA	7.1
43	Sunrise, FL	7.0
44	Huntington Beach, CA	6.9
45	Albany, GA	6.6
45	Hayward, CA	6.6
47	Anchorage, AK	6.2
48	Largo, FL	5.7
48	Santa Maria, CA	5.7
48	St. Louis, MO	5.7
51	Clinton Twnshp, MI	5.6
52	Plantation, FL	5.4
52	Sparks, NV	5.4
54	Canton, OH	5.2
54	Scottsdale, AZ	5.2
56	Lakeland, FL	5.1
57	Cary, NC	5.0
58	Gary, IN	4.8
58	Louisville, KY	4.8
58	Philadelphia, PA	4.8
61	Columbus, GA	4.5
61	Dayton, OH	4.5
63	Springfield, MO	4.4
64	Glendale, CA	4.3
64	Moreno Valley, CA	4.3
64	Shreveport, LA	4.3
67	Toms River Twnshp, NJ	4.2
68	San Jose, CA	4.1
69	North Las Vegas, NV	3.8
70	Lawton, OK	3.7
71	Grand Rapids, MI	3.6
71	Tuscaloosa, AL	3.6
73	New Bedford, MA	3.5
73	Paterson, NJ	3.5
73	Racine, WI	3.5
76	Macon, GA	3.3
77	Troy, MI	3.0
78	Ogden, UT	2.8
79	Lancaster, CA	2.6
79	Syracuse, NY	2.6
79	Yonkers, NY	2.6
82	Downey, CA	2.5
82	Fort Collins, CO	2.5
84	Carlsbad, CA	2.2
84	Kent, WA	2.2
86	Canton Twnshp, MI	2.1
86	Cleveland, OH	2.1
86	Napa, CA	2.1
89	Kenosha, WI	2.0
89	Livermore, CA	2.0
89	Yuma, AZ	2.0
92	Albuquerque, NM	1.9
92	Livonia, MI	1.9
94	Clifton, NJ	1.7
95	Danbury, CT	1.3
95	Stockton, CA	1.3
95	West Covina, CA	1.3
98	Clarksville, TN	1.2
98	Las Vegas, NV	1.2
98	Memphis, TN	1.2
98	Thousand Oaks, CA	1.2
102	Murfreesboro, TN	1.1
103	Tempe, AZ	1.0
104	Antioch, CA	0.9
105	Lee's Summit, MO	0.8
106	Boston, MA	0.7
106	Cincinnati, OH	0.7
106	Hawthorne, CA	0.7
109	Waterbury, CT	0.6
110	Chandler, AZ	0.5
110	Hialeah, FL	0.5
112	Pittsburgh, PA	0.3
112	Sacramento, CA	0.3
112	Southfield, MI	0.3
115	Charlotte, NC	0.2
115	Green Bay, WI	0.2
117	Buena Park, CA	0.1
117	Dearborn, MI	0.1
117	Greensboro, NC	0.1
117	St. Petersburg, FL	0.1
121	Athens-Clarke, GA	0.0
121	Huntsville, AL	0.0
121	Knoxville, TN	0.0
124	Colonie, NY	(0.1)
124	Pomona, CA	(0.1)
126	Gilbert, AZ	(0.2)
126	Oxnard, CA	(0.2)
128	Fort Smith, AR	(0.3)
128	Rochester, NY	(0.3)
130	Birmingham, AL	(0.4)
130	Irving, TX	(0.4)
130	Orlando, FL	(0.4)
133	Bridgeport, CT	(0.5)
133	West Palm Beach, FL	(0.5)
135	Henderson, NV	(0.7)
135	Houston, TX	(0.7)
137	Jacksonville, FL	(0.8)
138	North Charleston, SC	(0.9)
138	Salt Lake City, UT	(0.9)
140	Washington, DC	(1.0)
141	Lowell, MA	(1.1)
142	Chattanooga, TN	(1.2)
142	Woodbridge Twnshp, NJ	(1.2)
144	Albany, NY	(1.3)
144	Fairfield, CA	(1.3)
144	Newton, MA	(1.3)
144	Tacoma, WA	(1.3)
148	Indianapolis, IN	(1.4)
149	Manchester, NH	(1.5)
149	Omaha, NE	(1.5)
151	Amherst, NY	(1.6)
151	Madison, WI	(1.6)
151	Surprise, AZ	(1.6)
154	Burbank, CA	(1.7)
154	Columbia, MO	(1.7)
154	Edmond, OK	(1.7)
157	McKinney, TX	(1.8)
157	Virginia Beach, VA	(1.8)
159	Cambridge, MA	(1.9)
159	Palmdale, CA	(1.9)
159	San Diego, CA	(1.9)
162	Austin, TX	(2.0)
163	Sandy, UT	(2.2)
164	Miami Gardens, FL	(2.3)
164	Miramar, FL	(2.3)
164	Newport Beach, CA	(2.3)
164	Pasadena, TX	(2.3)
164	Torrance, CA	(2.3)
169	Laredo, TX	(2.4)
169	Montgomery, AL	(2.4)
169	Youngstown, OH	(2.4)
172	Baltimore, MD	(2.5)
172	Kansas City, KS	(2.5)
174	Orange, CA	(2.6)
174	Spokane, WA	(2.6)
176	Raleigh, NC	(2.7)
177	Edison Twnshp, NJ	(2.9)
177	Odessa, TX	(2.9)
177	Portsmouth, VA	(2.9)
180	Little Rock, AR	(3.0)
180	Vacaville, CA	(3.0)
182	Fullerton, CA	(3.1)
183	Murrieta, CA	(3.2)
183	Toledo, OH	(3.2)
185	Cheektowaga, NY	(3.3)
185	Elizabeth, NJ	(3.3)
185	Glendale, AZ	(3.3)
185	Grand Prairie, TX	(3.3)
189	Plano, TX	(3.4)
190	Norwalk, CA	(3.5)
190	Pasadena, CA	(3.5)
192	Inglewood, CA	(3.6)

RANK	CITY	% CHANGE
192	Santa Clara, CA	(3.6)
192	Santa Clarita, CA	(3.6)
192	Sunnyvale, CA	(3.6)
196	Arlington, TX	(3.7)
196	Baldwin Park, CA	(3.7)
196	Las Cruces, NM	(3.7)
196	Lynn, MA	(3.7)
196	Santa Monica, CA	(3.7)
201	Columbus, OH	(3.8)
201	Lansing, MI	(3.8)
203	Long Beach, CA	(3.9)
203	Richmond, CA	(3.9)
203	Temecula, CA	(3.9)
206	Hollywood, FL	(4.0)
206	South Gate, CA	(4.0)
206	Springfield, MA	(4.0)
209	Longview, TX	(4.1)
209	Mesquite, TX	(4.1)
209	Palm Bay, FL	(4.1)
212	Hartford, CT	(4.3)
212	Tulsa, OK	(4.3)
214	Midland, TX	(4.4)
215	Brownsville, TX	(4.5)
215	Reno, NV	(4.5)
217	Miami Beach, FL	(4.6)
217	Ventura, CA	(4.6)
219	Sioux City, IA	(4.7)
220	Worcester, MA	(4.8)
221	Alhambra, CA	(5.0)
221	Dallas, TX	(5.0)
221	Hesperia, CA	(5.0)
221	Roswell, GA	(5.0)
225	Lubbock, TX	(5.1)
225	Ontario, CA	(5.1)
225	Overland Park, KS	(5.1)
228	Buffalo, NY	(5.2)
228	Lincoln, NE	(5.2)
228	Vista, CA	(5.2)
231	Garland, TX	(5.3)
231	Newport News, VA	(5.3)
233	San Antonio, TX	(5.4)
233	Yakima, WA	(5.4)
235	Fort Worth, TX	(5.5)
235	Independence, MO	(5.5)
237	Thornton, CO	(5.6)
238	Clearwater, FL	(5.7)
238	Compton, CA	(5.7)
240	High Point, NC	(5.9)
240	New York, NY	(5.9)
240	Phoenix, AZ	(5.9)
243	Bellingham, WA	(6.1)
243	Colorado Springs, CO	(6.1)
245	Berkeley, CA	(6.3)
245	Boca Raton, FL	(6.3)
245	Corpus Christi, TX	(6.3)
245	Farmington Hills, MI	(6.3)
249	Wilmington, NC	(6.4)
250	Norfolk, VA	(6.5)
250	Providence, RI	(6.5)
250	Reading, PA	(6.5)
253	Anaheim, CA	(6.7)
254	Chino, CA	(6.9)
254	Garden Grove, CA	(6.9)
256	Amarillo, TX	(7.3)
257	Bakersfield, CA	(7.6)
258	Salinas, CA	(7.7)
259	Chula Vista, CA	(7.9)
259	Escondido, CA	(7.9)
259	Riverside, CA	(7.9)
262	Hammond, IN	(8.0)
262	Newark, NJ	(8.0)
264	Peoria, AZ	(8.1)
265	Modesto, CA	(8.3)
266	Victorville, CA	(8.5)
267	Alexandria, VA	(8.6)
267	Cranston, RI	(8.6)
267	Hampton, VA	(8.6)
267	Nashville, TN	(8.6)
271	Atlanta, GA	(8.7)
271	Cedar Rapids, IA	(8.7)
271	Columbia, SC	(8.7)
271	Fontana, CA	(8.7)
275	Clovis, CA	(8.8)
276	Abilene, TX	(8.9)
276	Bellevue, WA	(8.9)
276	Seattle, WA	(8.9)
276	Tallahassee, FL	(8.9)
280	Evansville, IN	(9.0)
280	Los Angeles, CA	(9.0)
282	Honolulu, HI	(9.1)
283	El Cajon, CA	(9.2)
283	Simi Valley, CA	(9.2)
285	El Monte, CA	(9.3)
286	Charleston, SC	(9.4)
286	Fresno, CA	(9.4)
286	Topeka, KS	(9.4)
289	Westminster, CA	(9.5)
290	Fort Lauderdale, FL	(9.7)
290	Salem, OR	(9.7)
292	Pueblo, CO	(9.8)
293	Davie, FL	(9.9)
293	Visalia, CA	(9.9)
295	Tampa, FL	(10.1)
296	Spokane Valley, WA	(10.2)
297	Killeen, TX	(10.3)
298	Carrollton, TX	(10.5)
299	Costa Mesa, CA	(10.9)
299	Irvine, CA	(10.9)
301	Corona, CA	(11.0)
302	Bellflower, CA	(11.1)
303	Richardson, TX	(11.3)
304	Tyler, TX	(11.5)
305	Deerfield Beach, FL	(11.6)
305	San Mateo, CA	(11.6)
307	Boise, ID	(11.7)
307	Jersey City, NJ	(11.7)
307	Suffolk, VA	(11.7)
310	Concord, CA	(12.0)
310	Miami, FL	(12.0)
310	Oceanside, CA	(12.0)
310	Santa Ana, CA	(12.0)
314	Ann Arbor, MI	(12.1)
315	Mesa, AZ	(13.0)
315	Parma, OH	(13.0)
317	Aurora, CO	(13.5)
318	Santa Rosa, CA	(13.7)
319	Portland, OR	(13.9)
319	Roanoke, VA	(13.9)
321	Chesapeake, VA	(14.0)
322	Lakewood, CO	(14.5)
322	San Angelo, TX	(14.5)
322	San Bernardino, CA	(14.5)
325	Beaumont, TX	(14.7)
325	Rancho Cucamon., CA	(14.7)
327	Santa Barbara, CA	(14.8)
328	Savannah, GA	(14.9)
329	Westminster, CO	(15.0)
330	Lakewood, CA	(15.3)
331	Boulder, CO	(15.4)
332	Sugar Land, TX	(15.5)
333	Waco, TX	(15.8)
334	Round Rock, TX	(16.3)
335	Federal Way, WA	(16.9)
335	Sioux Falls, SD	(16.9)
337	Warwick, RI	(17.6)
338	Tracy, CA	(17.7)
339	Pompano Beach, FL	(17.8)
340	McAllen, TX	(18.0)
340	Oklahoma City, OK	(18.0)
342	West Valley, UT	(18.1)
343	Arvada, CO	(18.2)
344	Eugene, OR	(18.4)
344	Vancouver, WA	(18.4)
346	Roseville, CA	(18.7)
347	Wichita Falls, TX	(19.2)
348	Broken Arrow, OK	(19.9)
349	Lewisville, TX	(20.0)
349	Redding, CA	(20.0)
351	Centennial, CO	(20.1)
352	Rialto, CA	(20.5)
353	Richmond, VA	(20.8)
354	Denver, CO	(20.9)
355	Gresham, OR	(22.4)
356	Billings, MT	(22.5)
357	Greeley, CO	(23.5)
357	Provo, UT	(23.5)
359	Hillsboro, OR	(25.4)
360	Trenton, NJ	(25.5)
361	Beaverton, OR	(26.1)
362	Orem, UT	(26.9)
363	Denton, TX	(27.3)
364	Olathe, KS	(32.1)
NA	Aurora, IL**	NA
NA	Bloomington, MN**	NA
NA	Brockton, MA**	NA
NA	Chicago, IL**	NA
NA	Clarkstown, NY**	NA
NA	Des Moines, IA**	NA
NA	Duluth, MN**	NA
NA	Durham, NC**	NA
NA	El Paso, TX**	NA
NA	Fort Wayne, IN**	NA
NA	Joliet, IL**	NA
NA	Kansas City, MO**	NA
NA	Lexington, KY**	NA
NA	Minneapolis, MN**	NA
NA	Naperville, IL**	NA
NA	New Orleans, LA**	NA
NA	Peoria, IL**	NA
NA	Rochester, MN**	NA
NA	Rockford, IL**	NA
NA	Springfield, IL**	NA
NA	St. Paul, MN**	NA
NA	Tucson, AZ**	NA
NA	Vallejo, CA**	NA
NA	Warren, MI**	NA
NA	West Jordan, UT**	NA
NA	Wichita, KS**	NA

Source: CQ Press using data from F.B.I. "Crime in the United States 2006"

**Includes murder, rape, robbery, aggravated assault, burglary, larceny-theft, and motor vehicle theft.*

***Not available.*

44. Percent Change in Crime Rate: 2002 to 2006

National Percent Change = 7.7% Decrease*

RANK	CITY	% CHANGE
59	Abilene, TX	6.5
31	Albany, GA	11.0
NA	Albany, NY**	NA
166	Albuquerque, NM	(7.3)
333	Alexandria, VA	(31.8)
49	Alhambra, CA	7.7
16	Allentown, PA	20.1
184	Amarillo, TX	(9.1)
83	Amherst, NY	3.1
235	Anaheim, CA	(13.9)
98	Anchorage, AK	0.8
205	Ann Arbor, MI	(10.5)
150	Antioch, CA	(5.3)
213	Arlington, TX	(11.5)
265	Arvada, CO	(17.3)
216	Athens-Clarke, GA	(11.7)
319	Atlanta, GA	(27.9)
295	Aurora, CO	(22.4)
NA	Aurora, IL**	NA
91	Austin, TX	1.7
8	Bakersfield, CA	26.8
12	Baldwin Park, CA	22.7
278	Baltimore, MD	(18.7)
95	Baton Rouge, LA	1.1
283	Beaumont, TX	(19.6)
342	Beaverton, OR	(35.3)
194	Bellevue, WA	(9.6)
178	Bellflower, CA	(8.5)
115	Bellingham, WA	(1.3)
278	Berkeley, CA	(18.7)
252	Billings, MT	(15.4)
42	Birmingham, AL	9.4
NA	Bloomington, MN**	NA
123	Boca Raton, FL	(2.1)
273	Boise, ID	(18.0)
134	Boston, MA	(3.1)
174	Boulder, CO	(7.9)
44	Brick Twnshp, NJ	8.9
93	Bridgeport, CT	1.5
NA	Brockton, MA**	NA
324	Broken Arrow, OK	(29.3)
348	Brownsville, TX	(38.6)
142	Buena Park, CA	(4.3)
50	Buffalo, NY	7.4
178	Burbank, CA	(8.5)
213	Cambridge, MA	(11.5)
48	Camden, NJ	7.8
121	Canton Twnshp, MI	(2.0)
NA	Canton, OH**	NA
126	Cape Coral, FL	(2.3)
46	Carlsbad, CA	8.5
226	Carrollton, TX	(12.4)
94	Carson, CA	1.4
166	Cary, NC	(7.3)
249	Cedar Rapids, IA	(15.1)
NA	Centennial, CO**	NA
338	Chandler, AZ	(33.5)
330	Charleston, SC	(30.6)
50	Charlotte, NC	7.4
189	Chattanooga, TN	(9.4)
NA	Cheektowaga, NY**	NA
261	Chesapeake, VA	(16.9)
NA	Chicago, IL**	NA
352	Chino Hills, CA	(50.4)
1	Chino, CA	103.1
189	Chula Vista, CA	(9.4)
144	Cincinnati, OH	(4.5)
292	Clarkstown, NY	(21.3)
277	Clarksville, TN	(18.6)
201	Clearwater, FL	(10.4)
26	Cleveland, OH	12.7
285	Clifton, NJ	(20.1)
70	Clinton Twnshp, MI	5.2
263	Clovis, CA	(17.2)
72	Colonie, NY	5.0
164	Colorado Springs, CO	(7.0)
235	Columbia, MO	(13.9)
281	Columbia, SC	(19.5)
10	Columbus, GA	23.2
239	Columbus, OH	(14.3)
192	Compton, CA	(9.5)
62	Concord, CA	5.9
295	Coral Springs, FL	(22.4)
250	Corona, CA	(15.2)
111	Corpus Christi, TX	(0.7)
121	Costa Mesa, CA	(2.0)
308	Cranston, RI	(23.9)
207	Dallas, TX	(10.7)
7	Daly City, CA	27.0
306	Danbury, CT	(23.7)
290	Davie, FL	(21.0)
208	Dayton, OH	(11.1)
102	Dearborn, MI	0.2
3	Deerfield Beach, FL	42.2
323	Denton, TX	(29.2)
129	Denver, CO	(2.7)
NA	Des Moines, IA**	NA
54	Detroit, MI	7.1
28	Downey, CA	12.0
NA	Duluth, MN**	NA
NA	Durham, NC**	NA
100	Edison Twnshp, NJ	0.6
57	Edmond, OK	6.7
197	El Cajon, CA	(9.9)
77	El Monte, CA	3.6
NA	El Paso, TX**	NA
298	Elizabeth, NJ	(22.5)
97	Erie, PA	0.9
146	Escondido, CA	(4.6)
218	Eugene, OR	(11.9)
101	Evansville, IN	0.3
4	Everett, WA	37.4
211	Fairfield, CA	(11.3)
223	Fargo, ND	(12.2)
129	Farmington Hills, MI	(2.7)
6	Fayetteville, NC	28.2
91	Federal Way, WA	1.7
11	Flint, MI	23.0
294	Fontana, CA	(21.8)
200	Fort Collins, CO	(10.2)
162	Fort Lauderdale, FL	(6.9)
263	Fort Smith, AR	(17.2)
NA	Fort Wayne, IN**	NA
290	Fort Worth, TX	(21.0)
52	Fremont, CA	7.2
310	Fresno, CA	(24.3)
120	Fullerton, CA	(1.8)
79	Gainesville, FL	3.4
178	Garden Grove, CA	(8.5)
219	Garland, TX	(12.0)
25	Gary, IN	13.0
345	Gilbert, AZ	(36.6)
267	Glendale, AZ	(17.5)
148	Glendale, CA	(5.0)
196	Grand Prairie, TX	(9.8)
38	Grand Rapids, MI	10.2
NA	Greece, NY**	NA
273	Greeley, CO	(18.0)
161	Green Bay, WI	(6.8)
61	Greensboro, NC	6.0
322	Gresham, OR	(29.1)
176	Hamilton Twnshp, NJ	(8.1)
155	Hammond, IN	(6.0)
201	Hampton, VA	(10.4)
147	Hartford, CT	(4.7)
201	Hawthorne, CA	(10.4)
14	Hayward, CA	21.2
106	Henderson, NV	(0.1)
192	Hesperia, CA	(9.5)
238	Hialeah, FL	(14.1)
189	High Point, NC	(9.4)
340	Hillsboro, OR	(34.2)
311	Hollywood, FL	(25.0)
324	Honolulu, HI	(29.3)
141	Houston, TX	(4.2)
30	Huntington Beach, CA	11.4
15	Huntsville, AL	21.0
89	Independence, MO	2.7
18	Indianapolis, IN	18.6
123	Inglewood, CA	(2.1)
331	Irvine, CA	(31.4)
128	Irving, TX	(2.5)
152	Jacksonville, FL	(5.7)
210	Jackson, MS	(11.2)
222	Jersey City, NJ	(12.1)
NA	Joliet, IL**	NA
NA	Kansas City, KS**	NA
NA	Kansas City, MO**	NA
27	Kenosha, WI	12.1
24	Kent, WA	14.4
251	Killeen, TX	(15.3)
72	Knoxville, TN	5.0
162	Lafayette, LA	(6.9)
224	Lake Forest, CA	(12.3)
127	Lakeland, FL	(2.4)
231	Lakewood, CA	(13.3)
188	Lakewood, CO	(9.3)
29	Lancaster, CA	11.9
172	Lansing, MI	(7.7)
184	Laredo, TX	(9.1)
107	Largo, FL	(0.4)
NA	Las Cruces, NM**	NA
22	Las Vegas, NV	14.7
5	Lawrence, KS	35.0
64	Lawton, OK	5.8
62	Lee's Summit, MO	5.9
337	Lewisville, TX	(32.7)
NA	Lexington, KY**	NA
246	Lincoln, NE	(14.8)
176	Little Rock, AR	(8.1)
281	Livermore, CA	(19.5)
164	Livonia, MI	(7.0)

RANK	CITY	% CHANGE
257	Long Beach, CA	(16.1)
138	Longview, TX	(4.0)
326	Los Angeles, CA	(29.7)
NA	Louisville, KY**	NA
86	Lowell, MA	3.0
125	Lubbock, TX	(2.2)
113	Lynn, MA	(0.9)
78	Macon, GA	3.5
184	Madison, WI	(9.1)
59	Manchester, NH	6.5
320	McAllen, TX	(28.9)
350	McKinney, TX	(45.4)
219	Melbourne, FL	(12.0)
75	Memphis, TN	4.1
344	Mesa, AZ	(35.9)
217	Mesquite, TX	(11.8)
235	Miami Beach, FL	(13.9)
NA	Miami Gardens, FL**	NA
314	Miami, FL	(25.5)
140	Midland, TX	(4.1)
79	Milwaukee, WI	3.4
NA	Minneapolis, MN**	NA
304	Miramar, FL	(23.0)
212	Mission Viejo, CA	(11.4)
131	Mobile, AL	(2.8)
144	Modesto, CA	(4.5)
276	Montgomery, AL	(18.4)
159	Moreno Valley, CA	(6.5)
45	Murfreesboro, TN	8.8
56	Murrieta, CA	6.8
52	Napa, CA	7.2
NA	Naperville, IL**	NA
NA	Nashua, NH**	NA
205	Nashville, TN	(10.5)
NA	New Bedford, MA**	NA
351	New Orleans, LA	(47.8)
280	New York, NY	(18.8)
286	Newark, NJ	(20.2)
194	Newport Beach, CA	(9.6)
170	Newport News, VA	(7.6)
NA	Newton, MA**	NA
199	Norfolk, VA	(10.0)
148	Norman, OK	(5.0)
156	North Charleston, SC	(6.3)
136	North Las Vegas, NV	(3.7)
208	Norwalk, CA	(11.1)
31	Oakland, CA	11.0
261	Oceanside, CA	(16.9)
318	Odessa, TX	(26.7)
95	Ogden, UT	1.1
316	Oklahoma City, OK	(26.1)
339	Olathe, KS	(33.7)
286	Omaha, NE	(20.2)
259	Ontario, CA	(16.7)
184	Orange, CA	(9.1)
335	Orem, UT	(32.1)
138	Orlando, FL	(4.0)
243	Overland Park, KS	(14.7)
168	Oxnard, CA	(7.4)
288	Palm Bay, FL	(20.3)
234	Palmdale, CA	(13.8)
47	Parma, OH	7.9
118	Pasadena, CA	(1.7)
308	Pasadena, TX	(23.9)
201	Paterson, NJ	(10.4)
76	Pembroke Pines, FL	3.8
267	Peoria, AZ	(17.5)
NA	Peoria, IL**	NA
57	Philadelphia, PA	6.7
243	Phoenix, AZ	(14.7)
103	Pittsburgh, PA	0.0
157	Plano, TX	(6.4)
219	Plantation, FL	(12.0)
66	Pomona, CA	5.6
19	Pompano Beach, FL	17.3
168	Port St. Lucie, FL	(7.4)
260	Portland, OR	(16.8)
233	Portsmouth, VA	(13.7)
328	Providence, RI	(30.4)
302	Provo, UT	(22.9)
22	Pueblo, CO	14.7
289	Quincy, MA	(20.5)
31	Racine, WI	11.0
332	Raleigh, NC	(31.7)
252	Rancho Cucamon., CA	(15.4)
181	Reading, PA	(8.6)
81	Redding, CA	3.3
117	Reno, NV	(1.5)
255	Rialto, CA	(15.8)
265	Richardson, TX	(17.3)
240	Richmond, CA	(14.5)
327	Richmond, VA	(29.9)
247	Riverside, CA	(14.9)
NA	Roanoke, VA**	NA
NA	Rochester, MN**	NA
132	Rochester, NY	(2.9)
NA	Rockford, IL**	NA
232	Roseville, CA	(13.5)
37	Roswell, GA	10.3
270	Round Rock, TX	(17.8)
152	Sacramento, CA	(5.7)
336	Salem, OR	(32.6)
34	Salinas, CA	10.8
183	Salt Lake City, UT	(9.0)
215	San Angelo, TX	(11.6)
247	San Antonio, TX	(14.9)
271	San Bernardino, CA	(17.9)
83	San Diego, CA	3.1
39	San Francisco, CA	10.1
20	San Jose, CA	16.1
40	San Leandro, CA	9.9
83	San Mateo, CA	3.1
182	Sandy, UT	(8.7)
197	Santa Ana, CA	(9.9)
65	Santa Barbara, CA	5.7
43	Santa Clara, CA	9.2
34	Santa Clarita, CA	10.8
NA	Santa Maria, CA**	NA
275	Santa Monica, CA	(18.3)
299	Santa Rosa, CA	(22.6)
347	Savannah, GA	(38.3)
284	Scottsdale, AZ	(20.0)
159	Seattle, WA	(6.5)
132	Shreveport, LA	(2.9)
9	Simi Valley, CA	24.0
341	Sioux City, IA	(34.9)
242	Sioux Falls, SD	(14.6)
174	Somerville, MA	(7.9)
82	South Bend, IN	3.2
142	South Gate, CA	(4.3)
66	Southfield, MI	5.6
228	Sparks, NV	(12.8)
NA	Spokane Valley, WA**	NA
269	Spokane, WA	(17.7)
NA	Springfield, IL**	NA
295	Springfield, MA	(22.4)
17	Springfield, MO	19.1
54	Sterling Heights, MI	7.1
111	Stockton, CA	(0.7)
107	St. Louis, MO	(0.4)
NA	St. Paul, MN**	NA
114	St. Petersburg, FL	(1.2)
320	Suffolk, VA	(28.9)
311	Sugar Land, TX	(25.0)
21	Sunnyvale, CA	15.1
240	Sunrise, FL	(14.5)
271	Surprise, AZ	(17.9)
226	Syracuse, NY	(12.4)
172	Tacoma, WA	(7.7)
305	Tallahassee, FL	(23.3)
349	Tampa, FL	(38.8)
109	Temecula, CA	(0.5)
299	Tempe, AZ	(22.6)
315	Thornton, CO	(25.7)
154	Thousand Oaks, CA	(5.9)
90	Toledo, OH	2.5
292	Toms River Twnshp, NJ	(21.3)
257	Topeka, KS	(16.1)
301	Torrance, CA	(22.7)
243	Tracy, CA	(14.7)
346	Trenton, NJ	(37.7)
88	Troy, MI	2.8
NA	Tucson, AZ**	NA
115	Tulsa, OK	(1.3)
135	Tuscaloosa, AL	(3.2)
334	Tyler, TX	(31.9)
2	Upper Darby Twnshp, PA	65.1
71	Vacaville, CA	5.1
86	Vallejo, CA	3.0
252	Vancouver, WA	(15.4)
40	Ventura, CA	9.9
157	Victorville, CA	(6.4)
229	Virginia Beach, VA	(13.2)
99	Visalia, CA	0.7
68	Vista, CA	5.3
317	Waco, TX	(26.2)
36	Warren, MI	10.7
302	Warwick, RI	(22.9)
307	Washington, DC	(23.8)
103	Waterbury, CT	0.0
74	West Covina, CA	4.8
313	West Jordan, UT	(25.2)
329	West Palm Beach, FL	(30.5)
224	West Valley, UT	(12.3)
68	Westland, MI	5.3
151	Westminster, CA	(5.5)
NA	Westminster, CO**	NA
13	Whittier, CA	21.3
255	Wichita Falls, TX	(15.8)
170	Wichita, KS	(7.6)
343	Wilmington, NC	(35.5)
103	Winston-Salem, NC	0.0
229	Woodbridge Twnshp, NJ	(13.2)
NA	Worcester, MA**	NA
109	Yakima, WA	(0.5)
136	Yonkers, NY	(3.7)
118	Youngstown, OH	(1.7)
NA	Yuma, AZ**	NA

Source: CQ Press using data from F.B.I. "Crime in the United States 2006"

**Includes murder, rape, robbery, aggravated assault, burglary, larceny-theft, and motor vehicle theft.*

***Not available.*

44. Percent Change in Crime Rate: 2002 to 2006 (continued)

National Percent Change = 7.7% Decrease*

RANK	CITY	% CHANGE
1	Chino, CA	103.1
2	Upper Darby Twnshp, PA	65.1
3	Deerfield Beach, FL	42.2
4	Everett, WA	37.4
5	Lawrence, KS	35.0
6	Fayetteville, NC	28.2
7	Daly City, CA	27.0
8	Bakersfield, CA	26.8
9	Simi Valley, CA	24.0
10	Columbus, GA	23.2
11	Flint, MI	23.0
12	Baldwin Park, CA	22.7
13	Whittier, CA	21.3
14	Hayward, CA	21.2
15	Huntsville, AL	21.0
16	Allentown, PA	20.1
17	Springfield, MO	19.1
18	Indianapolis, IN	18.6
19	Pompano Beach, FL	17.3
20	San Jose, CA	16.1
21	Sunnyvale, CA	15.1
22	Las Vegas, NV	14.7
22	Pueblo, CO	14.7
24	Kent, WA	14.4
25	Gary, IN	13.0
26	Cleveland, OH	12.7
27	Kenosha, WI	12.1
28	Downey, CA	12.0
29	Lancaster, CA	11.9
30	Huntington Beach, CA	11.4
31	Albany, GA	11.0
31	Oakland, CA	11.0
31	Racine, WI	11.0
34	Salinas, CA	10.8
34	Santa Clarita, CA	10.8
36	Warren, MI	10.7
37	Roswell, GA	10.3
38	Grand Rapids, MI	10.2
39	San Francisco, CA	10.1
40	San Leandro, CA	9.9
40	Ventura, CA	9.9
42	Birmingham, AL	9.4
43	Santa Clara, CA	9.2
44	Brick Twnshp, NJ	8.9
45	Murfreesboro, TN	8.8
46	Carlsbad, CA	8.5
47	Parma, OH	7.9
48	Camden, NJ	7.8
49	Alhambra, CA	7.7
50	Buffalo, NY	7.4
50	Charlotte, NC	7.4
52	Fremont, CA	7.2
52	Napa, CA	7.2
54	Detroit, MI	7.1
54	Sterling Heights, MI	7.1
56	Murrieta, CA	6.8
57	Edmond, OK	6.7
57	Philadelphia, PA	6.7
59	Abilene, TX	6.5
59	Manchester, NH	6.5
61	Greensboro, NC	6.0
62	Concord, CA	5.9
62	Lee's Summit, MO	5.9
64	Lawton, OK	5.8
65	Santa Barbara, CA	5.7
66	Pomona, CA	5.6
66	Southfield, MI	5.6
68	Vista, CA	5.3
68	Westland, MI	5.3
70	Clinton Twnshp, MI	5.2
71	Vacaville, CA	5.1
72	Colonie, NY	5.0
72	Knoxville, TN	5.0
74	West Covina, CA	4.8
75	Memphis, TN	4.1
76	Pembroke Pines, FL	3.8
77	El Monte, CA	3.6
78	Macon, GA	3.5
79	Gainesville, FL	3.4
79	Milwaukee, WI	3.4
81	Redding, CA	3.3
82	South Bend, IN	3.2
83	Amherst, NY	3.1
83	San Diego, CA	3.1
83	San Mateo, CA	3.1
86	Lowell, MA	3.0
86	Vallejo, CA	3.0
88	Troy, MI	2.8
89	Independence, MO	2.7
90	Toledo, OH	2.5
91	Austin, TX	1.7
91	Federal Way, WA	1.7
93	Bridgeport, CT	1.5
94	Carson, CA	1.4
95	Baton Rouge, LA	1.1
95	Ogden, UT	1.1
97	Erie, PA	0.9
98	Anchorage, AK	0.8
99	Visalia, CA	0.7
100	Edison Twnshp, NJ	0.6
101	Evansville, IN	0.3
102	Dearborn, MI	0.2
103	Pittsburgh, PA	0.0
103	Waterbury, CT	0.0
103	Winston-Salem, NC	0.0
106	Henderson, NV	(0.1)
107	Largo, FL	(0.4)
107	St. Louis, MO	(0.4)
109	Temecula, CA	(0.5)
109	Yakima, WA	(0.5)
111	Corpus Christi, TX	(0.7)
111	Stockton, CA	(0.7)
113	Lynn, MA	(0.9)
114	St. Petersburg, FL	(1.2)
115	Bellingham, WA	(1.3)
115	Tulsa, OK	(1.3)
117	Reno, NV	(1.5)
118	Pasadena, CA	(1.7)
118	Youngstown, OH	(1.7)
120	Fullerton, CA	(1.8)
121	Canton Twnshp, MI	(2.0)
121	Costa Mesa, CA	(2.0)
123	Boca Raton, FL	(2.1)
123	Inglewood, CA	(2.1)
125	Lubbock, TX	(2.2)
126	Cape Coral, FL	(2.3)
127	Lakeland, FL	(2.4)
128	Irving, TX	(2.5)
129	Denver, CO	(2.7)
129	Farmington Hills, MI	(2.7)
131	Mobile, AL	(2.8)
132	Rochester, NY	(2.9)
132	Shreveport, LA	(2.9)
134	Boston, MA	(3.1)
135	Tuscaloosa, AL	(3.2)
136	North Las Vegas, NV	(3.7)
136	Yonkers, NY	(3.7)
138	Longview, TX	(4.0)
138	Orlando, FL	(4.0)
140	Midland, TX	(4.1)
141	Houston, TX	(4.2)
142	Buena Park, CA	(4.3)
142	South Gate, CA	(4.3)
144	Cincinnati, OH	(4.5)
144	Modesto, CA	(4.5)
146	Escondido, CA	(4.6)
147	Hartford, CT	(4.7)
148	Glendale, CA	(5.0)
148	Norman, OK	(5.0)
150	Antioch, CA	(5.3)
151	Westminster, CA	(5.5)
152	Jacksonville, FL	(5.7)
152	Sacramento, CA	(5.7)
154	Thousand Oaks, CA	(5.9)
155	Hammond, IN	(6.0)
156	North Charleston, SC	(6.3)
157	Plano, TX	(6.4)
157	Victorville, CA	(6.4)
159	Moreno Valley, CA	(6.5)
159	Seattle, WA	(6.5)
161	Green Bay, WI	(6.8)
162	Fort Lauderdale, FL	(6.9)
162	Lafayette, LA	(6.9)
164	Colorado Springs, CO	(7.0)
164	Livonia, MI	(7.0)
166	Albuquerque, NM	(7.3)
166	Cary, NC	(7.3)
168	Oxnard, CA	(7.4)
168	Port St. Lucie, FL	(7.4)
170	Newport News, VA	(7.6)
170	Wichita, KS	(7.6)
172	Lansing, MI	(7.7)
172	Tacoma, WA	(7.7)
174	Boulder, CO	(7.9)
174	Somerville, MA	(7.9)
176	Hamilton Twnshp, NJ	(8.1)
176	Little Rock, AR	(8.1)
178	Bellflower, CA	(8.5)
178	Burbank, CA	(8.5)
178	Garden Grove, CA	(8.5)
181	Reading, PA	(8.6)
182	Sandy, UT	(8.7)
183	Salt Lake City, UT	(9.0)
184	Amarillo, TX	(9.1)
184	Laredo, TX	(9.1)
184	Madison, WI	(9.1)
184	Orange, CA	(9.1)
188	Lakewood, CO	(9.3)
189	Chattanooga, TN	(9.4)
189	Chula Vista, CA	(9.4)
189	High Point, NC	(9.4)
192	Compton, CA	(9.5)

RANK	CITY	% CHANGE
192	Hesperia, CA	(9.5)
194	Bellevue, WA	(9.6)
194	Newport Beach, CA	(9.6)
196	Grand Prairie, TX	(9.8)
197	El Cajon, CA	(9.9)
197	Santa Ana, CA	(9.9)
199	Norfolk, VA	(10.0)
200	Fort Collins, CO	(10.2)
201	Clearwater, FL	(10.4)
201	Hampton, VA	(10.4)
201	Hawthorne, CA	(10.4)
201	Paterson, NJ	(10.4)
205	Ann Arbor, MI	(10.5)
205	Nashville, TN	(10.5)
207	Dallas, TX	(10.7)
208	Dayton, OH	(11.1)
208	Norwalk, CA	(11.1)
210	Jackson, MS	(11.2)
211	Fairfield, CA	(11.3)
212	Mission Viejo, CA	(11.4)
213	Arlington, TX	(11.5)
213	Cambridge, MA	(11.5)
215	San Angelo, TX	(11.6)
216	Athens-Clarke, GA	(11.7)
217	Mesquite, TX	(11.8)
218	Eugene, OR	(11.9)
219	Garland, TX	(12.0)
219	Melbourne, FL	(12.0)
219	Plantation, FL	(12.0)
222	Jersey City, NJ	(12.1)
223	Fargo, ND	(12.2)
224	Lake Forest, CA	(12.3)
224	West Valley, UT	(12.3)
226	Carrollton, TX	(12.4)
226	Syracuse, NY	(12.4)
228	Sparks, NV	(12.8)
229	Virginia Beach, VA	(13.2)
229	Woodbridge Twnshp, NJ	(13.2)
231	Lakewood, CA	(13.3)
232	Roseville, CA	(13.5)
233	Portsmouth, VA	(13.7)
234	Palmdale, CA	(13.8)
235	Anaheim, CA	(13.9)
235	Columbia, MO	(13.9)
235	Miami Beach, FL	(13.9)
238	Hialeah, FL	(14.1)
239	Columbus, OH	(14.3)
240	Richmond, CA	(14.5)
240	Sunrise, FL	(14.5)
242	Sioux Falls, SD	(14.6)
243	Overland Park, KS	(14.7)
243	Phoenix, AZ	(14.7)
243	Tracy, CA	(14.7)
246	Lincoln, NE	(14.8)
247	Riverside, CA	(14.9)
247	San Antonio, TX	(14.9)
249	Cedar Rapids, IA	(15.1)
250	Corona, CA	(15.2)
251	Killeen, TX	(15.3)
252	Billings, MT	(15.4)
252	Rancho Cucamon., CA	(15.4)
252	Vancouver, WA	(15.4)
255	Rialto, CA	(15.8)
255	Wichita Falls, TX	(15.8)
257	Long Beach, CA	(16.1)
257	Topeka, KS	(16.1)
259	Ontario, CA	(16.7)
260	Portland, OR	(16.8)
261	Chesapeake, VA	(16.9)
261	Oceanside, CA	(16.9)
263	Clovis, CA	(17.2)
263	Fort Smith, AR	(17.2)
265	Arvada, CO	(17.3)
265	Richardson, TX	(17.3)
267	Glendale, AZ	(17.5)
267	Peoria, AZ	(17.5)
269	Spokane, WA	(17.7)
270	Round Rock, TX	(17.8)
271	San Bernardino, CA	(17.9)
271	Surprise, AZ	(17.9)
273	Boise, ID	(18.0)
273	Greeley, CO	(18.0)
275	Santa Monica, CA	(18.3)
276	Montgomery, AL	(18.4)
277	Clarksville, TN	(18.6)
278	Baltimore, MD	(18.7)
278	Berkeley, CA	(18.7)
280	New York, NY	(18.8)
281	Columbia, SC	(19.5)
281	Livermore, CA	(19.5)
283	Beaumont, TX	(19.6)
284	Scottsdale, AZ	(20.0)
285	Clifton, NJ	(20.1)
286	Newark, NJ	(20.2)
286	Omaha, NE	(20.2)
288	Palm Bay, FL	(20.3)
289	Quincy, MA	(20.5)
290	Davie, FL	(21.0)
290	Fort Worth, TX	(21.0)
292	Clarkstown, NY	(21.3)
292	Toms River Twnshp, NJ	(21.3)
294	Fontana, CA	(21.8)
295	Aurora, CO	(22.4)
295	Coral Springs, FL	(22.4)
295	Springfield, MA	(22.4)
298	Elizabeth, NJ	(22.5)
299	Santa Rosa, CA	(22.6)
299	Tempe, AZ	(22.6)
301	Torrance, CA	(22.7)
302	Provo, UT	(22.9)
302	Warwick, RI	(22.9)
304	Miramar, FL	(23.0)
305	Tallahassee, FL	(23.3)
306	Danbury, CT	(23.7)
307	Washington, DC	(23.8)
308	Cranston, RI	(23.9)
308	Pasadena, TX	(23.9)
310	Fresno, CA	(24.3)
311	Hollywood, FL	(25.0)
311	Sugar Land, TX	(25.0)
313	West Jordan, UT	(25.2)
314	Miami, FL	(25.5)
315	Thornton, CO	(25.7)
316	Oklahoma City, OK	(26.1)
317	Waco, TX	(26.2)
318	Odessa, TX	(26.7)
319	Atlanta, GA	(27.9)
320	McAllen, TX	(28.9)
320	Suffolk, VA	(28.9)
322	Gresham, OR	(29.1)
323	Denton, TX	(29.2)
324	Broken Arrow, OK	(29.3)
324	Honolulu, HI	(29.3)
326	Los Angeles, CA	(29.7)
327	Richmond, VA	(29.9)
328	Providence, RI	(30.4)
329	West Palm Beach, FL	(30.5)
330	Charleston, SC	(30.6)
331	Irvine, CA	(31.4)
332	Raleigh, NC	(31.7)
333	Alexandria, VA	(31.8)
334	Tyler, TX	(31.9)
335	Orem, UT	(32.1)
336	Salem, OR	(32.6)
337	Lewisville, TX	(32.7)
338	Chandler, AZ	(33.5)
339	Olathe, KS	(33.7)
340	Hillsboro, OR	(34.2)
341	Sioux City, IA	(34.9)
342	Beaverton, OR	(35.3)
343	Wilmington, NC	(35.5)
344	Mesa, AZ	(35.9)
345	Gilbert, AZ	(36.6)
346	Trenton, NJ	(37.7)
347	Savannah, GA	(38.3)
348	Brownsville, TX	(38.6)
349	Tampa, FL	(38.8)
350	McKinney, TX	(45.4)
351	New Orleans, LA	(47.8)
352	Chino Hills, CA	(50.4)
NA	Albany, NY**	NA
NA	Aurora, IL**	NA
NA	Bloomington, MN**	NA
NA	Brockton, MA**	NA
NA	Canton, OH**	NA
NA	Centennial, CO**	NA
NA	Cheektowaga, NY**	NA
NA	Chicago, IL**	NA
NA	Des Moines, IA**	NA
NA	Duluth, MN**	NA
NA	Durham, NC**	NA
NA	El Paso, TX**	NA
NA	Fort Wayne, IN**	NA
NA	Greece, NY**	NA
NA	Joliet, IL**	NA
NA	Kansas City, KS**	NA
NA	Kansas City, MO**	NA
NA	Las Cruces, NM**	NA
NA	Lexington, KY**	NA
NA	Louisville, KY**	NA
NA	Miami Gardens, FL**	NA
NA	Minneapolis, MN**	NA
NA	Naperville, IL**	NA
NA	Nashua, NH**	NA
NA	New Bedford, MA**	NA
NA	Newton, MA**	NA
NA	Peoria, IL**	NA
NA	Roanoke, VA**	NA
NA	Rochester, MN**	NA
NA	Rockford, IL**	NA
NA	Santa Maria, CA**	NA
NA	Spokane Valley, WA**	NA
NA	Springfield, IL**	NA
NA	St. Paul, MN**	NA
NA	Tucson, AZ**	NA
NA	Westminster, CO**	NA
NA	Worcester, MA**	NA
NA	Yuma, AZ**	NA

Source: CQ Press using data from F.B.I. "Crime in the United States 2006"

**Includes murder, rape, robbery, aggravated assault, burglary, larceny-theft, and motor vehicle theft.*

***Not available.*

45. Violent Crimes in 2006

National Total = 1,417,745 Violent Crimes*

RANK	CITY	CRIMES
225	Abilene, TX	554
227	Albany, GA	553
121	Albany, NY	1,217
31	Albuquerque, NM	4,550
251	Alexandria, VA	448
302	Alhambra, CA	297
138	Allentown, PA	1,081
94	Amarillo, TX	1,623
361	Amherst, NY	122
99	Anaheim, CA	1,524
60	Anchorage, AK	2,592
281	Ann Arbor, MI	344
196	Antioch, CA	657
58	Arlington, TX	2,728
334	Arvada, CO	193
271	Athens-Clarke, GA	373
18	Atlanta, GA	7,548
82	Aurora, CO	1,858
NA	Aurora, IL**	NA
44	Austin, TX	3,658
97	Bakersfield, CA	1,575
292	Baldwin Park, CA	323
10	Baltimore, MD	10,816
54	Baton Rouge, LA	2,954
131	Beaumont, TX	1,155
330	Beaverton, OR	208
337	Bellevue, WA	184
240	Bellflower, CA	474
333	Bellingham, WA	196
199	Berkeley, CA	646
329	Billings, MT	209
52	Birmingham, AL	3,175
NA	Bloomington, MN**	NA
320	Boca Raton, FL	238
180	Boise, ID	772
19	Boston, MA	7,533
323	Boulder, CO	229
375	Brick Twnshp, NJ	83
101	Bridgeport, CT	1,509
NA	Brockton, MA**	NA
343	Broken Arrow, OK	178
166	Brownsville, TX	867
312	Buena Park, CA	274
38	Buffalo, NY	3,957
318	Burbank, CA	252
246	Cambridge, MA	458
89	Camden, NJ	1,693
368	Canton Twnshp, MI	102
175	Canton, OH	813
261	Cape Coral, FL	406
287	Carlsbad, CA	329
323	Carrollton, TX	229
183	Carson, CA	738
355	Cary, NC	131
262	Cedar Rapids, IA	401
340	Centennial, CO	180
153	Chandler, AZ	959
152	Charleston, SC	960
20	Charlotte, NC	7,532
78	Chattanooga, TN	1,935
326	Cheektowaga, NY	221
151	Chesapeake, VA	963
NA	Chicago, IL**	NA
358	Chino Hills, CA	127
325	Chino, CA	228
156	Chula Vista, CA	947
42	Cincinnati, OH	3,766
377	Clarkstown, NY	66
141	Clarksville, TN	1,023
168	Clearwater, FL	862
21	Cleveland, OH	7,004
342	Clifton, NJ	179
289	Clinton Twnshp, MI	328
349	Clovis, CA	148
372	Colonie, NY	94
68	Colorado Springs, CO	2,145
245	Columbia, MO	460
112	Columbia, SC	1,290
125	Columbus, GA	1,187
26	Columbus, OH	5,948
91	Compton, CA	1,672
230	Concord, CA	520
306	Coral Springs, FL	292
289	Corona, CA	328
70	Corpus Christi, TX	2,070
299	Costa Mesa, CA	306
357	Cranston, RI	128
6	Dallas, TX	15,058
307	Daly City, CA	289
354	Danbury, CT	132
304	Davie, FL	295
86	Dayton, OH	1,721
248	Dearborn, MI	456
221	Deerfield Beach, FL	561
287	Denton, TX	329
32	Denver, CO	4,325
110	Des Moines, IA	1,306
5	Detroit, MI	21,394
249	Downey, CA	451
NA	Duluth, MN**	NA
77	Durham, NC	1,957
304	Edison Twnshp, NJ	295
374	Edmond, OK	91
241	El Cajon, CA	473
200	El Monte, CA	628
62	El Paso, TX	2,413
160	Elizabeth, NJ	894
225	Erie, PA	554
186	Escondido, CA	713
273	Eugene, OR	370
229	Evansville, IN	540
207	Everett, WA	602
197	Fairfield, CA	654
322	Fargo, ND	231
352	Farmington Hills, MI	134
111	Fayetteville, NC	1,299
286	Federal Way, WA	331
53	Flint, MI	3,070
167	Fontana, CA	863
236	Fort Collins, CO	493
90	Fort Lauderdale, FL	1,683
163	Fort Smith, AR	876
187	Fort Wayne, IN	708
36	Fort Worth, TX	4,209
216	Fremont, CA	569
46	Fresno, CA	3,524
243	Fullerton, CA	469
137	Gainesville, FL	1,090
193	Garden Grove, CA	695
214	Garland, TX	576
189	Gary, IN	707
317	Gilbert, AZ	254
98	Glendale, AZ	1,539
274	Glendale, CA	368
238	Grand Prairie, TX	490
79	Grand Rapids, MI	1,923
370	Greece, NY	97
244	Greeley, CO	467
223	Green Bay, WI	558
71	Greensboro, NC	2,062
220	Gresham, OR	562
330	Hamilton Twnshp, NJ	208
213	Hammond, IN	580
215	Hampton, VA	571
96	Hartford, CT	1,590
202	Hawthorne, CA	623
179	Hayward, CA	776
212	Henderson, NV	588
319	Hesperia, CA	241
115	Hialeah, FL	1,263
192	High Point, NC	699
335	Hillsboro, OR	192
183	Hollywood, FL	738
57	Honolulu, HI	2,745
3	Houston, TX	24,250
259	Huntington Beach, CA	407
106	Huntsville, AL	1,439
175	Independence, MO	813
16	Indianapolis, IN	7,689
139	Inglewood, CA	1,051
359	Irvine, CA	126
172	Irving, TX	850
22	Jacksonville, FL	6,663
85	Jackson, MS	1,736
55	Jersey City, NJ	2,890
NA	Joliet, IL**	NA
119	Kansas City, KS	1,245
24	Kansas City, MO	6,471
280	Kenosha, WI	347
218	Kent, WA	563
178	Killeen, TX	787
80	Knoxville, TN	1,894
133	Lafayette, LA	1,142
370	Lake Forest, CA	97
210	Lakeland, FL	593
259	Lakewood, CA	407
191	Lakewood, CO	702
113	Lancaster, CA	1,274
129	Lansing, MI	1,173
123	Laredo, TX	1,198
253	Largo, FL	439
231	Las Cruces, NM	515
8	Las Vegas, NV	12,931
234	Lawrence, KS	500
158	Lawton, OK	929
360	Lee's Summit, MO	125
327	Lewisville, TX	214
87	Lexington, KY	1,712
116	Lincoln, NE	1,256
50	Little Rock, AR	3,324
350	Livermore, CA	147
347	Livonia, MI	167

RANK	CITY	CRIMES
49	Long Beach, CA	3,420
185	Longview, TX	719
2	Los Angeles, CA	30,526
41	Louisville, KY	3,836
159	Lowell, MA	920
67	Lubbock, TX	2,169
171	Lynn, MA	852
170	Macon, GA	853
148	Madison, WI	973
296	Manchester, NH	313
268	McAllen, TX	383
313	McKinney, TX	264
162	Melbourne, FL	884
7	Memphis, TN	13,544
75	Mesa, AZ	2,003
235	Mesquite, TX	496
135	Miami Beach, FL	1,115
81	Miami Gardens, FL	1,868
27	Miami, FL	5,931
271	Midland, TX	373
15	Milwaukee, WI	7,698
NA	Minneapolis, MN**	NA
224	Miramar, FL	555
376	Mission Viejo, CA	70
130	Mobile, AL	1,167
108	Modesto, CA	1,418
126	Montgomery, AL	1,184
150	Moreno Valley, CA	968
190	Murfreesboro, TN	706
363	Murrieta, CA	113
283	Napa, CA	336
NA	Naperville, IL**	NA
336	Nashua, NH	190
12	Nashville, TN	8,565
132	New Bedford, MA	1,143
64	New Orleans, LA	2,255
1	New York, NY	52,086
56	Newark, NJ	2,839
356	Newport Beach, CA	130
107	Newport News, VA	1,422
351	Newton, MA	143
83	Norfolk, VA	1,844
328	Norman, OK	211
104	North Charleston, SC	1,481
88	North Las Vegas, NV	1,695
217	Norwalk, CA	567
17	Oakland, CA	7,599
157	Oceanside, CA	936
204	Odessa, TX	614
257	Ogden, UT	415
33	Oklahoma City, OK	4,301
308	Olathe, KS	288
61	Omaha, NE	2,505
142	Ontario, CA	1,011
301	Orange, CA	298
378	Orem, UT	60
34	Orlando, FL	4,300
285	Overland Park, KS	332
174	Oxnard, CA	841
208	Palm Bay, FL	601
146	Palmdale, CA	989
363	Parma, OH	113
205	Pasadena, CA	611
203	Pasadena, TX	620
91	Paterson, NJ	1,672
277	Pembroke Pines, FL	363
294	Peoria, AZ	317
NA	Peoria, IL**	NA
4	Philadelphia, PA	22,883
9	Phoenix, AZ	11,194
47	Pittsburgh, PA	3,473
181	Plano, TX	743
314	Plantation, FL	262
118	Pomona, CA	1,255
109	Pompano Beach, FL	1,367
282	Port St. Lucie, FL	340
39	Portland, OR	3,872
165	Portsmouth, VA	870
149	Providence, RI	972
346	Provo, UT	169
200	Pueblo, CO	628
300	Quincy, MA	305
239	Racine, WI	475
66	Raleigh, NC	2,223
278	Rancho Cucamon., CA	362
143	Reading, PA	1,001
267	Redding, CA	388
105	Reno, NV	1,478
187	Rialto, CA	708
321	Richardson, TX	234
120	Richmond, CA	1,224
72	Richmond, VA	2,041
74	Riverside, CA	2,014
154	Roanoke, VA	953
NA	Rochester, MN**	NA
59	Rochester, NY	2,666
84	Rockford, IL	1,841
270	Roseville, CA	378
343	Roswell, GA	178
367	Round Rock, TX	104
28	Sacramento, CA	5,556
194	Salem, OR	691
134	Salinas, CA	1,118
103	Salt Lake City, UT	1,494
264	San Angelo, TX	396
14	San Antonio, TX	7,977
73	San Bernardino, CA	2,017
25	San Diego, CA	6,391
23	San Francisco, CA	6,533
45	San Jose, CA	3,561
198	San Leandro, CA	650
291	San Mateo, CA	325
348	Sandy, UT	151
76	Santa Ana, CA	1,998
246	Santa Barbara, CA	458
340	Santa Clara, CA	180
266	Santa Clarita, CA	392
182	Santa Maria, CA	742
211	Santa Monica, CA	590
161	Santa Rosa, CA	891
126	Savannah, GA	1,184
233	Scottsdale, AZ	505
37	Seattle, WA	4,152
65	Shreveport, LA	2,249
332	Simi Valley, CA	199
263	Sioux City, IA	398
254	Sioux Falls, SD	426
293	Somerville, MA	322
177	South Bend, IN	805
232	South Gate, CA	506
140	Southfield, MI	1,041
269	Sparks, NV	380
303	Spokane Valley, WA	296
124	Spokane, WA	1,197
NA	Springfield, IL**	NA
63	Springfield, MA	2,260
143	Springfield, MO	1,001
316	Sterling Heights, MI	256
35	Stockton, CA	4,288
11	St. Louis, MO	8,605
NA	St. Paul, MN**	NA
43	St. Petersburg, FL	3,753
265	Suffolk, VA	395
369	Sugar Land, TX	101
337	Sunnyvale, CA	184
254	Sunrise, FL	426
366	Surprise, AZ	106
100	Syracuse, NY	1,515
69	Tacoma, WA	2,076
95	Tallahassee, FL	1,615
40	Tampa, FL	3,839
311	Temecula, CA	277
136	Tempe, AZ	1,094
276	Thornton, CO	366
339	Thousand Oaks, CA	182
48	Toledo, OH	3,461
365	Toms River Twnshp, NJ	112
195	Topeka, KS	669
279	Torrance, CA	354
352	Tracy, CA	134
113	Trenton, NJ	1,274
373	Troy, MI	93
30	Tucson, AZ	4,580
29	Tulsa, OK	4,816
206	Tuscaloosa, AL	604
218	Tyler, TX	563
298	Upper Darby Twnshp, PA	310
310	Vacaville, CA	280
122	Vallejo, CA	1,206
209	Vancouver, WA	598
284	Ventura, CA	335
222	Victorville, CA	560
116	Virginia Beach, VA	1,256
164	Visalia, CA	871
252	Vista, CA	446
155	Waco, TX	952
173	Warren, MI	842
362	Warwick, RI	114
13	Washington, DC	8,408
258	Waterbury, CT	408
256	West Covina, CA	419
345	West Jordan, UT	173
128	West Palm Beach, FL	1,174
241	West Valley, UT	473
275	Westland, MI	367
295	Westminster, CA	314
309	Westminster, CO	285
296	Whittier, CA	313
237	Wichita Falls, TX	491
51	Wichita, KS	3,319
169	Wilmington, NC	857
93	Winston-Salem, NC	1,654
315	Woodbridge Twnshp, NJ	260
102	Worcester, MA	1,496
250	Yakima, WA	449
147	Yonkers, NY	978
145	Youngstown, OH	993
228	Yuma, AZ	542

Source: Federal Bureau of Investigation "Crime in the United States 2006"
**Violent crimes are offenses of murder, forcible rape, robbery, and aggravated assault.*
***Not available.*

45. Violent Crimes in 2006 (continued)

National Total = 1,417,745 Violent Crimes*

RANK	CITY	CRIMES
1	New York, NY	52,086
2	Los Angeles, CA	30,526
3	Houston, TX	24,250
4	Philadelphia, PA	22,883
5	Detroit, MI	21,394
6	Dallas, TX	15,058
7	Memphis, TN	13,544
8	Las Vegas, NV	12,931
9	Phoenix, AZ	11,194
10	Baltimore, MD	10,816
11	St. Louis, MO	8,605
12	Nashville, TN	8,565
13	Washington, DC	8,408
14	San Antonio, TX	7,977
15	Milwaukee, WI	7,698
16	Indianapolis, IN	7,689
17	Oakland, CA	7,599
18	Atlanta, GA	7,548
19	Boston, MA	7,533
20	Charlotte, NC	7,532
21	Cleveland, OH	7,004
22	Jacksonville, FL	6,663
23	San Francisco, CA	6,533
24	Kansas City, MO	6,471
25	San Diego, CA	6,391
26	Columbus, OH	5,948
27	Miami, FL	5,931
28	Sacramento, CA	5,556
29	Tulsa, OK	4,816
30	Tucson, AZ	4,580
31	Albuquerque, NM	4,550
32	Denver, CO	4,325
33	Oklahoma City, OK	4,301
34	Orlando, FL	4,300
35	Stockton, CA	4,288
36	Fort Worth, TX	4,209
37	Seattle, WA	4,152
38	Buffalo, NY	3,957
39	Portland, OR	3,872
40	Tampa, FL	3,839
41	Louisville, KY	3,836
42	Cincinnati, OH	3,766
43	St. Petersburg, FL	3,753
44	Austin, TX	3,658
45	San Jose, CA	3,561
46	Fresno, CA	3,524
47	Pittsburgh, PA	3,473
48	Toledo, OH	3,461
49	Long Beach, CA	3,420
50	Little Rock, AR	3,324
51	Wichita, KS	3,319
52	Birmingham, AL	3,175
53	Flint, MI	3,070
54	Baton Rouge, LA	2,954
55	Jersey City, NJ	2,890
56	Newark, NJ	2,839
57	Honolulu, HI	2,745
58	Arlington, TX	2,728
59	Rochester, NY	2,666
60	Anchorage, AK	2,592
61	Omaha, NE	2,505
62	El Paso, TX	2,413
63	Springfield, MA	2,260
64	New Orleans, LA	2,255
65	Shreveport, LA	2,249
66	Raleigh, NC	2,223
67	Lubbock, TX	2,169
68	Colorado Springs, CO	2,145
69	Tacoma, WA	2,076
70	Corpus Christi, TX	2,070
71	Greensboro, NC	2,062
72	Richmond, VA	2,041
73	San Bernardino, CA	2,017
74	Riverside, CA	2,014
75	Mesa, AZ	2,003
76	Santa Ana, CA	1,998
77	Durham, NC	1,957
78	Chattanooga, TN	1,935
79	Grand Rapids, MI	1,923
80	Knoxville, TN	1,894
81	Miami Gardens, FL	1,868
82	Aurora, CO	1,858
83	Norfolk, VA	1,844
84	Rockford, IL	1,841
85	Jackson, MS	1,736
86	Dayton, OH	1,721
87	Lexington, KY	1,712
88	North Las Vegas, NV	1,695
89	Camden, NJ	1,693
90	Fort Lauderdale, FL	1,683
91	Compton, CA	1,672
91	Paterson, NJ	1,672
93	Winston-Salem, NC	1,654
94	Amarillo, TX	1,623
95	Tallahassee, FL	1,615
96	Hartford, CT	1,590
97	Bakersfield, CA	1,575
98	Glendale, AZ	1,539
99	Anaheim, CA	1,524
100	Syracuse, NY	1,515
101	Bridgeport, CT	1,509
102	Worcester, MA	1,496
103	Salt Lake City, UT	1,494
104	North Charleston, SC	1,481
105	Reno, NV	1,478
106	Huntsville, AL	1,439
107	Newport News, VA	1,422
108	Modesto, CA	1,418
109	Pompano Beach, FL	1,367
110	Des Moines, IA	1,306
111	Fayetteville, NC	1,299
112	Columbia, SC	1,290
113	Lancaster, CA	1,274
113	Trenton, NJ	1,274
115	Hialeah, FL	1,263
116	Lincoln, NE	1,256
116	Virginia Beach, VA	1,256
118	Pomona, CA	1,255
119	Kansas City, KS	1,245
120	Richmond, CA	1,224
121	Albany, NY	1,217
122	Vallejo, CA	1,206
123	Laredo, TX	1,198
124	Spokane, WA	1,197
125	Columbus, GA	1,187
126	Montgomery, AL	1,184
126	Savannah, GA	1,184
128	West Palm Beach, FL	1,174
129	Lansing, MI	1,173
130	Mobile, AL	1,167
131	Beaumont, TX	1,155
132	New Bedford, MA	1,143
133	Lafayette, LA	1,142
134	Salinas, CA	1,118
135	Miami Beach, FL	1,115
136	Tempe, AZ	1,094
137	Gainesville, FL	1,090
138	Allentown, PA	1,081
139	Inglewood, CA	1,051
140	Southfield, MI	1,041
141	Clarksville, TN	1,023
142	Ontario, CA	1,011
143	Reading, PA	1,001
143	Springfield, MO	1,001
145	Youngstown, OH	993
146	Palmdale, CA	989
147	Yonkers, NY	978
148	Madison, WI	973
149	Providence, RI	972
150	Moreno Valley, CA	968
151	Chesapeake, VA	963
152	Charleston, SC	960
153	Chandler, AZ	959
154	Roanoke, VA	953
155	Waco, TX	952
156	Chula Vista, CA	947
157	Oceanside, CA	936
158	Lawton, OK	929
159	Lowell, MA	920
160	Elizabeth, NJ	894
161	Santa Rosa, CA	891
162	Melbourne, FL	884
163	Fort Smith, AR	876
164	Visalia, CA	871
165	Portsmouth, VA	870
166	Brownsville, TX	867
167	Fontana, CA	863
168	Clearwater, FL	862
169	Wilmington, NC	857
170	Macon, GA	853
171	Lynn, MA	852
172	Irving, TX	850
173	Warren, MI	842
174	Oxnard, CA	841
175	Canton, OH	813
175	Independence, MO	813
177	South Bend, IN	805
178	Killeen, TX	787
179	Hayward, CA	776
180	Boise, ID	772
181	Plano, TX	743
182	Santa Maria, CA	742
183	Carson, CA	738
183	Hollywood, FL	738
185	Longview, TX	719
186	Escondido, CA	713
187	Fort Wayne, IN	708
187	Rialto, CA	708
189	Gary, IN	707
190	Murfreesboro, TN	706
191	Lakewood, CO	702
192	High Point, NC	699

RANK	CITY	CRIMES
193	Garden Grove, CA	695
194	Salem, OR	691
195	Topeka, KS	669
196	Antioch, CA	657
197	Fairfield, CA	654
198	San Leandro, CA	650
199	Berkeley, CA	646
200	El Monte, CA	628
200	Pueblo, CO	628
202	Hawthorne, CA	623
203	Pasadena, TX	620
204	Odessa, TX	614
205	Pasadena, CA	611
206	Tuscaloosa, AL	604
207	Everett, WA	602
208	Palm Bay, FL	601
209	Vancouver, WA	598
210	Lakeland, FL	593
211	Santa Monica, CA	590
212	Henderson, NV	588
213	Hammond, IN	580
214	Garland, TX	576
215	Hampton, VA	571
216	Fremont, CA	569
217	Norwalk, CA	567
218	Kent, WA	563
218	Tyler, TX	563
220	Gresham, OR	562
221	Deerfield Beach, FL	561
222	Victorville, CA	560
223	Green Bay, WI	558
224	Miramar, FL	555
225	Abilene, TX	554
225	Erie, PA	554
227	Albany, GA	553
228	Yuma, AZ	542
229	Evansville, IN	540
230	Concord, CA	520
231	Las Cruces, NM	515
232	South Gate, CA	506
233	Scottsdale, AZ	505
234	Lawrence, KS	500
235	Mesquite, TX	496
236	Fort Collins, CO	493
237	Wichita Falls, TX	491
238	Grand Prairie, TX	490
239	Racine, WI	475
240	Bellflower, CA	474
241	El Cajon, CA	473
241	West Valley, UT	473
243	Fullerton, CA	469
244	Greeley, CO	467
245	Columbia, MO	460
246	Cambridge, MA	458
246	Santa Barbara, CA	458
248	Dearborn, MI	456
249	Downey, CA	451
250	Yakima, WA	449
251	Alexandria, VA	448
252	Vista, CA	446
253	Largo, FL	439
254	Sioux Falls, SD	426
254	Sunrise, FL	426
256	West Covina, CA	419
257	Ogden, UT	415
258	Waterbury, CT	408
259	Huntington Beach, CA	407
259	Lakewood, CA	407
261	Cape Coral, FL	406
262	Cedar Rapids, IA	401
263	Sioux City, IA	398
264	San Angelo, TX	396
265	Suffolk, VA	395
266	Santa Clarita, CA	392
267	Redding, CA	388
268	McAllen, TX	383
269	Sparks, NV	380
270	Roseville, CA	378
271	Athens-Clarke, GA	373
271	Midland, TX	373
273	Eugene, OR	370
274	Glendale, CA	368
275	Westland, MI	367
276	Thornton, CO	366
277	Pembroke Pines, FL	363
278	Rancho Cucamon., CA	362
279	Torrance, CA	354
280	Kenosha, WI	347
281	Ann Arbor, MI	344
282	Port St. Lucie, FL	340
283	Napa, CA	336
284	Ventura, CA	335
285	Overland Park, KS	332
286	Federal Way, WA	331
287	Carlsbad, CA	329
287	Denton, TX	329
289	Clinton Twnshp, MI	328
289	Corona, CA	328
291	San Mateo, CA	325
292	Baldwin Park, CA	323
293	Somerville, MA	322
294	Peoria, AZ	317
295	Westminster, CA	314
296	Manchester, NH	313
296	Whittier, CA	313
298	Upper Darby Twnshp, PA	310
299	Costa Mesa, CA	306
300	Quincy, MA	305
301	Orange, CA	298
302	Alhambra, CA	297
303	Spokane Valley, WA	296
304	Davie, FL	295
304	Edison Twnshp, NJ	295
306	Coral Springs, FL	292
307	Daly City, CA	289
308	Olathe, KS	288
309	Westminster, CO	285
310	Vacaville, CA	280
311	Temecula, CA	277
312	Buena Park, CA	274
313	McKinney, TX	264
314	Plantation, FL	262
315	Woodbridge Twnshp, NJ	260
316	Sterling Heights, MI	256
317	Gilbert, AZ	254
318	Burbank, CA	252
319	Hesperia, CA	241
320	Boca Raton, FL	238
321	Richardson, TX	234
322	Fargo, ND	231
323	Boulder, CO	229
323	Carrollton, TX	229
325	Chino, CA	228
326	Cheektowaga, NY	221
327	Lewisville, TX	214
328	Norman, OK	211
329	Billings, MT	209
330	Beaverton, OR	208
330	Hamilton Twnshp, NJ	208
332	Simi Valley, CA	199
333	Bellingham, WA	196
334	Arvada, CO	193
335	Hillsboro, OR	192
336	Nashua, NH	190
337	Bellevue, WA	184
337	Sunnyvale, CA	184
339	Thousand Oaks, CA	182
340	Centennial, CO	180
340	Santa Clara, CA	180
342	Clifton, NJ	179
343	Broken Arrow, OK	178
343	Roswell, GA	178
345	West Jordan, UT	173
346	Provo, UT	169
347	Livonia, MI	167
348	Sandy, UT	151
349	Clovis, CA	148
350	Livermore, CA	147
351	Newton, MA	143
352	Farmington Hills, MI	134
352	Tracy, CA	134
354	Danbury, CT	132
355	Cary, NC	131
356	Newport Beach, CA	130
357	Cranston, RI	128
358	Chino Hills, CA	127
359	Irvine, CA	126
360	Lee's Summit, MO	125
361	Amherst, NY	122
362	Warwick, RI	114
363	Murrieta, CA	113
363	Parma, OH	113
365	Toms River Twnshp, NJ	112
366	Surprise, AZ	106
367	Round Rock, TX	104
368	Canton Twnshp, MI	102
369	Sugar Land, TX	101
370	Greece, NY	97
370	Lake Forest, CA	97
372	Colonie, NY	94
373	Troy, MI	93
374	Edmond, OK	91
375	Brick Twnshp, NJ	83
376	Mission Viejo, CA	70
377	Clarkstown, NY	66
378	Orem, UT	60
NA	Aurora, IL**	NA
NA	Bloomington, MN**	NA
NA	Brockton, MA**	NA
NA	Chicago, IL**	NA
NA	Duluth, MN**	NA
NA	Joliet, IL**	NA
NA	Minneapolis, MN**	NA
NA	Naperville, IL**	NA
NA	Peoria, IL**	NA
NA	Rochester, MN**	NA
NA	Springfield, IL**	NA
NA	St. Paul, MN**	NA

Source: Federal Bureau of Investigation "Crime in the United States 2006"

**Violent crimes are offenses of murder, forcible rape, robbery, and aggravated assault.*

***Not available.*

46. Violent Crime Rate in 2006

National Rate = 473.5 Violent Crimes per 100,000 Population*

RANK	CITY	RATE
221	Abilene, TX	469.5
138	Albany, GA	710.7
30	Albany, NY	1,297.8
90	Albuquerque, NM	908.3
276	Alexandria, VA	327.8
273	Alhambra, CA	336.7
70	Allentown, PA	1,009.5
99	Amarillo, TX	862.3
372	Amherst, NY	108.7
226	Anaheim, CA	455.2
85	Anchorage, AK	933.4
283	Ann Arbor, MI	304.5
152	Antioch, CA	647.1
128	Arlington, TX	731.2
339	Arvada, CO	182.2
267	Athens-Clarke, GA	349.6
14	Atlanta, GA	1,553.7
167	Aurora, CO	613.5
NA	Aurora, IL**	NA
203	Austin, TX	515.3
197	Bakersfield, CA	528.2
245	Baldwin Park, CA	405.9
11	Baltimore, MD	1,696.5
25	Baton Rouge, LA	1,403.4
73	Beaumont, TX	1,004.6
313	Beaverton, OR	238.6
354	Bellevue, WA	154.4
159	Bellflower, CA	630.0
303	Bellingham, WA	258.5
157	Berkeley, CA	635.5
328	Billings, MT	209.7
26	Birmingham, AL	1,359.3
NA	Bloomington, MN**	NA
299	Boca Raton, FL	270.2
250	Boise, ID	389.5
28	Boston, MA	1,339.5
310	Boulder, CO	245.1
373	Brick Twnshp, NJ	106.1
53	Bridgeport, CT	1,087.2
NA	Brockton, MA**	NA
331	Broken Arrow, OK	204.6
210	Brownsville, TX	503.4
270	Buena Park, CA	343.0
24	Buffalo, NY	1,410.7
312	Burbank, CA	239.9
227	Cambridge, MA	454.6
4	Camden, NJ	2,114.4
368	Canton Twnshp, MI	118.8
64	Canton, OH	1,021.7
293	Cape Coral, FL	285.2
262	Carlsbad, CA	359.2
335	Carrollton, TX	187.3
118	Carson, CA	778.5
366	Cary, NC	120.7
277	Cedar Rapids, IA	324.0
340	Centennial, CO	179.8
247	Chandler, AZ	393.2
93	Charleston, SC	885.8
56	Charlotte, NC	1,076.9
37	Chattanooga, TN	1,234.6
298	Cheektowaga, NY	272.9
235	Chesapeake, VA	435.5
NA	Chicago, IL**	NA
347	Chino Hills, CA	166.2
290	Chino, CA	291.3
230	Chula Vista, CA	445.9
39	Cincinnati, OH	1,218.4
375	Clarkstown, NY	83.9
91	Clarksville, TN	894.9
117	Clearwater, FL	779.9
15	Cleveland, OH	1,547.0
319	Clifton, NJ	223.8
272	Clinton Twnshp, MI	339.6
343	Clovis, CA	169.5
365	Colonie, NY	121.5
183	Colorado Springs, CO	569.3
213	Columbia, MO	497.4
54	Columbia, SC	1,084.9
161	Columbus, GA	620.7
108	Columbus, OH	813.1
10	Compton, CA	1,732.3
242	Concord, CA	418.1
321	Coral Springs, FL	222.9
324	Corona, CA	217.6
139	Corpus Christi, TX	710.1
297	Costa Mesa, CA	276.1
352	Cranston, RI	158.1
40	Dallas, TX	1,206.4
292	Daly City, CA	285.5
345	Danbury, CT	167.9
269	Davie, FL	344.5
55	Dayton, OH	1,081.9
218	Dearborn, MI	485.9
131	Deerfield Beach, FL	722.6
281	Denton, TX	307.2
121	Denver, CO	760.8
146	Des Moines, IA	669.1
3	Detroit, MI	2,418.9
244	Downey, CA	407.4
NA	Duluth, MN**	NA
84	Durham, NC	936.7
289	Edison Twnshp, NJ	293.3
367	Edmond, OK	120.5
208	El Cajon, CA	506.9
206	El Monte, CA	508.0
248	El Paso, TX	392.0
139	Elizabeth, NJ	710.1
193	Erie, PA	539.4
198	Escondido, CA	527.0
308	Eugene, OR	251.9
223	Evansville, IN	462.8
169	Everett, WA	612.6
162	Fairfield, CA	620.4
306	Fargo, ND	254.4
346	Farmington Hills, MI	167.5
79	Fayetteville, NC	980.2
249	Federal Way, WA	391.6
1	Flint, MI	2,596.1
202	Fontana, CA	522.0
256	Fort Collins, CO	377.9
77	Fort Lauderdale, FL	988.8
60	Fort Smith, AR	1,050.1
280	Fort Wayne, IN	314.9
150	Fort Worth, TX	655.9
296	Fremont, CA	281.3
123	Fresno, CA	757.4
266	Fullerton, CA	350.0
76	Gainesville, FL	990.8
243	Garden Grove, CA	414.7
302	Garland, TX	258.9
136	Gary, IN	711.5
358	Gilbert, AZ	140.6
163	Glendale, AZ	619.1
338	Glendale, CA	182.3
275	Grand Prairie, TX	330.1
75	Grand Rapids, MI	994.8
374	Greece, NY	102.9
199	Greeley, CO	523.2
189	Green Bay, WI	549.4
98	Greensboro, NC	871.5
182	Gresham, OR	575.5
315	Hamilton Twnshp, NJ	231.0
130	Hammond, IN	727.3
252	Hampton, VA	388.4
32	Hartford, CT	1,280.2
133	Hawthorne, CA	720.5
190	Hayward, CA	548.2
310	Henderson, NV	245.1
282	Hesperia, CA	306.3
184	Hialeah, FL	563.3
132	High Point, NC	720.7
320	Hillsboro, OR	223.5
212	Hollywood, FL	498.4
286	Honolulu, HI	300.8
48	Houston, TX	1,169.4
329	Huntington Beach, CA	207.4
101	Huntsville, AL	857.5
127	Independence, MO	732.3
81	Indianapolis, IN	960.0
89	Inglewood, CA	910.0
377	Irvine, CA	66.8
239	Irving, TX	426.8
105	Jacksonville, FL	837.2
80	Jackson, MS	978.9
42	Jersey City, NJ	1,205.2
NA	Joliet, IL**	NA
102	Kansas City, KS	857.3
23	Kansas City, MO	1,443.7
261	Kenosha, WI	363.0
145	Kent, WA	676.6
120	Killeen, TX	763.5
63	Knoxville, TN	1,038.3
57	Lafayette, LA	1,075.4
364	Lake Forest, CA	125.8
149	Lakeland, FL	657.4
211	Lakewood, CA	501.3
216	Lakewood, CO	489.8
83	Lancaster, CA	942.0
67	Lansing, MI	1,018.0
186	Laredo, TX	558.1
180	Largo, FL	579.7
166	Las Cruces, NM	614.6
78	Las Vegas, NV	982.9
171	Lawrence, KS	606.8
65	Lawton, OK	1,020.5
353	Lee's Summit, MO	154.5
317	Lewisville, TX	230.3
158	Lexington, KY	633.7
201	Lincoln, NE	522.2
9	Little Rock, AR	1,780.7
336	Livermore, CA	185.8
341	Livonia, MI	170.9

RANK	CITY	RATE
134	Long Beach, CA	715.1
88	Longview, TX	924.7
115	Los Angeles, CA	786.9
168	Louisville, KY	612.8
92	Lowell, MA	886.9
72	Lubbock, TX	1,005.7
82	Lynn, MA	953.9
95	Macon, GA	876.3
232	Madison, WI	437.6
294	Manchester, NH	284.3
285	McAllen, TX	301.3
301	McKinney, TX	265.8
51	Melbourne, FL	1,134.2
5	Memphis, TN	1,989.3
234	Mesa, AZ	435.7
258	Mesquite, TX	371.3
35	Miami Beach, FL	1,247.1
8	Miami Gardens, FL	1,847.4
17	Miami, FL	1,509.4
260	Midland, TX	365.5
29	Milwaukee, WI	1,324.9
NA	Minneapolis, MN**	NA
205	Miramar, FL	511.9
376	Mission Viejo, CA	73.0
222	Mobile, AL	466.5
144	Modesto, CA	678.9
177	Montgomery, AL	586.3
194	Moreno Valley, CA	537.9
111	Murfreesboro, TN	803.2
361	Murrieta, CA	135.3
231	Napa, CA	445.3
NA	Naperville, IL**	NA
325	Nashua, NH	216.8
16	Nashville, TN	1,527.2
38	New Bedford, MA	1,220.4
200	New Orleans, LA	523.0
155	New York, NY	637.9
69	Newark, NJ	1,010.8
351	Newport Beach, CA	161.4
116	Newport News, VA	782.6
341	Newton, MA	170.9
114	Norfolk, VA	787.1
330	Norman, OK	205.6
12	North Charleston, SC	1,689.6
87	North Las Vegas, NV	928.6
195	Norwalk, CA	531.0
7	Oakland, CA	1,905.3
185	Oceanside, CA	558.5
153	Odessa, TX	638.3
204	Ogden, UT	513.2
112	Oklahoma City, OK	802.4
305	Olathe, KS	256.9
172	Omaha, NE	601.1
179	Ontario, CA	580.3
323	Orange, CA	218.9
378	Orem, UT	64.8
6	Orlando, FL	1,983.2
334	Overland Park, KS	200.0
228	Oxnard, CA	453.9
156	Palm Bay, FL	636.7
129	Palmdale, CA	728.4
359	Parma, OH	138.5
240	Pasadena, CA	421.3
241	Pasadena, TX	419.1
52	Paterson, NJ	1,115.0
314	Pembroke Pines, FL	237.4

RANK	CITY	RATE
322	Peoria, AZ	220.9
NA	Peoria, IL**	NA
13	Philadelphia, PA	1,562.4
125	Phoenix, AZ	737.7
58	Pittsburgh, PA	1,069.9
291	Plano, TX	288.9
287	Plantation, FL	299.6
110	Pomona, CA	808.8
31	Pompano Beach, FL	1,290.4
307	Port St. Lucie, FL	253.9
135	Portland, OR	714.2
100	Portsmouth, VA	860.0
188	Providence, RI	554.0
356	Provo, UT	144.3
175	Pueblo, CO	595.5
274	Quincy, MA	335.9
174	Racine, WI	596.1
154	Raleigh, NC	638.2
327	Rancho Cucamon., CA	211.8
36	Reading, PA	1,236.9
237	Redding, CA	429.0
142	Reno, NV	702.6
141	Rialto, CA	705.1
318	Richardson, TX	229.4
46	Richmond, CA	1,187.1
61	Richmond, VA	1,042.9
143	Riverside, CA	688.1
66	Roanoke, VA	1,018.7
NA	Rochester, MN**	NA
33	Rochester, NY	1,259.6
43	Rockford, IL	1,197.5
264	Roseville, CA	353.6
332	Roswell, GA	200.7
370	Round Rock, TX	117.2
40	Sacramento, CA	1,206.4
225	Salem, OR	457.0
124	Salinas, CA	756.7
109	Salt Lake City, UT	812.4
233	San Angelo, TX	437.5
164	San Antonio, TX	617.4
71	San Bernardino, CA	1,006.8
209	San Diego, CA	504.5
96	San Francisco, CA	875.6
253	San Jose, CA	386.8
107	San Leandro, CA	824.0
264	San Mateo, CA	353.6
350	Sandy, UT	163.1
178	Santa Ana, CA	581.8
196	Santa Barbara, CA	528.4
344	Santa Clara, CA	169.3
316	Santa Clarita, CA	230.9
97	Santa Maria, CA	871.9
147	Santa Monica, CA	666.0
181	Santa Rosa, CA	576.6
187	Savannah, GA	554.6
326	Scottsdale, AZ	215.2
137	Seattle, WA	711.2
45	Shreveport, LA	1,193.1
347	Simi Valley, CA	166.2
220	Sioux City, IA	476.1
284	Sioux Falls, SD	303.0
238	Somerville, MA	427.0
122	South Bend, IN	759.7
207	South Gate, CA	507.1
27	Southfield, MI	1,358.5
229	Sparks, NV	448.1

RANK	CITY	RATE
263	Spokane Valley, WA	357.6
173	Spokane, WA	597.9
NA	Springfield, IL**	NA
21	Springfield, MA	1,480.6
148	Springfield, MO	661.2
333	Sterling Heights, MI	200.4
20	Stockton, CA	1,481.1
2	St. Louis, MO	2,480.7
NA	St. Paul, MN**	NA
19	St. Petersburg, FL	1,481.8
215	Suffolk, VA	495.1
363	Sugar Land, TX	129.7
357	Sunnyvale, CA	141.5
224	Sunrise, FL	462.5
360	Surprise, AZ	137.2
59	Syracuse, NY	1,066.4
62	Tacoma, WA	1,041.8
74	Tallahassee, FL	1,002.0
49	Tampa, FL	1,158.1
278	Temecula, CA	320.0
151	Tempe, AZ	653.9
271	Thornton, CO	341.5
355	Thousand Oaks, CA	145.0
50	Toledo, OH	1,147.3
369	Toms River Twnshp, NJ	118.2
191	Topeka, KS	544.8
309	Torrance, CA	246.4
349	Tracy, CA	166.1
18	Trenton, NJ	1,504.1
371	Troy, MI	114.9
103	Tucson, AZ	855.7
34	Tulsa, OK	1,248.2
126	Tuscaloosa, AL	735.7
175	Tyler, TX	595.5
251	Upper Darby Twnshp, PA	389.0
288	Vacaville, CA	298.4
68	Vallejo, CA	1,017.4
257	Vancouver, WA	373.3
279	Ventura, CA	319.2
170	Victorville, CA	608.1
295	Virginia Beach, VA	283.7
113	Visalia, CA	794.4
217	Vista, CA	488.9
119	Waco, TX	768.5
160	Warren, MI	623.8
362	Warwick, RI	131.7
22	Washington, DC	1,445.8
255	Waterbury, CT	378.7
254	West Covina, CA	383.8
337	West Jordan, UT	183.2
47	West Palm Beach, FL	1,184.2
246	West Valley, UT	404.3
236	Westland, MI	429.7
268	Westminster, CA	347.6
300	Westminster, CO	266.2
259	Whittier, CA	367.2
219	Wichita Falls, TX	478.2
86	Wichita, KS	928.7
94	Wilmington, NC	880.0
106	Winston-Salem, NC	837.0
304	Woodbridge Twnshp, NJ	258.3
104	Worcester, MA	845.4
192	Yakima, WA	543.5
214	Yonkers, NY	496.6
44	Youngstown, OH	1,197.3
165	Yuma, AZ	616.4

Source: CQ Press using data from F.B.I. "Crime in the United States 2006"

**Violent crimes are offenses of murder, forcible rape, robbery, and aggravated assault.*

***Not available.*

46. Violent Crime Rate in 2006 (continued)

National Rate = 473.5 Violent Crimes per 100,000 Population*

RANK	CITY	RATE
1	Flint, MI	2,596.1
2	St. Louis, MO	2,480.7
3	Detroit, MI	2,418.9
4	Camden, NJ	2,114.4
5	Memphis, TN	1,989.3
6	Orlando, FL	1,983.2
7	Oakland, CA	1,905.3
8	Miami Gardens, FL	1,847.4
9	Little Rock, AR	1,780.7
10	Compton, CA	1,732.3
11	Baltimore, MD	1,696.5
12	North Charleston, SC	1,689.6
13	Philadelphia, PA	1,562.4
14	Atlanta, GA	1,553.7
15	Cleveland, OH	1,547.0
16	Nashville, TN	1,527.2
17	Miami, FL	1,509.4
18	Trenton, NJ	1,504.1
19	St. Petersburg, FL	1,481.8
20	Stockton, CA	1,481.1
21	Springfield, MA	1,480.6
22	Washington, DC	1,445.8
23	Kansas City, MO	1,443.7
24	Buffalo, NY	1,410.7
25	Baton Rouge, LA	1,403.4
26	Birmingham, AL	1,359.3
27	Southfield, MI	1,358.5
28	Boston, MA	1,339.5
29	Milwaukee, WI	1,324.9
30	Albany, NY	1,297.8
31	Pompano Beach, FL	1,290.4
32	Hartford, CT	1,280.2
33	Rochester, NY	1,259.6
34	Tulsa, OK	1,248.2
35	Miami Beach, FL	1,247.1
36	Reading, PA	1,236.9
37	Chattanooga, TN	1,234.6
38	New Bedford, MA	1,220.4
39	Cincinnati, OH	1,218.4
40	Dallas, TX	1,206.4
40	Sacramento, CA	1,206.4
42	Jersey City, NJ	1,205.2
43	Rockford, IL	1,197.5
44	Youngstown, OH	1,197.3
45	Shreveport, LA	1,193.1
46	Richmond, CA	1,187.1
47	West Palm Beach, FL	1,184.2
48	Houston, TX	1,169.4
49	Tampa, FL	1,158.1
50	Toledo, OH	1,147.3
51	Melbourne, FL	1,134.2
52	Paterson, NJ	1,115.0
53	Bridgeport, CT	1,087.2
54	Columbia, SC	1,084.9
55	Dayton, OH	1,081.9
56	Charlotte, NC	1,076.9
57	Lafayette, LA	1,075.4
58	Pittsburgh, PA	1,069.9
59	Syracuse, NY	1,066.4
60	Fort Smith, AR	1,050.1
61	Richmond, VA	1,042.9
62	Tacoma, WA	1,041.8
63	Knoxville, TN	1,038.3
64	Canton, OH	1,021.7
65	Lawton, OK	1,020.5
66	Roanoke, VA	1,018.7
67	Lansing, MI	1,018.0
68	Vallejo, CA	1,017.4
69	Newark, NJ	1,010.8
70	Allentown, PA	1,009.5
71	San Bernardino, CA	1,006.8
72	Lubbock, TX	1,005.7
73	Beaumont, TX	1,004.6
74	Tallahassee, FL	1,002.0
75	Grand Rapids, MI	994.8
76	Gainesville, FL	990.8
77	Fort Lauderdale, FL	988.8
78	Las Vegas, NV	982.9
79	Fayetteville, NC	980.2
80	Jackson, MS	978.9
81	Indianapolis, IN	960.0
82	Lynn, MA	953.9
83	Lancaster, CA	942.0
84	Durham, NC	936.7
85	Anchorage, AK	933.4
86	Wichita, KS	928.7
87	North Las Vegas, NV	928.6
88	Longview, TX	924.7
89	Inglewood, CA	910.0
90	Albuquerque, NM	908.3
91	Clarksville, TN	894.9
92	Lowell, MA	886.9
93	Charleston, SC	885.8
94	Wilmington, NC	880.0
95	Macon, GA	876.3
96	San Francisco, CA	875.6
97	Santa Maria, CA	871.9
98	Greensboro, NC	871.5
99	Amarillo, TX	862.3
100	Portsmouth, VA	860.0
101	Huntsville, AL	857.5
102	Kansas City, KS	857.3
103	Tucson, AZ	855.7
104	Worcester, MA	845.4
105	Jacksonville, FL	837.2
106	Winston-Salem, NC	837.0
107	San Leandro, CA	824.0
108	Columbus, OH	813.1
109	Salt Lake City, UT	812.4
110	Pomona, CA	808.8
111	Murfreesboro, TN	803.2
112	Oklahoma City, OK	802.4
113	Visalia, CA	794.4
114	Norfolk, VA	787.1
115	Los Angeles, CA	786.9
116	Newport News, VA	782.6
117	Clearwater, FL	779.9
118	Carson, CA	778.5
119	Waco, TX	768.5
120	Killeen, TX	763.5
121	Denver, CO	760.8
122	South Bend, IN	759.7
123	Fresno, CA	757.4
124	Salinas, CA	756.7
125	Phoenix, AZ	737.7
126	Tuscaloosa, AL	735.7
127	Independence, MO	732.3
128	Arlington, TX	731.2
129	Palmdale, CA	728.4
130	Hammond, IN	727.3
131	Deerfield Beach, FL	722.6
132	High Point, NC	720.7
133	Hawthorne, CA	720.5
134	Long Beach, CA	715.1
135	Portland, OR	714.2
136	Gary, IN	711.5
137	Seattle, WA	711.2
138	Albany, GA	710.7
139	Corpus Christi, TX	710.1
139	Elizabeth, NJ	710.1
141	Rialto, CA	705.1
142	Reno, NV	702.6
143	Riverside, CA	688.1
144	Modesto, CA	678.9
145	Kent, WA	676.6
146	Des Moines, IA	669.1
147	Santa Monica, CA	666.0
148	Springfield, MO	661.2
149	Lakeland, FL	657.4
150	Fort Worth, TX	655.9
151	Tempe, AZ	653.9
152	Antioch, CA	647.1
153	Odessa, TX	638.3
154	Raleigh, NC	638.2
155	New York, NY	637.9
156	Palm Bay, FL	636.7
157	Berkeley, CA	635.5
158	Lexington, KY	633.7
159	Bellflower, CA	630.0
160	Warren, MI	623.8
161	Columbus, GA	620.7
162	Fairfield, CA	620.4
163	Glendale, AZ	619.1
164	San Antonio, TX	617.4
165	Yuma, AZ	616.4
166	Las Cruces, NM	614.6
167	Aurora, CO	613.5
168	Louisville, KY	612.8
169	Everett, WA	612.6
170	Victorville, CA	608.1
171	Lawrence, KS	606.8
172	Omaha, NE	601.1
173	Spokane, WA	597.9
174	Racine, WI	596.1
175	Pueblo, CO	595.5
175	Tyler, TX	595.5
177	Montgomery, AL	586.3
178	Santa Ana, CA	581.8
179	Ontario, CA	580.3
180	Largo, FL	579.7
181	Santa Rosa, CA	576.6
182	Gresham, OR	575.5
183	Colorado Springs, CO	569.3
184	Hialeah, FL	563.3
185	Oceanside, CA	558.5
186	Laredo, TX	558.1
187	Savannah, GA	554.6
188	Providence, RI	554.0
189	Green Bay, WI	549.4
190	Hayward, CA	548.2
191	Topeka, KS	544.8
192	Yakima, WA	543.5

RANK	CITY	RATE	RANK	CITY	RATE	RANK	CITY	RATE
193	Erie, PA	539.4	259	Whittier, CA	367.2	325	Nashua, NH	216.8
194	Moreno Valley, CA	537.9	260	Midland, TX	365.5	326	Scottsdale, AZ	215.2
195	Norwalk, CA	531.0	261	Kenosha, WI	363.0	327	Rancho Cucamon., CA	211.8
196	Santa Barbara, CA	528.4	262	Carlsbad, CA	359.2	328	Billings, MT	209.7
197	Bakersfield, CA	528.2	263	Spokane Valley, WA	357.6	329	Huntington Beach, CA	207.4
198	Escondido, CA	527.0	264	Roseville, CA	353.6	330	Norman, OK	205.6
199	Greeley, CO	523.2	264	San Mateo, CA	353.6	331	Broken Arrow, OK	204.6
200	New Orleans, LA	523.0	266	Fullerton, CA	350.0	332	Roswell, GA	200.7
201	Lincoln, NE	522.2	267	Athens-Clarke, GA	349.6	333	Sterling Heights, MI	200.4
202	Fontana, CA	522.0	268	Westminster, CA	347.6	334	Overland Park, KS	200.0
203	Austin, TX	515.3	269	Davie, FL	344.5	335	Carrollton, TX	187.3
204	Ogden, UT	513.2	270	Buena Park, CA	343.0	336	Livermore, CA	185.8
205	Miramar, FL	511.9	271	Thornton, CO	341.5	337	West Jordan, UT	183.2
206	El Monte, CA	508.0	272	Clinton Twnshp, MI	339.6	338	Glendale, CA	182.3
207	South Gate, CA	507.1	273	Alhambra, CA	336.7	339	Arvada, CO	182.2
208	El Cajon, CA	506.9	274	Quincy, MA	335.9	340	Centennial, CO	179.8
209	San Diego, CA	504.5	275	Grand Prairie, TX	330.1	341	Livonia, MI	170.9
210	Brownsville, TX	503.4	276	Alexandria, VA	327.8	341	Newton, MA	170.9
211	Lakewood, CA	501.3	277	Cedar Rapids, IA	324.0	343	Clovis, CA	169.5
212	Hollywood, FL	498.4	278	Temecula, CA	320.0	344	Santa Clara, CA	169.3
213	Columbia, MO	497.4	279	Ventura, CA	319.2	345	Danbury, CT	167.9
214	Yonkers, NY	496.6	280	Fort Wayne, IN	314.9	346	Farmington Hills, MI	167.5
215	Suffolk, VA	495.1	281	Denton, TX	307.2	347	Chino Hills, CA	166.2
216	Lakewood, CO	489.8	282	Hesperia, CA	306.3	347	Simi Valley, CA	166.2
217	Vista, CA	488.9	283	Ann Arbor, MI	304.5	349	Tracy, CA	166.1
218	Dearborn, MI	485.9	284	Sioux Falls, SD	303.0	350	Sandy, UT	163.1
219	Wichita Falls, TX	478.2	285	McAllen, TX	301.3	351	Newport Beach, CA	161.4
220	Sioux City, IA	476.1	286	Honolulu, HI	300.8	352	Cranston, RI	158.1
221	Abilene, TX	469.5	287	Plantation, FL	299.6	353	Lee's Summit, MO	154.5
222	Mobile, AL	466.5	288	Vacaville, CA	298.4	354	Bellevue, WA	154.4
223	Evansville, IN	462.8	289	Edison Twnshp, NJ	293.3	355	Thousand Oaks, CA	145.0
224	Sunrise, FL	462.5	290	Chino, CA	291.3	356	Provo, UT	144.3
225	Salem, OR	457.0	291	Plano, TX	288.9	357	Sunnyvale, CA	141.5
226	Anaheim, CA	455.2	292	Daly City, CA	285.5	358	Gilbert, AZ	140.6
227	Cambridge, MA	454.6	293	Cape Coral, FL	285.2	359	Parma, OH	138.5
228	Oxnard, CA	453.9	294	Manchester, NH	284.3	360	Surprise, AZ	137.2
229	Sparks, NV	448.1	295	Virginia Beach, VA	283.7	361	Murrieta, CA	135.3
230	Chula Vista, CA	445.9	296	Fremont, CA	281.3	362	Warwick, RI	131.7
231	Napa, CA	445.3	297	Costa Mesa, CA	276.1	363	Sugar Land, TX	129.7
232	Madison, WI	437.6	298	Cheektowaga, NY	272.9	364	Lake Forest, CA	125.8
233	San Angelo, TX	437.5	299	Boca Raton, FL	270.2	365	Colonie, NY	121.5
234	Mesa, AZ	435.7	300	Westminster, CO	266.2	366	Cary, NC	120.7
235	Chesapeake, VA	435.5	301	McKinney, TX	265.8	367	Edmond, OK	120.5
236	Westland, MI	429.7	302	Garland, TX	258.9	368	Canton Twnshp, MI	118.8
237	Redding, CA	429.0	303	Bellingham, WA	258.5	369	Toms River Twnshp, NJ	118.2
238	Somerville, MA	427.0	304	Woodbridge Twnshp, NJ	258.3	370	Round Rock, TX	117.2
239	Irving, TX	426.8	305	Olathe, KS	256.9	371	Troy, MI	114.9
240	Pasadena, CA	421.3	306	Fargo, ND	254.4	372	Amherst, NY	108.7
241	Pasadena, TX	419.1	307	Port St. Lucie, FL	253.9	373	Brick Twnshp, NJ	106.1
242	Concord, CA	418.1	308	Eugene, OR	251.9	374	Greece, NY	102.9
243	Garden Grove, CA	414.7	309	Torrance, CA	246.4	375	Clarkstown, NY	83.9
244	Downey, CA	407.4	310	Boulder, CO	245.1	376	Mission Viejo, CA	73.0
245	Baldwin Park, CA	405.9	310	Henderson, NV	245.1	377	Irvine, CA	66.8
246	West Valley, UT	404.3	312	Burbank, CA	239.9	378	Orem, UT	64.8
247	Chandler, AZ	393.2	313	Beaverton, OR	238.6	NA	Aurora, IL**	NA
248	El Paso, TX	392.0	314	Pembroke Pines, FL	237.4	NA	Bloomington, MN**	NA
249	Federal Way, WA	391.6	315	Hamilton Twnshp, NJ	231.0	NA	Brockton, MA**	NA
250	Boise, ID	389.5	316	Santa Clarita, CA	230.9	NA	Chicago, IL**	NA
251	Upper Darby Twnshp, PA	389.0	317	Lewisville, TX	230.3	NA	Duluth, MN**	NA
252	Hampton, VA	388.4	318	Richardson, TX	229.4	NA	Joliet, IL**	NA
253	San Jose, CA	386.8	319	Clifton, NJ	223.8	NA	Minneapolis, MN**	NA
254	West Covina, CA	383.8	320	Hillsboro, OR	223.5	NA	Naperville, IL**	NA
255	Waterbury, CT	378.7	321	Coral Springs, FL	222.9	NA	Peoria, IL**	NA
256	Fort Collins, CO	377.9	322	Peoria, AZ	220.9	NA	Rochester, MN**	NA
257	Vancouver, WA	373.3	323	Orange, CA	218.9	NA	Springfield, IL**	NA
258	Mesquite, TX	371.3	324	Corona, CA	217.6	NA	St. Paul, MN**	NA

Source: CQ Press using data from F.B.I. "Crime in the United States 2006"

**Violent crimes are offenses of murder, forcible rape, robbery, and aggravated assault.*

***Not available.*

47. Percent Change in Violent Crime Rate: 2005 to 2006

National Percent Change = 1.0% Increase*

RANK	CITY	% CHANGE
253	Abilene, TX	(4.9)
104	Albany, GA	7.9
240	Albany, NY	(4.0)
250	Albuquerque, NM	(4.6)
284	Alexandria, VA	(7.7)
276	Alhambra, CA	(7.1)
24	Allentown, PA	25.1
153	Amarillo, TX	3.1
45	Amherst, NY	18.5
258	Anaheim, CA	(5.4)
20	Anchorage, AK	26.9
231	Ann Arbor, MI	(3.3)
44	Antioch, CA	18.9
68	Arlington, TX	12.8
231	Arvada, CO	(3.3)
146	Athens-Clarke, GA	3.5
277	Atlanta, GA	(7.2)
214	Aurora, CO	(1.1)
NA	Aurora, IL**	NA
131	Austin, TX	5.2
310	Bakersfield, CA	(11.5)
290	Baldwin Park, CA	(8.7)
231	Baltimore, MD	(3.3)
50	Baton Rouge, LA	16.8
177	Beaumont, TX	1.5
127	Beaverton, OR	6.0
120	Bellevue, WA	6.3
310	Bellflower, CA	(11.5)
93	Bellingham, WA	9.9
62	Berkeley, CA	13.9
172	Billings, MT	2.1
280	Birmingham, AL	(7.5)
NA	Bloomington, MN**	NA
302	Boca Raton, FL	(10.5)
177	Boise, ID	1.5
174	Boston, MA	1.7
123	Boulder, CO	6.1
2	Brick Twnshp, NJ	89.8
184	Bridgeport, CT	1.1
NA	Brockton, MA**	NA
280	Broken Arrow, OK	(7.5)
288	Brownsville, TX	(8.6)
302	Buena Park, CA	(10.5)
177	Buffalo, NY	1.5
170	Burbank, CA	2.2
280	Cambridge, MA	(7.5)
192	Camden, NJ	0.8
363	Canton Twnshp, MI	(31.1)
29	Canton, OH	22.3
148	Cape Coral, FL	3.4
22	Carlsbad, CA	25.8
360	Carrollton, TX	(25.2)
63	Carson, CA	13.7
271	Cary, NC	(6.6)
251	Cedar Rapids, IA	(4.7)
338	Centennial, CO	(17.5)
88	Chandler, AZ	10.3
268	Charleston, SC	(6.1)
287	Charlotte, NC	(8.1)
90	Chattanooga, TN	10.1
271	Cheektowaga, NY	(6.6)
327	Chesapeake, VA	(15.1)
NA	Chicago, IL**	NA
21	Chino Hills, CA	26.5
122	Chino, CA	6.2
209	Chula Vista, CA	(0.8)
160	Cincinnati, OH	2.9
NA	Clarkstown, NY**	NA
76	Clarksville, TN	11.8
320	Clearwater, FL	(12.8)
86	Cleveland, OH	10.6
123	Clifton, NJ	6.1
299	Clinton Twnshp, MI	(9.4)
275	Clovis, CA	(6.9)
37	Colonie, NY	20.1
41	Colorado Springs, CO	19.0
262	Columbia, MO	(5.8)
220	Columbia, SC	(2.4)
47	Columbus, GA	17.6
225	Columbus, OH	(2.8)
228	Compton, CA	(3.1)
158	Concord, CA	3.0
15	Coral Springs, FL	30.6
209	Corona, CA	(0.8)
212	Corpus Christi, TX	(0.9)
196	Costa Mesa, CA	0.3
262	Cranston, RI	(5.8)
238	Dallas, TX	(3.8)
184	Daly City, CA	1.1
160	Danbury, CT	2.9
220	Davie, FL	(2.4)
67	Dayton, OH	13.2
344	Dearborn, MI	(18.7)
338	Deerfield Beach, FL	(17.5)
345	Denton, TX	(18.8)
247	Denver, CO	(4.4)
NA	Des Moines, IA**	NA
164	Detroit, MI	2.6
188	Downey, CA	1.0
NA	Duluth, MN**	NA
NA	Durham, NC**	NA
19	Edison Twnshp, NJ	27.4
352	Edmond, OK	(20.1)
279	El Cajon, CA	(7.4)
315	El Monte, CA	(12.2)
NA	El Paso, TX**	NA
104	Elizabeth, NJ	7.9
41	Erie, PA	19.0
145	Escondido, CA	3.8
82	Eugene, OR	11.0
60	Evansville, IN	14.0
79	Everett, WA	11.1
82	Fairfield, CA	11.0
1	Fargo, ND	123.6
358	Farmington Hills, MI	(23.9)
101	Fayetteville, NC	8.3
166	Federal Way, WA	2.5
58	Flint, MI	14.9
65	Fontana, CA	13.6
91	Fort Collins, CO	10.0
84	Fort Lauderdale, FL	10.7
196	Fort Smith, AR	0.3
NA	Fort Wayne, IN**	NA
164	Fort Worth, TX	2.6
91	Fremont, CA	10.0
302	Fresno, CA	(10.5)
34	Fullerton, CA	20.6
66	Gainesville, FL	13.4
269	Garden Grove, CA	(6.2)
318	Garland, TX	(12.7)
209	Gary, IN	(0.8)
123	Gilbert, AZ	6.1
108	Glendale, AZ	7.0
129	Glendale, CA	5.6
134	Grand Prairie, TX	4.9
213	Grand Rapids, MI	(1.0)
4	Greece, NY	45.3
347	Greeley, CO	(19.1)
68	Green Bay, WI	12.8
128	Greensboro, NC	5.7
78	Gresham, OR	11.2
27	Hamilton Twnshp, NJ	22.6
341	Hammond, IN	(17.8)
235	Hampton, VA	(3.4)
79	Hartford, CT	11.1
36	Hawthorne, CA	20.3
33	Hayward, CA	21.2
13	Henderson, NV	31.9
177	Hesperia, CA	1.5
242	Hialeah, FL	(4.1)
87	High Point, NC	10.5
63	Hillsboro, OR	13.7
251	Hollywood, FL	(4.7)
120	Honolulu, HI	6.3
204	Houston, TX	(0.3)
317	Huntington Beach, CA	(12.5)
54	Huntsville, AL	16.1
158	Independence, MO	3.0
231	Indianapolis, IN	(3.3)
203	Inglewood, CA	(0.1)
354	Irvine, CA	(20.6)
278	Irving, TX	(7.3)
189	Jacksonville, FL	0.9
5	Jackson, MS	44.2
286	Jersey City, NJ	(7.9)
NA	Joliet, IL**	NA
108	Kansas City, KS	7.0
NA	Kansas City, MO**	NA
7	Kenosha, WI	37.4
48	Kent, WA	16.9
273	Killeen, TX	(6.7)
102	Knoxville, TN	8.1
32	Lafayette, LA	21.7
349	Lake Forest, CA	(19.4)
8	Lakeland, FL	35.9
88	Lakewood, CA	10.3
141	Lakewood, CO	4.6
153	Lancaster, CA	3.1
330	Lansing, MI	(15.3)
97	Laredo, TX	9.4
31	Largo, FL	21.8
115	Las Cruces, NM	6.5
12	Las Vegas, NV	32.2
3	Lawrence, KS	80.6
10	Lawton, OK	35.5
288	Lee's Summit, MO	(8.6)
134	Lewisville, TX	4.9
NA	Lexington, KY**	NA
295	Lincoln, NE	(9.0)
194	Little Rock, AR	0.5
146	Livermore, CA	3.5
206	Livonia, MI	(0.5)

RANK	CITY	% CHANGE
189	Long Beach, CA	0.9
332	Longview, TX	(16.3)
242	Los Angeles, CA	(4.1)
218	Louisville, KY	(1.9)
296	Lowell, MA	(9.1)
247	Lubbock, TX	(4.4)
353	Lynn, MA	(20.4)
137	Macon, GA	4.8
57	Madison, WI	15.5
174	Manchester, NH	1.7
315	McAllen, TX	(12.2)
137	McKinney, TX	4.8
18	Melbourne, FL	27.8
108	Memphis, TN	7.0
321	Mesa, AZ	(13.6)
283	Mesquite, TX	(7.6)
228	Miami Beach, FL	(3.1)
205	Miami Gardens, FL	(0.4)
249	Miami, FL	(4.5)
305	Midland, TX	(10.7)
17	Milwaukee, WI	29.3
NA	Minneapolis, MN**	NA
98	Miramar, FL	9.3
366	Mission Viejo, CA	(35.7)
199	Mobile, AL	0.0
106	Modesto, CA	7.4
361	Montgomery, AL	(27.8)
41	Moreno Valley, CA	19.0
150	Murfreesboro, TN	3.2
334	Murrieta, CA	(16.8)
312	Napa, CA	(11.9)
NA	Naperville, IL**	NA
52	Nashua, NH	16.5
254	Nashville, TN	(5.2)
77	New Bedford, MA	11.7
NA	New Orleans, LA**	NA
254	New York, NY	(5.2)
193	Newark, NJ	0.7
115	Newport Beach, CA	6.5
195	Newport News, VA	0.4
23	Newton, MA	25.3
153	Norfolk, VA	3.1
290	Norman, OK	(8.7)
219	North Charleston, SC	(2.0)
72	North Las Vegas, NV	12.4
34	Norwalk, CA	20.6
11	Oakland, CA	34.1
245	Oceanside, CA	(4.2)
172	Odessa, TX	2.1
99	Ogden, UT	8.8
265	Oklahoma City, OK	(6.0)
335	Olathe, KS	(16.9)
115	Omaha, NE	6.5
59	Ontario, CA	14.7
14	Orange, CA	31.1
290	Orem, UT	(8.7)
94	Orlando, FL	9.7
365	Overland Park, KS	(33.9)
184	Oxnard, CA	1.1
39	Palm Bay, FL	19.9
284	Palmdale, CA	(7.7)
357	Parma, OH	(21.5)
358	Pasadena, CA	(23.9)
225	Pasadena, TX	(2.8)
50	Paterson, NJ	16.8
150	Pembroke Pines, FL	3.2

RANK	CITY	% CHANGE
140	Peoria, AZ	4.7
NA	Peoria, IL**	NA
115	Philadelphia, PA	6.5
183	Phoenix, AZ	1.2
141	Pittsburgh, PA	4.6
199	Plano, TX	0.0
55	Plantation, FL	15.9
166	Pomona, CA	2.5
327	Pompano Beach, FL	(15.1)
107	Port St. Lucie, FL	7.1
199	Portland, OR	0.0
239	Portsmouth, VA	(3.9)
343	Providence, RI	(18.6)
342	Provo, UT	(18.3)
294	Pueblo, CO	(8.8)
308	Quincy, MA	(11.2)
26	Racine, WI	22.7
149	Raleigh, NC	3.3
290	Rancho Cucamon., CA	(8.7)
111	Reading, PA	6.9
362	Redding, CA	(30.5)
254	Reno, NV	(5.2)
314	Rialto, CA	(12.0)
309	Richardson, TX	(11.3)
144	Richmond, CA	4.1
324	Richmond, VA	(14.6)
170	Riverside, CA	2.2
114	Roanoke, VA	6.6
NA	Rochester, MN**	NA
9	Rochester, NY	35.8
NA	Rockford, IL**	NA
176	Roseville, CA	1.6
37	Roswell, GA	20.1
348	Round Rock, TX	(19.2)
137	Sacramento, CA	4.8
245	Salem, OR	(4.2)
95	Salinas, CA	9.6
48	Salt Lake City, UT	16.9
133	San Angelo, TX	5.0
228	San Antonio, TX	(3.1)
351	San Bernardino, CA	(19.9)
225	San Diego, CA	(2.8)
95	San Francisco, CA	9.6
189	San Jose, CA	0.9
6	San Leandro, CA	41.2
349	San Mateo, CA	(19.4)
262	Sandy, UT	(5.8)
99	Santa Ana, CA	8.8
337	Santa Barbara, CA	(17.0)
273	Santa Clara, CA	(6.7)
60	Santa Clarita, CA	14.0
29	Santa Maria, CA	22.3
111	Santa Monica, CA	6.9
318	Santa Rosa, CA	(12.7)
325	Savannah, GA	(14.8)
123	Scottsdale, AZ	6.1
196	Seattle, WA	0.3
129	Shreveport, LA	5.6
56	Simi Valley, CA	15.7
199	Sioux City, IA	0.0
312	Sioux Falls, SD	(11.9)
25	Somerville, MA	22.9
177	South Bend, IN	1.5
237	South Gate, CA	(3.5)
73	Southfield, MI	12.2
141	Sparks, NV	4.6

RANK	CITY	% CHANGE
306	Spokane Valley, WA	(11.1)
119	Spokane, WA	6.4
NA	Springfield, IL**	NA
333	Springfield, MA	(16.5)
70	Springfield, MO	12.6
297	Sterling Heights, MI	(9.3)
208	Stockton, CA	(0.7)
153	St. Louis, MO	3.1
NA	St. Paul, MN**	NA
242	St. Petersburg, FL	(4.1)
338	Suffolk, VA	(17.5)
335	Sugar Land, TX	(16.9)
356	Sunnyvale, CA	(21.4)
75	Sunrise, FL	12.0
166	Surprise, AZ	2.5
224	Syracuse, NY	(2.7)
163	Tacoma, WA	2.8
223	Tallahassee, FL	(2.5)
346	Tampa, FL	(19.0)
217	Temecula, CA	(1.7)
166	Tempe, AZ	2.5
240	Thornton, CO	(4.0)
134	Thousand Oaks, CA	4.9
265	Toledo, OH	(6.0)
331	Toms River Twnshp, NJ	(16.0)
220	Topeka, KS	(2.4)
84	Torrance, CA	10.7
322	Tracy, CA	(13.7)
327	Trenton, NJ	(15.1)
16	Troy, MI	30.1
300	Tucson, AZ	(10.2)
235	Tulsa, OK	(3.4)
46	Tuscaloosa, AL	17.7
260	Tyler, TX	(5.6)
74	Upper Darby Twnshp, PA	12.1
102	Vacaville, CA	8.1
NA	Vallejo, CA**	NA
270	Vancouver, WA	(6.3)
70	Ventura, CA	12.6
52	Victorville, CA	16.5
79	Virginia Beach, VA	11.1
355	Visalia, CA	(20.7)
326	Vista, CA	(15.0)
153	Waco, TX	3.1
215	Warren, MI	(1.4)
261	Warwick, RI	(5.7)
150	Washington, DC	3.2
254	Waterbury, CT	(5.2)
39	West Covina, CA	19.9
NA	West Jordan, UT**	NA
258	West Palm Beach, FL	(5.4)
297	West Valley, UT	(9.3)
28	Westland, MI	22.5
301	Westminster, CA	(10.4)
306	Westminster, CO	(11.1)
160	Whittier, CA	2.9
364	Wichita Falls, TX	(33.1)
NA	Wichita, KS**	NA
132	Wilmington, NC	5.1
207	Winston-Salem, NC	(0.6)
323	Woodbridge Twnshp, NJ	(13.9)
113	Worcester, MA	6.7
215	Yakima, WA	(1.4)
184	Yonkers, NY	1.1
177	Youngstown, OH	1.5
265	Yuma, AZ	(6.0)

Source: CQ Press using data from F.B.I. "Crime in the United States 2006"

**Violent crimes are offenses of murder, forcible rape, robbery, and aggravated assault.*

***Not available.*

47. Percent Change in Violent Crime Rate: 2005 to 2006 (continued)

National Percent Change = 1.0% Increase*

RANK	CITY	% CHANGE
1	Fargo, ND	123.6
2	Brick Twnshp, NJ	89.8
3	Lawrence, KS	80.6
4	Greece, NY	45.3
5	Jackson, MS	44.2
6	San Leandro, CA	41.2
7	Kenosha, WI	37.4
8	Lakeland, FL	35.9
9	Rochester, NY	35.8
10	Lawton, OK	35.5
11	Oakland, CA	34.1
12	Las Vegas, NV	32.2
13	Henderson, NV	31.9
14	Orange, CA	31.1
15	Coral Springs, FL	30.6
16	Troy, MI	30.1
17	Milwaukee, WI	29.3
18	Melbourne, FL	27.8
19	Edison Twnshp, NJ	27.4
20	Anchorage, AK	26.9
21	Chino Hills, CA	26.5
22	Carlsbad, CA	25.8
23	Newton, MA	25.3
24	Allentown, PA	25.1
25	Somerville, MA	22.9
26	Racine, WI	22.7
27	Hamilton Twnshp, NJ	22.6
28	Westland, MI	22.5
29	Canton, OH	22.3
29	Santa Maria, CA	22.3
31	Largo, FL	21.8
32	Lafayette, LA	21.7
33	Hayward, CA	21.2
34	Fullerton, CA	20.6
34	Norwalk, CA	20.6
36	Hawthorne, CA	20.3
37	Colonie, NY	20.1
37	Roswell, GA	20.1
39	Palm Bay, FL	19.9
39	West Covina, CA	19.9
41	Colorado Springs, CO	19.0
41	Erie, PA	19.0
41	Moreno Valley, CA	19.0
44	Antioch, CA	18.9
45	Amherst, NY	18.5
46	Tuscaloosa, AL	17.7
47	Columbus, GA	17.6
48	Kent, WA	16.9
48	Salt Lake City, UT	16.9
50	Baton Rouge, LA	16.8
50	Paterson, NJ	16.8
52	Nashua, NH	16.5
52	Victorville, CA	16.5
54	Huntsville, AL	16.1
55	Plantation, FL	15.9
56	Simi Valley, CA	15.7
57	Madison, WI	15.5
58	Flint, MI	14.9
59	Ontario, CA	14.7
60	Evansville, IN	14.0
60	Santa Clarita, CA	14.0
62	Berkeley, CA	13.9
63	Carson, CA	13.7
63	Hillsboro, OR	13.7
65	Fontana, CA	13.6
66	Gainesville, FL	13.4
67	Dayton, OH	13.2
68	Arlington, TX	12.8
68	Green Bay, WI	12.8
70	Springfield, MO	12.6
70	Ventura, CA	12.6
72	North Las Vegas, NV	12.4
73	Southfield, MI	12.2
74	Upper Darby Twnshp, PA	12.1
75	Sunrise, FL	12.0
76	Clarksville, TN	11.8
77	New Bedford, MA	11.7
78	Gresham, OR	11.2
79	Everett, WA	11.1
79	Hartford, CT	11.1
79	Virginia Beach, VA	11.1
82	Eugene, OR	11.0
82	Fairfield, CA	11.0
84	Fort Lauderdale, FL	10.7
84	Torrance, CA	10.7
86	Cleveland, OH	10.6
87	High Point, NC	10.5
88	Chandler, AZ	10.3
88	Lakewood, CA	10.3
90	Chattanooga, TN	10.1
91	Fort Collins, CO	10.0
91	Fremont, CA	10.0
93	Bellingham, WA	9.9
94	Orlando, FL	9.7
95	Salinas, CA	9.6
95	San Francisco, CA	9.6
97	Laredo, TX	9.4
98	Miramar, FL	9.3
99	Ogden, UT	8.8
99	Santa Ana, CA	8.8
101	Fayetteville, NC	8.3
102	Knoxville, TN	8.1
102	Vacaville, CA	8.1
104	Albany, GA	7.9
104	Elizabeth, NJ	7.9
106	Modesto, CA	7.4
107	Port St. Lucie, FL	7.1
108	Glendale, AZ	7.0
108	Kansas City, KS	7.0
108	Memphis, TN	7.0
111	Reading, PA	6.9
111	Santa Monica, CA	6.9
113	Worcester, MA	6.7
114	Roanoke, VA	6.6
115	Las Cruces, NM	6.5
115	Newport Beach, CA	6.5
115	Omaha, NE	6.5
115	Philadelphia, PA	6.5
119	Spokane, WA	6.4
120	Bellevue, WA	6.3
120	Honolulu, HI	6.3
122	Chino, CA	6.2
123	Boulder, CO	6.1
123	Clifton, NJ	6.1
123	Gilbert, AZ	6.1
123	Scottsdale, AZ	6.1
127	Beaverton, OR	6.0
128	Greensboro, NC	5.7
129	Glendale, CA	5.6
129	Shreveport, LA	5.6
131	Austin, TX	5.2
132	Wilmington, NC	5.1
133	San Angelo, TX	5.0
134	Grand Prairie, TX	4.9
134	Lewisville, TX	4.9
134	Thousand Oaks, CA	4.9
137	Macon, GA	4.8
137	McKinney, TX	4.8
137	Sacramento, CA	4.8
140	Peoria, AZ	4.7
141	Lakewood, CO	4.6
141	Pittsburgh, PA	4.6
141	Sparks, NV	4.6
144	Richmond, CA	4.1
145	Escondido, CA	3.8
146	Athens-Clarke, GA	3.5
146	Livermore, CA	3.5
148	Cape Coral, FL	3.4
149	Raleigh, NC	3.3
150	Murfreesboro, TN	3.2
150	Pembroke Pines, FL	3.2
150	Washington, DC	3.2
153	Amarillo, TX	3.1
153	Lancaster, CA	3.1
153	Norfolk, VA	3.1
153	St. Louis, MO	3.1
153	Waco, TX	3.1
158	Concord, CA	3.0
158	Independence, MO	3.0
160	Cincinnati, OH	2.9
160	Danbury, CT	2.9
160	Whittier, CA	2.9
163	Tacoma, WA	2.8
164	Detroit, MI	2.6
164	Fort Worth, TX	2.6
166	Federal Way, WA	2.5
166	Pomona, CA	2.5
166	Surprise, AZ	2.5
166	Tempe, AZ	2.5
170	Burbank, CA	2.2
170	Riverside, CA	2.2
172	Billings, MT	2.1
172	Odessa, TX	2.1
174	Boston, MA	1.7
174	Manchester, NH	1.7
176	Roseville, CA	1.6
177	Beaumont, TX	1.5
177	Boise, ID	1.5
177	Buffalo, NY	1.5
177	Hesperia, CA	1.5
177	South Bend, IN	1.5
177	Youngstown, OH	1.5
183	Phoenix, AZ	1.2
184	Bridgeport, CT	1.1
184	Daly City, CA	1.1
184	Oxnard, CA	1.1
184	Yonkers, NY	1.1
188	Downey, CA	1.0
189	Jacksonville, FL	0.9
189	Long Beach, CA	0.9
189	San Jose, CA	0.9
192	Camden, NJ	0.8

RANK	CITY	% CHANGE
193	Newark, NJ	0.7
194	Little Rock, AR	0.5
195	Newport News, VA	0.4
196	Costa Mesa, CA	0.3
196	Fort Smith, AR	0.3
196	Seattle, WA	0.3
199	Mobile, AL	0.0
199	Plano, TX	0.0
199	Portland, OR	0.0
199	Sioux City, IA	0.0
203	Inglewood, CA	(0.1)
204	Houston, TX	(0.3)
205	Miami Gardens, FL	(0.4)
206	Livonia, MI	(0.5)
207	Winston-Salem, NC	(0.6)
208	Stockton, CA	(0.7)
209	Chula Vista, CA	(0.8)
209	Corona, CA	(0.8)
209	Gary, IN	(0.8)
212	Corpus Christi, TX	(0.9)
213	Grand Rapids, MI	(1.0)
214	Aurora, CO	(1.1)
215	Warren, MI	(1.4)
215	Yakima, WA	(1.4)
217	Temecula, CA	(1.7)
218	Louisville, KY	(1.9)
219	North Charleston, SC	(2.0)
220	Columbia, SC	(2.4)
220	Davie, FL	(2.4)
220	Topeka, KS	(2.4)
223	Tallahassee, FL	(2.5)
224	Syracuse, NY	(2.7)
225	Columbus, OH	(2.8)
225	Pasadena, TX	(2.8)
225	San Diego, CA	(2.8)
228	Compton, CA	(3.1)
228	Miami Beach, FL	(3.1)
228	San Antonio, TX	(3.1)
231	Ann Arbor, MI	(3.3)
231	Arvada, CO	(3.3)
231	Baltimore, MD	(3.3)
231	Indianapolis, IN	(3.3)
235	Hampton, VA	(3.4)
235	Tulsa, OK	(3.4)
237	South Gate, CA	(3.5)
238	Dallas, TX	(3.8)
239	Portsmouth, VA	(3.9)
240	Albany, NY	(4.0)
240	Thornton, CO	(4.0)
242	Hialeah, FL	(4.1)
242	Los Angeles, CA	(4.1)
242	St. Petersburg, FL	(4.1)
245	Oceanside, CA	(4.2)
245	Salem, OR	(4.2)
247	Denver, CO	(4.4)
247	Lubbock, TX	(4.4)
249	Miami, FL	(4.5)
250	Albuquerque, NM	(4.6)
251	Cedar Rapids, IA	(4.7)
251	Hollywood, FL	(4.7)
253	Abilene, TX	(4.9)
254	Nashville, TN	(5.2)
254	New York, NY	(5.2)
254	Reno, NV	(5.2)
254	Waterbury, CT	(5.2)
258	Anaheim, CA	(5.4)

RANK	CITY	% CHANGE
258	West Palm Beach, FL	(5.4)
260	Tyler, TX	(5.6)
261	Warwick, RI	(5.7)
262	Columbia, MO	(5.8)
262	Cranston, RI	(5.8)
262	Sandy, UT	(5.8)
265	Oklahoma City, OK	(6.0)
265	Toledo, OH	(6.0)
265	Yuma, AZ	(6.0)
268	Charleston, SC	(6.1)
269	Garden Grove, CA	(6.2)
270	Vancouver, WA	(6.3)
271	Cary, NC	(6.6)
271	Cheektowaga, NY	(6.6)
273	Killeen, TX	(6.7)
273	Santa Clara, CA	(6.7)
275	Clovis, CA	(6.9)
276	Alhambra, CA	(7.1)
277	Atlanta, GA	(7.2)
278	Irving, TX	(7.3)
279	El Cajon, CA	(7.4)
280	Birmingham, AL	(7.5)
280	Broken Arrow, OK	(7.5)
280	Cambridge, MA	(7.5)
283	Mesquite, TX	(7.6)
284	Alexandria, VA	(7.7)
284	Palmdale, CA	(7.7)
286	Jersey City, NJ	(7.9)
287	Charlotte, NC	(8.1)
288	Brownsville, TX	(8.6)
288	Lee's Summit, MO	(8.6)
290	Baldwin Park, CA	(8.7)
290	Norman, OK	(8.7)
290	Orem, UT	(8.7)
290	Rancho Cucamon., CA	(8.7)
294	Pueblo, CO	(8.8)
295	Lincoln, NE	(9.0)
296	Lowell, MA	(9.1)
297	Sterling Heights, MI	(9.3)
297	West Valley, UT	(9.3)
299	Clinton Twnshp, MI	(9.4)
300	Tucson, AZ	(10.2)
301	Westminster, CA	(10.4)
302	Boca Raton, FL	(10.5)
302	Buena Park, CA	(10.5)
302	Fresno, CA	(10.5)
305	Midland, TX	(10.7)
306	Spokane Valley, WA	(11.1)
306	Westminster, CO	(11.1)
308	Quincy, MA	(11.2)
309	Richardson, TX	(11.3)
310	Bakersfield, CA	(11.5)
310	Bellflower, CA	(11.5)
312	Napa, CA	(11.9)
312	Sioux Falls, SD	(11.9)
314	Rialto, CA	(12.0)
315	El Monte, CA	(12.2)
315	McAllen, TX	(12.2)
317	Huntington Beach, CA	(12.5)
318	Garland, TX	(12.7)
318	Santa Rosa, CA	(12.7)
320	Clearwater, FL	(12.8)
321	Mesa, AZ	(13.6)
322	Tracy, CA	(13.7)
323	Woodbridge Twnshp, NJ	(13.9)
324	Richmond, VA	(14.6)

RANK	CITY	% CHANGE
325	Savannah, GA	(14.8)
326	Vista, CA	(15.0)
327	Chesapeake, VA	(15.1)
327	Pompano Beach, FL	(15.1)
327	Trenton, NJ	(15.1)
330	Lansing, MI	(15.3)
331	Toms River Twnshp, NJ	(16.0)
332	Longview, TX	(16.3)
333	Springfield, MA	(16.5)
334	Murrieta, CA	(16.8)
335	Olathe, KS	(16.9)
335	Sugar Land, TX	(16.9)
337	Santa Barbara, CA	(17.0)
338	Centennial, CO	(17.5)
338	Deerfield Beach, FL	(17.5)
338	Suffolk, VA	(17.5)
341	Hammond, IN	(17.8)
342	Provo, UT	(18.3)
343	Providence, RI	(18.6)
344	Dearborn, MI	(18.7)
345	Denton, TX	(18.8)
346	Tampa, FL	(19.0)
347	Greeley, CO	(19.1)
348	Round Rock, TX	(19.2)
349	Lake Forest, CA	(19.4)
349	San Mateo, CA	(19.4)
351	San Bernardino, CA	(19.9)
352	Edmond, OK	(20.1)
353	Lynn, MA	(20.4)
354	Irvine, CA	(20.6)
355	Visalia, CA	(20.7)
356	Sunnyvale, CA	(21.4)
357	Parma, OH	(21.5)
358	Farmington Hills, MI	(23.9)
358	Pasadena, CA	(23.9)
360	Carrollton, TX	(25.2)
361	Montgomery, AL	(27.8)
362	Redding, CA	(30.5)
363	Canton Twnshp, MI	(31.1)
364	Wichita Falls, TX	(33.1)
365	Overland Park, KS	(33.9)
366	Mission Viejo, CA	(35.7)
NA	Aurora, IL**	NA
NA	Bloomington, MN**	NA
NA	Brockton, MA**	NA
NA	Chicago, IL**	NA
NA	Clarkstown, NY**	NA
NA	Des Moines, IA**	NA
NA	Duluth, MN**	NA
NA	Durham, NC**	NA
NA	El Paso, TX**	NA
NA	Fort Wayne, IN**	NA
NA	Joliet, IL**	NA
NA	Kansas City, MO**	NA
NA	Lexington, KY**	NA
NA	Minneapolis, MN**	NA
NA	Naperville, IL**	NA
NA	New Orleans, LA**	NA
NA	Peoria, IL**	NA
NA	Rochester, MN**	NA
NA	Rockford, IL**	NA
NA	Springfield, IL**	NA
NA	St. Paul, MN**	NA
NA	Vallejo, CA**	NA
NA	West Jordan, UT**	NA
NA	Wichita, KS**	NA

Source: CQ Press using data from F.B.I. "Crime in the United States 2006"

**Violent crimes are offenses of murder, forcible rape, robbery, and aggravated assault.*

***Not available.*

48. Percent Change in Violent Crime Rate: 2002 to 2006

National Percent Change = 4.2% Decrease*

RANK	CITY	% CHANGE
50	Abilene, TX	28.0
106	Albany, GA	11.2
NA	Albany, NY**	NA
279	Albuquerque, NM	(15.0)
130	Alexandria, VA	5.2
41	Alhambra, CA	31.4
7	Allentown, PA	75.8
126	Amarillo, TX	5.7
68	Amherst, NY	20.5
104	Anaheim, CA	11.4
20	Anchorage, AK	45.0
83	Ann Arbor, MI	16.7
251	Antioch, CA	(11.2)
87	Arlington, TX	15.5
102	Arvada, CO	12.1
289	Athens-Clarke, GA	(16.8)
332	Atlanta, GA	(32.1)
192	Aurora, CO	(4.1)
NA	Aurora, IL**	NA
111	Austin, TX	10.3
52	Bakersfield, CA	26.3
122	Baldwin Park, CA	6.4
291	Baltimore, MD	(17.4)
70	Baton Rouge, LA	20.1
139	Beaumont, TX	3.9
166	Beaverton, OR	0.5
59	Bellevue, WA	24.4
135	Bellflower, CA	4.1
113	Bellingham, WA	9.0
213	Berkeley, CA	(7.1)
256	Billings, MT	(11.7)
133	Birmingham, AL	4.5
NA	Bloomington, MN**	NA
144	Boca Raton, FL	3.1
110	Boise, ID	10.5
91	Boston, MA	14.9
130	Boulder, CO	5.2
240	Brick Twnshp, NJ	(10.4)
231	Bridgeport, CT	(9.1)
NA	Brockton, MA**	NA
209	Broken Arrow, OK	(6.6)
230	Brownsville, TX	(8.9)
77	Buena Park, CA	18.0
108	Buffalo, NY	10.9
225	Burbank, CA	(8.6)
208	Cambridge, MA	(6.2)
85	Camden, NJ	16.4
218	Canton Twnshp, MI	(7.3)
NA	Canton, OH**	NA
305	Cape Coral, FL	(21.6)
32	Carlsbad, CA	38.7
286	Carrollton, TX	(16.6)
184	Carson, CA	(2.8)
129	Cary, NC	5.3
228	Cedar Rapids, IA	(8.7)
NA	Centennial, CO**	NA
24	Chandler, AZ	42.3
144	Charleston, SC	3.1
222	Charlotte, NC	(8.1)
292	Chattanooga, TN	(18.4)
NA	Cheektowaga, NY**	NA
334	Chesapeake, VA	(34.7)
NA	Chicago, IL**	NA
353	Chino Hills, CA	(64.3)
1	Chino, CA	165.3
237	Chula Vista, CA	(10.0)
185	Cincinnati, OH	(3.2)
352	Clarkstown, NY	(57.0)
13	Clarksville, TN	58.8
303	Clearwater, FL	(21.0)
80	Cleveland, OH	17.0
262	Clifton, NJ	(12.7)
186	Clinton Twnshp, MI	(3.4)
149	Clovis, CA	2.9
70	Colonie, NY	20.1
125	Colorado Springs, CO	5.9
138	Columbia, MO	4.0
283	Columbia, SC	(16.1)
19	Columbus, GA	45.1
241	Columbus, OH	(10.5)
216	Compton, CA	(7.2)
61	Concord, CA	23.3
207	Coral Springs, FL	(6.1)
297	Corona, CA	(19.2)
173	Corpus Christi, TX	(0.3)
89	Costa Mesa, CA	15.3
264	Cranston, RI	(13.0)
259	Dallas, TX	(12.0)
157	Daly City, CA	1.6
286	Danbury, CT	(16.6)
272	Davie, FL	(13.9)
244	Dayton, OH	(10.9)
351	Dearborn, MI	(56.7)
9	Deerfield Beach, FL	70.0
329	Denton, TX	(30.9)
24	Denver, CO	42.3
NA	Des Moines, IA**	NA
83	Detroit, MI	16.7
141	Downey, CA	3.7
NA	Duluth, MN**	NA
NA	Durham, NC**	NA
42	Edison Twnshp, NJ	31.2
94	Edmond, OK	14.2
223	El Cajon, CA	(8.2)
292	El Monte, CA	(18.4)
NA	El Paso, TX**	NA
186	Elizabeth, NJ	(3.4)
58	Erie, PA	24.9
72	Escondido, CA	20.0
313	Eugene, OR	(23.8)
272	Evansville, IN	(13.9)
97	Everett, WA	13.8
117	Fairfield, CA	7.0
6	Fargo, ND	83.5
301	Farmington Hills, MI	(20.0)
116	Fayetteville, NC	7.3
54	Federal Way, WA	26.2
3	Flint, MI	91.5
310	Fontana, CA	(23.6)
115	Fort Collins, CO	7.8
103	Fort Lauderdale, FL	12.0
73	Fort Smith, AR	19.7
NA	Fort Wayne, IN**	NA
270	Fort Worth, TX	(13.7)
16	Fremont, CA	52.1
251	Fresno, CA	(11.2)
51	Fullerton, CA	26.7
47	Gainesville, FL	29.3
239	Garden Grove, CA	(10.3)
213	Garland, TX	(7.1)
179	Gary, IN	(2.2)
243	Gilbert, AZ	(10.8)
120	Glendale, AZ	6.5
320	Glendale, CA	(25.6)
282	Grand Prairie, TX	(16.0)
228	Grand Rapids, MI	(8.7)
NA	Greece, NY**	NA
39	Greeley, CO	33.9
17	Green Bay, WI	46.6
64	Greensboro, NC	23.1
109	Gresham, OR	10.8
44	Hamilton Twnshp, NJ	30.0
176	Hammond, IN	(1.0)
199	Hampton, VA	(4.9)
152	Hartford, CT	2.2
203	Hawthorne, CA	(5.7)
40	Hayward, CA	32.6
147	Henderson, NV	3.0
124	Hesperia, CA	6.3
248	Hialeah, FL	(11.1)
225	High Point, NC	(8.6)
257	Hillsboro, OR	(11.8)
325	Hollywood, FL	(29.0)
135	Honolulu, HI	4.1
194	Houston, TX	(4.4)
69	Huntington Beach, CA	20.2
23	Huntsville, AL	42.4
48	Independence, MO	29.0
150	Indianapolis, IN	2.7
93	Inglewood, CA	14.8
341	Irvine, CA	(38.4)
122	Irving, TX	6.4
225	Jacksonville, FL	(8.6)
163	Jackson, MS	1.0
157	Jersey City, NJ	1.6
NA	Joliet, IL**	NA
NA	Kansas City, KS**	NA
NA	Kansas City, MO**	NA
12	Kenosha, WI	60.8
2	Kent, WA	97.8
183	Killeen, TX	(2.5)
205	Knoxville, TN	(5.9)
95	Lafayette, LA	14.0
307	Lake Forest, CA	(22.0)
296	Lakeland, FL	(18.9)
66	Lakewood, CA	22.0
8	Lakewood, CO	71.2
278	Lancaster, CA	(14.9)
200	Lansing, MI	(5.1)
211	Laredo, TX	(7.0)
11	Largo, FL	61.7
NA	Las Cruces, NM**	NA
54	Las Vegas, NV	26.2
15	Lawrence, KS	53.0
21	Lawton, OK	43.9
10	Lee's Summit, MO	65.2
253	Lewisville, TX	(11.4)
NA	Lexington, KY**	NA
209	Lincoln, NE	(6.6)
33	Little Rock, AR	37.1
196	Livermore, CA	(4.5)
292	Livonia, MI	(18.4)

RANK	CITY	% CHANGE	RANK	CITY	% CHANGE	RANK	CITY	% CHANGE
202	Long Beach, CA	(5.6)	234	Peoria, AZ	(9.7)	NA	Spokane Valley, WA**	NA
63	Longview, TX	23.2	NA	Peoria, IL**	NA	221	Spokane, WA	(7.5)
345	Los Angeles, CA	(41.7)	75	Philadelphia, PA	18.7	NA	Springfield, IL**	NA
NA	Louisville, KY**	NA	160	Phoenix, AZ	1.4	322	Springfield, MA	(26.6)
106	Lowell, MA	11.2	186	Pittsburgh, PA	(3.4)	193	Springfield, MO	(4.2)
286	Lubbock, TX	(16.6)	170	Plano, TX	0.1	151	Sterling Heights, MI	2.6
168	Lynn, MA	0.3	172	Plantation, FL	(0.1)	160	Stockton, CA	1.4
27	Macon, GA	39.7	211	Pomona, CA	(7.0)	81	St. Louis, MO	16.8
65	Madison, WI	22.3	37	Pompano Beach, FL	34.6	NA	St. Paul, MN**	NA
46	Manchester, NH	29.7	262	Port St. Lucie, FL	(12.7)	264	St. Petersburg, FL	(13.0)
340	McAllen, TX	(37.2)	271	Portland, OR	(13.8)	317	Suffolk, VA	(24.5)
306	McKinney, TX	(21.8)	248	Portsmouth, VA	(11.1)	350	Sugar Land, TX	(52.6)
304	Melbourne, FL	(21.2)	319	Providence, RI	(24.6)	165	Sunnyvale, CA	0.6
54	Memphis, TN	26.2	197	Provo, UT	(4.6)	203	Sunrise, FL	(5.7)
339	Mesa, AZ	(36.4)	260	Pueblo, CO	(12.1)	343	Surprise, AZ	(40.0)
114	Mesquite, TX	8.0	100	Quincy, MA	13.4	134	Syracuse, NY	4.4
120	Miami Beach, FL	6.5	67	Racine, WI	21.9	198	Tacoma, WA	(4.8)
NA	Miami Gardens, FL**	NA	220	Raleigh, NC	(7.4)	180	Tallahassee, FL	(2.4)
302	Miami, FL	(20.8)	166	Rancho Cucamon., CA	0.5	344	Tampa, FL	(41.6)
335	Midland, TX	(35.4)	216	Reading, PA	(7.2)	253	Temecula, CA	(11.4)
31	Milwaukee, WI	38.8	281	Redding, CA	(15.6)	246	Tempe, AZ	(11.0)
NA	Minneapolis, MN**	NA	213	Reno, NV	(7.1)	333	Thornton, CO	(33.6)
274	Miramar, FL	(14.0)	317	Rialto, CA	(24.5)	105	Thousand Oaks, CA	11.3
342	Mission Viejo, CA	(39.3)	307	Richardson, TX	(22.0)	99	Toledo, OH	13.7
264	Mobile, AL	(13.0)	153	Richmond, CA	1.9	347	Toms River Twnshp, NJ	(42.7)
42	Modesto, CA	31.2	295	Richmond, VA	(18.6)	331	Topeka, KS	(31.9)
297	Montgomery, AL	(19.2)	238	Riverside, CA	(10.2)	324	Torrance, CA	(27.2)
338	Moreno Valley, CA	(36.1)	NA	Roanoke, VA**	NA	325	Tracy, CA	(29.0)
74	Murfreesboro, TN	19.1	NA	Rochester, MN**	NA	276	Trenton, NJ	(14.3)
154	Murrieta, CA	1.8	14	Rochester, NY	56.5	170	Troy, MI	0.1
45	Napa, CA	29.9	NA	Rockford, IL**	NA	205	Tucson, AZ	(5.9)
NA	Naperville, IL**	NA	35	Roseville, CA	36.3	91	Tulsa, OK	14.9
NA	Nashua, NH**	NA	321	Roswell, GA	(26.3)	61	Tuscaloosa, AL	23.3
177	Nashville, TN	(1.4)	336	Round Rock, TX	(35.5)	297	Tyler, TX	(19.2)
NA	New Bedford, MA**	NA	22	Sacramento, CA	43.5	4	Upper Darby Twnshp, PA	91.4
348	New Orleans, LA	(44.2)	5	Salem, OR	87.2	159	Vacaville, CA	1.5
297	New York, NY	(19.2)	135	Salinas, CA	4.1	97	Vallejo, CA	13.8
255	Newark, NJ	(11.6)	60	Salt Lake City, UT	24.2	141	Vancouver, WA	3.7
78	Newport Beach, CA	17.2	144	San Angelo, TX	3.1	81	Ventura, CA	16.8
118	Newport News, VA	6.9	316	San Antonio, TX	(24.4)	38	Victorville, CA	34.1
NA	Newton, MA**	NA	309	San Bernardino, CA	(22.1)	49	Virginia Beach, VA	28.7
28	Norfolk, VA	39.5	246	San Diego, CA	(11.0)	261	Visalia, CA	(12.5)
248	Norman, OK	(11.1)	85	San Francisco, CA	16.4	90	Vista, CA	15.0
156	North Charleston, SC	1.7	269	San Jose, CA	(13.2)	186	Waco, TX	(3.4)
236	North Las Vegas, NV	(9.9)	36	San Leandro, CA	36.0	154	Warren, MI	1.8
313	Norwalk, CA	(23.8)	175	San Mateo, CA	(0.9)	242	Warwick, RI	(10.6)
29	Oakland, CA	39.4	279	Sandy, UT	(15.0)	233	Washington, DC	(9.4)
285	Oceanside, CA	(16.5)	127	Santa Ana, CA	5.6	327	Waterbury, CT	(29.2)
101	Odessa, TX	12.5	180	Santa Barbara, CA	(2.4)	87	West Covina, CA	15.5
267	Ogden, UT	(13.1)	346	Santa Clara, CA	(42.2)	328	West Jordan, UT	(30.6)
180	Oklahoma City, OK	(2.4)	76	Santa Clarita, CA	18.6	277	West Palm Beach, FL	(14.6)
315	Olathe, KS	(24.1)	NA	Santa Maria, CA**	NA	132	West Valley, UT	5.0
284	Omaha, NE	(16.3)	258	Santa Monica, CA	(11.9)	52	Westland, MI	26.3
232	Ontario, CA	(9.3)	26	Santa Rosa, CA	41.2	224	Westminster, CA	(8.4)
128	Orange, CA	5.5	337	Savannah, GA	(35.9)	NA	Westminster, CO**	NA
275	Orem, UT	(14.2)	191	Scottsdale, AZ	(3.9)	140	Whittier, CA	3.8
119	Orlando, FL	6.6	164	Seattle, WA	0.8	349	Wichita Falls, TX	(47.9)
290	Overland Park, KS	(17.3)	78	Shreveport, LA	17.2	34	Wichita, KS	36.4
201	Oxnard, CA	(5.5)	30	Simi Valley, CA	39.1	329	Wilmington, NC	(30.9)
311	Palm Bay, FL	(23.7)	323	Sioux City, IA	(26.7)	174	Winston-Salem, NC	(0.4)
311	Palmdale, CA	(23.7)	194	Sioux Falls, SD	(4.4)	267	Woodbridge Twnshp, NJ	(13.1)
141	Parma, OH	3.7	190	Somerville, MA	(3.8)	NA	Worcester, MA**	NA
244	Pasadena, CA	(10.9)	162	South Bend, IN	1.2	96	Yakima, WA	13.9
169	Pasadena, TX	0.2	178	South Gate, CA	(2.0)	112	Yonkers, NY	10.1
18	Paterson, NJ	45.8	54	Southfield, MI	26.2	147	Youngstown, OH	3.0
234	Pembroke Pines, FL	(9.7)	218	Sparks, NV	(7.3)	NA	Yuma, AZ**	NA

Source: CQ Press using data from F.B.I. "Crime in the United States 2006"

**Violent crimes are offenses of murder, forcible rape, robbery, and aggravated assault.*

***Not available.*

48. Percent Change in Violent Crime Rate: 2002 to 2006 (continued)
National Percent Change = 4.2% Decrease*

RANK	CITY	% CHANGE
1	Chino, CA	165.3
2	Kent, WA	97.8
3	Flint, MI	91.5
4	Upper Darby Twnshp, PA	91.4
5	Salem, OR	87.2
6	Fargo, ND	83.5
7	Allentown, PA	75.8
8	Lakewood, CO	71.2
9	Deerfield Beach, FL	70.0
10	Lee's Summit, MO	65.2
11	Largo, FL	61.7
12	Kenosha, WI	60.8
13	Clarksville, TN	58.8
14	Rochester, NY	56.5
15	Lawrence, KS	53.0
16	Fremont, CA	52.1
17	Green Bay, WI	46.6
18	Paterson, NJ	45.8
19	Columbus, GA	45.1
20	Anchorage, AK	45.0
21	Lawton, OK	43.9
22	Sacramento, CA	43.5
23	Huntsville, AL	42.4
24	Chandler, AZ	42.3
24	Denver, CO	42.3
26	Santa Rosa, CA	41.2
27	Macon, GA	39.7
28	Norfolk, VA	39.5
29	Oakland, CA	39.4
30	Simi Valley, CA	39.1
31	Milwaukee, WI	38.8
32	Carlsbad, CA	38.7
33	Little Rock, AR	37.1
34	Wichita, KS	36.4
35	Roseville, CA	36.3
36	San Leandro, CA	36.0
37	Pompano Beach, FL	34.6
38	Victorville, CA	34.1
39	Greeley, CO	33.9
40	Hayward, CA	32.6
41	Alhambra, CA	31.4
42	Edison Twnshp, NJ	31.2
42	Modesto, CA	31.2
44	Hamilton Twnshp, NJ	30.0
45	Napa, CA	29.9
46	Manchester, NH	29.7
47	Gainesville, FL	29.3
48	Independence, MO	29.0
49	Virginia Beach, VA	28.7
50	Abilene, TX	28.0
51	Fullerton, CA	26.7
52	Bakersfield, CA	26.3
52	Westland, MI	26.3
54	Federal Way, WA	26.2
54	Las Vegas, NV	26.2
54	Memphis, TN	26.2
54	Southfield, MI	26.2
58	Erie, PA	24.9
59	Bellevue, WA	24.4
60	Salt Lake City, UT	24.2
61	Concord, CA	23.3
61	Tuscaloosa, AL	23.3
63	Longview, TX	23.2
64	Greensboro, NC	23.1
65	Madison, WI	22.3
66	Lakewood, CA	22.0
67	Racine, WI	21.9
68	Amherst, NY	20.5
69	Huntington Beach, CA	20.2
70	Baton Rouge, LA	20.1
70	Colonie, NY	20.1
72	Escondido, CA	20.0
73	Fort Smith, AR	19.7
74	Murfreesboro, TN	19.1
75	Philadelphia, PA	18.7
76	Santa Clarita, CA	18.6
77	Buena Park, CA	18.0
78	Newport Beach, CA	17.2
78	Shreveport, LA	17.2
80	Cleveland, OH	17.0
81	St. Louis, MO	16.8
81	Ventura, CA	16.8
83	Ann Arbor, MI	16.7
83	Detroit, MI	16.7
85	Camden, NJ	16.4
85	San Francisco, CA	16.4
87	Arlington, TX	15.5
87	West Covina, CA	15.5
89	Costa Mesa, CA	15.3
90	Vista, CA	15.0
91	Boston, MA	14.9
91	Tulsa, OK	14.9
93	Inglewood, CA	14.8
94	Edmond, OK	14.2
95	Lafayette, LA	14.0
96	Yakima, WA	13.9
97	Everett, WA	13.8
97	Vallejo, CA	13.8
99	Toledo, OH	13.7
100	Quincy, MA	13.4
101	Odessa, TX	12.5
102	Arvada, CO	12.1
103	Fort Lauderdale, FL	12.0
104	Anaheim, CA	11.4
105	Thousand Oaks, CA	11.3
106	Albany, GA	11.2
106	Lowell, MA	11.2
108	Buffalo, NY	10.9
109	Gresham, OR	10.8
110	Boise, ID	10.5
111	Austin, TX	10.3
112	Yonkers, NY	10.1
113	Bellingham, WA	9.0
114	Mesquite, TX	8.0
115	Fort Collins, CO	7.8
116	Fayetteville, NC	7.3
117	Fairfield, CA	7.0
118	Newport News, VA	6.9
119	Orlando, FL	6.6
120	Glendale, AZ	6.5
120	Miami Beach, FL	6.5
122	Baldwin Park, CA	6.4
122	Irving, TX	6.4
124	Hesperia, CA	6.3
125	Colorado Springs, CO	5.9
126	Amarillo, TX	5.7
127	Santa Ana, CA	5.6
128	Orange, CA	5.5
129	Cary, NC	5.3
130	Alexandria, VA	5.2
130	Boulder, CO	5.2
132	West Valley, UT	5.0
133	Birmingham, AL	4.5
134	Syracuse, NY	4.4
135	Bellflower, CA	4.1
135	Honolulu, HI	4.1
135	Salinas, CA	4.1
138	Columbia, MO	4.0
139	Beaumont, TX	3.9
140	Whittier, CA	3.8
141	Downey, CA	3.7
141	Parma, OH	3.7
141	Vancouver, WA	3.7
144	Boca Raton, FL	3.1
144	Charleston, SC	3.1
144	San Angelo, TX	3.1
147	Henderson, NV	3.0
147	Youngstown, OH	3.0
149	Clovis, CA	2.9
150	Indianapolis, IN	2.7
151	Sterling Heights, MI	2.6
152	Hartford, CT	2.2
153	Richmond, CA	1.9
154	Murrieta, CA	1.8
154	Warren, MI	1.8
156	North Charleston, SC	1.7
157	Daly City, CA	1.6
157	Jersey City, NJ	1.6
159	Vacaville, CA	1.5
160	Phoenix, AZ	1.4
160	Stockton, CA	1.4
162	South Bend, IN	1.2
163	Jackson, MS	1.0
164	Seattle, WA	0.8
165	Sunnyvale, CA	0.6
166	Beaverton, OR	0.5
166	Rancho Cucamon., CA	0.5
168	Lynn, MA	0.3
169	Pasadena, TX	0.2
170	Plano, TX	0.1
170	Troy, MI	0.1
172	Plantation, FL	(0.1)
173	Corpus Christi, TX	(0.3)
174	Winston-Salem, NC	(0.4)
175	San Mateo, CA	(0.9)
176	Hammond, IN	(1.0)
177	Nashville, TN	(1.4)
178	South Gate, CA	(2.0)
179	Gary, IN	(2.2)
180	Oklahoma City, OK	(2.4)
180	Santa Barbara, CA	(2.4)
180	Tallahassee, FL	(2.4)
183	Killeen, TX	(2.5)
184	Carson, CA	(2.8)
185	Cincinnati, OH	(3.2)
186	Clinton Twnshp, MI	(3.4)
186	Elizabeth, NJ	(3.4)
186	Pittsburgh, PA	(3.4)
186	Waco, TX	(3.4)
190	Somerville, MA	(3.8)
191	Scottsdale, AZ	(3.9)
192	Aurora, CO	(4.1)

RANK	CITY	% CHANGE
193	Springfield, MO	(4.2)
194	Houston, TX	(4.4)
194	Sioux Falls, SD	(4.4)
196	Livermore, CA	(4.5)
197	Provo, UT	(4.6)
198	Tacoma, WA	(4.8)
199	Hampton, VA	(4.9)
200	Lansing, MI	(5.1)
201	Oxnard, CA	(5.5)
202	Long Beach, CA	(5.6)
203	Hawthorne, CA	(5.7)
203	Sunrise, FL	(5.7)
205	Knoxville, TN	(5.9)
205	Tucson, AZ	(5.9)
207	Coral Springs, FL	(6.1)
208	Cambridge, MA	(6.2)
209	Broken Arrow, OK	(6.6)
209	Lincoln, NE	(6.6)
211	Laredo, TX	(7.0)
211	Pomona, CA	(7.0)
213	Berkeley, CA	(7.1)
213	Garland, TX	(7.1)
213	Reno, NV	(7.1)
216	Compton, CA	(7.2)
216	Reading, PA	(7.2)
218	Canton Twnshp, MI	(7.3)
218	Sparks, NV	(7.3)
220	Raleigh, NC	(7.4)
221	Spokane, WA	(7.5)
222	Charlotte, NC	(8.1)
223	El Cajon, CA	(8.2)
224	Westminster, CA	(8.4)
225	Burbank, CA	(8.6)
225	High Point, NC	(8.6)
225	Jacksonville, FL	(8.6)
228	Cedar Rapids, IA	(8.7)
228	Grand Rapids, MI	(8.7)
230	Brownsville, TX	(8.9)
231	Bridgeport, CT	(9.1)
232	Ontario, CA	(9.3)
233	Washington, DC	(9.4)
234	Pembroke Pines, FL	(9.7)
234	Peoria, AZ	(9.7)
236	North Las Vegas, NV	(9.9)
237	Chula Vista, CA	(10.0)
238	Riverside, CA	(10.2)
239	Garden Grove, CA	(10.3)
240	Brick Twnshp, NJ	(10.4)
241	Columbus, OH	(10.5)
242	Warwick, RI	(10.6)
243	Gilbert, AZ	(10.8)
244	Dayton, OH	(10.9)
244	Pasadena, CA	(10.9)
246	San Diego, CA	(11.0)
246	Tempe, AZ	(11.0)
248	Hialeah, FL	(11.1)
248	Norman, OK	(11.1)
248	Portsmouth, VA	(11.1)
251	Antioch, CA	(11.2)
251	Fresno, CA	(11.2)
253	Lewisville, TX	(11.4)
253	Temecula, CA	(11.4)
255	Newark, NJ	(11.6)
256	Billings, MT	(11.7)
257	Hillsboro, OR	(11.8)
258	Santa Monica, CA	(11.9)

RANK	CITY	% CHANGE
259	Dallas, TX	(12.0)
260	Pueblo, CO	(12.1)
261	Visalia, CA	(12.5)
262	Clifton, NJ	(12.7)
262	Port St. Lucie, FL	(12.7)
264	Cranston, RI	(13.0)
264	Mobile, AL	(13.0)
264	St. Petersburg, FL	(13.0)
267	Ogden, UT	(13.1)
267	Woodbridge Twnshp, NJ	(13.1)
269	San Jose, CA	(13.2)
270	Fort Worth, TX	(13.7)
271	Portland, OR	(13.8)
272	Davie, FL	(13.9)
272	Evansville, IN	(13.9)
274	Miramar, FL	(14.0)
275	Orem, UT	(14.2)
276	Trenton, NJ	(14.3)
277	West Palm Beach, FL	(14.6)
278	Lancaster, CA	(14.9)
279	Albuquerque, NM	(15.0)
279	Sandy, UT	(15.0)
281	Redding, CA	(15.6)
282	Grand Prairie, TX	(16.0)
283	Columbia, SC	(16.1)
284	Omaha, NE	(16.3)
285	Oceanside, CA	(16.5)
286	Carrollton, TX	(16.6)
286	Danbury, CT	(16.6)
286	Lubbock, TX	(16.6)
289	Athens-Clarke, GA	(16.8)
290	Overland Park, KS	(17.3)
291	Baltimore, MD	(17.4)
292	Chattanooga, TN	(18.4)
292	El Monte, CA	(18.4)
292	Livonia, MI	(18.4)
295	Richmond, VA	(18.6)
296	Lakeland, FL	(18.9)
297	Corona, CA	(19.2)
297	Montgomery, AL	(19.2)
297	New York, NY	(19.2)
297	Tyler, TX	(19.2)
301	Farmington Hills, MI	(20.0)
302	Miami, FL	(20.8)
303	Clearwater, FL	(21.0)
304	Melbourne, FL	(21.2)
305	Cape Coral, FL	(21.6)
306	McKinney, TX	(21.8)
307	Lake Forest, CA	(22.0)
307	Richardson, TX	(22.0)
309	San Bernardino, CA	(22.1)
310	Fontana, CA	(23.6)
311	Palm Bay, FL	(23.7)
311	Palmdale, CA	(23.7)
313	Eugene, OR	(23.8)
313	Norwalk, CA	(23.8)
315	Olathe, KS	(24.1)
316	San Antonio, TX	(24.4)
317	Rialto, CA	(24.5)
317	Suffolk, VA	(24.5)
319	Providence, RI	(24.6)
320	Glendale, CA	(25.6)
321	Roswell, GA	(26.3)
322	Springfield, MA	(26.6)
323	Sioux City, IA	(26.7)
324	Torrance, CA	(27.2)

RANK	CITY	% CHANGE
325	Hollywood, FL	(29.0)
325	Tracy, CA	(29.0)
327	Waterbury, CT	(29.2)
328	West Jordan, UT	(30.6)
329	Denton, TX	(30.9)
329	Wilmington, NC	(30.9)
331	Topeka, KS	(31.9)
332	Atlanta, GA	(32.1)
333	Thornton, CO	(33.6)
334	Chesapeake, VA	(34.7)
335	Midland, TX	(35.4)
336	Round Rock, TX	(35.5)
337	Savannah, GA	(35.9)
338	Moreno Valley, CA	(36.1)
339	Mesa, AZ	(36.4)
340	McAllen, TX	(37.2)
341	Irvine, CA	(38.4)
342	Mission Viejo, CA	(39.3)
343	Surprise, AZ	(40.0)
344	Tampa, FL	(41.6)
345	Los Angeles, CA	(41.7)
346	Santa Clara, CA	(42.2)
347	Toms River Twnshp, NJ	(42.7)
348	New Orleans, LA	(44.2)
349	Wichita Falls, TX	(47.9)
350	Sugar Land, TX	(52.6)
351	Dearborn, MI	(56.7)
352	Clarkstown, NY	(57.0)
353	Chino Hills, CA	(64.3)
NA	Albany, NY**	NA
NA	Aurora, IL**	NA
NA	Bloomington, MN**	NA
NA	Brockton, MA**	NA
NA	Canton, OH**	NA
NA	Centennial, CO**	NA
NA	Cheektowaga, NY**	NA
NA	Chicago, IL**	NA
NA	Des Moines, IA**	NA
NA	Duluth, MN**	NA
NA	Durham, NC**	NA
NA	El Paso, TX**	NA
NA	Fort Wayne, IN**	NA
NA	Greece, NY**	NA
NA	Joliet, IL**	NA
NA	Kansas City, KS**	NA
NA	Kansas City, MO**	NA
NA	Las Cruces, NM**	NA
NA	Lexington, KY**	NA
NA	Louisville, KY**	NA
NA	Miami Gardens, FL**	NA
NA	Minneapolis, MN**	NA
NA	Naperville, IL**	NA
NA	Nashua, NH**	NA
NA	New Bedford, MA**	NA
NA	Newton, MA**	NA
NA	Peoria, IL**	NA
NA	Roanoke, VA**	NA
NA	Rochester, MN**	NA
NA	Rockford, IL**	NA
NA	Santa Maria, CA**	NA
NA	Spokane Valley, WA**	NA
NA	Springfield, IL**	NA
NA	St. Paul, MN**	NA
NA	Westminster, CO**	NA
NA	Worcester, MA**	NA
NA	Yuma, AZ**	NA

Source: CQ Press using data from F.B.I. "Crime in the United States 2006"

**Violent crimes are offenses of murder, forcible rape, robbery, and aggravated assault.*

***Not available.*

49. Murders in 2006

National Total = 17,034 Murders*

RANK	CITY	MURDERS
212	Abilene, TX	5
163	Albany, GA	8
212	Albany, NY	5
61	Albuquerque, NM	34
176	Alexandria, VA	7
325	Alhambra, CA	1
115	Allentown, PA	16
212	Amarillo, TX	5
283	Amherst, NY	2
145	Anaheim, CA	10
106	Anchorage, AK	17
364	Ann Arbor, MI	0
145	Antioch, CA	10
126	Arlington, TX	14
364	Arvada, CO	0
212	Athens-Clarke, GA	5
19	Atlanta, GA	110
106	Aurora, CO	17
233	Aurora, IL	4
92	Austin, TX	20
79	Bakersfield, CA	24
192	Baldwin Park, CA	6
7	Baltimore, MD	276
36	Baton Rouge, LA	57
145	Beaumont, TX	10
325	Beaverton, OR	1
254	Bellevue, WA	3
212	Bellflower, CA	5
364	Bellingham, WA	0
233	Berkeley, CA	4
283	Billings, MT	2
22	Birmingham, AL	104
212	Bloomington, MN	5
254	Boca Raton, FL	3
192	Boise, ID	6
31	Boston, MA	75
325	Boulder, CO	1
364	Brick Twnshp, NJ	0
69	Bridgeport, CT	28
163	Brockton, MA	8
325	Broken Arrow, OK	1
212	Brownsville, TX	5
325	Buena Park, CA	1
33	Buffalo, NY	74
325	Burbank, CA	1
283	Cambridge, MA	2
64	Camden, NJ	32
254	Canton Twnshp, MI	3
154	Canton, OH	9
192	Cape Coral, FL	6
325	Carlsbad, CA	1
212	Carrollton, TX	5
119	Carson, CA	15
364	Cary, NC	0
192	Cedar Rapids, IA	6
364	Centennial, CO	0
154	Chandler, AZ	9
81	Charleston, SC	23
27	Charlotte, NC	83
106	Chattanooga, TN	17
283	Cheektowaga, NY	2
176	Chesapeake, VA	7
3	Chicago, IL	468
325	Chino Hills, CA	1
364	Chino, CA	0
176	Chula Vista, CA	7
25	Cincinnati, OH	89
325	Clarkstown, NY	1
192	Clarksville, TN	6
233	Clearwater, FL	4
31	Cleveland, OH	75
325	Clifton, NJ	1
325	Clinton Twnshp, MI	1
325	Clovis, CA	1
364	Colonie, NY	0
119	Colorado Springs, CO	15
283	Columbia, MO	2
176	Columbia, SC	7
106	Columbus, GA	17
22	Columbus, OH	104
56	Compton, CA	39
283	Concord, CA	2
283	Coral Springs, FL	2
325	Corona, CA	1
87	Corpus Christi, TX	21
192	Costa Mesa, CA	6
325	Cranston, RI	1
9	Dallas, TX	187
254	Daly City, CA	3
233	Danbury, CT	4
283	Davie, FL	2
57	Dayton, OH	37
283	Dearborn, MI	2
176	Deerfield Beach, FL	7
364	Denton, TX	0
44	Denver, CO	51
192	Des Moines, IA	6
4	Detroit, MI	418
233	Downey, CA	4
325	Duluth, MN	1
129	Durham, NC	13
325	Edison Twnshp, NJ	1
325	Edmond, OK	1
233	El Cajon, CA	4
212	El Monte, CA	5
129	El Paso, TX	13
106	Elizabeth, NJ	17
283	Erie, PA	2
254	Escondido, CA	3
254	Eugene, OR	3
192	Evansville, IN	6
254	Everett, WA	3
192	Fairfield, CA	6
283	Fargo, ND	2
364	Farmington Hills, MI	0
119	Fayetteville, NC	15
325	Federal Way, WA	1
41	Flint, MI	54
212	Fontana, CA	5
364	Fort Collins, CO	0
87	Fort Lauderdale, FL	21
139	Fort Smith, AR	11
101	Fort Wayne, IN	18
47	Fort Worth, TX	49
192	Fremont, CA	6
43	Fresno, CA	52
283	Fullerton, CA	2
176	Gainesville, FL	7
154	Garden Grove, CA	9
254	Garland, TX	3
50	Gary, IN	48
254	Gilbert, AZ	3
87	Glendale, AZ	21
283	Glendale, CA	2
254	Grand Prairie, TX	3
83	Grand Rapids, MI	22
283	Greece, NY	2
283	Greeley, CO	2
283	Green Bay, WI	2
73	Greensboro, NC	27
192	Gresham, OR	6
325	Hamilton Twnshp, NJ	1
163	Hammond, IN	8
139	Hampton, VA	11
79	Hartford, CT	24
154	Hawthorne, CA	9
233	Hayward, CA	4
212	Henderson, NV	5
176	Hesperia, CA	7
212	Hialeah, FL	5
163	High Point, NC	8
283	Hillsboro, OR	2
163	Hollywood, FL	8
106	Honolulu, HI	17
6	Houston, TX	377
283	Huntington Beach, CA	2
115	Huntsville, AL	16
283	Independence, MO	2
15	Indianapolis, IN	140
59	Inglewood, CA	36
233	Irvine, CA	4
254	Irving, TX	3
19	Jacksonville, FL	110
55	Jackson, MS	40
83	Jersey City, NJ	22
126	Joliet, IL	14
52	Kansas City, KS	45
18	Kansas City, MO	112
233	Kenosha, WI	4
283	Kent, WA	2
163	Killeen, TX	8
101	Knoxville, TN	18
145	Lafayette, LA	10
325	Lake Forest, CA	1
254	Lakeland, FL	3
233	Lakewood, CA	4
233	Lakewood, CO	4
95	Lancaster, CA	19
192	Lansing, MI	6
83	Laredo, TX	22
283	Largo, FL	2
254	Las Cruces, NM	3
12	Las Vegas, NV	152
254	Lawrence, KS	3
163	Lawton, OK	8
283	Lee's Summit, MO	2
283	Lewisville, TX	2
154	Lexington, KY	9
212	Lincoln, NE	5
35	Little Rock, AR	58
325	Livermore, CA	1
364	Livonia, MI	0

RANK	CITY	MURDERS
54	Long Beach, CA	41
145	Longview, TX	10
2	Los Angeles, CA	480
46	Louisville, KY	50
129	Lowell, MA	13
129	Lubbock, TX	13
233	Lynn, MA	4
135	Macon, GA	12
233	Madison, WI	4
233	Manchester, NH	4
233	McAllen, TX	4
283	McKinney, TX	2
283	Melbourne, FL	2
13	Memphis, TN	147
75	Mesa, AZ	26
212	Mesquite, TX	5
233	Miami Beach, FL	4
101	Miami Gardens, FL	18
29	Miami, FL	77
212	Midland, TX	5
24	Milwaukee, WI	103
36	Minneapolis, MN	57
192	Miramar, FL	6
364	Mission Viejo, CA	0
61	Mobile, AL	34
139	Modesto, CA	11
73	Montgomery, AL	27
115	Moreno Valley, CA	16
192	Murfreesboro, TN	6
283	Murrieta, CA	2
325	Napa, CA	1
364	Naperville, IL	0
325	Nashua, NH	1
28	Nashville, TN	80
176	New Bedford, MA	7
11	New Orleans, LA	162
1	New York, NY	596
21	Newark, NJ	105
325	Newport Beach, CA	1
95	Newport News, VA	19
325	Newton, MA	1
69	Norfolk, VA	28
212	Norman, OK	5
69	North Charleston, SC	28
83	North Las Vegas, NV	22
176	Norwalk, CA	7
14	Oakland, CA	145
163	Oceanside, CA	8
283	Odessa, TX	2
283	Ogden, UT	2
40	Oklahoma City, OK	55
254	Olathe, KS	3
63	Omaha, NE	33
129	Ontario, CA	13
325	Orange, CA	1
325	Orem, UT	1
47	Orlando, FL	49
364	Overland Park, KS	0
129	Oxnard, CA	13
325	Palm Bay, FL	1
119	Palmdale, CA	15
364	Parma, OH	0
139	Pasadena, CA	11
176	Pasadena, TX	7
119	Paterson, NJ	15
325	Pembroke Pines, FL	1
283	Peoria, AZ	2
106	Peoria, IL	17
5	Philadelphia, PA	406
8	Phoenix, AZ	234
39	Pittsburgh, PA	56
233	Plano, TX	4
254	Plantation, FL	3
95	Pomona, CA	19
145	Pompano Beach, FL	10
176	Port St. Lucie, FL	7
92	Portland, OR	20
101	Portsmouth, VA	18
139	Providence, RI	11
283	Provo, UT	2
192	Pueblo, CO	6
254	Quincy, MA	3
176	Racine, WI	7
95	Raleigh, NC	19
254	Rancho Cucamon., CA	3
145	Reading, PA	10
283	Redding, CA	2
81	Reno, NV	23
135	Rialto, CA	12
254	Richardson, TX	3
53	Richmond, CA	42
30	Richmond, VA	76
139	Riverside, CA	11
135	Roanoke, VA	12
283	Rochester, MN	2
47	Rochester, NY	49
95	Rockford, IL	19
254	Roseville, CA	3
364	Roswell, GA	0
364	Round Rock, TX	0
36	Sacramento, CA	57
154	Salem, OR	9
176	Salinas, CA	7
163	Salt Lake City, UT	8
254	San Angelo, TX	3
17	San Antonio, TX	119
51	San Bernardino, CA	46
34	San Diego, CA	68
26	San Francisco, CA	86
67	San Jose, CA	29
233	San Leandro, CA	4
283	San Mateo, CA	2
364	Sandy, UT	0
75	Santa Ana, CA	26
325	Santa Barbara, CA	1
254	Santa Clara, CA	3
254	Santa Clarita, CA	3
283	Santa Maria, CA	2
283	Santa Monica, CA	2
192	Santa Rosa, CA	6
67	Savannah, GA	29
212	Scottsdale, AZ	5
66	Seattle, WA	30
69	Shreveport, LA	28
254	Simi Valley, CA	3
364	Sioux City, IA	0
176	Sioux Falls, SD	7
283	Somerville, MA	2
126	South Bend, IN	14
115	South Gate, CA	16
325	Southfield, MI	1
254	Sparks, NV	3
325	Spokane Valley, WA	1
145	Spokane, WA	10
192	Springfield, IL	6
119	Springfield, MA	15
192	Springfield, MO	6
283	Sterling Heights, MI	2
57	Stockton, CA	37
16	St. Louis, MO	129
106	St. Paul, MN	17
87	St. Petersburg, FL	21
163	Suffolk, VA	8
364	Sugar Land, TX	0
325	Sunnyvale, CA	1
254	Sunrise, FL	3
364	Surprise, AZ	0
135	Syracuse, NY	12
87	Tacoma, WA	21
145	Tallahassee, FL	10
78	Tampa, FL	25
364	Temecula, CA	0
212	Tempe, AZ	5
233	Thornton, CO	4
364	Thousand Oaks, CA	0
60	Toledo, OH	35
364	Toms River Twnshp, NJ	0
154	Topeka, KS	9
325	Torrance, CA	1
364	Tracy, CA	0
101	Trenton, NJ	18
283	Troy, MI	2
44	Tucson, AZ	51
42	Tulsa, OK	53
119	Tuscaloosa, AL	15
212	Tyler, TX	5
283	Upper Darby Twnshp, PA	2
325	Vacaville, CA	1
192	Vallejo, CA	6
233	Vancouver, WA	4
325	Ventura, CA	1
163	Victorville, CA	8
95	Virginia Beach, VA	19
163	Visalia, CA	8
325	Vista, CA	1
154	Waco, TX	9
212	Warren, MI	5
283	Warwick, RI	2
10	Washington, DC	169
176	Waterbury, CT	7
283	West Covina, CA	2
325	West Jordan, UT	1
106	West Palm Beach, FL	17
254	West Valley, UT	3
283	Westland, MI	2
325	Westminster, CA	1
212	Westminster, CO	5
233	Whittier, CA	4
154	Wichita Falls, TX	9
75	Wichita, KS	26
176	Wilmington, NC	7
92	Winston-Salem, NC	20
364	Woodbridge Twnshp, NJ	0
192	Worcester, MA	6
254	Yakima, WA	3
163	Yonkers, NY	8
64	Youngstown, OH	32
254	Yuma, AZ	3

Source: Federal Bureau of Investigation "Crime in the United States 2006"
**Includes nonnegligent manslaughter.*

49. Murders in 2006 (continued)

National Total = 17,034 Murders*

RANK	CITY	MURDERS
1	New York, NY	596
2	Los Angeles, CA	480
3	Chicago, IL	468
4	Detroit, MI	418
5	Philadelphia, PA	406
6	Houston, TX	377
7	Baltimore, MD	276
8	Phoenix, AZ	234
9	Dallas, TX	187
10	Washington, DC	169
11	New Orleans, LA	162
12	Las Vegas, NV	152
13	Memphis, TN	147
14	Oakland, CA	145
15	Indianapolis, IN	140
16	St. Louis, MO	129
17	San Antonio, TX	119
18	Kansas City, MO	112
19	Atlanta, GA	110
19	Jacksonville, FL	110
21	Newark, NJ	105
22	Birmingham, AL	104
22	Columbus, OH	104
24	Milwaukee, WI	103
25	Cincinnati, OH	89
26	San Francisco, CA	86
27	Charlotte, NC	83
28	Nashville, TN	80
29	Miami, FL	77
30	Richmond, VA	76
31	Boston, MA	75
31	Cleveland, OH	75
33	Buffalo, NY	74
34	San Diego, CA	68
35	Little Rock, AR	58
36	Baton Rouge, LA	57
36	Minneapolis, MN	57
36	Sacramento, CA	57
39	Pittsburgh, PA	56
40	Oklahoma City, OK	55
41	Flint, MI	54
42	Tulsa, OK	53
43	Fresno, CA	52
44	Denver, CO	51
44	Tucson, AZ	51
46	Louisville, KY	50
47	Fort Worth, TX	49
47	Orlando, FL	49
47	Rochester, NY	49
50	Gary, IN	48
51	San Bernardino, CA	46
52	Kansas City, KS	45
53	Richmond, CA	42
54	Long Beach, CA	41
55	Jackson, MS	40
56	Compton, CA	39
57	Dayton, OH	37
57	Stockton, CA	37
59	Inglewood, CA	36
60	Toledo, OH	35
61	Albuquerque, NM	34
61	Mobile, AL	34
63	Omaha, NE	33
64	Camden, NJ	32
64	Youngstown, OH	32
66	Seattle, WA	30
67	San Jose, CA	29
67	Savannah, GA	29
69	Bridgeport, CT	28
69	Norfolk, VA	28
69	North Charleston, SC	28
69	Shreveport, LA	28
73	Greensboro, NC	27
73	Montgomery, AL	27
75	Mesa, AZ	26
75	Santa Ana, CA	26
75	Wichita, KS	26
78	Tampa, FL	25
79	Bakersfield, CA	24
79	Hartford, CT	24
81	Charleston, SC	23
81	Reno, NV	23
83	Grand Rapids, MI	22
83	Jersey City, NJ	22
83	Laredo, TX	22
83	North Las Vegas, NV	22
87	Corpus Christi, TX	21
87	Fort Lauderdale, FL	21
87	Glendale, AZ	21
87	St. Petersburg, FL	21
87	Tacoma, WA	21
92	Austin, TX	20
92	Portland, OR	20
92	Winston-Salem, NC	20
95	Lancaster, CA	19
95	Newport News, VA	19
95	Pomona, CA	19
95	Raleigh, NC	19
95	Rockford, IL	19
95	Virginia Beach, VA	19
101	Fort Wayne, IN	18
101	Knoxville, TN	18
101	Miami Gardens, FL	18
101	Portsmouth, VA	18
101	Trenton, NJ	18
106	Anchorage, AK	17
106	Aurora, CO	17
106	Chattanooga, TN	17
106	Columbus, GA	17
106	Elizabeth, NJ	17
106	Honolulu, HI	17
106	Peoria, IL	17
106	St. Paul, MN	17
106	West Palm Beach, FL	17
115	Allentown, PA	16
115	Huntsville, AL	16
115	Moreno Valley, CA	16
115	South Gate, CA	16
119	Carson, CA	15
119	Colorado Springs, CO	15
119	Fayetteville, NC	15
119	Palmdale, CA	15
119	Paterson, NJ	15
119	Springfield, MA	15
119	Tuscaloosa, AL	15
126	Arlington, TX	14
126	Joliet, IL	14
126	South Bend, IN	14
129	Durham, NC	13
129	El Paso, TX	13
129	Lowell, MA	13
129	Lubbock, TX	13
129	Ontario, CA	13
129	Oxnard, CA	13
135	Macon, GA	12
135	Rialto, CA	12
135	Roanoke, VA	12
135	Syracuse, NY	12
139	Fort Smith, AR	11
139	Hampton, VA	11
139	Modesto, CA	11
139	Pasadena, CA	11
139	Providence, RI	11
139	Riverside, CA	11
145	Anaheim, CA	10
145	Antioch, CA	10
145	Beaumont, TX	10
145	Lafayette, LA	10
145	Longview, TX	10
145	Pompano Beach, FL	10
145	Reading, PA	10
145	Spokane, WA	10
145	Tallahassee, FL	10
154	Canton, OH	9
154	Chandler, AZ	9
154	Garden Grove, CA	9
154	Hawthorne, CA	9
154	Lexington, KY	9
154	Salem, OR	9
154	Topeka, KS	9
154	Waco, TX	9
154	Wichita Falls, TX	9
163	Albany, GA	8
163	Brockton, MA	8
163	Hammond, IN	8
163	High Point, NC	8
163	Hollywood, FL	8
163	Killeen, TX	8
163	Lawton, OK	8
163	Oceanside, CA	8
163	Salt Lake City, UT	8
163	Suffolk, VA	8
163	Victorville, CA	8
163	Visalia, CA	8
163	Yonkers, NY	8
176	Alexandria, VA	7
176	Chesapeake, VA	7
176	Chula Vista, CA	7
176	Columbia, SC	7
176	Deerfield Beach, FL	7
176	Gainesville, FL	7
176	Hesperia, CA	7
176	New Bedford, MA	7
176	Norwalk, CA	7
176	Pasadena, TX	7
176	Port St. Lucie, FL	7
176	Racine, WI	7
176	Salinas, CA	7
176	Sioux Falls, SD	7
176	Waterbury, CT	7
176	Wilmington, NC	7
192	Baldwin Park, CA	6

RANK	CITY	MURDERS
192	Boise, ID	6
192	Cape Coral, FL	6
192	Cedar Rapids, IA	6
192	Clarksville, TN	6
192	Costa Mesa, CA	6
192	Des Moines, IA	6
192	Evansville, IN	6
192	Fairfield, CA	6
192	Fremont, CA	6
192	Gresham, OR	6
192	Lansing, MI	6
192	Miramar, FL	6
192	Murfreesboro, TN	6
192	Pueblo, CO	6
192	Santa Rosa, CA	6
192	Springfield, IL	6
192	Springfield, MO	6
192	Vallejo, CA	6
192	Worcester, MA	6
212	Abilene, TX	5
212	Albany, NY	5
212	Amarillo, TX	5
212	Athens-Clarke, GA	5
212	Bellflower, CA	5
212	Bloomington, MN	5
212	Brownsville, TX	5
212	Carrollton, TX	5
212	El Monte, CA	5
212	Fontana, CA	5
212	Henderson, NV	5
212	Hialeah, FL	5
212	Lincoln, NE	5
212	Mesquite, TX	5
212	Midland, TX	5
212	Norman, OK	5
212	Scottsdale, AZ	5
212	Tempe, AZ	5
212	Tyler, TX	5
212	Warren, MI	5
212	Westminster, CO	5
233	Aurora, IL	4
233	Berkeley, CA	4
233	Clearwater, FL	4
233	Danbury, CT	4
233	Downey, CA	4
233	El Cajon, CA	4
233	Hayward, CA	4
233	Irvine, CA	4
233	Kenosha, WI	4
233	Lakewood, CA	4
233	Lakewood, CO	4
233	Lynn, MA	4
233	Madison, WI	4
233	Manchester, NH	4
233	McAllen, TX	4
233	Miami Beach, FL	4
233	Plano, TX	4
233	San Leandro, CA	4
233	Thornton, CO	4
233	Vancouver, WA	4
233	Whittier, CA	4
254	Bellevue, WA	3
254	Boca Raton, FL	3
254	Canton Twnshp, MI	3
254	Daly City, CA	3
254	Escondido, CA	3
254	Eugene, OR	3
254	Everett, WA	3
254	Garland, TX	3
254	Gilbert, AZ	3
254	Grand Prairie, TX	3
254	Irving, TX	3
254	Lakeland, FL	3
254	Las Cruces, NM	3
254	Lawrence, KS	3
254	Olathe, KS	3
254	Plantation, FL	3
254	Quincy, MA	3
254	Rancho Cucamon., CA	3
254	Richardson, TX	3
254	Roseville, CA	3
254	San Angelo, TX	3
254	Santa Clara, CA	3
254	Santa Clarita, CA	3
254	Simi Valley, CA	3
254	Sparks, NV	3
254	Sunrise, FL	3
254	West Valley, UT	3
254	Yakima, WA	3
254	Yuma, AZ	3
283	Amherst, NY	2
283	Billings, MT	2
283	Cambridge, MA	2
283	Cheektowaga, NY	2
283	Columbia, MO	2
283	Concord, CA	2
283	Coral Springs, FL	2
283	Davie, FL	2
283	Dearborn, MI	2
283	Erie, PA	2
283	Fargo, ND	2
283	Fullerton, CA	2
283	Glendale, CA	2
283	Greece, NY	2
283	Greeley, CO	2
283	Green Bay, WI	2
283	Hillsboro, OR	2
283	Huntington Beach, CA	2
283	Independence, MO	2
283	Kent, WA	2
283	Largo, FL	2
283	Lee's Summit, MO	2
283	Lewisville, TX	2
283	McKinney, TX	2
283	Melbourne, FL	2
283	Murrieta, CA	2
283	Odessa, TX	2
283	Ogden, UT	2
283	Peoria, AZ	2
283	Provo, UT	2
283	Redding, CA	2
283	Rochester, MN	2
283	San Mateo, CA	2
283	Santa Maria, CA	2
283	Santa Monica, CA	2
283	Somerville, MA	2
283	Sterling Heights, MI	2
283	Troy, MI	2
283	Upper Darby Twnshp, PA	2
283	Warwick, RI	2
283	West Covina, CA	2
283	Westland, MI	2
325	Alhambra, CA	1
325	Beaverton, OR	1
325	Boulder, CO	1
325	Broken Arrow, OK	1
325	Buena Park, CA	1
325	Burbank, CA	1
325	Carlsbad, CA	1
325	Chino Hills, CA	1
325	Clarkstown, NY	1
325	Clifton, NJ	1
325	Clinton Twnshp, MI	1
325	Clovis, CA	1
325	Corona, CA	1
325	Cranston, RI	1
325	Duluth, MN	1
325	Edison Twnshp, NJ	1
325	Edmond, OK	1
325	Federal Way, WA	1
325	Hamilton Twnshp, NJ	1
325	Lake Forest, CA	1
325	Livermore, CA	1
325	Napa, CA	1
325	Nashua, NH	1
325	Newport Beach, CA	1
325	Newton, MA	1
325	Orange, CA	1
325	Orem, UT	1
325	Palm Bay, FL	1
325	Pembroke Pines, FL	1
325	Santa Barbara, CA	1
325	Southfield, MI	1
325	Spokane Valley, WA	1
325	Sunnyvale, CA	1
325	Torrance, CA	1
325	Vacaville, CA	1
325	Ventura, CA	1
325	Vista, CA	1
325	West Jordan, UT	1
325	Westminster, CA	1
364	Ann Arbor, MI	0
364	Arvada, CO	0
364	Bellingham, WA	0
364	Brick Twnshp, NJ	0
364	Cary, NC	0
364	Centennial, CO	0
364	Chino, CA	0
364	Colonie, NY	0
364	Denton, TX	0
364	Farmington Hills, MI	0
364	Fort Collins, CO	0
364	Livonia, MI	0
364	Mission Viejo, CA	0
364	Naperville, IL	0
364	Overland Park, KS	0
364	Parma, OH	0
364	Roswell, GA	0
364	Round Rock, TX	0
364	Sandy, UT	0
364	Sioux City, IA	0
364	Sugar Land, TX	0
364	Surprise, AZ	0
364	Temecula, CA	0
364	Thousand Oaks, CA	0
364	Toms River Twnshp, NJ	0
364	Tracy, CA	0
364	Woodbridge Twnshp, NJ	0

Source: Federal Bureau of Investigation "Crime in the United States 2006"

**Includes nonnegligent manslaughter.*

50. Murder Rate in 2006

National Rate = 5.7 Murders per 100,000 Population*

RANK	CITY	RATE
206	Abilene, TX	4.2
96	Albany, GA	10.3
176	Albany, NY	5.3
150	Albuquerque, NM	6.8
183	Alexandria, VA	5.1
339	Alhambra, CA	1.1
53	Allentown, PA	14.9
259	Amarillo, TX	2.7
307	Amherst, NY	1.8
246	Anaheim, CA	3.0
159	Anchorage, AK	6.1
364	Ann Arbor, MI	0.0
105	Antioch, CA	9.8
216	Arlington, TX	3.8
364	Arvada, CO	0.0
196	Athens-Clarke, GA	4.7
28	Atlanta, GA	22.6
169	Aurora, CO	5.6
273	Aurora, IL	2.4
254	Austin, TX	2.8
129	Bakersfield, CA	8.0
137	Baldwin Park, CA	7.5
5	Baltimore, MD	43.3
22	Baton Rouge, LA	27.1
121	Beaumont, TX	8.7
339	Beaverton, OR	1.1
265	Bellevue, WA	2.5
152	Bellflower, CA	6.6
364	Bellingham, WA	0.0
214	Berkeley, CA	3.9
299	Billings, MT	2.0
4	Birmingham, AL	44.5
159	Bloomington, MN	6.1
231	Boca Raton, FL	3.4
246	Boise, ID	3.0
64	Boston, MA	13.3
339	Boulder, CO	1.1
364	Brick Twnshp, NJ	0.0
34	Bridgeport, CT	20.2
124	Brockton, MA	8.4
339	Broken Arrow, OK	1.1
252	Brownsville, TX	2.9
322	Buena Park, CA	1.3
23	Buffalo, NY	26.4
353	Burbank, CA	1.0
299	Cambridge, MA	2.0
8	Camden, NJ	40.0
229	Canton Twnshp, MI	3.5
87	Canton, OH	11.3
206	Cape Coral, FL	4.2
339	Carlsbad, CA	1.1
209	Carrollton, TX	4.1
48	Carson, CA	15.8
364	Cary, NC	0.0
194	Cedar Rapids, IA	4.8
364	Centennial, CO	0.0
218	Chandler, AZ	3.7
33	Charleston, SC	21.2
81	Charlotte, NC	11.9
92	Chattanooga, TN	10.8
265	Cheektowaga, NY	2.5
241	Chesapeake, VA	3.2
46	Chicago, IL	16.4
322	Chino Hills, CA	1.3
364	Chino, CA	0.0
235	Chula Vista, CA	3.3
20	Cincinnati, OH	28.8
322	Clarkstown, NY	1.3
179	Clarksville, TN	5.2
223	Clearwater, FL	3.6
45	Cleveland, OH	16.6
322	Clifton, NJ	1.3
353	Clinton Twnshp, MI	1.0
339	Clovis, CA	1.1
364	Colonie, NY	0.0
211	Colorado Springs, CO	4.0
282	Columbia, MO	2.2
165	Columbia, SC	5.9
115	Columbus, GA	8.9
56	Columbus, OH	14.2
7	Compton, CA	40.4
315	Concord, CA	1.6
318	Coral Springs, FL	1.5
360	Corona, CA	0.7
147	Corpus Christi, TX	7.2
172	Costa Mesa, CA	5.4
332	Cranston, RI	1.2
51	Dallas, TX	15.0
246	Daly City, CA	3.0
183	Danbury, CT	5.1
277	Davie, FL	2.3
25	Dayton, OH	23.3
290	Dearborn, MI	2.1
113	Deerfield Beach, FL	9.0
364	Denton, TX	0.0
113	Denver, CO	9.0
243	Des Moines, IA	3.1
2	Detroit, MI	47.3
223	Downey, CA	3.6
332	Duluth, MN	1.2
157	Durham, NC	6.2
353	Edison Twnshp, NJ	1.0
322	Edmond, OK	1.3
204	El Cajon, CA	4.3
211	El Monte, CA	4.0
290	El Paso, TX	2.1
62	Elizabeth, NJ	13.5
305	Erie, PA	1.9
282	Escondido, CA	2.2
299	Eugene, OR	2.0
183	Evansville, IN	5.1
243	Everett, WA	3.1
166	Fairfield, CA	5.7
282	Fargo, ND	2.2
364	Farmington Hills, MI	0.0
87	Fayetteville, NC	11.3
332	Federal Way, WA	1.2
3	Flint, MI	45.7
246	Fontana, CA	3.0
364	Fort Collins, CO	0.0
75	Fort Lauderdale, FL	12.3
65	Fort Smith, AR	13.2
129	Fort Wayne, IN	8.0
134	Fort Worth, TX	7.6
246	Fremont, CA	3.0
89	Fresno, CA	11.2
318	Fullerton, CA	1.5
155	Gainesville, FL	6.4
172	Garden Grove, CA	5.4
322	Garland, TX	1.3
1	Gary, IN	48.3
313	Gilbert, AZ	1.7
124	Glendale, AZ	8.4
353	Glendale, CA	1.0
299	Grand Prairie, TX	2.0
85	Grand Rapids, MI	11.4
290	Greece, NY	2.1
282	Greeley, CO	2.2
299	Green Bay, WI	2.0
85	Greensboro, NC	11.4
159	Gresham, OR	6.1
339	Hamilton Twnshp, NJ	1.1
101	Hammond, IN	10.0
137	Hampton, VA	7.5
36	Hartford, CT	19.3
95	Hawthorne, CA	10.4
254	Hayward, CA	2.8
290	Henderson, NV	2.1
115	Hesperia, CA	8.9
282	Hialeah, FL	2.2
128	High Point, NC	8.2
277	Hillsboro, OR	2.3
172	Hollywood, FL	5.4
305	Honolulu, HI	1.9
38	Houston, TX	18.2
353	Huntington Beach, CA	1.0
107	Huntsville, AL	9.5
307	Independence, MO	1.8
42	Indianapolis, IN	17.5
16	Inglewood, CA	31.2
290	Irvine, CA	2.1
318	Irving, TX	1.5
58	Jacksonville, FL	13.8
28	Jackson, MS	22.6
111	Jersey City, NJ	9.2
98	Joliet, IL	10.2
18	Kansas City, KS	31.0
24	Kansas City, MO	25.0
206	Kenosha, WI	4.2
273	Kent, WA	2.4
133	Killeen, TX	7.8
104	Knoxville, TN	9.9
109	Lafayette, LA	9.4
322	Lake Forest, CA	1.3
235	Lakeland, FL	3.3
191	Lakewood, CA	4.9
254	Lakewood, CO	2.8
57	Lancaster, CA	14.0
179	Lansing, MI	5.2
98	Laredo, TX	10.2
262	Largo, FL	2.6
223	Las Cruces, NM	3.6
82	Las Vegas, NV	11.6
223	Lawrence, KS	3.6
118	Lawton, OK	8.8
265	Lee's Summit, MO	2.5
282	Lewisville, TX	2.2
235	Lexington, KY	3.3
290	Lincoln, NE	2.1
17	Little Rock, AR	31.1
322	Livermore, CA	1.3
364	Livonia, MI	0.0

RANK	CITY	RATE
123	Long Beach, CA	8.6
67	Longview, TX	12.9
71	Los Angeles, CA	12.4
129	Louisville, KY	8.0
70	Lowell, MA	12.5
163	Lubbock, TX	6.0
201	Lynn, MA	4.5
75	Macon, GA	12.3
307	Madison, WI	1.8
223	Manchester, NH	3.6
243	McAllen, TX	3.1
299	McKinney, TX	2.0
262	Melbourne, FL	2.6
31	Memphis, TN	21.6
166	Mesa, AZ	5.7
218	Mesquite, TX	3.7
201	Miami Beach, FL	4.5
39	Miami Gardens, FL	17.8
35	Miami, FL	19.6
191	Midland, TX	4.9
41	Milwaukee, WI	17.7
50	Minneapolis, MN	15.2
170	Miramar, FL	5.5
364	Mission Viejo, CA	0.0
60	Mobile, AL	13.6
176	Modesto, CA	5.3
63	Montgomery, AL	13.4
115	Moreno Valley, CA	8.9
150	Murfreesboro, TN	6.8
273	Murrieta, CA	2.4
322	Napa, CA	1.3
364	Naperville, IL	0.0
339	Nashua, NH	1.1
55	Nashville, TN	14.3
137	New Bedford, MA	7.5
11	New Orleans, LA	37.6
142	New York, NY	7.3
12	Newark, NJ	37.4
332	Newport Beach, CA	1.2
93	Newport News, VA	10.5
332	Newton, MA	1.2
79	Norfolk, VA	12.0
191	Norman, OK	4.9
15	North Charleston, SC	31.9
78	North Las Vegas, NV	12.1
152	Norwalk, CA	6.6
14	Oakland, CA	36.4
194	Oceanside, CA	4.8
290	Odessa, TX	2.1
265	Ogden, UT	2.5
96	Oklahoma City, OK	10.3
259	Olathe, KS	2.7
132	Omaha, NE	7.9
137	Ontario, CA	7.5
360	Orange, CA	0.7
339	Orem, UT	1.1
28	Orlando, FL	22.6
364	Overland Park, KS	0.0
149	Oxnard, CA	7.0
339	Palm Bay, FL	1.1
90	Palmdale, CA	11.0
364	Parma, OH	0.0
134	Pasadena, CA	7.6
196	Pasadena, TX	4.7
101	Paterson, NJ	10.0
360	Pembroke Pines, FL	0.7
321	Peoria, AZ	1.4
51	Peoria, IL	15.0
21	Philadelphia, PA	27.7
49	Phoenix, AZ	15.4
43	Pittsburgh, PA	17.3
315	Plano, TX	1.6
231	Plantation, FL	3.4
77	Pomona, CA	12.2
109	Pompano Beach, FL	9.4
179	Port St. Lucie, FL	5.2
218	Portland, OR	3.7
39	Portsmouth, VA	17.8
156	Providence, RI	6.3
313	Provo, UT	1.7
166	Pueblo, CO	5.7
235	Quincy, MA	3.3
118	Racine, WI	8.8
170	Raleigh, NC	5.5
307	Rancho Cucamon., CA	1.8
71	Reading, PA	12.4
282	Redding, CA	2.2
91	Reno, NV	10.9
79	Rialto, CA	12.0
252	Richardson, TX	2.9
6	Richmond, CA	40.7
9	Richmond, VA	38.8
216	Riverside, CA	3.8
68	Roanoke, VA	12.8
290	Rochester, MN	2.1
26	Rochester, NY	23.2
71	Rockford, IL	12.4
254	Roseville, CA	2.8
364	Roswell, GA	0.0
364	Round Rock, TX	0.0
71	Sacramento, CA	12.4
163	Salem, OR	6.0
196	Salinas, CA	4.7
203	Salt Lake City, UT	4.4
235	San Angelo, TX	3.3
111	San Antonio, TX	9.2
27	San Bernardino, CA	23.0
172	San Diego, CA	5.4
84	San Francisco, CA	11.5
241	San Jose, CA	3.2
183	San Leandro, CA	5.1
282	San Mateo, CA	2.2
364	Sandy, UT	0.0
134	Santa Ana, CA	7.6
332	Santa Barbara, CA	1.2
254	Santa Clara, CA	2.8
307	Santa Clarita, CA	1.8
273	Santa Maria, CA	2.4
277	Santa Monica, CA	2.3
214	Santa Rosa, CA	3.9
60	Savannah, GA	13.6
290	Scottsdale, AZ	2.1
183	Seattle, WA	5.1
53	Shreveport, LA	14.9
265	Simi Valley, CA	2.5
364	Sioux City, IA	0.0
189	Sioux Falls, SD	5.0
259	Somerville, MA	2.7
65	South Bend, IN	13.2
47	South Gate, CA	16.0
322	Southfield, MI	1.3
229	Sparks, NV	3.5
332	Spokane Valley, WA	1.2
189	Spokane, WA	5.0
179	Springfield, IL	5.2
105	Springfield, MA	9.8
211	Springfield, MO	4.0
315	Sterling Heights, MI	1.6
68	Stockton, CA	12.8
13	St. Louis, MO	37.2
159	St. Paul, MN	6.1
127	St. Petersburg, FL	8.3
101	Suffolk, VA	10.0
364	Sugar Land, TX	0.0
359	Sunnyvale, CA	0.8
235	Sunrise, FL	3.3
364	Surprise, AZ	0.0
124	Syracuse, NY	8.4
93	Tacoma, WA	10.5
157	Tallahassee, FL	6.2
137	Tampa, FL	7.5
364	Temecula, CA	0.0
246	Tempe, AZ	3.0
218	Thornton, CO	3.7
364	Thousand Oaks, CA	0.0
82	Toledo, OH	11.6
364	Toms River Twnshp, NJ	0.0
142	Topeka, KS	7.3
360	Torrance, CA	0.7
364	Tracy, CA	0.0
32	Trenton, NJ	21.3
265	Troy, MI	2.5
107	Tucson, AZ	9.5
59	Tulsa, OK	13.7
37	Tuscaloosa, AL	18.3
176	Tyler, TX	5.3
265	Upper Darby Twnshp, PA	2.5
339	Vacaville, CA	1.1
183	Vallejo, CA	5.1
265	Vancouver, WA	2.5
353	Ventura, CA	1.0
121	Victorville, CA	8.7
204	Virginia Beach, VA	4.3
142	Visalia, CA	7.3
339	Vista, CA	1.1
142	Waco, TX	7.3
218	Warren, MI	3.7
277	Warwick, RI	2.3
19	Washington, DC	29.1
154	Waterbury, CT	6.5
307	West Covina, CA	1.8
339	West Jordan, UT	1.1
44	West Palm Beach, FL	17.1
262	West Valley, UT	2.6
277	Westland, MI	2.3
339	Westminster, CA	1.1
196	Westminster, CO	4.7
196	Whittier, CA	4.7
118	Wichita Falls, TX	8.8
142	Wichita, KS	7.3
147	Wilmington, NC	7.2
100	Winston-Salem, NC	10.1
364	Woodbridge Twnshp, NJ	0.0
231	Worcester, MA	3.4
223	Yakima, WA	3.6
209	Yonkers, NY	4.1
10	Youngstown, OH	38.6
231	Yuma, AZ	3.4

Source: CQ Press using data from F.B.I. "Crime in the United States 2006"

**Includes nonnegligent manslaughter.*

50. Murder Rate in 2006 (continued)

National Rate = 5.7 Murders per 100,000 Population*

RANK	CITY	RATE
1	Gary, IN	48.3
2	Detroit, MI	47.3
3	Flint, MI	45.7
4	Birmingham, AL	44.5
5	Baltimore, MD	43.3
6	Richmond, CA	40.7
7	Compton, CA	40.4
8	Camden, NJ	40.0
9	Richmond, VA	38.8
10	Youngstown, OH	38.6
11	New Orleans, LA	37.6
12	Newark, NJ	37.4
13	St. Louis, MO	37.2
14	Oakland, CA	36.4
15	North Charleston, SC	31.9
16	Inglewood, CA	31.2
17	Little Rock, AR	31.1
18	Kansas City, KS	31.0
19	Washington, DC	29.1
20	Cincinnati, OH	28.8
21	Philadelphia, PA	27.7
22	Baton Rouge, LA	27.1
23	Buffalo, NY	26.4
24	Kansas City, MO	25.0
25	Dayton, OH	23.3
26	Rochester, NY	23.2
27	San Bernardino, CA	23.0
28	Atlanta, GA	22.6
28	Jackson, MS	22.6
28	Orlando, FL	22.6
31	Memphis, TN	21.6
32	Trenton, NJ	21.3
33	Charleston, SC	21.2
34	Bridgeport, CT	20.2
35	Miami, FL	19.6
36	Hartford, CT	19.3
37	Tuscaloosa, AL	18.3
38	Houston, TX	18.2
39	Miami Gardens, FL	17.8
39	Portsmouth, VA	17.8
41	Milwaukee, WI	17.7
42	Indianapolis, IN	17.5
43	Pittsburgh, PA	17.3
44	West Palm Beach, FL	17.1
45	Cleveland, OH	16.6
46	Chicago, IL	16.4
47	South Gate, CA	16.0
48	Carson, CA	15.8
49	Phoenix, AZ	15.4
50	Minneapolis, MN	15.2
51	Dallas, TX	15.0
51	Peoria, IL	15.0
53	Allentown, PA	14.9
53	Shreveport, LA	14.9
55	Nashville, TN	14.3
56	Columbus, OH	14.2
57	Lancaster, CA	14.0
58	Jacksonville, FL	13.8
59	Tulsa, OK	13.7
60	Mobile, AL	13.6
60	Savannah, GA	13.6
62	Elizabeth, NJ	13.5
63	Montgomery, AL	13.4
64	Boston, MA	13.3
65	Fort Smith, AR	13.2
65	South Bend, IN	13.2
67	Longview, TX	12.9
68	Roanoke, VA	12.8
68	Stockton, CA	12.8
70	Lowell, MA	12.5
71	Los Angeles, CA	12.4
71	Reading, PA	12.4
71	Rockford, IL	12.4
71	Sacramento, CA	12.4
75	Fort Lauderdale, FL	12.3
75	Macon, GA	12.3
77	Pomona, CA	12.2
78	North Las Vegas, NV	12.1
79	Norfolk, VA	12.0
79	Rialto, CA	12.0
81	Charlotte, NC	11.9
82	Las Vegas, NV	11.6
82	Toledo, OH	11.6
84	San Francisco, CA	11.5
85	Grand Rapids, MI	11.4
85	Greensboro, NC	11.4
87	Canton, OH	11.3
87	Fayetteville, NC	11.3
89	Fresno, CA	11.2
90	Palmdale, CA	11.0
91	Reno, NV	10.9
92	Chattanooga, TN	10.8
93	Newport News, VA	10.5
93	Tacoma, WA	10.5
95	Hawthorne, CA	10.4
96	Albany, GA	10.3
96	Oklahoma City, OK	10.3
98	Joliet, IL	10.2
98	Laredo, TX	10.2
100	Winston-Salem, NC	10.1
101	Hammond, IN	10.0
101	Paterson, NJ	10.0
101	Suffolk, VA	10.0
104	Knoxville, TN	9.9
105	Antioch, CA	9.8
105	Springfield, MA	9.8
107	Huntsville, AL	9.5
107	Tucson, AZ	9.5
109	Lafayette, LA	9.4
109	Pompano Beach, FL	9.4
111	Jersey City, NJ	9.2
111	San Antonio, TX	9.2
113	Deerfield Beach, FL	9.0
113	Denver, CO	9.0
115	Columbus, GA	8.9
115	Hesperia, CA	8.9
115	Moreno Valley, CA	8.9
118	Lawton, OK	8.8
118	Racine, WI	8.8
118	Wichita Falls, TX	8.8
121	Beaumont, TX	8.7
121	Victorville, CA	8.7
123	Long Beach, CA	8.6
124	Brockton, MA	8.4
124	Glendale, AZ	8.4
124	Syracuse, NY	8.4
127	St. Petersburg, FL	8.3
128	High Point, NC	8.2
129	Bakersfield, CA	8.0
129	Fort Wayne, IN	8.0
129	Louisville, KY	8.0
132	Omaha, NE	7.9
133	Killeen, TX	7.8
134	Fort Worth, TX	7.6
134	Pasadena, CA	7.6
134	Santa Ana, CA	7.6
137	Baldwin Park, CA	7.5
137	Hampton, VA	7.5
137	New Bedford, MA	7.5
137	Ontario, CA	7.5
137	Tampa, FL	7.5
142	New York, NY	7.3
142	Topeka, KS	7.3
142	Visalia, CA	7.3
142	Waco, TX	7.3
142	Wichita, KS	7.3
147	Corpus Christi, TX	7.2
147	Wilmington, NC	7.2
149	Oxnard, CA	7.0
150	Albuquerque, NM	6.8
150	Murfreesboro, TN	6.8
152	Bellflower, CA	6.6
152	Norwalk, CA	6.6
154	Waterbury, CT	6.5
155	Gainesville, FL	6.4
156	Providence, RI	6.3
157	Durham, NC	6.2
157	Tallahassee, FL	6.2
159	Anchorage, AK	6.1
159	Bloomington, MN	6.1
159	Gresham, OR	6.1
159	St. Paul, MN	6.1
163	Lubbock, TX	6.0
163	Salem, OR	6.0
165	Columbia, SC	5.9
166	Fairfield, CA	5.7
166	Mesa, AZ	5.7
166	Pueblo, CO	5.7
169	Aurora, CO	5.6
170	Miramar, FL	5.5
170	Raleigh, NC	5.5
172	Costa Mesa, CA	5.4
172	Garden Grove, CA	5.4
172	Hollywood, FL	5.4
172	San Diego, CA	5.4
176	Albany, NY	5.3
176	Modesto, CA	5.3
176	Tyler, TX	5.3
179	Clarksville, TN	5.2
179	Lansing, MI	5.2
179	Port St. Lucie, FL	5.2
179	Springfield, IL	5.2
183	Alexandria, VA	5.1
183	Danbury, CT	5.1
183	Evansville, IN	5.1
183	San Leandro, CA	5.1
183	Seattle, WA	5.1
183	Vallejo, CA	5.1
189	Sioux Falls, SD	5.0
189	Spokane, WA	5.0
191	Lakewood, CA	4.9
191	Midland, TX	4.9

RANK	CITY	RATE
191	Norman, OK	4.9
194	Cedar Rapids, IA	4.8
194	Oceanside, CA	4.8
196	Athens-Clarke, GA	4.7
196	Pasadena, TX	4.7
196	Salinas, CA	4.7
196	Westminster, CO	4.7
196	Whittier, CA	4.7
201	Lynn, MA	4.5
201	Miami Beach, FL	4.5
203	Salt Lake City, UT	4.4
204	El Cajon, CA	4.3
204	Virginia Beach, VA	4.3
206	Abilene, TX	4.2
206	Cape Coral, FL	4.2
206	Kenosha, WI	4.2
209	Carrollton, TX	4.1
209	Yonkers, NY	4.1
211	Colorado Springs, CO	4.0
211	El Monte, CA	4.0
211	Springfield, MO	4.0
214	Berkeley, CA	3.9
214	Santa Rosa, CA	3.9
216	Arlington, TX	3.8
216	Riverside, CA	3.8
218	Chandler, AZ	3.7
218	Mesquite, TX	3.7
218	Portland, OR	3.7
218	Thornton, CO	3.7
218	Warren, MI	3.7
223	Clearwater, FL	3.6
223	Downey, CA	3.6
223	Las Cruces, NM	3.6
223	Lawrence, KS	3.6
223	Manchester, NH	3.6
223	Yakima, WA	3.6
229	Canton Twnshp, MI	3.5
229	Sparks, NV	3.5
231	Boca Raton, FL	3.4
231	Plantation, FL	3.4
231	Worcester, MA	3.4
231	Yuma, AZ	3.4
235	Chula Vista, CA	3.3
235	Lakeland, FL	3.3
235	Lexington, KY	3.3
235	Quincy, MA	3.3
235	San Angelo, TX	3.3
235	Sunrise, FL	3.3
241	Chesapeake, VA	3.2
241	San Jose, CA	3.2
243	Des Moines, IA	3.1
243	Everett, WA	3.1
243	McAllen, TX	3.1
246	Anaheim, CA	3.0
246	Boise, ID	3.0
246	Daly City, CA	3.0
246	Fontana, CA	3.0
246	Fremont, CA	3.0
246	Tempe, AZ	3.0
252	Brownsville, TX	2.9
252	Richardson, TX	2.9
254	Austin, TX	2.8
254	Hayward, CA	2.8
254	Lakewood, CO	2.8
254	Roseville, CA	2.8
254	Santa Clara, CA	2.8

RANK	CITY	RATE
259	Amarillo, TX	2.7
259	Olathe, KS	2.7
259	Somerville, MA	2.7
262	Largo, FL	2.6
262	Melbourne, FL	2.6
262	West Valley, UT	2.6
265	Bellevue, WA	2.5
265	Cheektowaga, NY	2.5
265	Lee's Summit, MO	2.5
265	Ogden, UT	2.5
265	Simi Valley, CA	2.5
265	Troy, MI	2.5
265	Upper Darby Twnshp, PA	2.5
265	Vancouver, WA	2.5
273	Aurora, IL	2.4
273	Kent, WA	2.4
273	Murrieta, CA	2.4
273	Santa Maria, CA	2.4
277	Davie, FL	2.3
277	Hillsboro, OR	2.3
277	Santa Monica, CA	2.3
277	Warwick, RI	2.3
277	Westland, MI	2.3
282	Columbia, MO	2.2
282	Escondido, CA	2.2
282	Fargo, ND	2.2
282	Greeley, CO	2.2
282	Hialeah, FL	2.2
282	Lewisville, TX	2.2
282	Redding, CA	2.2
282	San Mateo, CA	2.2
290	Dearborn, MI	2.1
290	El Paso, TX	2.1
290	Greece, NY	2.1
290	Henderson, NV	2.1
290	Irvine, CA	2.1
290	Lincoln, NE	2.1
290	Odessa, TX	2.1
290	Rochester, MN	2.1
290	Scottsdale, AZ	2.1
299	Billings, MT	2.0
299	Cambridge, MA	2.0
299	Eugene, OR	2.0
299	Grand Prairie, TX	2.0
299	Green Bay, WI	2.0
299	McKinney, TX	2.0
305	Erie, PA	1.9
305	Honolulu, HI	1.9
307	Amherst, NY	1.8
307	Independence, MO	1.8
307	Madison, WI	1.8
307	Rancho Cucamon., CA	1.8
307	Santa Clarita, CA	1.8
307	West Covina, CA	1.8
313	Gilbert, AZ	1.7
313	Provo, UT	1.7
315	Concord, CA	1.6
315	Plano, TX	1.6
315	Sterling Heights, MI	1.6
318	Coral Springs, FL	1.5
318	Fullerton, CA	1.5
318	Irving, TX	1.5
321	Peoria, AZ	1.4
322	Buena Park, CA	1.3
322	Chino Hills, CA	1.3
322	Clarkstown, NY	1.3

RANK	CITY	RATE
322	Clifton, NJ	1.3
322	Edmond, OK	1.3
322	Garland, TX	1.3
322	Lake Forest, CA	1.3
322	Livermore, CA	1.3
322	Napa, CA	1.3
322	Southfield, MI	1.3
332	Cranston, RI	1.2
332	Duluth, MN	1.2
332	Federal Way, WA	1.2
332	Newport Beach, CA	1.2
332	Newton, MA	1.2
332	Santa Barbara, CA	1.2
332	Spokane Valley, WA	1.2
339	Alhambra, CA	1.1
339	Beaverton, OR	1.1
339	Boulder, CO	1.1
339	Broken Arrow, OK	1.1
339	Carlsbad, CA	1.1
339	Clovis, CA	1.1
339	Hamilton Twnshp, NJ	1.1
339	Nashua, NH	1.1
339	Orem, UT	1.1
339	Palm Bay, FL	1.1
339	Vacaville, CA	1.1
339	Vista, CA	1.1
339	West Jordan, UT	1.1
339	Westminster, CA	1.1
353	Burbank, CA	1.0
353	Clinton Twnshp, MI	1.0
353	Edison Twnshp, NJ	1.0
353	Glendale, CA	1.0
353	Huntington Beach, CA	1.0
353	Ventura, CA	1.0
359	Sunnyvale, CA	0.8
360	Corona, CA	0.7
360	Orange, CA	0.7
360	Pembroke Pines, FL	0.7
360	Torrance, CA	0.7
364	Ann Arbor, MI	0.0
364	Arvada, CO	0.0
364	Bellingham, WA	0.0
364	Brick Twnshp, NJ	0.0
364	Cary, NC	0.0
364	Centennial, CO	0.0
364	Chino, CA	0.0
364	Colonie, NY	0.0
364	Denton, TX	0.0
364	Farmington Hills, MI	0.0
364	Fort Collins, CO	0.0
364	Livonia, MI	0.0
364	Mission Viejo, CA	0.0
364	Naperville, IL	0.0
364	Overland Park, KS	0.0
364	Parma, OH	0.0
364	Roswell, GA	0.0
364	Round Rock, TX	0.0
364	Sandy, UT	0.0
364	Sioux City, IA	0.0
364	Sugar Land, TX	0.0
364	Surprise, AZ	0.0
364	Temecula, CA	0.0
364	Thousand Oaks, CA	0.0
364	Toms River Twnshp, NJ	0.0
364	Tracy, CA	0.0
364	Woodbridge Twnshp, NJ	0.0

Source: CQ Press using data from F.B.I. "Crime in the United States 2006"

**Includes nonnegligent manslaughter.*

51. Percent Change in Murder Rate: 2005 to 2006

National Percent Change = 0.8% Increase*

RANK	CITY	% CHANGE
182	Abilene, TX	(2.3)
146	Albany, GA	1.0
269	Albany, NY	(37.6)
267	Albuquerque, NM	(37.0)
22	Alexandria, VA	121.7
149	Alhambra, CA	0.0
241	Allentown, PA	(24.0)
290	Amarillo, TX	(50.0)
30	Amherst, NY	100.0
149	Anaheim, CA	0.0
135	Anchorage, AK	5.2
149	Ann Arbor, MI	0.0
149	Antioch, CA	0.0
280	Arlington, TX	(42.4)
338	Arvada, CO	(100.0)
149	Athens-Clarke, GA	0.0
127	Atlanta, GA	8.1
273	Aurora, CO	(41.1)
329	Aurora, IL	(71.4)
248	Austin, TX	(26.3)
251	Bakersfield, CA	(28.6)
103	Baldwin Park, CA	19.0
138	Baltimore, MD	3.1
87	Baton Rouge, LA	24.3
209	Beaumont, TX	(9.4)
201	Beaverton, OR	(8.3)
60	Bellevue, WA	47.1
284	Bellflower, CA	(44.5)
338	Bellingham, WA	(100.0)
76	Berkeley, CA	34.5
316	Billings, MT	(60.8)
148	Birmingham, AL	0.5
NA	Bloomington, MN**	NA
NA	Boca Raton, FL**	NA
110	Boise, ID	15.4
138	Boston, MA	3.1
NA	Boulder, CO**	NA
149	Brick Twnshp, NJ	0.0
59	Bridgeport, CT	48.5
235	Brockton, MA	(20.8)
NA	Broken Arrow, OK**	NA
100	Brownsville, TX	20.8
287	Buena Park, CA	(48.0)
77	Buffalo, NY	33.3
318	Burbank, CA	(65.5)
260	Cambridge, MA	(33.3)
186	Camden, NJ	(2.9)
62	Canton Twnshp, MI	45.8
20	Canton, OH	126.0
121	Cape Coral, FL	10.5
290	Carlsbad, CA	(50.0)
184	Carrollton, TX	(2.4)
25	Carson, CA	113.5
149	Cary, NC	0.0
3	Cedar Rapids, IA	500.0
338	Centennial, CO	(100.0)
132	Chandler, AZ	5.7
21	Charleston, SC	125.5
197	Charlotte, NC	(5.6)
249	Chattanooga, TN	(26.5)
NA	Cheektowaga, NY**	NA
290	Chesapeake, VA	(50.0)
136	Chicago, IL	5.1
319	Chino Hills, CA	(66.7)
338	Chino, CA	(100.0)
71	Chula Vista, CA	37.5
112	Cincinnati, OH	14.7
NA	Clarkstown, NY**	NA
109	Clarksville, TN	15.6
309	Clearwater, FL	(55.6)
257	Cleveland, OH	(30.3)
287	Clifton, NJ	(48.0)
NA	Clinton Twnshp, MI**	NA
334	Clovis, CA	(77.1)
149	Colonie, NY	0.0
85	Colorado Springs, CO	25.0
330	Columbia, MO	(71.8)
306	Columbia, SC	(53.5)
240	Columbus, GA	(23.9)
144	Columbus, OH	1.4
271	Compton, CA	(39.8)
30	Concord, CA	100.0
NA	Coral Springs, FL**	NA
331	Corona, CA	(74.1)
17	Corpus Christi, TX	157.1
30	Costa Mesa, CA	100.0
NA	Cranston, RI**	NA
203	Dallas, TX	(8.5)
53	Daly City, CA	50.0
6	Danbury, CT	292.3
193	Davie, FL	(4.2)
108	Dayton, OH	16.5
259	Dearborn, MI	(32.3)
8	Deerfield Beach, FL	200.0
338	Denton, TX	(100.0)
222	Denver, CO	(14.3)
NA	Des Moines, IA**	NA
101	Detroit, MI	20.4
281	Downey, CA	(42.9)
NA	Duluth, MN**	NA
NA	Durham, NC**	NA
NA	Edison Twnshp, NJ**	NA
200	Edmond, OK	(7.1)
29	El Cajon, CA	104.8
95	El Monte, CA	21.2
NA	El Paso, TX**	NA
178	Elizabeth, NJ	(0.7)
322	Erie, PA	(67.2)
61	Escondido, CA	46.7
281	Eugene, OR	(42.9)
245	Evansville, IN	(25.0)
149	Everett, WA	0.0
263	Fairfield, CA	(33.7)
149	Fargo, ND	0.0
338	Farmington Hills, MI	(100.0)
140	Fayetteville, NC	2.7
336	Federal Way, WA	(83.6)
114	Flint, MI	14.0
303	Fontana, CA	(52.4)
338	Fort Collins, CO	(100.0)
69	Fort Lauderdale, FL	38.2
23	Fort Smith, AR	116.4
NA	Fort Wayne, IN**	NA
236	Fort Worth, TX	(22.4)
3	Fremont, CA	500.0
132	Fresno, CA	5.7
NA	Fullerton, CA**	NA
64	Gainesville, FL	42.2
53	Garden Grove, CA	50.0
313	Garland, TX	(59.4)
225	Gary, IN	(16.7)
NA	Gilbert, AZ**	NA
128	Glendale, AZ	7.7
337	Glendale, CA	(89.4)
325	Grand Prairie, TX	(68.3)
15	Grand Rapids, MI	178.0
149	Greece, NY	0.0
195	Greeley, CO	(4.3)
312	Green Bay, WI	(59.2)
212	Greensboro, NC	(10.2)
38	Gresham, OR	96.8
290	Hamilton Twnshp, NJ	(50.0)
214	Hammond, IN	(10.7)
144	Hampton, VA	1.4
189	Hartford, CT	(3.5)
210	Hawthorne, CA	(9.6)
311	Hayward, CA	(56.3)
285	Henderson, NV	(46.2)
48	Hesperia, CA	64.8
268	Hialeah, FL	(37.1)
189	High Point, NC	(3.5)
193	Hillsboro, OR	(4.2)
79	Hollywood, FL	31.7
116	Honolulu, HI	11.8
118	Houston, TX	11.7
30	Huntington Beach, CA	100.0
251	Huntsville, AL	(28.6)
319	Independence, MO	(66.7)
81	Indianapolis, IN	29.6
68	Inglewood, CA	39.3
40	Irvine, CA	90.9
53	Irving, TX	50.0
97	Jacksonville, FL	21.1
129	Jackson, MS	7.1
279	Jersey City, NJ	(42.1)
102	Joliet, IL	20.0
93	Kansas City, KS	22.0
NA	Kansas City, MO**	NA
80	Kenosha, WI	31.2
260	Kent, WA	(33.3)
192	Killeen, TX	(3.7)
253	Knoxville, TN	(28.8)
78	Lafayette, LA	32.4
290	Lake Forest, CA	(50.0)
290	Lakeland, FL	(50.0)
NA	Lakewood, CA**	NA
233	Lakewood, CO	(20.0)
115	Lancaster, CA	13.8
239	Lansing, MI	(23.5)
106	Laredo, TX	17.2
304	Largo, FL	(52.7)
278	Las Cruces, NM	(41.9)
140	Las Vegas, NV	2.7
53	Lawrence, KS	50.0
82	Lawton, OK	29.4
39	Lee's Summit, MO	92.3
149	Lewisville, TX	0.0
NA	Lexington, KY**	NA
88	Lincoln, NE	23.5
66	Little Rock, AR	40.7
149	Livermore, CA	0.0
338	Livonia, MI	(100.0)

RANK	CITY	% CHANGE
182	Long Beach, CA	(2.3)
92	Longview, TX	22.9
180	Los Angeles, CA	(1.6)
208	Louisville, KY	(9.1)
1	Lowell, MA	557.9
110	Lubbock, TX	15.4
231	Lynn, MA	(19.6)
272	Macon, GA	(40.0)
30	Madison, WI	100.0
149	Manchester, NH	0.0
302	McAllen, TX	(52.3)
44	McKinney, TX	81.8
30	Melbourne, FL	100.0
131	Memphis, TN	6.9
215	Mesa, AZ	(10.9)
256	Mesquite, TX	(30.2)
72	Miami Beach, FL	36.4
47	Miami Gardens, FL	66.4
65	Miami, FL	41.0
5	Midland, TX	390.0
221	Milwaukee, WI	(14.1)
94	Minneapolis, MN	21.6
41	Miramar, FL	89.7
338	Mission Viejo, CA	(100.0)
186	Mobile, AL	(2.9)
67	Modesto, CA	39.5
198	Montgomery, AL	(6.3)
75	Moreno Valley, CA	34.8
13	Murfreesboro, TN	183.3
43	Murrieta, CA	84.6
NA	Napa, CA**	NA
338	Naperville, IL	(100.0)
301	Nashua, NH	(52.2)
224	Nashville, TN	(16.4)
218	New Bedford, MA	(11.8)
NA	New Orleans, LA**	NA
120	New York, NY	10.6
125	Newark, NJ	8.4
324	Newport Beach, CA	(67.6)
185	Newport News, VA	(2.8)
149	Newton, MA	0.0
299	Norfolk, VA	(51.0)
NA	Norman, OK**	NA
19	North Charleston, SC	147.3
179	North Las Vegas, NV	(0.8)
265	Norwalk, CA	(35.3)
50	Oakland, CA	56.9
113	Oceanside, CA	14.3
264	Odessa, TX	(34.4)
314	Ogden, UT	(59.7)
146	Oklahoma City, OK	1.0
8	Olathe, KS	200.0
134	Omaha, NE	5.3
129	Ontario, CA	7.1
305	Orange, CA	(53.3)
NA	Orem, UT**	NA
24	Orlando, FL	115.2
338	Overland Park, KS	(100.0)
258	Oxnard, CA	(32.0)
290	Palm Bay, FL	(50.0)
189	Palmdale, CA	(3.5)
149	Parma, OH	0.0
42	Pasadena, CA	85.4
69	Pasadena, TX	38.2
243	Paterson, NJ	(24.2)
335	Pembroke Pines, FL	(82.1)

RANK	CITY	% CHANGE
30	Peoria, AZ	100.0
98	Peoria, IL	21.0
126	Philadelphia, PA	8.2
140	Phoenix, AZ	2.7
206	Pittsburgh, PA	(8.9)
30	Plano, TX	100.0
247	Plantation, FL	(26.1)
207	Pomona, CA	(9.0)
46	Pompano Beach, FL	70.9
2	Port St. Lucie, FL	550.0
149	Portland, OR	0.0
228	Portsmouth, VA	(18.3)
283	Providence, RI	(44.2)
275	Provo, UT	(41.4)
307	Pueblo, CO	(54.0)
53	Quincy, MA	50.0
310	Racine, WI	(55.8)
201	Raleigh, NC	(8.3)
53	Rancho Cucamon., CA	50.0
308	Reading, PA	(54.4)
149	Redding, CA	0.0
14	Reno, NV	179.5
123	Rialto, CA	9.1
63	Richardson, TX	45.0
137	Richmond, CA	4.9
211	Richmond, VA	(9.8)
116	Riverside, CA	11.8
246	Roanoke, VA	(25.1)
NA	Rochester, MN**	NA
199	Rochester, NY	(6.8)
NA	Rockford, IL**	NA
NA	Roseville, CA**	NA
149	Roswell, GA	0.0
149	Round Rock, TX	0.0
124	Sacramento, CA	8.8
8	Salem, OR	200.0
149	Salinas, CA	0.0
229	Salt Lake City, UT	(18.5)
149	San Angelo, TX	0.0
73	San Antonio, TX	35.3
234	San Bernardino, CA	(20.7)
74	San Diego, CA	35.0
212	San Francisco, CA	(10.2)
122	San Jose, CA	10.3
143	San Leandro, CA	2.0
290	San Mateo, CA	(50.0)
338	Sandy, UT	(100.0)
51	Santa Ana, CA	55.1
NA	Santa Barbara, CA**	NA
276	Santa Clara, CA	(41.7)
149	Santa Clarita, CA	0.0
260	Santa Maria, CA	(33.3)
289	Santa Monica, CA	(48.9)
8	Santa Rosa, CA	200.0
186	Savannah, GA	(2.9)
88	Scottsdale, AZ	23.5
104	Seattle, WA	18.6
241	Shreveport, LA	(24.0)
NA	Simi Valley, CA**	NA
338	Sioux City, IA	(100.0)
45	Sioux Falls, SD	72.4
28	Somerville, MA	107.7
107	South Bend, IN	16.8
16	South Gate, CA	166.7
333	Southfield, MI	(75.0)
276	Sparks, NV	(41.7)

RANK	CITY	% CHANGE
149	Spokane Valley, WA	0.0
237	Spokane, WA	(23.1)
99	Springfield, IL	20.9
226	Springfield, MA	(17.6)
95	Springfield, MO	21.2
NA	Sterling Heights, MI**	NA
219	Stockton, CA	(12.3)
181	St. Louis, MO	(1.8)
254	St. Paul, MN	(29.1)
255	St. Petersburg, FL	(29.7)
220	Suffolk, VA	(13.8)
338	Sugar Land, TX	(100.0)
317	Sunnyvale, CA	(65.2)
8	Sunrise, FL	200.0
338	Surprise, AZ	(100.0)
266	Syracuse, NY	(36.8)
49	Tacoma, WA	61.5
119	Tallahassee, FL	10.7
91	Tampa, FL	23.0
338	Temecula, CA	(100.0)
85	Tempe, AZ	25.0
7	Thornton, CO	270.0
338	Thousand Oaks, CA	(100.0)
84	Toledo, OH	26.1
338	Toms River Twnshp, NJ	(100.0)
83	Topeka, KS	28.1
149	Torrance, CA	0.0
149	Tracy, CA	0.0
274	Trenton, NJ	(41.2)
27	Troy, MI	108.3
204	Tucson, AZ	(8.7)
204	Tulsa, OK	(8.7)
26	Tuscaloosa, AL	110.3
232	Tyler, TX	(19.7)
314	Upper Darby Twnshp, PA	(59.7)
286	Vacaville, CA	(47.6)
NA	Vallejo, CA**	NA
299	Vancouver, WA	(51.0)
149	Ventura, CA	0.0
270	Victorville, CA	(39.6)
196	Virginia Beach, VA	(4.4)
238	Visalia, CA	(23.2)
332	Vista, CA	(74.4)
250	Waco, TX	(27.0)
149	Warren, MI	0.0
290	Warwick, RI	(50.0)
227	Washington, DC	(17.8)
105	Waterbury, CT	18.2
323	West Covina, CA	(67.3)
NA	West Jordan, UT**	NA
244	West Palm Beach, FL	(24.3)
326	West Valley, UT	(69.8)
NA	Westland, MI**	NA
319	Westminster, CA	(66.7)
18	Westminster, CO	147.4
230	Whittier, CA	(19.0)
52	Wichita Falls, TX	51.7
NA	Wichita, KS**	NA
222	Wilmington, NC	(14.3)
90	Winston-Salem, NC	23.2
338	Woodbridge Twnshp, NJ	(100.0)
149	Worcester, MA	0.0
327	Yakima, WA	(70.5)
215	Yonkers, NY	(10.9)
217	Youngstown, OH	(11.7)
328	Yuma, AZ	(70.7)

Source: CQ Press using data from F.B.I. "Crime in the United States 2006"

**Includes nonnegligent manslaughter. **Not available. ***These cities had murder rates of 0 in 2005 but had at least one murder in 2006. Calculating percent increase from zero results in an infinite number. These are shown as "NA."*

51. Percent Change in Murder Rate: 2005 to 2006 (continued)

National Percent Change = 0.8% Increase*

RANK	CITY	% CHANGE
1	Lowell, MA	557.9
2	Port St. Lucie, FL	550.0
3	Cedar Rapids, IA	500.0
3	Fremont, CA	500.0
5	Midland, TX	390.0
6	Danbury, CT	292.3
7	Thornton, CO	270.0
8	Deerfield Beach, FL	200.0
8	Olathe, KS	200.0
8	Salem, OR	200.0
8	Santa Rosa, CA	200.0
8	Sunrise, FL	200.0
13	Murfreesboro, TN	183.3
14	Reno, NV	179.5
15	Grand Rapids, MI	178.0
16	South Gate, CA	166.7
17	Corpus Christi, TX	157.1
18	Westminster, CO	147.4
19	North Charleston, SC	147.3
20	Canton, OH	126.0
21	Charleston, SC	125.5
22	Alexandria, VA	121.7
23	Fort Smith, AR	116.4
24	Orlando, FL	115.2
25	Carson, CA	113.5
26	Tuscaloosa, AL	110.3
27	Troy, MI	108.3
28	Somerville, MA	107.7
29	El Cajon, CA	104.8
30	Amherst, NY	100.0
30	Concord, CA	100.0
30	Costa Mesa, CA	100.0
30	Huntington Beach, CA	100.0
30	Madison, WI	100.0
30	Melbourne, FL	100.0
30	Peoria, AZ	100.0
30	Plano, TX	100.0
38	Gresham, OR	96.8
39	Lee's Summit, MO	92.3
40	Irvine, CA	90.9
41	Miramar, FL	89.7
42	Pasadena, CA	85.4
43	Murrieta, CA	84.6
44	McKinney, TX	81.8
45	Sioux Falls, SD	72.4
46	Pompano Beach, FL	70.9
47	Miami Gardens, FL	66.4
48	Hesperia, CA	64.8
49	Tacoma, WA	61.5
50	Oakland, CA	56.9
51	Santa Ana, CA	55.1
52	Wichita Falls, TX	51.7
53	Daly City, CA	50.0
53	Garden Grove, CA	50.0
53	Irving, TX	50.0
53	Lawrence, KS	50.0
53	Quincy, MA	50.0
53	Rancho Cucamon., CA	50.0
59	Bridgeport, CT	48.5
60	Bellevue, WA	47.1
61	Escondido, CA	46.7
62	Canton Twnshp, MI	45.8
63	Richardson, TX	45.0
64	Gainesville, FL	42.2
65	Miami, FL	41.0
66	Little Rock, AR	40.7
67	Modesto, CA	39.5
68	Inglewood, CA	39.3
69	Fort Lauderdale, FL	38.2
69	Pasadena, TX	38.2
71	Chula Vista, CA	37.5
72	Miami Beach, FL	36.4
73	San Antonio, TX	35.3
74	San Diego, CA	35.0
75	Moreno Valley, CA	34.8
76	Berkeley, CA	34.5
77	Buffalo, NY	33.3
78	Lafayette, LA	32.4
79	Hollywood, FL	31.7
80	Kenosha, WI	31.2
81	Indianapolis, IN	29.6
82	Lawton, OK	29.4
83	Topeka, KS	28.1
84	Toledo, OH	26.1
85	Colorado Springs, CO	25.0
85	Tempe, AZ	25.0
87	Baton Rouge, LA	24.3
88	Lincoln, NE	23.5
88	Scottsdale, AZ	23.5
90	Winston-Salem, NC	23.2
91	Tampa, FL	23.0
92	Longview, TX	22.9
93	Kansas City, KS	22.0
94	Minneapolis, MN	21.6
95	El Monte, CA	21.2
95	Springfield, MO	21.2
97	Jacksonville, FL	21.1
98	Peoria, IL	21.0
99	Springfield, IL	20.9
100	Brownsville, TX	20.8
101	Detroit, MI	20.4
102	Joliet, IL	20.0
103	Baldwin Park, CA	19.0
104	Seattle, WA	18.6
105	Waterbury, CT	18.2
106	Laredo, TX	17.2
107	South Bend, IN	16.8
108	Dayton, OH	16.5
109	Clarksville, TN	15.6
110	Boise, ID	15.4
110	Lubbock, TX	15.4
112	Cincinnati, OH	14.7
113	Oceanside, CA	14.3
114	Flint, MI	14.0
115	Lancaster, CA	13.8
116	Honolulu, HI	11.8
116	Riverside, CA	11.8
118	Houston, TX	11.7
119	Tallahassee, FL	10.7
120	New York, NY	10.6
121	Cape Coral, FL	10.5
122	San Jose, CA	10.3
123	Rialto, CA	9.1
124	Sacramento, CA	8.8
125	Newark, NJ	8.4
126	Philadelphia, PA	8.2
127	Atlanta, GA	8.1
128	Glendale, AZ	7.7
129	Jackson, MS	7.1
129	Ontario, CA	7.1
131	Memphis, TN	6.9
132	Chandler, AZ	5.7
132	Fresno, CA	5.7
134	Omaha, NE	5.3
135	Anchorage, AK	5.2
136	Chicago, IL	5.1
137	Richmond, CA	4.9
138	Baltimore, MD	3.1
138	Boston, MA	3.1
140	Fayetteville, NC	2.7
140	Las Vegas, NV	2.7
140	Phoenix, AZ	2.7
143	San Leandro, CA	2.0
144	Columbus, OH	1.4
144	Hampton, VA	1.4
146	Albany, GA	1.0
146	Oklahoma City, OK	1.0
148	Birmingham, AL	0.5
149	Alhambra, CA	0.0
149	Anaheim, CA	0.0
149	Ann Arbor, MI	0.0
149	Antioch, CA	0.0
149	Athens-Clarke, GA	0.0
149	Brick Twnshp, NJ	0.0
149	Cary, NC	0.0
149	Colonie, NY	0.0
149	Everett, WA	0.0
149	Fargo, ND	0.0
149	Greece, NY	0.0
149	Lewisville, TX	0.0
149	Livermore, CA	0.0
149	Manchester, NH	0.0
149	Newton, MA	0.0
149	Parma, OH	0.0
149	Portland, OR	0.0
149	Redding, CA	0.0
149	Roswell, GA	0.0
149	Round Rock, TX	0.0
149	Salinas, CA	0.0
149	San Angelo, TX	0.0
149	Santa Clarita, CA	0.0
149	Spokane Valley, WA	0.0
149	Torrance, CA	0.0
149	Tracy, CA	0.0
149	Ventura, CA	0.0
149	Warren, MI	0.0
149	Worcester, MA	0.0
178	Elizabeth, NJ	(0.7)
179	North Las Vegas, NV	(0.8)
180	Los Angeles, CA	(1.6)
181	St. Louis, MO	(1.8)
182	Abilene, TX	(2.3)
182	Long Beach, CA	(2.3)
184	Carrollton, TX	(2.4)
185	Newport News, VA	(2.8)
186	Camden, NJ	(2.9)
186	Mobile, AL	(2.9)
186	Savannah, GA	(2.9)
189	Hartford, CT	(3.5)
189	High Point, NC	(3.5)
189	Palmdale, CA	(3.5)
192	Killeen, TX	(3.7)

RANK	CITY	% CHANGE
193	Davie, FL	(4.2)
193	Hillsboro, OR	(4.2)
195	Greeley, CO	(4.3)
196	Virginia Beach, VA	(4.4)
197	Charlotte, NC	(5.6)
198	Montgomery, AL	(6.3)
199	Rochester, NY	(6.8)
200	Edmond, OK	(7.1)
201	Beaverton, OR	(8.3)
201	Raleigh, NC	(8.3)
203	Dallas, TX	(8.5)
204	Tucson, AZ	(8.7)
204	Tulsa, OK	(8.7)
206	Pittsburgh, PA	(8.9)
207	Pomona, CA	(9.0)
208	Louisville, KY	(9.1)
209	Beaumont, TX	(9.4)
210	Hawthorne, CA	(9.6)
211	Richmond, VA	(9.8)
212	Greensboro, NC	(10.2)
212	San Francisco, CA	(10.2)
214	Hammond, IN	(10.7)
215	Mesa, AZ	(10.9)
215	Yonkers, NY	(10.9)
217	Youngstown, OH	(11.7)
218	New Bedford, MA	(11.8)
219	Stockton, CA	(12.3)
220	Suffolk, VA	(13.8)
221	Milwaukee, WI	(14.1)
222	Denver, CO	(14.3)
222	Wilmington, NC	(14.3)
224	Nashville, TN	(16.4)
225	Gary, IN	(16.7)
226	Springfield, MA	(17.6)
227	Washington, DC	(17.8)
228	Portsmouth, VA	(18.3)
229	Salt Lake City, UT	(18.5)
230	Whittier, CA	(19.0)
231	Lynn, MA	(19.6)
232	Tyler, TX	(19.7)
233	Lakewood, CO	(20.0)
234	San Bernardino, CA	(20.7)
235	Brockton, MA	(20.8)
236	Fort Worth, TX	(22.4)
237	Spokane, WA	(23.1)
238	Visalia, CA	(23.2)
239	Lansing, MI	(23.5)
240	Columbus, GA	(23.9)
241	Allentown, PA	(24.0)
241	Shreveport, LA	(24.0)
243	Paterson, NJ	(24.2)
244	West Palm Beach, FL	(24.3)
245	Evansville, IN	(25.0)
246	Roanoke, VA	(25.1)
247	Plantation, FL	(26.1)
248	Austin, TX	(26.3)
249	Chattanooga, TN	(26.5)
250	Waco, TX	(27.0)
251	Bakersfield, CA	(28.6)
251	Huntsville, AL	(28.6)
253	Knoxville, TN	(28.8)
254	St. Paul, MN	(29.1)
255	St. Petersburg, FL	(29.7)
256	Mesquite, TX	(30.2)
257	Cleveland, OH	(30.3)
258	Oxnard, CA	(32.0)

RANK	CITY	% CHANGE
259	Dearborn, MI	(32.3)
260	Cambridge, MA	(33.3)
260	Kent, WA	(33.3)
260	Santa Maria, CA	(33.3)
263	Fairfield, CA	(33.7)
264	Odessa, TX	(34.4)
265	Norwalk, CA	(35.3)
266	Syracuse, NY	(36.8)
267	Albuquerque, NM	(37.0)
268	Hialeah, FL	(37.1)
269	Albany, NY	(37.6)
270	Victorville, CA	(39.6)
271	Compton, CA	(39.8)
272	Macon, GA	(40.0)
273	Aurora, CO	(41.1)
274	Trenton, NJ	(41.2)
275	Provo, UT	(41.4)
276	Santa Clara, CA	(41.7)
276	Sparks, NV	(41.7)
278	Las Cruces, NM	(41.9)
279	Jersey City, NJ	(42.1)
280	Arlington, TX	(42.4)
281	Downey, CA	(42.9)
281	Eugene, OR	(42.9)
283	Providence, RI	(44.2)
284	Bellflower, CA	(44.5)
285	Henderson, NV	(46.2)
286	Vacaville, CA	(47.6)
287	Buena Park, CA	(48.0)
287	Clifton, NJ	(48.0)
289	Santa Monica, CA	(48.9)
290	Amarillo, TX	(50.0)
290	Carlsbad, CA	(50.0)
290	Chesapeake, VA	(50.0)
290	Hamilton Twnshp, NJ	(50.0)
290	Lake Forest, CA	(50.0)
290	Lakeland, FL	(50.0)
290	Palm Bay, FL	(50.0)
290	San Mateo, CA	(50.0)
290	Warwick, RI	(50.0)
299	Norfolk, VA	(51.0)
299	Vancouver, WA	(51.0)
301	Nashua, NH	(52.2)
302	McAllen, TX	(52.3)
303	Fontana, CA	(52.4)
304	Largo, FL	(52.7)
305	Orange, CA	(53.3)
306	Columbia, SC	(53.5)
307	Pueblo, CO	(54.0)
308	Reading, PA	(54.4)
309	Clearwater, FL	(55.6)
310	Racine, WI	(55.8)
311	Hayward, CA	(56.3)
312	Green Bay, WI	(59.2)
313	Garland, TX	(59.4)
314	Ogden, UT	(59.7)
314	Upper Darby Twnshp, PA	(59.7)
316	Billings, MT	(60.8)
317	Sunnyvale, CA	(65.2)
318	Burbank, CA	(65.5)
319	Chino Hills, CA	(66.7)
319	Independence, MO	(66.7)
319	Westminster, CA	(66.7)
322	Erie, PA	(67.2)
323	West Covina, CA	(67.3)
324	Newport Beach, CA	(67.6)

RANK	CITY	% CHANGE
325	Grand Prairie, TX	(68.3)
326	West Valley, UT	(69.8)
327	Yakima, WA	(70.5)
328	Yuma, AZ	(70.7)
329	Aurora, IL	(71.4)
330	Columbia, MO	(71.8)
331	Corona, CA	(74.1)
332	Vista, CA	(74.4)
333	Southfield, MI	(75.0)
334	Clovis, CA	(77.1)
335	Pembroke Pines, FL	(82.1)
336	Federal Way, WA	(83.6)
337	Glendale, CA	(89.4)
338	Arvada, CO	(100.0)
338	Bellingham, WA	(100.0)
338	Centennial, CO	(100.0)
338	Chino, CA	(100.0)
338	Denton, TX	(100.0)
338	Farmington Hills, MI	(100.0)
338	Fort Collins, CO	(100.0)
338	Livonia, MI	(100.0)
338	Mission Viejo, CA	(100.0)
338	Naperville, IL	(100.0)
338	Overland Park, KS	(100.0)
338	Sandy, UT	(100.0)
338	Sioux City, IA	(100.0)
338	Sugar Land, TX	(100.0)
338	Surprise, AZ	(100.0)
338	Temecula, CA	(100.0)
338	Thousand Oaks, CA	(100.0)
338	Toms River Twnshp, NJ	(100.0)
338	Woodbridge Twnshp, NJ	(100.0)
NA	Bloomington, MN**	NA
NA	Boca Raton, FL**	NA
NA	Boulder, CO**	NA
NA	Broken Arrow, OK**	NA
NA	Cheektowaga, NY**	NA
NA	Clarkstown, NY**	NA
NA	Clinton Twnshp, MI**	NA
NA	Coral Springs, FL**	NA
NA	Cranston, RI**	NA
NA	Des Moines, IA**	NA
NA	Duluth, MN**	NA
NA	Durham, NC**	NA
NA	Edison Twnshp, NJ**	NA
NA	El Paso, TX**	NA
NA	Fort Wayne, IN**	NA
NA	Fullerton, CA**	NA
NA	Gilbert, AZ**	NA
NA	Kansas City, MO**	NA
NA	Lakewood, CA**	NA
NA	Lexington, KY**	NA
NA	Napa, CA**	NA
NA	New Orleans, LA**	NA
NA	Norman, OK**	NA
NA	Orem, UT**	NA
NA	Rochester, MN**	NA
NA	Rockford, IL**	NA
NA	Roseville, CA**	NA
NA	Santa Barbara, CA**	NA
NA	Simi Valley, CA**	NA
NA	Sterling Heights, MI**	NA
NA	Vallejo, CA**	NA
NA	West Jordan, UT**	NA
NA	Westland, MI**	NA
NA	Wichita, KS**	NA

Source: CQ Press using data from F.B.I. "Crime in the United States 2006"

**Includes nonnegligent manslaughter. **Not available. ***These cities had murder rates of 0 in 2005 but had at least one murder in 2006. Calculating percent increase from zero results in an infinite number. These are shown as "NA."*

52. Percent Change in Murder Rate: 2002 to 2006

National Percent Change = 1.0% Increase*

RANK	CITY	% CHANGE
107	Abilene, TX	27.3
123	Albany, GA	18.4
NA	Albany, NY**	NA
270	Albuquerque, NM	(38.7)
36	Alexandria, VA	121.7
293	Alhambra, CA	(50.0)
59	Allentown, PA	77.4
253	Amarillo, TX	(30.8)
NA	Amherst, NY**	NA
272	Anaheim, CA	(40.0)
209	Anchorage, AK	(9.0)
328	Ann Arbor, MI	(100.0)
1	Antioch, CA	790.9
194	Arlington, TX	(5.0)
328	Arvada, CO	(100.0)
249	Athens-Clarke, GA	(29.9)
260	Atlanta, GA	(35.2)
155	Aurora, CO	1.8
326	Aurora, IL	(86.0)
231	Austin, TX	(22.2)
202	Bakersfield, CA	(7.0)
181	Baldwin Park, CA	(1.3)
131	Baltimore, MD	14.9
149	Baton Rouge, LA	5.0
78	Beaumont, TX	47.5
NA	Beaverton, OR**	NA
NA	Bellevue, WA**	NA
7	Bellflower, CA	407.7
328	Bellingham, WA	(100.0)
275	Berkeley, CA	(40.9)
NA	Billings, MT**	NA
62	Birmingham, AL	67.9
6	Bloomington, MN	408.3
101	Boca Raton, FL	30.8
187	Boise, ID	(3.2)
99	Boston, MA	31.7
324	Boulder, CO	(78.0)
157	Brick Twnshp, NJ	0.0
32	Bridgeport, CT	137.6
212	Brockton, MA	(10.6)
316	Broken Arrow, OK	(72.5)
12	Brownsville, TX	314.3
317	Buena Park, CA	(73.5)
57	Buffalo, NY	80.8
157	Burbank, CA	0.0
312	Cambridge, MA	(65.5)
180	Camden, NJ	(1.2)
NA	Canton Twnshp, MI**	NA
NA	Canton, OH**	NA
76	Cape Coral, FL	50.0
206	Carlsbad, CA	(8.3)
10	Carrollton, TX	355.6
138	Carson, CA	12.9
157	Cary, NC	0.0
29	Cedar Rapids, IA	182.4
NA	Centennial, CO**	NA
35	Chandler, AZ	131.3
68	Charleston, SC	61.8
133	Charlotte, NC	14.4
242	Chattanooga, TN	(28.5)
NA	Cheektowaga, NY**	NA
142	Chesapeake, VA	10.3
236	Chicago, IL	(25.8)
203	Chino Hills, CA	(7.1)
157	Chino, CA	0.0
127	Chula Vista, CA	17.9
76	Cincinnati, OH	50.0
157	Clarkstown, NY	0.0
208	Clarksville, TN	(8.8)
278	Clearwater, FL	(41.9)
157	Cleveland, OH	0.0
NA	Clifton, NJ**	NA
299	Clinton Twnshp, MI	(52.4)
NA	Clovis, CA**	NA
157	Colonie, NY	0.0
271	Colorado Springs, CO	(39.4)
192	Columbia, MO	(4.3)
248	Columbia, SC	(29.8)
218	Columbus, GA	(13.6)
112	Columbus, OH	25.7
234	Compton, CA	(24.6)
255	Concord, CA	(33.3)
200	Coral Springs, FL	(6.3)
327	Corona, CA	(88.7)
145	Corpus Christi, TX	9.1
24	Costa Mesa, CA	200.0
NA	Cranston, RI**	NA
197	Dallas, TX	(5.1)
71	Daly City, CA	57.9
46	Danbury, CT	96.2
309	Davie, FL	(63.5)
205	Dayton, OH	(7.2)
250	Dearborn, MI	(30.0)
119	Deerfield Beach, FL	21.6
328	Denton, TX	(100.0)
153	Denver, CO	2.3
NA	Des Moines, IA**	NA
137	Detroit, MI	13.2
14	Downey, CA	300.0
310	Duluth, MN	(64.7)
NA	Durham, NC**	NA
NA	Edison Twnshp, NJ**	NA
203	Edmond, OK	(7.1)
92	El Cajon, CA	38.7
254	El Monte, CA	(31.0)
NA	El Paso, TX**	NA
106	Elizabeth, NJ	27.4
293	Erie, PA	(50.0)
232	Escondido, CA	(24.1)
86	Eugene, OR	42.9
21	Evansville, IN	218.8
186	Everett, WA	(3.1)
194	Fairfield, CA	(5.0)
NA	Fargo, ND**	NA
157	Farmington Hills, MI	0.0
246	Fayetteville, NC	(29.4)
320	Federal Way, WA	(74.5)
47	Flint, MI	92.8
281	Fontana, CA	(42.3)
157	Fort Collins, CO	0.0
65	Fort Lauderdale, FL	64.0
97	Fort Smith, AR	34.7
NA	Fort Wayne, IN**	NA
228	Fort Worth, TX	(20.0)
37	Fremont, CA	114.3
126	Fresno, CA	17.9
54	Fullerton, CA	87.5
207	Gainesville, FL	(8.6)
73	Garden Grove, CA	54.3
317	Garland, TX	(73.5)
221	Gary, IN	(16.3)
306	Gilbert, AZ	(60.5)
130	Glendale, AZ	15.1
323	Glendale, CA	(77.8)
217	Grand Prairie, TX	(13.0)
28	Grand Rapids, MI	185.0
NA	Greece, NY**	NA
55	Greeley, CO	83.3
43	Green Bay, WI	100.0
199	Greensboro, NC	(5.8)
49	Gresham, OR	90.6
157	Hamilton Twnshp, NJ	0.0
251	Hammond, IN	(30.1)
114	Hampton, VA	25.0
193	Hartford, CT	(4.5)
56	Hawthorne, CA	82.5
302	Hayward, CA	(54.8)
157	Henderson, NV	0.0
4	Hesperia, CA	493.3
280	Hialeah, FL	(42.1)
80	High Point, NC	46.4
224	Hillsboro, OR	(17.9)
241	Hollywood, FL	(28.0)
194	Honolulu, HI	(5.0)
82	Houston, TX	45.6
255	Huntington Beach, CA	(33.3)
23	Huntsville, AL	206.5
311	Independence, MO	(65.4)
110	Indianapolis, IN	25.9
103	Inglewood, CA	30.0
24	Irvine, CA	200.0
272	Irving, TX	(40.0)
125	Jacksonville, FL	17.9
220	Jackson, MS	(14.1)
147	Jersey City, NJ	7.0
72	Joliet, IL	56.9
NA	Kansas City, KS**	NA
NA	Kansas City, MO**	NA
16	Kenosha, WI	281.8
297	Kent, WA	(51.0)
34	Killeen, TX	136.4
223	Knoxville, TN	(16.8)
19	Lafayette, LA	248.1
313	Lake Forest, CA	(65.8)
213	Lakeland, FL	(10.8)
13	Lakewood, CA	308.3
14	Lakewood, CO	300.0
83	Lancaster, CA	44.3
282	Lansing, MI	(42.9)
30	Laredo, TX	168.4
263	Largo, FL	(36.6)
NA	Las Cruces, NM**	NA
183	Las Vegas, NV	(2.5)
85	Lawrence, KS	44.0
94	Lawton, OK	37.5
58	Lee's Summit, MO	78.6
303	Lewisville, TX	(55.1)
NA	Lexington, KY**	NA
226	Lincoln, NE	(19.2)
88	Little Rock, AR	40.7
314	Livermore, CA	(66.7)
328	Livonia, MI	(100.0)

RANK	CITY	% CHANGE
269	Long Beach, CA	(38.6)
64	Longview, TX	65.4
239	Los Angeles, CA	(27.5)
NA	Louisville, KY**	NA
52	Lowell, MA	89.4
136	Lubbock, TX	13.2
96	Lynn, MA	36.4
230	Macon, GA	(21.7)
105	Madison, WI	28.6
NA	Manchester, NH**	NA
219	McAllen, TX	(13.9)
282	McKinney, TX	(42.9)
43	Melbourne, FL	100.0
198	Memphis, TN	(5.3)
143	Mesa, AZ	9.6
286	Mesquite, TX	(46.4)
274	Miami Beach, FL	(40.8)
NA	Miami Gardens, FL**	NA
132	Miami, FL	14.6
31	Midland, TX	145.0
188	Milwaukee, WI	(3.3)
108	Minneapolis, MN	26.7
252	Miramar, FL	(30.4)
328	Mission Viejo, CA	(100.0)
215	Mobile, AL	(12.8)
42	Modesto, CA	103.8
210	Montgomery, AL	(9.5)
53	Moreno Valley, CA	89.4
NA	Murfreesboro, TN**	NA
NA	Murrieta, CA**	NA
NA	Napa, CA**	NA
328	Naperville, IL	(100.0)
NA	Nashua, NH**	NA
100	Nashville, TN	31.2
NA	New Bedford, MA**	NA
245	New Orleans, LA	(29.2)
157	New York, NY	0.0
69	Newark, NJ	60.5
304	Newport Beach, CA	(57.1)
184	Newport News, VA	(2.8)
NA	Newton, MA**	NA
247	Norfolk, VA	(29.4)
8	Norman, OK	390.0
67	North Charleston, SC	62.8
227	North Las Vegas, NV	(19.9)
244	Norwalk, CA	(29.0)
90	Oakland, CA	39.5
70	Oceanside, CA	60.0
258	Odessa, TX	(34.4)
305	Ogden, UT	(59.7)
91	Oklahoma City, OK	39.2
265	Olathe, KS	(37.2)
121	Omaha, NE	19.7
61	Ontario, CA	74.4
157	Orange, CA	0.0
157	Orem, UT	0.0
26	Orlando, FL	193.5
328	Overland Park, KS	(100.0)
116	Oxnard, CA	22.8
301	Palm Bay, FL	(54.2)
51	Palmdale, CA	89.7
328	Parma, OH	(100.0)
20	Pasadena, CA	245.5
157	Pasadena, TX	0.0
154	Paterson, NJ	2.0
314	Pembroke Pines, FL	(66.7)
NA	Peoria, AZ**	NA
50	Peoria, IL	89.9
79	Philadelphia, PA	46.6
118	Phoenix, AZ	22.2
109	Pittsburgh, PA	26.3
268	Plano, TX	(38.5)
185	Plantation, FL	(2.9)
148	Pomona, CA	5.2
74	Pompano Beach, FL	54.1
9	Port St. Lucie, FL	372.7
157	Portland, OR	0.0
62	Portsmouth, VA	67.9
298	Providence, RI	(51.5)
NA	Provo, UT**	NA
156	Pueblo, CO	1.8
276	Quincy, MA	(41.1)
17	Racine, WI	266.7
225	Raleigh, NC	(17.9)
120	Rancho Cucamon., CA	20.0
288	Reading, PA	(46.8)
NA	Redding, CA**	NA
33	Reno, NV	137.0
262	Rialto, CA	(36.5)
NA	Richardson, TX**	NA
84	Richmond, CA	44.3
152	Richmond, VA	2.6
293	Riverside, CA	(50.0)
NA	Roanoke, VA**	NA
48	Rochester, MN	90.9
117	Rochester, NY	22.8
NA	Rockford, IL**	NA
NA	Roseville, CA**	NA
328	Roswell, GA	(100.0)
157	Round Rock, TX	0.0
140	Sacramento, CA	11.7
89	Salem, OR	39.5
308	Salinas, CA	(63.3)
232	Salt Lake City, UT	(24.1)
NA	San Angelo, TX**	NA
144	San Antonio, TX	9.5
150	San Bernardino, CA	5.0
81	San Diego, CA	45.9
95	San Francisco, CA	36.9
134	San Jose, CA	14.3
222	San Leandro, CA	(16.4)
NA	San Mateo, CA**	NA
328	Sandy, UT	(100.0)
129	Santa Ana, CA	15.2
307	Santa Barbara, CA	(61.3)
237	Santa Clara, CA	(26.3)
300	Santa Clarita, CA	(52.6)
NA	Santa Maria, CA**	NA
321	Santa Monica, CA	(75.0)
157	Santa Rosa, CA	0.0
277	Savannah, GA	(41.6)
11	Scottsdale, AZ	320.0
135	Seattle, WA	13.3
235	Shreveport, LA	(25.1)
NA	Simi Valley, CA**	NA
328	Sioux City, IA	(100.0)
2	Sioux Falls, SD	525.0
243	Somerville, MA	(28.9)
240	South Bend, IN	(27.9)
5	South Gate, CA	433.3
325	Southfield, MI	(82.9)
114	Sparks, NV	25.0
NA	Spokane Valley, WA**	NA
292	Spokane, WA	(49.5)
124	Springfield, IL	18.2
113	Springfield, MA	25.6
75	Springfield, MO	53.8
43	Sterling Heights, MI	100.0
211	Stockton, CA	(9.9)
122	St. Louis, MO	18.5
93	St. Paul, MN	38.6
201	St. Petersburg, FL	(6.7)
66	Suffolk, VA	63.9
328	Sugar Land, TX	(100.0)
287	Sunnyvale, CA	(46.7)
238	Sunrise, FL	(26.7)
328	Surprise, AZ	(100.0)
285	Syracuse, NY	(45.8)
141	Tacoma, WA	10.5
146	Tallahassee, FL	8.8
261	Tampa, FL	(35.9)
157	Temecula, CA	0.0
291	Tempe, AZ	(49.2)
22	Thornton, CO	208.3
157	Thousand Oaks, CA	0.0
102	Toledo, OH	30.3
328	Toms River Twnshp, NJ	(100.0)
139	Topeka, KS	12.3
293	Torrance, CA	(50.0)
328	Tracy, CA	(100.0)
182	Trenton, NJ	(2.3)
41	Troy, MI	108.3
151	Tucson, AZ	4.4
38	Tulsa, OK	110.8
27	Tuscaloosa, AL	185.9
128	Tyler, TX	15.2
290	Upper Darby Twnshp, PA	(49.0)
157	Vacaville, CA	0.0
214	Vallejo, CA	(12.1)
18	Vancouver, WA	257.1
289	Ventura, CA	(47.4)
189	Victorville, CA	(3.3)
3	Virginia Beach, VA	514.3
279	Visalia, CA	(42.1)
319	Vista, CA	(74.4)
267	Waco, TX	(38.1)
259	Warren, MI	(35.1)
157	Warwick, RI	0.0
264	Washington, DC	(37.0)
60	Waterbury, CT	75.7
157	West Covina, CA	0.0
229	West Jordan, UT	(21.4)
40	West Palm Beach, FL	108.5
191	West Valley, UT	(3.7)
39	Westland, MI	109.1
321	Westminster, CA	(75.0)
NA	Westminster, CO**	NA
98	Whittier, CA	34.3
216	Wichita Falls, TX	(12.9)
111	Wichita, KS	25.9
284	Wilmington, NC	(43.8)
104	Winston-Salem, NC	29.5
328	Woodbridge Twnshp, NJ	(100.0)
NA	Worcester, MA**	NA
255	Yakima, WA	(33.3)
266	Yonkers, NY	(37.9)
190	Youngstown, OH	(3.5)
87	Yuma, AZ	41.7

Source: CQ Press using data from F.B.I. "Crime in the United States 2006"

**Includes nonnegligent manslaughter. **Not available. ***These cities had murder rates of 0 in 2002 but had at least one murder in 2006. Calculating percent increase from zero results in an infinite number. These are shown as "NA."*

52. Percent Change in Murder Rate: 2002 to 2006 (continued)

National Percent Change = 1.0% Increase*

RANK	CITY	% CHANGE
1	Antioch, CA	790.9
2	Sioux Falls, SD	525.0
3	Virginia Beach, VA	514.3
4	Hesperia, CA	493.3
5	South Gate, CA	433.3
6	Bloomington, MN	408.3
7	Bellflower, CA	407.7
8	Norman, OK	390.0
9	Port St. Lucie, FL	372.7
10	Carrollton, TX	355.6
11	Scottsdale, AZ	320.0
12	Brownsville, TX	314.3
13	Lakewood, CA	308.3
14	Downey, CA	300.0
14	Lakewood, CO	300.0
16	Kenosha, WI	281.8
17	Racine, WI	266.7
18	Vancouver, WA	257.1
19	Lafayette, LA	248.1
20	Pasadena, CA	245.5
21	Evansville, IN	218.8
22	Thornton, CO	208.3
23	Huntsville, AL	206.5
24	Costa Mesa, CA	200.0
24	Irvine, CA	200.0
26	Orlando, FL	193.5
27	Tuscaloosa, AL	185.9
28	Grand Rapids, MI	185.0
29	Cedar Rapids, IA	182.4
30	Laredo, TX	168.4
31	Midland, TX	145.0
32	Bridgeport, CT	137.6
33	Reno, NV	137.0
34	Killeen, TX	136.4
35	Chandler, AZ	131.3
36	Alexandria, VA	121.7
37	Fremont, CA	114.3
38	Tulsa, OK	110.8
39	Westland, MI	109.1
40	West Palm Beach, FL	108.5
41	Troy, MI	108.3
42	Modesto, CA	103.8
43	Green Bay, WI	100.0
43	Melbourne, FL	100.0
43	Sterling Heights, MI	100.0
46	Danbury, CT	96.2
47	Flint, MI	92.8
48	Rochester, MN	90.9
49	Gresham, OR	90.6
50	Peoria, IL	89.9
51	Palmdale, CA	89.7
52	Lowell, MA	89.4
53	Moreno Valley, CA	89.4
54	Fullerton, CA	87.5
55	Greeley, CO	83.3
56	Hawthorne, CA	82.5
57	Buffalo, NY	80.8
58	Lee's Summit, MO	78.6
59	Allentown, PA	77.4
60	Waterbury, CT	75.7
61	Ontario, CA	74.4
62	Birmingham, AL	67.9
62	Portsmouth, VA	67.9
64	Longview, TX	65.4
65	Fort Lauderdale, FL	64.0
66	Suffolk, VA	63.9
67	North Charleston, SC	62.8
68	Charleston, SC	61.8
69	Newark, NJ	60.5
70	Oceanside, CA	60.0
71	Daly City, CA	57.9
72	Joliet, IL	56.9
73	Garden Grove, CA	54.3
74	Pompano Beach, FL	54.1
75	Springfield, MO	53.8
76	Cape Coral, FL	50.0
76	Cincinnati, OH	50.0
78	Beaumont, TX	47.5
79	Philadelphia, PA	46.6
80	High Point, NC	46.4
81	San Diego, CA	45.9
82	Houston, TX	45.6
83	Lancaster, CA	44.3
84	Richmond, CA	44.3
85	Lawrence, KS	44.0
86	Eugene, OR	42.9
87	Yuma, AZ	41.7
88	Little Rock, AR	40.7
89	Salem, OR	39.5
90	Oakland, CA	39.5
91	Oklahoma City, OK	39.2
92	El Cajon, CA	38.7
93	St. Paul, MN	38.6
94	Lawton, OK	37.5
95	San Francisco, CA	36.9
96	Lynn, MA	36.4
97	Fort Smith, AR	34.7
98	Whittier, CA	34.3
99	Boston, MA	31.7
100	Nashville, TN	31.2
101	Boca Raton, FL	30.8
102	Toledo, OH	30.3
103	Inglewood, CA	30.0
104	Winston-Salem, NC	29.5
105	Madison, WI	28.6
106	Elizabeth, NJ	27.4
107	Abilene, TX	27.3
108	Minneapolis, MN	26.7
109	Pittsburgh, PA	26.3
110	Indianapolis, IN	25.9
111	Wichita, KS	25.9
112	Columbus, OH	25.7
113	Springfield, MA	25.6
114	Hampton, VA	25.0
114	Sparks, NV	25.0
116	Oxnard, CA	22.8
117	Rochester, NY	22.8
118	Phoenix, AZ	22.2
119	Deerfield Beach, FL	21.6
120	Rancho Cucamon., CA	20.0
121	Omaha, NE	19.7
122	St. Louis, MO	18.5
123	Albany, GA	18.4
124	Springfield, IL	18.2
125	Jacksonville, FL	17.9
126	Fresno, CA	17.9
127	Chula Vista, CA	17.9
128	Tyler, TX	15.2
129	Santa Ana, CA	15.2
130	Glendale, AZ	15.1
131	Baltimore, MD	14.9
132	Miami, FL	14.6
133	Charlotte, NC	14.4
134	San Jose, CA	14.3
135	Seattle, WA	13.3
136	Lubbock, TX	13.2
137	Detroit, MI	13.2
138	Carson, CA	12.9
139	Topeka, KS	12.3
140	Sacramento, CA	11.7
141	Tacoma, WA	10.5
142	Chesapeake, VA	10.3
143	Mesa, AZ	9.6
144	San Antonio, TX	9.5
145	Corpus Christi, TX	9.1
146	Tallahassee, FL	8.8
147	Jersey City, NJ	7.0
148	Pomona, CA	5.2
149	Baton Rouge, LA	5.0
150	San Bernardino, CA	5.0
151	Tucson, AZ	4.4
152	Richmond, VA	2.6
153	Denver, CO	2.3
154	Paterson, NJ	2.0
155	Aurora, CO	1.8
156	Pueblo, CO	1.8
157	Brick Twnshp, NJ	0.0
157	Burbank, CA	0.0
157	Cary, NC	0.0
157	Chino, CA	0.0
157	Clarkstown, NY	0.0
157	Cleveland, OH	0.0
157	Colonie, NY	0.0
157	Farmington Hills, MI	0.0
157	Fort Collins, CO	0.0
157	Hamilton Twnshp, NJ	0.0
157	Henderson, NV	0.0
157	New York, NY	0.0
157	Orange, CA	0.0
157	Orem, UT	0.0
157	Pasadena, TX	0.0
157	Portland, OR	0.0
157	Round Rock, TX	0.0
157	Santa Rosa, CA	0.0
157	Temecula, CA	0.0
157	Thousand Oaks, CA	0.0
157	Vacaville, CA	0.0
157	Warwick, RI	0.0
157	West Covina, CA	0.0
180	Camden, NJ	(1.2)
181	Baldwin Park, CA	(1.3)
182	Trenton, NJ	(2.3)
183	Las Vegas, NV	(2.5)
184	Newport News, VA	(2.8)
185	Plantation, FL	(2.9)
186	Everett, WA	(3.1)
187	Boise, ID	(3.2)
188	Milwaukee, WI	(3.3)
189	Victorville, CA	(3.3)
190	Youngstown, OH	(3.5)
191	West Valley, UT	(3.7)
192	Columbia, MO	(4.3)

RANK	CITY	% CHANGE
193	Hartford, CT	(4.5)
194	Arlington, TX	(5.0)
194	Fairfield, CA	(5.0)
194	Honolulu, HI	(5.0)
197	Dallas, TX	(5.1)
198	Memphis, TN	(5.3)
199	Greensboro, NC	(5.8)
200	Coral Springs, FL	(6.3)
201	St. Petersburg, FL	(6.7)
202	Bakersfield, CA	(7.0)
203	Chino Hills, CA	(7.1)
203	Edmond, OK	(7.1)
205	Dayton, OH	(7.2)
206	Carlsbad, CA	(8.3)
207	Gainesville, FL	(8.6)
208	Clarksville, TN	(8.8)
209	Anchorage, AK	(9.0)
210	Montgomery, AL	(9.5)
211	Stockton, CA	(9.9)
212	Brockton, MA	(10.6)
213	Lakeland, FL	(10.8)
214	Vallejo, CA	(12.1)
215	Mobile, AL	(12.8)
216	Wichita Falls, TX	(12.9)
217	Grand Prairie, TX	(13.0)
218	Columbus, GA	(13.6)
219	McAllen, TX	(13.9)
220	Jackson, MS	(14.1)
221	Gary, IN	(16.3)
222	San Leandro, CA	(16.4)
223	Knoxville, TN	(16.8)
224	Hillsboro, OR	(17.9)
225	Raleigh, NC	(17.9)
226	Lincoln, NE	(19.2)
227	North Las Vegas, NV	(19.9)
228	Fort Worth, TX	(20.0)
229	West Jordan, UT	(21.4)
230	Macon, GA	(21.7)
231	Austin, TX	(22.2)
232	Escondido, CA	(24.1)
232	Salt Lake City, UT	(24.1)
234	Compton, CA	(24.6)
235	Shreveport, LA	(25.1)
236	Chicago, IL	(25.8)
237	Santa Clara, CA	(26.3)
238	Sunrise, FL	(26.7)
239	Los Angeles, CA	(27.5)
240	South Bend, IN	(27.9)
241	Hollywood, FL	(28.0)
242	Chattanooga, TN	(28.5)
243	Somerville, MA	(28.9)
244	Norwalk, CA	(29.0)
245	New Orleans, LA	(29.2)
246	Fayetteville, NC	(29.4)
247	Norfolk, VA	(29.4)
248	Columbia, SC	(29.8)
249	Athens-Clarke, GA	(29.9)
250	Dearborn, MI	(30.0)
251	Hammond, IN	(30.1)
252	Miramar, FL	(30.4)
253	Amarillo, TX	(30.8)
254	El Monte, CA	(31.0)
255	Concord, CA	(33.3)
255	Huntington Beach, CA	(33.3)
255	Yakima, WA	(33.3)
258	Odessa, TX	(34.4)
259	Warren, MI	(35.1)
260	Atlanta, GA	(35.2)
261	Tampa, FL	(35.9)
262	Rialto, CA	(36.5)
263	Largo, FL	(36.6)
264	Washington, DC	(37.0)
265	Olathe, KS	(37.2)
266	Yonkers, NY	(37.9)
267	Waco, TX	(38.1)
268	Plano, TX	(38.5)
269	Long Beach, CA	(38.6)
270	Albuquerque, NM	(38.7)
271	Colorado Springs, CO	(39.4)
272	Anaheim, CA	(40.0)
272	Irving, TX	(40.0)
274	Miami Beach, FL	(40.8)
275	Berkeley, CA	(40.9)
276	Quincy, MA	(41.1)
277	Savannah, GA	(41.6)
278	Clearwater, FL	(41.9)
279	Visalia, CA	(42.1)
280	Hialeah, FL	(42.1)
281	Fontana, CA	(42.3)
282	Lansing, MI	(42.9)
282	McKinney, TX	(42.9)
284	Wilmington, NC	(43.8)
285	Syracuse, NY	(45.8)
286	Mesquite, TX	(46.4)
287	Sunnyvale, CA	(46.7)
288	Reading, PA	(46.8)
289	Ventura, CA	(47.4)
290	Upper Darby Twnshp, PA	(49.0)
291	Tempe, AZ	(49.2)
292	Spokane, WA	(49.5)
293	Alhambra, CA	(50.0)
293	Erie, PA	(50.0)
293	Riverside, CA	(50.0)
293	Torrance, CA	(50.0)
297	Kent, WA	(51.0)
298	Providence, RI	(51.5)
299	Clinton Twnshp, MI	(52.4)
300	Santa Clarita, CA	(52.6)
301	Palm Bay, FL	(54.2)
302	Hayward, CA	(54.8)
303	Lewisville, TX	(55.1)
304	Newport Beach, CA	(57.1)
305	Ogden, UT	(59.7)
306	Gilbert, AZ	(60.5)
307	Santa Barbara, CA	(61.3)
308	Salinas, CA	(63.3)
309	Davie, FL	(63.5)
310	Duluth, MN	(64.7)
311	Independence, MO	(65.4)
312	Cambridge, MA	(65.5)
313	Lake Forest, CA	(65.8)
314	Livermore, CA	(66.7)
314	Pembroke Pines, FL	(66.7)
316	Broken Arrow, OK	(72.5)
317	Buena Park, CA	(73.5)
317	Garland, TX	(73.5)
319	Vista, CA	(74.4)
320	Federal Way, WA	(74.5)
321	Santa Monica, CA	(75.0)
321	Westminster, CA	(75.0)
323	Glendale, CA	(77.8)
324	Boulder, CO	(78.0)
325	Southfield, MI	(82.9)
326	Aurora, IL	(86.0)
327	Corona, CA	(88.7)
328	Ann Arbor, MI	(100.0)
328	Arvada, CO	(100.0)
328	Bellingham, WA	(100.0)
328	Denton, TX	(100.0)
328	Livonia, MI	(100.0)
328	Mission Viejo, CA	(100.0)
328	Naperville, IL	(100.0)
328	Overland Park, KS	(100.0)
328	Parma, OH	(100.0)
328	Roswell, GA	(100.0)
328	Sandy, UT	(100.0)
328	Sioux City, IA	(100.0)
328	Sugar Land, TX	(100.0)
328	Surprise, AZ	(100.0)
328	Toms River Twnshp, NJ	(100.0)
328	Tracy, CA	(100.0)
328	Woodbridge Twnshp, NJ	(100.0)
NA	Albany, NY**	NA
NA	Amherst, NY**	NA
NA	Beaverton, OR**	NA
NA	Bellevue, WA**	NA
NA	Billings, MT**	NA
NA	Canton Twnshp, MI**	NA
NA	Canton, OH**	NA
NA	Centennial, CO**	NA
NA	Cheektowaga, NY**	NA
NA	Clifton, NJ**	NA
NA	Clovis, CA**	NA
NA	Cranston, RI**	NA
NA	Des Moines, IA**	NA
NA	Durham, NC**	NA
NA	Edison Twnshp, NJ**	NA
NA	El Paso, TX**	NA
NA	Fargo, ND**	NA
NA	Fort Wayne, IN**	NA
NA	Greece, NY**	NA
NA	Kansas City, KS**	NA
NA	Kansas City, MO**	NA
NA	Las Cruces, NM**	NA
NA	Lexington, KY**	NA
NA	Louisville, KY**	NA
NA	Manchester, NH**	NA
NA	Miami Gardens, FL**	NA
NA	Murfreesboro, TN**	NA
NA	Murrieta, CA**	NA
NA	Napa, CA**	NA
NA	Nashua, NH**	NA
NA	New Bedford, MA**	NA
NA	Newton, MA**	NA
NA	Peoria, AZ**	NA
NA	Provo, UT**	NA
NA	Redding, CA**	NA
NA	Richardson, TX**	NA
NA	Roanoke, VA**	NA
NA	Rockford, IL**	NA
NA	Roseville, CA**	NA
NA	San Angelo, TX**	NA
NA	San Mateo, CA**	NA
NA	Santa Maria, CA**	NA
NA	Simi Valley, CA**	NA
NA	Spokane Valley, WA**	NA
NA	Westminster, CO**	NA
NA	Worcester, MA**	NA

Source: CQ Press using data from F.B.I. "Crime in the United States 2006"

**Includes nonnegligent manslaughter. **Not available. ***These cities had murder rates of 0 in 2002 but had at least one murder in 2006. Calculating percent increase from zero results in an infinite number. These are shown as "NA."*

53. Rapes in 2006

National Total = 92,455 Rapes*

RANK	CITY	RAPES
136	Abilene, TX	67
255	Albany, GA	31
184	Albany, NY	50
28	Albuquerque, NM	286
274	Alexandria, VA	27
306	Alhambra, CA	19
213	Allentown, PA	42
85	Amarillo, TX	98
352	Amherst, NY	11
75	Anaheim, CA	107
31	Anchorage, AK	248
253	Ann Arbor, MI	32
240	Antioch, CA	35
41	Arlington, TX	192
255	Arvada, CO	31
175	Athens-Clarke, GA	53
46	Atlanta, GA	171
37	Aurora, CO	217
NA	Aurora, IL**	NA
21	Austin, TX	319
210	Bakersfield, CA	43
352	Baldwin Park, CA	11
57	Baltimore, MD	138
94	Baton Rouge, LA	93
115	Beaumont, TX	75
312	Beaverton, OR	18
213	Bellevue, WA	42
323	Bellflower, CA	16
248	Bellingham, WA	33
294	Berkeley, CA	22
270	Billings, MT	28
35	Birmingham, AL	220
NA	Bloomington, MN**	NA
340	Boca Raton, FL	13
64	Boise, ID	127
29	Boston, MA	275
240	Boulder, CO	35
374	Brick Twnshp, NJ	3
131	Bridgeport, CT	69
213	Brockton, MA	42
340	Broken Arrow, OK	13
201	Brownsville, TX	46
306	Buena Park, CA	19
45	Buffalo, NY	174
360	Burbank, CA	10
352	Cambridge, MA	11
139	Camden, NJ	66
253	Canton Twnshp, MI	32
136	Canton, OH	67
180	Cape Coral, FL	52
352	Carlsbad, CA	11
368	Carrollton, TX	6
323	Carson, CA	16
334	Cary, NC	14
225	Cedar Rapids, IA	39
282	Centennial, CO	25
170	Chandler, AZ	56
203	Charleston, SC	45
15	Charlotte, NC	346
68	Chattanooga, TN	118
334	Cheektowaga, NY	14
159	Chesapeake, VA	60
NA	Chicago, IL**	NA
367	Chino Hills, CA	7
365	Chino, CA	8
130	Chula Vista, CA	70
25	Cincinnati, OH	291
371	Clarkstown, NY	5
184	Clarksville, TN	50
206	Clearwater, FL	44
12	Cleveland, OH	445
376	Clifton, NJ	2
295	Clinton Twnshp, MI	21
352	Clovis, CA	11
376	Colonie, NY	2
30	Colorado Springs, CO	251
289	Columbia, MO	23
170	Columbia, SC	56
306	Columbus, GA	19
8	Columbus, OH	586
184	Compton, CA	50
303	Concord, CA	20
376	Coral Springs, FL	2
255	Corona, CA	31
48	Corpus Christi, TX	167
262	Costa Mesa, CA	30
323	Cranston, RI	16
6	Dallas, TX	665
312	Daly City, CA	18
352	Danbury, CT	11
303	Davie, FL	20
67	Dayton, OH	120
295	Dearborn, MI	21
289	Deerfield Beach, FL	23
159	Denton, TX	60
16	Denver, CO	342
151	Des Moines, IA	62
7	Detroit, MI	593
295	Downey, CA	21
NA	Duluth, MN**	NA
85	Durham, NC	98
330	Edison Twnshp, NJ	15
262	Edmond, OK	30
270	El Cajon, CA	28
282	El Monte, CA	25
25	El Paso, TX	291
240	Elizabeth, NJ	35
131	Erie, PA	69
248	Escondido, CA	33
206	Eugene, OR	44
154	Evansville, IN	61
210	Everett, WA	43
236	Fairfield, CA	36
131	Fargo, ND	69
334	Farmington Hills, MI	14
154	Fayetteville, NC	61
146	Federal Way, WA	64
54	Flint, MI	143
222	Fontana, CA	40
113	Fort Collins, CO	76
102	Fort Lauderdale, FL	83
102	Fort Smith, AR	83
112	Fort Wayne, IN	80
32	Fort Worth, TX	247
266	Fremont, CA	29
59	Fresno, CA	133
198	Fullerton, CA	47
90	Gainesville, FL	96
266	Garden Grove, CA	29
184	Garland, TX	50
154	Gary, IN	61
230	Gilbert, AZ	37
115	Glendale, AZ	75
334	Glendale, CA	14
131	Grand Prairie, TX	69
143	Grand Rapids, MI	65
346	Greece, NY	12
175	Greeley, CO	53
184	Green Bay, WI	50
101	Greensboro, NC	86
126	Gresham, OR	72
363	Hamilton Twnshp, NJ	9
266	Hammond, IN	29
175	Hampton, VA	53
198	Hartford, CT	47
266	Hawthorne, CA	29
248	Hayward, CA	33
150	Henderson, NV	63
317	Hesperia, CA	17
278	Hialeah, FL	26
217	High Point, NC	41
244	Hillsboro, OR	34
163	Hollywood, FL	58
34	Honolulu, HI	229
4	Houston, TX	854
255	Huntington Beach, CA	31
81	Huntsville, AL	100
154	Independence, MO	61
10	Indianapolis, IN	549
236	Inglewood, CA	36
317	Irvine, CA	17
193	Irving, TX	48
36	Jacksonville, FL	218
50	Jackson, MS	160
159	Jersey City, NJ	60
NA	Joliet, IL**	NA
96	Kansas City, KS	91
19	Kansas City, MO	321
180	Kenosha, WI	52
102	Kent, WA	83
109	Killeen, TX	81
98	Knoxville, TN	89
123	Lafayette, LA	73
368	Lake Forest, CA	6
167	Lakeland, FL	57
352	Lakewood, CA	11
85	Lakewood, CO	98
170	Lancaster, CA	56
76	Lansing, MI	105
90	Laredo, TX	96
240	Largo, FL	35
93	Las Cruces, NM	94
5	Las Vegas, NV	718
193	Lawrence, KS	48
107	Lawton, OK	82
330	Lee's Summit, MO	15
230	Lewisville, TX	37
63	Lexington, KY	128
81	Lincoln, NE	100
53	Little Rock, AR	151
323	Livermore, CA	16
306	Livonia, MI	19

RANK	CITY	RAPES
58	Long Beach, CA	134
170	Longview, TX	56
2	Los Angeles, CA	1,059
44	Louisville, KY	175
222	Lowell, MA	40
85	Lubbock, TX	98
244	Lynn, MA	34
175	Macon, GA	53
146	Madison, WI	64
206	Manchester, NH	44
270	McAllen, TX	28
217	McKinney, TX	41
262	Melbourne, FL	30
13	Memphis, TN	425
39	Mesa, AZ	203
360	Mesquite, TX	10
109	Miami Beach, FL	81
139	Miami Gardens, FL	66
80	Miami, FL	101
163	Midland, TX	58
72	Milwaukee, WI	112
NA	Minneapolis, MN**	NA
203	Miramar, FL	45
379	Mission Viejo, CA	1
102	Mobile, AL	83
123	Modesto, CA	73
120	Montgomery, AL	74
154	Moreno Valley, CA	61
225	Murfreesboro, TN	39
363	Murrieta, CA	9
295	Napa, CA	21
NA	Naperville, IL**	NA
295	Nashua, NH	21
20	Nashville, TN	320
163	New Bedford, MA	58
99	New Orleans, LA	87
1	New York, NY	1,071
99	Newark, NJ	87
373	Newport Beach, CA	4
74	Newport News, VA	109
365	Newton, MA	8
81	Norfolk, VA	100
228	Norman, OK	38
109	North Charleston, SC	81
167	North Las Vegas, NV	57
295	Norwalk, CA	21
22	Oakland, CA	306
193	Oceanside, CA	48
346	Odessa, TX	12
230	Ogden, UT	37
18	Oklahoma City, OK	327
146	Olathe, KS	64
42	Omaha, NE	187
120	Ontario, CA	74
340	Orange, CA	13
323	Orem, UT	16
49	Orlando, FL	163
193	Overland Park, KS	48
244	Oxnard, CA	34
139	Palm Bay, FL	66
163	Palmdale, CA	58
334	Parma, OH	14
306	Pasadena, CA	19
191	Pasadena, TX	49
230	Paterson, NJ	37
330	Pembroke Pines, FL	15

RANK	CITY	RAPES
217	Peoria, AZ	41
NA	Peoria, IL**	NA
3	Philadelphia, PA	960
9	Phoenix, AZ	550
78	Pittsburgh, PA	102
213	Plano, TX	42
371	Plantation, FL	5
317	Pomona, CA	17
174	Pompano Beach, FL	54
236	Port St. Lucie, FL	36
24	Portland, OR	293
230	Portsmouth, VA	37
180	Providence, RI	52
228	Provo, UT	38
191	Pueblo, CO	49
289	Quincy, MA	23
323	Racine, WI	16
89	Raleigh, NC	97
282	Rancho Cucamon., CA	25
206	Reading, PA	44
126	Redding, CA	72
81	Reno, NV	100
262	Rialto, CA	30
352	Richardson, TX	11
217	Richmond, CA	41
113	Richmond, VA	76
102	Riverside, CA	83
159	Roanoke, VA	60
NA	Rochester, MN**	NA
95	Rochester, NY	92
61	Rockford, IL	132
287	Roseville, CA	24
346	Roswell, GA	12
289	Round Rock, TX	23
40	Sacramento, CA	196
120	Salem, OR	74
203	Salinas, CA	45
92	Salt Lake City, UT	95
175	San Angelo, TX	53
11	San Antonio, TX	514
184	San Bernardino, CA	50
14	San Diego, CA	348
52	San Francisco, CA	154
37	San Jose, CA	217
270	San Leandro, CA	28
312	San Mateo, CA	18
289	Sandy, UT	23
123	Santa Ana, CA	73
248	Santa Barbara, CA	33
323	Santa Clara, CA	16
278	Santa Clarita, CA	26
210	Santa Maria, CA	43
278	Santa Monica, CA	26
115	Santa Rosa, CA	75
143	Savannah, GA	65
143	Scottsdale, AZ	65
62	Seattle, WA	129
56	Shreveport, LA	140
295	Simi Valley, CA	21
183	Sioux City, IA	51
69	Sioux Falls, SD	115
306	Somerville, MA	19
136	South Bend, IN	67
334	South Gate, CA	14
236	Southfield, MI	36
222	Sparks, NV	40

RANK	CITY	RAPES
312	Spokane Valley, WA	18
96	Spokane, WA	91
NA	Springfield, IL**	NA
69	Springfield, MA	115
107	Springfield, MO	82
317	Sterling Heights, MI	17
78	Stockton, CA	102
17	St. Louis, MO	337
NA	St. Paul, MN**	NA
72	St. Petersburg, FL	112
282	Suffolk, VA	25
368	Sugar Land, TX	6
295	Sunnyvale, CA	21
330	Sunrise, FL	15
317	Surprise, AZ	17
139	Syracuse, NY	66
55	Tacoma, WA	142
51	Tallahassee, FL	155
59	Tampa, FL	133
340	Temecula, CA	13
129	Tempe, AZ	71
115	Thornton, CO	75
340	Thousand Oaks, CA	13
47	Toledo, OH	169
346	Toms River Twnshp, NJ	12
167	Topeka, KS	57
312	Torrance, CA	18
374	Tracy, CA	3
255	Trenton, NJ	31
360	Troy, MI	10
23	Tucson, AZ	294
27	Tulsa, OK	289
198	Tuscaloosa, AL	47
217	Tyler, TX	41
346	Upper Darby Twnshp, PA	12
282	Vacaville, CA	25
255	Vallejo, CA	31
77	Vancouver, WA	103
287	Ventura, CA	24
278	Victorville, CA	26
69	Virginia Beach, VA	115
184	Visalia, CA	50
244	Vista, CA	34
126	Waco, TX	72
115	Warren, MI	75
274	Warwick, RI	27
43	Washington, DC	182
225	Waterbury, CT	39
340	West Covina, CA	13
274	West Jordan, UT	27
201	West Palm Beach, FL	46
131	West Valley, UT	69
146	Westland, MI	64
303	Westminster, CA	20
230	Westminster, CO	37
346	Whittier, CA	12
274	Wichita Falls, TX	27
33	Wichita, KS	240
151	Wilmington, NC	62
65	Winston-Salem, NC	126
317	Woodbridge Twnshp, NJ	17
66	Worcester, MA	124
151	Yakima, WA	62
255	Yonkers, NY	31
193	Youngstown, OH	48
248	Yuma, AZ	33

Source: Federal Bureau of Investigation "Crime in the United States 2006"

**Forcible rape is the carnal knowledge of a female forcibly and against her will. Assaults or attempts to commit rape by force or threat of force are included. However, statutory rape without force and other sex offenses are excluded. **Not available.*

53. Rapes in 2006 (continued)

National Total = 92,455 Rapes*

RANK	CITY	RAPES
1	New York, NY	1,071
2	Los Angeles, CA	1,059
3	Philadelphia, PA	960
4	Houston, TX	854
5	Las Vegas, NV	718
6	Dallas, TX	665
7	Detroit, MI	593
8	Columbus, OH	586
9	Phoenix, AZ	550
10	Indianapolis, IN	549
11	San Antonio, TX	514
12	Cleveland, OH	445
13	Memphis, TN	425
14	San Diego, CA	348
15	Charlotte, NC	346
16	Denver, CO	342
17	St. Louis, MO	337
18	Oklahoma City, OK	327
19	Kansas City, MO	321
20	Nashville, TN	320
21	Austin, TX	319
22	Oakland, CA	306
23	Tucson, AZ	294
24	Portland, OR	293
25	Cincinnati, OH	291
25	El Paso, TX	291
27	Tulsa, OK	289
28	Albuquerque, NM	286
29	Boston, MA	275
30	Colorado Springs, CO	251
31	Anchorage, AK	248
32	Fort Worth, TX	247
33	Wichita, KS	240
34	Honolulu, HI	229
35	Birmingham, AL	220
36	Jacksonville, FL	218
37	Aurora, CO	217
37	San Jose, CA	217
39	Mesa, AZ	203
40	Sacramento, CA	196
41	Arlington, TX	192
42	Omaha, NE	187
43	Washington, DC	182
44	Louisville, KY	175
45	Buffalo, NY	174
46	Atlanta, GA	171
47	Toledo, OH	169
48	Corpus Christi, TX	167
49	Orlando, FL	163
50	Jackson, MS	160
51	Tallahassee, FL	155
52	San Francisco, CA	154
53	Little Rock, AR	151
54	Flint, MI	143
55	Tacoma, WA	142
56	Shreveport, LA	140
57	Baltimore, MD	138
58	Long Beach, CA	134
59	Fresno, CA	133
59	Tampa, FL	133
61	Rockford, IL	132
62	Seattle, WA	129
63	Lexington, KY	128
64	Boise, ID	127
65	Winston-Salem, NC	126
66	Worcester, MA	124
67	Dayton, OH	120
68	Chattanooga, TN	118
69	Sioux Falls, SD	115
69	Springfield, MA	115
69	Virginia Beach, VA	115
72	Milwaukee, WI	112
72	St. Petersburg, FL	112
74	Newport News, VA	109
75	Anaheim, CA	107
76	Lansing, MI	105
77	Vancouver, WA	103
78	Pittsburgh, PA	102
78	Stockton, CA	102
80	Miami, FL	101
81	Huntsville, AL	100
81	Lincoln, NE	100
81	Norfolk, VA	100
81	Reno, NV	100
85	Amarillo, TX	98
85	Durham, NC	98
85	Lakewood, CO	98
85	Lubbock, TX	98
89	Raleigh, NC	97
90	Gainesville, FL	96
90	Laredo, TX	96
92	Salt Lake City, UT	95
93	Las Cruces, NM	94
94	Baton Rouge, LA	93
95	Rochester, NY	92
96	Kansas City, KS	91
96	Spokane, WA	91
98	Knoxville, TN	89
99	New Orleans, LA	87
99	Newark, NJ	87
101	Greensboro, NC	86
102	Fort Lauderdale, FL	83
102	Fort Smith, AR	83
102	Kent, WA	83
102	Mobile, AL	83
102	Riverside, CA	83
107	Lawton, OK	82
107	Springfield, MO	82
109	Killeen, TX	81
109	Miami Beach, FL	81
109	North Charleston, SC	81
112	Fort Wayne, IN	80
113	Fort Collins, CO	76
113	Richmond, VA	76
115	Beaumont, TX	75
115	Glendale, AZ	75
115	Santa Rosa, CA	75
115	Thornton, CO	75
115	Warren, MI	75
120	Montgomery, AL	74
120	Ontario, CA	74
120	Salem, OR	74
123	Lafayette, LA	73
123	Modesto, CA	73
123	Santa Ana, CA	73
126	Gresham, OR	72
126	Redding, CA	72
126	Waco, TX	72
129	Tempe, AZ	71
130	Chula Vista, CA	70
131	Bridgeport, CT	69
131	Erie, PA	69
131	Fargo, ND	69
131	Grand Prairie, TX	69
131	West Valley, UT	69
136	Abilene, TX	67
136	Canton, OH	67
136	South Bend, IN	67
139	Camden, NJ	66
139	Miami Gardens, FL	66
139	Palm Bay, FL	66
139	Syracuse, NY	66
143	Grand Rapids, MI	65
143	Savannah, GA	65
143	Scottsdale, AZ	65
146	Federal Way, WA	64
146	Madison, WI	64
146	Olathe, KS	64
146	Westland, MI	64
150	Henderson, NV	63
151	Des Moines, IA	62
151	Wilmington, NC	62
151	Yakima, WA	62
154	Evansville, IN	61
154	Fayetteville, NC	61
154	Gary, IN	61
154	Independence, MO	61
154	Moreno Valley, CA	61
159	Chesapeake, VA	60
159	Denton, TX	60
159	Jersey City, NJ	60
159	Roanoke, VA	60
163	Hollywood, FL	58
163	Midland, TX	58
163	New Bedford, MA	58
163	Palmdale, CA	58
167	Lakeland, FL	57
167	North Las Vegas, NV	57
167	Topeka, KS	57
170	Chandler, AZ	56
170	Columbia, SC	56
170	Lancaster, CA	56
170	Longview, TX	56
174	Pompano Beach, FL	54
175	Athens-Clarke, GA	53
175	Greeley, CO	53
175	Hampton, VA	53
175	Macon, GA	53
175	San Angelo, TX	53
180	Cape Coral, FL	52
180	Kenosha, WI	52
180	Providence, RI	52
183	Sioux City, IA	51
184	Albany, NY	50
184	Clarksville, TN	50
184	Compton, CA	50
184	Garland, TX	50
184	Green Bay, WI	50
184	San Bernardino, CA	50
184	Visalia, CA	50
191	Pasadena, TX	49
191	Pueblo, CO	49

RANK	CITY	RAPES
193	Irving, TX	48
193	Lawrence, KS	48
193	Oceanside, CA	48
193	Overland Park, KS	48
193	Youngstown, OH	48
198	Fullerton, CA	47
198	Hartford, CT	47
198	Tuscaloosa, AL	47
201	Brownsville, TX	46
201	West Palm Beach, FL	46
203	Charleston, SC	45
203	Miramar, FL	45
203	Salinas, CA	45
206	Clearwater, FL	44
206	Eugene, OR	44
206	Manchester, NH	44
206	Reading, PA	44
210	Bakersfield, CA	43
210	Everett, WA	43
210	Santa Maria, CA	43
213	Allentown, PA	42
213	Bellevue, WA	42
213	Brockton, MA	42
213	Plano, TX	42
217	High Point, NC	41
217	McKinney, TX	41
217	Peoria, AZ	41
217	Richmond, CA	41
217	Tyler, TX	41
222	Fontana, CA	40
222	Lowell, MA	40
222	Sparks, NV	40
225	Cedar Rapids, IA	39
225	Murfreesboro, TN	39
225	Waterbury, CT	39
228	Norman, OK	38
228	Provo, UT	38
230	Gilbert, AZ	37
230	Lewisville, TX	37
230	Ogden, UT	37
230	Paterson, NJ	37
230	Portsmouth, VA	37
230	Westminster, CO	37
236	Fairfield, CA	36
236	Inglewood, CA	36
236	Port St. Lucie, FL	36
236	Southfield, MI	36
240	Antioch, CA	35
240	Boulder, CO	35
240	Elizabeth, NJ	35
240	Largo, FL	35
244	Hillsboro, OR	34
244	Lynn, MA	34
244	Oxnard, CA	34
244	Vista, CA	34
248	Bellingham, WA	33
248	Escondido, CA	33
248	Hayward, CA	33
248	Santa Barbara, CA	33
248	Yuma, AZ	33
253	Ann Arbor, MI	32
253	Canton Twnshp, MI	32
255	Albany, GA	31
255	Arvada, CO	31
255	Corona, CA	31
255	Huntington Beach, CA	31
255	Trenton, NJ	31
255	Vallejo, CA	31
255	Yonkers, NY	31
262	Costa Mesa, CA	30
262	Edmond, OK	30
262	Melbourne, FL	30
262	Rialto, CA	30
266	Fremont, CA	29
266	Garden Grove, CA	29
266	Hammond, IN	29
266	Hawthorne, CA	29
270	Billings, MT	28
270	El Cajon, CA	28
270	McAllen, TX	28
270	San Leandro, CA	28
274	Alexandria, VA	27
274	Warwick, RI	27
274	West Jordan, UT	27
274	Wichita Falls, TX	27
278	Hialeah, FL	26
278	Santa Clarita, CA	26
278	Santa Monica, CA	26
278	Victorville, CA	26
282	Centennial, CO	25
282	El Monte, CA	25
282	Rancho Cucamon., CA	25
282	Suffolk, VA	25
282	Vacaville, CA	25
287	Roseville, CA	24
287	Ventura, CA	24
289	Columbia, MO	23
289	Deerfield Beach, FL	23
289	Quincy, MA	23
289	Round Rock, TX	23
289	Sandy, UT	23
294	Berkeley, CA	22
295	Clinton Twnshp, MI	21
295	Dearborn, MI	21
295	Downey, CA	21
295	Napa, CA	21
295	Nashua, NH	21
295	Norwalk, CA	21
295	Simi Valley, CA	21
295	Sunnyvale, CA	21
303	Concord, CA	20
303	Davie, FL	20
303	Westminster, CA	20
306	Alhambra, CA	19
306	Buena Park, CA	19
306	Columbus, GA	19
306	Livonia, MI	19
306	Pasadena, CA	19
306	Somerville, MA	19
312	Beaverton, OR	18
312	Daly City, CA	18
312	San Mateo, CA	18
312	Spokane Valley, WA	18
312	Torrance, CA	18
317	Hesperia, CA	17
317	Irvine, CA	17
317	Pomona, CA	17
317	Sterling Heights, MI	17
317	Surprise, AZ	17
317	Woodbridge Twnshp, NJ	17
323	Bellflower, CA	16
323	Carson, CA	16
323	Cranston, RI	16
323	Livermore, CA	16
323	Orem, UT	16
323	Racine, WI	16
323	Santa Clara, CA	16
330	Edison Twnshp, NJ	15
330	Lee's Summit, MO	15
330	Pembroke Pines, FL	15
330	Sunrise, FL	15
334	Cary, NC	14
334	Cheektowaga, NY	14
334	Farmington Hills, MI	14
334	Glendale, CA	14
334	Parma, OH	14
334	South Gate, CA	14
340	Boca Raton, FL	13
340	Broken Arrow, OK	13
340	Orange, CA	13
340	Temecula, CA	13
340	Thousand Oaks, CA	13
340	West Covina, CA	13
346	Greece, NY	12
346	Odessa, TX	12
346	Roswell, GA	12
346	Toms River Twnshp, NJ	12
346	Upper Darby Twnshp, PA	12
346	Whittier, CA	12
352	Amherst, NY	11
352	Baldwin Park, CA	11
352	Cambridge, MA	11
352	Carlsbad, CA	11
352	Clovis, CA	11
352	Danbury, CT	11
352	Lakewood, CA	11
352	Richardson, TX	11
360	Burbank, CA	10
360	Mesquite, TX	10
360	Troy, MI	10
363	Hamilton Twnshp, NJ	9
363	Murrieta, CA	9
365	Chino, CA	8
365	Newton, MA	8
367	Chino Hills, CA	7
368	Carrollton, TX	6
368	Lake Forest, CA	6
368	Sugar Land, TX	6
371	Clarkstown, NY	5
371	Plantation, FL	5
373	Newport Beach, CA	4
374	Brick Twnshp, NJ	3
374	Tracy, CA	3
376	Clifton, NJ	2
376	Colonie, NY	2
376	Coral Springs, FL	2
379	Mission Viejo, CA	1
NA	Aurora, IL**	NA
NA	Bloomington, MN**	NA
NA	Chicago, IL**	NA
NA	Duluth, MN**	NA
NA	Joliet, IL**	NA
NA	Minneapolis, MN**	NA
NA	Naperville, IL**	NA
NA	Peoria, IL**	NA
NA	Rochester, MN**	NA
NA	Springfield, IL**	NA
NA	St. Paul, MN**	NA

Source: Federal Bureau of Investigation "Crime in the United States 2006"

**Forcible rape is the carnal knowledge of a female forcibly and against her will. Assaults or attempts to commit rape by force or threat of force are included. However, statutory rape without force and other sex offenses are excluded. **Not available.*

54. Rape Rate in 2006

National Rate = 30.9 Rapes per 100,000 Population*

RANK	CITY	RATE
83	Abilene, TX	56.8
159	Albany, GA	39.8
96	Albany, NY	53.3
80	Albuquerque, NM	57.1
298	Alexandria, VA	19.8
287	Alhambra, CA	21.5
166	Allentown, PA	39.2
99	Amarillo, TX	52.1
359	Amherst, NY	9.8
206	Anaheim, CA	32.0
15	Anchorage, AK	89.3
233	Ann Arbor, MI	28.3
197	Antioch, CA	34.5
102	Arlington, TX	51.5
224	Arvada, CO	29.3
105	Athens-Clarke, GA	49.7
191	Atlanta, GA	35.2
38	Aurora, CO	71.7
NA	Aurora, IL**	NA
132	Austin, TX	44.9
330	Bakersfield, CA	14.4
335	Baldwin Park, CA	13.8
284	Baltimore, MD	21.6
136	Baton Rouge, LA	44.2
53	Beaumont, TX	65.2
290	Beaverton, OR	20.6
191	Bellevue, WA	35.2
288	Bellflower, CA	21.3
142	Bellingham, WA	43.5
284	Berkeley, CA	21.6
235	Billings, MT	28.1
8	Birmingham, AL	94.2
NA	Bloomington, MN**	NA
328	Boca Raton, FL	14.8
55	Boise, ID	64.1
109	Boston, MA	48.9
175	Boulder, CO	37.5
374	Brick Twnshp, NJ	3.8
105	Bridgeport, CT	49.7
139	Brockton, MA	44.1
326	Broken Arrow, OK	14.9
248	Brownsville, TX	26.7
269	Buena Park, CA	23.8
63	Buffalo, NY	62.0
362	Burbank, CA	9.5
352	Cambridge, MA	10.9
19	Camden, NJ	82.4
177	Canton Twnshp, MI	37.3
18	Canton, OH	84.2
183	Cape Coral, FL	36.5
348	Carlsbad, CA	12.0
373	Carrollton, TX	4.9
314	Carson, CA	16.9
341	Cary, NC	12.9
208	Cedar Rapids, IA	31.5
259	Centennial, CO	25.0
273	Chandler, AZ	23.0
152	Charleston, SC	41.5
107	Charlotte, NC	49.5
29	Chattanooga, TN	75.3
310	Cheektowaga, NY	17.3
245	Chesapeake, VA	27.1
NA	Chicago, IL**	NA
364	Chino Hills, CA	9.2
356	Chino, CA	10.2
204	Chula Vista, CA	33.0
9	Cincinnati, OH	94.1
370	Clarkstown, NY	6.4
141	Clarksville, TN	43.7
159	Clearwater, FL	39.8
5	Cleveland, OH	98.3
377	Clifton, NJ	2.5
282	Clinton Twnshp, MI	21.7
344	Clovis, CA	12.6
376	Colonie, NY	2.6
50	Colorado Springs, CO	66.6
262	Columbia, MO	24.9
118	Columbia, SC	47.1
358	Columbus, GA	9.9
22	Columbus, OH	80.1
100	Compton, CA	51.8
318	Concord, CA	16.1
378	Coral Springs, FL	1.5
290	Corona, CA	20.6
78	Corpus Christi, TX	57.3
245	Costa Mesa, CA	27.1
298	Cranston, RI	19.8
96	Dallas, TX	53.3
307	Daly City, CA	17.8
333	Danbury, CT	14.0
271	Davie, FL	23.4
28	Dayton, OH	75.4
277	Dearborn, MI	22.4
222	Deerfield Beach, FL	29.6
85	Denton, TX	56.0
68	Denver, CO	60.2
207	Des Moines, IA	31.8
49	Detroit, MI	67.0
304	Downey, CA	19.0
NA	Duluth, MN**	NA
120	Durham, NC	46.9
326	Edison Twnshp, NJ	14.9
164	Edmond, OK	39.7
219	El Cajon, CA	30.0
294	El Monte, CA	20.2
116	El Paso, TX	47.3
238	Elizabeth, NJ	27.8
47	Erie, PA	67.2
265	Escondido, CA	24.4
219	Eugene, OR	30.0
98	Evansville, IN	52.3
140	Everett, WA	43.8
198	Fairfield, CA	34.2
26	Fargo, ND	76.0
308	Farmington Hills, MI	17.5
127	Fayetteville, NC	46.0
27	Federal Way, WA	75.7
1	Flint, MI	120.9
266	Fontana, CA	24.2
74	Fort Collins, CO	58.3
111	Fort Lauderdale, FL	48.8
4	Fort Smith, AR	99.5
189	Fort Wayne, IN	35.6
170	Fort Worth, TX	38.5
331	Fremont, CA	14.3
228	Fresno, CA	28.6
194	Fullerton, CA	35.1
16	Gainesville, FL	87.3
310	Garden Grove, CA	17.3
275	Garland, TX	22.5
65	Gary, IN	61.4
293	Gilbert, AZ	20.5
218	Glendale, AZ	30.2
369	Glendale, CA	6.9
121	Grand Prairie, TX	46.5
200	Grand Rapids, MI	33.6
342	Greece, NY	12.7
71	Greeley, CO	59.4
108	Green Bay, WI	49.2
185	Greensboro, NC	36.3
36	Gresham, OR	73.7
357	Hamilton Twnshp, NJ	10.0
184	Hammond, IN	36.4
188	Hampton, VA	36.0
174	Hartford, CT	37.8
201	Hawthorne, CA	33.5
272	Hayward, CA	23.3
250	Henderson, NV	26.3
284	Hesperia, CA	21.6
350	Hialeah, FL	11.6
150	High Point, NC	42.3
165	Hillsboro, OR	39.6
166	Hollywood, FL	39.2
258	Honolulu, HI	25.1
156	Houston, TX	41.2
320	Huntington Beach, CA	15.8
70	Huntsville, AL	59.6
88	Independence, MO	54.9
45	Indianapolis, IN	68.5
212	Inglewood, CA	31.2
365	Irvine, CA	9.0
267	Irving, TX	24.1
243	Jacksonville, FL	27.4
13	Jackson, MS	90.2
259	Jersey City, NJ	25.0
NA	Joliet, IL**	NA
61	Kansas City, KS	62.7
39	Kansas City, MO	71.6
91	Kenosha, WI	54.4
3	Kent, WA	99.8
24	Killeen, TX	78.6
111	Knoxville, TN	48.8
44	Lafayette, LA	68.7
366	Lake Forest, CA	7.8
59	Lakeland, FL	63.2
336	Lakewood, CA	13.5
46	Lakewood, CO	68.4
154	Lancaster, CA	41.4
11	Lansing, MI	91.1
134	Laredo, TX	44.7
126	Largo, FL	46.2
2	Las Cruces, NM	112.2
90	Las Vegas, NV	54.6
74	Lawrence, KS	58.3
14	Lawton, OK	90.1
305	Lee's Summit, MO	18.5
159	Lewisville, TX	39.8
115	Lexington, KY	47.4
151	Lincoln, NE	41.6
21	Little Rock, AR	80.9
294	Livermore, CA	20.2
302	Livonia, MI	19.4

RANK	CITY	RATE
236	Long Beach, CA	28.0
37	Longview, TX	72.0
244	Los Angeles, CA	27.3
236	Louisville, KY	28.0
169	Lowell, MA	38.6
131	Lubbock, TX	45.4
172	Lynn, MA	38.1
91	Macon, GA	54.4
227	Madison, WI	28.8
158	Manchester, NH	40.0
280	McAllen, TX	22.0
155	McKinney, TX	41.3
170	Melbourne, FL	38.5
62	Memphis, TN	62.4
136	Mesa, AZ	44.2
368	Mesquite, TX	7.5
12	Miami Beach, FL	90.6
52	Miami Gardens, FL	65.3
255	Miami, FL	25.7
83	Midland, TX	56.8
303	Milwaukee, WI	19.3
NA	Minneapolis, MN**	NA
152	Miramar, FL	41.5
379	Mission Viejo, CA	1.0
202	Mobile, AL	33.2
195	Modesto, CA	34.9
180	Montgomery, AL	36.6
199	Moreno Valley, CA	33.9
135	Murfreesboro, TN	44.4
353	Murrieta, CA	10.8
238	Napa, CA	27.8
NA	Naperville, IL**	NA
268	Nashua, NH	24.0
80	Nashville, TN	57.1
64	New Bedford, MA	61.9
294	New Orleans, LA	20.2
339	New York, NY	13.1
215	Newark, NJ	31.0
372	Newport Beach, CA	5.0
69	Newport News, VA	60.0
361	Newton, MA	9.6
145	Norfolk, VA	42.7
179	Norman, OK	37.0
10	North Charleston, SC	92.4
212	North Las Vegas, NV	31.2
300	Norwalk, CA	19.7
25	Oakland, CA	76.7
228	Oceanside, CA	28.6
345	Odessa, TX	12.5
128	Ogden, UT	45.8
66	Oklahoma City, OK	61.0
80	Olathe, KS	57.1
132	Omaha, NE	44.9
148	Ontario, CA	42.5
362	Orange, CA	9.5
310	Orem, UT	17.3
31	Orlando, FL	75.2
226	Overland Park, KS	28.9
306	Oxnard, CA	18.4
43	Palm Bay, FL	69.9
145	Palmdale, CA	42.7
313	Parma, OH	17.2
339	Pasadena, CA	13.1
203	Pasadena, TX	33.1
264	Paterson, NJ	24.7
359	Pembroke Pines, FL	9.8
228	Peoria, AZ	28.6
NA	Peoria, IL**	NA
51	Philadelphia, PA	65.5
186	Phoenix, AZ	36.2
209	Pittsburgh, PA	31.4
316	Plano, TX	16.3
371	Plantation, FL	5.7
351	Pomona, CA	11.0
103	Pompano Beach, FL	51.0
247	Port St. Lucie, FL	26.9
95	Portland, OR	54.0
180	Portsmouth, VA	36.6
222	Providence, RI	29.6
205	Provo, UT	32.4
121	Pueblo, CO	46.5
256	Quincy, MA	25.3
297	Racine, WI	20.1
238	Raleigh, NC	27.8
329	Rancho Cucamon., CA	14.6
91	Reading, PA	54.4
23	Redding, CA	79.6
114	Reno, NV	47.5
221	Rialto, CA	29.9
353	Richardson, TX	10.8
159	Richmond, CA	39.8
168	Richmond, VA	38.8
232	Riverside, CA	28.4
55	Roanoke, VA	64.1
NA	Rochester, MN**	NA
142	Rochester, NY	43.5
17	Rockford, IL	85.9
275	Roseville, CA	22.5
336	Roswell, GA	13.5
254	Round Rock, TX	25.9
147	Sacramento, CA	42.6
109	Salem, OR	48.9
216	Salinas, CA	30.5
101	Salt Lake City, UT	51.7
73	San Angelo, TX	58.6
159	San Antonio, TX	39.8
259	San Bernardino, CA	25.0
242	San Diego, CA	27.5
290	San Francisco, CA	20.6
270	San Jose, CA	23.6
190	San Leandro, CA	35.5
301	San Mateo, CA	19.6
263	Sandy, UT	24.8
288	Santa Ana, CA	21.3
172	Santa Barbara, CA	38.1
324	Santa Clara, CA	15.0
322	Santa Clarita, CA	15.3
104	Santa Maria, CA	50.5
224	Santa Monica, CA	29.3
113	Santa Rosa, CA	48.5
217	Savannah, GA	30.4
241	Scottsdale, AZ	27.7
278	Seattle, WA	22.1
35	Shreveport, LA	74.3
308	Simi Valley, CA	17.5
66	Sioux City, IA	61.0
20	Sioux Falls, SD	81.8
257	Somerville, MA	25.2
59	South Bend, IN	63.2
333	South Gate, CA	14.0
119	Southfield, MI	47.0
117	Sparks, NV	47.2
282	Spokane Valley, WA	21.7
130	Spokane, WA	45.5
NA	Springfield, IL**	NA
29	Springfield, MA	75.3
94	Springfield, MO	54.2
338	Sterling Heights, MI	13.3
191	Stockton, CA	35.2
6	St. Louis, MO	97.2
NA	St. Paul, MN**	NA
136	St. Petersburg, FL	44.2
210	Suffolk, VA	31.3
367	Sugar Land, TX	7.7
318	Sunnyvale, CA	16.1
316	Sunrise, FL	16.3
280	Surprise, AZ	22.0
121	Syracuse, NY	46.5
40	Tacoma, WA	71.3
7	Tallahassee, FL	96.2
157	Tampa, FL	40.1
324	Temecula, CA	15.0
149	Tempe, AZ	42.4
42	Thornton, CO	70.0
355	Thousand Oaks, CA	10.4
85	Toledo, OH	56.0
342	Toms River Twnshp, NJ	12.7
124	Topeka, KS	46.4
345	Torrance, CA	12.5
375	Tracy, CA	3.7
180	Trenton, NJ	36.6
347	Troy, MI	12.4
88	Tucson, AZ	54.9
33	Tulsa, OK	74.9
78	Tuscaloosa, AL	57.3
144	Tyler, TX	43.4
323	Upper Darby Twnshp, PA	15.1
249	Vacaville, CA	26.6
252	Vallejo, CA	26.2
54	Vancouver, WA	64.3
274	Ventura, CA	22.9
234	Victorville, CA	28.2
253	Virginia Beach, VA	26.0
129	Visalia, CA	45.6
177	Vista, CA	37.3
76	Waco, TX	58.1
87	Warren, MI	55.6
212	Warwick, RI	31.2
210	Washington, DC	31.3
186	Waterbury, CT	36.2
349	West Covina, CA	11.9
228	West Jordan, UT	28.6
124	West Palm Beach, FL	46.4
72	West Valley, UT	59.0
33	Westland, MI	74.9
278	Westminster, CA	22.1
196	Westminster, CO	34.6
332	Whittier, CA	14.1
250	Wichita Falls, TX	26.3
47	Wichita, KS	67.2
58	Wilmington, NC	63.7
57	Winston-Salem, NC	63.8
314	Woodbridge Twnshp, NJ	16.9
41	Worcester, MA	70.1
32	Yakima, WA	75.1
321	Yonkers, NY	15.7
77	Youngstown, OH	57.9
175	Yuma, AZ	37.5

Source: CQ Press using data from F.B.I. "Crime in the United States 2006"

**Forcible rape is the carnal knowledge of a female forcibly and against her will. Assaults or attempts to commit rape by force or threat of force are included. However, statutory rape without force and other sex offenses are excluded. **Not available.*

54. Rape Rate in 2006 (continued)

National Rate = 30.9 Rapes per 100,000 Population*

RANK	CITY	RATE
1	Flint, MI	120.9
2	Las Cruces, NM	112.2
3	Kent, WA	99.8
4	Fort Smith, AR	99.5
5	Cleveland, OH	98.3
6	St. Louis, MO	97.2
7	Tallahassee, FL	96.2
8	Birmingham, AL	94.2
9	Cincinnati, OH	94.1
10	North Charleston, SC	92.4
11	Lansing, MI	91.1
12	Miami Beach, FL	90.6
13	Jackson, MS	90.2
14	Lawton, OK	90.1
15	Anchorage, AK	89.3
16	Gainesville, FL	87.3
17	Rockford, IL	85.9
18	Canton, OH	84.2
19	Camden, NJ	82.4
20	Sioux Falls, SD	81.8
21	Little Rock, AR	80.9
22	Columbus, OH	80.1
23	Redding, CA	79.6
24	Killeen, TX	78.6
25	Oakland, CA	76.7
26	Fargo, ND	76.0
27	Federal Way, WA	75.7
28	Dayton, OH	75.4
29	Chattanooga, TN	75.3
29	Springfield, MA	75.3
31	Orlando, FL	75.2
32	Yakima, WA	75.1
33	Tulsa, OK	74.9
33	Westland, MI	74.9
35	Shreveport, LA	74.3
36	Gresham, OR	73.7
37	Longview, TX	72.0
38	Aurora, CO	71.7
39	Kansas City, MO	71.6
40	Tacoma, WA	71.3
41	Worcester, MA	70.1
42	Thornton, CO	70.0
43	Palm Bay, FL	69.9
44	Lafayette, LA	68.7
45	Indianapolis, IN	68.5
46	Lakewood, CO	68.4
47	Erie, PA	67.2
47	Wichita, KS	67.2
49	Detroit, MI	67.0
50	Colorado Springs, CO	66.6
51	Philadelphia, PA	65.5
52	Miami Gardens, FL	65.3
53	Beaumont, TX	65.2
54	Vancouver, WA	64.3
55	Boise, ID	64.1
55	Roanoke, VA	64.1
57	Winston-Salem, NC	63.8
58	Wilmington, NC	63.7
59	Lakeland, FL	63.2
59	South Bend, IN	63.2
61	Kansas City, KS	62.7
62	Memphis, TN	62.4
63	Buffalo, NY	62.0
64	New Bedford, MA	61.9
65	Gary, IN	61.4
66	Oklahoma City, OK	61.0
66	Sioux City, IA	61.0
68	Denver, CO	60.2
69	Newport News, VA	60.0
70	Huntsville, AL	59.6
71	Greeley, CO	59.4
72	West Valley, UT	59.0
73	San Angelo, TX	58.6
74	Fort Collins, CO	58.3
74	Lawrence, KS	58.3
76	Waco, TX	58.1
77	Youngstown, OH	57.9
78	Corpus Christi, TX	57.3
78	Tuscaloosa, AL	57.3
80	Albuquerque, NM	57.1
80	Nashville, TN	57.1
80	Olathe, KS	57.1
83	Abilene, TX	56.8
83	Midland, TX	56.8
85	Denton, TX	56.0
85	Toledo, OH	56.0
87	Warren, MI	55.6
88	Independence, MO	54.9
88	Tucson, AZ	54.9
90	Las Vegas, NV	54.6
91	Kenosha, WI	54.4
91	Macon, GA	54.4
91	Reading, PA	54.4
94	Springfield, MO	54.2
95	Portland, OR	54.0
96	Albany, NY	53.3
96	Dallas, TX	53.3
98	Evansville, IN	52.3
99	Amarillo, TX	52.1
100	Compton, CA	51.8
101	Salt Lake City, UT	51.7
102	Arlington, TX	51.5
103	Pompano Beach, FL	51.0
104	Santa Maria, CA	50.5
105	Athens-Clarke, GA	49.7
105	Bridgeport, CT	49.7
107	Charlotte, NC	49.5
108	Green Bay, WI	49.2
109	Boston, MA	48.9
109	Salem, OR	48.9
111	Fort Lauderdale, FL	48.8
111	Knoxville, TN	48.8
113	Santa Rosa, CA	48.5
114	Reno, NV	47.5
115	Lexington, KY	47.4
116	El Paso, TX	47.3
117	Sparks, NV	47.2
118	Columbia, SC	47.1
119	Southfield, MI	47.0
120	Durham, NC	46.9
121	Grand Prairie, TX	46.5
121	Pueblo, CO	46.5
121	Syracuse, NY	46.5
124	Topeka, KS	46.4
124	West Palm Beach, FL	46.4
126	Largo, FL	46.2
127	Fayetteville, NC	46.0
128	Ogden, UT	45.8
129	Visalia, CA	45.6
130	Spokane, WA	45.5
131	Lubbock, TX	45.4
132	Austin, TX	44.9
132	Omaha, NE	44.9
134	Laredo, TX	44.7
135	Murfreesboro, TN	44.4
136	Baton Rouge, LA	44.2
136	Mesa, AZ	44.2
136	St. Petersburg, FL	44.2
139	Brockton, MA	44.1
140	Everett, WA	43.8
141	Clarksville, TN	43.7
142	Bellingham, WA	43.5
142	Rochester, NY	43.5
144	Tyler, TX	43.4
145	Norfolk, VA	42.7
145	Palmdale, CA	42.7
147	Sacramento, CA	42.6
148	Ontario, CA	42.5
149	Tempe, AZ	42.4
150	High Point, NC	42.3
151	Lincoln, NE	41.6
152	Charleston, SC	41.5
152	Miramar, FL	41.5
154	Lancaster, CA	41.4
155	McKinney, TX	41.3
156	Houston, TX	41.2
157	Tampa, FL	40.1
158	Manchester, NH	40.0
159	Albany, GA	39.8
159	Clearwater, FL	39.8
159	Lewisville, TX	39.8
159	Richmond, CA	39.8
159	San Antonio, TX	39.8
164	Edmond, OK	39.7
165	Hillsboro, OR	39.6
166	Allentown, PA	39.2
166	Hollywood, FL	39.2
168	Richmond, VA	38.8
169	Lowell, MA	38.6
170	Fort Worth, TX	38.5
170	Melbourne, FL	38.5
172	Lynn, MA	38.1
172	Santa Barbara, CA	38.1
174	Hartford, CT	37.8
175	Boulder, CO	37.5
175	Yuma, AZ	37.5
177	Canton Twnshp, MI	37.3
177	Vista, CA	37.3
179	Norman, OK	37.0
180	Montgomery, AL	36.6
180	Portsmouth, VA	36.6
180	Trenton, NJ	36.6
183	Cape Coral, FL	36.5
184	Hammond, IN	36.4
185	Greensboro, NC	36.3
186	Phoenix, AZ	36.2
186	Waterbury, CT	36.2
188	Hampton, VA	36.0
189	Fort Wayne, IN	35.6
190	San Leandro, CA	35.5
191	Atlanta, GA	35.2
191	Bellevue, WA	35.2

Rank Order- City (continued)

RANK	CITY	RATE
191	Stockton, CA	35.2
194	Fullerton, CA	35.1
195	Modesto, CA	34.9
196	Westminster, CO	34.6
197	Antioch, CA	34.5
198	Fairfield, CA	34.2
199	Moreno Valley, CA	33.9
200	Grand Rapids, MI	33.6
201	Hawthorne, CA	33.5
202	Mobile, AL	33.2
203	Pasadena, TX	33.1
204	Chula Vista, CA	33.0
205	Provo, UT	32.4
206	Anaheim, CA	32.0
207	Des Moines, IA	31.8
208	Cedar Rapids, IA	31.5
209	Pittsburgh, PA	31.4
210	Suffolk, VA	31.3
210	Washington, DC	31.3
212	Inglewood, CA	31.2
212	North Las Vegas, NV	31.2
212	Warwick, RI	31.2
215	Newark, NJ	31.0
216	Salinas, CA	30.5
217	Savannah, GA	30.4
218	Glendale, AZ	30.2
219	El Cajon, CA	30.0
219	Eugene, OR	30.0
221	Rialto, CA	29.9
222	Deerfield Beach, FL	29.6
222	Providence, RI	29.6
224	Arvada, CO	29.3
224	Santa Monica, CA	29.3
226	Overland Park, KS	28.9
227	Madison, WI	28.8
228	Fresno, CA	28.6
228	Oceanside, CA	28.6
228	Peoria, AZ	28.6
228	West Jordan, UT	28.6
232	Riverside, CA	28.4
233	Ann Arbor, MI	28.3
234	Victorville, CA	28.2
235	Billings, MT	28.1
236	Long Beach, CA	28.0
236	Louisville, KY	28.0
238	Elizabeth, NJ	27.8
238	Napa, CA	27.8
238	Raleigh, NC	27.8
241	Scottsdale, AZ	27.7
242	San Diego, CA	27.5
243	Jacksonville, FL	27.4
244	Los Angeles, CA	27.3
245	Chesapeake, VA	27.1
245	Costa Mesa, CA	27.1
247	Port St. Lucie, FL	26.9
248	Brownsville, TX	26.7
249	Vacaville, CA	26.6
250	Henderson, NV	26.3
250	Wichita Falls, TX	26.3
252	Vallejo, CA	26.2
253	Virginia Beach, VA	26.0
254	Round Rock, TX	25.9
255	Miami, FL	25.7
256	Quincy, MA	25.3
257	Somerville, MA	25.2
258	Honolulu, HI	25.1

RANK	CITY	RATE
259	Centennial, CO	25.0
259	Jersey City, NJ	25.0
259	San Bernardino, CA	25.0
262	Columbia, MO	24.9
263	Sandy, UT	24.8
264	Paterson, NJ	24.7
265	Escondido, CA	24.4
266	Fontana, CA	24.2
267	Irving, TX	24.1
268	Nashua, NH	24.0
269	Buena Park, CA	23.8
270	San Jose, CA	23.6
271	Davie, FL	23.4
272	Hayward, CA	23.3
273	Chandler, AZ	23.0
274	Ventura, CA	22.9
275	Garland, TX	22.5
275	Roseville, CA	22.5
277	Dearborn, MI	22.4
278	Seattle, WA	22.1
278	Westminster, CA	22.1
280	McAllen, TX	22.0
280	Surprise, AZ	22.0
282	Clinton Twnshp, MI	21.7
282	Spokane Valley, WA	21.7
284	Baltimore, MD	21.6
284	Berkeley, CA	21.6
284	Hesperia, CA	21.6
287	Alhambra, CA	21.5
288	Bellflower, CA	21.3
288	Santa Ana, CA	21.3
290	Beaverton, OR	20.6
290	Corona, CA	20.6
290	San Francisco, CA	20.6
293	Gilbert, AZ	20.5
294	El Monte, CA	20.2
294	Livermore, CA	20.2
294	New Orleans, LA	20.2
297	Racine, WI	20.1
298	Alexandria, VA	19.8
298	Cranston, RI	19.8
300	Norwalk, CA	19.7
301	San Mateo, CA	19.6
302	Livonia, MI	19.4
303	Milwaukee, WI	19.3
304	Downey, CA	19.0
305	Lee's Summit, MO	18.5
306	Oxnard, CA	18.4
307	Daly City, CA	17.8
308	Farmington Hills, MI	17.5
308	Simi Valley, CA	17.5
310	Cheektowaga, NY	17.3
310	Garden Grove, CA	17.3
310	Orem, UT	17.3
313	Parma, OH	17.2
314	Carson, CA	16.9
314	Woodbridge Twnshp, NJ	16.9
316	Plano, TX	16.3
316	Sunrise, FL	16.3
318	Concord, CA	16.1
318	Sunnyvale, CA	16.1
320	Huntington Beach, CA	15.8
321	Yonkers, NY	15.7
322	Santa Clarita, CA	15.3
323	Upper Darby Twnshp, PA	15.1
324	Santa Clara, CA	15.0

RANK	CITY	RATE
324	Temecula, CA	15.0
326	Broken Arrow, OK	14.9
326	Edison Twnshp, NJ	14.9
328	Boca Raton, FL	14.8
329	Rancho Cucamon., CA	14.6
330	Bakersfield, CA	14.4
331	Fremont, CA	14.3
332	Whittier, CA	14.1
333	Danbury, CT	14.0
333	South Gate, CA	14.0
335	Baldwin Park, CA	13.8
336	Lakewood, CA	13.5
336	Roswell, GA	13.5
338	Sterling Heights, MI	13.3
339	New York, NY	13.1
339	Pasadena, CA	13.1
341	Cary, NC	12.9
342	Greece, NY	12.7
342	Toms River Twnshp, NJ	12.7
344	Clovis, CA	12.6
345	Odessa, TX	12.5
345	Torrance, CA	12.5
347	Troy, MI	12.4
348	Carlsbad, CA	12.0
349	West Covina, CA	11.9
350	Hialeah, FL	11.6
351	Pomona, CA	11.0
352	Cambridge, MA	10.9
353	Murrieta, CA	10.8
353	Richardson, TX	10.8
355	Thousand Oaks, CA	10.4
356	Chino, CA	10.2
357	Hamilton Twnshp, NJ	10.0
358	Columbus, GA	9.9
359	Amherst, NY	9.8
359	Pembroke Pines, FL	9.8
361	Newton, MA	9.6
362	Burbank, CA	9.5
362	Orange, CA	9.5
364	Chino Hills, CA	9.2
365	Irvine, CA	9.0
366	Lake Forest, CA	7.8
367	Sugar Land, TX	7.7
368	Mesquite, TX	7.5
369	Glendale, CA	6.9
370	Clarkstown, NY	6.4
371	Plantation, FL	5.7
372	Newport Beach, CA	5.0
373	Carrollton, TX	4.9
374	Brick Twnshp, NJ	3.8
375	Tracy, CA	3.7
376	Colonie, NY	2.6
377	Clifton, NJ	2.5
378	Coral Springs, FL	1.5
379	Mission Viejo, CA	1.0
NA	Aurora, IL**	NA
NA	Bloomington, MN**	NA
NA	Chicago, IL**	NA
NA	Duluth, MN**	NA
NA	Joliet, IL**	NA
NA	Minneapolis, MN**	NA
NA	Naperville, IL**	NA
NA	Peoria, IL**	NA
NA	Rochester, MN**	NA
NA	Springfield, IL**	NA
NA	St. Paul, MN**	NA

Source: CQ Press using data from F.B.I. "Crime in the United States 2006"

**Forcible rape is the carnal knowledge of a female forcibly and against her will. Assaults or attempts to commit rape by force or threat of force are included. However, statutory rape without force and other sex offenses are excluded. **Not available.*

55. Percent Change in Rape Rate: 2005 to 2006

National Percent Change = 3.0% Decrease*

RANK	CITY	% CHANGE
275	Abilene, TX	(15.0)
299	Albany, GA	(22.1)
320	Albany, NY	(26.1)
188	Albuquerque, NM	(1.7)
93	Alexandria, VA	17.2
18	Alhambra, CA	59.3
220	Allentown, PA	(6.9)
127	Amarillo, TX	8.8
21	Amherst, NY	55.6
49	Anaheim, CA	32.8
123	Anchorage, AK	10.1
265	Ann Arbor, MI	(13.2)
63	Antioch, CA	25.0
138	Arlington, TX	5.7
50	Arvada, CO	32.6
58	Athens-Clarke, GA	28.1
336	Atlanta, GA	(32.0)
208	Aurora, CO	(4.9)
NA	Aurora, IL**	NA
175	Austin, TX	(0.2)
229	Bakersfield, CA	(8.3)
296	Baldwin Park, CA	(21.6)
274	Baltimore, MD	(14.6)
82	Baton Rouge, LA	19.5
307	Beaumont, TX	(23.3)
352	Beaverton, OR	(45.9)
36	Bellevue, WA	43.7
105	Bellflower, CA	14.5
103	Bellingham, WA	15.1
74	Berkeley, CA	22.7
290	Billings, MT	(19.0)
229	Birmingham, AL	(8.3)
NA	Bloomington, MN**	NA
295	Boca Raton, FL	(21.3)
150	Boise, ID	4.2
154	Boston, MA	3.6
283	Boulder, CO	(16.5)
NA	Brick Twnshp, NJ***	NA
132	Bridgeport, CT	7.1
252	Brockton, MA	(11.1)
101	Broken Arrow, OK	15.5
284	Brownsville, TX	(17.3)
44	Buena Park, CA	36.0
205	Buffalo, NY	(4.6)
309	Burbank, CA	(23.4)
346	Cambridge, MA	(39.1)
38	Camden, NJ	40.4
165	Canton Twnshp, MI	1.9
88	Canton, OH	18.1
134	Cape Coral, FL	6.1
192	Carlsbad, CA	(2.4)
358	Carrollton, TX	(51.0)
280	Carson, CA	(15.9)
163	Cary, NC	2.4
273	Cedar Rapids, IA	(14.2)
313	Centennial, CO	(24.5)
186	Chandler, AZ	(1.3)
244	Charleston, SC	(10.0)
153	Charlotte, NC	3.8
166	Chattanooga, TN	1.6
56	Cheektowaga, NY	29.1
100	Chesapeake, VA	15.8
NA	Chicago, IL**	NA
261	Chino Hills, CA	(12.4)
267	Chino, CA	(13.6)
158	Chula Vista, CA	3.1
218	Cincinnati, OH	(6.1)
NA	Clarkstown, NY**	NA
226	Clarksville, TN	(7.4)
228	Clearwater, FL	(7.9)
214	Cleveland, OH	(5.7)
364	Clifton, NJ	(77.7)
148	Clinton Twnshp, MI	4.3
355	Clovis, CA	(50.2)
365	Colonie, NY	(77.8)
179	Colorado Springs, CO	(0.6)
83	Columbia, MO	18.6
183	Columbia, SC	(0.8)
302	Columbus, GA	(22.7)
112	Columbus, OH	13.0
62	Compton, CA	25.4
35	Concord, CA	43.8
366	Coral Springs, FL	(78.3)
231	Corona, CA	(8.4)
313	Corpus Christi, TX	(24.5)
170	Costa Mesa, CA	0.4
45	Cranston, RI	34.7
96	Dallas, TX	16.6
243	Daly City, CA	(9.6)
355	Danbury, CT	(50.2)
152	Davie, FL	4.0
267	Dayton, OH	(13.6)
327	Dearborn, MI	(28.7)
351	Deerfield Beach, FL	(42.7)
300	Denton, TX	(22.3)
154	Denver, CO	3.6
NA	Des Moines, IA**	NA
163	Detroit, MI	2.4
331	Downey, CA	(29.6)
NA	Duluth, MN**	NA
NA	Durham, NC**	NA
4	Edison Twnshp, NJ	148.3
114	Edmond, OK	12.5
328	El Cajon, CA	(29.1)
88	El Monte, CA	18.1
NA	El Paso, TX**	NA
8	Elizabeth, NJ	93.1
219	Erie, PA	(6.7)
130	Escondido, CA	7.5
292	Eugene, OR	(19.8)
147	Evansville, IN	4.4
253	Everett, WA	(11.2)
215	Fairfield, CA	(5.8)
12	Fargo, ND	65.2
345	Farmington Hills, MI	(38.4)
65	Fayetteville, NC	24.7
109	Federal Way, WA	13.5
40	Flint, MI	38.0
302	Fontana, CA	(22.7)
341	Fort Collins, CO	(36.4)
76	Fort Lauderdale, FL	22.6
266	Fort Smith, AR	(13.5)
NA	Fort Wayne, IN**	NA
311	Fort Worth, TX	(24.1)
321	Fremont, CA	(27.0)
257	Fresno, CA	(11.5)
59	Fullerton, CA	27.6
189	Gainesville, FL	(1.8)
52	Garden Grove, CA	32.1
79	Garland, TX	21.0
260	Gary, IN	(12.3)
67	Gilbert, AZ	23.5
262	Glendale, AZ	(12.5)
172	Glendale, CA	0.0
86	Grand Prairie, TX	18.3
179	Grand Rapids, MI	(0.6)
172	Greece, NY	0.0
133	Greeley, CO	6.5
269	Green Bay, WI	(13.8)
168	Greensboro, NC	0.6
156	Gresham, OR	3.2
172	Hamilton Twnshp, NJ	0.0
192	Hammond, IN	(2.4)
108	Hampton, VA	13.6
162	Hartford, CT	2.7
15	Hawthorne, CA	61.8
250	Hayward, CA	(10.7)
22	Henderson, NV	52.9
107	Hesperia, CA	13.7
332	Hialeah, FL	(30.1)
29	High Point, NC	47.9
125	Hillsboro, OR	9.4
200	Hollywood, FL	(3.4)
194	Honolulu, HI	(2.7)
199	Houston, TX	(3.3)
197	Huntington Beach, CA	(3.1)
118	Huntsville, AL	11.8
42	Independence, MO	36.6
151	Indianapolis, IN	4.1
269	Inglewood, CA	(13.8)
211	Irvine, CA	(5.3)
324	Irving, TX	(27.8)
103	Jacksonville, FL	15.1
159	Jackson, MS	3.0
39	Jersey City, NJ	39.7
NA	Joliet, IL**	NA
235	Kansas City, KS	(8.7)
NA	Kansas City, MO**	NA
31	Kenosha, WI	46.6
33	Kent, WA	44.8
237	Killeen, TX	(8.9)
254	Knoxville, TN	(11.3)
277	Lafayette, LA	(15.3)
312	Lake Forest, CA	(24.3)
6	Lakeland, FL	119.4
276	Lakewood, CA	(15.1)
140	Lakewood, CO	5.4
176	Lancaster, CA	(0.5)
225	Lansing, MI	(7.3)
34	Laredo, TX	44.2
53	Largo, FL	30.1
215	Las Cruces, NM	(5.8)
109	Las Vegas, NV	13.5
17	Lawrence, KS	59.7
7	Lawton, OK	95.0
77	Lee's Summit, MO	22.5
20	Lewisville, TX	56.7
NA	Lexington, KY**	NA
259	Lincoln, NE	(11.7)
55	Little Rock, AR	29.6
350	Livermore, CA	(41.3)
27	Livonia, MI	48.1

RANK	CITY	% CHANGE	RANK	CITY	% CHANGE	RANK	CITY	% CHANGE
57	Long Beach, CA	29.0	156	Peoria, AZ	3.2	352	Spokane Valley, WA	(45.9)
286	Longview, TX	(17.7)	NA	Peoria, IL**	NA	98	Spokane, WA	16.4
202	Los Angeles, CA	(4.2)	215	Philadelphia, PA	(5.8)	NA	Springfield, IL**	NA
282	Louisville, KY	(16.4)	176	Phoenix, AZ	(0.5)	145	Springfield, MA	4.7
195	Lowell, MA	(2.8)	254	Pittsburgh, PA	(11.3)	198	Springfield, MO	(3.2)
235	Lubbock, TX	(8.7)	313	Plano, TX	(24.5)	250	Sterling Heights, MI	(10.7)
2	Lynn, MA	184.3	362	Plantation, FL	(66.9)	239	Stockton, CA	(9.0)
231	Macon, GA	(8.4)	360	Pomona, CA	(60.9)	78	St. Louis, MO	21.8
293	Madison, WI	(20.2)	289	Pompano Beach, FL	(18.7)	NA	St. Paul, MN**	NA
348	Manchester, NH	(39.7)	9	Port St. Lucie, FL	92.1	120	St. Petersburg, FL	11.3
294	McAllen, TX	(20.6)	246	Portland, OR	(10.1)	326	Suffolk, VA	(28.5)
278	McKinney, TX	(15.7)	246	Portsmouth, VA	(10.1)	32	Sugar Land, TX	45.3
184	Melbourne, FL	(1.0)	357	Providence, RI	(50.5)	307	Sunnyvale, CA	(23.3)
136	Memphis, TN	5.9	347	Provo, UT	(39.3)	334	Sunrise, FL	(31.5)
159	Mesa, AZ	3.0	5	Pueblo, CO	122.5	102	Surprise, AZ	15.2
339	Mesquite, TX	(34.2)	263	Quincy, MA	(12.8)	234	Syracuse, NY	(8.6)
48	Miami Beach, FL	33.2	354	Racine, WI	(47.8)	91	Tacoma, WA	18.0
88	Miami Gardens, FL	18.1	143	Raleigh, NC	4.9	95	Tallahassee, FL	16.7
16	Miami, FL	60.6	338	Rancho Cucamon., CA	(33.0)	342	Tampa, FL	(37.1)
329	Midland, TX	(29.2)	269	Reading, PA	(13.8)	302	Temecula, CA	(22.7)
325	Milwaukee, WI	(28.3)	254	Redding, CA	(11.3)	190	Tempe, AZ	(2.1)
NA	Minneapolis, MN**	NA	257	Reno, NV	(11.5)	143	Thornton, CO	4.9
70	Miramar, FL	23.1	240	Rialto, CA	(9.1)	167	Thousand Oaks, CA	1.0
363	Mission Viejo, CA	(67.7)	241	Richardson, TX	(9.2)	205	Toledo, OH	(4.6)
115	Mobile, AL	12.2	94	Richmond, CA	17.1	46	Toms River Twnshp, NJ	33.7
117	Modesto, CA	11.9	213	Richmond, VA	(5.4)	111	Topeka, KS	13.4
337	Montgomery, AL	(32.1)	321	Riverside, CA	(27.0)	246	Torrance, CA	(10.1)
179	Moreno Valley, CA	(0.6)	126	Roanoke, VA	9.2	359	Tracy, CA	(58.9)
146	Murfreesboro, TN	4.5	NA	Rochester, MN**	NA	26	Trenton, NJ	49.4
244	Murrieta, CA	(10.0)	226	Rochester, NY	(7.4)	60	Troy, MI	26.5
121	Napa, CA	11.2	NA	Rockford, IL**	NA	306	Tucson, AZ	(23.1)
NA	Naperville, IL**	NA	281	Roseville, CA	(16.0)	204	Tulsa, OK	(4.5)
138	Nashua, NH	5.7	10	Roswell, GA	68.8	83	Tuscaloosa, AL	18.6
211	Nashville, TN	(5.3)	161	Round Rock, TX	2.8	310	Tyler, TX	(24.0)
119	New Bedford, MA	11.5	105	Sacramento, CA	14.5	313	Upper Darby Twnshp, PA	(24.5)
NA	New Orleans, LA**	NA	42	Salem, OR	36.6	124	Vacaville, CA	9.9
317	New York, NY	(24.7)	136	Salinas, CA	5.9	NA	Vallejo, CA**	NA
142	Newark, NJ	5.1	50	Salt Lake City, UT	32.6	237	Vancouver, WA	(8.9)
361	Newport Beach, CA	(66.4)	205	San Angelo, TX	(4.6)	60	Ventura, CA	26.5
130	Newport News, VA	7.5	278	San Antonio, TX	(15.7)	297	Victorville, CA	(21.7)
47	Newton, MA	33.3	333	San Bernardino, CA	(30.6)	80	Virginia Beach, VA	20.9
116	Norfolk, VA	12.1	222	San Diego, CA	(7.1)	68	Visalia, CA	23.2
122	Norman, OK	10.4	249	San Francisco, CA	(10.4)	14	Vista, CA	63.6
201	North Charleston, SC	(3.7)	288	San Jose, CA	(18.3)	99	Waco, TX	16.2
233	North Las Vegas, NV	(8.5)	73	San Leandro, CA	22.8	112	Warren, MI	13.0
65	Norwalk, CA	24.7	287	San Mateo, CA	(18.0)	23	Warwick, RI	51.5
170	Oakland, CA	0.4	13	Sandy, UT	64.2	148	Washington, DC	4.3
344	Oceanside, CA	(38.2)	176	Santa Ana, CA	(0.5)	74	Waterbury, CT	22.7
187	Odessa, TX	(1.6)	128	Santa Barbara, CA	8.2	335	West Covina, CA	(31.6)
222	Ogden, UT	(7.1)	263	Santa Clara, CA	(12.8)	NA	West Jordan, UT**	NA
242	Oklahoma City, OK	(9.4)	25	Santa Clarita, CA	50.0	340	West Palm Beach, FL	(36.3)
41	Olathe, KS	37.9	86	Santa Maria, CA	18.3	305	West Valley, UT	(22.8)
221	Omaha, NE	(7.0)	70	Santa Monica, CA	23.1	81	Westland, MI	19.8
54	Ontario, CA	30.0	70	Santa Rosa, CA	23.1	37	Westminster, CA	42.6
1	Orange, CA	533.3	298	Savannah, GA	(21.9)	30	Westminster, CO	47.2
185	Orem, UT	(1.1)	64	Scottsdale, AZ	24.8	290	Whittier, CA	(19.0)
202	Orlando, FL	(4.2)	222	Seattle, WA	(7.1)	343	Wichita Falls, TX	(37.2)
19	Overland Park, KS	57.1	190	Shreveport, LA	(2.1)	NA	Wichita, KS**	NA
323	Oxnard, CA	(27.6)	68	Simi Valley, CA	23.2	135	Wilmington, NC	6.0
24	Palm Bay, FL	51.0	210	Sioux City, IA	(5.1)	141	Winston-Salem, NC	5.3
92	Palmdale, CA	17.3	301	Sioux Falls, SD	(22.4)	168	Woodbridge Twnshp, NJ	0.6
83	Parma, OH	18.6	3	Somerville, MA	171.0	272	Worcester, MA	(14.0)
285	Pasadena, CA	(17.6)	195	South Bend, IN	(2.8)	182	Yakima, WA	(0.7)
208	Pasadena, TX	(4.9)	319	South Gate, CA	(25.9)	27	Yonkers, NY	48.1
97	Paterson, NJ	16.5	11	Southfield, MI	65.5	318	Youngstown, OH	(25.0)
349	Pembroke Pines, FL	(39.9)	330	Sparks, NV	(29.3)	129	Yuma, AZ	7.8

Source: CQ Press using data from F.B.I. "Crime in the United States 2006"

**Forcible rape is the carnal knowledge of a female forcibly and against her will. **Not available. ***Brick had a rape rate of 0 in 2005 but had three rapes in 2006. Calculating percent increase from zero results in an infinite number. This is shown as "NA."*

55. Percent Change in Rape Rate: 2005 to 2006 (continued)

National Percent Change = 3.0% Decrease*

RANK	CITY	% CHANGE
1	Orange, CA	533.3
2	Lynn, MA	184.3
3	Somerville, MA	171.0
4	Edison Twnshp, NJ	148.3
5	Pueblo, CO	122.5
6	Lakeland, FL	119.4
7	Lawton, OK	95.0
8	Elizabeth, NJ	93.1
9	Port St. Lucie, FL	92.1
10	Roswell, GA	68.8
11	Southfield, MI	65.5
12	Fargo, ND	65.2
13	Sandy, UT	64.2
14	Vista, CA	63.6
15	Hawthorne, CA	61.8
16	Miami, FL	60.6
17	Lawrence, KS	59.7
18	Alhambra, CA	59.3
19	Overland Park, KS	57.1
20	Lewisville, TX	56.7
21	Amherst, NY	55.6
22	Henderson, NV	52.9
23	Warwick, RI	51.5
24	Palm Bay, FL	51.0
25	Santa Clarita, CA	50.0
26	Trenton, NJ	49.4
27	Livonia, MI	48.1
27	Yonkers, NY	48.1
29	High Point, NC	47.9
30	Westminster, CO	47.2
31	Kenosha, WI	46.6
32	Sugar Land, TX	45.3
33	Kent, WA	44.8
34	Laredo, TX	44.2
35	Concord, CA	43.8
36	Bellevue, WA	43.7
37	Westminster, CA	42.6
38	Camden, NJ	40.4
39	Jersey City, NJ	39.7
40	Flint, MI	38.0
41	Olathe, KS	37.9
42	Independence, MO	36.6
42	Salem, OR	36.6
44	Buena Park, CA	36.0
45	Cranston, RI	34.7
46	Toms River Twnshp, NJ	33.7
47	Newton, MA	33.3
48	Miami Beach, FL	33.2
49	Anaheim, CA	32.8
50	Arvada, CO	32.6
50	Salt Lake City, UT	32.6
52	Garden Grove, CA	32.1
53	Largo, FL	30.1
54	Ontario, CA	30.0
55	Little Rock, AR	29.6
56	Cheektowaga, NY	29.1
57	Long Beach, CA	29.0
58	Athens-Clarke, GA	28.1
59	Fullerton, CA	27.6
60	Troy, MI	26.5
60	Ventura, CA	26.5
62	Compton, CA	25.4
63	Antioch, CA	25.0
64	Scottsdale, AZ	24.8
65	Fayetteville, NC	24.7
65	Norwalk, CA	24.7
67	Gilbert, AZ	23.5
68	Simi Valley, CA	23.2
68	Visalia, CA	23.2
70	Miramar, FL	23.1
70	Santa Monica, CA	23.1
70	Santa Rosa, CA	23.1
73	San Leandro, CA	22.8
74	Berkeley, CA	22.7
74	Waterbury, CT	22.7
76	Fort Lauderdale, FL	22.6
77	Lee's Summit, MO	22.5
78	St. Louis, MO	21.8
79	Garland, TX	21.0
80	Virginia Beach, VA	20.9
81	Westland, MI	19.8
82	Baton Rouge, LA	19.5
83	Columbia, MO	18.6
83	Parma, OH	18.6
83	Tuscaloosa, AL	18.6
86	Grand Prairie, TX	18.3
86	Santa Maria, CA	18.3
88	Canton, OH	18.1
88	El Monte, CA	18.1
88	Miami Gardens, FL	18.1
91	Tacoma, WA	18.0
92	Palmdale, CA	17.3
93	Alexandria, VA	17.2
94	Richmond, CA	17.1
95	Tallahassee, FL	16.7
96	Dallas, TX	16.6
97	Paterson, NJ	16.5
98	Spokane, WA	16.4
99	Waco, TX	16.2
100	Chesapeake, VA	15.8
101	Broken Arrow, OK	15.5
102	Surprise, AZ	15.2
103	Bellingham, WA	15.1
103	Jacksonville, FL	15.1
105	Bellflower, CA	14.5
105	Sacramento, CA	14.5
107	Hesperia, CA	13.7
108	Hampton, VA	13.6
109	Federal Way, WA	13.5
109	Las Vegas, NV	13.5
111	Topeka, KS	13.4
112	Columbus, OH	13.0
112	Warren, MI	13.0
114	Edmond, OK	12.5
115	Mobile, AL	12.2
116	Norfolk, VA	12.1
117	Modesto, CA	11.9
118	Huntsville, AL	11.8
119	New Bedford, MA	11.5
120	St. Petersburg, FL	11.3
121	Napa, CA	11.2
122	Norman, OK	10.4
123	Anchorage, AK	10.1
124	Vacaville, CA	9.9
125	Hillsboro, OR	9.4
126	Roanoke, VA	9.2
127	Amarillo, TX	8.8
128	Santa Barbara, CA	8.2
129	Yuma, AZ	7.8
130	Escondido, CA	7.5
130	Newport News, VA	7.5
132	Bridgeport, CT	7.1
133	Greeley, CO	6.5
134	Cape Coral, FL	6.1
135	Wilmington, NC	6.0
136	Memphis, TN	5.9
136	Salinas, CA	5.9
138	Arlington, TX	5.7
138	Nashua, NH	5.7
140	Lakewood, CO	5.4
141	Winston-Salem, NC	5.3
142	Newark, NJ	5.1
143	Raleigh, NC	4.9
143	Thornton, CO	4.9
145	Springfield, MA	4.7
146	Murfreesboro, TN	4.5
147	Evansville, IN	4.4
148	Clinton Twnshp, MI	4.3
148	Washington, DC	4.3
150	Boise, ID	4.2
151	Indianapolis, IN	4.1
152	Davie, FL	4.0
153	Charlotte, NC	3.8
154	Boston, MA	3.6
154	Denver, CO	3.6
156	Gresham, OR	3.2
156	Peoria, AZ	3.2
158	Chula Vista, CA	3.1
159	Jackson, MS	3.0
159	Mesa, AZ	3.0
161	Round Rock, TX	2.8
162	Hartford, CT	2.7
163	Cary, NC	2.4
163	Detroit, MI	2.4
165	Canton Twnshp, MI	1.9
166	Chattanooga, TN	1.6
167	Thousand Oaks, CA	1.0
168	Greensboro, NC	0.6
168	Woodbridge Twnshp, NJ	0.6
170	Costa Mesa, CA	0.4
170	Oakland, CA	0.4
172	Glendale, CA	0.0
172	Greece, NY	0.0
172	Hamilton Twnshp, NJ	0.0
175	Austin, TX	(0.2)
176	Lancaster, CA	(0.5)
176	Phoenix, AZ	(0.5)
176	Santa Ana, CA	(0.5)
179	Colorado Springs, CO	(0.6)
179	Grand Rapids, MI	(0.6)
179	Moreno Valley, CA	(0.6)
182	Yakima, WA	(0.7)
183	Columbia, SC	(0.8)
184	Melbourne, FL	(1.0)
185	Orem, UT	(1.1)
186	Chandler, AZ	(1.3)
187	Odessa, TX	(1.6)
188	Albuquerque, NM	(1.7)
189	Gainesville, FL	(1.8)
190	Shreveport, LA	(2.1)
190	Tempe, AZ	(2.1)
192	Carlsbad, CA	(2.4)

RANK	CITY	% CHANGE
192	Hammond, IN	(2.4)
194	Honolulu, HI	(2.7)
195	Lowell, MA	(2.8)
195	South Bend, IN	(2.8)
197	Huntington Beach, CA	(3.1)
198	Springfield, MO	(3.2)
199	Houston, TX	(3.3)
200	Hollywood, FL	(3.4)
201	North Charleston, SC	(3.7)
202	Los Angeles, CA	(4.2)
202	Orlando, FL	(4.2)
204	Tulsa, OK	(4.5)
205	Buffalo, NY	(4.6)
205	San Angelo, TX	(4.6)
205	Toledo, OH	(4.6)
208	Aurora, CO	(4.9)
208	Pasadena, TX	(4.9)
210	Sioux City, IA	(5.1)
211	Irvine, CA	(5.3)
211	Nashville, TN	(5.3)
213	Richmond, VA	(5.4)
214	Cleveland, OH	(5.7)
215	Fairfield, CA	(5.8)
215	Las Cruces, NM	(5.8)
215	Philadelphia, PA	(5.8)
218	Cincinnati, OH	(6.1)
219	Erie, PA	(6.7)
220	Allentown, PA	(6.9)
221	Omaha, NE	(7.0)
222	Ogden, UT	(7.1)
222	San Diego, CA	(7.1)
222	Seattle, WA	(7.1)
225	Lansing, MI	(7.3)
226	Clarksville, TN	(7.4)
226	Rochester, NY	(7.4)
228	Clearwater, FL	(7.9)
229	Bakersfield, CA	(8.3)
229	Birmingham, AL	(8.3)
231	Corona, CA	(8.4)
231	Macon, GA	(8.4)
233	North Las Vegas, NV	(8.5)
234	Syracuse, NY	(8.6)
235	Kansas City, KS	(8.7)
235	Lubbock, TX	(8.7)
237	Killeen, TX	(8.9)
237	Vancouver, WA	(8.9)
239	Stockton, CA	(9.0)
240	Rialto, CA	(9.1)
241	Richardson, TX	(9.2)
242	Oklahoma City, OK	(9.4)
243	Daly City, CA	(9.6)
244	Charleston, SC	(10.0)
244	Murrieta, CA	(10.0)
246	Portland, OR	(10.1)
246	Portsmouth, VA	(10.1)
246	Torrance, CA	(10.1)
249	San Francisco, CA	(10.4)
250	Hayward, CA	(10.7)
250	Sterling Heights, MI	(10.7)
252	Brockton, MA	(11.1)
253	Everett, WA	(11.2)
254	Knoxville, TN	(11.3)
254	Pittsburgh, PA	(11.3)
254	Redding, CA	(11.3)
257	Fresno, CA	(11.5)
257	Reno, NV	(11.5)

RANK	CITY	% CHANGE
259	Lincoln, NE	(11.7)
260	Gary, IN	(12.3)
261	Chino Hills, CA	(12.4)
262	Glendale, AZ	(12.5)
263	Quincy, MA	(12.8)
263	Santa Clara, CA	(12.8)
265	Ann Arbor, MI	(13.2)
266	Fort Smith, AR	(13.5)
267	Chino, CA	(13.6)
267	Dayton, OH	(13.6)
269	Green Bay, WI	(13.8)
269	Inglewood, CA	(13.8)
269	Reading, PA	(13.8)
272	Worcester, MA	(14.0)
273	Cedar Rapids, IA	(14.2)
274	Baltimore, MD	(14.6)
275	Abilene, TX	(15.0)
276	Lakewood, CA	(15.1)
277	Lafayette, LA	(15.3)
278	McKinney, TX	(15.7)
278	San Antonio, TX	(15.7)
280	Carson, CA	(15.9)
281	Roseville, CA	(16.0)
282	Louisville, KY	(16.4)
283	Boulder, CO	(16.5)
284	Brownsville, TX	(17.3)
285	Pasadena, CA	(17.6)
286	Longview, TX	(17.7)
287	San Mateo, CA	(18.0)
288	San Jose, CA	(18.3)
289	Pompano Beach, FL	(18.7)
290	Billings, MT	(19.0)
290	Whittier, CA	(19.0)
292	Eugene, OR	(19.8)
293	Madison, WI	(20.2)
294	McAllen, TX	(20.6)
295	Boca Raton, FL	(21.3)
296	Baldwin Park, CA	(21.6)
297	Victorville, CA	(21.7)
298	Savannah, GA	(21.9)
299	Albany, GA	(22.1)
300	Denton, TX	(22.3)
301	Sioux Falls, SD	(22.4)
302	Columbus, GA	(22.7)
302	Fontana, CA	(22.7)
302	Temecula, CA	(22.7)
305	West Valley, UT	(22.8)
306	Tucson, AZ	(23.1)
307	Beaumont, TX	(23.3)
307	Sunnyvale, CA	(23.3)
309	Burbank, CA	(23.4)
310	Tyler, TX	(24.0)
311	Fort Worth, TX	(24.1)
312	Lake Forest, CA	(24.3)
313	Centennial, CO	(24.5)
313	Corpus Christi, TX	(24.5)
313	Plano, TX	(24.5)
313	Upper Darby Twnshp, PA	(24.5)
317	New York, NY	(24.7)
318	Youngstown, OH	(25.0)
319	South Gate, CA	(25.9)
320	Albany, NY	(26.1)
321	Fremont, CA	(27.0)
321	Riverside, CA	(27.0)
323	Oxnard, CA	(27.6)
324	Irving, TX	(27.8)

RANK	CITY	% CHANGE
325	Milwaukee, WI	(28.3)
326	Suffolk, VA	(28.5)
327	Dearborn, MI	(28.7)
328	El Cajon, CA	(29.1)
329	Midland, TX	(29.2)
330	Sparks, NV	(29.3)
331	Downey, CA	(29.6)
332	Hialeah, FL	(30.1)
333	San Bernardino, CA	(30.6)
334	Sunrise, FL	(31.5)
335	West Covina, CA	(31.6)
336	Atlanta, GA	(32.0)
337	Montgomery, AL	(32.1)
338	Rancho Cucamon., CA	(33.0)
339	Mesquite, TX	(34.2)
340	West Palm Beach, FL	(36.3)
341	Fort Collins, CO	(36.4)
342	Tampa, FL	(37.1)
343	Wichita Falls, TX	(37.2)
344	Oceanside, CA	(38.2)
345	Farmington Hills, MI	(38.4)
346	Cambridge, MA	(39.1)
347	Provo, UT	(39.3)
348	Manchester, NH	(39.7)
349	Pembroke Pines, FL	(39.9)
350	Livermore, CA	(41.3)
351	Deerfield Beach, FL	(42.7)
352	Beaverton, OR	(45.9)
352	Spokane Valley, WA	(45.9)
354	Racine, WI	(47.8)
355	Clovis, CA	(50.2)
355	Danbury, CT	(50.2)
357	Providence, RI	(50.5)
358	Carrollton, TX	(51.0)
359	Tracy, CA	(58.9)
360	Pomona, CA	(60.9)
361	Newport Beach, CA	(66.4)
362	Plantation, FL	(66.9)
363	Mission Viejo, CA	(67.7)
364	Clifton, NJ	(77.7)
365	Colonie, NY	(77.8)
366	Coral Springs, FL	(78.3)
NA	Aurora, IL**	NA
NA	Bloomington, MN**	NA
NA	Brick Twnshp, NJ***	NA
NA	Chicago, IL**	NA
NA	Clarkstown, NY**	NA
NA	Des Moines, IA**	NA
NA	Duluth, MN**	NA
NA	Durham, NC**	NA
NA	El Paso, TX**	NA
NA	Fort Wayne, IN**	NA
NA	Joliet, IL**	NA
NA	Kansas City, MO**	NA
NA	Lexington, KY**	NA
NA	Minneapolis, MN**	NA
NA	Naperville, IL**	NA
NA	New Orleans, LA**	NA
NA	Peoria, IL**	NA
NA	Rochester, MN**	NA
NA	Rockford, IL**	NA
NA	Springfield, IL**	NA
NA	St. Paul, MN**	NA
NA	Vallejo, CA**	NA
NA	West Jordan, UT**	NA
NA	Wichita, KS**	NA

Source: CQ Press using data from F.B.I. "Crime in the United States 2006"

**Forcible rape is the carnal knowledge of a female forcibly and against her will. **Not available. ***Brick had a rape rate of 0 in 2005 but had three rapes in 2006. Calculating percent increase from zero results in an infinite number. This is shown as "NA."*

56. Percent Change in Rape Rate: 2002 to 2006

National Percent Change = 6.6% Decrease*

RANK	CITY	% CHANGE
112	Abilene, TX	9.2
308	Albany, GA	(34.6)
NA	Albany, NY**	NA
199	Albuquerque, NM	(10.8)
76	Alexandria, VA	24.5
28	Alhambra, CA	73.4
281	Allentown, PA	(27.7)
210	Amarillo, TX	(13.3)
80	Amherst, NY	22.5
54	Anaheim, CA	36.2
175	Anchorage, AK	(6.0)
72	Ann Arbor, MI	25.8
50	Antioch, CA	40.8
90	Arlington, TX	17.8
22	Arvada, CO	84.3
146	Athens-Clarke, GA	(1.6)
330	Atlanta, GA	(44.5)
234	Aurora, CO	(18.9)
NA	Aurora, IL**	NA
85	Austin, TX	20.4
251	Bakersfield, CA	(21.3)
328	Baldwin Park, CA	(43.0)
233	Baltimore, MD	(18.5)
264	Baton Rouge, LA	(24.1)
340	Beaumont, TX	(54.9)
216	Beaverton, OR	(14.9)
37	Bellevue, WA	53.0
194	Bellflower, CA	(10.5)
53	Bellingham, WA	36.8
227	Berkeley, CA	(17.9)
18	Billings, MT	95.1
155	Birmingham, AL	(3.5)
NA	Bloomington, MN**	NA
126	Boca Raton, FL	5.0
57	Boise, ID	34.1
248	Boston, MA	(21.0)
254	Boulder, CO	(22.5)
4	Brick Twnshp, NJ	192.3
113	Bridgeport, CT	8.5
160	Brockton, MA	(4.3)
346	Broken Arrow, OK	(63.6)
81	Brownsville, TX	21.9
152	Buena Park, CA	(3.3)
142	Buffalo, NY	(1.0)
143	Burbank, CA	(1.0)
133	Cambridge, MA	1.9
40	Camden, NJ	49.3
158	Canton Twnshp, MI	(3.9)
NA	Canton, OH**	NA
11	Cape Coral, FL	129.6
319	Carlsbad, CA	(39.1)
349	Carrollton, TX	(68.8)
268	Carson, CA	(25.2)
25	Cary, NC	79.2
300	Cedar Rapids, IA	(33.0)
NA	Centennial, CO**	NA
176	Chandler, AZ	(6.1)
106	Charleston, SC	11.0
107	Charlotte, NC	10.7
119	Chattanooga, TN	6.5
NA	Cheektowaga, NY**	NA
214	Chesapeake, VA	(14.5)
NA	Chicago, IL**	NA
331	Chino Hills, CA	(46.5)
10	Chino, CA	137.2
87	Chula Vista, CA	18.7
237	Cincinnati, OH	(19.2)
315	Clarkstown, NY	(37.3)
127	Clarksville, TN	4.8
202	Clearwater, FL	(11.2)
260	Cleveland, OH	(23.6)
350	Clifton, NJ	(71.3)
265	Clinton Twnshp, MI	(24.9)
321	Clovis, CA	(40.3)
351	Colonie, NY	(75.2)
185	Colorado Springs, CO	(8.4)
294	Columbia, MO	(31.2)
299	Columbia, SC	(32.4)
256	Columbus, GA	(23.3)
215	Columbus, OH	(14.8)
55	Compton, CA	35.6
179	Concord, CA	(7.5)
355	Coral Springs, FL	(92.6)
105	Corona, CA	11.4
296	Corpus Christi, TX	(31.7)
13	Costa Mesa, CA	118.5
325	Cranston, RI	(40.7)
136	Dallas, TX	0.9
288	Daly City, CA	(29.1)
339	Danbury, CT	(53.6)
29	Davie, FL	68.3
309	Dayton, OH	(34.7)
258	Dearborn, MI	(23.5)
75	Deerfield Beach, FL	24.9
280	Denton, TX	(27.6)
117	Denver, CO	7.9
NA	Des Moines, IA**	NA
187	Detroit, MI	(9.0)
77	Downey, CA	24.2
NA	Duluth, MN**	NA
NA	Durham, NC**	NA
141	Edison Twnshp, NJ	(0.7)
23	Edmond, OK	82.9
332	El Cajon, CA	(47.3)
318	El Monte, CA	(37.7)
NA	El Paso, TX**	NA
100	Elizabeth, NJ	13.9
144	Erie, PA	(1.5)
217	Escondido, CA	(15.6)
263	Eugene, OR	(24.1)
83	Evansville, IN	21.6
259	Everett, WA	(23.6)
82	Fairfield, CA	21.7
52	Fargo, ND	38.7
104	Farmington Hills, MI	11.5
120	Fayetteville, NC	6.5
20	Federal Way, WA	90.7
38	Flint, MI	51.3
284	Fontana, CA	(28.2)
274	Fort Collins, CO	(26.8)
16	Fort Lauderdale, FL	99.2
35	Fort Smith, AR	55.7
NA	Fort Wayne, IN**	NA
302	Fort Worth, TX	(33.0)
173	Fremont, CA	(5.9)
240	Fresno, CA	(19.7)
51	Fullerton, CA	38.7
56	Gainesville, FL	34.1
31	Garden Grove, CA	64.8
98	Garland, TX	15.4
111	Gary, IN	10.2
128	Gilbert, AZ	4.1
115	Glendale, AZ	8.2
305	Glendale, CA	(33.7)
188	Grand Prairie, TX	(9.0)
193	Grand Rapids, MI	(10.4)
NA	Greece, NY**	NA
209	Greeley, CO	(12.9)
235	Green Bay, WI	(18.9)
232	Greensboro, NC	(18.4)
110	Gresham, OR	10.3
69	Hamilton Twnshp, NJ	26.6
7	Hammond, IN	154.5
47	Hampton, VA	42.9
229	Hartford, CT	(18.0)
222	Hawthorne, CA	(16.5)
239	Hayward, CA	(19.4)
334	Henderson, NV	(51.7)
116	Hesperia, CA	8.0
327	Hialeah, FL	(42.9)
135	High Point, NC	1.4
255	Hillsboro, OR	(22.7)
63	Hollywood, FL	29.8
269	Honolulu, HI	(25.7)
171	Houston, TX	(5.7)
212	Huntington Beach, CA	(13.7)
95	Huntsville, AL	16.0
19	Independence, MO	91.3
74	Indianapolis, IN	25.0
323	Inglewood, CA	(40.3)
303	Irvine, CA	(33.3)
131	Irving, TX	2.6
262	Jacksonville, FL	(23.9)
182	Jackson, MS	(7.8)
285	Jersey City, NJ	(28.8)
NA	Joliet, IL**	NA
NA	Kansas City, KS**	NA
NA	Kansas City, MO**	NA
26	Kenosha, WI	78.4
2	Kent, WA	330.2
178	Killeen, TX	(7.3)
92	Knoxville, TN	16.7
197	Lafayette, LA	(10.7)
257	Lake Forest, CA	(23.5)
89	Lakeland, FL	17.9
247	Lakewood, CA	(20.6)
66	Lakewood, CO	29.1
196	Lancaster, CA	(10.6)
310	Lansing, MI	(35.1)
48	Laredo, TX	42.4
97	Largo, FL	15.5
NA	Las Cruces, NM**	NA
68	Las Vegas, NV	27.6
43	Lawrence, KS	47.6
42	Lawton, OK	48.4
45	Lee's Summit, MO	46.8
250	Lewisville, TX	(21.2)
NA	Lexington, KY**	NA
153	Lincoln, NE	(3.3)
65	Little Rock, AR	29.4
88	Livermore, CA	18.1
322	Livonia, MI	(40.3)

RANK	CITY	% CHANGE	RANK	CITY	% CHANGE	RANK	CITY	% CHANGE
177	Long Beach, CA	(7.0)	151	Peoria, AZ	(3.1)	NA	Spokane Valley, WA**	NA
345	Longview, TX	(62.5)	NA	Peoria, IL**	NA	109	Spokane, WA	10.4
272	Los Angeles, CA	(26.0)	156	Philadelphia, PA	(3.5)	NA	Springfield, IL**	NA
NA	Louisville, KY**	NA	78	Phoenix, AZ	24.0	114	Springfield, MA	8.3
206	Lowell, MA	(12.5)	278	Pittsburgh, PA	(27.3)	231	Springfield, MO	(18.4)
287	Lubbock, TX	(28.8)	169	Plano, TX	(5.2)	329	Sterling Heights, MI	(44.1)
3	Lynn, MA	281.0	344	Plantation, FL	(62.0)	314	Stockton, CA	(36.9)
204	Macon, GA	(12.1)	352	Pomona, CA	(77.9)	8	St. Louis, MO	152.5
298	Madison, WI	(32.4)	168	Pompano Beach, FL	(5.2)	NA	St. Paul, MN**	NA
138	Manchester, NH	0.3	61	Port St. Lucie, FL	31.2	180	St. Petersburg, FL	(7.5)
15	McAllen, TX	103.7	224	Portland, OR	(16.9)	213	Suffolk, VA	(14.5)
341	McKinney, TX	(56.6)	140	Portsmouth, VA	(0.3)	342	Sugar Land, TX	(57.5)
228	Melbourne, FL	(17.9)	335	Providence, RI	(51.9)	186	Sunnyvale, CA	(8.5)
241	Memphis, TN	(20.0)	161	Provo, UT	(4.4)	59	Sunrise, FL	32.5
46	Mesa, AZ	44.4	21	Pueblo, CO	84.5	1	Surprise, AZ	633.3
17	Mesquite, TX	97.4	60	Quincy, MA	32.5	33	Syracuse, NY	60.9
32	Miami Beach, FL	63.2	311	Racine, WI	(35.8)	223	Tacoma, WA	(16.9)
NA	Miami Gardens, FL**	NA	266	Raleigh, NC	(25.1)	137	Tallahassee, FL	0.3
134	Miami, FL	1.6	303	Rancho Cucamon., CA	(33.3)	317	Tampa, FL	(37.6)
230	Midland, TX	(18.3)	238	Reading, PA	(19.3)	337	Temecula, CA	(52.8)
348	Milwaukee, WI	(64.1)	91	Redding, CA	17.1	163	Tempe, AZ	(4.7)
NA	Minneapolis, MN**	NA	271	Reno, NV	(26.0)	44	Thornton, CO	47.4
205	Miramar, FL	(12.3)	166	Rialto, CA	(5.1)	292	Thousand Oaks, CA	(29.7)
354	Mission Viejo, CA	(86.3)	293	Richardson, TX	(30.8)	162	Toledo, OH	(4.4)
245	Mobile, AL	(20.4)	118	Richmond, CA	7.9	64	Toms River Twnshp, NJ	29.6
157	Modesto, CA	(3.9)	301	Richmond, VA	(33.0)	252	Topeka, KS	(21.4)
313	Montgomery, AL	(36.9)	241	Riverside, CA	(20.0)	253	Torrance, CA	(22.4)
148	Moreno Valley, CA	(2.0)	NA	Roanoke, VA**	NA	353	Tracy, CA	(78.1)
49	Murfreesboro, TN	41.4	NA	Rochester, MN**	NA	336	Trenton, NJ	(52.3)
9	Murrieta, CA	145.5	190	Rochester, NY	(9.8)	324	Troy, MI	(40.4)
164	Napa, CA	(4.8)	NA	Rockford, IL**	NA	220	Tucson, AZ	(15.9)
NA	Naperville, IL**	NA	129	Roseville, CA	3.7	79	Tulsa, OK	22.6
NA	Nashua, NH**	NA	12	Roswell, GA	125.0	184	Tuscaloosa, AL	(8.0)
246	Nashville, TN	(20.6)	225	Round Rock, TX	(17.3)	307	Tyler, TX	(34.6)
NA	New Bedford, MA**	NA	150	Sacramento, CA	(2.7)	27	Upper Darby Twnshp, PA	77.6
320	New Orleans, LA	(39.3)	208	Salem, OR	(12.8)	261	Vacaville, CA	(23.6)
316	New York, NY	(37.3)	236	Salinas, CA	(19.1)	290	Vallejo, CA	(29.6)
147	Newark, NJ	(1.6)	195	Salt Lake City, UT	(10.6)	165	Vancouver, WA	(5.0)
279	Newport Beach, CA	(27.5)	145	San Angelo, TX	(1.5)	243	Ventura, CA	(20.2)
125	Newport News, VA	5.1	130	San Antonio, TX	2.6	198	Victorville, CA	(10.8)
NA	Newton, MA**	NA	338	San Bernardino, CA	(52.9)	211	Virginia Beach, VA	(13.6)
192	Norfolk, VA	(10.3)	122	San Diego, CA	5.8	174	Visalia, CA	(6.0)
124	Norman, OK	5.4	249	San Francisco, CA	(21.1)	39	Vista, CA	51.0
275	North Charleston, SC	(26.8)	326	San Jose, CA	(42.2)	86	Waco, TX	19.1
295	North Las Vegas, NV	(31.3)	58	San Leandro, CA	33.0	99	Warren, MI	14.4
159	Norwalk, CA	(3.9)	108	San Mateo, CA	10.7	34	Warwick, RI	60.8
67	Oakland, CA	27.6	70	Sandy, UT	26.5	297	Washington, DC	(31.8)
312	Oceanside, CA	(36.3)	101	Santa Ana, CA	13.3	226	Waterbury, CT	(17.7)
347	Odessa, TX	(64.0)	200	Santa Barbara, CA	(11.0)	333	West Covina, CA	(48.0)
343	Ogden, UT	(58.8)	221	Santa Clara, CA	(16.2)	218	West Jordan, UT	(15.6)
291	Oklahoma City, OK	(29.7)	139	Santa Clarita, CA	0.0	286	West Palm Beach, FL	(28.8)
94	Olathe, KS	16.5	NA	Santa Maria, CA**	NA	102	West Valley, UT	13.0
132	Omaha, NE	2.3	276	Santa Monica, CA	(27.1)	24	Westland, MI	82.2
71	Ontario, CA	26.5	244	Santa Rosa, CA	(20.2)	121	Westminster, CA	6.3
267	Orange, CA	(25.2)	282	Savannah, GA	(28.0)	NA	Westminster, CO**	NA
170	Orem, UT	(5.5)	167	Scottsdale, AZ	(5.1)	36	Whittier, CA	53.3
84	Orlando, FL	20.9	219	Seattle, WA	(15.6)	181	Wichita Falls, TX	(7.7)
30	Overland Park, KS	67.1	73	Shreveport, LA	25.3	103	Wichita, KS	12.4
191	Oxnard, CA	(9.8)	5	Simi Valley, CA	186.9	149	Wilmington, NC	(2.2)
189	Palm Bay, FL	(9.3)	96	Sioux City, IA	15.8	123	Winston-Salem, NC	5.6
183	Palmdale, CA	(7.8)	201	Sioux Falls, SD	(11.1)	14	Woodbridge Twnshp, NJ	108.6
207	Parma, OH	(12.7)	273	Somerville, MA	(26.7)	NA	Worcester, MA**	NA
277	Pasadena, CA	(27.2)	270	South Bend, IN	(25.8)	172	Yakima, WA	(5.9)
283	Pasadena, TX	(28.0)	93	South Gate, CA	16.7	6	Yonkers, NY	180.4
62	Paterson, NJ	30.0	41	Southfield, MI	48.7	203	Youngstown, OH	(11.5)
289	Pembroke Pines, FL	(29.5)	306	Sparks, NV	(34.5)	154	Yuma, AZ	(3.4)

Source: CQ Press using data from F.B.I. "Crime in the United States 2006"

**Forcible rape is the carnal knowledge of a female forcibly and against her will. Assaults or attempts to commit rape by force or threat of force are included. However, statutory rape without force and other sex offenses are excluded. **Not available.*

56. Percent Change in Rape Rate: 2002 to 2006 (continued)

National Percent Change = 6.6% Decrease*

RANK	CITY	% CHANGE
1	Surprise, AZ	633.3
2	Kent, WA	330.2
3	Lynn, MA	281.0
4	Brick Twnshp, NJ	192.3
5	Simi Valley, CA	186.9
6	Yonkers, NY	180.4
7	Hammond, IN	154.5
8	St. Louis, MO	152.5
9	Murrieta, CA	145.5
10	Chino, CA	137.2
11	Cape Coral, FL	129.6
12	Roswell, GA	125.0
13	Costa Mesa, CA	118.5
14	Woodbridge Twnshp, NJ	108.6
15	McAllen, TX	103.7
16	Fort Lauderdale, FL	99.2
17	Mesquite, TX	97.4
18	Billings, MT	95.1
19	Independence, MO	91.3
20	Federal Way, WA	90.7
21	Pueblo, CO	84.5
22	Arvada, CO	84.3
23	Edmond, OK	82.9
24	Westland, MI	82.2
25	Cary, NC	79.2
26	Kenosha, WI	78.4
27	Upper Darby Twnshp, PA	77.6
28	Alhambra, CA	73.4
29	Davie, FL	68.3
30	Overland Park, KS	67.1
31	Garden Grove, CA	64.8
32	Miami Beach, FL	63.2
33	Syracuse, NY	60.9
34	Warwick, RI	60.8
35	Fort Smith, AR	55.7
36	Whittier, CA	53.3
37	Bellevue, WA	53.0
38	Flint, MI	51.3
39	Vista, CA	51.0
40	Camden, NJ	49.3
41	Southfield, MI	48.7
42	Lawton, OK	48.4
43	Lawrence, KS	47.6
44	Thornton, CO	47.4
45	Lee's Summit, MO	46.8
46	Mesa, AZ	44.4
47	Hampton, VA	42.9
48	Laredo, TX	42.4
49	Murfreesboro, TN	41.4
50	Antioch, CA	40.8
51	Fullerton, CA	38.7
52	Fargo, ND	38.7
53	Bellingham, WA	36.8
54	Anaheim, CA	36.2
55	Compton, CA	35.6
56	Gainesville, FL	34.1
57	Boise, ID	34.1
58	San Leandro, CA	33.0
59	Sunrise, FL	32.5
60	Quincy, MA	32.5
61	Port St. Lucie, FL	31.2
62	Paterson, NJ	30.0
63	Hollywood, FL	29.8
64	Toms River Twnshp, NJ	29.6
65	Little Rock, AR	29.4
66	Lakewood, CO	29.1
67	Oakland, CA	27.6
68	Las Vegas, NV	27.6
69	Hamilton Twnshp, NJ	26.6
70	Sandy, UT	26.5
71	Ontario, CA	26.5
72	Ann Arbor, MI	25.8
73	Shreveport, LA	25.3
74	Indianapolis, IN	25.0
75	Deerfield Beach, FL	24.9
76	Alexandria, VA	24.5
77	Downey, CA	24.2
78	Phoenix, AZ	24.0
79	Tulsa, OK	22.6
80	Amherst, NY	22.5
81	Brownsville, TX	21.9
82	Fairfield, CA	21.7
83	Evansville, IN	21.6
84	Orlando, FL	20.9
85	Austin, TX	20.4
86	Waco, TX	19.1
87	Chula Vista, CA	18.7
88	Livermore, CA	18.1
89	Lakeland, FL	17.9
90	Arlington, TX	17.8
91	Redding, CA	17.1
92	Knoxville, TN	16.7
93	South Gate, CA	16.7
94	Olathe, KS	16.5
95	Huntsville, AL	16.0
96	Sioux City, IA	15.8
97	Largo, FL	15.5
98	Garland, TX	15.4
99	Warren, MI	14.4
100	Elizabeth, NJ	13.9
101	Santa Ana, CA	13.3
102	West Valley, UT	13.0
103	Wichita, KS	12.4
104	Farmington Hills, MI	11.5
105	Corona, CA	11.4
106	Charleston, SC	11.0
107	Charlotte, NC	10.7
108	San Mateo, CA	10.7
109	Spokane, WA	10.4
110	Gresham, OR	10.3
111	Gary, IN	10.2
112	Abilene, TX	9.2
113	Bridgeport, CT	8.5
114	Springfield, MA	8.3
115	Glendale, AZ	8.2
116	Hesperia, CA	8.0
117	Denver, CO	7.9
118	Richmond, CA	7.9
119	Chattanooga, TN	6.5
120	Fayetteville, NC	6.5
121	Westminster, CA	6.3
122	San Diego, CA	5.8
123	Winston-Salem, NC	5.6
124	Norman, OK	5.4
125	Newport News, VA	5.1
126	Boca Raton, FL	5.0
127	Clarksville, TN	4.8
128	Gilbert, AZ	4.1
129	Roseville, CA	3.7
130	San Antonio, TX	2.6
131	Irving, TX	2.6
132	Omaha, NE	2.3
133	Cambridge, MA	1.9
134	Miami, FL	1.6
135	High Point, NC	1.4
136	Dallas, TX	0.9
137	Tallahassee, FL	0.3
138	Manchester, NH	0.3
139	Santa Clarita, CA	0.0
140	Portsmouth, VA	(0.3)
141	Edison Twnshp, NJ	(0.7)
142	Buffalo, NY	(1.0)
143	Burbank, CA	(1.0)
144	Erie, PA	(1.5)
145	San Angelo, TX	(1.5)
146	Athens-Clarke, GA	(1.6)
147	Newark, NJ	(1.6)
148	Moreno Valley, CA	(2.0)
149	Wilmington, NC	(2.2)
150	Sacramento, CA	(2.7)
151	Peoria, AZ	(3.1)
152	Buena Park, CA	(3.3)
153	Lincoln, NE	(3.3)
154	Yuma, AZ	(3.4)
155	Birmingham, AL	(3.5)
156	Philadelphia, PA	(3.5)
157	Modesto, CA	(3.9)
158	Canton Twnshp, MI	(3.9)
159	Norwalk, CA	(3.9)
160	Brockton, MA	(4.3)
161	Provo, UT	(4.4)
162	Toledo, OH	(4.4)
163	Tempe, AZ	(4.7)
164	Napa, CA	(4.8)
165	Vancouver, WA	(5.0)
166	Rialto, CA	(5.1)
167	Scottsdale, AZ	(5.1)
168	Pompano Beach, FL	(5.2)
169	Plano, TX	(5.2)
170	Orem, UT	(5.5)
171	Houston, TX	(5.7)
172	Yakima, WA	(5.9)
173	Fremont, CA	(5.9)
174	Visalia, CA	(6.0)
175	Anchorage, AK	(6.0)
176	Chandler, AZ	(6.1)
177	Long Beach, CA	(7.0)
178	Killeen, TX	(7.3)
179	Concord, CA	(7.5)
180	St. Petersburg, FL	(7.5)
181	Wichita Falls, TX	(7.7)
182	Jackson, MS	(7.8)
183	Palmdale, CA	(7.8)
184	Tuscaloosa, AL	(8.0)
185	Colorado Springs, CO	(8.4)
186	Sunnyvale, CA	(8.5)
187	Detroit, MI	(9.0)
188	Grand Prairie, TX	(9.0)
189	Palm Bay, FL	(9.3)
190	Rochester, NY	(9.8)
191	Oxnard, CA	(9.8)
192	Norfolk, VA	(10.3)

RANK	CITY	% CHANGE
193	Grand Rapids, MI	(10.4)
194	Bellflower, CA	(10.5)
195	Salt Lake City, UT	(10.6)
196	Lancaster, CA	(10.6)
197	Lafayette, LA	(10.7)
198	Victorville, CA	(10.8)
199	Albuquerque, NM	(10.8)
200	Santa Barbara, CA	(11.0)
201	Sioux Falls, SD	(11.1)
202	Clearwater, FL	(11.2)
203	Youngstown, OH	(11.5)
204	Macon, GA	(12.1)
205	Miramar, FL	(12.3)
206	Lowell, MA	(12.5)
207	Parma, OH	(12.7)
208	Salem, OR	(12.8)
209	Greeley, CO	(12.9)
210	Amarillo, TX	(13.3)
211	Virginia Beach, VA	(13.6)
212	Huntington Beach, CA	(13.7)
213	Suffolk, VA	(14.5)
214	Chesapeake, VA	(14.5)
215	Columbus, OH	(14.8)
216	Beaverton, OR	(14.9)
217	Escondido, CA	(15.6)
218	West Jordan, UT	(15.6)
219	Seattle, WA	(15.6)
220	Tucson, AZ	(15.9)
221	Santa Clara, CA	(16.2)
222	Hawthorne, CA	(16.5)
223	Tacoma, WA	(16.9)
224	Portland, OR	(16.9)
225	Round Rock, TX	(17.3)
226	Waterbury, CT	(17.7)
227	Berkeley, CA	(17.9)
228	Melbourne, FL	(17.9)
229	Hartford, CT	(18.0)
230	Midland, TX	(18.3)
231	Springfield, MO	(18.4)
232	Greensboro, NC	(18.4)
233	Baltimore, MD	(18.5)
234	Aurora, CO	(18.9)
235	Green Bay, WI	(18.9)
236	Salinas, CA	(19.1)
237	Cincinnati, OH	(19.2)
238	Reading, PA	(19.3)
239	Hayward, CA	(19.4)
240	Fresno, CA	(19.7)
241	Memphis, TN	(20.0)
241	Riverside, CA	(20.0)
243	Ventura, CA	(20.2)
244	Santa Rosa, CA	(20.2)
245	Mobile, AL	(20.4)
246	Nashville, TN	(20.6)
247	Lakewood, CA	(20.6)
248	Boston, MA	(21.0)
249	San Francisco, CA	(21.1)
250	Lewisville, TX	(21.2)
251	Bakersfield, CA	(21.3)
252	Topeka, KS	(21.4)
253	Torrance, CA	(22.4)
254	Boulder, CO	(22.5)
255	Hillsboro, OR	(22.7)
256	Columbus, GA	(23.3)
257	Lake Forest, CA	(23.5)
258	Dearborn, MI	(23.5)
259	Everett, WA	(23.6)
260	Cleveland, OH	(23.6)
261	Vacaville, CA	(23.6)
262	Jacksonville, FL	(23.9)
263	Eugene, OR	(24.1)
264	Baton Rouge, LA	(24.1)
265	Clinton Twnshp, MI	(24.9)
266	Raleigh, NC	(25.1)
267	Orange, CA	(25.2)
268	Carson, CA	(25.2)
269	Honolulu, HI	(25.7)
270	South Bend, IN	(25.8)
271	Reno, NV	(26.0)
272	Los Angeles, CA	(26.0)
273	Somerville, MA	(26.7)
274	Fort Collins, CO	(26.8)
275	North Charleston, SC	(26.8)
276	Santa Monica, CA	(27.1)
277	Pasadena, CA	(27.2)
278	Pittsburgh, PA	(27.3)
279	Newport Beach, CA	(27.5)
280	Denton, TX	(27.6)
281	Allentown, PA	(27.7)
282	Savannah, GA	(28.0)
283	Pasadena, TX	(28.0)
284	Fontana, CA	(28.2)
285	Jersey City, NJ	(28.8)
286	West Palm Beach, FL	(28.8)
287	Lubbock, TX	(28.8)
288	Daly City, CA	(29.1)
289	Pembroke Pines, FL	(29.5)
290	Vallejo, CA	(29.6)
291	Oklahoma City, OK	(29.7)
292	Thousand Oaks, CA	(29.7)
293	Richardson, TX	(30.8)
294	Columbia, MO	(31.2)
295	North Las Vegas, NV	(31.3)
296	Corpus Christi, TX	(31.7)
297	Washington, DC	(31.8)
298	Madison, WI	(32.4)
299	Columbia, SC	(32.4)
300	Cedar Rapids, IA	(33.0)
301	Richmond, VA	(33.0)
302	Fort Worth, TX	(33.0)
303	Irvine, CA	(33.3)
303	Rancho Cucamon., CA	(33.3)
305	Glendale, CA	(33.7)
306	Sparks, NV	(34.5)
307	Tyler, TX	(34.6)
308	Albany, GA	(34.6)
309	Dayton, OH	(34.7)
310	Lansing, MI	(35.1)
311	Racine, WI	(35.8)
312	Oceanside, CA	(36.3)
313	Montgomery, AL	(36.9)
314	Stockton, CA	(36.9)
315	Clarkstown, NY	(37.3)
316	New York, NY	(37.3)
317	Tampa, FL	(37.6)
318	El Monte, CA	(37.7)
319	Carlsbad, CA	(39.1)
320	New Orleans, LA	(39.3)
321	Clovis, CA	(40.3)
322	Livonia, MI	(40.3)
323	Inglewood, CA	(40.3)
324	Troy, MI	(40.4)
325	Cranston, RI	(40.7)
326	San Jose, CA	(42.2)
327	Hialeah, FL	(42.9)
328	Baldwin Park, CA	(43.0)
329	Sterling Heights, MI	(44.1)
330	Atlanta, GA	(44.5)
331	Chino Hills, CA	(46.5)
332	El Cajon, CA	(47.3)
333	West Covina, CA	(48.0)
334	Henderson, NV	(51.7)
335	Providence, RI	(51.9)
336	Trenton, NJ	(52.3)
337	Temecula, CA	(52.8)
338	San Bernardino, CA	(52.9)
339	Danbury, CT	(53.6)
340	Beaumont, TX	(54.9)
341	McKinney, TX	(56.6)
342	Sugar Land, TX	(57.5)
343	Ogden, UT	(58.8)
344	Plantation, FL	(62.0)
345	Longview, TX	(62.5)
346	Broken Arrow, OK	(63.6)
347	Odessa, TX	(64.0)
348	Milwaukee, WI	(64.1)
349	Carrollton, TX	(68.8)
350	Clifton, NJ	(71.3)
351	Colonie, NY	(75.2)
352	Pomona, CA	(77.9)
353	Tracy, CA	(78.1)
354	Mission Viejo, CA	(86.3)
355	Coral Springs, FL	(92.6)
NA	Albany, NY**	NA
NA	Aurora, IL**	NA
NA	Bloomington, MN**	NA
NA	Canton, OH**	NA
NA	Centennial, CO**	NA
NA	Cheektowaga, NY**	NA
NA	Chicago, IL**	NA
NA	Des Moines, IA**	NA
NA	Duluth, MN**	NA
NA	Durham, NC**	NA
NA	El Paso, TX**	NA
NA	Fort Wayne, IN**	NA
NA	Greece, NY**	NA
NA	Joliet, IL**	NA
NA	Kansas City, KS**	NA
NA	Kansas City, MO**	NA
NA	Las Cruces, NM**	NA
NA	Lexington, KY**	NA
NA	Louisville, KY**	NA
NA	Miami Gardens, FL**	NA
NA	Minneapolis, MN**	NA
NA	Naperville, IL**	NA
NA	Nashua, NH**	NA
NA	New Bedford, MA**	NA
NA	Newton, MA**	NA
NA	Peoria, IL**	NA
NA	Roanoke, VA**	NA
NA	Rochester, MN**	NA
NA	Rockford, IL**	NA
NA	Santa Maria, CA**	NA
NA	Spokane Valley, WA**	NA
NA	Springfield, IL**	NA
NA	St. Paul, MN**	NA
NA	Westminster, CO**	NA
NA	Worcester, MA**	NA

Source: CQ Press using data from F.B.I. "Crime in the United States 2006"

**Forcible rape is the carnal knowledge of a female forcibly and against her will. Assaults or attempts to commit rape by force or threat of force are included. However, statutory rape without force and other sex offenses are excluded. **Not available.*

57. Robberies in 2006

National Total = 447,403 Robberies*

RANK	CITY	ROBBERY
288	Abilene, TX	107
192	Albany, GA	243
142	Albany, NY	388
52	Albuquerque, NM	1,171
214	Alexandria, VA	206
240	Alhambra, CA	158
81	Allentown, PA	684
140	Amarillo, TX	401
367	Amherst, NY	31
93	Anaheim, CA	584
120	Anchorage, AK	465
301	Ann Arbor, MI	85
163	Antioch, CA	285
65	Arlington, TX	890
353	Arvada, CO	42
269	Athens-Clarke, GA	125
22	Atlanta, GA	2,959
91	Aurora, CO	600
224	Aurora, IL	178
43	Austin, TX	1,358
99	Bakersfield, CA	549
271	Baldwin Park, CA	123
12	Baltimore, MD	4,229
53	Baton Rouge, LA	1,049
156	Beaumont, TX	344
371	Beaverton, OR	30
322	Bellevue, WA	71
198	Bellflower, CA	236
316	Bellingham, WA	76
137	Berkeley, CA	414
351	Billings, MT	44
41	Birmingham, AL	1,429
332	Bloomington, MN	59
320	Boca Raton, FL	72
284	Boise, ID	111
23	Boston, MA	2,698
373	Boulder, CO	29
385	Brick Twnshp, NJ	19
86	Bridgeport, CT	659
172	Brockton, MA	266
381	Broken Arrow, OK	23
235	Brownsville, TX	168
279	Buena Park, CA	114
34	Buffalo, NY	1,708
318	Burbank, CA	75
213	Cambridge, MA	208
74	Camden, NJ	773
388	Canton Twnshp, MI	15
124	Canton, OH	459
304	Cape Coral, FL	83
312	Carlsbad, CA	77
298	Carrollton, TX	87
171	Carson, CA	268
353	Cary, NC	42
258	Cedar Rapids, IA	136
358	Centennial, CO	36
198	Chandler, AZ	236
189	Charleston, SC	245
19	Charlotte, NC	3,207
105	Chattanooga, TN	532
318	Cheektowaga, NY	75
165	Chesapeake, VA	278
2	Chicago, IL	15,863
376	Chino Hills, CA	26
287	Chino, CA	108
155	Chula Vista, CA	351
25	Cincinnati, OH	2,339
388	Clarkstown, NY	15
219	Clarksville, TN	195
217	Clearwater, FL	200
11	Cleveland, OH	4,288
311	Clifton, NJ	78
312	Clinton Twnshp, MI	77
332	Clovis, CA	59
367	Colonie, NY	31
90	Colorado Springs, CO	612
280	Columbia, MO	113
148	Columbia, SC	375
95	Columbus, GA	582
14	Columbus, OH	3,646
103	Compton, CA	534
185	Concord, CA	248
299	Coral Springs, FL	86
248	Corona, CA	152
118	Corpus Christi, TX	468
271	Costa Mesa, CA	123
349	Cranston, RI	45
7	Dallas, TX	6,914
259	Daly City, CA	134
330	Danbury, CT	62
308	Davie, FL	80
70	Dayton, OH	810
237	Dearborn, MI	164
254	Deerfield Beach, FL	141
327	Denton, TX	65
48	Denver, CO	1,280
149	Des Moines, IA	374
6	Detroit, MI	7,240
183	Downey, CA	249
278	Duluth, MN	116
59	Durham, NC	977
299	Edison Twnshp, NJ	86
390	Edmond, OK	14
245	El Cajon, CA	154
221	El Monte, CA	187
113	El Paso, TX	503
102	Elizabeth, NJ	536
166	Erie, PA	275
200	Escondido, CA	235
244	Eugene, OR	155
222	Evansville, IN	185
195	Everett, WA	240
193	Fairfield, CA	241
385	Fargo, ND	19
365	Farmington Hills, MI	32
108	Fayetteville, NC	510
252	Federal Way, WA	146
88	Flint, MI	627
180	Fontana, CA	254
358	Fort Collins, CO	36
68	Fort Lauderdale, FL	832
262	Fort Smith, AR	131
139	Fort Wayne, IN	404
42	Fort Worth, TX	1,417
178	Fremont, CA	256
47	Fresno, CA	1,282
228	Fullerton, CA	172
182	Gainesville, FL	250
186	Garden Grove, CA	247
204	Garland, TX	223
158	Gary, IN	336
340	Gilbert, AZ	53
119	Glendale, AZ	466
236	Glendale, CA	167
243	Grand Prairie, TX	156
77	Grand Rapids, MI	700
356	Greece, NY	40
343	Greeley, CO	50
289	Green Bay, WI	106
63	Greensboro, NC	901
231	Gresham, OR	170
286	Hamilton Twnshp, NJ	109
183	Hammond, IN	249
168	Hampton, VA	269
76	Hartford, CT	758
174	Hawthorne, CA	265
134	Hayward, CA	423
197	Henderson, NV	237
338	Hesperia, CA	56
149	Hialeah, FL	374
168	High Point, NC	269
312	Hillsboro, OR	77
145	Hollywood, FL	384
60	Honolulu, HI	956
4	Houston, TX	11,371
254	Huntington Beach, CA	141
89	Huntsville, AL	617
257	Independence, MO	138
18	Indianapolis, IN	3,249
115	Inglewood, CA	486
343	Irvine, CA	50
175	Irving, TX	264
27	Jacksonville, FL	2,304
56	Jackson, MS	1,022
37	Jersey City, NJ	1,553
220	Joliet, IL	191
127	Kansas City, KS	439
31	Kansas City, MO	2,044
248	Kenosha, WI	152
203	Kent, WA	224
188	Killeen, TX	246
101	Knoxville, TN	538
201	Lafayette, LA	231
378	Lake Forest, CA	25
216	Lakeland, FL	202
206	Lakewood, CA	220
226	Lakewood, CO	176
129	Lancaster, CA	432
176	Lansing, MI	262
172	Laredo, TX	266
292	Largo, FL	102
294	Las Cruces, NM	97
8	Las Vegas, NV	5,381
310	Lawrence, KS	79
233	Lawton, OK	169
381	Lee's Summit, MO	23
323	Lewisville, TX	70
111	Lexington, KY	505
239	Lincoln, NE	162
64	Little Rock, AR	899
336	Livermore, CA	57
327	Livonia, MI	65

RANK	CITY	ROBBERY
40	Long Beach, CA	1,440
276	Longview, TX	117
3	Los Angeles, CA	14,353
32	Louisville, KY	1,738
210	Lowell, MA	213
151	Lubbock, TX	367
168	Lynn, MA	269
152	Macon, GA	358
128	Madison, WI	434
242	Manchester, NH	157
271	McAllen, TX	123
357	McKinney, TX	37
212	Melbourne, FL	211
9	Memphis, TN	5,311
109	Mesa, AZ	508
229	Mesquite, TX	171
129	Miami Beach, FL	432
98	Miami Gardens, FL	550
30	Miami, FL	2,111
316	Midland, TX	76
15	Milwaukee, WI	3,608
21	Minneapolis, MN	3,028
268	Miramar, FL	127
373	Mission Viejo, CA	29
80	Mobile, AL	685
123	Modesto, CA	462
79	Montgomery, AL	686
116	Moreno Valley, CA	479
223	Murfreesboro, TN	179
367	Murrieta, CA	31
323	Napa, CA	70
378	Naperville, IL	25
346	Nashua, NH	47
24	Nashville, TN	2,425
164	New Bedford, MA	283
75	New Orleans, LA	761
1	New York, NY	23,511
46	Newark, NJ	1,288
365	Newport Beach, CA	32
117	Newport News, VA	473
381	Newton, MA	23
61	Norfolk, VA	948
343	Norman, OK	50
100	North Charleston, SC	544
93	North Las Vegas, NV	584
195	Norwalk, CA	240
17	Oakland, CA	3,534
189	Oceanside, CA	245
297	Odessa, TX	88
271	Ogden, UT	123
51	Oklahoma City, OK	1,179
364	Olathe, KS	33
67	Omaha, NE	848
135	Ontario, CA	418
251	Orange, CA	147
387	Orem, UT	18
38	Orlando, FL	1,528
329	Overland Park, KS	63
135	Oxnard, CA	418
320	Palm Bay, FL	72
157	Palmdale, CA	341
346	Parma, OH	47
186	Pasadena, CA	247
229	Pasadena, TX	171
71	Paterson, NJ	808
259	Pembroke Pines, FL	134

RANK	CITY	ROBBERY
312	Peoria, AZ	77
144	Peoria, IL	386
5	Philadelphia, PA	10,971
10	Phoenix, AZ	4,363
33	Pittsburgh, PA	1,722
245	Plano, TX	154
262	Plantation, FL	131
122	Pomona, CA	464
126	Pompano Beach, FL	441
362	Port St. Lucie, FL	34
45	Portland, OR	1,297
158	Portsmouth, VA	336
147	Providence, RI	379
380	Provo, UT	24
231	Pueblo, CO	170
296	Quincy, MA	92
189	Racine, WI	245
73	Raleigh, NC	782
253	Rancho Cucamon., CA	144
120	Reading, PA	465
325	Redding, CA	66
106	Reno, NV	523
162	Rialto, CA	299
293	Richardson, TX	98
112	Richmond, CA	504
58	Richmond, VA	987
69	Riverside, CA	814
206	Roanoke, VA	220
306	Rochester, MN	81
44	Rochester, NY	1,332
97	Rockford, IL	555
259	Roseville, CA	134
295	Roswell, GA	93
367	Round Rock, TX	31
28	Sacramento, CA	2,188
266	Salem, OR	129
146	Salinas, CA	383
110	Salt Lake City, UT	507
330	San Angelo, TX	62
26	San Antonio, TX	2,321
62	San Bernardino, CA	904
29	San Diego, CA	2,164
13	San Francisco, CA	3,858
55	San Jose, CA	1,030
161	San Leandro, CA	309
304	San Mateo, CA	83
373	Sandy, UT	29
72	Santa Ana, CA	787
291	Santa Barbara, CA	103
332	Santa Clara, CA	59
264	Santa Clarita, CA	130
280	Santa Maria, CA	113
178	Santa Monica, CA	256
227	Santa Rosa, CA	175
78	Savannah, GA	690
247	Scottsdale, AZ	153
36	Seattle, WA	1,667
92	Shreveport, LA	586
335	Simi Valley, CA	58
342	Sioux City, IA	51
362	Sioux Falls, SD	34
266	Somerville, MA	129
131	South Bend, IN	430
167	South Gate, CA	271
237	Southfield, MI	164
270	Sparks, NV	124

RANK	CITY	ROBBERY
338	Spokane Valley, WA	56
141	Spokane, WA	392
154	Springfield, IL	356
82	Springfield, MA	682
181	Springfield, MO	252
371	Sterling Heights, MI	30
39	Stockton, CA	1,519
20	St. Louis, MO	3,147
66	St. Paul, MN	849
54	St. Petersburg, FL	1,032
289	Suffolk, VA	106
349	Sugar Land, TX	45
306	Sunnyvale, CA	81
225	Sunrise, FL	177
384	Surprise, AZ	21
103	Syracuse, NY	534
83	Tacoma, WA	680
125	Tallahassee, FL	452
50	Tampa, FL	1,211
336	Temecula, CA	57
133	Tempe, AZ	426
348	Thornton, CO	46
355	Thousand Oaks, CA	41
49	Toledo, OH	1,248
351	Toms River Twnshp, NJ	44
160	Topeka, KS	310
215	Torrance, CA	203
325	Tracy, CA	66
87	Trenton, NJ	632
376	Troy, MI	26
35	Tucson, AZ	1,675
57	Tulsa, OK	997
205	Tuscaloosa, AL	221
285	Tyler, TX	110
201	Upper Darby Twnshp, PA	231
283	Vacaville, CA	112
131	Vallejo, CA	430
256	Vancouver, WA	139
264	Ventura, CA	130
208	Victorville, CA	219
84	Virginia Beach, VA	678
210	Visalia, CA	213
248	Vista, CA	152
177	Waco, TX	257
193	Warren, MI	241
358	Warwick, RI	36
16	Washington, DC	3,604
209	Waterbury, CT	216
217	West Covina, CA	200
358	West Jordan, UT	36
96	West Palm Beach, FL	574
280	West Valley, UT	113
301	Westland, MI	85
276	Westminster, CA	117
340	Westminster, CO	53
275	Whittier, CA	118
233	Wichita Falls, TX	169
107	Wichita, KS	520
138	Wilmington, NC	409
85	Winston-Salem, NC	669
308	Woodbridge Twnshp, NJ	80
142	Worcester, MA	388
240	Yakima, WA	158
114	Yonkers, NY	498
152	Youngstown, OH	358
303	Yuma, AZ	84

Source: Federal Bureau of Investigation "Crime in the United States 2006"

**Robbery is the taking of anything of value by force or threat of force. Attempts are included.*

57. Robberies in 2006 (continued)

National Total = 447,403 Robberies*

RANK	CITY	ROBBERY
1	New York, NY	23,511
2	Chicago, IL	15,863
3	Los Angeles, CA	14,353
4	Houston, TX	11,371
5	Philadelphia, PA	10,971
6	Detroit, MI	7,240
7	Dallas, TX	6,914
8	Las Vegas, NV	5,381
9	Memphis, TN	5,311
10	Phoenix, AZ	4,363
11	Cleveland, OH	4,288
12	Baltimore, MD	4,229
13	San Francisco, CA	3,858
14	Columbus, OH	3,646
15	Milwaukee, WI	3,608
16	Washington, DC	3,604
17	Oakland, CA	3,534
18	Indianapolis, IN	3,249
19	Charlotte, NC	3,207
20	St. Louis, MO	3,147
21	Minneapolis, MN	3,028
22	Atlanta, GA	2,959
23	Boston, MA	2,698
24	Nashville, TN	2,425
25	Cincinnati, OH	2,339
26	San Antonio, TX	2,321
27	Jacksonville, FL	2,304
28	Sacramento, CA	2,188
29	San Diego, CA	2,164
30	Miami, FL	2,111
31	Kansas City, MO	2,044
32	Louisville, KY	1,738
33	Pittsburgh, PA	1,722
34	Buffalo, NY	1,708
35	Tucson, AZ	1,675
36	Seattle, WA	1,667
37	Jersey City, NJ	1,553
38	Orlando, FL	1,528
39	Stockton, CA	1,519
40	Long Beach, CA	1,440
41	Birmingham, AL	1,429
42	Fort Worth, TX	1,417
43	Austin, TX	1,358
44	Rochester, NY	1,332
45	Portland, OR	1,297
46	Newark, NJ	1,288
47	Fresno, CA	1,282
48	Denver, CO	1,280
49	Toledo, OH	1,248
50	Tampa, FL	1,211
51	Oklahoma City, OK	1,179
52	Albuquerque, NM	1,171
53	Baton Rouge, LA	1,049
54	St. Petersburg, FL	1,032
55	San Jose, CA	1,030
56	Jackson, MS	1,022
57	Tulsa, OK	997
58	Richmond, VA	987
59	Durham, NC	977
60	Honolulu, HI	956
61	Norfolk, VA	948
62	San Bernardino, CA	904
63	Greensboro, NC	901
64	Little Rock, AR	899
65	Arlington, TX	890
66	St. Paul, MN	849
67	Omaha, NE	848
68	Fort Lauderdale, FL	832
69	Riverside, CA	814
70	Dayton, OH	810
71	Paterson, NJ	808
72	Santa Ana, CA	787
73	Raleigh, NC	782
74	Camden, NJ	773
75	New Orleans, LA	761
76	Hartford, CT	758
77	Grand Rapids, MI	700
78	Savannah, GA	690
79	Montgomery, AL	686
80	Mobile, AL	685
81	Allentown, PA	684
82	Springfield, MA	682
83	Tacoma, WA	680
84	Virginia Beach, VA	678
85	Winston-Salem, NC	669
86	Bridgeport, CT	659
87	Trenton, NJ	632
88	Flint, MI	627
89	Huntsville, AL	617
90	Colorado Springs, CO	612
91	Aurora, CO	600
92	Shreveport, LA	586
93	Anaheim, CA	584
93	North Las Vegas, NV	584
95	Columbus, GA	582
96	West Palm Beach, FL	574
97	Rockford, IL	555
98	Miami Gardens, FL	550
99	Bakersfield, CA	549
100	North Charleston, SC	544
101	Knoxville, TN	538
102	Elizabeth, NJ	536
103	Compton, CA	534
103	Syracuse, NY	534
105	Chattanooga, TN	532
106	Reno, NV	523
107	Wichita, KS	520
108	Fayetteville, NC	510
109	Mesa, AZ	508
110	Salt Lake City, UT	507
111	Lexington, KY	505
112	Richmond, CA	504
113	El Paso, TX	503
114	Yonkers, NY	498
115	Inglewood, CA	486
116	Moreno Valley, CA	479
117	Newport News, VA	473
118	Corpus Christi, TX	468
119	Glendale, AZ	466
120	Anchorage, AK	465
120	Reading, PA	465
122	Pomona, CA	464
123	Modesto, CA	462
124	Canton, OH	459
125	Tallahassee, FL	452
126	Pompano Beach, FL	441
127	Kansas City, KS	439
128	Madison, WI	434
129	Lancaster, CA	432
129	Miami Beach, FL	432
131	South Bend, IN	430
131	Vallejo, CA	430
133	Tempe, AZ	426
134	Hayward, CA	423
135	Ontario, CA	418
135	Oxnard, CA	418
137	Berkeley, CA	414
138	Wilmington, NC	409
139	Fort Wayne, IN	404
140	Amarillo, TX	401
141	Spokane, WA	392
142	Albany, NY	388
142	Worcester, MA	388
144	Peoria, IL	386
145	Hollywood, FL	384
146	Salinas, CA	383
147	Providence, RI	379
148	Columbia, SC	375
149	Des Moines, IA	374
149	Hialeah, FL	374
151	Lubbock, TX	367
152	Macon, GA	358
152	Youngstown, OH	358
154	Springfield, IL	356
155	Chula Vista, CA	351
156	Beaumont, TX	344
157	Palmdale, CA	341
158	Gary, IN	336
158	Portsmouth, VA	336
160	Topeka, KS	310
161	San Leandro, CA	309
162	Rialto, CA	299
163	Antioch, CA	285
164	New Bedford, MA	283
165	Chesapeake, VA	278
166	Erie, PA	275
167	South Gate, CA	271
168	Hampton, VA	269
168	High Point, NC	269
168	Lynn, MA	269
171	Carson, CA	268
172	Brockton, MA	266
172	Laredo, TX	266
174	Hawthorne, CA	265
175	Irving, TX	264
176	Lansing, MI	262
177	Waco, TX	257
178	Fremont, CA	256
178	Santa Monica, CA	256
180	Fontana, CA	254
181	Springfield, MO	252
182	Gainesville, FL	250
183	Downey, CA	249
183	Hammond, IN	249
185	Concord, CA	248
186	Garden Grove, CA	247
186	Pasadena, CA	247
188	Killeen, TX	246
189	Charleston, SC	245
189	Oceanside, CA	245
189	Racine, WI	245
192	Albany, GA	243

RANK	CITY	ROBBERY
193	Fairfield, CA	241
193	Warren, MI	241
195	Everett, WA	240
195	Norwalk, CA	240
197	Henderson, NV	237
198	Bellflower, CA	236
198	Chandler, AZ	236
200	Escondido, CA	235
201	Lafayette, LA	231
201	Upper Darby Twnshp, PA	231
203	Kent, WA	224
204	Garland, TX	223
205	Tuscaloosa, AL	221
206	Lakewood, CA	220
206	Roanoke, VA	220
208	Victorville, CA	219
209	Waterbury, CT	216
210	Lowell, MA	213
210	Visalia, CA	213
212	Melbourne, FL	211
213	Cambridge, MA	208
214	Alexandria, VA	206
215	Torrance, CA	203
216	Lakeland, FL	202
217	Clearwater, FL	200
217	West Covina, CA	200
219	Clarksville, TN	195
220	Joliet, IL	191
221	El Monte, CA	187
222	Evansville, IN	185
223	Murfreesboro, TN	179
224	Aurora, IL	178
225	Sunrise, FL	177
226	Lakewood, CO	176
227	Santa Rosa, CA	175
228	Fullerton, CA	172
229	Mesquite, TX	171
229	Pasadena, TX	171
231	Gresham, OR	170
231	Pueblo, CO	170
233	Lawton, OK	169
233	Wichita Falls, TX	169
235	Brownsville, TX	168
236	Glendale, CA	167
237	Dearborn, MI	164
237	Southfield, MI	164
239	Lincoln, NE	162
240	Alhambra, CA	158
240	Yakima, WA	158
242	Manchester, NH	157
243	Grand Prairie, TX	156
244	Eugene, OR	155
245	El Cajon, CA	154
245	Plano, TX	154
247	Scottsdale, AZ	153
248	Corona, CA	152
248	Kenosha, WI	152
248	Vista, CA	152
251	Orange, CA	147
252	Federal Way, WA	146
253	Rancho Cucamon., CA	144
254	Deerfield Beach, FL	141
254	Huntington Beach, CA	141
256	Vancouver, WA	139
257	Independence, MO	138
258	Cedar Rapids, IA	136
259	Daly City, CA	134
259	Pembroke Pines, FL	134
259	Roseville, CA	134
262	Fort Smith, AR	131
262	Plantation, FL	131
264	Santa Clarita, CA	130
264	Ventura, CA	130
266	Salem, OR	129
266	Somerville, MA	129
268	Miramar, FL	127
269	Athens-Clarke, GA	125
270	Sparks, NV	124
271	Baldwin Park, CA	123
271	Costa Mesa, CA	123
271	McAllen, TX	123
271	Ogden, UT	123
275	Whittier, CA	118
276	Longview, TX	117
276	Westminster, CA	117
278	Duluth, MN	116
279	Buena Park, CA	114
280	Columbia, MO	113
280	Santa Maria, CA	113
280	West Valley, UT	113
283	Vacaville, CA	112
284	Boise, ID	111
285	Tyler, TX	110
286	Hamilton Twnshp, NJ	109
287	Chino, CA	108
288	Abilene, TX	107
289	Green Bay, WI	106
289	Suffolk, VA	106
291	Santa Barbara, CA	103
292	Largo, FL	102
293	Richardson, TX	98
294	Las Cruces, NM	97
295	Roswell, GA	93
296	Quincy, MA	92
297	Odessa, TX	88
298	Carrollton, TX	87
299	Coral Springs, FL	86
299	Edison Twnshp, NJ	86
301	Ann Arbor, MI	85
301	Westland, MI	85
303	Yuma, AZ	84
304	Cape Coral, FL	83
304	San Mateo, CA	83
306	Rochester, MN	81
306	Sunnyvale, CA	81
308	Davie, FL	80
308	Woodbridge Twnshp, NJ	80
310	Lawrence, KS	79
311	Clifton, NJ	78
312	Carlsbad, CA	77
312	Clinton Twnshp, MI	77
312	Hillsboro, OR	77
312	Peoria, AZ	77
316	Bellingham, WA	76
316	Midland, TX	76
318	Burbank, CA	75
318	Cheektowaga, NY	75
320	Boca Raton, FL	72
320	Palm Bay, FL	72
322	Bellevue, WA	71
323	Lewisville, TX	70
323	Napa, CA	70
325	Redding, CA	66
325	Tracy, CA	66
327	Denton, TX	65
327	Livonia, MI	65
329	Overland Park, KS	63
330	Danbury, CT	62
330	San Angelo, TX	62
332	Bloomington, MN	59
332	Clovis, CA	59
332	Santa Clara, CA	59
335	Simi Valley, CA	58
336	Livermore, CA	57
336	Temecula, CA	57
338	Hesperia, CA	56
338	Spokane Valley, WA	56
340	Gilbert, AZ	53
340	Westminster, CO	53
342	Sioux City, IA	51
343	Greeley, CO	50
343	Irvine, CA	50
343	Norman, OK	50
346	Nashua, NH	47
346	Parma, OH	47
348	Thornton, CO	46
349	Cranston, RI	45
349	Sugar Land, TX	45
351	Billings, MT	44
351	Toms River Twnshp, NJ	44
353	Arvada, CO	42
353	Cary, NC	42
355	Thousand Oaks, CA	41
356	Greece, NY	40
357	McKinney, TX	37
358	Centennial, CO	36
358	Fort Collins, CO	36
358	Warwick, RI	36
358	West Jordan, UT	36
362	Port St. Lucie, FL	34
362	Sioux Falls, SD	34
364	Olathe, KS	33
365	Farmington Hills, MI	32
365	Newport Beach, CA	32
367	Amherst, NY	31
367	Colonie, NY	31
367	Murrieta, CA	31
367	Round Rock, TX	31
371	Beaverton, OR	30
371	Sterling Heights, MI	30
373	Boulder, CO	29
373	Mission Viejo, CA	29
373	Sandy, UT	29
376	Chino Hills, CA	26
376	Troy, MI	26
378	Lake Forest, CA	25
378	Naperville, IL	25
380	Provo, UT	24
381	Broken Arrow, OK	23
381	Lee's Summit, MO	23
381	Newton, MA	23
384	Surprise, AZ	21
385	Brick Twnshp, NJ	19
385	Fargo, ND	19
387	Orem, UT	18
388	Canton Twnshp, MI	15
388	Clarkstown, NY	15
390	Edmond, OK	14

Source: Federal Bureau of Investigation "Crime in the United States 2006"

**Robbery is the taking of anything of value by force or threat of force. Attempts are included.*

58. Robbery Rate in 2006

National Rate = 149.4 Robberies per 100,000 Population*

RANK	CITY	RATE
293	Abilene, TX	90.7
93	Albany, GA	312.3
61	Albany, NY	413.8
149	Albuquerque, NM	233.8
225	Alexandria, VA	150.7
194	Alhambra, CA	179.1
14	Allentown, PA	638.7
168	Amarillo, TX	213.1
374	Amherst, NY	27.6
198	Anaheim, CA	174.4
207	Anchorage, AK	167.5
313	Ann Arbor, MI	75.2
117	Antioch, CA	280.7
146	Arlington, TX	238.6
355	Arvada, CO	39.6
258	Athens-Clarke, GA	117.2
21	Atlanta, GA	609.1
176	Aurora, CO	198.1
270	Aurora, IL	105.3
182	Austin, TX	191.3
187	Bakersfield, CA	184.1
220	Baldwin Park, CA	154.6
12	Baltimore, MD	663.3
40	Baton Rouge, LA	498.4
105	Beaumont, TX	299.2
363	Beaverton, OR	34.4
334	Bellevue, WA	59.6
91	Bellflower, CA	313.7
277	Bellingham, WA	100.2
65	Berkeley, CA	407.3
348	Billings, MT	44.1
19	Birmingham, AL	611.8
316	Bloomington, MN	72.2
305	Boca Raton, FL	81.7
338	Boise, ID	56.0
46	Boston, MA	479.7
369	Boulder, CO	31.0
381	Brick Twnshp, NJ	24.3
48	Bridgeport, CT	474.8
119	Brockton, MA	279.4
379	Broken Arrow, OK	26.4
281	Brownsville, TX	97.5
232	Buena Park, CA	142.7
22	Buffalo, NY	608.9
319	Burbank, CA	71.4
170	Cambridge, MA	206.5
1	Camden, NJ	965.4
390	Canton Twnshp, MI	17.5
24	Canton, OH	576.8
335	Cape Coral, FL	58.3
302	Carlsbad, CA	84.1
320	Carrollton, TX	71.2
116	Carson, CA	282.7
356	Cary, NC	38.7
267	Cedar Rapids, IA	109.9
361	Centennial, CO	36.0
283	Chandler, AZ	96.8
154	Charleston, SC	226.1
51	Charlotte, NC	458.5
83	Chattanooga, TN	339.4
291	Cheektowaga, NY	92.6
248	Chesapeake, VA	125.7
27	Chicago, IL	555.1
364	Chino Hills, CA	34.0
237	Chino, CA	138.0
211	Chula Vista, CA	165.3
8	Cincinnati, OH	756.7
387	Clarkstown, NY	19.1
204	Clarksville, TN	170.6
191	Clearwater, FL	181.0
2	Cleveland, OH	947.1
281	Clifton, NJ	97.5
307	Clinton Twnshp, MI	79.7
324	Clovis, CA	67.6
352	Colonie, NY	40.1
214	Colorado Springs, CO	162.4
254	Columbia, MO	122.2
90	Columbia, SC	315.4
100	Columbus, GA	304.4
40	Columbus, OH	498.4
29	Compton, CA	553.3
175	Concord, CA	199.4
328	Coral Springs, FL	65.7
276	Corona, CA	100.8
216	Corpus Christi, TX	160.5
265	Costa Mesa, CA	111.0
340	Cranston, RI	55.6
28	Dallas, TX	553.9
243	Daly City, CA	132.4
309	Danbury, CT	78.9
289	Davie, FL	93.4
38	Dayton, OH	509.2
197	Dearborn, MI	174.7
190	Deerfield Beach, FL	181.6
332	Denton, TX	60.7
156	Denver, CO	225.2
181	Des Moines, IA	191.6
5	Detroit, MI	818.6
157	Downey, CA	224.9
238	Duluth, MN	135.7
49	Durham, NC	467.6
298	Edison Twnshp, NJ	85.5
388	Edmond, OK	18.5
212	El Cajon, CA	165.0
224	El Monte, CA	151.3
305	El Paso, TX	81.7
57	Elizabeth, NJ	425.7
131	Erie, PA	267.8
200	Escondido, CA	173.7
269	Eugene, OR	105.5
218	Evansville, IN	158.5
142	Everett, WA	244.2
151	Fairfield, CA	228.6
384	Fargo, ND	20.9
353	Farmington Hills, MI	40.0
70	Fayetteville, NC	384.8
201	Federal Way, WA	172.7
35	Flint, MI	530.2
221	Fontana, CA	153.6
374	Fort Collins, CO	27.6
42	Fort Lauderdale, FL	488.8
219	Fort Smith, AR	157.0
192	Fort Wayne, IN	179.7
162	Fort Worth, TX	220.8
247	Fremont, CA	126.6
124	Fresno, CA	275.5
245	Fullerton, CA	128.4
153	Gainesville, FL	227.3
228	Garden Grove, CA	147.4
277	Garland, TX	100.2
85	Gary, IN	338.1
372	Gilbert, AZ	29.3
184	Glendale, AZ	187.5
303	Glendale, CA	82.7
271	Grand Prairie, TX	105.1
78	Grand Rapids, MI	362.1
350	Greece, NY	42.4
338	Greeley, CO	56.0
274	Green Bay, WI	104.4
71	Greensboro, NC	380.8
199	Gresham, OR	174.1
255	Hamilton Twnshp, NJ	121.0
93	Hammond, IN	312.3
189	Hampton, VA	183.0
20	Hartford, CT	610.3
97	Hawthorne, CA	306.5
107	Hayward, CA	298.8
280	Henderson, NV	98.8
320	Hesperia, CA	71.2
208	Hialeah, FL	166.8
122	High Point, NC	277.4
295	Hillsboro, OR	89.6
134	Hollywood, FL	259.3
273	Honolulu, HI	104.7
30	Houston, TX	548.3
318	Huntington Beach, CA	71.9
75	Huntsville, AL	367.7
250	Independence, MO	124.3
67	Indianapolis, IN	405.6
58	Inglewood, CA	420.8
378	Irvine, CA	26.5
242	Irving, TX	132.6
111	Jacksonville, FL	289.5
25	Jackson, MS	576.3
13	Jersey City, NJ	647.6
235	Joliet, IL	139.5
101	Kansas City, KS	302.3
52	Kansas City, MO	456.0
217	Kenosha, WI	159.0
129	Kent, WA	269.2
145	Killeen, TX	238.7
109	Knoxville, TN	294.9
165	Lafayette, LA	217.5
366	Lake Forest, CA	32.4
160	Lakeland, FL	223.9
127	Lakewood, CA	271.0
253	Lakewood, CO	122.8
89	Lancaster, CA	319.4
152	Lansing, MI	227.4
251	Laredo, TX	123.9
239	Largo, FL	134.7
261	Las Cruces, NM	115.8
63	Las Vegas, NV	409.0
287	Lawrence, KS	95.9
186	Lawton, OK	185.7
373	Lee's Summit, MO	28.4
312	Lewisville, TX	75.3
185	Lexington, KY	186.9
325	Lincoln, NE	67.4
45	Little Rock, AR	481.6
317	Livermore, CA	72.0
326	Livonia, MI	66.5

RANK	CITY	RATE
104	Long Beach, CA	301.1
226	Longview, TX	150.5
73	Los Angeles, CA	370.0
121	Louisville, KY	277.6
171	Lowell, MA	205.3
206	Lubbock, TX	170.2
103	Lynn, MA	301.2
74	Macon, GA	367.8
178	Madison, WI	195.2
233	Manchester, NH	142.6
283	McAllen, TX	96.8
359	McKinney, TX	37.3
128	Melbourne, FL	270.7
7	Memphis, TN	780.1
266	Mesa, AZ	110.5
246	Mesquite, TX	128.0
44	Miami Beach, FL	483.2
31	Miami Gardens, FL	543.9
33	Miami, FL	537.2
314	Midland, TX	74.5
16	Milwaukee, WI	621.0
6	Minneapolis, MN	806.8
259	Miramar, FL	117.1
370	Mission Viejo, CA	30.3
125	Mobile, AL	273.8
161	Modesto, CA	221.2
82	Montgomery, AL	339.7
132	Moreno Valley, CA	266.2
172	Murfreesboro, TN	203.6
360	Murrieta, CA	37.1
290	Napa, CA	92.8
389	Naperville, IL	17.6
343	Nashua, NH	53.6
55	Nashville, TN	432.4
102	New Bedford, MA	302.2
196	New Orleans, LA	176.5
113	New York, NY	287.9
50	Newark, NJ	458.6
354	Newport Beach, CA	39.7
133	Newport News, VA	260.3
376	Newton, MA	27.5
68	Norfolk, VA	404.7
345	Norman, OK	48.7
17	North Charleston, SC	620.6
88	North Las Vegas, NV	319.9
158	Norwalk, CA	224.7
4	Oakland, CA	886.1
229	Oceanside, CA	146.2
292	Odessa, TX	91.5
223	Ogden, UT	152.1
163	Oklahoma City, OK	220.0
371	Olathe, KS	29.4
173	Omaha, NE	203.5
143	Ontario, CA	239.9
268	Orange, CA	108.0
386	Orem, UT	19.4
11	Orlando, FL	704.7
358	Overland Park, KS	38.0
155	Oxnard, CA	225.6
311	Palm Bay, FL	76.3
140	Palmdale, CA	251.1
337	Parma, OH	57.6
205	Pasadena, CA	170.3
262	Pasadena, TX	115.6
32	Paterson, NJ	538.8
296	Pembroke Pines, FL	87.6

RANK	CITY	RATE
342	Peoria, AZ	53.7
81	Peoria, IL	340.7
9	Philadelphia, PA	749.1
114	Phoenix, AZ	287.5
34	Pittsburgh, PA	530.5
333	Plano, TX	59.9
227	Plantation, FL	149.8
106	Pomona, CA	299.0
60	Pompano Beach, FL	416.3
380	Port St. Lucie, FL	25.4
144	Portland, OR	239.2
86	Portsmouth, VA	332.1
166	Providence, RI	216.0
385	Provo, UT	20.5
215	Pueblo, CO	161.2
275	Quincy, MA	101.3
96	Racine, WI	307.5
159	Raleigh, NC	224.5
301	Rancho Cucamon., CA	84.3
26	Reading, PA	574.6
315	Redding, CA	73.0
141	Reno, NV	248.6
108	Rialto, CA	297.8
286	Richardson, TX	96.1
42	Richmond, CA	488.8
39	Richmond, VA	504.3
120	Riverside, CA	278.1
148	Roanoke, VA	235.2
300	Rochester, MN	84.7
15	Rochester, NY	629.3
79	Rockford, IL	361.0
249	Roseville, CA	125.4
272	Roswell, GA	104.9
362	Round Rock, TX	34.9
47	Sacramento, CA	475.1
299	Salem, OR	85.3
135	Salinas, CA	259.2
123	Salt Lake City, UT	275.7
322	San Angelo, TX	68.5
193	San Antonio, TX	179.6
53	San Bernardino, CA	451.2
203	San Diego, CA	170.8
37	San Francisco, CA	517.1
264	San Jose, CA	111.9
69	San Leandro, CA	391.7
294	San Mateo, CA	90.3
368	Sandy, UT	31.3
150	Santa Ana, CA	229.2
257	Santa Barbara, CA	118.8
341	Santa Clara, CA	55.5
310	Santa Clarita, CA	76.6
241	Santa Maria, CA	132.8
112	Santa Monica, CA	289.0
263	Santa Rosa, CA	113.2
87	Savannah, GA	323.2
329	Scottsdale, AZ	65.2
115	Seattle, WA	285.6
95	Shreveport, LA	310.9
346	Simi Valley, CA	48.4
331	Sioux City, IA	61.0
382	Sioux Falls, SD	24.2
202	Somerville, MA	171.1
66	South Bend, IN	405.8
126	South Gate, CA	271.6
167	Southfield, MI	214.0
229	Sparks, NV	146.2

RANK	CITY	RATE
323	Spokane Valley, WA	67.7
177	Spokane, WA	195.8
99	Springfield, IL	306.1
54	Springfield, MA	446.8
210	Springfield, MO	166.4
383	Sterling Heights, MI	23.5
36	Stockton, CA	524.7
3	St. Louis, MO	907.2
97	St. Paul, MN	306.5
64	St. Petersburg, FL	407.5
240	Suffolk, VA	132.9
336	Sugar Land, TX	57.8
330	Sunnyvale, CA	62.3
180	Sunrise, FL	192.1
377	Surprise, AZ	27.2
72	Syracuse, NY	375.9
80	Tacoma, WA	341.3
118	Tallahassee, FL	280.4
76	Tampa, FL	365.3
327	Temecula, CA	65.8
137	Tempe, AZ	254.6
349	Thornton, CO	42.9
365	Thousand Oaks, CA	32.7
62	Toledo, OH	413.7
347	Toms River Twnshp, NJ	46.4
139	Topeka, KS	252.4
234	Torrance, CA	141.3
304	Tracy, CA	81.8
10	Trenton, NJ	746.1
367	Troy, MI	32.1
92	Tucson, AZ	312.9
136	Tulsa, OK	258.4
129	Tuscaloosa, AL	269.2
260	Tyler, TX	116.4
110	Upper Darby Twnshp, PA	289.9
256	Vacaville, CA	119.4
77	Vallejo, CA	362.7
297	Vancouver, WA	86.8
251	Ventura, CA	123.9
147	Victorville, CA	237.8
222	Virginia Beach, VA	153.1
179	Visalia, CA	194.3
209	Vista, CA	166.6
169	Waco, TX	207.5
195	Warren, MI	178.6
351	Warwick, RI	41.6
18	Washington, DC	619.7
174	Waterbury, CT	200.5
188	West Covina, CA	183.2
357	West Jordan, UT	38.1
23	West Palm Beach, FL	579.0
285	West Valley, UT	96.6
279	Westland, MI	99.5
244	Westminster, CA	129.5
344	Westminster, CO	49.5
236	Whittier, CA	138.4
213	Wichita Falls, TX	164.6
231	Wichita, KS	145.5
59	Wilmington, NC	420.0
84	Winston-Salem, NC	338.5
308	Woodbridge Twnshp, NJ	79.5
164	Worcester, MA	219.3
182	Yakima, WA	191.3
138	Yonkers, NY	252.9
56	Youngstown, OH	431.6
288	Yuma, AZ	95.5

Source: CQ Press using data from F.B.I. "Crime in the United States 2006"

**Robbery is the taking of anything of value by force or threat of force. Attempts are included.*

58. Robbery Rate in 2006 (continued)

National Rate = 149.4 Robberies per 100,000 Population*

RANK	CITY	RATE
1	Camden, NJ	965.4
2	Cleveland, OH	947.1
3	St. Louis, MO	907.2
4	Oakland, CA	886.1
5	Detroit, MI	818.6
6	Minneapolis, MN	806.8
7	Memphis, TN	780.1
8	Cincinnati, OH	756.7
9	Philadelphia, PA	749.1
10	Trenton, NJ	746.1
11	Orlando, FL	704.7
12	Baltimore, MD	663.3
13	Jersey City, NJ	647.6
14	Allentown, PA	638.7
15	Rochester, NY	629.3
16	Milwaukee, WI	621.0
17	North Charleston, SC	620.6
18	Washington, DC	619.7
19	Birmingham, AL	611.8
20	Hartford, CT	610.3
21	Atlanta, GA	609.1
22	Buffalo, NY	608.9
23	West Palm Beach, FL	579.0
24	Canton, OH	576.8
25	Jackson, MS	576.3
26	Reading, PA	574.6
27	Chicago, IL	555.1
28	Dallas, TX	553.9
29	Compton, CA	553.3
30	Houston, TX	548.3
31	Miami Gardens, FL	543.9
32	Paterson, NJ	538.8
33	Miami, FL	537.2
34	Pittsburgh, PA	530.5
35	Flint, MI	530.2
36	Stockton, CA	524.7
37	San Francisco, CA	517.1
38	Dayton, OH	509.2
39	Richmond, VA	504.3
40	Baton Rouge, LA	498.4
40	Columbus, OH	498.4
42	Fort Lauderdale, FL	488.8
42	Richmond, CA	488.8
44	Miami Beach, FL	483.2
45	Little Rock, AR	481.6
46	Boston, MA	479.7
47	Sacramento, CA	475.1
48	Bridgeport, CT	474.8
49	Durham, NC	467.6
50	Newark, NJ	458.6
51	Charlotte, NC	458.5
52	Kansas City, MO	456.0
53	San Bernardino, CA	451.2
54	Springfield, MA	446.8
55	Nashville, TN	432.4
56	Youngstown, OH	431.6
57	Elizabeth, NJ	425.7
58	Inglewood, CA	420.8
59	Wilmington, NC	420.0
60	Pompano Beach, FL	416.3
61	Albany, NY	413.8
62	Toledo, OH	413.7
63	Las Vegas, NV	409.0
64	St. Petersburg, FL	407.5
65	Berkeley, CA	407.3
66	South Bend, IN	405.8
67	Indianapolis, IN	405.6
68	Norfolk, VA	404.7
69	San Leandro, CA	391.7
70	Fayetteville, NC	384.8
71	Greensboro, NC	380.8
72	Syracuse, NY	375.9
73	Los Angeles, CA	370.0
74	Macon, GA	367.8
75	Huntsville, AL	367.7
76	Tampa, FL	365.3
77	Vallejo, CA	362.7
78	Grand Rapids, MI	362.1
79	Rockford, IL	361.0
80	Tacoma, WA	341.3
81	Peoria, IL	340.7
82	Montgomery, AL	339.7
83	Chattanooga, TN	339.4
84	Winston-Salem, NC	338.5
85	Gary, IN	338.1
86	Portsmouth, VA	332.1
87	Savannah, GA	323.2
88	North Las Vegas, NV	319.9
89	Lancaster, CA	319.4
90	Columbia, SC	315.4
91	Bellflower, CA	313.7
92	Tucson, AZ	312.9
93	Albany, GA	312.3
93	Hammond, IN	312.3
95	Shreveport, LA	310.9
96	Racine, WI	307.5
97	Hawthorne, CA	306.5
97	St. Paul, MN	306.5
99	Springfield, IL	306.1
100	Columbus, GA	304.4
101	Kansas City, KS	302.3
102	New Bedford, MA	302.2
103	Lynn, MA	301.2
104	Long Beach, CA	301.1
105	Beaumont, TX	299.2
106	Pomona, CA	299.0
107	Hayward, CA	298.8
108	Rialto, CA	297.8
109	Knoxville, TN	294.9
110	Upper Darby Twnshp, PA	289.9
111	Jacksonville, FL	289.5
112	Santa Monica, CA	289.0
113	New York, NY	287.9
114	Phoenix, AZ	287.5
115	Seattle, WA	285.6
116	Carson, CA	282.7
117	Antioch, CA	280.7
118	Tallahassee, FL	280.4
119	Brockton, MA	279.4
120	Riverside, CA	278.1
121	Louisville, KY	277.6
122	High Point, NC	277.4
123	Salt Lake City, UT	275.7
124	Fresno, CA	275.5
125	Mobile, AL	273.8
126	South Gate, CA	271.6
127	Lakewood, CA	271.0
128	Melbourne, FL	270.7
129	Kent, WA	269.2
129	Tuscaloosa, AL	269.2
131	Erie, PA	267.8
132	Moreno Valley, CA	266.2
133	Newport News, VA	260.3
134	Hollywood, FL	259.3
135	Salinas, CA	259.2
136	Tulsa, OK	258.4
137	Tempe, AZ	254.6
138	Yonkers, NY	252.9
139	Topeka, KS	252.4
140	Palmdale, CA	251.1
141	Reno, NV	248.6
142	Everett, WA	244.2
143	Ontario, CA	239.9
144	Portland, OR	239.2
145	Killeen, TX	238.7
146	Arlington, TX	238.6
147	Victorville, CA	237.8
148	Roanoke, VA	235.2
149	Albuquerque, NM	233.8
150	Santa Ana, CA	229.2
151	Fairfield, CA	228.6
152	Lansing, MI	227.4
153	Gainesville, FL	227.3
154	Charleston, SC	226.1
155	Oxnard, CA	225.6
156	Denver, CO	225.2
157	Downey, CA	224.9
158	Norwalk, CA	224.7
159	Raleigh, NC	224.5
160	Lakeland, FL	223.9
161	Modesto, CA	221.2
162	Fort Worth, TX	220.8
163	Oklahoma City, OK	220.0
164	Worcester, MA	219.3
165	Lafayette, LA	217.5
166	Providence, RI	216.0
167	Southfield, MI	214.0
168	Amarillo, TX	213.1
169	Waco, TX	207.5
170	Cambridge, MA	206.5
171	Lowell, MA	205.3
172	Murfreesboro, TN	203.6
173	Omaha, NE	203.5
174	Waterbury, CT	200.5
175	Concord, CA	199.4
176	Aurora, CO	198.1
177	Spokane, WA	195.8
178	Madison, WI	195.2
179	Visalia, CA	194.3
180	Sunrise, FL	192.1
181	Des Moines, IA	191.6
182	Austin, TX	191.3
182	Yakima, WA	191.3
184	Glendale, AZ	187.5
185	Lexington, KY	186.9
186	Lawton, OK	185.7
187	Bakersfield, CA	184.1
188	West Covina, CA	183.2
189	Hampton, VA	183.0
190	Deerfield Beach, FL	181.6
191	Clearwater, FL	181.0
192	Fort Wayne, IN	179.7

RANK	CITY	RATE
193	San Antonio, TX	179.6
194	Alhambra, CA	179.1
195	Warren, MI	178.6
196	New Orleans, LA	176.5
197	Dearborn, MI	174.7
198	Anaheim, CA	174.4
199	Gresham, OR	174.1
200	Escondido, CA	173.7
201	Federal Way, WA	172.7
202	Somerville, MA	171.1
203	San Diego, CA	170.8
204	Clarksville, TN	170.6
205	Pasadena, CA	170.3
206	Lubbock, TX	170.2
207	Anchorage, AK	167.5
208	Hialeah, FL	166.8
209	Vista, CA	166.6
210	Springfield, MO	166.4
211	Chula Vista, CA	165.3
212	El Cajon, CA	165.0
213	Wichita Falls, TX	164.6
214	Colorado Springs, CO	162.4
215	Pueblo, CO	161.2
216	Corpus Christi, TX	160.5
217	Kenosha, WI	159.0
218	Evansville, IN	158.5
219	Fort Smith, AR	157.0
220	Baldwin Park, CA	154.6
221	Fontana, CA	153.6
222	Virginia Beach, VA	153.1
223	Ogden, UT	152.1
224	El Monte, CA	151.3
225	Alexandria, VA	150.7
226	Longview, TX	150.5
227	Plantation, FL	149.8
228	Garden Grove, CA	147.4
229	Oceanside, CA	146.2
229	Sparks, NV	146.2
231	Wichita, KS	145.5
232	Buena Park, CA	142.7
233	Manchester, NH	142.6
234	Torrance, CA	141.3
235	Joliet, IL	139.5
236	Whittier, CA	138.4
237	Chino, CA	138.0
238	Duluth, MN	135.7
239	Largo, FL	134.7
240	Suffolk, VA	132.9
241	Santa Maria, CA	132.8
242	Irving, TX	132.6
243	Daly City, CA	132.4
244	Westminster, CA	129.5
245	Fullerton, CA	128.4
246	Mesquite, TX	128.0
247	Fremont, CA	126.6
248	Chesapeake, VA	125.7
249	Roseville, CA	125.4
250	Independence, MO	124.3
251	Laredo, TX	123.9
251	Ventura, CA	123.9
253	Lakewood, CO	122.8
254	Columbia, MO	122.2
255	Hamilton Twnshp, NJ	121.0
256	Vacaville, CA	119.4
257	Santa Barbara, CA	118.8
258	Athens-Clarke, GA	117.2
259	Miramar, FL	117.1
260	Tyler, TX	116.4
261	Las Cruces, NM	115.8
262	Pasadena, TX	115.6
263	Santa Rosa, CA	113.2
264	San Jose, CA	111.9
265	Costa Mesa, CA	111.0
266	Mesa, AZ	110.5
267	Cedar Rapids, IA	109.9
268	Orange, CA	108.0
269	Eugene, OR	105.5
270	Aurora, IL	105.3
271	Grand Prairie, TX	105.1
272	Roswell, GA	104.9
273	Honolulu, HI	104.7
274	Green Bay, WI	104.4
275	Quincy, MA	101.3
276	Corona, CA	100.8
277	Bellingham, WA	100.2
277	Garland, TX	100.2
279	Westland, MI	99.5
280	Henderson, NV	98.8
281	Brownsville, TX	97.5
281	Clifton, NJ	97.5
283	Chandler, AZ	96.8
283	McAllen, TX	96.8
285	West Valley, UT	96.6
286	Richardson, TX	96.1
287	Lawrence, KS	95.9
288	Yuma, AZ	95.5
289	Davie, FL	93.4
290	Napa, CA	92.8
291	Cheektowaga, NY	92.6
292	Odessa, TX	91.5
293	Abilene, TX	90.7
294	San Mateo, CA	90.3
295	Hillsboro, OR	89.6
296	Pembroke Pines, FL	87.6
297	Vancouver, WA	86.8
298	Edison Twnshp, NJ	85.5
299	Salem, OR	85.3
300	Rochester, MN	84.7
301	Rancho Cucamon., CA	84.3
302	Carlsbad, CA	84.1
303	Glendale, CA	82.7
304	Tracy, CA	81.8
305	Boca Raton, FL	81.7
305	El Paso, TX	81.7
307	Clinton Twnshp, MI	79.7
308	Woodbridge Twnshp, NJ	79.5
309	Danbury, CT	78.9
310	Santa Clarita, CA	76.6
311	Palm Bay, FL	76.3
312	Lewisville, TX	75.3
313	Ann Arbor, MI	75.2
314	Midland, TX	74.5
315	Redding, CA	73.0
316	Bloomington, MN	72.2
317	Livermore, CA	72.0
318	Huntington Beach, CA	71.9
319	Burbank, CA	71.4
320	Carrollton, TX	71.2
320	Hesperia, CA	71.2
322	San Angelo, TX	68.5
323	Spokane Valley, WA	67.7
324	Clovis, CA	67.6
325	Lincoln, NE	67.4
326	Livonia, MI	66.5
327	Temecula, CA	65.8
328	Coral Springs, FL	65.7
329	Scottsdale, AZ	65.2
330	Sunnyvale, CA	62.3
331	Sioux City, IA	61.0
332	Denton, TX	60.7
333	Plano, TX	59.9
334	Bellevue, WA	59.6
335	Cape Coral, FL	58.3
336	Sugar Land, TX	57.8
337	Parma, OH	57.6
338	Boise, ID	56.0
338	Greeley, CO	56.0
340	Cranston, RI	55.6
341	Santa Clara, CA	55.5
342	Peoria, AZ	53.7
343	Nashua, NH	53.6
344	Westminster, CO	49.5
345	Norman, OK	48.7
346	Simi Valley, CA	48.4
347	Toms River Twnshp, NJ	46.4
348	Billings, MT	44.1
349	Thornton, CO	42.9
350	Greece, NY	42.4
351	Warwick, RI	41.6
352	Colonie, NY	40.1
353	Farmington Hills, MI	40.0
354	Newport Beach, CA	39.7
355	Arvada, CO	39.6
356	Cary, NC	38.7
357	West Jordan, UT	38.1
358	Overland Park, KS	38.0
359	McKinney, TX	37.3
360	Murrieta, CA	37.1
361	Centennial, CO	36.0
362	Round Rock, TX	34.9
363	Beaverton, OR	34.4
364	Chino Hills, CA	34.0
365	Thousand Oaks, CA	32.7
366	Lake Forest, CA	32.4
367	Troy, MI	32.1
368	Sandy, UT	31.3
369	Boulder, CO	31.0
370	Mission Viejo, CA	30.3
371	Olathe, KS	29.4
372	Gilbert, AZ	29.3
373	Lee's Summit, MO	28.4
374	Amherst, NY	27.6
374	Fort Collins, CO	27.6
376	Newton, MA	27.5
377	Surprise, AZ	27.2
378	Irvine, CA	26.5
379	Broken Arrow, OK	26.4
380	Port St. Lucie, FL	25.4
381	Brick Twnshp, NJ	24.3
382	Sioux Falls, SD	24.2
383	Sterling Heights, MI	23.5
384	Fargo, ND	20.9
385	Provo, UT	20.5
386	Orem, UT	19.4
387	Clarkstown, NY	19.1
388	Edmond, OK	18.5
389	Naperville, IL	17.6
390	Canton Twnshp, MI	17.5

Source: CQ Press using data from F.B.I. "Crime in the United States 2006"

**Robbery is the taking of anything of value by force or threat of force. Attempts are included.*

59. Percent Change in Robbery Rate: 2005 to 2006

National Percent Change = 6.1% Increase*

RANK	CITY	% CHANGE
363	Abilene, TX	(27.5)
142	Albany, GA	13.3
321	Albany, NY	(11.0)
244	Albuquerque, NM	(0.3)
260	Alexandria, VA	(1.5)
220	Alhambra, CA	3.0
50	Allentown, PA	33.4
147	Amarillo, TX	12.9
364	Amherst, NY	(28.7)
195	Anaheim, CA	5.8
104	Anchorage, AK	20.4
339	Ann Arbor, MI	(16.2)
85	Antioch, CA	22.9
141	Arlington, TX	13.5
352	Arvada, CO	(20.8)
309	Athens-Clarke, GA	(8.2)
310	Atlanta, GA	(8.3)
314	Aurora, CO	(9.0)
240	Aurora, IL	0.1
152	Austin, TX	12.1
249	Bakersfield, CA	(0.7)
87	Baldwin Park, CA	22.8
174	Baltimore, MD	8.8
148	Baton Rouge, LA	12.7
234	Beaumont, TX	1.4
370	Beaverton, OR	(32.8)
26	Bellevue, WA	44.0
285	Bellflower, CA	(4.2)
30	Bellingham, WA	39.9
120	Berkeley, CA	17.6
332	Billings, MT	(13.7)
239	Birmingham, AL	0.4
NA	Bloomington, MN**	NA
83	Boca Raton, FL	23.0
66	Boise, ID	27.0
224	Boston, MA	2.8
335	Boulder, CO	(14.8)
1	Brick Twnshp, NJ	219.7
225	Bridgeport, CT	2.7
70	Brockton, MA	25.5
231	Broken Arrow, OK	1.9
73	Brownsville, TX	24.8
306	Buena Park, CA	(8.1)
216	Buffalo, NY	3.5
155	Burbank, CA	11.7
328	Cambridge, MA	(13.2)
162	Camden, NJ	10.2
373	Canton Twnshp, MI	(35.4)
98	Canton, OH	21.0
218	Cape Coral, FL	3.2
288	Carlsbad, CA	(4.5)
319	Carrollton, TX	(10.2)
102	Carson, CA	20.7
350	Cary, NC	(20.4)
156	Cedar Rapids, IA	11.5
293	Centennial, CO	(5.5)
153	Chandler, AZ	12.0
341	Charleston, SC	(17.1)
336	Charlotte, NC	(14.9)
105	Chattanooga, TN	20.1
340	Cheektowaga, NY	(16.8)
306	Chesapeake, VA	(8.1)
241	Chicago, IL	(0.1)
25	Chino Hills, CA	44.1
28	Chino, CA	40.8
237	Chula Vista, CA	0.9
226	Cincinnati, OH	2.6
NA	Clarkstown, NY**	NA
46	Clarksville, TN	36.2
286	Clearwater, FL	(4.3)
126	Cleveland, OH	16.1
306	Clifton, NJ	(8.1)
108	Clinton Twnshp, MI	19.7
113	Clovis, CA	19.2
298	Colonie, NY	(6.3)
34	Colorado Springs, CO	38.6
278	Columbia, MO	(3.2)
272	Columbia, SC	(2.4)
61	Columbus, GA	28.2
281	Columbus, OH	(3.6)
144	Compton, CA	13.1
67	Concord, CA	26.7
19	Coral Springs, FL	48.6
199	Corona, CA	5.3
289	Corpus Christi, TX	(4.6)
214	Costa Mesa, CA	3.6
292	Cranston, RI	(5.4)
252	Dallas, TX	(1.0)
167	Daly City, CA	10.0
188	Danbury, CT	6.6
157	Davie, FL	11.1
284	Dayton, OH	(4.1)
358	Dearborn, MI	(25.1)
334	Deerfield Beach, FL	(14.7)
349	Denton, TX	(20.2)
322	Denver, CO	(11.2)
NA	Des Moines, IA**	NA
182	Detroit, MI	8.1
241	Downey, CA	(0.1)
NA	Duluth, MN**	NA
NA	Durham, NC**	NA
99	Edison Twnshp, NJ	20.9
357	Edmond, OK	(24.5)
312	El Cajon, CA	(8.7)
354	El Monte, CA	(22.8)
NA	El Paso, TX**	NA
263	Elizabeth, NJ	(1.6)
33	Erie, PA	39.4
65	Escondido, CA	27.3
61	Eugene, OR	28.2
192	Evansville, IN	6.1
39	Everett, WA	37.5
170	Fairfield, CA	9.7
5	Fargo, ND	74.2
336	Farmington Hills, MI	(14.9)
135	Fayetteville, NC	14.2
301	Federal Way, WA	(7.0)
149	Flint, MI	12.2
195	Fontana, CA	5.8
374	Fort Collins, CO	(37.7)
158	Fort Lauderdale, FL	11.0
159	Fort Smith, AR	10.9
NA	Fort Wayne, IN**	NA
267	Fort Worth, TX	(1.8)
41	Fremont, CA	37.2
245	Fresno, CA	(0.4)
129	Fullerton, CA	15.8
16	Gainesville, FL	50.6
177	Garden Grove, CA	8.5
303	Garland, TX	(7.5)
160	Gary, IN	10.6
47	Gilbert, AZ	35.6
125	Glendale, AZ	16.2
80	Glendale, CA	23.2
324	Grand Prairie, TX	(11.8)
202	Grand Rapids, MI	4.9
222	Greece, NY	2.9
347	Greeley, CO	(19.8)
22	Green Bay, WI	47.2
136	Greensboro, NC	13.9
140	Gresham, OR	13.6
114	Hamilton Twnshp, NJ	18.7
318	Hammond, IN	(10.0)
267	Hampton, VA	(1.8)
161	Hartford, CT	10.3
118	Hawthorne, CA	18.3
29	Hayward, CA	40.7
7	Henderson, NV	72.7
372	Hesperia, CA	(35.1)
254	Hialeah, FL	(1.1)
102	High Point, NC	20.7
119	Hillsboro, OR	17.9
126	Hollywood, FL	16.1
144	Honolulu, HI	13.1
238	Houston, TX	0.8
12	Huntington Beach, CA	53.6
94	Huntsville, AL	21.4
144	Independence, MO	13.1
250	Indianapolis, IN	(0.9)
325	Inglewood, CA	(12.0)
143	Irvine, CA	13.2
276	Irving, TX	(2.9)
228	Jacksonville, FL	2.2
8	Jackson, MS	69.9
293	Jersey City, NJ	(5.5)
71	Joliet, IL	25.1
197	Kansas City, KS	5.7
NA	Kansas City, MO**	NA
99	Kenosha, WI	20.9
48	Kent, WA	35.0
201	Killeen, TX	5.0
273	Knoxville, TN	(2.6)
6	Lafayette, LA	73.0
355	Lake Forest, CA	(23.9)
24	Lakeland, FL	44.5
133	Lakewood, CA	14.6
297	Lakewood, CO	(5.9)
111	Lancaster, CA	19.4
203	Lansing, MI	4.8
211	Laredo, TX	4.0
60	Largo, FL	28.3
304	Las Cruces, NM	(7.7)
18	Las Vegas, NV	50.0
4	Lawrence, KS	92.2
89	Lawton, OK	22.2
368	Lee's Summit, MO	(29.7)
77	Lewisville, TX	24.1
NA	Lexington, KY**	NA
365	Lincoln, NE	(28.8)
210	Little Rock, AR	4.1
2	Livermore, CA	109.3
191	Livonia, MI	6.2

RANK	CITY	% CHANGE	RANK	CITY	% CHANGE	RANK	CITY	% CHANGE
222	Long Beach, CA	2.9	190	Peoria, AZ	6.5	235	Spokane Valley, WA	1.3
315	Longview, TX	(9.3)	233	Peoria, IL	1.5	44	Spokane, WA	36.5
213	Los Angeles, CA	3.8	171	Philadelphia, PA	9.6	42	Springfield, IL	36.7
291	Louisville, KY	(5.0)	247	Phoenix, AZ	(0.5)	326	Springfield, MA	(12.1)
245	Lowell, MA	(0.4)	177	Pittsburgh, PA	8.5	74	Springfield, MO	24.6
123	Lubbock, TX	16.3	69	Plano, TX	25.6	371	Sterling Heights, MI	(34.9)
247	Lynn, MA	(0.5)	132	Plantation, FL	14.9	173	Stockton, CA	8.9
182	Macon, GA	8.1	93	Pomona, CA	21.5	194	St. Louis, MO	5.9
53	Madison, WI	31.4	317	Pompano Beach, FL	(9.9)	169	St. Paul, MN	9.8
149	Manchester, NH	12.2	136	Port St. Lucie, FL	13.9	181	St. Petersburg, FL	8.2
305	McAllen, TX	(7.9)	139	Portland, OR	13.7	330	Suffolk, VA	(13.3)
343	McKinney, TX	(18.2)	311	Portsmouth, VA	(8.6)	369	Sugar Land, TX	(30.1)
10	Melbourne, FL	68.2	316	Providence, RI	(9.6)	165	Sunnyvale, CA	10.1
114	Memphis, TN	18.7	76	Provo, UT	24.2	35	Sunrise, FL	38.5
175	Mesa, AZ	8.7	205	Pueblo, CO	4.5	138	Surprise, AZ	13.8
243	Mesquite, TX	(0.2)	258	Quincy, MA	(1.3)	275	Syracuse, NY	(2.8)
333	Miami Beach, FL	(14.5)	227	Racine, WI	2.3	265	Tacoma, WA	(1.7)
212	Miami Gardens, FL	3.9	271	Raleigh, NC	(2.2)	123	Tallahassee, FL	16.3
217	Miami, FL	3.3	236	Rancho Cucamon., CA	1.0	214	Tampa, FL	3.6
20	Midland, TX	48.4	72	Reading, PA	24.9	359	Temecula, CA	(25.5)
75	Milwaukee, WI	24.4	328	Redding, CA	(13.2)	55	Tempe, AZ	29.8
121	Minneapolis, MN	17.5	99	Reno, NV	20.9	362	Thornton, CO	(27.2)
348	Miramar, FL	(20.1)	32	Rialto, CA	39.6	360	Thousand Oaks, CA	(26.5)
344	Mission Viejo, CA	(18.5)	252	Richardson, TX	(1.0)	300	Toledo, OH	(6.9)
133	Mobile, AL	14.6	286	Richmond, CA	(4.3)	205	Toms River Twnshp, NJ	4.5
114	Modesto, CA	18.7	342	Richmond, VA	(17.7)	149	Topeka, KS	12.2
345	Montgomery, AL	(18.9)	109	Riverside, CA	19.6	283	Torrance, CA	(3.7)
56	Moreno Valley, CA	29.5	280	Roanoke, VA	(3.4)	198	Tracy, CA	5.5
20	Murfreesboro, TN	48.4	153	Rochester, MN	12.0	351	Trenton, NJ	(20.7)
353	Murrieta, CA	(22.7)	54	Rochester, NY	30.5	38	Troy, MI	37.8
3	Napa, CA	107.1	NA	Rockford, IL**	NA	265	Tucson, AZ	(1.7)
254	Naperville, IL	(1.1)	17	Roseville, CA	50.4	313	Tulsa, OK	(8.9)
9	Nashua, NH	68.6	58	Roswell, GA	29.2	176	Tuscaloosa, AL	8.6
258	Nashville, TN	(1.3)	96	Round Rock, TX	21.2	375	Tyler, TX	(38.4)
162	New Bedford, MA	10.2	186	Sacramento, CA	7.7	37	Upper Darby Twnshp, PA	38.2
NA	New Orleans, LA**	NA	296	Salem, OR	(5.7)	11	Vacaville, CA	64.2
293	New York, NY	(5.5)	130	Salinas, CA	15.4	NA	Vallejo, CA**	NA
219	Newark, NJ	3.1	91	Salt Lake City, UT	22.0	338	Vancouver, WA	(15.2)
85	Newport Beach, CA	22.9	14	San Angelo, TX	53.2	94	Ventura, CA	21.4
323	Newport News, VA	(11.4)	203	San Antonio, TX	4.8	56	Victorville, CA	29.5
12	Newton, MA	53.6	257	San Bernardino, CA	(1.2)	168	Virginia Beach, VA	9.9
162	Norfolk, VA	10.2	122	San Diego, CA	16.7	188	Visalia, CA	6.6
79	Norman, OK	23.6	68	San Francisco, CA	25.8	346	Vista, CA	(19.2)
229	North Charleston, SC	2.1	131	San Jose, CA	15.2	277	Waco, TX	(3.1)
59	North Las Vegas, NV	28.7	52	San Leandro, CA	31.8	172	Warren, MI	9.1
63	Norwalk, CA	27.7	366	San Mateo, CA	(29.1)	15	Warwick, RI	51.3
51	Oakland, CA	32.8	185	Sandy, UT	7.9	273	Washington, DC	(2.6)
299	Oceanside, CA	(6.6)	87	Santa Ana, CA	22.8	232	Waterbury, CT	1.8
106	Odessa, TX	19.9	39	Santa Barbara, CA	37.5	49	West Covina, CA	33.6
230	Ogden, UT	2.0	117	Santa Clara, CA	18.6	NA	West Jordan, UT**	NA
270	Oklahoma City, OK	(2.0)	106	Santa Clarita, CA	19.9	187	West Palm Beach, FL	6.9
165	Olathe, KS	10.1	92	Santa Maria, CA	21.7	97	West Valley, UT	21.1
83	Omaha, NE	23.0	193	Santa Monica, CA	6.0	111	Westland, MI	19.4
31	Ontario, CA	39.7	208	Santa Rosa, CA	4.2	90	Westminster, CA	22.1
23	Orange, CA	45.6	269	Savannah, GA	(1.9)	361	Westminster, CO	(27.0)
43	Orem, UT	36.6	109	Scottsdale, AZ	19.6	290	Whittier, CA	(4.7)
82	Orlando, FL	23.1	220	Seattle, WA	3.0	367	Wichita Falls, TX	(29.4)
263	Overland Park, KS	(1.6)	260	Shreveport, LA	(1.5)	NA	Wichita, KS**	NA
184	Oxnard, CA	8.0	80	Simi Valley, CA	23.2	45	Wilmington, NC	36.4
327	Palm Bay, FL	(12.3)	260	Sioux City, IA	(1.5)	179	Winston-Salem, NC	8.4
208	Palmdale, CA	4.2	376	Sioux Falls, SD	(53.1)	250	Woodbridge Twnshp, NJ	(0.9)
356	Parma, OH	(24.4)	302	Somerville, MA	(7.2)	254	Worcester, MA	(1.1)
330	Pasadena, CA	(13.3)	78	South Bend, IN	23.7	199	Yakima, WA	5.3
126	Pasadena, TX	16.1	320	South Gate, CA	(10.7)	281	Yonkers, NY	(3.6)
35	Paterson, NJ	38.5	207	Southfield, MI	4.4	279	Youngstown, OH	(3.3)
27	Pembroke Pines, FL	41.5	64	Sparks, NV	27.6	180	Yuma, AZ	8.3

Source: CQ Press using data from F.B.I. "Crime in the United States 2006"

**Robbery is the taking of anything of value by force or threat of force. Attempts are included.*

***Not available.*

59. Percent Change in Robbery Rate: 2005 to 2006 (continued)

National Percent Change = 6.1% Increase*

RANK	CITY	% CHANGE
1	Brick Twnshp, NJ	219.7
2	Livermore, CA	109.3
3	Napa, CA	107.1
4	Lawrence, KS	92.2
5	Fargo, ND	74.2
6	Lafayette, LA	73.0
7	Henderson, NV	72.7
8	Jackson, MS	69.9
9	Nashua, NH	68.6
10	Melbourne, FL	68.2
11	Vacaville, CA	64.2
12	Huntington Beach, CA	53.6
12	Newton, MA	53.6
14	San Angelo, TX	53.2
15	Warwick, RI	51.3
16	Gainesville, FL	50.6
17	Roseville, CA	50.4
18	Las Vegas, NV	50.0
19	Coral Springs, FL	48.6
20	Midland, TX	48.4
20	Murfreesboro, TN	48.4
22	Green Bay, WI	47.2
23	Orange, CA	45.6
24	Lakeland, FL	44.5
25	Chino Hills, CA	44.1
26	Bellevue, WA	44.0
27	Pembroke Pines, FL	41.5
28	Chino, CA	40.8
29	Hayward, CA	40.7
30	Bellingham, WA	39.9
31	Ontario, CA	39.7
32	Rialto, CA	39.6
33	Erie, PA	39.4
34	Colorado Springs, CO	38.6
35	Paterson, NJ	38.5
35	Sunrise, FL	38.5
37	Upper Darby Twnshp, PA	38.2
38	Troy, MI	37.8
39	Everett, WA	37.5
39	Santa Barbara, CA	37.5
41	Fremont, CA	37.2
42	Springfield, IL	36.7
43	Orem, UT	36.6
44	Spokane, WA	36.5
45	Wilmington, NC	36.4
46	Clarksville, TN	36.2
47	Gilbert, AZ	35.6
48	Kent, WA	35.0
49	West Covina, CA	33.6
50	Allentown, PA	33.4
51	Oakland, CA	32.8
52	San Leandro, CA	31.8
53	Madison, WI	31.4
54	Rochester, NY	30.5
55	Tempe, AZ	29.8
56	Moreno Valley, CA	29.5
56	Victorville, CA	29.5
58	Roswell, GA	29.2
59	North Las Vegas, NV	28.7
60	Largo, FL	28.3
61	Columbus, GA	28.2
61	Eugene, OR	28.2
63	Norwalk, CA	27.7
64	Sparks, NV	27.6
65	Escondido, CA	27.3
66	Boise, ID	27.0
67	Concord, CA	26.7
68	San Francisco, CA	25.8
69	Plano, TX	25.6
70	Brockton, MA	25.5
71	Joliet, IL	25.1
72	Reading, PA	24.9
73	Brownsville, TX	24.8
74	Springfield, MO	24.6
75	Milwaukee, WI	24.4
76	Provo, UT	24.2
77	Lewisville, TX	24.1
78	South Bend, IN	23.7
79	Norman, OK	23.6
80	Glendale, CA	23.2
80	Simi Valley, CA	23.2
82	Orlando, FL	23.1
83	Boca Raton, FL	23.0
83	Omaha, NE	23.0
85	Antioch, CA	22.9
85	Newport Beach, CA	22.9
87	Baldwin Park, CA	22.8
87	Santa Ana, CA	22.8
89	Lawton, OK	22.2
90	Westminster, CA	22.1
91	Salt Lake City, UT	22.0
92	Santa Maria, CA	21.7
93	Pomona, CA	21.5
94	Huntsville, AL	21.4
94	Ventura, CA	21.4
96	Round Rock, TX	21.2
97	West Valley, UT	21.1
98	Canton, OH	21.0
99	Edison Twnshp, NJ	20.9
99	Kenosha, WI	20.9
99	Reno, NV	20.9
102	Carson, CA	20.7
102	High Point, NC	20.7
104	Anchorage, AK	20.4
105	Chattanooga, TN	20.1
106	Odessa, TX	19.9
106	Santa Clarita, CA	19.9
108	Clinton Twnshp, MI	19.7
109	Riverside, CA	19.6
109	Scottsdale, AZ	19.6
111	Lancaster, CA	19.4
111	Westland, MI	19.4
113	Clovis, CA	19.2
114	Hamilton Twnshp, NJ	18.7
114	Memphis, TN	18.7
114	Modesto, CA	18.7
117	Santa Clara, CA	18.6
118	Hawthorne, CA	18.3
119	Hillsboro, OR	17.9
120	Berkeley, CA	17.6
121	Minneapolis, MN	17.5
122	San Diego, CA	16.7
123	Lubbock, TX	16.3
123	Tallahassee, FL	16.3
125	Glendale, AZ	16.2
126	Cleveland, OH	16.1
126	Hollywood, FL	16.1
126	Pasadena, TX	16.1
129	Fullerton, CA	15.8
130	Salinas, CA	15.4
131	San Jose, CA	15.2
132	Plantation, FL	14.9
133	Lakewood, CA	14.6
133	Mobile, AL	14.6
135	Fayetteville, NC	14.2
136	Greensboro, NC	13.9
136	Port St. Lucie, FL	13.9
138	Surprise, AZ	13.8
139	Portland, OR	13.7
140	Gresham, OR	13.6
141	Arlington, TX	13.5
142	Albany, GA	13.3
143	Irvine, CA	13.2
144	Compton, CA	13.1
144	Honolulu, HI	13.1
144	Independence, MO	13.1
147	Amarillo, TX	12.9
148	Baton Rouge, LA	12.7
149	Flint, MI	12.2
149	Manchester, NH	12.2
149	Topeka, KS	12.2
152	Austin, TX	12.1
153	Chandler, AZ	12.0
153	Rochester, MN	12.0
155	Burbank, CA	11.7
156	Cedar Rapids, IA	11.5
157	Davie, FL	11.1
158	Fort Lauderdale, FL	11.0
159	Fort Smith, AR	10.9
160	Gary, IN	10.6
161	Hartford, CT	10.3
162	Camden, NJ	10.2
162	New Bedford, MA	10.2
162	Norfolk, VA	10.2
165	Olathe, KS	10.1
165	Sunnyvale, CA	10.1
167	Daly City, CA	10.0
168	Virginia Beach, VA	9.9
169	St. Paul, MN	9.8
170	Fairfield, CA	9.7
171	Philadelphia, PA	9.6
172	Warren, MI	9.1
173	Stockton, CA	8.9
174	Baltimore, MD	8.8
175	Mesa, AZ	8.7
176	Tuscaloosa, AL	8.6
177	Garden Grove, CA	8.5
177	Pittsburgh, PA	8.5
179	Winston-Salem, NC	8.4
180	Yuma, AZ	8.3
181	St. Petersburg, FL	8.2
182	Detroit, MI	8.1
182	Macon, GA	8.1
184	Oxnard, CA	8.0
185	Sandy, UT	7.9
186	Sacramento, CA	7.7
187	West Palm Beach, FL	6.9
188	Danbury, CT	6.6
188	Visalia, CA	6.6
190	Peoria, AZ	6.5
191	Livonia, MI	6.2
192	Evansville, IN	6.1

RANK	CITY	% CHANGE
193	Santa Monica, CA	6.0
194	St. Louis, MO	5.9
195	Anaheim, CA	5.8
195	Fontana, CA	5.8
197	Kansas City, KS	5.7
198	Tracy, CA	5.5
199	Corona, CA	5.3
199	Yakima, WA	5.3
201	Killeen, TX	5.0
202	Grand Rapids, MI	4.9
203	Lansing, MI	4.8
203	San Antonio, TX	4.8
205	Pueblo, CO	4.5
205	Toms River Twnshp, NJ	4.5
207	Southfield, MI	4.4
208	Palmdale, CA	4.2
208	Santa Rosa, CA	4.2
210	Little Rock, AR	4.1
211	Laredo, TX	4.0
212	Miami Gardens, FL	3.9
213	Los Angeles, CA	3.8
214	Costa Mesa, CA	3.6
214	Tampa, FL	3.6
216	Buffalo, NY	3.5
217	Miami, FL	3.3
218	Cape Coral, FL	3.2
219	Newark, NJ	3.1
220	Alhambra, CA	3.0
220	Seattle, WA	3.0
222	Greece, NY	2.9
222	Long Beach, CA	2.9
224	Boston, MA	2.8
225	Bridgeport, CT	2.7
226	Cincinnati, OH	2.6
227	Racine, WI	2.3
228	Jacksonville, FL	2.2
229	North Charleston, SC	2.1
230	Ogden, UT	2.0
231	Broken Arrow, OK	1.9
232	Waterbury, CT	1.8
233	Peoria, IL	1.5
234	Beaumont, TX	1.4
235	Spokane Valley, WA	1.3
236	Rancho Cucamon., CA	1.0
237	Chula Vista, CA	0.9
238	Houston, TX	0.8
239	Birmingham, AL	0.4
240	Aurora, IL	0.1
241	Chicago, IL	(0.1)
241	Downey, CA	(0.1)
243	Mesquite, TX	(0.2)
244	Albuquerque, NM	(0.3)
245	Fresno, CA	(0.4)
245	Lowell, MA	(0.4)
247	Lynn, MA	(0.5)
247	Phoenix, AZ	(0.5)
249	Bakersfield, CA	(0.7)
250	Indianapolis, IN	(0.9)
250	Woodbridge Twnshp, NJ	(0.9)
252	Dallas, TX	(1.0)
252	Richardson, TX	(1.0)
254	Hialeah, FL	(1.1)
254	Naperville, IL	(1.1)
254	Worcester, MA	(1.1)
257	San Bernardino, CA	(1.2)
258	Nashville, TN	(1.3)

RANK	CITY	% CHANGE
258	Quincy, MA	(1.3)
260	Alexandria, VA	(1.5)
260	Shreveport, LA	(1.5)
260	Sioux City, IA	(1.5)
263	Elizabeth, NJ	(1.6)
263	Overland Park, KS	(1.6)
265	Tacoma, WA	(1.7)
265	Tucson, AZ	(1.7)
267	Fort Worth, TX	(1.8)
267	Hampton, VA	(1.8)
269	Savannah, GA	(1.9)
270	Oklahoma City, OK	(2.0)
271	Raleigh, NC	(2.2)
272	Columbia, SC	(2.4)
273	Knoxville, TN	(2.6)
273	Washington, DC	(2.6)
275	Syracuse, NY	(2.8)
276	Irving, TX	(2.9)
277	Waco, TX	(3.1)
278	Columbia, MO	(3.2)
279	Youngstown, OH	(3.3)
280	Roanoke, VA	(3.4)
281	Columbus, OH	(3.6)
281	Yonkers, NY	(3.6)
283	Torrance, CA	(3.7)
284	Dayton, OH	(4.1)
285	Bellflower, CA	(4.2)
286	Clearwater, FL	(4.3)
286	Richmond, CA	(4.3)
288	Carlsbad, CA	(4.5)
289	Corpus Christi, TX	(4.6)
290	Whittier, CA	(4.7)
291	Louisville, KY	(5.0)
292	Cranston, RI	(5.4)
293	Centennial, CO	(5.5)
293	Jersey City, NJ	(5.5)
293	New York, NY	(5.5)
296	Salem, OR	(5.7)
297	Lakewood, CO	(5.9)
298	Colonie, NY	(6.3)
299	Oceanside, CA	(6.6)
300	Toledo, OH	(6.9)
301	Federal Way, WA	(7.0)
302	Somerville, MA	(7.2)
303	Garland, TX	(7.5)
304	Las Cruces, NM	(7.7)
305	McAllen, TX	(7.9)
306	Buena Park, CA	(8.1)
306	Chesapeake, VA	(8.1)
306	Clifton, NJ	(8.1)
309	Athens-Clarke, GA	(8.2)
310	Atlanta, GA	(8.3)
311	Portsmouth, VA	(8.6)
312	El Cajon, CA	(8.7)
313	Tulsa, OK	(8.9)
314	Aurora, CO	(9.0)
315	Longview, TX	(9.3)
316	Providence, RI	(9.6)
317	Pompano Beach, FL	(9.9)
318	Hammond, IN	(10.0)
319	Carrollton, TX	(10.2)
320	South Gate, CA	(10.7)
321	Albany, NY	(11.0)
322	Denver, CO	(11.2)
323	Newport News, VA	(11.4)
324	Grand Prairie, TX	(11.8)

RANK	CITY	% CHANGE
325	Inglewood, CA	(12.0)
326	Springfield, MA	(12.1)
327	Palm Bay, FL	(12.3)
328	Cambridge, MA	(13.2)
328	Redding, CA	(13.2)
330	Pasadena, CA	(13.3)
330	Suffolk, VA	(13.3)
332	Billings, MT	(13.7)
333	Miami Beach, FL	(14.5)
334	Deerfield Beach, FL	(14.7)
335	Boulder, CO	(14.8)
336	Charlotte, NC	(14.9)
336	Farmington Hills, MI	(14.9)
338	Vancouver, WA	(15.2)
339	Ann Arbor, MI	(16.2)
340	Cheektowaga, NY	(16.8)
341	Charleston, SC	(17.1)
342	Richmond, VA	(17.7)
343	McKinney, TX	(18.2)
344	Mission Viejo, CA	(18.5)
345	Montgomery, AL	(18.9)
346	Vista, CA	(19.2)
347	Greeley, CO	(19.8)
348	Miramar, FL	(20.1)
349	Denton, TX	(20.2)
350	Cary, NC	(20.4)
351	Trenton, NJ	(20.7)
352	Arvada, CO	(20.8)
353	Murrieta, CA	(22.7)
354	El Monte, CA	(22.8)
355	Lake Forest, CA	(23.9)
356	Parma, OH	(24.4)
357	Edmond, OK	(24.5)
358	Dearborn, MI	(25.1)
359	Temecula, CA	(25.5)
360	Thousand Oaks, CA	(26.5)
361	Westminster, CO	(27.0)
362	Thornton, CO	(27.2)
363	Abilene, TX	(27.5)
364	Amherst, NY	(28.7)
365	Lincoln, NE	(28.8)
366	San Mateo, CA	(29.1)
367	Wichita Falls, TX	(29.4)
368	Lee's Summit, MO	(29.7)
369	Sugar Land, TX	(30.1)
370	Beaverton, OR	(32.8)
371	Sterling Heights, MI	(34.9)
372	Hesperia, CA	(35.1)
373	Canton Twnshp, MI	(35.4)
374	Fort Collins, CO	(37.7)
375	Tyler, TX	(38.4)
376	Sioux Falls, SD	(53.1)
NA	Bloomington, MN**	NA
NA	Clarkstown, NY**	NA
NA	Des Moines, IA**	NA
NA	Duluth, MN**	NA
NA	Durham, NC**	NA
NA	El Paso, TX**	NA
NA	Fort Wayne, IN**	NA
NA	Kansas City, MO**	NA
NA	Lexington, KY**	NA
NA	New Orleans, LA**	NA
NA	Rockford, IL**	NA
NA	Vallejo, CA**	NA
NA	West Jordan, UT**	NA
NA	Wichita, KS**	NA

Source: CQ Press using data from F.B.I. "Crime in the United States 2006"

**Robbery is the taking of anything of value by force or threat of force. Attempts are included.*

***Not available.*

60. Percent Change in Robbery Rate: 2002 to 2006

National Percent Change = 2.3% Increase*

RANK	CITY	% CHANGE
223	Abilene, TX	(1.1)
147	Albany, GA	14.2
NA	Albany, NY**	NA
302	Albuquerque, NM	(17.4)
151	Alexandria, VA	13.1
159	Alhambra, CA	12.2
3	Allentown, PA	132.7
128	Amarillo, TX	17.1
341	Amherst, NY	(29.8)
85	Anaheim, CA	27.6
127	Anchorage, AK	17.2
220	Ann Arbor, MI	(0.3)
47	Antioch, CA	40.9
194	Arlington, TX	4.5
278	Arvada, CO	(11.6)
320	Athens-Clarke, GA	(22.1)
353	Atlanta, GA	(36.4)
194	Aurora, CO	4.5
232	Aurora, IL	(3.3)
161	Austin, TX	11.7
68	Bakersfield, CA	32.8
117	Baldwin Park, CA	20.3
249	Baltimore, MD	(5.6)
202	Baton Rouge, LA	2.9
285	Beaumont, TX	(12.8)
360	Beaverton, OR	(49.1)
51	Bellevue, WA	40.2
185	Bellflower, CA	6.8
228	Bellingham, WA	(2.4)
187	Berkeley, CA	6.6
347	Billings, MT	(32.3)
88	Birmingham, AL	26.4
278	Bloomington, MN	(11.6)
209	Boca Raton, FL	1.4
81	Boise, ID	28.4
153	Boston, MA	13.0
346	Boulder, CO	(31.7)
348	Brick Twnshp, NJ	(32.5)
114	Bridgeport, CT	21.3
188	Brockton, MA	6.3
300	Broken Arrow, OK	(16.7)
318	Brownsville, TX	(21.4)
78	Buena Park, CA	28.7
170	Buffalo, NY	10.6
332	Burbank, CA	(25.8)
176	Cambridge, MA	8.7
76	Camden, NJ	29.7
314	Canton Twnshp, MI	(20.5)
NA	Canton, OH**	NA
36	Cape Coral, FL	48.3
54	Carlsbad, CA	39.2
272	Carrollton, TX	(9.4)
91	Carson, CA	25.8
289	Cary, NC	(14.0)
83	Cedar Rapids, IA	28.1
NA	Centennial, CO**	NA
110	Chandler, AZ	22.1
287	Charleston, SC	(13.6)
204	Charlotte, NC	2.5
288	Chattanooga, TN	(13.9)
NA	Cheektowaga, NY**	NA
310	Chesapeake, VA	(19.6)
281	Chicago, IL	(12.0)
366	Chino Hills, CA	(76.6)

RANK	CITY	% CHANGE
1	Chino, CA	377.5
133	Chula Vista, CA	15.8
193	Cincinnati, OH	4.6
365	Clarkstown, NY	(68.8)
5	Clarksville, TN	119.3
326	Clearwater, FL	(23.7)
53	Cleveland, OH	39.7
350	Clifton, NJ	(33.1)
24	Clinton Twnshp, MI	67.4
119	Clovis, CA	19.9
241	Colonie, NY	(4.8)
105	Colorado Springs, CO	23.6
131	Columbia, MO	16.4
328	Columbia, SC	(24.5)
26	Columbus, GA	64.7
206	Columbus, OH	1.8
162	Compton, CA	11.3
18	Concord, CA	76.0
253	Coral Springs, FL	(7.2)
323	Corona, CA	(22.7)
270	Corpus Christi, TX	(9.0)
84	Costa Mesa, CA	27.7
205	Cranston, RI	2.2
292	Dallas, TX	(14.5)
89	Daly City, CA	25.9
271	Danbury, CT	(9.1)
237	Davie, FL	(3.9)
312	Dayton, OH	(20.2)
72	Dearborn, MI	31.8
10	Deerfield Beach, FL	88.8
351	Denton, TX	(34.5)
174	Denver, CO	9.7
NA	Des Moines, IA**	NA
96	Detroit, MI	25.2
82	Downey, CA	28.3
77	Duluth, MN	29.4
NA	Durham, NC**	NA
112	Edison Twnshp, NJ	21.8
267	Edmond, OK	(8.4)
74	El Cajon, CA	29.8
344	El Monte, CA	(31.4)
NA	El Paso, TX**	NA
266	Elizabeth, NJ	(8.2)
43	Erie, PA	42.4
38	Escondido, CA	45.7
233	Eugene, OR	(3.4)
38	Evansville, IN	45.7
102	Everett, WA	24.3
184	Fairfield, CA	7.0
62	Fargo, ND	34.0
259	Farmington Hills, MI	(7.8)
170	Fayetteville, NC	10.6
58	Federal Way, WA	37.1
34	Flint, MI	49.2
330	Fontana, CA	(25.1)
225	Fort Collins, CO	(2.1)
131	Fort Lauderdale, FL	16.4
298	Fort Smith, AR	(16.0)
NA	Fort Wayne, IN**	NA
331	Fort Worth, TX	(25.2)
9	Fremont, CA	99.4
302	Fresno, CA	(17.4)
60	Fullerton, CA	35.3
108	Gainesville, FL	22.6

RANK	CITY	% CHANGE
133	Garden Grove, CA	15.8
316	Garland, TX	(21.0)
299	Gary, IN	(16.2)
321	Gilbert, AZ	(22.3)
179	Glendale, AZ	7.8
274	Glendale, CA	(10.1)
336	Grand Prairie, TX	(27.5)
42	Grand Rapids, MI	42.6
NA	Greece, NY**	NA
262	Greeley, CO	(7.9)
35	Green Bay, WI	48.5
93	Greensboro, NC	25.6
144	Gresham, OR	14.6
116	Hamilton Twnshp, NJ	20.9
236	Hammond, IN	(3.8)
245	Hampton, VA	(5.1)
294	Hartford, CT	(15.4)
286	Hawthorne, CA	(13.0)
63	Hayward, CA	33.9
250	Henderson, NV	(5.7)
257	Hesperia, CA	(7.7)
267	Hialeah, FL	(8.4)
269	High Point, NC	(8.5)
179	Hillsboro, OR	7.8
234	Hollywood, FL	(3.6)
282	Honolulu, HI	(12.1)
218	Houston, TX	(0.2)
23	Huntington Beach, CA	68.4
12	Huntsville, AL	86.4
139	Independence, MO	15.1
164	Indianapolis, IN	11.0
230	Inglewood, CA	(3.1)
355	Irvine, CA	(36.6)
189	Irving, TX	6.2
173	Jacksonville, FL	10.5
218	Jackson, MS	(0.2)
142	Jersey City, NJ	14.9
305	Joliet, IL	(17.8)
NA	Kansas City, KS**	NA
NA	Kansas City, MO**	NA
13	Kenosha, WI	82.1
17	Kent, WA	76.3
52	Killeen, TX	39.8
248	Knoxville, TN	(5.5)
48	Lafayette, LA	40.7
340	Lake Forest, CA	(29.1)
333	Lakeland, FL	(26.5)
22	Lakewood, CA	68.8
78	Lakewood, CO	28.7
93	Lancaster, CA	25.6
160	Lansing, MI	11.8
157	Laredo, TX	12.5
16	Largo, FL	77.7
NA	Las Cruces, NM**	NA
98	Las Vegas, NV	25.0
15	Lawrence, KS	80.6
136	Lawton, OK	15.5
362	Lee's Summit, MO	(51.5)
277	Lewisville, TX	(11.4)
NA	Lexington, KY**	NA
290	Lincoln, NE	(14.1)
211	Little Rock, AR	1.1
86	Livermore, CA	27.4
168	Livonia, MI	10.8

Alpha Order- City (continued)

RANK	CITY	% CHANGE
240	Long Beach, CA	(4.3)
349	Longview, TX	(32.6)
304	Los Angeles, CA	(17.6)
NA	Louisville, KY**	NA
56	Lowell, MA	38.3
128	Lubbock, TX	17.1
32	Lynn, MA	50.8
27	Macon, GA	55.8
29	Madison, WI	54.9
59	Manchester, NH	35.7
358	McAllen, TX	(39.5)
363	McKinney, TX	(54.0)
107	Melbourne, FL	23.2
111	Memphis, TN	21.9
317	Mesa, AZ	(21.1)
106	Mesquite, TX	23.3
284	Miami Beach, FL	(12.4)
NA	Miami Gardens, FL**	NA
329	Miami, FL	(24.8)
217	Midland, TX	(0.1)
125	Milwaukee, WI	17.6
20	Minneapolis, MN	75.6
357	Miramar, FL	(38.6)
30	Mission Viejo, CA	53.8
252	Mobile, AL	(6.6)
89	Modesto, CA	25.9
222	Montgomery, AL	(1.0)
46	Moreno Valley, CA	41.4
4	Murfreesboro, TN	123.0
214	Murrieta, CA	0.3
6	Napa, CA	118.4
18	Naperville, IL	76.0
NA	Nashua, NH**	NA
130	Nashville, TN	16.5
NA	New Bedford, MA**	NA
364	New Orleans, LA	(57.0)
292	New York, NY	(14.5)
307	Newark, NJ	(18.3)
167	Newport Beach, CA	10.9
140	Newport News, VA	15.0
NA	Newton, MA**	NA
57	Norfolk, VA	37.8
181	Norman, OK	7.3
143	North Charleston, SC	14.7
275	North Las Vegas, NV	(10.5)
103	Norwalk, CA	24.0
33	Oakland, CA	49.7
291	Oceanside, CA	(14.4)
227	Odessa, TX	(2.3)
73	Ogden, UT	31.0
234	Oklahoma City, OK	(3.6)
224	Olathe, KS	(1.3)
310	Omaha, NE	(19.6)
213	Ontario, CA	0.5
64	Orange, CA	33.5
215	Orem, UT	0.0
69	Orlando, FL	32.5
101	Overland Park, KS	24.6
155	Oxnard, CA	12.9
339	Palm Bay, FL	(28.8)
104	Palmdale, CA	23.9
115	Parma, OH	21.0
253	Pasadena, CA	(7.2)
164	Pasadena, TX	11.0
92	Paterson, NJ	25.7
196	Pembroke Pines, FL	4.0

RANK	CITY	% CHANGE
231	Peoria, AZ	(3.2)
203	Peoria, IL	2.7
78	Philadelphia, PA	28.7
221	Phoenix, AZ	(0.9)
158	Pittsburgh, PA	12.4
238	Plano, TX	(4.2)
164	Plantation, FL	11.0
200	Pomona, CA	3.4
49	Pompano Beach, FL	40.6
318	Port St. Lucie, FL	(21.4)
212	Portland, OR	0.7
309	Portsmouth, VA	(19.0)
342	Providence, RI	(30.4)
229	Provo, UT	(2.8)
190	Pueblo, CO	5.2
192	Quincy, MA	5.0
153	Racine, WI	13.0
264	Raleigh, NC	(8.1)
156	Rancho Cucamon., CA	12.7
264	Reading, PA	(8.1)
322	Redding, CA	(22.5)
178	Reno, NV	8.5
168	Rialto, CA	10.8
243	Richardson, TX	(5.0)
186	Richmond, CA	6.7
313	Richmond, VA	(20.3)
122	Riverside, CA	19.4
NA	Roanoke, VA**	NA
21	Rochester, MN	72.5
41	Rochester, NY	43.6
NA	Rockford, IL**	NA
8	Roseville, CA	108.0
14	Roswell, GA	81.2
338	Round Rock, TX	(28.0)
135	Sacramento, CA	15.6
325	Salem, OR	(22.9)
170	Salinas, CA	10.6
176	Salt Lake City, UT	8.7
87	San Angelo, TX	26.6
207	San Antonio, TX	1.6
225	San Bernardino, CA	(2.1)
67	San Diego, CA	33.1
74	San Francisco, CA	29.8
93	San Jose, CA	25.6
44	San Leandro, CA	42.1
278	San Mateo, CA	(11.6)
255	Sandy, UT	(7.4)
259	Santa Ana, CA	(7.8)
70	Santa Barbara, CA	32.3
243	Santa Clara, CA	(5.0)
66	Santa Clarita, CA	33.2
NA	Santa Maria, CA**	NA
297	Santa Monica, CA	(15.7)
198	Santa Rosa, CA	3.8
345	Savannah, GA	(31.6)
305	Scottsdale, AZ	(17.8)
191	Seattle, WA	5.1
251	Shreveport, LA	(6.4)
7	Simi Valley, CA	115.1
337	Sioux City, IA	(27.7)
359	Sioux Falls, SD	(41.8)
181	Somerville, MA	7.3
96	South Bend, IN	25.2
308	South Gate, CA	(18.8)
70	Southfield, MI	32.3
199	Sparks, NV	3.5

RANK	CITY	% CHANGE
NA	Spokane Valley, WA**	NA
196	Spokane, WA	4.0
210	Springfield, IL	1.2
125	Springfield, MA	17.6
137	Springfield, MO	15.2
295	Sterling Heights, MI	(15.5)
150	Stockton, CA	13.3
149	St. Louis, MO	13.6
257	St. Paul, MN	(7.7)
201	St. Petersburg, FL	3.0
315	Suffolk, VA	(20.8)
356	Sugar Land, TX	(37.3)
113	Sunnyvale, CA	21.7
123	Sunrise, FL	18.9
343	Surprise, AZ	(31.3)
208	Syracuse, NY	1.5
242	Tacoma, WA	(4.9)
140	Tallahassee, FL	15.0
361	Tampa, FL	(50.3)
49	Temecula, CA	40.6
99	Tempe, AZ	24.9
352	Thornton, CO	(36.2)
151	Thousand Oaks, CA	13.1
247	Toledo, OH	(5.3)
256	Toms River Twnshp, NJ	(7.6)
326	Topeka, KS	(23.7)
238	Torrance, CA	(4.2)
283	Tracy, CA	(12.2)
262	Trenton, NJ	(7.9)
99	Troy, MI	24.9
118	Tucson, AZ	20.0
148	Tulsa, OK	14.1
145	Tuscaloosa, AL	14.4
335	Tyler, TX	(27.3)
2	Upper Darby Twnshp, PA	161.9
25	Vacaville, CA	66.3
61	Vallejo, CA	34.7
301	Vancouver, WA	(17.3)
40	Ventura, CA	44.1
137	Victorville, CA	15.2
31	Virginia Beach, VA	51.4
45	Visalia, CA	41.9
55	Vista, CA	38.6
276	Waco, TX	(11.0)
109	Warren, MI	22.4
183	Warwick, RI	7.2
246	Washington, DC	(5.2)
324	Waterbury, CT	(22.8)
37	West Covina, CA	46.8
295	West Jordan, UT	(15.5)
215	West Palm Beach, FL	0.0
162	West Valley, UT	11.3
28	Westland, MI	55.7
273	Westminster, CA	(9.6)
NA	Westminster, CO**	NA
145	Whittier, CA	14.4
334	Wichita Falls, TX	(27.2)
353	Wichita, KS	(36.4)
259	Wilmington, NC	(7.8)
124	Winston-Salem, NC	18.4
175	Woodbridge Twnshp, NJ	9.5
NA	Worcester, MA**	NA
64	Yakima, WA	33.5
120	Yonkers, NY	19.5
120	Youngstown, OH	19.5
11	Yuma, AZ	87.6

Source: CQ Press using data from F.B.I. "Crime in the United States 2006"

**Robbery is the taking of anything of value by force or threat of force. Attempts are included.*

***Not available.*

60. Percent Change in Robbery Rate: 2002 to 2006 (continued)

National Percent Change = 2.3% Increase*

RANK	CITY	% CHANGE
1	Chino, CA	377.5
2	Upper Darby Twnshp, PA	161.9
3	Allentown, PA	132.7
4	Murfreesboro, TN	123.0
5	Clarksville, TN	119.3
6	Napa, CA	118.4
7	Simi Valley, CA	115.1
8	Roseville, CA	108.0
9	Fremont, CA	99.4
10	Deerfield Beach, FL	88.8
11	Yuma, AZ	87.6
12	Huntsville, AL	86.4
13	Kenosha, WI	82.1
14	Roswell, GA	81.2
15	Lawrence, KS	80.6
16	Largo, FL	77.7
17	Kent, WA	76.3
18	Concord, CA	76.0
18	Naperville, IL	76.0
20	Minneapolis, MN	75.6
21	Rochester, MN	72.5
22	Lakewood, CA	68.8
23	Huntington Beach, CA	68.4
24	Clinton Twnshp, MI	67.4
25	Vacaville, CA	66.3
26	Columbus, GA	64.7
27	Macon, GA	55.8
28	Westland, MI	55.7
29	Madison, WI	54.9
30	Mission Viejo, CA	53.8
31	Virginia Beach, VA	51.4
32	Lynn, MA	50.8
33	Oakland, CA	49.7
34	Flint, MI	49.2
35	Green Bay, WI	48.5
36	Cape Coral, FL	48.3
37	West Covina, CA	46.8
38	Escondido, CA	45.7
38	Evansville, IN	45.7
40	Ventura, CA	44.1
41	Rochester, NY	43.6
42	Grand Rapids, MI	42.6
43	Erie, PA	42.4
44	San Leandro, CA	42.1
45	Visalia, CA	41.9
46	Moreno Valley, CA	41.4
47	Antioch, CA	40.9
48	Lafayette, LA	40.7
49	Pompano Beach, FL	40.6
49	Temecula, CA	40.6
51	Bellevue, WA	40.2
52	Killeen, TX	39.8
53	Cleveland, OH	39.7
54	Carlsbad, CA	39.2
55	Vista, CA	38.6
56	Lowell, MA	38.3
57	Norfolk, VA	37.8
58	Federal Way, WA	37.1
59	Manchester, NH	35.7
60	Fullerton, CA	35.3
61	Vallejo, CA	34.7
62	Fargo, ND	34.0
63	Hayward, CA	33.9
64	Orange, CA	33.5
64	Yakima, WA	33.5
66	Santa Clarita, CA	33.2
67	San Diego, CA	33.1
68	Bakersfield, CA	32.8
69	Orlando, FL	32.5
70	Santa Barbara, CA	32.3
70	Southfield, MI	32.3
72	Dearborn, MI	31.8
73	Ogden, UT	31.0
74	El Cajon, CA	29.8
74	San Francisco, CA	29.8
76	Camden, NJ	29.7
77	Duluth, MN	29.4
78	Buena Park, CA	28.7
78	Lakewood, CO	28.7
78	Philadelphia, PA	28.7
81	Boise, ID	28.4
82	Downey, CA	28.3
83	Cedar Rapids, IA	28.1
84	Costa Mesa, CA	27.7
85	Anaheim, CA	27.6
86	Livermore, CA	27.4
87	San Angelo, TX	26.6
88	Birmingham, AL	26.4
89	Daly City, CA	25.9
89	Modesto, CA	25.9
91	Carson, CA	25.8
92	Paterson, NJ	25.7
93	Greensboro, NC	25.6
93	Lancaster, CA	25.6
93	San Jose, CA	25.6
96	Detroit, MI	25.2
96	South Bend, IN	25.2
98	Las Vegas, NV	25.0
99	Tempe, AZ	24.9
99	Troy, MI	24.9
101	Overland Park, KS	24.6
102	Everett, WA	24.3
103	Norwalk, CA	24.0
104	Palmdale, CA	23.9
105	Colorado Springs, CO	23.6
106	Mesquite, TX	23.3
107	Melbourne, FL	23.2
108	Gainesville, FL	22.6
109	Warren, MI	22.4
110	Chandler, AZ	22.1
111	Memphis, TN	21.9
112	Edison Twnshp, NJ	21.8
113	Sunnyvale, CA	21.7
114	Bridgeport, CT	21.3
115	Parma, OH	21.0
116	Hamilton Twnshp, NJ	20.9
117	Baldwin Park, CA	20.3
118	Tucson, AZ	20.0
119	Clovis, CA	19.9
120	Yonkers, NY	19.5
120	Youngstown, OH	19.5
122	Riverside, CA	19.4
123	Sunrise, FL	18.9
124	Winston-Salem, NC	18.4
125	Milwaukee, WI	17.6
125	Springfield, MA	17.6
127	Anchorage, AK	17.2
128	Amarillo, TX	17.1
128	Lubbock, TX	17.1
130	Nashville, TN	16.5
131	Columbia, MO	16.4
131	Fort Lauderdale, FL	16.4
133	Chula Vista, CA	15.8
133	Garden Grove, CA	15.8
135	Sacramento, CA	15.6
136	Lawton, OK	15.5
137	Springfield, MO	15.2
137	Victorville, CA	15.2
139	Independence, MO	15.1
140	Newport News, VA	15.0
140	Tallahassee, FL	15.0
142	Jersey City, NJ	14.9
143	North Charleston, SC	14.7
144	Gresham, OR	14.6
145	Tuscaloosa, AL	14.4
145	Whittier, CA	14.4
147	Albany, GA	14.2
148	Tulsa, OK	14.1
149	St. Louis, MO	13.6
150	Stockton, CA	13.3
151	Alexandria, VA	13.1
151	Thousand Oaks, CA	13.1
153	Boston, MA	13.0
153	Racine, WI	13.0
155	Oxnard, CA	12.9
156	Rancho Cucamon., CA	12.7
157	Laredo, TX	12.5
158	Pittsburgh, PA	12.4
159	Alhambra, CA	12.2
160	Lansing, MI	11.8
161	Austin, TX	11.7
162	Compton, CA	11.3
162	West Valley, UT	11.3
164	Indianapolis, IN	11.0
164	Pasadena, TX	11.0
164	Plantation, FL	11.0
167	Newport Beach, CA	10.9
168	Livonia, MI	10.8
168	Rialto, CA	10.8
170	Buffalo, NY	10.6
170	Fayetteville, NC	10.6
170	Salinas, CA	10.6
173	Jacksonville, FL	10.5
174	Denver, CO	9.7
175	Woodbridge Twnshp, NJ	9.5
176	Cambridge, MA	8.7
176	Salt Lake City, UT	8.7
178	Reno, NV	8.5
179	Glendale, AZ	7.8
179	Hillsboro, OR	7.8
181	Norman, OK	7.3
181	Somerville, MA	7.3
183	Warwick, RI	7.2
184	Fairfield, CA	7.0
185	Bellflower, CA	6.8
186	Richmond, CA	6.7
187	Berkeley, CA	6.6
188	Brockton, MA	6.3
189	Irving, TX	6.2
190	Pueblo, CO	5.2
191	Seattle, WA	5.1
192	Quincy, MA	5.0

RANK	CITY	% CHANGE
193	Cincinnati, OH	4.6
194	Arlington, TX	4.5
194	Aurora, CO	4.5
196	Pembroke Pines, FL	4.0
196	Spokane, WA	4.0
198	Santa Rosa, CA	3.8
199	Sparks, NV	3.5
200	Pomona, CA	3.4
201	St. Petersburg, FL	3.0
202	Baton Rouge, LA	2.9
203	Peoria, IL	2.7
204	Charlotte, NC	2.5
205	Cranston, RI	2.2
206	Columbus, OH	1.8
207	San Antonio, TX	1.6
208	Syracuse, NY	1.5
209	Boca Raton, FL	1.4
210	Springfield, IL	1.2
211	Little Rock, AR	1.1
212	Portland, OR	0.7
213	Ontario, CA	0.5
214	Murrieta, CA	0.3
215	Orem, UT	0.0
215	West Palm Beach, FL	0.0
217	Midland, TX	(0.1)
218	Houston, TX	(0.2)
218	Jackson, MS	(0.2)
220	Ann Arbor, MI	(0.3)
221	Phoenix, AZ	(0.9)
222	Montgomery, AL	(1.0)
223	Abilene, TX	(1.1)
224	Olathe, KS	(1.3)
225	Fort Collins, CO	(2.1)
225	San Bernardino, CA	(2.1)
227	Odessa, TX	(2.3)
228	Bellingham, WA	(2.4)
229	Provo, UT	(2.8)
230	Inglewood, CA	(3.1)
231	Peoria, AZ	(3.2)
232	Aurora, IL	(3.3)
233	Eugene, OR	(3.4)
234	Hollywood, FL	(3.6)
234	Oklahoma City, OK	(3.6)
236	Hammond, IN	(3.8)
237	Davie, FL	(3.9)
238	Plano, TX	(4.2)
238	Torrance, CA	(4.2)
240	Long Beach, CA	(4.3)
241	Colonie, NY	(4.8)
242	Tacoma, WA	(4.9)
243	Richardson, TX	(5.0)
243	Santa Clara, CA	(5.0)
245	Hampton, VA	(5.1)
246	Washington, DC	(5.2)
247	Toledo, OH	(5.3)
248	Knoxville, TN	(5.5)
249	Baltimore, MD	(5.6)
250	Henderson, NV	(5.7)
251	Shreveport, LA	(6.4)
252	Mobile, AL	(6.6)
253	Coral Springs, FL	(7.2)
253	Pasadena, CA	(7.2)
255	Sandy, UT	(7.4)
256	Toms River Twnshp, NJ	(7.6)
257	Hesperia, CA	(7.7)
257	St. Paul, MN	(7.7)
259	Farmington Hills, MI	(7.8)
259	Santa Ana, CA	(7.8)
259	Wilmington, NC	(7.8)
262	Greeley, CO	(7.9)
262	Trenton, NJ	(7.9)
264	Raleigh, NC	(8.1)
264	Reading, PA	(8.1)
266	Elizabeth, NJ	(8.2)
267	Edmond, OK	(8.4)
267	Hialeah, FL	(8.4)
269	High Point, NC	(8.5)
270	Corpus Christi, TX	(9.0)
271	Danbury, CT	(9.1)
272	Carrollton, TX	(9.4)
273	Westminster, CA	(9.6)
274	Glendale, CA	(10.1)
275	North Las Vegas, NV	(10.5)
276	Waco, TX	(11.0)
277	Lewisville, TX	(11.4)
278	Arvada, CO	(11.6)
278	Bloomington, MN	(11.6)
278	San Mateo, CA	(11.6)
281	Chicago, IL	(12.0)
282	Honolulu, HI	(12.1)
283	Tracy, CA	(12.2)
284	Miami Beach, FL	(12.4)
285	Beaumont, TX	(12.8)
286	Hawthorne, CA	(13.0)
287	Charleston, SC	(13.6)
288	Chattanooga, TN	(13.9)
289	Cary, NC	(14.0)
290	Lincoln, NE	(14.1)
291	Oceanside, CA	(14.4)
292	Dallas, TX	(14.5)
292	New York, NY	(14.5)
294	Hartford, CT	(15.4)
295	Sterling Heights, MI	(15.5)
295	West Jordan, UT	(15.5)
297	Santa Monica, CA	(15.7)
298	Fort Smith, AR	(16.0)
299	Gary, IN	(16.2)
300	Broken Arrow, OK	(16.7)
301	Vancouver, WA	(17.3)
302	Albuquerque, NM	(17.4)
302	Fresno, CA	(17.4)
304	Los Angeles, CA	(17.6)
305	Joliet, IL	(17.8)
305	Scottsdale, AZ	(17.8)
307	Newark, NJ	(18.3)
308	South Gate, CA	(18.8)
309	Portsmouth, VA	(19.0)
310	Chesapeake, VA	(19.6)
310	Omaha, NE	(19.6)
312	Dayton, OH	(20.2)
313	Richmond, VA	(20.3)
314	Canton Twnshp, MI	(20.5)
315	Suffolk, VA	(20.8)
316	Garland, TX	(21.0)
317	Mesa, AZ	(21.1)
318	Brownsville, TX	(21.4)
318	Port St. Lucie, FL	(21.4)
320	Athens-Clarke, GA	(22.1)
321	Gilbert, AZ	(22.3)
322	Redding, CA	(22.5)
323	Corona, CA	(22.7)
324	Waterbury, CT	(22.8)
325	Salem, OR	(22.9)
326	Clearwater, FL	(23.7)
326	Topeka, KS	(23.7)
328	Columbia, SC	(24.5)
329	Miami, FL	(24.8)
330	Fontana, CA	(25.1)
331	Fort Worth, TX	(25.2)
332	Burbank, CA	(25.8)
333	Lakeland, FL	(26.5)
334	Wichita Falls, TX	(27.2)
335	Tyler, TX	(27.3)
336	Grand Prairie, TX	(27.5)
337	Sioux City, IA	(27.7)
338	Round Rock, TX	(28.0)
339	Palm Bay, FL	(28.8)
340	Lake Forest, CA	(29.1)
341	Amherst, NY	(29.8)
342	Providence, RI	(30.4)
343	Surprise, AZ	(31.3)
344	El Monte, CA	(31.4)
345	Savannah, GA	(31.6)
346	Boulder, CO	(31.7)
347	Billings, MT	(32.3)
348	Brick Twnshp, NJ	(32.5)
349	Longview, TX	(32.6)
350	Clifton, NJ	(33.1)
351	Denton, TX	(34.5)
352	Thornton, CO	(36.2)
353	Atlanta, GA	(36.4)
353	Wichita, KS	(36.4)
355	Irvine, CA	(36.6)
356	Sugar Land, TX	(37.3)
357	Miramar, FL	(38.6)
358	McAllen, TX	(39.5)
359	Sioux Falls, SD	(41.8)
360	Beaverton, OR	(49.1)
361	Tampa, FL	(50.3)
362	Lee's Summit, MO	(51.5)
363	McKinney, TX	(54.0)
364	New Orleans, LA	(57.0)
365	Clarkstown, NY	(68.8)
366	Chino Hills, CA	(76.6)
NA	Albany, NY**	NA
NA	Canton, OH**	NA
NA	Centennial, CO**	NA
NA	Cheektowaga, NY**	NA
NA	Des Moines, IA**	NA
NA	Durham, NC**	NA
NA	El Paso, TX**	NA
NA	Fort Wayne, IN**	NA
NA	Greece, NY**	NA
NA	Kansas City, KS**	NA
NA	Kansas City, MO**	NA
NA	Las Cruces, NM**	NA
NA	Lexington, KY**	NA
NA	Louisville, KY**	NA
NA	Miami Gardens, FL**	NA
NA	Nashua, NH**	NA
NA	New Bedford, MA**	NA
NA	Newton, MA**	NA
NA	Roanoke, VA**	NA
NA	Rockford, IL**	NA
NA	Santa Maria, CA**	NA
NA	Spokane Valley, WA**	NA
NA	Westminster, CO**	NA
NA	Worcester, MA**	NA

Source: CQ Press using data from F.B.I. "Crime in the United States 2006"

**Robbery is the taking of anything of value by force or threat of force. Attempts are included.*

***Not available.*

61. Aggravated Assaults in 2006

National Total = 860,853 Aggravated Assaults*

RANK	CITY	ASSAULTS
203	Abilene, TX	375
244	Albany, GA	271
116	Albany, NY	774
28	Albuquerque, NM	3,059
281	Alexandria, VA	208
338	Alhambra, CA	119
210	Allentown, PA	339
80	Amarillo, TX	1,119
360	Amherst, NY	78
109	Anaheim, CA	823
51	Anchorage, AK	1,862
269	Ann Arbor, MI	227
213	Antioch, CA	327
55	Arlington, TX	1,632
336	Arvada, CO	120
295	Athens-Clarke, GA	190
17	Atlanta, GA	4,308
88	Aurora, CO	1,024
164	Aurora, IL	531
49	Austin, TX	1,961
94	Bakersfield, CA	959
302	Baldwin Park, CA	183
10	Baltimore, MD	6,173
53	Baton Rouge, LA	1,755
127	Beaumont, TX	726
315	Beaverton, OR	159
368	Bellevue, WA	68
276	Bellflower, CA	217
355	Bellingham, WA	87
286	Berkeley, CA	206
327	Billings, MT	135
63	Birmingham, AL	1,422
361	Bloomington, MN	77
317	Boca Raton, FL	150
166	Boise, ID	528
15	Boston, MA	4,485
311	Boulder, CO	164
374	Brick Twnshp, NJ	61
123	Bridgeport, CT	753
NA	Brockton, MA**	NA
322	Broken Arrow, OK	141
139	Brownsville, TX	648
324	Buena Park, CA	140
48	Buffalo, NY	2,001
310	Burbank, CA	166
262	Cambridge, MA	237
110	Camden, NJ	822
380	Canton Twnshp, MI	52
241	Canton, OH	278
247	Cape Coral, FL	265
260	Carlsbad, CA	240
330	Carrollton, TX	131
183	Carson, CA	439
363	Cary, NC	75
275	Cedar Rapids, IA	220
338	Centennial, CO	119
136	Chandler, AZ	658
140	Charleston, SC	647
20	Charlotte, NC	3,896
69	Chattanooga, TN	1,268
331	Cheektowaga, NY	130
145	Chesapeake, VA	618
2	Chicago, IL	17,445
351	Chino Hills, CA	93
342	Chino, CA	112
168	Chula Vista, CA	519
86	Cincinnati, OH	1,047
386	Clarkstown, NY	45
117	Clarksville, TN	772
146	Clearwater, FL	614
45	Cleveland, OH	2,196
350	Clifton, NJ	98
267	Clinton Twnshp, MI	229
361	Clovis, CA	77
374	Colonie, NY	61
70	Colorado Springs, CO	1,267
214	Columbia, MO	322
103	Columbia, SC	852
155	Columbus, GA	569
56	Columbus, OH	1,612
84	Compton, CA	1,049
255	Concord, CA	250
291	Coral Springs, FL	202
320	Corona, CA	144
64	Corpus Christi, TX	1,414
318	Costa Mesa, CA	147
370	Cranston, RI	66
8	Dallas, TX	7,292
328	Daly City, CA	134
377	Danbury, CT	55
293	Davie, FL	193
122	Dayton, OH	754
246	Dearborn, MI	269
196	Deerfield Beach, FL	390
289	Denton, TX	204
31	Denver, CO	2,652
100	Des Moines, IA	864
4	Detroit, MI	13,143
305	Downey, CA	177
271	Duluth, MN	224
99	Durham, NC	869
293	Edison Twnshp, NJ	193
385	Edmond, OK	46
237	El Cajon, CA	287
188	El Monte, CA	411
57	El Paso, TX	1,606
225	Elizabeth, NJ	306
281	Erie, PA	208
181	Escondido, CA	442
309	Eugene, OR	168
234	Evansville, IN	288
219	Everett, WA	316
204	Fairfield, CA	371
322	Fargo, ND	141
354	Farmington Hills, MI	88
128	Fayetteville, NC	713
336	Federal Way, WA	120
43	Flint, MI	2,246
156	Fontana, CA	564
198	Fort Collins, CO	381
124	Fort Lauderdale, FL	747
138	Fort Smith, AR	651
286	Fort Wayne, IN	206
37	Fort Worth, TX	2,496
241	Fremont, CA	278
46	Fresno, CA	2,057
256	Fullerton, CA	248
126	Gainesville, FL	737
189	Garden Grove, CA	410
227	Garland, TX	300
249	Gary, IN	262
313	Gilbert, AZ	161
93	Glendale, AZ	977
300	Glendale, CA	185
249	Grand Prairie, TX	262
78	Grand Rapids, MI	1,136
387	Greece, NY	43
208	Greeley, CO	362
192	Green Bay, WI	400
85	Greensboro, NC	1,048
221	Gresham, OR	314
353	Hamilton Twnshp, NJ	89
231	Hammond, IN	294
261	Hampton, VA	238
120	Hartford, CT	761
218	Hawthorne, CA	320
219	Hayward, CA	316
239	Henderson, NV	283
313	Hesperia, CA	161
102	Hialeah, FL	858
198	High Point, NC	381
359	Hillsboro, OR	79
234	Hollywood, FL	288
59	Honolulu, HI	1,543
5	Houston, TX	11,648
264	Huntington Beach, CA	233
129	Huntsville, AL	706
148	Independence, MO	612
23	Indianapolis, IN	3,751
172	Inglewood, CA	493
377	Irvine, CA	55
163	Irving, TX	535
18	Jacksonville, FL	4,031
169	Jackson, MS	514
72	Jersey City, NJ	1,255
197	Joliet, IL	387
132	Kansas City, KS	670
19	Kansas City, MO	3,994
325	Kenosha, WI	139
253	Kent, WA	254
179	Killeen, TX	452
73	Knoxville, TN	1,249
107	Lafayette, LA	828
371	Lake Forest, CA	65
212	Lakeland, FL	331
307	Lakewood, CA	172
185	Lakewood, CO	424
119	Lancaster, CA	767
114	Lansing, MI	800
112	Laredo, TX	814
227	Largo, FL	300
215	Las Cruces, NM	321
9	Las Vegas, NV	6,680
205	Lawrence, KS	370
132	Lawton, OK	670
356	Lee's Summit, MO	85
346	Lewisville, TX	105
83	Lexington, KY	1,070
91	Lincoln, NE	989
44	Little Rock, AR	2,216
365	Livermore, CA	73
357	Livonia, MI	83

RANK	CITY	ASSAULTS
52	Long Beach, CA	1,805
162	Longview, TX	536
3	Los Angeles, CA	14,634
50	Louisville, KY	1,873
137	Lowell, MA	654
54	Lubbock, TX	1,691
159	Lynn, MA	545
184	Macon, GA	430
177	Madison, WI	471
345	Manchester, NH	108
268	McAllen, TX	228
301	McKinney, TX	184
141	Melbourne, FL	641
7	Memphis, TN	7,661
71	Mesa, AZ	1,266
222	Mesquite, TX	310
150	Miami Beach, FL	598
75	Miami Gardens, FL	1,234
24	Miami, FL	3,642
263	Midland, TX	234
21	Milwaukee, WI	3,875
29	Minneapolis, MN	2,836
201	Miramar, FL	377
388	Mission Viejo, CA	40
207	Mobile, AL	365
98	Modesto, CA	872
194	Montgomery, AL	397
187	Moreno Valley, CA	412
173	Murfreesboro, TN	482
367	Murrieta, CA	71
258	Napa, CA	244
363	Naperville, IL	75
335	Nashua, NH	121
12	Nashville, TN	5,740
115	New Bedford, MA	795
74	New Orleans, LA	1,245
1	New York, NY	26,908
66	Newark, NJ	1,359
351	Newport Beach, CA	93
111	Newport News, VA	821
343	Newton, MA	111
118	Norfolk, VA	768
340	Norman, OK	118
107	North Charleston, SC	828
87	North Las Vegas, NV	1,032
229	Norwalk, CA	299
25	Oakland, CA	3,614
143	Oceanside, CA	635
170	Odessa, TX	512
254	Ogden, UT	253
30	Oklahoma City, OK	2,740
298	Olathe, KS	188
62	Omaha, NE	1,437
171	Ontario, CA	506
326	Orange, CA	137
389	Orem, UT	25
34	Orlando, FL	2,560
273	Overland Park, KS	221
202	Oxnard, CA	376
178	Palm Bay, FL	462
154	Palmdale, CA	575
381	Parma, OH	52
211	Pasadena, CA	334
195	Pasadena, TX	393
113	Paterson, NJ	812
279	Pembroke Pines, FL	213

RANK	CITY	ASSAULTS
292	Peoria, AZ	197
158	Peoria, IL	554
6	Philadelphia, PA	10,546
11	Phoenix, AZ	6,047
58	Pittsburgh, PA	1,593
160	Plano, TX	543
333	Plantation, FL	123
121	Pomona, CA	755
101	Pompano Beach, FL	862
248	Port St. Lucie, FL	263
42	Portland, OR	2,262
175	Portsmouth, VA	479
165	Providence, RI	530
346	Provo, UT	105
191	Pueblo, CO	403
299	Quincy, MA	187
283	Racine, WI	207
68	Raleigh, NC	1,325
295	Rancho Cucamon., CA	190
173	Reading, PA	482
256	Redding, CA	248
106	Reno, NV	832
206	Rialto, CA	367
334	Richardson, TX	122
142	Richmond, CA	637
96	Richmond, VA	902
82	Riverside, CA	1,106
134	Roanoke, VA	661
316	Rochester, MN	152
77	Rochester, NY	1,193
79	Rockford, IL	1,135
276	Roseville, CA	217
365	Roswell, GA	73
382	Round Rock, TX	50
27	Sacramento, CA	3,115
175	Salem, OR	479
131	Salinas, CA	683
97	Salt Lake City, UT	884
241	San Angelo, TX	278
13	San Antonio, TX	5,023
89	San Bernardino, CA	1,017
22	San Diego, CA	3,811
39	San Francisco, CA	2,435
41	San Jose, CA	2,285
223	San Leandro, CA	309
272	San Mateo, CA	222
349	Sandy, UT	99
81	Santa Ana, CA	1,112
215	Santa Barbara, CA	321
348	Santa Clara, CA	102
264	Santa Clarita, CA	233
153	Santa Maria, CA	584
225	Santa Monica, CA	306
143	Santa Rosa, CA	635
192	Savannah, GA	400
240	Scottsdale, AZ	282
40	Seattle, WA	2,326
60	Shreveport, LA	1,495
341	Simi Valley, CA	117
230	Sioux City, IA	296
245	Sioux Falls, SD	270
307	Somerville, MA	172
231	South Bend, IN	294
288	South Gate, CA	205
104	Southfield, MI	840
279	Sparks, NV	213

RANK	CITY	ASSAULTS
273	Spokane Valley, WA	221
130	Spokane, WA	704
67	Springfield, IL	1,329
61	Springfield, MA	1,448
134	Springfield, MO	661
283	Sterling Heights, MI	207
32	Stockton, CA	2,630
14	St. Louis, MO	4,992
65	St. Paul, MN	1,403
33	St. Petersburg, FL	2,588
252	Suffolk, VA	256
382	Sugar Land, TX	50
358	Sunnyvale, CA	81
266	Sunrise, FL	231
368	Surprise, AZ	68
95	Syracuse, NY	903
76	Tacoma, WA	1,233
90	Tallahassee, FL	998
38	Tampa, FL	2,470
283	Temecula, CA	207
152	Tempe, AZ	592
259	Thornton, CO	241
332	Thousand Oaks, CA	128
47	Toledo, OH	2,009
376	Toms River Twnshp, NJ	56
233	Topeka, KS	293
329	Torrance, CA	132
371	Tracy, CA	65
151	Trenton, NJ	593
377	Troy, MI	55
34	Tucson, AZ	2,560
26	Tulsa, OK	3,477
215	Tuscaloosa, AL	321
190	Tyler, TX	407
371	Upper Darby Twnshp, PA	65
321	Vacaville, CA	142
125	Vallejo, CA	739
209	Vancouver, WA	352
303	Ventura, CA	180
224	Victorville, CA	307
180	Virginia Beach, VA	444
149	Visalia, CA	600
251	Vista, CA	259
146	Waco, TX	614
167	Warren, MI	521
384	Warwick, RI	49
16	Washington, DC	4,453
319	Waterbury, CT	146
289	West Covina, CA	204
344	West Jordan, UT	109
161	West Palm Beach, FL	537
234	West Valley, UT	288
278	Westland, MI	216
306	Westminster, CA	176
295	Westminster, CO	190
304	Whittier, CA	179
238	Wichita Falls, TX	286
36	Wichita, KS	2,533
200	Wilmington, NC	379
105	Winston-Salem, NC	839
312	Woodbridge Twnshp, NJ	163
92	Worcester, MA	978
270	Yakima, WA	226
182	Yonkers, NY	441
157	Youngstown, OH	555
186	Yuma, AZ	422

Source: Federal Bureau of Investigation "Crime in the United States 2006"
**Aggravated assault is an attack for the purpose of inflicting severe bodily injury.*
***Not available.*

61. Aggravated Assaults in 2006 (continued)

National Total = 860,853 Aggravated Assaults*

RANK	CITY	ASSAULTS	RANK	CITY	ASSAULTS	RANK	CITY	ASSAULTS
1	New York, NY	26,908	65	St. Paul, MN	1,403	129	Huntsville, AL	706
2	Chicago, IL	17,445	66	Newark, NJ	1,359	130	Spokane, WA	704
3	Los Angeles, CA	14,634	67	Springfield, IL	1,329	131	Salinas, CA	683
4	Detroit, MI	13,143	68	Raleigh, NC	1,325	132	Kansas City, KS	670
5	Houston, TX	11,648	69	Chattanooga, TN	1,268	132	Lawton, OK	670
6	Philadelphia, PA	10,546	70	Colorado Springs, CO	1,267	134	Roanoke, VA	661
7	Memphis, TN	7,661	71	Mesa, AZ	1,266	134	Springfield, MO	661
8	Dallas, TX	7,292	72	Jersey City, NJ	1,255	136	Chandler, AZ	658
9	Las Vegas, NV	6,680	73	Knoxville, TN	1,249	137	Lowell, MA	654
10	Baltimore, MD	6,173	74	New Orleans, LA	1,245	138	Fort Smith, AR	651
11	Phoenix, AZ	6,047	75	Miami Gardens, FL	1,234	139	Brownsville, TX	648
12	Nashville, TN	5,740	76	Tacoma, WA	1,233	140	Charleston, SC	647
13	San Antonio, TX	5,023	77	Rochester, NY	1,193	141	Melbourne, FL	641
14	St. Louis, MO	4,992	78	Grand Rapids, MI	1,136	142	Richmond, CA	637
15	Boston, MA	4,485	79	Rockford, IL	1,135	143	Oceanside, CA	635
16	Washington, DC	4,453	80	Amarillo, TX	1,119	143	Santa Rosa, CA	635
17	Atlanta, GA	4,308	81	Santa Ana, CA	1,112	145	Chesapeake, VA	618
18	Jacksonville, FL	4,031	82	Riverside, CA	1,106	146	Clearwater, FL	614
19	Kansas City, MO	3,994	83	Lexington, KY	1,070	146	Waco, TX	614
20	Charlotte, NC	3,896	84	Compton, CA	1,049	148	Independence, MO	612
21	Milwaukee, WI	3,875	85	Greensboro, NC	1,048	149	Visalia, CA	600
22	San Diego, CA	3,811	86	Cincinnati, OH	1,047	150	Miami Beach, FL	598
23	Indianapolis, IN	3,751	87	North Las Vegas, NV	1,032	151	Trenton, NJ	593
24	Miami, FL	3,642	88	Aurora, CO	1,024	152	Tempe, AZ	592
25	Oakland, CA	3,614	89	San Bernardino, CA	1,017	153	Santa Maria, CA	584
26	Tulsa, OK	3,477	90	Tallahassee, FL	998	154	Palmdale, CA	575
27	Sacramento, CA	3,115	91	Lincoln, NE	989	155	Columbus, GA	569
28	Albuquerque, NM	3,059	92	Worcester, MA	978	156	Fontana, CA	564
29	Minneapolis, MN	2,836	93	Glendale, AZ	977	157	Youngstown, OH	555
30	Oklahoma City, OK	2,740	94	Bakersfield, CA	959	158	Peoria, IL	554
31	Denver, CO	2,652	95	Syracuse, NY	903	159	Lynn, MA	545
32	Stockton, CA	2,630	96	Richmond, VA	902	160	Plano, TX	543
33	St. Petersburg, FL	2,588	97	Salt Lake City, UT	884	161	West Palm Beach, FL	537
34	Orlando, FL	2,560	98	Modesto, CA	872	162	Longview, TX	536
34	Tucson, AZ	2,560	99	Durham, NC	869	163	Irving, TX	535
36	Wichita, KS	2,533	100	Des Moines, IA	864	164	Aurora, IL	531
37	Fort Worth, TX	2,496	101	Pompano Beach, FL	862	165	Providence, RI	530
38	Tampa, FL	2,470	102	Hialeah, FL	858	166	Boise, ID	528
39	San Francisco, CA	2,435	103	Columbia, SC	852	167	Warren, MI	521
40	Seattle, WA	2,326	104	Southfield, MI	840	168	Chula Vista, CA	519
41	San Jose, CA	2,285	105	Winston-Salem, NC	839	169	Jackson, MS	514
42	Portland, OR	2,262	106	Reno, NV	832	170	Odessa, TX	512
43	Flint, MI	2,246	107	Lafayette, LA	828	171	Ontario, CA	506
44	Little Rock, AR	2,216	107	North Charleston, SC	828	172	Inglewood, CA	493
45	Cleveland, OH	2,196	109	Anaheim, CA	823	173	Murfreesboro, TN	482
46	Fresno, CA	2,057	110	Camden, NJ	822	173	Reading, PA	482
47	Toledo, OH	2,009	111	Newport News, VA	821	175	Portsmouth, VA	479
48	Buffalo, NY	2,001	112	Laredo, TX	814	175	Salem, OR	479
49	Austin, TX	1,961	113	Paterson, NJ	812	177	Madison, WI	471
50	Louisville, KY	1,873	114	Lansing, MI	800	178	Palm Bay, FL	462
51	Anchorage, AK	1,862	115	New Bedford, MA	795	179	Killeen, TX	452
52	Long Beach, CA	1,805	116	Albany, NY	774	180	Virginia Beach, VA	444
53	Baton Rouge, LA	1,755	117	Clarksville, TN	772	181	Escondido, CA	442
54	Lubbock, TX	1,691	118	Norfolk, VA	768	182	Yonkers, NY	441
55	Arlington, TX	1,632	119	Lancaster, CA	767	183	Carson, CA	439
56	Columbus, OH	1,612	120	Hartford, CT	761	184	Macon, GA	430
57	El Paso, TX	1,606	121	Pomona, CA	755	185	Lakewood, CO	424
58	Pittsburgh, PA	1,593	122	Dayton, OH	754	186	Yuma, AZ	422
59	Honolulu, HI	1,543	123	Bridgeport, CT	753	187	Moreno Valley, CA	412
60	Shreveport, LA	1,495	124	Fort Lauderdale, FL	747	188	El Monte, CA	411
61	Springfield, MA	1,448	125	Vallejo, CA	739	189	Garden Grove, CA	410
62	Omaha, NE	1,437	126	Gainesville, FL	737	190	Tyler, TX	407
63	Birmingham, AL	1,422	127	Beaumont, TX	726	191	Pueblo, CO	403
64	Corpus Christi, TX	1,414	128	Fayetteville, NC	713	192	Green Bay, WI	400

RANK	CITY	ASSAULTS
192	Savannah, GA	400
194	Montgomery, AL	397
195	Pasadena, TX	393
196	Deerfield Beach, FL	390
197	Joliet, IL	387
198	Fort Collins, CO	381
198	High Point, NC	381
200	Wilmington, NC	379
201	Miramar, FL	377
202	Oxnard, CA	376
203	Abilene, TX	375
204	Fairfield, CA	371
205	Lawrence, KS	370
206	Rialto, CA	367
207	Mobile, AL	365
208	Greeley, CO	362
209	Vancouver, WA	352
210	Allentown, PA	339
211	Pasadena, CA	334
212	Lakeland, FL	331
213	Antioch, CA	327
214	Columbia, MO	322
215	Las Cruces, NM	321
215	Santa Barbara, CA	321
215	Tuscaloosa, AL	321
218	Hawthorne, CA	320
219	Everett, WA	316
219	Hayward, CA	316
221	Gresham, OR	314
222	Mesquite, TX	310
223	San Leandro, CA	309
224	Victorville, CA	307
225	Elizabeth, NJ	306
225	Santa Monica, CA	306
227	Garland, TX	300
227	Largo, FL	300
229	Norwalk, CA	299
230	Sioux City, IA	296
231	Hammond, IN	294
231	South Bend, IN	294
233	Topeka, KS	293
234	Evansville, IN	288
234	Hollywood, FL	288
234	West Valley, UT	288
237	El Cajon, CA	287
238	Wichita Falls, TX	286
239	Henderson, NV	283
240	Scottsdale, AZ	282
241	Canton, OH	278
241	Fremont, CA	278
241	San Angelo, TX	278
244	Albany, GA	271
245	Sioux Falls, SD	270
246	Dearborn, MI	269
247	Cape Coral, FL	265
248	Port St. Lucie, FL	263
249	Gary, IN	262
249	Grand Prairie, TX	262
251	Vista, CA	259
252	Suffolk, VA	256
253	Kent, WA	254
254	Ogden, UT	253
255	Concord, CA	250
256	Fullerton, CA	248
256	Redding, CA	248
258	Napa, CA	244
259	Thornton, CO	241
260	Carlsbad, CA	240
261	Hampton, VA	238
262	Cambridge, MA	237
263	Midland, TX	234
264	Huntington Beach, CA	233
264	Santa Clarita, CA	233
266	Sunrise, FL	231
267	Clinton Twnshp, MI	229
268	McAllen, TX	228
269	Ann Arbor, MI	227
270	Yakima, WA	226
271	Duluth, MN	224
272	San Mateo, CA	222
273	Overland Park, KS	221
273	Spokane Valley, WA	221
275	Cedar Rapids, IA	220
276	Bellflower, CA	217
276	Roseville, CA	217
278	Westland, MI	216
279	Pembroke Pines, FL	213
279	Sparks, NV	213
281	Alexandria, VA	208
281	Erie, PA	208
283	Racine, WI	207
283	Sterling Heights, MI	207
283	Temecula, CA	207
286	Berkeley, CA	206
286	Fort Wayne, IN	206
288	South Gate, CA	205
289	Denton, TX	204
289	West Covina, CA	204
291	Coral Springs, FL	202
292	Peoria, AZ	197
293	Davie, FL	193
293	Edison Twnshp, NJ	193
295	Athens-Clarke, GA	190
295	Rancho Cucamon., CA	190
295	Westminster, CO	190
298	Olathe, KS	188
299	Quincy, MA	187
300	Glendale, CA	185
301	McKinney, TX	184
302	Baldwin Park, CA	183
303	Ventura, CA	180
304	Whittier, CA	179
305	Downey, CA	177
306	Westminster, CA	176
307	Lakewood, CA	172
307	Somerville, MA	172
309	Eugene, OR	168
310	Burbank, CA	166
311	Boulder, CO	164
312	Woodbridge Twnshp, NJ	163
313	Gilbert, AZ	161
313	Hesperia, CA	161
315	Beaverton, OR	159
316	Rochester, MN	152
317	Boca Raton, FL	150
318	Costa Mesa, CA	147
319	Waterbury, CT	146
320	Corona, CA	144
321	Vacaville, CA	142
322	Broken Arrow, OK	141
322	Fargo, ND	141
324	Buena Park, CA	140
325	Kenosha, WI	139
326	Orange, CA	137
327	Billings, MT	135
328	Daly City, CA	134
329	Torrance, CA	132
330	Carrollton, TX	131
331	Cheektowaga, NY	130
332	Thousand Oaks, CA	128
333	Plantation, FL	123
334	Richardson, TX	122
335	Nashua, NH	121
336	Arvada, CO	120
336	Federal Way, WA	120
338	Alhambra, CA	119
338	Centennial, CO	119
340	Norman, OK	118
341	Simi Valley, CA	117
342	Chino, CA	112
343	Newton, MA	111
344	West Jordan, UT	109
345	Manchester, NH	108
346	Lewisville, TX	105
346	Provo, UT	105
348	Santa Clara, CA	102
349	Sandy, UT	99
350	Clifton, NJ	98
351	Chino Hills, CA	93
351	Newport Beach, CA	93
353	Hamilton Twnshp, NJ	89
354	Farmington Hills, MI	88
355	Bellingham, WA	87
356	Lee's Summit, MO	85
357	Livonia, MI	83
358	Sunnyvale, CA	81
359	Hillsboro, OR	79
360	Amherst, NY	78
361	Bloomington, MN	77
361	Clovis, CA	77
363	Cary, NC	75
363	Naperville, IL	75
365	Livermore, CA	73
365	Roswell, GA	73
367	Murrieta, CA	71
368	Bellevue, WA	68
368	Surprise, AZ	68
370	Cranston, RI	66
371	Lake Forest, CA	65
371	Tracy, CA	65
371	Upper Darby Twnshp, PA	65
374	Brick Twnshp, NJ	61
374	Colonie, NY	61
376	Toms River Twnshp, NJ	56
377	Danbury, CT	55
377	Irvine, CA	55
377	Troy, MI	55
380	Canton Twnshp, MI	52
381	Parma, OH	52
382	Round Rock, TX	50
382	Sugar Land, TX	50
384	Warwick, RI	49
385	Edmond, OK	46
386	Clarkstown, NY	45
387	Greece, NY	43
388	Mission Viejo, CA	40
389	Orem, UT	25
NA	Brockton, MA**	NA

Source: Federal Bureau of Investigation "Crime in the United States 2006"

**Aggravated assault is an attack for the purpose of inflicting severe bodily injury.*

***Not available.*

62. Aggravated Assault Rate in 2006

National Rate = 287.5 Aggravated Assaults per 100,000 Population*

RANK	CITY	RATE
192	Abilene, TX	317.8
170	Albany, GA	348.3
25	Albany, NY	825.4
65	Albuquerque, NM	610.6
305	Alexandria, VA	152.2
319	Alhambra, CA	134.9
194	Allentown, PA	316.6
71	Amarillo, TX	594.6
372	Amherst, NY	69.5
237	Anaheim, CA	245.8
51	Anchorage, AK	670.5
270	Ann Arbor, MI	200.9
187	Antioch, CA	322.1
123	Arlington, TX	437.4
337	Arvada, CO	113.3
285	Athens-Clarke, GA	178.1
22	Atlanta, GA	886.8
177	Aurora, CO	338.1
195	Aurora, IL	314.0
217	Austin, TX	276.3
188	Bakersfield, CA	321.6
248	Baldwin Park, CA	230.0
14	Baltimore, MD	968.2
24	Baton Rouge, LA	833.8
58	Beaumont, TX	631.5
283	Beaverton, OR	182.4
382	Bellevue, WA	57.1
209	Bellflower, CA	288.4
335	Bellingham, WA	114.7
267	Berkeley, CA	202.7
317	Billings, MT	135.5
68	Birmingham, AL	608.8
352	Bloomington, MN	94.2
292	Boca Raton, FL	170.3
224	Boise, ID	266.4
29	Boston, MA	797.5
289	Boulder, CO	175.6
370	Brick Twnshp, NJ	78.0
84	Bridgeport, CT	542.5
NA	Brockton, MA**	NA
295	Broken Arrow, OK	162.1
159	Brownsville, TX	376.2
290	Buena Park, CA	175.2
41	Buffalo, NY	713.4
302	Burbank, CA	158.0
245	Cambridge, MA	235.3
11	Camden, NJ	1,026.6
379	Canton Twnshp, MI	60.6
169	Canton, OH	349.4
280	Cape Coral, FL	186.1
228	Carlsbad, CA	262.0
341	Carrollton, TX	107.2
111	Carson, CA	463.1
373	Cary, NC	69.1
286	Cedar Rapids, IA	177.7
329	Centennial, CO	118.9
221	Chandler, AZ	269.8
69	Charleston, SC	597.0
78	Charlotte, NC	557.1
28	Chattanooga, TN	809.0
299	Cheektowaga, NY	160.5
214	Chesapeake, VA	279.4
66	Chicago, IL	610.4
326	Chino Hills, CA	121.7
309	Chino, CA	143.1
239	Chula Vista, CA	244.4
176	Cincinnati, OH	338.7
381	Clarkstown, NY	57.2
50	Clarksville, TN	675.3
79	Clearwater, FL	555.6
102	Cleveland, OH	485.0
325	Clifton, NJ	122.5
244	Clinton Twnshp, MI	237.1
360	Clovis, CA	88.2
369	Colonie, NY	78.9
178	Colorado Springs, CO	336.2
171	Columbia, MO	348.2
40	Columbia, SC	716.5
203	Columbus, GA	297.6
256	Columbus, OH	220.4
10	Compton, CA	1,086.8
269	Concord, CA	201.0
304	Coral Springs, FL	154.2
351	Corona, CA	95.5
101	Corpus Christi, TX	485.1
323	Costa Mesa, CA	132.6
367	Cranston, RI	81.5
73	Dallas, TX	584.2
324	Daly City, CA	132.4
371	Danbury, CT	70.0
252	Davie, FL	225.4
107	Dayton, OH	474.0
210	Dearborn, MI	286.6
95	Deerfield Beach, FL	502.3
277	Denton, TX	190.5
110	Denver, CO	466.5
118	Des Moines, IA	442.6
2	Detroit, MI	1,486.0
300	Downey, CA	159.9
227	Duluth, MN	262.1
132	Durham, NC	415.9
276	Edison Twnshp, NJ	191.9
378	Edmond, OK	60.9
197	El Cajon, CA	307.5
180	El Monte, CA	332.5
229	El Paso, TX	260.9
240	Elizabeth, NJ	243.0
268	Erie, PA	202.5
183	Escondido, CA	326.7
336	Eugene, OR	114.4
235	Evansville, IN	246.8
188	Everett, WA	321.6
167	Fairfield, CA	351.9
303	Fargo, ND	155.3
340	Farmington Hills, MI	110.0
87	Fayetteville, NC	538.0
310	Federal Way, WA	142.0
1	Flint, MI	1,899.3
175	Fontana, CA	341.1
205	Fort Collins, CO	292.1
121	Fort Lauderdale, FL	438.9
32	Fort Smith, AR	780.4
356	Fort Wayne, IN	91.6
147	Fort Worth, TX	388.9
314	Fremont, CA	137.4
119	Fresno, CA	442.1
282	Fullerton, CA	185.1
52	Gainesville, FL	669.9
238	Garden Grove, CA	244.7
320	Garland, TX	134.8
226	Gary, IN	263.7
359	Gilbert, AZ	89.1
142	Glendale, AZ	393.0
356	Glendale, CA	91.6
288	Grand Prairie, TX	176.5
72	Grand Rapids, MI	587.7
386	Greece, NY	45.6
135	Greeley, CO	405.6
141	Green Bay, WI	393.8
117	Greensboro, NC	443.0
188	Gresham, OR	321.6
347	Hamilton Twnshp, NJ	98.8
162	Hammond, IN	368.7
297	Hampton, VA	161.9
64	Hartford, CT	612.7
161	Hawthorne, CA	370.1
255	Hayward, CA	223.2
331	Henderson, NV	118.0
264	Hesperia, CA	204.6
151	Hialeah, FL	382.7
143	High Point, NC	392.9
354	Hillsboro, OR	91.9
274	Hollywood, FL	194.5
293	Honolulu, HI	169.1
77	Houston, TX	561.7
330	Huntington Beach, CA	118.8
129	Huntsville, AL	420.7
81	Independence, MO	551.3
109	Indianapolis, IN	468.3
126	Inglewood, CA	426.8
388	Irvine, CA	29.2
222	Irving, TX	268.7
93	Jacksonville, FL	506.5
207	Jackson, MS	289.8
89	Jersey City, NJ	523.4
212	Joliet, IL	282.6
113	Kansas City, KS	461.3
21	Kansas City, MO	891.1
308	Kenosha, WI	145.4
199	Kent, WA	305.3
122	Killeen, TX	438.5
48	Knoxville, TN	684.7
33	Lafayette, LA	779.7
364	Lake Forest, CA	84.3
163	Lakeland, FL	366.9
258	Lakewood, CA	211.8
204	Lakewood, CO	295.8
74	Lancaster, CA	567.1
45	Lansing, MI	694.3
154	Laredo, TX	379.2
138	Largo, FL	396.1
150	Las Cruces, NM	383.1
91	Las Vegas, NV	507.7
116	Lawrence, KS	449.1
38	Lawton, OK	736.0
343	Lee's Summit, MO	105.0
338	Lewisville, TX	113.0
139	Lexington, KY	396.0
133	Lincoln, NE	411.2
5	Little Rock, AR	1,187.1
353	Livermore, CA	92.3
363	Livonia, MI	84.9

RANK	CITY	RATE
157	Long Beach, CA	377.4
46	Longview, TX	689.4
158	Los Angeles, CA	377.2
202	Louisville, KY	299.2
59	Lowell, MA	630.5
31	Lubbock, TX	784.0
67	Lynn, MA	610.2
120	Macon, GA	441.7
258	Madison, WI	211.8
348	Manchester, NH	98.1
284	McAllen, TX	179.4
281	McKinney, TX	185.3
26	Melbourne, FL	822.4
8	Memphis, TN	1,125.2
218	Mesa, AZ	275.4
246	Mesquite, TX	232.1
54	Miami Beach, FL	668.8
4	Miami Gardens, FL	1,220.4
17	Miami, FL	926.9
249	Midland, TX	229.3
55	Milwaukee, WI	666.9
35	Minneapolis, MN	755.7
172	Miramar, FL	347.7
387	Mission Viejo, CA	41.7
307	Mobile, AL	145.9
130	Modesto, CA	417.5
271	Montgomery, AL	196.6
250	Moreno Valley, CA	228.9
82	Murfreesboro, TN	548.4
362	Murrieta, CA	85.0
186	Napa, CA	323.4
385	Naperville, IL	52.7
313	Nashua, NH	138.0
12	Nashville, TN	1,023.5
23	New Bedford, MA	848.8
208	New Orleans, LA	288.8
181	New York, NY	329.6
103	Newark, NJ	483.8
332	Newport Beach, CA	115.5
115	Newport News, VA	451.9
322	Newton, MA	132.7
182	Norfolk, VA	327.8
334	Norman, OK	115.0
16	North Charleston, SC	944.6
75	North Las Vegas, NV	565.4
213	Norwalk, CA	280.0
19	Oakland, CA	906.1
155	Oceanside, CA	378.9
88	Odessa, TX	532.2
196	Ogden, UT	312.9
90	Oklahoma City, OK	511.2
294	Olathe, KS	167.7
174	Omaha, NE	344.8
206	Ontario, CA	290.4
345	Orange, CA	100.6
389	Orem, UT	27.0
6	Orlando, FL	1,180.7
321	Overland Park, KS	133.2
266	Oxnard, CA	202.9
98	Palm Bay, FL	489.4
128	Palmdale, CA	423.5
376	Parma, OH	63.8
247	Pasadena, CA	230.3
225	Pasadena, TX	265.7
86	Paterson, NJ	541.5
312	Pembroke Pines, FL	139.3
315	Peoria, AZ	137.3
99	Peoria, IL	489.0
39	Philadelphia, PA	720.1
136	Phoenix, AZ	398.5
97	Pittsburgh, PA	490.8
260	Plano, TX	211.1
311	Plantation, FL	140.7
100	Pomona, CA	486.6
27	Pompano Beach, FL	813.7
272	Port St. Lucie, FL	196.4
131	Portland, OR	417.2
108	Portsmouth, VA	473.5
200	Providence, RI	302.1
358	Provo, UT	89.6
152	Pueblo, CO	382.2
262	Quincy, MA	206.0
230	Racine, WI	259.8
153	Raleigh, NC	380.4
339	Rancho Cucamon., CA	111.2
70	Reading, PA	595.6
219	Redding, CA	274.2
140	Reno, NV	395.5
164	Rialto, CA	365.5
328	Richardson, TX	119.6
63	Richmond, CA	617.8
114	Richmond, VA	460.9
156	Riverside, CA	377.9
43	Roanoke, VA	706.5
301	Rochester, MN	159.0
76	Rochester, NY	563.7
37	Rockford, IL	738.3
265	Roseville, CA	203.0
365	Roswell, GA	82.3
384	Round Rock, TX	56.3
49	Sacramento, CA	676.4
193	Salem, OR	316.8
112	Salinas, CA	462.3
104	Salt Lake City, UT	480.7
198	San Angelo, TX	307.2
148	San Antonio, TX	388.7
92	San Bernardino, CA	507.6
201	San Diego, CA	300.8
184	San Francisco, CA	326.4
234	San Jose, CA	248.2
144	San Leandro, CA	391.7
241	San Mateo, CA	241.6
342	Sandy, UT	106.9
185	Santa Ana, CA	323.8
160	Santa Barbara, CA	370.4
350	Santa Clara, CA	95.9
316	Santa Clarita, CA	137.2
47	Santa Maria, CA	686.2
173	Santa Monica, CA	345.4
134	Santa Rosa, CA	410.9
278	Savannah, GA	187.4
327	Scottsdale, AZ	120.2
137	Seattle, WA	398.4
30	Shreveport, LA	793.1
349	Simi Valley, CA	97.7
165	Sioux City, IA	354.1
275	Sioux Falls, SD	192.0
251	Somerville, MA	228.1
216	South Bend, IN	277.5
263	South Gate, CA	205.4
9	Southfield, MI	1,096.2
232	Sparks, NV	251.2
223	Spokane Valley, WA	267.0
168	Spokane, WA	351.6
7	Springfield, IL	1,142.8
15	Springfield, MA	948.6
124	Springfield, MO	436.6
295	Sterling Heights, MI	162.1
18	Stockton, CA	908.4
3	St. Louis, MO	1,439.1
93	St. Paul, MN	506.5
13	St. Petersburg, FL	1,021.8
191	Suffolk, VA	320.9
375	Sugar Land, TX	64.2
377	Sunnyvale, CA	62.3
233	Sunrise, FL	250.8
361	Surprise, AZ	88.0
57	Syracuse, NY	635.6
62	Tacoma, WA	618.8
61	Tallahassee, FL	619.2
36	Tampa, FL	745.1
242	Temecula, CA	239.1
166	Tempe, AZ	353.8
253	Thornton, CO	224.9
344	Thousand Oaks, CA	102.0
56	Toledo, OH	666.0
380	Toms River Twnshp, NJ	59.1
243	Topeka, KS	238.6
354	Torrance, CA	91.9
368	Tracy, CA	80.6
44	Trenton, NJ	700.1
374	Troy, MI	67.9
106	Tucson, AZ	478.3
20	Tulsa, OK	901.2
145	Tuscaloosa, AL	391.0
125	Tyler, TX	430.5
366	Upper Darby Twnshp, PA	81.6
306	Vacaville, CA	151.4
60	Vallejo, CA	623.4
257	Vancouver, WA	219.7
291	Ventura, CA	171.5
179	Victorville, CA	333.4
346	Virginia Beach, VA	100.3
83	Visalia, CA	547.2
211	Vista, CA	283.9
96	Waco, TX	495.6
149	Warren, MI	386.0
383	Warwick, RI	56.6
34	Washington, DC	765.7
317	Waterbury, CT	135.5
279	West Covina, CA	186.9
333	West Jordan, UT	115.4
85	West Palm Beach, FL	541.6
236	West Valley, UT	246.2
231	Westland, MI	252.9
273	Westminster, CA	194.8
287	Westminster, CO	177.5
261	Whittier, CA	210.0
215	Wichita Falls, TX	278.5
42	Wichita, KS	708.8
146	Wilmington, NC	389.2
127	Winston-Salem, NC	424.6
297	Woodbridge Twnshp, NJ	161.9
80	Worcester, MA	552.7
220	Yakima, WA	273.6
254	Yonkers, NY	223.9
53	Youngstown, OH	669.2
105	Yuma, AZ	480.0

Source: CQ Press using data from F.B.I. "Crime in the United States 2006"

**Aggravated assault is an attack for the purpose of inflicting severe bodily injury.*

***Not available.*

62. Aggravated Assault Rate in 2006 (continued)

National Rate = 287.5 Aggravated Assaults per 100,000 Population*

RANK	CITY	RATE
1	Flint, MI	1,899.3
2	Detroit, MI	1,486.0
3	St. Louis, MO	1,439.1
4	Miami Gardens, FL	1,220.4
5	Little Rock, AR	1,187.1
6	Orlando, FL	1,180.7
7	Springfield, IL	1,142.8
8	Memphis, TN	1,125.2
9	Southfield, MI	1,096.2
10	Compton, CA	1,086.8
11	Camden, NJ	1,026.6
12	Nashville, TN	1,023.5
13	St. Petersburg, FL	1,021.8
14	Baltimore, MD	968.2
15	Springfield, MA	948.6
16	North Charleston, SC	944.6
17	Miami, FL	926.9
18	Stockton, CA	908.4
19	Oakland, CA	906.1
20	Tulsa, OK	901.2
21	Kansas City, MO	891.1
22	Atlanta, GA	886.8
23	New Bedford, MA	848.8
24	Baton Rouge, LA	833.8
25	Albany, NY	825.4
26	Melbourne, FL	822.4
27	Pompano Beach, FL	813.7
28	Chattanooga, TN	809.0
29	Boston, MA	797.5
30	Shreveport, LA	793.1
31	Lubbock, TX	784.0
32	Fort Smith, AR	780.4
33	Lafayette, LA	779.7
34	Washington, DC	765.7
35	Minneapolis, MN	755.7
36	Tampa, FL	745.1
37	Rockford, IL	738.3
38	Lawton, OK	736.0
39	Philadelphia, PA	720.1
40	Columbia, SC	716.5
41	Buffalo, NY	713.4
42	Wichita, KS	708.8
43	Roanoke, VA	706.5
44	Trenton, NJ	700.1
45	Lansing, MI	694.3
46	Longview, TX	689.4
47	Santa Maria, CA	686.2
48	Knoxville, TN	684.7
49	Sacramento, CA	676.4
50	Clarksville, TN	675.3
51	Anchorage, AK	670.5
52	Gainesville, FL	669.9
53	Youngstown, OH	669.2
54	Miami Beach, FL	668.8
55	Milwaukee, WI	666.9
56	Toledo, OH	666.0
57	Syracuse, NY	635.6
58	Beaumont, TX	631.5
59	Lowell, MA	630.5
60	Vallejo, CA	623.4
61	Tallahassee, FL	619.2
62	Tacoma, WA	618.8
63	Richmond, CA	617.8
64	Hartford, CT	612.7
65	Albuquerque, NM	610.6
66	Chicago, IL	610.4
67	Lynn, MA	610.2
68	Birmingham, AL	608.8
69	Charleston, SC	597.0
70	Reading, PA	595.6
71	Amarillo, TX	594.6
72	Grand Rapids, MI	587.7
73	Dallas, TX	584.2
74	Lancaster, CA	567.1
75	North Las Vegas, NV	565.4
76	Rochester, NY	563.7
77	Houston, TX	561.7
78	Charlotte, NC	557.1
79	Clearwater, FL	555.6
80	Worcester, MA	552.7
81	Independence, MO	551.3
82	Murfreesboro, TN	548.4
83	Visalia, CA	547.2
84	Bridgeport, CT	542.5
85	West Palm Beach, FL	541.6
86	Paterson, NJ	541.5
87	Fayetteville, NC	538.0
88	Odessa, TX	532.2
89	Jersey City, NJ	523.4
90	Oklahoma City, OK	511.2
91	Las Vegas, NV	507.7
92	San Bernardino, CA	507.6
93	Jacksonville, FL	506.5
93	St. Paul, MN	506.5
95	Deerfield Beach, FL	502.3
96	Waco, TX	495.6
97	Pittsburgh, PA	490.8
98	Palm Bay, FL	489.4
99	Peoria, IL	489.0
100	Pomona, CA	486.6
101	Corpus Christi, TX	485.1
102	Cleveland, OH	485.0
103	Newark, NJ	483.8
104	Salt Lake City, UT	480.7
105	Yuma, AZ	480.0
106	Tucson, AZ	478.3
107	Dayton, OH	474.0
108	Portsmouth, VA	473.5
109	Indianapolis, IN	468.3
110	Denver, CO	466.5
111	Carson, CA	463.1
112	Salinas, CA	462.3
113	Kansas City, KS	461.3
114	Richmond, VA	460.9
115	Newport News, VA	451.9
116	Lawrence, KS	449.1
117	Greensboro, NC	443.0
118	Des Moines, IA	442.6
119	Fresno, CA	442.1
120	Macon, GA	441.7
121	Fort Lauderdale, FL	438.9
122	Killeen, TX	438.5
123	Arlington, TX	437.4
124	Springfield, MO	436.6
125	Tyler, TX	430.5
126	Inglewood, CA	426.8
127	Winston-Salem, NC	424.6
128	Palmdale, CA	423.5
129	Huntsville, AL	420.7
130	Modesto, CA	417.5
131	Portland, OR	417.2
132	Durham, NC	415.9
133	Lincoln, NE	411.2
134	Santa Rosa, CA	410.9
135	Greeley, CO	405.6
136	Phoenix, AZ	398.5
137	Seattle, WA	398.4
138	Largo, FL	396.1
139	Lexington, KY	396.0
140	Reno, NV	395.5
141	Green Bay, WI	393.8
142	Glendale, AZ	393.0
143	High Point, NC	392.9
144	San Leandro, CA	391.7
145	Tuscaloosa, AL	391.0
146	Wilmington, NC	389.2
147	Fort Worth, TX	388.9
148	San Antonio, TX	388.7
149	Warren, MI	386.0
150	Las Cruces, NM	383.1
151	Hialeah, FL	382.7
152	Pueblo, CO	382.2
153	Raleigh, NC	380.4
154	Laredo, TX	379.2
155	Oceanside, CA	378.9
156	Riverside, CA	377.9
157	Long Beach, CA	377.4
158	Los Angeles, CA	377.2
159	Brownsville, TX	376.2
160	Santa Barbara, CA	370.4
161	Hawthorne, CA	370.1
162	Hammond, IN	368.7
163	Lakeland, FL	366.9
164	Rialto, CA	365.5
165	Sioux City, IA	354.1
166	Tempe, AZ	353.8
167	Fairfield, CA	351.9
168	Spokane, WA	351.6
169	Canton, OH	349.4
170	Albany, GA	348.3
171	Columbia, MO	348.2
172	Miramar, FL	347.7
173	Santa Monica, CA	345.4
174	Omaha, NE	344.8
175	Fontana, CA	341.1
176	Cincinnati, OH	338.7
177	Aurora, CO	338.1
178	Colorado Springs, CO	336.2
179	Victorville, CA	333.4
180	El Monte, CA	332.5
181	New York, NY	329.6
182	Norfolk, VA	327.8
183	Escondido, CA	326.7
184	San Francisco, CA	326.4
185	Santa Ana, CA	323.8
186	Napa, CA	323.4
187	Antioch, CA	322.1
188	Bakersfield, CA	321.6
188	Everett, WA	321.6
188	Gresham, OR	321.6
191	Suffolk, VA	320.9
192	Abilene, TX	317.8

Rank Order- City (continued)

RANK	CITY	RATE
193	Salem, OR	316.8
194	Allentown, PA	316.6
195	Aurora, IL	314.0
196	Ogden, UT	312.9
197	El Cajon, CA	307.5
198	San Angelo, TX	307.2
199	Kent, WA	305.3
200	Providence, RI	302.1
201	San Diego, CA	300.8
202	Louisville, KY	299.2
203	Columbus, GA	297.6
204	Lakewood, CO	295.8
205	Fort Collins, CO	292.1
206	Ontario, CA	290.4
207	Jackson, MS	289.8
208	New Orleans, LA	288.8
209	Bellflower, CA	288.4
210	Dearborn, MI	286.6
211	Vista, CA	283.9
212	Joliet, IL	282.6
213	Norwalk, CA	280.0
214	Chesapeake, VA	279.4
215	Wichita Falls, TX	278.5
216	South Bend, IN	277.5
217	Austin, TX	276.3
218	Mesa, AZ	275.4
219	Redding, CA	274.2
220	Yakima, WA	273.6
221	Chandler, AZ	269.8
222	Irving, TX	268.7
223	Spokane Valley, WA	267.0
224	Boise, ID	266.4
225	Pasadena, TX	265.7
226	Gary, IN	263.7
227	Duluth, MN	262.1
228	Carlsbad, CA	262.0
229	El Paso, TX	260.9
230	Racine, WI	259.8
231	Westland, MI	252.9
232	Sparks, NV	251.2
233	Sunrise, FL	250.8
234	San Jose, CA	248.2
235	Evansville, IN	246.8
236	West Valley, UT	246.2
237	Anaheim, CA	245.8
238	Garden Grove, CA	244.7
239	Chula Vista, CA	244.4
240	Elizabeth, NJ	243.0
241	San Mateo, CA	241.6
242	Temecula, CA	239.1
243	Topeka, KS	238.6
244	Clinton Twnshp, MI	237.1
245	Cambridge, MA	235.3
246	Mesquite, TX	232.1
247	Pasadena, CA	230.3
248	Baldwin Park, CA	230.0
249	Midland, TX	229.3
250	Moreno Valley, CA	228.9
251	Somerville, MA	228.1
252	Davie, FL	225.4
253	Thornton, CO	224.9
254	Yonkers, NY	223.9
255	Hayward, CA	223.2
256	Columbus, OH	220.4
257	Vancouver, WA	219.7
258	Lakewood, CA	211.8
258	Madison, WI	211.8
260	Plano, TX	211.1
261	Whittier, CA	210.0
262	Quincy, MA	206.0
263	South Gate, CA	205.4
264	Hesperia, CA	204.6
265	Roseville, CA	203.0
266	Oxnard, CA	202.9
267	Berkeley, CA	202.7
268	Erie, PA	202.5
269	Concord, CA	201.0
270	Ann Arbor, MI	200.9
271	Montgomery, AL	196.6
272	Port St. Lucie, FL	196.4
273	Westminster, CA	194.8
274	Hollywood, FL	194.5
275	Sioux Falls, SD	192.0
276	Edison Twnshp, NJ	191.9
277	Denton, TX	190.5
278	Savannah, GA	187.4
279	West Covina, CA	186.9
280	Cape Coral, FL	186.1
281	McKinney, TX	185.3
282	Fullerton, CA	185.1
283	Beaverton, OR	182.4
284	McAllen, TX	179.4
285	Athens-Clarke, GA	178.1
286	Cedar Rapids, IA	177.7
287	Westminster, CO	177.5
288	Grand Prairie, TX	176.5
289	Boulder, CO	175.6
290	Buena Park, CA	175.2
291	Ventura, CA	171.5
292	Boca Raton, FL	170.3
293	Honolulu, HI	169.1
294	Olathe, KS	167.7
295	Broken Arrow, OK	162.1
295	Sterling Heights, MI	162.1
297	Hampton, VA	161.9
297	Woodbridge Twnshp, NJ	161.9
299	Cheektowaga, NY	160.5
300	Downey, CA	159.9
301	Rochester, MN	159.0
302	Burbank, CA	158.0
303	Fargo, ND	155.3
304	Coral Springs, FL	154.2
305	Alexandria, VA	152.2
306	Vacaville, CA	151.4
307	Mobile, AL	145.9
308	Kenosha, WI	145.4
309	Chino, CA	143.1
310	Federal Way, WA	142.0
311	Plantation, FL	140.7
312	Pembroke Pines, FL	139.3
313	Nashua, NH	138.0
314	Fremont, CA	137.4
315	Peoria, AZ	137.3
316	Santa Clarita, CA	137.2
317	Billings, MT	135.5
317	Waterbury, CT	135.5
319	Alhambra, CA	134.9
320	Garland, TX	134.8
321	Overland Park, KS	133.2
322	Newton, MA	132.7
323	Costa Mesa, CA	132.6
324	Daly City, CA	132.4
325	Clifton, NJ	122.5
326	Chino Hills, CA	121.7
327	Scottsdale, AZ	120.2
328	Richardson, TX	119.6
329	Centennial, CO	118.9
330	Huntington Beach, CA	118.8
331	Henderson, NV	118.0
332	Newport Beach, CA	115.5
333	West Jordan, UT	115.4
334	Norman, OK	115.0
335	Bellingham, WA	114.7
336	Eugene, OR	114.4
337	Arvada, CO	113.3
338	Lewisville, TX	113.0
339	Rancho Cucamon., CA	111.2
340	Farmington Hills, MI	110.0
341	Carrollton, TX	107.2
342	Sandy, UT	106.9
343	Lee's Summit, MO	105.0
344	Thousand Oaks, CA	102.0
345	Orange, CA	100.6
346	Virginia Beach, VA	100.3
347	Hamilton Twnshp, NJ	98.8
348	Manchester, NH	98.1
349	Simi Valley, CA	97.7
350	Santa Clara, CA	95.9
351	Corona, CA	95.5
352	Bloomington, MN	94.2
353	Livermore, CA	92.3
354	Hillsboro, OR	91.9
354	Torrance, CA	91.9
356	Fort Wayne, IN	91.6
356	Glendale, CA	91.6
358	Provo, UT	89.6
359	Gilbert, AZ	89.1
360	Clovis, CA	88.2
361	Surprise, AZ	88.0
362	Murrieta, CA	85.0
363	Livonia, MI	84.9
364	Lake Forest, CA	84.3
365	Roswell, GA	82.3
366	Upper Darby Twnshp, PA	81.6
367	Cranston, RI	81.5
368	Tracy, CA	80.6
369	Colonie, NY	78.9
370	Brick Twnshp, NJ	78.0
371	Danbury, CT	70.0
372	Amherst, NY	69.5
373	Cary, NC	69.1
374	Troy, MI	67.9
375	Sugar Land, TX	64.2
376	Parma, OH	63.8
377	Sunnyvale, CA	62.3
378	Edmond, OK	60.9
379	Canton Twnshp, MI	60.6
380	Toms River Twnshp, NJ	59.1
381	Clarkstown, NY	57.2
382	Bellevue, WA	57.1
383	Warwick, RI	56.6
384	Round Rock, TX	56.3
385	Naperville, IL	52.7
386	Greece, NY	45.6
387	Mission Viejo, CA	41.7
388	Irvine, CA	29.2
389	Orem, UT	27.0
NA	Brockton, MA**	NA

Source: CQ Press using data from F.B.I. "Crime in the United States 2006"

**Aggravated assault is an attack for the purpose of inflicting severe bodily injury.*

***Not available.*

63. Percent Change in Aggravated Assault Rate: 2005 to 2006

National Percent Change = 1.1% Decrease*

RANK	CITY	% CHANGE
119	Abilene, TX	6.9
109	Albany, GA	8.3
152	Albany, NY	2.5
238	Albuquerque, NM	(5.9)
314	Alexandria, VA	(16.8)
342	Alhambra, CA	(22.4)
50	Allentown, PA	18.8
174	Amarillo, TX	0.1
10	Amherst, NY	51.4
297	Anaheim, CA	(14.9)
24	Anchorage, AK	31.6
140	Ann Arbor, MI	4.3
66	Antioch, CA	15.6
71	Arlington, TX	14.2
186	Arvada, CO	(1.0)
117	Athens-Clarke, GA	7.0
229	Atlanta, GA	(5.4)
125	Aurora, CO	6.3
103	Aurora, IL	9.4
155	Austin, TX	2.2
311	Bakersfield, CA	(16.4)
339	Baldwin Park, CA	(22.0)
270	Baltimore, MD	(10.1)
48	Baton Rouge, LA	19.0
131	Beaumont, TX	5.2
19	Beaverton, OR	35.5
351	Bellevue, WA	(26.4)
326	Bellflower, CA	(18.5)
235	Bellingham, WA	(5.8)
126	Berkeley, CA	6.2
52	Billings, MT	18.4
296	Birmingham, AL	(14.7)
NA	Bloomington, MN**	NA
337	Boca Raton, FL	(21.4)
212	Boise, ID	(3.3)
165	Boston, MA	0.8
57	Boulder, CO	17.2
7	Brick Twnshp, NJ	61.5
200	Bridgeport, CT	(2.0)
NA	Brockton, MA**	NA
273	Broken Arrow, OK	(11.1)
292	Brownsville, TX	(14.1)
305	Buena Park, CA	(15.7)
179	Buffalo, NY	(0.5)
160	Burbank, CA	1.6
163	Cambridge, MA	1.0
260	Camden, NJ	(8.4)
374	Canton Twnshp, MI	(42.9)
34	Canton, OH	23.6
149	Cape Coral, FL	2.8
15	Carlsbad, CA	43.2
362	Carrollton, TX	(31.7)
101	Carson, CA	9.5
160	Cary, NC	1.6
284	Cedar Rapids, IA	(12.8)
316	Centennial, CO	(17.2)
91	Chandler, AZ	10.8
209	Charleston, SC	(3.0)
205	Charlotte, NC	(2.7)
111	Chattanooga, TN	7.9
219	Cheektowaga, NY	(4.2)
330	Chesapeake, VA	(19.3)
202	Chicago, IL	(2.2)
25	Chino Hills, CA	30.4
279	Chino, CA	(11.7)
205	Chula Vista, CA	(2.7)
130	Cincinnati, OH	5.4
NA	Clarkstown, NY**	NA
107	Clarksville, TN	8.4
299	Clearwater, FL	(15.0)
121	Cleveland, OH	6.7
20	Clifton, NJ	34.5
318	Clinton Twnshp, MI	(17.5)
251	Clovis, CA	(7.5)
5	Colonie, NY	69.0
67	Colorado Springs, CO	15.5
244	Columbia, MO	(6.7)
194	Columbia, SC	(1.6)
83	Columbus, GA	11.8
240	Columbus, OH	(6.1)
261	Compton, CA	(8.6)
299	Concord, CA	(15.0)
26	Coral Springs, FL	28.9
207	Corona, CA	(2.9)
145	Corpus Christi, TX	3.3
220	Costa Mesa, CA	(4.3)
287	Cranston, RI	(13.6)
253	Dallas, TX	(7.7)
232	Daly City, CA	(5.6)
59	Danbury, CT	16.9
252	Davie, FL	(7.6)
14	Dayton, OH	49.1
285	Dearborn, MI	(13.1)
318	Deerfield Beach, FL	(17.5)
301	Denton, TX	(15.4)
193	Denver, CO	(1.5)
NA	Des Moines, IA**	NA
182	Detroit, MI	(0.7)
94	Downey, CA	10.3
NA	Duluth, MN**	NA
NA	Durham, NC**	NA
29	Edison Twnshp, NJ	25.1
364	Edmond, OK	(32.1)
224	El Cajon, CA	(4.6)
258	El Monte, CA	(8.1)
NA	El Paso, TX**	NA
39	Elizabeth, NJ	23.0
93	Erie, PA	10.4
235	Escondido, CA	(5.8)
96	Eugene, OR	10.2
32	Evansville, IN	23.7
174	Everett, WA	0.1
68	Fairfield, CA	15.1
2	Fargo, ND	189.7
339	Farmington Hills, MI	(22.0)
144	Fayetteville, NC	3.5
64	Federal Way, WA	15.9
70	Flint, MI	14.4
36	Fontana, CA	23.3
16	Fort Collins, CO	41.9
106	Fort Lauderdale, FL	8.6
179	Fort Smith, AR	(0.5)
NA	Fort Wayne, IN**	NA
97	Fort Worth, TX	9.9
218	Fremont, CA	(4.1)
308	Fresno, CA	(16.0)
41	Fullerton, CA	21.9
124	Gainesville, FL	6.4
303	Garden Grove, CA	(15.5)
328	Garland, TX	(19.1)
245	Gary, IN	(7.1)
230	Gilbert, AZ	(5.5)
133	Glendale, AZ	4.9
151	Glendale, CA	2.6
53	Grand Prairie, TX	17.7
230	Grand Rapids, MI	(5.5)
1	Greece, NY	208.1
338	Greeley, CO	(21.8)
86	Green Bay, WI	11.1
171	Greensboro, NC	0.4
89	Gresham, OR	11.0
22	Hamilton Twnshp, NJ	33.2
346	Hammond, IN	(24.7)
259	Hampton, VA	(8.2)
77	Hartford, CT	12.9
45	Hawthorne, CA	20.4
114	Hayward, CA	7.6
98	Henderson, NV	9.8
41	Hesperia, CA	21.9
217	Hialeah, FL	(4.0)
157	High Point, NC	1.9
81	Hillsboro, OR	12.1
343	Hollywood, FL	(23.8)
143	Honolulu, HI	3.8
190	Houston, TX	(1.4)
361	Huntington Beach, CA	(31.5)
73	Huntsville, AL	13.9
184	Independence, MO	(0.8)
247	Indianapolis, IN	(7.2)
72	Inglewood, CA	14.1
373	Irvine, CA	(41.7)
245	Irving, TX	(7.1)
186	Jacksonville, FL	(1.0)
28	Jackson, MS	25.4
274	Jersey City, NJ	(11.2)
49	Joliet, IL	18.9
101	Kansas City, KS	9.5
NA	Kansas City, MO**	NA
8	Kenosha, WI	57.5
181	Kent, WA	(0.6)
278	Killeen, TX	(11.6)
62	Knoxville, TN	16.4
62	Lafayette, LA	16.4
310	Lake Forest, CA	(16.2)
29	Lakeland, FL	25.1
134	Lakewood, CA	4.8
98	Lakewood, CO	9.8
220	Lancaster, CA	(4.3)
336	Lansing, MI	(21.1)
111	Laredo, TX	7.9
46	Largo, FL	20.0
54	Las Cruces, NM	17.4
36	Las Vegas, NV	23.3
4	Lawrence, KS	81.7
21	Lawton, OK	34.2
242	Lee's Summit, MO	(6.5)
290	Lewisville, TX	(13.9)
NA	Lexington, KY**	NA
223	Lincoln, NE	(4.5)
211	Little Rock, AR	(3.1)
307	Livermore, CA	(15.8)
261	Livonia, MI	(8.6)

RANK	CITY	% CHANGE
201	Long Beach, CA	(2.1)
324	Longview, TX	(18.1)
272	Los Angeles, CA	(10.8)
147	Louisville, KY	3.1
286	Lowell, MA	(13.5)
254	Lubbock, TX	(7.8)
358	Lynn, MA	(30.5)
126	Macon, GA	6.2
100	Madison, WI	9.6
50	Manchester, NH	18.8
280	McAllen, TX	(11.9)
56	McKinney, TX	17.3
47	Melbourne, FL	19.8
173	Memphis, TN	0.2
339	Mesa, AZ	(22.0)
268	Mesquite, TX	(9.7)
149	Miami Beach, FL	2.8
214	Miami Gardens, FL	(3.5)
269	Miami, FL	(10.0)
318	Midland, TX	(17.5)
17	Milwaukee, WI	39.5
61	Minneapolis, MN	16.6
41	Miramar, FL	21.9
372	Mission Viejo, CA	(41.4)
335	Mobile, AL	(20.6)
160	Modesto, CA	1.6
371	Montgomery, AL	(39.4)
86	Moreno Valley, CA	11.1
257	Murfreesboro, TN	(8.0)
309	Murrieta, CA	(16.1)
348	Napa, CA	(25.8)
6	Naperville, IL	64.7
122	Nashua, NH	6.6
243	Nashville, TN	(6.6)
79	New Bedford, MA	12.5
NA	New Orleans, LA**	NA
220	New York, NY	(4.3)
202	Newark, NJ	(2.2)
69	Newport Beach, CA	14.8
113	Newport News, VA	7.7
44	Newton, MA	20.5
194	Norfolk, VA	(1.6)
345	Norman, OK	(24.6)
241	North Charleston, SC	(6.3)
123	North Las Vegas, NV	6.5
54	Norwalk, CA	17.4
18	Oakland, CA	38.5
167	Oceanside, CA	0.7
177	Odessa, TX	(0.2)
58	Ogden, UT	17.0
248	Oklahoma City, OK	(7.3)
355	Olathe, KS	(30.1)
171	Omaha, NE	0.4
190	Ontario, CA	(1.4)
82	Orange, CA	12.0
360	Orem, UT	(31.3)
148	Orlando, FL	3.0
375	Overland Park, KS	(45.5)
184	Oxnard, CA	(0.8)
32	Palm Bay, FL	23.7
301	Palmdale, CA	(15.4)
347	Parma, OH	(25.6)
362	Pasadena, CA	(31.7)
267	Pasadena, TX	(9.4)
159	Paterson, NJ	1.8
235	Pembroke Pines, FL	(5.8)

RANK	CITY	% CHANGE
142	Peoria, AZ	3.9
134	Peoria, IL	4.8
137	Philadelphia, PA	4.6
152	Phoenix, AZ	2.5
155	Pittsburgh, PA	2.2
215	Plano, TX	(3.6)
23	Plantation, FL	32.2
209	Pomona, CA	(3.0)
321	Pompano Beach, FL	(17.8)
197	Port St. Lucie, FL	(1.8)
227	Portland, OR	(5.1)
163	Portsmouth, VA	1.0
325	Providence, RI	(18.4)
289	Provo, UT	(13.8)
322	Pueblo, CO	(17.9)
305	Quincy, MA	(15.7)
3	Racine, WI	105.1
117	Raleigh, NC	7.0
275	Rancho Cucamon., CA	(11.3)
199	Reading, PA	(1.9)
368	Redding, CA	(37.8)
317	Reno, NV	(17.3)
365	Rialto, CA	(32.8)
327	Richardson, TX	(19.0)
86	Richmond, CA	11.1
282	Richmond, VA	(12.2)
227	Riverside, CA	(5.1)
89	Roanoke, VA	11.0
115	Rochester, MN	7.4
11	Rochester, NY	50.9
NA	Rockford, IL**	NA
294	Roseville, CA	(14.6)
128	Roswell, GA	5.8
370	Round Rock, TX	(38.2)
154	Sacramento, CA	2.3
265	Salem, OR	(9.1)
119	Salinas, CA	6.9
76	Salt Lake City, UT	13.2
176	San Angelo, TX	0.0
232	San Antonio, TX	(5.6)
359	San Bernardino, CA	(30.9)
275	San Diego, CA	(11.3)
250	San Francisco, CA	(7.4)
204	San Jose, CA	(2.6)
9	San Leandro, CA	55.3
294	San Mateo, CA	(14.6)
311	Sandy, UT	(16.4)
167	Santa Ana, CA	0.7
353	Santa Barbara, CA	(28.1)
297	Santa Clara, CA	(14.9)
107	Santa Clarita, CA	8.4
38	Santa Maria, CA	23.1
116	Santa Monica, CA	7.1
333	Santa Rosa, CA	(19.6)
357	Savannah, GA	(30.2)
212	Scottsdale, AZ	(3.3)
188	Seattle, WA	(1.3)
94	Shreveport, LA	10.3
109	Simi Valley, CA	8.3
157	Sioux City, IA	1.9
139	Sioux Falls, SD	4.4
13	Somerville, MA	49.6
331	South Bend, IN	(19.4)
137	South Gate, CA	4.6
78	Southfield, MI	12.8
141	Sparks, NV	4.2

RANK	CITY	% CHANGE
266	Spokane Valley, WA	(9.2)
232	Spokane, WA	(5.6)
165	Springfield, IL	0.8
334	Springfield, MA	(19.8)
92	Springfield, MO	10.7
225	Sterling Heights, MI	(4.7)
226	Stockton, CA	(5.0)
169	St. Louis, MO	0.6
182	St. Paul, MN	(0.7)
261	St. Petersburg, FL	(8.6)
323	Suffolk, VA	(18.0)
216	Sugar Land, TX	(3.7)
368	Sunnyvale, CA	(37.8)
169	Sunrise, FL	0.6
188	Surprise, AZ	(1.3)
190	Syracuse, NY	(1.4)
145	Tacoma, WA	3.3
277	Tallahassee, FL	(11.4)
350	Tampa, FL	(26.1)
80	Temecula, CA	12.3
271	Tempe, AZ	(10.7)
197	Thornton, CO	(1.8)
31	Thousand Oaks, CA	24.7
239	Toledo, OH	(6.0)
355	Toms River Twnshp, NJ	(30.1)
313	Topeka, KS	(16.7)
12	Torrance, CA	50.2
344	Tracy, CA	(23.9)
264	Trenton, NJ	(9.0)
27	Troy, MI	25.7
287	Tucson, AZ	(13.6)
194	Tulsa, OK	(1.6)
40	Tuscaloosa, AL	22.3
73	Tyler, TX	13.9
352	Upper Darby Twnshp, PA	(26.6)
293	Vacaville, CA	(14.5)
NA	Vallejo, CA**	NA
177	Vancouver, WA	(0.2)
129	Ventura, CA	5.7
65	Victorville, CA	15.8
85	Virginia Beach, VA	11.4
354	Visalia, CA	(29.2)
315	Vista, CA	(16.9)
132	Waco, TX	5.1
248	Warren, MI	(7.3)
366	Warwick, RI	(34.9)
103	Washington, DC	9.4
328	Waterbury, CT	(19.1)
60	West Covina, CA	16.8
NA	West Jordan, UT**	NA
281	West Palm Beach, FL	(12.0)
283	West Valley, UT	(12.3)
35	Westland, MI	23.4
349	Westminster, CA	(26.0)
290	Westminster, CO	(13.9)
84	Whittier, CA	11.6
367	Wichita Falls, TX	(35.8)
NA	Wichita, KS**	NA
303	Wilmington, NC	(15.5)
254	Winston-Salem, NC	(7.8)
332	Woodbridge Twnshp, NJ	(19.5)
75	Worcester, MA	13.8
207	Yakima, WA	(2.9)
136	Yonkers, NY	4.7
105	Youngstown, OH	9.3
256	Yuma, AZ	(7.9)

Source: CQ Press using data from F.B.I. "Crime in the United States 2006"

**Aggravated assault is an attack for the purpose of inflicting severe bodily injury.*

***Not available.*

63. Percent Change in Aggravated Assault Rate: 2005 to 2006 (continued)

National Percent Change = 1.1% Decrease*

RANK	CITY	% CHANGE	RANK	CITY	% CHANGE	RANK	CITY	% CHANGE
1	Greece, NY	208.1	65	Victorville, CA	15.8	129	Ventura, CA	5.7
2	Fargo, ND	189.7	66	Antioch, CA	15.6	130	Cincinnati, OH	5.4
3	Racine, WI	105.1	67	Colorado Springs, CO	15.5	131	Beaumont, TX	5.2
4	Lawrence, KS	81.7	68	Fairfield, CA	15.1	132	Waco, TX	5.1
5	Colonie, NY	69.0	69	Newport Beach, CA	14.8	133	Glendale, AZ	4.9
6	Naperville, IL	64.7	70	Flint, MI	14.4	134	Lakewood, CA	4.8
7	Brick Twnshp, NJ	61.5	71	Arlington, TX	14.2	134	Peoria, IL	4.8
8	Kenosha, WI	57.5	72	Inglewood, CA	14.1	136	Yonkers, NY	4.7
9	San Leandro, CA	55.3	73	Huntsville, AL	13.9	137	Philadelphia, PA	4.6
10	Amherst, NY	51.4	73	Tyler, TX	13.9	137	South Gate, CA	4.6
11	Rochester, NY	50.9	75	Worcester, MA	13.8	139	Sioux Falls, SD	4.4
12	Torrance, CA	50.2	76	Salt Lake City, UT	13.2	140	Ann Arbor, MI	4.3
13	Somerville, MA	49.6	77	Hartford, CT	12.9	141	Sparks, NV	4.2
14	Dayton, OH	49.1	78	Southfield, MI	12.8	142	Peoria, AZ	3.9
15	Carlsbad, CA	43.2	79	New Bedford, MA	12.5	143	Honolulu, HI	3.8
16	Fort Collins, CO	41.9	80	Temecula, CA	12.3	144	Fayetteville, NC	3.5
17	Milwaukee, WI	39.5	81	Hillsboro, OR	12.1	145	Corpus Christi, TX	3.3
18	Oakland, CA	38.5	82	Orange, CA	12.0	145	Tacoma, WA	3.3
19	Beaverton, OR	35.5	83	Columbus, GA	11.8	147	Louisville, KY	3.1
20	Clifton, NJ	34.5	84	Whittier, CA	11.6	148	Orlando, FL	3.0
21	Lawton, OK	34.2	85	Virginia Beach, VA	11.4	149	Cape Coral, FL	2.8
22	Hamilton Twnshp, NJ	33.2	86	Green Bay, WI	11.1	149	Miami Beach, FL	2.8
23	Plantation, FL	32.2	86	Moreno Valley, CA	11.1	151	Glendale, CA	2.6
24	Anchorage, AK	31.6	86	Richmond, CA	11.1	152	Albany, NY	2.5
25	Chino Hills, CA	30.4	89	Gresham, OR	11.0	152	Phoenix, AZ	2.5
26	Coral Springs, FL	28.9	89	Roanoke, VA	11.0	154	Sacramento, CA	2.3
27	Troy, MI	25.7	91	Chandler, AZ	10.8	155	Austin, TX	2.2
28	Jackson, MS	25.4	92	Springfield, MO	10.7	155	Pittsburgh, PA	2.2
29	Edison Twnshp, NJ	25.1	93	Erie, PA	10.4	157	High Point, NC	1.9
29	Lakeland, FL	25.1	94	Downey, CA	10.3	157	Sioux City, IA	1.9
31	Thousand Oaks, CA	24.7	94	Shreveport, LA	10.3	159	Paterson, NJ	1.8
32	Evansville, IN	23.7	96	Eugene, OR	10.2	160	Burbank, CA	1.6
32	Palm Bay, FL	23.7	97	Fort Worth, TX	9.9	160	Cary, NC	1.6
34	Canton, OH	23.6	98	Henderson, NV	9.8	160	Modesto, CA	1.6
35	Westland, MI	23.4	98	Lakewood, CO	9.8	163	Cambridge, MA	1.0
36	Fontana, CA	23.3	100	Madison, WI	9.6	163	Portsmouth, VA	1.0
36	Las Vegas, NV	23.3	101	Carson, CA	9.5	165	Boston, MA	0.8
38	Santa Maria, CA	23.1	101	Kansas City, KS	9.5	165	Springfield, IL	0.8
39	Elizabeth, NJ	23.0	103	Aurora, IL	9.4	167	Oceanside, CA	0.7
40	Tuscaloosa, AL	22.3	103	Washington, DC	9.4	167	Santa Ana, CA	0.7
41	Fullerton, CA	21.9	105	Youngstown, OH	9.3	169	St. Louis, MO	0.6
41	Hesperia, CA	21.9	106	Fort Lauderdale, FL	8.6	169	Sunrise, FL	0.6
41	Miramar, FL	21.9	107	Clarksville, TN	8.4	171	Greensboro, NC	0.4
44	Newton, MA	20.5	107	Santa Clarita, CA	8.4	171	Omaha, NE	0.4
45	Hawthorne, CA	20.4	109	Albany, GA	8.3	173	Memphis, TN	0.2
46	Largo, FL	20.0	109	Simi Valley, CA	8.3	174	Amarillo, TX	0.1
47	Melbourne, FL	19.8	111	Chattanooga, TN	7.9	174	Everett, WA	0.1
48	Baton Rouge, LA	19.0	111	Laredo, TX	7.9	176	San Angelo, TX	0.0
49	Joliet, IL	18.9	113	Newport News, VA	7.7	177	Odessa, TX	(0.2)
50	Allentown, PA	18.8	114	Hayward, CA	7.6	177	Vancouver, WA	(0.2)
50	Manchester, NH	18.8	115	Rochester, MN	7.4	179	Buffalo, NY	(0.5)
52	Billings, MT	18.4	116	Santa Monica, CA	7.1	179	Fort Smith, AR	(0.5)
53	Grand Prairie, TX	17.7	117	Athens-Clarke, GA	7.0	181	Kent, WA	(0.6)
54	Las Cruces, NM	17.4	117	Raleigh, NC	7.0	182	Detroit, MI	(0.7)
54	Norwalk, CA	17.4	119	Abilene, TX	6.9	182	St. Paul, MN	(0.7)
56	McKinney, TX	17.3	119	Salinas, CA	6.9	184	Independence, MO	(0.8)
57	Boulder, CO	17.2	121	Cleveland, OH	6.7	184	Oxnard, CA	(0.8)
58	Ogden, UT	17.0	122	Nashua, NH	6.6	186	Arvada, CO	(1.0)
59	Danbury, CT	16.9	123	North Las Vegas, NV	6.5	186	Jacksonville, FL	(1.0)
60	West Covina, CA	16.8	124	Gainesville, FL	6.4	188	Seattle, WA	(1.3)
61	Minneapolis, MN	16.6	125	Aurora, CO	6.3	188	Surprise, AZ	(1.3)
62	Knoxville, TN	16.4	126	Berkeley, CA	6.2	190	Houston, TX	(1.4)
62	Lafayette, LA	16.4	126	Macon, GA	6.2	190	Ontario, CA	(1.4)
64	Federal Way, WA	15.9	128	Roswell, GA	5.8	190	Syracuse, NY	(1.4)

RANK	CITY	% CHANGE	RANK	CITY	% CHANGE	RANK	CITY	% CHANGE
193	Denver, CO	(1.5)	259	Hampton, VA	(8.2)	325	Providence, RI	(18.4)
194	Columbia, SC	(1.6)	260	Camden, NJ	(8.4)	326	Bellflower, CA	(18.5)
194	Norfolk, VA	(1.6)	261	Compton, CA	(8.6)	327	Richardson, TX	(19.0)
194	Tulsa, OK	(1.6)	261	Livonia, MI	(8.6)	328	Garland, TX	(19.1)
197	Port St. Lucie, FL	(1.8)	261	St. Petersburg, FL	(8.6)	328	Waterbury, CT	(19.1)
197	Thornton, CO	(1.8)	264	Trenton, NJ	(9.0)	330	Chesapeake, VA	(19.3)
199	Reading, PA	(1.9)	265	Salem, OR	(9.1)	331	South Bend, IN	(19.4)
200	Bridgeport, CT	(2.0)	266	Spokane Valley, WA	(9.2)	332	Woodbridge Twnshp, NJ	(19.5)
201	Long Beach, CA	(2.1)	267	Pasadena, TX	(9.4)	333	Santa Rosa, CA	(19.6)
202	Chicago, IL	(2.2)	268	Mesquite, TX	(9.7)	334	Springfield, MA	(19.8)
202	Newark, NJ	(2.2)	269	Miami, FL	(10.0)	335	Mobile, AL	(20.6)
204	San Jose, CA	(2.6)	270	Baltimore, MD	(10.1)	336	Lansing, MI	(21.1)
205	Charlotte, NC	(2.7)	271	Tempe, AZ	(10.7)	337	Boca Raton, FL	(21.4)
205	Chula Vista, CA	(2.7)	272	Los Angeles, CA	(10.8)	338	Greeley, CO	(21.8)
207	Corona, CA	(2.9)	273	Broken Arrow, OK	(11.1)	339	Baldwin Park, CA	(22.0)
207	Yakima, WA	(2.9)	274	Jersey City, NJ	(11.2)	339	Farmington Hills, MI	(22.0)
209	Charleston, SC	(3.0)	275	Rancho Cucamon., CA	(11.3)	339	Mesa, AZ	(22.0)
209	Pomona, CA	(3.0)	275	San Diego, CA	(11.3)	342	Alhambra, CA	(22.4)
211	Little Rock, AR	(3.1)	277	Tallahassee, FL	(11.4)	343	Hollywood, FL	(23.8)
212	Boise, ID	(3.3)	278	Killeen, TX	(11.6)	344	Tracy, CA	(23.9)
212	Scottsdale, AZ	(3.3)	279	Chino, CA	(11.7)	345	Norman, OK	(24.6)
214	Miami Gardens, FL	(3.5)	280	McAllen, TX	(11.9)	346	Hammond, IN	(24.7)
215	Plano, TX	(3.6)	281	West Palm Beach, FL	(12.0)	347	Parma, OH	(25.6)
216	Sugar Land, TX	(3.7)	282	Richmond, VA	(12.2)	348	Napa, CA	(25.8)
217	Hialeah, FL	(4.0)	283	West Valley, UT	(12.3)	349	Westminster, CA	(26.0)
218	Fremont, CA	(4.1)	284	Cedar Rapids, IA	(12.8)	350	Tampa, FL	(26.1)
219	Cheektowaga, NY	(4.2)	285	Dearborn, MI	(13.1)	351	Bellevue, WA	(26.4)
220	Costa Mesa, CA	(4.3)	286	Lowell, MA	(13.5)	352	Upper Darby Twnshp, PA	(26.6)
220	Lancaster, CA	(4.3)	287	Cranston, RI	(13.6)	353	Santa Barbara, CA	(28.1)
220	New York, NY	(4.3)	287	Tucson, AZ	(13.6)	354	Visalia, CA	(29.2)
223	Lincoln, NE	(4.5)	289	Provo, UT	(13.8)	355	Olathe, KS	(30.1)
224	El Cajon, CA	(4.6)	290	Lewisville, TX	(13.9)	355	Toms River Twnshp, NJ	(30.1)
225	Sterling Heights, MI	(4.7)	290	Westminster, CO	(13.9)	357	Savannah, GA	(30.2)
226	Stockton, CA	(5.0)	292	Brownsville, TX	(14.1)	358	Lynn, MA	(30.5)
227	Portland, OR	(5.1)	293	Vacaville, CA	(14.5)	359	San Bernardino, CA	(30.9)
227	Riverside, CA	(5.1)	294	Roseville, CA	(14.6)	360	Orem, UT	(31.3)
229	Atlanta, GA	(5.4)	294	San Mateo, CA	(14.6)	361	Huntington Beach, CA	(31.5)
230	Gilbert, AZ	(5.5)	296	Birmingham, AL	(14.7)	362	Carrollton, TX	(31.7)
230	Grand Rapids, MI	(5.5)	297	Anaheim, CA	(14.9)	362	Pasadena, CA	(31.7)
232	Daly City, CA	(5.6)	297	Santa Clara, CA	(14.9)	364	Edmond, OK	(32.1)
232	San Antonio, TX	(5.6)	299	Clearwater, FL	(15.0)	365	Rialto, CA	(32.8)
232	Spokane, WA	(5.6)	299	Concord, CA	(15.0)	366	Warwick, RI	(34.9)
235	Bellingham, WA	(5.8)	301	Denton, TX	(15.4)	367	Wichita Falls, TX	(35.8)
235	Escondido, CA	(5.8)	301	Palmdale, CA	(15.4)	368	Redding, CA	(37.8)
235	Pembroke Pines, FL	(5.8)	303	Garden Grove, CA	(15.5)	368	Sunnyvale, CA	(37.8)
238	Albuquerque, NM	(5.9)	303	Wilmington, NC	(15.5)	370	Round Rock, TX	(38.2)
239	Toledo, OH	(6.0)	305	Buena Park, CA	(15.7)	371	Montgomery, AL	(39.4)
240	Columbus, OH	(6.1)	305	Quincy, MA	(15.7)	372	Mission Viejo, CA	(41.4)
241	North Charleston, SC	(6.3)	307	Livermore, CA	(15.8)	373	Irvine, CA	(41.7)
242	Lee's Summit, MO	(6.5)	308	Fresno, CA	(16.0)	374	Canton Twnshp, MI	(42.9)
243	Nashville, TN	(6.6)	309	Murrieta, CA	(16.1)	375	Overland Park, KS	(45.5)
244	Columbia, MO	(6.7)	310	Lake Forest, CA	(16.2)	NA	Bloomington, MN**	NA
245	Gary, IN	(7.1)	311	Bakersfield, CA	(16.4)	NA	Brockton, MA**	NA
245	Irving, TX	(7.1)	311	Sandy, UT	(16.4)	NA	Clarkstown, NY**	NA
247	Indianapolis, IN	(7.2)	313	Topeka, KS	(16.7)	NA	Des Moines, IA**	NA
248	Oklahoma City, OK	(7.3)	314	Alexandria, VA	(16.8)	NA	Duluth, MN**	NA
248	Warren, MI	(7.3)	315	Vista, CA	(16.9)	NA	Durham, NC**	NA
250	San Francisco, CA	(7.4)	316	Centennial, CO	(17.2)	NA	El Paso, TX**	NA
251	Clovis, CA	(7.5)	317	Reno, NV	(17.3)	NA	Fort Wayne, IN**	NA
252	Davie, FL	(7.6)	318	Clinton Twnshp, MI	(17.5)	NA	Kansas City, MO**	NA
253	Dallas, TX	(7.7)	318	Deerfield Beach, FL	(17.5)	NA	Lexington, KY**	NA
254	Lubbock, TX	(7.8)	318	Midland, TX	(17.5)	NA	New Orleans, LA**	NA
254	Winston-Salem, NC	(7.8)	321	Pompano Beach, FL	(17.8)	NA	Rockford, IL**	NA
256	Yuma, AZ	(7.9)	322	Pueblo, CO	(17.9)	NA	Vallejo, CA**	NA
257	Murfreesboro, TN	(8.0)	323	Suffolk, VA	(18.0)	NA	West Jordan, UT**	NA
258	El Monte, CA	(8.1)	324	Longview, TX	(18.1)	NA	Wichita, KS**	NA

Source: CQ Press using data from F.B.I. "Crime in the United States 2006"

**Aggravated assault is an attack for the purpose of inflicting severe bodily injury.*

***Not available.*

64. Percent Change in Aggravated Assault Rate: 2002 to 2006

National Percent Change = 7.1% Decrease*

RANK	CITY	% CHANGE
36	Abilene, TX	44.7
86	Albany, GA	17.7
NA	Albany, NY**	NA
240	Albuquerque, NM	(14.0)
192	Alexandria, VA	(5.1)
19	Alhambra, CA	64.3
50	Allentown, PA	33.5
135	Amarillo, TX	4.4
20	Amherst, NY	62.4
156	Anaheim, CA	1.1
17	Anchorage, AK	68.0
66	Ann Arbor, MI	26.6
330	Antioch, CA	(36.1)
74	Arlington, TX	22.5
102	Arvada, CO	13.3
257	Athens-Clarke, GA	(16.1)
314	Atlanta, GA	(28.1)
190	Aurora, CO	(5.0)
252	Aurora, IL	(15.3)
116	Austin, TX	8.4
64	Bakersfield, CA	27.3
137	Baldwin Park, CA	3.9
302	Baltimore, MD	(24.8)
42	Baton Rouge, LA	39.0
51	Beaumont, TX	33.4
70	Beaverton, OR	25.4
175	Bellevue, WA	(2.4)
160	Bellflower, CA	0.9
93	Bellingham, WA	14.9
302	Berkeley, CA	(24.8)
243	Billings, MT	(14.2)
231	Birmingham, AL	(12.1)
146	Bloomington, MN	2.3
138	Boca Raton, FL	3.2
138	Boise, ID	3.2
82	Boston, MA	19.1
59	Boulder, CO	30.9
185	Brick Twnshp, NJ	(3.8)
311	Bridgeport, CT	(27.6)
NA	Brockton, MA**	NA
98	Broken Arrow, OK	13.8
207	Brownsville, TX	(7.2)
90	Buena Park, CA	16.6
106	Buffalo, NY	10.8
152	Burbank, CA	1.4
252	Cambridge, MA	(15.3)
131	Camden, NJ	5.1
223	Canton Twnshp, MI	(10.0)
NA	Canton, OH**	NA
335	Cape Coral, FL	(39.1)
35	Carlsbad, CA	47.6
267	Carrollton, TX	(17.1)
243	Carson, CA	(14.2)
107	Cary, NC	10.7
274	Cedar Rapids, IA	(19.3)
NA	Centennial, CO**	NA
26	Chandler, AZ	57.9
112	Charleston, SC	9.2
265	Charlotte, NC	(16.9)
289	Chattanooga, TN	(21.7)
NA	Cheektowaga, NY**	NA
342	Chesapeake, VA	(41.3)
312	Chicago, IL	(27.8)
360	Chino Hills, CA	(59.6)
10	Chino, CA	87.1
299	Chula Vista, CA	(24.1)
250	Cincinnati, OH	(15.1)
354	Clarkstown, NY	(53.3)
29	Clarksville, TN	54.1
281	Clearwater, FL	(20.5)
177	Cleveland, OH	(2.8)
80	Clifton, NJ	20.0
235	Clinton Twnshp, MI	(13.1)
158	Clovis, CA	1.0
21	Colonie, NY	62.3
142	Colorado Springs, CO	2.9
136	Columbia, MO	4.0
224	Columbia, SC	(10.1)
46	Columbus, GA	35.4
316	Columbus, OH	(29.6)
249	Compton, CA	(15.0)
175	Concord, CA	(2.4)
124	Coral Springs, FL	6.5
258	Corona, CA	(16.4)
113	Corpus Christi, TX	9.0
188	Costa Mesa, CA	(4.2)
236	Cranston, RI	(13.3)
227	Dallas, TX	(10.7)
228	Daly City, CA	(11.1)
242	Danbury, CT	(14.1)
280	Davie, FL	(20.3)
114	Dayton, OH	8.8
364	Dearborn, MI	(70.0)
16	Deerfield Beach, FL	68.8
318	Denton, TX	(30.0)
14	Denver, CO	76.2
NA	Des Moines, IA**	NA
97	Detroit, MI	14.0
282	Downey, CA	(20.6)
164	Duluth, MN	(0.2)
NA	Durham, NC**	NA
43	Edison Twnshp, NJ	38.7
172	Edmond, OK	(2.1)
255	El Cajon, CA	(15.8)
214	El Monte, CA	(8.5)
NA	El Paso, TX**	NA
144	Elizabeth, NJ	2.8
84	Erie, PA	17.9
100	Escondido, CA	13.4
333	Eugene, OR	(36.6)
329	Evansville, IN	(35.7)
96	Everett, WA	14.3
126	Fairfield, CA	6.0
3	Fargo, ND	127.7
310	Farmington Hills, MI	(26.9)
125	Fayetteville, NC	6.2
152	Federal Way, WA	1.4
5	Flint, MI	111.8
291	Fontana, CA	(22.3)
77	Fort Collins, CO	20.3
151	Fort Lauderdale, FL	1.8
67	Fort Smith, AR	26.5
NA	Fort Wayne, IN**	NA
174	Fort Worth, TX	(2.2)
58	Fremont, CA	31.1
203	Fresno, CA	(6.7)
82	Fullerton, CA	19.1
56	Gainesville, FL	31.6
298	Garden Grove, CA	(23.8)
127	Garland, TX	5.9
71	Gary, IN	25.3
207	Gilbert, AZ	(7.2)
128	Glendale, AZ	5.6
324	Glendale, CA	(33.6)
220	Grand Prairie, TX	(9.3)
305	Grand Rapids, MI	(26.0)
NA	Greece, NY**	NA
27	Greeley, CO	55.7
22	Green Bay, WI	62.2
65	Greensboro, NC	27.2
117	Gresham, OR	8.2
37	Hamilton Twnshp, NJ	44.0
180	Hammond, IN	(3.4)
231	Hampton, VA	(12.1)
54	Hartford, CT	31.9
155	Hawthorne, CA	1.2
37	Hayward, CA	44.0
28	Henderson, NV	54.2
120	Hesperia, CA	7.9
226	Hialeah, FL	(10.5)
225	High Point, NC	(10.4)
286	Hillsboro, OR	(21.0)
352	Hollywood, FL	(50.8)
68	Honolulu, HI	26.2
218	Houston, TX	(9.0)
118	Huntington Beach, CA	8.1
78	Huntsville, AL	20.1
61	Independence, MO	29.5
200	Indianapolis, IN	(6.5)
33	Inglewood, CA	51.4
346	Irvine, CA	(44.5)
121	Irving, TX	7.4
258	Jacksonville, FL	(16.4)
115	Jackson, MS	8.5
221	Jersey City, NJ	(9.6)
302	Joliet, IL	(24.8)
NA	Kansas City, KS**	NA
NA	Kansas City, MO**	NA
45	Kenosha, WI	36.0
7	Kent, WA	89.4
258	Killeen, TX	(16.4)
207	Knoxville, TN	(7.2)
109	Lafayette, LA	10.0
265	Lake Forest, CA	(16.9)
271	Lakeland, FL	(18.2)
217	Lakewood, CA	(8.8)
4	Lakewood, CO	115.8
315	Lancaster, CA	(28.8)
183	Lansing, MI	(3.5)
261	Laredo, TX	(16.6)
18	Largo, FL	66.1
NA	Las Cruces, NM**	NA
63	Las Vegas, NV	28.0
34	Lawrence, KS	49.0
31	Lawton, OK	52.9
1	Lee's Summit, MO	402.4
194	Lewisville, TX	(5.4)
NA	Lexington, KY**	NA
195	Lincoln, NE	(5.5)
24	Little Rock, AR	60.9
287	Livermore, CA	(21.1)
296	Livonia, MI	(23.0)

RANK	CITY	% CHANGE
195	Long Beach, CA	(5.5)
6	Longview, TX	110.4
357	Los Angeles, CA	(55.4)
NA	Louisville, KY**	NA
129	Lowell, MA	5.4
285	Lubbock, TX	(20.9)
269	Lynn, MA	(17.3)
41	Macon, GA	40.8
104	Madison, WI	12.9
52	Manchester, NH	32.0
341	McAllen, TX	(41.2)
92	McKinney, TX	15.7
317	Melbourne, FL	(29.8)
48	Memphis, TN	34.6
349	Mesa, AZ	(45.9)
154	Mesquite, TX	1.3
78	Miami Beach, FL	20.1
NA	Miami Gardens, FL**	NA
275	Miami, FL	(19.4)
348	Midland, TX	(45.3)
9	Milwaukee, WI	88.0
30	Minneapolis, MN	53.7
165	Miramar, FL	(0.6)
355	Mission Viejo, CA	(54.8)
288	Mobile, AL	(21.5)
44	Modesto, CA	37.8
332	Montgomery, AL	(36.4)
363	Moreno Valley, CA	(62.7)
165	Murfreesboro, TN	(0.6)
205	Murrieta, CA	(7.1)
81	Napa, CA	19.3
107	Naperville, IL	10.7
NA	Nashua, NH**	NA
200	Nashville, TN	(6.5)
NA	New Bedford, MA**	NA
326	New Orleans, LA	(34.5)
292	New York, NY	(22.4)
213	Newark, NJ	(8.3)
73	Newport Beach, CA	25.1
138	Newport News, VA	3.2
NA	Newton, MA**	NA
25	Norfolk, VA	59.0
297	Norman, OK	(23.2)
178	North Charleston, SC	(3.0)
211	North Las Vegas, NV	(7.6)
343	Norwalk, CA	(42.3)
56	Oakland, CA	31.6
255	Oceanside, CA	(15.8)
76	Odessa, TX	22.1
233	Ogden, UT	(12.4)
148	Oklahoma City, OK	2.2
325	Olathe, KS	(34.4)
262	Omaha, NE	(16.7)
277	Ontario, CA	(20.0)
228	Orange, CA	(11.1)
306	Orem, UT	(26.2)
198	Orlando, FL	(6.2)
320	Overland Park, KS	(30.8)
279	Oxnard, CA	(20.2)
301	Palm Bay, FL	(24.5)
337	Palmdale, CA	(39.5)
163	Parma, OH	0.0
247	Pasadena, CA	(14.5)
161	Pasadena, TX	0.8
13	Paterson, NJ	76.3
246	Pembroke Pines, FL	(14.4)

RANK	CITY	% CHANGE
240	Peoria, AZ	(14.0)
62	Peoria, IL	28.2
105	Philadelphia, PA	11.3
162	Phoenix, AZ	0.7
251	Pittsburgh, PA	(15.2)
145	Plano, TX	2.4
187	Plantation, FL	(3.9)
199	Pomona, CA	(6.3)
47	Pompano Beach, FL	35.0
267	Port St. Lucie, FL	(17.1)
278	Portland, OR	(20.1)
205	Portsmouth, VA	(7.1)
239	Providence, RI	(13.7)
204	Provo, UT	(7.0)
293	Pueblo, CO	(22.6)
86	Quincy, MA	17.7
40	Racine, WI	42.0
192	Raleigh, NC	(5.1)
169	Rancho Cucamon., CA	(1.2)
180	Reading, PA	(3.4)
283	Redding, CA	(20.7)
237	Reno, NV	(13.6)
339	Rialto, CA	(40.6)
321	Richardson, TX	(32.5)
184	Richmond, CA	(3.7)
262	Richmond, VA	(16.7)
294	Riverside, CA	(22.9)
NA	Roanoke, VA**	NA
179	Rochester, MN	(3.3)
8	Rochester, NY	88.1
NA	Rockford, IL**	NA
95	Roseville, CA	14.4
361	Roswell, GA	(60.3)
347	Round Rock, TX	(44.7)
12	Sacramento, CA	80.5
2	Salem, OR	333.4
133	Salinas, CA	4.6
39	Salt Lake City, UT	42.7
167	San Angelo, TX	(1.1)
326	San Antonio, TX	(34.5)
322	San Bernardino, CA	(32.9)
309	San Diego, CA	(26.5)
148	San Francisco, CA	2.2
283	San Jose, CA	(20.7)
55	San Leandro, CA	31.7
150	San Mateo, CA	2.0
290	Sandy, UT	(22.2)
89	Santa Ana, CA	17.0
216	Santa Barbara, CA	(8.6)
356	Santa Clara, CA	(55.0)
91	Santa Clarita, CA	16.2
NA	Santa Maria, CA**	NA
190	Santa Monica, CA	(5.0)
15	Santa Rosa, CA	75.1
344	Savannah, GA	(42.6)
134	Scottsdale, AZ	4.5
167	Seattle, WA	(1.1)
60	Shreveport, LA	30.7
121	Simi Valley, CA	7.4
319	Sioux City, IA	(30.4)
130	Sioux Falls, SD	5.3
210	Somerville, MA	(7.3)
243	South Bend, IN	(14.2)
75	South Gate, CA	22.2
71	Southfield, MI	25.3
197	Sparks, NV	(6.1)

RANK	CITY	% CHANGE
NA	Spokane Valley, WA**	NA
237	Spokane, WA	(13.6)
32	Springfield, IL	52.8
335	Springfield, MA	(39.1)
214	Springfield, MO	(8.5)
100	Sterling Heights, MI	13.4
172	Stockton, CA	(2.1)
94	St. Louis, MO	14.6
69	St. Paul, MN	25.7
272	St. Petersburg, FL	(18.4)
313	Suffolk, VA	(27.9)
361	Sugar Land, TX	(60.3)
230	Sunnyvale, CA	(11.4)
276	Sunrise, FL	(19.6)
353	Surprise, AZ	(51.9)
132	Syracuse, NY	4.8
180	Tacoma, WA	(3.4)
219	Tallahassee, FL	(9.1)
331	Tampa, FL	(36.3)
252	Temecula, CA	(15.3)
308	Tempe, AZ	(26.4)
345	Thornton, CO	(43.6)
85	Thousand Oaks, CA	17.8
52	Toledo, OH	32.0
358	Toms River Twnshp, NJ	(56.0)
340	Topeka, KS	(40.9)
350	Torrance, CA	(47.0)
323	Tracy, CA	(33.0)
270	Trenton, NJ	(17.4)
158	Troy, MI	1.0
264	Tucson, AZ	(16.8)
99	Tulsa, OK	13.7
49	Tuscaloosa, AL	33.6
248	Tyler, TX	(14.9)
138	Upper Darby Twnshp, PA	3.2
273	Vacaville, CA	(18.6)
123	Vallejo, CA	7.2
86	Vancouver, WA	17.7
111	Ventura, CA	9.4
23	Victorville, CA	61.5
102	Virginia Beach, VA	13.3
294	Visalia, CA	(22.9)
142	Vista, CA	2.9
169	Waco, TX	(1.2)
200	Warren, MI	(6.5)
328	Warwick, RI	(34.8)
222	Washington, DC	(9.9)
338	Waterbury, CT	(40.4)
146	West Covina, CA	2.3
334	West Jordan, UT	(37.1)
306	West Palm Beach, FL	(26.2)
156	West Valley, UT	1.1
119	Westland, MI	8.0
212	Westminster, CA	(7.7)
NA	Westminster, CO**	NA
189	Whittier, CA	(4.6)
359	Wichita Falls, TX	(57.3)
11	Wichita, KS	83.4
351	Wilmington, NC	(47.4)
234	Winston-Salem, NC	(12.7)
300	Woodbridge Twnshp, NJ	(24.2)
NA	Worcester, MA**	NA
109	Yakima, WA	10.0
171	Yonkers, NY	(1.5)
185	Youngstown, OH	(3.8)
NA	Yuma, AZ**	NA

Source: CQ Press using data from F.B.I. "Crime in the United States 2006"

**Aggravated assault is an attack for the purpose of inflicting severe bodily injury.*

***Not available.*

64. Percent Change in Aggravated Assault Rate: 2002 to 2006 (continued)

National Percent Change = 7.1% Decrease*

RANK	CITY	% CHANGE
1	Lee's Summit, MO	402.4
2	Salem, OR	333.4
3	Fargo, ND	127.7
4	Lakewood, CO	115.8
5	Flint, MI	111.8
6	Longview, TX	110.4
7	Kent, WA	89.4
8	Rochester, NY	88.1
9	Milwaukee, WI	88.0
10	Chino, CA	87.1
11	Wichita, KS	83.4
12	Sacramento, CA	80.5
13	Paterson, NJ	76.3
14	Denver, CO	76.2
15	Santa Rosa, CA	75.1
16	Deerfield Beach, FL	68.8
17	Anchorage, AK	68.0
18	Largo, FL	66.1
19	Alhambra, CA	64.3
20	Amherst, NY	62.4
21	Colonie, NY	62.3
22	Green Bay, WI	62.2
23	Victorville, CA	61.5
24	Little Rock, AR	60.9
25	Norfolk, VA	59.0
26	Chandler, AZ	57.9
27	Greeley, CO	55.7
28	Henderson, NV	54.2
29	Clarksville, TN	54.1
30	Minneapolis, MN	53.7
31	Lawton, OK	52.9
32	Springfield, IL	52.8
33	Inglewood, CA	51.4
34	Lawrence, KS	49.0
35	Carlsbad, CA	47.6
36	Abilene, TX	44.7
37	Hamilton Twnshp, NJ	44.0
37	Hayward, CA	44.0
39	Salt Lake City, UT	42.7
40	Racine, WI	42.0
41	Macon, GA	40.8
42	Baton Rouge, LA	39.0
43	Edison Twnshp, NJ	38.7
44	Modesto, CA	37.8
45	Kenosha, WI	36.0
46	Columbus, GA	35.4
47	Pompano Beach, FL	35.0
48	Memphis, TN	34.6
49	Tuscaloosa, AL	33.6
50	Allentown, PA	33.5
51	Beaumont, TX	33.4
52	Manchester, NH	32.0
52	Toledo, OH	32.0
54	Hartford, CT	31.9
55	San Leandro, CA	31.7
56	Gainesville, FL	31.6
56	Oakland, CA	31.6
58	Fremont, CA	31.1
59	Boulder, CO	30.9
60	Shreveport, LA	30.7
61	Independence, MO	29.5
62	Peoria, IL	28.2
63	Las Vegas, NV	28.0
64	Bakersfield, CA	27.3
65	Greensboro, NC	27.2
66	Ann Arbor, MI	26.6
67	Fort Smith, AR	26.5
68	Honolulu, HI	26.2
69	St. Paul, MN	25.7
70	Beaverton, OR	25.4
71	Gary, IN	25.3
71	Southfield, MI	25.3
73	Newport Beach, CA	25.1
74	Arlington, TX	22.5
75	South Gate, CA	22.2
76	Odessa, TX	22.1
77	Fort Collins, CO	20.3
78	Huntsville, AL	20.1
78	Miami Beach, FL	20.1
80	Clifton, NJ	20.0
81	Napa, CA	19.3
82	Boston, MA	19.1
82	Fullerton, CA	19.1
84	Erie, PA	17.9
85	Thousand Oaks, CA	17.8
86	Albany, GA	17.7
86	Quincy, MA	17.7
86	Vancouver, WA	17.7
89	Santa Ana, CA	17.0
90	Buena Park, CA	16.6
91	Santa Clarita, CA	16.2
92	McKinney, TX	15.7
93	Bellingham, WA	14.9
94	St. Louis, MO	14.6
95	Roseville, CA	14.4
96	Everett, WA	14.3
97	Detroit, MI	14.0
98	Broken Arrow, OK	13.8
99	Tulsa, OK	13.7
100	Escondido, CA	13.4
100	Sterling Heights, MI	13.4
102	Arvada, CO	13.3
102	Virginia Beach, VA	13.3
104	Madison, WI	12.9
105	Philadelphia, PA	11.3
106	Buffalo, NY	10.8
107	Cary, NC	10.7
107	Naperville, IL	10.7
109	Lafayette, LA	10.0
109	Yakima, WA	10.0
111	Ventura, CA	9.4
112	Charleston, SC	9.2
113	Corpus Christi, TX	9.0
114	Dayton, OH	8.8
115	Jackson, MS	8.5
116	Austin, TX	8.4
117	Gresham, OR	8.2
118	Huntington Beach, CA	8.1
119	Westland, MI	8.0
120	Hesperia, CA	7.9
121	Irving, TX	7.4
121	Simi Valley, CA	7.4
123	Vallejo, CA	7.2
124	Coral Springs, FL	6.5
125	Fayetteville, NC	6.2
126	Fairfield, CA	6.0
127	Garland, TX	5.9
128	Glendale, AZ	5.6
129	Lowell, MA	5.4
130	Sioux Falls, SD	5.3
131	Camden, NJ	5.1
132	Syracuse, NY	4.8
133	Salinas, CA	4.6
134	Scottsdale, AZ	4.5
135	Amarillo, TX	4.4
136	Columbia, MO	4.0
137	Baldwin Park, CA	3.9
138	Boca Raton, FL	3.2
138	Boise, ID	3.2
138	Newport News, VA	3.2
138	Upper Darby Twnshp, PA	3.2
142	Colorado Springs, CO	2.9
142	Vista, CA	2.9
144	Elizabeth, NJ	2.8
145	Plano, TX	2.4
146	Bloomington, MN	2.3
146	West Covina, CA	2.3
148	Oklahoma City, OK	2.2
148	San Francisco, CA	2.2
150	San Mateo, CA	2.0
151	Fort Lauderdale, FL	1.8
152	Burbank, CA	1.4
152	Federal Way, WA	1.4
154	Mesquite, TX	1.3
155	Hawthorne, CA	1.2
156	Anaheim, CA	1.1
156	West Valley, UT	1.1
158	Clovis, CA	1.0
158	Troy, MI	1.0
160	Bellflower, CA	0.9
161	Pasadena, TX	0.8
162	Phoenix, AZ	0.7
163	Parma, OH	0.0
164	Duluth, MN	(0.2)
165	Miramar, FL	(0.6)
165	Murfreesboro, TN	(0.6)
167	San Angelo, TX	(1.1)
167	Seattle, WA	(1.1)
169	Rancho Cucamon., CA	(1.2)
169	Waco, TX	(1.2)
171	Yonkers, NY	(1.5)
172	Edmond, OK	(2.1)
172	Stockton, CA	(2.1)
174	Fort Worth, TX	(2.2)
175	Bellevue, WA	(2.4)
175	Concord, CA	(2.4)
177	Cleveland, OH	(2.8)
178	North Charleston, SC	(3.0)
179	Rochester, MN	(3.3)
180	Hammond, IN	(3.4)
180	Reading, PA	(3.4)
180	Tacoma, WA	(3.4)
183	Lansing, MI	(3.5)
184	Richmond, CA	(3.7)
185	Brick Twnshp, NJ	(3.8)
185	Youngstown, OH	(3.8)
187	Plantation, FL	(3.9)
188	Costa Mesa, CA	(4.2)
189	Whittier, CA	(4.6)
190	Aurora, CO	(5.0)
190	Santa Monica, CA	(5.0)
192	Alexandria, VA	(5.1)

RANK	CITY	% CHANGE
192	Raleigh, NC	(5.1)
194	Lewisville, TX	(5.4)
195	Lincoln, NE	(5.5)
195	Long Beach, CA	(5.5)
197	Sparks, NV	(6.1)
198	Orlando, FL	(6.2)
199	Pomona, CA	(6.3)
200	Indianapolis, IN	(6.5)
200	Nashville, TN	(6.5)
200	Warren, MI	(6.5)
203	Fresno, CA	(6.7)
204	Provo, UT	(7.0)
205	Murrieta, CA	(7.1)
205	Portsmouth, VA	(7.1)
207	Brownsville, TX	(7.2)
207	Gilbert, AZ	(7.2)
207	Knoxville, TN	(7.2)
210	Somerville, MA	(7.3)
211	North Las Vegas, NV	(7.6)
212	Westminster, CA	(7.7)
213	Newark, NJ	(8.3)
214	El Monte, CA	(8.5)
214	Springfield, MO	(8.5)
216	Santa Barbara, CA	(8.6)
217	Lakewood, CA	(8.8)
218	Houston, TX	(9.0)
219	Tallahassee, FL	(9.1)
220	Grand Prairie, TX	(9.3)
221	Jersey City, NJ	(9.6)
222	Washington, DC	(9.9)
223	Canton Twnshp, MI	(10.0)
224	Columbia, SC	(10.1)
225	High Point, NC	(10.4)
226	Hialeah, FL	(10.5)
227	Dallas, TX	(10.7)
228	Daly City, CA	(11.1)
228	Orange, CA	(11.1)
230	Sunnyvale, CA	(11.4)
231	Birmingham, AL	(12.1)
231	Hampton, VA	(12.1)
233	Ogden, UT	(12.4)
234	Winston-Salem, NC	(12.7)
235	Clinton Twnshp, MI	(13.1)
236	Cranston, RI	(13.3)
237	Reno, NV	(13.6)
237	Spokane, WA	(13.6)
239	Providence, RI	(13.7)
240	Albuquerque, NM	(14.0)
240	Peoria, AZ	(14.0)
242	Danbury, CT	(14.1)
243	Billings, MT	(14.2)
243	Carson, CA	(14.2)
243	South Bend, IN	(14.2)
246	Pembroke Pines, FL	(14.4)
247	Pasadena, CA	(14.5)
248	Tyler, TX	(14.9)
249	Compton, CA	(15.0)
250	Cincinnati, OH	(15.1)
251	Pittsburgh, PA	(15.2)
252	Aurora, IL	(15.3)
252	Cambridge, MA	(15.3)
252	Temecula, CA	(15.3)
255	El Cajon, CA	(15.8)
255	Oceanside, CA	(15.8)
257	Athens-Clarke, GA	(16.1)
258	Corona, CA	(16.4)
258	Jacksonville, FL	(16.4)
258	Killeen, TX	(16.4)
261	Laredo, TX	(16.6)
262	Omaha, NE	(16.7)
262	Richmond, VA	(16.7)
264	Tucson, AZ	(16.8)
265	Charlotte, NC	(16.9)
265	Lake Forest, CA	(16.9)
267	Carrollton, TX	(17.1)
267	Port St. Lucie, FL	(17.1)
269	Lynn, MA	(17.3)
270	Trenton, NJ	(17.4)
271	Lakeland, FL	(18.2)
272	St. Petersburg, FL	(18.4)
273	Vacaville, CA	(18.6)
274	Cedar Rapids, IA	(19.3)
275	Miami, FL	(19.4)
276	Sunrise, FL	(19.6)
277	Ontario, CA	(20.0)
278	Portland, OR	(20.1)
279	Oxnard, CA	(20.2)
280	Davie, FL	(20.3)
281	Clearwater, FL	(20.5)
282	Downey, CA	(20.6)
283	Redding, CA	(20.7)
283	San Jose, CA	(20.7)
285	Lubbock, TX	(20.9)
286	Hillsboro, OR	(21.0)
287	Livermore, CA	(21.1)
288	Mobile, AL	(21.5)
289	Chattanooga, TN	(21.7)
290	Sandy, UT	(22.2)
291	Fontana, CA	(22.3)
292	New York, NY	(22.4)
293	Pueblo, CO	(22.6)
294	Riverside, CA	(22.9)
294	Visalia, CA	(22.9)
296	Livonia, MI	(23.0)
297	Norman, OK	(23.2)
298	Garden Grove, CA	(23.8)
299	Chula Vista, CA	(24.1)
300	Woodbridge Twnshp, NJ	(24.2)
301	Palm Bay, FL	(24.5)
302	Baltimore, MD	(24.8)
302	Berkeley, CA	(24.8)
302	Joliet, IL	(24.8)
305	Grand Rapids, MI	(26.0)
306	Orem, UT	(26.2)
306	West Palm Beach, FL	(26.2)
308	Tempe, AZ	(26.4)
309	San Diego, CA	(26.5)
310	Farmington Hills, MI	(26.9)
311	Bridgeport, CT	(27.6)
312	Chicago, IL	(27.8)
313	Suffolk, VA	(27.9)
314	Atlanta, GA	(28.1)
315	Lancaster, CA	(28.8)
316	Columbus, OH	(29.6)
317	Melbourne, FL	(29.8)
318	Denton, TX	(30.0)
319	Sioux City, IA	(30.4)
320	Overland Park, KS	(30.8)
321	Richardson, TX	(32.5)
322	San Bernardino, CA	(32.9)
323	Tracy, CA	(33.0)
324	Glendale, CA	(33.6)
325	Olathe, KS	(34.4)
326	New Orleans, LA	(34.5)
326	San Antonio, TX	(34.5)
328	Warwick, RI	(34.8)
329	Evansville, IN	(35.7)
330	Antioch, CA	(36.1)
331	Tampa, FL	(36.3)
332	Montgomery, AL	(36.4)
333	Eugene, OR	(36.6)
334	West Jordan, UT	(37.1)
335	Cape Coral, FL	(39.1)
335	Springfield, MA	(39.1)
337	Palmdale, CA	(39.5)
338	Waterbury, CT	(40.4)
339	Rialto, CA	(40.6)
340	Topeka, KS	(40.9)
341	McAllen, TX	(41.2)
342	Chesapeake, VA	(41.3)
343	Norwalk, CA	(42.3)
344	Savannah, GA	(42.6)
345	Thornton, CO	(43.6)
346	Irvine, CA	(44.5)
347	Round Rock, TX	(44.7)
348	Midland, TX	(45.3)
349	Mesa, AZ	(45.9)
350	Torrance, CA	(47.0)
351	Wilmington, NC	(47.4)
352	Hollywood, FL	(50.8)
353	Surprise, AZ	(51.9)
354	Clarkstown, NY	(53.3)
355	Mission Viejo, CA	(54.8)
356	Santa Clara, CA	(55.0)
357	Los Angeles, CA	(55.4)
358	Toms River Twnshp, NJ	(56.0)
359	Wichita Falls, TX	(57.3)
360	Chino Hills, CA	(59.6)
361	Roswell, GA	(60.3)
361	Sugar Land, TX	(60.3)
363	Moreno Valley, CA	(62.7)
364	Dearborn, MI	(70.0)
NA	Albany, NY**	NA
NA	Brockton, MA**	NA
NA	Canton, OH**	NA
NA	Centennial, CO**	NA
NA	Cheektowaga, NY**	NA
NA	Des Moines, IA**	NA
NA	Durham, NC**	NA
NA	El Paso, TX**	NA
NA	Fort Wayne, IN**	NA
NA	Greece, NY**	NA
NA	Kansas City, KS**	NA
NA	Kansas City, MO**	NA
NA	Las Cruces, NM**	NA
NA	Lexington, KY**	NA
NA	Louisville, KY**	NA
NA	Miami Gardens, FL**	NA
NA	Nashua, NH**	NA
NA	New Bedford, MA**	NA
NA	Newton, MA**	NA
NA	Roanoke, VA**	NA
NA	Rockford, IL**	NA
NA	Santa Maria, CA**	NA
NA	Spokane Valley, WA**	NA
NA	Westminster, CO**	NA
NA	Worcester, MA**	NA
NA	Yuma, AZ**	NA

Source: CQ Press using data from F.B.I. "Crime in the United States 2006"

**Aggravated assault is an attack for the purpose of inflicting severe bodily injury.*

***Not available.*

65. Property Crimes in 2006
National Total = 9,983,568 Property Crimes*

RANK	CITY	CRIMES
191	Abilene, TX	5,045
186	Albany, GA	5,279
209	Albany, NY	4,820
29	Albuquerque, NM	31,757
284	Alexandria, VA	3,194
332	Alhambra, CA	2,472
164	Allentown, PA	6,059
97	Amarillo, TX	11,080
371	Amherst, NY	1,882
112	Anaheim, CA	8,817
92	Anchorage, AK	11,721
301	Ann Arbor, MI	2,923
308	Antioch, CA	2,844
49	Arlington, TX	19,666
282	Arvada, CO	3,202
175	Athens-Clarke, GA	5,634
27	Atlanta, GA	32,231
75	Aurora, CO	12,805
197	Aurora, IL	4,936
17	Austin, TX	41,573
58	Bakersfield, CA	15,915
361	Baldwin Park, CA	2,046
26	Baltimore, MD	32,321
64	Baton Rouge, LA	14,684
145	Beaumont, TX	6,962
354	Beaverton, OR	2,205
233	Bellevue, WA	4,245
351	Bellflower, CA	2,219
182	Bellingham, WA	5,334
139	Berkeley, CA	7,323
232	Billings, MT	4,304
52	Birmingham, AL	19,007
303	Bloomington, MN	2,892
298	Boca Raton, FL	2,951
151	Boise, ID	6,616
36	Boston, MA	25,094
295	Boulder, CO	3,016
385	Brick Twnshp, NJ	1,463
144	Bridgeport, CT	6,987
265	Brockton, MA	3,498
379	Broken Arrow, OK	1,673
121	Brownsville, TX	8,385
367	Buena Park, CA	1,960
61	Buffalo, NY	15,436
319	Burbank, CA	2,721
280	Cambridge, MA	3,283
210	Camden, NJ	4,787
375	Canton Twnshp, MI	1,708
162	Canton, OH	6,222
200	Cape Coral, FL	4,908
334	Carlsbad, CA	2,455
252	Carrollton, TX	3,782
311	Carson, CA	2,823
355	Cary, NC	2,189
168	Cedar Rapids, IA	5,872
380	Centennial, CO	1,618
115	Chandler, AZ	8,724
227	Charleston, SC	4,358
14	Charlotte, NC	48,886
82	Chattanooga, TN	12,275
336	Cheektowaga, NY	2,419
148	Chesapeake, VA	6,888
2	Chicago, IL	129,718
387	Chino Hills, CA	1,214
339	Chino, CA	2,390
141	Chula Vista, CA	7,034
43	Cincinnati, OH	22,107
382	Clarkstown, NY	1,602
234	Clarksville, TN	4,242
208	Clearwater, FL	4,837
32	Cleveland, OH	28,220
370	Clifton, NJ	1,911
333	Clinton Twnshp, MI	2,461
288	Clovis, CA	3,154
304	Colonie, NY	2,890
55	Colorado Springs, CO	18,076
292	Columbia, MO	3,105
143	Columbia, SC	6,994
66	Columbus, GA	13,825
12	Columbus, OH	52,098
337	Compton, CA	2,411
180	Concord, CA	5,386
299	Coral Springs, FL	2,949
244	Corona, CA	4,042
51	Corpus Christi, TX	19,138
272	Costa Mesa, CA	3,380
372	Cranston, RI	1,876
6	Dallas, TX	85,592
341	Daly City, CA	2,344
383	Danbury, CT	1,601
306	Davie, FL	2,865
91	Dayton, OH	11,759
196	Dearborn, MI	4,947
325	Deerfield Beach, FL	2,591
286	Denton, TX	3,168
33	Denver, CO	26,266
67	Des Moines, IA	13,505
9	Detroit, MI	62,338
257	Downey, CA	3,616
242	Duluth, MN	4,057
88	Durham, NC	11,866
343	Edison Twnshp, NJ	2,320
366	Edmond, OK	1,961
258	El Cajon, CA	3,612
283	El Monte, CA	3,199
46	El Paso, TX	20,576
211	Elizabeth, NJ	4,774
297	Erie, PA	2,987
221	Escondido, CA	4,407
125	Eugene, OR	8,113
183	Evansville, IN	5,307
110	Everett, WA	9,063
225	Fairfield, CA	4,363
321	Fargo, ND	2,679
384	Farmington Hills, MI	1,553
71	Fayetteville, NC	13,091
189	Federal Way, WA	5,182
124	Flint, MI	8,117
278	Fontana, CA	3,309
217	Fort Collins, CO	4,570
105	Fort Lauderdale, FL	9,937
178	Fort Smith, AR	5,491
100	Fort Wayne, IN	10,767
23	Fort Worth, TX	36,473
184	Fremont, CA	5,298
40	Fresno, CA	23,407
228	Fullerton, CA	4,337
170	Gainesville, FL	5,763
239	Garden Grove, CA	4,165
126	Garland, TX	7,884
176	Gary, IN	5,564
198	Gilbert, AZ	4,935
87	Glendale, AZ	12,094
249	Glendale, CA	3,935
135	Grand Prairie, TX	7,479
103	Grand Rapids, MI	10,103
342	Greece, NY	2,321
229	Greeley, CO	4,324
305	Green Bay, WI	2,874
65	Greensboro, NC	14,336
246	Gresham, OR	4,026
373	Hamilton Twnshp, NJ	1,871
235	Hammond, IN	4,226
205	Hampton, VA	4,861
111	Hartford, CT	8,824
359	Hawthorne, CA	2,101
171	Hayward, CA	5,736
150	Henderson, NV	6,674
362	Hesperia, CA	2,040
116	Hialeah, FL	8,674
174	High Point, NC	5,652
317	Hillsboro, OR	2,752
160	Hollywood, FL	6,254
20	Honolulu, HI	38,310
3	Houston, TX	121,053
220	Huntington Beach, CA	4,468
94	Huntsville, AL	11,495
129	Independence, MO	7,608
13	Indianapolis, IN	49,599
300	Inglewood, CA	2,926
294	Irvine, CA	3,034
108	Irving, TX	9,644
16	Jacksonville, FL	43,103
69	Jackson, MS	13,208
130	Jersey City, NJ	7,590
243	Joliet, IL	4,049
102	Kansas City, KS	10,281
30	Kansas City, MO	31,100
302	Kenosha, WI	2,909
161	Kent, WA	6,252
179	Killeen, TX	5,471
98	Knoxville, TN	11,063
155	Lafayette, LA	6,393
388	Lake Forest, CA	1,104
190	Lakeland, FL	5,158
347	Lakewood, CA	2,255
142	Lakewood, CO	6,995
194	Lancaster, CA	5,027
214	Lansing, MI	4,656
80	Laredo, TX	12,511
318	Largo, FL	2,733
250	Las Cruces, NM	3,906
10	Las Vegas, NV	61,405
199	Lawrence, KS	4,914
212	Lawton, OK	4,727
345	Lee's Summit, MO	2,315
293	Lewisville, TX	3,045
101	Lexington, KY	10,437
84	Lincoln, NE	12,237
60	Little Rock, AR	15,789
376	Livermore, CA	1,703
344	Livonia, MI	2,318

Alpha Order- City (continued)

RANK	CITY	CRIMES
76	Long Beach, CA	12,778
201	Longview, TX	4,902
4	Los Angeles, CA	105,459
31	Louisville, KY	29,136
274	Lowell, MA	3,352
81	Lubbock, TX	12,373
296	Lynn, MA	3,000
109	Macon, GA	9,486
134	Madison, WI	7,498
266	Manchester, NH	3,454
146	McAllen, TX	6,926
353	McKinney, TX	2,217
247	Melbourne, FL	4,010
11	Memphis, TN	56,905
45	Mesa, AZ	21,304
181	Mesquite, TX	5,374
131	Miami Beach, FL	7,582
159	Miami Gardens, FL	6,281
47	Miami, FL	20,288
253	Midland, TX	3,712
21	Milwaukee, WI	38,233
42	Minneapolis, MN	22,561
281	Miramar, FL	3,219
386	Mission Viejo, CA	1,399
59	Mobile, AL	15,849
89	Modesto, CA	11,804
72	Montgomery, AL	13,086
147	Moreno Valley, CA	6,899
229	Murfreesboro, TN	4,324
364	Murrieta, CA	1,974
356	Napa, CA	2,164
350	Naperville, IL	2,231
349	Nashua, NH	2,241
25	Nashville, TN	32,625
290	New Bedford, MA	3,140
85	New Orleans, LA	12,178
1	New York, NY	153,436
95	Newark, NJ	11,456
335	Newport Beach, CA	2,431
132	Newport News, VA	7,578
389	Newton, MA	1,055
93	Norfolk, VA	11,683
261	Norman, OK	3,582
136	North Charleston, SC	7,470
119	North Las Vegas, NV	8,617
323	Norwalk, CA	2,602
37	Oakland, CA	24,344
204	Oceanside, CA	4,873
256	Odessa, TX	3,654
193	Ogden, UT	5,029
24	Oklahoma City, OK	34,292
346	Olathe, KS	2,277
44	Omaha, NE	21,787
156	Ontario, CA	6,337
279	Orange, CA	3,291
326	Orem, UT	2,564
54	Orlando, FL	18,318
219	Overland Park, KS	4,541
223	Oxnard, CA	4,376
289	Palm Bay, FL	3,141
236	Palmdale, CA	4,212
377	Parma, OH	1,699
222	Pasadena, CA	4,398
207	Pasadena, TX	4,848
226	Paterson, NJ	4,360
202	Pembroke Pines, FL	4,886
172	Peoria, AZ	5,719
152	Peoria, IL	6,547
8	Philadelphia, PA	62,612
5	Phoenix, AZ	90,050
63	Pittsburgh, PA	15,236
118	Plano, TX	8,618
255	Plantation, FL	3,675
188	Pomona, CA	5,227
195	Pompano Beach, FL	4,985
262	Port St. Lucie, FL	3,563
28	Portland, OR	31,996
191	Portsmouth, VA	5,045
120	Providence, RI	8,585
307	Provo, UT	2,859
157	Pueblo, CO	6,317
378	Quincy, MA	1,684
216	Racine, WI	4,594
78	Raleigh, NC	12,650
248	Rancho Cucamon., CA	3,966
215	Reading, PA	4,637
270	Redding, CA	3,389
99	Reno, NV	10,797
320	Rialto, CA	2,708
291	Richardson, TX	3,118
177	Richmond, CA	5,495
104	Richmond, VA	10,092
83	Riverside, CA	12,267
185	Roanoke, VA	5,295
327	Rochester, MN	2,525
73	Rochester, NY	12,999
96	Rockford, IL	11,240
251	Roseville, CA	3,884
352	Roswell, GA	2,218
365	Round Rock, TX	1,968
34	Sacramento, CA	26,112
123	Salem, OR	8,267
166	Salinas, CA	6,023
62	Salt Lake City, UT	15,420
218	San Angelo, TX	4,557
7	San Antonio, TX	78,621
107	San Bernardino, CA	9,760
15	San Diego, CA	45,209
22	San Francisco, CA	36,992
38	San Jose, CA	24,240
238	San Leandro, CA	4,196
329	San Mateo, CA	2,488
287	Sandy, UT	3,161
117	Santa Ana, CA	8,630
330	Santa Barbara, CA	2,483
273	Santa Clara, CA	3,354
268	Santa Clarita, CA	3,444
338	Santa Maria, CA	2,410
277	Santa Monica, CA	3,314
236	Santa Rosa, CA	4,212
106	Savannah, GA	9,924
122	Scottsdale, AZ	8,315
19	Seattle, WA	39,532
77	Shreveport, LA	12,693
360	Simi Valley, CA	2,060
271	Sioux City, IA	3,384
260	Sioux Falls, SD	3,596
369	Somerville, MA	1,954
137	South Bend, IN	7,411
314	South Gate, CA	2,764
259	Southfield, MI	3,604
267	Sparks, NV	3,452
263	Spokane Valley, WA	3,527
89	Spokane, WA	11,804
127	Springfield, IL	7,747
114	Springfield, MA	8,747
70	Springfield, MO	13,161
269	Sterling Heights, MI	3,415
48	Stockton, CA	19,719
18	St. Louis, MO	40,751
86	St. Paul, MN	12,103
57	St. Petersburg, FL	16,409
328	Suffolk, VA	2,515
381	Sugar Land, TX	1,609
322	Sunnyvale, CA	2,632
275	Sunrise, FL	3,343
348	Surprise, AZ	2,253
149	Syracuse, NY	6,677
56	Tacoma, WA	16,540
128	Tallahassee, FL	7,709
53	Tampa, FL	18,789
312	Temecula, CA	2,820
79	Tempe, AZ	12,589
213	Thornton, CO	4,711
374	Thousand Oaks, CA	1,794
41	Toledo, OH	22,711
368	Toms River Twnshp, NJ	1,958
113	Topeka, KS	8,748
285	Torrance, CA	3,171
310	Tracy, CA	2,825
331	Trenton, NJ	2,477
363	Troy, MI	2,018
NA	Tucson, AZ**	NA
39	Tulsa, OK	24,011
187	Tuscaloosa, AL	5,234
231	Tyler, TX	4,313
357	Upper Darby Twnshp, PA	2,158
340	Vacaville, CA	2,384
167	Vallejo, CA	5,971
153	Vancouver, WA	6,527
254	Ventura, CA	3,686
240	Victorville, CA	4,157
74	Virginia Beach, VA	12,855
154	Visalia, CA	6,466
309	Vista, CA	2,838
133	Waco, TX	7,512
203	Warren, MI	4,883
358	Warwick, RI	2,120
35	Washington, DC	26,015
165	Waterbury, CT	6,039
245	West Covina, CA	4,030
276	West Jordan, UT	3,329
138	West Palm Beach, FL	7,332
169	West Valley, UT	5,783
316	Westland, MI	2,758
324	Westminster, CA	2,594
224	Westminster, CO	4,366
315	Whittier, CA	2,760
158	Wichita Falls, TX	6,285
50	Wichita, KS	19,562
163	Wilmington, NC	6,207
68	Winston-Salem, NC	13,449
313	Woodbridge Twnshp, NJ	2,804
173	Worcester, MA	5,671
140	Yakima, WA	7,159
264	Yonkers, NY	3,502
206	Youngstown, OH	4,854
241	Yuma, AZ	4,066

Source: Federal Bureau of Investigation "Crime in the United States 2006"

**Property crimes are offenses of burglary, larceny-theft, and motor vehicle theft. Attempts are included.*

***Not available.*

65. Property Crimes in 2006 (continued)

National Total = 9,983,568 Property Crimes*

RANK	CITY	CRIMES
1	New York, NY	153,436
2	Chicago, IL	129,718
3	Houston, TX	121,053
4	Los Angeles, CA	105,459
5	Phoenix, AZ	90,050
6	Dallas, TX	85,592
7	San Antonio, TX	78,621
8	Philadelphia, PA	62,612
9	Detroit, MI	62,338
10	Las Vegas, NV	61,405
11	Memphis, TN	56,905
12	Columbus, OH	52,098
13	Indianapolis, IN	49,599
14	Charlotte, NC	48,886
15	San Diego, CA	45,209
16	Jacksonville, FL	43,103
17	Austin, TX	41,573
18	St. Louis, MO	40,751
19	Seattle, WA	39,532
20	Honolulu, HI	38,310
21	Milwaukee, WI	38,233
22	San Francisco, CA	36,992
23	Fort Worth, TX	36,473
24	Oklahoma City, OK	34,292
25	Nashville, TN	32,625
26	Baltimore, MD	32,321
27	Atlanta, GA	32,231
28	Portland, OR	31,996
29	Albuquerque, NM	31,757
30	Kansas City, MO	31,100
31	Louisville, KY	29,136
32	Cleveland, OH	28,220
33	Denver, CO	26,266
34	Sacramento, CA	26,112
35	Washington, DC	26,015
36	Boston, MA	25,094
37	Oakland, CA	24,344
38	San Jose, CA	24,240
39	Tulsa, OK	24,011
40	Fresno, CA	23,407
41	Toledo, OH	22,711
42	Minneapolis, MN	22,561
43	Cincinnati, OH	22,107
44	Omaha, NE	21,787
45	Mesa, AZ	21,304
46	El Paso, TX	20,576
47	Miami, FL	20,288
48	Stockton, CA	19,719
49	Arlington, TX	19,666
50	Wichita, KS	19,562
51	Corpus Christi, TX	19,138
52	Birmingham, AL	19,007
53	Tampa, FL	18,789
54	Orlando, FL	18,318
55	Colorado Springs, CO	18,076
56	Tacoma, WA	16,540
57	St. Petersburg, FL	16,409
58	Bakersfield, CA	15,915
59	Mobile, AL	15,849
60	Little Rock, AR	15,789
61	Buffalo, NY	15,436
62	Salt Lake City, UT	15,420
63	Pittsburgh, PA	15,236
64	Baton Rouge, LA	14,684
65	Greensboro, NC	14,336
66	Columbus, GA	13,825
67	Des Moines, IA	13,505
68	Winston-Salem, NC	13,449
69	Jackson, MS	13,208
70	Springfield, MO	13,161
71	Fayetteville, NC	13,091
72	Montgomery, AL	13,086
73	Rochester, NY	12,999
74	Virginia Beach, VA	12,855
75	Aurora, CO	12,805
76	Long Beach, CA	12,778
77	Shreveport, LA	12,693
78	Raleigh, NC	12,650
79	Tempe, AZ	12,589
80	Laredo, TX	12,511
81	Lubbock, TX	12,373
82	Chattanooga, TN	12,275
83	Riverside, CA	12,267
84	Lincoln, NE	12,237
85	New Orleans, LA	12,178
86	St. Paul, MN	12,103
87	Glendale, AZ	12,094
88	Durham, NC	11,866
89	Modesto, CA	11,804
89	Spokane, WA	11,804
91	Dayton, OH	11,759
92	Anchorage, AK	11,721
93	Norfolk, VA	11,683
94	Huntsville, AL	11,495
95	Newark, NJ	11,456
96	Rockford, IL	11,240
97	Amarillo, TX	11,080
98	Knoxville, TN	11,063
99	Reno, NV	10,797
100	Fort Wayne, IN	10,767
101	Lexington, KY	10,437
102	Kansas City, KS	10,281
103	Grand Rapids, MI	10,103
104	Richmond, VA	10,092
105	Fort Lauderdale, FL	9,937
106	Savannah, GA	9,924
107	San Bernardino, CA	9,760
108	Irving, TX	9,644
109	Macon, GA	9,486
110	Everett, WA	9,063
111	Hartford, CT	8,824
112	Anaheim, CA	8,817
113	Topeka, KS	8,748
114	Springfield, MA	8,747
115	Chandler, AZ	8,724
116	Hialeah, FL	8,674
117	Santa Ana, CA	8,630
118	Plano, TX	8,618
119	North Las Vegas, NV	8,617
120	Providence, RI	8,585
121	Brownsville, TX	8,385
122	Scottsdale, AZ	8,315
123	Salem, OR	8,267
124	Flint, MI	8,117
125	Eugene, OR	8,113
126	Garland, TX	7,884
127	Springfield, IL	7,747
128	Tallahassee, FL	7,709
129	Independence, MO	7,608
130	Jersey City, NJ	7,590
131	Miami Beach, FL	7,582
132	Newport News, VA	7,578
133	Waco, TX	7,512
134	Madison, WI	7,498
135	Grand Prairie, TX	7,479
136	North Charleston, SC	7,470
137	South Bend, IN	7,411
138	West Palm Beach, FL	7,332
139	Berkeley, CA	7,323
140	Yakima, WA	7,159
141	Chula Vista, CA	7,034
142	Lakewood, CO	6,995
143	Columbia, SC	6,994
144	Bridgeport, CT	6,987
145	Beaumont, TX	6,962
146	McAllen, TX	6,926
147	Moreno Valley, CA	6,899
148	Chesapeake, VA	6,888
149	Syracuse, NY	6,677
150	Henderson, NV	6,674
151	Boise, ID	6,616
152	Peoria, IL	6,547
153	Vancouver, WA	6,527
154	Visalia, CA	6,466
155	Lafayette, LA	6,393
156	Ontario, CA	6,337
157	Pueblo, CO	6,317
158	Wichita Falls, TX	6,285
159	Miami Gardens, FL	6,281
160	Hollywood, FL	6,254
161	Kent, WA	6,252
162	Canton, OH	6,222
163	Wilmington, NC	6,207
164	Allentown, PA	6,059
165	Waterbury, CT	6,039
166	Salinas, CA	6,023
167	Vallejo, CA	5,971
168	Cedar Rapids, IA	5,872
169	West Valley, UT	5,783
170	Gainesville, FL	5,763
171	Hayward, CA	5,736
172	Peoria, AZ	5,719
173	Worcester, MA	5,671
174	High Point, NC	5,652
175	Athens-Clarke, GA	5,634
176	Gary, IN	5,564
177	Richmond, CA	5,495
178	Fort Smith, AR	5,491
179	Killeen, TX	5,471
180	Concord, CA	5,386
181	Mesquite, TX	5,374
182	Bellingham, WA	5,334
183	Evansville, IN	5,307
184	Fremont, CA	5,298
185	Roanoke, VA	5,295
186	Albany, GA	5,279
187	Tuscaloosa, AL	5,234
188	Pomona, CA	5,227
189	Federal Way, WA	5,182
190	Lakeland, FL	5,158
191	Abilene, TX	5,045
191	Portsmouth, VA	5,045

RANK	CITY	CRIMES
193	Ogden, UT	5,029
194	Lancaster, CA	5,027
195	Pompano Beach, FL	4,985
196	Dearborn, MI	4,947
197	Aurora, IL	4,936
198	Gilbert, AZ	4,935
199	Lawrence, KS	4,914
200	Cape Coral, FL	4,908
201	Longview, TX	4,902
202	Pembroke Pines, FL	4,886
203	Warren, MI	4,883
204	Oceanside, CA	4,873
205	Hampton, VA	4,861
206	Youngstown, OH	4,854
207	Pasadena, TX	4,848
208	Clearwater, FL	4,837
209	Albany, NY	4,820
210	Camden, NJ	4,787
211	Elizabeth, NJ	4,774
212	Lawton, OK	4,727
213	Thornton, CO	4,711
214	Lansing, MI	4,656
215	Reading, PA	4,637
216	Racine, WI	4,594
217	Fort Collins, CO	4,570
218	San Angelo, TX	4,557
219	Overland Park, KS	4,541
220	Huntington Beach, CA	4,468
221	Escondido, CA	4,407
222	Pasadena, CA	4,398
223	Oxnard, CA	4,376
224	Westminster, CO	4,366
225	Fairfield, CA	4,363
226	Paterson, NJ	4,360
227	Charleston, SC	4,358
228	Fullerton, CA	4,337
229	Greeley, CO	4,324
229	Murfreesboro, TN	4,324
231	Tyler, TX	4,313
232	Billings, MT	4,304
233	Bellevue, WA	4,245
234	Clarksville, TN	4,242
235	Hammond, IN	4,226
236	Palmdale, CA	4,212
236	Santa Rosa, CA	4,212
238	San Leandro, CA	4,196
239	Garden Grove, CA	4,165
240	Victorville, CA	4,157
241	Yuma, AZ	4,066
242	Duluth, MN	4,057
243	Joliet, IL	4,049
244	Corona, CA	4,042
245	West Covina, CA	4,030
246	Gresham, OR	4,026
247	Melbourne, FL	4,010
248	Rancho Cucamon., CA	3,966
249	Glendale, CA	3,935
250	Las Cruces, NM	3,906
251	Roseville, CA	3,884
252	Carrollton, TX	3,782
253	Midland, TX	3,712
254	Ventura, CA	3,686
255	Plantation, FL	3,675
256	Odessa, TX	3,654
257	Downey, CA	3,616
258	El Cajon, CA	3,612
259	Southfield, MI	3,604
260	Sioux Falls, SD	3,596
261	Norman, OK	3,582
262	Port St. Lucie, FL	3,563
263	Spokane Valley, WA	3,527
264	Yonkers, NY	3,502
265	Brockton, MA	3,498
266	Manchester, NH	3,454
267	Sparks, NV	3,452
268	Santa Clarita, CA	3,444
269	Sterling Heights, MI	3,415
270	Redding, CA	3,389
271	Sioux City, IA	3,384
272	Costa Mesa, CA	3,380
273	Santa Clara, CA	3,354
274	Lowell, MA	3,352
275	Sunrise, FL	3,343
276	West Jordan, UT	3,329
277	Santa Monica, CA	3,314
278	Fontana, CA	3,309
279	Orange, CA	3,291
280	Cambridge, MA	3,283
281	Miramar, FL	3,219
282	Arvada, CO	3,202
283	El Monte, CA	3,199
284	Alexandria, VA	3,194
285	Torrance, CA	3,171
286	Denton, TX	3,168
287	Sandy, UT	3,161
288	Clovis, CA	3,154
289	Palm Bay, FL	3,141
290	New Bedford, MA	3,140
291	Richardson, TX	3,118
292	Columbia, MO	3,105
293	Lewisville, TX	3,045
294	Irvine, CA	3,034
295	Boulder, CO	3,016
296	Lynn, MA	3,000
297	Erie, PA	2,987
298	Boca Raton, FL	2,951
299	Coral Springs, FL	2,949
300	Inglewood, CA	2,926
301	Ann Arbor, MI	2,923
302	Kenosha, WI	2,909
303	Bloomington, MN	2,892
304	Colonie, NY	2,890
305	Green Bay, WI	2,874
306	Davie, FL	2,865
307	Provo, UT	2,859
308	Antioch, CA	2,844
309	Vista, CA	2,838
310	Tracy, CA	2,825
311	Carson, CA	2,823
312	Temecula, CA	2,820
313	Woodbridge Twnshp, NJ	2,804
314	South Gate, CA	2,764
315	Whittier, CA	2,760
316	Westland, MI	2,758
317	Hillsboro, OR	2,752
318	Largo, FL	2,733
319	Burbank, CA	2,721
320	Rialto, CA	2,708
321	Fargo, ND	2,679
322	Sunnyvale, CA	2,632
323	Norwalk, CA	2,602
324	Westminster, CA	2,594
325	Deerfield Beach, FL	2,591
326	Orem, UT	2,564
327	Rochester, MN	2,525
328	Suffolk, VA	2,515
329	San Mateo, CA	2,488
330	Santa Barbara, CA	2,483
331	Trenton, NJ	2,477
332	Alhambra, CA	2,472
333	Clinton Twnshp, MI	2,461
334	Carlsbad, CA	2,455
335	Newport Beach, CA	2,431
336	Cheektowaga, NY	2,419
337	Compton, CA	2,411
338	Santa Maria, CA	2,410
339	Chino, CA	2,390
340	Vacaville, CA	2,384
341	Daly City, CA	2,344
342	Greece, NY	2,321
343	Edison Twnshp, NJ	2,320
344	Livonia, MI	2,318
345	Lee's Summit, MO	2,315
346	Olathe, KS	2,277
347	Lakewood, CA	2,255
348	Surprise, AZ	2,253
349	Nashua, NH	2,241
350	Naperville, IL	2,231
351	Bellflower, CA	2,219
352	Roswell, GA	2,218
353	McKinney, TX	2,217
354	Beaverton, OR	2,205
355	Cary, NC	2,189
356	Napa, CA	2,164
357	Upper Darby Twnshp, PA	2,158
358	Warwick, RI	2,120
359	Hawthorne, CA	2,101
360	Simi Valley, CA	2,060
361	Baldwin Park, CA	2,046
362	Hesperia, CA	2,040
363	Troy, MI	2,018
364	Murrieta, CA	1,974
365	Round Rock, TX	1,968
366	Edmond, OK	1,961
367	Buena Park, CA	1,960
368	Toms River Twnshp, NJ	1,958
369	Somerville, MA	1,954
370	Clifton, NJ	1,911
371	Amherst, NY	1,882
372	Cranston, RI	1,876
373	Hamilton Twnshp, NJ	1,871
374	Thousand Oaks, CA	1,794
375	Canton Twnshp, MI	1,708
376	Livermore, CA	1,703
377	Parma, OH	1,699
378	Quincy, MA	1,684
379	Broken Arrow, OK	1,673
380	Centennial, CO	1,618
381	Sugar Land, TX	1,609
382	Clarkstown, NY	1,602
383	Danbury, CT	1,601
384	Farmington Hills, MI	1,553
385	Brick Twnshp, NJ	1,463
386	Mission Viejo, CA	1,399
387	Chino Hills, CA	1,214
388	Lake Forest, CA	1,104
389	Newton, MA	1,055
NA	Tucson, AZ**	NA

Source: Federal Bureau of Investigation "Crime in the United States 2006"

**Property crimes are offenses of burglary, larceny-theft, and motor vehicle theft. Attempts are included.*

***Not available.*

66. Property Crime Rate in 2006

National Rate = 3,334.5 Property Crimes per 100,000 Population*

RANK	CITY	RATE
177	Abilene, TX	4,275.1
44	Albany, GA	6,784.0
128	Albany, NY	5,140.1
57	Albuquerque, NM	6,339.3
350	Alexandria, VA	2,336.7
298	Alhambra, CA	2,802.8
103	Allentown, PA	5,658.0
83	Amarillo, TX	5,887.1
381	Amherst, NY	1,676.1
318	Anaheim, CA	2,633.6
182	Anchorage, AK	4,220.9
326	Ann Arbor, MI	2,587.0
299	Antioch, CA	2,800.9
119	Arlington, TX	5,271.2
275	Arvada, CO	3,022.7
118	Athens-Clarke, GA	5,280.2
48	Atlanta, GA	6,634.6
180	Aurora, CO	4,228.1
285	Aurora, IL	2,919.2
85	Austin, TX	5,856.9
113	Bakersfield, CA	5,337.1
327	Baldwin Park, CA	2,571.3
131	Baltimore, MD	5,069.5
35	Baton Rouge, LA	6,976.2
73	Beaumont, TX	6,055.7
333	Beaverton, OR	2,529.2
223	Bellevue, WA	3,562.7
283	Bellflower, CA	2,949.2
32	Bellingham, WA	7,034.3
25	Berkeley, CA	7,204.1
176	Billings, MT	4,318.4
14	Birmingham, AL	8,137.4
226	Bloomington, MN	3,539.5
240	Boca Raton, FL	3,349.9
243	Boise, ID	3,337.8
171	Boston, MA	4,462.0
258	Boulder, CO	3,228.5
377	Brick Twnshp, NJ	1,870.5
135	Bridgeport, CT	5,034.2
212	Brockton, MA	3,674.4
375	Broken Arrow, OK	1,923.2
145	Brownsville, TX	4,868.2
340	Buena Park, CA	2,453.5
108	Buffalo, NY	5,503.1
324	Burbank, CA	2,590.3
251	Cambridge, MA	3,259.0
77	Camden, NJ	5,978.4
372	Canton Twnshp, MI	1,989.2
16	Canton, OH	7,819.0
232	Cape Coral, FL	3,447.3
313	Carlsbad, CA	2,680.4
269	Carrollton, TX	3,093.9
278	Carson, CA	2,977.8
370	Cary, NC	2,016.3
153	Cedar Rapids, IA	4,744.2
382	Centennial, CO	1,616.4
221	Chandler, AZ	3,576.6
198	Charleston, SC	4,021.4
34	Charlotte, NC	6,989.7
15	Chattanooga, TN	7,831.9
277	Cheektowaga, NY	2,986.6
266	Chesapeake, VA	3,114.6
168	Chicago, IL	4,539.1
384	Chino Hills, CA	1,588.9
271	Chino, CA	3,053.3
246	Chula Vista, CA	3,311.8
26	Cincinnati, OH	7,152.0
365	Clarkstown, NY	2,037.1
210	Clarksville, TN	3,710.8
173	Clearwater, FL	4,376.6
60	Cleveland, OH	6,232.9
346	Clifton, NJ	2,389.3
330	Clinton Twnshp, MI	2,548.0
219	Clovis, CA	3,612.6
208	Colonie, NY	3,735.9
149	Colorado Springs, CO	4,797.2
237	Columbia, MO	3,357.3
84	Columbia, SC	5,881.8
24	Columbus, GA	7,229.9
28	Columbus, OH	7,121.6
336	Compton, CA	2,497.9
175	Concord, CA	4,330.9
356	Coral Springs, FL	2,251.6
312	Corona, CA	2,681.6
51	Corpus Christi, TX	6,565.2
272	Costa Mesa, CA	3,050.0
352	Cranston, RI	2,317.1
39	Dallas, TX	6,857.1
353	Daly City, CA	2,315.2
366	Danbury, CT	2,036.6
241	Davie, FL	3,346.0
22	Dayton, OH	7,392.5
120	Dearborn, MI	5,270.8
244	Deerfield Beach, FL	3,337.4
280	Denton, TX	2,957.8
165	Denver, CO	4,620.5
37	Des Moines, IA	6,918.8
31	Detroit, MI	7,048.1
250	Downey, CA	3,266.3
152	Duluth, MN	4,747.1
99	Durham, NC	5,679.4
354	Edison Twnshp, NJ	2,306.7
321	Edmond, OK	2,595.9
200	El Cajon, CA	3,870.6
325	El Monte, CA	2,587.9
242	El Paso, TX	3,342.7
205	Elizabeth, NJ	3,791.7
287	Erie, PA	2,908.4
252	Escondido, CA	3,257.4
107	Eugene, OR	5,523.4
167	Evansville, IN	4,548.1
4	Everett, WA	9,223.1
187	Fairfield, CA	4,138.8
282	Fargo, ND	2,949.9
374	Farmington Hills, MI	1,940.7
2	Fayetteville, NC	9,878.4
66	Federal Way, WA	6,131.4
38	Flint, MI	6,863.9
371	Fontana, CA	2,001.4
229	Fort Collins, CO	3,503.4
87	Fort Lauderdale, FL	5,838.3
49	Fort Smith, AR	6,582.2
150	Fort Wayne, IN	4,789.2
98	Fort Worth, TX	5,683.3
320	Fremont, CA	2,619.2
136	Fresno, CA	5,030.9
255	Fullerton, CA	3,237.0
121	Gainesville, FL	5,238.7
338	Garden Grove, CA	2,485.5
224	Garland, TX	3,543.7
106	Gary, IN	5,599.3
306	Gilbert, AZ	2,732.0
146	Glendale, AZ	4,865.1
373	Glendale, CA	1,949.3
132	Grand Prairie, TX	5,038.8
123	Grand Rapids, MI	5,226.7
339	Greece, NY	2,463.0
147	Greeley, CO	4,844.7
296	Green Bay, WI	2,829.5
72	Greensboro, NC	6,059.4
188	Gresham, OR	4,123.0
362	Hamilton Twnshp, NJ	2,077.5
117	Hammond, IN	5,299.6
247	Hampton, VA	3,306.1
29	Hartford, CT	7,104.5
344	Hawthorne, CA	2,429.8
194	Hayward, CA	4,052.1
301	Henderson, NV	2,781.9
322	Hesperia, CA	2,592.6
201	Hialeah, FL	3,868.8
90	High Point, NC	5,827.8
260	Hillsboro, OR	3,203.0
181	Hollywood, FL	4,223.3
184	Honolulu, HI	4,197.5
88	Houston, TX	5,837.5
355	Huntington Beach, CA	2,277.2
41	Huntsville, AL	6,849.7
40	Independence, MO	6,853.2
64	Indianapolis, IN	6,192.4
332	Inglewood, CA	2,533.4
383	Irvine, CA	1,609.3
148	Irving, TX	4,842.9
112	Jacksonville, FL	5,416.2
20	Jackson, MS	7,448.1
262	Jersey City, NJ	3,165.2
281	Joliet, IL	2,956.8
30	Kansas City, KS	7,079.2
36	Kansas City, MO	6,938.6
273	Kenosha, WI	3,043.2
19	Kent, WA	7,513.9
116	Killeen, TX	5,307.9
70	Knoxville, TN	6,064.5
74	Lafayette, LA	6,020.4
387	Lake Forest, CA	1,431.9
97	Lakeland, FL	5,717.8
302	Lakewood, CA	2,777.4
143	Lakewood, CO	4,880.3
209	Lancaster, CA	3,717.1
196	Lansing, MI	4,040.6
89	Laredo, TX	5,828.0
220	Largo, FL	3,608.9
160	Las Cruces, NM	4,661.4
159	Las Vegas, NV	4,667.4
78	Lawrence, KS	5,964.0
124	Lawton, OK	5,192.7
294	Lee's Summit, MO	2,860.7
248	Lewisville, TX	3,277.4
202	Lexington, KY	3,863.0
130	Lincoln, NE	5,087.9
9	Little Rock, AR	8,458.2
360	Livermore, CA	2,152.6
347	Livonia, MI	2,371.8

RANK	CITY	RATE
315	Long Beach, CA	2,671.6
59	Longview, TX	6,304.7
308	Los Angeles, CA	2,718.4
161	Louisville, KY	4,654.2
256	Lowell, MA	3,231.5
94	Lubbock, TX	5,736.7
236	Lynn, MA	3,358.6
3	Macon, GA	9,744.7
234	Madison, WI	3,371.9
265	Manchester, NH	3,137.0
111	McAllen, TX	5,448.2
357	McKinney, TX	2,232.2
127	Melbourne, FL	5,145.0
12	Memphis, TN	8,358.2
163	Mesa, AZ	4,634.3
197	Mesquite, TX	4,023.0
8	Miami Beach, FL	8,480.2
63	Miami Gardens, FL	6,211.7
125	Miami, FL	5,163.2
213	Midland, TX	3,637.8
50	Milwaukee, WI	6,580.5
75	Minneapolis, MN	6,011.4
279	Miramar, FL	2,969.0
386	Mission Viejo, CA	1,459.8
58	Mobile, AL	6,335.7
104	Modesto, CA	5,651.2
52	Montgomery, AL	6,480.2
203	Moreno Valley, CA	3,833.4
141	Murfreesboro, TN	4,919.4
348	Murrieta, CA	2,363.4
292	Napa, CA	2,867.9
385	Naperville, IL	1,567.4
329	Nashua, NH	2,556.7
91	Nashville, TN	5,817.4
238	New Bedford, MA	3,352.5
297	New Orleans, LA	2,824.5
376	New York, NY	1,879.2
189	Newark, NJ	4,078.7
276	Newport Beach, CA	3,017.9
186	Newport News, VA	4,170.8
389	Newton, MA	1,261.1
137	Norfolk, VA	4,987.1
231	Norman, OK	3,490.6
7	North Charleston, SC	8,522.0
154	North Las Vegas, NV	4,720.6
343	Norwalk, CA	2,436.6
68	Oakland, CA	6,103.8
289	Oceanside, CA	2,907.4
204	Odessa, TX	3,798.5
62	Ogden, UT	6,219.3
54	Oklahoma City, OK	6,397.6
367	Olathe, KS	2,030.9
122	Omaha, NE	5,227.6
214	Ontario, CA	3,637.1
345	Orange, CA	2,416.9
304	Orem, UT	2,767.8
10	Orlando, FL	8,448.5
305	Overland Park, KS	2,736.0
349	Oxnard, CA	2,361.8
245	Palm Bay, FL	3,327.4
268	Palmdale, CA	3,102.0
361	Parma, OH	2,082.9
274	Pasadena, CA	3,032.6
249	Pasadena, TX	3,277.2
288	Paterson, NJ	2,907.5
261	Pembroke Pines, FL	3,195.2
199	Peoria, AZ	3,985.8
92	Peoria, IL	5,778.9
177	Philadelphia, PA	4,275.1
79	Phoenix, AZ	5,934.3
158	Pittsburgh, PA	4,693.7
239	Plano, TX	3,350.9
183	Plantation, FL	4,202.9
235	Pomona, CA	3,368.5
155	Pompano Beach, FL	4,705.7
316	Port St. Lucie, FL	2,660.7
80	Portland, OR	5,901.4
138	Portsmouth, VA	4,986.8
142	Providence, RI	4,893.1
342	Provo, UT	2,440.3
76	Pueblo, CO	5,990.4
378	Quincy, MA	1,854.8
93	Racine, WI	5,765.3
216	Raleigh, NC	3,631.5
351	Rancho Cucamon., CA	2,321.0
96	Reading, PA	5,729.9
206	Redding, CA	3,746.9
129	Reno, NV	5,132.8
311	Rialto, CA	2,697.0
270	Richardson, TX	3,056.9
114	Richmond, CA	5,329.5
126	Richmond, VA	5,156.7
185	Riverside, CA	4,191.0
102	Roanoke, VA	5,659.8
317	Rochester, MN	2,641.6
65	Rochester, NY	6,141.6
23	Rockford, IL	7,311.1
215	Roseville, CA	3,633.5
335	Roswell, GA	2,501.2
358	Round Rock, TX	2,217.2
100	Sacramento, CA	5,669.7
110	Salem, OR	5,468.0
191	Salinas, CA	4,076.5
11	Salt Lake City, UT	8,384.9
134	San Angelo, TX	5,034.9
69	San Antonio, TX	6,084.7
144	San Bernardino, CA	4,871.8
222	San Diego, CA	3,568.6
139	San Francisco, CA	4,958.1
319	San Jose, CA	2,633.2
115	San Leandro, CA	5,319.3
310	San Mateo, CA	2,707.3
233	Sandy, UT	3,414.1
334	Santa Ana, CA	2,512.9
293	Santa Barbara, CA	2,864.8
263	Santa Clara, CA	3,153.7
368	Santa Clarita, CA	2,028.7
295	Santa Maria, CA	2,831.8
207	Santa Monica, CA	3,740.8
307	Santa Rosa, CA	2,725.6
162	Savannah, GA	4,648.5
225	Scottsdale, AZ	3,543.5
45	Seattle, WA	6,771.8
46	Shreveport, LA	6,733.5
380	Simi Valley, CA	1,720.2
195	Sioux City, IA	4,048.3
328	Sioux Falls, SD	2,557.7
323	Somerville, MA	2,591.1
33	South Bend, IN	6,994.2
303	South Gate, CA	2,769.9
156	Southfield, MI	4,703.3
193	Sparks, NV	4,071.0
179	Spokane Valley, WA	4,260.8
82	Spokane, WA	5,896.1
47	Springfield, IL	6,661.8
95	Springfield, MA	5,730.3
5	Springfield, MO	8,693.0
314	Sterling Heights, MI	2,673.9
42	Stockton, CA	6,811.2
1	St. Louis, MO	11,747.9
174	St. Paul, MN	4,369.5
53	St. Petersburg, FL	6,478.6
264	Suffolk, VA	3,152.4
364	Sugar Land, TX	2,065.4
369	Sunnyvale, CA	2,023.6
217	Sunrise, FL	3,629.1
286	Surprise, AZ	2,916.3
157	Syracuse, NY	4,700.1
13	Tacoma, WA	8,300.5
151	Tallahassee, FL	4,783.1
101	Tampa, FL	5,668.1
252	Temecula, CA	3,257.4
18	Tempe, AZ	7,524.7
172	Thornton, CO	4,395.8
388	Thousand Oaks, CA	1,429.7
17	Toledo, OH	7,528.9
363	Toms River Twnshp, NJ	2,066.9
27	Topeka, KS	7,123.4
359	Torrance, CA	2,207.2
230	Tracy, CA	3,501.3
284	Trenton, NJ	2,924.3
337	Troy, MI	2,492.4
NA	Tucson, AZ**	NA
61	Tulsa, OK	6,223.1
55	Tuscaloosa, AL	6,375.6
166	Tyler, TX	4,562.0
309	Upper Darby Twnshp, PA	2,708.0
331	Vacaville, CA	2,541.0
133	Vallejo, CA	5,037.1
192	Vancouver, WA	4,074.3
228	Ventura, CA	3,512.0
169	Victorville, CA	4,514.3
290	Virginia Beach, VA	2,903.2
81	Visalia, CA	5,897.1
267	Vista, CA	3,111.3
71	Waco, TX	6,064.0
218	Warren, MI	3,617.7
341	Warwick, RI	2,449.8
170	Washington, DC	4,473.5
105	Waterbury, CT	5,605.5
211	West Covina, CA	3,691.9
227	West Jordan, UT	3,525.6
21	West Palm Beach, FL	7,395.5
140	West Valley, UT	4,943.1
257	Westland, MI	3,229.1
291	Westminster, CA	2,871.7
190	Westminster, CO	4,077.7
254	Whittier, CA	3,238.1
67	Wichita Falls, TX	6,121.3
109	Wichita, KS	5,473.8
56	Wilmington, NC	6,373.9
43	Winston-Salem, NC	6,805.5
300	Woodbridge Twnshp, NJ	2,785.8
259	Worcester, MA	3,204.8
6	Yakima, WA	8,666.1
379	Yonkers, NY	1,778.1
86	Youngstown, OH	5,852.6
164	Yuma, AZ	4,624.4

Source: CQ Press using data from F.B.I. "Crime in the United States 2006"

**Property crimes are offenses of burglary, larceny-theft, and motor vehicle theft. Attempts are included.*

***Not available.*

66. Property Crime Rate in 2006 (continued)

National Rate = 3,334.5 Property Crimes per 100,000 Population*

RANK	CITY	RATE
1	St. Louis, MO	11,747.9
2	Fayetteville, NC	9,878.4
3	Macon, GA	9,744.7
4	Everett, WA	9,223.1
5	Springfield, MO	8,693.0
6	Yakima, WA	8,666.1
7	North Charleston, SC	8,522.0
8	Miami Beach, FL	8,480.2
9	Little Rock, AR	8,458.2
10	Orlando, FL	8,448.5
11	Salt Lake City, UT	8,384.9
12	Memphis, TN	8,358.2
13	Tacoma, WA	8,300.5
14	Birmingham, AL	8,137.4
15	Chattanooga, TN	7,831.9
16	Canton, OH	7,819.0
17	Toledo, OH	7,528.9
18	Tempe, AZ	7,524.7
19	Kent, WA	7,513.9
20	Jackson, MS	7,448.1
21	West Palm Beach, FL	7,395.5
22	Dayton, OH	7,392.5
23	Rockford, IL	7,311.1
24	Columbus, GA	7,229.9
25	Berkeley, CA	7,204.1
26	Cincinnati, OH	7,152.0
27	Topeka, KS	7,123.4
28	Columbus, OH	7,121.6
29	Hartford, CT	7,104.5
30	Kansas City, KS	7,079.2
31	Detroit, MI	7,048.1
32	Bellingham, WA	7,034.3
33	South Bend, IN	6,994.2
34	Charlotte, NC	6,989.7
35	Baton Rouge, LA	6,976.2
36	Kansas City, MO	6,938.6
37	Des Moines, IA	6,918.8
38	Flint, MI	6,863.9
39	Dallas, TX	6,857.1
40	Independence, MO	6,853.2
41	Huntsville, AL	6,849.7
42	Stockton, CA	6,811.2
43	Winston-Salem, NC	6,805.5
44	Albany, GA	6,784.0
45	Seattle, WA	6,771.8
46	Shreveport, LA	6,733.5
47	Springfield, IL	6,661.8
48	Atlanta, GA	6,634.6
49	Fort Smith, AR	6,582.2
50	Milwaukee, WI	6,580.5
51	Corpus Christi, TX	6,565.2
52	Montgomery, AL	6,480.2
53	St. Petersburg, FL	6,478.6
54	Oklahoma City, OK	6,397.6
55	Tuscaloosa, AL	6,375.6
56	Wilmington, NC	6,373.9
57	Albuquerque, NM	6,339.3
58	Mobile, AL	6,335.7
59	Longview, TX	6,304.7
60	Cleveland, OH	6,232.9
61	Tulsa, OK	6,223.1
62	Ogden, UT	6,219.3
63	Miami Gardens, FL	6,211.7
64	Indianapolis, IN	6,192.4
65	Rochester, NY	6,141.6
66	Federal Way, WA	6,131.4
67	Wichita Falls, TX	6,121.3
68	Oakland, CA	6,103.8
69	San Antonio, TX	6,084.7
70	Knoxville, TN	6,064.5
71	Waco, TX	6,064.0
72	Greensboro, NC	6,059.4
73	Beaumont, TX	6,055.7
74	Lafayette, LA	6,020.4
75	Minneapolis, MN	6,011.4
76	Pueblo, CO	5,990.4
77	Camden, NJ	5,978.4
78	Lawrence, KS	5,964.0
79	Phoenix, AZ	5,934.3
80	Portland, OR	5,901.4
81	Visalia, CA	5,897.1
82	Spokane, WA	5,896.1
83	Amarillo, TX	5,887.1
84	Columbia, SC	5,881.8
85	Austin, TX	5,856.9
86	Youngstown, OH	5,852.6
87	Fort Lauderdale, FL	5,838.3
88	Houston, TX	5,837.5
89	Laredo, TX	5,828.0
90	High Point, NC	5,827.8
91	Nashville, TN	5,817.4
92	Peoria, IL	5,778.9
93	Racine, WI	5,765.3
94	Lubbock, TX	5,736.7
95	Springfield, MA	5,730.3
96	Reading, PA	5,729.9
97	Lakeland, FL	5,717.8
98	Fort Worth, TX	5,683.3
99	Durham, NC	5,679.4
100	Sacramento, CA	5,669.7
101	Tampa, FL	5,668.1
102	Roanoke, VA	5,659.8
103	Allentown, PA	5,658.0
104	Modesto, CA	5,651.2
105	Waterbury, CT	5,605.5
106	Gary, IN	5,599.3
107	Eugene, OR	5,523.4
108	Buffalo, NY	5,503.1
109	Wichita, KS	5,473.8
110	Salem, OR	5,468.0
111	McAllen, TX	5,448.2
112	Jacksonville, FL	5,416.2
113	Bakersfield, CA	5,337.1
114	Richmond, CA	5,329.5
115	San Leandro, CA	5,319.3
116	Killeen, TX	5,307.9
117	Hammond, IN	5,299.6
118	Athens-Clarke, GA	5,280.2
119	Arlington, TX	5,271.2
120	Dearborn, MI	5,270.8
121	Gainesville, FL	5,238.7
122	Omaha, NE	5,227.6
123	Grand Rapids, MI	5,226.7
124	Lawton, OK	5,192.7
125	Miami, FL	5,163.2
126	Richmond, VA	5,156.7
127	Melbourne, FL	5,145.0
128	Albany, NY	5,140.1
129	Reno, NV	5,132.8
130	Lincoln, NE	5,087.9
131	Baltimore, MD	5,069.5
132	Grand Prairie, TX	5,038.8
133	Vallejo, CA	5,037.1
134	San Angelo, TX	5,034.9
135	Bridgeport, CT	5,034.2
136	Fresno, CA	5,030.9
137	Norfolk, VA	4,987.1
138	Portsmouth, VA	4,986.8
139	San Francisco, CA	4,958.1
140	West Valley, UT	4,943.1
141	Murfreesboro, TN	4,919.4
142	Providence, RI	4,893.1
143	Lakewood, CO	4,880.3
144	San Bernardino, CA	4,871.8
145	Brownsville, TX	4,868.2
146	Glendale, AZ	4,865.1
147	Greeley, CO	4,844.7
148	Irving, TX	4,842.9
149	Colorado Springs, CO	4,797.2
150	Fort Wayne, IN	4,789.2
151	Tallahassee, FL	4,783.1
152	Duluth, MN	4,747.1
153	Cedar Rapids, IA	4,744.2
154	North Las Vegas, NV	4,720.6
155	Pompano Beach, FL	4,705.7
156	Southfield, MI	4,703.3
157	Syracuse, NY	4,700.1
158	Pittsburgh, PA	4,693.7
159	Las Vegas, NV	4,667.4
160	Las Cruces, NM	4,661.4
161	Louisville, KY	4,654.2
162	Savannah, GA	4,648.5
163	Mesa, AZ	4,634.3
164	Yuma, AZ	4,624.4
165	Denver, CO	4,620.5
166	Tyler, TX	4,562.0
167	Evansville, IN	4,548.1
168	Chicago, IL	4,539.1
169	Victorville, CA	4,514.3
170	Washington, DC	4,473.5
171	Boston, MA	4,462.0
172	Thornton, CO	4,395.8
173	Clearwater, FL	4,376.6
174	St. Paul, MN	4,369.5
175	Concord, CA	4,330.9
176	Billings, MT	4,318.4
177	Abilene, TX	4,275.1
177	Philadelphia, PA	4,275.1
179	Spokane Valley, WA	4,260.8
180	Aurora, CO	4,228.1
181	Hollywood, FL	4,223.3
182	Anchorage, AK	4,220.9
183	Plantation, FL	4,202.9
184	Honolulu, HI	4,197.5
185	Riverside, CA	4,191.0
186	Newport News, VA	4,170.8
187	Fairfield, CA	4,138.8
188	Gresham, OR	4,123.0
189	Newark, NJ	4,078.7
190	Westminster, CO	4,077.7
191	Salinas, CA	4,076.5
192	Vancouver, WA	4,074.3

RANK	CITY	RATE	RANK	CITY	RATE	RANK	CITY	RATE
193	Sparks, NV	4,071.0	259	Worcester, MA	3,204.8	325	El Monte, CA	2,587.9
194	Hayward, CA	4,052.1	260	Hillsboro, OR	3,203.0	326	Ann Arbor, MI	2,587.0
195	Sioux City, IA	4,048.3	261	Pembroke Pines, FL	3,195.2	327	Baldwin Park, CA	2,571.3
196	Lansing, MI	4,040.6	262	Jersey City, NJ	3,165.2	328	Sioux Falls, SD	2,557.7
197	Mesquite, TX	4,023.0	263	Santa Clara, CA	3,153.7	329	Nashua, NH	2,556.7
198	Charleston, SC	4,021.4	264	Suffolk, VA	3,152.4	330	Clinton Twnshp, MI	2,548.0
199	Peoria, AZ	3,985.8	265	Manchester, NH	3,137.0	331	Vacaville, CA	2,541.0
200	El Cajon, CA	3,870.6	266	Chesapeake, VA	3,114.6	332	Inglewood, CA	2,533.4
201	Hialeah, FL	3,868.8	267	Vista, CA	3,111.3	333	Beaverton, OR	2,529.2
202	Lexington, KY	3,863.0	268	Palmdale, CA	3,102.0	334	Santa Ana, CA	2,512.9
203	Moreno Valley, CA	3,833.4	269	Carrollton, TX	3,093.9	335	Roswell, GA	2,501.2
204	Odessa, TX	3,798.5	270	Richardson, TX	3,056.9	336	Compton, CA	2,497.9
205	Elizabeth, NJ	3,791.7	271	Chino, CA	3,053.3	337	Troy, MI	2,492.4
206	Redding, CA	3,746.9	272	Costa Mesa, CA	3,050.0	338	Garden Grove, CA	2,485.5
207	Santa Monica, CA	3,740.8	273	Kenosha, WI	3,043.2	339	Greece, NY	2,463.0
208	Colonie, NY	3,735.9	274	Pasadena, CA	3,032.6	340	Buena Park, CA	2,453.5
209	Lancaster, CA	3,717.1	275	Arvada, CO	3,022.7	341	Warwick, RI	2,449.8
210	Clarksville, TN	3,710.8	276	Newport Beach, CA	3,017.9	342	Provo, UT	2,440.3
211	West Covina, CA	3,691.9	277	Cheektowaga, NY	2,986.6	343	Norwalk, CA	2,436.6
212	Brockton, MA	3,674.4	278	Carson, CA	2,977.8	344	Hawthorne, CA	2,429.8
213	Midland, TX	3,637.8	279	Miramar, FL	2,969.0	345	Orange, CA	2,416.9
214	Ontario, CA	3,637.1	280	Denton, TX	2,957.8	346	Clifton, NJ	2,389.3
215	Roseville, CA	3,633.5	281	Joliet, IL	2,956.8	347	Livonia, MI	2,371.8
216	Raleigh, NC	3,631.5	282	Fargo, ND	2,949.9	348	Murrieta, CA	2,363.4
217	Sunrise, FL	3,629.1	283	Bellflower, CA	2,949.2	349	Oxnard, CA	2,361.8
218	Warren, MI	3,617.7	284	Trenton, NJ	2,924.3	350	Alexandria, VA	2,336.7
219	Clovis, CA	3,612.6	285	Aurora, IL	2,919.2	351	Rancho Cucamon., CA	2,321.0
220	Largo, FL	3,608.9	286	Surprise, AZ	2,916.3	352	Cranston, RI	2,317.1
221	Chandler, AZ	3,576.6	287	Erie, PA	2,908.4	353	Daly City, CA	2,315.2
222	San Diego, CA	3,568.6	288	Paterson, NJ	2,907.5	354	Edison Twnshp, NJ	2,306.7
223	Bellevue, WA	3,562.7	289	Oceanside, CA	2,907.4	355	Huntington Beach, CA	2,277.2
224	Garland, TX	3,543.7	290	Virginia Beach, VA	2,903.2	356	Coral Springs, FL	2,251.6
225	Scottsdale, AZ	3,543.5	291	Westminster, CA	2,871.7	357	McKinney, TX	2,232.2
226	Bloomington, MN	3,539.5	292	Napa, CA	2,867.9	358	Round Rock, TX	2,217.2
227	West Jordan, UT	3,525.6	293	Santa Barbara, CA	2,864.8	359	Torrance, CA	2,207.2
228	Ventura, CA	3,512.0	294	Lee's Summit, MO	2,860.7	360	Livermore, CA	2,152.6
229	Fort Collins, CO	3,503.4	295	Santa Maria, CA	2,831.8	361	Parma, OH	2,082.9
230	Tracy, CA	3,501.3	296	Green Bay, WI	2,829.5	362	Hamilton Twnshp, NJ	2,077.5
231	Norman, OK	3,490.6	297	New Orleans, LA	2,824.5	363	Toms River Twnshp, NJ	2,066.9
232	Cape Coral, FL	3,447.3	298	Alhambra, CA	2,802.8	364	Sugar Land, TX	2,065.4
233	Sandy, UT	3,414.1	299	Antioch, CA	2,800.9	365	Clarkstown, NY	2,037.1
234	Madison, WI	3,371.9	300	Woodbridge Twnshp, NJ	2,785.8	366	Danbury, CT	2,036.6
235	Pomona, CA	3,368.5	301	Henderson, NV	2,781.9	367	Olathe, KS	2,030.9
236	Lynn, MA	3,358.6	302	Lakewood, CA	2,777.4	368	Santa Clarita, CA	2,028.7
237	Columbia, MO	3,357.3	303	South Gate, CA	2,769.9	369	Sunnyvale, CA	2,023.6
238	New Bedford, MA	3,352.5	304	Orem, UT	2,767.8	370	Cary, NC	2,016.3
239	Plano, TX	3,350.9	305	Overland Park, KS	2,736.0	371	Fontana, CA	2,001.4
240	Boca Raton, FL	3,349.9	306	Gilbert, AZ	2,732.0	372	Canton Twnshp, MI	1,989.2
241	Davie, FL	3,346.0	307	Santa Rosa, CA	2,725.6	373	Glendale, CA	1,949.3
242	El Paso, TX	3,342.7	308	Los Angeles, CA	2,718.4	374	Farmington Hills, MI	1,940.7
243	Boise, ID	3,337.8	309	Upper Darby Twnshp, PA	2,708.0	375	Broken Arrow, OK	1,923.2
244	Deerfield Beach, FL	3,337.4	310	San Mateo, CA	2,707.3	376	New York, NY	1,879.2
245	Palm Bay, FL	3,327.4	311	Rialto, CA	2,697.0	377	Brick Twnshp, NJ	1,870.5
246	Chula Vista, CA	3,311.8	312	Corona, CA	2,681.6	378	Quincy, MA	1,854.8
247	Hampton, VA	3,306.1	313	Carlsbad, CA	2,680.4	379	Yonkers, NY	1,778.1
248	Lewisville, TX	3,277.4	314	Sterling Heights, MI	2,673.9	380	Simi Valley, CA	1,720.2
249	Pasadena, TX	3,277.2	315	Long Beach, CA	2,671.6	381	Amherst, NY	1,676.1
250	Downey, CA	3,266.3	316	Port St. Lucie, FL	2,660.7	382	Centennial, CO	1,616.4
251	Cambridge, MA	3,259.0	317	Rochester, MN	2,641.6	383	Irvine, CA	1,609.3
252	Escondido, CA	3,257.4	318	Anaheim, CA	2,633.6	384	Chino Hills, CA	1,588.9
252	Temecula, CA	3,257.4	319	San Jose, CA	2,633.2	385	Naperville, IL	1,567.4
254	Whittier, CA	3,238.1	320	Fremont, CA	2,619.2	386	Mission Viejo, CA	1,459.8
255	Fullerton, CA	3,237.0	321	Edmond, OK	2,595.9	387	Lake Forest, CA	1,431.9
256	Lowell, MA	3,231.5	322	Hesperia, CA	2,592.6	388	Thousand Oaks, CA	1,429.7
257	Westland, MI	3,229.1	323	Somerville, MA	2,591.1	389	Newton, MA	1,261.1
258	Boulder, CO	3,228.5	324	Burbank, CA	2,590.3	NA	Tucson, AZ**	NA

Source: CQ Press using data from F.B.I. "Crime in the United States 2006"

**Property crimes are offenses of burglary, larceny-theft, and motor vehicle theft. Attempts are included.*

***Not available.*

67. Percent Change in Property Crime Rate: 2005 to 2006

National Percent Change = 2.8% Decrease*

RANK	CITY	% CHANGE
278	Abilene, TX	(9.4)
39	Albany, GA	6.5
131	Albany, NY	(0.7)
73	Albuquerque, NM	2.8
267	Alexandria, VA	(8.8)
212	Alhambra, CA	(4.8)
54	Allentown, PA	4.8
265	Amarillo, TX	(8.7)
169	Amherst, NY	(2.7)
249	Anaheim, CA	(7.0)
75	Anchorage, AK	2.5
319	Ann Arbor, MI	(13.0)
166	Antioch, CA	(2.6)
229	Arlington, TX	(5.6)
354	Arvada, CO	(18.9)
119	Athens-Clarke, GA	(0.2)
273	Atlanta, GA	(9.0)
331	Aurora, CO	(15.0)
97	Aurora, IL	1.1
166	Austin, TX	(2.6)
251	Bakersfield, CA	(7.2)
176	Baldwin Park, CA	(2.9)
159	Baltimore, MD	(2.2)
31	Baton Rouge, LA	8.9
342	Beaumont, TX	(16.9)
372	Beaverton, OR	(28.2)
282	Bellevue, WA	(9.5)
307	Bellflower, CA	(11.0)
243	Bellingham, WA	(6.6)
257	Berkeley, CA	(7.7)
365	Billings, MT	(23.4)
102	Birmingham, AL	0.9
NA	Bloomington, MN**	NA
236	Boca Raton, FL	(6.0)
319	Boise, ID	(13.0)
110	Boston, MA	0.5
340	Boulder, CO	(16.7)
26	Brick Twnshp, NJ	10.1
139	Bridgeport, CT	(0.9)
237	Brockton, MA	(6.1)
360	Broken Arrow, OK	(21.0)
200	Brownsville, TX	(4.0)
87	Buena Park, CA	1.8
246	Buffalo, NY	(6.8)
154	Burbank, CA	(2.0)
141	Cambridge, MA	(1.0)
20	Camden, NJ	11.2
51	Canton Twnshp, MI	5.1
68	Canton, OH	3.3
13	Cape Coral, FL	15.7
122	Carlsbad, CA	(0.4)
278	Carrollton, TX	(9.4)
10	Carson, CA	17.0
46	Cary, NC	5.7
272	Cedar Rapids, IA	(8.9)
359	Centennial, CO	(20.4)
125	Chandler, AZ	(0.5)
293	Charleston, SC	(10.1)
91	Charlotte, NC	1.6
173	Chattanooga, TN	(2.8)
176	Cheektowaga, NY	(2.9)
326	Chesapeake, VA	(13.8)
128	Chicago, IL	(0.6)
23	Chino Hills, CA	10.8
260	Chino, CA	(7.9)
267	Chula Vista, CA	(8.8)
112	Cincinnati, OH	0.3
NA	Clarkstown, NY**	NA
141	Clarksville, TN	(1.0)
206	Clearwater, FL	(4.3)
114	Cleveland, OH	0.2
95	Clifton, NJ	1.3
35	Clinton Twnshp, MI	8.0
267	Clovis, CA	(8.8)
131	Colonie, NY	(0.7)
264	Colorado Springs, CO	(8.4)
145	Columbia, MO	(1.1)
286	Columbia, SC	(9.7)
66	Columbus, GA	3.5
197	Columbus, OH	(3.9)
252	Compton, CA	(7.5)
323	Concord, CA	(13.2)
18	Coral Springs, FL	11.9
312	Corona, CA	(11.8)
246	Corpus Christi, TX	(6.8)
312	Costa Mesa, CA	(11.8)
265	Cranston, RI	(8.7)
222	Dallas, TX	(5.2)
32	Daly City, CA	8.7
97	Danbury, CT	1.1
302	Davie, FL	(10.6)
68	Dayton, OH	3.3
81	Dearborn, MI	2.3
297	Deerfield Beach, FL	(10.3)
371	Denton, TX	(28.1)
364	Denver, CO	(23.1)
NA	Des Moines, IA**	NA
7	Detroit, MI	17.7
74	Downey, CA	2.7
NA	Duluth, MN**	NA
NA	Durham, NC**	NA
231	Edison Twnshp, NJ	(5.7)
128	Edmond, OK	(0.6)
282	El Cajon, CA	(9.5)
267	El Monte, CA	(8.8)
NA	El Paso, TX**	NA
219	Elizabeth, NJ	(5.1)
48	Erie, PA	5.6
285	Escondido, CA	(9.6)
356	Eugene, OR	(19.4)
304	Evansville, IN	(10.8)
6	Everett, WA	18.2
176	Fairfield, CA	(2.9)
14	Fargo, ND	14.8
207	Farmington Hills, MI	(4.4)
5	Fayetteville, NC	19.2
346	Federal Way, WA	(17.9)
37	Flint, MI	6.7
321	Fontana, CA	(13.1)
89	Fort Collins, CO	1.7
315	Fort Lauderdale, FL	(12.4)
122	Fort Smith, AR	(0.4)
NA	Fort Wayne, IN**	NA
239	Fort Worth, TX	(6.3)
21	Fremont, CA	11.1
277	Fresno, CA	(9.3)
219	Fullerton, CA	(5.1)
3	Gainesville, FL	19.7
250	Garden Grove, CA	(7.1)
211	Garland, TX	(4.7)
49	Gary, IN	5.5
125	Gilbert, AZ	(0.5)
209	Glendale, AZ	(4.5)
60	Glendale, CA	4.2
196	Grand Prairie, TX	(3.8)
58	Grand Rapids, MI	4.5
9	Greece, NY	17.3
367	Greeley, CO	(23.9)
153	Green Bay, WI	(1.9)
131	Greensboro, NC	(0.7)
368	Gresham, OR	(25.5)
21	Hamilton Twnshp, NJ	11.1
241	Hammond, IN	(6.4)
276	Hampton, VA	(9.2)
243	Hartford, CT	(6.6)
197	Hawthorne, CA	(3.9)
53	Hayward, CA	4.9
173	Henderson, NV	(2.8)
234	Hesperia, CA	(5.8)
95	Hialeah, FL	1.3
254	High Point, NC	(7.6)
369	Hillsboro, OR	(27.2)
197	Hollywood, FL	(3.9)
292	Honolulu, HI	(10.0)
137	Houston, TX	(0.8)
30	Huntington Beach, CA	9.1
148	Huntsville, AL	(1.7)
241	Independence, MO	(6.4)
141	Indianapolis, IN	(1.0)
215	Inglewood, CA	(4.9)
300	Irvine, CA	(10.4)
112	Irving, TX	0.3
141	Jacksonville, FL	(1.0)
18	Jackson, MS	11.9
321	Jersey City, NJ	(13.1)
275	Joliet, IL	(9.1)
184	Kansas City, KS	(3.5)
NA	Kansas City, MO**	NA
145	Kenosha, WI	(1.1)
100	Kent, WA	1.0
304	Killeen, TX	(10.8)
147	Knoxville, TN	(1.3)
39	Lafayette, LA	6.5
15	Lake Forest, CA	14.3
79	Lakeland, FL	2.4
352	Lakewood, CA	(18.7)
338	Lakewood, CO	(16.1)
75	Lancaster, CA	2.5
120	Lansing, MI	(0.3)
182	Laredo, TX	(3.4)
66	Largo, FL	3.5
215	Las Cruces, NM	(4.9)
184	Las Vegas, NV	(3.5)
1	Lawrence, KS	40.3
139	Lawton, OK	(0.9)
92	Lee's Summit, MO	1.4
361	Lewisville, TX	(21.3)
NA	Lexington, KY**	NA
212	Lincoln, NE	(4.8)
191	Little Rock, AR	(3.7)
86	Livermore, CA	1.9
84	Livonia, MI	2.1

RANK	CITY	% CHANGE
219	Long Beach, CA	(5.1)
154	Longview, TX	(2.0)
297	Los Angeles, CA	(10.3)
45	Louisville, KY	5.8
92	Lowell, MA	1.4
222	Lubbock, TX	(5.2)
75	Lynn, MA	2.5
70	Macon, GA	3.2
184	Madison, WI	(3.5)
148	Manchester, NH	(1.7)
349	McAllen, TX	(18.3)
166	McKinney, TX	(2.6)
33	Melbourne, FL	8.4
117	Memphis, TN	(0.1)
318	Mesa, AZ	(12.9)
191	Mesquite, TX	(3.7)
215	Miami Beach, FL	(4.9)
176	Miami Gardens, FL	(2.9)
327	Miami, FL	(14.0)
191	Midland, TX	(3.7)
8	Milwaukee, WI	17.6
102	Minneapolis, MN	0.9
202	Miramar, FL	(4.1)
16	Mission Viejo, CA	12.3
25	Mobile, AL	10.3
287	Modesto, CA	(9.8)
105	Montgomery, AL	0.8
75	Moreno Valley, CA	2.5
105	Murfreesboro, TN	0.8
160	Murrieta, CA	(2.3)
55	Napa, CA	4.7
304	Naperville, IL	(10.8)
28	Nashua, NH	9.3
282	Nashville, TN	(9.5)
105	New Bedford, MA	0.8
NA	New Orleans, LA**	NA
238	New York, NY	(6.2)
289	Newark, NJ	(9.9)
169	Newport Beach, CA	(2.7)
239	Newport News, VA	(6.3)
200	Newton, MA	(4.0)
260	Norfolk, VA	(7.9)
24	Norman, OK	10.4
131	North Charleston, SC	(0.7)
82	North Las Vegas, NV	2.2
254	Norwalk, CA	(7.6)
44	Oakland, CA	6.2
325	Oceanside, CA	(13.4)
190	Odessa, TX	(3.6)
79	Ogden, UT	2.4
355	Oklahoma City, OK	(19.3)
374	Olathe, KS	(33.6)
160	Omaha, NE	(2.3)
257	Ontario, CA	(7.7)
212	Orange, CA	(4.8)
369	Orem, UT	(27.2)
165	Orlando, FL	(2.5)
154	Overland Park, KS	(2.0)
122	Oxnard, CA	(0.4)
254	Palm Bay, FL	(7.6)
125	Palmdale, CA	(0.5)
315	Parma, OH	(12.4)
114	Pasadena, CA	0.2
160	Pasadena, TX	(2.3)
137	Paterson, NJ	(0.8)
27	Pembroke Pines, FL	9.7
267	Peoria, AZ	(8.8)
317	Peoria, IL	(12.5)
60	Philadelphia, PA	4.2
246	Phoenix, AZ	(6.8)
131	Pittsburgh, PA	(0.7)
191	Plano, TX	(3.7)
55	Plantation, FL	4.7
131	Pomona, CA	(0.7)
350	Pompano Beach, FL	(18.5)
4	Port St. Lucie, FL	19.4
333	Portland, OR	(15.3)
169	Portsmouth, VA	(2.7)
215	Providence, RI	(4.9)
366	Provo, UT	(23.8)
289	Pueblo, CO	(9.9)
11	Quincy, MA	16.9
87	Racine, WI	1.8
191	Raleigh, NC	(3.7)
333	Rancho Cucamon., CA	(15.3)
273	Reading, PA	(9.0)
351	Redding, CA	(18.6)
207	Reno, NV	(4.4)
363	Rialto, CA	(22.5)
311	Richardson, TX	(11.3)
227	Richmond, CA	(5.5)
362	Richmond, VA	(21.9)
278	Riverside, CA	(9.4)
340	Roanoke, VA	(16.7)
109	Rochester, MN	0.6
227	Rochester, NY	(5.5)
NA	Rockford, IL**	NA
358	Roseville, CA	(20.2)
243	Roswell, GA	(6.6)
338	Round Rock, TX	(16.1)
128	Sacramento, CA	(0.6)
293	Salem, OR	(10.1)
297	Salinas, CA	(10.3)
164	Salt Lake City, UT	(2.4)
336	San Angelo, TX	(15.8)
229	San Antonio, TX	(5.6)
324	San Bernardino, CA	(13.3)
150	San Diego, CA	(1.8)
33	San Francisco, CA	8.4
57	San Jose, CA	4.6
60	San Leandro, CA	4.2
301	San Mateo, CA	(10.5)
154	Sandy, UT	(2.0)
336	Santa Ana, CA	(15.8)
329	Santa Barbara, CA	(14.4)
184	Santa Clara, CA	(3.5)
222	Santa Clarita, CA	(5.2)
92	Santa Maria, CA	1.4
226	Santa Monica, CA	(5.4)
327	Santa Rosa, CA	(14.0)
330	Savannah, GA	(14.9)
51	Scottsdale, AZ	5.1
287	Seattle, WA	(9.8)
63	Shreveport, LA	4.1
309	Simi Valley, CA	(11.1)
225	Sioux City, IA	(5.3)
343	Sioux Falls, SD	(17.5)
12	Somerville, MA	16.8
17	South Bend, IN	12.2
202	South Gate, CA	(4.1)
169	Southfield, MI	(2.7)
50	Sparks, NV	5.4
293	Spokane Valley, WA	(10.1)
182	Spokane, WA	(3.4)
58	Springfield, IL	4.5
117	Springfield, MA	(0.1)
64	Springfield, MO	3.8
2	Sterling Heights, MI	20.1
89	Stockton, CA	1.7
43	St. Louis, MO	6.3
309	St. Paul, MN	(11.1)
97	St. Petersburg, FL	1.1
303	Suffolk, VA	(10.7)
335	Sugar Land, TX	(15.4)
154	Sunnyvale, CA	(2.0)
42	Sunrise, FL	6.4
150	Surprise, AZ	(1.8)
64	Syracuse, NY	3.8
150	Tacoma, WA	(1.8)
293	Tallahassee, FL	(10.1)
262	Tampa, FL	(8.0)
202	Temecula, CA	(4.1)
105	Tempe, AZ	0.8
231	Thornton, CO	(5.7)
102	Thousand Oaks, CA	0.9
173	Toledo, OH	(2.8)
46	Toms River Twnshp, NJ	5.7
289	Topeka, KS	(9.9)
184	Torrance, CA	(3.5)
346	Tracy, CA	(17.9)
373	Trenton, NJ	(30.0)
85	Troy, MI	2.0
NA	Tucson, AZ**	NA
209	Tulsa, OK	(4.5)
82	Tuscaloosa, AL	2.2
314	Tyler, TX	(12.2)
37	Upper Darby Twnshp, PA	6.7
205	Vacaville, CA	(4.2)
NA	Vallejo, CA**	NA
356	Vancouver, WA	(19.4)
235	Ventura, CA	(5.9)
307	Victorville, CA	(11.0)
176	Virginia Beach, VA	(2.9)
263	Visalia, CA	(8.2)
184	Vista, CA	(3.5)
344	Waco, TX	(17.7)
NA	Warren, MI**	NA
348	Warwick, RI	(18.2)
160	Washington, DC	(2.3)
100	Waterbury, CT	1.0
120	West Covina, CA	(0.3)
NA	West Jordan, UT**	NA
111	West Palm Beach, FL	0.4
352	West Valley, UT	(18.7)
39	Westland, MI	6.5
278	Westminster, CA	(9.4)
332	Westminster, CO	(15.2)
36	Whittier, CA	7.5
345	Wichita Falls, TX	(17.8)
NA	Wichita, KS**	NA
259	Wilmington, NC	(7.8)
28	Winston-Salem, NC	9.3
114	Woodbridge Twnshp, NJ	0.2
252	Worcester, MA	(7.5)
231	Yakima, WA	(5.7)
71	Yonkers, NY	3.1
181	Youngstown, OH	(3.1)
71	Yuma, AZ	3.1

Source: CQ Press using data from F.B.I. "Crime in the United States 2006"

**Property crimes are offenses of burglary, larceny-theft, and motor vehicle theft. Attempts are included.*

***Not available.*

67. Percent Change in Property Crime Rate: 2005 to 2006 (continued)

National Percent Change = 2.8% Decrease*

RANK	CITY	% CHANGE
1	Lawrence, KS	40.3
2	Sterling Heights, MI	20.1
3	Gainesville, FL	19.7
4	Port St. Lucie, FL	19.4
5	Fayetteville, NC	19.2
6	Everett, WA	18.2
7	Detroit, MI	17.7
8	Milwaukee, WI	17.6
9	Greece, NY	17.3
10	Carson, CA	17.0
11	Quincy, MA	16.9
12	Somerville, MA	16.8
13	Cape Coral, FL	15.7
14	Fargo, ND	14.8
15	Lake Forest, CA	14.3
16	Mission Viejo, CA	12.3
17	South Bend, IN	12.2
18	Coral Springs, FL	11.9
18	Jackson, MS	11.9
20	Camden, NJ	11.2
21	Fremont, CA	11.1
21	Hamilton Twnshp, NJ	11.1
23	Chino Hills, CA	10.8
24	Norman, OK	10.4
25	Mobile, AL	10.3
26	Brick Twnshp, NJ	10.1
27	Pembroke Pines, FL	9.7
28	Nashua, NH	9.3
28	Winston-Salem, NC	9.3
30	Huntington Beach, CA	9.1
31	Baton Rouge, LA	8.9
32	Daly City, CA	8.7
33	Melbourne, FL	8.4
33	San Francisco, CA	8.4
35	Clinton Twnshp, MI	8.0
36	Whittier, CA	7.5
37	Flint, MI	6.7
37	Upper Darby Twnshp, PA	6.7
39	Albany, GA	6.5
39	Lafayette, LA	6.5
39	Westland, MI	6.5
42	Sunrise, FL	6.4
43	St. Louis, MO	6.3
44	Oakland, CA	6.2
45	Louisville, KY	5.8
46	Cary, NC	5.7
46	Toms River Twnshp, NJ	5.7
48	Erie, PA	5.6
49	Gary, IN	5.5
50	Sparks, NV	5.4
51	Canton Twnshp, MI	5.1
51	Scottsdale, AZ	5.1
53	Hayward, CA	4.9
54	Allentown, PA	4.8
55	Napa, CA	4.7
55	Plantation, FL	4.7
57	San Jose, CA	4.6
58	Grand Rapids, MI	4.5
58	Springfield, IL	4.5
60	Glendale, CA	4.2
60	Philadelphia, PA	4.2
60	San Leandro, CA	4.2
63	Shreveport, LA	4.1
64	Springfield, MO	3.8
64	Syracuse, NY	3.8
66	Columbus, GA	3.5
66	Largo, FL	3.5
68	Canton, OH	3.3
68	Dayton, OH	3.3
70	Macon, GA	3.2
71	Yonkers, NY	3.1
71	Yuma, AZ	3.1
73	Albuquerque, NM	2.8
74	Downey, CA	2.7
75	Anchorage, AK	2.5
75	Lancaster, CA	2.5
75	Lynn, MA	2.5
75	Moreno Valley, CA	2.5
79	Lakeland, FL	2.4
79	Ogden, UT	2.4
81	Dearborn, MI	2.3
82	North Las Vegas, NV	2.2
82	Tuscaloosa, AL	2.2
84	Livonia, MI	2.1
85	Troy, MI	2.0
86	Livermore, CA	1.9
87	Buena Park, CA	1.8
87	Racine, WI	1.8
89	Fort Collins, CO	1.7
89	Stockton, CA	1.7
91	Charlotte, NC	1.6
92	Lee's Summit, MO	1.4
92	Lowell, MA	1.4
92	Santa Maria, CA	1.4
95	Clifton, NJ	1.3
95	Hialeah, FL	1.3
97	Aurora, IL	1.1
97	Danbury, CT	1.1
97	St. Petersburg, FL	1.1
100	Kent, WA	1.0
100	Waterbury, CT	1.0
102	Birmingham, AL	0.9
102	Minneapolis, MN	0.9
102	Thousand Oaks, CA	0.9
105	Montgomery, AL	0.8
105	Murfreesboro, TN	0.8
105	New Bedford, MA	0.8
105	Tempe, AZ	0.8
109	Rochester, MN	0.6
110	Boston, MA	0.5
111	West Palm Beach, FL	0.4
112	Cincinnati, OH	0.3
112	Irving, TX	0.3
114	Cleveland, OH	0.2
114	Pasadena, CA	0.2
114	Woodbridge Twnshp, NJ	0.2
117	Memphis, TN	(0.1)
117	Springfield, MA	(0.1)
119	Athens-Clarke, GA	(0.2)
120	Lansing, MI	(0.3)
120	West Covina, CA	(0.3)
122	Carlsbad, CA	(0.4)
122	Fort Smith, AR	(0.4)
122	Oxnard, CA	(0.4)
125	Chandler, AZ	(0.5)
125	Gilbert, AZ	(0.5)
125	Palmdale, CA	(0.5)
128	Chicago, IL	(0.6)
128	Edmond, OK	(0.6)
128	Sacramento, CA	(0.6)
131	Albany, NY	(0.7)
131	Colonie, NY	(0.7)
131	Greensboro, NC	(0.7)
131	North Charleston, SC	(0.7)
131	Pittsburgh, PA	(0.7)
131	Pomona, CA	(0.7)
137	Houston, TX	(0.8)
137	Paterson, NJ	(0.8)
139	Bridgeport, CT	(0.9)
139	Lawton, OK	(0.9)
141	Cambridge, MA	(1.0)
141	Clarksville, TN	(1.0)
141	Indianapolis, IN	(1.0)
141	Jacksonville, FL	(1.0)
145	Columbia, MO	(1.1)
145	Kenosha, WI	(1.1)
147	Knoxville, TN	(1.3)
148	Huntsville, AL	(1.7)
148	Manchester, NH	(1.7)
150	San Diego, CA	(1.8)
150	Surprise, AZ	(1.8)
150	Tacoma, WA	(1.8)
153	Green Bay, WI	(1.9)
154	Burbank, CA	(2.0)
154	Longview, TX	(2.0)
154	Overland Park, KS	(2.0)
154	Sandy, UT	(2.0)
154	Sunnyvale, CA	(2.0)
159	Baltimore, MD	(2.2)
160	Murrieta, CA	(2.3)
160	Omaha, NE	(2.3)
160	Pasadena, TX	(2.3)
160	Washington, DC	(2.3)
164	Salt Lake City, UT	(2.4)
165	Orlando, FL	(2.5)
166	Antioch, CA	(2.6)
166	Austin, TX	(2.6)
166	McKinney, TX	(2.6)
169	Amherst, NY	(2.7)
169	Newport Beach, CA	(2.7)
169	Portsmouth, VA	(2.7)
169	Southfield, MI	(2.7)
173	Chattanooga, TN	(2.8)
173	Henderson, NV	(2.8)
173	Toledo, OH	(2.8)
176	Baldwin Park, CA	(2.9)
176	Cheektowaga, NY	(2.9)
176	Fairfield, CA	(2.9)
176	Miami Gardens, FL	(2.9)
176	Virginia Beach, VA	(2.9)
181	Youngstown, OH	(3.1)
182	Laredo, TX	(3.4)
182	Spokane, WA	(3.4)
184	Kansas City, KS	(3.5)
184	Las Vegas, NV	(3.5)
184	Madison, WI	(3.5)
184	Santa Clara, CA	(3.5)
184	Torrance, CA	(3.5)
184	Vista, CA	(3.5)
190	Odessa, TX	(3.6)
191	Little Rock, AR	(3.7)
191	Mesquite, TX	(3.7)

RANK	CITY	% CHANGE
191	Midland, TX	(3.7)
191	Plano, TX	(3.7)
191	Raleigh, NC	(3.7)
196	Grand Prairie, TX	(3.8)
197	Columbus, OH	(3.9)
197	Hawthorne, CA	(3.9)
197	Hollywood, FL	(3.9)
200	Brownsville, TX	(4.0)
200	Newton, MA	(4.0)
202	Miramar, FL	(4.1)
202	South Gate, CA	(4.1)
202	Temecula, CA	(4.1)
205	Vacaville, CA	(4.2)
206	Clearwater, FL	(4.3)
207	Farmington Hills, MI	(4.4)
207	Reno, NV	(4.4)
209	Glendale, AZ	(4.5)
209	Tulsa, OK	(4.5)
211	Garland, TX	(4.7)
212	Alhambra, CA	(4.8)
212	Lincoln, NE	(4.8)
212	Orange, CA	(4.8)
215	Inglewood, CA	(4.9)
215	Las Cruces, NM	(4.9)
215	Miami Beach, FL	(4.9)
215	Providence, RI	(4.9)
219	Elizabeth, NJ	(5.1)
219	Fullerton, CA	(5.1)
219	Long Beach, CA	(5.1)
222	Dallas, TX	(5.2)
222	Lubbock, TX	(5.2)
222	Santa Clarita, CA	(5.2)
225	Sioux City, IA	(5.3)
226	Santa Monica, CA	(5.4)
227	Richmond, CA	(5.5)
227	Rochester, NY	(5.5)
229	Arlington, TX	(5.6)
229	San Antonio, TX	(5.6)
231	Edison Twnshp, NJ	(5.7)
231	Thornton, CO	(5.7)
231	Yakima, WA	(5.7)
234	Hesperia, CA	(5.8)
235	Ventura, CA	(5.9)
236	Boca Raton, FL	(6.0)
237	Brockton, MA	(6.1)
238	New York, NY	(6.2)
239	Fort Worth, TX	(6.3)
239	Newport News, VA	(6.3)
241	Hammond, IN	(6.4)
241	Independence, MO	(6.4)
243	Bellingham, WA	(6.6)
243	Hartford, CT	(6.6)
243	Roswell, GA	(6.6)
246	Buffalo, NY	(6.8)
246	Corpus Christi, TX	(6.8)
246	Phoenix, AZ	(6.8)
249	Anaheim, CA	(7.0)
250	Garden Grove, CA	(7.1)
251	Bakersfield, CA	(7.2)
252	Compton, CA	(7.5)
252	Worcester, MA	(7.5)
254	High Point, NC	(7.6)
254	Norwalk, CA	(7.6)
254	Palm Bay, FL	(7.6)
257	Berkeley, CA	(7.7)
257	Ontario, CA	(7.7)
259	Wilmington, NC	(7.8)
260	Chino, CA	(7.9)
260	Norfolk, VA	(7.9)
262	Tampa, FL	(8.0)
263	Visalia, CA	(8.2)
264	Colorado Springs, CO	(8.4)
265	Amarillo, TX	(8.7)
265	Cranston, RI	(8.7)
267	Alexandria, VA	(8.8)
267	Chula Vista, CA	(8.8)
267	Clovis, CA	(8.8)
267	El Monte, CA	(8.8)
267	Peoria, AZ	(8.8)
272	Cedar Rapids, IA	(8.9)
273	Atlanta, GA	(9.0)
273	Reading, PA	(9.0)
275	Joliet, IL	(9.1)
276	Hampton, VA	(9.2)
277	Fresno, CA	(9.3)
278	Abilene, TX	(9.4)
278	Carrollton, TX	(9.4)
278	Riverside, CA	(9.4)
278	Westminster, CA	(9.4)
282	Bellevue, WA	(9.5)
282	El Cajon, CA	(9.5)
282	Nashville, TN	(9.5)
285	Escondido, CA	(9.6)
286	Columbia, SC	(9.7)
287	Modesto, CA	(9.8)
287	Seattle, WA	(9.8)
289	Newark, NJ	(9.9)
289	Pueblo, CO	(9.9)
289	Topeka, KS	(9.9)
292	Honolulu, HI	(10.0)
293	Charleston, SC	(10.1)
293	Salem, OR	(10.1)
293	Spokane Valley, WA	(10.1)
293	Tallahassee, FL	(10.1)
297	Deerfield Beach, FL	(10.3)
297	Los Angeles, CA	(10.3)
297	Salinas, CA	(10.3)
300	Irvine, CA	(10.4)
301	San Mateo, CA	(10.5)
302	Davie, FL	(10.6)
303	Suffolk, VA	(10.7)
304	Evansville, IN	(10.8)
304	Killeen, TX	(10.8)
304	Naperville, IL	(10.8)
307	Bellflower, CA	(11.0)
307	Victorville, CA	(11.0)
309	Simi Valley, CA	(11.1)
309	St. Paul, MN	(11.1)
311	Richardson, TX	(11.3)
312	Corona, CA	(11.8)
312	Costa Mesa, CA	(11.8)
314	Tyler, TX	(12.2)
315	Fort Lauderdale, FL	(12.4)
315	Parma, OH	(12.4)
317	Peoria, IL	(12.5)
318	Mesa, AZ	(12.9)
319	Ann Arbor, MI	(13.0)
319	Boise, ID	(13.0)
321	Fontana, CA	(13.1)
321	Jersey City, NJ	(13.1)
323	Concord, CA	(13.2)
324	San Bernardino, CA	(13.3)
325	Oceanside, CA	(13.4)
326	Chesapeake, VA	(13.8)
327	Miami, FL	(14.0)
327	Santa Rosa, CA	(14.0)
329	Santa Barbara, CA	(14.4)
330	Savannah, GA	(14.9)
331	Aurora, CO	(15.0)
332	Westminster, CO	(15.2)
333	Portland, OR	(15.3)
333	Rancho Cucamon., CA	(15.3)
335	Sugar Land, TX	(15.4)
336	San Angelo, TX	(15.8)
336	Santa Ana, CA	(15.8)
338	Lakewood, CO	(16.1)
338	Round Rock, TX	(16.1)
340	Boulder, CO	(16.7)
340	Roanoke, VA	(16.7)
342	Beaumont, TX	(16.9)
343	Sioux Falls, SD	(17.5)
344	Waco, TX	(17.7)
345	Wichita Falls, TX	(17.8)
346	Federal Way, WA	(17.9)
346	Tracy, CA	(17.9)
348	Warwick, RI	(18.2)
349	McAllen, TX	(18.3)
350	Pompano Beach, FL	(18.5)
351	Redding, CA	(18.6)
352	Lakewood, CA	(18.7)
352	West Valley, UT	(18.7)
354	Arvada, CO	(18.9)
355	Oklahoma City, OK	(19.3)
356	Eugene, OR	(19.4)
356	Vancouver, WA	(19.4)
358	Roseville, CA	(20.2)
359	Centennial, CO	(20.4)
360	Broken Arrow, OK	(21.0)
361	Lewisville, TX	(21.3)
362	Richmond, VA	(21.9)
363	Rialto, CA	(22.5)
364	Denver, CO	(23.1)
365	Billings, MT	(23.4)
366	Provo, UT	(23.8)
367	Greeley, CO	(23.9)
368	Gresham, OR	(25.5)
369	Hillsboro, OR	(27.2)
369	Orem, UT	(27.2)
371	Denton, TX	(28.1)
372	Beaverton, OR	(28.2)
373	Trenton, NJ	(30.0)
374	Olathe, KS	(33.6)
NA	Bloomington, MN**	NA
NA	Clarkstown, NY**	NA
NA	Des Moines, IA**	NA
NA	Duluth, MN**	NA
NA	Durham, NC**	NA
NA	El Paso, TX**	NA
NA	Fort Wayne, IN**	NA
NA	Kansas City, MO**	NA
NA	Lexington, KY**	NA
NA	New Orleans, LA**	NA
NA	Rockford, IL**	NA
NA	Tucson, AZ**	NA
NA	Vallejo, CA**	NA
NA	Warren, MI**	NA
NA	West Jordan, UT**	NA
NA	Wichita, KS**	NA

Source: CQ Press using data from F.B.I. "Crime in the United States 2006"

**Property crimes are offenses of burglary, larceny-theft, and motor vehicle theft. Attempts are included.*

***Not available.*

68. Percent Change in Property Crime Rate: 2002 to 2006

National Percent Change = 8.2% Decrease*

RANK	CITY	% CHANGE
66	Abilene, TX	4.6
34	Albany, GA	11.0
NA	Albany, NY**	NA
146	Albuquerque, NM	(6.1)
349	Alexandria, VA	(35.0)
60	Alhambra, CA	5.4
27	Allentown, PA	13.7
196	Amarillo, TX	(11.0)
88	Amherst, NY	2.1
268	Anaheim, CA	(17.1)
142	Anchorage, AK	(5.6)
220	Ann Arbor, MI	(12.9)
132	Antioch, CA	(3.8)
236	Arlington, TX	(14.3)
279	Arvada, CO	(18.6)
203	Athens-Clarke, GA	(11.3)
326	Atlanta, GA	(26.8)
315	Aurora, CO	(24.5)
291	Aurora, IL	(20.3)
92	Austin, TX	1.0
8	Bakersfield, CA	26.9
9	Baldwin Park, CA	25.7
282	Baltimore, MD	(19.1)
122	Baton Rouge, LA	(2.1)
307	Beaumont, TX	(22.5)
357	Beaverton, OR	(37.4)
193	Bellevue, WA	(10.7)
195	Bellflower, CA	(10.8)
118	Bellingham, WA	(1.6)
284	Berkeley, CA	(19.6)
246	Billings, MT	(15.5)
36	Birmingham, AL	10.3
288	Bloomington, MN	(19.9)
125	Boca Raton, FL	(2.5)
291	Boise, ID	(20.3)
157	Boston, MA	(7.4)
176	Boulder, CO	(8.8)
36	Brick Twnshp, NJ	10.3
73	Bridgeport, CT	4.1
237	Brockton, MA	(14.4)
339	Broken Arrow, OK	(31.1)
361	Brownsville, TX	(40.6)
149	Buena Park, CA	(6.7)
55	Buffalo, NY	6.5
174	Burbank, CA	(8.5)
212	Cambridge, MA	(12.2)
63	Camden, NJ	5.0
119	Canton Twnshp, MI	(1.7)
NA	Canton, OH**	NA
108	Cape Coral, FL	(0.3)
60	Carlsbad, CA	5.4
212	Carrollton, TX	(12.2)
86	Carson, CA	2.6
167	Cary, NC	(8.0)
246	Cedar Rapids, IA	(15.5)
NA	Centennial, CO**	NA
356	Chandler, AZ	(37.1)
350	Charleston, SC	(35.3)
38	Charlotte, NC	10.2
163	Chattanooga, TN	(7.8)
NA	Cheektowaga, NY**	NA
230	Chesapeake, VA	(13.6)
181	Chicago, IL	(9.4)
364	Chino Hills, CA	(48.3)
1	Chino, CA	98.7
178	Chula Vista, CA	(9.3)
137	Cincinnati, OH	(4.7)
277	Clarkstown, NY	(18.5)
328	Clarksville, TN	(27.1)
169	Clearwater, FL	(8.2)
33	Cleveland, OH	11.7
295	Clifton, NJ	(20.7)
55	Clinton Twnshp, MI	6.5
274	Clovis, CA	(17.9)
66	Colonie, NY	4.6
171	Colorado Springs, CO	(8.3)
253	Columbia, MO	(16.0)
289	Columbia, SC	(20.1)
13	Columbus, GA	21.6
241	Columbus, OH	(14.7)
196	Compton, CA	(11.0)
68	Concord, CA	4.5
311	Coral Springs, FL	(23.7)
243	Corona, CA	(14.9)
113	Corpus Christi, TX	(0.8)
130	Costa Mesa, CA	(3.3)
317	Cranston, RI	(24.6)
192	Dallas, TX	(10.4)
6	Daly City, CA	31.1
313	Danbury, CT	(24.3)
301	Davie, FL	(21.7)
200	Dayton, OH	(11.1)
26	Dearborn, MI	14.0
4	Deerfield Beach, FL	37.4
333	Denton, TX	(29.0)
159	Denver, CO	(7.5)
NA	Des Moines, IA**	NA
72	Detroit, MI	4.2
29	Downey, CA	13.1
244	Duluth, MN	(15.1)
NA	Durham, NC**	NA
123	Edison Twnshp, NJ	(2.3)
57	Edmond, OK	6.4
189	El Cajon, CA	(10.1)
42	El Monte, CA	9.4
NA	El Paso, TX**	NA
322	Elizabeth, NJ	(25.3)
127	Erie, PA	(2.6)
161	Escondido, CA	(7.7)
203	Eugene, OR	(11.3)
89	Evansville, IN	2.0
3	Everett, WA	39.3
230	Fairfield, CA	(13.6)
253	Fargo, ND	(16.0)
113	Farmington Hills, MI	(0.8)
7	Fayetteville, NC	30.7
102	Federal Way, WA	0.5
46	Flint, MI	8.4
299	Fontana, CA	(21.3)
208	Fort Collins, CO	(11.7)
181	Fort Lauderdale, FL	(9.4)
297	Fort Smith, AR	(21.1)
NA	Fort Wayne, IN**	NA
301	Fort Worth, TX	(21.7)
76	Fremont, CA	3.9
323	Fresno, CA	(26.0)
134	Fullerton, CA	(4.2)
110	Gainesville, FL	(0.4)
169	Garden Grove, CA	(8.2)
214	Garland, TX	(12.3)
22	Gary, IN	15.3
358	Gilbert, AZ	(37.5)
287	Glendale, AZ	(19.8)
125	Glendale, CA	(2.5)
181	Grand Prairie, TX	(9.4)
24	Grand Rapids, MI	14.7
NA	Greece, NY**	NA
299	Greeley, CO	(21.3)
220	Green Bay, WI	(12.9)
74	Greensboro, NC	4.0
343	Gresham, OR	(32.5)
196	Hamilton Twnshp, NJ	(11.0)
149	Hammond, IN	(6.7)
196	Hampton, VA	(11.0)
144	Hartford, CT	(5.9)
209	Hawthorne, CA	(11.8)
17	Hayward, CA	19.9
110	Henderson, NV	(0.4)
200	Hesperia, CA	(11.1)
238	Hialeah, FL	(14.5)
184	High Point, NC	(9.5)
350	Hillsboro, OR	(35.3)
315	Hollywood, FL	(24.5)
337	Honolulu, HI	(30.9)
134	Houston, TX	(4.2)
35	Huntington Beach, CA	10.6
19	Huntsville, AL	18.8
102	Independence, MO	0.5
15	Indianapolis, IN	21.5
155	Inglewood, CA	(7.1)
339	Irvine, CA	(31.1)
129	Irving, TX	(3.2)
140	Jacksonville, FL	(5.3)
216	Jackson, MS	(12.6)
256	Jersey City, NJ	(16.4)
310	Joliet, IL	(23.5)
NA	Kansas City, KS**	NA
NA	Kansas City, MO**	NA
47	Kenosha, WI	8.2
38	Kent, WA	10.2
263	Killeen, TX	(16.8)
52	Knoxville, TN	7.2
187	Lafayette, LA	(9.9)
206	Lake Forest, CA	(11.4)
106	Lakeland, FL	(0.1)
272	Lakewood, CA	(17.6)
227	Lakewood, CO	(13.4)
13	Lancaster, CA	21.6
171	Lansing, MI	(8.3)
178	Laredo, TX	(9.3)
147	Largo, FL	(6.2)
NA	Las Cruces, NM**	NA
30	Las Vegas, NV	12.6
5	Lawrence, KS	33.4
101	Lawton, OK	0.6
76	Lee's Summit, MO	3.9
346	Lewisville, TX	(33.8)
NA	Lexington, KY**	NA
246	Lincoln, NE	(15.5)
234	Little Rock, AR	(14.0)
293	Livermore, CA	(20.6)
145	Livonia, MI	(6.0)

RANK	CITY	% CHANGE
277	Long Beach, CA	(18.5)
153	Longview, TX	(7.0)
321	Los Angeles, CA	(25.2)
NA	Louisville, KY**	NA
94	Lowell, MA	0.9
94	Lubbock, TX	0.9
117	Lynn, MA	(1.3)
91	Macon, GA	1.2
210	Madison, WI	(12.1)
65	Manchester, NH	4.9
330	McAllen, TX	(28.3)
363	McKinney, TX	(47.2)
185	Melbourne, FL	(9.7)
106	Memphis, TN	(0.1)
352	Mesa, AZ	(35.8)
226	Mesquite, TX	(13.3)
255	Miami Beach, FL	(16.3)
NA	Miami Gardens, FL**	NA
326	Miami, FL	(26.8)
98	Midland, TX	0.8
119	Milwaukee, WI	(1.7)
71	Minneapolis, MN	4.3
313	Miramar, FL	(24.3)
178	Mission Viejo, CA	(9.3)
121	Mobile, AL	(1.9)
159	Modesto, CA	(7.5)
276	Montgomery, AL	(18.4)
105	Moreno Valley, CA	0.0
51	Murfreesboro, TN	7.3
53	Murrieta, CA	7.1
69	Napa, CA	4.4
223	Naperville, IL	(13.1)
NA	Nashua, NH**	NA
217	Nashville, TN	(12.7)
NA	New Bedford, MA**	NA
365	New Orleans, LA	(48.5)
281	New York, NY	(18.7)
304	Newark, NJ	(22.1)
193	Newport Beach, CA	(10.7)
186	Newport News, VA	(9.8)
NA	Newton, MA**	NA
241	Norfolk, VA	(14.7)
136	Norman, OK	(4.6)
161	North Charleston, SC	(7.7)
124	North Las Vegas, NV	(2.4)
163	Norwalk, CA	(7.8)
69	Oakland, CA	4.4
266	Oceanside, CA	(17.0)
336	Odessa, TX	(30.7)
87	Ogden, UT	2.5
330	Oklahoma City, OK	(28.3)
347	Olathe, KS	(34.7)
293	Omaha, NE	(20.6)
273	Ontario, CA	(17.8)
191	Orange, CA	(10.2)
342	Orem, UT	(32.4)
147	Orlando, FL	(6.2)
238	Overland Park, KS	(14.5)
163	Oxnard, CA	(7.8)
284	Palm Bay, FL	(19.6)
200	Palmdale, CA	(11.1)
47	Parma, OH	8.2
108	Pasadena, CA	(0.3)
324	Pasadena, TX	(26.1)
303	Paterson, NJ	(22.0)
63	Pembroke Pines, FL	5.0

RANK	CITY	% CHANGE
274	Peoria, AZ	(17.9)
289	Peoria, IL	(20.1)
82	Philadelphia, PA	2.9
256	Phoenix, AZ	(16.4)
98	Pittsburgh, PA	0.8
151	Plano, TX	(6.9)
217	Plantation, FL	(12.7)
44	Pomona, CA	9.1
28	Pompano Beach, FL	13.4
151	Port St. Lucie, FL	(6.9)
270	Portland, OR	(17.2)
235	Portsmouth, VA	(14.2)
338	Providence, RI	(31.0)
312	Provo, UT	(23.8)
20	Pueblo, CO	18.3
317	Quincy, MA	(24.6)
40	Racine, WI	10.0
347	Raleigh, NC	(34.7)
261	Rancho Cucamon., CA	(16.6)
177	Reading, PA	(8.9)
58	Redding, CA	6.0
112	Reno, NV	(0.7)
223	Rialto, CA	(13.1)
266	Richardson, TX	(17.0)
271	Richmond, CA	(17.4)
341	Richmond, VA	(31.8)
250	Riverside, CA	(15.6)
NA	Roanoke, VA**	NA
259	Rochester, MN	(16.5)
187	Rochester, NY	(9.9)
NA	Rockford, IL**	NA
259	Roseville, CA	(16.5)
23	Roswell, GA	14.8
261	Round Rock, TX	(16.6)
210	Sacramento, CA	(12.1)
354	Salem, OR	(36.0)
32	Salinas, CA	12.1
203	Salt Lake City, UT	(11.3)
217	San Angelo, TX	(12.7)
232	San Antonio, TX	(13.8)
265	San Bernardino, CA	(16.9)
60	San Diego, CA	5.4
44	San Francisco, CA	9.1
12	San Jose, CA	22.1
54	San Leandro, CA	6.7
79	San Mateo, CA	3.7
173	Sandy, UT	(8.4)
220	Santa Ana, CA	(12.9)
50	Santa Barbara, CA	7.4
24	Santa Clara, CA	14.7
40	Santa Clarita, CA	10.0
NA	Santa Maria, CA**	NA
283	Santa Monica, CA	(19.3)
334	Santa Rosa, CA	(29.4)
360	Savannah, GA	(38.6)
296	Scottsdale, AZ	(20.8)
156	Seattle, WA	(7.2)
143	Shreveport, LA	(5.8)
11	Simi Valley, CA	22.7
352	Sioux City, IA	(35.8)
251	Sioux Falls, SD	(15.7)
174	Somerville, MA	(8.5)
80	South Bend, IN	3.4
138	South Gate, CA	(4.8)
94	Southfield, MI	0.9
227	Sparks, NV	(13.4)

RANK	CITY	% CHANGE
NA	Spokane Valley, WA**	NA
279	Spokane, WA	(18.6)
166	Springfield, IL	(7.9)
298	Springfield, MA	(21.2)
16	Springfield, MO	21.4
49	Sterling Heights, MI	7.5
115	Stockton, CA	(1.2)
131	St. Louis, MO	(3.4)
268	St. Paul, MN	(17.1)
89	St. Petersburg, FL	2.0
335	Suffolk, VA	(29.6)
305	Sugar Land, TX	(22.2)
21	Sunnyvale, CA	16.3
245	Sunrise, FL	(15.4)
256	Surprise, AZ	(16.4)
246	Syracuse, NY	(15.5)
168	Tacoma, WA	(8.1)
325	Tallahassee, FL	(26.6)
359	Tampa, FL	(38.2)
100	Temecula, CA	0.7
308	Tempe, AZ	(23.4)
320	Thornton, CO	(25.0)
157	Thousand Oaks, CA	(7.4)
94	Toledo, OH	0.9
284	Toms River Twnshp, NJ	(19.6)
238	Topeka, KS	(14.5)
305	Torrance, CA	(22.2)
233	Tracy, CA	(13.9)
362	Trenton, NJ	(45.4)
82	Troy, MI	2.9
NA	Tucson, AZ**	NA
133	Tulsa, OK	(4.0)
141	Tuscaloosa, AL	(5.5)
345	Tyler, TX	(33.2)
2	Upper Darby Twnshp, PA	61.9
59	Vacaville, CA	5.5
92	Vallejo, CA	1.0
263	Vancouver, WA	(16.8)
43	Ventura, CA	9.3
189	Victorville, CA	(10.1)
252	Virginia Beach, VA	(15.8)
84	Visalia, CA	2.8
74	Vista, CA	4.0
332	Waco, TX	(28.4)
31	Warren, MI	12.4
308	Warwick, RI	(23.4)
329	Washington, DC	(27.5)
84	Waterbury, CT	2.8
78	West Covina, CA	3.8
319	West Jordan, UT	(24.9)
343	West Palm Beach, FL	(32.5)
229	West Valley, UT	(13.5)
81	Westland, MI	3.1
139	Westminster, CA	(5.1)
NA	Westminster, CO**	NA
10	Whittier, CA	23.7
207	Wichita Falls, TX	(11.6)
215	Wichita, KS	(12.4)
354	Wilmington, NC	(36.0)
104	Winston-Salem, NC	0.1
225	Woodbridge Twnshp, NJ	(13.2)
NA	Worcester, MA**	NA
115	Yakima, WA	(1.2)
153	Yonkers, NY	(7.0)
127	Youngstown, OH	(2.6)
18	Yuma, AZ	19.7

Source: CQ Press using data from F.B.I. "Crime in the United States 2006"

**Property crimes are offenses of burglary, larceny-theft, and motor vehicle theft. Attempts are included.*

***Not available.*

68. Percent Change in Property Crime Rate: 2002 to 2006 (continued)

National Percent Change = 8.2% Decrease*

RANK	CITY	% CHANGE	RANK	CITY	% CHANGE	RANK	CITY	% CHANGE
1	Chino, CA	98.7	65	Manchester, NH	4.9	129	Irving, TX	(3.2)
2	Upper Darby Twnshp, PA	61.9	66	Abilene, TX	4.6	130	Costa Mesa, CA	(3.3)
3	Everett, WA	39.3	66	Colonie, NY	4.6	131	St. Louis, MO	(3.4)
4	Deerfield Beach, FL	37.4	68	Concord, CA	4.5	132	Antioch, CA	(3.8)
5	Lawrence, KS	33.4	69	Napa, CA	4.4	133	Tulsa, OK	(4.0)
6	Daly City, CA	31.1	69	Oakland, CA	4.4	134	Fullerton, CA	(4.2)
7	Fayetteville, NC	30.7	71	Minneapolis, MN	4.3	134	Houston, TX	(4.2)
8	Bakersfield, CA	26.9	72	Detroit, MI	4.2	136	Norman, OK	(4.6)
9	Baldwin Park, CA	25.7	73	Bridgeport, CT	4.1	137	Cincinnati, OH	(4.7)
10	Whittier, CA	23.7	74	Greensboro, NC	4.0	138	South Gate, CA	(4.8)
11	Simi Valley, CA	22.7	74	Vista, CA	4.0	139	Westminster, CA	(5.1)
12	San Jose, CA	22.1	76	Fremont, CA	3.9	140	Jacksonville, FL	(5.3)
13	Columbus, GA	21.6	76	Lee's Summit, MO	3.9	141	Tuscaloosa, AL	(5.5)
13	Lancaster, CA	21.6	78	West Covina, CA	3.8	142	Anchorage, AK	(5.6)
15	Indianapolis, IN	21.5	79	San Mateo, CA	3.7	143	Shreveport, LA	(5.8)
16	Springfield, MO	21.4	80	South Bend, IN	3.4	144	Hartford, CT	(5.9)
17	Hayward, CA	19.9	81	Westland, MI	3.1	145	Livonia, MI	(6.0)
18	Yuma, AZ	19.7	82	Philadelphia, PA	2.9	146	Albuquerque, NM	(6.1)
19	Huntsville, AL	18.8	82	Troy, MI	2.9	147	Largo, FL	(6.2)
20	Pueblo, CO	18.3	84	Visalia, CA	2.8	147	Orlando, FL	(6.2)
21	Sunnyvale, CA	16.3	84	Waterbury, CT	2.8	149	Buena Park, CA	(6.7)
22	Gary, IN	15.3	86	Carson, CA	2.6	149	Hammond, IN	(6.7)
23	Roswell, GA	14.8	87	Ogden, UT	2.5	151	Plano, TX	(6.9)
24	Grand Rapids, MI	14.7	88	Amherst, NY	2.1	151	Port St. Lucie, FL	(6.9)
24	Santa Clara, CA	14.7	89	Evansville, IN	2.0	153	Longview, TX	(7.0)
26	Dearborn, MI	14.0	89	St. Petersburg, FL	2.0	153	Yonkers, NY	(7.0)
27	Allentown, PA	13.7	91	Macon, GA	1.2	155	Inglewood, CA	(7.1)
28	Pompano Beach, FL	13.4	92	Austin, TX	1.0	156	Seattle, WA	(7.2)
29	Downey, CA	13.1	92	Vallejo, CA	1.0	157	Boston, MA	(7.4)
30	Las Vegas, NV	12.6	94	Lowell, MA	0.9	157	Thousand Oaks, CA	(7.4)
31	Warren, MI	12.4	94	Lubbock, TX	0.9	159	Denver, CO	(7.5)
32	Salinas, CA	12.1	94	Southfield, MI	0.9	159	Modesto, CA	(7.5)
33	Cleveland, OH	11.7	94	Toledo, OH	0.9	161	Escondido, CA	(7.7)
34	Albany, GA	11.0	98	Midland, TX	0.8	161	North Charleston, SC	(7.7)
35	Huntington Beach, CA	10.6	98	Pittsburgh, PA	0.8	163	Chattanooga, TN	(7.8)
36	Birmingham, AL	10.3	100	Temecula, CA	0.7	163	Norwalk, CA	(7.8)
36	Brick Twnshp, NJ	10.3	101	Lawton, OK	0.6	163	Oxnard, CA	(7.8)
38	Charlotte, NC	10.2	102	Federal Way, WA	0.5	166	Springfield, IL	(7.9)
38	Kent, WA	10.2	102	Independence, MO	0.5	167	Cary, NC	(8.0)
40	Racine, WI	10.0	104	Winston-Salem, NC	0.1	168	Tacoma, WA	(8.1)
40	Santa Clarita, CA	10.0	105	Moreno Valley, CA	0.0	169	Clearwater, FL	(8.2)
42	El Monte, CA	9.4	106	Lakeland, FL	(0.1)	169	Garden Grove, CA	(8.2)
43	Ventura, CA	9.3	106	Memphis, TN	(0.1)	171	Colorado Springs, CO	(8.3)
44	Pomona, CA	9.1	108	Cape Coral, FL	(0.3)	171	Lansing, MI	(8.3)
44	San Francisco, CA	9.1	108	Pasadena, CA	(0.3)	173	Sandy, UT	(8.4)
46	Flint, MI	8.4	110	Gainesville, FL	(0.4)	174	Burbank, CA	(8.5)
47	Kenosha, WI	8.2	110	Henderson, NV	(0.4)	174	Somerville, MA	(8.5)
47	Parma, OH	8.2	112	Reno, NV	(0.7)	176	Boulder, CO	(8.8)
49	Sterling Heights, MI	7.5	113	Corpus Christi, TX	(0.8)	177	Reading, PA	(8.9)
50	Santa Barbara, CA	7.4	113	Farmington Hills, MI	(0.8)	178	Chula Vista, CA	(9.3)
51	Murfreesboro, TN	7.3	115	Stockton, CA	(1.2)	178	Laredo, TX	(9.3)
52	Knoxville, TN	7.2	115	Yakima, WA	(1.2)	178	Mission Viejo, CA	(9.3)
53	Murrieta, CA	7.1	117	Lynn, MA	(1.3)	181	Chicago, IL	(9.4)
54	San Leandro, CA	6.7	118	Bellingham, WA	(1.6)	181	Fort Lauderdale, FL	(9.4)
55	Buffalo, NY	6.5	119	Canton Twnshp, MI	(1.7)	181	Grand Prairie, TX	(9.4)
55	Clinton Twnshp, MI	6.5	119	Milwaukee, WI	(1.7)	184	High Point, NC	(9.5)
57	Edmond, OK	6.4	121	Mobile, AL	(1.9)	185	Melbourne, FL	(9.7)
58	Redding, CA	6.0	122	Baton Rouge, LA	(2.1)	186	Newport News, VA	(9.8)
59	Vacaville, CA	5.5	123	Edison Twnshp, NJ	(2.3)	187	Lafayette, LA	(9.9)
60	Alhambra, CA	5.4	124	North Las Vegas, NV	(2.4)	187	Rochester, NY	(9.9)
60	Carlsbad, CA	5.4	125	Boca Raton, FL	(2.5)	189	El Cajon, CA	(10.1)
60	San Diego, CA	5.4	125	Glendale, CA	(2.5)	189	Victorville, CA	(10.1)
63	Camden, NJ	5.0	127	Erie, PA	(2.6)	191	Orange, CA	(10.2)
63	Pembroke Pines, FL	5.0	127	Youngstown, OH	(2.6)	192	Dallas, TX	(10.4)

RANK	CITY	% CHANGE
193	Bellevue, WA	(10.7)
193	Newport Beach, CA	(10.7)
195	Bellflower, CA	(10.8)
196	Amarillo, TX	(11.0)
196	Compton, CA	(11.0)
196	Hamilton Twnshp, NJ	(11.0)
196	Hampton, VA	(11.0)
200	Dayton, OH	(11.1)
200	Hesperia, CA	(11.1)
200	Palmdale, CA	(11.1)
203	Athens-Clarke, GA	(11.3)
203	Eugene, OR	(11.3)
203	Salt Lake City, UT	(11.3)
206	Lake Forest, CA	(11.4)
207	Wichita Falls, TX	(11.6)
208	Fort Collins, CO	(11.7)
209	Hawthorne, CA	(11.8)
210	Madison, WI	(12.1)
210	Sacramento, CA	(12.1)
212	Cambridge, MA	(12.2)
212	Carrollton, TX	(12.2)
214	Garland, TX	(12.3)
215	Wichita, KS	(12.4)
216	Jackson, MS	(12.6)
217	Nashville, TN	(12.7)
217	Plantation, FL	(12.7)
217	San Angelo, TX	(12.7)
220	Ann Arbor, MI	(12.9)
220	Green Bay, WI	(12.9)
220	Santa Ana, CA	(12.9)
223	Naperville, IL	(13.1)
223	Rialto, CA	(13.1)
225	Woodbridge Twnshp, NJ	(13.2)
226	Mesquite, TX	(13.3)
227	Lakewood, CO	(13.4)
227	Sparks, NV	(13.4)
229	West Valley, UT	(13.5)
230	Chesapeake, VA	(13.6)
230	Fairfield, CA	(13.6)
232	San Antonio, TX	(13.8)
233	Tracy, CA	(13.9)
234	Little Rock, AR	(14.0)
235	Portsmouth, VA	(14.2)
236	Arlington, TX	(14.3)
237	Brockton, MA	(14.4)
238	Hialeah, FL	(14.5)
238	Overland Park, KS	(14.5)
238	Topeka, KS	(14.5)
241	Columbus, OH	(14.7)
241	Norfolk, VA	(14.7)
243	Corona, CA	(14.9)
244	Duluth, MN	(15.1)
245	Sunrise, FL	(15.4)
246	Billings, MT	(15.5)
246	Cedar Rapids, IA	(15.5)
246	Lincoln, NE	(15.5)
246	Syracuse, NY	(15.5)
250	Riverside, CA	(15.6)
251	Sioux Falls, SD	(15.7)
252	Virginia Beach, VA	(15.8)
253	Columbia, MO	(16.0)
253	Fargo, ND	(16.0)
255	Miami Beach, FL	(16.3)
256	Jersey City, NJ	(16.4)
256	Phoenix, AZ	(16.4)
256	Surprise, AZ	(16.4)

RANK	CITY	% CHANGE
259	Rochester, MN	(16.5)
259	Roseville, CA	(16.5)
261	Rancho Cucamon., CA	(16.6)
261	Round Rock, TX	(16.6)
263	Killeen, TX	(16.8)
263	Vancouver, WA	(16.8)
265	San Bernardino, CA	(16.9)
266	Oceanside, CA	(17.0)
266	Richardson, TX	(17.0)
268	Anaheim, CA	(17.1)
268	St. Paul, MN	(17.1)
270	Portland, OR	(17.2)
271	Richmond, CA	(17.4)
272	Lakewood, CA	(17.6)
273	Ontario, CA	(17.8)
274	Clovis, CA	(17.9)
274	Peoria, AZ	(17.9)
276	Montgomery, AL	(18.4)
277	Clarkstown, NY	(18.5)
277	Long Beach, CA	(18.5)
279	Arvada, CO	(18.6)
279	Spokane, WA	(18.6)
281	New York, NY	(18.7)
282	Baltimore, MD	(19.1)
283	Santa Monica, CA	(19.3)
284	Berkeley, CA	(19.6)
284	Palm Bay, FL	(19.6)
284	Toms River Twnshp, NJ	(19.6)
287	Glendale, AZ	(19.8)
288	Bloomington, MN	(19.9)
289	Columbia, SC	(20.1)
289	Peoria, IL	(20.1)
291	Aurora, IL	(20.3)
291	Boise, ID	(20.3)
293	Livermore, CA	(20.6)
293	Omaha, NE	(20.6)
295	Clifton, NJ	(20.7)
296	Scottsdale, AZ	(20.8)
297	Fort Smith, AR	(21.1)
298	Springfield, MA	(21.2)
299	Fontana, CA	(21.3)
299	Greeley, CO	(21.3)
301	Davie, FL	(21.7)
301	Fort Worth, TX	(21.7)
303	Paterson, NJ	(22.0)
304	Newark, NJ	(22.1)
305	Sugar Land, TX	(22.2)
305	Torrance, CA	(22.2)
307	Beaumont, TX	(22.5)
308	Tempe, AZ	(23.4)
308	Warwick, RI	(23.4)
310	Joliet, IL	(23.5)
311	Coral Springs, FL	(23.7)
312	Provo, UT	(23.8)
313	Danbury, CT	(24.3)
313	Miramar, FL	(24.3)
315	Aurora, CO	(24.5)
315	Hollywood, FL	(24.5)
317	Cranston, RI	(24.6)
317	Quincy, MA	(24.6)
319	West Jordan, UT	(24.9)
320	Thornton, CO	(25.0)
321	Los Angeles, CA	(25.2)
322	Elizabeth, NJ	(25.3)
323	Fresno, CA	(26.0)
324	Pasadena, TX	(26.1)

RANK	CITY	% CHANGE
325	Tallahassee, FL	(26.6)
326	Atlanta, GA	(26.8)
326	Miami, FL	(26.8)
328	Clarksville, TN	(27.1)
329	Washington, DC	(27.5)
330	McAllen, TX	(28.3)
330	Oklahoma City, OK	(28.3)
332	Waco, TX	(28.4)
333	Denton, TX	(29.0)
334	Santa Rosa, CA	(29.4)
335	Suffolk, VA	(29.6)
336	Odessa, TX	(30.7)
337	Honolulu, HI	(30.9)
338	Providence, RI	(31.0)
339	Broken Arrow, OK	(31.1)
339	Irvine, CA	(31.1)
341	Richmond, VA	(31.8)
342	Orem, UT	(32.4)
343	Gresham, OR	(32.5)
343	West Palm Beach, FL	(32.5)
345	Tyler, TX	(33.2)
346	Lewisville, TX	(33.8)
347	Olathe, KS	(34.7)
347	Raleigh, NC	(34.7)
349	Alexandria, VA	(35.0)
350	Charleston, SC	(35.3)
350	Hillsboro, OR	(35.3)
352	Mesa, AZ	(35.8)
352	Sioux City, IA	(35.8)
354	Salem, OR	(36.0)
354	Wilmington, NC	(36.0)
356	Chandler, AZ	(37.1)
357	Beaverton, OR	(37.4)
358	Gilbert, AZ	(37.5)
359	Tampa, FL	(38.2)
360	Savannah, GA	(38.6)
361	Brownsville, TX	(40.6)
362	Trenton, NJ	(45.4)
363	McKinney, TX	(47.2)
364	Chino Hills, CA	(48.3)
365	New Orleans, LA	(48.5)
NA	Albany, NY**	NA
NA	Canton, OH**	NA
NA	Centennial, CO**	NA
NA	Cheektowaga, NY**	NA
NA	Des Moines, IA**	NA
NA	Durham, NC**	NA
NA	El Paso, TX**	NA
NA	Fort Wayne, IN**	NA
NA	Greece, NY**	NA
NA	Kansas City, KS**	NA
NA	Kansas City, MO**	NA
NA	Las Cruces, NM**	NA
NA	Lexington, KY**	NA
NA	Louisville, KY**	NA
NA	Miami Gardens, FL**	NA
NA	Nashua, NH**	NA
NA	New Bedford, MA**	NA
NA	Newton, MA**	NA
NA	Roanoke, VA**	NA
NA	Rockford, IL**	NA
NA	Santa Maria, CA**	NA
NA	Spokane Valley, WA**	NA
NA	Tucson, AZ**	NA
NA	Westminster, CO**	NA
NA	Worcester, MA**	NA

Source: CQ Press using data from F.B.I. "Crime in the United States 2006"

**Property crimes are offenses of burglary, larceny-theft, and motor vehicle theft. Attempts are included.*

***Not available.*

69. Burglaries in 2006

National Total = 2,183,746 Burglaries*

RANK	CITY	BURGLARY
165	Abilene, TX	1,282
132	Albany, GA	1,645
196	Albany, NY	1,058
31	Albuquerque, NM	6,352
349	Alexandria, VA	380
335	Alhambra, CA	443
147	Allentown, PA	1,433
86	Amarillo, TX	2,412
377	Amherst, NY	277
118	Anaheim, CA	1,886
124	Anchorage, AK	1,733
283	Ann Arbor, MI	631
229	Antioch, CA	840
51	Arlington, TX	4,042
310	Arvada, CO	539
185	Athens-Clarke, GA	1,116
25	Atlanta, GA	7,401
85	Aurora, CO	2,470
215	Aurora, IL	917
24	Austin, TX	7,467
59	Bakersfield, CA	3,729
356	Baldwin Park, CA	363
21	Baltimore, MD	7,608
52	Baton Rouge, LA	4,021
117	Beaumont, TX	1,887
370	Beaverton, OR	311
292	Bellevue, WA	591
329	Bellflower, CA	476
238	Bellingham, WA	791
181	Berkeley, CA	1,152
332	Billings, MT	465
41	Birmingham, AL	4,813
363	Bloomington, MN	331
305	Boca Raton, FL	551
178	Boise, ID	1,165
49	Boston, MA	4,121
324	Boulder, CO	487
373	Brick Twnshp, NJ	303
154	Bridgeport, CT	1,362
272	Brockton, MA	673
341	Broken Arrow, OK	420
151	Brownsville, TX	1,377
345	Buena Park, CA	410
43	Buffalo, NY	4,447
301	Burbank, CA	567
267	Cambridge, MA	684
175	Camden, NJ	1,179
372	Canton Twnshp, MI	309
120	Canton, OH	1,812
145	Cape Coral, FL	1,462
294	Carlsbad, CA	587
234	Carrollton, TX	815
288	Carson, CA	619
304	Cary, NC	554
186	Cedar Rapids, IA	1,114
361	Centennial, CO	340
149	Chandler, AZ	1,401
262	Charleston, SC	707
12	Charlotte, NC	13,582
91	Chattanooga, TN	2,273
343	Cheektowaga, NY	415
158	Chesapeake, VA	1,345
2	Chicago, IL	24,153
379	Chino Hills, CA	275

RANK	CITY	BURGLARY
311	Chino, CA	530
173	Chula Vista, CA	1,184
34	Cincinnati, OH	6,009
390	Clarkstown, NY	103
157	Clarksville, TN	1,348
221	Clearwater, FL	882
15	Cleveland, OH	9,650
357	Clifton, NJ	361
316	Clinton Twnshp, MI	522
284	Clovis, CA	630
371	Colonie, NY	310
68	Colorado Springs, CO	3,347
307	Columbia, MO	544
167	Columbia, SC	1,254
80	Columbus, GA	2,773
10	Columbus, OH	14,816
297	Compton, CA	578
212	Concord, CA	941
324	Coral Springs, FL	487
255	Corona, CA	730
75	Corpus Christi, TX	3,005
313	Costa Mesa, CA	524
374	Cranston, RI	299
4	Dallas, TX	21,653
385	Daly City, CA	243
383	Danbury, CT	257
333	Davie, FL	450
63	Dayton, OH	3,525
274	Dearborn, MI	670
328	Deerfield Beach, FL	478
276	Denton, TX	664
28	Denver, CO	6,543
97	Des Moines, IA	2,189
6	Detroit, MI	18,134
299	Downey, CA	575
284	Duluth, MN	630
72	Durham, NC	3,098
352	Edison Twnshp, NJ	368
351	Edmond, OK	370
280	El Cajon, CA	638
231	El Monte, CA	831
96	El Paso, TX	2,212
268	Elizabeth, NJ	682
253	Erie, PA	740
249	Escondido, CA	758
140	Eugene, OR	1,561
183	Evansville, IN	1,131
156	Everett, WA	1,352
252	Fairfield, CA	745
312	Fargo, ND	525
364	Farmington Hills, MI	325
64	Fayetteville, NC	3,519
250	Federal Way, WA	753
74	Flint, MI	3,058
241	Fontana, CA	779
264	Fort Collins, CO	701
94	Fort Lauderdale, FL	2,239
191	Fort Smith, AR	1,089
104	Fort Wayne, IN	2,128
18	Fort Worth, TX	8,998
161	Fremont, CA	1,325
46	Fresno, CA	4,366
247	Fullerton, CA	764
148	Gainesville, FL	1,420

RANK	CITY	BURGLARY
260	Garden Grove, CA	715
116	Garland, TX	1,889
119	Gary, IN	1,818
210	Gilbert, AZ	949
58	Glendale, AZ	3,756
273	Glendale, CA	672
137	Grand Prairie, TX	1,591
84	Grand Rapids, MI	2,484
384	Greece, NY	255
228	Greeley, CO	841
265	Green Bay, WI	687
48	Greensboro, NC	4,129
279	Gresham, OR	645
336	Hamilton Twnshp, NJ	440
207	Hammond, IN	970
245	Hampton, VA	767
179	Hartford, CT	1,158
322	Hawthorne, CA	491
172	Hayward, CA	1,196
136	Henderson, NV	1,600
303	Hesperia, CA	562
129	Hialeah, FL	1,673
126	High Point, NC	1,697
374	Hillsboro, OR	299
159	Hollywood, FL	1,338
38	Honolulu, HI	5,482
1	Houston, TX	26,869
209	Huntington Beach, CA	961
83	Huntsville, AL	2,493
169	Independence, MO	1,236
13	Indianapolis, IN	11,734
270	Inglewood, CA	675
282	Irvine, CA	634
128	Irving, TX	1,674
16	Jacksonville, FL	9,615
56	Jackson, MS	3,817
130	Jersey City, NJ	1,670
221	Joliet, IL	882
92	Kansas City, KS	2,265
26	Kansas City, MO	7,399
286	Kenosha, WI	626
171	Kent, WA	1,223
105	Killeen, TX	2,121
90	Knoxville, TN	2,281
162	Lafayette, LA	1,296
387	Lake Forest, CA	205
182	Lakeland, FL	1,140
348	Lakewood, CA	394
174	Lakewood, CO	1,182
142	Lancaster, CA	1,539
168	Lansing, MI	1,249
133	Laredo, TX	1,643
327	Largo, FL	485
248	Las Cruces, NM	760
9	Las Vegas, NV	14,913
290	Lawrence, KS	603
141	Lawton, OK	1,550
368	Lee's Summit, MO	314
319	Lewisville, TX	508
99	Lexington, KY	2,184
114	Lincoln, NE	1,922
53	Little Rock, AR	3,866
347	Livermore, CA	395
354	Livonia, MI	366

RANK	CITY	BURGLARY
79	Long Beach, CA	2,896
188	Longview, TX	1,103
5	Los Angeles, CA	20,359
22	Louisville, KY	7,587
250	Lowell, MA	753
73	Lubbock, TX	3,070
203	Lynn, MA	980
88	Macon, GA	2,355
134	Madison, WI	1,619
240	Manchester, NH	781
281	McAllen, TX	637
323	McKinney, TX	490
213	Melbourne, FL	928
7	Memphis, TN	16,450
69	Mesa, AZ	3,283
214	Mesquite, TX	926
152	Miami Beach, FL	1,372
164	Miami Gardens, FL	1,287
44	Miami, FL	4,442
225	Midland, TX	861
36	Milwaukee, WI	5,651
35	Minneapolis, MN	5,826
237	Miramar, FL	800
382	Mission Viejo, CA	260
61	Mobile, AL	3,662
122	Modesto, CA	1,762
66	Montgomery, AL	3,380
94	Moreno Valley, CA	2,239
217	Murfreesboro, TN	895
302	Murrieta, CA	563
346	Napa, CA	401
389	Naperville, IL	185
362	Nashua, NH	333
30	Nashville, TN	6,370
226	New Bedford, MA	842
50	New Orleans, LA	4,087
3	New York, NY	22,137
110	Newark, NJ	1,982
299	Newport Beach, CA	575
131	Newport News, VA	1,661
388	Newton, MA	189
135	Norfolk, VA	1,614
223	Norman, OK	881
160	North Charleston, SC	1,331
82	North Las Vegas, NV	2,523
320	Norwalk, CA	504
40	Oakland, CA	5,070
204	Oceanside, CA	979
242	Odessa, TX	774
233	Ogden, UT	820
17	Oklahoma City, OK	9,304
360	Olathe, KS	353
71	Omaha, NE	3,172
208	Ontario, CA	967
306	Orange, CA	549
381	Orem, UT	269
61	Orlando, FL	3,662
295	Overland Park, KS	584
211	Oxnard, CA	946
189	Palm Bay, FL	1,101
177	Palmdale, CA	1,169
321	Parma, OH	496
220	Pasadena, CA	892
201	Pasadena, TX	1,017
155	Paterson, NJ	1,361
231	Pembroke Pines, FL	831

RANK	CITY	BURGLARY
192	Peoria, AZ	1,075
139	Peoria, IL	1,590
14	Philadelphia, PA	11,542
8	Phoenix, AZ	16,150
60	Pittsburgh, PA	3,713
150	Plano, TX	1,394
287	Plantation, FL	622
200	Pomona, CA	1,027
197	Pompano Beach, FL	1,049
195	Port St. Lucie, FL	1,065
37	Portland, OR	5,485
190	Portsmouth, VA	1,100
123	Providence, RI	1,746
309	Provo, UT	541
146	Pueblo, CO	1,453
330	Quincy, MA	473
187	Racine, WI	1,113
77	Raleigh, NC	2,978
260	Rancho Cucamon., CA	715
184	Reading, PA	1,128
259	Redding, CA	719
106	Reno, NV	2,105
289	Rialto, CA	607
266	Richardson, TX	685
199	Richmond, CA	1,031
89	Richmond, VA	2,284
87	Riverside, CA	2,372
205	Roanoke, VA	978
326	Rochester, MN	486
81	Rochester, NY	2,673
76	Rockford, IL	2,986
293	Roseville, CA	588
334	Roswell, GA	445
377	Round Rock, TX	277
33	Sacramento, CA	6,175
194	Salem, OR	1,073
216	Salinas, CA	907
93	Salt Lake City, UT	2,244
206	San Angelo, TX	974
11	San Antonio, TX	14,629
103	San Bernardino, CA	2,135
20	San Diego, CA	7,746
29	San Francisco, CA	6,465
45	San Jose, CA	4,423
243	San Leandro, CA	773
380	San Mateo, CA	274
316	Sandy, UT	522
193	Santa Ana, CA	1,074
307	Santa Barbara, CA	544
291	Santa Clara, CA	595
246	Santa Clarita, CA	766
350	Santa Maria, CA	372
254	Santa Monica, CA	733
230	Santa Rosa, CA	833
108	Savannah, GA	2,039
125	Scottsdale, AZ	1,721
23	Seattle, WA	7,505
78	Shreveport, LA	2,922
339	Simi Valley, CA	425
263	Sioux City, IA	702
244	Sioux Falls, SD	768
337	Somerville, MA	434
113	South Bend, IN	1,930
342	South Gate, CA	416
218	Southfield, MI	894
219	Sparks, NV	893

RANK	CITY	BURGLARY
296	Spokane Valley, WA	581
102	Spokane, WA	2,165
112	Springfield, IL	1,953
100	Springfield, MA	2,178
111	Springfield, MO	1,972
359	Sterling Heights, MI	356
54	Stockton, CA	3,836
19	St. Louis, MO	8,510
67	St. Paul, MN	3,349
65	St. Petersburg, FL	3,466
338	Suffolk, VA	427
386	Sugar Land, TX	212
313	Sunnyvale, CA	524
298	Sunrise, FL	576
358	Surprise, AZ	360
115	Syracuse, NY	1,904
70	Tacoma, WA	3,276
101	Tallahassee, FL	2,168
42	Tampa, FL	4,451
271	Temecula, CA	674
121	Tempe, AZ	1,795
258	Thornton, CO	722
353	Thousand Oaks, CA	367
27	Toledo, OH	6,915
369	Toms River Twnshp, NJ	312
143	Topeka, KS	1,478
275	Torrance, CA	666
354	Tracy, CA	366
236	Trenton, NJ	806
365	Troy, MI	321
39	Tucson, AZ	5,121
32	Tulsa, OK	6,315
166	Tuscaloosa, AL	1,256
226	Tyler, TX	842
376	Upper Darby Twnshp, PA	287
366	Vacaville, CA	320
180	Vallejo, CA	1,155
202	Vancouver, WA	1,001
255	Ventura, CA	730
176	Victorville, CA	1,173
107	Virginia Beach, VA	2,048
153	Visalia, CA	1,368
257	Vista, CA	729
98	Waco, TX	2,188
239	Warren, MI	790
367	Warwick, RI	316
55	Washington, DC	3,826
198	Waterbury, CT	1,045
269	West Covina, CA	679
331	West Jordan, UT	466
137	West Palm Beach, FL	1,591
224	West Valley, UT	877
315	Westland, MI	523
318	Westminster, CA	509
277	Westminster, CO	653
340	Whittier, CA	421
163	Wichita Falls, TX	1,291
57	Wichita, KS	3,800
127	Wilmington, NC	1,694
47	Winston-Salem, NC	4,289
343	Woodbridge Twnshp, NJ	415
170	Worcester, MA	1,231
144	Yakima, WA	1,469
278	Yonkers, NY	651
109	Youngstown, OH	2,017
235	Yuma, AZ	809

Source: Federal Bureau of Investigation "Crime in the United States 2006"

**Burglary is the unlawful entry of a structure to commit a felony or theft. Attempts are included.*

69. Burglaries in 2006 (continued)
National Total = 2,183,746 Burglaries*

RANK	CITY	BURGLARY
1	Houston, TX	26,869
2	Chicago, IL	24,153
3	New York, NY	22,137
4	Dallas, TX	21,653
5	Los Angeles, CA	20,359
6	Detroit, MI	18,134
7	Memphis, TN	16,450
8	Phoenix, AZ	16,150
9	Las Vegas, NV	14,913
10	Columbus, OH	14,816
11	San Antonio, TX	14,629
12	Charlotte, NC	13,582
13	Indianapolis, IN	11,734
14	Philadelphia, PA	11,542
15	Cleveland, OH	9,650
16	Jacksonville, FL	9,615
17	Oklahoma City, OK	9,304
18	Fort Worth, TX	8,998
19	St. Louis, MO	8,510
20	San Diego, CA	7,746
21	Baltimore, MD	7,608
22	Louisville, KY	7,587
23	Seattle, WA	7,505
24	Austin, TX	7,467
25	Atlanta, GA	7,401
26	Kansas City, MO	7,399
27	Toledo, OH	6,915
28	Denver, CO	6,543
29	San Francisco, CA	6,465
30	Nashville, TN	6,370
31	Albuquerque, NM	6,352
32	Tulsa, OK	6,315
33	Sacramento, CA	6,175
34	Cincinnati, OH	6,009
35	Minneapolis, MN	5,826
36	Milwaukee, WI	5,651
37	Portland, OR	5,485
38	Honolulu, HI	5,482
39	Tucson, AZ	5,121
40	Oakland, CA	5,070
41	Birmingham, AL	4,813
42	Tampa, FL	4,451
43	Buffalo, NY	4,447
44	Miami, FL	4,442
45	San Jose, CA	4,423
46	Fresno, CA	4,366
47	Winston-Salem, NC	4,289
48	Greensboro, NC	4,129
49	Boston, MA	4,121
50	New Orleans, LA	4,087
51	Arlington, TX	4,042
52	Baton Rouge, LA	4,021
53	Little Rock, AR	3,866
54	Stockton, CA	3,836
55	Washington, DC	3,826
56	Jackson, MS	3,817
57	Wichita, KS	3,800
58	Glendale, AZ	3,756
59	Bakersfield, CA	3,729
60	Pittsburgh, PA	3,713
61	Mobile, AL	3,662
61	Orlando, FL	3,662
63	Dayton, OH	3,525
64	Fayetteville, NC	3,519
65	St. Petersburg, FL	3,466
66	Montgomery, AL	3,380
67	St. Paul, MN	3,349
68	Colorado Springs, CO	3,347
69	Mesa, AZ	3,283
70	Tacoma, WA	3,276
71	Omaha, NE	3,172
72	Durham, NC	3,098
73	Lubbock, TX	3,070
74	Flint, MI	3,058
75	Corpus Christi, TX	3,005
76	Rockford, IL	2,986
77	Raleigh, NC	2,978
78	Shreveport, LA	2,922
79	Long Beach, CA	2,896
80	Columbus, GA	2,773
81	Rochester, NY	2,673
82	North Las Vegas, NV	2,523
83	Huntsville, AL	2,493
84	Grand Rapids, MI	2,484
85	Aurora, CO	2,470
86	Amarillo, TX	2,412
87	Riverside, CA	2,372
88	Macon, GA	2,355
89	Richmond, VA	2,284
90	Knoxville, TN	2,281
91	Chattanooga, TN	2,273
92	Kansas City, KS	2,265
93	Salt Lake City, UT	2,244
94	Fort Lauderdale, FL	2,239
94	Moreno Valley, CA	2,239
96	El Paso, TX	2,212
97	Des Moines, IA	2,189
98	Waco, TX	2,188
99	Lexington, KY	2,184
100	Springfield, MA	2,178
101	Tallahassee, FL	2,168
102	Spokane, WA	2,165
103	San Bernardino, CA	2,135
104	Fort Wayne, IN	2,128
105	Killeen, TX	2,121
106	Reno, NV	2,105
107	Virginia Beach, VA	2,048
108	Savannah, GA	2,039
109	Youngstown, OH	2,017
110	Newark, NJ	1,982
111	Springfield, MO	1,972
112	Springfield, IL	1,953
113	South Bend, IN	1,930
114	Lincoln, NE	1,922
115	Syracuse, NY	1,904
116	Garland, TX	1,889
117	Beaumont, TX	1,887
118	Anaheim, CA	1,886
119	Gary, IN	1,818
120	Canton, OH	1,812
121	Tempe, AZ	1,795
122	Modesto, CA	1,762
123	Providence, RI	1,746
124	Anchorage, AK	1,733
125	Scottsdale, AZ	1,721
126	High Point, NC	1,697
127	Wilmington, NC	1,694
128	Irving, TX	1,674
129	Hialeah, FL	1,673
130	Jersey City, NJ	1,670
131	Newport News, VA	1,661
132	Albany, GA	1,645
133	Laredo, TX	1,643
134	Madison, WI	1,619
135	Norfolk, VA	1,614
136	Henderson, NV	1,600
137	Grand Prairie, TX	1,591
137	West Palm Beach, FL	1,591
139	Peoria, IL	1,590
140	Eugene, OR	1,561
141	Lawton, OK	1,550
142	Lancaster, CA	1,539
143	Topeka, KS	1,478
144	Yakima, WA	1,469
145	Cape Coral, FL	1,462
146	Pueblo, CO	1,453
147	Allentown, PA	1,433
148	Gainesville, FL	1,420
149	Chandler, AZ	1,401
150	Plano, TX	1,394
151	Brownsville, TX	1,377
152	Miami Beach, FL	1,372
153	Visalia, CA	1,368
154	Bridgeport, CT	1,362
155	Paterson, NJ	1,361
156	Everett, WA	1,352
157	Clarksville, TN	1,348
158	Chesapeake, VA	1,345
159	Hollywood, FL	1,338
160	North Charleston, SC	1,331
161	Fremont, CA	1,325
162	Lafayette, LA	1,296
163	Wichita Falls, TX	1,291
164	Miami Gardens, FL	1,287
165	Abilene, TX	1,282
166	Tuscaloosa, AL	1,256
167	Columbia, SC	1,254
168	Lansing, MI	1,249
169	Independence, MO	1,236
170	Worcester, MA	1,231
171	Kent, WA	1,223
172	Hayward, CA	1,196
173	Chula Vista, CA	1,184
174	Lakewood, CO	1,182
175	Camden, NJ	1,179
176	Victorville, CA	1,173
177	Palmdale, CA	1,169
178	Boise, ID	1,165
179	Hartford, CT	1,158
180	Vallejo, CA	1,155
181	Berkeley, CA	1,152
182	Lakeland, FL	1,140
183	Evansville, IN	1,131
184	Reading, PA	1,128
185	Athens-Clarke, GA	1,116
186	Cedar Rapids, IA	1,114
187	Racine, WI	1,113
188	Longview, TX	1,103
189	Palm Bay, FL	1,101
190	Portsmouth, VA	1,100
191	Fort Smith, AR	1,089
192	Peoria, AZ	1,075

RANK	CITY	BURGLARY
193	Santa Ana, CA	1,074
194	Salem, OR	1,073
195	Port St. Lucie, FL	1,065
196	Albany, NY	1,058
197	Pompano Beach, FL	1,049
198	Waterbury, CT	1,045
199	Richmond, CA	1,031
200	Pomona, CA	1,027
201	Pasadena, TX	1,017
202	Vancouver, WA	1,001
203	Lynn, MA	980
204	Oceanside, CA	979
205	Roanoke, VA	978
206	San Angelo, TX	974
207	Hammond, IN	970
208	Ontario, CA	967
209	Huntington Beach, CA	961
210	Gilbert, AZ	949
211	Oxnard, CA	946
212	Concord, CA	941
213	Melbourne, FL	928
214	Mesquite, TX	926
215	Aurora, IL	917
216	Salinas, CA	907
217	Murfreesboro, TN	895
218	Southfield, MI	894
219	Sparks, NV	893
220	Pasadena, CA	892
221	Clearwater, FL	882
221	Joliet, IL	882
223	Norman, OK	881
224	West Valley, UT	877
225	Midland, TX	861
226	New Bedford, MA	842
226	Tyler, TX	842
228	Greeley, CO	841
229	Antioch, CA	840
230	Santa Rosa, CA	833
231	El Monte, CA	831
231	Pembroke Pines, FL	831
233	Ogden, UT	820
234	Carrollton, TX	815
235	Yuma, AZ	809
236	Trenton, NJ	806
237	Miramar, FL	800
238	Bellingham, WA	791
239	Warren, MI	790
240	Manchester, NH	781
241	Fontana, CA	779
242	Odessa, TX	774
243	San Leandro, CA	773
244	Sioux Falls, SD	768
245	Hampton, VA	767
246	Santa Clarita, CA	766
247	Fullerton, CA	764
248	Las Cruces, NM	760
249	Escondido, CA	758
250	Federal Way, WA	753
250	Lowell, MA	753
252	Fairfield, CA	745
253	Erie, PA	740
254	Santa Monica, CA	733
255	Corona, CA	730
255	Ventura, CA	730
257	Vista, CA	729
258	Thornton, CO	722
259	Redding, CA	719
260	Garden Grove, CA	715
260	Rancho Cucamon., CA	715
262	Charleston, SC	707
263	Sioux City, IA	702
264	Fort Collins, CO	701
265	Green Bay, WI	687
266	Richardson, TX	685
267	Cambridge, MA	684
268	Elizabeth, NJ	682
269	West Covina, CA	679
270	Inglewood, CA	675
271	Temecula, CA	674
272	Brockton, MA	673
273	Glendale, CA	672
274	Dearborn, MI	670
275	Torrance, CA	666
276	Denton, TX	664
277	Westminster, CO	653
278	Yonkers, NY	651
279	Gresham, OR	645
280	El Cajon, CA	638
281	McAllen, TX	637
282	Irvine, CA	634
283	Ann Arbor, MI	631
284	Clovis, CA	630
284	Duluth, MN	630
286	Kenosha, WI	626
287	Plantation, FL	622
288	Carson, CA	619
289	Rialto, CA	607
290	Lawrence, KS	603
291	Santa Clara, CA	595
292	Bellevue, WA	591
293	Roseville, CA	588
294	Carlsbad, CA	587
295	Overland Park, KS	584
296	Spokane Valley, WA	581
297	Compton, CA	578
298	Sunrise, FL	576
299	Downey, CA	575
299	Newport Beach, CA	575
301	Burbank, CA	567
302	Murrieta, CA	563
303	Hesperia, CA	562
304	Cary, NC	554
305	Boca Raton, FL	551
306	Orange, CA	549
307	Columbia, MO	544
307	Santa Barbara, CA	544
309	Provo, UT	541
310	Arvada, CO	539
311	Chino, CA	530
312	Fargo, ND	525
313	Costa Mesa, CA	524
313	Sunnyvale, CA	524
315	Westland, MI	523
316	Clinton Twnshp, MI	522
316	Sandy, UT	522
318	Westminster, CA	509
319	Lewisville, TX	508
320	Norwalk, CA	504
321	Parma, OH	496
322	Hawthorne, CA	491
323	McKinney, TX	490
324	Boulder, CO	487
324	Coral Springs, FL	487
326	Rochester, MN	486
327	Largo, FL	485
328	Deerfield Beach, FL	478
329	Bellflower, CA	476
330	Quincy, MA	473
331	West Jordan, UT	466
332	Billings, MT	465
333	Davie, FL	450
334	Roswell, GA	445
335	Alhambra, CA	443
336	Hamilton Twnshp, NJ	440
337	Somerville, MA	434
338	Suffolk, VA	427
339	Simi Valley, CA	425
340	Whittier, CA	421
341	Broken Arrow, OK	420
342	South Gate, CA	416
343	Cheektowaga, NY	415
343	Woodbridge Twnshp, NJ	415
345	Buena Park, CA	410
346	Napa, CA	401
347	Livermore, CA	395
348	Lakewood, CA	394
349	Alexandria, VA	380
350	Santa Maria, CA	372
351	Edmond, OK	370
352	Edison Twnshp, NJ	368
353	Thousand Oaks, CA	367
354	Livonia, MI	366
354	Tracy, CA	366
356	Baldwin Park, CA	363
357	Clifton, NJ	361
358	Surprise, AZ	360
359	Sterling Heights, MI	356
360	Olathe, KS	353
361	Centennial, CO	340
362	Nashua, NH	333
363	Bloomington, MN	331
364	Farmington Hills, MI	325
365	Troy, MI	321
366	Vacaville, CA	320
367	Warwick, RI	316
368	Lee's Summit, MO	314
369	Toms River Twnshp, NJ	312
370	Beaverton, OR	311
371	Colonie, NY	310
372	Canton Twnshp, MI	309
373	Brick Twnshp, NJ	303
374	Cranston, RI	299
374	Hillsboro, OR	299
376	Upper Darby Twnshp, PA	287
377	Amherst, NY	277
377	Round Rock, TX	277
379	Chino Hills, CA	275
380	San Mateo, CA	274
381	Orem, UT	269
382	Mission Viejo, CA	260
383	Danbury, CT	257
384	Greece, NY	255
385	Daly City, CA	243
386	Sugar Land, TX	212
387	Lake Forest, CA	205
388	Newton, MA	189
389	Naperville, IL	185
390	Clarkstown, NY	103

Source: Federal Bureau of Investigation "Crime in the United States 2006"

**Burglary is the unlawful entry of a structure to commit a felony or theft. Attempts are included.*

70. Burglary Rate in 2006

National Rate = 729.4 Burglaries per 100,000 Population*

RANK	CITY	RATE
120	Abilene, TX	1,086.4
13	Albany, GA	2,114.0
115	Albany, NY	1,128.3
86	Albuquerque, NM	1,268.0
380	Alexandria, VA	278.0
312	Alhambra, CA	502.3
73	Allentown, PA	1,338.2
82	Amarillo, TX	1,281.6
386	Amherst, NY	246.7
280	Anaheim, CA	563.3
253	Anchorage, AK	624.1
283	Ann Arbor, MI	558.5
182	Antioch, CA	827.3
122	Arlington, TX	1,083.4
310	Arvada, CO	508.8
134	Athens-Clarke, GA	1,045.9
47	Atlanta, GA	1,523.5
184	Aurora, CO	815.6
290	Aurora, IL	542.3
133	Austin, TX	1,052.0
90	Bakersfield, CA	1,250.5
335	Baldwin Park, CA	456.2
101	Baltimore, MD	1,193.3
22	Baton Rouge, LA	1,910.3
38	Beaumont, TX	1,641.3
362	Beaverton, OR	356.7
316	Bellevue, WA	496.0
248	Bellflower, CA	632.6
136	Bellingham, WA	1,043.2
112	Berkeley, CA	1,133.3
330	Billings, MT	466.6
15	Birmingham, AL	2,060.6
345	Bloomington, MN	405.1
250	Boca Raton, FL	625.5
269	Boise, ID	587.8
205	Boston, MA	732.8
303	Boulder, CO	521.3
351	Brick Twnshp, NJ	387.4
146	Bridgeport, CT	981.3
218	Brockton, MA	706.9
325	Broken Arrow, OK	482.8
188	Brownsville, TX	799.5
306	Buena Park, CA	513.2
41	Buffalo, NY	1,585.4
294	Burbank, CA	539.8
229	Cambridge, MA	679.0
52	Camden, NJ	1,472.4
359	Canton Twnshp, MI	359.9
8	Canton, OH	2,277.1
138	Cape Coral, FL	1,026.9
246	Carlsbad, CA	640.9
237	Carrollton, TX	666.7
243	Carson, CA	652.9
309	Cary, NC	510.3
165	Cedar Rapids, IA	900.0
367	Centennial, CO	339.7
275	Chandler, AZ	574.4
244	Charleston, SC	652.4
21	Charlotte, NC	1,942.0
56	Chattanooga, TN	1,450.3
307	Cheektowaga, NY	512.4
262	Chesapeake, VA	608.2
175	Chicago, IL	845.2
359	Chino Hills, CA	359.9
230	Chino, CA	677.1
284	Chula Vista, CA	557.5
19	Cincinnati, OH	1,944.0
389	Clarkstown, NY	131.0
103	Clarksville, TN	1,179.2
191	Clearwater, FL	798.0
12	Cleveland, OH	2,131.4
337	Clifton, NJ	451.3
293	Clinton Twnshp, MI	540.4
209	Clovis, CA	721.6
348	Colonie, NY	400.7
169	Colorado Springs, CO	888.3
268	Columbia, MO	588.2
131	Columbia, SC	1,054.6
57	Columbus, GA	1,450.2
18	Columbus, OH	2,025.3
267	Compton, CA	598.8
198	Concord, CA	756.7
354	Coral Springs, FL	371.8
324	Corona, CA	484.3
137	Corpus Christi, TX	1,030.9
327	Costa Mesa, CA	472.8
355	Cranston, RI	369.3
31	Dallas, TX	1,734.7
387	Daly City, CA	240.0
372	Danbury, CT	326.9
299	Davie, FL	525.6
9	Dayton, OH	2,216.0
213	Dearborn, MI	713.9
256	Deerfield Beach, FL	615.7
255	Denton, TX	620.0
107	Denver, CO	1,151.0
116	Des Moines, IA	1,121.4
17	Detroit, MI	2,050.3
305	Downey, CA	519.4
203	Duluth, MN	737.2
51	Durham, NC	1,482.8
356	Edison Twnshp, NJ	365.9
320	Edmond, OK	489.8
228	El Cajon, CA	683.7
234	El Monte, CA	672.2
361	El Paso, TX	359.4
292	Elizabeth, NJ	541.7
210	Erie, PA	720.5
281	Escondido, CA	560.3
130	Eugene, OR	1,062.7
151	Evansville, IN	969.3
67	Everett, WA	1,375.9
219	Fairfield, CA	706.7
273	Fargo, ND	578.1
344	Farmington Hills, MI	406.1
1	Fayetteville, NC	2,655.4
167	Federal Way, WA	891.0
2	Flint, MI	2,585.9
329	Fontana, CA	471.2
296	Fort Collins, CO	537.4
75	Fort Lauderdale, FL	1,315.5
76	Fort Smith, AR	1,305.4
156	Fort Wayne, IN	946.5
62	Fort Worth, TX	1,402.1
241	Fremont, CA	655.1
158	Fresno, CA	938.4
276	Fullerton, CA	570.2
79	Gainesville, FL	1,290.8
340	Garden Grove, CA	426.7
174	Garland, TX	849.1
23	Gary, IN	1,829.5
300	Gilbert, AZ	525.4
49	Glendale, AZ	1,510.9
369	Glendale, CA	332.9
126	Grand Prairie, TX	1,071.9
81	Grand Rapids, MI	1,285.1
384	Greece, NY	270.6
157	Greeley, CO	942.3
231	Green Bay, WI	676.4
28	Greensboro, NC	1,745.2
239	Gresham, OR	660.5
322	Hamilton Twnshp, NJ	488.6
96	Hammond, IN	1,216.4
302	Hampton, VA	521.7
159	Hartford, CT	932.3
277	Hawthorne, CA	567.8
176	Hayward, CA	844.9
236	Henderson, NV	666.9
211	Hesperia, CA	714.2
201	Hialeah, FL	746.2
27	High Point, NC	1,749.8
365	Hillsboro, OR	348.0
164	Hollywood, FL	903.5
266	Honolulu, HI	600.6
78	Houston, TX	1,295.7
320	Huntington Beach, CA	489.8
50	Huntsville, AL	1,485.5
117	Independence, MO	1,113.4
54	Indianapolis, IN	1,465.0
271	Inglewood, CA	584.4
368	Irvine, CA	336.3
179	Irving, TX	840.6
99	Jacksonville, FL	1,208.2
11	Jackson, MS	2,152.4
222	Jersey City, NJ	696.4
245	Joliet, IL	644.1
42	Kansas City, KS	1,559.6
36	Kansas City, MO	1,650.8
242	Kenosha, WI	654.9
53	Kent, WA	1,469.8
16	Killeen, TX	2,057.8
91	Knoxville, TN	1,250.4
94	Lafayette, LA	1,220.5
385	Lake Forest, CA	265.9
87	Lakeland, FL	1,263.7
323	Lakewood, CA	485.3
183	Lakewood, CO	824.7
109	Lancaster, CA	1,138.0
121	Lansing, MI	1,083.9
196	Laredo, TX	765.4
247	Largo, FL	640.4
163	Las Cruces, NM	907.0
111	Las Vegas, NV	1,133.5
206	Lawrence, KS	731.8
32	Lawton, OK	1,702.7
350	Lee's Summit, MO	388.0
287	Lewisville, TX	546.8
186	Lexington, KY	808.4
190	Lincoln, NE	799.1
14	Little Rock, AR	2,071.0
315	Livermore, CA	499.3
353	Livonia, MI	374.5

RANK	CITY	RATE	RANK	CITY	RATE	RANK	CITY	RATE
264	Long Beach, CA	605.5	200	Peoria, AZ	749.2	221	Spokane Valley, WA	701.9
60	Longview, TX	1,418.6	61	Peoria, IL	1,403.5	123	Spokane, WA	1,081.4
301	Los Angeles, CA	524.8	194	Philadelphia, PA	788.1	34	Springfield, IL	1,679.4
97	Louisville, KY	1,211.9	128	Phoenix, AZ	1,064.3	58	Springfield, MA	1,426.8
208	Lowell, MA	725.9	108	Pittsburgh, PA	1,143.9	77	Springfield, MO	1,302.5
59	Lubbock, TX	1,423.4	291	Plano, TX	542.0	379	Sterling Heights, MI	278.7
118	Lynn, MA	1,097.2	215	Plantation, FL	711.4	74	Stockton, CA	1,325.0
5	Macon, GA	2,419.2	238	Pomona, CA	661.8	3	St. Louis, MO	2,453.3
207	Madison, WI	728.1	145	Pompano Beach, FL	990.2	98	St. Paul, MN	1,209.1
217	Manchester, NH	709.3	192	Port St. Lucie, FL	795.3	68	St. Petersburg, FL	1,368.4
314	McAllen, TX	501.1	141	Portland, OR	1,011.7	297	Suffolk, VA	535.2
319	McKinney, TX	493.4	119	Portsmouth, VA	1,087.3	381	Sugar Land, TX	272.1
102	Melbourne, FL	1,190.7	144	Providence, RI	995.1	347	Sunnyvale, CA	402.9
6	Memphis, TN	2,416.2	334	Provo, UT	461.8	251	Sunrise, FL	625.3
211	Mesa, AZ	714.2	66	Pueblo, CO	1,377.9	331	Surprise, AZ	466.0
225	Mesquite, TX	693.2	304	Quincy, MA	521.0	72	Syracuse, NY	1,340.3
45	Miami Beach, FL	1,534.5	63	Racine, WI	1,396.8	37	Tacoma, WA	1,644.1
84	Miami Gardens, FL	1,272.8	173	Raleigh, NC	854.9	69	Tallahassee, FL	1,345.1
114	Miami, FL	1,130.5	341	Rancho Cucamon., CA	418.4	70	Tampa, FL	1,342.7
177	Midland, TX	843.8	64	Reading, PA	1,393.8	195	Temecula, CA	778.5
149	Milwaukee, WI	972.6	193	Redding, CA	794.9	125	Tempe, AZ	1,072.9
43	Minneapolis, MN	1,552.3	142	Reno, NV	1,000.7	233	Thornton, CO	673.7
202	Miramar, FL	737.9	265	Rialto, CA	604.5	377	Thousand Oaks, CA	292.5
382	Mission Viejo, CA	271.3	235	Richardson, TX	671.6	7	Toledo, OH	2,292.4
55	Mobile, AL	1,463.9	143	Richmond, CA	999.9	371	Toms River Twnshp, NJ	329.4
178	Modesto, CA	843.6	104	Richmond, VA	1,167.0	100	Topeka, KS	1,203.5
35	Montgomery, AL	1,673.8	185	Riverside, CA	810.4	332	Torrance, CA	463.6
93	Moreno Valley, CA	1,244.1	135	Roanoke, VA	1,045.4	336	Tracy, CA	453.6
139	Murfreesboro, TN	1,018.2	311	Rochester, MN	508.4	154	Trenton, NJ	951.6
232	Murrieta, CA	674.1	88	Rochester, NY	1,262.9	349	Troy, MI	396.5
298	Napa, CA	531.4	20	Rockford, IL	1,942.3	152	Tucson, AZ	956.8
390	Naperville, IL	130.0	286	Roseville, CA	550.1	39	Tulsa, OK	1,636.7
352	Nashua, NH	379.9	313	Roswell, GA	501.8	46	Tuscaloosa, AL	1,530.0
110	Nashville, TN	1,135.9	375	Round Rock, TX	312.1	168	Tyler, TX	890.6
166	New Bedford, MA	899.0	71	Sacramento, CA	1,340.8	358	Upper Darby Twnshp, PA	360.1
155	New Orleans, LA	947.9	216	Salem, OR	709.7	366	Vacaville, CA	341.1
383	New York, NY	271.1	258	Salinas, CA	613.9	148	Vallejo, CA	974.3
220	Newark, NJ	705.6	95	Salt Lake City, UT	1,220.2	252	Vancouver, WA	624.8
214	Newport Beach, CA	713.8	124	San Angelo, TX	1,076.1	224	Ventura, CA	695.5
161	Newport News, VA	914.2	113	San Antonio, TX	1,132.2	83	Victorville, CA	1,273.8
388	Newton, MA	225.9	127	San Bernardino, CA	1,065.7	333	Virginia Beach, VA	462.5
226	Norfolk, VA	689.0	260	San Diego, CA	611.4	92	Visalia, CA	1,247.6
172	Norman, OK	858.5	170	San Francisco, CA	866.5	189	Vista, CA	799.2
48	North Charleston, SC	1,518.5	326	San Jose, CA	480.5	26	Waco, TX	1,766.2
65	North Las Vegas, NV	1,382.2	147	San Leandro, CA	979.9	270	Warren, MI	585.3
328	Norwalk, CA	472.0	376	San Mateo, CA	298.1	357	Warwick, RI	365.2
85	Oakland, CA	1,271.2	278	Sandy, UT	563.8	240	Washington, DC	657.9
272	Oceanside, CA	584.1	374	Santa Ana, CA	312.7	150	Waterbury, CT	970.0
187	Odessa, TX	804.6	249	Santa Barbara, CA	627.6	254	West Covina, CA	622.0
140	Ogden, UT	1,014.1	282	Santa Clara, CA	559.5	318	West Jordan, UT	493.5
30	Oklahoma City, OK	1,735.8	338	Santa Clarita, CA	451.2	40	West Palm Beach, FL	1,604.8
373	Olathe, KS	314.8	339	Santa Maria, CA	437.1	199	West Valley, UT	749.6
197	Omaha, NE	761.1	181	Santa Monica, CA	827.4	259	Westland, MI	612.3
285	Ontario, CA	555.0	295	Santa Rosa, CA	539.0	279	Westminster, CA	563.5
346	Orange, CA	403.2	153	Savannah, GA	955.1	261	Westminster, CO	609.9
378	Orem, UT	290.4	204	Scottsdale, AZ	733.4	317	Whittier, CA	493.9
33	Orlando, FL	1,689.0	80	Seattle, WA	1,285.6	89	Wichita Falls, TX	1,257.4
364	Overland Park, KS	351.9	44	Shreveport, LA	1,550.1	129	Wichita, KS	1,063.3
308	Oxnard, CA	510.6	363	Simi Valley, CA	354.9	29	Wilmington, NC	1,739.6
106	Palm Bay, FL	1,166.3	180	Sioux City, IA	839.8	10	Winston-Salem, NC	2,170.3
171	Palmdale, CA	860.9	288	Sioux Falls, SD	546.3	343	Woodbridge Twnshp, NJ	412.3
263	Parma, OH	608.1	274	Somerville, MA	575.5	223	Worcester, MA	695.7
257	Pasadena, CA	615.1	24	South Bend, IN	1,821.5	25	Yakima, WA	1,778.3
227	Pasadena, TX	687.5	342	South Gate, CA	416.9	370	Yonkers, NY	330.5
162	Paterson, NJ	907.6	105	Southfield, MI	1,166.7	4	Youngstown, OH	2,431.9
289	Pembroke Pines, FL	543.4	132	Sparks, NV	1,053.1	160	Yuma, AZ	920.1

Source: CQ Press using data from F.B.I. "Crime in the United States 2006"

**Burglary is the unlawful entry of a structure to commit a felony or theft. Attempts are included.*

70. Burglary Rate in 2006 (continued)

National Rate = 729.4 Burglaries per 100,000 Population*

RANK	CITY	RATE
1	Fayetteville, NC	2,655.4
2	Flint, MI	2,585.9
3	St. Louis, MO	2,453.3
4	Youngstown, OH	2,431.9
5	Macon, GA	2,419.2
6	Memphis, TN	2,416.2
7	Toledo, OH	2,292.4
8	Canton, OH	2,277.1
9	Dayton, OH	2,216.0
10	Winston-Salem, NC	2,170.3
11	Jackson, MS	2,152.4
12	Cleveland, OH	2,131.4
13	Albany, GA	2,114.0
14	Little Rock, AR	2,071.0
15	Birmingham, AL	2,060.6
16	Killeen, TX	2,057.8
17	Detroit, MI	2,050.3
18	Columbus, OH	2,025.3
19	Cincinnati, OH	1,944.0
20	Rockford, IL	1,942.3
21	Charlotte, NC	1,942.0
22	Baton Rouge, LA	1,910.3
23	Gary, IN	1,829.5
24	South Bend, IN	1,821.5
25	Yakima, WA	1,778.3
26	Waco, TX	1,766.2
27	High Point, NC	1,749.8
28	Greensboro, NC	1,745.2
29	Wilmington, NC	1,739.6
30	Oklahoma City, OK	1,735.8
31	Dallas, TX	1,734.7
32	Lawton, OK	1,702.7
33	Orlando, FL	1,689.0
34	Springfield, IL	1,679.4
35	Montgomery, AL	1,673.8
36	Kansas City, MO	1,650.8
37	Tacoma, WA	1,644.1
38	Beaumont, TX	1,641.3
39	Tulsa, OK	1,636.7
40	West Palm Beach, FL	1,604.8
41	Buffalo, NY	1,585.4
42	Kansas City, KS	1,559.6
43	Minneapolis, MN	1,552.3
44	Shreveport, LA	1,550.1
45	Miami Beach, FL	1,534.5
46	Tuscaloosa, AL	1,530.0
47	Atlanta, GA	1,523.5
48	North Charleston, SC	1,518.5
49	Glendale, AZ	1,510.9
50	Huntsville, AL	1,485.5
51	Durham, NC	1,482.8
52	Camden, NJ	1,472.4
53	Kent, WA	1,469.8
54	Indianapolis, IN	1,465.0
55	Mobile, AL	1,463.9
56	Chattanooga, TN	1,450.3
57	Columbus, GA	1,450.2
58	Springfield, MA	1,426.8
59	Lubbock, TX	1,423.4
60	Longview, TX	1,418.6
61	Peoria, IL	1,403.5
62	Fort Worth, TX	1,402.1
63	Racine, WI	1,396.8
64	Reading, PA	1,393.8
65	North Las Vegas, NV	1,382.2
66	Pueblo, CO	1,377.9
67	Everett, WA	1,375.9
68	St. Petersburg, FL	1,368.4
69	Tallahassee, FL	1,345.1
70	Tampa, FL	1,342.7
71	Sacramento, CA	1,340.8
72	Syracuse, NY	1,340.3
73	Allentown, PA	1,338.2
74	Stockton, CA	1,325.0
75	Fort Lauderdale, FL	1,315.5
76	Fort Smith, AR	1,305.4
77	Springfield, MO	1,302.5
78	Houston, TX	1,295.7
79	Gainesville, FL	1,290.8
80	Seattle, WA	1,285.6
81	Grand Rapids, MI	1,285.1
82	Amarillo, TX	1,281.6
83	Victorville, CA	1,273.8
84	Miami Gardens, FL	1,272.8
85	Oakland, CA	1,271.2
86	Albuquerque, NM	1,268.0
87	Lakeland, FL	1,263.7
88	Rochester, NY	1,262.9
89	Wichita Falls, TX	1,257.4
90	Bakersfield, CA	1,250.5
91	Knoxville, TN	1,250.4
92	Visalia, CA	1,247.6
93	Moreno Valley, CA	1,244.1
94	Lafayette, LA	1,220.5
95	Salt Lake City, UT	1,220.2
96	Hammond, IN	1,216.4
97	Louisville, KY	1,211.9
98	St. Paul, MN	1,209.1
99	Jacksonville, FL	1,208.2
100	Topeka, KS	1,203.5
101	Baltimore, MD	1,193.3
102	Melbourne, FL	1,190.7
103	Clarksville, TN	1,179.2
104	Richmond, VA	1,167.0
105	Southfield, MI	1,166.7
106	Palm Bay, FL	1,166.3
107	Denver, CO	1,151.0
108	Pittsburgh, PA	1,143.9
109	Lancaster, CA	1,138.0
110	Nashville, TN	1,135.9
111	Las Vegas, NV	1,133.5
112	Berkeley, CA	1,133.3
113	San Antonio, TX	1,132.2
114	Miami, FL	1,130.5
115	Albany, NY	1,128.3
116	Des Moines, IA	1,121.4
117	Independence, MO	1,113.4
118	Lynn, MA	1,097.2
119	Portsmouth, VA	1,087.3
120	Abilene, TX	1,086.4
121	Lansing, MI	1,083.9
122	Arlington, TX	1,083.4
123	Spokane, WA	1,081.4
124	San Angelo, TX	1,076.1
125	Tempe, AZ	1,072.9
126	Grand Prairie, TX	1,071.9
127	San Bernardino, CA	1,065.7
128	Phoenix, AZ	1,064.3
129	Wichita, KS	1,063.3
130	Eugene, OR	1,062.7
131	Columbia, SC	1,054.6
132	Sparks, NV	1,053.1
133	Austin, TX	1,052.0
134	Athens-Clarke, GA	1,045.9
135	Roanoke, VA	1,045.4
136	Bellingham, WA	1,043.2
137	Corpus Christi, TX	1,030.9
138	Cape Coral, FL	1,026.9
139	Murfreesboro, TN	1,018.2
140	Ogden, UT	1,014.1
141	Portland, OR	1,011.7
142	Reno, NV	1,000.7
143	Richmond, CA	999.9
144	Providence, RI	995.1
145	Pompano Beach, FL	990.2
146	Bridgeport, CT	981.3
147	San Leandro, CA	979.9
148	Vallejo, CA	974.3
149	Milwaukee, WI	972.6
150	Waterbury, CT	970.0
151	Evansville, IN	969.3
152	Tucson, AZ	956.8
153	Savannah, GA	955.1
154	Trenton, NJ	951.6
155	New Orleans, LA	947.9
156	Fort Wayne, IN	946.5
157	Greeley, CO	942.3
158	Fresno, CA	938.4
159	Hartford, CT	932.3
160	Yuma, AZ	920.1
161	Newport News, VA	914.2
162	Paterson, NJ	907.6
163	Las Cruces, NM	907.0
164	Hollywood, FL	903.5
165	Cedar Rapids, IA	900.0
166	New Bedford, MA	899.0
167	Federal Way, WA	891.0
168	Tyler, TX	890.6
169	Colorado Springs, CO	888.3
170	San Francisco, CA	866.5
171	Palmdale, CA	860.9
172	Norman, OK	858.5
173	Raleigh, NC	854.9
174	Garland, TX	849.1
175	Chicago, IL	845.2
176	Hayward, CA	844.9
177	Midland, TX	843.8
178	Modesto, CA	843.6
179	Irving, TX	840.6
180	Sioux City, IA	839.8
181	Santa Monica, CA	827.4
182	Antioch, CA	827.3
183	Lakewood, CO	824.7
184	Aurora, CO	815.6
185	Riverside, CA	810.4
186	Lexington, KY	808.4
187	Odessa, TX	804.6
188	Brownsville, TX	799.5
189	Vista, CA	799.2
190	Lincoln, NE	799.1
191	Clearwater, FL	798.0
192	Port St. Lucie, FL	795.3

Rank Order- City (continued)

RANK	CITY	RATE
193	Redding, CA	794.9
194	Philadelphia, PA	788.1
195	Temecula, CA	778.5
196	Laredo, TX	765.4
197	Omaha, NE	761.1
198	Concord, CA	756.7
199	West Valley, UT	749.6
200	Peoria, AZ	749.2
201	Hialeah, FL	746.2
202	Miramar, FL	737.9
203	Duluth, MN	737.2
204	Scottsdale, AZ	733.4
205	Boston, MA	732.8
206	Lawrence, KS	731.8
207	Madison, WI	728.1
208	Lowell, MA	725.9
209	Clovis, CA	721.6
210	Erie, PA	720.5
211	Hesperia, CA	714.2
211	Mesa, AZ	714.2
213	Dearborn, MI	713.9
214	Newport Beach, CA	713.8
215	Plantation, FL	711.4
216	Salem, OR	709.7
217	Manchester, NH	709.3
218	Brockton, MA	706.9
219	Fairfield, CA	706.7
220	Newark, NJ	705.6
221	Spokane Valley, WA	701.9
222	Jersey City, NJ	696.4
223	Worcester, MA	695.7
224	Ventura, CA	695.5
225	Mesquite, TX	693.2
226	Norfolk, VA	689.0
227	Pasadena, TX	687.5
228	El Cajon, CA	683.7
229	Cambridge, MA	679.0
230	Chino, CA	677.1
231	Green Bay, WI	676.4
232	Murrieta, CA	674.1
233	Thornton, CO	673.7
234	El Monte, CA	672.2
235	Richardson, TX	671.6
236	Henderson, NV	666.9
237	Carrollton, TX	666.7
238	Pomona, CA	661.8
239	Gresham, OR	660.5
240	Washington, DC	657.9
241	Fremont, CA	655.1
242	Kenosha, WI	654.9
243	Carson, CA	652.9
244	Charleston, SC	652.4
245	Joliet, IL	644.1
246	Carlsbad, CA	640.9
247	Largo, FL	640.4
248	Bellflower, CA	632.6
249	Santa Barbara, CA	627.6
250	Boca Raton, FL	625.5
251	Sunrise, FL	625.3
252	Vancouver, WA	624.8
253	Anchorage, AK	624.1
254	West Covina, CA	622.0
255	Denton, TX	620.0
256	Deerfield Beach, FL	615.7
257	Pasadena, CA	615.1
258	Salinas, CA	613.9
259	Westland, MI	612.3
260	San Diego, CA	611.4
261	Westminster, CO	609.9
262	Chesapeake, VA	608.2
263	Parma, OH	608.1
264	Long Beach, CA	605.5
265	Rialto, CA	604.5
266	Honolulu, HI	600.6
267	Compton, CA	598.8
268	Columbia, MO	588.2
269	Boise, ID	587.8
270	Warren, MI	585.3
271	Inglewood, CA	584.4
272	Oceanside, CA	584.1
273	Fargo, ND	578.1
274	Somerville, MA	575.5
275	Chandler, AZ	574.4
276	Fullerton, CA	570.2
277	Hawthorne, CA	567.8
278	Sandy, UT	563.8
279	Westminster, CA	563.5
280	Anaheim, CA	563.3
281	Escondido, CA	560.3
282	Santa Clara, CA	559.5
283	Ann Arbor, MI	558.5
284	Chula Vista, CA	557.5
285	Ontario, CA	555.0
286	Roseville, CA	550.1
287	Lewisville, TX	546.8
288	Sioux Falls, SD	546.3
289	Pembroke Pines, FL	543.4
290	Aurora, IL	542.3
291	Plano, TX	542.0
292	Elizabeth, NJ	541.7
293	Clinton Twnshp, MI	540.4
294	Burbank, CA	539.8
295	Santa Rosa, CA	539.0
296	Fort Collins, CO	537.4
297	Suffolk, VA	535.2
298	Napa, CA	531.4
299	Davie, FL	525.6
300	Gilbert, AZ	525.4
301	Los Angeles, CA	524.8
302	Hampton, VA	521.7
303	Boulder, CO	521.3
304	Quincy, MA	521.0
305	Downey, CA	519.4
306	Buena Park, CA	513.2
307	Cheektowaga, NY	512.4
308	Oxnard, CA	510.6
309	Cary, NC	510.3
310	Arvada, CO	508.8
311	Rochester, MN	508.4
312	Alhambra, CA	502.3
313	Roswell, GA	501.8
314	McAllen, TX	501.1
315	Livermore, CA	499.3
316	Bellevue, WA	496.0
317	Whittier, CA	493.9
318	West Jordan, UT	493.5
319	McKinney, TX	493.4
320	Edmond, OK	489.8
320	Huntington Beach, CA	489.8
322	Hamilton Twnshp, NJ	488.6
323	Lakewood, CA	485.3
324	Corona, CA	484.3
325	Broken Arrow, OK	482.8
326	San Jose, CA	480.5
327	Costa Mesa, CA	472.8
328	Norwalk, CA	472.0
329	Fontana, CA	471.2
330	Billings, MT	466.6
331	Surprise, AZ	466.0
332	Torrance, CA	463.6
333	Virginia Beach, VA	462.5
334	Provo, UT	461.8
335	Baldwin Park, CA	456.2
336	Tracy, CA	453.6
337	Clifton, NJ	451.3
338	Santa Clarita, CA	451.2
339	Santa Maria, CA	437.1
340	Garden Grove, CA	426.7
341	Rancho Cucamon., CA	418.4
342	South Gate, CA	416.9
343	Woodbridge Twnshp, NJ	412.3
344	Farmington Hills, MI	406.1
345	Bloomington, MN	405.1
346	Orange, CA	403.2
347	Sunnyvale, CA	402.9
348	Colonie, NY	400.7
349	Troy, MI	396.5
350	Lee's Summit, MO	388.0
351	Brick Twnshp, NJ	387.4
352	Nashua, NH	379.9
353	Livonia, MI	374.5
354	Coral Springs, FL	371.8
355	Cranston, RI	369.3
356	Edison Twnshp, NJ	365.9
357	Warwick, RI	365.2
358	Upper Darby Twnshp, PA	360.1
359	Canton Twnshp, MI	359.9
359	Chino Hills, CA	359.9
361	El Paso, TX	359.4
362	Beaverton, OR	356.7
363	Simi Valley, CA	354.9
364	Overland Park, KS	351.9
365	Hillsboro, OR	348.0
366	Vacaville, CA	341.1
367	Centennial, CO	339.7
368	Irvine, CA	336.3
369	Glendale, CA	332.9
370	Yonkers, NY	330.5
371	Toms River Twnshp, NJ	329.4
372	Danbury, CT	326.9
373	Olathe, KS	314.8
374	Santa Ana, CA	312.7
375	Round Rock, TX	312.1
376	San Mateo, CA	298.1
377	Thousand Oaks, CA	292.5
378	Orem, UT	290.4
379	Sterling Heights, MI	278.7
380	Alexandria, VA	278.0
381	Sugar Land, TX	272.1
382	Mission Viejo, CA	271.3
383	New York, NY	271.1
384	Greece, NY	270.6
385	Lake Forest, CA	265.9
386	Amherst, NY	246.7
387	Daly City, CA	240.0
388	Newton, MA	225.9
389	Clarkstown, NY	131.0
390	Naperville, IL	130.0

Source: CQ Press using data from F.B.I. "Crime in the United States 2006"

**Burglary is the unlawful entry of a structure to commit a felony or theft. Attempts are included.*

71. Percent Change in Burglary Rate: 2005 to 2006

National Percent Change = 0.3% Increase*

RANK	CITY	% CHANGE
339	Abilene, TX	(16.6)
207	Albany, GA	(2.8)
351	Albany, NY	(19.8)
90	Albuquerque, NM	8.3
17	Alexandria, VA	23.0
355	Alhambra, CA	(22.6)
143	Allentown, PA	2.7
270	Amarillo, TX	(7.6)
2	Amherst, NY	39.9
195	Anaheim, CA	(1.9)
216	Anchorage, AK	(3.4)
364	Ann Arbor, MI	(26.1)
50	Antioch, CA	14.7
176	Arlington, TX	(0.6)
158	Arvada, CO	1.0
108	Athens-Clarke, GA	5.6
188	Atlanta, GA	(1.3)
201	Aurora, CO	(2.5)
143	Aurora, IL	2.7
169	Austin, TX	0.1
235	Bakersfield, CA	(4.6)
342	Baldwin Park, CA	(17.5)
120	Baltimore, MD	4.3
86	Baton Rouge, LA	8.8
280	Beaumont, TX	(8.9)
308	Beaverton, OR	(11.9)
186	Bellevue, WA	(1.2)
169	Bellflower, CA	0.1
86	Bellingham, WA	8.8
246	Berkeley, CA	(5.8)
358	Billings, MT	(23.6)
197	Birmingham, AL	(2.0)
NA	Bloomington, MN**	NA
331	Boca Raton, FL	(15.5)
332	Boise, ID	(15.6)
273	Boston, MA	(8.2)
305	Boulder, CO	(11.6)
1	Brick Twnshp, NJ	58.7
174	Bridgeport, CT	(0.5)
201	Brockton, MA	(2.5)
184	Broken Arrow, OK	(1.1)
100	Brownsville, TX	6.0
279	Buena Park, CA	(8.7)
102	Buffalo, NY	5.9
217	Burbank, CA	(3.5)
83	Cambridge, MA	9.5
43	Camden, NJ	15.7
308	Canton Twnshp, MI	(11.9)
42	Canton, OH	16.2
8	Cape Coral, FL	31.0
71	Carlsbad, CA	11.1
319	Carrollton, TX	(12.8)
55	Carson, CA	13.4
21	Cary, NC	21.6
135	Cedar Rapids, IA	3.5
351	Centennial, CO	(19.8)
269	Chandler, AZ	(7.5)
324	Charleston, SC	(14.4)
141	Charlotte, NC	2.9
133	Chattanooga, TN	3.6
140	Cheektowaga, NY	3.2
264	Chesapeake, VA	(7.1)
226	Chicago, IL	(4.1)
105	Chino Hills, CA	5.8
174	Chino, CA	(0.5)
263	Chula Vista, CA	(6.9)
61	Cincinnati, OH	12.5
NA	Clarkstown, NY**	NA
23	Clarksville, TN	21.2
255	Clearwater, FL	(6.6)
53	Cleveland, OH	13.8
32	Clifton, NJ	18.5
9	Clinton Twnshp, MI	27.8
261	Clovis, CA	(6.8)
245	Colonie, NY	(5.3)
289	Colorado Springs, CO	(9.5)
112	Columbia, MO	5.0
255	Columbia, SC	(6.6)
149	Columbus, GA	1.6
153	Columbus, OH	1.3
284	Compton, CA	(9.1)
327	Concord, CA	(15.0)
44	Coral Springs, FL	15.1
357	Corona, CA	(23.5)
315	Corpus Christi, TX	(12.2)
307	Costa Mesa, CA	(11.8)
254	Cranston, RI	(6.4)
235	Dallas, TX	(4.6)
213	Daly City, CA	(3.1)
47	Danbury, CT	14.9
353	Davie, FL	(20.2)
80	Dayton, OH	10.1
115	Dearborn, MI	4.8
323	Deerfield Beach, FL	(14.1)
288	Denton, TX	(9.4)
306	Denver, CO	(11.7)
NA	Des Moines, IA**	NA
25	Detroit, MI	20.7
173	Downey, CA	(0.4)
NA	Duluth, MN**	NA
NA	Durham, NC**	NA
354	Edison Twnshp, NJ	(21.9)
267	Edmond, OK	(7.3)
334	El Cajon, CA	(15.9)
33	El Monte, CA	17.7
NA	El Paso, TX**	NA
116	Elizabeth, NJ	4.7
31	Erie, PA	18.7
235	Escondido, CA	(4.6)
230	Eugene, OR	(4.2)
283	Evansville, IN	(9.0)
110	Everett, WA	5.4
184	Fairfield, CA	(1.1)
27	Fargo, ND	20.6
347	Farmington Hills, MI	(18.5)
5	Fayetteville, NC	33.6
273	Federal Way, WA	(8.2)
36	Flint, MI	17.6
219	Fontana, CA	(3.7)
289	Fort Collins, CO	(9.5)
321	Fort Lauderdale, FL	(13.4)
71	Fort Smith, AR	11.1
NA	Fort Wayne, IN**	NA
181	Fort Worth, TX	(1.0)
7	Fremont, CA	32.3
130	Fresno, CA	3.7
239	Fullerton, CA	(4.9)
20	Gainesville, FL	22.0
297	Garden Grove, CA	(10.5)
261	Garland, TX	(6.8)
47	Gary, IN	14.9
317	Gilbert, AZ	(12.6)
77	Glendale, AZ	10.5
259	Glendale, CA	(6.7)
98	Grand Prairie, TX	6.2
16	Grand Rapids, MI	23.1
97	Greece, NY	6.3
370	Greeley, CO	(29.5)
54	Green Bay, WI	13.6
125	Greensboro, NC	3.9
367	Gresham, OR	(27.7)
52	Hamilton Twnshp, NJ	13.9
255	Hammond, IN	(6.6)
320	Hampton, VA	(12.9)
339	Hartford, CT	(16.6)
375	Hawthorne, CA	(37.2)
118	Hayward, CA	4.4
172	Henderson, NV	(0.3)
85	Hesperia, CA	9.0
71	Hialeah, FL	11.1
336	High Point, NC	(16.1)
376	Hillsboro, OR	(39.0)
149	Hollywood, FL	1.6
312	Honolulu, HI	(12.1)
220	Houston, TX	(3.8)
19	Huntington Beach, CA	22.1
166	Huntsville, AL	0.3
234	Independence, MO	(4.5)
151	Indianapolis, IN	1.5
342	Inglewood, CA	(17.5)
326	Irvine, CA	(14.9)
223	Irving, TX	(3.9)
96	Jacksonville, FL	6.8
14	Jackson, MS	23.7
360	Jersey City, NJ	(24.7)
64	Joliet, IL	12.4
15	Kansas City, KS	23.2
NA	Kansas City, MO**	NA
94	Kenosha, WI	7.4
146	Kent, WA	2.4
198	Killeen, TX	(2.1)
280	Knoxville, TN	(8.9)
74	Lafayette, LA	11.0
122	Lake Forest, CA	4.1
11	Lakeland, FL	25.2
242	Lakewood, CA	(5.2)
253	Lakewood, CO	(6.2)
38	Lancaster, CA	17.2
64	Lansing, MI	12.4
147	Laredo, TX	1.9
166	Largo, FL	0.3
205	Las Cruces, NM	(2.6)
156	Las Vegas, NV	1.1
78	Lawrence, KS	10.3
74	Lawton, OK	11.0
312	Lee's Summit, MO	(12.1)
208	Lewisville, TX	(2.9)
NA	Lexington, KY**	NA
163	Lincoln, NE	0.4
154	Little Rock, AR	1.2
264	Livermore, CA	(7.1)
338	Livonia, MI	(16.5)

RANK	CITY	% CHANGE
192	Long Beach, CA	(1.7)
171	Longview, TX	(0.1)
294	Los Angeles, CA	(10.1)
105	Louisville, KY	5.8
59	Lowell, MA	13.0
68	Lubbock, TX	11.5
28	Lynn, MA	20.0
41	Macon, GA	16.4
70	Madison, WI	11.3
60	Manchester, NH	12.8
337	McAllen, TX	(16.2)
192	McKinney, TX	(1.7)
128	Melbourne, FL	3.8
135	Memphis, TN	3.5
287	Mesa, AZ	(9.3)
84	Mesquite, TX	9.2
232	Miami Beach, FL	(4.4)
249	Miami Gardens, FL	(5.9)
345	Miami, FL	(18.4)
93	Midland, TX	8.0
13	Milwaukee, WI	24.8
109	Minneapolis, MN	5.5
345	Miramar, FL	(18.4)
39	Mission Viejo, CA	16.8
235	Mobile, AL	(4.6)
160	Modesto, CA	0.8
226	Montgomery, AL	(4.1)
4	Moreno Valley, CA	36.8
98	Murfreesboro, TN	6.2
137	Murrieta, CA	3.4
64	Napa, CA	12.4
374	Naperville, IL	(37.0)
88	Nashua, NH	8.7
195	Nashville, TN	(1.9)
223	New Bedford, MA	(3.9)
NA	New Orleans, LA**	NA
242	New York, NY	(5.2)
217	Newark, NJ	(3.5)
201	Newport Beach, CA	(2.5)
49	Newport News, VA	14.8
371	Newton, MA	(29.8)
250	Norfolk, VA	(6.0)
6	Norman, OK	33.4
240	North Charleston, SC	(5.0)
21	North Las Vegas, NV	21.6
286	Norwalk, CA	(9.2)
308	Oakland, CA	(11.9)
270	Oceanside, CA	(7.6)
163	Odessa, TX	0.4
139	Ogden, UT	3.3
137	Oklahoma City, OK	3.4
3	Olathe, KS	37.5
179	Omaha, NE	(0.9)
226	Ontario, CA	(4.1)
154	Orange, CA	1.2
372	Orem, UT	(32.1)
277	Orlando, FL	(8.5)
33	Overland Park, KS	17.7
166	Oxnard, CA	0.3
145	Palm Bay, FL	2.6
37	Palmdale, CA	17.5
315	Parma, OH	(12.2)
57	Pasadena, CA	13.2
242	Pasadena, TX	(5.2)
208	Paterson, NJ	(2.9)
67	Pembroke Pines, FL	12.2
280	Peoria, AZ	(8.9)
322	Peoria, IL	(13.6)
102	Philadelphia, PA	5.9
225	Phoenix, AZ	(4.0)
10	Pittsburgh, PA	25.4
181	Plano, TX	(1.0)
100	Plantation, FL	6.0
125	Pomona, CA	3.9
252	Pompano Beach, FL	(6.1)
12	Port St. Lucie, FL	25.0
299	Portland, OR	(10.7)
118	Portsmouth, VA	4.4
220	Providence, RI	(3.8)
369	Provo, UT	(29.3)
241	Pueblo, CO	(5.1)
25	Quincy, MA	20.7
51	Racine, WI	14.5
255	Raleigh, NC	(6.6)
317	Rancho Cucamon., CA	(12.6)
362	Reading, PA	(25.4)
361	Redding, CA	(24.8)
95	Reno, NV	6.9
328	Rialto, CA	(15.2)
302	Richardson, TX	(11.3)
212	Richmond, CA	(3.0)
292	Richmond, VA	(9.9)
246	Riverside, CA	(5.8)
213	Roanoke, VA	(3.1)
55	Rochester, MN	13.4
205	Rochester, NY	(2.6)
NA	Rockford, IL**	NA
373	Roseville, CA	(32.7)
177	Roswell, GA	(0.8)
268	Round Rock, TX	(7.4)
112	Sacramento, CA	5.0
296	Salem, OR	(10.2)
198	Salinas, CA	(2.1)
130	Salt Lake City, UT	3.7
328	San Angelo, TX	(15.2)
181	San Antonio, TX	(1.0)
333	San Bernardino, CA	(15.7)
121	San Diego, CA	4.2
117	San Francisco, CA	4.6
91	San Jose, CA	8.1
69	San Leandro, CA	11.4
356	San Mateo, CA	(22.9)
76	Sandy, UT	10.6
291	Santa Ana, CA	(9.7)
348	Santa Barbara, CA	(18.8)
102	Santa Clara, CA	5.9
299	Santa Clarita, CA	(10.7)
220	Santa Maria, CA	(3.8)
266	Santa Monica, CA	(7.2)
128	Santa Rosa, CA	3.8
349	Savannah, GA	(19.4)
293	Scottsdale, AZ	(10.0)
80	Seattle, WA	10.1
125	Shreveport, LA	3.9
365	Simi Valley, CA	(27.1)
303	Sioux City, IA	(11.5)
79	Sioux Falls, SD	10.2
341	Somerville, MA	(16.7)
44	South Bend, IN	15.1
246	South Gate, CA	(5.8)
24	Southfield, MI	21.0
30	Sparks, NV	19.3
273	Spokane Valley, WA	(8.2)
303	Spokane, WA	(11.5)
61	Springfield, IL	12.5
156	Springfield, MA	1.1
61	Springfield, MO	12.5
57	Sterling Heights, MI	13.2
88	Stockton, CA	8.7
33	St. Louis, MO	17.7
215	St. Paul, MN	(3.3)
189	St. Petersburg, FL	(1.4)
230	Suffolk, VA	(4.2)
368	Sugar Land, TX	(28.5)
114	Sunnyvale, CA	4.9
122	Sunrise, FL	4.1
160	Surprise, AZ	0.8
141	Syracuse, NY	2.9
163	Tacoma, WA	0.4
344	Tallahassee, FL	(17.6)
294	Tampa, FL	(10.1)
250	Temecula, CA	(6.0)
208	Tempe, AZ	(2.9)
130	Thornton, CO	3.7
208	Thousand Oaks, CA	(2.9)
190	Toledo, OH	(1.5)
190	Toms River Twnshp, NJ	(1.5)
324	Topeka, KS	(14.4)
124	Torrance, CA	4.0
363	Tracy, CA	(25.8)
330	Trenton, NJ	(15.4)
40	Troy, MI	16.7
186	Tucson, AZ	(1.2)
226	Tulsa, OK	(4.1)
133	Tuscaloosa, AL	3.6
366	Tyler, TX	(27.6)
159	Upper Darby Twnshp, PA	0.9
276	Vacaville, CA	(8.3)
NA	Vallejo, CA**	NA
349	Vancouver, WA	(19.4)
298	Ventura, CA	(10.6)
18	Victorville, CA	22.7
259	Virginia Beach, VA	(6.7)
91	Visalia, CA	8.1
232	Vista, CA	(4.4)
312	Waco, TX	(12.1)
194	Warren, MI	(1.8)
44	Warwick, RI	15.1
152	Washington, DC	1.4
311	Waterbury, CT	(12.0)
277	West Covina, CA	(8.5)
NA	West Jordan, UT**	NA
201	West Palm Beach, FL	(2.5)
335	West Valley, UT	(16.0)
177	Westland, MI	(0.8)
284	Westminster, CA	(9.1)
270	Westminster, CO	(7.6)
179	Whittier, CA	(0.9)
359	Wichita Falls, TX	(24.3)
NA	Wichita, KS**	NA
301	Wilmington, NC	(11.1)
111	Winston-Salem, NC	5.2
28	Woodbridge Twnshp, NJ	20.0
200	Worcester, MA	(2.2)
162	Yakima, WA	0.5
148	Yonkers, NY	1.8
80	Youngstown, OH	10.1
105	Yuma, AZ	5.8

Source: CQ Press using data from F.B.I. "Crime in the United States 2006"

**Burglary is the unlawful entry of a structure to commit a felony or theft. Attempts are included.*

***Not available.*

71. Percent Change in Burglary Rate: 2005 to 2006 (continued)

National Percent Change = 0.3% Increase*

RANK	CITY	% CHANGE
1	Brick Twnshp, NJ	58.7
2	Amherst, NY	39.9
3	Olathe, KS	37.5
4	Moreno Valley, CA	36.8
5	Fayetteville, NC	33.6
6	Norman, OK	33.4
7	Fremont, CA	32.3
8	Cape Coral, FL	31.0
9	Clinton Twnshp, MI	27.8
10	Pittsburgh, PA	25.4
11	Lakeland, FL	25.2
12	Port St. Lucie, FL	25.0
13	Milwaukee, WI	24.8
14	Jackson, MS	23.7
15	Kansas City, KS	23.2
16	Grand Rapids, MI	23.1
17	Alexandria, VA	23.0
18	Victorville, CA	22.7
19	Huntington Beach, CA	22.1
20	Gainesville, FL	22.0
21	Cary, NC	21.6
21	North Las Vegas, NV	21.6
23	Clarksville, TN	21.2
24	Southfield, MI	21.0
25	Detroit, MI	20.7
25	Quincy, MA	20.7
27	Fargo, ND	20.6
28	Lynn, MA	20.0
28	Woodbridge Twnshp, NJ	20.0
30	Sparks, NV	19.3
31	Erie, PA	18.7
32	Clifton, NJ	18.5
33	El Monte, CA	17.7
33	Overland Park, KS	17.7
33	St. Louis, MO	17.7
36	Flint, MI	17.6
37	Palmdale, CA	17.5
38	Lancaster, CA	17.2
39	Mission Viejo, CA	16.8
40	Troy, MI	16.7
41	Macon, GA	16.4
42	Canton, OH	16.2
43	Camden, NJ	15.7
44	Coral Springs, FL	15.1
44	South Bend, IN	15.1
44	Warwick, RI	15.1
47	Danbury, CT	14.9
47	Gary, IN	14.9
49	Newport News, VA	14.8
50	Antioch, CA	14.7
51	Racine, WI	14.5
52	Hamilton Twnshp, NJ	13.9
53	Cleveland, OH	13.8
54	Green Bay, WI	13.6
55	Carson, CA	13.4
55	Rochester, MN	13.4
57	Pasadena, CA	13.2
57	Sterling Heights, MI	13.2
59	Lowell, MA	13.0
60	Manchester, NH	12.8
61	Cincinnati, OH	12.5
61	Springfield, IL	12.5
61	Springfield, MO	12.5
64	Joliet, IL	12.4
64	Lansing, MI	12.4
64	Napa, CA	12.4
67	Pembroke Pines, FL	12.2
68	Lubbock, TX	11.5
69	San Leandro, CA	11.4
70	Madison, WI	11.3
71	Carlsbad, CA	11.1
71	Fort Smith, AR	11.1
71	Hialeah, FL	11.1
74	Lafayette, LA	11.0
74	Lawton, OK	11.0
76	Sandy, UT	10.6
77	Glendale, AZ	10.5
78	Lawrence, KS	10.3
79	Sioux Falls, SD	10.2
80	Dayton, OH	10.1
80	Seattle, WA	10.1
80	Youngstown, OH	10.1
83	Cambridge, MA	9.5
84	Mesquite, TX	9.2
85	Hesperia, CA	9.0
86	Baton Rouge, LA	8.8
86	Bellingham, WA	8.8
88	Nashua, NH	8.7
88	Stockton, CA	8.7
90	Albuquerque, NM	8.3
91	San Jose, CA	8.1
91	Visalia, CA	8.1
93	Midland, TX	8.0
94	Kenosha, WI	7.4
95	Reno, NV	6.9
96	Jacksonville, FL	6.8
97	Greece, NY	6.3
98	Grand Prairie, TX	6.2
98	Murfreesboro, TN	6.2
100	Brownsville, TX	6.0
100	Plantation, FL	6.0
102	Buffalo, NY	5.9
102	Philadelphia, PA	5.9
102	Santa Clara, CA	5.9
105	Chino Hills, CA	5.8
105	Louisville, KY	5.8
105	Yuma, AZ	5.8
108	Athens-Clarke, GA	5.6
109	Minneapolis, MN	5.5
110	Everett, WA	5.4
111	Winston-Salem, NC	5.2
112	Columbia, MO	5.0
112	Sacramento, CA	5.0
114	Sunnyvale, CA	4.9
115	Dearborn, MI	4.8
116	Elizabeth, NJ	4.7
117	San Francisco, CA	4.6
118	Hayward, CA	4.4
118	Portsmouth, VA	4.4
120	Baltimore, MD	4.3
121	San Diego, CA	4.2
122	Lake Forest, CA	4.1
122	Sunrise, FL	4.1
124	Torrance, CA	4.0
125	Greensboro, NC	3.9
125	Pomona, CA	3.9
125	Shreveport, LA	3.9
128	Melbourne, FL	3.8
128	Santa Rosa, CA	3.8
130	Fresno, CA	3.7
130	Salt Lake City, UT	3.7
130	Thornton, CO	3.7
133	Chattanooga, TN	3.6
133	Tuscaloosa, AL	3.6
135	Cedar Rapids, IA	3.5
135	Memphis, TN	3.5
137	Murrieta, CA	3.4
137	Oklahoma City, OK	3.4
139	Ogden, UT	3.3
140	Cheektowaga, NY	3.2
141	Charlotte, NC	2.9
141	Syracuse, NY	2.9
143	Allentown, PA	2.7
143	Aurora, IL	2.7
145	Palm Bay, FL	2.6
146	Kent, WA	2.4
147	Laredo, TX	1.9
148	Yonkers, NY	1.8
149	Columbus, GA	1.6
149	Hollywood, FL	1.6
151	Indianapolis, IN	1.5
152	Washington, DC	1.4
153	Columbus, OH	1.3
154	Little Rock, AR	1.2
154	Orange, CA	1.2
156	Las Vegas, NV	1.1
156	Springfield, MA	1.1
158	Arvada, CO	1.0
159	Upper Darby Twnshp, PA	0.9
160	Modesto, CA	0.8
160	Surprise, AZ	0.8
162	Yakima, WA	0.5
163	Lincoln, NE	0.4
163	Odessa, TX	0.4
163	Tacoma, WA	0.4
166	Huntsville, AL	0.3
166	Largo, FL	0.3
166	Oxnard, CA	0.3
169	Austin, TX	0.1
169	Bellflower, CA	0.1
171	Longview, TX	(0.1)
172	Henderson, NV	(0.3)
173	Downey, CA	(0.4)
174	Bridgeport, CT	(0.5)
174	Chino, CA	(0.5)
176	Arlington, TX	(0.6)
177	Roswell, GA	(0.8)
177	Westland, MI	(0.8)
179	Omaha, NE	(0.9)
179	Whittier, CA	(0.9)
181	Fort Worth, TX	(1.0)
181	Plano, TX	(1.0)
181	San Antonio, TX	(1.0)
184	Broken Arrow, OK	(1.1)
184	Fairfield, CA	(1.1)
186	Bellevue, WA	(1.2)
186	Tucson, AZ	(1.2)
188	Atlanta, GA	(1.3)
189	St. Petersburg, FL	(1.4)
190	Toledo, OH	(1.5)
190	Toms River Twnshp, NJ	(1.5)
192	Long Beach, CA	(1.7)

RANK	CITY	% CHANGE
192	McKinney, TX	(1.7)
194	Warren, MI	(1.8)
195	Anaheim, CA	(1.9)
195	Nashville, TN	(1.9)
197	Birmingham, AL	(2.0)
198	Killeen, TX	(2.1)
198	Salinas, CA	(2.1)
200	Worcester, MA	(2.2)
201	Aurora, CO	(2.5)
201	Brockton, MA	(2.5)
201	Newport Beach, CA	(2.5)
201	West Palm Beach, FL	(2.5)
205	Las Cruces, NM	(2.6)
205	Rochester, NY	(2.6)
207	Albany, GA	(2.8)
208	Lewisville, TX	(2.9)
208	Paterson, NJ	(2.9)
208	Tempe, AZ	(2.9)
208	Thousand Oaks, CA	(2.9)
212	Richmond, CA	(3.0)
213	Daly City, CA	(3.1)
213	Roanoke, VA	(3.1)
215	St. Paul, MN	(3.3)
216	Anchorage, AK	(3.4)
217	Burbank, CA	(3.5)
217	Newark, NJ	(3.5)
219	Fontana, CA	(3.7)
220	Houston, TX	(3.8)
220	Providence, RI	(3.8)
220	Santa Maria, CA	(3.8)
223	Irving, TX	(3.9)
223	New Bedford, MA	(3.9)
225	Phoenix, AZ	(4.0)
226	Chicago, IL	(4.1)
226	Montgomery, AL	(4.1)
226	Ontario, CA	(4.1)
226	Tulsa, OK	(4.1)
230	Eugene, OR	(4.2)
230	Suffolk, VA	(4.2)
232	Miami Beach, FL	(4.4)
232	Vista, CA	(4.4)
234	Independence, MO	(4.5)
235	Bakersfield, CA	(4.6)
235	Dallas, TX	(4.6)
235	Escondido, CA	(4.6)
235	Mobile, AL	(4.6)
239	Fullerton, CA	(4.9)
240	North Charleston, SC	(5.0)
241	Pueblo, CO	(5.1)
242	Lakewood, CA	(5.2)
242	New York, NY	(5.2)
242	Pasadena, TX	(5.2)
245	Colonie, NY	(5.3)
246	Berkeley, CA	(5.8)
246	Riverside, CA	(5.8)
246	South Gate, CA	(5.8)
249	Miami Gardens, FL	(5.9)
250	Norfolk, VA	(6.0)
250	Temecula, CA	(6.0)
252	Pompano Beach, FL	(6.1)
253	Lakewood, CO	(6.2)
254	Cranston, RI	(6.4)
255	Clearwater, FL	(6.6)
255	Columbia, SC	(6.6)
255	Hammond, IN	(6.6)
255	Raleigh, NC	(6.6)

RANK	CITY	% CHANGE
259	Glendale, CA	(6.7)
259	Virginia Beach, VA	(6.7)
261	Clovis, CA	(6.8)
261	Garland, TX	(6.8)
263	Chula Vista, CA	(6.9)
264	Chesapeake, VA	(7.1)
264	Livermore, CA	(7.1)
266	Santa Monica, CA	(7.2)
267	Edmond, OK	(7.3)
268	Round Rock, TX	(7.4)
269	Chandler, AZ	(7.5)
270	Amarillo, TX	(7.6)
270	Oceanside, CA	(7.6)
270	Westminster, CO	(7.6)
273	Boston, MA	(8.2)
273	Federal Way, WA	(8.2)
273	Spokane Valley, WA	(8.2)
276	Vacaville, CA	(8.3)
277	Orlando, FL	(8.5)
277	West Covina, CA	(8.5)
279	Buena Park, CA	(8.7)
280	Beaumont, TX	(8.9)
280	Knoxville, TN	(8.9)
280	Peoria, AZ	(8.9)
283	Evansville, IN	(9.0)
284	Compton, CA	(9.1)
284	Westminster, CA	(9.1)
286	Norwalk, CA	(9.2)
287	Mesa, AZ	(9.3)
288	Denton, TX	(9.4)
289	Colorado Springs, CO	(9.5)
289	Fort Collins, CO	(9.5)
291	Santa Ana, CA	(9.7)
292	Richmond, VA	(9.9)
293	Scottsdale, AZ	(10.0)
294	Los Angeles, CA	(10.1)
294	Tampa, FL	(10.1)
296	Salem, OR	(10.2)
297	Garden Grove, CA	(10.5)
298	Ventura, CA	(10.6)
299	Portland, OR	(10.7)
299	Santa Clarita, CA	(10.7)
301	Wilmington, NC	(11.1)
302	Richardson, TX	(11.3)
303	Sioux City, IA	(11.5)
303	Spokane, WA	(11.5)
305	Boulder, CO	(11.6)
306	Denver, CO	(11.7)
307	Costa Mesa, CA	(11.8)
308	Beaverton, OR	(11.9)
308	Canton Twnshp, MI	(11.9)
308	Oakland, CA	(11.9)
311	Waterbury, CT	(12.0)
312	Honolulu, HI	(12.1)
312	Lee's Summit, MO	(12.1)
312	Waco, TX	(12.1)
315	Corpus Christi, TX	(12.2)
315	Parma, OH	(12.2)
317	Gilbert, AZ	(12.6)
317	Rancho Cucamon., CA	(12.6)
319	Carrollton, TX	(12.8)
320	Hampton, VA	(12.9)
321	Fort Lauderdale, FL	(13.4)
322	Peoria, IL	(13.6)
323	Deerfield Beach, FL	(14.1)
324	Charleston, SC	(14.4)

RANK	CITY	% CHANGE
324	Topeka, KS	(14.4)
326	Irvine, CA	(14.9)
327	Concord, CA	(15.0)
328	Rialto, CA	(15.2)
328	San Angelo, TX	(15.2)
330	Trenton, NJ	(15.4)
331	Boca Raton, FL	(15.5)
332	Boise, ID	(15.6)
333	San Bernardino, CA	(15.7)
334	El Cajon, CA	(15.9)
335	West Valley, UT	(16.0)
336	High Point, NC	(16.1)
337	McAllen, TX	(16.2)
338	Livonia, MI	(16.5)
339	Abilene, TX	(16.6)
339	Hartford, CT	(16.6)
341	Somerville, MA	(16.7)
342	Baldwin Park, CA	(17.5)
342	Inglewood, CA	(17.5)
344	Tallahassee, FL	(17.6)
345	Miami, FL	(18.4)
345	Miramar, FL	(18.4)
347	Farmington Hills, MI	(18.5)
348	Santa Barbara, CA	(18.8)
349	Savannah, GA	(19.4)
349	Vancouver, WA	(19.4)
351	Albany, NY	(19.8)
351	Centennial, CO	(19.8)
353	Davie, FL	(20.2)
354	Edison Twnshp, NJ	(21.9)
355	Alhambra, CA	(22.6)
356	San Mateo, CA	(22.9)
357	Corona, CA	(23.5)
358	Billings, MT	(23.6)
359	Wichita Falls, TX	(24.3)
360	Jersey City, NJ	(24.7)
361	Redding, CA	(24.8)
362	Reading, PA	(25.4)
363	Tracy, CA	(25.8)
364	Ann Arbor, MI	(26.1)
365	Simi Valley, CA	(27.1)
366	Tyler, TX	(27.6)
367	Gresham, OR	(27.7)
368	Sugar Land, TX	(28.5)
369	Provo, UT	(29.3)
370	Greeley, CO	(29.5)
371	Newton, MA	(29.8)
372	Orem, UT	(32.1)
373	Roseville, CA	(32.7)
374	Naperville, IL	(37.0)
375	Hawthorne, CA	(37.2)
376	Hillsboro, OR	(39.0)
NA	Bloomington, MN**	NA
NA	Clarkstown, NY**	NA
NA	Des Moines, IA**	NA
NA	Duluth, MN**	NA
NA	Durham, NC**	NA
NA	El Paso, TX**	NA
NA	Fort Wayne, IN**	NA
NA	Kansas City, MO**	NA
NA	Lexington, KY**	NA
NA	New Orleans, LA**	NA
NA	Rockford, IL**	NA
NA	Vallejo, CA**	NA
NA	West Jordan, UT**	NA
NA	Wichita, KS**	NA

Source: CQ Press using data from F.B.I. "Crime in the United States 2006"

**Burglary is the unlawful entry of a structure to commit a felony or theft. Attempts are included.*

***Not available.*

72. Percent Change in Burglary Rate: 2002 to 2006

National Percent Change = 2.4% Decrease*

RANK	CITY	% CHANGE
149	Abilene, TX	2.1
31	Albany, GA	31.1
NA	Albany, NY**	NA
117	Albuquerque, NM	6.4
315	Alexandria, VA	(23.8)
242	Alhambra, CA	(11.0)
69	Allentown, PA	18.3
211	Amarillo, TX	(5.8)
17	Amherst, NY	42.4
196	Anaheim, CA	(4.0)
98	Anchorage, AK	9.7
319	Ann Arbor, MI	(25.0)
19	Antioch, CA	40.4
140	Arlington, TX	3.6
127	Arvada, CO	4.9
125	Athens-Clarke, GA	5.4
307	Atlanta, GA	(22.4)
103	Aurora, CO	9.3
309	Aurora, IL	(22.6)
131	Austin, TX	4.3
30	Bakersfield, CA	31.5
170	Baldwin Park, CA	(1.5)
225	Baltimore, MD	(8.6)
112	Baton Rouge, LA	7.3
85	Beaumont, TX	13.4
344	Beaverton, OR	(33.5)
222	Bellevue, WA	(7.7)
250	Bellflower, CA	(11.8)
117	Bellingham, WA	6.4
297	Berkeley, CA	(20.3)
136	Billings, MT	3.8
80	Birmingham, AL	15.0
159	Bloomington, MN	0.6
235	Boca Raton, FL	(10.3)
262	Boise, ID	(14.1)
81	Boston, MA	14.1
194	Boulder, CO	(3.5)
26	Brick Twnshp, NJ	36.2
165	Bridgeport, CT	(0.7)
166	Brockton, MA	(0.9)
264	Broken Arrow, OK	(14.3)
191	Brownsville, TX	(3.3)
210	Buena Park, CA	(5.6)
59	Buffalo, NY	21.4
91	Burbank, CA	12.1
189	Cambridge, MA	(3.2)
133	Camden, NJ	4.0
126	Canton Twnshp, MI	5.3
NA	Canton, OH**	NA
154	Cape Coral, FL	1.6
57	Carlsbad, CA	22.1
218	Carrollton, TX	(6.8)
161	Carson, CA	0.2
36	Cary, NC	29.8
174	Cedar Rapids, IA	(1.8)
NA	Centennial, CO**	NA
359	Chandler, AZ	(43.0)
351	Charleston, SC	(36.8)
64	Charlotte, NC	19.5
238	Chattanooga, TN	(10.7)
NA	Cheektowaga, NY**	NA
258	Chesapeake, VA	(13.2)
185	Chicago, IL	(2.8)
362	Chino Hills, CA	(46.5)
1	Chino, CA	126.5
213	Chula Vista, CA	(6.1)
160	Cincinnati, OH	0.3
361	Clarkstown, NY	(44.2)
6	Clarksville, TN	61.9
312	Clearwater, FL	(23.1)
43	Cleveland, OH	26.7
257	Clifton, NJ	(13.1)
53	Clinton Twnshp, MI	23.3
236	Clovis, CA	(10.6)
278	Colonie, NY	(16.3)
285	Colorado Springs, CO	(17.3)
74	Columbia, MO	16.7
314	Columbia, SC	(23.4)
14	Columbus, GA	45.4
231	Columbus, OH	(9.8)
305	Compton, CA	(21.4)
48	Concord, CA	24.6
342	Coral Springs, FL	(32.9)
268	Corona, CA	(14.8)
279	Corpus Christi, TX	(16.6)
131	Costa Mesa, CA	4.3
346	Cranston, RI	(34.2)
121	Dallas, TX	5.8
74	Daly City, CA	16.7
246	Danbury, CT	(11.5)
355	Davie, FL	(40.7)
203	Dayton, OH	(5.1)
29	Dearborn, MI	31.7
11	Deerfield Beach, FL	48.0
308	Denton, TX	(22.5)
103	Denver, CO	9.3
NA	Des Moines, IA**	NA
24	Detroit, MI	37.0
134	Downey, CA	3.9
277	Duluth, MN	(16.2)
NA	Durham, NC**	NA
150	Edison Twnshp, NJ	1.9
251	Edmond, OK	(12.0)
264	El Cajon, CA	(14.3)
45	El Monte, CA	24.9
NA	El Paso, TX**	NA
350	Elizabeth, NJ	(36.5)
115	Erie, PA	6.9
290	Escondido, CA	(19.2)
46	Eugene, OR	24.8
111	Evansville, IN	7.4
8	Everett, WA	54.5
134	Fairfield, CA	3.9
33	Fargo, ND	30.6
180	Farmington Hills, MI	(2.3)
13	Fayetteville, NC	46.1
88	Federal Way, WA	12.8
15	Flint, MI	44.5
320	Fontana, CA	(25.3)
228	Fort Collins, CO	(9.5)
275	Fort Lauderdale, FL	(15.5)
234	Fort Smith, AR	(10.2)
NA	Fort Wayne, IN**	NA
293	Fort Worth, TX	(19.6)
27	Fremont, CA	35.7
220	Fresno, CA	(7.1)
198	Fullerton, CA	(4.3)
142	Gainesville, FL	3.2
261	Garden Grove, CA	(13.8)
147	Garland, TX	2.4
52	Gary, IN	23.4
366	Gilbert, AZ	(55.5)
16	Glendale, AZ	44.2
325	Glendale, CA	(26.3)
96	Grand Prairie, TX	10.5
94	Grand Rapids, MI	11.3
NA	Greece, NY**	NA
65	Greeley, CO	19.2
95	Green Bay, WI	10.6
23	Greensboro, NC	37.1
318	Gresham, OR	(24.9)
186	Hamilton Twnshp, NJ	(3.0)
61	Hammond, IN	20.1
287	Hampton, VA	(18.1)
328	Hartford, CT	(26.7)
295	Hawthorne, CA	(19.9)
7	Hayward, CA	55.1
260	Henderson, NV	(13.5)
300	Hesperia, CA	(20.7)
97	Hialeah, FL	9.8
128	High Point, NC	4.7
343	Hillsboro, OR	(33.1)
103	Hollywood, FL	9.3
354	Honolulu, HI	(39.5)
171	Houston, TX	(1.7)
90	Huntington Beach, CA	12.5
21	Huntsville, AL	38.3
122	Independence, MO	5.7
58	Indianapolis, IN	21.9
167	Inglewood, CA	(1.2)
358	Irvine, CA	(42.5)
146	Irving, TX	3.0
156	Jacksonville, FL	1.3
224	Jackson, MS	(8.5)
320	Jersey City, NJ	(25.3)
289	Joliet, IL	(18.4)
NA	Kansas City, KS**	NA
NA	Kansas City, MO**	NA
63	Kenosha, WI	19.6
28	Kent, WA	32.3
117	Killeen, TX	6.4
136	Knoxville, TN	3.8
186	Lafayette, LA	(3.0)
240	Lake Forest, CA	(10.9)
151	Lakeland, FL	1.8
200	Lakewood, CA	(4.7)
182	Lakewood, CO	(2.5)
66	Lancaster, CA	18.8
56	Lansing, MI	22.6
323	Laredo, TX	(25.6)
271	Largo, FL	(15.1)
NA	Las Cruces, NM**	NA
70	Las Vegas, NV	17.4
245	Lawrence, KS	(11.4)
46	Lawton, OK	24.8
91	Lee's Summit, MO	12.1
333	Lewisville, TX	(28.0)
NA	Lexington, KY**	NA
229	Lincoln, NE	(9.6)
297	Little Rock, AR	(20.3)
231	Livermore, CA	(9.8)
201	Livonia, MI	(4.8)

RANK	CITY	% CHANGE	RANK	CITY	% CHANGE	RANK	CITY	% CHANGE
269	Long Beach, CA	(14.9)	229	Peoria, AZ	(9.6)	NA	Spokane Valley, WA**	NA
136	Longview, TX	3.8	256	Peoria, IL	(12.6)	287	Spokane, WA	(18.1)
302	Los Angeles, CA	(20.8)	116	Philadelphia, PA	6.8	102	Springfield, IL	9.4
NA	Louisville, KY**	NA	244	Phoenix, AZ	(11.3)	357	Springfield, MA	(42.3)
54	Lowell, MA	22.7	66	Pittsburgh, PA	18.8	117	Springfield, MO	6.4
164	Lubbock, TX	(0.4)	205	Plano, TX	(5.2)	249	Sterling Heights, MI	(11.6)
3	Lynn, MA	76.3	201	Plantation, FL	(4.8)	86	Stockton, CA	12.9
110	Macon, GA	7.5	76	Pomona, CA	15.8	54	St. Louis, MO	22.7
171	Madison, WI	(1.7)	50	Pompano Beach, FL	24.0	99	St. Paul, MN	9.6
41	Manchester, NH	26.9	161	Port St. Lucie, FL	0.2	177	St. Petersburg, FL	(2.1)
364	McAllen, TX	(48.1)	193	Portland, OR	(3.4)	329	Suffolk, VA	(27.1)
363	McKinney, TX	(46.9)	266	Portsmouth, VA	(14.4)	338	Sugar Land, TX	(29.7)
91	Melbourne, FL	12.1	291	Providence, RI	(19.4)	4	Sunnyvale, CA	70.9
175	Memphis, TN	(2.0)	175	Provo, UT	(2.0)	151	Sunrise, FL	1.8
353	Mesa, AZ	(39.3)	37	Pueblo, CO	28.9	352	Surprise, AZ	(37.6)
32	Mesquite, TX	30.9	113	Quincy, MA	7.0	141	Syracuse, NY	3.3
195	Miami Beach, FL	(3.6)	62	Racine, WI	19.9	109	Tacoma, WA	8.1
NA	Miami Gardens, FL**	NA	349	Raleigh, NC	(36.4)	215	Tallahassee, FL	(6.3)
334	Miami, FL	(28.1)	322	Rancho Cucamon., CA	(25.5)	341	Tampa, FL	(32.2)
163	Midland, TX	(0.2)	317	Reading, PA	(24.4)	144	Temecula, CA	3.1
269	Milwaukee, WI	(14.9)	281	Redding, CA	(16.8)	313	Tempe, AZ	(23.3)
25	Minneapolis, MN	36.7	9	Reno, NV	52.5	284	Thornton, CO	(17.2)
347	Miramar, FL	(34.4)	184	Rialto, CA	(2.6)	182	Thousand Oaks, CA	(2.5)
60	Mission Viejo, CA	21.2	233	Richardson, TX	(10.1)	49	Toledo, OH	24.5
130	Mobile, AL	4.6	177	Richmond, CA	(2.1)	339	Toms River Twnshp, NJ	(30.2)
227	Modesto, CA	(9.2)	294	Richmond, VA	(19.8)	276	Topeka, KS	(15.8)
238	Montgomery, AL	(10.7)	271	Riverside, CA	(15.1)	216	Torrance, CA	(6.4)
39	Moreno Valley, CA	27.0	NA	Roanoke, VA**	NA	332	Tracy, CA	(27.4)
10	Murfreesboro, TN	51.6	179	Rochester, MN	(2.2)	336	Trenton, NJ	(29.3)
151	Murrieta, CA	1.8	84	Rochester, NY	13.6	214	Troy, MI	(6.2)
20	Napa, CA	40.3	NA	Rockford, IL**	NA	325	Tucson, AZ	(26.3)
365	Naperville, IL	(49.3)	282	Roseville, CA	(17.0)	142	Tulsa, OK	3.2
NA	Nashua, NH**	NA	100	Roswell, GA	9.5	66	Tuscaloosa, AL	18.8
267	Nashville, TN	(14.7)	335	Round Rock, TX	(28.3)	310	Tyler, TX	(22.8)
NA	New Bedford, MA**	NA	89	Sacramento, CA	12.7	2	Upper Darby Twnshp, PA	113.0
189	New Orleans, LA	(3.2)	336	Salem, OR	(29.3)	144	Vacaville, CA	3.1
330	New York, NY	(27.2)	39	Salinas, CA	27.0	167	Vallejo, CA	(1.2)
254	Newark, NJ	(12.5)	223	Salt Lake City, UT	(8.4)	310	Vancouver, WA	(22.8)
188	Newport Beach, CA	(3.1)	203	San Angelo, TX	(5.1)	73	Ventura, CA	17.2
139	Newport News, VA	3.7	156	San Antonio, TX	1.3	71	Victorville, CA	17.3
NA	Newton, MA**	NA	254	San Bernardino, CA	(12.5)	246	Virginia Beach, VA	(11.5)
207	Norfolk, VA	(5.3)	155	San Diego, CA	1.5	108	Visalia, CA	8.3
304	Norman, OK	(21.3)	71	San Francisco, CA	17.3	207	Vista, CA	(5.3)
226	North Charleston, SC	(8.8)	12	San Jose, CA	47.3	199	Waco, TX	(4.5)
82	North Las Vegas, NV	13.9	34	San Leandro, CA	30.4	212	Warren, MI	(5.9)
303	Norwalk, CA	(20.9)	286	San Mateo, CA	(17.9)	280	Warwick, RI	(16.7)
51	Oakland, CA	23.8	209	Sandy, UT	(5.5)	331	Washington, DC	(27.3)
252	Oceanside, CA	(12.1)	236	Santa Ana, CA	(10.6)	271	Waterbury, CT	(15.1)
291	Odessa, TX	(19.4)	191	Santa Barbara, CA	(3.3)	38	West Covina, CA	27.4
243	Ogden, UT	(11.1)	17	Santa Clara, CA	42.4	306	West Jordan, UT	(21.6)
113	Oklahoma City, OK	7.0	77	Santa Clarita, CA	15.7	297	West Palm Beach, FL	(20.3)
83	Olathe, KS	13.7	NA	Santa Maria, CA**	NA	197	West Valley, UT	(4.1)
219	Omaha, NE	(6.9)	181	Santa Monica, CA	(2.4)	158	Westland, MI	0.8
296	Ontario, CA	(20.2)	274	Santa Rosa, CA	(15.3)	171	Westminster, CA	(1.7)
263	Orange, CA	(14.2)	345	Savannah, GA	(33.8)	NA	Westminster, CO**	NA
340	Orem, UT	(31.7)	360	Scottsdale, AZ	(43.2)	35	Whittier, CA	30.2
246	Orlando, FL	(11.5)	148	Seattle, WA	2.3	300	Wichita Falls, TX	(20.7)
205	Overland Park, KS	(5.2)	220	Shreveport, LA	(7.1)	283	Wichita, KS	(17.1)
167	Oxnard, CA	(1.2)	79	Simi Valley, CA	15.4	325	Wilmington, NC	(26.3)
124	Palm Bay, FL	5.6	356	Sioux City, IA	(42.0)	44	Winston-Salem, NC	25.9
107	Palmdale, CA	8.4	128	Sioux Falls, SD	4.7	315	Woodbridge Twnshp, NJ	(23.8)
22	Parma, OH	37.2	122	Somerville, MA	5.7	NA	Worcester, MA**	NA
240	Pasadena, CA	(10.9)	106	South Bend, IN	8.9	217	Yakima, WA	(6.5)
324	Pasadena, TX	(26.2)	348	South Gate, CA	(35.0)	253	Yonkers, NY	(12.3)
259	Paterson, NJ	(13.3)	5	Southfield, MI	62.9	100	Youngstown, OH	9.5
77	Pembroke Pines, FL	15.7	86	Sparks, NV	12.9	42	Yuma, AZ	26.8

Source: CQ Press using data from F.B.I. "Crime in the United States 2006"

**Burglary is the unlawful entry of a structure to commit a felony or theft. Attempts are included.*

***Not available.*

72. Percent Change in Burglary Rate: 2002 to 2006 (continued)

National Percent Change = 2.4% Decrease*

RANK	CITY	% CHANGE
1	Chino, CA	126.5
2	Upper Darby Twnshp, PA	113.0
3	Lynn, MA	76.3
4	Sunnyvale, CA	70.9
5	Southfield, MI	62.9
6	Clarksville, TN	61.9
7	Hayward, CA	55.1
8	Everett, WA	54.5
9	Reno, NV	52.5
10	Murfreesboro, TN	51.6
11	Deerfield Beach, FL	48.0
12	San Jose, CA	47.3
13	Fayetteville, NC	46.1
14	Columbus, GA	45.4
15	Flint, MI	44.5
16	Glendale, AZ	44.2
17	Amherst, NY	42.4
17	Santa Clara, CA	42.4
19	Antioch, CA	40.4
20	Napa, CA	40.3
21	Huntsville, AL	38.3
22	Parma, OH	37.2
23	Greensboro, NC	37.1
24	Detroit, MI	37.0
25	Minneapolis, MN	36.7
26	Brick Twnshp, NJ	36.2
27	Fremont, CA	35.7
28	Kent, WA	32.3
29	Dearborn, MI	31.7
30	Bakersfield, CA	31.5
31	Albany, GA	31.1
32	Mesquite, TX	30.9
33	Fargo, ND	30.6
34	San Leandro, CA	30.4
35	Whittier, CA	30.2
36	Cary, NC	29.8
37	Pueblo, CO	28.9
38	West Covina, CA	27.4
39	Moreno Valley, CA	27.0
39	Salinas, CA	27.0
41	Manchester, NH	26.9
42	Yuma, AZ	26.8
43	Cleveland, OH	26.7
44	Winston-Salem, NC	25.9
45	El Monte, CA	24.9
46	Eugene, OR	24.8
46	Lawton, OK	24.8
48	Concord, CA	24.6
49	Toledo, OH	24.5
50	Pompano Beach, FL	24.0
51	Oakland, CA	23.8
52	Gary, IN	23.4
53	Clinton Twnshp, MI	23.3
54	Lowell, MA	22.7
54	St. Louis, MO	22.7
56	Lansing, MI	22.6
57	Carlsbad, CA	22.1
58	Indianapolis, IN	21.9
59	Buffalo, NY	21.4
60	Mission Viejo, CA	21.2
61	Hammond, IN	20.1
62	Racine, WI	19.9
63	Kenosha, WI	19.6
64	Charlotte, NC	19.5
65	Greeley, CO	19.2
66	Lancaster, CA	18.8
66	Pittsburgh, PA	18.8
66	Tuscaloosa, AL	18.8
69	Allentown, PA	18.3
70	Las Vegas, NV	17.4
71	San Francisco, CA	17.3
71	Victorville, CA	17.3
73	Ventura, CA	17.2
74	Columbia, MO	16.7
74	Daly City, CA	16.7
76	Pomona, CA	15.8
77	Pembroke Pines, FL	15.7
77	Santa Clarita, CA	15.7
79	Simi Valley, CA	15.4
80	Birmingham, AL	15.0
81	Boston, MA	14.1
82	North Las Vegas, NV	13.9
83	Olathe, KS	13.7
84	Rochester, NY	13.6
85	Beaumont, TX	13.4
86	Sparks, NV	12.9
86	Stockton, CA	12.9
88	Federal Way, WA	12.8
89	Sacramento, CA	12.7
90	Huntington Beach, CA	12.5
91	Burbank, CA	12.1
91	Lee's Summit, MO	12.1
91	Melbourne, FL	12.1
94	Grand Rapids, MI	11.3
95	Green Bay, WI	10.6
96	Grand Prairie, TX	10.5
97	Hialeah, FL	9.8
98	Anchorage, AK	9.7
99	St. Paul, MN	9.6
100	Roswell, GA	9.5
100	Youngstown, OH	9.5
102	Springfield, IL	9.4
103	Aurora, CO	9.3
103	Denver, CO	9.3
103	Hollywood, FL	9.3
106	South Bend, IN	8.9
107	Palmdale, CA	8.4
108	Visalia, CA	8.3
109	Tacoma, WA	8.1
110	Macon, GA	7.5
111	Evansville, IN	7.4
112	Baton Rouge, LA	7.3
113	Oklahoma City, OK	7.0
113	Quincy, MA	7.0
115	Erie, PA	6.9
116	Philadelphia, PA	6.8
117	Albuquerque, NM	6.4
117	Bellingham, WA	6.4
117	Killeen, TX	6.4
117	Springfield, MO	6.4
121	Dallas, TX	5.8
122	Independence, MO	5.7
122	Somerville, MA	5.7
124	Palm Bay, FL	5.6
125	Athens-Clarke, GA	5.4
126	Canton Twnshp, MI	5.3
127	Arvada, CO	4.9
128	High Point, NC	4.7
128	Sioux Falls, SD	4.7
130	Mobile, AL	4.6
131	Austin, TX	4.3
131	Costa Mesa, CA	4.3
133	Camden, NJ	4.0
134	Downey, CA	3.9
134	Fairfield, CA	3.9
136	Billings, MT	3.8
136	Knoxville, TN	3.8
136	Longview, TX	3.8
139	Newport News, VA	3.7
140	Arlington, TX	3.6
141	Syracuse, NY	3.3
142	Gainesville, FL	3.2
142	Tulsa, OK	3.2
144	Temecula, CA	3.1
144	Vacaville, CA	3.1
146	Irving, TX	3.0
147	Garland, TX	2.4
148	Seattle, WA	2.3
149	Abilene, TX	2.1
150	Edison Twnshp, NJ	1.9
151	Lakeland, FL	1.8
151	Murrieta, CA	1.8
151	Sunrise, FL	1.8
154	Cape Coral, FL	1.6
155	San Diego, CA	1.5
156	Jacksonville, FL	1.3
156	San Antonio, TX	1.3
158	Westland, MI	0.8
159	Bloomington, MN	0.6
160	Cincinnati, OH	0.3
161	Carson, CA	0.2
161	Port St. Lucie, FL	0.2
163	Midland, TX	(0.2)
164	Lubbock, TX	(0.4)
165	Bridgeport, CT	(0.7)
166	Brockton, MA	(0.9)
167	Inglewood, CA	(1.2)
167	Oxnard, CA	(1.2)
167	Vallejo, CA	(1.2)
170	Baldwin Park, CA	(1.5)
171	Houston, TX	(1.7)
171	Madison, WI	(1.7)
171	Westminster, CA	(1.7)
174	Cedar Rapids, IA	(1.8)
175	Memphis, TN	(2.0)
175	Provo, UT	(2.0)
177	Richmond, CA	(2.1)
177	St. Petersburg, FL	(2.1)
179	Rochester, MN	(2.2)
180	Farmington Hills, MI	(2.3)
181	Santa Monica, CA	(2.4)
182	Lakewood, CO	(2.5)
182	Thousand Oaks, CA	(2.5)
184	Rialto, CA	(2.6)
185	Chicago, IL	(2.8)
186	Hamilton Twnshp, NJ	(3.0)
186	Lafayette, LA	(3.0)
188	Newport Beach, CA	(3.1)
189	Cambridge, MA	(3.2)
189	New Orleans, LA	(3.2)
191	Brownsville, TX	(3.3)
191	Santa Barbara, CA	(3.3)

RANK	CITY	% CHANGE	RANK	CITY	% CHANGE	RANK	CITY	% CHANGE
193	Portland, OR	(3.4)	259	Paterson, NJ	(13.3)	325	Glendale, CA	(26.3)
194	Boulder, CO	(3.5)	260	Henderson, NV	(13.5)	325	Tucson, AZ	(26.3)
195	Miami Beach, FL	(3.6)	261	Garden Grove, CA	(13.8)	325	Wilmington, NC	(26.3)
196	Anaheim, CA	(4.0)	262	Boise, ID	(14.1)	328	Hartford, CT	(26.7)
197	West Valley, UT	(4.1)	263	Orange, CA	(14.2)	329	Suffolk, VA	(27.1)
198	Fullerton, CA	(4.3)	264	Broken Arrow, OK	(14.3)	330	New York, NY	(27.2)
199	Waco, TX	(4.5)	264	El Cajon, CA	(14.3)	331	Washington, DC	(27.3)
200	Lakewood, CA	(4.7)	266	Portsmouth, VA	(14.4)	332	Tracy, CA	(27.4)
201	Livonia, MI	(4.8)	267	Nashville, TN	(14.7)	333	Lewisville, TX	(28.0)
201	Plantation, FL	(4.8)	268	Corona, CA	(14.8)	334	Miami, FL	(28.1)
203	Dayton, OH	(5.1)	269	Long Beach, CA	(14.9)	335	Round Rock, TX	(28.3)
203	San Angelo, TX	(5.1)	269	Milwaukee, WI	(14.9)	336	Salem, OR	(29.3)
205	Overland Park, KS	(5.2)	271	Largo, FL	(15.1)	336	Trenton, NJ	(29.3)
205	Plano, TX	(5.2)	271	Riverside, CA	(15.1)	338	Sugar Land, TX	(29.7)
207	Norfolk, VA	(5.3)	271	Waterbury, CT	(15.1)	339	Toms River Twnshp, NJ	(30.2)
207	Vista, CA	(5.3)	274	Santa Rosa, CA	(15.3)	340	Orem, UT	(31.7)
209	Sandy, UT	(5.5)	275	Fort Lauderdale, FL	(15.5)	341	Tampa, FL	(32.2)
210	Buena Park, CA	(5.6)	276	Topeka, KS	(15.8)	342	Coral Springs, FL	(32.9)
211	Amarillo, TX	(5.8)	277	Duluth, MN	(16.2)	343	Hillsboro, OR	(33.1)
212	Warren, MI	(5.9)	278	Colonie, NY	(16.3)	344	Beaverton, OR	(33.5)
213	Chula Vista, CA	(6.1)	279	Corpus Christi, TX	(16.6)	345	Savannah, GA	(33.8)
214	Troy, MI	(6.2)	280	Warwick, RI	(16.7)	346	Cranston, RI	(34.2)
215	Tallahassee, FL	(6.3)	281	Redding, CA	(16.8)	347	Miramar, FL	(34.4)
216	Torrance, CA	(6.4)	282	Roseville, CA	(17.0)	348	South Gate, CA	(35.0)
217	Yakima, WA	(6.5)	283	Wichita, KS	(17.1)	349	Raleigh, NC	(36.4)
218	Carrollton, TX	(6.8)	284	Thornton, CO	(17.2)	350	Elizabeth, NJ	(36.5)
219	Omaha, NE	(6.9)	285	Colorado Springs, CO	(17.3)	351	Charleston, SC	(36.8)
220	Fresno, CA	(7.1)	286	San Mateo, CA	(17.9)	352	Surprise, AZ	(37.6)
220	Shreveport, LA	(7.1)	287	Hampton, VA	(18.1)	353	Mesa, AZ	(39.3)
222	Bellevue, WA	(7.7)	287	Spokane, WA	(18.1)	354	Honolulu, HI	(39.5)
223	Salt Lake City, UT	(8.4)	289	Joliet, IL	(18.4)	355	Davie, FL	(40.7)
224	Jackson, MS	(8.5)	290	Escondido, CA	(19.2)	356	Sioux City, IA	(42.0)
225	Baltimore, MD	(8.6)	291	Odessa, TX	(19.4)	357	Springfield, MA	(42.3)
226	North Charleston, SC	(8.8)	291	Providence, RI	(19.4)	358	Irvine, CA	(42.5)
227	Modesto, CA	(9.2)	293	Fort Worth, TX	(19.6)	359	Chandler, AZ	(43.0)
228	Fort Collins, CO	(9.5)	294	Richmond, VA	(19.8)	360	Scottsdale, AZ	(43.2)
229	Lincoln, NE	(9.6)	295	Hawthorne, CA	(19.9)	361	Clarkstown, NY	(44.2)
229	Peoria, AZ	(9.6)	296	Ontario, CA	(20.2)	362	Chino Hills, CA	(46.5)
231	Columbus, OH	(9.8)	297	Berkeley, CA	(20.3)	363	McKinney, TX	(46.9)
231	Livermore, CA	(9.8)	297	Little Rock, AR	(20.3)	364	McAllen, TX	(48.1)
233	Richardson, TX	(10.1)	297	West Palm Beach, FL	(20.3)	365	Naperville, IL	(49.3)
234	Fort Smith, AR	(10.2)	300	Hesperia, CA	(20.7)	366	Gilbert, AZ	(55.5)
235	Boca Raton, FL	(10.3)	300	Wichita Falls, TX	(20.7)	NA	Albany, NY**	NA
236	Clovis, CA	(10.6)	302	Los Angeles, CA	(20.8)	NA	Canton, OH**	NA
236	Santa Ana, CA	(10.6)	303	Norwalk, CA	(20.9)	NA	Centennial, CO**	NA
238	Chattanooga, TN	(10.7)	304	Norman, OK	(21.3)	NA	Cheektowaga, NY**	NA
238	Montgomery, AL	(10.7)	305	Compton, CA	(21.4)	NA	Des Moines, IA**	NA
240	Lake Forest, CA	(10.9)	306	West Jordan, UT	(21.6)	NA	Durham, NC**	NA
240	Pasadena, CA	(10.9)	307	Atlanta, GA	(22.4)	NA	El Paso, TX**	NA
242	Alhambra, CA	(11.0)	308	Denton, TX	(22.5)	NA	Fort Wayne, IN**	NA
243	Ogden, UT	(11.1)	309	Aurora, IL	(22.6)	NA	Greece, NY**	NA
244	Phoenix, AZ	(11.3)	310	Tyler, TX	(22.8)	NA	Kansas City, KS**	NA
245	Lawrence, KS	(11.4)	310	Vancouver, WA	(22.8)	NA	Kansas City, MO**	NA
246	Danbury, CT	(11.5)	312	Clearwater, FL	(23.1)	NA	Las Cruces, NM**	NA
246	Orlando, FL	(11.5)	313	Tempe, AZ	(23.3)	NA	Lexington, KY**	NA
246	Virginia Beach, VA	(11.5)	314	Columbia, SC	(23.4)	NA	Louisville, KY**	NA
249	Sterling Heights, MI	(11.6)	315	Alexandria, VA	(23.8)	NA	Miami Gardens, FL**	NA
250	Bellflower, CA	(11.8)	315	Woodbridge Twnshp, NJ	(23.8)	NA	Nashua, NH**	NA
251	Edmond, OK	(12.0)	317	Reading, PA	(24.4)	NA	New Bedford, MA**	NA
252	Oceanside, CA	(12.1)	318	Gresham, OR	(24.9)	NA	Newton, MA**	NA
253	Yonkers, NY	(12.3)	319	Ann Arbor, MI	(25.0)	NA	Roanoke, VA**	NA
254	Newark, NJ	(12.5)	320	Fontana, CA	(25.3)	NA	Rockford, IL**	NA
254	San Bernardino, CA	(12.5)	320	Jersey City, NJ	(25.3)	NA	Santa Maria, CA**	NA
256	Peoria, IL	(12.6)	322	Rancho Cucamon., CA	(25.5)	NA	Spokane Valley, WA**	NA
257	Clifton, NJ	(13.1)	323	Laredo, TX	(25.6)	NA	Westminster, CO**	NA
258	Chesapeake, VA	(13.2)	324	Pasadena, TX	(26.2)	NA	Worcester, MA**	NA

Source: CQ Press using data from F.B.I. "Crime in the United States 2006"

**Burglary is the unlawful entry of a structure to commit a felony or theft. Attempts are included.*

***Not available.*

73. Larcenies and Thefts in 2006

National Total = 6,607,013 Larcenies and Thefts*

RANK	CITY	THEFTS
189	Abilene, TX	3,460
204	Albany, GA	3,235
185	Albany, NY	3,521
27	Albuquerque, NM	19,890
253	Alexandria, VA	2,439
341	Alhambra, CA	1,572
156	Allentown, PA	4,131
88	Amarillo, TX	7,617
342	Amherst, NY	1,571
123	Anaheim, CA	5,277
78	Anchorage, AK	8,543
291	Ann Arbor, MI	2,119
371	Antioch, CA	1,124
40	Arlington, TX	13,905
268	Arvada, CO	2,303
155	Athens-Clarke, GA	4,154
28	Atlanta, GA	18,952
81	Aurora, CO	8,292
171	Aurora, IL	3,734
10	Austin, TX	31,562
66	Bakersfield, CA	9,623
386	Baldwin Park, CA	882
29	Baltimore, MD	18,451
67	Baton Rouge, LA	9,209
145	Beaumont, TX	4,525
335	Beaverton, OR	1,634
207	Bellevue, WA	3,178
378	Bellflower, CA	1,060
153	Bellingham, WA	4,267
127	Berkeley, CA	5,096
186	Billings, MT	3,518
51	Birmingham, AL	12,113
260	Bloomington, MN	2,398
275	Boca Raton, FL	2,232
130	Boise, ID	5,074
32	Boston, MA	16,897
262	Boulder, CO	2,372
375	Brick Twnshp, NJ	1,100
149	Bridgeport, CT	4,400
283	Brockton, MA	2,163
373	Broken Arrow, OK	1,118
104	Brownsville, TX	6,483
376	Buena Park, CA	1,091
72	Buffalo, NY	8,864
327	Burbank, CA	1,683
261	Cambridge, MA	2,376
255	Camden, NJ	2,430
363	Canton Twnshp, MI	1,258
165	Canton, OH	3,871
212	Cape Coral, FL	3,115
330	Carlsbad, CA	1,648
248	Carrollton, TX	2,489
349	Carson, CA	1,502
348	Cary, NC	1,520
146	Cedar Rapids, IA	4,460
372	Centennial, CO	1,122
107	Chandler, AZ	6,152
214	Charleston, SC	3,108
14	Charlotte, NC	28,154
71	Chattanooga, TN	8,876
313	Cheektowaga, NY	1,867
129	Chesapeake, VA	5,082
2	Chicago, IL	83,737
389	Chino Hills, CA	776
356	Chino, CA	1,426
167	Chula Vista, CA	3,817
42	Cincinnati, OH	13,523
353	Clarkstown, NY	1,436
240	Clarksville, TN	2,611
184	Clearwater, FL	3,527
52	Cleveland, OH	12,036
362	Clifton, NJ	1,259
336	Clinton Twnshp, MI	1,623
287	Clovis, CA	2,139
249	Colonie, NY	2,472
46	Colorado Springs, CO	12,940
266	Columbia, MO	2,335
128	Columbia, SC	5,086
68	Columbus, GA	9,202
11	Columbus, OH	30,882
384	Compton, CA	931
202	Concord, CA	3,258
278	Coral Springs, FL	2,209
246	Corona, CA	2,492
33	Corpus Christi, TX	15,261
250	Costa Mesa, CA	2,449
359	Cranston, RI	1,309
6	Dallas, TX	50,009
339	Daly City, CA	1,587
368	Danbury, CT	1,191
295	Davie, FL	2,102
108	Dayton, OH	6,037
203	Dearborn, MI	3,242
317	Deerfield Beach, FL	1,835
269	Denton, TX	2,295
43	Denver, CO	13,376
59	Des Moines, IA	10,331
25	Detroit, MI	21,287
311	Downey, CA	1,897
206	Duluth, MN	3,214
88	Durham, NC	7,617
326	Edison Twnshp, NJ	1,684
350	Edmond, OK	1,499
306	El Cajon, CA	1,954
354	El Monte, CA	1,435
36	El Paso, TX	14,845
225	Elizabeth, NJ	2,860
293	Erie, PA	2,106
233	Escondido, CA	2,687
119	Eugene, OR	5,386
162	Evansville, IN	3,933
116	Everett, WA	5,468
221	Fairfield, CA	2,912
309	Fargo, ND	1,930
378	Farmington Hills, MI	1,060
77	Fayetteville, NC	8,549
205	Federal Way, WA	3,230
183	Flint, MI	3,538
357	Fontana, CA	1,375
180	Fort Collins, CO	3,585
98	Fort Lauderdale, FL	6,678
160	Fort Smith, AR	4,039
84	Fort Wayne, IN	7,934
18	Fort Worth, TX	24,128
213	Fremont, CA	3,113
39	Fresno, CA	14,097
219	Fullerton, CA	2,962
164	Gainesville, FL	3,877
236	Garden Grove, CA	2,665
122	Garland, TX	5,278
235	Gary, IN	2,680
187	Gilbert, AZ	3,516
113	Glendale, AZ	5,625
234	Glendale, CA	2,685
137	Grand Prairie, TX	4,844
96	Grand Rapids, MI	6,922
306	Greece, NY	1,954
208	Greeley, CO	3,163
304	Green Bay, WI	1,986
70	Greensboro, NC	9,000
244	Gresham, OR	2,525
364	Hamilton Twnshp, NJ	1,246
232	Hammond, IN	2,694
177	Hampton, VA	3,594
109	Hartford, CT	5,957
383	Hawthorne, CA	961
265	Hayward, CA	2,343
176	Henderson, NV	3,614
385	Hesperia, CA	930
117	Hialeah, FL	5,416
192	High Point, NC	3,449
279	Hillsboro, OR	2,204
157	Hollywood, FL	4,113
16	Honolulu, HI	26,540
3	Houston, TX	73,091
216	Huntington Beach, CA	3,044
87	Huntsville, AL	7,643
114	Independence, MO	5,538
13	Indianapolis, IN	28,929
367	Inglewood, CA	1,194
286	Irvine, CA	2,147
97	Irving, TX	6,728
12	Jacksonville, FL	29,167
91	Jackson, MS	7,534
147	Jersey City, NJ	4,425
217	Joliet, IL	3,016
112	Kansas City, KS	5,691
30	Kansas City, MO	18,186
296	Kenosha, WI	2,084
188	Kent, WA	3,466
214	Killeen, TX	3,108
86	Knoxville, TN	7,684
144	Lafayette, LA	4,566
388	Lake Forest, CA	793
175	Lakeland, FL	3,666
355	Lakewood, CA	1,427
139	Lakewood, CO	4,710
252	Lancaster, CA	2,440
220	Lansing, MI	2,928
64	Laredo, TX	9,661
299	Largo, FL	2,016
224	Las Cruces, NM	2,864
15	Las Vegas, NV	26,815
158	Lawrence, KS	4,106
223	Lawton, OK	2,886
316	Lee's Summit, MO	1,856
285	Lewisville, TX	2,150
90	Lexington, KY	7,550
62	Lincoln, NE	9,884
57	Little Rock, AR	10,611
377	Livermore, CA	1,083
332	Livonia, MI	1,639

RANK	CITY	THEFTS	RANK	CITY	THEFTS	RANK	CITY	THEFTS
103	Long Beach, CA	6,598	174	Peoria, AZ	3,672	273	Spokane Valley, WA	2,268
197	Longview, TX	3,318	150	Peoria, IL	4,395	94	Spokane, WA	7,340
4	Los Angeles, CA	59,711	8	Philadelphia, PA	39,413	120	Springfield, IL	5,373
31	Louisville, KY	17,855	7	Phoenix, AZ	49,811	132	Springfield, MA	4,963
297	Lowell, MA	2,073	65	Pittsburgh, PA	9,658	58	Springfield, MO	10,358
75	Lubbock, TX	8,610	101	Plano, TX	6,642	230	Sterling Heights, MI	2,716
352	Lynn, MA	1,439	231	Plantation, FL	2,708	50	Stockton, CA	12,202
110	Macon, GA	5,891	228	Pomona, CA	2,781	22	St. Louis, MO	23,596
118	Madison, WI	5,404	193	Pompano Beach, FL	3,398	102	St. Paul, MN	6,616
256	Manchester, NH	2,423	263	Port St. Lucie, FL	2,355	61	St. Petersburg, FL	10,182
111	McAllen, TX	5,820	24	Portland, OR	22,033	308	Suffolk, VA	1,943
337	McKinney, TX	1,616	179	Portsmouth, VA	3,591	358	Sugar Land, TX	1,322
226	Melbourne, FL	2,840	126	Providence, RI	5,106	324	Sunnyvale, CA	1,699
9	Memphis, TN	33,736	289	Provo, UT	2,121	250	Sunrise, FL	2,449
38	Mesa, AZ	14,367	148	Pueblo, CO	4,409	338	Surprise, AZ	1,610
170	Mesquite, TX	3,743	380	Quincy, MA	1,058	161	Syracuse, NY	4,037
121	Miami Beach, FL	5,357	211	Racine, WI	3,116	63	Tacoma, WA	9,663
154	Miami Gardens, FL	4,181	74	Raleigh, NC	8,666	134	Tallahassee, FL	4,935
53	Miami, FL	11,967	243	Rancho Cucamon., CA	2,550	54	Tampa, FL	11,251
238	Midland, TX	2,619	270	Reading, PA	2,288	319	Temecula, CA	1,789
17	Milwaukee, WI	24,343	282	Redding, CA	2,174	80	Tempe, AZ	8,374
45	Minneapolis, MN	13,110	95	Reno, NV	7,061	196	Thornton, CO	3,339
303	Miramar, FL	1,988	370	Rialto, CA	1,141	361	Thousand Oaks, CA	1,296
382	Mission Viejo, CA	1,016	289	Richardson, TX	2,121	44	Toledo, OH	13,239
56	Mobile, AL	10,857	277	Richmond, CA	2,211	346	Toms River Twnshp, NJ	1,548
83	Modesto, CA	8,018	106	Richmond, VA	6,351	100	Topeka, KS	6,645
76	Montgomery, AL	8,579	93	Riverside, CA	7,471	301	Torrance, CA	1,998
200	Moreno Valley, CA	3,272	163	Roanoke, VA	3,887	298	Tracy, CA	2,018
209	Murfreesboro, TN	3,144	312	Rochester, MN	1,892	365	Trenton, NJ	1,211
369	Murrieta, CA	1,187	85	Rochester, NY	7,913	344	Troy, MI	1,550
343	Napa, CA	1,563	92	Rockford, IL	7,476	NA	Tucson, AZ**	NA
305	Naperville, IL	1,972	229	Roseville, CA	2,722	37	Tulsa, OK	14,523
318	Nashua, NH	1,801	340	Roswell, GA	1,586	173	Tuscaloosa, AL	3,709
23	Nashville, TN	23,234	331	Round Rock, TX	1,642	199	Tyler, TX	3,280
314	New Bedford, MA	1,866	47	Sacramento, CA	12,762	334	Upper Darby Twnshp, PA	1,635
124	New Orleans, LA	5,228	105	Salem, OR	6,363	323	Vacaville, CA	1,733
1	New York, NY	115,363	172	Salinas, CA	3,718	198	Vallejo, CA	3,300
151	Newark, NJ	4,377	55	Salt Lake City, UT	11,136	142	Vancouver, WA	4,584
328	Newport Beach, CA	1,682	195	San Angelo, TX	3,359	241	Ventura, CA	2,604
125	Newport News, VA	5,160	5	San Antonio, TX	57,377	276	Victorville, CA	2,218
387	Newton, MA	829	140	San Bernardino, CA	4,708	60	Virginia Beach, VA	10,212
69	Norfolk, VA	9,032	19	San Diego, CA	24,125	167	Visalia, CA	3,817
257	Norman, OK	2,415	20	San Francisco, CA	23,891	347	Vista, CA	1,522
131	North Charleston, SC	5,040	48	San Jose, CA	12,678	136	Waco, TX	4,869
190	North Las Vegas, NV	3,456	281	San Leandro, CA	2,176	270	Warren, MI	2,288
360	Norwalk, CA	1,301	310	San Mateo, CA	1,920	332	Warwick, RI	1,639
73	Oakland, CA	8,725	258	Sandy, UT	2,404	35	Washington, DC	15,132
201	Oceanside, CA	3,261	133	Santa Ana, CA	4,956	152	Waterbury, CT	4,374
237	Odessa, TX	2,624	321	Santa Barbara, CA	1,781	253	West Covina, CA	2,439
169	Ogden, UT	3,773	272	Santa Clara, CA	2,283	242	West Jordan, UT	2,560
26	Oklahoma City, OK	20,169	274	Santa Clarita, CA	2,253	138	West Palm Beach, FL	4,775
325	Olathe, KS	1,689	344	Santa Maria, CA	1,550	159	West Valley, UT	4,047
34	Omaha, NE	15,172	280	Santa Monica, CA	2,187	319	Westland, MI	1,789
178	Ontario, CA	3,592	222	Santa Rosa, CA	2,887	329	Westminster, CA	1,664
267	Orange, CA	2,309	99	Savannah, GA	6,665	210	Westminster, CO	3,121
284	Orem, UT	2,152	115	Scottsdale, AZ	5,476	315	Whittier, CA	1,865
49	Orlando, FL	12,320	21	Seattle, WA	23,880	143	Wichita Falls, TX	4,574
182	Overland Park, KS	3,571	79	Shreveport, LA	8,508	41	Wichita, KS	13,786
227	Oxnard, CA	2,816	351	Simi Valley, CA	1,475	166	Wilmington, NC	3,865
322	Palm Bay, FL	1,754	247	Sioux City, IA	2,491	82	Winston-Salem, NC	8,126
264	Palmdale, CA	2,353	239	Sioux Falls, SD	2,616	292	Woodbridge Twnshp, NJ	2,113
381	Parma, OH	1,049	366	Somerville, MA	1,204	191	Worcester, MA	3,452
218	Pasadena, CA	2,998	135	South Bend, IN	4,895	141	Yakima, WA	4,687
194	Pasadena, TX	3,395	374	South Gate, CA	1,102	259	Yonkers, NY	2,400
302	Paterson, NJ	1,994	300	Southfield, MI	2,003	288	Youngstown, OH	2,136
181	Pembroke Pines, FL	3,581	294	Sparks, NV	2,104	245	Yuma, AZ	2,512

Source: Federal Bureau of Investigation "Crime in the United States 2006"

**Larceny and theft is the unlawful taking of property. Attempts are included.*

***Not available.*

73. Larcenies and Thefts in 2006 (continued)

National Total = 6,607,013 Larcenies and Thefts*

RANK	CITY	THEFTS	RANK	CITY	THEFTS	RANK	CITY	THEFTS
1	New York, NY	115,363	65	Pittsburgh, PA	9,658	129	Chesapeake, VA	5,082
2	Chicago, IL	83,737	66	Bakersfield, CA	9,623	130	Boise, ID	5,074
3	Houston, TX	73,091	67	Baton Rouge, LA	9,209	131	North Charleston, SC	5,040
4	Los Angeles, CA	59,711	68	Columbus, GA	9,202	132	Springfield, MA	4,963
5	San Antonio, TX	57,377	69	Norfolk, VA	9,032	133	Santa Ana, CA	4,956
6	Dallas, TX	50,009	70	Greensboro, NC	9,000	134	Tallahassee, FL	4,935
7	Phoenix, AZ	49,811	71	Chattanooga, TN	8,876	135	South Bend, IN	4,895
8	Philadelphia, PA	39,413	72	Buffalo, NY	8,864	136	Waco, TX	4,869
9	Memphis, TN	33,736	73	Oakland, CA	8,725	137	Grand Prairie, TX	4,844
10	Austin, TX	31,562	74	Raleigh, NC	8,666	138	West Palm Beach, FL	4,775
11	Columbus, OH	30,882	75	Lubbock, TX	8,610	139	Lakewood, CO	4,710
12	Jacksonville, FL	29,167	76	Montgomery, AL	8,579	140	San Bernardino, CA	4,708
13	Indianapolis, IN	28,929	77	Fayetteville, NC	8,549	141	Yakima, WA	4,687
14	Charlotte, NC	28,154	78	Anchorage, AK	8,543	142	Vancouver, WA	4,584
15	Las Vegas, NV	26,815	79	Shreveport, LA	8,508	143	Wichita Falls, TX	4,574
16	Honolulu, HI	26,540	80	Tempe, AZ	8,374	144	Lafayette, LA	4,566
17	Milwaukee, WI	24,343	81	Aurora, CO	8,292	145	Beaumont, TX	4,525
18	Fort Worth, TX	24,128	82	Winston-Salem, NC	8,126	146	Cedar Rapids, IA	4,460
19	San Diego, CA	24,125	83	Modesto, CA	8,018	147	Jersey City, NJ	4,425
20	San Francisco, CA	23,891	84	Fort Wayne, IN	7,934	148	Pueblo, CO	4,409
21	Seattle, WA	23,880	85	Rochester, NY	7,913	149	Bridgeport, CT	4,400
22	St. Louis, MO	23,596	86	Knoxville, TN	7,684	150	Peoria, IL	4,395
23	Nashville, TN	23,234	87	Huntsville, AL	7,643	151	Newark, NJ	4,377
24	Portland, OR	22,033	88	Amarillo, TX	7,617	152	Waterbury, CT	4,374
25	Detroit, MI	21,287	88	Durham, NC	7,617	153	Bellingham, WA	4,267
26	Oklahoma City, OK	20,169	90	Lexington, KY	7,550	154	Miami Gardens, FL	4,181
27	Albuquerque, NM	19,890	91	Jackson, MS	7,534	155	Athens-Clarke, GA	4,154
28	Atlanta, GA	18,952	92	Rockford, IL	7,476	156	Allentown, PA	4,131
29	Baltimore, MD	18,451	93	Riverside, CA	7,471	157	Hollywood, FL	4,113
30	Kansas City, MO	18,186	94	Spokane, WA	7,340	158	Lawrence, KS	4,106
31	Louisville, KY	17,855	95	Reno, NV	7,061	159	West Valley, UT	4,047
32	Boston, MA	16,897	96	Grand Rapids, MI	6,922	160	Fort Smith, AR	4,039
33	Corpus Christi, TX	15,261	97	Irving, TX	6,728	161	Syracuse, NY	4,037
34	Omaha, NE	15,172	98	Fort Lauderdale, FL	6,678	162	Evansville, IN	3,933
35	Washington, DC	15,132	99	Savannah, GA	6,665	163	Roanoke, VA	3,887
36	El Paso, TX	14,845	100	Topeka, KS	6,645	164	Gainesville, FL	3,877
37	Tulsa, OK	14,523	101	Plano, TX	6,642	165	Canton, OH	3,871
38	Mesa, AZ	14,367	102	St. Paul, MN	6,616	166	Wilmington, NC	3,865
39	Fresno, CA	14,097	103	Long Beach, CA	6,598	167	Chula Vista, CA	3,817
40	Arlington, TX	13,905	104	Brownsville, TX	6,483	167	Visalia, CA	3,817
41	Wichita, KS	13,786	105	Salem, OR	6,363	169	Ogden, UT	3,773
42	Cincinnati, OH	13,523	106	Richmond, VA	6,351	170	Mesquite, TX	3,743
43	Denver, CO	13,376	107	Chandler, AZ	6,152	171	Aurora, IL	3,734
44	Toledo, OH	13,239	108	Dayton, OH	6,037	172	Salinas, CA	3,718
45	Minneapolis, MN	13,110	109	Hartford, CT	5,957	173	Tuscaloosa, AL	3,709
46	Colorado Springs, CO	12,940	110	Macon, GA	5,891	174	Peoria, AZ	3,672
47	Sacramento, CA	12,762	111	McAllen, TX	5,820	175	Lakeland, FL	3,666
48	San Jose, CA	12,678	112	Kansas City, KS	5,691	176	Henderson, NV	3,614
49	Orlando, FL	12,320	113	Glendale, AZ	5,625	177	Hampton, VA	3,594
50	Stockton, CA	12,202	114	Independence, MO	5,538	178	Ontario, CA	3,592
51	Birmingham, AL	12,113	115	Scottsdale, AZ	5,476	179	Portsmouth, VA	3,591
52	Cleveland, OH	12,036	116	Everett, WA	5,468	180	Fort Collins, CO	3,585
53	Miami, FL	11,967	117	Hialeah, FL	5,416	181	Pembroke Pines, FL	3,581
54	Tampa, FL	11,251	118	Madison, WI	5,404	182	Overland Park, KS	3,571
55	Salt Lake City, UT	11,136	119	Eugene, OR	5,386	183	Flint, MI	3,538
56	Mobile, AL	10,857	120	Springfield, IL	5,373	184	Clearwater, FL	3,527
57	Little Rock, AR	10,611	121	Miami Beach, FL	5,357	185	Albany, NY	3,521
58	Springfield, MO	10,358	122	Garland, TX	5,278	186	Billings, MT	3,518
59	Des Moines, IA	10,331	123	Anaheim, CA	5,277	187	Gilbert, AZ	3,516
60	Virginia Beach, VA	10,212	124	New Orleans, LA	5,228	188	Kent, WA	3,466
61	St. Petersburg, FL	10,182	125	Newport News, VA	5,160	189	Abilene, TX	3,460
62	Lincoln, NE	9,884	126	Providence, RI	5,106	190	North Las Vegas, NV	3,456
63	Tacoma, WA	9,663	127	Berkeley, CA	5,096	191	Worcester, MA	3,452
64	Laredo, TX	9,661	128	Columbia, SC	5,086	192	High Point, NC	3,449

RANK	CITY	THEFTS
193	Pompano Beach, FL	3,398
194	Pasadena, TX	3,395
195	San Angelo, TX	3,359
196	Thornton, CO	3,339
197	Longview, TX	3,318
198	Vallejo, CA	3,300
199	Tyler, TX	3,280
200	Moreno Valley, CA	3,272
201	Oceanside, CA	3,261
202	Concord, CA	3,258
203	Dearborn, MI	3,242
204	Albany, GA	3,235
205	Federal Way, WA	3,230
206	Duluth, MN	3,214
207	Bellevue, WA	3,178
208	Greeley, CO	3,163
209	Murfreesboro, TN	3,144
210	Westminster, CO	3,121
211	Racine, WI	3,116
212	Cape Coral, FL	3,115
213	Fremont, CA	3,113
214	Charleston, SC	3,108
214	Killeen, TX	3,108
216	Huntington Beach, CA	3,044
217	Joliet, IL	3,016
218	Pasadena, CA	2,998
219	Fullerton, CA	2,962
220	Lansing, MI	2,928
221	Fairfield, CA	2,912
222	Santa Rosa, CA	2,887
223	Lawton, OK	2,886
224	Las Cruces, NM	2,864
225	Elizabeth, NJ	2,860
226	Melbourne, FL	2,840
227	Oxnard, CA	2,816
228	Pomona, CA	2,781
229	Roseville, CA	2,722
230	Sterling Heights, MI	2,716
231	Plantation, FL	2,708
232	Hammond, IN	2,694
233	Escondido, CA	2,687
234	Glendale, CA	2,685
235	Gary, IN	2,680
236	Garden Grove, CA	2,665
237	Odessa, TX	2,624
238	Midland, TX	2,619
239	Sioux Falls, SD	2,616
240	Clarksville, TN	2,611
241	Ventura, CA	2,604
242	West Jordan, UT	2,560
243	Rancho Cucamon., CA	2,550
244	Gresham, OR	2,525
245	Yuma, AZ	2,512
246	Corona, CA	2,492
247	Sioux City, IA	2,491
248	Carrollton, TX	2,489
249	Colonie, NY	2,472
250	Costa Mesa, CA	2,449
250	Sunrise, FL	2,449
252	Lancaster, CA	2,440
253	Alexandria, VA	2,439
253	West Covina, CA	2,439
255	Camden, NJ	2,430
256	Manchester, NH	2,423
257	Norman, OK	2,415
258	Sandy, UT	2,404

RANK	CITY	THEFTS
259	Yonkers, NY	2,400
260	Bloomington, MN	2,398
261	Cambridge, MA	2,376
262	Boulder, CO	2,372
263	Port St. Lucie, FL	2,355
264	Palmdale, CA	2,353
265	Hayward, CA	2,343
266	Columbia, MO	2,335
267	Orange, CA	2,309
268	Arvada, CO	2,303
269	Denton, TX	2,295
270	Reading, PA	2,288
270	Warren, MI	2,288
272	Santa Clara, CA	2,283
273	Spokane Valley, WA	2,268
274	Santa Clarita, CA	2,253
275	Boca Raton, FL	2,232
276	Victorville, CA	2,218
277	Richmond, CA	2,211
278	Coral Springs, FL	2,209
279	Hillsboro, OR	2,204
280	Santa Monica, CA	2,187
281	San Leandro, CA	2,176
282	Redding, CA	2,174
283	Brockton, MA	2,163
284	Orem, UT	2,152
285	Lewisville, TX	2,150
286	Irvine, CA	2,147
287	Clovis, CA	2,139
288	Youngstown, OH	2,136
289	Provo, UT	2,121
289	Richardson, TX	2,121
291	Ann Arbor, MI	2,119
292	Woodbridge Twnshp, NJ	2,113
293	Erie, PA	2,106
294	Sparks, NV	2,104
295	Davie, FL	2,102
296	Kenosha, WI	2,084
297	Lowell, MA	2,073
298	Tracy, CA	2,018
299	Largo, FL	2,016
300	Southfield, MI	2,003
301	Torrance, CA	1,998
302	Paterson, NJ	1,994
303	Miramar, FL	1,988
304	Green Bay, WI	1,986
305	Naperville, IL	1,972
306	El Cajon, CA	1,954
306	Greece, NY	1,954
308	Suffolk, VA	1,943
309	Fargo, ND	1,930
310	San Mateo, CA	1,920
311	Downey, CA	1,897
312	Rochester, MN	1,892
313	Cheektowaga, NY	1,867
314	New Bedford, MA	1,866
315	Whittier, CA	1,865
316	Lee's Summit, MO	1,856
317	Deerfield Beach, FL	1,835
318	Nashua, NH	1,801
319	Temecula, CA	1,789
319	Westland, MI	1,789
321	Santa Barbara, CA	1,781
322	Palm Bay, FL	1,754
323	Vacaville, CA	1,733
324	Sunnyvale, CA	1,699

RANK	CITY	THEFTS
325	Olathe, KS	1,689
326	Edison Twnshp, NJ	1,684
327	Burbank, CA	1,683
328	Newport Beach, CA	1,682
329	Westminster, CA	1,664
330	Carlsbad, CA	1,648
331	Round Rock, TX	1,642
332	Livonia, MI	1,639
332	Warwick, RI	1,639
334	Upper Darby Twnshp, PA	1,635
335	Beaverton, OR	1,634
336	Clinton Twnshp, MI	1,623
337	McKinney, TX	1,616
338	Surprise, AZ	1,610
339	Daly City, CA	1,587
340	Roswell, GA	1,586
341	Alhambra, CA	1,572
342	Amherst, NY	1,571
343	Napa, CA	1,563
344	Santa Maria, CA	1,550
344	Troy, MI	1,550
346	Toms River Twnshp, NJ	1,548
347	Vista, CA	1,522
348	Cary, NC	1,520
349	Carson, CA	1,502
350	Edmond, OK	1,499
351	Simi Valley, CA	1,475
352	Lynn, MA	1,439
353	Clarkstown, NY	1,436
354	El Monte, CA	1,435
355	Lakewood, CA	1,427
356	Chino, CA	1,426
357	Fontana, CA	1,375
358	Sugar Land, TX	1,322
359	Cranston, RI	1,309
360	Norwalk, CA	1,301
361	Thousand Oaks, CA	1,296
362	Clifton, NJ	1,259
363	Canton Twnshp, MI	1,258
364	Hamilton Twnshp, NJ	1,246
365	Trenton, NJ	1,211
366	Somerville, MA	1,204
367	Inglewood, CA	1,194
368	Danbury, CT	1,191
369	Murrieta, CA	1,187
370	Rialto, CA	1,141
371	Antioch, CA	1,124
372	Centennial, CO	1,122
373	Broken Arrow, OK	1,118
374	South Gate, CA	1,102
375	Brick Twnshp, NJ	1,100
376	Buena Park, CA	1,091
377	Livermore, CA	1,083
378	Bellflower, CA	1,060
378	Farmington Hills, MI	1,060
380	Quincy, MA	1,058
381	Parma, OH	1,049
382	Mission Viejo, CA	1,016
383	Hawthorne, CA	961
384	Compton, CA	931
385	Hesperia, CA	930
386	Baldwin Park, CA	882
387	Newton, MA	829
388	Lake Forest, CA	793
389	Chino Hills, CA	776
NA	Tucson, AZ**	NA

Source: Federal Bureau of Investigation "Crime in the United States 2006"

**Larceny and theft is the unlawful taking of property. Attempts are included.*

***Not available.*

74. Larceny and Theft Rate in 2006

National Rate = 2,206.8 Larcenies and Thefts per 100,000 Population*

RANK	CITY	RATE
156	Abilene, TX	2,932.0
57	Albany, GA	4,157.3
95	Albany, NY	3,754.8
73	Albuquerque, NM	3,970.4
309	Alexandria, VA	1,784.4
310	Alhambra, CA	1,782.4
83	Allentown, PA	3,857.6
68	Amarillo, TX	4,047.1
353	Amherst, NY	1,399.1
333	Anaheim, CA	1,576.2
145	Anchorage, AK	3,076.4
289	Ann Arbor, MI	1,875.4
380	Antioch, CA	1,107.0
97	Arlington, TX	3,727.0
251	Arvada, CO	2,174.0
81	Athens-Clarke, GA	3,893.2
80	Atlanta, GA	3,901.2
178	Aurora, CO	2,737.9
244	Aurora, IL	2,208.4
39	Austin, TX	4,446.5
133	Bakersfield, CA	3,227.1
379	Baldwin Park, CA	1,108.4
161	Baltimore, MD	2,894.0
42	Baton Rouge, LA	4,375.1
75	Beaumont, TX	3,935.9
290	Beaverton, OR	1,874.3
183	Bellevue, WA	2,667.2
350	Bellflower, CA	1,408.8
12	Bellingham, WA	5,627.2
18	Berkeley, CA	5,013.2
112	Billings, MT	3,529.8
17	Birmingham, AL	5,185.9
155	Bloomington, MN	2,934.9
202	Boca Raton, FL	2,533.7
196	Boise, ID	2,559.9
151	Boston, MA	3,004.5
201	Boulder, CO	2,539.1
351	Brick Twnshp, NJ	1,406.4
139	Bridgeport, CT	3,170.2
238	Brockton, MA	2,272.1
367	Broken Arrow, OK	1,285.2
91	Brownsville, TX	3,764.0
360	Buena Park, CA	1,365.7
140	Buffalo, NY	3,160.1
329	Burbank, CA	1,602.2
224	Cambridge, MA	2,358.6
148	Camden, NJ	3,034.8
345	Canton Twnshp, MI	1,465.1
23	Canton, OH	4,864.6
248	Cape Coral, FL	2,187.9
305	Carlsbad, CA	1,799.3
275	Carrollton, TX	2,036.2
332	Carson, CA	1,584.4
352	Cary, NC	1,400.1
106	Cedar Rapids, IA	3,603.4
377	Centennial, CO	1,120.9
204	Chandler, AZ	2,522.1
162	Charleston, SC	2,867.9
69	Charlotte, NC	4,025.5
11	Chattanooga, TN	5,663.2
233	Cheektowaga, NY	2,305.1
234	Chesapeake, VA	2,298.0
157	Chicago, IL	2,930.1
386	Chino Hills, CA	1,015.7
300	Chino, CA	1,821.7
306	Chula Vista, CA	1,797.1
43	Cincinnati, OH	4,374.9
299	Clarkstown, NY	1,826.0
237	Clarksville, TN	2,284.1
137	Clearwater, FL	3,191.3
186	Cleveland, OH	2,658.4
334	Clifton, NJ	1,574.1
319	Clinton Twnshp, MI	1,680.4
212	Clovis, CA	2,450.0
136	Colonie, NY	3,195.6
121	Colorado Springs, CO	3,434.1
203	Columbia, MO	2,524.7
46	Columbia, SC	4,277.2
28	Columbus, GA	4,812.2
50	Columbus, OH	4,221.5
388	Compton, CA	964.6
187	Concord, CA	2,619.8
318	Coral Springs, FL	1,686.6
324	Corona, CA	1,653.3
16	Corpus Christi, TX	5,235.2
243	Costa Mesa, CA	2,209.9
327	Cranston, RI	1,616.8
71	Dallas, TX	4,006.4
335	Daly City, CA	1,567.5
341	Danbury, CT	1,515.0
211	Davie, FL	2,454.9
89	Dayton, OH	3,795.3
120	Dearborn, MI	3,454.2
223	Deerfield Beach, FL	2,363.6
255	Denton, TX	2,142.8
226	Denver, CO	2,353.0
15	Des Moines, IA	5,292.7
219	Detroit, MI	2,406.8
314	Downey, CA	1,713.5
93	Duluth, MN	3,760.7
102	Durham, NC	3,645.7
321	Edison Twnshp, NJ	1,674.4
279	Edmond, OK	1,984.3
260	El Cajon, CA	2,093.9
374	El Monte, CA	1,160.9
217	El Paso, TX	2,411.7
239	Elizabeth, NJ	2,271.6
273	Erie, PA	2,050.6
278	Escondido, CA	1,986.1
99	Eugene, OR	3,666.8
126	Evansville, IN	3,370.6
13	Everett, WA	5,564.6
174	Fairfield, CA	2,762.4
257	Fargo, ND	2,125.1
364	Farmington Hills, MI	1,324.6
3	Fayetteville, NC	6,451.1
87	Federal Way, WA	3,821.8
152	Flint, MI	2,991.8
389	Fontana, CA	831.6
176	Fort Collins, CO	2,748.3
77	Fort Lauderdale, FL	3,923.6
26	Fort Smith, AR	4,841.6
113	Fort Wayne, IN	3,529.0
94	Fort Worth, TX	3,759.7
339	Fremont, CA	1,539.0
149	Fresno, CA	3,029.9
242	Fullerton, CA	2,210.7
115	Gainesville, FL	3,524.3
331	Garden Grove, CA	1,590.4
222	Garland, TX	2,372.4
181	Gary, IN	2,697.0
283	Gilbert, AZ	1,946.4
240	Glendale, AZ	2,262.8
361	Glendale, CA	1,330.1
130	Grand Prairie, TX	3,263.6
107	Grand Rapids, MI	3,581.0
265	Greece, NY	2,073.6
111	Greeley, CO	3,543.9
281	Green Bay, WI	1,955.2
88	Greensboro, NC	3,804.0
191	Gresham, OR	2,585.8
356	Hamilton Twnshp, NJ	1,383.5
125	Hammond, IN	3,378.4
213	Hampton, VA	2,444.4
29	Hartford, CT	4,796.2
378	Hawthorne, CA	1,111.4
323	Hayward, CA	1,655.2
342	Henderson, NV	1,506.4
372	Hesperia, CA	1,181.9
216	Hialeah, FL	2,415.7
109	High Point, NC	3,556.3
195	Hillsboro, OR	2,565.2
172	Hollywood, FL	2,777.5
160	Honolulu, HI	2,907.9
114	Houston, TX	3,524.6
337	Huntington Beach, CA	1,551.4
34	Huntsville, AL	4,554.4
20	Independence, MO	4,988.6
105	Indianapolis, IN	3,611.8
383	Inglewood, CA	1,033.8
375	Irvine, CA	1,138.8
124	Irving, TX	3,378.6
101	Jacksonville, FL	3,665.0
48	Jackson, MS	4,248.5
296	Jersey City, NJ	1,845.3
245	Joliet, IL	2,202.4
78	Kansas City, KS	3,918.6
67	Kansas City, MO	4,057.4
250	Kenosha, WI	2,180.2
56	Kent, WA	4,165.6
150	Killeen, TX	3,015.3
52	Knoxville, TN	4,212.2
45	Lafayette, LA	4,299.9
385	Lake Forest, CA	1,028.5
64	Lakeland, FL	4,063.9
312	Lakewood, CA	1,757.6
128	Lakewood, CO	3,286.1
304	Lancaster, CA	1,804.2
200	Lansing, MI	2,541.0
37	Laredo, TX	4,500.4
184	Largo, FL	2,662.1
122	Las Cruces, NM	3,417.9
274	Las Vegas, NV	2,038.2
21	Lawrence, KS	4,983.4
138	Lawton, OK	3,170.3
236	Lee's Summit, MO	2,293.5
231	Lewisville, TX	2,314.1
170	Lexington, KY	2,794.4
62	Lincoln, NE	4,109.6
8	Little Rock, AR	5,684.4
359	Livermore, CA	1,368.9
320	Livonia, MI	1,677.0

RANK	CITY	RATE
357	Long Beach, CA	1,379.5
47	Longview, TX	4,267.4
338	Los Angeles, CA	1,539.2
165	Louisville, KY	2,852.2
276	Lowell, MA	1,998.5
72	Lubbock, TX	3,992.0
328	Lynn, MA	1,611.0
5	Macon, GA	6,051.7
215	Madison, WI	2,430.2
246	Manchester, NH	2,200.6
33	McAllen, TX	4,578.2
326	McKinney, TX	1,627.1
103	Melbourne, FL	3,643.9
22	Memphis, TN	4,955.1
141	Mesa, AZ	3,125.3
169	Mesquite, TX	2,802.0
6	Miami Beach, FL	5,991.6
60	Miami Gardens, FL	4,134.9
147	Miami, FL	3,045.5
194	Midland, TX	2,566.7
54	Milwaukee, WI	4,189.8
116	Minneapolis, MN	3,493.2
298	Miramar, FL	1,833.6
382	Mission Viejo, CA	1,060.1
44	Mobile, AL	4,340.2
86	Modesto, CA	3,838.7
49	Montgomery, AL	4,248.4
302	Moreno Valley, CA	1,818.1
108	Murfreesboro, TN	3,576.9
348	Murrieta, CA	1,421.2
266	Napa, CA	2,071.4
355	Naperville, IL	1,385.4
271	Nashua, NH	2,054.7
59	Nashville, TN	4,142.9
277	New Bedford, MA	1,992.3
371	New Orleans, LA	1,212.6
349	New York, NY	1,412.9
336	Newark, NJ	1,558.3
262	Newport Beach, CA	2,088.1
167	Newport News, VA	2,840.0
387	Newton, MA	990.9
85	Norfolk, VA	3,855.4
225	Norman, OK	2,353.4
7	North Charleston, SC	5,749.8
288	North Las Vegas, NV	1,893.3
370	Norwalk, CA	1,218.3
249	Oakland, CA	2,187.6
284	Oceanside, CA	1,945.7
179	Odessa, TX	2,727.7
30	Ogden, UT	4,666.0
92	Oklahoma City, OK	3,762.8
342	Olathe, KS	1,506.4
104	Omaha, NE	3,640.4
269	Ontario, CA	2,061.6
316	Orange, CA	1,695.7
230	Orem, UT	2,323.0
9	Orlando, FL	5,682.2
252	Overland Park, KS	2,151.5
340	Oxnard, CA	1,519.8
293	Palm Bay, FL	1,858.1
313	Palmdale, CA	1,732.9
366	Parma, OH	1,286.0
267	Pasadena, CA	2,067.2
235	Pasadena, TX	2,295.0
362	Paterson, NJ	1,329.7
228	Pembroke Pines, FL	2,341.8

RANK	CITY	RATE
197	Peoria, AZ	2,559.2
82	Peoria, IL	3,879.4
182	Philadelphia, PA	2,691.1
129	Phoenix, AZ	3,282.6
154	Pittsburgh, PA	2,975.3
192	Plano, TX	2,582.6
144	Plantation, FL	3,097.0
307	Pomona, CA	1,792.2
134	Pompano Beach, FL	3,207.6
311	Port St. Lucie, FL	1,758.6
65	Portland, OR	4,063.8
110	Portsmouth, VA	3,549.6
159	Providence, RI	2,910.2
303	Provo, UT	1,810.4
55	Pueblo, CO	4,181.0
373	Quincy, MA	1,165.3
79	Racine, WI	3,910.5
207	Raleigh, NC	2,487.8
344	Rancho Cucamon., CA	1,492.3
168	Reading, PA	2,827.2
220	Redding, CA	2,403.6
127	Reno, NV	3,356.7
376	Rialto, CA	1,136.4
264	Richardson, TX	2,079.5
254	Richmond, CA	2,144.4
132	Richmond, VA	3,245.1
198	Riverside, CA	2,552.5
58	Roanoke, VA	4,154.8
280	Rochester, MN	1,979.4
96	Rochester, NY	3,738.6
24	Rockford, IL	4,862.8
199	Roseville, CA	2,546.4
308	Roswell, GA	1,788.5
294	Round Rock, TX	1,849.9
173	Sacramento, CA	2,771.0
53	Salem, OR	4,208.6
205	Salinas, CA	2,516.4
4	Salt Lake City, UT	6,055.4
98	San Angelo, TX	3,711.3
40	San Antonio, TX	4,440.5
227	San Bernardino, CA	2,350.0
286	San Diego, CA	1,904.3
135	San Francisco, CA	3,202.2
358	San Jose, CA	1,377.2
175	San Leandro, CA	2,758.6
261	San Mateo, CA	2,089.2
190	Sandy, UT	2,596.5
346	Santa Ana, CA	1,443.1
270	Santa Barbara, CA	2,054.8
253	Santa Clara, CA	2,146.7
363	Santa Clarita, CA	1,327.1
301	Santa Maria, CA	1,821.3
210	Santa Monica, CA	2,468.6
291	Santa Rosa, CA	1,868.2
142	Savannah, GA	3,122.0
229	Scottsdale, AZ	2,333.7
63	Seattle, WA	4,090.6
36	Shreveport, LA	4,513.4
368	Simi Valley, CA	1,231.7
153	Sioux City, IA	2,980.0
292	Sioux Falls, SD	1,860.7
330	Somerville, MA	1,596.5
32	South Bend, IN	4,619.7
381	South Gate, CA	1,104.3
188	Southfield, MI	2,614.0
208	Sparks, NV	2,481.3

RANK	CITY	RATE
177	Spokane Valley, WA	2,739.9
100	Spokane, WA	3,666.3
31	Springfield, IL	4,620.3
131	Springfield, MA	3,251.4
1	Springfield, MO	6,841.6
256	Sterling Heights, MI	2,126.6
51	Stockton, CA	4,214.7
2	St. Louis, MO	6,802.4
221	St. Paul, MN	2,388.5
70	St. Petersburg, FL	4,020.1
214	Suffolk, VA	2,435.4
315	Sugar Land, TX	1,697.0
365	Sunnyvale, CA	1,306.3
185	Sunrise, FL	2,658.6
263	Surprise, AZ	2,084.0
166	Syracuse, NY	2,841.7
25	Tacoma, WA	4,849.3
146	Tallahassee, FL	3,061.9
123	Tampa, FL	3,394.1
268	Temecula, CA	2,066.5
19	Tempe, AZ	5,005.3
143	Thornton, CO	3,115.6
384	Thousand Oaks, CA	1,032.8
41	Toledo, OH	4,388.8
325	Toms River Twnshp, NJ	1,634.1
14	Topeka, KS	5,410.9
354	Torrance, CA	1,390.7
206	Tracy, CA	2,501.1
347	Trenton, NJ	1,429.7
285	Troy, MI	1,914.4
NA	Tucson, AZ**	NA
90	Tulsa, OK	3,764.1
35	Tuscaloosa, AL	4,518.0
118	Tyler, TX	3,469.4
272	Upper Darby Twnshp, PA	2,051.7
295	Vacaville, CA	1,847.1
171	Vallejo, CA	2,783.8
163	Vancouver, WA	2,861.4
209	Ventura, CA	2,481.1
218	Victorville, CA	2,408.6
232	Virginia Beach, VA	2,306.3
117	Visalia, CA	3,481.1
322	Vista, CA	1,668.6
76	Waco, TX	3,930.4
317	Warren, MI	1,695.1
287	Warwick, RI	1,894.0
189	Washington, DC	2,602.1
66	Waterbury, CT	4,060.0
241	West Covina, CA	2,234.4
180	West Jordan, UT	2,711.2
27	West Palm Beach, FL	4,816.3
119	West Valley, UT	3,459.2
259	Westland, MI	2,094.6
297	Westminster, CA	1,842.2
158	Westminster, CO	2,914.9
247	Whittier, CA	2,188.1
38	Wichita Falls, TX	4,454.8
83	Wichita, KS	3,857.6
74	Wilmington, NC	3,968.9
61	Winston-Salem, NC	4,111.9
258	Woodbridge Twnshp, NJ	2,099.2
282	Worcester, MA	1,950.8
10	Yakima, WA	5,673.7
369	Yonkers, NY	1,218.6
193	Youngstown, OH	2,575.4
164	Yuma, AZ	2,857.0

Source: CQ Press using data from F.B.I. "Crime in the United States 2006"

**Larceny and theft is the unlawful taking of property. Attempts are included.*

***Not available.*

74. Larceny and Theft Rate in 2006 (continued)

National Rate = 2,206.8 Larcenies and Thefts per 100,000 Population*

RANK	CITY	RATE	RANK	CITY	RATE	RANK	CITY	RATE
1	Springfield, MO	6,841.6	65	Portland, OR	4,063.8	129	Phoenix, AZ	3,282.6
2	St. Louis, MO	6,802.4	66	Waterbury, CT	4,060.0	130	Grand Prairie, TX	3,263.6
3	Fayetteville, NC	6,451.1	67	Kansas City, MO	4,057.4	131	Springfield, MA	3,251.4
4	Salt Lake City, UT	6,055.4	68	Amarillo, TX	4,047.1	132	Richmond, VA	3,245.1
5	Macon, GA	6,051.7	69	Charlotte, NC	4,025.5	133	Bakersfield, CA	3,227.1
6	Miami Beach, FL	5,991.6	70	St. Petersburg, FL	4,020.1	134	Pompano Beach, FL	3,207.6
7	North Charleston, SC	5,749.8	71	Dallas, TX	4,006.4	135	San Francisco, CA	3,202.2
8	Little Rock, AR	5,684.4	72	Lubbock, TX	3,992.0	136	Colonie, NY	3,195.6
9	Orlando, FL	5,682.2	73	Albuquerque, NM	3,970.4	137	Clearwater, FL	3,191.3
10	Yakima, WA	5,673.7	74	Wilmington, NC	3,968.9	138	Lawton, OK	3,170.3
11	Chattanooga, TN	5,663.2	75	Beaumont, TX	3,935.9	139	Bridgeport, CT	3,170.2
12	Bellingham, WA	5,627.2	76	Waco, TX	3,930.4	140	Buffalo, NY	3,160.1
13	Everett, WA	5,564.6	77	Fort Lauderdale, FL	3,923.6	141	Mesa, AZ	3,125.3
14	Topeka, KS	5,410.9	78	Kansas City, KS	3,918.6	142	Savannah, GA	3,122.0
15	Des Moines, IA	5,292.7	79	Racine, WI	3,910.5	143	Thornton, CO	3,115.6
16	Corpus Christi, TX	5,235.2	80	Atlanta, GA	3,901.2	144	Plantation, FL	3,097.0
17	Birmingham, AL	5,185.9	81	Athens-Clarke, GA	3,893.2	145	Anchorage, AK	3,076.4
18	Berkeley, CA	5,013.2	82	Peoria, IL	3,879.4	146	Tallahassee, FL	3,061.9
19	Tempe, AZ	5,005.3	83	Allentown, PA	3,857.6	147	Miami, FL	3,045.5
20	Independence, MO	4,988.6	83	Wichita, KS	3,857.6	148	Camden, NJ	3,034.8
21	Lawrence, KS	4,983.4	85	Norfolk, VA	3,855.4	149	Fresno, CA	3,029.9
22	Memphis, TN	4,955.1	86	Modesto, CA	3,838.7	150	Killeen, TX	3,015.3
23	Canton, OH	4,864.6	87	Federal Way, WA	3,821.8	151	Boston, MA	3,004.5
24	Rockford, IL	4,862.8	88	Greensboro, NC	3,804.0	152	Flint, MI	2,991.8
25	Tacoma, WA	4,849.3	89	Dayton, OH	3,795.3	153	Sioux City, IA	2,980.0
26	Fort Smith, AR	4,841.6	90	Tulsa, OK	3,764.1	154	Pittsburgh, PA	2,975.3
27	West Palm Beach, FL	4,816.3	91	Brownsville, TX	3,764.0	155	Bloomington, MN	2,934.9
28	Columbus, GA	4,812.2	92	Oklahoma City, OK	3,762.8	156	Abilene, TX	2,932.0
29	Hartford, CT	4,796.2	93	Duluth, MN	3,760.7	157	Chicago, IL	2,930.1
30	Ogden, UT	4,666.0	94	Fort Worth, TX	3,759.7	158	Westminster, CO	2,914.9
31	Springfield, IL	4,620.3	95	Albany, NY	3,754.8	159	Providence, RI	2,910.2
32	South Bend, IN	4,619.7	96	Rochester, NY	3,738.6	160	Honolulu, HI	2,907.9
33	McAllen, TX	4,578.2	97	Arlington, TX	3,727.0	161	Baltimore, MD	2,894.0
34	Huntsville, AL	4,554.4	98	San Angelo, TX	3,711.3	162	Charleston, SC	2,867.9
35	Tuscaloosa, AL	4,518.0	99	Eugene, OR	3,666.8	163	Vancouver, WA	2,861.4
36	Shreveport, LA	4,513.4	100	Spokane, WA	3,666.3	164	Yuma, AZ	2,857.0
37	Laredo, TX	4,500.4	101	Jacksonville, FL	3,665.0	165	Louisville, KY	2,852.2
38	Wichita Falls, TX	4,454.8	102	Durham, NC	3,645.7	166	Syracuse, NY	2,841.7
39	Austin, TX	4,446.5	103	Melbourne, FL	3,643.9	167	Newport News, VA	2,840.0
40	San Antonio, TX	4,440.5	104	Omaha, NE	3,640.4	168	Reading, PA	2,827.2
41	Toledo, OH	4,388.8	105	Indianapolis, IN	3,611.8	169	Mesquite, TX	2,802.0
42	Baton Rouge, LA	4,375.1	106	Cedar Rapids, IA	3,603.4	170	Lexington, KY	2,794.4
43	Cincinnati, OH	4,374.9	107	Grand Rapids, MI	3,581.0	171	Vallejo, CA	2,783.8
44	Mobile, AL	4,340.2	108	Murfreesboro, TN	3,576.9	172	Hollywood, FL	2,777.5
45	Lafayette, LA	4,299.9	109	High Point, NC	3,556.3	173	Sacramento, CA	2,771.0
46	Columbia, SC	4,277.2	110	Portsmouth, VA	3,549.6	174	Fairfield, CA	2,762.4
47	Longview, TX	4,267.4	111	Greeley, CO	3,543.9	175	San Leandro, CA	2,758.6
48	Jackson, MS	4,248.5	112	Billings, MT	3,529.8	176	Fort Collins, CO	2,748.3
49	Montgomery, AL	4,248.4	113	Fort Wayne, IN	3,529.0	177	Spokane Valley, WA	2,739.9
50	Columbus, OH	4,221.5	114	Houston, TX	3,524.6	178	Aurora, CO	2,737.9
51	Stockton, CA	4,214.7	115	Gainesville, FL	3,524.3	179	Odessa, TX	2,727.7
52	Knoxville, TN	4,212.2	116	Minneapolis, MN	3,493.2	180	West Jordan, UT	2,711.2
53	Salem, OR	4,208.6	117	Visalia, CA	3,481.1	181	Gary, IN	2,697.0
54	Milwaukee, WI	4,189.8	118	Tyler, TX	3,469.4	182	Philadelphia, PA	2,691.1
55	Pueblo, CO	4,181.0	119	West Valley, UT	3,459.2	183	Bellevue, WA	2,667.2
56	Kent, WA	4,165.6	120	Dearborn, MI	3,454.2	184	Largo, FL	2,662.1
57	Albany, GA	4,157.3	121	Colorado Springs, CO	3,434.1	185	Sunrise, FL	2,658.6
58	Roanoke, VA	4,154.8	122	Las Cruces, NM	3,417.9	186	Cleveland, OH	2,658.4
59	Nashville, TN	4,142.9	123	Tampa, FL	3,394.1	187	Concord, CA	2,619.8
60	Miami Gardens, FL	4,134.9	124	Irving, TX	3,378.6	188	Southfield, MI	2,614.0
61	Winston-Salem, NC	4,111.9	125	Hammond, IN	3,378.4	189	Washington, DC	2,602.1
62	Lincoln, NE	4,109.6	126	Evansville, IN	3,370.6	190	Sandy, UT	2,596.5
63	Seattle, WA	4,090.6	127	Reno, NV	3,356.7	191	Gresham, OR	2,585.8
64	Lakeland, FL	4,063.9	128	Lakewood, CO	3,286.1	192	Plano, TX	2,582.6

RANK	CITY	RATE
193	Youngstown, OH	2,575.4
194	Midland, TX	2,566.7
195	Hillsboro, OR	2,565.2
196	Boise, ID	2,559.9
197	Peoria, AZ	2,559.2
198	Riverside, CA	2,552.5
199	Roseville, CA	2,546.4
200	Lansing, MI	2,541.0
201	Boulder, CO	2,539.1
202	Boca Raton, FL	2,533.7
203	Columbia, MO	2,524.7
204	Chandler, AZ	2,522.1
205	Salinas, CA	2,516.4
206	Tracy, CA	2,501.1
207	Raleigh, NC	2,487.8
208	Sparks, NV	2,481.3
209	Ventura, CA	2,481.1
210	Santa Monica, CA	2,468.6
211	Davie, FL	2,454.9
212	Clovis, CA	2,450.0
213	Hampton, VA	2,444.4
214	Suffolk, VA	2,435.4
215	Madison, WI	2,430.2
216	Hialeah, FL	2,415.7
217	El Paso, TX	2,411.7
218	Victorville, CA	2,408.6
219	Detroit, MI	2,406.8
220	Redding, CA	2,403.6
221	St. Paul, MN	2,388.5
222	Garland, TX	2,372.4
223	Deerfield Beach, FL	2,363.6
224	Cambridge, MA	2,358.6
225	Norman, OK	2,353.4
226	Denver, CO	2,353.0
227	San Bernardino, CA	2,350.0
228	Pembroke Pines, FL	2,341.8
229	Scottsdale, AZ	2,333.7
230	Orem, UT	2,323.0
231	Lewisville, TX	2,314.1
232	Virginia Beach, VA	2,306.3
233	Cheektowaga, NY	2,305.1
234	Chesapeake, VA	2,298.0
235	Pasadena, TX	2,295.0
236	Lee's Summit, MO	2,293.5
237	Clarksville, TN	2,284.1
238	Brockton, MA	2,272.1
239	Elizabeth, NJ	2,271.6
240	Glendale, AZ	2,262.8
241	West Covina, CA	2,234.4
242	Fullerton, CA	2,210.7
243	Costa Mesa, CA	2,209.9
244	Aurora, IL	2,208.4
245	Joliet, IL	2,202.4
246	Manchester, NH	2,200.6
247	Whittier, CA	2,188.1
248	Cape Coral, FL	2,187.9
249	Oakland, CA	2,187.6
250	Kenosha, WI	2,180.2
251	Arvada, CO	2,174.0
252	Overland Park, KS	2,151.5
253	Santa Clara, CA	2,146.7
254	Richmond, CA	2,144.4
255	Denton, TX	2,142.8
256	Sterling Heights, MI	2,126.6
257	Fargo, ND	2,125.1
258	Woodbridge Twnshp, NJ	2,099.2

RANK	CITY	RATE
259	Westland, MI	2,094.6
260	El Cajon, CA	2,093.9
261	San Mateo, CA	2,089.2
262	Newport Beach, CA	2,088.1
263	Surprise, AZ	2,084.0
264	Richardson, TX	2,079.5
265	Greece, NY	2,073.6
266	Napa, CA	2,071.4
267	Pasadena, CA	2,067.2
268	Temecula, CA	2,066.5
269	Ontario, CA	2,061.6
270	Santa Barbara, CA	2,054.8
271	Nashua, NH	2,054.7
272	Upper Darby Twnshp, PA	2,051.7
273	Erie, PA	2,050.6
274	Las Vegas, NV	2,038.2
275	Carrollton, TX	2,036.2
276	Lowell, MA	1,998.5
277	New Bedford, MA	1,992.3
278	Escondido, CA	1,986.1
279	Edmond, OK	1,984.3
280	Rochester, MN	1,979.4
281	Green Bay, WI	1,955.2
282	Worcester, MA	1,950.8
283	Gilbert, AZ	1,946.4
284	Oceanside, CA	1,945.7
285	Troy, MI	1,914.4
286	San Diego, CA	1,904.3
287	Warwick, RI	1,894.0
288	North Las Vegas, NV	1,893.3
289	Ann Arbor, MI	1,875.4
290	Beaverton, OR	1,874.3
291	Santa Rosa, CA	1,868.2
292	Sioux Falls, SD	1,860.7
293	Palm Bay, FL	1,858.1
294	Round Rock, TX	1,849.9
295	Vacaville, CA	1,847.1
296	Jersey City, NJ	1,845.3
297	Westminster, CA	1,842.2
298	Miramar, FL	1,833.6
299	Clarkstown, NY	1,826.0
300	Chino, CA	1,821.7
301	Santa Maria, CA	1,821.3
302	Moreno Valley, CA	1,818.1
303	Provo, UT	1,810.4
304	Lancaster, CA	1,804.2
305	Carlsbad, CA	1,799.3
306	Chula Vista, CA	1,797.1
307	Pomona, CA	1,792.2
308	Roswell, GA	1,788.5
309	Alexandria, VA	1,784.4
310	Alhambra, CA	1,782.4
311	Port St. Lucie, FL	1,758.6
312	Lakewood, CA	1,757.6
313	Palmdale, CA	1,732.9
314	Downey, CA	1,713.5
315	Sugar Land, TX	1,697.0
316	Orange, CA	1,695.7
317	Warren, MI	1,695.1
318	Coral Springs, FL	1,686.6
319	Clinton Twnshp, MI	1,680.4
320	Livonia, MI	1,677.0
321	Edison Twnshp, NJ	1,674.4
322	Vista, CA	1,668.6
323	Hayward, CA	1,655.2
324	Corona, CA	1,653.3

RANK	CITY	RATE
325	Toms River Twnshp, NJ	1,634.1
326	McKinney, TX	1,627.1
327	Cranston, RI	1,616.8
328	Lynn, MA	1,611.0
329	Burbank, CA	1,602.2
330	Somerville, MA	1,596.5
331	Garden Grove, CA	1,590.4
332	Carson, CA	1,584.4
333	Anaheim, CA	1,576.2
334	Clifton, NJ	1,574.1
335	Daly City, CA	1,567.5
336	Newark, NJ	1,558.3
337	Huntington Beach, CA	1,551.4
338	Los Angeles, CA	1,539.2
339	Fremont, CA	1,539.0
340	Oxnard, CA	1,519.8
341	Danbury, CT	1,515.0
342	Henderson, NV	1,506.4
342	Olathe, KS	1,506.4
344	Rancho Cucamon., CA	1,492.3
345	Canton Twnshp, MI	1,465.1
346	Santa Ana, CA	1,443.1
347	Trenton, NJ	1,429.7
348	Murrieta, CA	1,421.2
349	New York, NY	1,412.9
350	Bellflower, CA	1,408.8
351	Brick Twnshp, NJ	1,406.4
352	Cary, NC	1,400.1
353	Amherst, NY	1,399.1
354	Torrance, CA	1,390.7
355	Naperville, IL	1,385.4
356	Hamilton Twnshp, NJ	1,383.5
357	Long Beach, CA	1,379.5
358	San Jose, CA	1,377.2
359	Livermore, CA	1,368.9
360	Buena Park, CA	1,365.7
361	Glendale, CA	1,330.1
362	Paterson, NJ	1,329.7
363	Santa Clarita, CA	1,327.1
364	Farmington Hills, MI	1,324.6
365	Sunnyvale, CA	1,306.3
366	Parma, OH	1,286.0
367	Broken Arrow, OK	1,285.2
368	Simi Valley, CA	1,231.7
369	Yonkers, NY	1,218.6
370	Norwalk, CA	1,218.3
371	New Orleans, LA	1,212.6
372	Hesperia, CA	1,181.9
373	Quincy, MA	1,165.3
374	El Monte, CA	1,160.9
375	Irvine, CA	1,138.8
376	Rialto, CA	1,136.4
377	Centennial, CO	1,120.9
378	Hawthorne, CA	1,111.4
379	Baldwin Park, CA	1,108.4
380	Antioch, CA	1,107.0
381	South Gate, CA	1,104.3
382	Mission Viejo, CA	1,060.1
383	Inglewood, CA	1,033.8
384	Thousand Oaks, CA	1,032.8
385	Lake Forest, CA	1,028.5
386	Chino Hills, CA	1,015.7
387	Newton, MA	990.9
388	Compton, CA	964.6
389	Fontana, CA	831.6
NA	Tucson, AZ**	NA

Source: CQ Press using data from F.B.I. "Crime in the United States 2006"
**Larceny and theft is the unlawful taking of property. Attempts are included.*
***Not available.*

75. Percent Change in Larceny and Theft Rate: 2005 to 2006

National Percent Change = 3.5% Decrease*

RANK	CITY	% CHANGE
240	Abilene, TX	(7.2)
33	Albany, GA	10.1
31	Albany, NY	11.2
218	Albuquerque, NM	(5.9)
282	Alexandria, VA	(9.7)
43	Alhambra, CA	7.3
52	Allentown, PA	5.6
285	Amarillo, TX	(9.8)
248	Amherst, NY	(7.5)
189	Anaheim, CA	(4.4)
74	Anchorage, AK	3.0
230	Ann Arbor, MI	(6.6)
302	Antioch, CA	(11.4)
233	Arlington, TX	(6.8)
347	Arvada, CO	(18.4)
137	Athens-Clarke, GA	(1.6)
303	Atlanta, GA	(11.5)
323	Aurora, CO	(14.7)
92	Aurora, IL	1.4
167	Austin, TX	(3.2)
258	Bakersfield, CA	(8.1)
326	Baldwin Park, CA	(15.0)
214	Baltimore, MD	(5.8)
36	Baton Rouge, LA	9.8
358	Beaumont, TX	(21.7)
372	Beaverton, OR	(31.6)
285	Bellevue, WA	(9.8)
272	Bellflower, CA	(9.1)
264	Bellingham, WA	(8.6)
237	Berkeley, CA	(6.9)
365	Billings, MT	(24.3)
87	Birmingham, AL	1.7
NA	Bloomington, MN**	NA
152	Boca Raton, FL	(2.3)
299	Boise, ID	(11.3)
45	Boston, MA	6.9
334	Boulder, CO	(15.9)
105	Brick Twnshp, NJ	0.6
115	Bridgeport, CT	(0.2)
208	Brockton, MA	(5.7)
366	Broken Arrow, OK	(26.4)
240	Brownsville, TX	(7.2)
57	Buena Park, CA	4.7
299	Buffalo, NY	(11.3)
121	Burbank, CA	(0.6)
128	Cambridge, MA	(1.1)
60	Camden, NJ	4.3
28	Canton Twnshp, MI	11.5
130	Canton, OH	(1.3)
28	Cape Coral, FL	11.5
147	Carlsbad, CA	(2.1)
267	Carrollton, TX	(8.8)
12	Carson, CA	17.7
99	Cary, NC	0.9
307	Cedar Rapids, IA	(12.0)
351	Centennial, CO	(20.2)
76	Chandler, AZ	2.8
307	Charleston, SC	(12.0)
84	Charlotte, NC	2.1
203	Chattanooga, TN	(5.4)
152	Cheektowaga, NY	(2.3)
330	Chesapeake, VA	(15.2)
97	Chicago, IL	1.0
38	Chino Hills, CA	9.7
303	Chino, CA	(11.5)
132	Chula Vista, CA	(1.4)
143	Cincinnati, OH	(2.0)
NA	Clarkstown, NY**	NA
289	Clarksville, TN	(10.2)
184	Clearwater, FL	(4.1)
240	Cleveland, OH	(7.2)
141	Clifton, NJ	(1.9)
65	Clinton Twnshp, MI	3.4
264	Clovis, CA	(8.6)
110	Colonie, NY	0.3
273	Colorado Springs, CO	(9.2)
189	Columbia, MO	(4.4)
262	Columbia, SC	(8.5)
72	Columbus, GA	3.2
163	Columbus, OH	(2.8)
176	Compton, CA	(3.8)
339	Concord, CA	(17.5)
22	Coral Springs, FL	12.1
227	Corona, CA	(6.5)
208	Corpus Christi, TX	(5.7)
267	Costa Mesa, CA	(8.8)
292	Cranston, RI	(10.8)
214	Dallas, TX	(5.8)
32	Daly City, CA	10.3
157	Danbury, CT	(2.6)
280	Davie, FL	(9.6)
99	Dayton, OH	0.9
65	Dearborn, MI	3.4
279	Deerfield Beach, FL	(9.5)
373	Denton, TX	(32.7)
369	Denver, CO	(28.3)
NA	Des Moines, IA**	NA
4	Detroit, MI	24.7
76	Downey, CA	2.8
NA	Duluth, MN**	NA
NA	Durham, NC**	NA
143	Edison Twnshp, NJ	(2.0)
107	Edmond, OK	0.5
244	El Cajon, CA	(7.4)
317	El Monte, CA	(13.5)
NA	El Paso, TX**	NA
148	Elizabeth, NJ	(2.2)
110	Erie, PA	0.3
291	Escondido, CA	(10.6)
351	Eugene, OR	(20.2)
297	Evansville, IN	(11.2)
3	Everett, WA	27.7
107	Fairfield, CA	0.5
15	Fargo, ND	14.4
132	Farmington Hills, MI	(1.4)
20	Fayetteville, NC	13.5
338	Federal Way, WA	(16.8)
80	Flint, MI	2.7
297	Fontana, CA	(11.2)
40	Fort Collins, CO	9.2
312	Fort Lauderdale, FL	(12.7)
168	Fort Smith, AR	(3.5)
NA	Fort Wayne, IN**	NA
239	Fort Worth, TX	(7.1)
69	Fremont, CA	3.3
316	Fresno, CA	(13.2)
214	Fullerton, CA	(5.8)
7	Gainesville, FL	20.3
65	Garden Grove, CA	3.4
176	Garland, TX	(3.8)
52	Gary, IN	5.6
69	Gilbert, AZ	3.3
255	Glendale, AZ	(7.8)
35	Glendale, CA	9.9
227	Grand Prairie, TX	(6.5)
123	Grand Rapids, MI	(0.8)
5	Greece, NY	21.7
357	Greeley, CO	(21.4)
203	Green Bay, WI	(5.4)
157	Greensboro, NC	(2.6)
359	Gresham, OR	(22.3)
30	Hamilton Twnshp, NJ	11.3
117	Hammond, IN	(0.4)
259	Hampton, VA	(8.2)
184	Hartford, CT	(4.1)
14	Hawthorne, CA	14.8
110	Hayward, CA	0.3
179	Henderson, NV	(3.9)
250	Hesperia, CA	(7.6)
160	Hialeah, FL	(2.7)
187	High Point, NC	(4.3)
364	Hillsboro, OR	(24.2)
221	Hollywood, FL	(6.0)
288	Honolulu, HI	(10.1)
118	Houston, TX	(0.5)
39	Huntington Beach, CA	9.6
208	Huntsville, AL	(5.7)
226	Independence, MO	(6.3)
148	Indianapolis, IN	(2.2)
293	Inglewood, CA	(10.9)
248	Irvine, CA	(7.5)
110	Irving, TX	0.3
135	Jacksonville, FL	(1.5)
33	Jackson, MS	10.1
198	Jersey City, NJ	(5.1)
317	Joliet, IL	(13.5)
176	Kansas City, KS	(3.8)
NA	Kansas City, MO**	NA
168	Kenosha, WI	(3.5)
130	Kent, WA	(1.3)
348	Killeen, TX	(18.5)
75	Knoxville, TN	2.9
76	Lafayette, LA	2.8
11	Lake Forest, CA	18.1
148	Lakeland, FL	(2.2)
363	Lakewood, CA	(23.7)
335	Lakewood, CO	(16.7)
179	Lancaster, CA	(3.9)
240	Lansing, MI	(7.2)
230	Laredo, TX	(6.6)
55	Largo, FL	4.9
233	Las Cruces, NM	(6.8)
208	Las Vegas, NV	(5.7)
1	Lawrence, KS	46.4
262	Lawton, OK	(8.5)
80	Lee's Summit, MO	2.7
368	Lewisville, TX	(28.0)
NA	Lexington, KY**	NA
221	Lincoln, NE	(6.0)
244	Little Rock, AR	(7.4)
46	Livermore, CA	6.8
54	Livonia, MI	5.5

RANK	CITY	% CHANGE
163	Long Beach, CA	(2.8)
115	Longview, TX	(0.2)
282	Los Angeles, CA	(9.7)
64	Louisville, KY	3.7
48	Lowell, MA	6.4
277	Lubbock, TX	(9.4)
218	Lynn, MA	(5.9)
168	Macon, GA	(3.5)
202	Madison, WI	(5.3)
208	Manchester, NH	(5.7)
346	McAllen, TX	(18.3)
118	McKinney, TX	(0.5)
36	Melbourne, FL	9.8
73	Memphis, TN	3.1
315	Mesa, AZ	(13.1)
233	Mesquite, TX	(6.8)
179	Miami Beach, FL	(3.9)
103	Miami Gardens, FL	0.7
327	Miami, FL	(15.1)
269	Midland, TX	(8.9)
19	Milwaukee, WI	13.7
94	Minneapolis, MN	1.2
63	Miramar, FL	3.9
42	Mission Viejo, CA	7.8
13	Mobile, AL	15.4
172	Modesto, CA	(3.6)
87	Montgomery, AL	1.7
238	Moreno Valley, CA	(7.0)
137	Murfreesboro, TN	(1.6)
102	Murrieta, CA	0.8
93	Napa, CA	1.3
250	Naperville, IL	(7.6)
26	Nashua, NH	11.6
293	Nashville, TN	(10.9)
165	New Bedford, MA	(3.0)
NA	New Orleans, LA**	NA
200	New York, NY	(5.2)
306	Newark, NJ	(11.9)
143	Newport Beach, CA	(2.0)
295	Newport News, VA	(11.0)
49	Newton, MA	5.8
260	Norfolk, VA	(8.4)
62	Norman, OK	4.0
155	North Charleston, SC	(2.4)
187	North Las Vegas, NV	(4.3)
227	Norwalk, CA	(6.5)
47	Oakland, CA	6.5
323	Oceanside, CA	(14.7)
250	Odessa, TX	(7.6)
87	Ogden, UT	1.7
371	Oklahoma City, OK	(30.1)
375	Olathe, KS	(41.9)
118	Omaha, NE	(0.5)
197	Ontario, CA	(5.0)
122	Orange, CA	(0.7)
367	Orem, UT	(26.8)
141	Orlando, FL	(1.9)
182	Overland Park, KS	(4.0)
56	Oxnard, CA	4.8
331	Palm Bay, FL	(15.6)
182	Palmdale, CA	(4.0)
311	Parma, OH	(12.5)
132	Pasadena, CA	(1.4)
126	Pasadena, TX	(1.0)
193	Paterson, NJ	(4.6)
41	Pembroke Pines, FL	9.1

RANK	CITY	% CHANGE
205	Peoria, AZ	(5.5)
277	Peoria, IL	(9.4)
61	Philadelphia, PA	4.2
260	Phoenix, AZ	(8.4)
194	Pittsburgh, PA	(4.8)
186	Plano, TX	(4.2)
57	Plantation, FL	4.7
96	Pomona, CA	1.1
353	Pompano Beach, FL	(20.7)
8	Port St. Lucie, FL	19.4
325	Portland, OR	(14.9)
172	Portsmouth, VA	(3.6)
80	Providence, RI	2.7
361	Provo, UT	(22.9)
305	Pueblo, CO	(11.8)
10	Quincy, MA	18.3
160	Racine, WI	(2.7)
157	Raleigh, NC	(2.6)
343	Rancho Cucamon., CA	(18.1)
275	Reading, PA	(9.3)
350	Redding, CA	(19.6)
269	Reno, NV	(8.9)
370	Rialto, CA	(28.8)
321	Richardson, TX	(13.9)
221	Richmond, CA	(6.0)
360	Richmond, VA	(22.4)
273	Riverside, CA	(9.2)
354	Roanoke, VA	(20.8)
166	Rochester, MN	(3.1)
287	Rochester, NY	(9.9)
NA	Rockford, IL**	NA
335	Roseville, CA	(16.7)
275	Roswell, GA	(9.3)
340	Round Rock, TX	(17.6)
195	Sacramento, CA	(4.9)
253	Salem, OR	(7.7)
317	Salinas, CA	(13.5)
175	Salt Lake City, UT	(3.7)
333	San Angelo, TX	(15.7)
257	San Antonio, TX	(8.0)
327	San Bernardino, CA	(15.1)
137	San Diego, CA	(1.6)
6	San Francisco, CA	20.6
224	San Jose, CA	(6.2)
205	San Leandro, CA	(5.5)
314	San Mateo, CA	(12.9)
191	Sandy, UT	(4.5)
282	Santa Ana, CA	(9.7)
309	Santa Barbara, CA	(12.3)
271	Santa Clara, CA	(9.0)
114	Santa Clarita, CA	0.1
15	Santa Maria, CA	14.4
191	Santa Monica, CA	(4.5)
340	Santa Rosa, CA	(17.6)
309	Savannah, GA	(12.3)
17	Scottsdale, AZ	13.8
312	Seattle, WA	(12.7)
97	Shreveport, LA	1.0
160	Simi Valley, CA	(2.7)
152	Sioux City, IA	(2.3)
356	Sioux Falls, SD	(21.3)
2	Somerville, MA	44.5
21	South Bend, IN	12.2
195	South Gate, CA	(4.9)
208	Southfield, MI	(5.7)
87	Sparks, NV	1.7

RANK	CITY	% CHANGE
335	Spokane Valley, WA	(16.7)
255	Spokane, WA	(7.8)
105	Springfield, IL	0.6
125	Springfield, MA	(0.9)
69	Springfield, MO	3.3
9	Sterling Heights, MI	18.6
65	Stockton, CA	3.4
76	St. Louis, MO	2.8
322	St. Paul, MN	(14.2)
135	St. Petersburg, FL	(1.5)
320	Suffolk, VA	(13.7)
299	Sugar Land, TX	(11.3)
224	Sunnyvale, CA	(6.2)
44	Sunrise, FL	7.2
140	Surprise, AZ	(1.8)
25	Syracuse, NY	11.9
168	Tacoma, WA	(3.5)
205	Tallahassee, FL	(5.5)
296	Tampa, FL	(11.1)
126	Temecula, CA	(1.0)
103	Tempe, AZ	0.7
200	Thornton, CO	(5.2)
99	Thousand Oaks, CA	0.9
109	Toledo, OH	0.4
50	Toms River Twnshp, NJ	5.7
266	Topeka, KS	(8.7)
232	Torrance, CA	(6.7)
344	Tracy, CA	(18.2)
374	Trenton, NJ	(36.9)
128	Troy, MI	(1.1)
NA	Tucson, AZ**	NA
143	Tulsa, OK	(2.0)
87	Tuscaloosa, AL	1.7
244	Tyler, TX	(7.4)
23	Upper Darby Twnshp, PA	12.0
253	Vacaville, CA	(7.7)
NA	Vallejo, CA**	NA
349	Vancouver, WA	(19.3)
172	Ventura, CA	(3.6)
354	Victorville, CA	(20.8)
123	Virginia Beach, VA	(0.8)
331	Visalia, CA	(15.6)
198	Vista, CA	(5.1)
342	Waco, TX	(17.8)
83	Warren, MI	2.6
344	Warwick, RI	(18.2)
94	Washington, DC	1.2
57	Waterbury, CT	4.7
85	West Covina, CA	1.9
NA	West Jordan, UT**	NA
85	West Palm Beach, FL	1.9
362	West Valley, UT	(23.0)
26	Westland, MI	11.6
214	Westminster, CA	(5.8)
290	Westminster, CO	(10.3)
17	Whittier, CA	13.8
327	Wichita Falls, TX	(15.1)
NA	Wichita, KS**	NA
218	Wilmington, NC	(5.9)
23	Winston-Salem, NC	12.0
148	Woodbridge Twnshp, NJ	(2.2)
233	Worcester, MA	(6.8)
244	Yakima, WA	(7.4)
50	Yonkers, NY	5.7
280	Youngstown, OH	(9.6)
155	Yuma, AZ	(2.4)

Source: CQ Press using data from F.B.I. "Crime in the United States 2006"

**Larceny and theft is the unlawful taking of property. Attempts are included.*

***Not available.*

75. Percent Change in Larceny and Theft Rate: 2005 to 2006 (continued)

National Percent Change = 3.5% Decrease*

RANK	CITY	% CHANGE
1	Lawrence, KS	46.4
2	Somerville, MA	44.5
3	Everett, WA	27.7
4	Detroit, MI	24.7
5	Greece, NY	21.7
6	San Francisco, CA	20.6
7	Gainesville, FL	20.3
8	Port St. Lucie, FL	19.4
9	Sterling Heights, MI	18.6
10	Quincy, MA	18.3
11	Lake Forest, CA	18.1
12	Carson, CA	17.7
13	Mobile, AL	15.4
14	Hawthorne, CA	14.8
15	Fargo, ND	14.4
15	Santa Maria, CA	14.4
17	Scottsdale, AZ	13.8
17	Whittier, CA	13.8
19	Milwaukee, WI	13.7
20	Fayetteville, NC	13.5
21	South Bend, IN	12.2
22	Coral Springs, FL	12.1
23	Upper Darby Twnshp, PA	12.0
23	Winston-Salem, NC	12.0
25	Syracuse, NY	11.9
26	Nashua, NH	11.6
26	Westland, MI	11.6
28	Canton Twnshp, MI	11.5
28	Cape Coral, FL	11.5
30	Hamilton Twnshp, NJ	11.3
31	Albany, NY	11.2
32	Daly City, CA	10.3
33	Albany, GA	10.1
33	Jackson, MS	10.1
35	Glendale, CA	9.9
36	Baton Rouge, LA	9.8
36	Melbourne, FL	9.8
38	Chino Hills, CA	9.7
39	Huntington Beach, CA	9.6
40	Fort Collins, CO	9.2
41	Pembroke Pines, FL	9.1
42	Mission Viejo, CA	7.8
43	Alhambra, CA	7.3
44	Sunrise, FL	7.2
45	Boston, MA	6.9
46	Livermore, CA	6.8
47	Oakland, CA	6.5
48	Lowell, MA	6.4
49	Newton, MA	5.8
50	Toms River Twnshp, NJ	5.7
50	Yonkers, NY	5.7
52	Allentown, PA	5.6
52	Gary, IN	5.6
54	Livonia, MI	5.5
55	Largo, FL	4.9
56	Oxnard, CA	4.8
57	Buena Park, CA	4.7
57	Plantation, FL	4.7
57	Waterbury, CT	4.7
60	Camden, NJ	4.3
61	Philadelphia, PA	4.2
62	Norman, OK	4.0
63	Miramar, FL	3.9
64	Louisville, KY	3.7

RANK	CITY	% CHANGE
65	Clinton Twnshp, MI	3.4
65	Dearborn, MI	3.4
65	Garden Grove, CA	3.4
65	Stockton, CA	3.4
69	Fremont, CA	3.3
69	Gilbert, AZ	3.3
69	Springfield, MO	3.3
72	Columbus, GA	3.2
73	Memphis, TN	3.1
74	Anchorage, AK	3.0
75	Knoxville, TN	2.9
76	Chandler, AZ	2.8
76	Downey, CA	2.8
76	Lafayette, LA	2.8
76	St. Louis, MO	2.8
80	Flint, MI	2.7
80	Lee's Summit, MO	2.7
80	Providence, RI	2.7
83	Warren, MI	2.6
84	Charlotte, NC	2.1
85	West Covina, CA	1.9
85	West Palm Beach, FL	1.9
87	Birmingham, AL	1.7
87	Montgomery, AL	1.7
87	Ogden, UT	1.7
87	Sparks, NV	1.7
87	Tuscaloosa, AL	1.7
92	Aurora, IL	1.4
93	Napa, CA	1.3
94	Minneapolis, MN	1.2
94	Washington, DC	1.2
96	Pomona, CA	1.1
97	Chicago, IL	1.0
97	Shreveport, LA	1.0
99	Cary, NC	0.9
99	Dayton, OH	0.9
99	Thousand Oaks, CA	0.9
102	Murrieta, CA	0.8
103	Miami Gardens, FL	0.7
103	Tempe, AZ	0.7
105	Brick Twnshp, NJ	0.6
105	Springfield, IL	0.6
107	Edmond, OK	0.5
107	Fairfield, CA	0.5
109	Toledo, OH	0.4
110	Colonie, NY	0.3
110	Erie, PA	0.3
110	Hayward, CA	0.3
110	Irving, TX	0.3
114	Santa Clarita, CA	0.1
115	Bridgeport, CT	(0.2)
115	Longview, TX	(0.2)
117	Hammond, IN	(0.4)
118	Houston, TX	(0.5)
118	McKinney, TX	(0.5)
118	Omaha, NE	(0.5)
121	Burbank, CA	(0.6)
122	Orange, CA	(0.7)
123	Grand Rapids, MI	(0.8)
123	Virginia Beach, VA	(0.8)
125	Springfield, MA	(0.9)
126	Pasadena, TX	(1.0)
126	Temecula, CA	(1.0)
128	Cambridge, MA	(1.1)

RANK	CITY	% CHANGE
128	Troy, MI	(1.1)
130	Canton, OH	(1.3)
130	Kent, WA	(1.3)
132	Chula Vista, CA	(1.4)
132	Farmington Hills, MI	(1.4)
132	Pasadena, CA	(1.4)
135	Jacksonville, FL	(1.5)
135	St. Petersburg, FL	(1.5)
137	Athens-Clarke, GA	(1.6)
137	Murfreesboro, TN	(1.6)
137	San Diego, CA	(1.6)
140	Surprise, AZ	(1.8)
141	Clifton, NJ	(1.9)
141	Orlando, FL	(1.9)
143	Cincinnati, OH	(2.0)
143	Edison Twnshp, NJ	(2.0)
143	Newport Beach, CA	(2.0)
143	Tulsa, OK	(2.0)
147	Carlsbad, CA	(2.1)
148	Elizabeth, NJ	(2.2)
148	Indianapolis, IN	(2.2)
148	Lakeland, FL	(2.2)
148	Woodbridge Twnshp, NJ	(2.2)
152	Boca Raton, FL	(2.3)
152	Cheektowaga, NY	(2.3)
152	Sioux City, IA	(2.3)
155	North Charleston, SC	(2.4)
155	Yuma, AZ	(2.4)
157	Danbury, CT	(2.6)
157	Greensboro, NC	(2.6)
157	Raleigh, NC	(2.6)
160	Hialeah, FL	(2.7)
160	Racine, WI	(2.7)
160	Simi Valley, CA	(2.7)
163	Columbus, OH	(2.8)
163	Long Beach, CA	(2.8)
165	New Bedford, MA	(3.0)
166	Rochester, MN	(3.1)
167	Austin, TX	(3.2)
168	Fort Smith, AR	(3.5)
168	Kenosha, WI	(3.5)
168	Macon, GA	(3.5)
168	Tacoma, WA	(3.5)
172	Modesto, CA	(3.6)
172	Portsmouth, VA	(3.6)
172	Ventura, CA	(3.6)
175	Salt Lake City, UT	(3.7)
176	Compton, CA	(3.8)
176	Garland, TX	(3.8)
176	Kansas City, KS	(3.8)
179	Henderson, NV	(3.9)
179	Lancaster, CA	(3.9)
179	Miami Beach, FL	(3.9)
182	Overland Park, KS	(4.0)
182	Palmdale, CA	(4.0)
184	Clearwater, FL	(4.1)
184	Hartford, CT	(4.1)
186	Plano, TX	(4.2)
187	High Point, NC	(4.3)
187	North Las Vegas, NV	(4.3)
189	Anaheim, CA	(4.4)
189	Columbia, MO	(4.4)
191	Sandy, UT	(4.5)
191	Santa Monica, CA	(4.5)

RANK	CITY	% CHANGE
193	Paterson, NJ	(4.6)
194	Pittsburgh, PA	(4.8)
195	Sacramento, CA	(4.9)
195	South Gate, CA	(4.9)
197	Ontario, CA	(5.0)
198	Jersey City, NJ	(5.1)
198	Vista, CA	(5.1)
200	New York, NY	(5.2)
200	Thornton, CO	(5.2)
202	Madison, WI	(5.3)
203	Chattanooga, TN	(5.4)
203	Green Bay, WI	(5.4)
205	Peoria, AZ	(5.5)
205	San Leandro, CA	(5.5)
205	Tallahassee, FL	(5.5)
208	Brockton, MA	(5.7)
208	Corpus Christi, TX	(5.7)
208	Huntsville, AL	(5.7)
208	Las Vegas, NV	(5.7)
208	Manchester, NH	(5.7)
208	Southfield, MI	(5.7)
214	Baltimore, MD	(5.8)
214	Dallas, TX	(5.8)
214	Fullerton, CA	(5.8)
214	Westminster, CA	(5.8)
218	Albuquerque, NM	(5.9)
218	Lynn, MA	(5.9)
218	Wilmington, NC	(5.9)
221	Hollywood, FL	(6.0)
221	Lincoln, NE	(6.0)
221	Richmond, CA	(6.0)
224	San Jose, CA	(6.2)
224	Sunnyvale, CA	(6.2)
226	Independence, MO	(6.3)
227	Corona, CA	(6.5)
227	Grand Prairie, TX	(6.5)
227	Norwalk, CA	(6.5)
230	Ann Arbor, MI	(6.6)
230	Laredo, TX	(6.6)
232	Torrance, CA	(6.7)
233	Arlington, TX	(6.8)
233	Las Cruces, NM	(6.8)
233	Mesquite, TX	(6.8)
233	Worcester, MA	(6.8)
237	Berkeley, CA	(6.9)
238	Moreno Valley, CA	(7.0)
239	Fort Worth, TX	(7.1)
240	Abilene, TX	(7.2)
240	Brownsville, TX	(7.2)
240	Cleveland, OH	(7.2)
240	Lansing, MI	(7.2)
244	El Cajon, CA	(7.4)
244	Little Rock, AR	(7.4)
244	Tyler, TX	(7.4)
244	Yakima, WA	(7.4)
248	Amherst, NY	(7.5)
248	Irvine, CA	(7.5)
250	Hesperia, CA	(7.6)
250	Naperville, IL	(7.6)
250	Odessa, TX	(7.6)
253	Salem, OR	(7.7)
253	Vacaville, CA	(7.7)
255	Glendale, AZ	(7.8)
255	Spokane, WA	(7.8)
257	San Antonio, TX	(8.0)
258	Bakersfield, CA	(8.1)
259	Hampton, VA	(8.2)
260	Norfolk, VA	(8.4)
260	Phoenix, AZ	(8.4)
262	Columbia, SC	(8.5)
262	Lawton, OK	(8.5)
264	Bellingham, WA	(8.6)
264	Clovis, CA	(8.6)
266	Topeka, KS	(8.7)
267	Carrollton, TX	(8.8)
267	Costa Mesa, CA	(8.8)
269	Midland, TX	(8.9)
269	Reno, NV	(8.9)
271	Santa Clara, CA	(9.0)
272	Bellflower, CA	(9.1)
273	Colorado Springs, CO	(9.2)
273	Riverside, CA	(9.2)
275	Reading, PA	(9.3)
275	Roswell, GA	(9.3)
277	Lubbock, TX	(9.4)
277	Peoria, IL	(9.4)
279	Deerfield Beach, FL	(9.5)
280	Davie, FL	(9.6)
280	Youngstown, OH	(9.6)
282	Alexandria, VA	(9.7)
282	Los Angeles, CA	(9.7)
282	Santa Ana, CA	(9.7)
285	Amarillo, TX	(9.8)
285	Bellevue, WA	(9.8)
287	Rochester, NY	(9.9)
288	Honolulu, HI	(10.1)
289	Clarksville, TN	(10.2)
290	Westminster, CO	(10.3)
291	Escondido, CA	(10.6)
292	Cranston, RI	(10.8)
293	Inglewood, CA	(10.9)
293	Nashville, TN	(10.9)
295	Newport News, VA	(11.0)
296	Tampa, FL	(11.1)
297	Evansville, IN	(11.2)
297	Fontana, CA	(11.2)
299	Boise, ID	(11.3)
299	Buffalo, NY	(11.3)
299	Sugar Land, TX	(11.3)
302	Antioch, CA	(11.4)
303	Atlanta, GA	(11.5)
303	Chino, CA	(11.5)
305	Pueblo, CO	(11.8)
306	Newark, NJ	(11.9)
307	Cedar Rapids, IA	(12.0)
307	Charleston, SC	(12.0)
309	Santa Barbara, CA	(12.3)
309	Savannah, GA	(12.3)
311	Parma, OH	(12.5)
312	Fort Lauderdale, FL	(12.7)
312	Seattle, WA	(12.7)
314	San Mateo, CA	(12.9)
315	Mesa, AZ	(13.1)
316	Fresno, CA	(13.2)
317	El Monte, CA	(13.5)
317	Joliet, IL	(13.5)
317	Salinas, CA	(13.5)
320	Suffolk, VA	(13.7)
321	Richardson, TX	(13.9)
322	St. Paul, MN	(14.2)
323	Aurora, CO	(14.7)
323	Oceanside, CA	(14.7)
325	Portland, OR	(14.9)
326	Baldwin Park, CA	(15.0)
327	Miami, FL	(15.1)
327	San Bernardino, CA	(15.1)
327	Wichita Falls, TX	(15.1)
330	Chesapeake, VA	(15.2)
331	Palm Bay, FL	(15.6)
331	Visalia, CA	(15.6)
333	San Angelo, TX	(15.7)
334	Boulder, CO	(15.9)
335	Lakewood, CO	(16.7)
335	Roseville, CA	(16.7)
335	Spokane Valley, WA	(16.7)
338	Federal Way, WA	(16.8)
339	Concord, CA	(17.5)
340	Round Rock, TX	(17.6)
340	Santa Rosa, CA	(17.6)
342	Waco, TX	(17.8)
343	Rancho Cucamon., CA	(18.1)
344	Tracy, CA	(18.2)
344	Warwick, RI	(18.2)
346	McAllen, TX	(18.3)
347	Arvada, CO	(18.4)
348	Killeen, TX	(18.5)
349	Vancouver, WA	(19.3)
350	Redding, CA	(19.6)
351	Centennial, CO	(20.2)
351	Eugene, OR	(20.2)
353	Pompano Beach, FL	(20.7)
354	Roanoke, VA	(20.8)
354	Victorville, CA	(20.8)
356	Sioux Falls, SD	(21.3)
357	Greeley, CO	(21.4)
358	Beaumont, TX	(21.7)
359	Gresham, OR	(22.3)
360	Richmond, VA	(22.4)
361	Provo, UT	(22.9)
362	West Valley, UT	(23.0)
363	Lakewood, CA	(23.7)
364	Hillsboro, OR	(24.2)
365	Billings, MT	(24.3)
366	Broken Arrow, OK	(26.4)
367	Orem, UT	(26.8)
368	Lewisville, TX	(28.0)
369	Denver, CO	(28.3)
370	Rialto, CA	(28.8)
371	Oklahoma City, OK	(30.1)
372	Beaverton, OR	(31.6)
373	Denton, TX	(32.7)
374	Trenton, NJ	(36.9)
375	Olathe, KS	(41.9)
NA	Bloomington, MN**	NA
NA	Clarkstown, NY**	NA
NA	Des Moines, IA**	NA
NA	Duluth, MN**	NA
NA	Durham, NC**	NA
NA	El Paso, TX**	NA
NA	Fort Wayne, IN**	NA
NA	Kansas City, MO**	NA
NA	Lexington, KY**	NA
NA	New Orleans, LA**	NA
NA	Rockford, IL**	NA
NA	Tucson, AZ**	NA
NA	Vallejo, CA**	NA
NA	West Jordan, UT**	NA
NA	Wichita, KS**	NA

Source: CQ Press using data from F.B.I. "Crime in the United States 2006"

**Larceny and theft is the unlawful taking of property. Attempts are included.*

***Not available.*

76. Percent Change in Larceny and Theft Rate: 2002 to 2006

National Percent Change = 10.0% Decrease*

RANK	CITY	% CHANGE
63	Abilene, TX	3.4
74	Albany, GA	0.8
NA	Albany, NY**	NA
214	Albuquerque, NM	(15.0)
336	Alexandria, VA	(33.2)
14	Alhambra, CA	18.9
23	Allentown, PA	14.3
207	Amarillo, TX	(14.3)
78	Amherst, NY	0.6
286	Anaheim, CA	(22.8)
175	Anchorage, AK	(11.2)
159	Ann Arbor, MI	(9.3)
295	Antioch, CA	(23.9)
239	Arlington, TX	(17.7)
299	Arvada, CO	(24.9)
211	Athens-Clarke, GA	(14.5)
319	Atlanta, GA	(28.3)
306	Aurora, CO	(26.2)
260	Aurora, IL	(19.5)
68	Austin, TX	2.6
13	Bakersfield, CA	19.1
18	Baldwin Park, CA	16.0
311	Baltimore, MD	(27.3)
142	Baton Rouge, LA	(7.1)
338	Beaumont, TX	(33.3)
355	Beaverton, OR	(39.1)
166	Bellevue, WA	(10.1)
222	Bellflower, CA	(15.9)
95	Bellingham, WA	(2.0)
266	Berkeley, CA	(20.1)
251	Billings, MT	(18.9)
34	Birmingham, AL	9.1
278	Bloomington, MN	(21.5)
67	Boca Raton, FL	2.8
270	Boise, ID	(20.6)
79	Boston, MA	0.5
161	Boulder, CO	(9.6)
52	Brick Twnshp, NJ	5.2
22	Bridgeport, CT	14.7
115	Brockton, MA	(3.7)
350	Broken Arrow, OK	(36.4)
363	Brownsville, TX	(46.5)
166	Buena Park, CA	(10.1)
69	Buffalo, NY	2.4
165	Burbank, CA	(10.0)
158	Cambridge, MA	(9.2)
66	Camden, NJ	2.9
98	Canton Twnshp, MI	(2.2)
NA	Canton, OH**	NA
98	Cape Coral, FL	(2.2)
56	Carlsbad, CA	4.6
229	Carrollton, TX	(16.8)
49	Carson, CA	5.9
235	Cary, NC	(17.3)
251	Cedar Rapids, IA	(18.9)
NA	Centennial, CO**	NA
350	Chandler, AZ	(36.4)
338	Charleston, SC	(33.3)
77	Charlotte, NC	0.7
129	Chattanooga, TN	(5.1)
NA	Cheektowaga, NY**	NA
182	Chesapeake, VA	(11.9)
172	Chicago, IL	(10.7)
360	Chino Hills, CA	(43.1)
1	Chino, CA	75.7
198	Chula Vista, CA	(13.4)
80	Cincinnati, OH	0.4
211	Clarkstown, NY	(14.5)
361	Clarksville, TN	(44.4)
120	Clearwater, FL	(4.4)
112	Cleveland, OH	(3.4)
262	Clifton, NJ	(19.6)
74	Clinton Twnshp, MI	0.8
237	Clovis, CA	(17.6)
41	Colonie, NY	7.3
150	Colorado Springs, CO	(8.1)
286	Columbia, MO	(22.8)
244	Columbia, SC	(18.1)
36	Columbus, GA	8.8
225	Columbus, OH	(16.2)
275	Compton, CA	(21.3)
130	Concord, CA	(5.2)
271	Coral Springs, FL	(20.7)
223	Corona, CA	(16.0)
43	Corpus Christi, TX	7.2
126	Costa Mesa, CA	(4.9)
300	Cranston, RI	(25.1)
181	Dallas, TX	(11.7)
6	Daly City, CA	36.7
310	Danbury, CT	(26.9)
223	Davie, FL	(16.0)
193	Dayton, OH	(13.2)
31	Dearborn, MI	10.2
4	Deerfield Beach, FL	40.8
329	Denton, TX	(32.1)
179	Denver, CO	(11.6)
NA	Des Moines, IA**	NA
203	Detroit, MI	(13.7)
12	Downey, CA	19.6
203	Duluth, MN	(13.7)
NA	Durham, NC**	NA
57	Edison Twnshp, NJ	4.4
29	Edmond, OK	11.7
258	El Cajon, CA	(19.4)
81	El Monte, CA	0.3
NA	El Paso, TX**	NA
242	Elizabeth, NJ	(17.8)
124	Erie, PA	(4.7)
179	Escondido, CA	(11.6)
294	Eugene, OR	(23.7)
71	Evansville, IN	2.1
4	Everett, WA	40.8
262	Fairfield, CA	(19.6)
301	Fargo, ND	(25.4)
135	Farmington Hills, MI	(6.1)
9	Fayetteville, NC	24.5
96	Federal Way, WA	(2.1)
205	Flint, MI	(14.0)
230	Fontana, CA	(16.9)
209	Fort Collins, CO	(14.4)
105	Fort Lauderdale, FL	(2.6)
302	Fort Smith, AR	(25.6)
NA	Fort Wayne, IN**	NA
282	Fort Worth, TX	(21.9)
184	Fremont, CA	(12.0)
311	Fresno, CA	(27.3)
133	Fullerton, CA	(5.5)
85	Gainesville, FL	(0.4)
131	Garden Grove, CA	(5.3)
220	Garland, TX	(15.8)
11	Gary, IN	23.6
324	Gilbert, AZ	(30.1)
338	Glendale, AZ	(33.3)
27	Glendale, CA	12.4
161	Grand Prairie, TX	(9.6)
16	Grand Rapids, MI	17.0
NA	Greece, NY**	NA
318	Greeley, CO	(28.1)
242	Green Bay, WI	(17.8)
138	Greensboro, NC	(6.3)
356	Gresham, OR	(39.3)
169	Hamilton Twnshp, NJ	(10.3)
188	Hammond, IN	(12.1)
103	Hampton, VA	(2.3)
47	Hartford, CT	6.4
234	Hawthorne, CA	(17.1)
190	Hayward, CA	(12.8)
48	Henderson, NV	6.2
281	Hesperia, CA	(21.7)
248	Hialeah, FL	(18.6)
196	High Point, NC	(13.3)
332	Hillsboro, OR	(32.7)
327	Hollywood, FL	(31.6)
322	Honolulu, HI	(29.7)
96	Houston, TX	(2.1)
28	Huntington Beach, CA	12.3
39	Huntsville, AL	8.2
92	Independence, MO	(1.8)
16	Indianapolis, IN	17.0
271	Inglewood, CA	(20.7)
315	Irvine, CA	(27.8)
121	Irving, TX	(4.5)
118	Jacksonville, FL	(4.1)
154	Jackson, MS	(8.8)
115	Jersey City, NJ	(3.7)
278	Joliet, IL	(21.5)
NA	Kansas City, KS**	NA
NA	Kansas City, MO**	NA
52	Kenosha, WI	5.2
60	Kent, WA	3.9
304	Killeen, TX	(26.0)
29	Knoxville, TN	11.7
201	Lafayette, LA	(13.6)
184	Lake Forest, CA	(12.0)
83	Lakeland, FL	0.1
275	Lakewood, CA	(21.3)
246	Lakewood, CO	(18.4)
15	Lancaster, CA	17.3
267	Lansing, MI	(20.2)
153	Laredo, TX	(8.4)
143	Largo, FL	(7.3)
NA	Las Cruces, NM**	NA
107	Las Vegas, NV	(2.9)
3	Lawrence, KS	45.3
151	Lawton, OK	(8.3)
65	Lee's Summit, MO	3.1
349	Lewisville, TX	(36.3)
NA	Lexington, KY**	NA
226	Lincoln, NE	(16.3)
177	Little Rock, AR	(11.5)
297	Livermore, CA	(24.5)
184	Livonia, MI	(12.0)

RANK	CITY	% CHANGE
285	Long Beach, CA	(22.6)
170	Longview, TX	(10.5)
305	Los Angeles, CA	(26.1)
NA	Louisville, KY**	NA
37	Lowell, MA	8.7
82	Lubbock, TX	0.2
87	Lynn, MA	(0.7)
103	Macon, GA	(2.3)
191	Madison, WI	(13.0)
86	Manchester, NH	(0.5)
295	McAllen, TX	(23.9)
362	McKinney, TX	(46.1)
217	Melbourne, FL	(15.5)
33	Memphis, TN	10.0
346	Mesa, AZ	(35.4)
260	Mesquite, TX	(19.5)
232	Miami Beach, FL	(17.0)
NA	Miami Gardens, FL**	NA
311	Miami, FL	(27.3)
83	Midland, TX	0.1
117	Milwaukee, WI	(4.0)
140	Minneapolis, MN	(6.9)
254	Miramar, FL	(19.0)
236	Mission Viejo, CA	(17.5)
114	Mobile, AL	(3.5)
173	Modesto, CA	(10.8)
250	Montgomery, AL	(18.8)
192	Moreno Valley, CA	(13.1)
90	Murfreesboro, TN	(1.4)
45	Murrieta, CA	7.0
92	Napa, CA	(1.8)
135	Naperville, IL	(6.1)
NA	Nashua, NH**	NA
144	Nashville, TN	(7.4)
NA	New Bedford, MA**	NA
365	New Orleans, LA	(58.8)
182	New York, NY	(11.9)
316	Newark, NJ	(27.9)
198	Newport Beach, CA	(13.4)
145	Newport News, VA	(7.8)
NA	Newton, MA**	NA
196	Norfolk, VA	(13.3)
109	Norman, OK	(3.1)
119	North Charleston, SC	(4.2)
278	North Las Vegas, NV	(21.5)
105	Norwalk, CA	(2.6)
343	Oakland, CA	(33.9)
216	Oceanside, CA	(15.1)
347	Odessa, TX	(35.5)
46	Ogden, UT	6.6
359	Oklahoma City, OK	(42.8)
358	Olathe, KS	(41.4)
284	Omaha, NE	(22.4)
289	Ontario, CA	(23.1)
141	Orange, CA	(7.0)
336	Orem, UT	(33.2)
125	Orlando, FL	(4.8)
189	Overland Park, KS	(12.7)
177	Oxnard, CA	(11.5)
344	Palm Bay, FL	(34.1)
230	Palmdale, CA	(16.9)
112	Parma, OH	(3.4)
69	Pasadena, CA	2.4
286	Pasadena, TX	(22.8)
292	Paterson, NJ	(23.4)
35	Pembroke Pines, FL	8.9

RANK	CITY	% CHANGE
206	Peoria, AZ	(14.2)
269	Peoria, IL	(20.5)
50	Philadelphia, PA	5.7
258	Phoenix, AZ	(19.4)
74	Pittsburgh, PA	0.8
148	Plano, TX	(7.9)
193	Plantation, FL	(13.2)
62	Pomona, CA	3.6
21	Pompano Beach, FL	14.8
164	Port St. Lucie, FL	(9.9)
273	Portland, OR	(20.8)
160	Portsmouth, VA	(9.4)
326	Providence, RI	(31.4)
321	Provo, UT	(29.2)
19	Pueblo, CO	14.9
327	Quincy, MA	(31.6)
41	Racine, WI	7.3
342	Raleigh, NC	(33.6)
228	Rancho Cucamon., CA	(16.7)
239	Reading, PA	(17.7)
24	Redding, CA	12.7
214	Reno, NV	(15.0)
275	Rialto, CA	(21.3)
264	Richardson, TX	(19.8)
353	Richmond, CA	(37.6)
341	Richmond, VA	(33.5)
232	Riverside, CA	(17.0)
NA	Roanoke, VA**	NA
251	Rochester, MN	(18.9)
220	Rochester, NY	(15.8)
NA	Rockford, IL**	NA
265	Roseville, CA	(19.9)
19	Roswell, GA	14.9
193	Round Rock, TX	(13.2)
298	Sacramento, CA	(24.8)
348	Salem, OR	(36.1)
92	Salinas, CA	(1.8)
209	Salt Lake City, UT	(14.4)
217	San Angelo, TX	(15.5)
248	San Antonio, TX	(18.6)
314	San Bernardino, CA	(27.4)
91	San Diego, CA	(1.7)
51	San Francisco, CA	5.4
138	San Jose, CA	(6.3)
156	San Leandro, CA	(8.9)
63	San Mateo, CA	3.4
166	Sandy, UT	(10.1)
283	Santa Ana, CA	(22.0)
32	Santa Barbara, CA	10.1
58	Santa Clara, CA	4.1
24	Santa Clarita, CA	12.7
NA	Santa Maria, CA**	NA
292	Santa Monica, CA	(23.4)
329	Santa Rosa, CA	(32.1)
353	Savannah, GA	(37.6)
151	Scottsdale, AZ	(8.3)
176	Seattle, WA	(11.3)
109	Shreveport, LA	(3.1)
7	Simi Valley, CA	29.3
331	Sioux City, IA	(32.6)
274	Sioux Falls, SD	(21.1)
149	Somerville, MA	(8.0)
73	South Bend, IN	1.2
72	South Gate, CA	1.9
174	Southfield, MI	(11.1)
302	Sparks, NV	(25.6)

RANK	CITY	% CHANGE
NA	Spokane Valley, WA**	NA
316	Spokane, WA	(27.9)
207	Springfield, IL	(14.3)
98	Springfield, MA	(2.2)
8	Springfield, MO	25.9
40	Sterling Heights, MI	7.5
111	Stockton, CA	(3.2)
145	St. Louis, MO	(7.8)
325	St. Paul, MN	(30.3)
89	St. Petersburg, FL	(1.1)
323	Suffolk, VA	(30.0)
255	Sugar Land, TX	(19.1)
107	Sunnyvale, CA	(2.9)
239	Sunrise, FL	(17.7)
154	Surprise, AZ	(8.8)
227	Syracuse, NY	(16.5)
237	Tacoma, WA	(17.6)
334	Tallahassee, FL	(32.9)
335	Tampa, FL	(33.1)
88	Temecula, CA	(1.0)
291	Tempe, AZ	(23.3)
309	Thornton, CO	(26.8)
145	Thousand Oaks, CA	(7.8)
122	Toledo, OH	(4.6)
245	Toms River Twnshp, NJ	(18.2)
213	Topeka, KS	(14.9)
308	Torrance, CA	(26.7)
200	Tracy, CA	(13.5)
364	Trenton, NJ	(48.1)
61	Troy, MI	3.7
NA	Tucson, AZ**	NA
134	Tulsa, OK	(5.9)
184	Tuscaloosa, AL	(12.0)
333	Tyler, TX	(32.8)
2	Upper Darby Twnshp, PA	63.7
58	Vacaville, CA	4.1
171	Vallejo, CA	(10.6)
247	Vancouver, WA	(18.5)
55	Ventura, CA	4.8
290	Victorville, CA	(23.2)
219	Virginia Beach, VA	(15.7)
135	Visalia, CA	(6.1)
98	Vista, CA	(2.2)
345	Waco, TX	(34.6)
122	Warren, MI	(4.6)
268	Warwick, RI	(20.4)
320	Washington, DC	(28.9)
24	Waterbury, CT	12.7
132	West Covina, CA	(5.4)
307	West Jordan, UT	(26.5)
352	West Palm Beach, FL	(36.6)
257	West Valley, UT	(19.3)
54	Westland, MI	5.1
126	Westminster, CA	(4.9)
NA	Westminster, CO**	NA
10	Whittier, CA	24.1
157	Wichita Falls, TX	(9.0)
201	Wichita, KS	(13.6)
357	Wilmington, NC	(40.3)
163	Winston-Salem, NC	(9.8)
98	Woodbridge Twnshp, NJ	(2.2)
NA	Worcester, MA**	NA
126	Yakima, WA	(4.9)
38	Yonkers, NY	8.4
256	Youngstown, OH	(19.2)
44	Yuma, AZ	7.1

Source: CQ Press using data from F.B.I. "Crime in the United States 2006"

**Larceny and theft is the unlawful taking of property. Attempts are included.*

***Not available.*

76. Percent Change in Larceny and Theft Rate: 2002 to 2006 (continued)

National Percent Change = 10.0% Decrease*

RANK	CITY	% CHANGE
1	Chino, CA	75.7
2	Upper Darby Twnshp, PA	63.7
3	Lawrence, KS	45.3
4	Deerfield Beach, FL	40.8
4	Everett, WA	40.8
6	Daly City, CA	36.7
7	Simi Valley, CA	29.3
8	Springfield, MO	25.9
9	Fayetteville, NC	24.5
10	Whittier, CA	24.1
11	Gary, IN	23.6
12	Downey, CA	19.6
13	Bakersfield, CA	19.1
14	Alhambra, CA	18.9
15	Lancaster, CA	17.3
16	Grand Rapids, MI	17.0
16	Indianapolis, IN	17.0
18	Baldwin Park, CA	16.0
19	Pueblo, CO	14.9
19	Roswell, GA	14.9
21	Pompano Beach, FL	14.8
22	Bridgeport, CT	14.7
23	Allentown, PA	14.3
24	Redding, CA	12.7
24	Santa Clarita, CA	12.7
24	Waterbury, CT	12.7
27	Glendale, CA	12.4
28	Huntington Beach, CA	12.3
29	Edmond, OK	11.7
29	Knoxville, TN	11.7
31	Dearborn, MI	10.2
32	Santa Barbara, CA	10.1
33	Memphis, TN	10.0
34	Birmingham, AL	9.1
35	Pembroke Pines, FL	8.9
36	Columbus, GA	8.8
37	Lowell, MA	8.7
38	Yonkers, NY	8.4
39	Huntsville, AL	8.2
40	Sterling Heights, MI	7.5
41	Colonie, NY	7.3
41	Racine, WI	7.3
43	Corpus Christi, TX	7.2
44	Yuma, AZ	7.1
45	Murrieta, CA	7.0
46	Ogden, UT	6.6
47	Hartford, CT	6.4
48	Henderson, NV	6.2
49	Carson, CA	5.9
50	Philadelphia, PA	5.7
51	San Francisco, CA	5.4
52	Brick Twnshp, NJ	5.2
52	Kenosha, WI	5.2
54	Westland, MI	5.1
55	Ventura, CA	4.8
56	Carlsbad, CA	4.6
57	Edison Twnshp, NJ	4.4
58	Santa Clara, CA	4.1
58	Vacaville, CA	4.1
60	Kent, WA	3.9
61	Troy, MI	3.7
62	Pomona, CA	3.6
63	Abilene, TX	3.4
63	San Mateo, CA	3.4
65	Lee's Summit, MO	3.1
66	Camden, NJ	2.9
67	Boca Raton, FL	2.8
68	Austin, TX	2.6
69	Buffalo, NY	2.4
69	Pasadena, CA	2.4
71	Evansville, IN	2.1
72	South Gate, CA	1.9
73	South Bend, IN	1.2
74	Albany, GA	0.8
74	Clinton Twnshp, MI	0.8
74	Pittsburgh, PA	0.8
77	Charlotte, NC	0.7
78	Amherst, NY	0.6
79	Boston, MA	0.5
80	Cincinnati, OH	0.4
81	El Monte, CA	0.3
82	Lubbock, TX	0.2
83	Lakeland, FL	0.1
83	Midland, TX	0.1
85	Gainesville, FL	(0.4)
86	Manchester, NH	(0.5)
87	Lynn, MA	(0.7)
88	Temecula, CA	(1.0)
89	St. Petersburg, FL	(1.1)
90	Murfreesboro, TN	(1.4)
91	San Diego, CA	(1.7)
92	Independence, MO	(1.8)
92	Napa, CA	(1.8)
92	Salinas, CA	(1.8)
95	Bellingham, WA	(2.0)
96	Federal Way, WA	(2.1)
96	Houston, TX	(2.1)
98	Canton Twnshp, MI	(2.2)
98	Cape Coral, FL	(2.2)
98	Springfield, MA	(2.2)
98	Vista, CA	(2.2)
98	Woodbridge Twnshp, NJ	(2.2)
103	Hampton, VA	(2.3)
103	Macon, GA	(2.3)
105	Fort Lauderdale, FL	(2.6)
105	Norwalk, CA	(2.6)
107	Las Vegas, NV	(2.9)
107	Sunnyvale, CA	(2.9)
109	Norman, OK	(3.1)
109	Shreveport, LA	(3.1)
111	Stockton, CA	(3.2)
112	Cleveland, OH	(3.4)
112	Parma, OH	(3.4)
114	Mobile, AL	(3.5)
115	Brockton, MA	(3.7)
115	Jersey City, NJ	(3.7)
117	Milwaukee, WI	(4.0)
118	Jacksonville, FL	(4.1)
119	North Charleston, SC	(4.2)
120	Clearwater, FL	(4.4)
121	Irving, TX	(4.5)
122	Toledo, OH	(4.6)
122	Warren, MI	(4.6)
124	Erie, PA	(4.7)
125	Orlando, FL	(4.8)
126	Costa Mesa, CA	(4.9)
126	Westminster, CA	(4.9)
126	Yakima, WA	(4.9)
129	Chattanooga, TN	(5.1)
130	Concord, CA	(5.2)
131	Garden Grove, CA	(5.3)
132	West Covina, CA	(5.4)
133	Fullerton, CA	(5.5)
134	Tulsa, OK	(5.9)
135	Farmington Hills, MI	(6.1)
135	Naperville, IL	(6.1)
135	Visalia, CA	(6.1)
138	Greensboro, NC	(6.3)
138	San Jose, CA	(6.3)
140	Minneapolis, MN	(6.9)
141	Orange, CA	(7.0)
142	Baton Rouge, LA	(7.1)
143	Largo, FL	(7.3)
144	Nashville, TN	(7.4)
145	Newport News, VA	(7.8)
145	St. Louis, MO	(7.8)
145	Thousand Oaks, CA	(7.8)
148	Plano, TX	(7.9)
149	Somerville, MA	(8.0)
150	Colorado Springs, CO	(8.1)
151	Lawton, OK	(8.3)
151	Scottsdale, AZ	(8.3)
153	Laredo, TX	(8.4)
154	Jackson, MS	(8.8)
154	Surprise, AZ	(8.8)
156	San Leandro, CA	(8.9)
157	Wichita Falls, TX	(9.0)
158	Cambridge, MA	(9.2)
159	Ann Arbor, MI	(9.3)
160	Portsmouth, VA	(9.4)
161	Boulder, CO	(9.6)
161	Grand Prairie, TX	(9.6)
163	Winston-Salem, NC	(9.8)
164	Port St. Lucie, FL	(9.9)
165	Burbank, CA	(10.0)
166	Bellevue, WA	(10.1)
166	Buena Park, CA	(10.1)
166	Sandy, UT	(10.1)
169	Hamilton Twnshp, NJ	(10.3)
170	Longview, TX	(10.5)
171	Vallejo, CA	(10.6)
172	Chicago, IL	(10.7)
173	Modesto, CA	(10.8)
174	Southfield, MI	(11.1)
175	Anchorage, AK	(11.2)
176	Seattle, WA	(11.3)
177	Little Rock, AR	(11.5)
177	Oxnard, CA	(11.5)
179	Denver, CO	(11.6)
179	Escondido, CA	(11.6)
181	Dallas, TX	(11.7)
182	Chesapeake, VA	(11.9)
182	New York, NY	(11.9)
184	Fremont, CA	(12.0)
184	Lake Forest, CA	(12.0)
184	Livonia, MI	(12.0)
184	Tuscaloosa, AL	(12.0)
188	Hammond, IN	(12.1)
189	Overland Park, KS	(12.7)
190	Hayward, CA	(12.8)
191	Madison, WI	(13.0)
192	Moreno Valley, CA	(13.1)

RANK	CITY	% CHANGE
193	Dayton, OH	(13.2)
193	Plantation, FL	(13.2)
193	Round Rock, TX	(13.2)
196	High Point, NC	(13.3)
196	Norfolk, VA	(13.3)
198	Chula Vista, CA	(13.4)
198	Newport Beach, CA	(13.4)
200	Tracy, CA	(13.5)
201	Lafayette, LA	(13.6)
201	Wichita, KS	(13.6)
203	Detroit, MI	(13.7)
203	Duluth, MN	(13.7)
205	Flint, MI	(14.0)
206	Peoria, AZ	(14.2)
207	Amarillo, TX	(14.3)
207	Springfield, IL	(14.3)
209	Fort Collins, CO	(14.4)
209	Salt Lake City, UT	(14.4)
211	Athens-Clarke, GA	(14.5)
211	Clarkstown, NY	(14.5)
213	Topeka, KS	(14.9)
214	Albuquerque, NM	(15.0)
214	Reno, NV	(15.0)
216	Oceanside, CA	(15.1)
217	Melbourne, FL	(15.5)
217	San Angelo, TX	(15.5)
219	Virginia Beach, VA	(15.7)
220	Garland, TX	(15.8)
220	Rochester, NY	(15.8)
222	Bellflower, CA	(15.9)
223	Corona, CA	(16.0)
223	Davie, FL	(16.0)
225	Columbus, OH	(16.2)
226	Lincoln, NE	(16.3)
227	Syracuse, NY	(16.5)
228	Rancho Cucamon., CA	(16.7)
229	Carrollton, TX	(16.8)
230	Fontana, CA	(16.9)
230	Palmdale, CA	(16.9)
232	Miami Beach, FL	(17.0)
232	Riverside, CA	(17.0)
234	Hawthorne, CA	(17.1)
235	Cary, NC	(17.3)
236	Mission Viejo, CA	(17.5)
237	Clovis, CA	(17.6)
237	Tacoma, WA	(17.6)
239	Arlington, TX	(17.7)
239	Reading, PA	(17.7)
239	Sunrise, FL	(17.7)
242	Elizabeth, NJ	(17.8)
242	Green Bay, WI	(17.8)
244	Columbia, SC	(18.1)
245	Toms River Twnshp, NJ	(18.2)
246	Lakewood, CO	(18.4)
247	Vancouver, WA	(18.5)
248	Hialeah, FL	(18.6)
248	San Antonio, TX	(18.6)
250	Montgomery, AL	(18.8)
251	Billings, MT	(18.9)
251	Cedar Rapids, IA	(18.9)
251	Rochester, MN	(18.9)
254	Miramar, FL	(19.0)
255	Sugar Land, TX	(19.1)
256	Youngstown, OH	(19.2)
257	West Valley, UT	(19.3)
258	El Cajon, CA	(19.4)

RANK	CITY	% CHANGE
258	Phoenix, AZ	(19.4)
260	Aurora, IL	(19.5)
260	Mesquite, TX	(19.5)
262	Clifton, NJ	(19.6)
262	Fairfield, CA	(19.6)
264	Richardson, TX	(19.8)
265	Roseville, CA	(19.9)
266	Berkeley, CA	(20.1)
267	Lansing, MI	(20.2)
268	Warwick, RI	(20.4)
269	Peoria, IL	(20.5)
270	Boise, ID	(20.6)
271	Coral Springs, FL	(20.7)
271	Inglewood, CA	(20.7)
273	Portland, OR	(20.8)
274	Sioux Falls, SD	(21.1)
275	Compton, CA	(21.3)
275	Lakewood, CA	(21.3)
275	Rialto, CA	(21.3)
278	Bloomington, MN	(21.5)
278	Joliet, IL	(21.5)
278	North Las Vegas, NV	(21.5)
281	Hesperia, CA	(21.7)
282	Fort Worth, TX	(21.9)
283	Santa Ana, CA	(22.0)
284	Omaha, NE	(22.4)
285	Long Beach, CA	(22.6)
286	Anaheim, CA	(22.8)
286	Columbia, MO	(22.8)
286	Pasadena, TX	(22.8)
289	Ontario, CA	(23.1)
290	Victorville, CA	(23.2)
291	Tempe, AZ	(23.3)
292	Paterson, NJ	(23.4)
292	Santa Monica, CA	(23.4)
294	Eugene, OR	(23.7)
295	Antioch, CA	(23.9)
295	McAllen, TX	(23.9)
297	Livermore, CA	(24.5)
298	Sacramento, CA	(24.8)
299	Arvada, CO	(24.9)
300	Cranston, RI	(25.1)
301	Fargo, ND	(25.4)
302	Fort Smith, AR	(25.6)
302	Sparks, NV	(25.6)
304	Killeen, TX	(26.0)
305	Los Angeles, CA	(26.1)
306	Aurora, CO	(26.2)
307	West Jordan, UT	(26.5)
308	Torrance, CA	(26.7)
309	Thornton, CO	(26.8)
310	Danbury, CT	(26.9)
311	Baltimore, MD	(27.3)
311	Fresno, CA	(27.3)
311	Miami, FL	(27.3)
314	San Bernardino, CA	(27.4)
315	Irvine, CA	(27.8)
316	Newark, NJ	(27.9)
316	Spokane, WA	(27.9)
318	Greeley, CO	(28.1)
319	Atlanta, GA	(28.3)
320	Washington, DC	(28.9)
321	Provo, UT	(29.2)
322	Honolulu, HI	(29.7)
323	Suffolk, VA	(30.0)
324	Gilbert, AZ	(30.1)

RANK	CITY	% CHANGE
325	St. Paul, MN	(30.3)
326	Providence, RI	(31.4)
327	Hollywood, FL	(31.6)
327	Quincy, MA	(31.6)
329	Denton, TX	(32.1)
329	Santa Rosa, CA	(32.1)
331	Sioux City, IA	(32.6)
332	Hillsboro, OR	(32.7)
333	Tyler, TX	(32.8)
334	Tallahassee, FL	(32.9)
335	Tampa, FL	(33.1)
336	Alexandria, VA	(33.2)
336	Orem, UT	(33.2)
338	Beaumont, TX	(33.3)
338	Charleston, SC	(33.3)
338	Glendale, AZ	(33.3)
341	Richmond, VA	(33.5)
342	Raleigh, NC	(33.6)
343	Oakland, CA	(33.9)
344	Palm Bay, FL	(34.1)
345	Waco, TX	(34.6)
346	Mesa, AZ	(35.4)
347	Odessa, TX	(35.5)
348	Salem, OR	(36.1)
349	Lewisville, TX	(36.3)
350	Broken Arrow, OK	(36.4)
350	Chandler, AZ	(36.4)
352	West Palm Beach, FL	(36.6)
353	Richmond, CA	(37.6)
353	Savannah, GA	(37.6)
355	Beaverton, OR	(39.1)
356	Gresham, OR	(39.3)
357	Wilmington, NC	(40.3)
358	Olathe, KS	(41.4)
359	Oklahoma City, OK	(42.8)
360	Chino Hills, CA	(43.1)
361	Clarksville, TN	(44.4)
362	McKinney, TX	(46.1)
363	Brownsville, TX	(46.5)
364	Trenton, NJ	(48.1)
365	New Orleans, LA	(58.8)
NA	Albany, NY**	NA
NA	Canton, OH**	NA
NA	Centennial, CO**	NA
NA	Cheektowaga, NY**	NA
NA	Des Moines, IA**	NA
NA	Durham, NC**	NA
NA	El Paso, TX**	NA
NA	Fort Wayne, IN**	NA
NA	Greece, NY**	NA
NA	Kansas City, KS**	NA
NA	Kansas City, MO**	NA
NA	Las Cruces, NM**	NA
NA	Lexington, KY**	NA
NA	Louisville, KY**	NA
NA	Miami Gardens, FL**	NA
NA	Nashua, NH**	NA
NA	New Bedford, MA**	NA
NA	Newton, MA**	NA
NA	Roanoke, VA**	NA
NA	Rockford, IL**	NA
NA	Santa Maria, CA**	NA
NA	Spokane Valley, WA**	NA
NA	Tucson, AZ**	NA
NA	Westminster, CO**	NA
NA	Worcester, MA**	NA

Source: CQ Press using data from F.B.I. "Crime in the United States 2006"

**Larceny and theft is the unlawful taking of property. Attempts are included.*

***Not available.*

77. Motor Vehicle Thefts in 2006

National Total = 1,192,809 Motor Vehicle Thefts*

RANK	CITY	THEFTS
295	Abilene, TX	303
268	Albany, GA	399
324	Albany, NY	241
30	Albuquerque, NM	5,515
274	Alexandria, VA	375
245	Alhambra, CA	457
226	Allentown, PA	495
135	Amarillo, TX	1,051
390	Amherst, NY	34
88	Anaheim, CA	1,654
99	Anchorage, AK	1,445
350	Ann Arbor, MI	173
157	Antioch, CA	880
86	Arlington, TX	1,719
278	Arvada, CO	360
276	Athens-Clarke, GA	364
29	Atlanta, GA	5,878
74	Aurora, CO	2,043
303	Aurora, IL	285
60	Austin, TX	2,544
58	Bakersfield, CA	2,563
169	Baldwin Park, CA	801
28	Baltimore, MD	6,262
98	Baton Rouge, LA	1,454
212	Beaumont, TX	550
315	Beaverton, OR	260
232	Bellevue, WA	476
189	Bellflower, CA	683
310	Bellingham, WA	276
132	Berkeley, CA	1,075
287	Billings, MT	321
73	Birmingham, AL	2,081
354	Bloomington, MN	163
351	Boca Raton, FL	168
273	Boise, ID	377
37	Boston, MA	4,076
358	Boulder, CO	157
387	Brick Twnshp, NJ	60
113	Bridgeport, CT	1,225
191	Brockton, MA	662
373	Broken Arrow, OK	135
219	Brownsville, TX	525
244	Buena Park, CA	459
72	Buffalo, NY	2,125
237	Burbank, CA	471
335	Cambridge, MA	223
120	Camden, NJ	1,178
370	Canton Twnshp, MI	141
215	Canton, OH	539
285	Cape Coral, FL	331
336	Carlsbad, CA	220
231	Carrollton, TX	478
183	Carson, CA	702
376	Cary, NC	115
297	Cedar Rapids, IA	298
359	Centennial, CO	156
121	Chandler, AZ	1,171
214	Charleston, SC	543
18	Charlotte, NC	7,150
127	Chattanooga, TN	1,126
372	Cheektowaga, NY	137
242	Chesapeake, VA	461
4	Chicago, IL	21,828
354	Chino Hills, CA	163

RANK	CITY	THEFTS
254	Chino, CA	434
76	Chula Vista, CA	2,033
57	Cincinnati, OH	2,575
386	Clarkstown, NY	63
306	Clarksville, TN	283
261	Clearwater, FL	428
24	Cleveland, OH	6,534
299	Clifton, NJ	291
290	Clinton Twnshp, MI	316
272	Clovis, CA	385
379	Colonie, NY	108
83	Colorado Springs, CO	1,789
330	Columbia, MO	226
192	Columbia, SC	654
81	Columbus, GA	1,850
25	Columbus, OH	6,400
156	Compton, CA	902
119	Concord, CA	1,187
317	Coral Springs, FL	253
166	Corona, CA	820
158	Corpus Christi, TX	872
267	Costa Mesa, CA	407
313	Cranston, RI	268
8	Dallas, TX	13,930
220	Daly City, CA	514
361	Danbury, CT	153
292	Davie, FL	313
69	Dayton, OH	2,197
139	Dearborn, MI	1,035
309	Deerfield Beach, FL	278
339	Denton, TX	209
26	Denver, CO	6,347
148	Des Moines, IA	985
3	Detroit, MI	22,917
125	Downey, CA	1,144
337	Duluth, MN	213
124	Durham, NC	1,151
313	Edison Twnshp, NJ	268
383	Edmond, OK	92
142	El Cajon, CA	1,020
154	El Monte, CA	933
44	El Paso, TX	3,519
112	Elizabeth, NJ	1,232
370	Erie, PA	141
151	Escondido, CA	962
122	Eugene, OR	1,166
321	Evansville, IN	243
68	Everett, WA	2,243
179	Fairfield, CA	706
332	Fargo, ND	224
351	Farmington Hills, MI	168
141	Fayetteville, NC	1,023
118	Federal Way, WA	1,199
93	Flint, MI	1,521
123	Fontana, CA	1,155
305	Fort Collins, CO	284
142	Fort Lauderdale, FL	1,020
277	Fort Smith, AR	363
180	Fort Wayne, IN	705
46	Fort Worth, TX	3,347
159	Fremont, CA	860
33	Fresno, CA	4,944
200	Fullerton, CA	611
240	Gainesville, FL	466

RANK	CITY	THEFTS
171	Garden Grove, CA	785
177	Garland, TX	717
133	Gary, IN	1,066
238	Gilbert, AZ	470
54	Glendale, AZ	2,713
208	Glendale, CA	578
137	Grand Prairie, TX	1,044
186	Grand Rapids, MI	697
377	Greece, NY	112
288	Greeley, CO	320
341	Green Bay, WI	201
116	Greensboro, NC	1,207
161	Gresham, OR	856
348	Hamilton Twnshp, NJ	185
210	Hammond, IN	562
224	Hampton, VA	500
87	Hartford, CT	1,709
194	Hawthorne, CA	649
69	Hayward, CA	2,197
96	Henderson, NV	1,460
213	Hesperia, CA	548
91	Hialeah, FL	1,585
223	High Point, NC	506
320	Hillsboro, OR	249
168	Hollywood, FL	803
27	Honolulu, HI	6,288
5	Houston, TX	21,093
241	Huntington Beach, CA	463
103	Huntsville, AL	1,359
163	Independence, MO	834
12	Indianapolis, IN	8,936
134	Inglewood, CA	1,057
317	Irvine, CA	253
110	Irving, TX	1,242
36	Jacksonville, FL	4,321
80	Jackson, MS	1,857
95	Jersey City, NJ	1,495
363	Joliet, IL	151
65	Kansas City, KS	2,325
30	Kansas City, MO	5,515
343	Kenosha, WI	199
92	Kent, WA	1,563
322	Killeen, TX	242
131	Knoxville, TN	1,098
217	Lafayette, LA	531
380	Lake Forest, CA	106
281	Lakeland, FL	352
254	Lakewood, CA	434
129	Lakewood, CO	1,103
136	Lancaster, CA	1,048
230	Lansing, MI	479
116	Laredo, TX	1,207
328	Largo, FL	232
308	Las Cruces, NM	282
6	Las Vegas, NV	19,677
340	Lawrence, KS	205
299	Lawton, OK	291
366	Lee's Summit, MO	145
270	Lewisville, TX	387
182	Lexington, KY	703
258	Lincoln, NE	431
105	Little Rock, AR	1,312
331	Livermore, CA	225
292	Livonia, MI	313

RANK	CITY	THEFTS
47	Long Beach, CA	3,284
229	Longview, TX	481
1	Los Angeles, CA	25,389
39	Louisville, KY	3,694
218	Lowell, MA	526
187	Lubbock, TX	693
207	Lynn, MA	581
111	Macon, GA	1,240
234	Madison, WI	475
319	Manchester, NH	250
239	McAllen, TX	469
378	McKinney, TX	111
322	Melbourne, FL	242
21	Memphis, TN	6,719
41	Mesa, AZ	3,654
180	Mesquite, TX	705
162	Miami Beach, FL	853
167	Miami Gardens, FL	813
38	Miami, FL	3,879
328	Midland, TX	232
14	Milwaukee, WI	8,239
42	Minneapolis, MN	3,625
258	Miramar, FL	431
375	Mission Viejo, CA	123
104	Mobile, AL	1,330
77	Modesto, CA	2,024
126	Montgomery, AL	1,127
102	Moreno Valley, CA	1,388
303	Murfreesboro, TN	285
332	Murrieta, CA	224
342	Napa, CA	200
385	Naperville, IL	74
380	Nashua, NH	107
50	Nashville, TN	3,021
257	New Bedford, MA	432
52	New Orleans, LA	2,863
7	New York, NY	15,936
32	Newark, NJ	5,097
349	Newport Beach, CA	174
174	Newport News, VA	757
389	Newton, MA	37
138	Norfolk, VA	1,037
301	Norman, OK	286
130	North Charleston, SC	1,099
55	North Las Vegas, NV	2,638
170	Norwalk, CA	797
11	Oakland, CA	10,549
196	Oceanside, CA	633
316	Odessa, TX	256
252	Ogden, UT	436
34	Oklahoma City, OK	4,819
326	Olathe, KS	235
45	Omaha, NE	3,443
84	Ontario, CA	1,778
256	Orange, CA	433
368	Orem, UT	143
64	Orlando, FL	2,336
271	Overland Park, KS	386
199	Oxnard, CA	614
301	Palm Bay, FL	286
188	Palmdale, CA	690
360	Parma, OH	154
221	Pasadena, CA	508
252	Pasadena, TX	436
145	Paterson, NJ	1,005
235	Pembroke Pines, FL	474

RANK	CITY	THEFTS
149	Peoria, AZ	972
210	Peoria, IL	562
10	Philadelphia, PA	11,657
2	Phoenix, AZ	24,089
79	Pittsburgh, PA	1,865
206	Plano, TX	582
283	Plantation, FL	345
100	Pomona, CA	1,419
216	Pompano Beach, FL	538
368	Port St. Lucie, FL	143
35	Portland, OR	4,478
280	Portsmouth, VA	354
85	Providence, RI	1,733
344	Provo, UT	197
246	Pueblo, CO	455
361	Quincy, MA	153
275	Racine, WI	365
144	Raleigh, NC	1,006
184	Rancho Cucamon., CA	701
114	Reading, PA	1,221
225	Redding, CA	496
89	Reno, NV	1,631
152	Rialto, CA	960
294	Richardson, TX	312
67	Richmond, CA	2,253
97	Richmond, VA	1,457
61	Riverside, CA	2,424
260	Roanoke, VA	430
364	Rochester, MN	147
63	Rochester, NY	2,413
172	Rockford, IL	778
209	Roseville, CA	574
347	Roswell, GA	187
388	Round Rock, TX	49
17	Sacramento, CA	7,175
164	Salem, OR	831
101	Salinas, CA	1,398
75	Salt Lake City, UT	2,040
332	San Angelo, TX	224
23	San Antonio, TX	6,615
51	San Bernardino, CA	2,917
9	San Diego, CA	13,338
22	San Francisco, CA	6,636
19	San Jose, CA	7,139
108	San Leandro, CA	1,247
298	San Mateo, CA	294
326	Sandy, UT	235
56	Santa Ana, CA	2,600
357	Santa Barbara, CA	158
232	Santa Clara, CA	476
262	Santa Clarita, CA	425
228	Santa Maria, CA	488
269	Santa Monica, CA	394
227	Santa Rosa, CA	492
115	Savannah, GA	1,220
128	Scottsdale, AZ	1,118
15	Seattle, WA	8,147
107	Shreveport, LA	1,263
356	Simi Valley, CA	160
345	Sioux City, IA	191
338	Sioux Falls, SD	212
290	Somerville, MA	316
205	South Bend, IN	586
109	South Gate, CA	1,246
178	Southfield, MI	707
246	Sparks, NV	455

RANK	CITY	THEFTS
190	Spokane Valley, WA	678
66	Spokane, WA	2,299
263	Springfield, IL	421
90	Springfield, MA	1,606
164	Springfield, MO	831
284	Sterling Heights, MI	343
40	Stockton, CA	3,681
13	St. Louis, MO	8,645
71	St. Paul, MN	2,138
53	St. Petersburg, FL	2,761
366	Suffolk, VA	145
384	Sugar Land, TX	75
266	Sunnyvale, CA	409
289	Sunrise, FL	318
306	Surprise, AZ	283
176	Syracuse, NY	736
43	Tacoma, WA	3,601
201	Tallahassee, FL	606
49	Tampa, FL	3,087
279	Temecula, CA	357
62	Tempe, AZ	2,420
193	Thornton, CO	650
374	Thousand Oaks, CA	131
59	Toledo, OH	2,557
382	Toms River Twnshp, NJ	98
197	Topeka, KS	625
222	Torrance, CA	507
251	Tracy, CA	441
243	Trenton, NJ	460
364	Troy, MI	147
16	Tucson, AZ	7,376
48	Tulsa, OK	3,173
312	Tuscaloosa, AL	269
345	Tyler, TX	191
325	Upper Darby Twnshp, PA	236
285	Vacaville, CA	331
94	Vallejo, CA	1,516
153	Vancouver, WA	942
281	Ventura, CA	352
173	Victorville, CA	766
202	Virginia Beach, VA	595
106	Visalia, CA	1,281
204	Vista, CA	587
246	Waco, TX	455
82	Warren, MI	1,805
353	Warwick, RI	165
20	Washington, DC	7,057
198	Waterbury, CT	620
155	West Covina, CA	912
295	West Jordan, UT	303
150	West Palm Beach, FL	966
160	West Valley, UT	859
250	Westland, MI	446
263	Westminster, CA	421
203	Westminster, CO	592
235	Whittier, CA	474
265	Wichita Falls, TX	420
78	Wichita, KS	1,976
195	Wilmington, NC	648
140	Winston-Salem, NC	1,034
310	Woodbridge Twnshp, NJ	276
147	Worcester, MA	988
146	Yakima, WA	1,003
249	Yonkers, NY	451
184	Youngstown, OH	701
175	Yuma, AZ	745

Source: Federal Bureau of Investigation "Crime in the United States 2006"

**Motor vehicle theft includes the theft or attempted theft of a self-propelled vehicle. Excludes motorboats, construction equipment, airplanes, and farming equipment.*

77. Motor Vehicle Thefts in 2006 (continued)

National Total = 1,192,809 Motor Vehicle Thefts*

RANK	CITY	THEFTS
1	Los Angeles, CA	25,389
2	Phoenix, AZ	24,089
3	Detroit, MI	22,917
4	Chicago, IL	21,828
5	Houston, TX	21,093
6	Las Vegas, NV	19,677
7	New York, NY	15,936
8	Dallas, TX	13,930
9	San Diego, CA	13,338
10	Philadelphia, PA	11,657
11	Oakland, CA	10,549
12	Indianapolis, IN	8,936
13	St. Louis, MO	8,645
14	Milwaukee, WI	8,239
15	Seattle, WA	8,147
16	Tucson, AZ	7,376
17	Sacramento, CA	7,175
18	Charlotte, NC	7,150
19	San Jose, CA	7,139
20	Washington, DC	7,057
21	Memphis, TN	6,719
22	San Francisco, CA	6,636
23	San Antonio, TX	6,615
24	Cleveland, OH	6,534
25	Columbus, OH	6,400
26	Denver, CO	6,347
27	Honolulu, HI	6,288
28	Baltimore, MD	6,262
29	Atlanta, GA	5,878
30	Albuquerque, NM	5,515
30	Kansas City, MO	5,515
32	Newark, NJ	5,097
33	Fresno, CA	4,944
34	Oklahoma City, OK	4,819
35	Portland, OR	4,478
36	Jacksonville, FL	4,321
37	Boston, MA	4,076
38	Miami, FL	3,879
39	Louisville, KY	3,694
40	Stockton, CA	3,681
41	Mesa, AZ	3,654
42	Minneapolis, MN	3,625
43	Tacoma, WA	3,601
44	El Paso, TX	3,519
45	Omaha, NE	3,443
46	Fort Worth, TX	3,347
47	Long Beach, CA	3,284
48	Tulsa, OK	3,173
49	Tampa, FL	3,087
50	Nashville, TN	3,021
51	San Bernardino, CA	2,917
52	New Orleans, LA	2,863
53	St. Petersburg, FL	2,761
54	Glendale, AZ	2,713
55	North Las Vegas, NV	2,638
56	Santa Ana, CA	2,600
57	Cincinnati, OH	2,575
58	Bakersfield, CA	2,563
59	Toledo, OH	2,557
60	Austin, TX	2,544
61	Riverside, CA	2,424
62	Tempe, AZ	2,420
63	Rochester, NY	2,413
64	Orlando, FL	2,336
65	Kansas City, KS	2,325
66	Spokane, WA	2,299
67	Richmond, CA	2,253
68	Everett, WA	2,243
69	Dayton, OH	2,197
69	Hayward, CA	2,197
71	St. Paul, MN	2,138
72	Buffalo, NY	2,125
73	Birmingham, AL	2,081
74	Aurora, CO	2,043
75	Salt Lake City, UT	2,040
76	Chula Vista, CA	2,033
77	Modesto, CA	2,024
78	Wichita, KS	1,976
79	Pittsburgh, PA	1,865
80	Jackson, MS	1,857
81	Columbus, GA	1,850
82	Warren, MI	1,805
83	Colorado Springs, CO	1,789
84	Ontario, CA	1,778
85	Providence, RI	1,733
86	Arlington, TX	1,719
87	Hartford, CT	1,709
88	Anaheim, CA	1,654
89	Reno, NV	1,631
90	Springfield, MA	1,606
91	Hialeah, FL	1,585
92	Kent, WA	1,563
93	Flint, MI	1,521
94	Vallejo, CA	1,516
95	Jersey City, NJ	1,495
96	Henderson, NV	1,460
97	Richmond, VA	1,457
98	Baton Rouge, LA	1,454
99	Anchorage, AK	1,445
100	Pomona, CA	1,419
101	Salinas, CA	1,398
102	Moreno Valley, CA	1,388
103	Huntsville, AL	1,359
104	Mobile, AL	1,330
105	Little Rock, AR	1,312
106	Visalia, CA	1,281
107	Shreveport, LA	1,263
108	San Leandro, CA	1,247
109	South Gate, CA	1,246
110	Irving, TX	1,242
111	Macon, GA	1,240
112	Elizabeth, NJ	1,232
113	Bridgeport, CT	1,225
114	Reading, PA	1,221
115	Savannah, GA	1,220
116	Greensboro, NC	1,207
116	Laredo, TX	1,207
118	Federal Way, WA	1,199
119	Concord, CA	1,187
120	Camden, NJ	1,178
121	Chandler, AZ	1,171
122	Eugene, OR	1,166
123	Fontana, CA	1,155
124	Durham, NC	1,151
125	Downey, CA	1,144
126	Montgomery, AL	1,127
127	Chattanooga, TN	1,126
128	Scottsdale, AZ	1,118
129	Lakewood, CO	1,103
130	North Charleston, SC	1,099
131	Knoxville, TN	1,098
132	Berkeley, CA	1,075
133	Gary, IN	1,066
134	Inglewood, CA	1,057
135	Amarillo, TX	1,051
136	Lancaster, CA	1,048
137	Grand Prairie, TX	1,044
138	Norfolk, VA	1,037
139	Dearborn, MI	1,035
140	Winston-Salem, NC	1,034
141	Fayetteville, NC	1,023
142	El Cajon, CA	1,020
142	Fort Lauderdale, FL	1,020
144	Raleigh, NC	1,006
145	Paterson, NJ	1,005
146	Yakima, WA	1,003
147	Worcester, MA	988
148	Des Moines, IA	985
149	Peoria, AZ	972
150	West Palm Beach, FL	966
151	Escondido, CA	962
152	Rialto, CA	960
153	Vancouver, WA	942
154	El Monte, CA	933
155	West Covina, CA	912
156	Compton, CA	902
157	Antioch, CA	880
158	Corpus Christi, TX	872
159	Fremont, CA	860
160	West Valley, UT	859
161	Gresham, OR	856
162	Miami Beach, FL	853
163	Independence, MO	834
164	Salem, OR	831
164	Springfield, MO	831
166	Corona, CA	820
167	Miami Gardens, FL	813
168	Hollywood, FL	803
169	Baldwin Park, CA	801
170	Norwalk, CA	797
171	Garden Grove, CA	785
172	Rockford, IL	778
173	Victorville, CA	766
174	Newport News, VA	757
175	Yuma, AZ	745
176	Syracuse, NY	736
177	Garland, TX	717
178	Southfield, MI	707
179	Fairfield, CA	706
180	Fort Wayne, IN	705
180	Mesquite, TX	705
182	Lexington, KY	703
183	Carson, CA	702
184	Rancho Cucamon., CA	701
184	Youngstown, OH	701
186	Grand Rapids, MI	697
187	Lubbock, TX	693
188	Palmdale, CA	690
189	Bellflower, CA	683
190	Spokane Valley, WA	678
191	Brockton, MA	662
192	Columbia, SC	654

RANK	CITY	THEFTS
193	Thornton, CO	650
194	Hawthorne, CA	649
195	Wilmington, NC	648
196	Oceanside, CA	633
197	Topeka, KS	625
198	Waterbury, CT	620
199	Oxnard, CA	614
200	Fullerton, CA	611
201	Tallahassee, FL	606
202	Virginia Beach, VA	595
203	Westminster, CO	592
204	Vista, CA	587
205	South Bend, IN	586
206	Plano, TX	582
207	Lynn, MA	581
208	Glendale, CA	578
209	Roseville, CA	574
210	Hammond, IN	562
210	Peoria, IL	562
212	Beaumont, TX	550
213	Hesperia, CA	548
214	Charleston, SC	543
215	Canton, OH	539
216	Pompano Beach, FL	538
217	Lafayette, LA	531
218	Lowell, MA	526
219	Brownsville, TX	525
220	Daly City, CA	514
221	Pasadena, CA	508
222	Torrance, CA	507
223	High Point, NC	506
224	Hampton, VA	500
225	Redding, CA	496
226	Allentown, PA	495
227	Santa Rosa, CA	492
228	Santa Maria, CA	488
229	Longview, TX	481
230	Lansing, MI	479
231	Carrollton, TX	478
232	Bellevue, WA	476
232	Santa Clara, CA	476
234	Madison, WI	475
235	Pembroke Pines, FL	474
235	Whittier, CA	474
237	Burbank, CA	471
238	Gilbert, AZ	470
239	McAllen, TX	469
240	Gainesville, FL	466
241	Huntington Beach, CA	463
242	Chesapeake, VA	461
243	Trenton, NJ	460
244	Buena Park, CA	459
245	Alhambra, CA	457
246	Pueblo, CO	455
246	Sparks, NV	455
246	Waco, TX	455
249	Yonkers, NY	451
250	Westland, MI	446
251	Tracy, CA	441
252	Ogden, UT	436
252	Pasadena, TX	436
254	Chino, CA	434
254	Lakewood, CA	434
256	Orange, CA	433
257	New Bedford, MA	432
258	Lincoln, NE	431
258	Miramar, FL	431
260	Roanoke, VA	430
261	Clearwater, FL	428
262	Santa Clarita, CA	425
263	Springfield, IL	421
263	Westminster, CA	421
265	Wichita Falls, TX	420
266	Sunnyvale, CA	409
267	Costa Mesa, CA	407
268	Albany, GA	399
269	Santa Monica, CA	394
270	Lewisville, TX	387
271	Overland Park, KS	386
272	Clovis, CA	385
273	Boise, ID	377
274	Alexandria, VA	375
275	Racine, WI	365
276	Athens-Clarke, GA	364
277	Fort Smith, AR	363
278	Arvada, CO	360
279	Temecula, CA	357
280	Portsmouth, VA	354
281	Lakeland, FL	352
281	Ventura, CA	352
283	Plantation, FL	345
284	Sterling Heights, MI	343
285	Cape Coral, FL	331
285	Vacaville, CA	331
287	Billings, MT	321
288	Greeley, CO	320
289	Sunrise, FL	318
290	Clinton Twnshp, MI	316
290	Somerville, MA	316
292	Davie, FL	313
292	Livonia, MI	313
294	Richardson, TX	312
295	Abilene, TX	303
295	West Jordan, UT	303
297	Cedar Rapids, IA	298
298	San Mateo, CA	294
299	Clifton, NJ	291
299	Lawton, OK	291
301	Norman, OK	286
301	Palm Bay, FL	286
303	Aurora, IL	285
303	Murfreesboro, TN	285
305	Fort Collins, CO	284
306	Clarksville, TN	283
306	Surprise, AZ	283
308	Las Cruces, NM	282
309	Deerfield Beach, FL	278
310	Bellingham, WA	276
310	Woodbridge Twnshp, NJ	276
312	Tuscaloosa, AL	269
313	Cranston, RI	268
313	Edison Twnshp, NJ	268
315	Beaverton, OR	260
316	Odessa, TX	256
317	Coral Springs, FL	253
317	Irvine, CA	253
319	Manchester, NH	250
320	Hillsboro, OR	249
321	Evansville, IN	243
322	Killeen, TX	242
322	Melbourne, FL	242
324	Albany, NY	241
325	Upper Darby Twnshp, PA	236
326	Olathe, KS	235
326	Sandy, UT	235
328	Largo, FL	232
328	Midland, TX	232
330	Columbia, MO	226
331	Livermore, CA	225
332	Fargo, ND	224
332	Murrieta, CA	224
332	San Angelo, TX	224
335	Cambridge, MA	223
336	Carlsbad, CA	220
337	Duluth, MN	213
338	Sioux Falls, SD	212
339	Denton, TX	209
340	Lawrence, KS	205
341	Green Bay, WI	201
342	Napa, CA	200
343	Kenosha, WI	199
344	Provo, UT	197
345	Sioux City, IA	191
345	Tyler, TX	191
347	Roswell, GA	187
348	Hamilton Twnshp, NJ	185
349	Newport Beach, CA	174
350	Ann Arbor, MI	173
351	Boca Raton, FL	168
351	Farmington Hills, MI	168
353	Warwick, RI	165
354	Bloomington, MN	163
354	Chino Hills, CA	163
356	Simi Valley, CA	160
357	Santa Barbara, CA	158
358	Boulder, CO	157
359	Centennial, CO	156
360	Parma, OH	154
361	Danbury, CT	153
361	Quincy, MA	153
363	Joliet, IL	151
364	Rochester, MN	147
364	Troy, MI	147
366	Lee's Summit, MO	145
366	Suffolk, VA	145
368	Orem, UT	143
368	Port St. Lucie, FL	143
370	Canton Twnshp, MI	141
370	Erie, PA	141
372	Cheektowaga, NY	137
373	Broken Arrow, OK	135
374	Thousand Oaks, CA	131
375	Mission Viejo, CA	123
376	Cary, NC	115
377	Greece, NY	112
378	McKinney, TX	111
379	Colonie, NY	108
380	Nashua, NH	107
380	Lake Forest, CA	106
382	Toms River Twnshp, NJ	98
383	Edmond, OK	92
384	Sugar Land, TX	75
385	Naperville, IL	74
386	Clarkstown, NY	63
387	Brick Twnshp, NJ	60
388	Round Rock, TX	49
389	Newton, MA	37
390	Amherst, NY	34

Source: Federal Bureau of Investigation "Crime in the United States 2006"

**Motor vehicle theft includes the theft or attempted theft of a self-propelled vehicle. Excludes motorboats, construction equipment, airplanes, and farming equipment.*

78. Motor Vehicle Theft Rate in 2006

National Rate = 398.4 Motor Vehicle Thefts per 100,000 Population*

RANK	CITY	RATE
308	Abilene, TX	256.8
195	Albany, GA	512.8
307	Albany, NY	257.0
46	Albuquerque, NM	1,100.9
298	Alexandria, VA	274.4
193	Alhambra, CA	518.2
215	Allentown, PA	462.2
163	Amarillo, TX	558.4
390	Amherst, NY	30.3
208	Anaheim, CA	494.0
192	Anchorage, AK	520.4
366	Ann Arbor, MI	153.1
88	Antioch, CA	866.7
217	Arlington, TX	460.8
264	Arvada, CO	339.8
262	Athens-Clarke, GA	341.1
37	Atlanta, GA	1,210.0
138	Aurora, CO	674.6
357	Aurora, IL	168.6
255	Austin, TX	358.4
89	Bakersfield, CA	859.5
61	Baldwin Park, CA	1,006.6
65	Baltimore, MD	982.2
133	Baton Rouge, LA	690.8
210	Beaumont, TX	478.4
290	Beaverton, OR	298.2
237	Bellevue, WA	399.5
81	Bellflower, CA	907.7
250	Bellingham, WA	364.0
53	Berkeley, CA	1,057.5
273	Billings, MT	322.1
83	Birmingham, AL	890.9
341	Bloomington, MN	199.5
347	Boca Raton, FL	190.7
349	Boise, ID	190.2
123	Boston, MA	724.8
360	Boulder, CO	168.1
386	Brick Twnshp, NJ	76.7
85	Bridgeport, CT	882.6
132	Brockton, MA	695.4
363	Broken Arrow, OK	155.2
287	Brownsville, TX	304.8
157	Buena Park, CA	574.6
114	Buffalo, NY	757.6
221	Burbank, CA	448.4
328	Cambridge, MA	221.4
16	Camden, NJ	1,471.2
361	Canton Twnshp, MI	164.2
137	Canton, OH	677.3
322	Cape Coral, FL	232.5
318	Carlsbad, CA	240.2
240	Carrollton, TX	391.0
121	Carson, CA	740.5
381	Cary, NC	105.9
317	Cedar Rapids, IA	240.8
362	Centennial, CO	155.8
209	Chandler, AZ	480.1
205	Charleston, SC	501.1
58	Charlotte, NC	1,022.3
124	Chattanooga, TN	718.4
356	Cheektowaga, NY	169.1
336	Chesapeake, VA	208.5
113	Chicago, IL	763.8
332	Chino Hills, CA	213.3
167	Chino, CA	554.4
71	Chula Vista, CA	957.2
94	Cincinnati, OH	833.1
385	Clarkstown, NY	80.1
313	Clarksville, TN	247.6
242	Clearwater, FL	387.3
20	Cleveland, OH	1,443.2
251	Clifton, NJ	363.8
270	Clinton Twnshp, MI	327.2
225	Clovis, CA	441.0
368	Colonie, NY	139.6
212	Colorado Springs, CO	474.8
316	Columbia, MO	244.4
172	Columbia, SC	550.0
69	Columbus, GA	967.5
87	Columbus, OH	874.9
76	Compton, CA	934.5
73	Concord, CA	954.5
346	Coral Springs, FL	193.2
177	Corona, CA	544.0
289	Corpus Christi, TX	299.1
246	Costa Mesa, CA	367.3
268	Cranston, RI	331.0
42	Dallas, TX	1,116.0
201	Daly City, CA	507.7
345	Danbury, CT	194.6
249	Davie, FL	365.6
24	Dayton, OH	1,381.2
45	Dearborn, MI	1,102.8
256	Deerfield Beach, FL	358.1
344	Denton, TX	195.1
41	Denver, CO	1,116.5
204	Des Moines, IA	504.6
2	Detroit, MI	2,591.1
57	Downey, CA	1,033.4
311	Duluth, MN	249.2
171	Durham, NC	550.9
302	Edison Twnshp, NJ	266.5
376	Edmond, OK	121.8
47	El Cajon, CA	1,093.0
116	El Monte, CA	754.8
160	El Paso, TX	571.7
66	Elizabeth, NJ	978.5
370	Erie, PA	137.3
125	Escondido, CA	711.0
105	Eugene, OR	793.8
337	Evansville, IN	208.3
4	Everett, WA	2,282.6
141	Fairfield, CA	669.7
315	Fargo, ND	246.6
334	Farmington Hills, MI	209.9
109	Fayetteville, NC	772.0
21	Federal Way, WA	1,418.7
28	Flint, MI	1,286.2
130	Fontana, CA	698.6
329	Fort Collins, CO	217.7
153	Fort Lauderdale, FL	599.3
226	Fort Smith, AR	435.1
282	Fort Wayne, IN	313.6
191	Fort Worth, TX	521.5
228	Fremont, CA	425.2
52	Fresno, CA	1,062.6
220	Fullerton, CA	456.0
229	Gainesville, FL	423.6
213	Garden Grove, CA	468.5
272	Garland, TX	322.3
51	Gary, IN	1,072.8
305	Gilbert, AZ	260.2
48	Glendale, AZ	1,091.4
295	Glendale, CA	286.3
128	Grand Prairie, TX	703.4
253	Grand Rapids, MI	360.6
377	Greece, NY	118.9
254	Greeley, CO	358.5
342	Green Bay, WI	197.9
197	Greensboro, NC	510.2
86	Gresham, OR	876.6
339	Hamilton Twnshp, NJ	205.4
127	Hammond, IN	704.8
263	Hampton, VA	340.1
26	Hartford, CT	1,376.0
118	Hawthorne, CA	750.6
13	Hayward, CA	1,552.0
150	Henderson, NV	608.6
131	Hesperia, CA	696.4
126	Hialeah, FL	706.9
190	High Point, NC	521.7
293	Hillsboro, OR	289.8
180	Hollywood, FL	542.3
134	Honolulu, HI	689.0
60	Houston, TX	1,017.2
319	Huntington Beach, CA	236.0
101	Huntsville, AL	809.8
117	Independence, MO	751.3
43	Indianapolis, IN	1,115.6
79	Inglewood, CA	915.2
372	Irvine, CA	134.2
147	Irving, TX	623.7
179	Jacksonville, FL	543.0
56	Jackson, MS	1,047.2
148	Jersey City, NJ	623.5
379	Joliet, IL	110.3
9	Kansas City, KS	1,600.9
34	Kansas City, MO	1,230.4
338	Kenosha, WI	208.2
6	Kent, WA	1,878.5
320	Killeen, TX	234.8
152	Knoxville, TN	601.9
206	Lafayette, LA	500.1
369	Lake Forest, CA	137.5
241	Lakeland, FL	390.2
185	Lakewood, CA	534.5
112	Lakewood, CO	769.5
108	Lancaster, CA	774.9
233	Lansing, MI	415.7
162	Laredo, TX	562.3
285	Largo, FL	306.4
265	Las Cruces, NM	336.5
15	Las Vegas, NV	1,495.6
312	Lawrence, KS	248.8
278	Lawton, OK	319.7
354	Lee's Summit, MO	179.2
232	Lewisville, TX	416.5
305	Lexington, KY	260.2
354	Lincoln, NE	179.2
129	Little Rock, AR	702.8
296	Livermore, CA	284.4
276	Livonia, MI	320.3

RANK	CITY	RATE	RANK	CITY	RATE	RANK	CITY	RATE
135	Long Beach, CA	686.6	136	Peoria, AZ	677.4	100	Spokane Valley, WA	819.1
149	Longview, TX	618.6	207	Peoria, IL	496.1	39	Spokane, WA	1,148.4
144	Los Angeles, CA	654.4	103	Philadelphia, PA	795.9	252	Springfield, IL	362.0
154	Louisville, KY	590.1	10	Phoenix, AZ	1,587.5	55	Springfield, MA	1,052.1
202	Lowell, MA	507.1	158	Pittsburgh, PA	574.5	174	Springfield, MO	548.9
274	Lubbock, TX	321.3	327	Plano, TX	226.3	300	Sterling Heights, MI	268.6
145	Lynn, MA	650.5	239	Plantation, FL	394.6	31	Stockton, CA	1,271.5
30	Macon, GA	1,273.8	80	Pomona, CA	914.5	3	St. Louis, MO	2,492.2
331	Madison, WI	213.6	200	Pompano Beach, FL	507.9	110	St. Paul, MN	771.9
326	Manchester, NH	227.1	380	Port St. Lucie, FL	106.8	49	St. Petersburg, FL	1,090.1
245	McAllen, TX	368.9	98	Portland, OR	825.9	352	Suffolk, VA	181.7
378	McKinney, TX	111.8	260	Portsmouth, VA	349.9	384	Sugar Land, TX	96.3
283	Melbourne, FL	310.5	62	Providence, RI	987.7	281	Sunnyvale, CA	314.5
64	Memphis, TN	986.9	359	Provo, UT	168.2	261	Sunrise, FL	345.2
104	Mesa, AZ	794.9	227	Pueblo, CO	431.5	248	Surprise, AZ	366.3
187	Mesquite, TX	527.8	358	Quincy, MA	168.5	194	Syracuse, NY	518.1
74	Miami Beach, FL	954.1	219	Racine, WI	458.1	8	Tacoma, WA	1,807.2
102	Miami Gardens, FL	804.0	294	Raleigh, NC	288.8	244	Tallahassee, FL	376.0
63	Miami, FL	987.2	235	Rancho Cucamon., CA	410.2	77	Tampa, FL	931.3
325	Midland, TX	227.4	14	Reading, PA	1,508.8	234	Temecula, CA	412.4
22	Milwaukee, WI	1,418.1	175	Redding, CA	548.4	18	Tempe, AZ	1,446.5
70	Minneapolis, MN	965.9	107	Reno, NV	775.4	151	Thornton, CO	606.5
238	Miramar, FL	397.5	72	Rialto, CA	956.1	382	Thousand Oaks, CA	104.4
374	Mission Viejo, CA	128.3	286	Richardson, TX	305.9	90	Toledo, OH	847.7
186	Mobile, AL	531.7	5	Richmond, CA	2,185.1	383	Toms River Twnshp, NJ	103.4
68	Modesto, CA	969.0	120	Richmond, VA	744.5	198	Topeka, KS	508.9
165	Montgomery, AL	558.1	96	Riverside, CA	828.2	257	Torrance, CA	352.9
111	Moreno Valley, CA	771.2	218	Roanoke, VA	459.6	176	Tracy, CA	546.6
271	Murfreesboro, TN	324.2	365	Rochester, MN	153.8	178	Trenton, NJ	543.1
301	Murrieta, CA	268.2	40	Rochester, NY	1,140.1	353	Troy, MI	181.6
304	Napa, CA	265.1	203	Rockford, IL	506.1	25	Tucson, AZ	1,378.1
388	Naperville, IL	52.0	183	Roseville, CA	537.0	99	Tulsa, OK	822.4
375	Nashua, NH	122.1	333	Roswell, GA	210.9	269	Tuscaloosa, AL	327.7
182	Nashville, TN	538.7	387	Round Rock, TX	55.2	340	Tyler, TX	202.0
216	New Bedford, MA	461.2	12	Sacramento, CA	1,557.9	291	Upper Darby Twnshp, PA	296.1
143	New Orleans, LA	664.0	173	Salem, OR	549.6	258	Vacaville, CA	352.8
343	New York, NY	195.2	75	Salinas, CA	946.2	29	Vallejo, CA	1,278.9
7	Newark, NJ	1,814.7	44	Salt Lake City, UT	1,109.3	155	Vancouver, WA	588.0
330	Newport Beach, CA	216.0	314	San Angelo, TX	247.5	266	Ventura, CA	335.4
231	Newport News, VA	416.6	196	San Antonio, TX	512.0	95	Victorville, CA	831.8
389	Newton, MA	44.2	17	San Bernardino, CA	1,456.0	371	Virginia Beach, VA	134.4
224	Norfolk, VA	442.7	54	San Diego, CA	1,052.9	38	Visalia, CA	1,168.3
297	Norman, OK	278.7	84	San Francisco, CA	889.4	146	Vista, CA	643.5
32	North Charleston, SC	1,253.8	106	San Jose, CA	775.5	246	Waco, TX	367.3
19	North Las Vegas, NV	1,445.2	11	San Leandro, CA	1,580.8	27	Warren, MI	1,337.3
119	Norwalk, CA	746.3	277	San Mateo, CA	319.9	347	Warwick, RI	190.7
1	Oakland, CA	2,645.0	309	Sandy, UT	253.8	36	Washington, DC	1,213.5
243	Oceanside, CA	377.7	115	Santa Ana, CA	757.1	156	Waterbury, CT	575.5
303	Odessa, TX	266.1	351	Santa Barbara, CA	182.3	93	West Covina, CA	835.5
181	Ogden, UT	539.2	222	Santa Clara, CA	447.6	275	West Jordan, UT	320.9
82	Oklahoma City, OK	899.0	310	Santa Clarita, CA	250.3	67	West Palm Beach, FL	974.4
335	Olathe, KS	209.6	159	Santa Maria, CA	573.4	122	West Valley, UT	734.2
97	Omaha, NE	826.1	223	Santa Monica, CA	444.7	189	Westland, MI	522.2
59	Ontario, CA	1,020.5	279	Santa Rosa, CA	318.4	214	Westminster, CA	466.1
280	Orange, CA	318.0	161	Savannah, GA	571.5	169	Westminster, CO	552.9
364	Orem, UT	154.4	211	Scottsdale, AZ	476.5	166	Whittier, CA	556.1
50	Orlando, FL	1,077.4	23	Seattle, WA	1,395.6	236	Wichita Falls, TX	409.1
321	Overland Park, KS	232.6	140	Shreveport, LA	670.0	169	Wichita, KS	552.9
267	Oxnard, CA	331.4	373	Simi Valley, CA	133.6	142	Wilmington, NC	665.4
288	Palm Bay, FL	303.0	324	Sioux City, IA	228.5	188	Winston-Salem, NC	523.2
199	Palmdale, CA	508.2	367	Sioux Falls, SD	150.8	299	Woodbridge Twnshp, NJ	274.2
350	Parma, OH	188.8	230	Somerville, MA	419.0	164	Worcester, MA	558.3
259	Pasadena, CA	350.3	168	South Bend, IN	553.0	35	Yakima, WA	1,214.2
292	Pasadena, TX	294.7	33	South Gate, CA	1,248.6	323	Yonkers, NY	229.0
139	Paterson, NJ	670.2	78	Southfield, MI	922.7	92	Youngstown, OH	845.2
284	Pembroke Pines, FL	310.0	184	Sparks, NV	536.6	91	Yuma, AZ	847.3

Source: CQ Press using data from F.B.I. "Crime in the United States 2006"

**Motor vehicle theft includes the theft or attempted theft of a self-propelled vehicle. Excludes motorboats, construction equipment, airplanes, and farming equipment.*

78. Motor Vehicle Theft Rate in 2006 (continued)

National Rate = 398.4 Motor Vehicle Thefts per 100,000 Population*

RANK	CITY	RATE
1	Oakland, CA	2,645.0
2	Detroit, MI	2,591.1
3	St. Louis, MO	2,492.2
4	Everett, WA	2,282.6
5	Richmond, CA	2,185.1
6	Kent, WA	1,878.5
7	Newark, NJ	1,814.7
8	Tacoma, WA	1,807.2
9	Kansas City, KS	1,600.9
10	Phoenix, AZ	1,587.5
11	San Leandro, CA	1,580.8
12	Sacramento, CA	1,557.9
13	Hayward, CA	1,552.0
14	Reading, PA	1,508.8
15	Las Vegas, NV	1,495.6
16	Camden, NJ	1,471.2
17	San Bernardino, CA	1,456.0
18	Tempe, AZ	1,446.5
19	North Las Vegas, NV	1,445.2
20	Cleveland, OH	1,443.2
21	Federal Way, WA	1,418.7
22	Milwaukee, WI	1,418.1
23	Seattle, WA	1,395.6
24	Dayton, OH	1,381.2
25	Tucson, AZ	1,378.1
26	Hartford, CT	1,376.0
27	Warren, MI	1,337.3
28	Flint, MI	1,286.2
29	Vallejo, CA	1,278.9
30	Macon, GA	1,273.8
31	Stockton, CA	1,271.5
32	North Charleston, SC	1,253.8
33	South Gate, CA	1,248.6
34	Kansas City, MO	1,230.4
35	Yakima, WA	1,214.2
36	Washington, DC	1,213.5
37	Atlanta, GA	1,210.0
38	Visalia, CA	1,168.3
39	Spokane, WA	1,148.4
40	Rochester, NY	1,140.1
41	Denver, CO	1,116.5
42	Dallas, TX	1,116.0
43	Indianapolis, IN	1,115.6
44	Salt Lake City, UT	1,109.3
45	Dearborn, MI	1,102.8
46	Albuquerque, NM	1,100.9
47	El Cajon, CA	1,093.0
48	Glendale, AZ	1,091.4
49	St. Petersburg, FL	1,090.1
50	Orlando, FL	1,077.4
51	Gary, IN	1,072.8
52	Fresno, CA	1,062.6
53	Berkeley, CA	1,057.5
54	San Diego, CA	1,052.9
55	Springfield, MA	1,052.1
56	Jackson, MS	1,047.2
57	Downey, CA	1,033.4
58	Charlotte, NC	1,022.3
59	Ontario, CA	1,020.5
60	Houston, TX	1,017.2
61	Baldwin Park, CA	1,006.6
62	Providence, RI	987.7
63	Miami, FL	987.2
64	Memphis, TN	986.9
65	Baltimore, MD	982.2
66	Elizabeth, NJ	978.5
67	West Palm Beach, FL	974.4
68	Modesto, CA	969.0
69	Columbus, GA	967.5
70	Minneapolis, MN	965.9
71	Chula Vista, CA	957.2
72	Rialto, CA	956.1
73	Concord, CA	954.5
74	Miami Beach, FL	954.1
75	Salinas, CA	946.2
76	Compton, CA	934.5
77	Tampa, FL	931.3
78	Southfield, MI	922.7
79	Inglewood, CA	915.2
80	Pomona, CA	914.5
81	Bellflower, CA	907.7
82	Oklahoma City, OK	899.0
83	Birmingham, AL	890.9
84	San Francisco, CA	889.4
85	Bridgeport, CT	882.6
86	Gresham, OR	876.6
87	Columbus, OH	874.9
88	Antioch, CA	866.7
89	Bakersfield, CA	859.5
90	Toledo, OH	847.7
91	Yuma, AZ	847.3
92	Youngstown, OH	845.2
93	West Covina, CA	835.5
94	Cincinnati, OH	833.1
95	Victorville, CA	831.8
96	Riverside, CA	828.2
97	Omaha, NE	826.1
98	Portland, OR	825.9
99	Tulsa, OK	822.4
100	Spokane Valley, WA	819.1
101	Huntsville, AL	809.8
102	Miami Gardens, FL	804.0
103	Philadelphia, PA	795.9
104	Mesa, AZ	794.9
105	Eugene, OR	793.8
106	San Jose, CA	775.5
107	Reno, NV	775.4
108	Lancaster, CA	774.9
109	Fayetteville, NC	772.0
110	St. Paul, MN	771.9
111	Moreno Valley, CA	771.2
112	Lakewood, CO	769.5
113	Chicago, IL	763.8
114	Buffalo, NY	757.6
115	Santa Ana, CA	757.1
116	El Monte, CA	754.8
117	Independence, MO	751.3
118	Hawthorne, CA	750.6
119	Norwalk, CA	746.3
120	Richmond, VA	744.5
121	Carson, CA	740.5
122	West Valley, UT	734.2
123	Boston, MA	724.8
124	Chattanooga, TN	718.4
125	Escondido, CA	711.0
126	Hialeah, FL	706.9
127	Hammond, IN	704.8
128	Grand Prairie, TX	703.4
129	Little Rock, AR	702.8
130	Fontana, CA	698.6
131	Hesperia, CA	696.4
132	Brockton, MA	695.4
133	Baton Rouge, LA	690.8
134	Honolulu, HI	689.0
135	Long Beach, CA	686.6
136	Peoria, AZ	677.4
137	Canton, OH	677.3
138	Aurora, CO	674.6
139	Paterson, NJ	670.2
140	Shreveport, LA	670.0
141	Fairfield, CA	669.7
142	Wilmington, NC	665.4
143	New Orleans, LA	664.0
144	Los Angeles, CA	654.4
145	Lynn, MA	650.5
146	Vista, CA	643.5
147	Irving, TX	623.7
148	Jersey City, NJ	623.5
149	Longview, TX	618.6
150	Henderson, NV	608.6
151	Thornton, CO	606.5
152	Knoxville, TN	601.9
153	Fort Lauderdale, FL	599.3
154	Louisville, KY	590.1
155	Vancouver, WA	588.0
156	Waterbury, CT	575.5
157	Buena Park, CA	574.6
158	Pittsburgh, PA	574.5
159	Santa Maria, CA	573.4
160	El Paso, TX	571.7
161	Savannah, GA	571.5
162	Laredo, TX	562.3
163	Amarillo, TX	558.4
164	Worcester, MA	558.3
165	Montgomery, AL	558.1
166	Whittier, CA	556.1
167	Chino, CA	554.4
168	South Bend, IN	553.0
169	Westminster, CO	552.9
169	Wichita, KS	552.9
171	Durham, NC	550.9
172	Columbia, SC	550.0
173	Salem, OR	549.6
174	Springfield, MO	548.9
175	Redding, CA	548.4
176	Tracy, CA	546.6
177	Corona, CA	544.0
178	Trenton, NJ	543.1
179	Jacksonville, FL	543.0
180	Hollywood, FL	542.3
181	Ogden, UT	539.2
182	Nashville, TN	538.7
183	Roseville, CA	537.0
184	Sparks, NV	536.6
185	Lakewood, CA	534.5
186	Mobile, AL	531.7
187	Mesquite, TX	527.8
188	Winston-Salem, NC	523.2
189	Westland, MI	522.2
190	High Point, NC	521.7
191	Fort Worth, TX	521.5
192	Anchorage, AK	520.4

RANK	CITY	RATE
193	Alhambra, CA	518.2
194	Syracuse, NY	518.1
195	Albany, GA	512.8
196	San Antonio, TX	512.0
197	Greensboro, NC	510.2
198	Topeka, KS	508.9
199	Palmdale, CA	508.2
200	Pompano Beach, FL	507.9
201	Daly City, CA	507.7
202	Lowell, MA	507.1
203	Rockford, IL	506.1
204	Des Moines, IA	504.6
205	Charleston, SC	501.1
206	Lafayette, LA	500.1
207	Peoria, IL	496.1
208	Anaheim, CA	494.0
209	Chandler, AZ	480.1
210	Beaumont, TX	478.4
211	Scottsdale, AZ	476.5
212	Colorado Springs, CO	474.8
213	Garden Grove, CA	468.5
214	Westminster, CA	466.1
215	Allentown, PA	462.2
216	New Bedford, MA	461.2
217	Arlington, TX	460.8
218	Roanoke, VA	459.6
219	Racine, WI	458.1
220	Fullerton, CA	456.0
221	Burbank, CA	448.4
222	Santa Clara, CA	447.6
223	Santa Monica, CA	444.7
224	Norfolk, VA	442.7
225	Clovis, CA	441.0
226	Fort Smith, AR	435.1
227	Pueblo, CO	431.5
228	Fremont, CA	425.2
229	Gainesville, Fl	423.6
230	Somerville, MA	419.0
231	Newport News, VA	416.6
232	Lewisville, TX	416.5
233	Lansing, MI	415.7
234	Temecula, CA	412.4
235	Rancho Cucamon., CA	410.2
236	Wichita Falls, TX	409.1
237	Bellevue, WA	399.5
238	Miramar, FL	397.5
239	Plantation, FL	394.6
240	Carrollton, TX	391.0
241	Lakeland, FL	390.2
242	Clearwater, FL	387.3
243	Oceanside, CA	377.7
244	Tallahassee, FL	376.0
245	McAllen, TX	368.9
246	Costa Mesa, CA	367.3
246	Waco, TX	367.3
248	Surprise, AZ	366.3
249	Davie, FL	365.6
250	Bellingham, WA	364.0
251	Clifton, NJ	363.8
252	Springfield, IL	362.0
253	Grand Rapids, MI	360.6
254	Greeley, CO	358.5
255	Austin, TX	358.4
256	Deerfield Beach, FL	358.1
257	Torrance, CA	352.9
258	Vacaville, CA	352.8
259	Pasadena, CA	350.3
260	Portsmouth, VA	349.9
261	Sunrise, FL	345.2
262	Athens-Clarke, GA	341.1
263	Hampton, VA	340.1
264	Arvada, CO	339.8
265	Las Cruces, NM	336.5
266	Ventura, CA	335.4
267	Oxnard, CA	331.4
268	Cranston, RI	331.0
269	Tuscaloosa, AL	327.7
270	Clinton Twnshp, MI	327.2
271	Murfreesboro, TN	324.2
272	Garland, TX	322.3
273	Billings, MT	322.1
274	Lubbock, TX	321.3
275	West Jordan, UT	320.9
276	Livonia, MI	320.3
277	San Mateo, CA	319.9
278	Lawton, OK	319.7
279	Santa Rosa, CA	318.4
280	Orange, CA	318.0
281	Sunnyvale, CA	314.5
282	Fort Wayne, IN	313.6
283	Melbourne, FL	310.5
284	Pembroke Pines, FL	310.0
285	Largo, FL	306.4
286	Richardson, TX	305.9
287	Brownsville, TX	304.8
288	Palm Bay, FL	303.0
289	Corpus Christi, TX	299.1
290	Beaverton, OR	298.2
291	Upper Darby Twnshp, PA	296.1
292	Pasadena, TX	294.7
293	Hillsboro, OR	289.8
294	Raleigh, NC	288.8
295	Glendale, CA	286.3
296	Livermore, CA	284.4
297	Norman, OK	278.7
298	Alexandria, VA	274.4
299	Woodbridge Twnshp, NJ	274.2
300	Sterling Heights, MI	268.6
301	Murrieta, CA	268.2
302	Edison Twnshp, NJ	266.5
303	Odessa, TX	266.1
304	Napa, CA	265.1
305	Gilbert, AZ	260.2
305	Lexington, KY	260.2
307	Albany, NY	257.0
308	Abilene, TX	256.8
309	Sandy, UT	253.8
310	Santa Clarita, CA	250.3
311	Duluth, MN	249.2
312	Lawrence, KS	248.8
313	Clarksville, TN	247.6
314	San Angelo, TX	247.5
315	Fargo, ND	246.6
316	Columbia, MO	244.4
317	Cedar Rapids, IA	240.8
318	Carlsbad, CA	240.2
319	Huntington Beach, CA	236.0
320	Killeen, TX	234.8
321	Overland Park, KS	232.6
322	Cape Coral, FL	232.5
323	Yonkers, NY	229.0
324	Sioux City, IA	228.5
325	Midland, TX	227.4
326	Manchester, NH	227.1
327	Plano, TX	226.3
328	Cambridge, MA	221.4
329	Fort Collins, CO	217.7
330	Newport Beach, CA	216.0
331	Madison, WI	213.6
332	Chino Hills, CA	213.3
333	Roswell, GA	210.9
334	Farmington Hills, MI	209.9
335	Olathe, KS	209.6
336	Chesapeake, VA	208.5
337	Evansville, IN	208.3
338	Kenosha, WI	208.2
339	Hamilton Twnshp, NJ	205.4
340	Tyler, TX	202.0
341	Bloomington, MN	199.5
342	Green Bay, WI	197.9
343	New York, NY	195.2
344	Denton, TX	195.1
345	Danbury, CT	194.6
346	Coral Springs, FL	193.2
347	Boca Raton, FL	190.7
347	Warwick, RI	190.7
349	Boise, ID	190.2
350	Parma, OH	188.8
351	Santa Barbara, CA	182.3
352	Suffolk, VA	181.7
353	Troy, MI	181.6
354	Lee's Summit, MO	179.2
354	Lincoln, NE	179.2
356	Cheektowaga, NY	169.1
357	Aurora, IL	168.6
358	Quincy, MA	168.5
359	Provo, UT	168.2
360	Boulder, CO	168.1
361	Canton Twnshp, MI	164.2
362	Centennial, CO	155.8
363	Broken Arrow, OK	155.2
364	Orem, UT	154.4
365	Rochester, MN	153.8
366	Ann Arbor, MI	153.1
367	Sioux Falls, SD	150.8
368	Colonie, NY	139.6
369	Lake Forest, CA	137.5
370	Erie, PA	137.3
371	Virginia Beach, VA	134.4
372	Irvine, CA	134.2
373	Simi Valley, CA	133.6
374	Mission Viejo, CA	128.3
375	Nashua, NH	122.1
376	Edmond, OK	121.8
377	Greece, NY	118.9
378	McKinney, TX	111.8
379	Joliet, IL	110.3
380	Port St. Lucie, FL	106.8
381	Cary, NC	105.9
382	Thousand Oaks, CA	104.4
383	Toms River Twnshp, NJ	103.4
384	Sugar Land, TX	96.3
385	Clarkstown, NY	80.1
386	Brick Twnshp, NJ	76.7
387	Round Rock, TX	55.2
388	Naperville, IL	52.0
389	Newton, MA	44.2
390	Amherst, NY	30.3

Source: CQ Press using data from F.B.I. "Crime in the United States 2006"

**Motor vehicle theft includes the theft or attempted theft of a self-propelled vehicle. Excludes motorboats, construction equipment, airplanes, and farming equipment.*

79. Percent Change in Motor Vehicle Theft Rate: 2005 to 2006

National Percent Change = 4.4% Decrease*

RANK	CITY	% CHANGE
126	Abilene, TX	0.5
28	Albany, GA	22.1
366	Albany, NY	(34.3)
4	Albuquerque, NM	42.3
340	Alexandria, VA	(23.6)
301	Alhambra, CA	(18.0)
97	Allentown, PA	4.5
166	Amarillo, TX	(2.8)
246	Amherst, NY	(11.4)
306	Anaheim, CA	(18.9)
79	Anchorage, AK	7.7
353	Ann Arbor, MI	(26.9)
177	Antioch, CA	(4.1)
206	Arlington, TX	(7.0)
374	Arvada, CO	(39.2)
131	Athens-Clarke, GA	(0.1)
227	Atlanta, GA	(9.5)
355	Aurora, CO	(27.2)
216	Aurora, IL	(8.1)
159	Austin, TX	(2.5)
213	Bakersfield, CA	(7.6)
18	Baldwin Park, CA	27.3
120	Baltimore, MD	1.4
102	Baton Rouge, LA	4.1
108	Beaumont, TX	3.4
320	Beaverton, OR	(20.8)
296	Bellevue, WA	(16.5)
314	Bellflower, CA	(19.7)
262	Bellingham, WA	(12.9)
264	Berkeley, CA	(13.1)
253	Billings, MT	(12.2)
110	Birmingham, AL	3.0
NA	Bloomington, MN**	NA
292	Boca Raton, FL	(16.4)
349	Boise, ID	(25.7)
261	Boston, MA	(12.8)
372	Boulder, CO	(37.6)
11	Brick Twnshp, NJ	34.1
171	Bridgeport, CT	(3.6)
239	Brockton, MA	(10.7)
337	Broken Arrow, OK	(22.9)
43	Brownsville, TX	16.2
92	Buena Park, CA	5.5
238	Buffalo, NY	(10.6)
184	Burbank, CA	(5.1)
339	Cambridge, MA	(23.3)
25	Camden, NJ	23.4
175	Canton Twnshp, MI	(4.0)
143	Canton, OH	(0.8)
144	Cape Coral, FL	(0.9)
256	Carlsbad, CA	(12.5)
196	Carrollton, TX	(6.2)
35	Carson, CA	18.6
87	Cary, NC	5.9
156	Cedar Rapids, IA	(2.2)
333	Centennial, CO	(22.4)
207	Chandler, AZ	(7.3)
65	Charleston, SC	10.5
159	Charlotte, NC	(2.5)
81	Chattanooga, TN	7.0
342	Cheektowaga, NY	(24.0)
286	Chesapeake, VA	(15.7)
158	Chicago, IL	(2.4)
20	Chino Hills, CA	26.9
175	Chino, CA	(4.0)
323	Chula Vista, CA	(20.9)
244	Cincinnati, OH	(11.3)
NA	Clarkstown, NY**	NA
84	Clarksville, TN	6.5
140	Clearwater, FL	(0.7)
162	Cleveland, OH	(2.6)
159	Clifton, NJ	(2.5)
93	Clinton Twnshp, MI	5.4
266	Clovis, CA	(13.3)
222	Colonie, NY	(8.9)
131	Colorado Springs, CO	(0.1)
16	Columbia, MO	27.6
334	Columbia, SC	(22.5)
76	Columbus, GA	8.1
302	Columbus, OH	(18.2)
230	Compton, CA	(10.0)
114	Concord, CA	2.8
99	Coral Springs, FL	4.4
278	Corona, CA	(14.8)
190	Corpus Christi, TX	(5.6)
352	Costa Mesa, CA	(26.5)
135	Cranston, RI	(0.3)
172	Dallas, TX	(3.8)
66	Daly City, CA	9.9
54	Danbury, CT	12.2
140	Davie, FL	(0.7)
129	Dayton, OH	0.2
162	Dearborn, MI	(2.6)
221	Deerfield Beach, FL	(8.5)
320	Denton, TX	(20.8)
327	Denver, CO	(21.4)
NA	Des Moines, IA**	NA
68	Detroit, MI	9.7
102	Downey, CA	4.1
NA	Duluth, MN**	NA
NA	Durham, NC**	NA
149	Edison Twnshp, NJ	(1.3)
55	Edmond, OK	12.1
223	El Cajon, CA	(9.0)
302	El Monte, CA	(18.2)
NA	El Paso, TX**	NA
282	Elizabeth, NJ	(15.4)
9	Erie, PA	34.9
231	Escondido, CA	(10.1)
360	Eugene, OR	(30.9)
268	Evansville, IN	(13.6)
82	Everett, WA	6.6
290	Fairfield, CA	(16.2)
91	Fargo, ND	5.8
60	Farmington Hills, MI	10.9
23	Fayetteville, NC	25.1
348	Federal Way, WA	(25.6)
162	Flint, MI	(2.6)
318	Fontana, CA	(20.4)
369	Fort Collins, CO	(35.0)
216	Fort Lauderdale, FL	(8.1)
95	Fort Smith, AR	5.1
NA	Fort Wayne, IN**	NA
270	Fort Worth, TX	(13.9)
50	Fremont, CA	14.1
208	Fresno, CA	(7.4)
157	Fullerton, CA	(2.3)
68	Gainesville, FL	9.7
359	Garden Grove, CA	(29.0)
186	Garland, TX	(5.2)
211	Gary, IN	(7.5)
134	Gilbert, AZ	(0.2)
272	Glendale, AZ	(14.3)
189	Glendale, CA	(5.5)
179	Grand Prairie, TX	(4.5)
106	Grand Rapids, MI	3.9
282	Greece, NY	(15.4)
362	Greeley, CO	(31.2)
246	Green Bay, WI	(11.4)
138	Greensboro, NC	(0.6)
363	Gresham, OR	(32.2)
107	Hamilton Twnshp, NJ	3.6
355	Hammond, IN	(27.2)
231	Hampton, VA	(10.1)
211	Hartford, CT	(7.5)
49	Hawthorne, CA	14.4
63	Hayward, CA	10.6
162	Henderson, NV	(2.6)
276	Hesperia, CA	(14.7)
87	Hialeah, FL	5.9
110	High Point, NC	3.0
368	Hillsboro, OR	(34.5)
155	Hollywood, FL	(2.0)
215	Honolulu, HI	(7.9)
118	Houston, TX	2.0
258	Huntington Beach, CA	(12.6)
27	Huntsville, AL	22.9
228	Independence, MO	(9.6)
140	Indianapolis, IN	(0.7)
46	Inglewood, CA	15.2
324	Irvine, CA	(21.0)
86	Irving, TX	6.3
256	Jacksonville, FL	(12.5)
146	Jackson, MS	(1.0)
311	Jersey City, NJ	(19.5)
289	Joliet, IL	(16.1)
316	Kansas City, KS	(20.0)
NA	Kansas City, MO**	NA
122	Kenosha, WI	1.2
93	Kent, WA	5.4
1	Killeen, TX	57.4
244	Knoxville, TN	(11.3)
10	Lafayette, LA	34.2
73	Lake Forest, CA	8.8
200	Lakeland, FL	(6.7)
241	Lakewood, CA	(11.0)
334	Lakewood, CO	(22.5)
137	Lancaster, CA	(0.5)
37	Lansing, MI	18.1
29	Laredo, TX	21.4
150	Largo, FL	(1.5)
62	Las Cruces, NM	10.7
174	Las Vegas, NV	(3.9)
8	Lawrence, KS	35.4
13	Lawton, OK	33.3
29	Lee's Summit, MO	21.4
76	Lewisville, TX	8.1
NA	Lexington, KY**	NA
123	Lincoln, NE	1.0
39	Little Rock, AR	17.7
169	Livermore, CA	(3.4)
55	Livonia, MI	12.1

RANK	CITY	% CHANGE	RANK	CITY	% CHANGE	RANK	CITY	% CHANGE
251	Long Beach, CA	(12.0)	307	Peoria, AZ	(19.1)	34	Spokane Valley, WA	19.7
296	Longview, TX	(16.5)	358	Peoria, IL	(28.3)	19	Spokane, WA	27.1
248	Los Angeles, CA	(11.8)	115	Philadelphia, PA	2.7	25	Springfield, IL	23.4
41	Louisville, KY	16.9	184	Phoenix, AZ	(5.1)	126	Springfield, MA	0.5
341	Lowell, MA	(23.9)	292	Pittsburgh, PA	(16.4)	214	Springfield, MO	(7.8)
258	Lubbock, TX	(12.6)	178	Plano, TX	(4.2)	3	Sterling Heights, MI	43.4
135	Lynn, MA	(0.3)	110	Plantation, FL	3.0	224	Stockton, CA	(9.1)
42	Macon, GA	16.7	204	Pomona, CA	(6.8)	87	St. Louis, MO	5.9
330	Madison, WI	(22.0)	345	Pompano Beach, FL	(24.8)	252	St. Paul, MN	(12.1)
153	Manchester, NH	(1.9)	233	Port St. Lucie, FL	(10.2)	44	St. Petersburg, FL	16.0
327	McAllen, TX	(21.4)	331	Portland, OR	(22.1)	32	Suffolk, VA	20.7
357	McKinney, TX	(27.7)	267	Portsmouth, VA	(13.4)	367	Sugar Land, TX	(34.4)
61	Melbourne, FL	10.8	336	Providence, RI	(22.6)	71	Sunnyvale, CA	8.9
310	Memphis, TN	(19.3)	298	Provo, UT	(16.7)	102	Sunrise, FL	4.1
282	Mesa, AZ	(15.4)	186	Pueblo, CO	(5.2)	181	Surprise, AZ	(4.6)
153	Mesquite, TX	(1.9)	138	Quincy, MA	(0.6)	344	Syracuse, NY	(24.2)
241	Miami Beach, FL	(11.0)	75	Racine, WI	8.5	124	Tacoma, WA	0.9
272	Miami Gardens, FL	(14.3)	182	Raleigh, NC	(4.8)	286	Tallahassee, FL	(15.7)
179	Miami, FL	(4.5)	199	Rancho Cucamon., CA	(6.5)	68	Tampa, FL	9.7
17	Midland, TX	27.4	48	Reading, PA	15.0	275	Temecula, CA	(14.6)
22	Milwaukee, WI	25.4	146	Redding, CA	(1.0)	100	Tempe, AZ	4.3
200	Minneapolis, MN	(6.7)	105	Reno, NV	4.0	292	Thornton, CO	(16.4)
200	Miramar, FL	(6.7)	302	Rialto, CA	(18.2)	52	Thousand Oaks, CA	13.4
2	Mission Viejo, CA	53.5	58	Richardson, TX	11.4	307	Toledo, OH	(19.1)
36	Mobile, AL	18.5	194	Richmond, CA	(6.1)	7	Toms River Twnshp, NJ	35.7
364	Modesto, CA	(33.1)	365	Richmond, VA	(34.0)	241	Topeka, KS	(11.0)
63	Montgomery, AL	10.6	265	Riverside, CA	(13.2)	126	Torrance, CA	0.5
248	Moreno Valley, CA	(11.8)	170	Roanoke, VA	(3.5)	219	Tracy, CA	(8.4)
53	Murfreesboro, TN	12.7	51	Rochester, MN	13.7	360	Trenton, NJ	(30.9)
347	Murrieta, CA	(24.9)	76	Rochester, NY	8.1	73	Troy, MI	8.8
33	Napa, CA	19.8	NA	Rockford, IL**	NA	57	Tucson, AZ	11.8
148	Naperville, IL	(1.1)	325	Roseville, CA	(21.1)	278	Tulsa, OK	(14.8)
300	Nashua, NH	(17.9)	87	Roswell, GA	5.9	119	Tuscaloosa, AL	1.7
263	Nashville, TN	(13.0)	229	Round Rock, TX	(9.8)	200	Tyler, TX	(6.7)
6	New Bedford, MA	37.2	113	Sacramento, CA	2.9	280	Upper Darby Twnshp, PA	(15.3)
NA	New Orleans, LA**	NA	345	Salem, OR	(24.8)	21	Vacaville, CA	25.9
269	New York, NY	(13.8)	196	Salinas, CA	(6.2)	NA	Vallejo, CA**	NA
235	Newark, NJ	(10.4)	150	Salt Lake City, UT	(1.5)	315	Vancouver, WA	(19.8)
226	Newport Beach, CA	(9.4)	320	San Angelo, TX	(20.8)	255	Ventura, CA	(12.4)
236	Newport News, VA	(10.5)	79	San Antonio, TX	7.7	291	Victorville, CA	(16.3)
312	Newton, MA	(19.6)	219	San Bernardino, CA	(8.4)	317	Virginia Beach, VA	(20.3)
196	Norfolk, VA	(6.2)	188	San Diego, CA	(5.3)	117	Visalia, CA	2.4
71	Norman, OK	8.9	305	San Francisco, CA	(18.5)	116	Vista, CA	2.5
46	North Charleston, SC	15.2	15	San Jose, CA	28.2	370	Waco, TX	(36.3)
172	North Las Vegas, NV	(3.8)	31	San Leandro, CA	21.2	NA	Warren, MI**	NA
218	Norwalk, CA	(8.3)	12	San Mateo, CA	33.6	375	Warwick, RI	(47.3)
40	Oakland, CA	17.5	130	Sandy, UT	0.0	236	Washington, DC	(10.5)
276	Oceanside, CA	(14.7)	354	Santa Ana, CA	(27.1)	121	Waterbury, CT	1.3
5	Odessa, TX	40.3	327	Santa Barbara, CA	(21.4)	125	West Covina, CA	0.7
84	Ogden, UT	6.5	38	Santa Clara, CA	18.0	NA	West Jordan, UT**	NA
100	Oklahoma City, OK	4.3	309	Santa Clarita, CA	(19.2)	152	West Palm Beach, FL	(1.8)
260	Olathe, KS	(12.7)	338	Santa Maria, CA	(23.1)	95	West Valley, UT	5.1
239	Omaha, NE	(10.7)	204	Santa Monica, CA	(6.8)	168	Westland, MI	(3.0)
272	Ontario, CA	(14.3)	292	Santa Rosa, CA	(16.4)	326	Westminster, CA	(21.3)
350	Orange, CA	(26.3)	319	Savannah, GA	(20.6)	373	Westminster, CO	(38.5)
332	Orem, UT	(22.3)	193	Scottsdale, AZ	(5.9)	191	Whittier, CA	(5.8)
97	Orlando, FL	4.5	285	Seattle, WA	(15.5)	342	Wichita Falls, TX	(24.0)
208	Overland Park, KS	(7.4)	14	Shreveport, LA	31.2	NA	Wichita, KS**	NA
312	Oxnard, CA	(19.6)	350	Simi Valley, CA	(26.3)	233	Wilmington, NC	(10.2)
45	Palm Bay, FL	15.6	299	Sioux City, IA	(16.9)	82	Winston-Salem, NC	6.6
253	Palmdale, CA	(12.2)	371	Sioux Falls, SD	(36.9)	191	Woodbridge Twnshp, NJ	(5.8)
248	Parma, OH	(11.8)	144	Somerville, MA	(0.9)	280	Worcester, MA	(15.3)
225	Pasadena, CA	(9.3)	109	South Bend, IN	3.3	194	Yakima, WA	(6.1)
183	Pasadena, TX	(4.9)	167	South Gate, CA	(2.9)	208	Yonkers, NY	(7.4)
59	Paterson, NJ	11.0	288	Southfield, MI	(15.8)	271	Youngstown, OH	(14.0)
66	Pembroke Pines, FL	9.9	131	Sparks, NV	(0.1)	24	Yuma, AZ	23.5

Source: CQ Press using data from F.B.I. "Crime in the United States 2006"

**Motor vehicle theft includes the theft or attempted theft of a self-propelled vehicle. Excludes motorboats, construction equipment, airplanes, and farming equipment. **Not available.*

79. Percent Change in Motor Vehicle Theft Rate: 2005 to 2006 (continued)

National Percent Change = 4.4% Decrease*

RANK	CITY	% CHANGE
1	Killeen, TX	57.4
2	Mission Viejo, CA	53.5
3	Sterling Heights, MI	43.4
4	Albuquerque, NM	42.3
5	Odessa, TX	40.3
6	New Bedford, MA	37.2
7	Toms River Twnshp, NJ	35.7
8	Lawrence, KS	35.4
9	Erie, PA	34.9
10	Lafayette, LA	34.2
11	Brick Twnshp, NJ	34.1
12	San Mateo, CA	33.6
13	Lawton, OK	33.3
14	Shreveport, LA	31.2
15	San Jose, CA	28.2
16	Columbia, MO	27.6
17	Midland, TX	27.4
18	Baldwin Park, CA	27.3
19	Spokane, WA	27.1
20	Chino Hills, CA	26.9
21	Vacaville, CA	25.9
22	Milwaukee, WI	25.4
23	Fayetteville, NC	25.1
24	Yuma, AZ	23.5
25	Camden, NJ	23.4
25	Springfield, IL	23.4
27	Huntsville, AL	22.9
28	Albany, GA	22.1
29	Laredo, TX	21.4
29	Lee's Summit, MO	21.4
31	San Leandro, CA	21.2
32	Suffolk, VA	20.7
33	Napa, CA	19.8
34	Spokane Valley, WA	19.7
35	Carson, CA	18.6
36	Mobile, AL	18.5
37	Lansing, MI	18.1
38	Santa Clara, CA	18.0
39	Little Rock, AR	17.7
40	Oakland, CA	17.5
41	Louisville, KY	16.9
42	Macon, GA	16.7
43	Brownsville, TX	16.2
44	St. Petersburg, FL	16.0
45	Palm Bay, FL	15.6
46	Inglewood, CA	15.2
46	North Charleston, SC	15.2
48	Reading, PA	15.0
49	Hawthorne, CA	14.4
50	Fremont, CA	14.1
51	Rochester, MN	13.7
52	Thousand Oaks, CA	13.4
53	Murfreesboro, TN	12.7
54	Danbury, CT	12.2
55	Edmond, OK	12.1
55	Livonia, MI	12.1
57	Tucson, AZ	11.8
58	Richardson, TX	11.4
59	Paterson, NJ	11.0
60	Farmington Hills, MI	10.9
61	Melbourne, FL	10.8
62	Las Cruces, NM	10.7
63	Hayward, CA	10.6
63	Montgomery, AL	10.6
65	Charleston, SC	10.5
66	Daly City, CA	9.9
66	Pembroke Pines, FL	9.9
68	Detroit, MI	9.7
68	Gainesville, FL	9.7
68	Tampa, FL	9.7
71	Norman, OK	8.9
71	Sunnyvale, CA	8.9
73	Lake Forest, CA	8.8
73	Troy, MI	8.8
75	Racine, WI	8.5
76	Columbus, GA	8.1
76	Lewisville, TX	8.1
76	Rochester, NY	8.1
79	Anchorage, AK	7.7
79	San Antonio, TX	7.7
81	Chattanooga, TN	7.0
82	Everett, WA	6.6
82	Winston-Salem, NC	6.6
84	Clarksville, TN	6.5
84	Ogden, UT	6.5
86	Irving, TX	6.3
87	Cary, NC	5.9
87	Hialeah, FL	5.9
87	Roswell, GA	5.9
87	St. Louis, MO	5.9
91	Fargo, ND	5.8
92	Buena Park, CA	5.5
93	Clinton Twnshp, MI	5.4
93	Kent, WA	5.4
95	Fort Smith, AR	5.1
95	West Valley, UT	5.1
97	Allentown, PA	4.5
97	Orlando, FL	4.5
99	Coral Springs, FL	4.4
100	Oklahoma City, OK	4.3
100	Tempe, AZ	4.3
102	Baton Rouge, LA	4.1
102	Downey, CA	4.1
102	Sunrise, FL	4.1
105	Reno, NV	4.0
106	Grand Rapids, MI	3.9
107	Hamilton Twnshp, NJ	3.6
108	Beaumont, TX	3.4
109	South Bend, IN	3.3
110	Birmingham, AL	3.0
110	High Point, NC	3.0
110	Plantation, FL	3.0
113	Sacramento, CA	2.9
114	Concord, CA	2.8
115	Philadelphia, PA	2.7
116	Vista, CA	2.5
117	Visalia, CA	2.4
118	Houston, TX	2.0
119	Tuscaloosa, AL	1.7
120	Baltimore, MD	1.4
121	Waterbury, CT	1.3
122	Kenosha, WI	1.2
123	Lincoln, NE	1.0
124	Tacoma, WA	0.9
125	West Covina, CA	0.7
126	Abilene, TX	0.5
126	Springfield, MA	0.5
126	Torrance, CA	0.5
129	Dayton, OH	0.2
130	Sandy, UT	0.0
131	Athens-Clarke, GA	(0.1)
131	Colorado Springs, CO	(0.1)
131	Sparks, NV	(0.1)
134	Gilbert, AZ	(0.2)
135	Cranston, RI	(0.3)
135	Lynn, MA	(0.3)
137	Lancaster, CA	(0.5)
138	Greensboro, NC	(0.6)
138	Quincy, MA	(0.6)
140	Clearwater, FL	(0.7)
140	Davie, FL	(0.7)
140	Indianapolis, IN	(0.7)
143	Canton, OH	(0.8)
144	Cape Coral, FL	(0.9)
144	Somerville, MA	(0.9)
146	Jackson, MS	(1.0)
146	Redding, CA	(1.0)
148	Naperville, IL	(1.1)
149	Edison Twnshp, NJ	(1.3)
150	Largo, FL	(1.5)
150	Salt Lake City, UT	(1.5)
152	West Palm Beach, FL	(1.8)
153	Manchester, NH	(1.9)
153	Mesquite, TX	(1.9)
155	Hollywood, FL	(2.0)
156	Cedar Rapids, IA	(2.2)
157	Fullerton, CA	(2.3)
158	Chicago, IL	(2.4)
159	Austin, TX	(2.5)
159	Charlotte, NC	(2.5)
159	Clifton, NJ	(2.5)
162	Cleveland, OH	(2.6)
162	Dearborn, MI	(2.6)
162	Flint, MI	(2.6)
162	Henderson, NV	(2.6)
166	Amarillo, TX	(2.8)
167	South Gate, CA	(2.9)
168	Westland, MI	(3.0)
169	Livermore, CA	(3.4)
170	Roanoke, VA	(3.5)
171	Bridgeport, CT	(3.6)
172	Dallas, TX	(3.8)
172	North Las Vegas, NV	(3.8)
174	Las Vegas, NV	(3.9)
175	Canton Twnshp, MI	(4.0)
175	Chino, CA	(4.0)
177	Antioch, CA	(4.1)
178	Plano, TX	(4.2)
179	Grand Prairie, TX	(4.5)
179	Miami, FL	(4.5)
181	Surprise, AZ	(4.6)
182	Raleigh, NC	(4.8)
183	Pasadena, TX	(4.9)
184	Burbank, CA	(5.1)
184	Phoenix, AZ	(5.1)
186	Garland, TX	(5.2)
186	Pueblo, CO	(5.2)
188	San Diego, CA	(5.3)
189	Glendale, CA	(5.5)
190	Corpus Christi, TX	(5.6)
191	Whittier, CA	(5.8)
191	Woodbridge Twnshp, NJ	(5.8)

RANK	CITY	% CHANGE
193	Scottsdale, AZ	(5.9)
194	Richmond, CA	(6.1)
194	Yakima, WA	(6.1)
196	Carrollton, TX	(6.2)
196	Norfolk, VA	(6.2)
196	Salinas, CA	(6.2)
199	Rancho Cucamon., CA	(6.5)
200	Lakeland, FL	(6.7)
200	Minneapolis, MN	(6.7)
200	Miramar, FL	(6.7)
200	Tyler, TX	(6.7)
204	Pomona, CA	(6.8)
204	Santa Monica, CA	(6.8)
206	Arlington, TX	(7.0)
207	Chandler, AZ	(7.3)
208	Fresno, CA	(7.4)
208	Overland Park, KS	(7.4)
208	Yonkers, NY	(7.4)
211	Gary, IN	(7.5)
211	Hartford, CT	(7.5)
213	Bakersfield, CA	(7.6)
214	Springfield, MO	(7.8)
215	Honolulu, HI	(7.9)
216	Aurora, IL	(8.1)
216	Fort Lauderdale, FL	(8.1)
218	Norwalk, CA	(8.3)
219	San Bernardino, CA	(8.4)
219	Tracy, CA	(8.4)
221	Deerfield Beach, FL	(8.5)
222	Colonie, NY	(8.9)
223	El Cajon, CA	(9.0)
224	Stockton, CA	(9.1)
225	Pasadena, CA	(9.3)
226	Newport Beach, CA	(9.4)
227	Atlanta, GA	(9.5)
228	Independence, MO	(9.6)
229	Round Rock, TX	(9.8)
230	Compton, CA	(10.0)
231	Escondido, CA	(10.1)
231	Hampton, VA	(10.1)
233	Port St. Lucie, FL	(10.2)
233	Wilmington, NC	(10.2)
235	Newark, NJ	(10.4)
236	Newport News, VA	(10.5)
236	Washington, DC	(10.5)
238	Buffalo, NY	(10.6)
239	Brockton, MA	(10.7)
239	Omaha, NE	(10.7)
241	Lakewood, CA	(11.0)
241	Miami Beach, FL	(11.0)
241	Topeka, KS	(11.0)
244	Cincinnati, OH	(11.3)
244	Knoxville, TN	(11.3)
246	Amherst, NY	(11.4)
246	Green Bay, WI	(11.4)
248	Los Angeles, CA	(11.8)
248	Moreno Valley, CA	(11.8)
248	Parma, OH	(11.8)
251	Long Beach, CA	(12.0)
252	St. Paul, MN	(12.1)
253	Billings, MT	(12.2)
253	Palmdale, CA	(12.2)
255	Ventura, CA	(12.4)
256	Carlsbad, CA	(12.5)
256	Jacksonville, FL	(12.5)
258	Huntington Beach, CA	(12.6)
258	Lubbock, TX	(12.6)
260	Olathe, KS	(12.7)
261	Boston, MA	(12.8)
262	Bellingham, WA	(12.9)
263	Nashville, TN	(13.0)
264	Berkeley, CA	(13.1)
265	Riverside, CA	(13.2)
266	Clovis, CA	(13.3)
267	Portsmouth, VA	(13.4)
268	Evansville, IN	(13.6)
269	New York, NY	(13.8)
270	Fort Worth, TX	(13.9)
271	Youngstown, OH	(14.0)
272	Glendale, AZ	(14.3)
272	Miami Gardens, FL	(14.3)
272	Ontario, CA	(14.3)
275	Temecula, CA	(14.6)
276	Hesperia, CA	(14.7)
276	Oceanside, CA	(14.7)
278	Corona, CA	(14.8)
278	Tulsa, OK	(14.8)
280	Upper Darby Twnshp, PA	(15.3)
280	Worcester, MA	(15.3)
282	Elizabeth, NJ	(15.4)
282	Greece, NY	(15.4)
282	Mesa, AZ	(15.4)
285	Seattle, WA	(15.5)
286	Chesapeake, VA	(15.7)
286	Tallahassee, FL	(15.7)
288	Southfield, MI	(15.8)
289	Joliet, IL	(16.1)
290	Fairfield, CA	(16.2)
291	Victorville, CA	(16.3)
292	Boca Raton, FL	(16.4)
292	Pittsburgh, PA	(16.4)
292	Santa Rosa, CA	(16.4)
292	Thornton, CO	(16.4)
296	Bellevue, WA	(16.5)
296	Longview, TX	(16.5)
298	Provo, UT	(16.7)
299	Sioux City, IA	(16.9)
300	Nashua, NH	(17.9)
301	Alhambra, CA	(18.0)
302	Columbus, OH	(18.2)
302	El Monte, CA	(18.2)
302	Rialto, CA	(18.2)
305	San Francisco, CA	(18.5)
306	Anaheim, CA	(18.9)
307	Peoria, AZ	(19.1)
307	Toledo, OH	(19.1)
309	Santa Clarita, CA	(19.2)
310	Memphis, TN	(19.3)
311	Jersey City, NJ	(19.5)
312	Newton, MA	(19.6)
312	Oxnard, CA	(19.6)
314	Bellflower, CA	(19.7)
315	Vancouver, WA	(19.8)
316	Kansas City, KS	(20.0)
317	Virginia Beach, VA	(20.3)
318	Fontana, CA	(20.4)
319	Savannah, GA	(20.6)
320	Beaverton, OR	(20.8)
320	Denton, TX	(20.8)
320	San Angelo, TX	(20.8)
323	Chula Vista, CA	(20.9)
324	Irvine, CA	(21.0)
325	Roseville, CA	(21.1)
326	Westminster, CA	(21.3)
327	Denver, CO	(21.4)
327	McAllen, TX	(21.4)
327	Santa Barbara, CA	(21.4)
330	Madison, WI	(22.0)
331	Portland, OR	(22.1)
332	Orem, UT	(22.3)
333	Centennial, CO	(22.4)
334	Columbia, SC	(22.5)
334	Lakewood, CO	(22.5)
336	Providence, RI	(22.6)
337	Broken Arrow, OK	(22.9)
338	Santa Maria, CA	(23.1)
339	Cambridge, MA	(23.3)
340	Alexandria, VA	(23.6)
341	Lowell, MA	(23.9)
342	Cheektowaga, NY	(24.0)
342	Wichita Falls, TX	(24.0)
344	Syracuse, NY	(24.2)
345	Pompano Beach, FL	(24.8)
345	Salem, OR	(24.8)
347	Murrieta, CA	(24.9)
348	Federal Way, WA	(25.6)
349	Boise, ID	(25.7)
350	Orange, CA	(26.3)
350	Simi Valley, CA	(26.3)
352	Costa Mesa, CA	(26.5)
353	Ann Arbor, MI	(26.9)
354	Santa Ana, CA	(27.1)
355	Aurora, CO	(27.2)
355	Hammond, IN	(27.2)
357	McKinney, TX	(27.7)
358	Peoria, IL	(28.3)
359	Garden Grove, CA	(29.0)
360	Eugene, OR	(30.9)
360	Trenton, NJ	(30.9)
362	Greeley, CO	(31.2)
363	Gresham, OR	(32.2)
364	Modesto, CA	(33.1)
365	Richmond, VA	(34.0)
366	Albany, NY	(34.3)
367	Sugar Land, TX	(34.4)
368	Hillsboro, OR	(34.5)
369	Fort Collins, CO	(35.0)
370	Waco, TX	(36.3)
371	Sioux Falls, SD	(36.9)
372	Boulder, CO	(37.6)
373	Westminster, CO	(38.5)
374	Arvada, CO	(39.2)
375	Warwick, RI	(47.3)
NA	Bloomington, MN**	NA
NA	Clarkstown, NY**	NA
NA	Des Moines, IA**	NA
NA	Duluth, MN**	NA
NA	Durham, NC**	NA
NA	El Paso, TX**	NA
NA	Fort Wayne, IN**	NA
NA	Kansas City, MO**	NA
NA	Lexington, KY**	NA
NA	New Orleans, LA**	NA
NA	Rockford, IL**	NA
NA	Vallejo, CA**	NA
NA	Warren, MI**	NA
NA	West Jordan, UT**	NA
NA	Wichita, KS**	NA

Source: CQ Press using data from F.B.I. "Crime in the United States 2006"

**Motor vehicle theft includes the theft or attempted theft of a self-propelled vehicle. Excludes motorboats, construction equipment, airplanes, and farming equipment. **Not available.*

80. Percent Change in Motor Vehicle Theft Rate: 2002 to 2006

National Percent Change = 8.0% Decrease*

RANK	CITY	% CHANGE
36	Abilene, TX	35.8
34	Albany, GA	37.5
NA	Albany, NY**	NA
48	Albuquerque, NM	24.4
357	Alexandria, VA	(50.9)
213	Alhambra, CA	(13.0)
154	Allentown, PA	(1.4)
115	Amarillo, TX	5.5
365	Amherst, NY	(61.0)
200	Anaheim, CA	(10.1)
66	Anchorage, AK	18.6
167	Ann Arbor, MI	(3.0)
150	Antioch, CA	(0.3)
244	Arlington, TX	(20.2)
135	Arvada, CO	1.9
229	Athens-Clarke, GA	(16.9)
284	Atlanta, GA	(27.0)
341	Aurora, CO	(41.1)
262	Aurora, IL	(22.8)
257	Austin, TX	(21.6)
14	Bakersfield, CA	57.5
12	Baldwin Park, CA	60.5
147	Baltimore, MD	0.5
102	Baton Rouge, LA	9.2
133	Beaumont, TX	2.3
301	Beaverton, OR	(30.0)
231	Bellevue, WA	(17.3)
152	Bellflower, CA	(0.5)
221	Bellingham, WA	(14.4)
226	Berkeley, CA	(16.0)
126	Billings, MT	3.8
111	Birmingham, AL	6.5
290	Bloomington, MN	(28.4)
301	Boca Raton, FL	(30.0)
311	Boise, ID	(32.4)
334	Boston, MA	(39.1)
208	Boulder, CO	(11.8)
129	Brick Twnshp, NJ	2.8
238	Bridgeport, CT	(18.5)
345	Brockton, MA	(42.9)
274	Broken Arrow, OK	(24.6)
186	Brownsville, TX	(7.3)
142	Buena Park, CA	1.2
160	Buffalo, NY	(2.2)
252	Burbank, CA	(21.1)
352	Cambridge, MA	(46.5)
91	Camden, NJ	11.0
200	Canton Twnshp, MI	(10.1)
NA	Canton, OH**	NA
88	Cape Coral, FL	12.0
239	Carlsbad, CA	(19.2)
103	Carrollton, TX	8.9
158	Carson, CA	(2.0)
140	Cary, NC	1.4
172	Cedar Rapids, IA	(4.3)
NA	Centennial, CO**	NA
315	Chandler, AZ	(33.0)
346	Charleston, SC	(43.1)
21	Charlotte, NC	42.6
247	Chattanooga, TN	(20.5)
NA	Cheektowaga, NY**	NA
299	Chesapeake, VA	(29.2)
205	Chicago, IL	(11.1)
366	Chino Hills, CA	(65.3)
1	Chino, CA	176.2
164	Chula Vista, CA	(2.8)
307	Cincinnati, OH	(31.0)
329	Clarkstown, NY	(37.2)
168	Clarksville, TN	(3.3)
149	Clearwater, FL	(0.1)
45	Cleveland, OH	26.3
311	Clifton, NJ	(32.4)
83	Clinton Twnshp, MI	13.8
296	Clovis, CA	(29.0)
63	Colonie, NY	19.3
86	Colorado Springs, CO	13.3
105	Columbia, MO	8.0
292	Columbia, SC	(28.5)
5	Columbus, GA	84.5
233	Columbus, OH	(18.0)
80	Compton, CA	14.1
52	Concord, CA	23.5
292	Coral Springs, FL	(28.5)
206	Corona, CA	(11.2)
339	Corpus Christi, TX	(40.1)
162	Costa Mesa, CA	(2.6)
180	Cranston, RI	(6.4)
274	Dallas, TX	(24.6)
55	Daly City, CA	22.8
251	Danbury, CT	(20.9)
252	Davie, FL	(21.1)
218	Dayton, OH	(14.1)
75	Dearborn, MI	16.4
107	Deerfield Beach, FL	7.0
189	Denton, TX	(7.8)
212	Denver, CO	(12.8)
NA	Des Moines, IA**	NA
123	Detroit, MI	4.5
104	Downey, CA	8.1
295	Duluth, MN	(28.7)
NA	Durham, NC**	NA
316	Edison Twnshp, NJ	(33.1)
83	Edmond, OK	13.8
59	El Cajon, CA	20.5
87	El Monte, CA	12.7
NA	El Paso, TX**	NA
314	Elizabeth, NJ	(32.9)
220	Erie, PA	(14.3)
58	Escondido, CA	20.7
25	Eugene, OR	39.8
234	Evansville, IN	(18.1)
43	Everett, WA	28.4
152	Fairfield, CA	(0.5)
92	Fargo, ND	10.8
11	Farmington Hills, MI	61.3
27	Fayetteville, NC	38.4
145	Federal Way, WA	0.8
57	Flint, MI	21.1
269	Fontana, CA	(23.4)
41	Fort Collins, CO	30.8
306	Fort Lauderdale, FL	(30.5)
76	Fort Smith, AR	16.1
NA	Fort Wayne, IN**	NA
280	Fort Worth, TX	(26.0)
17	Fremont, CA	47.0
321	Fresno, CA	(34.3)
130	Fullerton, CA	2.7
204	Gainesville, FL	(10.6)
211	Garden Grove, CA	(12.3)
235	Garland, TX	(18.3)
199	Gary, IN	(10.0)
325	Gilbert, AZ	(35.8)
316	Glendale, AZ	(33.1)
255	Glendale, CA	(21.3)
289	Grand Prairie, TX	(28.3)
113	Grand Rapids, MI	6.1
NA	Greece, NY**	NA
232	Greeley, CO	(17.7)
270	Green Bay, WI	(23.9)
131	Greensboro, NC	2.6
195	Gresham, OR	(9.5)
299	Hamilton Twnshp, NJ	(29.2)
218	Hammond, IN	(14.1)
341	Hampton, VA	(41.1)
258	Hartford, CT	(22.0)
109	Hawthorne, CA	6.6
9	Hayward, CA	65.5
145	Henderson, NV	0.8
32	Hesperia, CA	37.8
240	Hialeah, FL	(19.5)
256	High Point, NC	(21.4)
358	Hillsboro, OR	(53.0)
264	Hollywood, FL	(23.0)
283	Honolulu, HI	(26.9)
216	Houston, TX	(13.3)
161	Huntington Beach, CA	(2.4)
8	Huntsville, AL	67.0
99	Independence, MO	9.5
31	Indianapolis, IN	37.9
95	Inglewood, CA	10.1
261	Irvine, CA	(22.6)
170	Irving, TX	(3.8)
262	Jacksonville, FL	(22.8)
305	Jackson, MS	(30.4)
318	Jersey City, NJ	(33.5)
362	Joliet, IL	(59.0)
NA	Kansas City, KS**	NA
NA	Kansas City, MO**	NA
106	Kenosha, WI	7.8
93	Kent, WA	10.7
327	Killeen, TX	(36.9)
209	Knoxville, TN	(12.0)
88	Lafayette, LA	12.0
187	Lake Forest, CA	(7.4)
185	Lakeland, FL	(7.2)
224	Lakewood, CA	(15.3)
138	Lakewood, CO	1.5
27	Lancaster, CA	38.4
53	Lansing, MI	23.1
69	Laredo, TX	17.4
26	Largo, FL	38.9
NA	Las Cruces, NM**	NA
29	Las Vegas, NV	38.1
78	Lawrence, KS	15.0
181	Lawton, OK	(6.5)
158	Lee's Summit, MO	(2.0)
277	Lewisville, TX	(25.3)
NA	Lexington, KY**	NA
259	Lincoln, NE	(22.4)
217	Little Rock, AR	(13.8)
230	Livermore, CA	(17.1)
20	Livonia, MI	42.9

RANK	CITY	% CHANGE
210	Long Beach, CA	(12.2)
172	Longview, TX	(4.3)
281	Los Angeles, CA	(26.5)
NA	Louisville, KY**	NA
321	Lowell, MA	(34.3)
70	Lubbock, TX	17.3
349	Lynn, MA	(43.8)
107	Macon, GA	7.0
290	Madison, WI	(28.4)
133	Manchester, NH	2.3
340	McAllen, TX	(40.7)
363	McKinney, TX	(60.3)
176	Melbourne, FL	(5.0)
298	Memphis, TN	(29.1)
320	Mesa, AZ	(34.1)
225	Mesquite, TX	(15.9)
287	Miami Beach, FL	(27.5)
NA	Miami Gardens, FL**	NA
267	Miami, FL	(23.3)
81	Midland, TX	14.0
61	Milwaukee, WI	19.5
97	Minneapolis, MN	9.8
279	Miramar, FL	(25.7)
44	Mission Viejo, CA	27.7
178	Mobile, AL	(5.9)
95	Modesto, CA	10.1
313	Montgomery, AL	(32.8)
143	Moreno Valley, CA	1.1
85	Murfreesboro, TN	13.7
48	Murrieta, CA	24.4
136	Napa, CA	1.8
285	Naperville, IL	(27.2)
NA	Nashua, NH**	NA
327	Nashville, TN	(36.9)
NA	New Bedford, MA**	NA
361	New Orleans, LA	(57.3)
343	New York, NY	(41.6)
242	Newark, NJ	(20.0)
182	Newport Beach, CA	(6.7)
331	Newport News, VA	(37.4)
NA	Newton, MA**	NA
321	Norfolk, VA	(34.3)
3	Norman, OK	98.5
246	North Charleston, SC	(20.3)
61	North Las Vegas, NV	19.5
179	Norwalk, CA	(6.1)
7	Oakland, CA	75.0
308	Oceanside, CA	(31.1)
118	Odessa, TX	5.3
156	Ogden, UT	(1.8)
51	Oklahoma City, OK	24.0
248	Olathe, KS	(20.6)
267	Omaha, NE	(23.3)
164	Ontario, CA	(2.8)
244	Orange, CA	(20.2)
243	Orem, UT	(20.1)
174	Orlando, FL	(4.9)
326	Overland Park, KS	(36.4)
141	Oxnard, CA	1.3
23	Palm Bay, FL	40.6
227	Palmdale, CA	(16.6)
46	Parma, OH	25.1
118	Pasadena, CA	5.3
351	Pasadena, TX	(44.4)
296	Paterson, NJ	(29.0)
282	Pembroke Pines, FL	(26.6)
324	Peoria, AZ	(35.0)
319	Peoria, IL	(33.9)
193	Philadelphia, PA	(8.8)
213	Phoenix, AZ	(13.0)
259	Pittsburgh, PA	(22.4)
144	Plano, TX	0.9
248	Plantation, FL	(20.6)
74	Pomona, CA	16.5
194	Pompano Beach, FL	(8.9)
170	Port St. Lucie, FL	(3.8)
215	Portland, OR	(13.2)
348	Portsmouth, VA	(43.7)
333	Providence, RI	(38.8)
166	Provo, UT	(2.9)
59	Pueblo, CO	20.5
329	Quincy, MA	(37.2)
112	Racine, WI	6.3
332	Raleigh, NC	(38.4)
174	Rancho Cucamon., CA	(4.9)
16	Reading, PA	49.0
54	Redding, CA	22.9
33	Reno, NV	37.6
190	Rialto, CA	(8.1)
202	Richardson, TX	(10.3)
100	Richmond, CA	9.4
337	Richmond, VA	(39.5)
207	Riverside, CA	(11.3)
NA	Roanoke, VA**	NA
276	Rochester, MN	(25.2)
197	Rochester, NY	(9.8)
NA	Rockford, IL**	NA
121	Roseville, CA	5.2
42	Roswell, GA	28.7
336	Round Rock, TX	(39.2)
154	Sacramento, CA	(1.4)
344	Salem, OR	(42.8)
13	Salinas, CA	60.0
114	Salt Lake City, UT	5.8
132	San Angelo, TX	2.5
109	San Antonio, TX	6.6
127	San Bernardino, CA	3.5
47	San Diego, CA	24.6
77	San Francisco, CA	15.6
2	San Jose, CA	115.6
40	San Leandro, CA	30.9
24	San Mateo, CA	40.1
118	Sandy, UT	5.3
94	Santa Ana, CA	10.6
65	Santa Barbara, CA	18.7
15	Santa Clara, CA	52.2
198	Santa Clarita, CA	(9.9)
NA	Santa Maria, CA**	NA
254	Santa Monica, CA	(21.2)
310	Santa Rosa, CA	(32.2)
355	Savannah, GA	(48.9)
278	Scottsdale, AZ	(25.5)
162	Seattle, WA	(2.6)
236	Shreveport, LA	(18.4)
177	Simi Valley, CA	(5.4)
354	Sioux City, IA	(47.9)
168	Sioux Falls, SD	(3.3)
271	Somerville, MA	(24.1)
121	South Bend, IN	5.2
115	South Gate, CA	5.5
190	Southfield, MI	(8.1)
50	Sparks, NV	24.1
NA	Spokane Valley, WA**	NA
35	Spokane, WA	37.3
70	Springfield, IL	17.3
294	Springfield, MA	(28.6)
100	Springfield, MO	9.4
30	Sterling Heights, MI	38.0
184	Stockton, CA	(6.9)
203	St. Louis, MO	(10.5)
124	St. Paul, MN	4.2
56	St. Petersburg, FL	22.3
309	Suffolk, VA	(31.5)
347	Sugar Land, TX	(43.6)
4	Sunnyvale, CA	97.1
266	Sunrise, FL	(23.2)
241	Surprise, AZ	(19.9)
338	Syracuse, NY	(39.9)
90	Tacoma, WA	11.2
285	Tallahassee, FL	(27.2)
359	Tampa, FL	(56.0)
117	Temecula, CA	5.4
271	Tempe, AZ	(24.1)
264	Thornton, CO	(23.0)
223	Thousand Oaks, CA	(15.0)
228	Toledo, OH	(16.8)
128	Toms River Twnshp, NJ	2.9
183	Topeka, KS	(6.8)
250	Torrance, CA	(20.8)
151	Tracy, CA	(0.4)
360	Trenton, NJ	(56.8)
64	Troy, MI	18.9
79	Tucson, AZ	14.9
192	Tulsa, OK	(8.2)
148	Tuscaloosa, AL	0.2
364	Tyler, TX	(60.8)
67	Upper Darby Twnshp, PA	18.1
73	Vacaville, CA	16.6
19	Vallejo, CA	44.3
138	Vancouver, WA	1.5
38	Ventura, CA	33.4
124	Victorville, CA	4.2
303	Virginia Beach, VA	(30.1)
39	Visalia, CA	33.3
18	Vista, CA	45.5
334	Waco, TX	(39.1)
10	Warren, MI	62.9
356	Warwick, RI	(50.0)
273	Washington, DC	(24.4)
236	Waterbury, CT	(18.4)
67	West Covina, CA	18.1
222	West Jordan, UT	(14.5)
288	West Palm Beach, FL	(27.8)
82	West Valley, UT	13.9
157	Westland, MI	(1.9)
195	Westminster, CA	(9.5)
NA	Westminster, CO**	NA
72	Whittier, CA	17.1
187	Wichita Falls, TX	(7.4)
98	Wichita, KS	9.6
304	Wilmington, NC	(30.2)
136	Winston-Salem, NC	1.8
353	Woodbridge Twnshp, NJ	(47.6)
NA	Worcester, MA**	NA
37	Yakima, WA	34.1
350	Yonkers, NY	(44.2)
22	Youngstown, OH	41.5
6	Yuma, AZ	79.6

Source: CQ Press using data from F.B.I. "Crime in the United States 2006"

**Motor vehicle theft includes the theft or attempted theft of a self-propelled vehicle. Excludes motorboats, construction equipment, airplanes, and farming equipment. **Not available.*

80. Percent Change in Motor Vehicle Theft Rate: 2002 to 2006 (continued)

National Percent Change = 8.0% Decrease*

RANK	CITY	% CHANGE
1	Chino, CA	176.2
2	San Jose, CA	115.6
3	Norman, OK	98.5
4	Sunnyvale, CA	97.1
5	Columbus, GA	84.5
6	Yuma, AZ	79.6
7	Oakland, CA	75.0
8	Huntsville, AL	67.0
9	Hayward, CA	65.5
10	Warren, MI	62.9
11	Farmington Hills, MI	61.3
12	Baldwin Park, CA	60.5
13	Salinas, CA	60.0
14	Bakersfield, CA	57.5
15	Santa Clara, CA	52.2
16	Reading, PA	49.0
17	Fremont, CA	47.0
18	Vista, CA	45.5
19	Vallejo, CA	44.3
20	Livonia, MI	42.9
21	Charlotte, NC	42.6
22	Youngstown, OH	41.5
23	Palm Bay, FL	40.6
24	San Mateo, CA	40.1
25	Eugene, OR	39.8
26	Largo, FL	38.9
27	Fayetteville, NC	38.4
27	Lancaster, CA	38.4
29	Las Vegas, NV	38.1
30	Sterling Heights, MI	38.0
31	Indianapolis, IN	37.9
32	Hesperia, CA	37.8
33	Reno, NV	37.6
34	Albany, GA	37.5
35	Spokane, WA	37.3
36	Abilene, TX	35.8
37	Yakima, WA	34.1
38	Ventura, CA	33.4
39	Visalia, CA	33.3
40	San Leandro, CA	30.9
41	Fort Collins, CO	30.8
42	Roswell, GA	28.7
43	Everett, WA	28.4
44	Mission Viejo, CA	27.7
45	Cleveland, OH	26.3
46	Parma, OH	25.1
47	San Diego, CA	24.6
48	Albuquerque, NM	24.4
48	Murrieta, CA	24.4
50	Sparks, NV	24.1
51	Oklahoma City, OK	24.0
52	Concord, CA	23.5
53	Lansing, MI	23.1
54	Redding, CA	22.9
55	Daly City, CA	22.8
56	St. Petersburg, FL	22.3
57	Flint, MI	21.1
58	Escondido, CA	20.7
59	El Cajon, CA	20.5
59	Pueblo, CO	20.5
61	Milwaukee, WI	19.5
61	North Las Vegas, NV	19.5
63	Colonie, NY	19.3
64	Troy, MI	18.9
65	Santa Barbara, CA	18.7
66	Anchorage, AK	18.6
67	Upper Darby Twnshp, PA	18.1
67	West Covina, CA	18.1
69	Laredo, TX	17.4
70	Lubbock, TX	17.3
70	Springfield, IL	17.3
72	Whittier, CA	17.1
73	Vacaville, CA	16.6
74	Pomona, CA	16.5
75	Dearborn, MI	16.4
76	Fort Smith, AR	16.1
77	San Francisco, CA	15.6
78	Lawrence, KS	15.0
79	Tucson, AZ	14.9
80	Compton, CA	14.1
81	Midland, TX	14.0
82	West Valley, UT	13.9
83	Clinton Twnshp, MI	13.8
83	Edmond, OK	13.8
85	Murfreesboro, TN	13.7
86	Colorado Springs, CO	13.3
87	El Monte, CA	12.7
88	Cape Coral, FL	12.0
88	Lafayette, LA	12.0
90	Tacoma, WA	11.2
91	Camden, NJ	11.0
92	Fargo, ND	10.8
93	Kent, WA	10.7
94	Santa Ana, CA	10.6
95	Inglewood, CA	10.1
95	Modesto, CA	10.1
97	Minneapolis, MN	9.8
98	Wichita, KS	9.6
99	Independence, MO	9.5
100	Richmond, CA	9.4
100	Springfield, MO	9.4
102	Baton Rouge, LA	9.2
103	Carrollton, TX	8.9
104	Downey, CA	8.1
105	Columbia, MO	8.0
106	Kenosha, WI	7.8
107	Deerfield Beach, FL	7.0
107	Macon, GA	7.0
109	Hawthorne, CA	6.6
109	San Antonio, TX	6.6
111	Birmingham, AL	6.5
112	Racine, WI	6.3
113	Grand Rapids, MI	6.1
114	Salt Lake City, UT	5.8
115	Amarillo, TX	5.5
115	South Gate, CA	5.5
117	Temecula, CA	5.4
118	Odessa, TX	5.3
118	Pasadena, CA	5.3
118	Sandy, UT	5.3
121	Roseville, CA	5.2
121	South Bend, IN	5.2
123	Detroit, MI	4.5
124	St. Paul, MN	4.2
124	Victorville, CA	4.2
126	Billings, MT	3.8
127	San Bernardino, CA	3.5
128	Toms River Twnshp, NJ	2.9
129	Brick Twnshp, NJ	2.8
130	Fullerton, CA	2.7
131	Greensboro, NC	2.6
132	San Angelo, TX	2.5
133	Beaumont, TX	2.3
133	Manchester, NH	2.3
135	Arvada, CO	1.9
136	Napa, CA	1.8
136	Winston-Salem, NC	1.8
138	Lakewood, CO	1.5
138	Vancouver, WA	1.5
140	Cary, NC	1.4
141	Oxnard, CA	1.3
142	Buena Park, CA	1.2
143	Moreno Valley, CA	1.1
144	Plano, TX	0.9
145	Federal Way, WA	0.8
145	Henderson, NV	0.8
147	Baltimore, MD	0.5
148	Tuscaloosa, AL	0.2
149	Clearwater, FL	(0.1)
150	Antioch, CA	(0.3)
151	Tracy, CA	(0.4)
152	Bellflower, CA	(0.5)
152	Fairfield, CA	(0.5)
154	Allentown, PA	(1.4)
154	Sacramento, CA	(1.4)
156	Ogden, UT	(1.8)
157	Westland, MI	(1.9)
158	Carson, CA	(2.0)
158	Lee's Summit, MO	(2.0)
160	Buffalo, NY	(2.2)
161	Huntington Beach, CA	(2.4)
162	Costa Mesa, CA	(2.6)
162	Seattle, WA	(2.6)
164	Chula Vista, CA	(2.8)
164	Ontario, CA	(2.8)
166	Provo, UT	(2.9)
167	Ann Arbor, MI	(3.0)
168	Clarksville, TN	(3.3)
168	Sioux Falls, SD	(3.3)
170	Irving, TX	(3.8)
170	Port St. Lucie, FL	(3.8)
172	Cedar Rapids, IA	(4.3)
172	Longview, TX	(4.3)
174	Orlando, FL	(4.9)
174	Rancho Cucamon., CA	(4.9)
176	Melbourne, FL	(5.0)
177	Simi Valley, CA	(5.4)
178	Mobile, AL	(5.9)
179	Norwalk, CA	(6.1)
180	Cranston, RI	(6.4)
181	Lawton, OK	(6.5)
182	Newport Beach, CA	(6.7)
183	Topeka, KS	(6.8)
184	Stockton, CA	(6.9)
185	Lakeland, FL	(7.2)
186	Brownsville, TX	(7.3)
187	Lake Forest, CA	(7.4)
187	Wichita Falls, TX	(7.4)
189	Denton, TX	(7.8)
190	Rialto, CA	(8.1)
190	Southfield, MI	(8.1)
192	Tulsa, OK	(8.2)

RANK	CITY	% CHANGE
193	Philadelphia, PA	(8.8)
194	Pompano Beach, FL	(8.9)
195	Gresham, OR	(9.5)
195	Westminster, CA	(9.5)
197	Rochester, NY	(9.8)
198	Santa Clarita, CA	(9.9)
199	Gary, IN	(10.0)
200	Anaheim, CA	(10.1)
200	Canton Twnshp, MI	(10.1)
202	Richardson, TX	(10.3)
203	St. Louis, MO	(10.5)
204	Gainesville, FL	(10.6)
205	Chicago, IL	(11.1)
206	Corona, CA	(11.2)
207	Riverside, CA	(11.3)
208	Boulder, CO	(11.8)
209	Knoxville, TN	(12.0)
210	Long Beach, CA	(12.2)
211	Garden Grove, CA	(12.3)
212	Denver, CO	(12.8)
213	Alhambra, CA	(13.0)
213	Phoenix, AZ	(13.0)
215	Portland, OR	(13.2)
216	Houston, TX	(13.3)
217	Little Rock, AR	(13.8)
218	Dayton, OH	(14.1)
218	Hammond, IN	(14.1)
220	Erie, PA	(14.3)
221	Bellingham, WA	(14.4)
222	West Jordan, UT	(14.5)
223	Thousand Oaks, CA	(15.0)
224	Lakewood, CA	(15.3)
225	Mesquite, TX	(15.9)
226	Berkeley, CA	(16.0)
227	Palmdale, CA	(16.6)
228	Toledo, OH	(16.8)
229	Athens-Clarke, GA	(16.9)
230	Livermore, CA	(17.1)
231	Bellevue, WA	(17.3)
232	Greeley, CO	(17.7)
233	Columbus, OH	(18.0)
234	Evansville, IN	(18.1)
235	Garland, TX	(18.3)
236	Shreveport, LA	(18.4)
236	Waterbury, CT	(18.4)
238	Bridgeport, CT	(18.5)
239	Carlsbad, CA	(19.2)
240	Hialeah, FL	(19.5)
241	Surprise, AZ	(19.9)
242	Newark, NJ	(20.0)
243	Orem, UT	(20.1)
244	Arlington, TX	(20.2)
244	Orange, CA	(20.2)
246	North Charleston, SC	(20.3)
247	Chattanooga, TN	(20.5)
248	Olathe, KS	(20.6)
248	Plantation, FL	(20.6)
250	Torrance, CA	(20.8)
251	Danbury, CT	(20.9)
252	Burbank, CA	(21.1)
252	Davie, FL	(21.1)
254	Santa Monica, CA	(21.2)
255	Glendale, CA	(21.3)
256	High Point, NC	(21.4)
257	Austin, TX	(21.6)
258	Hartford, CT	(22.0)
259	Lincoln, NE	(22.4)
259	Pittsburgh, PA	(22.4)
261	Irvine, CA	(22.6)
262	Aurora, IL	(22.8)
262	Jacksonville, FL	(22.8)
264	Hollywood, FL	(23.0)
264	Thornton, CO	(23.0)
266	Sunrise, FL	(23.2)
267	Miami, FL	(23.3)
267	Omaha, NE	(23.3)
269	Fontana, CA	(23.4)
270	Green Bay, WI	(23.9)
271	Somerville, MA	(24.1)
271	Tempe, AZ	(24.1)
273	Washington, DC	(24.4)
274	Broken Arrow, OK	(24.6)
274	Dallas, TX	(24.6)
276	Rochester, MN	(25.2)
277	Lewisville, TX	(25.3)
278	Scottsdale, AZ	(25.5)
279	Miramar, FL	(25.7)
280	Fort Worth, TX	(26.0)
281	Los Angeles, CA	(26.5)
282	Pembroke Pines, FL	(26.6)
283	Honolulu, HI	(26.9)
284	Atlanta, GA	(27.0)
285	Naperville, IL	(27.2)
285	Tallahassee, FL	(27.2)
287	Miami Beach, FL	(27.5)
288	West Palm Beach, FL	(27.8)
289	Grand Prairie, TX	(28.3)
290	Bloomington, MN	(28.4)
290	Madison, WI	(28.4)
292	Columbia, SC	(28.5)
292	Coral Springs, FL	(28.5)
294	Springfield, MA	(28.6)
295	Duluth, MN	(28.7)
296	Clovis, CA	(29.0)
296	Paterson, NJ	(29.0)
298	Memphis, TN	(29.1)
299	Chesapeake, VA	(29.2)
299	Hamilton Twnshp, NJ	(29.2)
301	Beaverton, OR	(30.0)
301	Boca Raton, FL	(30.0)
303	Virginia Beach, VA	(30.1)
304	Wilmington, NC	(30.2)
305	Jackson, MS	(30.4)
306	Fort Lauderdale, FL	(30.5)
307	Cincinnati, OH	(31.0)
308	Oceanside, CA	(31.1)
309	Suffolk, VA	(31.5)
310	Santa Rosa, CA	(32.2)
311	Boise, ID	(32.4)
311	Clifton, NJ	(32.4)
313	Montgomery, AL	(32.8)
314	Elizabeth, NJ	(32.9)
315	Chandler, AZ	(33.0)
316	Edison Twnshp, NJ	(33.1)
316	Glendale, AZ	(33.1)
318	Jersey City, NJ	(33.5)
319	Peoria, IL	(33.9)
320	Mesa, AZ	(34.1)
321	Fresno, CA	(34.3)
321	Lowell, MA	(34.3)
321	Norfolk, VA	(34.3)
324	Peoria, AZ	(35.0)
325	Gilbert, AZ	(35.8)
326	Overland Park, KS	(36.4)
327	Killeen, TX	(36.9)
327	Nashville, TN	(36.9)
329	Clarkstown, NY	(37.2)
329	Quincy, MA	(37.2)
331	Newport News, VA	(37.4)
332	Raleigh, NC	(38.4)
333	Providence, RI	(38.8)
334	Boston, MA	(39.1)
334	Waco, TX	(39.1)
336	Round Rock, TX	(39.2)
337	Richmond, VA	(39.5)
338	Syracuse, NY	(39.9)
339	Corpus Christi, TX	(40.1)
340	McAllen, TX	(40.7)
341	Aurora, CO	(41.1)
341	Hampton, VA	(41.1)
343	New York, NY	(41.6)
344	Salem, OR	(42.8)
345	Brockton, MA	(42.9)
346	Charleston, SC	(43.1)
347	Sugar Land, TX	(43.6)
348	Portsmouth, VA	(43.7)
349	Lynn, MA	(43.8)
350	Yonkers, NY	(44.2)
351	Pasadena, TX	(44.4)
352	Cambridge, MA	(46.5)
353	Woodbridge Twnshp, NJ	(47.6)
354	Sioux City, IA	(47.9)
355	Savannah, GA	(48.9)
356	Warwick, RI	(50.0)
357	Alexandria, VA	(50.9)
358	Hillsboro, OR	(53.0)
359	Tampa, FL	(56.0)
360	Trenton, NJ	(56.8)
361	New Orleans, LA	(57.3)
362	Joliet, IL	(59.0)
363	McKinney, TX	(60.3)
364	Tyler, TX	(60.8)
365	Amherst, NY	(61.0)
366	Chino Hills, CA	(65.3)
NA	Albany, NY**	NA
NA	Canton, OH**	NA
NA	Centennial, CO**	NA
NA	Cheektowaga, NY**	NA
NA	Des Moines, IA**	NA
NA	Durham, NC**	NA
NA	El Paso, TX**	NA
NA	Fort Wayne, IN**	NA
NA	Greece, NY**	NA
NA	Kansas City, KS**	NA
NA	Kansas City, MO**	NA
NA	Las Cruces, NM**	NA
NA	Lexington, KY**	NA
NA	Louisville, KY**	NA
NA	Miami Gardens, FL**	NA
NA	Nashua, NH**	NA
NA	New Bedford, MA**	NA
NA	Newton, MA**	NA
NA	Roanoke, VA**	NA
NA	Rockford, IL**	NA
NA	Santa Maria, CA**	NA
NA	Spokane Valley, WA**	NA
NA	Westminster, CO**	NA
NA	Worcester, MA**	NA

Source: CQ Press using data from F.B.I. "Crime in the United States 2006"

**Motor vehicle theft includes the theft or attempted theft of a self-propelled vehicle. Excludes motorboats, construction equipment, airplanes, and farming equipment. **Not available.*

81. Police Officers in 2006

National Total = 683,396 Officers*

RANK	CITY	OFFICERS
214	Abilene, TX	186
219	Albany, GA	184
118	Albany, NY	338
42	Albuquerque, NM	972
126	Alexandria, VA	322
364	Alhambra, CA	82
205	Allentown, PA	191
135	Amarillo, TX	295
280	Amherst, NY	149
90	Anaheim, CA	410
104	Anchorage, AK	367
267	Ann Arbor, MI	155
343	Antioch, CA	105
69	Arlington, TX	559
301	Arvada, CO	130
182	Athens-Clarke, GA	225
21	Atlanta, GA	1,669
65	Aurora, CO	631
142	Aurora, IL	286
28	Austin, TX	1,373
127	Bakersfield, CA	321
369	Baldwin Park, CA	70
9	Baltimore, MD	2,974
56	Baton Rouge, LA	699
162	Beaumont, TX	252
322	Beaverton, OR	120
243	Bellevue, WA	167
NA	Bellflower, CA**	NA
340	Bellingham, WA	109
219	Berkeley, CA	184
297	Billings, MT	132
51	Birmingham, AL	791
329	Bloomington, MN	116
212	Boca Raton, FL	188
150	Boise, ID	268
13	Boston, MA	2,056
250	Boulder, CO	163
307	Brick Twnshp, NJ	127
90	Bridgeport, CT	410
217	Brockton, MA	185
318	Broken Arrow, OK	123
177	Brownsville, TX	232
359	Buena Park, CA	91
53	Buffalo, NY	753
267	Burbank, CA	155
152	Cambridge, MA	265
88	Camden, NJ	423
367	Canton Twnshp, MI	76
231	Canton, OH	176
190	Cape Coral, FL	209
335	Carlsbad, CA	112
265	Carrollton, TX	157
NA	Carson, CA**	NA
272	Cary, NC	152
211	Cedar Rapids, IA	189
NA	Centennial, CO**	NA
133	Chandler, AZ	306
104	Charleston, SC	367
24	Charlotte, NC	1,558
87	Chattanooga, TN	429
313	Cheektowaga, NY	125
117	Chesapeake, VA	343
2	Chicago, IL	13,624
NA	Chino Hills, CA**	NA
351	Chino, CA	95
168	Chula Vista, CA	241
37	Cincinnati, OH	1,086
238	Clarkstown, NY	172
174	Clarksville, TN	237
161	Clearwater, FL	255
22	Cleveland, OH	1,591
260	Clifton, NJ	158
345	Clinton Twnshp, MI	103
346	Clovis, CA	102
340	Colonie, NY	109
62	Colorado Springs, CO	681
283	Columbia, MO	147
122	Columbia, SC	328
116	Columbus, GA	349
19	Columbus, OH	1,829
NA	Compton, CA**	NA
269	Concord, CA	154
200	Coral Springs, FL	197
238	Corona, CA	172
86	Corpus Christi, TX	439
276	Costa Mesa, CA	151
272	Cranston, RI	152
8	Dallas, TX	3,043
343	Daly City, CA	105
283	Danbury, CT	147
233	Davie, FL	174
NA	Dayton, OH**	NA
205	Dearborn, MI	191
322	Deerfield Beach, FL	120
282	Denton, TX	148
25	Denver, CO	1,497
101	Des Moines, IA	373
7	Detroit, MI	3,164
339	Downey, CA	110
287	Duluth, MN	143
81	Durham, NC	458
193	Edison Twnshp, NJ	204
335	Edmond, OK	112
290	El Cajon, CA	141
258	El Monte, CA	159
36	El Paso, TX	1,098
110	Elizabeth, NJ	357
236	Erie, PA	173
250	Escondido, CA	163
225	Eugene, OR	178
140	Evansville, IN	287
224	Everett, WA	180
319	Fairfield, CA	122
309	Fargo, ND	126
322	Farmington Hills, MI	120
130	Fayetteville, NC	308
329	Federal Way, WA	116
156	Flint, MI	258
233	Fontana, CA	174
266	Fort Collins, CO	156
78	Fort Lauderdale, FL	483
248	Fort Smith, AR	164
89	Fort Wayne, IN	422
30	Fort Worth, TX	1,368
212	Fremont, CA	188
50	Fresno, CA	798
260	Fullerton, CA	158
145	Gainesville, FL	278
260	Garden Grove, CA	158
121	Garland, TX	329
153	Gary, IN	264
205	Gilbert, AZ	191
102	Glendale, AZ	370
158	Glendale, CA	257
192	Grand Prairie, TX	205
120	Grand Rapids, MI	332
357	Greece, NY	92
297	Greeley, CO	132
222	Green Bay, WI	182
72	Greensboro, NC	530
325	Gresham, OR	119
222	Hamilton Twnshp, NJ	182
195	Hammond, IN	201
144	Hampton, VA	284
90	Hartford, CT	410
354	Hawthorne, CA	93
205	Hayward, CA	191
127	Henderson, NV	321
NA	Hesperia, CA**	NA
115	Hialeah, FL	352
184	High Point, NC	222
331	Hillsboro, OR	115
123	Hollywood, FL	327
14	Honolulu, HI	2,053
5	Houston, TX	4,781
188	Huntington Beach, CA	217
110	Huntsville, AL	357
202	Independence, MO	194
23	Indianapolis, IN	1,581
204	Inglewood, CA	192
250	Irvine, CA	163
124	Irving, TX	323
20	Jacksonville, FL	1,690
83	Jackson, MS	452
44	Jersey City, NJ	870
138	Joliet, IL	292
110	Kansas City, KS	357
31	Kansas City, MO	1,357
214	Kenosha, WI	186
313	Kent, WA	125
228	Killeen, TX	177
108	Knoxville, TN	359
179	Lafayette, LA	228
NA	Lake Forest, CA**	NA
175	Lakeland, FL	235
NA	Lakewood, CA**	NA
154	Lakewood, CO	263
NA	Lancaster, CA**	NA
166	Lansing, MI	243
95	Laredo, TX	399
296	Largo, FL	134
246	Las Cruces, NM	165
11	Las Vegas, NV	2,231
292	Lawrence, KS	139
258	Lawton, OK	159
332	Lee's Summit, MO	114
300	Lewisville, TX	131
70	Lexington, KY	553
132	Lincoln, NE	307
73	Little Rock, AR	519
351	Livermore, CA	95
283	Livonia, MI	147

RANK	CITY	OFFICERS
43	Long Beach, CA	901
276	Longview, TX	151
3	Los Angeles, CA	9,393
35	Louisville, KY	1,206
169	Lowell, MA	240
103	Lubbock, TX	368
221	Lynn, MA	183
148	Macon, GA	272
98	Madison, WI	388
197	Manchester, NH	200
155	McAllen, TX	261
303	McKinney, TX	129
256	Melbourne, FL	160
16	Memphis, TN	1,990
46	Mesa, AZ	829
185	Mesquite, TX	220
99	Miami Beach, FL	386
287	Miami Gardens, FL	143
38	Miami, FL	1,058
260	Midland, TX	158
17	Milwaukee, WI	1,951
47	Minneapolis, MN	818
242	Miramar, FL	168
NA	Mission Viejo, CA**	NA
74	Mobile, AL	514
151	Modesto, CA	266
83	Montgomery, AL	452
NA	Moreno Valley, CA**	NA
233	Murfreesboro, TN	174
365	Murrieta, CA	78
368	Napa, CA	71
209	Naperville, IL	190
244	Nashua, NH	166
34	Nashville, TN	1,213
138	New Bedford, MA	292
26	New Orleans, LA	1,424
1	New York, NY	35,690
32	Newark, NJ	1,286
290	Newport Beach, CA	141
96	Newport News, VA	392
272	Newton, MA	152
54	Norfolk, VA	729
303	Norman, OK	129
143	North Charleston, SC	285
145	North Las Vegas, NV	278
NA	Norwalk, CA**	NA
61	Oakland, CA	688
199	Oceanside, CA	199
272	Odessa, TX	152
307	Ogden, UT	127
39	Oklahoma City, OK	994
248	Olathe, KS	164
52	Omaha, NE	774
182	Ontario, CA	225
260	Orange, CA	158
360	Orem, UT	88
57	Orlando, FL	695
169	Overland Park, KS	240
177	Oxnard, CA	232
269	Palm Bay, FL	154
NA	Palmdale, CA**	NA
363	Parma, OH	84
169	Pasadena, CA	240
160	Pasadena, TX	256
82	Paterson, NJ	457
166	Pembroke Pines, FL	243

RANK	CITY	OFFICERS
244	Peoria, AZ	166
165	Peoria, IL	246
4	Philadelphia, PA	6,665
10	Phoenix, AZ	2,896
45	Pittsburgh, PA	848
119	Plano, TX	333
231	Plantation, FL	176
214	Pomona, CA	186
187	Pompano Beach, FL	218
179	Port St. Lucie, FL	228
NA	Portland, OR**	NA
164	Portsmouth, VA	248
79	Providence, RI	480
354	Provo, UT	93
209	Pueblo, CO	190
197	Quincy, MA	200
200	Racine, WI	197
58	Raleigh, NC	691
NA	Rancho Cucamon., CA**	NA
191	Reading, PA	206
327	Redding, CA	117
106	Reno, NV	365
360	Rialto, CA	88
289	Richardson, TX	142
271	Richmond, CA	153
59	Richmond, VA	690
97	Riverside, CA	389
156	Roanoke, VA	258
327	Rochester, MN	117
55	Rochester, NY	725
134	Rockford, IL	304
297	Roseville, CA	132
303	Roswell, GA	129
309	Round Rock, TX	126
63	Sacramento, CA	663
217	Salem, OR	185
255	Salinas, CA	161
94	Salt Lake City, UT	401
279	San Angelo, TX	150
15	San Antonio, TX	1,993
130	San Bernardino, CA	308
18	San Diego, CA	1,911
12	San Francisco, CA	2,202
28	San Jose, CA	1,373
354	San Leandro, CA	93
334	San Mateo, CA	113
332	Sandy, UT	114
107	Santa Ana, CA	360
293	Santa Barbara, CA	138
303	Santa Clara, CA	129
NA	Santa Clarita, CA**	NA
342	Santa Maria, CA	106
193	Santa Monica, CA	204
254	Santa Rosa, CA	162
71	Savannah, GA	539
100	Scottsdale, AZ	382
33	Seattle, WA	1,276
67	Shreveport, LA	598
321	Simi Valley, CA	121
313	Sioux City, IA	125
189	Sioux Falls, SD	216
301	Somerville, MA	130
158	South Bend, IN	257
362	South Gate, CA	86
280	Southfield, MI	149
338	Sparks, NV	111

RANK	CITY	OFFICERS
348	Spokane Valley, WA	100
145	Spokane, WA	278
149	Springfield, IL	271
85	Springfield, MA	445
127	Springfield, MO	321
250	Sterling Heights, MI	163
93	Stockton, CA	404
27	St. Louis, MO	1,407
68	St. Paul, MN	563
75	St. Petersburg, FL	504
256	Suffolk, VA	160
309	Sugar Land, TX	126
186	Sunnyvale, CA	219
240	Sunrise, FL	170
351	Surprise, AZ	95
76	Syracuse, NY	485
110	Tacoma, WA	357
114	Tallahassee, FL	354
41	Tampa, FL	983
NA	Temecula, CA**	NA
124	Tempe, AZ	323
286	Thornton, CO	144
NA	Thousand Oaks, CA**	NA
59	Toledo, OH	690
246	Toms River Twnshp, NJ	165
136	Topeka, KS	294
169	Torrance, CA	240
366	Tracy, CA	77
108	Trenton, NJ	359
295	Troy, MI	135
39	Tucson, AZ	994
48	Tulsa, OK	816
162	Tuscaloosa, AL	252
225	Tyler, TX	178
317	Upper Darby Twnshp, PA	124
347	Vacaville, CA	101
294	Vallejo, CA	136
203	Vancouver, WA	193
313	Ventura, CA	125
NA	Victorville, CA**	NA
49	Virginia Beach, VA	800
319	Visalia, CA	122
NA	Vista, CA**	NA
179	Waco, TX	228
175	Warren, MI	235
228	Warwick, RI	177
6	Washington, DC	3,799
136	Waterbury, CT	294
335	West Covina, CA	112
357	West Jordan, UT	92
140	West Palm Beach, FL	287
228	West Valley, UT	177
348	Westland, MI	100
350	Westminster, CA	99
236	Westminster, CO	173
325	Whittier, CA	119
241	Wichita Falls, TX	169
64	Wichita, KS	640
169	Wilmington, NC	240
76	Winston-Salem, NC	485
195	Woodbridge Twnshp, NJ	201
80	Worcester, MA	464
309	Yakima, WA	126
66	Yonkers, NY	609
225	Youngstown, OH	178
276	Yuma, AZ	151

Source: Federal Bureau of Investigation "Crime in the United States 2006"
**Sworn officers only, does not include civilian employees.*
***Not available*

81. Police Officers in 2006 (continued)

National Total = 683,396 Officers*

RANK	CITY	OFFICERS
1	New York, NY	35,690
2	Chicago, IL	13,624
3	Los Angeles, CA	9,393
4	Philadelphia, PA	6,665
5	Houston, TX	4,781
6	Washington, DC	3,799
7	Detroit, MI	3,164
8	Dallas, TX	3,043
9	Baltimore, MD	2,974
10	Phoenix, AZ	2,896
11	Las Vegas, NV	2,231
12	San Francisco, CA	2,202
13	Boston, MA	2,056
14	Honolulu, HI	2,053
15	San Antonio, TX	1,993
16	Memphis, TN	1,990
17	Milwaukee, WI	1,951
18	San Diego, CA	1,911
19	Columbus, OH	1,829
20	Jacksonville, FL	1,690
21	Atlanta, GA	1,669
22	Cleveland, OH	1,591
23	Indianapolis, IN	1,581
24	Charlotte, NC	1,558
25	Denver, CO	1,497
26	New Orleans, LA	1,424
27	St. Louis, MO	1,407
28	Austin, TX	1,373
28	San Jose, CA	1,373
30	Fort Worth, TX	1,368
31	Kansas City, MO	1,357
32	Newark, NJ	1,286
33	Seattle, WA	1,276
34	Nashville, TN	1,213
35	Louisville, KY	1,206
36	El Paso, TX	1,098
37	Cincinnati, OH	1,086
38	Miami, FL	1,058
39	Oklahoma City, OK	994
39	Tucson, AZ	994
41	Tampa, FL	983
42	Albuquerque, NM	972
43	Long Beach, CA	901
44	Jersey City, NJ	870
45	Pittsburgh, PA	848
46	Mesa, AZ	829
47	Minneapolis, MN	818
48	Tulsa, OK	816
49	Virginia Beach, VA	800
50	Fresno, CA	798
51	Birmingham, AL	791
52	Omaha, NE	774
53	Buffalo, NY	753
54	Norfolk, VA	729
55	Rochester, NY	725
56	Baton Rouge, LA	699
57	Orlando, FL	695
58	Raleigh, NC	691
59	Richmond, VA	690
59	Toledo, OH	690
61	Oakland, CA	688
62	Colorado Springs, CO	681
63	Sacramento, CA	663
64	Wichita, KS	640
65	Aurora, CO	631
66	Yonkers, NY	609
67	Shreveport, LA	598
68	St. Paul, MN	563
69	Arlington, TX	559
70	Lexington, KY	553
71	Savannah, GA	539
72	Greensboro, NC	530
73	Little Rock, AR	519
74	Mobile, AL	514
75	St. Petersburg, FL	504
76	Syracuse, NY	485
76	Winston-Salem, NC	485
78	Fort Lauderdale, FL	483
79	Providence, RI	480
80	Worcester, MA	464
81	Durham, NC	458
82	Paterson, NJ	457
83	Jackson, MS	452
83	Montgomery, AL	452
85	Springfield, MA	445
86	Corpus Christi, TX	439
87	Chattanooga, TN	429
88	Camden, NJ	423
89	Fort Wayne, IN	422
90	Anaheim, CA	410
90	Bridgeport, CT	410
90	Hartford, CT	410
93	Stockton, CA	404
94	Salt Lake City, UT	401
95	Laredo, TX	399
96	Newport News, VA	392
97	Riverside, CA	389
98	Madison, WI	388
99	Miami Beach, FL	386
100	Scottsdale, AZ	382
101	Des Moines, IA	373
102	Glendale, AZ	370
103	Lubbock, TX	368
104	Anchorage, AK	367
104	Charleston, SC	367
106	Reno, NV	365
107	Santa Ana, CA	360
108	Knoxville, TN	359
108	Trenton, NJ	359
110	Elizabeth, NJ	357
110	Huntsville, AL	357
110	Kansas City, KS	357
110	Tacoma, WA	357
114	Tallahassee, FL	354
115	Hialeah, FL	352
116	Columbus, GA	349
117	Chesapeake, VA	343
118	Albany, NY	338
119	Plano, TX	333
120	Grand Rapids, MI	332
121	Garland, TX	329
122	Columbia, SC	328
123	Hollywood, FL	327
124	Irving, TX	323
124	Tempe, AZ	323
126	Alexandria, VA	322
127	Bakersfield, CA	321
127	Henderson, NV	321
127	Springfield, MO	321
130	Fayetteville, NC	308
130	San Bernardino, CA	308
132	Lincoln, NE	307
133	Chandler, AZ	306
134	Rockford, IL	304
135	Amarillo, TX	295
136	Topeka, KS	294
136	Waterbury, CT	294
138	Joliet, IL	292
138	New Bedford, MA	292
140	Evansville, IN	287
140	West Palm Beach, FL	287
142	Aurora, IL	286
143	North Charleston, SC	285
144	Hampton, VA	284
145	Gainesville, FL	278
145	North Las Vegas, NV	278
145	Spokane, WA	278
148	Macon, GA	272
149	Springfield, IL	271
150	Boise, ID	268
151	Modesto, CA	266
152	Cambridge, MA	265
153	Gary, IN	264
154	Lakewood, CO	263
155	McAllen, TX	261
156	Flint, MI	258
156	Roanoke, VA	258
158	Glendale, CA	257
158	South Bend, IN	257
160	Pasadena, TX	256
161	Clearwater, FL	255
162	Beaumont, TX	252
162	Tuscaloosa, AL	252
164	Portsmouth, VA	248
165	Peoria, IL	246
166	Lansing, MI	243
166	Pembroke Pines, FL	243
168	Chula Vista, CA	241
169	Lowell, MA	240
169	Overland Park, KS	240
169	Pasadena, CA	240
169	Torrance, CA	240
169	Wilmington, NC	240
174	Clarksville, TN	237
175	Lakeland, FL	235
175	Warren, MI	235
177	Brownsville, TX	232
177	Oxnard, CA	232
179	Lafayette, LA	228
179	Port St. Lucie, FL	228
179	Waco, TX	228
182	Athens-Clarke, GA	225
182	Ontario, CA	225
184	High Point, NC	222
185	Mesquite, TX	220
186	Sunnyvale, CA	219
187	Pompano Beach, FL	218
188	Huntington Beach, CA	217
189	Sioux Falls, SD	216
190	Cape Coral, FL	209
191	Reading, PA	206
192	Grand Prairie, TX	205

RANK	CITY	OFFICERS
193	Edison Twnshp, NJ	204
193	Santa Monica, CA	204
195	Hammond, IN	201
195	Woodbridge Twnshp, NJ	201
197	Manchester, NH	200
197	Quincy, MA	200
199	Oceanside, CA	199
200	Coral Springs, FL	197
200	Racine, WI	197
202	Independence, MO	194
203	Vancouver, WA	193
204	Inglewood, CA	192
205	Allentown, PA	191
205	Dearborn, MI	191
205	Gilbert, AZ	191
205	Hayward, CA	191
209	Naperville, IL	190
209	Pueblo, CO	190
211	Cedar Rapids, IA	189
212	Boca Raton, FL	188
212	Fremont, CA	188
214	Abilene, TX	186
214	Kenosha, WI	186
214	Pomona, CA	186
217	Brockton, MA	185
217	Salem, OR	185
219	Albany, GA	184
219	Berkeley, CA	184
221	Lynn, MA	183
222	Green Bay, WI	182
222	Hamilton Twnshp, NJ	182
224	Everett, WA	180
225	Eugene, OR	178
225	Tyler, TX	178
225	Youngstown, OH	178
228	Killeen, TX	177
228	Warwick, RI	177
228	West Valley, UT	177
231	Canton, OH	176
231	Plantation, FL	176
233	Davie, FL	174
233	Fontana, CA	174
233	Murfreesboro, TN	174
236	Erie, PA	173
236	Westminster, CO	173
238	Clarkstown, NY	172
238	Corona, CA	172
240	Sunrise, FL	170
241	Wichita Falls, TX	169
242	Miramar, FL	168
243	Bellevue, WA	167
244	Nashua, NH	166
244	Peoria, AZ	166
246	Las Cruces, NM	165
246	Toms River Twnshp, NJ	165
248	Fort Smith, AR	164
248	Olathe, KS	164
250	Boulder, CO	163
250	Escondido, CA	163
250	Irvine, CA	163
250	Sterling Heights, MI	163
254	Santa Rosa, CA	162
255	Salinas, CA	161
256	Melbourne, FL	160
256	Suffolk, VA	160
258	El Monte, CA	159
258	Lawton, OK	159
260	Clifton, NJ	158
260	Fullerton, CA	158
260	Garden Grove, CA	158
260	Midland, TX	158
260	Orange, CA	158
265	Carrollton, TX	157
266	Fort Collins, CO	156
267	Ann Arbor, MI	155
267	Burbank, CA	155
269	Concord, CA	154
269	Palm Bay, FL	154
271	Richmond, CA	153
272	Cary, NC	152
272	Cranston, RI	152
272	Newton, MA	152
272	Odessa, TX	152
276	Costa Mesa, CA	151
276	Longview, TX	151
276	Yuma, AZ	151
279	San Angelo, TX	150
280	Amherst, NY	149
280	Southfield, MI	149
282	Denton, TX	148
283	Columbia, MO	147
283	Danbury, CT	147
283	Livonia, MI	147
286	Thornton, CO	144
287	Duluth, MN	143
287	Miami Gardens, FL	143
289	Richardson, TX	142
290	El Cajon, CA	141
290	Newport Beach, CA	141
292	Lawrence, KS	139
293	Santa Barbara, CA	138
294	Vallejo, CA	136
295	Troy, MI	135
296	Largo, FL	134
297	Billings, MT	132
297	Greeley, CO	132
297	Roseville, CA	132
300	Lewisville, TX	131
301	Arvada, CO	130
301	Somerville, MA	130
303	McKinney, TX	129
303	Norman, OK	129
303	Roswell, GA	129
303	Santa Clara, CA	129
307	Brick Twnshp, NJ	127
307	Ogden, UT	127
309	Fargo, ND	126
309	Round Rock, TX	126
309	Sugar Land, TX	126
309	Yakima, WA	126
313	Cheektowaga, NY	125
313	Kent, WA	125
313	Sioux City, IA	125
313	Ventura, CA	125
317	Upper Darby Twnshp, PA	124
318	Broken Arrow, OK	123
319	Fairfield, CA	122
319	Visalia, CA	122
321	Simi Valley, CA	121
322	Beaverton, OR	120
322	Deerfield Beach, FL	120
322	Farmington Hills, MI	120
325	Gresham, OR	119
325	Whittier, CA	119
327	Redding, CA	117
327	Rochester, MN	117
329	Bloomington, MN	116
329	Federal Way, WA	116
331	Hillsboro, OR	115
332	Lee's Summit, MO	114
332	Sandy, UT	114
334	San Mateo, CA	113
335	Carlsbad, CA	112
335	Edmond, OK	112
335	West Covina, CA	112
338	Sparks, NV	111
339	Downey, CA	110
340	Bellingham, WA	109
340	Colonie, NY	109
342	Santa Maria, CA	106
343	Antioch, CA	105
343	Daly City, CA	105
345	Clinton Twnshp, MI	103
346	Clovis, CA	102
347	Vacaville, CA	101
348	Spokane Valley, WA	100
348	Westland, MI	100
350	Westminster, CA	99
351	Chino, CA	95
351	Livermore, CA	95
351	Surprise, AZ	95
354	Hawthorne, CA	93
354	Provo, UT	93
354	San Leandro, CA	93
357	Greece, NY	92
357	West Jordan, UT	92
359	Buena Park, CA	91
360	Orem, UT	88
360	Rialto, CA	88
362	South Gate, CA	86
363	Parma, OH	84
364	Alhambra, CA	82
365	Murrieta, CA	78
366	Tracy, CA	77
367	Canton Twnshp, MI	76
368	Napa, CA	71
369	Baldwin Park, CA	70
NA	Bellflower, CA**	NA
NA	Carson, CA**	NA
NA	Centennial, CO**	NA
NA	Chino Hills, CA**	NA
NA	Compton, CA**	NA
NA	Dayton, OH**	NA
NA	Hesperia, CA**	NA
NA	Lake Forest, CA**	NA
NA	Lakewood, CA**	NA
NA	Lancaster, CA**	NA
NA	Mission Viejo, CA**	NA
NA	Moreno Valley, CA**	NA
NA	Norwalk, CA**	NA
NA	Palmdale, CA**	NA
NA	Portland, OR**	NA
NA	Rancho Cucamon., CA**	NA
NA	Santa Clarita, CA**	NA
NA	Temecula, CA**	NA
NA	Thousand Oaks, CA**	NA
NA	Victorville, CA**	NA
NA	Vista, CA**	NA

Source: Federal Bureau of Investigation "Crime in the United States 2006"
**Sworn officers only, does not include civilian employees.*
***Not available*

82. Rate of Police Officers in 2006

National Rate = 241 Officers per 100,000 Population*

RANK	CITY	RATE
218	Abilene, TX	158
75	Albany, GA	236
13	Albany, NY	360
141	Albuquerque, NM	194
75	Alexandria, VA	236
361	Alhambra, CA	93
176	Allentown, PA	178
220	Amarillo, TX	157
284	Amherst, NY	133
310	Anaheim, CA	122
287	Anchorage, AK	132
275	Ann Arbor, MI	137
350	Antioch, CA	103
239	Arlington, TX	150
305	Arvada, CO	123
111	Athens-Clarke, GA	211
18	Atlanta, GA	344
114	Aurora, CO	208
197	Aurora, IL	169
145	Austin, TX	193
341	Bakersfield, CA	108
365	Baldwin Park, CA	88
4	Baltimore, MD	466
24	Baton Rouge, LA	332
93	Beaumont, TX	219
272	Beaverton, OR	138
265	Bellevue, WA	140
NA	Bellflower, CA**	NA
256	Bellingham, WA	144
168	Berkeley, CA	181
287	Billings, MT	132
21	Birmingham, AL	339
258	Bloomington, MN	142
105	Boca Raton, FL	213
278	Boise, ID	135
11	Boston, MA	366
182	Boulder, CO	174
211	Brick Twnshp, NJ	162
37	Bridgeport, CT	295
141	Brockton, MA	194
260	Broken Arrow, OK	141
278	Brownsville, TX	135
334	Buena Park, CA	114
52	Buffalo, NY	268
247	Burbank, CA	148
54	Cambridge, MA	263
2	Camden, NJ	528
364	Canton Twnshp, MI	89
89	Canton, OH	221
252	Cape Coral, FL	147
310	Carlsbad, CA	122
295	Carrollton, TX	128
NA	Carson, CA**	NA
265	Cary, NC	140
232	Cedar Rapids, IA	153
NA	Centennial, CO**	NA
301	Chandler, AZ	125
21	Charleston, SC	339
88	Charlotte, NC	223
48	Chattanooga, TN	274
228	Cheektowaga, NY	154
224	Chesapeake, VA	155
3	Chicago, IL	477
NA	Chino Hills, CA**	NA
315	Chino, CA	121
336	Chula Vista, CA	113
16	Cincinnati, OH	351
93	Clarkstown, NY	219
115	Clarksville, TN	207
79	Clearwater, FL	231
16	Cleveland, OH	351
132	Clifton, NJ	198
344	Clinton Twnshp, MI	107
328	Clovis, CA	117
260	Colonie, NY	141
168	Colorado Springs, CO	181
215	Columbia, MO	159
46	Columbia, SC	276
163	Columbus, GA	183
64	Columbus, OH	250
NA	Compton, CA**	NA
304	Concord, CA	124
239	Coral Springs, FL	150
334	Corona, CA	114
235	Corpus Christi, TX	151
277	Costa Mesa, CA	136
152	Cranston, RI	188
71	Dallas, TX	244
349	Daly City, CA	104
156	Danbury, CT	187
124	Davie, FL	203
NA	Dayton, OH**	NA
123	Dearborn, MI	204
224	Deerfield Beach, FL	155
272	Denton, TX	138
54	Denver, CO	263
149	Des Moines, IA	191
14	Detroit, MI	358
354	Downey, CA	99
201	Duluth, MN	167
93	Durham, NC	219
124	Edison Twnshp, NJ	203
247	Edmond, OK	148
235	El Cajon, CA	151
291	El Monte, CA	129
176	El Paso, TX	178
42	Elizabeth, NJ	284
199	Erie, PA	168
319	Escondido, CA	120
315	Eugene, OR	121
66	Evansville, IN	246
163	Everett, WA	183
330	Fairfield, CA	116
269	Fargo, ND	139
239	Farmington Hills, MI	150
78	Fayetteville, NC	232
275	Federal Way, WA	137
97	Flint, MI	218
346	Fontana, CA	105
319	Fort Collins, CO	120
42	Fort Lauderdale, FL	284
136	Fort Smith, AR	197
152	Fort Wayne, IN	188
105	Fort Worth, TX	213
361	Fremont, CA	93
189	Fresno, CA	172
326	Fullerton, CA	118
61	Gainesville, FL	253
359	Garden Grove, CA	94
247	Garland, TX	148
53	Gary, IN	266
345	Gilbert, AZ	106
245	Glendale, AZ	149
298	Glendale, CA	127
272	Grand Prairie, TX	138
189	Grand Rapids, MI	172
355	Greece, NY	98
247	Greeley, CO	148
173	Green Bay, WI	179
86	Greensboro, NC	224
310	Gresham, OR	122
127	Hamilton Twnshp, NJ	202
62	Hammond, IN	252
145	Hampton, VA	193
25	Hartford, CT	330
341	Hawthorne, CA	108
278	Hayward, CA	135
281	Henderson, NV	134
NA	Hesperia, CA**	NA
220	Hialeah, FL	157
83	High Point, NC	229
281	Hillsboro, OR	134
89	Hollywood, FL	221
85	Honolulu, HI	225
79	Houston, TX	231
337	Huntington Beach, CA	111
105	Huntsville, AL	213
179	Independence, MO	175
136	Indianapolis, IN	197
204	Inglewood, CA	166
367	Irvine, CA	86
211	Irving, TX	162
109	Jacksonville, FL	212
59	Jackson, MS	255
12	Jersey City, NJ	363
105	Joliet, IL	213
66	Kansas City, KS	246
35	Kansas City, MO	303
140	Kenosha, WI	195
239	Kent, WA	150
189	Killeen, TX	172
136	Knoxville, TN	197
103	Lafayette, LA	215
NA	Lake Forest, CA**	NA
57	Lakeland, FL	261
NA	Lakewood, CA**	NA
163	Lakewood, CO	183
NA	Lancaster, CA**	NA
111	Lansing, MI	211
157	Laredo, TX	186
178	Largo, FL	177
136	Las Cruces, NM	197
195	Las Vegas, NV	170
197	Lawrence, KS	169
179	Lawton, OK	175
260	Lee's Summit, MO	141
260	Lewisville, TX	141
117	Lexington, KY	205
295	Lincoln, NE	128
45	Little Rock, AR	278
319	Livermore, CA	120
239	Livonia, MI	150

RANK	CITY	RATE	RANK	CITY	RATE	RANK	CITY	RATE
152	Long Beach, CA	188	330	Peoria, AZ	116	315	Spokane Valley, WA	121
141	Longview, TX	194	100	Peoria, IL	217	269	Spokane, WA	139
73	Los Angeles, CA	242	6	Philadelphia, PA	455	77	Springfield, IL	233
145	Louisville, KY	193	149	Phoenix, AZ	191	39	Springfield, MA	292
79	Lowell, MA	231	57	Pittsburgh, PA	261	109	Springfield, MO	212
194	Lubbock, TX	171	291	Plano, TX	129	295	Sterling Heights, MI	128
117	Lynn, MA	205	128	Plantation, FL	201	265	Stockton, CA	140
44	Macon, GA	279	319	Pomona, CA	120	10	St. Louis, MO	406
182	Madison, WI	174	116	Pompano Beach, FL	206	124	St. Paul, MN	203
166	Manchester, NH	182	195	Port St. Lucie, FL	170	131	St. Petersburg, FL	199
117	McAllen, TX	205	NA	Portland, OR**	NA	128	Suffolk, VA	201
290	McKinney, TX	130	69	Portsmouth, VA	245	211	Sugar Land, TX	162
117	Melbourne, FL	205	48	Providence, RI	274	199	Sunnyvale, CA	168
39	Memphis, TN	292	369	Provo, UT	79	160	Sunrise, FL	185
171	Mesa, AZ	180	171	Pueblo, CO	180	305	Surprise, AZ	123
206	Mesquite, TX	165	91	Quincy, MA	220	20	Syracuse, NY	341
8	Miami Beach, FL	432	65	Racine, WI	247	173	Tacoma, WA	179
260	Miami Gardens, FL	141	132	Raleigh, NC	198	91	Tallahassee, FL	220
51	Miami, FL	269	NA	Rancho Cucamon., CA**	NA	36	Tampa, FL	297
224	Midland, TX	155	59	Reading, PA	255	NA	Temecula, CA**	NA
23	Milwaukee, WI	336	291	Redding, CA	129	145	Tempe, AZ	193
97	Minneapolis, MN	218	182	Reno, NV	174	281	Thornton, CO	134
224	Miramar, FL	155	365	Rialto, CA	88	NA	Thousand Oaks, CA**	NA
NA	Mission Viejo, CA**	NA	269	Richardson, TX	139	83	Toledo, OH	229
117	Mobile, AL	205	247	Richmond, CA	148	182	Toms River Twnshp, NJ	174
298	Modesto, CA	127	15	Richmond, VA	353	74	Topeka, KS	239
86	Montgomery, AL	224	284	Riverside, CA	133	201	Torrance, CA	167
NA	Moreno Valley, CA**	NA	46	Roanoke, VA	276	357	Tracy, CA	95
132	Murfreesboro, TN	198	310	Rochester, MN	122	9	Trenton, NJ	424
361	Murrieta, CA	93	19	Rochester, NY	343	201	Troy, MI	167
359	Napa, CA	94	132	Rockford, IL	198	157	Tucson, AZ	186
284	Naperville, IL	133	305	Roseville, CA	123	111	Tulsa, OK	211
151	Nashua, NH	189	254	Roswell, GA	145	33	Tuscaloosa, AL	307
101	Nashville, TN	216	258	Round Rock, TX	142	152	Tyler, TX	188
30	New Bedford, MA	312	256	Sacramento, CA	144	223	Upper Darby Twnshp, PA	156
25	New Orleans, LA	330	310	Salem, OR	122	341	Vacaville, CA	108
7	New York, NY	437	340	Salinas, CA	109	333	Vallejo, CA	115
5	Newark, NJ	458	97	Salt Lake City, UT	218	319	Vancouver, WA	120
179	Newport Beach, CA	175	204	San Angelo, TX	166	324	Ventura, CA	119
101	Newport News, VA	216	228	San Antonio, TX	154	NA	Victorville, CA**	NA
166	Newton, MA	182	228	San Bernardino, CA	154	168	Virginia Beach, VA	181
31	Norfolk, VA	311	235	San Diego, CA	151	337	Visalia, CA	111
300	Norman, OK	126	37	San Francisco, CA	295	NA	Vista, CA**	NA
27	North Charleston, SC	325	245	San Jose, CA	149	162	Waco, TX	184
234	North Las Vegas, NV	152	326	San Leandro, CA	118	182	Warren, MI	174
NA	Norwalk, CA**	NA	305	San Mateo, CA	123	117	Warwick, RI	205
187	Oakland, CA	173	305	Sandy, UT	123	1	Washington, DC	653
324	Oceanside, CA	119	346	Santa Ana, CA	105	50	Waterbury, CT	273
218	Odessa, TX	158	215	Santa Barbara, CA	159	350	West Covina, CA	103
220	Ogden, UT	157	315	Santa Clara, CA	121	356	West Jordan, UT	97
160	Oklahoma City, OK	185	NA	Santa Clarita, CA**	NA	41	West Palm Beach, FL	289
253	Olathe, KS	146	301	Santa Maria, CA	125	235	West Valley, UT	151
157	Omaha, NE	186	82	Santa Monica, CA	230	328	Westland, MI	117
291	Ontario, CA	129	346	Santa Rosa, CA	105	339	Westminster, CA	110
330	Orange, CA	116	62	Savannah, GA	252	211	Westminster, CO	162
357	Orem, UT	95	209	Scottsdale, AZ	163	265	Whittier, CA	140
28	Orlando, FL	321	93	Seattle, WA	219	206	Wichita Falls, TX	165
254	Overland Park, KS	145	29	Shreveport, LA	317	173	Wichita, KS	179
301	Oxnard, CA	125	353	Simi Valley, CA	101	66	Wilmington, NC	246
209	Palm Bay, FL	163	239	Sioux City, IA	150	69	Winston-Salem, NC	245
NA	Palmdale, CA**	NA	228	Sioux Falls, SD	154	130	Woodbridge Twnshp, NJ	200
350	Parma, OH	103	189	Somerville, MA	172	56	Worcester, MA	262
206	Pasadena, CA	165	72	South Bend, IN	243	232	Yakima, WA	153
187	Pasadena, TX	173	367	South Gate, CA	86	32	Yonkers, NY	309
34	Paterson, NJ	305	141	Southfield, MI	194	103	Youngstown, OH	215
215	Pembroke Pines, FL	159	289	Sparks, NV	131	189	Yuma, AZ	172

Source: CQ Press using data from F.B.I. "Crime in the United States 2006"
**Sworn officers only, does not include civilian employees.*
***Not available*

82. Rate of Police Officers in 2006 (continued)

National Rate = 241 Officers per 100,000 Population*

RANK	CITY	RATE
1	Washington, DC	653
2	Camden, NJ	528
3	Chicago, IL	477
4	Baltimore, MD	466
5	Newark, NJ	458
6	Philadelphia, PA	455
7	New York, NY	437
8	Miami Beach, FL	432
9	Trenton, NJ	424
10	St. Louis, MO	406
11	Boston, MA	366
12	Jersey City, NJ	363
13	Albany, NY	360
14	Detroit, MI	358
15	Richmond, VA	353
16	Cincinnati, OH	351
16	Cleveland, OH	351
18	Atlanta, GA	344
19	Rochester, NY	343
20	Syracuse, NY	341
21	Birmingham, AL	339
21	Charleston, SC	339
23	Milwaukee, WI	336
24	Baton Rouge, LA	332
25	Hartford, CT	330
25	New Orleans, LA	330
27	North Charleston, SC	325
28	Orlando, FL	321
29	Shreveport, LA	317
30	New Bedford, MA	312
31	Norfolk, VA	311
32	Yonkers, NY	309
33	Tuscaloosa, AL	307
34	Paterson, NJ	305
35	Kansas City, MO	303
36	Tampa, FL	297
37	Bridgeport, CT	295
37	San Francisco, CA	295
39	Memphis, TN	292
39	Springfield, MA	292
41	West Palm Beach, FL	289
42	Elizabeth, NJ	284
42	Fort Lauderdale, FL	284
44	Macon, GA	279
45	Little Rock, AR	278
46	Columbia, SC	276
46	Roanoke, VA	276
48	Chattanooga, TN	274
48	Providence, RI	274
50	Waterbury, CT	273
51	Miami, FL	269
52	Buffalo, NY	268
53	Gary, IN	266
54	Cambridge, MA	263
54	Denver, CO	263
56	Worcester, MA	262
57	Lakeland, FL	261
57	Pittsburgh, PA	261
59	Jackson, MS	255
59	Reading, PA	255
61	Gainesville, FL	253
62	Hammond, IN	252
62	Savannah, GA	252
64	Columbus, OH	250
65	Racine, WI	247
66	Evansville, IN	246
66	Kansas City, KS	246
66	Wilmington, NC	246
69	Portsmouth, VA	245
69	Winston-Salem, NC	245
71	Dallas, TX	244
72	South Bend, IN	243
73	Los Angeles, CA	242
74	Topeka, KS	239
75	Albany, GA	236
75	Alexandria, VA	236
77	Springfield, IL	233
78	Fayetteville, NC	232
79	Clearwater, FL	231
79	Houston, TX	231
79	Lowell, MA	231
82	Santa Monica, CA	230
83	High Point, NC	229
83	Toledo, OH	229
85	Honolulu, HI	225
86	Greensboro, NC	224
86	Montgomery, AL	224
88	Charlotte, NC	223
89	Canton, OH	221
89	Hollywood, FL	221
91	Quincy, MA	220
91	Tallahassee, FL	220
93	Beaumont, TX	219
93	Clarkstown, NY	219
93	Durham, NC	219
93	Seattle, WA	219
97	Flint, MI	218
97	Minneapolis, MN	218
97	Salt Lake City, UT	218
100	Peoria, IL	217
101	Nashville, TN	216
101	Newport News, VA	216
103	Lafayette, LA	215
103	Youngstown, OH	215
105	Boca Raton, FL	213
105	Fort Worth, TX	213
105	Huntsville, AL	213
105	Joliet, IL	213
109	Jacksonville, FL	212
109	Springfield, MO	212
111	Athens-Clarke, GA	211
111	Lansing, MI	211
111	Tulsa, OK	211
114	Aurora, CO	208
115	Clarksville, TN	207
116	Pompano Beach, FL	206
117	Lexington, KY	205
117	Lynn, MA	205
117	McAllen, TX	205
117	Melbourne, FL	205
117	Mobile, AL	205
117	Warwick, RI	205
123	Dearborn, MI	204
124	Davie, FL	203
124	Edison Twnshp, NJ	203
124	St. Paul, MN	203
127	Hamilton Twnshp, NJ	202
128	Plantation, FL	201
128	Suffolk, VA	201
130	Woodbridge Twnshp, NJ	200
131	St. Petersburg, FL	199
132	Clifton, NJ	198
132	Murfreesboro, TN	198
132	Raleigh, NC	198
132	Rockford, IL	198
136	Fort Smith, AR	197
136	Indianapolis, IN	197
136	Knoxville, TN	197
136	Las Cruces, NM	197
140	Kenosha, WI	195
141	Albuquerque, NM	194
141	Brockton, MA	194
141	Longview, TX	194
141	Southfield, MI	194
145	Austin, TX	193
145	Hampton, VA	193
145	Louisville, KY	193
145	Tempe, AZ	193
149	Des Moines, IA	191
149	Phoenix, AZ	191
151	Nashua, NH	189
152	Cranston, RI	188
152	Fort Wayne, IN	188
152	Long Beach, CA	188
152	Tyler, TX	188
156	Danbury, CT	187
157	Laredo, TX	186
157	Omaha, NE	186
157	Tucson, AZ	186
160	Oklahoma City, OK	185
160	Sunrise, FL	185
162	Waco, TX	184
163	Columbus, GA	183
163	Everett, WA	183
163	Lakewood, CO	183
166	Manchester, NH	182
166	Newton, MA	182
168	Berkeley, CA	181
168	Colorado Springs, CO	181
168	Virginia Beach, VA	181
171	Mesa, AZ	180
171	Pueblo, CO	180
173	Green Bay, WI	179
173	Tacoma, WA	179
173	Wichita, KS	179
176	Allentown, PA	178
176	El Paso, TX	178
178	Largo, FL	177
179	Independence, MO	175
179	Lawton, OK	175
179	Newport Beach, CA	175
182	Boulder, CO	174
182	Madison, WI	174
182	Reno, NV	174
182	Toms River Twnshp, NJ	174
182	Warren, MI	174
187	Oakland, CA	173
187	Pasadena, TX	173
189	Fresno, CA	172
189	Grand Rapids, MI	172
189	Killeen, TX	172
189	Somerville, MA	172

RANK	CITY	RATE
189	Yuma, AZ	172
194	Lubbock, TX	171
195	Las Vegas, NV	170
195	Port St. Lucie, FL	170
197	Aurora, IL	169
197	Lawrence, KS	169
199	Erie, PA	168
199	Sunnyvale, CA	168
201	Duluth, MN	167
201	Torrance, CA	167
201	Troy, MI	167
204	Inglewood, CA	166
204	San Angelo, TX	166
206	Mesquite, TX	165
206	Pasadena, CA	165
206	Wichita Falls, TX	165
209	Palm Bay, FL	163
209	Scottsdale, AZ	163
211	Brick Twnshp, NJ	162
211	Irving, TX	162
211	Sugar Land, TX	162
211	Westminster, CO	162
215	Columbia, MO	159
215	Pembroke Pines, FL	159
215	Santa Barbara, CA	159
218	Abilene, TX	158
218	Odessa, TX	158
220	Amarillo, TX	157
220	Hialeah, FL	157
220	Ogden, UT	157
223	Upper Darby Twnshp, PA	156
224	Chesapeake, VA	155
224	Deerfield Beach, FL	155
224	Midland, TX	155
224	Miramar, FL	155
228	Cheektowaga, NY	154
228	San Antonio, TX	154
228	San Bernardino, CA	154
228	Sioux Falls, SD	154
232	Cedar Rapids, IA	153
232	Yakima, WA	153
234	North Las Vegas, NV	152
235	Corpus Christi, TX	151
235	El Cajon, CA	151
235	San Diego, CA	151
235	West Valley, UT	151
239	Arlington, TX	150
239	Coral Springs, FL	150
239	Farmington Hills, MI	150
239	Kent, WA	150
239	Livonia, MI	150
239	Sioux City, IA	150
245	Glendale, AZ	149
245	San Jose, CA	149
247	Burbank, CA	148
247	Edmond, OK	148
247	Garland, TX	148
247	Greeley, CO	148
247	Richmond, CA	148
252	Cape Coral, FL	147
253	Olathe, KS	146
254	Overland Park, KS	145
254	Roswell, GA	145
256	Bellingham, WA	144
256	Sacramento, CA	144
258	Bloomington, MN	142
258	Round Rock, TX	142
260	Broken Arrow, OK	141
260	Colonie, NY	141
260	Lee's Summit, MO	141
260	Lewisville, TX	141
260	Miami Gardens, FL	141
265	Bellevue, WA	140
265	Cary, NC	140
265	Stockton, CA	140
265	Whittier, CA	140
269	Fargo, ND	139
269	Richardson, TX	139
269	Spokane, WA	139
272	Beaverton, OR	138
272	Denton, TX	138
272	Grand Prairie, TX	138
275	Ann Arbor, MI	137
275	Federal Way, WA	137
277	Costa Mesa, CA	136
278	Boise, ID	135
278	Brownsville, TX	135
278	Hayward, CA	135
281	Henderson, NV	134
281	Hillsboro, OR	134
281	Thornton, CO	134
284	Amherst, NY	133
284	Naperville, IL	133
284	Riverside, CA	133
287	Anchorage, AK	132
287	Billings, MT	132
289	Sparks, NV	131
290	McKinney, TX	130
291	El Monte, CA	129
291	Ontario, CA	129
291	Plano, TX	129
291	Redding, CA	129
295	Carrollton, TX	128
295	Lincoln, NE	128
295	Sterling Heights, MI	128
298	Glendale, CA	127
298	Modesto, CA	127
300	Norman, OK	126
301	Chandler, AZ	125
301	Oxnard, CA	125
301	Santa Maria, CA	125
304	Concord, CA	124
305	Arvada, CO	123
305	Roseville, CA	123
305	San Mateo, CA	123
305	Sandy, UT	123
305	Surprise, AZ	123
310	Anaheim, CA	122
310	Carlsbad, CA	122
310	Gresham, OR	122
310	Rochester, MN	122
310	Salem, OR	122
315	Chino, CA	121
315	Eugene, OR	121
315	Santa Clara, CA	121
315	Spokane Valley, WA	121
319	Escondido, CA	120
319	Fort Collins, CO	120
319	Livermore, CA	120
319	Pomona, CA	120
319	Vancouver, WA	120
324	Oceanside, CA	119
324	Ventura, CA	119
326	Fullerton, CA	118
326	San Leandro, CA	118
328	Clovis, CA	117
328	Westland, MI	117
330	Fairfield, CA	116
330	Orange, CA	116
330	Peoria, AZ	116
333	Vallejo, CA	115
334	Buena Park, CA	114
334	Corona, CA	114
336	Chula Vista, CA	113
337	Huntington Beach, CA	111
337	Visalia, CA	111
339	Westminster, CA	110
340	Salinas, CA	109
341	Bakersfield, CA	108
341	Hawthorne, CA	108
341	Vacaville, CA	108
344	Clinton Twnshp, MI	107
345	Gilbert, AZ	106
346	Fontana, CA	105
346	Santa Ana, CA	105
346	Santa Rosa, CA	105
349	Daly City, CA	104
350	Antioch, CA	103
350	Parma, OH	103
350	West Covina, CA	103
353	Simi Valley, CA	101
354	Downey, CA	99
355	Greece, NY	98
356	West Jordan, UT	97
357	Orem, UT	95
357	Tracy, CA	95
359	Garden Grove, CA	94
359	Napa, CA	94
361	Alhambra, CA	93
361	Fremont, CA	93
361	Murrieta, CA	93
364	Canton Twnshp, MI	89
365	Baldwin Park, CA	88
365	Rialto, CA	88
367	Irvine, CA	86
367	South Gate, CA	86
369	Provo, UT	79
NA	Bellflower, CA**	NA
NA	Carson, CA**	NA
NA	Centennial, CO**	NA
NA	Chino Hills, CA**	NA
NA	Compton, CA**	NA
NA	Dayton, OH**	NA
NA	Hesperia, CA**	NA
NA	Lake Forest, CA**	NA
NA	Lakewood, CA**	NA
NA	Lancaster, CA**	NA
NA	Mission Viejo, CA**	NA
NA	Moreno Valley, CA**	NA
NA	Norwalk, CA**	NA
NA	Palmdale, CA**	NA
NA	Portland, OR**	NA
NA	Rancho Cucamon., CA**	NA
NA	Santa Clarita, CA**	NA
NA	Temecula, CA**	NA
NA	Thousand Oaks, CA**	NA
NA	Victorville, CA**	NA
NA	Vista, CA**	NA

Source: CQ Press using data from F.B.I. "Crime in the United States 2006"
**Sworn officers only, does not include civilian employees.*
***Not available*

83. Percent Change in Rate of Police Officers: 2005 to 2006

National Percent Change = 0.0% Change*

RANK	CITY	% CHANGE
74	Abilene, TX	3.9
3	Albany, GA	15.7
137	Albany, NY	1.7
286	Albuquerque, NM	(2.5)
273	Alexandria, VA	(2.1)
119	Alhambra, CA	2.2
5	Allentown, PA	13.4
212	Amarillo, TX	(0.6)
324	Amherst, NY	(4.3)
86	Anaheim, CA	3.4
42	Anchorage, AK	5.6
119	Ann Arbor, MI	2.2
342	Antioch, CA	(5.5)
166	Arlington, TX	0.7
284	Arvada, CO	(2.4)
185	Athens-Clarke, GA	0.0
359	Atlanta, GA	(11.3)
52	Aurora, CO	5.1
185	Aurora, IL	0.0
248	Austin, TX	(1.5)
259	Bakersfield, CA	(1.8)
354	Baldwin Park, CA	(8.3)
248	Baltimore, MD	(1.5)
1	Baton Rouge, LA	22.1
259	Beaumont, TX	(1.8)
309	Beaverton, OR	(3.5)
306	Bellevue, WA	(3.4)
NA	Bellflower, CA**	NA
124	Bellingham, WA	2.1
117	Berkeley, CA	2.3
74	Billings, MT	3.9
281	Birmingham, AL	(2.3)
218	Bloomington, MN	(0.7)
346	Boca Raton, FL	(6.2)
248	Boise, ID	(1.5)
185	Boston, MA	0.0
277	Boulder, CO	(2.2)
150	Brick Twnshp, NJ	1.3
255	Bridgeport, CT	(1.7)
317	Brockton, MA	(4.0)
79	Broken Arrow, OK	3.7
324	Brownsville, TX	(4.3)
185	Buena Park, CA	0.0
294	Buffalo, NY	(2.9)
185	Burbank, CA	0.0
34	Cambridge, MA	6.5
137	Camden, NJ	1.7
340	Canton Twnshp, MI	(5.3)
41	Canton, OH	5.7
8	Cape Coral, FL	12.2
68	Carlsbad, CA	4.3
140	Carrollton, TX	1.6
NA	Carson, CA**	NA
166	Cary, NC	0.7
266	Cedar Rapids, IA	(1.9)
NA	Centennial, CO**	NA
281	Chandler, AZ	(2.3)
151	Charleston, SC	1.2
185	Charlotte, NC	0.0
233	Chattanooga, TN	(1.1)
NA	Cheektowaga, NY**	NA
350	Chesapeake, VA	(7.2)
94	Chicago, IL	3.2
NA	Chino Hills, CA**	NA
352	Chino, CA	(7.6)
42	Chula Vista, CA	5.6
126	Cincinnati, OH	2.0
17	Clarkstown, NY	7.4
206	Clarksville, TN	(0.5)
72	Clearwater, FL	4.1
204	Cleveland, OH	(0.3)
97	Clifton, NJ	3.1
259	Clinton Twnshp, MI	(1.8)
255	Clovis, CA	(1.7)
185	Colonie, NY	0.0
173	Colorado Springs, CO	0.6
61	Columbia, MO	4.6
14	Columbia, SC	8.2
338	Columbus, GA	(5.2)
126	Columbus, OH	2.0
NA	Compton, CA**	NA
185	Concord, CA	0.0
107	Coral Springs, FL	2.7
107	Corona, CA	2.7
42	Corpus Christi, TX	5.6
322	Costa Mesa, CA	(4.2)
26	Cranston, RI	6.8
151	Dallas, TX	1.2
357	Daly City, CA	(8.8)
63	Danbury, CT	4.5
113	Davie, FL	2.5
NA	Dayton, OH**	NA
50	Dearborn, MI	5.2
361	Deerfield Beach, FL	(11.9)
185	Denton, TX	0.0
145	Denver, CO	1.5
206	Des Moines, IA	(0.5)
296	Detroit, MI	(3.0)
48	Downey, CA	5.3
173	Duluth, MN	0.6
92	Durham, NC	3.3
303	Edison Twnshp, NJ	(3.3)
9	Edmond, OK	11.3
53	El Cajon, CA	4.9
248	El Monte, CA	(1.5)
277	El Paso, TX	(2.2)
83	Elizabeth, NJ	3.6
259	Erie, PA	(1.8)
185	Escondido, CA	0.0
300	Eugene, OR	(3.2)
77	Evansville, IN	3.8
86	Everett, WA	3.4
35	Fairfield, CA	6.4
218	Fargo, ND	(0.7)
23	Farmington Hills, MI	7.1
345	Fayetteville, NC	(6.1)
145	Federal Way, WA	1.5
25	Flint, MI	6.9
10	Fontana, CA	9.4
185	Fort Collins, CO	0.0
73	Fort Lauderdale, FL	4.0
97	Fort Smith, AR	3.1
320	Fort Wayne, IN	(4.1)
290	Fort Worth, TX	(2.7)
63	Fremont, CA	4.5
212	Fresno, CA	(0.6)
85	Fullerton, CA	3.5
126	Gainesville, FL	2.0
273	Garden Grove, CA	(2.1)
20	Garland, TX	7.2
277	Gary, IN	(2.2)
353	Gilbert, AZ	(7.8)
218	Glendale, AZ	(0.7)
330	Glendale, CA	(4.5)
243	Grand Prairie, TX	(1.4)
151	Grand Rapids, MI	1.2
185	Greece, NY	0.0
102	Greeley, CO	2.8
335	Green Bay, WI	(4.8)
94	Greensboro, NC	3.2
113	Gresham, OR	2.5
178	Hamilton Twnshp, NJ	0.5
330	Hammond, IN	(4.5)
38	Hampton, VA	6.0
228	Hartford, CT	(0.9)
340	Hawthorne, CA	(5.3)
166	Hayward, CA	0.7
45	Henderson, NV	5.5
NA	Hesperia, CA**	NA
46	Hialeah, FL	5.4
348	High Point, NC	(6.5)
165	Hillsboro, OR	0.8
240	Hollywood, FL	(1.3)
133	Honolulu, HI	1.8
240	Houston, TX	(1.3)
79	Huntington Beach, CA	3.7
311	Huntsville, AL	(3.6)
212	Independence, MO	(0.6)
248	Indianapolis, IN	(1.5)
332	Inglewood, CA	(4.6)
233	Irvine, CA	(1.1)
185	Irving, TX	0.0
16	Jacksonville, FL	7.6
336	Jackson, MS	(4.9)
79	Jersey City, NJ	3.7
243	Joliet, IL	(1.4)
151	Kansas City, KS	1.2
30	Kansas City, MO	6.7
178	Kenosha, WI	0.5
23	Kent, WA	7.1
26	Killeen, TX	6.8
344	Knoxville, TN	(5.7)
40	Lafayette, LA	5.9
NA	Lake Forest, CA**	NA
83	Lakeland, FL	3.6
NA	Lakewood, CA**	NA
155	Lakewood, CO	1.1
NA	Lancaster, CA**	NA
147	Lansing, MI	1.4
343	Laredo, TX	(5.6)
303	Largo, FL	(3.3)
328	Las Cruces, NM	(4.4)
36	Las Vegas, NV	6.3
68	Lawrence, KS	4.3
30	Lawton, OK	6.7
26	Lee's Summit, MO	6.8
166	Lewisville, TX	0.7
18	Lexington, KY	7.3
314	Lincoln, NE	(3.8)
119	Little Rock, AR	2.2
11	Livermore, CA	9.1
218	Livonia, MI	(0.7)

RANK	CITY	% CHANGE
178	Long Beach, CA	0.5
158	Longview, TX	1.0
185	Los Angeles, CA	0.0
53	Louisville, KY	4.9
255	Lowell, MA	(1.7)
173	Lubbock, TX	0.6
126	Lynn, MA	2.0
NA	Macon, GA**	NA
233	Madison, WI	(1.1)
206	Manchester, NH	(0.5)
314	McAllen, TX	(3.8)
6	McKinney, TX	13.0
284	Melbourne, FL	(2.4)
183	Memphis, TN	0.3
137	Mesa, AZ	1.7
77	Mesquite, TX	3.8
NA	Miami Beach, FL**	NA
166	Miami Gardens, FL	0.7
97	Miami, FL	3.1
312	Midland, TX	(3.7)
116	Milwaukee, WI	2.4
102	Minneapolis, MN	2.8
297	Miramar, FL	(3.1)
NA	Mission Viejo, CA**	NA
243	Mobile, AL	(1.4)
140	Modesto, CA	1.6
277	Montgomery, AL	(2.2)
NA	Moreno Valley, CA**	NA
286	Murfreesboro, TN	(2.5)
119	Murrieta, CA	2.2
66	Napa, CA	4.4
60	Naperville, IL	4.7
107	Nashua, NH	2.7
297	Nashville, TN	(3.1)
26	New Bedford, MA	6.8
NA	New Orleans, LA**	NA
233	New York, NY	(1.1)
273	Newark, NJ	(2.1)
328	Newport Beach, CA	(4.4)
92	Newport News, VA	3.3
119	Newton, MA	2.2
20	Norfolk, VA	7.2
7	Norman, OK	12.5
212	North Charleston, SC	(0.6)
126	North Las Vegas, NV	2.0
NA	Norwalk, CA**	NA
336	Oakland, CA	(4.9)
20	Oceanside, CA	7.2
212	Odessa, TX	(0.6)
312	Ogden, UT	(3.7)
206	Oklahoma City, OK	(0.5)
102	Olathe, KS	2.8
233	Omaha, NE	(1.1)
140	Ontario, CA	1.6
63	Orange, CA	4.5
155	Orem, UT	1.1
290	Orlando, FL	(2.7)
303	Overland Park, KS	(3.3)
113	Oxnard, CA	2.5
50	Palm Bay, FL	5.2
NA	Palmdale, CA**	NA
347	Parma, OH	(6.4)
185	Pasadena, CA	0.0
185	Pasadena, TX	0.0
79	Paterson, NJ	3.7
61	Pembroke Pines, FL	4.6

RANK	CITY	% CHANGE
185	Peoria, AZ	0.0
102	Peoria, IL	2.8
161	Philadelphia, PA	0.9
309	Phoenix, AZ	(3.5)
266	Pittsburgh, PA	(1.9)
248	Plano, TX	(1.5)
338	Plantation, FL	(5.2)
68	Pomona, CA	4.3
362	Pompano Beach, FL	(15.6)
12	Port St. Lucie, FL	9.0
NA	Portland, OR**	NA
124	Portsmouth, VA	2.1
155	Providence, RI	1.1
358	Provo, UT	(10.2)
233	Pueblo, CO	(1.1)
290	Quincy, MA	(2.7)
140	Racine, WI	1.6
306	Raleigh, NC	(3.4)
NA	Rancho Cucamon., CA**	NA
223	Reading, PA	(0.8)
140	Redding, CA	1.6
173	Reno, NV	0.6
364	Rialto, CA	(20.7)
48	Richardson, TX	5.3
271	Richmond, CA	(2.0)
223	Richmond, VA	(0.8)
74	Riverside, CA	3.9
133	Roanoke, VA	1.8
334	Rochester, MN	(4.7)
15	Rochester, NY	7.9
178	Rockford, IL	0.5
86	Roseville, CA	3.4
271	Roswell, GA	(2.0)
NA	Round Rock, TX**	NA
243	Sacramento, CA	(1.4)
300	Salem, OR	(3.2)
228	Salinas, CA	(0.9)
259	Salt Lake City, UT	(1.8)
173	San Angelo, TX	0.6
266	San Antonio, TX	(1.9)
126	San Bernardino, CA	2.0
351	San Diego, CA	(7.4)
166	San Francisco, CA	0.7
166	San Jose, CA	0.7
46	San Leandro, CA	5.4
86	San Mateo, CA	3.4
13	Sandy, UT	8.8
132	Santa Ana, CA	1.9
38	Santa Barbara, CA	6.0
317	Santa Clara, CA	(4.0)
NA	Santa Clarita, CA**	NA
223	Santa Maria, CA	(0.8)
107	Santa Monica, CA	2.7
37	Santa Rosa, CA	6.1
223	Savannah, GA	(0.8)
320	Scottsdale, AZ	(4.1)
228	Seattle, WA	(0.9)
2	Shreveport, LA	18.3
266	Simi Valley, CA	(1.9)
53	Sioux City, IA	4.9
86	Sioux Falls, SD	3.4
4	Somerville, MA	15.4
254	South Bend, IN	(1.6)
233	South Gate, CA	(1.1)
158	Southfield, MI	1.0
97	Sparks, NV	3.1

RANK	CITY	% CHANGE
223	Spokane Valley, WA	(0.8)
243	Spokane, WA	(1.4)
185	Springfield, IL	0.0
231	Springfield, MA	(1.0)
293	Springfield, MO	(2.8)
314	Sterling Heights, MI	(3.8)
147	Stockton, CA	1.4
32	St. Louis, MO	6.6
231	St. Paul, MN	(1.0)
286	St. Petersburg, FL	(2.5)
356	Suffolk, VA	(8.6)
18	Sugar Land, TX	7.3
259	Sunnyvale, CA	(1.8)
86	Sunrise, FL	3.4
363	Surprise, AZ	(18.5)
183	Syracuse, NY	0.3
324	Tacoma, WA	(4.3)
117	Tallahassee, FL	2.3
218	Tampa, FL	(0.7)
NA	Temecula, CA**	NA
286	Tempe, AZ	(2.5)
294	Thornton, CO	(2.9)
NA	Thousand Oaks, CA**	NA
94	Toledo, OH	3.2
56	Toms River Twnshp, NJ	4.8
112	Topeka, KS	2.6
66	Torrance, CA	4.4
317	Tracy, CA	(4.0)
158	Trenton, NJ	1.0
133	Troy, MI	1.8
273	Tucson, AZ	(2.1)
147	Tulsa, OK	1.4
56	Tuscaloosa, AL	4.8
178	Tyler, TX	0.5
266	Upper Darby Twnshp, PA	(1.9)
161	Vacaville, CA	0.9
322	Vallejo, CA	(4.2)
300	Vancouver, WA	(3.2)
255	Ventura, CA	(1.7)
NA	Victorville, CA**	NA
102	Virginia Beach, VA	2.8
161	Visalia, CA	0.9
NA	Vista, CA**	NA
206	Waco, TX	(0.5)
212	Warren, MI	(0.6)
206	Warwick, RI	(0.5)
324	Washington, DC	(4.3)
32	Waterbury, CT	6.6
332	West Covina, CA	(4.6)
349	West Jordan, UT	(6.7)
133	West Palm Beach, FL	1.8
240	West Valley, UT	(1.3)
161	Westland, MI	0.9
56	Westminster, CA	4.8
259	Westminster, CO	(1.8)
306	Whittier, CA	(3.4)
354	Wichita Falls, TX	(8.3)
185	Wichita, KS	0.0
297	Wilmington, NC	(3.1)
68	Winston-Salem, NC	4.3
97	Woodbridge Twnshp, NJ	3.1
107	Worcester, MA	2.7
56	Yakima, WA	4.8
204	Yonkers, NY	(0.3)
360	Youngstown, OH	(11.5)
281	Yuma, AZ	(2.3)

Source: CQ Press using data from F.B.I. "Crime in the United States 2006"
**Sworn officers only, does not include civilian employees.*
***Not available*

83. Percent Change in Rate of Police Officers: 2005 to 2006 (continued)

National Percent Change = 0.0% Change*

RANK	CITY	% CHANGE
1	Baton Rouge, LA	22.1
2	Shreveport, LA	18.3
3	Albany, GA	15.7
4	Somerville, MA	15.4
5	Allentown, PA	13.4
6	McKinney, TX	13.0
7	Norman, OK	12.5
8	Cape Coral, FL	12.2
9	Edmond, OK	11.3
10	Fontana, CA	9.4
11	Livermore, CA	9.1
12	Port St. Lucie, FL	9.0
13	Sandy, UT	8.8
14	Columbia, SC	8.2
15	Rochester, NY	7.9
16	Jacksonville, FL	7.6
17	Clarkstown, NY	7.4
18	Lexington, KY	7.3
18	Sugar Land, TX	7.3
20	Garland, TX	7.2
20	Norfolk, VA	7.2
20	Oceanside, CA	7.2
23	Farmington Hills, MI	7.1
23	Kent, WA	7.1
25	Flint, MI	6.9
26	Cranston, RI	6.8
26	Killeen, TX	6.8
26	Lee's Summit, MO	6.8
26	New Bedford, MA	6.8
30	Kansas City, MO	6.7
30	Lawton, OK	6.7
32	St. Louis, MO	6.6
32	Waterbury, CT	6.6
34	Cambridge, MA	6.5
35	Fairfield, CA	6.4
36	Las Vegas, NV	6.3
37	Santa Rosa, CA	6.1
38	Hampton, VA	6.0
38	Santa Barbara, CA	6.0
40	Lafayette, LA	5.9
41	Canton, OH	5.7
42	Anchorage, AK	5.6
42	Chula Vista, CA	5.6
42	Corpus Christi, TX	5.6
45	Henderson, NV	5.5
46	Hialeah, FL	5.4
46	San Leandro, CA	5.4
48	Downey, CA	5.3
48	Richardson, TX	5.3
50	Dearborn, MI	5.2
50	Palm Bay, FL	5.2
52	Aurora, CO	5.1
53	El Cajon, CA	4.9
53	Louisville, KY	4.9
53	Sioux City, IA	4.9
56	Toms River Twnshp, NJ	4.8
56	Tuscaloosa, AL	4.8
56	Westminster, CA	4.8
56	Yakima, WA	4.8
60	Naperville, IL	4.7
61	Columbia, MO	4.6
61	Pembroke Pines, FL	4.6
63	Danbury, CT	4.5
63	Fremont, CA	4.5
63	Orange, CA	4.5
66	Napa, CA	4.4
66	Torrance, CA	4.4
68	Carlsbad, CA	4.3
68	Lawrence, KS	4.3
68	Pomona, CA	4.3
68	Winston-Salem, NC	4.3
72	Clearwater, FL	4.1
73	Fort Lauderdale, FL	4.0
74	Abilene, TX	3.9
74	Billings, MT	3.9
74	Riverside, CA	3.9
77	Evansville, IN	3.8
77	Mesquite, TX	3.8
79	Broken Arrow, OK	3.7
79	Huntington Beach, CA	3.7
79	Jersey City, NJ	3.7
79	Paterson, NJ	3.7
83	Elizabeth, NJ	3.6
83	Lakeland, FL	3.6
85	Fullerton, CA	3.5
86	Anaheim, CA	3.4
86	Everett, WA	3.4
86	Roseville, CA	3.4
86	San Mateo, CA	3.4
86	Sioux Falls, SD	3.4
86	Sunrise, FL	3.4
92	Durham, NC	3.3
92	Newport News, VA	3.3
94	Chicago, IL	3.2
94	Greensboro, NC	3.2
94	Toledo, OH	3.2
97	Clifton, NJ	3.1
97	Fort Smith, AR	3.1
97	Miami, FL	3.1
97	Sparks, NV	3.1
97	Woodbridge Twnshp, NJ	3.1
102	Greeley, CO	2.8
102	Minneapolis, MN	2.8
102	Olathe, KS	2.8
102	Peoria, IL	2.8
102	Virginia Beach, VA	2.8
107	Coral Springs, FL	2.7
107	Corona, CA	2.7
107	Nashua, NH	2.7
107	Santa Monica, CA	2.7
107	Worcester, MA	2.7
112	Topeka, KS	2.6
113	Davie, FL	2.5
113	Gresham, OR	2.5
113	Oxnard, CA	2.5
116	Milwaukee, WI	2.4
117	Berkeley, CA	2.3
117	Tallahassee, FL	2.3
119	Alhambra, CA	2.2
119	Ann Arbor, MI	2.2
119	Little Rock, AR	2.2
119	Murrieta, CA	2.2
119	Newton, MA	2.2
124	Bellingham, WA	2.1
124	Portsmouth, VA	2.1
126	Cincinnati, OH	2.0
126	Columbus, OH	2.0
126	Gainesville, FL	2.0
126	Lynn, MA	2.0
126	North Las Vegas, NV	2.0
126	San Bernardino, CA	2.0
132	Santa Ana, CA	1.9
133	Honolulu, HI	1.8
133	Roanoke, VA	1.8
133	Troy, MI	1.8
133	West Palm Beach, FL	1.8
137	Albany, NY	1.7
137	Camden, NJ	1.7
137	Mesa, AZ	1.7
140	Carrollton, TX	1.6
140	Modesto, CA	1.6
140	Ontario, CA	1.6
140	Racine, WI	1.6
140	Redding, CA	1.6
145	Denver, CO	1.5
145	Federal Way, WA	1.5
147	Lansing, MI	1.4
147	Stockton, CA	1.4
147	Tulsa, OK	1.4
150	Brick Twnshp, NJ	1.3
151	Charleston, SC	1.2
151	Dallas, TX	1.2
151	Grand Rapids, MI	1.2
151	Kansas City, KS	1.2
155	Lakewood, CO	1.1
155	Orem, UT	1.1
155	Providence, RI	1.1
158	Longview, TX	1.0
158	Southfield, MI	1.0
158	Trenton, NJ	1.0
161	Philadelphia, PA	0.9
161	Vacaville, CA	0.9
161	Visalia, CA	0.9
161	Westland, MI	0.9
165	Hillsboro, OR	0.8
166	Arlington, TX	0.7
166	Cary, NC	0.7
166	Hayward, CA	0.7
166	Lewisville, TX	0.7
166	Miami Gardens, FL	0.7
166	San Francisco, CA	0.7
166	San Jose, CA	0.7
173	Colorado Springs, CO	0.6
173	Duluth, MN	0.6
173	Lubbock, TX	0.6
173	Reno, NV	0.6
173	San Angelo, TX	0.6
178	Hamilton Twnshp, NJ	0.5
178	Kenosha, WI	0.5
178	Long Beach, CA	0.5
178	Rockford, IL	0.5
178	Tyler, TX	0.5
183	Memphis, TN	0.3
183	Syracuse, NY	0.3
185	Athens-Clarke, GA	0.0
185	Aurora, IL	0.0
185	Boston, MA	0.0
185	Buena Park, CA	0.0
185	Burbank, CA	0.0
185	Charlotte, NC	0.0
185	Colonie, NY	0.0
185	Concord, CA	0.0

RANK	CITY	% CHANGE
185	Denton, TX	0.0
185	Escondido, CA	0.0
185	Fort Collins, CO	0.0
185	Greece, NY	0.0
185	Irving, TX	0.0
185	Los Angeles, CA	0.0
185	Pasadena, CA	0.0
185	Pasadena, TX	0.0
185	Peoria, AZ	0.0
185	Springfield, IL	0.0
185	Wichita, KS	0.0
204	Cleveland, OH	(0.3)
204	Yonkers, NY	(0.3)
206	Clarksville, TN	(0.5)
206	Des Moines, IA	(0.5)
206	Manchester, NH	(0.5)
206	Oklahoma City, OK	(0.5)
206	Waco, TX	(0.5)
206	Warwick, RI	(0.5)
212	Amarillo, TX	(0.6)
212	Fresno, CA	(0.6)
212	Independence, MO	(0.6)
212	North Charleston, SC	(0.6)
212	Odessa, TX	(0.6)
212	Warren, MI	(0.6)
218	Bloomington, MN	(0.7)
218	Fargo, ND	(0.7)
218	Glendale, AZ	(0.7)
218	Livonia, MI	(0.7)
218	Tampa, FL	(0.7)
223	Reading, PA	(0.8)
223	Richmond, VA	(0.8)
223	Santa Maria, CA	(0.8)
223	Savannah, GA	(0.8)
223	Spokane Valley, WA	(0.8)
228	Hartford, CT	(0.9)
228	Salinas, CA	(0.9)
228	Seattle, WA	(0.9)
231	Springfield, MA	(1.0)
231	St. Paul, MN	(1.0)
233	Chattanooga, TN	(1.1)
233	Irvine, CA	(1.1)
233	Madison, WI	(1.1)
233	New York, NY	(1.1)
233	Omaha, NE	(1.1)
233	Pueblo, CO	(1.1)
233	South Gate, CA	(1.1)
240	Hollywood, FL	(1.3)
240	Houston, TX	(1.3)
240	West Valley, UT	(1.3)
243	Grand Prairie, TX	(1.4)
243	Joliet, IL	(1.4)
243	Mobile, AL	(1.4)
243	Sacramento, CA	(1.4)
243	Spokane, WA	(1.4)
248	Austin, TX	(1.5)
248	Baltimore, MD	(1.5)
248	Boise, ID	(1.5)
248	El Monte, CA	(1.5)
248	Indianapolis, IN	(1.5)
248	Plano, TX	(1.5)
254	South Bend, IN	(1.6)
255	Bridgeport, CT	(1.7)
255	Clovis, CA	(1.7)
255	Lowell, MA	(1.7)
255	Ventura, CA	(1.7)
259	Bakersfield, CA	(1.8)
259	Beaumont, TX	(1.8)
259	Clinton Twnshp, MI	(1.8)
259	Erie, PA	(1.8)
259	Salt Lake City, UT	(1.8)
259	Sunnyvale, CA	(1.8)
259	Westminster, CO	(1.8)
266	Cedar Rapids, IA	(1.9)
266	Pittsburgh, PA	(1.9)
266	San Antonio, TX	(1.9)
266	Simi Valley, CA	(1.9)
266	Upper Darby Twnshp, PA	(1.9)
271	Richmond, CA	(2.0)
271	Roswell, GA	(2.0)
273	Alexandria, VA	(2.1)
273	Garden Grove, CA	(2.1)
273	Newark, NJ	(2.1)
273	Tucson, AZ	(2.1)
277	Boulder, CO	(2.2)
277	El Paso, TX	(2.2)
277	Gary, IN	(2.2)
277	Montgomery, AL	(2.2)
281	Birmingham, AL	(2.3)
281	Chandler, AZ	(2.3)
281	Yuma, AZ	(2.3)
284	Arvada, CO	(2.4)
284	Melbourne, FL	(2.4)
286	Albuquerque, NM	(2.5)
286	Murfreesboro, TN	(2.5)
286	St. Petersburg, FL	(2.5)
286	Tempe, AZ	(2.5)
290	Fort Worth, TX	(2.7)
290	Orlando, FL	(2.7)
290	Quincy, MA	(2.7)
293	Springfield, MO	(2.8)
294	Buffalo, NY	(2.9)
294	Thornton, CO	(2.9)
296	Detroit, MI	(3.0)
297	Miramar, FL	(3.1)
297	Nashville, TN	(3.1)
297	Wilmington, NC	(3.1)
300	Eugene, OR	(3.2)
300	Salem, OR	(3.2)
300	Vancouver, WA	(3.2)
303	Edison Twnshp, NJ	(3.3)
303	Largo, FL	(3.3)
303	Overland Park, KS	(3.3)
306	Bellevue, WA	(3.4)
306	Raleigh, NC	(3.4)
306	Whittier, CA	(3.4)
309	Beaverton, OR	(3.5)
309	Phoenix, AZ	(3.5)
311	Huntsville, AL	(3.6)
312	Midland, TX	(3.7)
312	Ogden, UT	(3.7)
314	Lincoln, NE	(3.8)
314	McAllen, TX	(3.8)
314	Sterling Heights, MI	(3.8)
317	Brockton, MA	(4.0)
317	Santa Clara, CA	(4.0)
317	Tracy, CA	(4.0)
320	Fort Wayne, IN	(4.1)
320	Scottsdale, AZ	(4.1)
322	Costa Mesa, CA	(4.2)
322	Vallejo, CA	(4.2)
324	Amherst, NY	(4.3)
324	Brownsville, TX	(4.3)
324	Tacoma, WA	(4.3)
324	Washington, DC	(4.3)
328	Las Cruces, NM	(4.4)
328	Newport Beach, CA	(4.4)
330	Glendale, CA	(4.5)
330	Hammond, IN	(4.5)
332	Inglewood, CA	(4.6)
332	West Covina, CA	(4.6)
334	Rochester, MN	(4.7)
335	Green Bay, WI	(4.8)
336	Jackson, MS	(4.9)
336	Oakland, CA	(4.9)
338	Columbus, GA	(5.2)
338	Plantation, FL	(5.2)
340	Canton Twnshp, MI	(5.3)
340	Hawthorne, CA	(5.3)
342	Antioch, CA	(5.5)
343	Laredo, TX	(5.6)
344	Knoxville, TN	(5.7)
345	Fayetteville, NC	(6.1)
346	Boca Raton, FL	(6.2)
347	Parma, OH	(6.4)
348	High Point, NC	(6.5)
349	West Jordan, UT	(6.7)
350	Chesapeake, VA	(7.2)
351	San Diego, CA	(7.4)
352	Chino, CA	(7.6)
353	Gilbert, AZ	(7.8)
354	Baldwin Park, CA	(8.3)
354	Wichita Falls, TX	(8.3)
356	Suffolk, VA	(8.6)
357	Daly City, CA	(8.8)
358	Provo, UT	(10.2)
359	Atlanta, GA	(11.3)
360	Youngstown, OH	(11.5)
361	Deerfield Beach, FL	(11.9)
362	Pompano Beach, FL	(15.6)
363	Surprise, AZ	(18.5)
364	Rialto, CA	(20.7)
NA	Bellflower, CA**	NA
NA	Carson, CA**	NA
NA	Centennial, CO**	NA
NA	Cheektowaga, NY**	NA
NA	Chino Hills, CA**	NA
NA	Compton, CA**	NA
NA	Dayton, OH**	NA
NA	Hesperia, CA**	NA
NA	Lake Forest, CA**	NA
NA	Lakewood, CA**	NA
NA	Lancaster, CA**	NA
NA	Macon, GA**	NA
NA	Miami Beach, FL**	NA
NA	Mission Viejo, CA**	NA
NA	Moreno Valley, CA**	NA
NA	New Orleans, LA**	NA
NA	Norwalk, CA**	NA
NA	Palmdale, CA**	NA
NA	Portland, OR**	NA
NA	Rancho Cucamon., CA**	NA
NA	Round Rock, TX**	NA
NA	Santa Clarita, CA**	NA
NA	Temecula, CA**	NA
NA	Thousand Oaks, CA**	NA
NA	Victorville, CA**	NA
NA	Vista, CA**	NA

Source: CQ Press using data from F.B.I. "Crime in the United States 2006"

**Sworn officers only, does not include civilian employees.*

***Not available*

84. Percent Change in Rate of Police Officers: 2002 to 2006

National Percent Change = 1.6% Decrease*

RANK	CITY	% CHANGE	RANK	CITY	% CHANGE	RANK	CITY	% CHANGE
31	Abilene, TX	10.5	300	Chino, CA	(7.6)	226	Garden Grove, CA	(2.1)
226	Albany, GA	(2.1)	325	Chula Vista, CA	(10.3)	11	Garland, TX	14.7
123	Albany, NY	2.9	6	Cincinnati, OH	18.2	236	Gary, IN	(2.6)
187	Albuquerque, NM	(0.5)	112	Clarkstown, NY	3.3	54	Gilbert, AZ	7.1
58	Alexandria, VA	6.8	131	Clarksville, TN	2.5	1	Glendale, AZ	28.4
168	Alhambra, CA	0.0	95	Clearwater, FL	4.1	41	Glendale, CA	8.5
346	Allentown, PA	(14.4)	322	Cleveland, OH	(10.0)	239	Grand Prairie, TX	(2.8)
112	Amarillo, TX	3.3	49	Clifton, NJ	7.6	285	Grand Rapids, MI	(6.0)
210	Amherst, NY	(1.5)	289	Clinton Twnshp, MI	(6.1)	39	Greece, NY	8.9
110	Anaheim, CA	3.4	7	Clovis, CA	17.0	62	Greeley, CO	6.5
16	Anchorage, AK	12.8	168	Colonie, NY	0.0	163	Green Bay, WI	0.6
282	Ann Arbor, MI	(5.5)	83	Colorado Springs, CO	5.2	103	Greensboro, NC	3.7
168	Antioch, CA	0.0	168	Columbia, MO	0.0	83	Gresham, OR	5.2
298	Arlington, TX	(7.4)	12	Columbia, SC	14.0	168	Hamilton Twnshp, NJ	0.0
234	Arvada, CO	(2.4)	278	Columbus, GA	(5.2)	135	Hammond, IN	2.4
25	Athens-Clarke, GA	11.6	200	Columbus, OH	(1.2)	10	Hampton, VA	14.9
231	Atlanta, GA	(2.3)	NA	Compton, CA**	NA	125	Hartford, CT	2.8
14	Aurora, CO	13.7	168	Concord, CA	0.0	220	Hawthorne, CA	(1.8)
314	Aurora, IL	(8.6)	168	Coral Springs, FL	0.0	264	Hayward, CA	(4.3)
72	Austin, TX	6.0	250	Corona, CA	(3.4)	323	Henderson, NV	(10.1)
331	Bakersfield, CA	(12.2)	223	Corpus Christi, TX	(1.9)	NA	Hesperia, CA**	NA
298	Baldwin Park, CA	(7.4)	251	Costa Mesa, CA	(3.5)	58	Hialeah, FL	6.8
284	Baltimore, MD	(5.7)	33	Cranston, RI	9.9	56	High Point, NC	7.0
2	Baton Rouge, LA	27.7	61	Dallas, TX	6.6	328	Hillsboro, OR	(11.3)
138	Beaumont, TX	2.3	223	Daly City, CA	(1.9)	156	Hollywood, FL	1.4
271	Beaverton, OR	(4.8)	236	Danbury, CT	(2.6)	128	Honolulu, HI	2.7
292	Bellevue, WA	(6.7)	248	Davie, FL	(3.3)	331	Houston, TX	(12.2)
NA	Bellflower, CA**	NA	NA	Dayton, OH**	NA	220	Huntington Beach, CA	(1.8)
297	Bellingham, WA	(7.1)	86	Dearborn, MI	4.6	207	Huntsville, AL	(1.4)
62	Berkeley, CA	6.5	130	Deerfield Beach, FL	2.6	69	Independence, MO	6.1
264	Billings, MT	(4.3)	329	Denton, TX	(11.5)	187	Indianapolis, IN	(0.5)
186	Birmingham, AL	(0.3)	83	Denver, CO	5.2	118	Inglewood, CA	3.1
22	Bloomington, MN	11.8	69	Des Moines, IA	6.1	326	Irvine, CA	(10.4)
45	Boca Raton, FL	8.1	343	Detroit, MI	(13.9)	28	Irving, TX	11.0
193	Boise, ID	(0.7)	161	Downey, CA	1.0	90	Jacksonville, FL	4.4
145	Boston, MA	1.9	200	Duluth, MN	(1.2)	37	Jackson, MS	9.0
105	Boulder, CO	3.6	271	Durham, NC	(4.8)	48	Jersey City, NJ	7.7
101	Brick Twnshp, NJ	3.8	198	Edison Twnshp, NJ	(1.0)	336	Joliet, IL	(12.3)
311	Bridgeport, CT	(8.4)	142	Edmond, OK	2.1	62	Kansas City, KS	6.5
210	Brockton, MA	(1.5)	54	El Cajon, CA	7.1	22	Kansas City, MO	11.8
123	Broken Arrow, OK	2.9	194	El Monte, CA	(0.8)	255	Kenosha, WI	(3.9)
264	Brownsville, TX	(4.3)	309	El Paso, TX	(8.2)	156	Kent, WA	1.4
218	Buena Park, CA	(1.7)	148	Elizabeth, NJ	1.8	50	Killeen, TX	7.5
NA	Buffalo, NY**	NA	347	Erie, PA	(14.7)	305	Knoxville, TN	(7.9)
314	Burbank, CA	(8.6)	110	Escondido, CA	3.4	20	Lafayette, LA	12.0
NA	Cambridge, MA**	NA	168	Eugene, OR	0.0	NA	Lake Forest, CA**	NA
131	Camden, NJ	2.5	62	Evansville, IN	6.5	303	Lakeland, FL	(7.8)
337	Canton Twnshp, MI	(12.7)	263	Everett, WA	(4.2)	NA	Lakewood, CA**	NA
236	Canton, OH	(2.6)	42	Fairfield, CA	8.4	98	Lakewood, CO	4.0
45	Cape Coral, FL	8.1	19	Fargo, ND	12.1	NA	Lancaster, CA**	NA
295	Carlsbad, CA	(6.9)	80	Farmington Hills, MI	5.6	207	Lansing, MI	(1.4)
194	Carrollton, TX	(0.8)	118	Fayetteville, NC	3.1	165	Laredo, TX	0.5
NA	Carson, CA**	NA	47	Federal Way, WA	7.9	40	Largo, FL	8.6
35	Cary, NC	9.4	8	Flint, MI	16.0	103	Las Cruces, NM	3.7
283	Cedar Rapids, IA	(5.6)	168	Fontana, CA	0.0	163	Las Vegas, NV	0.6
NA	Centennial, CO**	NA	194	Fort Collins, CO	(0.8)	91	Lawrence, KS	4.3
351	Chandler, AZ	(17.8)	311	Fort Lauderdale, FL	(8.4)	52	Lawton, OK	7.4
291	Charleston, SC	(6.6)	17	Fort Smith, AR	12.6	226	Lee's Summit, MO	(2.1)
255	Charlotte, NC	(3.9)	276	Fort Wayne, IN	(5.1)	239	Lewisville, TX	(2.8)
301	Chattanooga, TN	(7.7)	269	Fort Worth, TX	(4.5)	37	Lexington, KY	9.0
NA	Cheektowaga, NY**	NA	199	Fremont, CA	(1.1)	243	Lincoln, NE	(3.0)
321	Chesapeake, VA	(9.9)	28	Fresno, CA	11.0	271	Little Rock, AR	(4.8)
121	Chicago, IL	3.0	150	Fullerton, CA	1.7	215	Livermore, CA	(1.6)
NA	Chino Hills, CA**	NA	308	Gainesville, FL	(8.0)	294	Livonia, MI	(6.8)

RANK	CITY	% CHANGE
112	Long Beach, CA	3.3
72	Longview, TX	6.0
131	Los Angeles, CA	2.5
NA	Louisville, KY**	NA
202	Lowell, MA	(1.3)
5	Lubbock, TX	18.8
234	Lynn, MA	(2.4)
253	Macon, GA	(3.8)
255	Madison, WI	(3.9)
187	Manchester, NH	(0.5)
239	McAllen, TX	(2.8)
331	McKinney, TX	(12.2)
207	Melbourne, FL	(1.4)
168	Memphis, TN	0.0
215	Mesa, AZ	(1.6)
62	Mesquite, TX	6.5
50	Miami Beach, FL	7.5
NA	Miami Gardens, FL**	NA
281	Miami, FL	(5.3)
158	Midland, TX	1.3
118	Milwaukee, WI	3.1
145	Minneapolis, MN	1.9
356	Miramar, FL	(22.5)
NA	Mission Viejo, CA**	NA
168	Mobile, AL	0.0
194	Modesto, CA	(0.8)
138	Montgomery, AL	2.3
NA	Moreno Valley, CA**	NA
342	Murfreesboro, TN	(13.2)
NA	Murrieta, CA**	NA
285	Napa, CA	(6.0)
252	Naperville, IL	(3.6)
NA	Nashua, NH**	NA
247	Nashville, TN	(3.1)
43	New Bedford, MA	8.3
191	New Orleans, LA	(0.6)
278	New York, NY	(5.2)
285	Newark, NJ	(6.0)
345	Newport Beach, CA	(14.2)
91	Newport News, VA	4.3
98	Newton, MA	4.0
202	Norfolk, VA	(1.3)
231	Norman, OK	(2.3)
125	North Charleston, SC	2.8
292	North Las Vegas, NV	(6.7)
NA	Norwalk, CA**	NA
331	Oakland, CA	(12.2)
27	Oceanside, CA	11.2
290	Odessa, TX	(6.5)
202	Ogden, UT	(1.3)
324	Oklahoma City, OK	(10.2)
255	Olathe, KS	(3.9)
261	Omaha, NE	(4.1)
210	Ontario, CA	(1.5)
162	Orange, CA	0.9
160	Orem, UT	1.1
310	Orlando, FL	(8.3)
79	Overland Park, KS	5.8
77	Oxnard, CA	5.9
117	Palm Bay, FL	3.2
NA	Palmdale, CA**	NA
337	Parma, OH	(12.7)
303	Pasadena, CA	(7.8)
274	Pasadena, TX	(4.9)
44	Paterson, NJ	8.2
82	Pembroke Pines, FL	5.3

RANK	CITY	% CHANGE
168	Peoria, AZ	0.0
67	Peoria, IL	6.4
168	Philadelphia, PA	0.0
243	Phoenix, AZ	(3.0)
349	Pittsburgh, PA	(16.6)
313	Plano, TX	(8.5)
264	Plantation, FL	(4.3)
15	Pomona, CA	13.2
353	Pompano Beach, FL	(19.8)
34	Port St. Lucie, FL	9.7
NA	Portland, OR**	NA
4	Portsmouth, VA	18.9
167	Providence, RI	0.4
344	Provo, UT	(14.1)
191	Pueblo, CO	(0.6)
255	Quincy, MA	(3.9)
NA	Racine, WI**	NA
317	Raleigh, NC	(8.8)
NA	Rancho Cucamon., CA**	NA
95	Reading, PA	4.1
231	Redding, CA	(2.3)
32	Reno, NV	10.1
340	Rialto, CA	(12.9)
226	Richardson, TX	(2.1)
357	Richmond, CA	(22.9)
13	Richmond, VA	13.9
210	Riverside, CA	(1.5)
26	Roanoke, VA	11.3
330	Rochester, MN	(11.6)
30	Rochester, NY	10.6
155	Rockford, IL	1.5
9	Roseville, CA	15.0
NA	Roswell, GA**	NA
348	Round Rock, TX	(15.5)
327	Sacramento, CA	(10.6)
215	Salem, OR	(1.6)
57	Salinas, CA	6.9
112	Salt Lake City, UT	3.3
131	San Angelo, TX	2.5
318	San Antonio, TX	(9.4)
68	San Bernardino, CA	6.2
320	San Diego, CA	(9.6)
86	San Francisco, CA	4.6
168	San Jose, CA	0.0
107	San Leandro, CA	3.5
93	San Mateo, CA	4.2
72	Sandy, UT	6.0
98	Santa Ana, CA	4.0
72	Santa Barbara, CA	6.0
340	Santa Clara, CA	(12.9)
NA	Santa Clarita, CA**	NA
93	Santa Maria, CA	4.2
243	Santa Monica, CA	(3.0)
305	Santa Rosa, CA	(7.9)
350	Savannah, GA	(17.4)
159	Scottsdale, AZ	1.2
165	Seattle, WA	0.5
3	Shreveport, LA	27.3
270	Simi Valley, CA	(4.7)
253	Sioux City, IA	(3.8)
81	Sioux Falls, SD	5.5
135	Somerville, MA	2.4
101	South Bend, IN	3.8
105	South Gate, CA	3.6
210	Southfield, MI	(1.5)
153	Sparks, NV	1.6

RANK	CITY	% CHANGE
NA	Spokane Valley, WA**	NA
261	Spokane, WA	(4.1)
248	Springfield, IL	(3.3)
352	Springfield, MA	(18.7)
168	Springfield, MO	0.0
243	Sterling Heights, MI	(3.0)
305	Stockton, CA	(7.9)
223	St. Louis, MO	(1.9)
95	St. Paul, MN	4.1
142	St. Petersburg, FL	2.1
278	Suffolk, VA	(5.2)
77	Sugar Land, TX	5.9
20	Sunnyvale, CA	12.0
153	Sunrise, FL	1.6
359	Surprise, AZ	(38.8)
53	Syracuse, NY	7.2
150	Tacoma, WA	1.7
112	Tallahassee, FL	3.3
202	Tampa, FL	(1.3)
NA	Temecula, CA**	NA
260	Tempe, AZ	(4.0)
319	Thornton, CO	(9.5)
NA	Thousand Oaks, CA**	NA
86	Toledo, OH	4.6
60	Toms River Twnshp, NJ	6.7
107	Topeka, KS	3.5
148	Torrance, CA	1.8
354	Tracy, CA	(22.1)
135	Trenton, NJ	2.4
168	Troy, MI	0.0
187	Tucson, AZ	(0.5)
72	Tulsa, OK	6.0
138	Tuscaloosa, AL	2.3
316	Tyler, TX	(8.7)
69	Upper Darby Twnshp, PA	6.1
295	Vacaville, CA	(6.9)
331	Vallejo, CA	(12.2)
150	Vancouver, WA	1.7
168	Ventura, CA	0.0
NA	Victorville, CA**	NA
86	Virginia Beach, VA	4.6
276	Visalia, CA	(5.1)
NA	Vista, CA**	NA
125	Waco, TX	2.8
218	Warren, MI	(1.7)
121	Warwick, RI	3.0
144	Washington, DC	2.0
339	Waterbury, CT	(12.8)
239	West Covina, CA	(2.8)
358	West Jordan, UT	(26.0)
301	West Palm Beach, FL	(7.7)
275	West Valley, UT	(5.0)
107	Westland, MI	3.5
145	Westminster, CA	1.9
24	Westminster, CO	11.7
285	Whittier, CA	(6.0)
220	Wichita Falls, TX	(1.8)
230	Wichita, KS	(2.2)
355	Wilmington, NC	(22.2)
35	Winston-Salem, NC	9.4
168	Woodbridge Twnshp, NJ	0.0
138	Worcester, MA	2.3
128	Yakima, WA	2.7
202	Yonkers, NY	(1.3)
268	Youngstown, OH	(4.4)
18	Yuma, AZ	12.4

Source: CQ Press using data from F.B.I. "Crime in the United States 2006"
**Sworn officers only, does not include civilian employees.*
***Not available*

84. Percent Change in Rate of Police Officers: 2002 to 2006 (continued)

National Percent Change = 1.6% Decrease*

RANK	CITY	% CHANGE
1	Glendale, AZ	28.4
2	Baton Rouge, LA	27.7
3	Shreveport, LA	27.3
4	Portsmouth, VA	18.9
5	Lubbock, TX	18.8
6	Cincinnati, OH	18.2
7	Clovis, CA	17.0
8	Flint, MI	16.0
9	Roseville, CA	15.0
10	Hampton, VA	14.9
11	Garland, TX	14.7
12	Columbia, SC	14.0
13	Richmond, VA	13.9
14	Aurora, CO	13.7
15	Pomona, CA	13.2
16	Anchorage, AK	12.8
17	Fort Smith, AR	12.6
18	Yuma, AZ	12.4
19	Fargo, ND	12.1
20	Lafayette, LA	12.0
20	Sunnyvale, CA	12.0
22	Bloomington, MN	11.8
22	Kansas City, MO	11.8
24	Westminster, CO	11.7
25	Athens-Clarke, GA	11.6
26	Roanoke, VA	11.3
27	Oceanside, CA	11.2
28	Fresno, CA	11.0
28	Irving, TX	11.0
30	Rochester, NY	10.6
31	Abilene, TX	10.5
32	Reno, NV	10.1
33	Cranston, RI	9.9
34	Port St. Lucie, FL	9.7
35	Cary, NC	9.4
35	Winston-Salem, NC	9.4
37	Jackson, MS	9.0
37	Lexington, KY	9.0
39	Greece, NY	8.9
40	Largo, FL	8.6
41	Glendale, CA	8.5
42	Fairfield, CA	8.4
43	New Bedford, MA	8.3
44	Paterson, NJ	8.2
45	Boca Raton, FL	8.1
45	Cape Coral, FL	8.1
47	Federal Way, WA	7.9
48	Jersey City, NJ	7.7
49	Clifton, NJ	7.6
50	Killeen, TX	7.5
50	Miami Beach, FL	7.5
52	Lawton, OK	7.4
53	Syracuse, NY	7.2
54	El Cajon, CA	7.1
54	Gilbert, AZ	7.1
56	High Point, NC	7.0
57	Salinas, CA	6.9
58	Alexandria, VA	6.8
58	Hialeah, FL	6.8
60	Toms River Twnshp, NJ	6.7
61	Dallas, TX	6.6
62	Berkeley, CA	6.5
62	Evansville, IN	6.5
62	Greeley, CO	6.5
62	Kansas City, KS	6.5
62	Mesquite, TX	6.5
67	Peoria, IL	6.4
68	San Bernardino, CA	6.2
69	Des Moines, IA	6.1
69	Independence, MO	6.1
69	Upper Darby Twnshp, PA	6.1
72	Austin, TX	6.0
72	Longview, TX	6.0
72	Sandy, UT	6.0
72	Santa Barbara, CA	6.0
72	Tulsa, OK	6.0
77	Oxnard, CA	5.9
77	Sugar Land, TX	5.9
79	Overland Park, KS	5.8
80	Farmington Hills, MI	5.6
81	Sioux Falls, SD	5.5
82	Pembroke Pines, FL	5.3
83	Colorado Springs, CO	5.2
83	Denver, CO	5.2
83	Gresham, OR	5.2
86	Dearborn, MI	4.6
86	San Francisco, CA	4.6
86	Toledo, OH	4.6
86	Virginia Beach, VA	4.6
90	Jacksonville, FL	4.4
91	Lawrence, KS	4.3
91	Newport News, VA	4.3
93	San Mateo, CA	4.2
93	Santa Maria, CA	4.2
95	Clearwater, FL	4.1
95	Reading, PA	4.1
95	St. Paul, MN	4.1
98	Lakewood, CO	4.0
98	Newton, MA	4.0
98	Santa Ana, CA	4.0
101	Brick Twnshp, NJ	3.8
101	South Bend, IN	3.8
103	Greensboro, NC	3.7
103	Las Cruces, NM	3.7
105	Boulder, CO	3.6
105	South Gate, CA	3.6
107	San Leandro, CA	3.5
107	Topeka, KS	3.5
107	Westland, MI	3.5
110	Anaheim, CA	3.4
110	Escondido, CA	3.4
112	Amarillo, TX	3.3
112	Clarkstown, NY	3.3
112	Long Beach, CA	3.3
112	Salt Lake City, UT	3.3
112	Tallahassee, FL	3.3
117	Palm Bay, FL	3.2
118	Fayetteville, NC	3.1
118	Inglewood, CA	3.1
118	Milwaukee, WI	3.1
121	Chicago, IL	3.0
121	Warwick, RI	3.0
123	Albany, NY	2.9
123	Broken Arrow, OK	2.9
125	Hartford, CT	2.8
125	North Charleston, SC	2.8
125	Waco, TX	2.8
128	Honolulu, HI	2.7
128	Yakima, WA	2.7
130	Deerfield Beach, FL	2.6
131	Camden, NJ	2.5
131	Clarksville, TN	2.5
131	Los Angeles, CA	2.5
131	San Angelo, TX	2.5
135	Hammond, IN	2.4
135	Somerville, MA	2.4
135	Trenton, NJ	2.4
138	Beaumont, TX	2.3
138	Montgomery, AL	2.3
138	Tuscaloosa, AL	2.3
138	Worcester, MA	2.3
142	Edmond, OK	2.1
142	St. Petersburg, FL	2.1
144	Washington, DC	2.0
145	Boston, MA	1.9
145	Minneapolis, MN	1.9
145	Westminster, CA	1.9
148	Elizabeth, NJ	1.8
148	Torrance, CA	1.8
150	Fullerton, CA	1.7
150	Tacoma, WA	1.7
150	Vancouver, WA	1.7
153	Sparks, NV	1.6
153	Sunrise, FL	1.6
155	Rockford, IL	1.5
156	Hollywood, FL	1.4
156	Kent, WA	1.4
158	Midland, TX	1.3
159	Scottsdale, AZ	1.2
160	Orem, UT	1.1
161	Downey, CA	1.0
162	Orange, CA	0.9
163	Green Bay, WI	0.6
163	Las Vegas, NV	0.6
165	Laredo, TX	0.5
165	Seattle, WA	0.5
167	Providence, RI	0.4
168	Alhambra, CA	0.0
168	Antioch, CA	0.0
168	Colonie, NY	0.0
168	Columbia, MO	0.0
168	Concord, CA	0.0
168	Coral Springs, FL	0.0
168	Eugene, OR	0.0
168	Fontana, CA	0.0
168	Hamilton Twnshp, NJ	0.0
168	Memphis, TN	0.0
168	Mobile, AL	0.0
168	Peoria, AZ	0.0
168	Philadelphia, PA	0.0
168	San Jose, CA	0.0
168	Springfield, MO	0.0
168	Troy, MI	0.0
168	Ventura, CA	0.0
168	Woodbridge Twnshp, NJ	0.0
186	Birmingham, AL	(0.3)
187	Albuquerque, NM	(0.5)
187	Indianapolis, IN	(0.5)
187	Manchester, NH	(0.5)
187	Tucson, AZ	(0.5)
191	New Orleans, LA	(0.6)
191	Pueblo, CO	(0.6)

RANK	CITY	% CHANGE
193	Boise, ID	(0.7)
194	Carrollton, TX	(0.8)
194	El Monte, CA	(0.8)
194	Fort Collins, CO	(0.8)
194	Modesto, CA	(0.8)
198	Edison Twnshp, NJ	(1.0)
199	Fremont, CA	(1.1)
200	Columbus, OH	(1.2)
200	Duluth, MN	(1.2)
202	Lowell, MA	(1.3)
202	Norfolk, VA	(1.3)
202	Ogden, UT	(1.3)
202	Tampa, FL	(1.3)
202	Yonkers, NY	(1.3)
207	Huntsville, AL	(1.4)
207	Lansing, MI	(1.4)
207	Melbourne, FL	(1.4)
210	Amherst, NY	(1.5)
210	Brockton, MA	(1.5)
210	Ontario, CA	(1.5)
210	Riverside, CA	(1.5)
210	Southfield, MI	(1.5)
215	Livermore, CA	(1.6)
215	Mesa, AZ	(1.6)
215	Salem, OR	(1.6)
218	Buena Park, CA	(1.7)
218	Warren, MI	(1.7)
220	Hawthorne, CA	(1.8)
220	Huntington Beach, CA	(1.8)
220	Wichita Falls, TX	(1.8)
223	Corpus Christi, TX	(1.9)
223	Daly City, CA	(1.9)
223	St. Louis, MO	(1.9)
226	Albany, GA	(2.1)
226	Garden Grove, CA	(2.1)
226	Lee's Summit, MO	(2.1)
226	Richardson, TX	(2.1)
230	Wichita, KS	(2.2)
231	Atlanta, GA	(2.3)
231	Norman, OK	(2.3)
231	Redding, CA	(2.3)
234	Arvada, CO	(2.4)
234	Lynn, MA	(2.4)
236	Canton, OH	(2.6)
236	Danbury, CT	(2.6)
236	Gary, IN	(2.6)
239	Grand Prairie, TX	(2.8)
239	Lewisville, TX	(2.8)
239	McAllen, TX	(2.8)
239	West Covina, CA	(2.8)
243	Lincoln, NE	(3.0)
243	Phoenix, AZ	(3.0)
243	Santa Monica, CA	(3.0)
243	Sterling Heights, MI	(3.0)
247	Nashville, TN	(3.1)
248	Davie, FL	(3.3)
248	Springfield, IL	(3.3)
250	Corona, CA	(3.4)
251	Costa Mesa, CA	(3.5)
252	Naperville, IL	(3.6)
253	Macon, GA	(3.8)
253	Sioux City, IA	(3.8)
255	Charlotte, NC	(3.9)
255	Kenosha, WI	(3.9)
255	Madison, WI	(3.9)
255	Olathe, KS	(3.9)
255	Quincy, MA	(3.9)
260	Tempe, AZ	(4.0)
261	Omaha, NE	(4.1)
261	Spokane, WA	(4.1)
263	Everett, WA	(4.2)
264	Billings, MT	(4.3)
264	Brownsville, TX	(4.3)
264	Hayward, CA	(4.3)
264	Plantation, FL	(4.3)
268	Youngstown, OH	(4.4)
269	Fort Worth, TX	(4.5)
270	Simi Valley, CA	(4.7)
271	Beaverton, OR	(4.8)
271	Durham, NC	(4.8)
271	Little Rock, AR	(4.8)
274	Pasadena, TX	(4.9)
275	West Valley, UT	(5.0)
276	Fort Wayne, IN	(5.1)
276	Visalia, CA	(5.1)
278	Columbus, GA	(5.2)
278	New York, NY	(5.2)
278	Suffolk, VA	(5.2)
281	Miami, FL	(5.3)
282	Ann Arbor, MI	(5.5)
283	Cedar Rapids, IA	(5.6)
284	Baltimore, MD	(5.7)
285	Grand Rapids, MI	(6.0)
285	Napa, CA	(6.0)
285	Newark, NJ	(6.0)
285	Whittier, CA	(6.0)
289	Clinton Twnshp, MI	(6.1)
290	Odessa, TX	(6.5)
291	Charleston, SC	(6.6)
292	Bellevue, WA	(6.7)
292	North Las Vegas, NV	(6.7)
294	Livonia, MI	(6.8)
295	Carlsbad, CA	(6.9)
295	Vacaville, CA	(6.9)
297	Bellingham, WA	(7.1)
298	Arlington, TX	(7.4)
298	Baldwin Park, CA	(7.4)
300	Chino, CA	(7.6)
301	Chattanooga, TN	(7.7)
301	West Palm Beach, FL	(7.7)
303	Lakeland, FL	(7.8)
303	Pasadena, CA	(7.8)
305	Knoxville, TN	(7.9)
305	Santa Rosa, CA	(7.9)
305	Stockton, CA	(7.9)
308	Gainesville, FL	(8.0)
309	El Paso, TX	(8.2)
310	Orlando, FL	(8.3)
311	Bridgeport, CT	(8.4)
311	Fort Lauderdale, FL	(8.4)
313	Plano, TX	(8.5)
314	Aurora, IL	(8.6)
314	Burbank, CA	(8.6)
316	Tyler, TX	(8.7)
317	Raleigh, NC	(8.8)
318	San Antonio, TX	(9.4)
319	Thornton, CO	(9.5)
320	San Diego, CA	(9.6)
321	Chesapeake, VA	(9.9)
322	Cleveland, OH	(10.0)
323	Henderson, NV	(10.1)
324	Oklahoma City, OK	(10.2)
325	Chula Vista, CA	(10.3)
326	Irvine, CA	(10.4)
327	Sacramento, CA	(10.6)
328	Hillsboro, OR	(11.3)
329	Denton, TX	(11.5)
330	Rochester, MN	(11.6)
331	Bakersfield, CA	(12.2)
331	Houston, TX	(12.2)
331	McKinney, TX	(12.2)
331	Oakland, CA	(12.2)
331	Vallejo, CA	(12.2)
336	Joliet, IL	(12.3)
337	Canton Twnshp, MI	(12.7)
337	Parma, OH	(12.7)
339	Waterbury, CT	(12.8)
340	Rialto, CA	(12.9)
340	Santa Clara, CA	(12.9)
342	Murfreesboro, TN	(13.2)
343	Detroit, MI	(13.9)
344	Provo, UT	(14.1)
345	Newport Beach, CA	(14.2)
346	Allentown, PA	(14.4)
347	Erie, PA	(14.7)
348	Round Rock, TX	(15.5)
349	Pittsburgh, PA	(16.6)
350	Savannah, GA	(17.4)
351	Chandler, AZ	(17.8)
352	Springfield, MA	(18.7)
353	Pompano Beach, FL	(19.8)
354	Tracy, CA	(22.1)
355	Wilmington, NC	(22.2)
356	Miramar, FL	(22.5)
357	Richmond, CA	(22.9)
358	West Jordan, UT	(26.0)
359	Surprise, AZ	(38.8)
NA	Bellflower, CA**	NA
NA	Buffalo, NY**	NA
NA	Cambridge, MA**	NA
NA	Carson, CA**	NA
NA	Centennial, CO**	NA
NA	Cheektowaga, NY**	NA
NA	Chino Hills, CA**	NA
NA	Compton, CA**	NA
NA	Dayton, OH**	NA
NA	Hesperia, CA**	NA
NA	Lake Forest, CA**	NA
NA	Lakewood, CA**	NA
NA	Lancaster, CA**	NA
NA	Louisville, KY**	NA
NA	Miami Gardens, FL**	NA
NA	Mission Viejo, CA**	NA
NA	Moreno Valley, CA**	NA
NA	Murrieta, CA**	NA
NA	Nashua, NH**	NA
NA	Norwalk, CA**	NA
NA	Palmdale, CA**	NA
NA	Portland, OR**	NA
NA	Racine, WI**	NA
NA	Rancho Cucamon., CA**	NA
NA	Roswell, GA**	NA
NA	Santa Clarita, CA**	NA
NA	Spokane Valley, WA**	NA
NA	Temecula, CA**	NA
NA	Thousand Oaks, CA**	NA
NA	Victorville, CA**	NA
NA	Vista, CA**	NA

Source: CQ Press using data from F.B.I. "Crime in the United States 2006"

**Sworn officers only, does not include civilian employees.*

***Not available*

APPENDICES

85. Metropolitan Population in 2006

National Total = 299,398,484*

RANK	METROPOLITAN AREA	POP
234	Abilene, TX	162,776
73	Albany-Schenectady-Troy, NY	851,151
229	Albany, GA	168,071
76	Albuquerque, NM	808,790
268	Alexandria, LA	140,250
290	Altoona, PA	126,907
181	Amarillo, TX	245,428
341	Ames, IA	80,377
163	Anchorage, AK	294,862
225	Anderson, SC	178,243
149	Ann Arbor, MI	340,995
197	Appleton, WI	215,932
136	Asheville, NC	400,669
223	Athens-Clarke County, GA	180,707
10	Atlanta, GA	5,075,647
171	Atlantic City, NJ	271,221
106	Augusta, GA-SC	534,131
52	Austin-Round Rock, TX	1,493,692
81	Bakersfield, CA	763,641
25	Baltimore-Towson, MD	2,662,948
257	Bangor, ME	147,076
194	Barnstable Town, MA	227,875
85	Baton Rouge, LA	695,541
270	Battle Creek, MI	138,844
316	Bay City, MI	108,757
138	Beaumont-Port Arthur, TX	394,399
215	Bellingham, WA	186,623
262	Bend, OR	143,700
62	Bethesda-Frederick, MD M.D.	1,151,428
256	Billings, MT	147,997
178	Binghamton, NY	249,087
64	Birmingham-Hoover, AL	1,099,986
332	Bismarck, ND	99,220
250	Blacksburg, VA	152,562
224	Bloomington, IN	178,886
100	Boise City-Nampa, ID	558,432
311	Bowling Green, KY	111,859
182	Bremerton-Silverdale, WA	244,796
139	Brownsville-Harlingen, TX	389,032
326	Brunswick, GA	101,593
63	Buffalo-Niagara Falls, NY	1,150,784
264	Burlington, NC	143,337
58	Camden, NJ M.D.	1,246,850
101	Cape Coral-Fort Myers, FL	553,945
348	Carson City, NV	57,936
346	Casper, WY	70,582
179	Cedar Rapids, IA	247,720
96	Charleston-North Charleston, SC	604,149
158	Charleston, WV	306,706
50	Charlotte-Gastonia, NC-SC	1,550,796
212	Charlottesville, VA	190,302
113	Chattanooga, TN-GA	501,115
340	Cheyenne, WY	86,117
NA	Chicago, IL**	NA
196	Chico, CA	216,114
36	Cincinnati-Middletown, OH-KY-IN	2,076,054
180	Clarksville, TN-KY	246,355
35	Cleveland-Elyria-Mentor, OH	2,128,904
314	Cleveland, TN	109,410
279	Coeur d'Alene, ID	131,006
208	College Station-Bryan, TX	195,111
98	Colorado Springs, CO	598,605
246	Columbia, MO	154,404
83	Columbia, SC	700,605
164	Columbus, GA-AL	292,291
345	Columbus, IN	74,027
46	Columbus, OH	1,710,708
125	Corpus Christi, TX	425,272
328	Cumberland, MD-WV	100,893
5	Dallas (greater), TX	5,984,390
15	Dallas-Plano-Irving, TX M.D.	4,003,448
273	Dalton, GA	135,931
315	Danville, VA	109,073
114	Daytona Beach, FL	498,320
74	Dayton, OH	844,605
252	Decatur, AL	149,687
30	Denver-Aurora, CO	2,404,612
107	Des Moines-West Des Moines, IA	525,225
11	Detroit (greater), MI	4,477,154
38	Detroit-Livonia-Dearborn, MI M.D.	1,993,241
271	Dothan, AL	137,829
258	Dover, DE	145,667
337	Dubuque, IA	92,118
169	Duluth, MN-WI	277,120
118	Durham, NC	465,289
245	Eau Claire, WI	154,604
32	Edison, NJ M.D.	2,305,462
242	El Centro, CA	157,226
82	El Paso, TX	742,047
312	Elizabethtown, KY	111,512
205	Elkhart-Goshen, IN	196,656
338	Elmira, NY	89,752
168	Erie, PA	280,694
150	Eugene-Springfield, OR	340,676
148	Evansville, IN-KY	351,930
349	Fairbanks, AK	33,421
217	Fargo, ND-MN	185,052
288	Farmington, NM	127,924
129	Fayetteville, AR-MO	409,630
147	Fayetteville, NC	352,430
286	Flagstaff, AZ	128,601
123	Flint, MI	442,777
202	Florence, SC	201,529
330	Fond du Lac, WI	99,701
170	Fort Collins-Loveland, CO	277,068
43	Fort Lauderdale, FL M.D.	1,807,618
165	Fort Smith, AR-OK	288,013
216	Fort Walton Beach, FL	185,244
131	Fort Wayne, IN	407,093
39	Fort Worth-Arlington, TX M.D.	1,980,942
72	Fresno, CA	885,487
323	Gadsden, AL	104,122
183	Gainesville, FL	244,306
228	Gainesville, GA	171,095
284	Glens Falls, NY	128,917
299	Goldsboro, NC	116,732
335	Grand Forks, ND-MN	97,197
276	Grand Junction, CO	132,327
79	Grand Rapids-Wyoming, MI	769,263
342	Great Falls, MT	80,331
188	Greeley, CO	233,271
161	Green Bay, WI	298,584
88	Greensboro-High Point, NC	687,959
231	Greenville, NC	165,841
97	Greenville, SC	600,445
177	Hagerstown-Martinsburg, MD-WV	251,797
260	Hanford-Corcoran, CA	144,712
108	Harrisburg-Carlisle, PA	522,275
309	Harrisonburg, VA	112,802
67	Hartford, CT	1,001,896
278	Hattiesburg, MS	131,395
175	Holland-Grand Haven, MI	254,770
70	Honolulu, HI	912,693
336	Hot Springs, AR	94,619
213	Houma, LA	189,259
8	Houston, TX	5,429,705
166	Huntington-Ashland, WV-KY-OH	286,889
142	Huntsville, AL	371,995
302	Idaho Falls, ID	116,402
49	Indianapolis, IN	1,651,458
269	Iowa City, IA	139,260
329	Ithaca, NY	100,286
56	Jacksonville, FL	1,269,424
244	Jacksonville, NC	155,482
233	Jackson, MI	163,221
109	Jackson, MS	520,697
310	Jackson, TN	112,267
240	Janesville, WI	158,116
259	Jefferson City, MO	144,919
211	Johnson City, TN	191,348
255	Johnstown, PA	148,204
308	Jonesboro, AR	113,363
230	Joplin, MO	167,393
155	Kalamazoo-Portage, MI	318,553
41	Kansas City, MO-KS	1,961,734
195	Kennewick-Richland-Pasco, WA	224,758
145	Killeen-Temple-Fort Hood, TX	361,489
159	Kingsport, TN-VA	304,872
220	Kingston, NY	183,182
92	Knoxville, TN	663,737
325	Kokomo, IN	102,034
282	La Crosse, WI-MN	129,432
219	Lafayette, IN	184,554
218	Lake Charles, LA	184,811
209	Lake Havasu City-Kingman, AZ	194,356
102	Lakeland, FL	552,068
115	Lancaster, PA	490,996
120	Lansing-East Lansing, MI	454,180
190	Laredo, TX	231,062
210	Las Cruces, NM	192,019
45	Las Vegas-Paradise, NV	1,767,730

Note: All listings are for Metropolitan Statistical Areas (M.S.A.s) except for those ending with "M.D." Listings with "M.D." are Metropolitan Divisions which are smaller parts of ten large M.S.A.s. See explanatory note at beginning of metropolitan area section on page 23.

RANK	METROPOLITAN AREA	POP
324	Lawrence, KS	103,641
307	Lawton, OK	113,422
291	Lebanon, PA	125,689
318	Lewiston-Auburn, ME	108,045
347	Lewiston, ID-WA	60,465
124	Lexington-Fayette, KY	433,254
321	Lima, OH	106,363
167	Lincoln, NE	283,081
95	Little Rock, AR	650,613
306	Logan, UT-ID	113,944
200	Longview, TX	207,210
333	Longview, WA	98,997
4	Los Angeles County, CA M.D.	10,024,953
2	Los Angeles (greater), CA	13,039,935
59	Louisville, KY-IN	1,217,627
173	Lubbock, TX	266,308
185	Lynchburg, VA	239,271
186	Macon, GA	236,057
261	Madera, CA	144,074
105	Madison, WI	539,008
134	Manchester-Nashua, NH	402,810
287	Mansfield, OH	128,105
84	McAllen-Edinburg-Mission, TX	697,496
204	Medford, OR	198,525
55	Memphis, TN-MS-AR	1,273,452
184	Merced, CA	243,883
7	Miami (greater), FL	5,513,643
29	Miami-Dade County, FL M.D.	2,416,083
313	Michigan City-La Porte, IN	111,244
292	Midland, TX	124,810
51	Milwaukee, WI	1,518,404
19	Minneapolis-St. Paul, MN-WI	3,163,432
327	Missoula, MT	101,045
132	Mobile, AL	405,058
111	Modesto, CA	510,058
236	Monroe, LA	162,215
248	Monroe, MI	153,551
146	Montgomery, AL	360,475
305	Morgantown, WV	114,603
277	Morristown, TN	132,236
303	Mount Vernon-Anacortes, WA	115,116
298	Muncie, IN	117,133
227	Muskegon-Norton Shores, MI	175,117
193	Myrtle Beach, SC	230,522
274	Napa, CA	133,960
156	Naples-Marco Island, FL	312,424
53	Nashville-Davidson, TN	1,440,638
22	Nassau-Suffolk, NY M.D.	2,815,582
57	New Orleans, LA	1,250,582
1	New York (greater), NY-NJ-PA	18,785,139
3	New York-W. Plains NY-NJ M.D.	11,509,472
33	Newark-Union, NJ-PA M.D.	2,154,623
237	Niles-Benton Harbor, MI	162,206
27	Oakland-Fremont, CA M.D.	2,488,907
157	Ocala, FL	308,560
331	Ocean City, NJ	99,362
285	Odessa, TX	128,891
112	Ogden-Clearfield, UT	502,708
61	Oklahoma City, OK	1,167,026
189	Olympia, WA	232,799
75	Omaha-Council Bluffs, NE-IA	817,568
40	Orlando, FL	1,965,859
239	Oshkosh-Neenah, WI	160,067
77	Oxnard-Thousand Oaks, CA	803,276
104	Palm Bay-Melbourne, FL	540,209
344	Palm Coast, FL	77,699
232	Panama City-Lynn Haven, FL	164,283
243	Pascagoula, MS	156,631
122	Pensacola, FL	447,295
6	Philadelphia (greater) PA-NJ-DE	5,834,113
17	Philadelphia, PA M.D.	3,893,625
14	Phoenix-Mesa-Scottsdale, AZ	4,012,817
322	Pine Bluff, AR	106,062
31	Pittsburgh, PA	2,388,185
275	Pittsfield, MA	132,660
339	Pocatello, ID	88,155
140	Port St. Lucie, FL	387,459
34	Portland-Vancouver, OR-WA	2,130,553
110	Portland, ME	514,252
91	Poughkeepsie, NY	669,529
201	Prescott, AZ	206,296
117	Provo-Orem, UT	467,608
247	Pueblo, CO	154,183
238	Punta Gorda, FL	160,193
206	Racine, WI	196,426
68	Raleigh-Cary, NC	968,631
295	Rapid City, SD	119,115
137	Reading, PA	396,665
222	Redding, CA	181,524
130	Reno-Sparks, NV	407,115
60	Richmond, VA	1,187,370
16	Riverside-San Bernardino, CA	3,945,166
162	Roanoke, VA	295,903
226	Rochester, MN	178,166
66	Rochester, NY	1,041,811
254	Rocky Mount, NC	148,410
334	Rome, GA	97,223
37	Sacramento, CA	2,060,675
199	Saginaw, MI	207,837
141	Salem, OR	381,718
126	Salinas, CA	415,815
301	Salisbury, MD	116,566
65	Salt Lake City, UT	1,068,196
317	San Angelo, TX	108,353
42	San Antonio, TX	1,943,351
21	San Diego, CA	2,959,880
12	San Francisco (greater), CA	4,190,087
47	San Francisco-S. Mateo, CA M.D.	1,701,180
44	San Jose, CA	1,770,793
174	San Luis Obispo, CA	257,779
343	Sandusky, OH	78,761
20	Santa Ana-Anaheim, CA M.D.	3,014,982
133	Santa Barbara-Santa Maria, CA	404,371
176	Santa Cruz-Watsonville, CA	251,914
265	Santa Fe, NM	142,770
116	Santa Rosa-Petaluma, CA	470,678
89	Sarasota-Bradenton-Venice, FL	684,386
152	Savannah, GA	323,964
103	Scranton--Wilkes-Barre, PA	551,034
18	Seattle (greater), WA	3,258,355
26	Seattle-Bellevue, WA M.D.	2,491,616
280	Sebastian-Vero Beach, FL	130,763
304	Sheboygan, WI	115,030
294	Sherman-Denison, TX	120,145
144	Shreveport-Bossier City, LA	363,251
263	Sioux City, IA-NE-SD	143,363
198	Sioux Falls, SD	209,523
154	South Bend-Mishawaka, IN-MI	319,789
172	Spartanburg, SC	270,958
121	Spokane, WA	448,278
87	Springfield, MA	691,394
135	Springfield, MO	401,034
266	Springfield, OH	142,549
267	State College, PA	140,685
90	Stockton, CA	670,097
221	St. Cloud, MN	182,369
293	St. Joseph, MO-KS	122,851
23	St. Louis, MO-IL	2,798,956
319	Sumter, SC	107,158
94	Syracuse, NY	653,507
80	Tacoma, WA M.D.	766,739
151	Tallahassee, FL	340,534
24	Tampa-St Petersburg, FL	2,692,311
272	Texarkana, TX-Texarkana, AR	136,867
93	Toledo, OH	657,496
192	Topeka, KS	230,694
143	Trenton-Ewing, NJ	366,535
69	Tucson, AZ	960,135
71	Tulsa, OK	895,554
203	Tuscaloosa, AL	198,666
207	Tyler, TX	195,995
160	Utica-Rome, NY	298,683
289	Valdosta, GA	127,788
127	Vallejo-Fairfield, CA	415,300
300	Victoria, TX	116,568
249	Vineland, NJ	153,369
48	Virginia Beach-Norfolk, VA-NC	1,663,994
128	Visalia-Porterville, CA	414,574
191	Waco, TX	231,035
281	Warner Robins, GA	130,215
28	Warren-Farmington Hills, MI M.D.	2,483,913
9	Washington (greater) DC-VA-MD	5,275,654
13	Washington, DC-VA-MD-WV M.D.	4,124,226
235	Waterloo-Cedar Falls, IA	162,756
283	Wausau, WI	129,414
320	Wenatchee, WA	106,568
54	West Palm Beach, FL M.D.	1,289,942
253	Wheeling, WV-OH	148,832
251	Wichita Falls, TX	150,422
99	Wichita, KS	591,201
296	Williamsport, PA	118,500
86	Wilmington, DE-MD-NJ M.D.	693,638
153	Wilmington, NC	321,432
297	Winchester, VA-WV	117,226
119	Winston-Salem, NC	457,581
78	Worcester, MA	787,969
187	Yakima, WA	235,565
241	Yuba City, CA	157,434
214	Yuma, AZ	188,206

Source: Federal Bureau of Investigation
"Crime in the United States 2006" (Uniform Crime Reports, September 24, 2007)
**Estimates as of July 2006 based on U.S. Bureau of the Census figures.*
***Not available.*

85. Metropolitan Population in 2006 (continued)

National Total = 299,398,484*

RANK	METROPOLITAN AREA	POP
1	New York (greater), NY-NJ-PA	18,785,139
2	Los Angeles (greater), CA	13,039,935
3	New York-W. Plains NY-NJ M.D.	11,509,472
4	Los Angeles County, CA M.D.	10,024,953
5	Dallas (greater), TX	5,984,390
6	Philadelphia (greater) PA-NJ-DE	5,834,113
7	Miami (greater), FL	5,513,643
8	Houston, TX	5,429,705
9	Washington (greater) DC-VA-MD	5,275,654
10	Atlanta, GA	5,075,647
11	Detroit (greater), MI	4,477,154
12	San Francisco (greater), CA	4,190,087
13	Washington, DC-VA-MD-WV M.D.	4,124,226
14	Phoenix-Mesa-Scottsdale, AZ	4,012,817
15	Dallas-Plano-Irving, TX M.D.	4,003,448
16	Riverside-San Bernardino, CA	3,945,166
17	Philadelphia, PA M.D.	3,893,625
18	Seattle (greater), WA	3,258,355
19	Minneapolis-St. Paul, MN-WI	3,163,432
20	Santa Ana-Anaheim, CA M.D.	3,014,982
21	San Diego, CA	2,959,880
22	Nassau-Suffolk, NY M.D.	2,815,582
23	St. Louis, MO-IL	2,798,956
24	Tampa-St Petersburg, FL	2,692,311
25	Baltimore-Towson, MD	2,662,948
26	Seattle-Bellevue, WA M.D.	2,491,616
27	Oakland-Fremont, CA M.D.	2,488,907
28	Warren-Farmington Hills, MI M.D.	2,483,913
29	Miami-Dade County, FL M.D.	2,416,083
30	Denver-Aurora, CO	2,404,612
31	Pittsburgh, PA	2,388,185
32	Edison, NJ M.D.	2,305,462
33	Newark-Union, NJ-PA M.D.	2,154,623
34	Portland-Vancouver, OR-WA	2,130,553
35	Cleveland-Elyria-Mentor, OH	2,128,904
36	Cincinnati-Middletown, OH-KY-IN	2,076,054
37	Sacramento, CA	2,060,675
38	Detroit-Livonia-Dearborn, MI M.D.	1,993,241
39	Fort Worth-Arlington, TX M.D.	1,980,942
40	Orlando, FL	1,965,859
41	Kansas City, MO-KS	1,961,734
42	San Antonio, TX	1,943,351
43	Fort Lauderdale, FL M.D.	1,807,618
44	San Jose, CA	1,770,793
45	Las Vegas-Paradise, NV	1,767,730
46	Columbus, OH	1,710,708
47	San Francisco-S. Mateo, CA M.D.	1,701,180
48	Virginia Beach-Norfolk, VA-NC	1,663,994
49	Indianapolis, IN	1,651,458
50	Charlotte-Gastonia, NC-SC	1,550,796
51	Milwaukee, WI	1,518,404
52	Austin-Round Rock, TX	1,493,692
53	Nashville-Davidson, TN	1,440,638
54	West Palm Beach, FL M.D.	1,289,942
55	Memphis, TN-MS-AR	1,273,452
56	Jacksonville, FL	1,269,424
57	New Orleans, LA	1,250,582
58	Camden, NJ M.D.	1,246,850
59	Louisville, KY-IN	1,217,627
60	Richmond, VA	1,187,370
61	Oklahoma City, OK	1,167,026
62	Bethesda-Frederick, MD M.D.	1,151,428
63	Buffalo-Niagara Falls, NY	1,150,784
64	Birmingham-Hoover, AL	1,099,986
65	Salt Lake City, UT	1,068,196
66	Rochester, NY	1,041,811
67	Hartford, CT	1,001,896
68	Raleigh-Cary, NC	968,631
69	Tucson, AZ	960,135
70	Honolulu, HI	912,693
71	Tulsa, OK	895,554
72	Fresno, CA	885,487
73	Albany-Schenectady-Troy, NY	851,151
74	Dayton, OH	844,605
75	Omaha-Council Bluffs, NE-IA	817,568
76	Albuquerque, NM	808,790
77	Oxnard-Thousand Oaks, CA	803,276
78	Worcester, MA	787,969
79	Grand Rapids-Wyoming, MI	769,263
80	Tacoma, WA M.D.	766,739
81	Bakersfield, CA	763,641
82	El Paso, TX	742,047
83	Columbia, SC	700,605
84	McAllen-Edinburg-Mission, TX	697,496
85	Baton Rouge, LA	695,541
86	Wilmington, DE-MD-NJ M.D.	693,638
87	Springfield, MA	691,394
88	Greensboro-High Point, NC	687,959
89	Sarasota-Bradenton-Venice, FL	684,386
90	Stockton, CA	670,097
91	Poughkeepsie, NY	669,529
92	Knoxville, TN	663,737
93	Toledo, OH	657,496
94	Syracuse, NY	653,507
95	Little Rock, AR	650,613
96	Charleston-North Charleston, SC	604,149
97	Greenville, SC	600,445
98	Colorado Springs, CO	598,605
99	Wichita, KS	591,201
100	Boise City-Nampa, ID	558,432
101	Cape Coral-Fort Myers, FL	553,945
102	Lakeland, FL	552,068
103	Scranton--Wilkes-Barre, PA	551,034
104	Palm Bay-Melbourne, FL	540,209
105	Madison, WI	539,008
106	Augusta, GA-SC	534,131
107	Des Moines-West Des Moines, IA	525,225
108	Harrisburg-Carlisle, PA	522,275
109	Jackson, MS	520,697
110	Portland, ME	514,252
111	Modesto, CA	510,058
112	Ogden-Clearfield, UT	502,708
113	Chattanooga, TN-GA	501,115
114	Daytona Beach, FL	498,320
115	Lancaster, PA	490,996
116	Santa Rosa-Petaluma, CA	470,678
117	Provo-Orem, UT	467,608
118	Durham, NC	465,289
119	Winston-Salem, NC	457,581
120	Lansing-East Lansing, MI	454,180
121	Spokane, WA	448,278
122	Pensacola, FL	447,295
123	Flint, MI	442,777
124	Lexington-Fayette, KY	433,254
125	Corpus Christi, TX	425,272
126	Salinas, CA	415,815
127	Vallejo-Fairfield, CA	415,300
128	Visalia-Porterville, CA	414,574
129	Fayetteville, AR-MO	409,630
130	Reno-Sparks, NV	407,115
131	Fort Wayne, IN	407,093
132	Mobile, AL	405,058
133	Santa Barbara-Santa Maria, CA	404,371
134	Manchester-Nashua, NH	402,810
135	Springfield, MO	401,034
136	Asheville, NC	400,669
137	Reading, PA	396,665
138	Beaumont-Port Arthur, TX	394,399
139	Brownsville-Harlingen, TX	389,032
140	Port St. Lucie, FL	387,459
141	Salem, OR	381,718
142	Huntsville, AL	371,995
143	Trenton-Ewing, NJ	366,535
144	Shreveport-Bossier City, LA	363,251
145	Killeen-Temple-Fort Hood, TX	361,489
146	Montgomery, AL	360,475
147	Fayetteville, NC	352,430
148	Evansville, IN-KY	351,930
149	Ann Arbor, MI	340,995
150	Eugene-Springfield, OR	340,676
151	Tallahassee, FL	340,534
152	Savannah, GA	323,964
153	Wilmington, NC	321,432
154	South Bend-Mishawaka, IN-MI	319,789
155	Kalamazoo-Portage, MI	318,553
156	Naples-Marco Island, FL	312,424
157	Ocala, FL	308,560
158	Charleston, WV	306,706
159	Kingsport, TN-VA	304,872
160	Utica-Rome, NY	298,683
161	Green Bay, WI	298,584
162	Roanoke, VA	295,903
163	Anchorage, AK	294,862
164	Columbus, GA-AL	292,291
165	Fort Smith, AR-OK	288,013
166	Huntington-Ashland, WV-KY-OH	286,889
167	Lincoln, NE	283,081
168	Erie, PA	280,694
169	Duluth, MN-WI	277,120
170	Fort Collins-Loveland, CO	277,068
171	Atlantic City, NJ	271,221

Note: All listings are for Metropolitan Statistical Areas (M.S.A.s) except for those ending with "M.D." Listings with "M.D." are Metropolitan Divisions which are smaller parts of ten large M.S.A.s. See explanatory note at beginning of metropolitan area section on page 23.

RANK	METROPOLITAN AREA	POP
172	Spartanburg, SC	270,958
173	Lubbock, TX	266,308
174	San Luis Obispo, CA	257,779
175	Holland-Grand Haven, MI	254,770
176	Santa Cruz-Watsonville, CA	251,914
177	Hagerstown-Martinsburg, MD-WV	251,797
178	Binghamton, NY	249,087
179	Cedar Rapids, IA	247,720
180	Clarksville, TN-KY	246,355
181	Amarillo, TX	245,428
182	Bremerton-Silverdale, WA	244,796
183	Gainesville, FL	244,306
184	Merced, CA	243,883
185	Lynchburg, VA	239,271
186	Macon, GA	236,057
187	Yakima, WA	235,565
188	Greeley, CO	233,271
189	Olympia, WA	232,799
190	Laredo, TX	231,062
191	Waco, TX	231,035
192	Topeka, KS	230,694
193	Myrtle Beach, SC	230,522
194	Barnstable Town, MA	227,875
195	Kennewick-Richland-Pasco, WA	224,758
196	Chico, CA	216,114
197	Appleton, WI	215,932
198	Sioux Falls, SD	209,523
199	Saginaw, MI	207,837
200	Longview, TX	207,210
201	Prescott, AZ	206,296
202	Florence, SC	201,529
203	Tuscaloosa, AL	198,666
204	Medford, OR	198,525
205	Elkhart-Goshen, IN	196,656
206	Racine, WI	196,426
207	Tyler, TX	195,995
208	College Station-Bryan, TX	195,111
209	Lake Havasu City-Kingman, AZ	194,356
210	Las Cruces, NM	192,019
211	Johnson City, TN	191,348
212	Charlottesville, VA	190,302
213	Houma, LA	189,259
214	Yuma, AZ	188,206
215	Bellingham, WA	186,623
216	Fort Walton Beach, FL	185,244
217	Fargo, ND-MN	185,052
218	Lake Charles, LA	184,811
219	Lafayette, IN	184,554
220	Kingston, NY	183,182
221	St. Cloud, MN	182,369
222	Redding, CA	181,524
223	Athens-Clarke County, GA	180,707
224	Bloomington, IN	178,886
225	Anderson, SC	178,243
226	Rochester, MN	178,166
227	Muskegon-Norton Shores, MI	175,117
228	Gainesville, GA	171,095
229	Albany, GA	168,071
230	Joplin, MO	167,393
231	Greenville, NC	165,841

RANK	METROPOLITAN AREA	POP
232	Panama City-Lynn Haven, FL	164,283
233	Jackson, MI	163,221
234	Abilene, TX	162,776
235	Waterloo-Cedar Falls, IA	162,756
236	Monroe, LA	162,215
237	Niles-Benton Harbor, MI	162,206
238	Punta Gorda, FL	160,193
239	Oshkosh-Neenah, WI	160,067
240	Janesville, WI	158,116
241	Yuba City, CA	157,434
242	El Centro, CA	157,226
243	Pascagoula, MS	156,631
244	Jacksonville, NC	155,482
245	Eau Claire, WI	154,604
246	Columbia, MO	154,404
247	Pueblo, CO	154,183
248	Monroe, MI	153,551
249	Vineland, NJ	153,369
250	Blacksburg, VA	152,562
251	Wichita Falls, TX	150,422
252	Decatur, AL	149,687
253	Wheeling, WV-OH	148,832
254	Rocky Mount, NC	148,410
255	Johnstown, PA	148,204
256	Billings, MT	147,997
257	Bangor, ME	147,076
258	Dover, DE	145,667
259	Jefferson City, MO	144,919
260	Hanford-Corcoran, CA	144,712
261	Madera, CA	144,074
262	Bend, OR	143,700
263	Sioux City, IA-NE-SD	143,363
264	Burlington, NC	143,337
265	Santa Fe, NM	142,770
266	Springfield, OH	142,549
267	State College, PA	140,685
268	Alexandria, LA	140,250
269	Iowa City, IA	139,260
270	Battle Creek, MI	138,844
271	Dothan, AL	137,829
272	Texarkana, TX-Texarkana, AR	136,867
273	Dalton, GA	135,931
274	Napa, CA	133,960
275	Pittsfield, MA	132,660
276	Grand Junction, CO	132,327
277	Morristown, TN	132,236
278	Hattiesburg, MS	131,395
279	Coeur d'Alene, ID	131,006
280	Sebastian-Vero Beach, FL	130,763
281	Warner Robins, GA	130,215
282	La Crosse, WI-MN	129,432
283	Wausau, WI	129,414
284	Glens Falls, NY	128,917
285	Odessa, TX	128,891
286	Flagstaff, AZ	128,601
287	Mansfield, OH	128,105
288	Farmington, NM	127,924
289	Valdosta, GA	127,788
290	Altoona, PA	126,907
291	Lebanon, PA	125,689

RANK	METROPOLITAN AREA	POP
292	Midland, TX	124,810
293	St. Joseph, MO-KS	122,851
294	Sherman-Denison, TX	120,145
295	Rapid City, SD	119,115
296	Williamsport, PA	118,500
297	Winchester, VA-WV	117,226
298	Muncie, IN	117,133
299	Goldsboro, NC	116,732
300	Victoria, TX	116,568
301	Salisbury, MD	116,566
302	Idaho Falls, ID	116,402
303	Mount Vernon-Anacortes, WA	115,116
304	Sheboygan, WI	115,030
305	Morgantown, WV	114,603
306	Logan, UT-ID	113,944
307	Lawton, OK	113,422
308	Jonesboro, AR	113,363
309	Harrisonburg, VA	112,802
310	Jackson, TN	112,267
311	Bowling Green, KY	111,859
312	Elizabethtown, KY	111,512
313	Michigan City-La Porte, IN	111,244
314	Cleveland, TN	109,410
315	Danville, VA	109,073
316	Bay City, MI	108,757
317	San Angelo, TX	108,353
318	Lewiston-Auburn, ME	108,045
319	Sumter, SC	107,158
320	Wenatchee, WA	106,568
321	Lima, OH	106,363
322	Pine Bluff, AR	106,062
323	Gadsden, AL	104,122
324	Lawrence, KS	103,641
325	Kokomo, IN	102,034
326	Brunswick, GA	101,593
327	Missoula, MT	101,045
328	Cumberland, MD-WV	100,893
329	Ithaca, NY	100,286
330	Fond du Lac, WI	99,701
331	Ocean City, NJ	99,362
332	Bismarck, ND	99,220
333	Longview, WA	98,997
334	Rome, GA	97,223
335	Grand Forks, ND-MN	97,197
336	Hot Springs, AR	94,619
337	Dubuque, IA	92,118
338	Elmira, NY	89,752
339	Pocatello, ID	88,155
340	Cheyenne, WY	86,117
341	Ames, IA	80,377
342	Great Falls, MT	80,331
343	Sandusky, OH	78,761
344	Palm Coast, FL	77,699
345	Columbus, IN	74,027
346	Casper, WY	70,582
347	Lewiston, ID-WA	60,465
348	Carson City, NV	57,936
349	Fairbanks, AK	33,421
NA	Chicago, IL**	NA

Source: Federal Bureau of Investigation
"Crime in the United States 2006" (Uniform Crime Reports, September 24, 2007)
**Estimates as of July 2006 based on U.S. Bureau of the Census figures.*
***Not available.*

86. Metropolitan Population in 2005

National Total = 296,507,061*

RANK	METROPOLITAN AREA	POP
227	Abilene, TX	161,123
69	Albany-Schenectady-Troy, NY	846,480
219	Albany, GA	167,284
73	Albuquerque, NM	791,750
245	Alexandria, LA	147,408
268	Altoona, PA	127,708
175	Amarillo, TX	239,998
324	Ames, IA	80,727
156	Anchorage, AK	291,624
216	Anderson, SC	175,907
142	Ann Arbor, MI	339,467
189	Appleton, WI	214,153
129	Asheville, NC	393,687
214	Athens-Clarke County, GA	178,545
10	Atlanta, GA	4,837,981
163	Atlantic City, NJ	269,281
99	Augusta, GA-SC	527,083
50	Austin-Round Rock, TX	1,435,502
77	Bakersfield, CA	739,726
23	Baltimore-Towson, MD	2,659,312
242	Bangor, ME	148,674
181	Barnstable Town, MA	228,050
78	Baton Rouge, LA	729,999
256	Battle Creek, MI	139,180
300	Bay City, MI	109,569
131	Beaumont-Port Arthur, TX	389,750
206	Bellingham, WA	182,606
258	Bend, OR	136,218
60	Bethesda-Frederick, MD M.D.	1,148,021
246	Billings, MT	145,842
169	Binghamton, NY	249,588
NA	Birmingham-Hoover, AL**	NA
315	Bismarck, ND	98,280
234	Blacksburg, VA	153,046
213	Bloomington, IN	178,566
NA	Boise City-Nampa, ID**	NA
298	Bowling Green, KY	109,812
173	Bremerton-Silverdale, WA	242,375
133	Brownsville-Harlingen, TX	377,941
312	Brunswick, GA	100,737
58	Buffalo-Niagara Falls, NY	1,156,031
252	Burlington, NC	140,764
55	Camden, NJ M.D.	1,240,483
100	Cape Coral-Fort Myers, FL	525,904
330	Carson City, NV	57,893
328	Casper, WY	69,387
171	Cedar Rapids, IA	245,529
93	Charleston-North Charleston, SC	591,358
149	Charleston, WV	308,017
49	Charlotte-Gastonia, NC-SC	1,498,697
205	Charlottesville, VA	183,511
106	Chattanooga, TN-GA	497,125
322	Cheyenne, WY	85,764
NA	Chicago, IL**	NA
188	Chico, CA	214,382
34	Cincinnati-Middletown, OH-KY-IN	2,061,977
174	Clarksville, TN-KY	241,081
NA	Cleveland-Elyria-Mentor, OH**	NA
NA	Cleveland, TN**	NA
275	Coeur d'Alene, ID	125,497
200	College Station-Bryan, TX	192,585
94	Colorado Springs, CO	584,237
236	Columbia, MO	152,508
81	Columbia, SC	688,684
158	Columbus, GA-AL	286,160
327	Columbus, IN	73,390
45	Columbus, OH	1,694,651
120	Corpus Christi, TX	416,481
310	Cumberland, MD-WV	101,601
6	Dallas (greater), TX	5,794,020
15	Dallas-Plano-Irving, TX M.D.	3,875,593
NA	Dalton, GA**	NA
299	Danville, VA	109,683
108	Daytona Beach, FL	489,475
70	Dayton, OH	846,018
243	Decatur, AL	148,529
30	Denver-Aurora, CO	2,362,441
103	Des Moines-West Des Moines, IA	513,940
11	Detroit (greater), MI	4,496,826
36	Detroit-Livonia-Dearborn, MI M.D.	2,017,845
259	Dothan, AL	136,070
251	Dover, DE	140,951
320	Dubuque, IA	91,366
NA	Duluth, MN-WI**	NA
111	Durham, NC	458,714
232	Eau Claire, WI	153,906
31	Edison, NJ M.D.	2,296,411
233	El Centro, CA	153,460
79	El Paso, TX	724,856
297	Elizabethtown, KY	110,277
199	Elkhart-Goshen, IN	192,826
321	Elmira, NY	90,113
160	Erie, PA	282,886
144	Eugene-Springfield, OR	335,881
141	Evansville, IN-KY	350,443
331	Fairbanks, AK	32,497
208	Fargo, ND-MN	182,319
274	Farmington, NM	125,803
127	Fayetteville, AR-MO	394,610
139	Fayetteville, NC	353,533
270	Flagstaff, AZ	126,931
115	Flint, MI	444,309
193	Florence, SC	199,935
314	Fond du Lac, WI	99,150
162	Fort Collins-Loveland, CO	272,598
41	Fort Lauderdale, FL M.D.	1,794,506
159	Fort Smith, AR-OK	284,640
204	Fort Walton Beach, FL	185,556
122	Fort Wayne, IN	404,303
38	Fort Worth-Arlington, TX M.D.	1,918,427
68	Fresno, CA	872,528
307	Gadsden, AL	103,880
172	Gainesville, FL	244,512
221	Gainesville, GA	165,357
NA	Glens Falls, NY**	NA
283	Goldsboro, NC	116,145
318	Grand Forks, ND-MN	96,477
265	Grand Junction, CO	129,017
75	Grand Rapids-Wyoming, MI	768,164
325	Great Falls, MT	80,608
185	Greeley, CO	222,296
154	Green Bay, WI	296,931
83	Greensboro-High Point, NC	678,641
222	Greenville, NC	163,480
92	Greenville, SC	591,797
170	Hagerstown-Martinsburg, MD-WV	245,946
249	Hanford-Corcoran, CA	143,508
102	Harrisburg-Carlisle, PA	520,307
291	Harrisonburg, VA	112,890
63	Hartford, CT	1,002,799
NA	Hattiesburg, MS**	NA
167	Holland-Grand Haven, MI	252,557
66	Honolulu, HI	908,521
319	Hot Springs, AR	93,029
194	Houma, LA	199,025
8	Houston, TX	5,265,657
157	Huntington-Ashland, WV-KY-OH	287,756
137	Huntsville, AL	364,669
289	Idaho Falls, ID	113,276
47	Indianapolis, IN	1,630,558
257	Iowa City, IA	137,950
NA	Ithaca, NY**	NA
54	Jacksonville, FL	1,253,042
NA	Jacksonville, NC**	NA
224	Jackson, MI	163,106
101	Jackson, MS	520,502
294	Jackson, TN	111,328
230	Janesville, WI	157,284
248	Jefferson City, MO	143,579
202	Johnson City, TN	189,289
NA	Johnstown, PA**	NA
292	Jonesboro, AR	112,605
220	Joplin, MO	165,539
146	Kalamazoo-Portage, MI	319,525
37	Kansas City, MO-KS	1,936,981
187	Kennewick-Richland-Pasco, WA	218,379
140	Killeen-Temple-Fort Hood, TX	351,810
150	Kingsport, TN-VA	304,191
210	Kingston, NY	182,039
90	Knoxville, TN	653,969
309	Kokomo, IN	101,779
264	La Crosse, WI-MN	129,304
207	Lafayette, IN	182,513
198	Lake Charles, LA	194,981
NA	Lake Havasu City-Kingman, AZ**	NA
96	Lakeland, FL	536,226
109	Lancaster, PA	488,248
112	Lansing-East Lansing, MI	456,300
184	Laredo, TX	223,074
203	Las Cruces, NM	188,549
43	Las Vegas-Paradise, NV	1,707,257

Note: All listings are for Metropolitan Statistical Areas (M.S.A.s) except for those ending with "M.D." Listings with "M.D." are Metropolitan Divisions which are smaller parts of ten large M.S.A.s. See explanatory note at beginning of metropolitan area section on page 23.

RANK	METROPOLITAN AREA	POP
308	Lawrence, KS	103,131
295	Lawton, OK	111,277
276	Lebanon, PA	124,723
302	Lewiston-Auburn, ME	107,367
329	Lewiston, ID-WA	59,909
117	Lexington-Fayette, KY	427,476
304	Lima, OH	106,920
161	Lincoln, NE	280,043
91	Little Rock, AR	642,769
290	Logan, UT-ID	113,266
192	Longview, TX	203,701
316	Longview, WA	97,491
4	Los Angeles County, CA M.D.	10,003,731
2	Los Angeles (greater), CA	13,011,161
56	Louisville, KY-IN	1,208,545
165	Lubbock, TX	261,901
177	Lynchburg, VA	235,893
178	Macon, GA	234,455
255	Madera, CA	139,874
97	Madison, WI	534,388
125	Manchester-Nashua, NH	401,776
267	Mansfield, OH	128,152
84	McAllen-Edinburg-Mission, TX	669,076
196	Medford, OR	195,487
53	Memphis, TN-MS-AR	1,262,520
176	Merced, CA	238,579
7	Miami (greater), FL	5,482,749
28	Miami-Dade County, FL M.D.	2,416,950
296	Michigan City-La Porte, IN	110,360
278	Midland, TX	122,324
48	Milwaukee, WI	1,523,217
NA	Minneapolis-St. Paul, MN-WI**	NA
313	Missoula, MT	99,959
124	Mobile, AL	402,968
105	Modesto, CA	501,664
218	Monroe, LA	171,547
235	Monroe, MI	152,676
138	Montgomery, AL	357,347
288	Morgantown, WV	113,868
263	Morristown, TN	130,365
293	Mount Vernon-Anacortes, WA	112,567
280	Muncie, IN	118,424
217	Muskegon-Norton Shores, MI	174,543
186	Myrtle Beach, SC	220,563
261	Napa, CA	133,218
151	Naples-Marco Island, FL	303,375
51	Nashville-Davidson, TN	1,410,545
21	Nassau-Suffolk, NY M.D.	2,819,162
NA	New Orleans, LA**	NA
1	New York (greater), NY-NJ-PA	18,741,475
3	New York-W. Plains NY-NJ M.D.	11,468,310
32	Newark-Union, NJ-PA M.D.	2,157,592
223	Niles-Benton Harbor, MI	163,258
25	Oakland-Fremont, CA M.D.	2,480,743
153	Ocala, FL	297,898
311	Ocean City, NJ	100,979
272	Odessa, TX	126,536
107	Ogden-Clearfield, UT	493,553
59	Oklahoma City, OK	1,152,229
182	Olympia, WA	227,714
71	Omaha-Council Bluffs, NE-IA	808,810
39	Orlando, FL	1,903,731
229	Oshkosh-Neenah, WI	159,792
72	Oxnard-Thousand Oaks, CA	802,996
98	Palm Bay-Melbourne, FL	531,111
NA	Palm Coast, FL**	NA
226	Panama City-Lynn Haven, FL	161,514
231	Pascagoula, MS	157,249
114	Pensacola, FL	447,002
5	Philadelphia (greater) PA-NJ-DE	5,819,726
14	Philadelphia, PA M.D.	3,889,872
16	Phoenix-Mesa-Scottsdale, AZ	3,841,790
305	Pine Bluff, AR	106,885
29	Pittsburgh, PA	2,406,091
262	Pittsfield, MA	132,119
323	Pocatello, ID	85,293
135	Port St. Lucie, FL	373,006
33	Portland-Vancouver, OR-WA	2,091,269
104	Portland, ME	512,440
86	Poughkeepsie, NY	664,698
195	Prescott, AZ	197,115
118	Provo-Orem, UT	426,264
238	Pueblo, CO	152,252
228	Punta Gorda, FL	160,681
197	Racine, WI	195,146
65	Raleigh-Cary, NC	929,889
281	Rapid City, SD	118,257
130	Reading, PA	392,376
212	Redding, CA	178,997
126	Reno-Sparks, NV	397,671
57	Richmond, VA	1,170,973
17	Riverside-San Bernardino, CA	3,818,268
155	Roanoke, VA	295,336
215	Rochester, MN	175,945
62	Rochester, NY	1,042,990
244	Rocky Mount, NC	147,841
317	Rome, GA	96,598
35	Sacramento, CA	2,030,094
190	Saginaw, MI	209,232
134	Salem, OR	374,181
119	Salinas, CA	417,382
284	Salisbury, MD	115,518
61	Salt Lake City, UT	1,053,174
303	San Angelo, TX	107,246
40	San Antonio, TX	1,884,548
20	San Diego, CA	2,951,182
12	San Francisco (greater), CA	4,181,453
44	San Francisco-S. Mateo, CA M.D.	1,700,710
42	San Jose, CA	1,752,994
166	San Luis Obispo, CA	256,256
326	Sandusky, OH	79,027
19	Santa Ana-Anaheim, CA M.D.	3,007,430
121	Santa Barbara-Santa Maria, CA	404,519
168	Santa Cruz-Watsonville, CA	252,297
254	Santa Fe, NM	140,534
110	Santa Rosa-Petaluma, CA	471,561
85	Sarasota-Bradenton-Venice, FL	666,576
147	Savannah, GA	319,272
95	Scranton--Wilkes-Barre, PA	552,568
18	Seattle (greater), WA	3,209,692
27	Seattle-Bellevue, WA M.D.	2,454,192
271	Sebastian-Vero Beach, FL	126,916
286	Sheboygan, WI	114,520
282	Sherman-Denison, TX	117,840
132	Shreveport-Bossier City, LA	382,482
247	Sioux City, IA-NE-SD	143,872
191	Sioux Falls, SD	204,654
145	South Bend-Mishawaka, IN-MI	319,704
164	Spartanburg, SC	267,819
116	Spokane, WA	441,541
82	Springfield, MA	678,672
128	Springfield, MO	394,091
250	Springfield, OH	142,676
253	State College, PA	140,740
89	Stockton, CA	654,183
211	St. Cloud, MN	180,272
277	St. Joseph, MO-KS	123,143
22	St. Louis, MO-IL	2,784,658
301	Sumter, SC	107,382
88	Syracuse, NY	654,925
76	Tacoma, WA M.D.	755,500
143	Tallahassee, FL	339,142
24	Tampa-St Petersburg, FL	2,646,385
260	Texarkana, TX-Texarkana, AR	134,610
87	Toledo, OH	658,525
180	Topeka, KS	228,584
136	Trenton-Ewing, NJ	366,071
64	Tucson, AZ	937,925
67	Tulsa, OK	887,903
NA	Tuscaloosa, AL**	NA
201	Tyler, TX	189,480
152	Utica-Rome, NY	299,248
273	Valdosta, GA	126,064
NA	Vallejo-Fairfield, CA**	NA
285	Victoria, TX	115,316
239	Vineland, NJ	151,514
46	Virginia Beach-Norfolk, VA-NC	1,668,025
123	Visalia-Porterville, CA	404,168
183	Waco, TX	226,098
269	Warner Robins, GA	127,162
26	Warren-Farmington Hills, MI M.D.	2,478,981
9	Washington (greater) DC-VA-MD	5,187,049
13	Washington, DC-VA-MD-WV M.D.	4,039,028
225	Waterloo-Cedar Falls, IA	162,564
266	Wausau, WI	128,363
306	Wenatchee, WA	104,814
52	West Palm Beach, FL M.D.	1,271,293
241	Wheeling, WV-OH	149,595
240	Wichita Falls, TX	150,258
NA	Wichita, KS**	NA
279	Williamsport, PA	118,765
80	Wilmington, DE-MD-NJ M.D.	689,371
148	Wilmington, NC	308,288
287	Winchester, VA-WV	114,269
113	Winston-Salem, NC	448,950
74	Worcester, MA	777,330
179	Yakima, WA	232,195
237	Yuba City, CA	152,396
209	Yuma, AZ	182,075

Source: Federal Bureau of Investigation
"Crime in the United States 2005"
**Estimates as of July 2005 based on U.S. Bureau of the Census figures.*
***Not available (comparable metro area not included in 2005 crime statistics).*

86. Metropolitan Population in 2005 (continued)

National Total = 296,507,061*

RANK	METROPOLITAN AREA	POP
1	New York (greater), NY-NJ-PA	18,741,475
2	Los Angeles (greater), CA	13,011,161
3	New York-W. Plains NY-NJ M.D.	11,468,310
4	Los Angeles County, CA M.D.	10,003,731
5	Philadelphia (greater) PA-NJ-DE	5,819,726
6	Dallas (greater), TX	5,794,020
7	Miami (greater), FL	5,482,749
8	Houston, TX	5,265,657
9	Washington (greater) DC-VA-MD	5,187,049
10	Atlanta, GA	4,837,981
11	Detroit (greater), MI	4,496,826
12	San Francisco (greater), CA	4,181,453
13	Washington, DC-VA-MD-WV M.D.	4,039,028
14	Philadelphia, PA M.D.	3,889,872
15	Dallas-Plano-Irving, TX M.D.	3,875,593
16	Phoenix-Mesa-Scottsdale, AZ	3,841,790
17	Riverside-San Bernardino, CA	3,818,268
18	Seattle (greater), WA	3,209,692
19	Santa Ana-Anaheim, CA M.D.	3,007,430
20	San Diego, CA	2,951,182
21	Nassau-Suffolk, NY M.D.	2,819,162
22	St. Louis, MO-IL	2,784,658
23	Baltimore-Towson, MD	2,659,312
24	Tampa-St Petersburg, FL	2,646,385
25	Oakland-Fremont, CA M.D.	2,480,743
26	Warren-Farmington Hills, MI M.D.	2,478,981
27	Seattle-Bellevue, WA M.D.	2,454,192
28	Miami-Dade County, FL M.D.	2,416,950
29	Pittsburgh, PA	2,406,091
30	Denver-Aurora, CO	2,362,441
31	Edison, NJ M.D.	2,296,411
32	Newark-Union, NJ-PA M.D.	2,157,592
33	Portland-Vancouver, OR-WA	2,091,269
34	Cincinnati-Middletown, OH-KY-IN	2,061,977
35	Sacramento, CA	2,030,094
36	Detroit-Livonia-Dearborn, MI M.D.	2,017,845
37	Kansas City, MO-KS	1,936,981
38	Fort Worth-Arlington, TX M.D.	1,918,427
39	Orlando, FL	1,903,731
40	San Antonio, TX	1,884,548
41	Fort Lauderdale, FL M.D.	1,794,506
42	San Jose, CA	1,752,994
43	Las Vegas-Paradise, NV	1,707,257
44	San Francisco-S. Mateo, CA M.D.	1,700,710
45	Columbus, OH	1,694,651
46	Virginia Beach-Norfolk, VA-NC	1,668,025
47	Indianapolis, IN	1,630,558
48	Milwaukee, WI	1,523,217
49	Charlotte-Gastonia, NC-SC	1,498,697
50	Austin-Round Rock, TX	1,435,502
51	Nashville-Davidson, TN	1,410,545
52	West Palm Beach, FL M.D.	1,271,293
53	Memphis, TN-MS-AR	1,262,520
54	Jacksonville, FL	1,253,042
55	Camden, NJ M.D.	1,240,483
56	Louisville, KY-IN	1,208,545
57	Richmond, VA	1,170,973
58	Buffalo-Niagara Falls, NY	1,156,031
59	Oklahoma City, OK	1,152,229
60	Bethesda-Frederick, MD M.D.	1,148,021
61	Salt Lake City, UT	1,053,174
62	Rochester, NY	1,042,990
63	Hartford, CT	1,002,799
64	Tucson, AZ	937,925
65	Raleigh-Cary, NC	929,889
66	Honolulu, HI	908,521
67	Tulsa, OK	887,903
68	Fresno, CA	872,528
69	Albany-Schenectady-Troy, NY	846,480
70	Dayton, OH	846,018
71	Omaha-Council Bluffs, NE-IA	808,810
72	Oxnard-Thousand Oaks, CA	802,996
73	Albuquerque, NM	791,750
74	Worcester, MA	777,330
75	Grand Rapids-Wyoming, MI	768,164
76	Tacoma, WA M.D.	755,500
77	Bakersfield, CA	739,726
78	Baton Rouge, LA	729,999
79	El Paso, TX	724,856
80	Wilmington, DE-MD-NJ M.D.	689,371
81	Columbia, SC	688,684
82	Springfield, MA	678,672
83	Greensboro-High Point, NC	678,641
84	McAllen-Edinburg-Mission, TX	669,076
85	Sarasota-Bradenton-Venice, FL	666,576
86	Poughkeepsie, NY	664,698
87	Toledo, OH	658,525
88	Syracuse, NY	654,925
89	Stockton, CA	654,183
90	Knoxville, TN	653,969
91	Little Rock, AR	642,769
92	Greenville, SC	591,797
93	Charleston-North Charleston, SC	591,358
94	Colorado Springs, CO	584,237
95	Scranton--Wilkes-Barre, PA	552,568
96	Lakeland, FL	536,226
97	Madison, WI	534,388
98	Palm Bay-Melbourne, FL	531,111
99	Augusta, GA-SC	527,083
100	Cape Coral-Fort Myers, FL	525,904
101	Jackson, MS	520,502
102	Harrisburg-Carlisle, PA	520,307
103	Des Moines-West Des Moines, IA	513,940
104	Portland, ME	512,440
105	Modesto, CA	501,664
106	Chattanooga, TN-GA	497,125
107	Ogden-Clearfield, UT	493,553
108	Daytona Beach, FL	489,475
109	Lancaster, PA	488,248
110	Santa Rosa-Petaluma, CA	471,561
111	Durham, NC	458,714
112	Lansing-East Lansing, MI	456,300
113	Winston-Salem, NC	448,950
114	Pensacola, FL	447,002
115	Flint, MI	444,309
116	Spokane, WA	441,541
117	Lexington-Fayette, KY	427,476
118	Provo-Orem, UT	426,264
119	Salinas, CA	417,382
120	Corpus Christi, TX	416,481
121	Santa Barbara-Santa Maria, CA	404,519
122	Fort Wayne, IN	404,303
123	Visalia-Porterville, CA	404,168
124	Mobile, AL	402,968
125	Manchester-Nashua, NH	401,776
126	Reno-Sparks, NV	397,671
127	Fayetteville, AR-MO	394,610
128	Springfield, MO	394,091
129	Asheville, NC	393,687
130	Reading, PA	392,376
131	Beaumont-Port Arthur, TX	389,750
132	Shreveport-Bossier City, LA	382,482
133	Brownsville-Harlingen, TX	377,941
134	Salem, OR	374,181
135	Port St. Lucie, FL	373,006
136	Trenton-Ewing, NJ	366,071
137	Huntsville, AL	364,669
138	Montgomery, AL	357,347
139	Fayetteville, NC	353,533
140	Killeen-Temple-Fort Hood, TX	351,810
141	Evansville, IN-KY	350,443
142	Ann Arbor, MI	339,467
143	Tallahassee, FL	339,142
144	Eugene-Springfield, OR	335,881
145	South Bend-Mishawaka, IN-MI	319,704
146	Kalamazoo-Portage, MI	319,525
147	Savannah, GA	319,272
148	Wilmington, NC	308,288
149	Charleston, WV	308,017
150	Kingsport, TN-VA	304,191
151	Naples-Marco Island, FL	303,375
152	Utica-Rome, NY	299,248
153	Ocala, FL	297,898
154	Green Bay, WI	296,931
155	Roanoke, VA	295,336
156	Anchorage, AK	291,624
157	Huntington-Ashland, WV-KY-OH	287,756
158	Columbus, GA-AL	286,160
159	Fort Smith, AR-OK	284,640
160	Erie, PA	282,886
161	Lincoln, NE	280,043
162	Fort Collins-Loveland, CO	272,598
163	Atlantic City, NJ	269,281
164	Spartanburg, SC	267,819
165	Lubbock, TX	261,901
166	San Luis Obispo, CA	256,256
167	Holland-Grand Haven, MI	252,557
168	Santa Cruz-Watsonville, CA	252,297
169	Binghamton, NY	249,588
170	Hagerstown-Martinsburg, MD-WV	245,946
171	Cedar Rapids, IA	245,529

Note: All listings are for Metropolitan Statistical Areas (M.S.A.s) except for those ending with "M.D." Listings with "M.D." are Metropolitan Divisions which are smaller parts of ten large M.S.A.s. See explanatory note at beginning of metropolitan area section on page 23.

RANK	METROPOLITAN AREA	POP
172	Gainesville, FL	244,512
173	Bremerton-Silverdale, WA	242,375
174	Clarksville, TN-KY	241,081
175	Amarillo, TX	239,998
176	Merced, CA	238,579
177	Lynchburg, VA	235,893
178	Macon, GA	234,455
179	Yakima, WA	232,195
180	Topeka, KS	228,584
181	Barnstable Town, MA	228,050
182	Olympia, WA	227,714
183	Waco, TX	226,098
184	Laredo, TX	223,074
185	Greeley, CO	222,296
186	Myrtle Beach, SC	220,563
187	Kennewick-Richland-Pasco, WA	218,379
188	Chico, CA	214,382
189	Appleton, WI	214,153
190	Saginaw, MI	209,232
191	Sioux Falls, SD	204,654
192	Longview, TX	203,701
193	Florence, SC	199,935
194	Houma, LA	199,025
195	Prescott, AZ	197,115
196	Medford, OR	195,487
197	Racine, WI	195,146
198	Lake Charles, LA	194,981
199	Elkhart-Goshen, IN	192,826
200	College Station-Bryan, TX	192,585
201	Tyler, TX	189,480
202	Johnson City, TN	189,289
203	Las Cruces, NM	188,549
204	Fort Walton Beach, FL	185,556
205	Charlottesville, VA	183,511
206	Bellingham, WA	182,606
207	Lafayette, IN	182,513
208	Fargo, ND-MN	182,319
209	Yuma, AZ	182,075
210	Kingston, NY	182,039
211	St. Cloud, MN	180,272
212	Redding, CA	178,997
213	Bloomington, IN	178,566
214	Athens-Clarke County, GA	178,545
215	Rochester, MN	175,945
216	Anderson, SC	175,907
217	Muskegon-Norton Shores, MI	174,543
218	Monroe, LA	171,547
219	Albany, GA	167,284
220	Joplin, MO	165,539
221	Gainesville, GA	165,357
222	Greenville, NC	163,480
223	Niles-Benton Harbor, MI	163,258
224	Jackson, MI	163,106
225	Waterloo-Cedar Falls, IA	162,564
226	Panama City-Lynn Haven, FL	161,514
227	Abilene, TX	161,123
228	Punta Gorda, FL	160,681
229	Oshkosh-Neenah, WI	159,792
230	Janesville, WI	157,284
231	Pascagoula, MS	157,249

RANK	METROPOLITAN AREA	POP
232	Eau Claire, WI	153,906
233	El Centro, CA	153,460
234	Blacksburg, VA	153,046
235	Monroe, MI	152,676
236	Columbia, MO	152,508
237	Yuba City, CA	152,396
238	Pueblo, CO	152,252
239	Vineland, NJ	151,514
240	Wichita Falls, TX	150,258
241	Wheeling, WV-OH	149,595
242	Bangor, ME	148,674
243	Decatur, AL	148,529
244	Rocky Mount, NC	147,841
245	Alexandria, LA	147,408
246	Billings, MT	145,842
247	Sioux City, IA-NE-SD	143,872
248	Jefferson City, MO	143,579
249	Hanford-Corcoran, CA	143,508
250	Springfield, OH	142,676
251	Dover, DE	140,951
252	Burlington, NC	140,764
253	State College, PA	140,740
254	Santa Fe, NM	140,534
255	Madera, CA	139,874
256	Battle Creek, MI	139,180
257	Iowa City, IA	137,950
258	Bend, OR	136,218
259	Dothan, AL	136,070
260	Texarkana, TX-Texarkana, AR	134,610
261	Napa, CA	133,218
262	Pittsfield, MA	132,119
263	Morristown, TN	130,365
264	La Crosse, WI-MN	129,304
265	Grand Junction, CO	129,017
266	Wausau, WI	128,363
267	Mansfield, OH	128,152
268	Altoona, PA	127,708
269	Warner Robins, GA	127,162
270	Flagstaff, AZ	126,931
271	Sebastian-Vero Beach, FL	126,916
272	Odessa, TX	126,536
273	Valdosta, GA	126,064
274	Farmington, NM	125,803
275	Coeur d'Alene, ID	125,497
276	Lebanon, PA	124,723
277	St. Joseph, MO-KS	123,143
278	Midland, TX	122,324
279	Williamsport, PA	118,765
280	Muncie, IN	118,424
281	Rapid City, SD	118,257
282	Sherman-Denison, TX	117,840
283	Goldsboro, NC	116,145
284	Salisbury, MD	115,518
285	Victoria, TX	115,316
286	Sheboygan, WI	114,520
287	Winchester, VA-WV	114,269
288	Morgantown, WV	113,868
289	Idaho Falls, ID	113,276
290	Logan, UT-ID	113,266
291	Harrisonburg, VA	112,890

RANK	METROPOLITAN AREA	POP
292	Jonesboro, AR	112,605
293	Mount Vernon-Anacortes, WA	112,567
294	Jackson, TN	111,328
295	Lawton, OK	111,277
296	Michigan City-La Porte, IN	110,360
297	Elizabethtown, KY	110,277
298	Bowling Green, KY	109,812
299	Danville, VA	109,683
300	Bay City, MI	109,569
301	Sumter, SC	107,382
302	Lewiston-Auburn, ME	107,367
303	San Angelo, TX	107,246
304	Lima, OH	106,920
305	Pine Bluff, AR	106,885
306	Wenatchee, WA	104,814
307	Gadsden, AL	103,880
308	Lawrence, KS	103,131
309	Kokomo, IN	101,779
310	Cumberland, MD-WV	101,601
311	Ocean City, NJ	100,979
312	Brunswick, GA	100,737
313	Missoula, MT	99,959
314	Fond du Lac, WI	99,150
315	Bismarck, ND	98,280
316	Longview, WA	97,491
317	Rome, GA	96,598
318	Grand Forks, ND-MN	96,477
319	Hot Springs, AR	93,029
320	Dubuque, IA	91,366
321	Elmira, NY	90,113
322	Cheyenne, WY	85,764
323	Pocatello, ID	85,293
324	Ames, IA	80,727
325	Great Falls, MT	80,608
326	Sandusky, OH	79,027
327	Columbus, IN	73,390
328	Casper, WY	69,387
329	Lewiston, ID-WA	59,909
330	Carson City, NV	57,893
331	Fairbanks, AK	32,497
NA	Birmingham-Hoover, AL**	NA
NA	Boise City-Nampa, ID**	NA
NA	Chicago, IL**	NA
NA	Cleveland-Elyria-Mentor, OH**	NA
NA	Cleveland, TN**	NA
NA	Dalton, GA**	NA
NA	Duluth, MN-WI**	NA
NA	Glens Falls, NY**	NA
NA	Hattiesburg, MS**	NA
NA	Ithaca, NY**	NA
NA	Jacksonville, NC**	NA
NA	Johnstown, PA**	NA
NA	Lake Havasu City-Kingman, AZ**	NA
NA	Minneapolis-St. Paul, MN-WI**	NA
NA	New Orleans, LA**	NA
NA	Palm Coast, FL**	NA
NA	Tuscaloosa, AL**	NA
NA	Vallejo-Fairfield, CA**	NA
NA	Wichita, KS**	NA

Source: Federal Bureau of Investigation "Crime in the United States 2005"

**Estimates as of July 2005 based on U.S. Bureau of the Census figures.*

***Not available (comparable metro area not included in 2005 crime statistics).*

87. Metropolitan Population in 2002

National Total = 287,973,924*

RANK	METROPOLITAN AREA	POP
175	Abilene, TX	132,188
NA	Albany-Schenectady-Troy, NY**	NA
186	Albany, GA	126,341
50	Albuquerque, NM	726,846
185	Alexandria, LA	126,723
179	Altoona, PA	129,712
125	Amarillo, TX	227,555
NA	Ames, IA**	NA
109	Anchorage, AK	267,280
NA	Anderson, SC**	NA
NA	Ann Arbor, MI**	NA
NA	Appleton, WI**	NA
121	Asheville, NC	233,567
156	Athens-Clarke County, GA	160,451
7	Atlanta, GA	4,299,988
NA	Atlantic City, NJ**	NA
70	Augusta, GA-SC	495,578
35	Austin-Round Rock, TX	1,305,388
55	Bakersfield, CA	685,953
14	Baltimore-Towson, MD	2,630,914
NA	Bangor, ME**	NA
NA	Barnstable Town, MA**	NA
59	Baton Rouge, LA	604,739
NA	Battle Creek, MI**	NA
NA	Bay City, MI**	NA
85	Beaumont-Port Arthur, TX	402,229
150	Bellingham, WA	171,763
NA	Bend, OR**	NA
NA	Bethesda-Frederick, MD M.D.**	NA
177	Billings, MT	130,387
114	Binghamton, NY	254,727
46	Birmingham-Hoover, AL	929,271
210	Bismarck, ND	93,525
NA	Blacksburg, VA**	NA
189	Bloomington, IN	122,121
78	Boise City-Nampa, ID	448,110
NA	Bowling Green, KY**	NA
120	Bremerton-Silverdale, WA	238,852
94	Brownsville-Harlingen, TX	350,147
NA	Brunswick, GA**	NA
38	Buffalo-Niagara Falls, NY	1,181,277
NA	Burlington, NC**	NA
NA	Camden, NJ M.D.**	NA
75	Cape Coral-Fort Myers, FL	461,047
NA	Carson City, NV**	NA
219	Casper, WY	67,196
138	Cedar Rapids, IA	192,385
63	Charleston-North Charleston, SC	562,057
117	Charleston, WV	250,758
NA	Charlotte-Gastonia, NC-SC**	NA
NA	Charlottesville, VA**	NA
71	Chattanooga, TN-GA	477,446
216	Cheyenne, WY	82,418
NA	Chicago, IL**	NA
131	Chico, CA	210,636
31	Cincinnati-Middletown, OH-KY-IN	1,659,096
132	Clarksville, TN-KY	210,505
NA	Cleveland-Elyria-Mentor, OH**	NA
NA	Cleveland, TN**	NA
NA	Coeur d'Alene, ID**	NA
NA	College Station-Bryan, TX**	NA
66	Colorado Springs, CO	541,600
172	Columbia, MO	137,327
65	Columbia, SC	549,421
105	Columbus, GA-AL	285,336
NA	Columbus, IN**	NA
33	Columbus, OH	1,549,398
86	Corpus Christi, TX	397,732
204	Cumberland, MD-WV	104,197
NA	Dallas (greater), TX**	NA
8	Dallas-Plano-Irving, TX M.D.	3,675,809
NA	Dalton, GA**	NA
197	Danville, VA	113,502
67	Daytona Beach, FL	515,725
NA	Dayton, OH**	NA
168	Decatur, AL	147,160
20	Denver-Aurora, CO	2,232,454
76	Des Moines-West Des Moines, IA	457,650
5	Detroit (greater), MI	4,491,605
NA	Detroit-Livonia-Dearborn, MI M.D.*	NA
NA	Dothan, AL**	NA
176	Dover, DE	130,543
211	Dubuque, IA	89,461
118	Duluth, MN-WI	248,526
NA	Durham, NC**	NA
163	Eau Claire, WI	150,481
NA	Edison, NJ M.D.**	NA
NA	El Centro, CA**	NA
53	El Paso, TX	709,871
NA	Elizabethtown, KY**	NA
143	Elkhart-Goshen, IN	185,154
NA	Elmira, NY**	NA
106	Erie, PA	282,078
98	Eugene-Springfield, OR	332,409
NA	Evansville, IN-KY**	NA
NA	Fairbanks, AK**	NA
148	Fargo, ND-MN	173,858
NA	Farmington, NM**	NA
NA	Fayetteville, AR-MO**	NA
101	Fayetteville, NC	313,156
178	Flagstaff, AZ	129,978
80	Flint, MI	441,056
181	Florence, SC	128,744
NA	Fond du Lac, WI**	NA
111	Fort Collins-Loveland, CO	263,497
27	Fort Lauderdale, FL M.D.	1,697,228
133	Fort Smith, AR-OK	210,086
146	Fort Walton Beach, FL	178,294
NA	Fort Wayne, IN**	NA
24	Fort Worth-Arlington, TX M.D.	1,778,405
45	Fresno, CA	956,408
203	Gadsden, AL	104,375
124	Gainesville, FL	227,920
NA	Gainesville, GA**	NA
187	Glens Falls, NY	125,531
193	Goldsboro, NC	117,143
209	Grand Forks, ND-MN	97,284
190	Grand Junction, CO	121,803
NA	Grand Rapids-Wyoming, MI**	NA
217	Great Falls, MT	81,004
140	Greeley, CO	189,571
122	Green Bay, WI	230,055
NA	Greensboro-High Point, NC**	NA
171	Greenville, NC	138,300
NA	Greenville, SC**	NA
NA	Hagerstown-Martinsburg, MD-WV*	NA
NA	Hanford-Corcoran, CA**	NA
NA	Harrisburg-Carlisle, PA**	NA
NA	Harrisonburg, VA**	NA
44	Hartford, CT	992,269
198	Hattiesburg, MS	112,739
NA	Holland-Grand Haven, MI**	NA
47	Honolulu, HI	900,433
NA	Hot Springs, AR**	NA
137	Houma, LA	195,072
6	Houston, TX	4,363,586
NA	Huntington-Ashland, WV-KY-OH**	NA
95	Huntsville, AL	345,410
NA	Idaho Falls, ID**	NA
NA	Indianapolis, IN**	NA
199	Iowa City, IA	111,402
NA	Ithaca, NY**	NA
39	Jacksonville, FL	1,150,811
159	Jacksonville, NC	155,414
157	Jackson, MI	160,207
79	Jackson, MS	445,012
200	Jackson, TN	109,415
162	Janesville, WI	154,508
NA	Jefferson City, MO**	NA
NA	Johnson City, TN**	NA
NA	Johnstown, PA**	NA
215	Jonesboro, AR	83,275
158	Joplin, MO	159,498
NA	Kalamazoo-Portage, MI**	NA
NA	Kansas City, MO-KS**	NA
136	Kennewick-Richland-Pasco, WA	197,514
100	Killeen-Temple-Fort Hood, TX	326,881
NA	Kingsport, TN-VA**	NA
NA	Kingston, NY**	NA
54	Knoxville, TN	700,296
206	Kokomo, IN	102,853
180	La Crosse, WI-MN	128,788
142	Lafayette, IN	185,184
144	Lake Charles, LA	184,138
NA	Lake Havasu City-Kingman, AZ**	NA
68	Lakeland, FL	506,050
73	Lancaster, PA	472,729
77	Lansing-East Lansing, MI	452,774
134	Laredo, TX	201,712
NA	Las Cruces, NM**	NA
28	Las Vegas-Paradise, NV	1,696,624

Note: All listings are for Metropolitan Statistical Areas (M.S.A.s) except for those ending with "M.D." Listings with "M.D." are Metropolitan Divisions which are smaller parts of ten large M.S.A.s. See explanatory note at beginning of metropolitan area section on page 23.

RANK	METROPOLITAN AREA	POP
208	Lawrence, KS	100,984
195	Lawton, OK	115,396
NA	Lebanon, PA**	NA
207	Lewiston-Auburn, ME	102,108
NA	Lewiston, ID-WA**	NA
NA	Lexington-Fayette, KY**	NA
NA	Lima, OH**	NA
116	Lincoln, NE	252,912
61	Little Rock, AR	591,859
NA	Logan, UT-ID**	NA
129	Longview, TX	218,072
NA	Longview, WA**	NA
1	Los Angeles County, CA M.D.	9,869,056
NA	Los Angeles (greater), CA**	NA
42	Louisville, KY-IN	1,038,641
115	Lubbock, TX	253,427
127	Lynchburg, VA	221,438
NA	Macon, GA**	NA
NA	Madera, CA**	NA
81	Madison, WI	432,691
NA	Manchester-Nashua, NH**	NA
147	Mansfield, OH	176,873
60	McAllen-Edinburg-Mission, TX	594,808
141	Medford, OR	186,573
NA	Memphis, TN-MS-AR**	NA
128	Merced, CA	218,289
NA	Miami (greater), FL**	NA
19	Miami-Dade County, FL M.D.	2,356,396
NA	Michigan City-La Porte, IN**	NA
NA	Midland, TX**	NA
NA	Milwaukee, WI**	NA
11	Minneapolis-St. Paul, MN-WI	3,028,704
NA	Missoula, MT**	NA
NA	Mobile, AL**	NA
74	Modesto, CA	463,419
NA	Monroe, LA**	NA
NA	Monroe, MI**	NA
96	Montgomery, AL	336,006
NA	Morgantown, WV**	NA
NA	Morristown, TN**	NA
NA	Mount Vernon-Anacortes, WA**	NA
192	Muncie, IN	120,304
NA	Muskegon-Norton Shores, MI**	NA
135	Myrtle Beach, SC	201,293
NA	Napa, CA**	NA
112	Naples-Marco Island, FL	262,871
36	Nashville-Davidson, TN	1,254,684
NA	Nassau-Suffolk, NY M.D.**	NA
34	New Orleans, LA	1,341,821
NA	New York (greater), NY-NJ-PA**	NA
2	New York-W. Plains NY-NJ M.D.	9,403,110
21	Newark-Union, NJ-PA M.D.	2,075,500
NA	Niles-Benton Harbor, MI**	NA
17	Oakland-Fremont, CA M.D.	2,480,456
107	Ocala, FL	270,754
NA	Ocean City, NJ**	NA
NA	Odessa, TX**	NA
NA	Ogden-Clearfield, UT**	NA
41	Oklahoma City, OK	1,096,867
130	Olympia, WA	213,507
51	Omaha-Council Bluffs, NE-IA	723,899
26	Orlando, FL	1,719,756
NA	Oshkosh-Neenah, WI**	NA
NA	Oxnard-Thousand Oaks, CA**	NA
69	Palm Bay-Melbourne, FL	498,005
NA	Palm Coast, FL**	NA
161	Panama City-Lynn Haven, FL	154,994
NA	Pascagoula, MS**	NA
82	Pensacola, FL	430,998
3	Philadelphia (greater) PA-NJ-DE	5,144,034
NA	Philadelphia, PA M.D.**	NA
9	Phoenix-Mesa-Scottsdale, AZ	3,458,385
214	Pine Bluff, AR	85,434
18	Pittsburgh, PA	2,369,073
NA	Pittsfield, MA**	NA
218	Pocatello, ID	78,320
97	Port St. Lucie, FL	334,032
22	Portland-Vancouver, OR-WA	1,974,272
NA	Portland, ME**	NA
NA	Poughkeepsie, NY**	NA
NA	Prescott, AZ**	NA
88	Provo-Orem, UT	382,248
165	Pueblo, CO	148,224
166	Punta Gorda, FL	148,102
139	Racine, WI	191,560
NA	Raleigh-Cary, NC**	NA
212	Rapid City, SD	89,294
90	Reading, PA	375,282
154	Redding, CA	169,254
91	Reno-Sparks, NV	369,256
43	Richmond, VA	1,026,785
10	Riverside-San Bernardino, CA	3,374,398
NA	Roanoke, VA**	NA
184	Rochester, MN	126,809
40	Rochester, NY	1,108,681
167	Rocky Mount, NC	147,839
NA	Rome, GA**	NA
29	Sacramento, CA	1,688,014
NA	Saginaw, MI**	NA
93	Salem, OR	357,375
84	Salinas, CA	416,522
NA	Salisbury, MD**	NA
NA	Salt Lake City, UT**	NA
201	San Angelo, TX	108,640
30	San Antonio, TX	1,663,258
13	San Diego, CA	2,917,208
NA	San Francisco (greater), CA**	NA
23	San Francisco-S. Mateo, CA M.D.	1,794,784
25	San Jose, CA	1,744,400
113	San Luis Obispo, CA	255,744
NA	Sandusky, OH**	NA
12	Santa Ana-Anaheim, CA M.D.	2,950,856
NA	Santa Barbara-Santa Maria, CA**	NA
110	Santa Cruz-Watsonville, CA	264,993
160	Santa Fe, NM	155,169
72	Santa Rosa-Petaluma, CA	475,463
58	Sarasota-Bradenton-Venice, FL	616,934
102	Savannah, GA	306,380
56	Scranton--Wilkes-Barre, PA	627,525
NA	Seattle (greater), WA**	NA
16	Seattle-Bellevue, WA M.D.	2,486,255
NA	Sebastian-Vero Beach, FL**	NA
196	Sheboygan, WI	114,274
194	Sherman-Denison, TX	115,518
87	Shreveport-Bossier City, LA	393,503
188	Sioux City, IA-NE-SD	124,712
149	Sioux Falls, SD	173,837
108	South Bend-Mishawaka, IN-MI	268,991
NA	Spartanburg, SC**	NA
83	Spokane, WA	430,339
NA	Springfield, MA**	NA
99	Springfield, MO	330,225
NA	Springfield, OH**	NA
173	State College, PA	136,356
62	Stockton, CA	584,304
152	St. Cloud, MN	170,803
205	St. Joseph, MO-KS	103,907
NA	St. Louis, MO-IL**	NA
202	Sumter, SC	107,128
NA	Syracuse, NY**	NA
52	Tacoma, WA M.D.	721,613
104	Tallahassee, FL	297,549
15	Tampa-St Petersburg, FL	2,505,551
174	Texarkana, TX-Texarkana, AR	134,279
57	Toledo, OH	621,914
151	Topeka, KS	171,606
92	Trenton-Ewing, NJ	358,096
48	Tucson, AZ	897,329
49	Tulsa, OK	813,257
155	Tuscaloosa, AL	166,336
145	Tyler, TX	182,482
103	Utica-Rome, NY	302,757
NA	Valdosta, GA**	NA
NA	Vallejo-Fairfield, CA**	NA
213	Victoria, TX	87,831
164	Vineland, NJ	149,500
32	Virginia Beach-Norfolk, VA-NC	1,617,279
89	Visalia-Porterville, CA	381,542
126	Waco, TX	223,020
NA	Warner Robins, GA**	NA
NA	Warren-Farmington Hills, MI M.D.*	NA
4	Washington (greater) DC-VA-MD	5,050,449
NA	Washington, DC-VA-MD-WV M.D.*	NA
182	Waterloo-Cedar Falls, IA	128,469
183	Wausau, WI	127,653
NA	Wenatchee, WA**	NA
37	West Palm Beach, FL M.D.	1,182,905
NA	Wheeling, WV-OH**	NA
169	Wichita Falls, TX	146,772
64	Wichita, KS	550,790
191	Williamsport, PA	120,573
NA	Wilmington, DE-MD-NJ M.D.**	NA
119	Wilmington, NC	241,305
NA	Winchester, VA-WV**	NA
NA	Winston-Salem, NC**	NA
NA	Worcester, MA**	NA
123	Yakima, WA	229,185
170	Yuba City, CA	144,261
153	Yuma, AZ	170,189

Source: Federal Bureau of Investigation
"Crime in the United States 2002"
**Estimates as of July 2002 based on U.S. Bureau of the Census figures.*
***Not available (comparable metro area not included in 2002 crime statistics).*

87. Metropolitan Population in 2002 (continued)

National Total = 287,973,924*

RANK	METROPOLITAN AREA	POP	RANK	METROPOLITAN AREA	POP	RANK	METROPOLITAN AREA	POP
1	Los Angeles County, CA M.D.	9,869,056	58	Sarasota-Bradenton-Venice, FL	616,934	115	Lubbock, TX	253,427
2	New York-W. Plains NY-NJ M.D.	9,403,110	59	Baton Rouge, LA	604,739	116	Lincoln, NE	252,912
3	Philadelphia (greater) PA-NJ-DE	5,144,034	60	McAllen-Edinburg-Mission, TX	594,808	117	Charleston, WV	250,758
4	Washington (greater) DC-VA-MD	5,050,449	61	Little Rock, AR	591,859	118	Duluth, MN-WI	248,526
5	Detroit (greater), MI	4,491,605	62	Stockton, CA	584,304	119	Wilmington, NC	241,305
6	Houston, TX	4,363,586	63	Charleston-North Charleston, SC	562,057	120	Bremerton-Silverdale, WA	238,852
7	Atlanta, GA	4,299,988	64	Wichita, KS	550,790	121	Asheville, NC	233,567
8	Dallas-Plano-Irving, TX M.D.	3,675,809	65	Columbia, SC	549,421	122	Green Bay, WI	230,055
9	Phoenix-Mesa-Scottsdale, AZ	3,458,385	66	Colorado Springs, CO	541,600	123	Yakima, WA	229,185
10	Riverside-San Bernardino, CA	3,374,398	67	Daytona Beach, FL	515,725	124	Gainesville, FL	227,920
11	Minneapolis-St. Paul, MN-WI	3,028,704	68	Lakeland, FL	506,050	125	Amarillo, TX	227,555
12	Santa Ana-Anaheim, CA M.D.	2,950,856	69	Palm Bay-Melbourne, FL	498,005	126	Waco, TX	223,020
13	San Diego, CA	2,917,208	70	Augusta, GA-SC	495,578	127	Lynchburg, VA	221,438
14	Baltimore-Towson, MD	2,630,914	71	Chattanooga, TN-GA	477,446	128	Merced, CA	218,289
15	Tampa-St Petersburg, FL	2,505,551	72	Santa Rosa-Petaluma, CA	475,463	129	Longview, TX	218,072
16	Seattle-Bellevue, WA M.D.	2,486,255	73	Lancaster, PA	472,729	130	Olympia, WA	213,507
17	Oakland-Fremont, CA M.D.	2,480,456	74	Modesto, CA	463,419	131	Chico, CA	210,636
18	Pittsburgh, PA	2,369,073	75	Cape Coral-Fort Myers, FL	461,047	132	Clarksville, TN-KY	210,505
19	Miami-Dade County, FL M.D.	2,356,396	76	Des Moines-West Des Moines, IA	457,650	133	Fort Smith, AR-OK	210,086
20	Denver-Aurora, CO	2,232,454	77	Lansing-East Lansing, MI	452,774	134	Laredo, TX	201,712
21	Newark-Union, NJ-PA M.D.	2,075,500	78	Boise City-Nampa, ID	448,110	135	Myrtle Beach, SC	201,293
22	Portland-Vancouver, OR-WA	1,974,272	79	Jackson, MS	445,012	136	Kennewick-Richland-Pasco, WA	197,514
23	San Francisco-S. Mateo, CA M.D.	1,794,784	80	Flint, MI	441,056	137	Houma, LA	195,072
24	Fort Worth-Arlington, TX M.D.	1,778,405	81	Madison, WI	432,691	138	Cedar Rapids, IA	192,385
25	San Jose, CA	1,744,400	82	Pensacola, FL	430,998	139	Racine, WI	191,560
26	Orlando, FL	1,719,756	83	Spokane, WA	430,339	140	Greeley, CO	189,571
27	Fort Lauderdale, FL M.D.	1,697,228	84	Salinas, CA	416,522	141	Medford, OR	186,573
28	Las Vegas-Paradise, NV	1,696,624	85	Beaumont-Port Arthur, TX	402,229	142	Lafayette, IN	185,184
29	Sacramento, CA	1,688,014	86	Corpus Christi, TX	397,732	143	Elkhart-Goshen, IN	185,154
30	San Antonio, TX	1,663,258	87	Shreveport-Bossier City, LA	393,503	144	Lake Charles, LA	184,138
31	Cincinnati-Middletown, OH-KY-IN	1,659,096	88	Provo-Orem, UT	382,248	145	Tyler, TX	182,482
32	Virginia Beach-Norfolk, VA-NC	1,617,279	89	Visalia-Porterville, CA	381,542	146	Fort Walton Beach, FL	178,294
33	Columbus, OH	1,549,398	90	Reading, PA	375,282	147	Mansfield, OH	176,873
34	New Orleans, LA	1,341,821	91	Reno-Sparks, NV	369,256	148	Fargo, ND-MN	173,858
35	Austin-Round Rock, TX	1,305,388	92	Trenton-Ewing, NJ	358,096	149	Sioux Falls, SD	173,837
36	Nashville-Davidson, TN	1,254,684	93	Salem, OR	357,375	150	Bellingham, WA	171,763
37	West Palm Beach, FL M.D.	1,182,905	94	Brownsville-Harlingen, TX	350,147	151	Topeka, KS	171,606
38	Buffalo-Niagara Falls, NY	1,181,277	95	Huntsville, AL	345,410	152	St. Cloud, MN	170,803
39	Jacksonville, FL	1,150,811	96	Montgomery, AL	336,006	153	Yuma, AZ	170,189
40	Rochester, NY	1,108,681	97	Port St. Lucie, FL	334,032	154	Redding, CA	169,254
41	Oklahoma City, OK	1,096,867	98	Eugene-Springfield, OR	332,409	155	Tuscaloosa, AL	166,336
42	Louisville, KY-IN	1,038,641	99	Springfield, MO	330,225	156	Athens-Clarke County, GA	160,451
43	Richmond, VA	1,026,785	100	Killeen-Temple-Fort Hood, TX	326,881	157	Jackson, MI	160,207
44	Hartford, CT	992,269	101	Fayetteville, NC	313,156	158	Joplin, MO	159,498
45	Fresno, CA	956,408	102	Savannah, GA	306,380	159	Jacksonville, NC	155,414
46	Birmingham-Hoover, AL	929,271	103	Utica-Rome, NY	302,757	160	Santa Fe, NM	155,169
47	Honolulu, HI	900,433	104	Tallahassee, FL	297,549	161	Panama City-Lynn Haven, FL	154,994
48	Tucson, AZ	897,329	105	Columbus, GA-AL	285,336	162	Janesville, WI	154,508
49	Tulsa, OK	813,257	106	Erie, PA	282,078	163	Eau Claire, WI	150,481
50	Albuquerque, NM	726,846	107	Ocala, FL	270,754	164	Vineland, NJ	149,500
51	Omaha-Council Bluffs, NE-IA	723,899	108	South Bend-Mishawaka, IN-MI	268,991	165	Pueblo, CO	148,224
52	Tacoma, WA M.D.	721,613	109	Anchorage, AK	267,280	166	Punta Gorda, FL	148,102
53	El Paso, TX	709,871	110	Santa Cruz-Watsonville, CA	264,993	167	Rocky Mount, NC	147,839
54	Knoxville, TN	700,296	111	Fort Collins-Loveland, CO	263,497	168	Decatur, AL	147,160
55	Bakersfield, CA	685,953	112	Naples-Marco Island, FL	262,871	169	Wichita Falls, TX	146,772
56	Scranton--Wilkes-Barre, PA	627,525	113	San Luis Obispo, CA	255,744	170	Yuba City, CA	144,261
57	Toledo, OH	621,914	114	Binghamton, NY	254,727	171	Greenville, NC	138,300

Note: All listings are for Metropolitan Statistical Areas (M.S.A.s) except for those ending with "M.D." Listings with "M.D." are Metropolitan Divisions which are smaller parts of ten large M.S.A.s. See explanatory note at beginning of metropolitan area section on page 23.

RANK	METROPOLITAN AREA	POP
172	Columbia, MO	137,327
173	State College, PA	136,356
174	Texarkana, TX-Texarkana, AR	134,279
175	Abilene, TX	132,188
176	Dover, DE	130,543
177	Billings, MT	130,387
178	Flagstaff, AZ	129,978
179	Altoona, PA	129,712
180	La Crosse, WI-MN	128,788
181	Florence, SC	128,744
182	Waterloo-Cedar Falls, IA	128,469
183	Wausau, WI	127,653
184	Rochester, MN	126,809
185	Alexandria, LA	126,723
186	Albany, GA	126,341
187	Glens Falls, NY	125,531
188	Sioux City, IA-NE-SD	124,712
189	Bloomington, IN	122,121
190	Grand Junction, CO	121,803
191	Williamsport, PA	120,573
192	Muncie, IN	120,304
193	Goldsboro, NC	117,143
194	Sherman-Denison, TX	115,518
195	Lawton, OK	115,396
196	Sheboygan, WI	114,274
197	Danville, VA	113,502
198	Hattiesburg, MS	112,739
199	Iowa City, IA	111,402
200	Jackson, TN	109,415
201	San Angelo, TX	108,640
202	Sumter, SC	107,128
203	Gadsden, AL	104,375
204	Cumberland, MD-WV	104,197
205	St. Joseph, MO-KS	103,907
206	Kokomo, IN	102,853
207	Lewiston-Auburn, ME	102,108
208	Lawrence, KS	100,984
209	Grand Forks, ND-MN	97,284
210	Bismarck, ND	93,525
211	Dubuque, IA	89,461
212	Rapid City, SD	89,294
213	Victoria, TX	87,831
214	Pine Bluff, AR	85,434
215	Jonesboro, AR	83,275
216	Cheyenne, WY	82,418
217	Great Falls, MT	81,004
218	Pocatello, ID	78,320
219	Casper, WY	67,196
NA	Albany-Schenectady-Troy, NY**	NA
NA	Ames, IA**	NA
NA	Anderson, SC**	NA
NA	Ann Arbor, MI**	NA
NA	Appleton, WI**	NA
NA	Atlantic City, NJ**	NA
NA	Bangor, ME**	NA
NA	Barnstable Town, MA**	NA
NA	Battle Creek, MI**	NA
NA	Bay City, MI**	NA
NA	Bend, OR**	NA
NA	Bethesda-Frederick, MD M.D.**	NA

RANK	METROPOLITAN AREA	POP
NA	Blacksburg, VA**	NA
NA	Bowling Green, KY**	NA
NA	Brunswick, GA**	NA
NA	Burlington, NC**	NA
NA	Camden, NJ M.D.**	NA
NA	Carson City, NV**	NA
NA	Charlotte-Gastonia, NC-SC**	NA
NA	Charlottesville, VA**	NA
NA	Chicago, IL**	NA
NA	Cleveland-Elyria-Mentor, OH**	NA
NA	Cleveland, TN**	NA
NA	Coeur d'Alene, ID**	NA
NA	College Station-Bryan, TX**	NA
NA	Columbus, IN**	NA
NA	Dallas (greater), TX**	NA
NA	Dalton, GA**	NA
NA	Dayton, OH**	NA
NA	Detroit-Livonia-Dearborn, MI M.D.*	NA
NA	Dothan, AL**	NA
NA	Durham, NC**	NA
NA	Edison, NJ M.D.**	NA
NA	El Centro, CA**	NA
NA	Elizabethtown, KY**	NA
NA	Elmira, NY**	NA
NA	Evansville, IN-KY**	NA
NA	Fairbanks, AK**	NA
NA	Farmington, NM**	NA
NA	Fayetteville, AR-MO**	NA
NA	Fond du Lac, WI**	NA
NA	Fort Wayne, IN**	NA
NA	Gainesville, GA**	NA
NA	Grand Rapids-Wyoming, MI**	NA
NA	Greensboro-High Point, NC**	NA
NA	Greenville, SC**	NA
NA	Hagerstown-Martinsburg, MD-WV*	NA
NA	Hanford-Corcoran, CA**	NA
NA	Harrisburg-Carlisle, PA**	NA
NA	Harrisonburg, VA**	NA
NA	Holland-Grand Haven, MI**	NA
NA	Hot Springs, AR**	NA
NA	Huntington-Ashland, WV-KY-OH**	NA
NA	Idaho Falls, ID**	NA
NA	Indianapolis, IN**	NA
NA	Ithaca, NY**	NA
NA	Jefferson City, MO**	NA
NA	Johnson City, TN**	NA
NA	Johnstown, PA**	NA
NA	Kalamazoo-Portage, MI**	NA
NA	Kansas City, MO-KS**	NA
NA	Kingsport, TN-VA**	NA
NA	Kingston, NY**	NA
NA	Lake Havasu City-Kingman, AZ**	NA
NA	Las Cruces, NM**	NA
NA	Lebanon, PA**	NA
NA	Lewiston, ID-WA**	NA
NA	Lexington-Fayette, KY**	NA
NA	Lima, OH**	NA
NA	Logan, UT-ID**	NA
NA	Longview, WA**	NA
NA	Los Angeles (greater), CA**	NA

RANK	METROPOLITAN AREA	POP
NA	Macon, GA**	NA
NA	Madera, CA**	NA
NA	Manchester-Nashua, NH**	NA
NA	Memphis, TN-MS-AR**	NA
NA	Miami (greater), FL**	NA
NA	Michigan City-La Porte, IN**	NA
NA	Midland, TX**	NA
NA	Milwaukee, WI**	NA
NA	Missoula, MT**	NA
NA	Mobile, AL**	NA
NA	Monroe, LA**	NA
NA	Monroe, MI**	NA
NA	Morgantown, WV**	NA
NA	Morristown, TN**	NA
NA	Mount Vernon-Anacortes, WA**	NA
NA	Muskegon-Norton Shores, MI**	NA
NA	Napa, CA**	NA
NA	Nassau-Suffolk, NY M.D.**	NA
NA	New York (greater), NY-NJ-PA**	NA
NA	Niles-Benton Harbor, MI**	NA
NA	Ocean City, NJ**	NA
NA	Odessa, TX**	NA
NA	Ogden-Clearfield, UT**	NA
NA	Oshkosh-Neenah, WI**	NA
NA	Oxnard-Thousand Oaks, CA**	NA
NA	Palm Coast, FL**	NA
NA	Pascagoula, MS**	NA
NA	Philadelphia, PA M.D.**	NA
NA	Pittsfield, MA**	NA
NA	Portland, ME**	NA
NA	Poughkeepsie, NY**	NA
NA	Prescott, AZ**	NA
NA	Raleigh-Cary, NC**	NA
NA	Roanoke, VA**	NA
NA	Rome, GA**	NA
NA	Saginaw, MI**	NA
NA	Salisbury, MD**	NA
NA	Salt Lake City, UT**	NA
NA	San Francisco (greater), CA**	NA
NA	Sandusky, OH**	NA
NA	Santa Barbara-Santa Maria, CA**	NA
NA	Seattle (greater), WA**	NA
NA	Sebastian-Vero Beach, FL**	NA
NA	Spartanburg, SC**	NA
NA	Springfield, MA**	NA
NA	Springfield, OH**	NA
NA	St. Louis, MO-IL**	NA
NA	Syracuse, NY**	NA
NA	Valdosta, GA**	NA
NA	Vallejo-Fairfield, CA**	NA
NA	Warner Robins, GA**	NA
NA	Warren-Farmington Hills, MI M.D.**	NA
NA	Washington, DC-VA-MD-WV M.D.**	NA
NA	Wenatchee, WA**	NA
NA	Wheeling, WV-OH**	NA
NA	Wilmington, DE-MD-NJ M.D.**	NA
NA	Winchester, VA-WV**	NA
NA	Winston-Salem, NC**	NA
NA	Worcester, MA**	NA

Source: Federal Bureau of Investigation "Crime in the United States 2002"

**Estimates as of July 2002 based on U.S. Bureau of the Census figures.*

***Not available (comparable metro area not included in 2002 crime statistics).*

88. City Population in 2006

National Total = 299,398,484*

RANK	CITY	POP
198	Abilene, TX	118,009
377	Albany, GA	77,815
284	Albany, NY	93,773
34	Albuquerque, NM	500,955
169	Alexandria, VA	136,686
312	Alhambra, CA	88,197
225	Allentown, PA	107,087
114	Amarillo, TX	188,208
209	Amherst, NY	112,284
55	Anaheim, CA	334,792
67	Anchorage, AK	277,692
208	Ann Arbor, MI	112,989
249	Antioch, CA	101,537
50	Arlington, TX	373,086
234	Arvada, CO	105,932
229	Athens-Clarke, GA	106,700
35	Atlanta, GA	485,804
59	Aurora, CO	302,855
131	Aurora, IL	169,085
18	Austin, TX	709,813
61	Bakersfield, CA	298,198
367	Baldwin Park, CA	79,571
22	Baltimore, MD	637,556
93	Baton Rouge, LA	210,486
205	Beaumont, TX	114,967
320	Beaverton, OR	87,181
194	Bellevue, WA	119,150
390	Bellflower, CA	75,242
385	Bellingham, WA	75,828
247	Berkeley, CA	101,651
259	Billings, MT	99,667
81	Birmingham, AL	233,577
347	Bloomington, MN	81,706
313	Boca Raton, FL	88,093
104	Boise, ID	198,212
29	Boston, MA	562,393
287	Boulder, CO	93,418
374	Brick Twnshp, NJ	78,214
167	Bridgeport, CT	138,791
275	Brockton, MA	95,200
321	Broken Arrow, OK	86,989
127	Brownsville, TX	172,239
361	Buena Park, CA	79,887
66	Buffalo, NY	280,494
237	Burbank, CA	105,046
253	Cambridge, MA	100,737
358	Camden, NJ	80,071
327	Canton Twnshp, MI	85,862
366	Canton, OH	79,575
162	Cape Coral, FL	142,371
296	Carlsbad, CA	91,590
192	Carrollton, TX	122,239
276	Carson, CA	94,801
219	Cary, NC	108,563
189	Cedar Rapids, IA	123,773
257	Centennial, CO	100,100
74	Chandler, AZ	243,919
221	Charleston, SC	108,371
19	Charlotte, NC	699,398
141	Chattanooga, TN	156,730
350	Cheektowaga, NY	80,995
86	Chesapeake, VA	221,150
3	Chicago, IL	2,857,796
384	Chino Hills, CA	76,404
373	Chino, CA	78,277
91	Chula Vista, CA	212,393
58	Cincinnati, OH	309,104
371	Clarkstown, NY	78,642
206	Clarksville, TN	114,314
214	Clearwater, FL	110,520
40	Cleveland, OH	452,759
360	Clifton, NJ	79,983
269	Clinton Twnshp, MI	96,587
319	Clovis, CA	87,306
380	Colonie, NY	77,357
48	Colorado Springs, CO	376,807
292	Columbia, MO	92,485
195	Columbia, SC	118,909
111	Columbus, GA	191,221
17	Columbus, OH	731,547
270	Compton, CA	96,520
186	Concord, CA	124,362
179	Coral Springs, FL	130,976
149	Corona, CA	150,732
63	Corpus Christi, TX	291,507
212	Costa Mesa, CA	110,819
352	Cranston, RI	80,963
10	Dallas, TX	1,248,223
250	Daly City, CA	101,243
372	Danbury, CT	78,613
328	Davie, FL	85,624
140	Dayton, OH	159,067
282	Dearborn, MI	93,856
379	Deerfield Beach, FL	77,636
224	Denton, TX	107,105
28	Denver, CO	568,465
109	Des Moines, IA	195,194
13	Detroit, MI	884,462
213	Downey, CA	110,706
329	Duluth, MN	85,463
95	Durham, NC	208,932
255	Edison Twnshp, NJ	100,575
387	Edmond, OK	75,542
288	El Cajon, CA	93,320
190	El Monte, CA	123,616
24	El Paso, TX	615,553
184	Elizabeth, NJ	125,905
242	Erie, PA	102,703
172	Escondido, CA	135,293
156	Eugene, OR	146,885
201	Evansville, IN	116,686
263	Everett, WA	98,264
236	Fairfield, CA	105,417
299	Fargo, ND	90,818
359	Farmington Hills, MI	80,023
178	Fayetteville, NC	132,521
335	Federal Way, WA	84,516
197	Flint, MI	118,256
137	Fontana, CA	165,336
180	Fort Collins, CO	130,446
129	Fort Lauderdale, FL	170,203
340	Fort Smith, AR	83,422
82	Fort Wayne, IN	224,820
21	Fort Worth, TX	641,752
97	Fremont, CA	202,273
37	Fresno, CA	465,269
175	Fullerton, CA	133,983
216	Gainesville, FL	110,009
134	Garden Grove, CA	167,571
84	Garland, TX	222,477
260	Gary, IN	99,369
121	Gilbert, AZ	180,640
73	Glendale, AZ	248,587
99	Glendale, CA	201,867
151	Grand Prairie, TX	148,427
110	Grand Rapids, MI	193,297
281	Greece, NY	94,233
308	Greeley, CO	89,252
248	Green Bay, WI	101,574
78	Greensboro, NC	236,591
265	Gresham, OR	97,647
305	Hamilton Twnshp, NJ	90,062
363	Hammond, IN	79,742
155	Hampton, VA	147,030
187	Hartford, CT	124,203
325	Hawthorne, CA	86,469
165	Hayward, CA	141,556
76	Henderson, NV	239,906
370	Hesperia, CA	78,686
83	Hialeah, FL	224,203
268	High Point, NC	96,983
326	Hillsboro, OR	85,919
152	Hollywood, FL	148,085
12	Honolulu, HI	912,693
4	Houston, TX	2,073,729
107	Huntington Beach, CA	196,208
132	Huntsville, AL	167,817
211	Independence, MO	111,014
14	Indianapolis, IN	800,969
203	Inglewood, CA	115,498
112	Irvine, CA	188,535
103	Irving, TX	199,137
15	Jacksonville, FL	795,822
123	Jackson, MS	177,334
77	Jersey City, NJ	239,794
168	Joliet, IL	136,940
157	Kansas City, KS	145,229
41	Kansas City, MO	448,218
273	Kenosha, WI	95,589
341	Kent, WA	83,206
241	Killeen, TX	103,073
119	Knoxville, TN	182,421
231	Lafayette, LA	106,189
382	Lake Forest, CA	77,100
304	Lakeland, FL	90,209
349	Lakewood, CA	81,192
161	Lakewood, CO	143,331
173	Lancaster, CA	135,239
204	Lansing, MI	115,230
89	Laredo, TX	214,670
386	Largo, FL	75,729
336	Las Cruces, NM	83,795
7	Las Vegas, NV	1,315,625
345	Lawrence, KS	82,394
298	Lawton, OK	91,031
354	Lee's Summit, MO	80,925
289	Lewisville, TX	92,908
69	Lexington, KY	270,179
75	Lincoln, NE	240,511
115	Little Rock, AR	186,670
368	Livermore, CA	79,115
264	Livonia, MI	97,733

Alpha Order- City (continued)

RANK	CITY	POP
36	Long Beach, CA	478,283
378	Longview, TX	77,752
2	Los Angeles, CA	3,879,455
23	Louisville, KY	626,018
239	Lowell, MA	103,729
88	Lubbock, TX	215,681
307	Lynn, MA	89,322
267	Macon, GA	97,345
85	Madison, WI	222,364
215	Manchester, NH	110,106
183	McAllen, TX	127,125
261	McKinney, TX	99,318
375	Melbourne, FL	77,939
20	Memphis, TN	680,828
39	Mesa, AZ	459,705
177	Mesquite, TX	133,583
306	Miami Beach, FL	89,408
252	Miami Gardens, FL	101,115
46	Miami, FL	392,934
245	Midland, TX	102,039
27	Milwaukee, WI	581,005
49	Minneapolis, MN	375,302
220	Miramar, FL	108,421
272	Mission Viejo, CA	95,837
72	Mobile, AL	250,152
96	Modesto, CA	208,875
98	Montgomery, AL	201,937
122	Moreno Valley, CA	179,973
315	Murfreesboro, TN	87,897
339	Murrieta, CA	83,523
388	Napa, CA	75,455
163	Naperville, IL	142,340
317	Nashua, NH	87,651
30	Nashville, TN	560,813
285	New Bedford, MA	93,661
43	New Orleans, LA	431,153
1	New York, NY	8,165,001
65	Newark, NJ	280,877
357	Newport Beach, CA	80,553
120	Newport News, VA	181,692
337	Newton, MA	83,658
80	Norfolk, VA	234,266
244	Norman, OK	102,617
316	North Charleston, SC	87,655
118	North Las Vegas, NV	182,540
228	Norwalk, CA	106,787
45	Oakland, CA	398,834
133	Oceanside, CA	167,604
271	Odessa, TX	96,197
355	Ogden, UT	80,861
32	Oklahoma City, OK	536,016
210	Olathe, KS	112,120
44	Omaha, NE	416,770
126	Ontario, CA	174,234
170	Orange, CA	136,165
290	Orem, UT	92,637
87	Orlando, FL	216,819
136	Overland Park, KS	165,975
116	Oxnard, CA	185,282
280	Palm Bay, FL	94,399
171	Palmdale, CA	135,782
348	Parma, OH	81,568
158	Pasadena, CA	145,025
153	Pasadena, TX	147,929
150	Paterson, NJ	149,957
145	Pembroke Pines, FL	152,916
160	Peoria, AZ	143,483
207	Peoria, IL	113,291
6	Philadelphia, PA	1,464,576
5	Phoenix, AZ	1,517,443
57	Pittsburgh, PA	324,604
70	Plano, TX	257,183
318	Plantation, FL	87,439
142	Pomona, CA	155,172
233	Pompano Beach, FL	105,936
176	Port St. Lucie, FL	133,913
31	Portland, OR	542,174
251	Portsmouth, VA	101,167
125	Providence, RI	175,452
199	Provo, UT	117,156
235	Pueblo, CO	105,452
300	Quincy, MA	90,792
365	Racine, WI	79,683
52	Raleigh, NC	348,345
128	Rancho Cucamon., CA	170,878
353	Reading, PA	80,927
302	Redding, CA	90,448
94	Reno, NV	210,354
256	Rialto, CA	100,409
246	Richardson, TX	101,998
240	Richmond, CA	103,106
108	Richmond, VA	195,708
62	Riverside, CA	292,698
286	Roanoke, VA	93,554
274	Rochester, MN	95,585
92	Rochester, NY	211,656
144	Rockford, IL	153,738
227	Roseville, CA	106,894
310	Roswell, GA	88,679
309	Round Rock, TX	88,762
38	Sacramento, CA	460,552
148	Salem, OR	151,190
154	Salinas, CA	147,750
117	Salt Lake City, UT	183,901
301	San Angelo, TX	90,508
8	San Antonio, TX	1,292,116
100	San Bernardino, CA	200,338
9	San Diego, CA	1,266,847
16	San Francisco, CA	746,085
11	San Jose, CA	920,548
369	San Leandro, CA	78,882
295	San Mateo, CA	91,901
291	Sandy, UT	92,586
54	Santa Ana, CA	343,433
322	Santa Barbara, CA	86,673
230	Santa Clara, CA	106,351
130	Santa Clarita, CA	169,768
332	Santa Maria, CA	85,106
311	Santa Monica, CA	88,591
143	Santa Rosa, CA	154,537
90	Savannah, GA	213,488
79	Scottsdale, AZ	234,652
25	Seattle, WA	583,772
113	Shreveport, LA	188,505
193	Simi Valley, CA	119,756
338	Sioux City, IA	83,590
166	Sioux Falls, SD	140,593
389	Somerville, MA	75,413
232	South Bend, IN	105,959
258	South Gate, CA	99,788
383	Southfield, MI	76,627
333	Sparks, NV	84,794
343	Spokane Valley, WA	82,778
101	Spokane, WA	200,200
202	Springfield, IL	116,290
146	Springfield, MA	152,644
147	Springfield, MO	151,397
182	Sterling Heights, MI	127,715
64	Stockton, CA	289,510
53	St. Louis, MO	346,879
68	St. Paul, MN	276,989
71	St. Petersburg, FL	253,280
362	Suffolk, VA	79,781
376	Sugar Land, TX	77,901
181	Sunnyvale, CA	130,063
293	Sunrise, FL	92,117
381	Surprise, AZ	77,255
164	Syracuse, NY	142,062
102	Tacoma, WA	199,264
138	Tallahassee, FL	161,173
56	Tampa, FL	331,487
323	Temecula, CA	86,572
135	Tempe, AZ	167,303
223	Thornton, CO	107,171
185	Thousand Oaks, CA	125,479
60	Toledo, OH	301,652
277	Toms River Twnshp, NJ	94,732
191	Topeka, KS	122,807
159	Torrance, CA	143,666
356	Tracy, CA	80,684
334	Trenton, NJ	84,703
351	Troy, MI	80,966
33	Tucson, AZ	535,232
47	Tulsa, OK	385,834
346	Tuscaloosa, AL	82,094
278	Tyler, TX	94,541
364	Upper Darby Twnshp, PA	79,690
283	Vacaville, CA	93,822
196	Vallejo, CA	118,541
139	Vancouver, WA	160,199
238	Ventura, CA	104,954
294	Victorville, CA	92,086
42	Virginia Beach, VA	442,784
217	Visalia, CA	109,648
297	Vista, CA	91,216
188	Waco, TX	123,879
174	Warren, MI	134,974
324	Warwick, RI	86,538
26	Washington, DC	581,530
222	Waterbury, CT	107,733
218	West Covina, CA	109,159
279	West Jordan, UT	94,424
262	West Palm Beach, FL	99,142
200	West Valley, UT	116,992
330	Westland, MI	85,410
303	Westminster, CA	90,329
226	Westminster, CO	107,071
331	Whittier, CA	85,234
243	Wichita Falls, TX	102,675
51	Wichita, KS	357,372
266	Wilmington, NC	97,381
105	Winston-Salem, NC	197,621
254	Woodbridge Twnshp, NJ	100,655
124	Worcester, MA	176,956
344	Yakima, WA	82,609
106	Yonkers, NY	196,951
342	Youngstown, OH	82,938
314	Yuma, AZ	87,925

Source: Federal Bureau of Investigation "Crime in the United States 2006"

**Estimates as of July 2006 based on U.S. Bureau of the Census figures. Charlotte, Honolulu, Indianapolis, Las Vegas, Louisville, Mobile and Savannah include areas under their police department but outside the city limits. All populations are for area covered by police department.*

88. City Population in 2006 (continued)

National Total = 299,398,484*

RANK	CITY	POP
1	New York, NY	8,165,001
2	Los Angeles, CA	3,879,455
3	Chicago, IL	2,857,796
4	Houston, TX	2,073,729
5	Phoenix, AZ	1,517,443
6	Philadelphia, PA	1,464,576
7	Las Vegas, NV	1,315,625
8	San Antonio, TX	1,292,116
9	San Diego, CA	1,266,847
10	Dallas, TX	1,248,223
11	San Jose, CA	920,548
12	Honolulu, HI	912,693
13	Detroit, MI	884,462
14	Indianapolis, IN	800,969
15	Jacksonville, FL	795,822
16	San Francisco, CA	746,085
17	Columbus, OH	731,547
18	Austin, TX	709,813
19	Charlotte, NC	699,398
20	Memphis, TN	680,828
21	Fort Worth, TX	641,752
22	Baltimore, MD	637,556
23	Louisville, KY	626,018
24	El Paso, TX	615,553
25	Seattle, WA	583,772
26	Washington, DC	581,530
27	Milwaukee, WI	581,005
28	Denver, CO	568,465
29	Boston, MA	562,393
30	Nashville, TN	560,813
31	Portland, OR	542,174
32	Oklahoma City, OK	536,016
33	Tucson, AZ	535,232
34	Albuquerque, NM	500,955
35	Atlanta, GA	485,804
36	Long Beach, CA	478,283
37	Fresno, CA	465,269
38	Sacramento, CA	460,552
39	Mesa, AZ	459,705
40	Cleveland, OH	452,759
41	Kansas City, MO	448,218
42	Virginia Beach, VA	442,784
43	New Orleans, LA	431,153
44	Omaha, NE	416,770
45	Oakland, CA	398,834
46	Miami, FL	392,934
47	Tulsa, OK	385,834
48	Colorado Springs, CO	376,807
49	Minneapolis, MN	375,302
50	Arlington, TX	373,086
51	Wichita, KS	357,372
52	Raleigh, NC	348,345
53	St. Louis, MO	346,879
54	Santa Ana, CA	343,433
55	Anaheim, CA	334,792
56	Tampa, FL	331,487
57	Pittsburgh, PA	324,604
58	Cincinnati, OH	309,104
59	Aurora, CO	302,855
60	Toledo, OH	301,652
61	Bakersfield, CA	298,198
62	Riverside, CA	292,698
63	Corpus Christi, TX	291,507
64	Stockton, CA	289,510
65	Newark, NJ	280,877
66	Buffalo, NY	280,494
67	Anchorage, AK	277,692
68	St. Paul, MN	276,989
69	Lexington, KY	270,179
70	Plano, TX	257,183
71	St. Petersburg, FL	253,280
72	Mobile, AL	250,152
73	Glendale, AZ	248,587
74	Chandler, AZ	243,919
75	Lincoln, NE	240,511
76	Henderson, NV	239,906
77	Jersey City, NJ	239,794
78	Greensboro, NC	236,591
79	Scottsdale, AZ	234,652
80	Norfolk, VA	234,266
81	Birmingham, AL	233,577
82	Fort Wayne, IN	224,820
83	Hialeah, FL	224,203
84	Garland, TX	222,477
85	Madison, WI	222,364
86	Chesapeake, VA	221,150
87	Orlando, FL	216,819
88	Lubbock, TX	215,681
89	Laredo, TX	214,670
90	Savannah, GA	213,488
91	Chula Vista, CA	212,393
92	Rochester, NY	211,656
93	Baton Rouge, LA	210,486
94	Reno, NV	210,354
95	Durham, NC	208,932
96	Modesto, CA	208,875
97	Fremont, CA	202,273
98	Montgomery, AL	201,937
99	Glendale, CA	201,867
100	San Bernardino, CA	200,338
101	Spokane, WA	200,200
102	Tacoma, WA	199,264
103	Irving, TX	199,137
104	Boise, ID	198,212
105	Winston-Salem, NC	197,621
106	Yonkers, NY	196,951
107	Huntington Beach, CA	196,208
108	Richmond, VA	195,708
109	Des Moines, IA	195,194
110	Grand Rapids, MI	193,297
111	Columbus, GA	191,221
112	Irvine, CA	188,535
113	Shreveport, LA	188,505
114	Amarillo, TX	188,208
115	Little Rock, AR	186,670
116	Oxnard, CA	185,282
117	Salt Lake City, UT	183,901
118	North Las Vegas, NV	182,540
119	Knoxville, TN	182,421
120	Newport News, VA	181,692
121	Gilbert, AZ	180,640
122	Moreno Valley, CA	179,973
123	Jackson, MS	177,334
124	Worcester, MA	176,956
125	Providence, RI	175,452
126	Ontario, CA	174,234
127	Brownsville, TX	172,239
128	Rancho Cucamon., CA	170,878
129	Fort Lauderdale, FL	170,203
130	Santa Clarita, CA	169,768
131	Aurora, IL	169,085
132	Huntsville, AL	167,817
133	Oceanside, CA	167,604
134	Garden Grove, CA	167,571
135	Tempe, AZ	167,303
136	Overland Park, KS	165,975
137	Fontana, CA	165,336
138	Tallahassee, FL	161,173
139	Vancouver, WA	160,199
140	Dayton, OH	159,067
141	Chattanooga, TN	156,730
142	Pomona, CA	155,172
143	Santa Rosa, CA	154,537
144	Rockford, IL	153,738
145	Pembroke Pines, FL	152,916
146	Springfield, MA	152,644
147	Springfield, MO	151,397
148	Salem, OR	151,190
149	Corona, CA	150,732
150	Paterson, NJ	149,957
151	Grand Prairie, TX	148,427
152	Hollywood, FL	148,085
153	Pasadena, TX	147,929
154	Salinas, CA	147,750
155	Hampton, VA	147,030
156	Eugene, OR	146,885
157	Kansas City, KS	145,229
158	Pasadena, CA	145,025
159	Torrance, CA	143,666
160	Peoria, AZ	143,483
161	Lakewood, CO	143,331
162	Cape Coral, FL	142,371
163	Naperville, IL	142,340
164	Syracuse, NY	142,062
165	Hayward, CA	141,556
166	Sioux Falls, SD	140,593
167	Bridgeport, CT	138,791
168	Joliet, IL	136,940
169	Alexandria, VA	136,686
170	Orange, CA	136,165
171	Palmdale, CA	135,782
172	Escondido, CA	135,293
173	Lancaster, CA	135,239
174	Warren, MI	134,974
175	Fullerton, CA	133,983
176	Port St. Lucie, FL	133,913
177	Mesquite, TX	133,583
178	Fayetteville, NC	132,521
179	Coral Springs, FL	130,976
180	Fort Collins, CO	130,446
181	Sunnyvale, CA	130,063
182	Sterling Heights, MI	127,715
183	McAllen, TX	127,125
184	Elizabeth, NJ	125,905
185	Thousand Oaks, CA	125,479
186	Concord, CA	124,362
187	Hartford, CT	124,203
188	Waco, TX	123,879
189	Cedar Rapids, IA	123,773
190	El Monte, CA	123,616
191	Topeka, KS	122,807
192	Carrollton, TX	122,239

RANK	CITY	POP
193	Simi Valley, CA	119,756
194	Bellevue, WA	119,150
195	Columbia, SC	118,909
196	Vallejo, CA	118,541
197	Flint, MI	118,256
198	Abilene, TX	118,009
199	Provo, UT	117,156
200	West Valley, UT	116,992
201	Evansville, IN	116,686
202	Springfield, IL	116,290
203	Inglewood, CA	115,498
204	Lansing, MI	115,230
205	Beaumont, TX	114,967
206	Clarksville, TN	114,314
207	Peoria, IL	113,291
208	Ann Arbor, MI	112,989
209	Amherst, NY	112,284
210	Olathe, KS	112,120
211	Independence, MO	111,014
212	Costa Mesa, CA	110,819
213	Downey, CA	110,706
214	Clearwater, FL	110,520
215	Manchester, NH	110,106
216	Gainesville, FL	110,009
217	Visalia, CA	109,648
218	West Covina, CA	109,159
219	Cary, NC	108,563
220	Miramar, FL	108,421
221	Charleston, SC	108,371
222	Waterbury, CT	107,733
223	Thornton, CO	107,171
224	Denton, TX	107,105
225	Allentown, PA	107,087
226	Westminster, CO	107,071
227	Roseville, CA	106,894
228	Norwalk, CA	106,787
229	Athens-Clarke, GA	106,700
230	Santa Clara, CA	106,351
231	Lafayette, LA	106,189
232	South Bend, IN	105,959
233	Pompano Beach, FL	105,936
234	Arvada, CO	105,932
235	Pueblo, CO	105,452
236	Fairfield, CA	105,417
237	Burbank, CA	105,046
238	Ventura, CA	104,954
239	Lowell, MA	103,729
240	Richmond, CA	103,106
241	Killeen, TX	103,073
242	Erie, PA	102,703
243	Wichita Falls, TX	102,675
244	Norman, OK	102,617
245	Midland, TX	102,039
246	Richardson, TX	101,998
247	Berkeley, CA	101,651
248	Green Bay, WI	101,574
249	Antioch, CA	101,537
250	Daly City, CA	101,243
251	Portsmouth, VA	101,167
252	Miami Gardens, FL	101,115
253	Cambridge, MA	100,737
254	Woodbridge Twnshp, NJ	100,655
255	Edison Twnshp, NJ	100,575
256	Rialto, CA	100,409
257	Centennial, CO	100,100
258	South Gate, CA	99,788
259	Billings, MT	99,667
260	Gary, IN	99,369
261	McKinney, TX	99,318
262	West Palm Beach, FL	99,142
263	Everett, WA	98,264
264	Livonia, MI	97,733
265	Gresham, OR	97,647
266	Wilmington, NC	97,381
267	Macon, GA	97,345
268	High Point, NC	96,983
269	Clinton Twnshp, MI	96,587
270	Compton, CA	96,520
271	Odessa, TX	96,197
272	Mission Viejo, CA	95,837
273	Kenosha, WI	95,589
274	Rochester, MN	95,585
275	Brockton, MA	95,200
276	Carson, CA	94,801
277	Toms River Twnshp, NJ	94,732
278	Tyler, TX	94,541
279	West Jordan, UT	94,424
280	Palm Bay, FL	94,399
281	Greece, NY	94,233
282	Dearborn, MI	93,856
283	Vacaville, CA	93,822
284	Albany, NY	93,773
285	New Bedford, MA	93,661
286	Roanoke, VA	93,554
287	Boulder, CO	93,418
288	El Cajon, CA	93,320
289	Lewisville, TX	92,908
290	Orem, UT	92,637
291	Sandy, UT	92,586
292	Columbia, MO	92,485
293	Sunrise, FL	92,117
294	Victorville, CA	92,086
295	San Mateo, CA	91,901
296	Carlsbad, CA	91,590
297	Vista, CA	91,216
298	Lawton, OK	91,031
299	Fargo, ND	90,818
300	Quincy, MA	90,792
301	San Angelo, TX	90,508
302	Redding, CA	90,448
303	Westminster, CA	90,329
304	Lakeland, FL	90,209
305	Hamilton Twnshp, NJ	90,062
306	Miami Beach, FL	89,408
307	Lynn, MA	89,322
308	Greeley, CO	89,252
309	Round Rock, TX	88,762
310	Roswell, GA	88,679
311	Santa Monica, CA	88,591
312	Alhambra, CA	88,197
313	Boca Raton, FL	88,093
314	Yuma, AZ	87,925
315	Murfreesboro, TN	87,897
316	North Charleston, SC	87,655
317	Nashua, NH	87,651
318	Plantation, FL	87,439
319	Clovis, CA	87,306
320	Beaverton, OR	87,181
321	Broken Arrow, OK	86,989
322	Santa Barbara, CA	86,673
323	Temecula, CA	86,572
324	Warwick, RI	86,538
325	Hawthorne, CA	86,469
326	Hillsboro, OR	85,919
327	Canton Twnshp, MI	85,862
328	Davie, FL	85,624
329	Duluth, MN	85,463
330	Westland, MI	85,410
331	Whittier, CA	85,234
332	Santa Maria, CA	85,106
333	Sparks, NV	84,794
334	Trenton, NJ	84,703
335	Federal Way, WA	84,516
336	Las Cruces, NM	83,795
337	Newton, MA	83,658
338	Sioux City, IA	83,590
339	Murrieta, CA	83,523
340	Fort Smith, AR	83,422
341	Kent, WA	83,206
342	Youngstown, OH	82,938
343	Spokane Valley, WA	82,778
344	Yakima, WA	82,609
345	Lawrence, KS	82,394
346	Tuscaloosa, AL	82,094
347	Bloomington, MN	81,706
348	Parma, OH	81,568
349	Lakewood, CA	81,192
350	Cheektowaga, NY	80,995
351	Troy, MI	80,966
352	Cranston, RI	80,963
353	Reading, PA	80,927
354	Lee's Summit, MO	80,925
355	Ogden, UT	80,861
356	Tracy, CA	80,684
357	Newport Beach, CA	80,553
358	Camden, NJ	80,071
359	Farmington Hills, MI	80,023
360	Clifton, NJ	79,983
361	Buena Park, CA	79,887
362	Suffolk, VA	79,781
363	Hammond, IN	79,742
364	Upper Darby Twnshp, PA	79,690
365	Racine, WI	79,683
366	Canton, OH	79,575
367	Baldwin Park, CA	79,571
368	Livermore, CA	79,115
369	San Leandro, CA	78,882
370	Hesperia, CA	78,686
371	Clarkstown, NY	78,642
372	Danbury, CT	78,613
373	Chino, CA	78,277
374	Brick Twnshp, NJ	78,214
375	Melbourne, FL	77,939
376	Sugar Land, TX	77,901
377	Albany, GA	77,815
378	Longview, TX	77,752
379	Deerfield Beach, FL	77,636
380	Colonie, NY	77,357
381	Surprise, AZ	77,255
382	Lake Forest, CA	77,100
383	Southfield, MI	76,627
384	Chino Hills, CA	76,404
385	Bellingham, WA	75,828
386	Largo, FL	75,729
387	Edmond, OK	75,542
388	Napa, CA	75,455
389	Somerville, MA	75,413
390	Bellflower, CA	75,242

Source: Federal Bureau of Investigation "Crime in the United States 2006"

**Estimates as of July 2006 based on U.S. Bureau of the Census figures. Charlotte, Honolulu, Indianapolis, Las Vegas, Louisville, Mobile and Savannah include areas under their police department but outside the city limits. All populations are for area covered by police department.*

89. City Population in 2005

National Total = 296,507,061*

RANK	CITY	POP
199	Abilene, TX	116,695
368	Albany, GA	78,353
276	Albany, NY	94,361
34	Albuquerque, NM	490,631
174	Alexandria, VA	130,056
306	Alhambra, CA	88,579
219	Allentown, PA	106,933
116	Amarillo, TX	183,765
209	Amherst, NY	111,178
53	Anaheim, CA	335,992
67	Anchorage, AK	276,109
204	Ann Arbor, MI	113,660
244	Antioch, CA	101,593
49	Arlington, TX	365,380
232	Arvada, CO	103,983
223	Athens-Clarke, GA	105,727
42	Atlanta, GA	430,666
59	Aurora, CO	295,888
127	Aurora, IL	167,266
18	Austin, TX	693,019
61	Bakersfield, CA	285,821
363	Baldwin Park, CA	79,411
21	Baltimore, MD	641,097
82	Baton Rouge, LA	224,487
203	Beaumont, TX	114,141
326	Beaverton, OR	83,979
194	Bellevue, WA	118,496
380	Bellflower, CA	75,462
384	Bellingham, WA	73,980
241	Berkeley, CA	102,191
259	Billings, MT	97,898
77	Birmingham, AL	234,571
348	Bloomington, MN	81,068
361	Boca Raton, FL	79,831
109	Boise, ID	195,012
27	Boston, MA	567,589
282	Boulder, CO	93,474
365	Brick Twnshp, NJ	78,646
163	Bridgeport, CT	140,177
270	Brockton, MA	94,746
320	Broken Arrow, OK	84,982
132	Brownsville, TX	163,877
360	Buena Park, CA	79,884
63	Buffalo, NY	283,269
226	Burbank, CA	104,805
249	Cambridge, MA	100,492
356	Camden, NJ	80,125
322	Canton Twnshp, MI	84,723
359	Canton, OH	79,940
173	Cape Coral, FL	130,874
301	Carlsbad, CA	89,633
192	Carrollton, TX	119,761
277	Carson, CA	94,355
239	Cary, NC	102,949
187	Cedar Rapids, IA	122,698
256	Centennial, CO	99,607
79	Chandler, AZ	231,613
220	Charleston, SC	106,307
20	Charlotte, NC	677,122
140	Chattanooga, TN	156,480
343	Cheektowaga, NY	81,793
86	Chesapeake, VA	217,823
3	Chicago, IL	2,873,441
378	Chino Hills, CA	76,124
376	Chino, CA	76,547
93	Chula Vista, CA	206,239
57	Cincinnati, OH	314,292
331	Clarkstown, NY	82,928
214	Clarksville, TN	110,117
211	Clearwater, FL	111,058
37	Cleveland, OH	458,885
357	Clifton, NJ	80,119
266	Clinton Twnshp, MI	96,028
332	Clovis, CA	82,921
375	Colonie, NY	77,048
48	Colorado Springs, CO	374,482
297	Columbia, MO	90,304
195	Columbia, SC	117,911
111	Columbus, GA	187,886
17	Columbus, OH	730,329
264	Compton, CA	96,874
182	Concord, CA	125,154
172	Coral Springs, FL	131,252
153	Corona, CA	146,363
61	Corpus Christi, TX	285,821
210	Costa Mesa, CA	111,144
344	Cranston, RI	81,649
10	Dallas, TX	1,230,303
245	Daly City, CA	101,288
367	Danbury, CT	78,413
323	Davie, FL	84,443
136	Dayton, OH	160,363
267	Dearborn, MI	95,548
388	Deerfield Beach, FL	67,683
254	Denton, TX	99,905
28	Denver, CO	564,552
108	Des Moines, IA	195,093
13	Detroit, MI	900,932
212	Downey, CA	111,051
321	Duluth, MN	84,781
94	Durham, NC	205,080
250	Edison Twnshp, NJ	100,361
386	Edmond, OK	73,585
272	El Cajon, CA	94,611
185	El Monte, CA	122,934
24	El Paso, TX	601,839
184	Elizabeth, NJ	124,997
231	Erie, PA	104,120
166	Escondido, CA	136,362
156	Eugene, OR	144,526
196	Evansville, IN	117,802
262	Everett, WA	97,402
229	Fairfield, CA	104,639
289	Fargo, ND	91,380
350	Farmington Hills, MI	80,853
180	Fayetteville, NC	127,323
338	Federal Way, WA	82,457
191	Flint, MI	119,814
138	Fontana, CA	159,769
178	Fort Collins, CO	128,727
125	Fort Lauderdale, FL	168,293
336	Fort Smith, AR	82,638
85	Fort Wayne, IN	220,561
23	Fort Worth, TX	613,261
96	Fremont, CA	203,717
36	Fresno, CA	460,758
169	Fullerton, CA	134,325
208	Gainesville, FL	111,313
124	Garden Grove, CA	168,458
84	Garland, TX	220,748
253	Gary, IN	100,065
134	Gilbert, AZ	162,257
72	Glendale, AZ	243,608
97	Glendale, CA	202,663
160	Grand Prairie, TX	142,628
106	Grand Rapids, MI	195,274
271	Greece, NY	94,688
317	Greeley, CO	85,991
243	Green Bay, WI	101,599
76	Greensboro, NC	235,393
265	Gresham, OR	96,609
298	Hamilton Twnshp, NJ	90,255
355	Hammond, IN	80,426
149	Hampton, VA	148,057
183	Hartford, CT	125,086
313	Hawthorne, CA	86,852
161	Hayward, CA	141,730
78	Henderson, NV	232,536
385	Hesperia, CA	73,863
80	Hialeah, FL	229,590
274	High Point, NC	94,401
333	Hillsboro, OR	82,912
151	Hollywood, FL	147,798
12	Honolulu, HI	908,521
4	Houston, TX	2,045,732
105	Huntington Beach, CA	196,602
130	Huntsville, AL	165,147
207	Independence, MO	111,905
14	Indianapolis, IN	800,304
201	Inglewood, CA	116,079
119	Irvine, CA	179,501
103	Irving, TX	197,747
15	Jacksonville, FL	795,259
117	Jackson, MS	180,417
74	Jersey City, NJ	239,603
175	Joliet, IL	130,026
154	Kansas City, KS	145,491
40	Kansas City, MO	447,915
278	Kenosha, WI	94,261
334	Kent, WA	82,736
258	Killeen, TX	98,538
118	Knoxville, TN	179,989
206	Lafayette, LA	112,161
372	Lake Forest, CA	77,523
296	Lakeland, FL	90,351
345	Lakewood, CA	81,626
159	Lakewood, CO	143,259
176	Lancaster, CA	129,784
198	Lansing, MI	117,036
92	Laredo, TX	206,555
387	Largo, FL	73,323
352	Las Cruces, NM	80,573
7	Las Vegas, NV	1,281,698
341	Lawrence, KS	82,148
305	Lawton, OK	88,823
364	Lee's Summit, MO	79,284
294	Lewisville, TX	90,608
68	Lexington, KY	268,124
75	Lincoln, NE	237,710
112	Little Rock, AR	185,855
366	Livermore, CA	78,501
257	Livonia, MI	99,017

RANK	CITY	POP
35	Long Beach, CA	479,729
377	Longview, TX	76,545
2	Los Angeles, CA	3,871,077
22	Louisville, KY	623,735
235	Lowell, MA	103,370
89	Lubbock, TX	211,271
303	Lynn, MA	89,234
260	Macon, GA	97,606
83	Madison, WI	221,419
213	Manchester, NH	110,188
186	McAllen, TX	122,729
299	McKinney, TX	89,863
374	Melbourne, FL	77,067
19	Memphis, TN	678,988
39	Mesa, AZ	452,340
171	Mesquite, TX	131,844
290	Miami Beach, FL	91,115
236	Miami Gardens, FL	103,164
45	Miami, FL	388,295
255	Midland, TX	99,695
25	Milwaukee, WI	586,500
47	Minneapolis, MN	376,277
233	Miramar, FL	103,777
263	Mission Viejo, CA	96,892
70	Mobile, AL	249,798
91	Modesto, CA	208,142
98	Montgomery, AL	202,209
126	Moreno Valley, CA	167,394
339	Murfreesboro, TN	82,367
382	Murrieta, CA	75,008
379	Napa, CA	75,966
162	Naperville, IL	140,654
308	Nashua, NH	88,113
29	Nashville, TN	557,034
280	New Bedford, MA	93,720
NA	New Orleans, LA**	NA
1	New York, NY	8,115,690
65	Newark, NJ	281,063
354	Newport Beach, CA	80,488
115	Newport News, VA	184,538
328	Newton, MA	83,570
73	Norfolk, VA	241,267
242	Norman, OK	101,620
319	North Charleston, SC	85,416
131	North Las Vegas, NV	164,190
218	Norwalk, CA	107,391
44	Oakland, CA	400,619
123	Oceanside, CA	168,550
275	Odessa, TX	94,371
347	Ogden, UT	81,166
32	Oklahoma City, OK	531,688
216	Olathe, KS	108,754
43	Omaha, NE	412,128
122	Ontario, CA	171,186
168	Orange, CA	134,708
287	Orem, UT	91,607
90	Orlando, FL	210,290
133	Overland Park, KS	163,274
113	Oxnard, CA	184,806
293	Palm Bay, FL	90,762
170	Palmdale, CA	132,024
335	Parma, OH	82,708
155	Pasadena, CA	145,025
152	Pasadena, TX	146,546
147	Paterson, NJ	151,200
143	Pembroke Pines, FL	153,492
165	Peoria, AZ	136,995
205	Peoria, IL	113,161
5	Philadelphia, PA	1,472,915
6	Phoenix, AZ	1,466,296
55	Pittsburgh, PA	330,780
71	Plano, TX	249,448
310	Plantation, FL	87,427
140	Pomona, CA	156,480
292	Pompano Beach, FL	90,880
189	Port St. Lucie, FL	121,069
31	Portland, OR	540,389
248	Portsmouth, VA	100,724
120	Providence, RI	177,392
238	Provo, UT	102,983
225	Pueblo, CO	105,057
300	Quincy, MA	89,661
353	Racine, WI	80,503
54	Raleigh, NC	332,084
135	Rancho Cucamon., CA	160,404
349	Reading, PA	80,879
304	Redding, CA	89,161
95	Reno, NV	204,749
251	Rialto, CA	100,321
247	Richardson, TX	100,896
237	Richmond, CA	102,997
107	Richmond, VA	195,271
60	Riverside, CA	290,299
281	Roanoke, VA	93,685
279	Rochester, MN	93,866
88	Rochester, NY	212,785
144	Rockford, IL	153,048
230	Roseville, CA	104,297
311	Roswell, GA	87,386
329	Round Rock, TX	83,390
38	Sacramento, CA	457,347
150	Salem, OR	148,009
148	Salinas, CA	149,167
114	Salt Lake City, UT	184,627
302	San Angelo, TX	89,561
9	San Antonio, TX	1,256,584
99	San Bernardino, CA	199,723
8	San Diego, CA	1,272,148
16	San Francisco, CA	749,172
11	San Jose, CA	910,528
362	San Leandro, CA	79,709
286	San Mateo, CA	91,881
283	Sandy, UT	93,013
52	Santa Ana, CA	344,991
309	Santa Barbara, CA	87,950
228	Santa Clara, CA	104,692
129	Santa Clarita, CA	165,894
324	Santa Maria, CA	84,312
307	Santa Monica, CA	88,406
142	Santa Rosa, CA	154,656
87	Savannah, GA	213,587
81	Scottsdale, AZ	229,339
26	Seattle, WA	579,215
101	Shreveport, LA	199,021
193	Simi Valley, CA	119,682
325	Sioux City, IA	84,017
164	Sioux Falls, SD	137,590
381	Somerville, MA	75,412
222	South Bend, IN	106,076
252	South Gate, CA	100,289
371	Southfield, MI	77,554
327	Sparks, NV	83,791
340	Spokane Valley, WA	82,288
100	Spokane, WA	199,384
202	Springfield, IL	115,187
146	Springfield, MA	151,670
145	Springfield, MO	151,901
179	Sterling Heights, MI	127,580
64	Stockton, CA	281,747
51	St. Louis, MO	346,005
66	St. Paul, MN	278,692
69	St. Petersburg, FL	254,713
370	Suffolk, VA	77,691
383	Sugar Land, TX	74,934
177	Sunnyvale, CA	128,862
284	Sunrise, FL	92,264
389	Surprise, AZ	62,751
158	Syracuse, NY	143,306
102	Tacoma, WA	198,748
137	Tallahassee, FL	160,147
56	Tampa, FL	329,035
337	Temecula, CA	82,628
128	Tempe, AZ	166,144
234	Thornton, CO	103,487
181	Thousand Oaks, CA	125,884
58	Toledo, OH	305,107
273	Toms River Twnshp, NJ	94,527
188	Topeka, KS	122,218
157	Torrance, CA	143,790
373	Tracy, CA	77,411
318	Trenton, NJ	85,566
346	Troy, MI	81,498
33	Tucson, AZ	529,447
46	Tulsa, OK	386,414
351	Tuscaloosa, AL	80,670
291	Tyler, TX	91,025
358	Upper Darby Twnshp, PA	80,104
268	Vacaville, CA	94,929
197	Vallejo, CA	117,351
139	Vancouver, WA	157,152
227	Ventura, CA	104,759
330	Victorville, CA	83,340
41	Virginia Beach, VA	446,448
224	Visalia, CA	105,350
285	Vista, CA	92,193
190	Waco, TX	120,036
167	Warren, MI	136,229
312	Warwick, RI	87,322
30	Washington, DC	550,521
217	Waterbury, CT	108,636
215	West Covina, CA	109,390
288	West Jordan, UT	91,543
261	West Palm Beach, FL	97,496
200	West Valley, UT	116,477
314	Westland, MI	86,386
295	Westminster, CA	90,452
221	Westminster, CO	106,211
316	Whittier, CA	86,077
240	Wichita Falls, TX	102,589
50	Wichita, KS	355,029
269	Wilmington, NC	94,843
110	Winston-Salem, NC	194,708
246	Woodbridge Twnshp, NJ	100,998
121	Worcester, MA	175,479
342	Yakima, WA	81,986
104	Yonkers, NY	197,408
369	Youngstown, OH	77,747
315	Yuma, AZ	86,157

Source: Federal Bureau of Investigation "Crime in the United States 2005"

**Updated estimates as of July 2005 based on U.S. Bureau of the Census figures. Charlotte, Honolulu, Indianapolis, Las Vegas, Louisville and Mobile include areas under their police department but outside the city limits. **Not available (not included in 2005 crime statistics).*

89. City Population in 2005 (continued)

National Total = 296,507,061*

RANK	CITY	POP	RANK	CITY	POP	RANK	CITY	POP
1	New York, NY	8,115,690	65	Newark, NJ	281,063	129	Santa Clarita, CA	165,894
2	Los Angeles, CA	3,871,077	66	St. Paul, MN	278,692	130	Huntsville, AL	165,147
3	Chicago, IL	2,873,441	67	Anchorage, AK	276,109	131	North Las Vegas, NV	164,190
4	Houston, TX	2,045,732	68	Lexington, KY	268,124	132	Brownsville, TX	163,877
5	Philadelphia, PA	1,472,915	69	St. Petersburg, FL	254,713	133	Overland Park, KS	163,274
6	Phoenix, AZ	1,466,296	70	Mobile, AL	249,798	134	Gilbert, AZ	162,257
7	Las Vegas, NV	1,281,698	71	Plano, TX	249,448	135	Rancho Cucamon., CA	160,404
8	San Diego, CA	1,272,148	72	Glendale, AZ	243,608	136	Dayton, OH	160,363
9	San Antonio, TX	1,256,584	73	Norfolk, VA	241,267	137	Tallahassee, FL	160,147
10	Dallas, TX	1,230,303	74	Jersey City, NJ	239,603	138	Fontana, CA	159,769
11	San Jose, CA	910,528	75	Lincoln, NE	237,710	139	Vancouver, WA	157,152
12	Honolulu, HI	908,521	76	Greensboro, NC	235,393	140	Chattanooga, TN	156,480
13	Detroit, MI	900,932	77	Birmingham, AL	234,571	140	Pomona, CA	156,480
14	Indianapolis, IN	800,304	78	Henderson, NV	232,536	142	Santa Rosa, CA	154,656
15	Jacksonville, FL	795,259	79	Chandler, AZ	231,613	143	Pembroke Pines, FL	153,492
16	San Francisco, CA	749,172	80	Hialeah, FL	229,590	144	Rockford, IL	153,048
17	Columbus, OH	730,329	81	Scottsdale, AZ	229,339	145	Springfield, MO	151,901
18	Austin, TX	693,019	82	Baton Rouge, LA	224,487	146	Springfield, MA	151,670
19	Memphis, TN	678,988	83	Madison, WI	221,419	147	Paterson, NJ	151,200
20	Charlotte, NC	677,122	84	Garland, TX	220,748	148	Salinas, CA	149,167
21	Baltimore, MD	641,097	85	Fort Wayne, IN	220,561	149	Hampton, VA	148,057
22	Louisville, KY	623,735	86	Chesapeake, VA	217,823	150	Salem, OR	148,009
23	Fort Worth, TX	613,261	87	Savannah, GA	213,587	151	Hollywood, FL	147,798
24	El Paso, TX	601,839	88	Rochester, NY	212,785	152	Pasadena, TX	146,546
25	Milwaukee, WI	586,500	89	Lubbock, TX	211,271	153	Corona, CA	146,363
26	Seattle, WA	579,215	90	Orlando, FL	210,290	154	Kansas City, KS	145,491
27	Boston, MA	567,589	91	Modesto, CA	208,142	155	Pasadena, CA	145,025
28	Denver, CO	564,552	92	Laredo, TX	206,555	156	Eugene, OR	144,526
29	Nashville, TN	557,034	93	Chula Vista, CA	206,239	157	Torrance, CA	143,790
30	Washington, DC	550,521	94	Durham, NC	205,080	158	Syracuse, NY	143,306
31	Portland, OR	540,389	95	Reno, NV	204,749	159	Lakewood, CO	143,259
32	Oklahoma City, OK	531,688	96	Fremont, CA	203,717	160	Grand Prairie, TX	142,628
33	Tucson, AZ	529,447	97	Glendale, CA	202,663	161	Hayward, CA	141,730
34	Albuquerque, NM	490,631	98	Montgomery, AL	202,209	162	Naperville, IL	140,654
35	Long Beach, CA	479,729	99	San Bernardino, CA	199,723	163	Bridgeport, CT	140,177
36	Fresno, CA	460,758	100	Spokane, WA	199,384	164	Sioux Falls, SD	137,590
37	Cleveland, OH	458,885	101	Shreveport, LA	199,021	165	Peoria, AZ	136,995
38	Sacramento, CA	457,347	102	Tacoma, WA	198,748	166	Escondido, CA	136,362
39	Mesa, AZ	452,340	103	Irving, TX	197,747	167	Warren, MI	136,229
40	Kansas City, MO	447,915	104	Yonkers, NY	197,408	168	Orange, CA	134,708
41	Virginia Beach, VA	446,448	105	Huntington Beach, CA	196,602	169	Fullerton, CA	134,325
42	Atlanta, GA	430,666	106	Grand Rapids, MI	195,274	170	Palmdale, CA	132,024
43	Omaha, NE	412,128	107	Richmond, VA	195,271	171	Mesquite, TX	131,844
44	Oakland, CA	400,619	108	Des Moines, IA	195,093	172	Coral Springs, FL	131,252
45	Miami, FL	388,295	109	Boise, ID	195,012	173	Cape Coral, FL	130,874
46	Tulsa, OK	386,414	110	Winston-Salem, NC	194,708	174	Alexandria, VA	130,056
47	Minneapolis, MN	376,277	111	Columbus, GA	187,886	175	Joliet, IL	130,026
48	Colorado Springs, CO	374,482	112	Little Rock, AR	185,855	176	Lancaster, CA	129,784
49	Arlington, TX	365,380	113	Oxnard, CA	184,806	177	Sunnyvale, CA	128,862
50	Wichita, KS	355,029	114	Salt Lake City, UT	184,627	178	Fort Collins, CO	128,727
51	St. Louis, MO	346,005	115	Newport News, VA	184,538	179	Sterling Heights, MI	127,580
52	Santa Ana, CA	344,991	116	Amarillo, TX	183,765	180	Fayetteville, NC	127,323
53	Anaheim, CA	335,992	117	Jackson, MS	180,417	181	Thousand Oaks, CA	125,884
54	Raleigh, NC	332,084	118	Knoxville, TN	179,989	182	Concord, CA	125,154
55	Pittsburgh, PA	330,780	119	Irvine, CA	179,501	183	Hartford, CT	125,086
56	Tampa, FL	329,035	120	Providence, RI	177,392	184	Elizabeth, NJ	124,997
57	Cincinnati, OH	314,292	121	Worcester, MA	175,479	185	El Monte, CA	122,934
58	Toledo, OH	305,107	122	Ontario, CA	171,186	186	McAllen, TX	122,729
59	Aurora, CO	295,888	123	Oceanside, CA	168,550	187	Cedar Rapids, IA	122,698
60	Riverside, CA	290,299	124	Garden Grove, CA	168,458	188	Topeka, KS	122,218
61	Bakersfield, CA	285,821	125	Fort Lauderdale, FL	168,293	189	Port St. Lucie, FL	121,069
61	Corpus Christi, TX	285,821	126	Moreno Valley, CA	167,394	190	Waco, TX	120,036
63	Buffalo, NY	283,269	127	Aurora, IL	167,266	191	Flint, MI	119,814
64	Stockton, CA	281,747	128	Tempe, AZ	166,144	192	Carrollton, TX	119,761

RANK	CITY	POP
193	Simi Valley, CA	119,682
194	Bellevue, WA	118,496
195	Columbia, SC	117,911
196	Evansville, IN	117,802
197	Vallejo, CA	117,351
198	Lansing, MI	117,036
199	Abilene, TX	116,695
200	West Valley, UT	116,477
201	Inglewood, CA	116,079
202	Springfield, IL	115,187
203	Beaumont, TX	114,141
204	Ann Arbor, MI	113,660
205	Peoria, IL	113,161
206	Lafayette, LA	112,161
207	Independence, MO	111,905
208	Gainesville, FL	111,313
209	Amherst, NY	111,178
210	Costa Mesa, CA	111,144
211	Clearwater, FL	111,058
212	Downey, CA	111,051
213	Manchester, NH	110,188
214	Clarksville, TN	110,117
215	West Covina, CA	109,390
216	Olathe, KS	108,754
217	Waterbury, CT	108,636
218	Norwalk, CA	107,391
219	Allentown, PA	106,933
220	Charleston, SC	106,307
221	Westminster, CO	106,211
222	South Bend, IN	106,076
223	Athens-Clarke, GA	105,727
224	Visalia, CA	105,350
225	Pueblo, CO	105,057
226	Burbank, CA	104,805
227	Ventura, CA	104,759
228	Santa Clara, CA	104,692
229	Fairfield, CA	104,639
230	Roseville, CA	104,297
231	Erie, PA	104,120
232	Arvada, CO	103,983
233	Miramar, FL	103,777
234	Thornton, CO	103,487
235	Lowell, MA	103,370
236	Miami Gardens, FL	103,164
237	Richmond, CA	102,997
238	Provo, UT	102,983
239	Cary, NC	102,949
240	Wichita Falls, TX	102,589
241	Berkeley, CA	102,191
242	Norman, OK	101,620
243	Green Bay, WI	101,599
244	Antioch, CA	101,593
245	Daly City, CA	101,288
246	Woodbridge Twnshp, NJ	100,998
247	Richardson, TX	100,896
248	Portsmouth, VA	100,724
249	Cambridge, MA	100,492
250	Edison Twnshp, NJ	100,361
251	Rialto, CA	100,321
252	South Gate, CA	100,289
253	Gary, IN	100,065
254	Denton, TX	99,905
255	Midland, TX	99,695
256	Centennial, CO	99,607
257	Livonia, MI	99,017
258	Killeen, TX	98,538
259	Billings, MT	97,898
260	Macon, GA	97,606
261	West Palm Beach, FL	97,496
262	Everett, WA	97,402
263	Mission Viejo, CA	96,892
264	Compton, CA	96,874
265	Gresham, OR	96,609
266	Clinton Twnshp, MI	96,028
267	Dearborn, MI	95,548
268	Vacaville, CA	94,929
269	Wilmington, NC	94,843
270	Brockton, MA	94,746
271	Greece, NY	94,688
272	El Cajon, CA	94,611
273	Toms River Twnshp, NJ	94,527
274	High Point, NC	94,401
275	Odessa, TX	94,371
276	Albany, NY	94,361
277	Carson, CA	94,355
278	Kenosha, WI	94,261
279	Rochester, MN	93,866
280	New Bedford, MA	93,720
281	Roanoke, VA	93,685
282	Boulder, CO	93,474
283	Sandy, UT	93,013
284	Sunrise, FL	92,264
285	Vista, CA	92,193
286	San Mateo, CA	91,881
287	Orem, UT	91,607
288	West Jordan, UT	91,543
289	Fargo, ND	91,380
290	Miami Beach, FL	91,115
291	Tyler, TX	91,025
292	Pompano Beach, FL	90,880
293	Palm Bay, FL	90,762
294	Lewisville, TX	90,608
295	Westminster, CA	90,452
296	Lakeland, FL	90,351
297	Columbia, MO	90,304
298	Hamilton Twnshp, NJ	90,255
299	McKinney, TX	89,863
300	Quincy, MA	89,661
301	Carlsbad, CA	89,633
302	San Angelo, TX	89,561
303	Lynn, MA	89,234
304	Redding, CA	89,161
305	Lawton, OK	88,823
306	Alhambra, CA	88,579
307	Santa Monica, CA	88,406
308	Nashua, NH	88,113
309	Santa Barbara, CA	87,950
310	Plantation, FL	87,427
311	Roswell, GA	87,386
312	Warwick, RI	87,322
313	Hawthorne, CA	86,852
314	Westland, MI	86,386
315	Yuma, AZ	86,157
316	Whittier, CA	86,077
317	Greeley, CO	85,991
318	Trenton, NJ	85,566
319	North Charleston, SC	85,416
320	Broken Arrow, OK	84,982
321	Duluth, MN	84,781
322	Canton Twnshp, MI	84,723
323	Davie, FL	84,443
324	Santa Maria, CA	84,312
325	Sioux City, IA	84,017
326	Beaverton, OR	83,979
327	Sparks, NV	83,791
328	Newton, MA	83,570
329	Round Rock, TX	83,390
330	Victorville, CA	83,340
331	Clarkstown, NY	82,928
332	Clovis, CA	82,921
333	Hillsboro, OR	82,912
334	Kent, WA	82,736
335	Parma, OH	82,708
336	Fort Smith, AR	82,638
337	Temecula, CA	82,628
338	Federal Way, WA	82,457
339	Murfreesboro, TN	82,367
340	Spokane Valley, WA	82,288
341	Lawrence, KS	82,148
342	Yakima, WA	81,986
343	Cheektowaga, NY	81,793
344	Cranston, RI	81,649
345	Lakewood, CA	81,626
346	Troy, MI	81,498
347	Ogden, UT	81,166
348	Bloomington, MN	81,068
349	Reading, PA	80,879
350	Farmington Hills, MI	80,853
351	Tuscaloosa, AL	80,670
352	Las Cruces, NM	80,573
353	Racine, WI	80,503
354	Newport Beach, CA	80,488
355	Hammond, IN	80,426
356	Camden, NJ	80,125
357	Clifton, NJ	80,119
358	Upper Darby Twnshp, PA	80,104
359	Canton, OH	79,940
360	Buena Park, CA	79,884
361	Boca Raton, FL	79,831
362	San Leandro, CA	79,709
363	Baldwin Park, CA	79,411
364	Lee's Summit, MO	79,284
365	Brick Twnshp, NJ	78,646
366	Livermore, CA	78,501
367	Danbury, CT	78,413
368	Albany, GA	78,353
369	Youngstown, OH	77,747
370	Suffolk, VA	77,691
371	Southfield, MI	77,554
372	Lake Forest, CA	77,523
373	Tracy, CA	77,411
374	Melbourne, FL	77,067
375	Colonie, NY	77,048
376	Chino, CA	76,547
377	Longview, TX	76,545
378	Chino Hills, CA	76,124
379	Napa, CA	75,966
380	Bellflower, CA	75,462
381	Somerville, MA	75,412
382	Murrieta, CA	75,008
383	Sugar Land, TX	74,934
384	Bellingham, WA	73,980
385	Hesperia, CA	73,863
386	Edmond, OK	73,585
387	Largo, FL	73,323
388	Deerfield Beach, FL	67,683
389	Surprise, AZ	62,751
NA	New Orleans, LA**	NA

Source: Federal Bureau of Investigation "Crime in the United States 2005"

**Updated estimates as of July 2005 based on U.S. Bureau of the Census figures. Charlotte, Honolulu, Indianapolis, Las Vegas, Louisville and Mobile include areas under their police department but outside the city limits. **Not available (not included in 2005 crime statistics).*

90. City Population in 2002

National Total = 287,973,924*

RANK	CITY	POP
184	Abilene, TX	121,089
334	Albany, GA	80,452
262	Albany, NY	93,915
36	Albuquerque, NM	457,488
164	Alexandria, VA	132,180
285	Alhambra, CA	88,956
217	Allentown, PA	107,101
114	Amarillo, TX	181,355
205	Amherst, NY	112,024
54	Anaheim, CA	340,065
64	Anchorage, AK	267,280
195	Ann Arbor, MI	115,309
265	Antioch, CA	93,858
52	Arlington, TX	347,789
219	Arvada, CO	107,028
226	Athens-Clarke, GA	105,007
40	Atlanta, GA	435,494
61	Aurora, CO	289,584
149	Aurora, IL	145,078
18	Austin, TX	685,784
69	Bakersfield, CA	256,134
342	Baldwin Park, CA	78,623
19	Baltimore, MD	671,028
78	Baton Rouge, LA	228,515
190	Beaumont, TX	118,934
347	Beaverton, OR	78,357
203	Bellevue, WA	112,819
357	Bellflower, CA	75,555
373	Bellingham, WA	69,164
222	Berkeley, CA	106,518
280	Billings, MT	90,569
72	Birmingham, AL	244,972
297	Bloomington, MN	86,907
348	Boca Raton, FL	78,183
104	Boise, ID	192,561
23	Boston, MA	596,444
244	Boulder, CO	99,191
349	Brick Twnshp, NJ	77,710
153	Bridgeport, CT	141,780
256	Brockton, MA	95,473
356	Broken Arrow, OK	75,794
146	Brownsville, TX	145,941
329	Buena Park, CA	81,158
58	Buffalo, NY	295,441
231	Burbank, CA	104,001
235	Cambridge, MA	102,611
324	Camden, NJ	81,575
350	Canton Twnshp, MI	77,226
335	Canton, OH	80,353
221	Cape Coral, FL	106,963
330	Carlsbad, CA	81,122
199	Carrollton, TX	114,453
269	Carson, CA	93,027
248	Cary, NC	97,716
183	Cedar Rapids, IA	121,189
NA	Centennial, CO**	NA
109	Chandler, AZ	187,795
245	Charleston, SC	98,942
21	Charlotte, NC	646,864
127	Chattanooga, TN	158,507
NA	Cheektowaga, NY**	NA
87	Chesapeake, VA	205,235
3	Chicago, IL	2,938,299
370	Chino Hills, CA	69,635
371	Chino, CA	69,241
115	Chula Vista, CA	179,932
55	Cincinnati, OH	333,273
345	Clarkstown, NY	78,409
225	Clarksville, TN	105,419
200	Clearwater, FL	113,761
34	Cleveland, OH	481,274
336	Clifton, NJ	80,317
251	Clinton Twnshp, MI	96,726
367	Clovis, CA	70,983
352	Colonie, NY	76,068
48	Colorado Springs, CO	378,114
304	Columbia, MO	85,700
189	Columbia, SC	119,036
102	Columbus, GA	194,265
17	Columbus, OH	715,739
249	Compton, CA	96,928
170	Concord, CA	126,254
181	Coral Springs, FL	122,923
168	Corona, CA	129,557
60	Corpus Christi, TX	289,803
204	Costa Mesa, CA	112,718
332	Cranston, RI	80,887
8	Dallas, TX	1,241,481
216	Daly City, CA	107,428
354	Danbury, CT	76,055
339	Davie, FL	79,182
122	Dayton, OH	167,176
246	Dearborn, MI	98,877
374	Deerfield Beach, FL	67,536
306	Denton, TX	84,121
25	Denver, CO	581,105
95	Des Moines, IA	199,390
11	Detroit, MI	961,987
206	Downey, CA	111,266
288	Duluth, MN	88,689
103	Durham, NC	193,328
240	Edison Twnshp, NJ	99,731
372	Edmond, OK	69,168
247	El Cajon, CA	98,354
188	El Monte, CA	120,225
24	El Paso, TX	588,750
179	Elizabeth, NJ	123,088
228	Erie, PA	104,173
157	Escondido, CA	138,466
152	Eugene, OR	141,928
178	Evansville, IN	123,153
260	Everett, WA	94,203
241	Fairfield, CA	99,711
283	Fargo, ND	89,458
312	Farmington Hills, MI	83,036
173	Fayetteville, NC	125,087
303	Federal Way, WA	85,729
169	Flint, MI	126,351
160	Fontana, CA	133,665
175	Fort Collins, CO	124,315
126	Fort Lauderdale, FL	159,365
327	Fort Smith, AR	81,369
86	Fort Wayne, IN	208,386
29	Fort Worth, TX	558,493
84	Fremont, CA	210,886
38	Fresno, CA	443,363
165	Fullerton, CA	130,632
239	Gainesville, FL	99,811
120	Garden Grove, CA	171,266
80	Garland, TX	225,371
229	Gary, IN	104,074
193	Gilbert, AZ	116,663
75	Glendale, AZ	232,707
90	Glendale, CA	202,136
162	Grand Prairie, TX	133,099
94	Grand Rapids, MI	200,029
266	Greece, NY	93,650
333	Greeley, CO	80,601
232	Green Bay, WI	103,791
77	Greensboro, NC	231,424
270	Gresham, OR	92,844
286	Hamilton Twnshp, NJ	88,931
306	Hammond, IN	84,121
138	Hampton, VA	150,885
177	Hartford, CT	123,540
294	Hawthorne, CA	87,202
148	Hayward, CA	145,174
107	Henderson, NV	190,761
378	Hesperia, CA	64,882
74	Hialeah, FL	236,772
287	High Point, NC	88,727
364	Hillsboro, OR	72,240
147	Hollywood, FL	145,729
13	Honolulu, HI	900,433
4	Houston, TX	2,040,583
98	Huntington Beach, CA	196,559
125	Huntsville, AL	159,618
197	Independence, MO	114,854
15	Indianapolis, IN	804,034
192	Inglewood, CA	116,716
141	Irvine, CA	148,328
93	Irving, TX	200,144
16	Jacksonville, FL	769,253
110	Jackson, MS	186,012
71	Jersey City, NJ	245,075
215	Joliet, IL	107,772
145	Kansas City, KS	146,352
37	Kansas City, MO	447,650
276	Kenosha, WI	91,658
321	Kent, WA	81,883
279	Killeen, TX	90,779
116	Knoxville, TN	177,191
208	Lafayette, LA	110,594
341	Lake Forest, CA	78,790
320	Lakeland, FL	82,039
318	Lakewood, CA	82,260
137	Lakewood, CO	151,005
180	Lancaster, CA	123,079
187	Lansing, MI	120,471
113	Laredo, TX	184,435
363	Largo, FL	72,543
359	Las Cruces, NM	75,077
10	Las Vegas, NV	1,153,546
331	Lawrence, KS	80,916
262	Lawton, OK	93,915
366	Lee's Summit, MO	71,678
328	Lewisville, TX	81,196
66	Lexington, KY	263,807
79	Lincoln, NE	227,943
111	Little Rock, AR	185,646
355	Livermore, CA	76,039
237	Livonia, MI	101,678

RANK	CITY	POP
35	Long Beach, CA	478,478
351	Longview, TX	76,608
2	Los Angeles, CA	3,830,561
NA	Louisville, KY**	NA
223	Lowell, MA	106,472
85	Lubbock, TX	208,447
281	Lynn, MA	90,156
236	Macon, GA	101,696
83	Madison, WI	211,061
209	Manchester, NH	110,406
207	McAllen, TX	111,150
382	McKinney, TX	56,789
360	Melbourne, FL	74,646
20	Memphis, TN	662,441
42	Mesa, AZ	421,547
167	Mesquite, TX	130,065
273	Miami Beach, FL	91,954
NA	Miami Gardens, FL**	NA
47	Miami, FL	379,044
243	Midland, TX	99,224
22	Milwaukee, WI	605,600
46	Minneapolis, MN	390,415
353	Miramar, FL	76,065
252	Mission Viejo, CA	96,522
68	Mobile, AL	256,542
100	Modesto, CA	195,795
89	Montgomery, AL	203,355
144	Moreno Valley, CA	147,612
369	Murfreesboro, TN	70,122
383	Murrieta, CA	45,909
358	Napa, CA	75,252
166	Naperville, IL	130,232
NA	Nashua, NH**	NA
28	Nashville, TN	560,596
261	New Bedford, MA	94,130
33	New Orleans, LA	486,157
1	New York, NY	8,084,693
63	Newark, NJ	279,269
362	Newport Beach, CA	72,605
112	Newport News, VA	185,622
309	Newton, MA	83,643
73	Norfolk, VA	241,523
250	Norman, OK	96,888
326	North Charleston, SC	81,530
172	North Las Vegas, NV	125,616
218	Norwalk, CA	107,093
43	Oakland, CA	414,161
123	Oceanside, CA	166,945
258	Odessa, TX	94,990
337	Ogden, UT	80,099
32	Oklahoma City, OK	512,448
264	Olathe, KS	93,912
45	Omaha, NE	394,090
124	Ontario, CA	163,812
161	Orange, CA	133,554
292	Orem, UT	87,462
101	Orlando, FL	194,454
139	Overland Park, KS	150,603
118	Oxnard, CA	176,617
310	Palm Bay, FL	83,044
186	Palmdale, CA	120,956
301	Parma, OH	86,169
156	Pasadena, CA	138,857
142	Pasadena, TX	147,979
135	Paterson, NJ	152,340
150	Pembroke Pines, FL	143,711
196	Peoria, AZ	115,245
198	Peoria, IL	114,585
5	Philadelphia, PA	1,524,226
6	Phoenix, AZ	1,404,938
53	Pittsburgh, PA	342,529
76	Plano, TX	231,912
299	Plantation, FL	86,726
131	Pomona, CA	154,964
323	Pompano Beach, FL	81,767
271	Port St. Lucie, FL	92,827
30	Portland, OR	544,604
233	Portsmouth, VA	103,620
117	Providence, RI	177,162
211	Provo, UT	109,079
220	Pueblo, CO	106,995
284	Quincy, MA	89,118
311	Racine, WI	83,038
62	Raleigh, NC	285,383
163	Rancho Cucamon., CA	132,436
325	Reading, PA	81,565
308	Redding, CA	83,836
99	Reno, NV	196,307
257	Rialto, CA	95,248
253	Richardson, TX	95,888
234	Richmond, CA	102,861
88	Richmond, VA	203,799
65	Riverside, CA	264,540
268	Roanoke, VA	93,104
291	Rochester, MN	87,555
81	Rochester, NY	221,871
136	Rockford, IL	152,307
314	Roseville, CA	82,858
313	Roswell, GA	82,957
379	Round Rock, TX	63,857
41	Sacramento, CA	421,971
154	Salem, OR	140,931
130	Salinas, CA	156,609
108	Salt Lake City, UT	188,504
272	San Angelo, TX	92,375
9	San Antonio, TX	1,195,592
105	San Bernardino, CA	192,212
7	San Diego, CA	1,268,346
14	San Francisco, CA	805,269
12	San Jose, CA	927,821
317	San Leandro, CA	82,371
254	San Mateo, CA	95,880
275	Sandy, UT	91,707
50	Santa Ana, CA	350,393
255	Santa Barbara, CA	95,717
224	Santa Clara, CA	106,121
129	Santa Clarita, CA	156,639
338	Santa Maria, CA	79,432
296	Santa Monica, CA	87,173
134	Santa Rosa, CA	153,018
158	Savannah, GA	137,516
82	Scottsdale, AZ	215,578
26	Seattle, WA	580,089
92	Shreveport, LA	200,757
194	Simi Valley, CA	115,442
305	Sioux City, IA	85,316
174	Sioux Falls, SD	124,997
344	Somerville, MA	78,438
210	South Bend, IN	109,182
238	South Gate, CA	99,916
340	Southfield, MI	79,178
365	Sparks, NV	72,164
NA	Spokane Valley, WA**	NA
91	Spokane, WA	201,433
201	Springfield, IL	113,081
132	Springfield, MA	153,967
133	Springfield, MO	153,675
171	Sterling Heights, MI	125,873
70	Stockton, CA	252,727
49	St. Louis, MO	353,004
59	St. Paul, MN	293,002
67	St. Petersburg, FL	259,582
377	Suffolk, VA	65,612
376	Sugar Land, TX	66,147
159	Sunnyvale, CA	136,601
282	Sunrise, FL	89,701
384	Surprise, AZ	32,807
140	Syracuse, NY	148,712
96	Tacoma, WA	199,299
128	Tallahassee, FL	157,511
56	Tampa, FL	317,322
380	Temecula, CA	59,837
121	Tempe, AZ	168,699
300	Thornton, CO	86,316
182	Thousand Oaks, CA	121,304
57	Toledo, OH	315,501
277	Toms River Twnshp, NJ	91,582
176	Topeka, KS	123,627
151	Torrance, CA	143,014
381	Tracy, CA	59,021
295	Trenton, NJ	87,189
322	Troy, MI	81,871
31	Tucson, AZ	517,607
44	Tulsa, OK	397,953
343	Tuscaloosa, AL	78,596
293	Tyler, TX	87,373
319	Upper Darby Twnshp, PA	82,181
274	Vacaville, CA	91,881
185	Vallejo, CA	121,049
143	Vancouver, WA	147,819
227	Ventura, CA	104,623
375	Victorville, CA	66,382
39	Virginia Beach, VA	438,175
259	Visalia, CA	94,929
267	Vista, CA	93,158
191	Waco, TX	118,788
155	Warren, MI	139,805
290	Warwick, RI	87,560
27	Washington, DC	570,898
212	Waterbury, CT	109,002
213	West Covina, CA	108,940
368	West Jordan, UT	70,879
302	West Palm Beach, FL	85,857
202	West Valley, UT	112,948
289	Westland, MI	87,578
278	Westminster, CA	91,448
230	Westminster, CO	104,018
298	Whittier, CA	86,755
214	Wichita Falls, TX	108,834
51	Wichita, KS	347,801
346	Wilmington, NC	78,389
106	Winston-Salem, NC	192,027
242	Woodbridge Twnshp, NJ	99,236
119	Worcester, MA	175,091
361	Yakima, WA	73,977
97	Yonkers, NY	197,957
315	Youngstown, OH	82,518
316	Yuma, AZ	82,437

Source: Federal Bureau of Investigation "Crime in the United States 2002"

**Updated estimates as of July 2002 based on U.S. Bureau of the Census figures. Charlotte, Honolulu, Indianapolis, Las Vegas, Louisville and Mobile include areas under their police department but outside the city limits. **Not available (cities not included in 2002 crime statistics)*

90. City Population in 2002 (continued)

National Total = 287,973,924*

RANK	CITY	POP
1	New York, NY	8,084,693
2	Los Angeles, CA	3,830,561
3	Chicago, IL	2,938,299
4	Houston, TX	2,040,583
5	Philadelphia, PA	1,524,226
6	Phoenix, AZ	1,404,938
7	San Diego, CA	1,268,346
8	Dallas, TX	1,241,481
9	San Antonio, TX	1,195,592
10	Las Vegas, NV	1,153,546
11	Detroit, MI	961,987
12	San Jose, CA	927,821
13	Honolulu, HI	900,433
14	San Francisco, CA	805,269
15	Indianapolis, IN	804,034
16	Jacksonville, FL	769,253
17	Columbus, OH	715,739
18	Austin, TX	685,784
19	Baltimore, MD	671,028
20	Memphis, TN	662,441
21	Charlotte, NC	646,864
22	Milwaukee, WI	605,600
23	Boston, MA	596,444
24	El Paso, TX	588,750
25	Denver, CO	581,105
26	Seattle, WA	580,089
27	Washington, DC	570,898
28	Nashville, TN	560,596
29	Fort Worth, TX	558,493
30	Portland, OR	544,604
31	Tucson, AZ	517,607
32	Oklahoma City, OK	512,448
33	New Orleans, LA	486,157
34	Cleveland, OH	481,274
35	Long Beach, CA	478,478
36	Albuquerque, NM	457,488
37	Kansas City, MO	447,650
38	Fresno, CA	443,363
39	Virginia Beach, VA	438,175
40	Atlanta, GA	435,494
41	Sacramento, CA	421,971
42	Mesa, AZ	421,547
43	Oakland, CA	414,161
44	Tulsa, OK	397,953
45	Omaha, NE	394,090
46	Minneapolis, MN	390,415
47	Miami, FL	379,044
48	Colorado Springs, CO	378,114
49	St. Louis, MO	353,004
50	Santa Ana, CA	350,393
51	Wichita, KS	347,801
52	Arlington, TX	347,789
53	Pittsburgh, PA	342,529
54	Anaheim, CA	340,065
55	Cincinnati, OH	333,273
56	Tampa, FL	317,322
57	Toledo, OH	315,501
58	Buffalo, NY	295,441
59	St. Paul, MN	293,002
60	Corpus Christi, TX	289,803
61	Aurora, CO	289,584
62	Raleigh, NC	285,383
63	Newark, NJ	279,269
64	Anchorage, AK	267,280
65	Riverside, CA	264,540
66	Lexington, KY	263,807
67	St. Petersburg, FL	259,582
68	Mobile, AL	256,542
69	Bakersfield, CA	256,134
70	Stockton, CA	252,727
71	Jersey City, NJ	245,075
72	Birmingham, AL	244,972
73	Norfolk, VA	241,523
74	Hialeah, FL	236,772
75	Glendale, AZ	232,707
76	Plano, TX	231,912
77	Greensboro, NC	231,424
78	Baton Rouge, LA	228,515
79	Lincoln, NE	227,943
80	Garland, TX	225,371
81	Rochester, NY	221,871
82	Scottsdale, AZ	215,578
83	Madison, WI	211,061
84	Fremont, CA	210,886
85	Lubbock, TX	208,447
86	Fort Wayne, IN	208,386
87	Chesapeake, VA	205,235
88	Richmond, VA	203,799
89	Montgomery, AL	203,355
90	Glendale, CA	202,136
91	Spokane, WA	201,433
92	Shreveport, LA	200,757
93	Irving, TX	200,144
94	Grand Rapids, MI	200,029
95	Des Moines, IA	199,390
96	Tacoma, WA	199,299
97	Yonkers, NY	197,957
98	Huntington Beach, CA	196,559
99	Reno, NV	196,307
100	Modesto, CA	195,795
101	Orlando, FL	194,454
102	Columbus, GA	194,265
103	Durham, NC	193,328
104	Boise, ID	192,561
105	San Bernardino, CA	192,212
106	Winston-Salem, NC	192,027
107	Henderson, NV	190,761
108	Salt Lake City, UT	188,504
109	Chandler, AZ	187,795
110	Jackson, MS	186,012
111	Little Rock, AR	185,646
112	Newport News, VA	185,622
113	Laredo, TX	184,435
114	Amarillo, TX	181,355
115	Chula Vista, CA	179,932
116	Knoxville, TN	177,191
117	Providence, RI	177,162
118	Oxnard, CA	176,617
119	Worcester, MA	175,091
120	Garden Grove, CA	171,266
121	Tempe, AZ	168,699
122	Dayton, OH	167,176
123	Oceanside, CA	166,945
124	Ontario, CA	163,812
125	Huntsville, AL	159,618
126	Fort Lauderdale, FL	159,365
127	Chattanooga, TN	158,507
128	Tallahassee, FL	157,511
129	Santa Clarita, CA	156,639
130	Salinas, CA	156,609
131	Pomona, CA	154,964
132	Springfield, MA	153,967
133	Springfield, MO	153,675
134	Santa Rosa, CA	153,018
135	Paterson, NJ	152,340
136	Rockford, IL	152,307
137	Lakewood, CO	151,005
138	Hampton, VA	150,885
139	Overland Park, KS	150,603
140	Syracuse, NY	148,712
141	Irvine, CA	148,328
142	Pasadena, TX	147,979
143	Vancouver, WA	147,819
144	Moreno Valley, CA	147,612
145	Kansas City, KS	146,352
146	Brownsville, TX	145,941
147	Hollywood, FL	145,729
148	Hayward, CA	145,174
149	Aurora, IL	145,078
150	Pembroke Pines, FL	143,711
151	Torrance, CA	143,014
152	Eugene, OR	141,928
153	Bridgeport, CT	141,780
154	Salem, OR	140,931
155	Warren, MI	139,805
156	Pasadena, CA	138,857
157	Escondido, CA	138,466
158	Savannah, GA	137,516
159	Sunnyvale, CA	136,601
160	Fontana, CA	133,665
161	Orange, CA	133,554
162	Grand Prairie, TX	133,099
163	Rancho Cucamon., CA	132,436
164	Alexandria, VA	132,180
165	Fullerton, CA	130,632
166	Naperville, IL	130,232
167	Mesquite, TX	130,065
168	Corona, CA	129,557
169	Flint, MI	126,351
170	Concord, CA	126,254
171	Sterling Heights, MI	125,873
172	North Las Vegas, NV	125,616
173	Fayetteville, NC	125,087
174	Sioux Falls, SD	124,997
175	Fort Collins, CO	124,315
176	Topeka, KS	123,627
177	Hartford, CT	123,540
178	Evansville, IN	123,153
179	Elizabeth, NJ	123,088
180	Lancaster, CA	123,079
181	Coral Springs, FL	122,923
182	Thousand Oaks, CA	121,304
183	Cedar Rapids, IA	121,189
184	Abilene, TX	121,089
185	Vallejo, CA	121,049
186	Palmdale, CA	120,956
187	Lansing, MI	120,471
188	El Monte, CA	120,225
189	Columbia, SC	119,036
190	Beaumont, TX	118,934
191	Waco, TX	118,788
192	Inglewood, CA	116,716

RANK	CITY	POP
193	Gilbert, AZ	116,663
194	Simi Valley, CA	115,442
195	Ann Arbor, MI	115,309
196	Peoria, AZ	115,245
197	Independence, MO	114,854
198	Peoria, IL	114,585
199	Carrollton, TX	114,453
200	Clearwater, FL	113,761
201	Springfield, IL	113,081
202	West Valley, UT	112,948
203	Bellevue, WA	112,819
204	Costa Mesa, CA	112,718
205	Amherst, NY	112,024
206	Downey, CA	111,266
207	McAllen, TX	111,150
208	Lafayette, LA	110,594
209	Manchester, NH	110,406
210	South Bend, IN	109,182
211	Provo, UT	109,079
212	Waterbury, CT	109,002
213	West Covina, CA	108,940
214	Wichita Falls, TX	108,834
215	Joliet, IL	107,772
216	Daly City, CA	107,428
217	Allentown, PA	107,101
218	Norwalk, CA	107,093
219	Arvada, CO	107,028
220	Pueblo, CO	106,995
221	Cape Coral, FL	106,963
222	Berkeley, CA	106,518
223	Lowell, MA	106,472
224	Santa Clara, CA	106,121
225	Clarksville, TN	105,419
226	Athens-Clarke, GA	105,007
227	Ventura, CA	104,623
228	Erie, PA	104,173
229	Gary, IN	104,074
230	Westminster, CO	104,018
231	Burbank, CA	104,001
232	Green Bay, WI	103,791
233	Portsmouth, VA	103,620
234	Richmond, CA	102,861
235	Cambridge, MA	102,611
236	Macon, GA	101,696
237	Livonia, MI	101,678
238	South Gate, CA	99,916
239	Gainesville, FL	99,811
240	Edison Twnshp, NJ	99,731
241	Fairfield, CA	99,711
242	Woodbridge Twnshp, NJ	99,236
243	Midland, TX	99,224
244	Boulder, CO	99,191
245	Charleston, SC	98,942
246	Dearborn, MI	98,877
247	El Cajon, CA	98,354
248	Cary, NC	97,716
249	Compton, CA	96,928
250	Norman, OK	96,888
251	Clinton Twnshp, MI	96,726
252	Mission Viejo, CA	96,522
253	Richardson, TX	95,888
254	San Mateo, CA	95,880
255	Santa Barbara, CA	95,717
256	Brockton, MA	95,473
257	Rialto, CA	95,248
258	Odessa, TX	94,990

RANK	CITY	POP
259	Visalia, CA	94,929
260	Everett, WA	94,203
261	New Bedford, MA	94,130
262	Albany, NY	93,915
262	Lawton, OK	93,915
264	Olathe, KS	93,912
265	Antioch, CA	93,858
266	Greece, NY	93,650
267	Vista, CA	93,158
268	Roanoke, VA	93,104
269	Carson, CA	93,027
270	Gresham, OR	92,844
271	Port St. Lucie, FL	92,827
272	San Angelo, TX	92,375
273	Miami Beach, FL	91,954
274	Vacaville, CA	91,881
275	Sandy, UT	91,707
276	Kenosha, WI	91,658
277	Toms River Twnshp, NJ	91,582
278	Westminster, CA	91,448
279	Killeen, TX	90,779
280	Billings, MT	90,569
281	Lynn, MA	90,156
282	Sunrise, FL	89,701
283	Fargo, ND	89,458
284	Quincy, MA	89,118
285	Alhambra, CA	88,956
286	Hamilton Twnshp, NJ	88,931
287	High Point, NC	88,727
288	Duluth, MN	88,689
289	Westland, MI	87,578
290	Warwick, RI	87,560
291	Rochester, MN	87,555
292	Orem, UT	87,462
293	Tyler, TX	87,373
294	Hawthorne, CA	87,202
295	Trenton, NJ	87,189
296	Santa Monica, CA	87,173
297	Bloomington, MN	86,907
298	Whittier, CA	86,755
299	Plantation, FL	86,726
300	Thornton, CO	86,316
301	Parma, OH	86,169
302	West Palm Beach, FL	85,857
303	Federal Way, WA	85,729
304	Columbia, MO	85,700
305	Sioux City, IA	85,316
306	Denton, TX	84,121
306	Hammond, IN	84,121
308	Redding, CA	83,836
309	Newton, MA	83,643
310	Palm Bay, FL	83,044
311	Racine, WI	83,038
312	Farmington Hills, MI	83,036
313	Roswell, GA	82,957
314	Roseville, CA	82,858
315	Youngstown, OH	82,518
316	Yuma, AZ	82,437
317	San Leandro, CA	82,371
318	Lakewood, CA	82,260
319	Upper Darby Twnshp, PA	82,181
320	Lakeland, FL	82,039
321	Kent, WA	81,883
322	Troy, MI	81,871
323	Pompano Beach, FL	81,767
324	Camden, NJ	81,575

RANK	CITY	POP
325	Reading, PA	81,565
326	North Charleston, SC	81,530
327	Fort Smith, AR	81,369
328	Lewisville, TX	81,196
329	Buena Park, CA	81,158
330	Carlsbad, CA	81,122
331	Lawrence, KS	80,916
332	Cranston, RI	80,887
333	Greeley, CO	80,601
334	Albany, GA	80,452
335	Canton, OH	80,353
336	Clifton, NJ	80,317
337	Ogden, UT	80,099
338	Santa Maria, CA	79,432
339	Davie, FL	79,182
340	Southfield, MI	79,178
341	Lake Forest, CA	78,790
342	Baldwin Park, CA	78,623
343	Tuscaloosa, AL	78,596
344	Somerville, MA	78,438
345	Clarkstown, NY	78,409
346	Wilmington, NC	78,389
347	Beaverton, OR	78,357
348	Boca Raton, FL	78,183
349	Brick Twnshp, NJ	77,710
350	Canton Twnshp, MI	77,226
351	Longview, TX	76,608
352	Colonie, NY	76,068
353	Miramar, FL	76,065
354	Danbury, CT	76,055
355	Livermore, CA	76,039
356	Broken Arrow, OK	75,794
357	Bellflower, CA	75,555
358	Napa, CA	75,252
359	Las Cruces, NM	75,077
360	Melbourne, FL	74,646
361	Yakima, WA	73,977
362	Newport Beach, CA	72,605
363	Largo, FL	72,543
364	Hillsboro, OR	72,240
365	Sparks, NV	72,164
366	Lee's Summit, MO	71,678
367	Clovis, CA	70,983
368	West Jordan, UT	70,879
369	Murfreesboro, TN	70,122
370	Chino Hills, CA	69,635
371	Chino, CA	69,241
372	Edmond, OK	69,168
373	Bellingham, WA	69,164
374	Deerfield Beach, FL	67,536
375	Victorville, CA	66,382
376	Sugar Land, TX	66,147
377	Suffolk, VA	65,612
378	Hesperia, CA	64,882
379	Round Rock, TX	63,857
380	Temecula, CA	59,837
381	Tracy, CA	59,021
382	McKinney, TX	56,789
383	Murrieta, CA	45,909
384	Surprise, AZ	32,807
NA	Centennial, CO**	NA
NA	Cheektowaga, NY**	NA
NA	Louisville, KY**	NA
NA	Miami Gardens, FL**	NA
NA	Nashua, NH**	NA
NA	Spokane Valley, WA**	NA

Source: Federal Bureau of Investigation "Crime in the United States 2002"

**Updated estimates as of July 2002 based on U.S. Bureau of the Census figures. Charlotte, Honolulu, Indianapolis, Las Vegas, Louisville and Mobile include areas under their police department but outside the city limits. **Not available (cities not included in 2002 crime statistics)*

DESCRIPTIONS OF METROPOLITAN AREAS IN 2006

Abilene, TX includes Callahan, Jones and Taylor counties

Akron, OH includes Portage and Summit counties

Albany, GA includes Baker, Dougherty, Lee, Terrell and Worth counties

Albany-Schenectady-Troy, NY includes Albany, Rensselaer, Saratoga, Schenectady and Schoharie counties

Albuquerque, NM includes Bernalillo, Sandoval, Torrance and Valencia counties

Alexandria, LA includes Grant and Rapides parishes

Allentown-Bethlehem-Easton, PA-NJ includes Warren, NJ, Carbon, PA, Lehigh, PA and Northampton, PA counties

Altoona, PA includes Blair County

Amarillo, TX includes Armstrong, Carson, Potter and Randall counties

Ames, IA includes Story County

Anchorage, AK includes Anchorage Municipality and Matanuska-Susitna Borough

Anderson, IN includes Madison County

Anderson, SC includes Anderson County

Ann Arbor, MI includes Washtenaw County

Anniston-Oxford, AL includes Calhoun County

Appleton, WI includes Calumet and Outagamie counties

Asheville, NC includes Buncombe, Haywood, Henderson and Madison counties

Athens-Clarke, GA includes, Clarke, Madison, Oconee and Oglethorpe counties

Atlanta-Sandy Springs-Marietta, GA includes Barrow, Bartow, Butts, Carroll, Cherokee, Clayton, Cobb, Coweta, Dawson, DeKalb, Douglas, Fayette, Forsyth, Fulton, Gwinnett, Haralson, Heard, Henry, Jasper, Lamar, Meriwether, Newton, Paulding, Pickens, Pike, Rockdale, Spalding and Walton counties

Atlantic City, NJ includes Atlantic County

Auburn-Opelika, AL includes Lee County

Augusta-Richmond, GA-SC includes Burke, GA, Columbia, GA, McDuffie, GA, Richmond, GA and Aiken, SC and Edgefield, SC counties

Austin-Round Rock, TX includes Bastrop, Caldwell, Hays, Travis and Williamson counties

Bakersfield, CA includes Kern County

Baltimore-Towson, MD includes Anne Arundel, Baltimore, Carroll, Harford, Howard and Queen Anne's counties and Baltimore city

Bangor, ME includes Penobscot County

Barnstable Town, MA includes Barnstable County

Baton Rouge, LA includes Ascension, East Baton Rouge, East Feliciana, Iberville, Livingston, Pointe Coupee, St. Helena, West Baton Rouge and West Feliciana parishes

Battle Creek, MI includes Calhoun County

Bay City, MI includes Bay County

Beaumont-Port Arthur, TX includes Hardin, Jefferson and Orange counties

Bellingham, WA includes Whatcom County

Bend, OR includes Deschutes County

Bethesda, MD see Washington, DC

Billings, MT includes Carbon and Yellowstone counties

Binghamton, NY includes Broome and Tioga counties

Birmingham-Hoover, AL includes Bibb, Blount, Chilton, Jefferson, St. Clair, Shelby and Walker counties

Bismarck, ND includes Burleigh and Morton counties

Blacksburg-Christiansburg-Radford, VA includes Giles, Montgomery and Pulaski counties and Radford city

Bloomington, IN includes Greene, Monroe and Owen counties

Bloomington-Normal, IL includes McLean County

Boise City-Nampa, ID includes Ada, Boise, Canyon, Gem and Owyhee counties

Boston-Cambridge-Quincy, MA-NH includes:

- Boston-Quincy, MA Metropolitan Division includes Norfolk, Plymouth, and Suffolk counties
- Cambridge-Newton-Framingham, MA Metropolitan Division includes Middlesex County
- Essex Metropolitan Division, MA includes Essex County
- Rockingham County-Strafford Metropolitan Division includes Rockingham and Strafford counties

Boulder, CO includes Boulder County

Bowling Green, KY includes Edmonson and Warren counties

Bremerton-Silverdale, WA includes Kitsap County

Bridgeport-Stamford-Norwalk, CT includes Fairfield County

Brownsville-Harlingen, TX includes Cameron County

Brunswick, GA includes Brantley, Glynn and McIntosh counties

Buffalo-Niagara Falls, NY includes Erie and Niagara counties

Burlington, NC includes Alamance County

Burlington-South Burlington, VT includes Chittenden, Franklin and Grand Isle counties

Cambridge, MA see Boston, MA

Camden, NJ see Philadelphia, PA

Canton-Massillon, OH includes Carroll and Stark counties

Cape Coral-Fort Myers, FL includes Lee County

Carson City, NV includes Carson City

DESCRIPTIONS OF METROPOLITAN AREAS IN 2006 (continued)

Casper, WY includes Natrona County

Cedar Rapids, IA includes Benton, Jones and Linn counties

Champaign-Urbana, IL includes Champaign, Ford and Piatt counties

Charleston, WV includes Boone, Clay, Kanawha, Lincoln and Putnam counties

Charleston-North Charleston, SC includes Berkeley, Charleston and Dorchester counties

Charlotte-Gastonia-Concord, NC-SC includes Anson, Cabarrus, Gaston, Mecklenburg, Union and York, SC counties

Charlottesville, VA includes Albemarle, Fluvanna, Greene and Nelson counties and Charlottesville city

Chattanooga, TN-GA includes Catoosa, GA, Dade, GA, Walker, GA, Hamilton, TN, Marion, TN and Sequatchie, TN counties

Cheyenne, WY includes Laramie County

Chicago-Naperville-Joliet, IL-IN-WI includes:

- Chicago-Naperville-Joliet, IL Metropolitan Division includes Cook, DeKalb, DuPage, Grundy, Kane, Kendall, McHenry and Will counties,
- Gary, IN Metropolitan Division includes Jasper, Lake, Newton and Porter counties, and
- Lake County-Kenosha-WI Metropolitan Division includes Lake, IL and Kenosha, WI counties

Chico, CA includes Butte County

Cincinnati-Middletown, OH-KY-IN includes Dearborn, IN, Franklin, IN, Ohio, IN, Boone KY, Bracken KY, Campbell, KY, Gallatin, KY, Grant, KY, Kenton, KY, Pendleton, KY, Brown, OH, Butler, OH, Clermont, OH, Hamilton, OH and Warren, OH counties

Clarksville, TN-KY includes Christian, KY, Trigg, KY, Montgomery, TN and Stewart, TN counties

Cleveland, TN includes Bradley and Polk counties

Cleveland-Elyria-Mentor, OH includes Cuyahoga, Geauga, Lake, Lorain and Medina counties

Coeur d'Alene, ID includes Kootenai County

College Station-Bryan, TX includes Brazos, Burleson and Robertson counties

Colorado Springs, CO includes El Paso and Teller counties

Columbia, MO includes Boone and Howard counties

Columbia, SC includes Calhoun, Fairfield, Kershaw, Lexington, Richland and Saluda counties

Columbus, GA-AL includes Russell, AL, Chattahoochee, GA, Harris, GA, Marion, GA and Muscogee, GA counties

Columbus, IN includes Bartholomew County

Columbus, OH includes Delaware, Fairfield, Franklin, Licking, Madison, Morrow, Pickaway and Union counties

Corpus Christi, TX includes Aransas, Nueces and San Patricio counties

Corvallis, OR includes Benton County

Cumberland, MD-WV includes Allegany, MD and Mineral, WV counties

Dallas-Fort Worth-Arlington, TX includes

- Dallas-Plano-Irving, TX Metropolitan Division includes Collin, Dallas, Delta, Denton, Ellis, Hunt, Kaufman and Rockwall counties and
- Fort Worth-Arlington, TX Metropolitan Division includes Johnson, Parker, Tarrant and Wise counties

Dalton, GA includes Murray and Whitfield counties

Danville, IL includes Vermilion County

Danville, VA includes Pittsylvania County and Danville city

Davenport-Moline-Rock Island, IA-IL includes Henry, IL, Mercer, IL, Rock Island, IL and Scott, IA counties

Dayton, OH includes Greene, Miami, Montgomery and Preble counties

Decatur, AL includes Lawrence and Morgan counties

Decatur, IL includes Macon County

Deltona-Daytona Beach-Ormond Beach, FL includes Volusia County

Denver-Aurora, CO includes Adams, Arapahoe, Broomfield, Clear Creek, Denver, Douglas, Elbert, Gilpin, Jefferson and Park counties

Des Moines, IA includes Dallas, Guthrie, Madison, Polk and Warren counties

Detroit-Warren-Livonia, MI includes

- Detroit-Livonia-Dearborn, MI Metropolitan Division includes Wayne County and
- Warren-Farmington Hills-Troy, MI Metropolitan Division includes Lapeer, Livingston, Macomb, Oakland and St. Clair counties

Dothan, AL includes Geneva, Henry and Houston counties

Dover, DE includes Kent County

Dubuque, IA includes Dubuque County

Duluth, MN-WI includes Carlton, MN, St. Louis, MN and Douglas, WI counties

Durham, NC includes Chatham, Durham, Orange and Person counties

Eau Claire, WI includes Chippewa and Eau Claire counties

Edison, NJ see New York, NY

El Centro, CA includes Imperial County

Elizabethtown, KY includes Hardin and Larue counties

Elkhart-Goshen, IN includes Elkhart County

Elmira, NY includes Chemung County

El Paso, TX includes El Paso County

Erie, PA includes Erie County

Essex County, MA see Boston, MA

Eugene-Springfield, OR includes Lane County

DESCRIPTIONS OF METROPOLITAN AREAS IN 2006 (continued)

Evansville, IN-KY includes Gibson, IN, Posey, IN, Vanderburgh, IN, Warrick, IN, Henderson, KY and Webster, KY counties

Fairbanks, AK includes Fairbanks North Star Borough

Fargo, ND-MN includes Clay, MN and Cass, ND counties

Farmington, NM includes San Juan County

Fayetteville, NC includes Cumberland and Hoke counties

Fayetteville-Springdale-Rogers, AR-MO includes Benton, AR, Madison, AR, Washington, AR and McDonald, MO counties

Flagstaff, AZ includes Coconino County

Flint, MI includes Genesee County

Florence, SC includes Darlington and Florence counties

Florence-Muscle Shoals, AL includes Colbert and Lauderdale counties

Fond du Lac, WI includes Fond du Lac County

Fort Collins-Loveland, CO includes Larimer County

Fort Lauderdale, FL see Miami, FL

Fort Smith, AR-OK includes Crawford, AR, Franklin, AR, Sebastian, AR, Le Flore, OK and Sequoyah, OK counties

Fort Walton Beach-Crestview-Destin, FL includes Okaloosa County

Fort Wayne, IN includes Allen, Wells and Whitley counties

Fort Worth, TX see Dallas, TX

Fresno, CA includes Fresno County

Gadsden, AL includes Etowah County

Gainesville, FL includes Alachua and Gilchrist counties

Gainesville, GA includes Hall County

Glens Falls, NY includes Warren and Washington counties

Goldsboro, NC includes Wayne County

Grand Forks, ND-MN includes Polk, MN and Grand Forks, ND counties

Grand Junction, CO includes Mesa County

Grand Rapids-Wyoming, MI includes Barry, Ionia, Kent and Newaygo counties

Great Falls, MT includes Cascade County

Greeley, CO includes Weld County

Green Bay, WI includes Brown, Kewaunee and Oconto counties

Greensboro-High Point, NC includes Guilford, Randolph and Rockingham counties

Greenville, NC includes Greene and Pitt counties

Greenville, SC includes Greenville, Laurens and Pickens counties

Gulfport-Biloxi, MS includes Hancock, Harrison and Stone counties

Hagerstown-Martinsburg, MD-WV includes Washington, MD, Berkeley, WV and Morgan, WV counties

Hanford-Corcoran, CA includes Kings County

Harrisburg-Carlisle, PA includes Cumberland, Dauphin and Perry counties

Harrisonburg, VA includes Rockingham County and Harrisonburg city

Hartford-West Hartford-East Hartford, CT includes Hartford, Middlesex and Tolland counties

Hattiesburg, MS includes Forrest, Lamar and Perry counties

Hickory-Lenoir-Morganton, NC includes Alexander, Burke, Caldwell and Catawba counties

Hinesville-Fort Stewart, GA includes Liberty and Long counties

Holland-Grand Haven, MI includes Ottawa County

Honolulu, HI includes Honolulu County

Hot Springs, AR includes Garland County

Houma-Bayou Cane-Thibodaux, LA includes Lafourche and Terrebonne parishes

Houston-Baytown-Sugar Land, TX includes Austin, Brazoria, Chambers, Fort Bend, Galveston, Harris, Liberty, Montgomery, San Jacinto and Waller counties

Huntington-Ashland, WV-KY-OH includes Boyd, KY, Greenup, KY, Lawrence, OH, Cabell, WV and Wayne, WV counties

Huntsville, AL includes Limestone and Madison counties

Idaho Falls, ID includes Bonneville and Jefferson counties

Indianapolis, IN includes Boone, Brown, Hamilton, Hancock, Hendricks, Johnson, Marion, Morgan, Putnam and Shelby counties

Iowa City, IA includes Johnson and Washington counties

Ithaca, NY includes Tompkins County

Jackson, MI includes Jackson County

Jackson, MS includes Copiah, Hinds, Madison, Rankin and Simpson counties

Jackson, TN includes Chester and Madison counties

Jacksonville, FL includes Baker, Clay, Duval, Nassau and St. Johns counties

Jacksonville, NC includes Onslow County

Janesville, WI includes Rock County

Jefferson City, MO includes Callaway, Cole, Moniteau and Osage counties

Johnson City, TN includes Carter, Unicoi and Washington counties

Johnstown, PA includes Cambria County

Jonesboro, AR includes Craighead and Poinsett counties

Joplin, MO includes Jasper and Newton counties

DESCRIPTIONS OF METROPOLITAN AREAS IN 2006 (continued)

Kalamazoo-Portage, MI includes Kalamazoo and Van Buren counties

Kankakee-Bradley, IL includes Kankakee County

Kansas City, MO-KS includes Franklin, KS, Johnson, KS, Leavenworth, KS, Linn, KS, Miami, KS, Wyandotte, KS, Bates, MO, Caldwell, MO, Cass, MO, Clay, MO, Clinton, MO, Jackson, MO, Lafayette, MO, Platte, MO and Ray, MO counties

Kennewick-Richland-Pasco, WA includes Benton and Franklin counties

Killeen-Temple-Fort Hood, TX includes Bell, Coryell and Lampasas counties

Kingsport-Bristol-Bristol, TN-VA includes Hawkins, TN, Sullivan, TN, Scott, VA, and Washington, VA counties and Bristol city, VA

Kingston, NY includes Ulster County

Knoxville, TN includes Anderson, Blount, Knox, Loudon and Union counties

Kokomo, IN includes Howard and Tipton counties

La Crosse, WI-MN includes Houston, MN and La Crosse, WI counties

Lafayette, IN includes Benton, Carroll and Tippecanoe counties

Lafayette, LA includes Lafayette and St. Martin parishes

Lake Charles, LA includes Calcasieu and Cameron parishes

Lake Havasu City-Kingman, AZ includes Mohave County

Lakeland, FL includes Polk County

Lancaster, PA includes Lancaster County

Lansing-East Lansing, MI includes Clinton, Eaton and Ingham counties

Laredo, TX includes Webb County

Las Cruces, NM includes Dona Ana County

Las Vegas-Paradise, NV includes Clark County

Lawrence, KS includes Douglas County

Lawton, OK includes Comanche County

Lebanon, PA includes Lebanon County

Lewiston, ID-WA includes Nez Perce, ID and Asotin, WA counties

Lewiston-Auburn, ME includes Androscoggin County

Lexington-Fayette, KY includes Bourbon, Clark, Fayette, Jessamine, Scott and Woodford counties

Lima, OH includes Allen County

Lincoln, NE includes Lancaster and Seward counties

Little Rock-North Little Rock, AR includes Faulkner, Grant, Lonoke, Perry, Pulaski and Saline counties

Logan, UT-ID includes Franklin, ID and Cache, UT counties

Longview, TX includes Gregg, Rusk and Upshur counties

Longview, WA includes Cowlitz County

Los Angeles-Long Beach-Santa Ana, CA includes:
- Los Angeles-Long Beach-Glendale, CA Metropolitan Division includes Los Angeles County and
- Santa Ana-Anaheim-Irvine, CA Metropolitan Division includes Orange County

Louisville, KY-IN includes Clark, IN, Floyd, IN, Harrison, IN, Washington, IN, Bullitt, KY, Henry, KY, Jefferson, KY, Meade, KY, Nelson, KY, Oldham, KY, Shelby, KY, Spencer, KY and Trimble, KY counties

Lubbock, TX includes Crosby and Lubbock counties

Lynchburg, VA includes Amherst, Appomattox, Bedford and Campbell counties and Bedford and Lynchburg cities

Macon, GA includes Bibb, Crawford, Jones, Monroe and Twiggs counties

Madera, CA includes Madera County

Madison, WI includes Columbia, Dane and Iowa counties

Manchester-Nashua, NH includes Hillsborough County

Mansfield, OH includes Richland County

McAllen-Edinburg-Pharr, TX includes Hidalgo County

Medford, OR includes Jackson County

Memphis, TN-MS-AR includes Crittenden, AR, DeSoto, MS, Marshall, MS, Tate, MS, Tunica, MS, Fayette, TN, Shelby, TN and Tipton, TN counties

Merced, CA includes Merced County

Miami-Fort Lauderdale-Miami Beach, FL includes:
- Fort Lauderdale-Pompano Beach-Deerfield Beach, FL Metropolitan Division includes Broward County,
- Miami-Miami Beach-Kendall, FL Metropolitan Division includes Miami-Dade County and
- West Palm Beach-Boca Raton-Boynton Beach, FL Metropolitan Division includes Palm Beach County

Michigan City-La Porte, IN includes LaPorte County

Midland, TX includes Midland County

Milwaukee-Waukesha-West Allis, WI includes Milwaukee, Ozaukee, Washington and Waukesha counties

Minneapolis-St. Paul-Bloomington, MN-WI includes Anoka, MN, Carver, MN, Chisago, MN, Dakota, MN, Hennepin, MN, Isanti, MN, Ramsey, MN, Scott, MN, Sherburne, MN, Washington, MN, Wright, MN, Pierce, WI and St. Croix, WI counties

Missoula, MT includes Missoula County

Mobile, AL includes Mobile County

Modesto, CA includes Stanislaus County

Monroe, LA includes Ouachita and Union parishes

Monroe, MI includes Monroe County

Montgomery, AL includes Autauga, Elmore, Lowndes and Montgomery counties

DESCRIPTIONS OF METROPOLITAN AREAS IN 2006 (continued)

Morgantown, WV includes Monongalia and Preston counties

Morristown, TN includes Grainger, Hamblen and Jefferson counties

Mount Vernon-Anacortes, WA includes Skagit County

Muncie, IN includes Delaware County

Muskegon-Norton Shores, MI includes Muskegon County

Myrtle Beach-Conway-North Myrtle Beach, SC includes Horry County

Napa, CA includes Napa County

Naples-Marco Island, FL includes Collier County

Nashville-Davidson--Murfreesboro, TN includes Cannon, Cheatham, Davidson, Dickson, Hickman, Macon, Robertson, Rutherford, Smith, Sumner, Trousdale, Williamson and Wilson counties

Nassau, NY see New York, NY

New Haven-Milford, CT includes New Haven County

New Orleans-Metairie-Kenner, LA includes Jefferson, Orleans, Plaquemines, St. Bernard, St. Charles, St. John the Baptist and St. Tammany parishes

New York-Northern New Jersey-Long Island, NY-NJ-PA includes:
- Edison, NJ, Metropolitan Division includes Middlesex, Monmouth, Ocean and Somerset counties,
- Nassau-Suffolk, NY Metropolitan Division includes Nassau and Suffolk counties,
- New York-Wayne-White Plains, NY-NJ Metropolitan Division includes Bergen, NJ, Hudson, NJ, Passaic, NJ, Bronx, NY, Kings, NY, New York, NY, Putnam, NY, Queens, NY, Richmond, NY, Rockland, NY and Westchester, NY counties and
- Newark-Union, NJ-PA Metropolitan Division includes Essex, NJ, Hunterdon, NJ, Morris, NJ Sussex, NJ, Union, NJ and Pike, PA counties

Niles-Benton Harbor, MI includes Berrien County

Norwich-New London, CT includes New London County

Oakland, CA see San Francisco, CA

Ocala, FL includes Marion County

Ocean City, NJ includes Cape May County

Odessa, TX includes Ector County

Ogden-Clearfield, UT includes Davis, Morgan and Weber counties

Oklahoma City, OK includes Canadian, Cleveland, Grady, Lincoln, Logan, McClain and Oklahoma counties

Olympia, WA includes Thurston County

Omaha-Council Bluffs, NE-IA includes Harrison, IA, Mills, IA, Pottawattamie, IA, Cass, NE, Douglas, NE, Sarpy, NE, Saunders, NE and Washington, NE counties

Orlando, FL includes Lake, Orange, Osceola and Seminole counties

Oshkosh-Neenah, WI includes Winnebago County

Owensboro, KY includes Daviess, Hancock and McLean counties

Oxnard-Thousand Oaks-Ventura, CA includes Ventura County

Palm Bay-Melbourne-Titusville, FL includes Brevard County

Palm Coast, FL includes Flagler County

Panama City-Lynn Haven, FL includes Bay County

Parkersburg-Marietta, WV-OH includes Washington, OH, Pleasants, WV, Wirt, WV and Wood, WV counties

Pascagoula, MS includes George and Jackson counties

Pensacola-Ferry Pass-Brent, FL includes Escambia and Santa Rosa counties

Peoria, IL includes Marshall, Peoria, Stark, Tazewell and Woodford counties

Philadelphia-Camden-Wilmington, PA-NJ-DE-MD includes:
- Camden, NJ Metropolitan Division includes Burlington, Camden, and Gloucester counties,
- Philadelphia, PA Metropolitan Division includes Bucks, Chester, Delaware, Montgomery and Philadelphia counties and
- Wilmington, DE-MD-NJ Metropolitan Division includes New Castle, DE, Cecil, MD and Salem, NJ counties

Phoenix-Mesa-Scottsdale, AZ includes Maricopa and Pinal counties

Pine Bluff, AR includes Cleveland, Jefferson and Lincoln counties

Pittsburgh, PA includes Allegheny, Armstrong, Beaver, Butler, Fayette, Washington and Westmoreland counties

Pittsfield, MA includes Berkshire County

Pocatello, ID includes Bannock and Power counties

Portland-South Portland-Biddeford, ME includes Cumberland, Sagadahoc and York counties

Portland-Vancouver-Beaverton, OR-WA includes Clackamas, Columbia, OR, Multnomah, OR, Washington, OR, Yamhill, OR, Clark, WA and Skamania, WA counties

Port St. Lucie-Fort Pierce, FL includes Martin and St. Lucie counties

Poughkeepsie-Newburgh-Middletown, NY includes Dutchess and Orange counties

Prescott, AZ includes Yavapai County

Providence-New Bedford-Fall River, RI-MA includes Bristol, MA, Bristol, RI, Kent, RI, Newport, RI, Providence, RI and Washington, RI counties

Provo-Orem, UT includes Juab and Utah counties

Pueblo, CO includes Pueblo County

Punta Gorda, FL includes Charlotte County

Racine, WI includes Racine County

Raleigh-Cary, NC includes Franklin, Johnston and Wake counties

Rapid City, SD includes Meade and Pennington counties

DESCRIPTIONS OF METROPOLITAN AREAS IN 2006 (continued)

Reading, PA includes Berks County

Redding, CA includes Shasta County

Reno-Sparks, NV includes Storey and Washoe counties

Richmond, VA includes Amelia, Caroline, Charles city, Chesterfield, Cumberland, Dinwiddie, Goochland, Hanover, Henrico, King and Queen, King William, Louisa, New, Kent, Powhatan, Prince George and Sussex counties and Colonial Heights, Hopewell, Petersburg and Richmond cities

Riverside-San Bernardino-Ontario, CA includes Riverside and San Bernardino counties

Roanoke, VA includes Botetourt, Craig, Franklin and Roanoke counties and Roanoke and Salem cities

Rochester, MN includes Dodge, Olmsted and Wabasha counties

Rochester, NY includes Livingston, Monroe, Ontario, Orleans and Wayne counties

Rockford, IL includes Boone and Winnebago counties

Rockingham County, NH see Boston, MA

Rocky Mount, NC includes Edgecombe and Nash counties

Rome, GA includes Floyd County

Sacramento--Arden-Arcade--Roseville, CA includes El Dorado, Placer, Sacramento and Yolo counties

Saginaw-Saginaw Township North, MI includes Saginaw County

St. Cloud, MN includes Benton and Stearns counties

St. George, UT includes Washington County

St. Joseph, MO-KS includes Doniphan, KS, Andrew, MO, Buchanan, MO and DeKalb, MO counties

St. Louis, MO-IL includes, Bond, IL, Calhoun, IL, Clinton, IL, Jersey, IL, Macoupin, IL, Madison, IL, Monroe, IL, St. Clair, IL, Crawford, MO (pt.), Franklin, MO, Jefferson, MO, Lincoln, MO, St. Charles, MO, St. Louis, MO, Warren, MO and Washington, MO counties and St. Louis city, MO

Salem, OR includes Marion and Polk counties

Salinas, CA includes Monterey County

Salisbury, MD includes Somerset and Wicomico counties

Salt Lake City, UT includes Salt Lake, Summit and Tooele counties

San Angelo, TX includes Irion and Tom Green counties

San Antonio, TX includes Atascosa, Bandera, Bexar, Comal, Guadalupe, Kendall, Medina and Wilson counties

San Diego-Carlsbad-San Marcos, CA includes San Diego County

Sandusky, OH includes Erie County

San Francisco-Oakland-Fremont, CA includes:

- Oakland-Fremont-Hayward, CA Metropolitan Division includes Alameda and Contra Costa counties and
- San Francisco-San Mateo-Redwood City, CA Metropolitan Division includes Marin, San Francisco and San Mateo counties

San Jose-Sunnyvale-Santa Clara, CA includes San Benito and Santa Clara counties

San Luis Obispo-Paso Robles, CA includes San Luis Obispo County

Santa Ana, CA see Los Angeles, CA

Santa Barbara-Santa Maria-Goleta, CA includes Santa Barbara County

Santa Cruz-Watsonville, CA includes Santa Cruz County

Santa Fe, NM includes Santa Fe County

Santa Rosa-Petaluma, CA includes Sonoma County

Sarasota-Bradenton-Venice, FL includes Manatee and Sarasota counties

Savannah, GA includes Bryan, Chatham and Effingham counties

Scranton--Wilkes-Barre, PA includes Lackawanna, Luzerne, Wyoming counties

Seattle-Tacoma-Bellevue, WA includes:

- Seattle-Bellevue-Everett, WA Metropolitan Division includes King and Snohomish counties and
- Tacoma, WA Metropolitan Division includes Pierce County

Sebastian-Vero Beach, FL includes Indian River County

Sheboygan, WI includes Sheboygan County

Sherman-Denison, TX includes Grayson County

Shreveport-Bossier City, LA includes Bossier, Caddo and De Soto parishes

Sioux City, IA-NE-SD includes Woodbury, IA, Dakota, NE, Dixon, NE and Union, SD counties

Sioux Falls, SD includes Lincoln, McCook, Minnehaha and Turner counties

South Bend-Mishawaka, IN-MI includes St. Joseph, IN and Cass, MI counties

Spartanburg, SC includes Spartanburg County

Spokane, WA includes Spokane County

Springfield, IL includes Menard and Sangamon counties

Springfield, MA includes Franklin, Hampden and Hampshire counties

Springfield, MO includes Christian, Dallas, Greene, Polk and Webster counties

Springfield, OH includes Clark County

State College, PA includes Centre County

Stockton, CA includes San Joaquin County

Sumter, SC includes Sumter County

Syracuse, NY includes Madison, Onondaga and Oswego counties

Tacoma, WA see Seattle, WA

DESCRIPTIONS OF METROPOLITAN AREAS IN 2006 (continued)

Tallahassee, FL includes Gadsden, Jefferson, Leon and Wakulla counties

Tampa-St. Petersburg-Clearwater, FL includes Hernando, Hillsborough, Pasco and Pinellas counties

Terre Haute, IN includes Clay, Sullivan, Vermillion and Vigo counties

Texarkana, TX-Texarkana, AR includes Miller, AR and Bowie, TX counties

Toledo, OH includes Fulton, Lucas, Ottawa and Wood counties

Topeka, KS includes Jackson, Jefferson, Osage, Shawnee and Wabaunsee counties

Trenton-Ewing, NJ includes Mercer County

Tucson, AZ includes Pima County

Tulsa, OK includes Creek, Okmulgee, Osage, Pawnee, Rogers, Tulsa and Wagoner counties

Tuscaloosa, AL includes Greene, Hale and Tuscaloosa counties

Tyler, TX includes Smith County

Utica-Rome, NY includes Herkimer and Oneida counties

Valdosta, GA includes Brooks, Echols, Lanier and Lowndes counties

Vallejo-Fairfield, CA includes Solano County

Victoria, TX includes Calhoun, Goliad and Victoria counties

Vineland-Millville-Bridgeton, NJ includes Cumberland County

Virginia Beach-Norfolk-Newport News, VA-NC includes Currituck, NC, Gloucester, VA, Isle of Wight, VA, James city, VA, Mathews, VA, Surry, VA and York, VA counties and Chesapeake, VA, Hampton, VA, Newport News, VA, Norfolk, VA, Poquoson, VA, Portsmouth, VA, Suffolk, VA, Virginia Beach, VA and Williamsburg, VA cities

Visalia-Porterville, CA includes Tulare County

Waco, TX includes McLennan County

Warner Robins, GA includes Houston County

Warren, MI see Detroit, MI

Washington-Arlington-Alexandria, DC-VA-MD-WV includes:

- Bethesda-Frederick-Gaithersburg, MD Metropolitan Division includes Frederick and Montgomery counties,
- Washington-Arlington-Alexandria, DC-VA-MD-WV Metropolitan Division includes District of Columbia, DC and Calvert, MD, Charles, MD, Prince George's, MD, Arlington, VA, Clarke, VA, Fairfax, VA, Fauquier, VA, Loudoun, VA, Prince William, VA, Spotsylvania, VA, Stafford, VA and Warren, VA counties and Alexandria, VA, Fairfax, VA, Falls Church, VA, Fredericksburg, VA, Manassas, VA and Manassas Park, VA cities and Jefferson WV County

Waterloo-Cedar Falls, IA includes Black Hawk, Bremer and Grundy counties

Wausau, WI includes Marathon County

Weirton-Steubenville, WV-OH includes Jefferson, OH, Brooke, WV and Hancock, WV counties

Wenatchee, WA includes Chelan and Douglas counties

West Palm Beach, FL see Miami, FL

Wheeling, WV-OH includes Belmont, OH, Marshall, WV and Ohio, WV

Wichita, KS includes Butler, Harvey, Sedgwick and Sumner counties

Wichita Falls, TX includes Archer, Clay and Wichita counties

Williamsport, PA includes Lycoming County

Wilmington, DE see Philadelphia, PA

Wilmington, NC includes Brunswick, New Hanover and Pender counties

Winchester, VA-WV includes Frederick, VA County, Winchester city, VA and Hampshire, WV County

Winston-Salem, NC includes Davie, Forsyth, Stokes and Yadkin counties

Worcester, MA includes Worcester County

Yakima, WA includes Yakima County

York-Hanover, PA includes York County

Youngstown-Warren-Boardman, OH-PA includes Mahoning, OH, Trumbull, OH and Mercer, PA counties

Yuba City, CA includes Sutter and Yuba counties

Yuma, AZ includes Yuma County

COUNTY INDEX: 2006

COUNTY:	IS IN METROPOLITAN:
Adams, CO	Denver-Aurora, CO
Ada, ID	Boise City-Nampa, ID
Aiken, SC	Augusta-Richmond County, GA-SC
Alachua, FL	Gainesville, FL
Alamance, NC	Burlington, NC
Alameda, CA	San Francisco-Oakland-Fremont, CA
Albany, NY	Albany-Schenectady-Troy, NY
Albemarle, VA	Charlottesville, VA
Alexander, NC	Hickory-Lenoir-Morganton, NC
Alexandria city, VA	Washington, DC-VA-MD-WV
Allegany, MD	Cumberland, MD-WV
Allegheny, PA	Pittsburgh, PA
Allen, IN	Fort Wayne, IN
Allen, OH	Lima, OH
Amelia, VA	Richmond, VA
Amherst, VA	Lynchburg, VA
Anchorage city, AK	Anchorage, AK
Anderson, SC	Anderson, SC
Anderson, TN	Knoxville, TN
Andrew, MO	St. Joseph, MO-KS
Androscoggin, ME	Lewiston-Auburn, ME
Anne Arundel, MD	Baltimore-Towson, MD
Anoka, MN	Minneapolis-St. Paul-Bloomington, MN-WI
Anson, NC	Charlotte-Gastonia-Concord, NC-SC
Appomattox, VA	Lynchburg, VA
Aransas, TX	Corpus Christi, TX
Arapahoe, CO	Denver-Aurora, CO
Archer, TX	Wichita Falls, TX
Arlington, VA	Washington, DC-VA-MD-WV
Armstrong, PA	Pittsburgh, PA
Armstrong, TX	Amarillo, TX
Ascension, LA	Baton Rouge, LA
Asotin, WA	Lewiston, ID-WA
Atascosa, TX	San Antonio, TX
Atlantic, NJ	Atlantic City, NJ
Austin, TX	Houston-Baytown-Sugar Land, TX
Autauga, AL	Montgomery, AL
Baker, FL	Jacksonville, FL
Baker, GA	Albany, GA
Baltimore city, MD	Baltimore-Towson, MD
Baltimore, MD	Baltimore-Towson, MD
Bandera, TX	San Antonio, TX
Bannock, ID	Pocatello, ID
Barnstable, MA	Barnstable Town, MA
Barrow, GA	Atlanta-Sandy Springs-Marietta, GA
Barry, MI	Grand Rapids-Wyoming, MI
Bartholomew, IN	Columbus, IN
Bartow, GA	Atlanta-Sandy Springs-Marietta, GA
Bastrop, TX	Austin-Round Rock, TX
Bates, MO	Kansas City, MO-KS
Bay, FL	Panama City-Lynn Haven, FL
Bay, MI	Bay City, MI
Beaver, PA	Pittsburgh, PA
Bedford city, VA	Lynchburg, VA
Bedford, VA	Lynchburg, VA
Bell, TX	Killeen-Temple-Fort Hood, TX
Belmont, OH	Wheeling, WV-OH
Benton, AR	Fayetteville-Springdale-Rogers, AR-MO
Benton, IA	Cedar Rapids, IA
Benton, IN	Lafayette, IN
Benton, MN	St. Cloud, MN
Benton, OR	Corvallis, OR
Benton, WA	Kennewick-Richland-Pasco, WA
Bergen, NJ	New York, NY-NJ-PA
Berkeley, SC	Charleston-North Charleston, SC
Berkeley, WV	Hagerstown-Martinsburg, MD-WV
Berkshire, MA	Pittsfield, MA
Berks, PA	Reading, PA
Bernalillo, NM	Albuquerque, NM
Berrien, MI	Niles-Benton Harbor, MI
Bexar, TX	San Antonio, TX
Bibb, AL	Birmingham-Hoover, AL
Bibb, GA	Macon, GA
Black Hawk, IA	Waterloo-Cedar Falls, IA
Blair, PA	Altoona, PA
Blount, AL	Birmingham-Hoover, AL
Blount, TN	Knoxville, TN
Boise, ID	Boise City-Nampa, ID
Bond, IL	St. Louis, MO-IL
Bonneville, ID	Idaho Falls, ID
Boone, IL	Rockford, IL
Boone, IN	Indianapolis, IN
Boone, KY	Cincinnati-Middletown, OH-KY-IN
Boone, MO	Columbia, MO
Boone, WV	Charleston, WV
Bossier, LA	Shreveport-Bossier City, LA
Botetourt, VA	Roanoke, VA
Boulder, CO	Boulder, CO
Bourbon, KY	Lexington-Fayette, KY
Bowie, TX	Texarkana, TX-Texarkana, AR
Boyd, KY	Huntington-Ashland, WV-KY-OH
Bracken, KY	Cincinnati-Middletown, OH-KY-IN
Bradley, TN	Cleveland, TN
Brantley, GA	Brunswick, GA
Brazoria, TX	Houston-Baytown-Sugar Land, TX
Brazos, TX	College Station-Bryan, TX
Bremer, IA	Waterloo-Cedar Falls, IA
Brevard, FL	Palm Bay-Melbourne-Titusville, FL
Bristol city, VA	Kingsport-Bristol-Bristol, TN-VA
Bristol, MA	Providence-New Bedford-Fall River, RI-MA
Bristol, RI	Providence-New Bedford-Fall River, RI-MA
Bronx, NY	New York, NY-NJ-PA
Brooke, WV	Weirton-Steubenville, WV-OH
Brooks, GA	Valdosta, GA
Broome, NY	Binghamton, NY
Broomfield, CO	Denver-Aurora, CO
Broward, FL	Miami-Fort Lauderdale-Miami Beach, FL
Brown, IN	Indianapolis, IN
Brown, OH	Cincinnati-Middletown, OH-KY-IN
Brown, WI	Green Bay, WI
Brunswick, NC	Wilmington, NC
Bryan, GA	Savannah, GA
Buchanan, MO	St. Joseph, MO-KS
Bucks, PA	Philadelphia, PA-NJ-DE-MD
Bullitt, KY	Louisville, KY-IN
Buncombe, NC	Asheville, NC
Burke, GA	Augusta-Richmond County, GA-SC
Burke, NC	Hickory-Lenoir-Morganton, NC
Burleigh, ND	Bismarck, ND
Burleson, TX	College Station-Bryan, TX
Burlington, NJ	Philadelphia, PA-NJ-DE-MD
Butler, KS	Wichita, KS
Butler, OH	Cincinnati-Middletown, OH-KY-IN
Butler, PA	Pittsburgh, PA
Butte, CA	Chico, CA
Butts, GA	Atlanta-Sandy Springs-Marietta, GA
Cabarrus, NC	Charlotte-Gastonia-Concord, NC-SC
Cabell, WV	Huntington-Ashland, WV-KY-OH
Cache, UT	Logan, UT-ID
Caddo, LA	Shreveport-Bossier City, LA
Calcasieu, LA	Lake Charles, LA
Caldwell, MO	Kansas City, MO-KS
Caldwell, NC	Hickory-Lenoir-Morganton, NC
Caldwell, TX	Austin-Round Rock, TX
Calhoun, AL	Anniston-Oxford, AL
Calhoun, IL	St. Louis, MO-IL
Calhoun, MI	Battle Creek, MI
Calhoun, SC	Columbia, SC
Calhoun, TX	Victoria, TX
Callahan, TX	Abilene, TX
Callaway, MO	Jefferson City, MO
Calumet, WI	Appleton, WI
Calvert, MD	Washington, DC-VA-MD-WV
Cambria, PA	Johnstown, PA
Camden, NJ	Philadelphia, PA-NJ-DE-MD
Cameron, LA	Lake Charles, LA
Cameron, TX	Brownsville-Harlingen, TX
Campbell, KY	Cincinnati-Middletown, OH-KY-IN
Campbell, VA	Lynchburg, VA
Canadian, OK	Oklahoma City, OK
Cannon, TN	Nashville-Davidson--Murfreesboro, TN
Canyon, ID	Boise City-Nampa, ID
Cape May, NJ	Ocean City, NJ
Carbon, MT	Billings, MT
Carbon, PA	Allentown-Bethlehem-Easton, PA-NJ
Carlton, MN	Duluth, MN-WI

COUNTY:	IS IN METROPOLITAN:
Caroline, VA	Richmond, VA
Carroll, GA	Atlanta-Sandy Springs-Marietta, GA
Carroll, IN	Lafayette, IN
Carroll, MD	Baltimore-Towson, MD
Carroll, OH	Canton-Massillon, OH
Carson City, NV	Carson City, NV
Carson, TX	Amarillo, TX
Carter, TN	Johnson City, TN
Carver, MN	Minneapolis-St. Paul-Bloomington, MN-WI
Cascade, MT	Great Falls, MT
Cass, MI	South Bend-Mishawaka, IN-MI
Cass, MO	Kansas City, MO-KS
Cass, ND	Fargo, ND-MN
Cass, NE	Omaha-Council Bluffs, NE-IA
Catawba, NC	Hickory-Lenoir-Morganton, NC
Catoosa, GA	Chattanooga, TN-GA
Cecil, MD	Philadelphia, PA-NJ-DE-MD
Centre, PA	State College, PA
Chambers, TX	Houston-Baytown-Sugar Land, TX
Champaign, IL	Champaign-Urbana, IL
Charles City, VA	Richmond, VA
Charleston, SC	Charleston-North Charleston, SC
Charles, MD	Washington, DC-VA-MD-WV
Charlottesville city, VA	Charlottesville, VA
Charlotte, FL	Punta Gorda, FL
Chatham, GA	Savannah, GA
Chatham, NC	Durham, NC
Chattahoochee, GA	Columbus, GA-AL
Cheatham, TN	Nashville-Davidson--Murfreesboro, TN
Chelan, WA	Wenatchee, WA
Chemung, NY	Elmira, NY
Cherokee, GA	Atlanta-Sandy Springs-Marietta, GA
Chesapeake city, VA	Virginia Beach-Norfolk, VA-NC
Chesterfield, VA	Richmond, VA
Chester, PA	Philadelphia, PA-NJ-DE-MD
Chester, TN	Jackson, TN
Chilton, AL	Birmingham-Hoover, AL
Chippewa, WI	Eau Claire, WI
Chisago, MN	Minneapolis-St. Paul-Bloomington, MN-WI
Chittenden, VT	Burlington-South Burlington, VT
Christian, KY	Clarksville, TN-KY
Christian, MO	Springfield, MO
Clackamas, OR	Portland-Vancouver-Beaverton, OR-WA
Clarke, GA	Athens-Clarke County, GA
Clarke, VA	Washington, DC-VA-MD-WV
Clark, IN	Louisville, KY-IN
Clark, KY	Lexington-Fayette, KY
Clark, NV	Las Vegas-Paradise, NV
Clark, OH	Springfield, OH
Clark, WA	Portland-Vancouver-Beaverton, OR-WA
Clayton, GA	Atlanta-Sandy Springs-Marietta, GA
Clay, FL	Jacksonville, FL
Clay, IN	Terre Haute, IN
Clay, MN	Fargo, ND-MN
Clay, MO	Kansas City, MO-KS
Clay, TX	Wichita Falls, TX
Clay, WV	Charleston, WV
Clear Creek, CO	Denver-Aurora, CO
Clermont, OH	Cincinnati-Middletown, OH-KY-IN
Cleveland, AR	Pine Bluff, AR
Cleveland, OK	Oklahoma City, OK
Clinton, IL	St. Louis, MO-IL
Clinton, MI	Lansing-East Lansing, MI
Clinton, MO	Kansas City, MO-KS
Cobb, GA	Atlanta-Sandy Springs-Marietta, GA
Coconino, AZ	Flagstaff, AZ
Colbert, AL	Florence-Muscle Shoals, AL
Cole, MO	Jefferson City, MO
Collier, FL	Naples-Marco Island, FL
Collin, TX	Dallas-Fort Worth-Arlington, TX
Colonial Heights city, VA	Richmond, VA
Columbia, GA	Augusta-Richmond County, GA-SC
Columbia, OR	Portland-Vancouver-Beaverton, OR-WA
Columbia, WI	Madison, WI
Comal, TX	San Antonio, TX
Comanche, OK	Lawton, OK
Contra Costa, CA	San Francisco-Oakland-Fremont, CA
Cook, IL	Chicago-Naperville-Joliet, IL-IN-WI

COUNTY:	IS IN METROPOLITAN:
Copiah, MS	Jackson, MS
Coryell, TX	Killeen-Temple-Fort Hood, TX
Coweta, GA	Atlanta-Sandy Springs-Marietta, GA
Cowlitz, WA	Longview, WA
Craighead, AR	Jonesboro, AR
Craig, VA	Roanoke, VA
Crawford, AR	Fort Smith, AR-OK
Crawford, GA	Macon, GA
Creek, OK	Tulsa, OK
Crittenden, AR	Memphis, TN-MS-AR
Crosby, TX	Lubbock, TX
Cumberland, ME	Portland-South Portland-Biddeford, ME
Cumberland, NC	Fayetteville, NC
Cumberland, NJ	Vineland-Millville-Bridgeton, NJ
Cumberland, PA	Harrisburg-Carlisle, PA
Cumberland, VA	Richmond, VA
Currituck, NC	Virginia Beach-Norfolk, VA-NC
Cuyahoga, OH	Cleveland-Elyria-Mentor, OH
Dade, GA	Chattanooga, TN-GA
Dakota, MN	Minneapolis-St. Paul-Bloomington, MN-WI
Dakota, NE	Sioux City, IA-NE-SD
Dallas, IA	Des Moines, IA
Dallas, MO	Springfield, MO
Dallas, TX	Dallas-Fort Worth-Arlington, TX
Dane, WI	Madison, WI
Danville city, VA	Danville, VA
Darlington, SC	Florence, SC
Dauphin, PA	Harrisburg-Carlisle, PA
Davidson, TN	Nashville-Davidson--Murfreesboro, TN
Daviess, KY	Owensboro, KY
Davie, NC	Winston-Salem, NC
Davis, UT	Ogden-Clearfield, UT
Dawson, GA	Atlanta-Sandy Springs-Marietta, GA
De Soto, LA	Shreveport-Bossier City, LA
Dearborn, IN	Cincinnati-Middletown, OH-KY-IN
DeKalb, GA	Atlanta-Sandy Springs-Marietta, GA
DeKalb, IL	Chicago-Naperville-Joliet, IL-IN-WI
DeKalb, MO	St. Joseph, MO-KS
Delaware, IN	Muncie, IN
Delaware, OH	Columbus, OH
Delaware, PA	Philadelphia, PA-NJ-DE-MD
Delta, TX	Dallas-Fort Worth-Arlington, TX
Denton, TX	Dallas-Fort Worth-Arlington, TX
Denver, CO	Denver-Aurora, CO
Deschutes, OR	Bend, OR
DeSoto, MS	Memphis, TN-MS-AR
Dickson, TN	Nashville-Davidson--Murfreesboro, TN
Dinwiddie, VA	Richmond, VA
District of Columbia, DC	Washington, DC-VA-MD-WV
Dixon, NE	Sioux City, IA-NE-SD
Dodge, MN	Rochester, MN
Dona Ana, NM	Las Cruces, NM
Doniphan, KS	St. Joseph, MO-KS
Dorchester, SC	Charleston-North Charleston, SC
Dougherty, GA	Albany, GA
Douglas, CO	Denver-Aurora, CO
Douglas, GA	Atlanta-Sandy Springs-Marietta, GA
Douglas, KS	Lawrence, KS
Douglas, NE	Omaha-Council Bluffs, NE-IA
Douglas, WA	Wenatchee, WA
Douglas, WI	Duluth, MN-WI
Dubuque, IA	Dubuque, IA
DuPage, IL	Chicago-Naperville-Joliet, IL-IN-WI
Durham, NC	Durham, NC
Dutchess, NY	Poughkeepsie-Newburgh-Middletown, NY
Duval, FL	Jacksonville, FL
East Baton Rouge, LA	Baton Rouge, LA
East Feliciana, LA	Baton Rouge, LA
Eaton, MI	Lansing-East Lansing, MI
Eau Claire, WI	Eau Claire, WI
Echols, GA	Valdosta, GA
Ector, TX	Odessa, TX
Edgecombe, NC	Rocky Mount, NC
Edgefield, SC	Augusta-Richmond County, GA-SC
Edmonson, KY	Bowling Green, KY
Effingham, GA	Savannah, GA
El Dorado, CA	Sacramento--Arden-Arcade--Roseville, CA
El Paso, CO	Colorado Springs, CO

COUNTY INDEX: 2006 (continued)

COUNTY:	IS IN METROPOLITAN:	COUNTY:	IS IN METROPOLITAN:
El Paso, TX	El Paso, TX	Grant, LA	Alexandria, LA
Elbert, CO	Denver-Aurora, CO	Grayson, TX	Sherman-Denison, TX
Elkhart, IN	Elkhart-Goshen, IN	Greene, AL	Tuscaloosa, AL
Ellis, TX	Dallas-Fort Worth-Arlington, TX	Greene, IN	Bloomington, IN
Elmore, AL	Montgomery, AL	Greene, MO	Springfield, MO
Erie, NY	Buffalo-Niagara Falls, NY	Greene, NC	Greenville, NC
Erie, OH	Sandusky, OH	Greene, OH	Dayton, OH
Erie, PA	Erie, PA	Greene, VA	Charlottesville, VA
Escambia, FL	Pensacola-Ferry Pass-Brent, FL	Greenup, KY	Huntington-Ashland, WV-KY-OH
Essex, MA	Boston-Cambridge-Quincy, MA-NH	Greenville, SC	Greenville, SC
Essex, NJ	New York, NY-NJ-PA	Gregg, TX	Longview, TX
Etowah, AL	Gadsden, AL	Grundy, IA	Waterloo-Cedar Falls, IA
Fairbanks North Star, AK	Fairbanks, AK	Grundy, IL	Chicago-Naperville-Joliet, IL-IN-WI
Fairfax city, VA	Washington, DC-VA-MD-WV	Guadalupe, TX	San Antonio, TX
Fairfax, VA	Washington, DC-VA-MD-WV	Guilford, NC	Greensboro-High Point, NC
Fairfield, CT	Bridgeport-Stamford-Norwalk, CT	Guthrie, IA	Des Moines, IA
Fairfield, OH	Columbus, OH	Gwinnett, GA	Atlanta-Sandy Springs-Marietta, GA
Fairfield, SC	Columbia, SC	Hale, AL	Tuscaloosa, AL
Falls Church city, VA	Washington, DC-VA-MD-WV	Hall, GA	Gainesville, GA
Faulkner, AR	Little Rock-North Little Rock, AR	Hamblen, TN	Morristown, TN
Fauquier, VA	Washington, DC-VA-MD-WV	Hamilton, IN	Indianapolis, IN
Fayette, GA	Atlanta-Sandy Springs-Marietta, GA	Hamilton, OH	Cincinnati-Middletown, OH-KY-IN
Fayette, KY	Lexington-Fayette, KY	Hamilton, TN	Chattanooga, TN-GA
Fayette, PA	Pittsburgh, PA	Hampden, MA	Springfield, MA
Fayette, TN	Memphis, TN-MS-AR	Hampshire, MA	Springfield, MA
Flagler, FL	Palm Coast, FL	Hampshire, WV	Winchester, VA-WV
Florence, SC	Florence, SC	Hampton city, VA	Virginia Beach-Norfolk, VA-NC
Floyd, GA	Rome, GA	Hancock, IN	Indianapolis, IN
Floyd, IN	Louisville, KY-IN	Hancock, KY	Owensboro, KY
Fluvanna, VA	Charlottesville, VA	Hancock, MS	Gulfport-Biloxi, MS
Fond du Lac, WI	Fond du Lac, WI	Hancock, WV	Weirton-Steubenville, WV-OH
Ford, IL	Champaign-Urbana, IL	Hanover, VA	Richmond, VA
Forrest, MS	Hattiesburg, MS	Haralson, GA	Atlanta-Sandy Springs-Marietta, GA
Forsyth, GA	Atlanta-Sandy Springs-Marietta, GA	Hardin, KY	Elizabethtown, KY
Forsyth, NC	Winston-Salem, NC	Hardin, TX	Beaumont-Port Arthur, TX
Fort Bend, TX	Houston-Baytown-Sugar Land, TX	Harford, MD	Baltimore-Towson, MD
Franklin, AR	Fort Smith, AR-OK	Harrisonburg city, VA	Harrisonburg, VA
Franklin, ID	Logan, UT-ID	Harrison, IA	Omaha-Council Bluffs, NE-IA
Franklin, IN	Cincinnati-Middletown, OH-KY-IN	Harrison, IN	Louisville, KY-IN
Franklin, KS	Kansas City, MO-KS	Harrison, MS	Gulfport-Biloxi, MS
Franklin, MA	Springfield, MA	Harris, GA	Columbus, GA-AL
Franklin, MO	St. Louis, MO-IL	Harris, TX	Houston-Baytown-Sugar Land, TX
Franklin, NC	Raleigh-Cary, NC	Hartford, CT	Hartford-West Hartford-East Hartford, CT
Franklin, OH	Columbus, OH	Harvey, KS	Wichita, KS
Franklin, VA	Roanoke, VA	Hawkins, TN	Kingsport-Bristol-Bristol, TN-VA
Franklin, VT	Burlington-South Burlington, VT	Hays, TX	Austin-Round Rock, TX
Franklin, WA	Kennewick-Richland-Pasco, WA	Haywood, NC	Asheville, NC
Fredericksburg city, VA	Washington, DC-VA-MD-WV	Heard, GA	Atlanta-Sandy Springs-Marietta, GA
Frederick, MD	Washington, DC-VA-MD-WV	Henderson, KY	Evansville, IN-KY
Frederick, VA	Winchester, VA-WV	Henderson, NC	Asheville, NC
Fresno, CA	Fresno, CA	Hendricks, IN	Indianapolis, IN
Fulton, GA	Atlanta-Sandy Springs-Marietta, GA	Hennepin, MN	Minneapolis-St. Paul-Bloomington, MN-WI
Fulton, OH	Toledo, OH	Henrico, VA	Richmond, VA
Gadsden, FL	Tallahassee, FL	Henry, AL	Dothan, AL
Gallatin, KY	Cincinnati-Middletown, OH-KY-IN	Henry, GA	Atlanta-Sandy Springs-Marietta, GA
Galveston, TX	Houston-Baytown-Sugar Land, TX	Henry, IL	Davenport-Moline-Rock Island, IA-IL
Garland, AR	Hot Springs, AR	Henry, KY	Louisville, KY-IN
Gaston, NC	Charlotte-Gastonia-Concord, NC-SC	Herkimer, NY	Utica-Rome, NY
Geauga, OH	Cleveland-Elyria-Mentor, OH	Hernando, FL	Tampa-St. Petersburg-Clearwater, FL
Gem, ID	Boise City-Nampa, ID	Hickman, TN	Nashville-Davidson--Murfreesboro, TN
Genesee, MI	Flint, MI	Hidalgo, TX	McAllen-Edinburg-Pharr, TX
Geneva, AL	Dothan, AL	Hillsborough, FL	Tampa-St. Petersburg-Clearwater, FL
George, MS	Pascagoula, MS	Hillsborough, NH	Manchester-Nashua, NH
Gibson, IN	Evansville, IN-KY	Hinds, MS	Jackson, MS
Gilchrist, FL	Gainesville, FL	Hoke, NC	Fayetteville, NC
Giles, VA	Blacksburg-Christiansburg-Radford, VA	Honolulu, HI	Honolulu, HI
Gilpin, CO	Denver-Aurora, CO	Hopewell city, VA	Richmond, VA
Gloucester, NJ	Philadelphia, PA-NJ-DE-MD	Horry, SC	Myrtle Beach-Conway, SC
Gloucester, VA	Virginia Beach-Norfolk, VA-NC	Houston, AL	Dothan, AL
Glynn, GA	Brunswick, GA	Houston, GA	Warner Robins, GA
Goliad, TX	Victoria, TX	Houston, MN	La Crosse, WI-MN
Goochland, VA	Richmond, VA	Howard, IN	Kokomo, IN
Grady, OK	Oklahoma City, OK	Howard, MD	Baltimore-Towson, MD
Grainger, TN	Morristown, TN	Howard, MO	Columbia, MO
Grand Forks, ND	Grand Forks, ND-MN	Hudson, NJ	New York, NY-NJ-PA
Grand Isle, VT	Burlington-South Burlington, VT	Hunterdon, NJ	New York, NY-NJ-PA
Grant, AR	Little Rock-North Little Rock, AR	Hunt, TX	Dallas-Fort Worth-Arlington, TX
Grant, KY	Cincinnati-Middletown, OH-KY-IN	Iberville, LA	Baton Rouge, LA

COUNTY INDEX: 2006 (continued)

COUNTY:	IS IN METROPOLITAN:
Imperial, CA	El Centro, CA
Indian River, FL	Sebastian-Vero Beach, FL
Ingham, MI	Lansing-East Lansing, MI
Ionia, MI	Grand Rapids-Wyoming, MI
Iowa, WI	Madison, WI
Irion, TX	San Angelo, TX
Isanti, MN	Minneapolis-St. Paul-Bloomington, MN-WI
Isle of Wight, VA	Virginia Beach-Norfolk, VA-NC
Jackson, KS	Topeka, KS
Jackson, MI	Jackson, MI
Jackson, MO	Kansas City, MO-KS
Jackson, MS	Pascagoula, MS
Jackson, OR	Medford, OR
James City, VA	Virginia Beach-Norfolk, VA-NC
Jasper, GA	Atlanta-Sandy Springs-Marietta, GA
Jasper, IN	Chicago-Naperville-Joliet, IL-IN-WI
Jasper, MO	Joplin, MO
Jefferson, AL	Birmingham-Hoover, AL
Jefferson, AR	Pine Bluff, AR
Jefferson, CO	Denver-Aurora, CO
Jefferson, FL	Tallahassee, FL
Jefferson, ID	Idaho Falls, ID
Jefferson, KS	Topeka, KS
Jefferson, KY	Louisville, KY-IN
Jefferson, LA	New Orleans-Metairie-Kenner, LA
Jefferson, MO	St. Louis, MO-IL
Jefferson, OH	Weirton-Steubenville, WV-OH
Jefferson, TN	Morristown, TN
Jefferson, TX	Beaumont-Port Arthur, TX
Jefferson, WV	Washington, DC-VA-MD-WV
Jersey, IL	St. Louis, MO-IL
Jessamine, KY	Lexington-Fayette, KY
Johnson, IA	Iowa City, IA
Johnson, IN	Indianapolis, IN
Johnson, KS	Kansas City, MO-KS
Johnson, TX	Dallas-Fort Worth-Arlington, TX
Johnston, NC	Raleigh-Cary, NC
Jones, GA	Macon, GA
Jones, IA	Cedar Rapids, IA
Jones, TX	Abilene, TX
Juab, UT	Provo-Orem, UT
Kalamazoo, MI	Kalamazoo-Portage, MI
Kanawha, WV	Charleston, WV
Kane, IL	Chicago-Naperville-Joliet, IL-IN-WI
Kankakee, IL	Kankakee-Bradley, IL
Kaufman, TX	Dallas-Fort Worth-Arlington, TX
Kendall, IL	Chicago-Naperville-Joliet, IL-IN-WI
Kendall, TX	San Antonio, TX
Kenosha, WI	Chicago-Naperville-Joliet, IL-IN-WI
Kenton, KY	Cincinnati-Middletown, OH-KY-IN
Kent, DE	Dover, DE
Kent, MI	Grand Rapids-Wyoming, MI
Kent, RI	Providence-New Bedford-Fall River, RI-MA
Kern, CA	Bakersfield, CA
Kershaw, SC	Columbia, SC
Kewaunee, WI	Green Bay, WI
King and Queen, VA	Richmond, VA
King William, VA	Richmond, VA
Kings, CA	Hanford-Corcoran, CA
Kings, NY	New York, NY-NJ-PA
King, WA	Seattle-Tacoma-Bellevue, WA
Kitsap, WA	Bremerton-Silverdale, WA
Knox, TN	Knoxville, TN
Kootenai, ID	Coeur d'Alene, ID
La Crosse, WI	La Crosse, WI-MN
Lackawanna, PA	Scranton--Wilkes-Barre, PA
Lafayette, LA	Lafayette, LA
Lafayette, MO	Kansas City, MO-KS
Lafourche, LA	Houma-Bayou Cane-Thibodaux, LA
Lake, FL	Orlando, FL
Lake, IL	Chicago-Naperville-Joliet, IL-IN-WI
Lake, IN	Chicago-Naperville-Joliet, IL-IN-WI
Lake, OH	Cleveland-Elyria-Mentor, OH
Lamar, GA	Atlanta-Sandy Springs-Marietta, GA
Lamar, MS	Hattiesburg, MS
Lampasas, TX	Killeen-Temple-Fort Hood, TX
Lancaster, NE	Lincoln, NE
Lancaster, PA	Lancaster, PA
Lane, OR	Eugene-Springfield, OR
Lanier, GA	Valdosta, GA
Lapeer, MI	Detroit-Warren-Livonia, MI
LaPorte, IN	Michigan City-La Porte, IN
Laramie, WY	Cheyenne, WY
Larimer, CO	Fort Collins-Loveland, CO
Larue, KY	Elizabethtown, KY
Lauderdale, AL	Florence-Muscle Shoals, AL
Laurens, SC	Greenville, SC
Lawrence, AL	Decatur, AL
Lawrence, OH	Huntington-Ashland, WV-KY-OH
Le Flore, OK	Fort Smith, AR-OK
Leavenworth, KS	Kansas City, MO-KS
Lebanon, PA	Lebanon, PA
Lee, AL	Auburn-Opelika, AL
Lee, FL	Cape Coral-Fort Myers, FL
Lee, GA	Albany, GA
Lehigh, PA	Allentown-Bethlehem-Easton, PA-NJ
Leon, FL	Tallahassee, FL
Lexington, SC	Columbia, SC
Liberty, GA	Hinesville-Fort Stewart, GA
Liberty, TX	Houston-Baytown-Sugar Land, TX
Licking, OH	Columbus, OH
Limestone, AL	Huntsville, AL
Lincoln, AR	Pine Bluff, AR
Lincoln, MO	St. Louis, MO-IL
Lincoln, OK	Oklahoma City, OK
Lincoln, SD	Sioux Falls, SD
Lincoln, WV	Charleston, WV
Linn, IA	Cedar Rapids, IA
Linn, KS	Kansas City, MO-KS
Livingston, LA	Baton Rouge, LA
Livingston, MI	Detroit-Warren-Livonia, MI
Livingston, NY	Rochester, NY
Logan, OK	Oklahoma City, OK
Long, GA	Hinesville-Fort Stewart, GA
Lonoke, AR	Little Rock-North Little Rock, AR
Lorain, OH	Cleveland-Elyria-Mentor, OH
Los Angeles, CA	Los Angeles-Long Beach-Santa Ana, CA
Loudon, TN	Knoxville, TN
Loudoun, VA	Washington, DC-VA-MD-WV
Louisa, VA	Richmond, VA
Lowndes, AL	Montgomery, AL
Lowndes, GA	Valdosta, GA
Lubbock, TX	Lubbock, TX
Lucas, OH	Toledo, OH
Luzerne, PA	Scranton--Wilkes-Barre, PA
Lycoming, PA	Williamsport, PA
Lynchburg city, VA	Lynchburg, VA
Macomb, MI	Detroit-Warren-Livonia, MI
Macon, IL	Decatur, IL
Macon, TN	Nashville-Davidson--Murfreesboro, TN
Macoupin, IL	St. Louis, MO-IL
Madera, CA	Madera, CA
Madison, AL	Huntsville, AL
Madison, AR	Fayetteville-Springdale-Rogers, AR-MO
Madison, GA	Athens-Clarke County, GA
Madison, IA	Des Moines, IA
Madison, IL	St. Louis, MO-IL
Madison, IN	Anderson, IN
Madison, MS	Jackson, MS
Madison, NC	Asheville, NC
Madison, NY	Syracuse, NY
Madison, OH	Columbus, OH
Madison, TN	Jackson, TN
Mahoning, OH	Youngstown-Warren-Boardman, OH-PA
Manassas city, VA	Washington, DC-VA-MD-WV
Manassas Park city, VA	Washington, DC-VA-MD-WV
Manatee, FL	Sarasota-Bradenton-Venice, FL
Marathon, WI	Wausau, WI
Maricopa, AZ	Phoenix-Mesa-Scottsdale, AZ
Marin, CA	San Francisco-Oakland-Fremont, CA
Marion, FL	Ocala, FL
Marion, GA	Columbus, GA-AL
Marion, IN	Indianapolis, IN
Marion, OR	Salem, OR
Marion, TN	Chattanooga, TN-GA
Marshall, IL	Peoria, IL

COUNTY INDEX: 2006 (continued)

COUNTY:	IS IN METROPOLITAN:
Marshall, MS	Memphis, TN-MS-AR
Marshall, WV	Wheeling, WV-OH
Martin, FL	Port St. Lucie-Fort Pierce, FL
Matanuska-Susitna, AK	Anchorage, AK
Mathews, VA	Virginia Beach-Norfolk, VA-NC
McClain, OK	Oklahoma City, OK
McCook, SD	Sioux Falls, SD
McDonald, MO	Fayetteville-Springdale-Rogers, AR-MO
McDuffie, GA	Augusta-Richmond County, GA-SC
McHenry, IL	Chicago-Naperville-Joliet, IL-IN-WI
McIntosh, GA	Brunswick, GA
McLean, IL	Bloomington-Normal, IL
McLean, KY	Owensboro, KY
McLennan, TX	Waco, TX
Meade, KY	Louisville, KY-IN
Meade, SD	Rapid City, SD
Mecklenburg, NC	Charlotte-Gastonia-Concord, NC-SC
Medina, OH	Cleveland-Elyria-Mentor, OH
Medina, TX	San Antonio, TX
Menard, IL	Springfield, IL
Merced, CA	Merced, CA
Mercer, IL	Davenport-Moline-Rock Island, IA-IL
Mercer, NJ	Trenton-Ewing, NJ
Mercer, PA	Youngstown-Warren-Boardman, OH-PA
Meriwether, GA	Atlanta-Sandy Springs-Marietta, GA
Mesa, CO	Grand Junction, CO
Miami-Dade, FL	Miami-Fort Lauderdale-Miami Beach, FL
Miami, KS	Kansas City, MO-KS
Miami, OH	Dayton, OH
Middlesex, CT	Hartford-West Hartford-East Hartford, CT
Middlesex, MA	Boston-Cambridge-Quincy, MA-NH
Middlesex, NJ	New York, NY-NJ-PA
Midland, TX	Midland, TX
Miller, AR	Texarkana, TX-Texarkana, AR
Mills, IA	Omaha-Council Bluffs, NE-IA
Milwaukee, WI	Milwaukee-Waukesha-West Allis, WI
Mineral, WV	Cumberland, MD-WV
Minnehaha, SD	Sioux Falls, SD
Missoula, MT	Missoula, MT
Mobile, AL	Mobile, AL
Mohave, AZ	Lake Havasu City-Kingman, AZ
Moniteau, MO	Jefferson City, MO
Monmouth, NJ	New York, NY-NJ-PA
Monongalia, WV	Morgantown, WV
Monroe, GA	Macon, GA
Monroe, IL	St. Louis, MO-IL
Monroe, IN	Bloomington, IN
Monroe, MI	Monroe, MI
Monroe, NY	Rochester, NY
Monterey, CA	Salinas, CA
Montgomery, AL	Montgomery, AL
Montgomery, MD	Washington, DC-VA-MD-WV
Montgomery, OH	Dayton, OH
Montgomery, PA	Philadelphia, PA-NJ-DE-MD
Montgomery, TN	Clarksville, TN-KY
Montgomery, TX	Houston-Baytown-Sugar Land, TX
Montgomery, VA	Blacksburg-Christiansburg-Radford, VA
Morgan, AL	Decatur, AL
Morgan, IN	Indianapolis, IN
Morgan, UT	Ogden-Clearfield, UT
Morgan, WV	Hagerstown-Martinsburg, MD-WV
Morris, NJ	New York, NY-NJ-PA
Morrow, OH	Columbus, OH
Morton, ND	Bismarck, ND
Multnomah, OR	Portland-Vancouver-Beaverton, OR-WA
Murray, GA	Dalton, GA
Muscogee, GA	Columbus, GA-AL
Muskegon, MI	Muskegon-Norton Shores, MI
Napa, CA	Napa, CA
Nash, NC	Rocky Mount, NC
Nassau, FL	Jacksonville, FL
Nassau, NY	New York, NY-NJ-PA
Natrona, WY	Casper, WY
Nelson, KY	Louisville, KY-IN
Nelson, VA	Charlottesville, VA
New Castle, DE	Philadelphia, PA-NJ-DE-MD
New Hanover, NC	Wilmington, NC
New Haven, CT	New Haven-Milford, CT
New Kent, VA	Richmond, VA
New London, CT	Norwich-New London, CT
New York, NY	New York, NY-NJ-PA
Newaygo, MI	Grand Rapids-Wyoming, MI
Newport News city, VA	Virginia Beach-Norfolk, VA-NC
Newport, RI	Providence-New Bedford-Fall River, RI-MA
Newton, GA	Atlanta-Sandy Springs-Marietta, GA
Newton, IN	Chicago-Naperville-Joliet, IL-IN-WI
Newton, MO	Joplin, MO
Nez Perce, ID	Lewiston, ID-WA
Niagara, NY	Buffalo-Niagara Falls, NY
Norfolk city, VA	Virginia Beach-Norfolk, VA-NC
Norfolk, MA	Boston-Cambridge-Quincy, MA-NH
Northampton, PA	Allentown-Bethlehem-Easton, PA-NJ
Nueces, TX	Corpus Christi, TX
Oakland, MI	Detroit-Warren-Livonia, MI
Ocean, NJ	New York, NY-NJ-PA
Oconee, GA	Athens-Clarke County, GA
Oconto, WI	Green Bay, WI
Oglethorpe, GA	Athens-Clarke County, GA
Ohio, IN	Cincinnati-Middletown, OH-KY-IN
Ohio, WV	Wheeling, WV-OH
Okaloosa, FL	Fort Walton Beach-Crestview-Destin, FL
Oklahoma, OK	Oklahoma City, OK
Okmulgee, OK	Tulsa, OK
Oldham, KY	Louisville, KY-IN
Olmsted, MN	Rochester, MN
Oneida, NY	Utica-Rome, NY
Onondaga, NY	Syracuse, NY
Onslow, NC	Jacksonville, NC
Ontario, NY	Rochester, NY
Orange, CA	Los Angeles-Long Beach-Santa Ana, CA
Orange, FL	Orlando, FL
Orange, NC	Durham, NC
Orange, NY	Poughkeepsie-Newburgh-Middletown, NY
Orange, TX	Beaumont-Port Arthur, TX
Orleans, LA	New Orleans-Metairie-Kenner, LA
Orleans, NY	Rochester, NY
Osage, KS	Topeka, KS
Osage, MO	Jefferson City, MO
Osage, OK	Tulsa, OK
Osceola, FL	Orlando, FL
Oswego, NY	Syracuse, NY
Ottawa, MI	Holland-Grand Haven, MI
Ottawa, OH	Toledo, OH
Ouachita, LA	Monroe, LA
Outagamie, WI	Appleton, WI
Owen, IN	Bloomington, IN
Owyhee, ID	Boise City-Nampa, ID
Ozaukee, WI	Milwaukee-Waukesha-West Allis, WI
Palm Beach, FL	Miami-Fort Lauderdale-Miami Beach, FL
Parker, TX	Dallas-Fort Worth-Arlington, TX
Park, CO	Denver-Aurora, CO
Pasco, FL	Tampa-St. Petersburg-Clearwater, FL
Passaic, NJ	New York, NY-NJ-PA
Paulding, GA	Atlanta-Sandy Springs-Marietta, GA
Pawnee, OK	Tulsa, OK
Pender, NC	Wilmington, NC
Pendleton, KY	Cincinnati-Middletown, OH-KY-IN
Pennington, SD	Rapid City, SD
Penobscot, ME	Bangor, ME
Peoria, IL	Peoria, IL
Perry, AR	Little Rock-North Little Rock, AR
Perry, MS	Hattiesburg, MS
Perry, PA	Harrisburg-Carlisle, PA
Person, NC	Durham, NC
Petersburg city, VA	Richmond, VA
Philadelphia, PA	Philadelphia, PA-NJ-DE-MD
Piatt, IL	Champaign-Urbana, IL
Pickaway, OH	Columbus, OH
Pickens, GA	Atlanta-Sandy Springs-Marietta, GA
Pickens, SC	Greenville, SC
Pierce, WA	Seattle-Tacoma-Bellevue, WA
Pierce, WI	Minneapolis-St. Paul-Bloomington, MN-WI
Pike, GA	Atlanta-Sandy Springs-Marietta, GA
Pike, PA	New York, NY-NJ-PA
Pima, AZ	Tucson, AZ
Pinal, AZ	Phoenix-Mesa-Scottsdale, AZ

COUNTY INDEX: 2006 (continued)

COUNTY:	IS IN METROPOLITAN:	COUNTY:	IS IN METROPOLITAN:
Pinellas, FL	Tampa-St. Petersburg-Clearwater, FL	San Benito, CA	San Jose-Sunnyvale-Santa Clara, CA
Pittsylvania, VA	Danville, VA	San Bernardino, CA	Riverside-San Bernardino-Ontario, CA
Pitt, NC	Greenville, NC	San Diego, CA	San Diego-Carlsbad-San Marcos, CA
Placer, CA	Sacramento--Arden-Arcade--Roseville, CA	San Francisco, CA	San Francisco-Oakland-Fremont, CA
Plaquemines, LA	New Orleans-Metairie-Kenner, LA	San Jacinto, TX	Houston-Baytown-Sugar Land, TX
Platte, MO	Kansas City, MO-KS	San Joaquin, CA	Stockton, CA
Pleasants, WV	Parkersburg-Marietta, WV-OH	San Juan, NM	Farmington, NM
Plymouth, MA	Boston-Cambridge-Quincy, MA-NH	San Luis Obispo, CA	San Luis Obispo-Paso Robles, CA
Poinsett, AR	Jonesboro, AR	San Mateo, CA	San Francisco-Oakland-Fremont, CA
Pointe Coupee, LA	Baton Rouge, LA	San Patricio, TX	Corpus Christi, TX
Polk, FL	Lakeland, FL	Sandoval, NM	Albuquerque, NM
Polk, IA	Des Moines, IA	Sangamon, IL	Springfield, IL
Polk, MN	Grand Forks, ND-MN	Santa Barbara, CA	Santa Barbara-Santa Maria-Goleta, CA
Polk, MO	Springfield, MO	Santa Clara, CA	San Jose-Sunnyvale-Santa Clara, CA
Polk, OR	Salem, OR	Santa Cruz, CA	Santa Cruz-Watsonville, CA
Polk, TN	Cleveland, TN	Santa Fe, NM	Santa Fe, NM
Poquoson city , VA	Virginia Beach-Norfolk, VA-NC	Santa Rosa, FL	Pensacola-Ferry Pass-Brent, FL
Portage, OH	Akron, OH	Sarasota, FL	Sarasota-Bradenton-Venice, FL
Porter, IN	Chicago-Naperville-Joliet, IL-IN-WI	Saratoga, NY	Albany-Schenectady-Troy, NY
Portsmouth city, VA	Virginia Beach-Norfolk, VA-NC	Sarpy, NE	Omaha-Council Bluffs, NE-IA
Posey, IN	Evansville, IN-KY	Saunders, NE	Omaha-Council Bluffs, NE-IA
Pottawattamie, IA	Omaha-Council Bluffs, NE-IA	Schenectady, NY	Albany-Schenectady-Troy, NY
Potter, TX	Amarillo, TX	Schoharie, NY	Albany-Schenectady-Troy, NY
Power, ID	Pocatello, ID	Scott, IA	Davenport-Moline-Rock Island, IA-IL
Powhatan, VA	Richmond, VA	Scott, KY	Lexington-Fayette, KY
Preble, OH	Dayton, OH	Scott, MN	Minneapolis-St. Paul-Bloomington, MN-WI
Preston, WV	Morgantown, WV	Scott, VA	Kingsport-Bristol-Bristol, TN-VA
Prince George's, MD	Washington, DC-VA-MD-WV	Sebastian, AR	Fort Smith, AR-OK
Prince George, VA	Richmond, VA	Sedgwick, KS	Wichita, KS
Prince William, VA	Washington, DC-VA-MD-WV	Seminole, FL	Orlando, FL
Providence, RI	Providence-New Bedford-Fall River, RI-MA	Sequatchie, TN	Chattanooga, TN-GA
Pueblo, CO	Pueblo, CO	Sequoyah, OK	Fort Smith, AR-OK
Pulaski, AR	Little Rock-North Little Rock, AR	Seward, NE	Lincoln, NE
Pulaski, VA	Blacksburg-Christiansburg-Radford, VA	Shasta, CA	Redding, CA
Putnam, IN	Indianapolis, IN	Shawnee, KS	Topeka, KS
Putnam, NY	New York, NY-NJ-PA	Sheboygan, WI	Sheboygan, WI
Putnam, WV	Charleston, WV	Shelby, AL	Birmingham-Hoover, AL
Queen Anne's, MD	Baltimore-Towson, MD	Shelby, IN	Indianapolis, IN
Queens, NY	New York, NY-NJ-PA	Shelby, KY	Louisville, KY-IN
Racine, WI	Racine, WI	Shelby, TN	Memphis, TN-MS-AR
Radford city, VA	Blacksburg-Christiansburg-Radford, VA	Sherburne, MN	Minneapolis-St. Paul-Bloomington, MN-WI
Ramsey, MN	Minneapolis-St. Paul-Bloomington, MN-WI	Simpson, MS	Jackson, MS
Randall, TX	Amarillo, TX	Skagit, WA	Mount Vernon-Anacortes, WA
Randolph, NC	Greensboro-High Point, NC	Skamania, WA	Portland-Vancouver-Beaverton, OR-WA
Rankin, MS	Jackson, MS	Smith, TN	Nashville-Davidson--Murfreesboro, TN
Rapides, LA	Alexandria, LA	Smith, TX	Tyler, TX
Ray, MO	Kansas City, MO-KS	Snohomish, WA	Seattle-Tacoma-Bellevue, WA
Rensselaer, NY	Albany-Schenectady-Troy, NY	Solano, CA	Vallejo-Fairfield, CA
Richland, OH	Mansfield, OH	Somerset, MD	Salisbury, MD
Richland, SC	Columbia, SC	Somerset, NJ	New York, NY-NJ-PA
Richmond city, VA	Richmond, VA	Sonoma, CA	Santa Rosa-Petaluma, CA
Richmond, GA	Augusta-Richmond County, GA-SC	Spalding, GA	Atlanta-Sandy Springs-Marietta, GA
Richmond, NY	New York, NY-NJ-PA	Spartanburg, SC	Spartanburg, SC
Riverside, CA	Riverside-San Bernardino-Ontario, CA	Spencer, KY	Louisville, KY-IN
Roanoke city, VA	Roanoke, VA	Spokane, WA	Spokane, WA
Roanoke, VA	Roanoke, VA	Spotsylvania, VA	Washington, DC-VA-MD-WV
Robertson, TN	Nashville-Davidson--Murfreesboro, TN	Stafford, VA	Washington, DC-VA-MD-WV
Robertson, TX	College Station-Bryan, TX	Stanislaus, CA	Modesto, CA
Rock Island, IL	Davenport-Moline-Rock Island, IA-IL	Stark, IL	Peoria, IL
Rockdale, GA	Atlanta-Sandy Springs-Marietta, GA	Stark, OH	Canton-Massillon, OH
Rockingham, NC	Greensboro-High Point, NC	Stearns, MN	St. Cloud, MN
Rockingham, NH	Boston-Cambridge-Quincy, MA-NH	Stewart, TN	Clarksville, TN-KY
Rockingham, VA	Harrisonburg, VA	Stokes, NC	Winston-Salem, NC
Rockland, NY	New York, NY-NJ-PA	Stone, MS	Gulfport-Biloxi, MS
Rockwall, TX	Dallas-Fort Worth-Arlington, TX	Storey, NV	Reno-Sparks, NV
Rock, WI	Janesville, WI	Story, IA	Ames, IA
Rogers, OK	Tulsa, OK	Strafford, NH	Boston-Cambridge-Quincy, MA-NH
Rusk, TX	Longview, TX	St. Bernard, LA	New Orleans-Metairie-Kenner, LA
Russell, AL	Columbus, GA-AL	St. Charles, LA	New Orleans-Metairie-Kenner, LA
Rutherford, TN	Nashville-Davidson--Murfreesboro, TN	St. Charles, MO	St. Louis, MO-IL
Sacramento, CA	Sacramento--Arden-Arcade--Roseville, CA	St. Clair, AL	Birmingham-Hoover, AL
Sagadahoc, ME	Portland-South Portland-Biddeford, ME	St. Clair, IL	St. Louis, MO-IL
Saginaw, MI	Saginaw-Saginaw Township North, MI	St. Clair, MI	Detroit-Warren-Livonia, MI
Salem city, VA	Roanoke, VA	St. Croix, WI	Minneapolis-St. Paul-Bloomington, MN-WI
Salem, NJ	Philadelphia, PA-NJ-DE-MD	St. Helena, LA	Baton Rouge, LA
Saline, AR	Little Rock-North Little Rock, AR	St. John the Baptist, LA	New Orleans-Metairie-Kenner, LA
Salt Lake, UT	Salt Lake City, UT	St. Johns, FL	Jacksonville, FL
Saluda, SC	Columbia, SC	St. Joseph, IN	South Bend-Mishawaka, IN-MI

COUNTY INDEX: 2006 (continued)

National Crime Trends: 1987 to 2006

In the 20 years from 1987 to 2006, crime rates in the United States fell significantly. The total crime rate dropped 31.7%: from 5,575.5 crimes per 100,000 population in 1987 to a rate of 3,808.0 in 2006. Violent crime rates also decreased, falling 22.7% from 1987 to 2006. In addition, property crime rates dropped 32.8%.

Among individual crime categories, each recorded declines from 1987 to 2006. The nation's burglary rate posted the largest decrease, falling 45.4% from 1987 to 2006. The smallest decline was in the rape rate, which dropped 17.8% during that same 20-year time frame.

The table below shows rates for each category of crime for every year since 1987. Trends for each individual crime are shown in graphs on the following pages. Violent crimes are murder, rape, robbery and aggravated assault. Property crimes consist of burglary, larceny-theft and motor vehicle theft. The total crime rate is simply the sum of the seven specific crimes and was calculated by the editors. All rates are crimes per 100,000 population for the year shown.

Year	Crime	Violent Crime	Property Crime	Murder	Rape	Robbery	Assault	Burglary	Larceny-Theft	Motor Vehicle Theft
1987	5,575.5	612.5	4,963.0	8.3	37.6	213.7	352.9	1,335.7	3,095.4	531.9
1988	5,694.6	640.6	5,054.0	8.5	37.8	222.1	372.2	1,316.2	3,151.7	586.1
1989	5,774.0	666.9	5,107.1	8.7	38.3	234.3	385.6	1,283.6	3,189.6	634.0
1990	5,802.7	729.6	5,073.1	9.4	41.1	256.3	422.9	1,232.2	3,185.1	655.8
1991	5,898.4	758.2	5,140.2	9.8	42.3	272.7	433.4	1,252.1	3,229.1	659.0
1992	5,661.4	757.7	4,903.7	9.3	42.8	263.7	441.9	1,168.4	3,103.6	631.6
1993	5,487.1	747.1	4,740.0	9.5	41.1	256.0	440.5	1,099.7	3,033.9	606.3
1994	5,373.8	713.6	4,660.2	9.0	39.3	237.8	427.6	1,042.1	3,026.9	591.3
1995	5,275.0	684.5	4,590.5	8.2	37.1	220.9	418.3	987.0	3,043.2	560.3
1996	5,087.6	636.6	4,451.0	7.4	36.3	201.9	391.0	945.0	2,980.3	525.7
1997	4,927.3	611.0	4,316.3	6.8	35.9	186.2	382.1	918.8	2,891.8	505.7
1998	4,620.1	567.6	4,052.5	6.3	34.5	165.5	361.4	863.2	2,729.5	459.9
1999	4,266.6	523.0	3,743.6	5.7	32.8	150.1	334.3	770.4	2,550.7	422.5
2000	4,124.8	506.5	3,618.3	5.5	32.0	145.0	324.0	728.8	2,477.3	412.2
2001	4,162.6	504.5	3,658.1	5.6	31.8	148.5	318.6	741.8	2,485.7	430.5
2002	4,125.0	494.4	3,630.6	5.6	33.1	146.1	309.5	747.0	2,450.7	432.9
2003	4,067.0	475.8	3,591.2	5.7	32.3	142.5	295.4	741.0	2,416.5	433.7
2004	3,977.3	463.2	3,514.1	5.5	32.4	136.7	288.6	730.3	2,362.3	421.5
2005	3,900.5	469.0	3,431.5	5.6	31.8	140.8	290.8	726.9	2,287.8	416.8
2006	3,808.0	473.5	3,334.5	5.7	30.9	149.4	287.5	729.4	2,206.8	398.4

Source: Federal Bureau of Investigation
"Crime in the United States 2006" (Uniform Crime Reports, September 24, 2007)

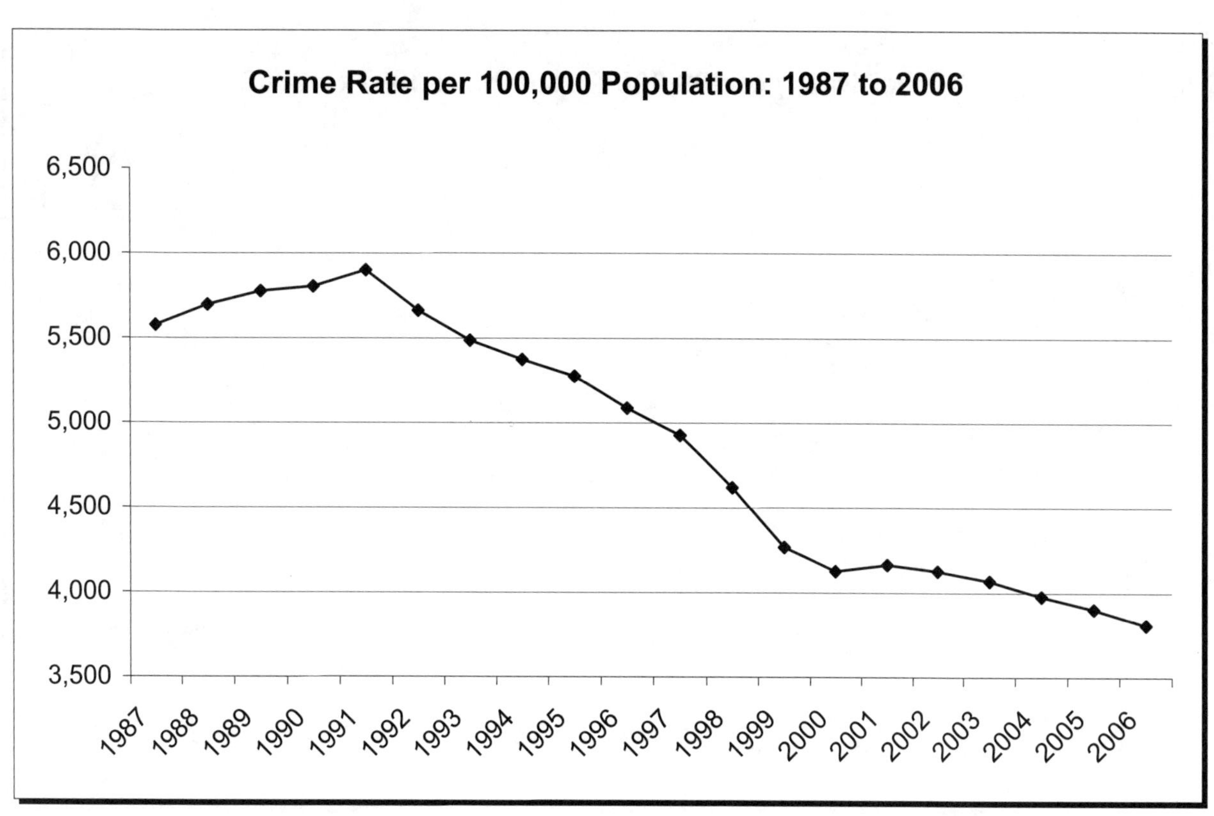

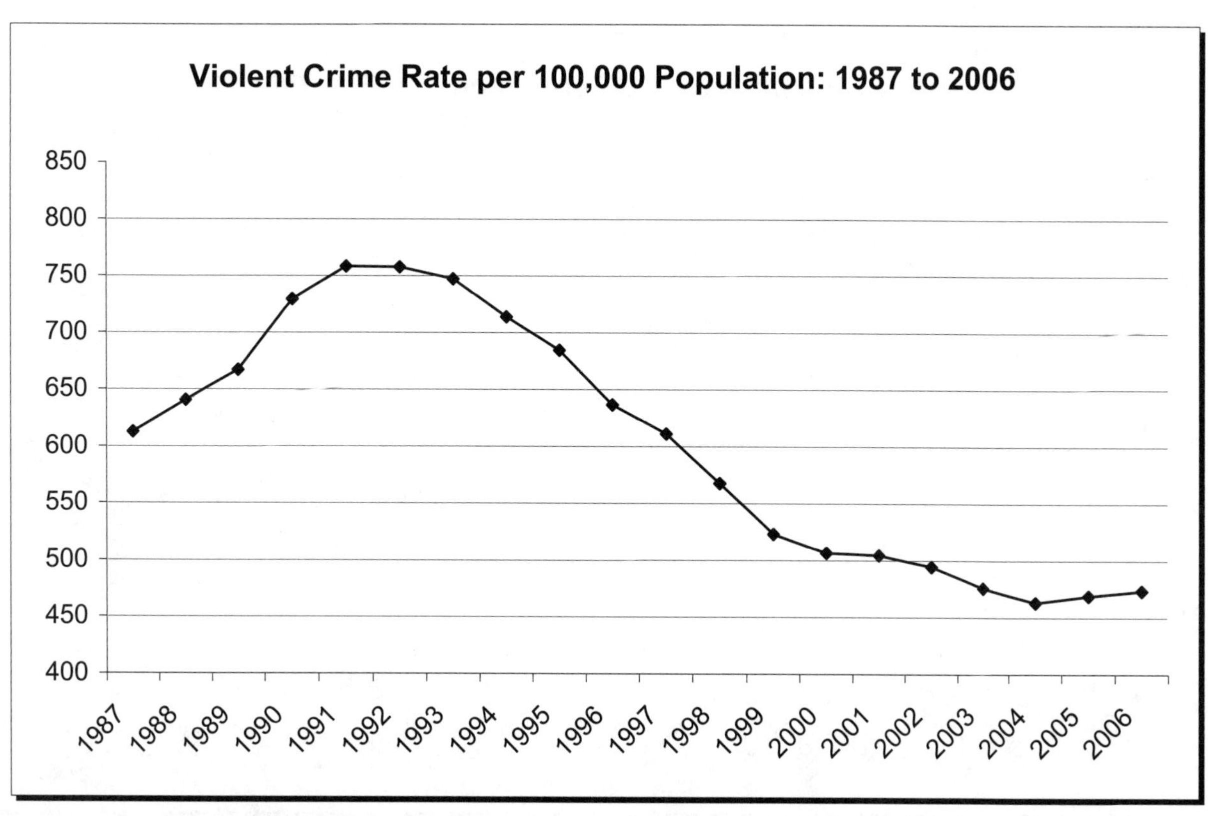

Source: Federal Bureau of Investigation
"Crime in the United States 2006" (Uniform Crime Reports, September 24, 2007)

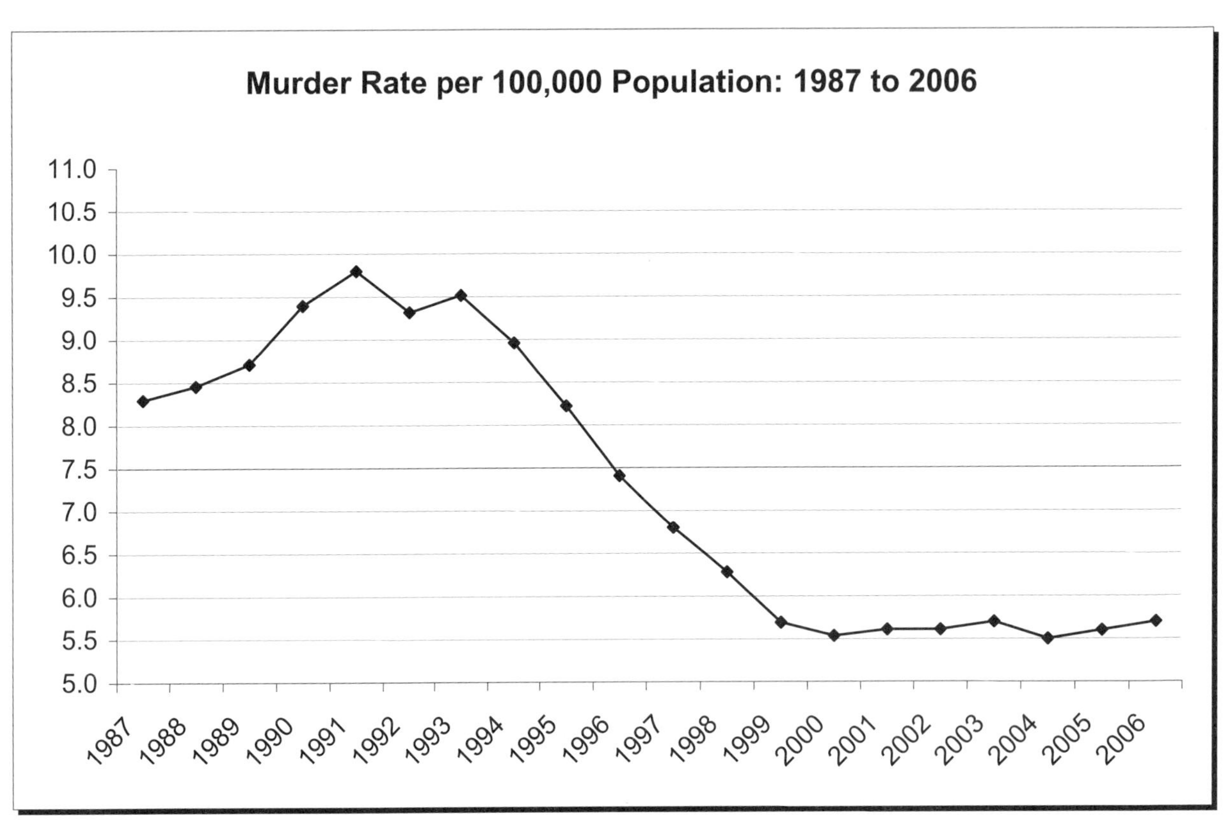

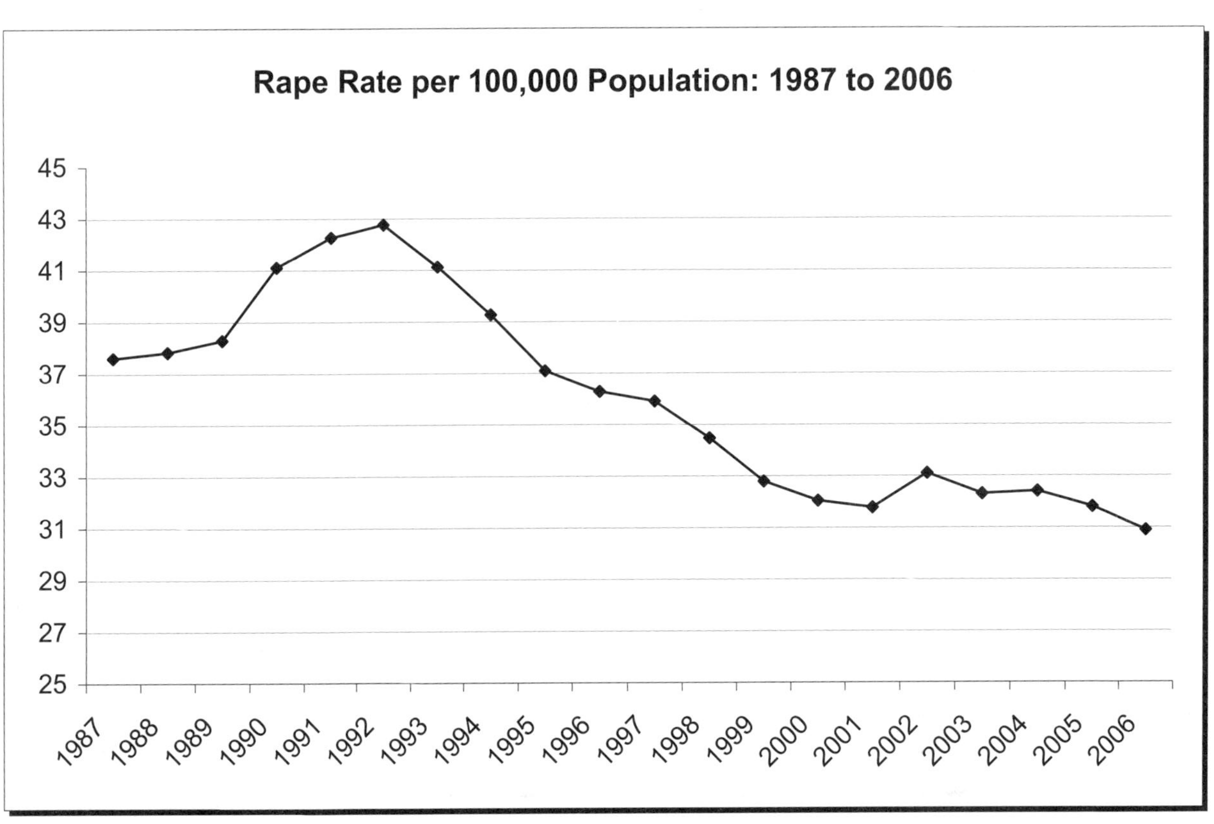

Source: Federal Bureau of Investigation
"Crime in the United States 2006" (Uniform Crime Reports, September 24, 2007)

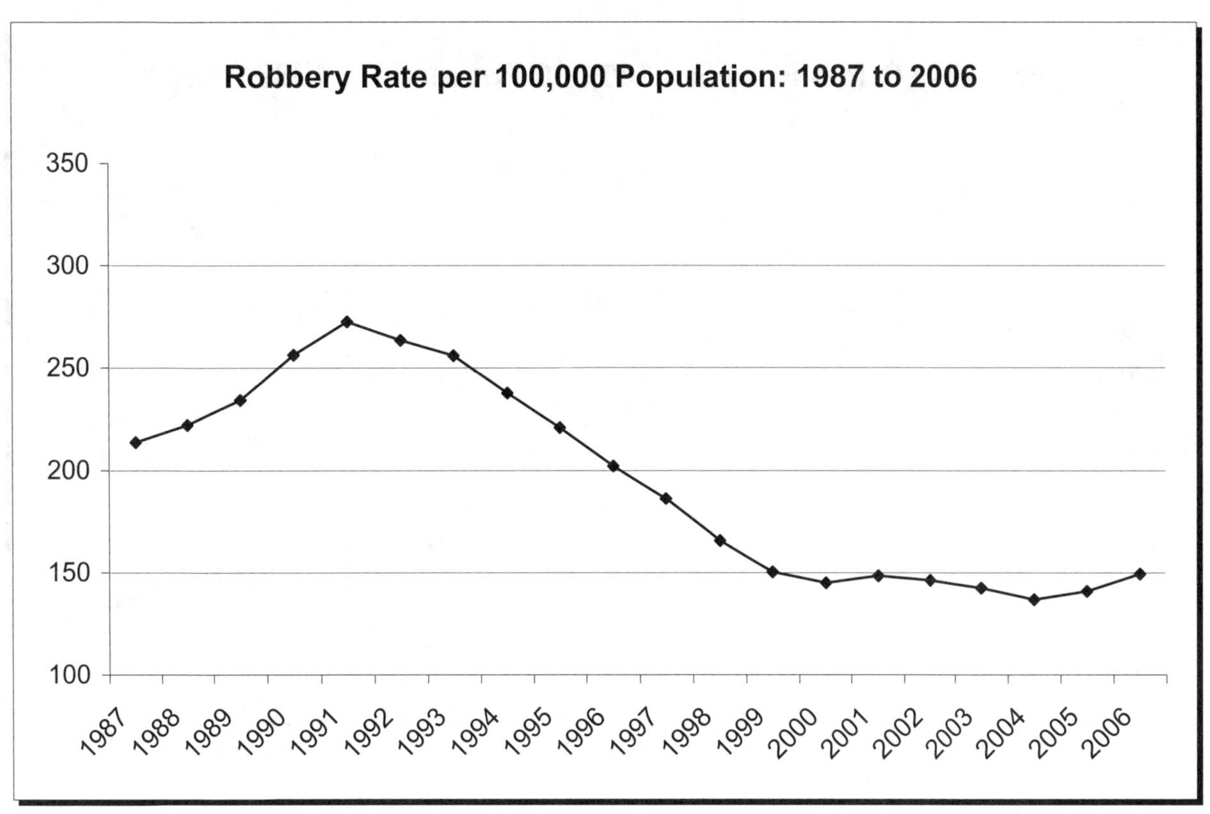

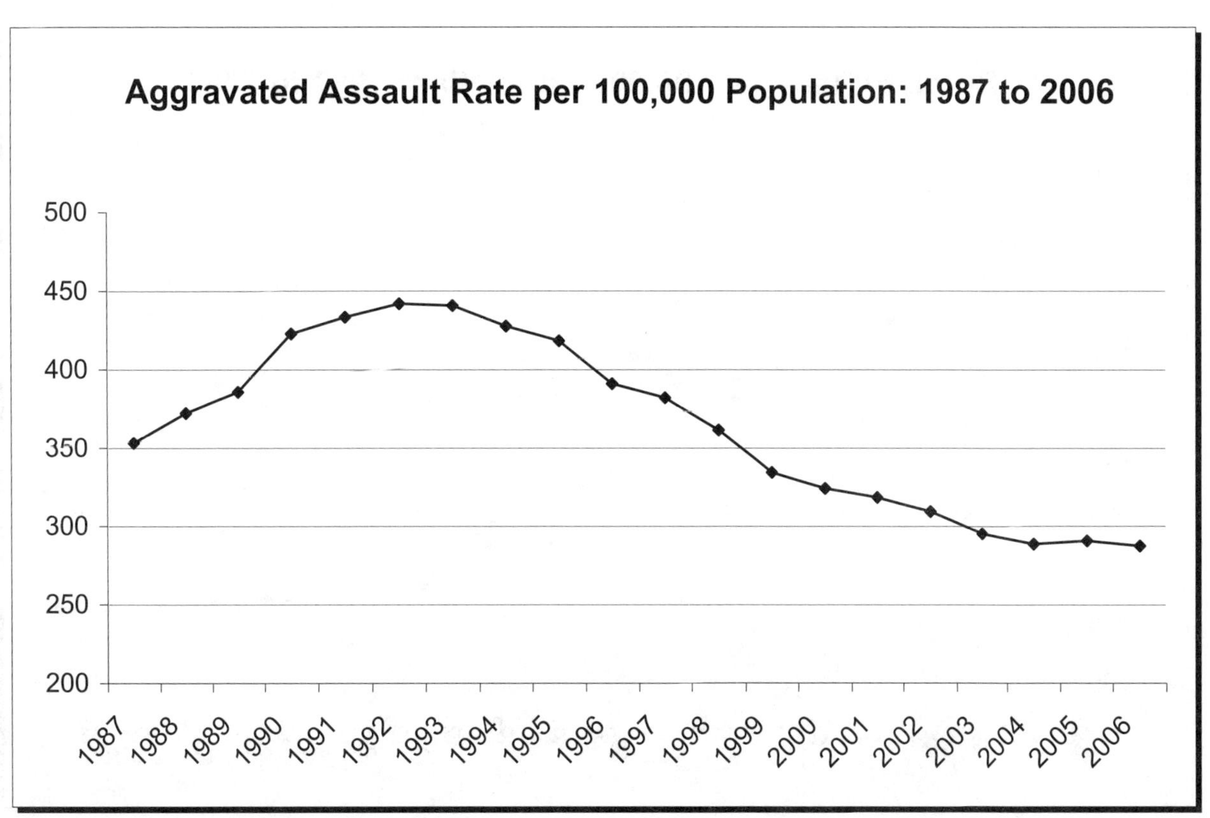

Source: Federal Bureau of Investigation
"Crime in the United States 2006" (Uniform Crime Reports, September 24, 2007)

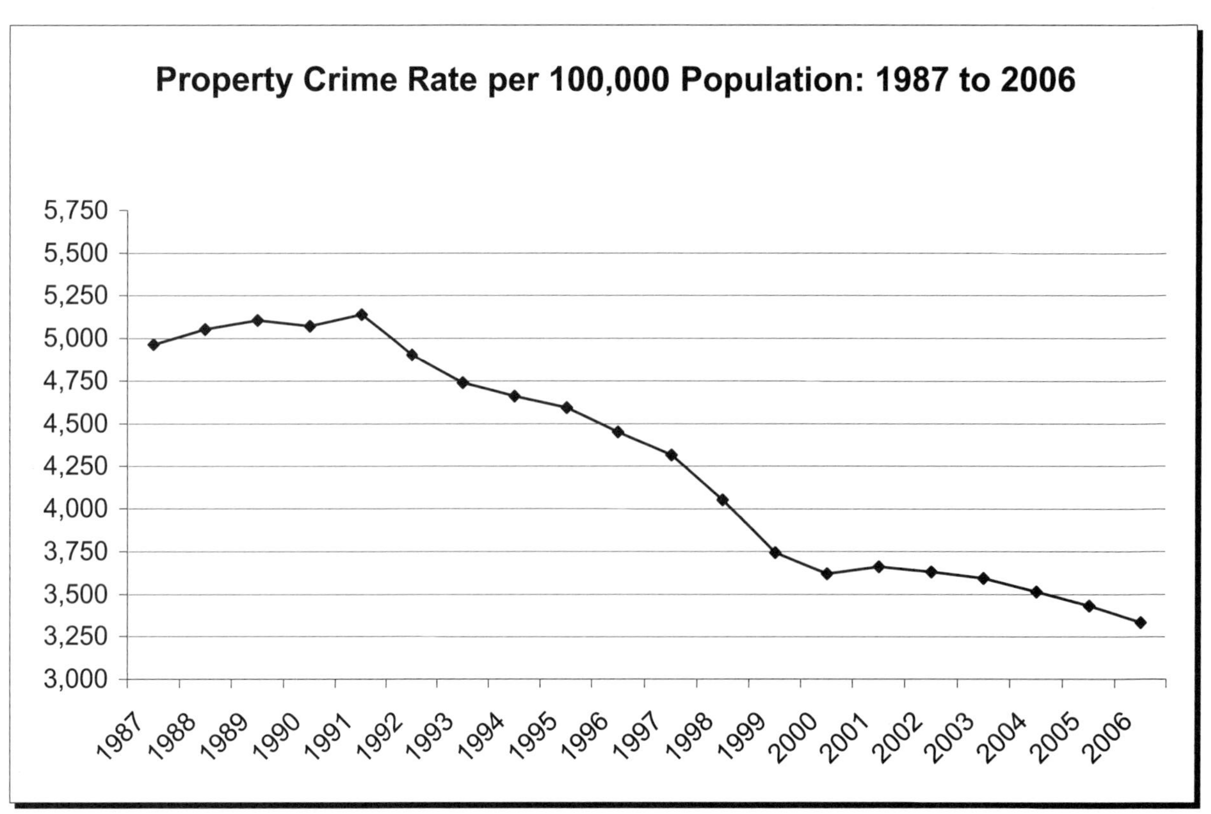

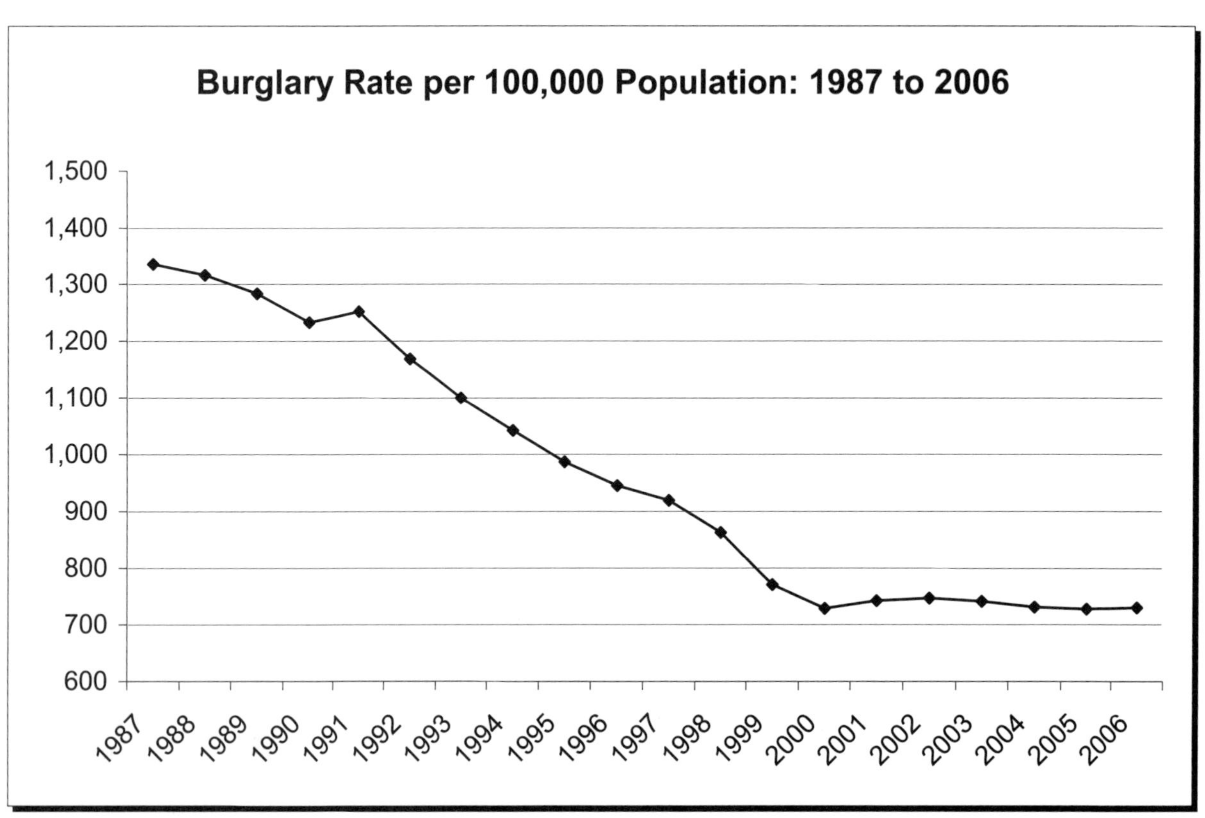

Source: Federal Bureau of Investigation
"Crime in the United States 2006" (Uniform Crime Reports, September 24, 2007)

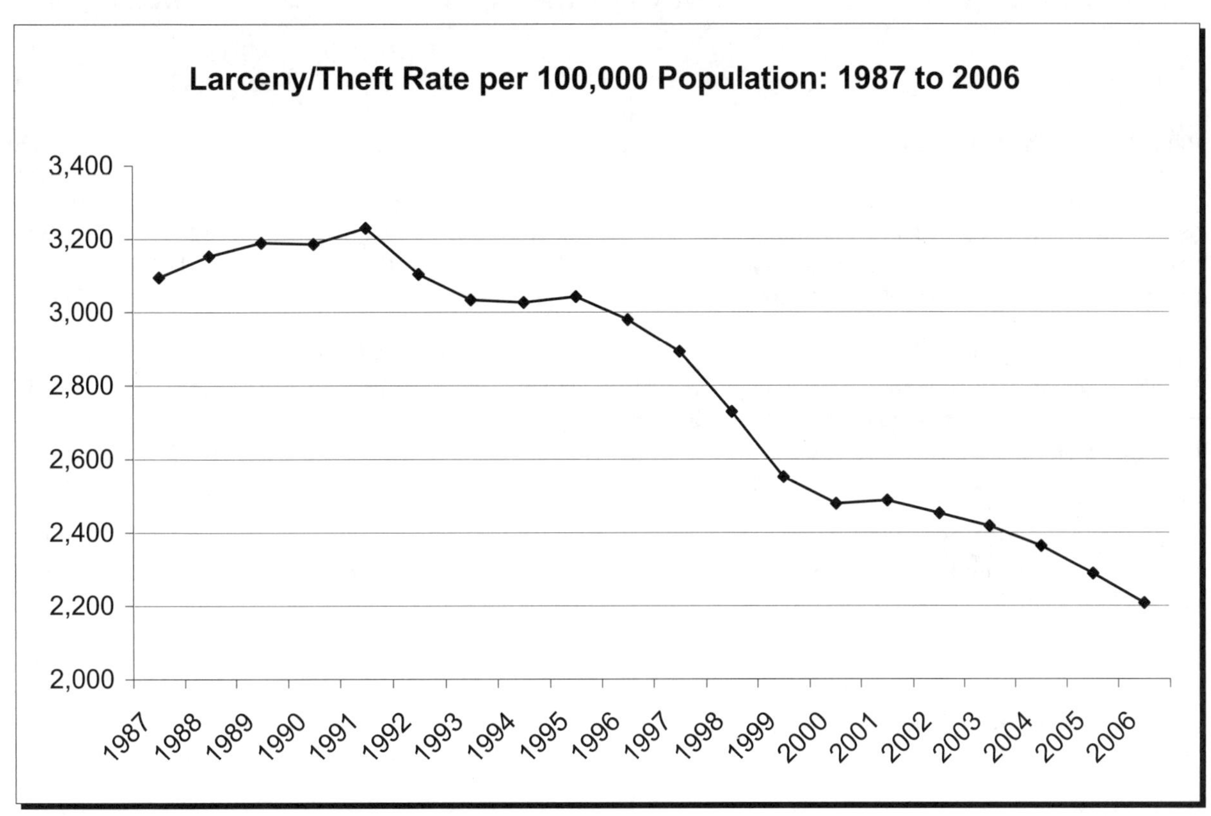

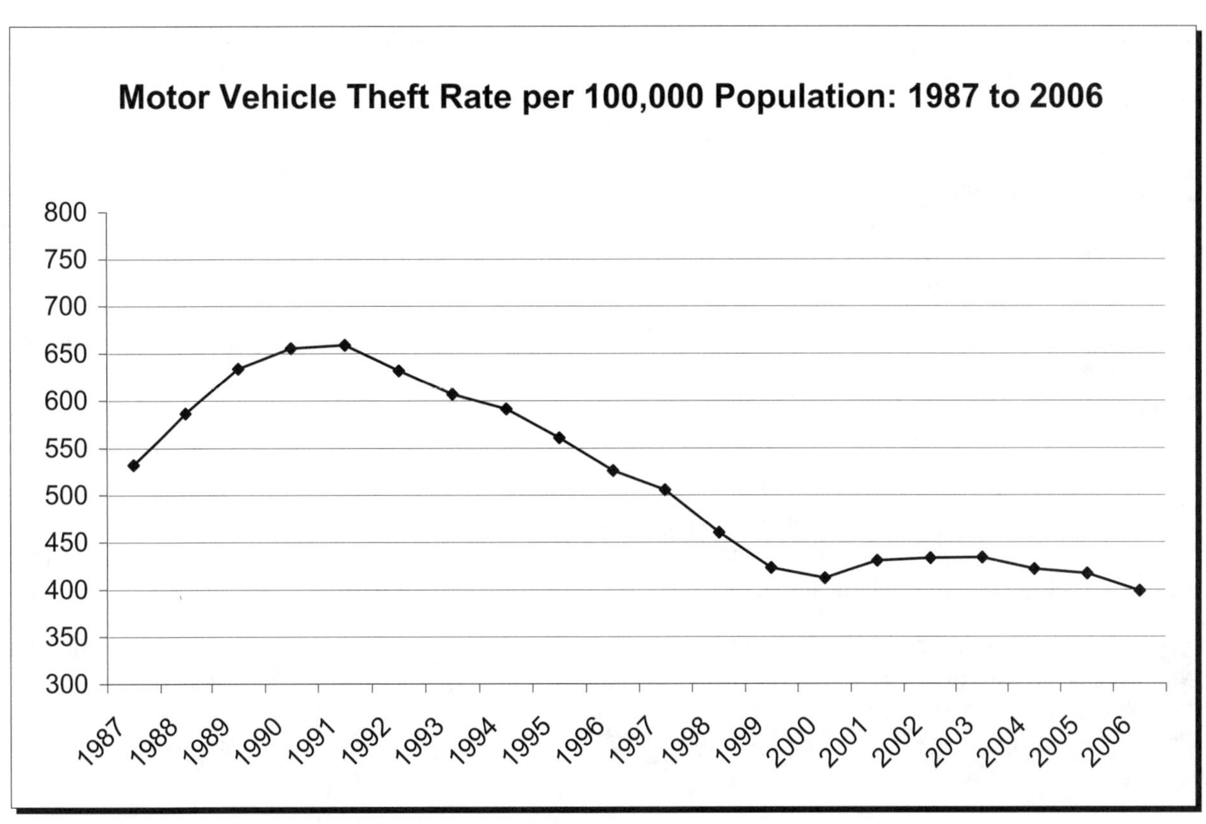

Source: Federal Bureau of Investigation

"Crime in the United States 2006" (Uniform Crime Reports, September 24, 2007)

NATIONAL, METROPOLITAN AND CITY CRIME STATISTICS SUMMARY: 2006

	NATIONAL	METRO*	CITY*
Population 2006	299,398,484	248,798,842	81,395,450
Police (Sworn Officers)	683,396		202,334
Rate of Police Officers (per 100,000 Population)	241		250
Crimes in 2006	11,401,313	9,987,412	4,357,577
Crime Rate in 2006 (per 100,000 Population)	3,808.0	4,014.3	5,353.6
Percent Change in Crime Rate: 2005 to 2006	(2.4)	(2.3)	(2.7)
Percent Change in Crime Rate: 2002 to 2006	(7.7)	(9.0)	(11.2)
Violent Crimes in 2006	1,417,745	1,280,264	671,662
Violent Crime Rate in 2006 (per 100,000 Population)	473.5	514.6	825.2
Percent Change in Violent Crime Rate: 2005 to 2006	1.0	1.0	2.7
Percent Change in Violent Crime Rate: 2002 to 2006	(4.2)	(5.7)	(8.1)
Murders in 2006	17,034	15,429	9,032
Murder Rate in 2006 (per 100,000 Population)	5.7	6.2	11.1
Percent Change in Murder Rate: 2005 to 2006	0.8	1.6	0.0
Percent Change in Murder Rate: 2002 to 2006	1.0	0.0	(2.6)
Rapes in 2006	92,455	77,384	30,019
Rape Rate in 2006 (per 100,000 Population)	30.9	31.1	36.9
Percent Change in Rape Rate: 2005 to 2006	(3.0)	(2.2)	(4.2)
Percent Change in Rape Rate: 2002 to 2006	(6.6)	(8.0)	(11.1)
Robberies in 2006	447,403	430,003	266,911
Robbery Rate in 2006 (per 100,000 Population)	149.4	172.8	327.9
Percent Change in Robbery Rate: 2005 to 2006	6.1	5.9	4.3
Percent Change in Robbery Rate: 2002 to 2006	2.3	(0.3)	(3.0)
Aggravated Assaults in 2006	860,853	757,448	365,700
Aggravated Assault Rate in 2006 (per 100,000 Population)	287.5	304.4	449.3
Percent Change in Aggravated Assault Rate: 2005 to 2006	(1.1)	(1.4)	2.2
Percent Change in Aggravated Assault Rate: 2002 to 2006	(7.1)	(8.4)	(11.5)
Property Crimes in 2006	9,983,568	8,707,148	3,685,915
Property Crime Rate in 2006 (per 100,000 Population)	3,334.5	3,499.7	4,528.4
Percent Change in Property Crime Rate: 2005 to 2006	(2.8)	(2.8)	(3.6)
Percent Change in Property Crime Rate: 2002 to 2006	(8.2)	(9.4)	(11.8)
Burglaries in 2006	2,183,746	1,862,416	782,079
Burglary Rate in 2006 (per 100,000 Population)	729.4	748.6	960.8
Percent Change in Burglary Rate: 2005 to 2006	0.3	0.7	0.2
Percent Change in Burglary Rate: 2002 to 2006	(2.4)	(2.6)	(3.1)
Larcenies and Thefts in 2006	6,607,013	5,730,014	2,302,537
Larceny and Theft Rate in 2006 (per 100,000 Population)	2,206.8	2,303.1	2,828.8
Percent Change in Larceny and Theft Rate: 2005 to 2006	(3.5)	(3.5)	(4.4)
Percent Change in Larceny and Theft Rate: 2002 to 2006	(10.0)	(11.3)	(14.4)
Motor Vehicle Thefts in 2006	1,192,809	1,114,718	601,299
Motor Vehicle Theft Rate in 2006 (per 100,000 Population)	398.4	448.0	738.7
Percent Change in Motor Vehicle Theft Rate: 2005 to 2006	(4.4)	(4.5)	(5.4)
Percent Change in Motor Vehicle Theft Rate: 2002 to 2006	(8.0)	(10.1)	(11.6)

Source: CQ Press using data from Federal Bureau of Investigation
"Crime in the United States 2006" (Uniform Crime Reports, September 24, 2007)
**Metro includes population and crime for all metropolitan statistical areas. City statistics are for cities of 100,000 or more in population.*